# INTRODUCTORY ECONOMICS

Craig Baker

RONALD A. WYKSTRA
*Colorado State University*

**HARPER & ROW, PUBLISHERS**
*New York, Evanston, San Francisco, London*

TO NANCY

*Graig Baker*

**INTRODUCTORY ECONOMICS**

# Preface

The meaningful question today is not, "What are the basic principles of economics?" but rather, "Why is economics important *now*?" The basic purpose of writing this book is to demonstrate that economics is a "now" subject—that the facts and theory comprising the body of economic knowledge are useful and pragmatic. Indeed, perhaps more than any other branch of the social sciences, economics is about the real world, if for no other reason than that it confronts a wide variety of current problems daily.

Economics has systematically developed as a science, but it remains firmly rooted in the realm of social values and practical problems. As a science, economics tests hypotheses and compares theory to real-world observations. Try as one might, economics as a science is not and cannot be made a pure or value-free subject, nor can its theory prove what should be. Thus, the subject matter of economics is a combination of practical problems, scientific analysis, and political economy.

## CONTENT

This text is organized around five basic parts: Part 1 is an introduction to economics and a survey of the private and public sectors of the American economy (Chapters 1–5); Part 2 analyzes economic instability—the problems of unemployment, inflation, and economic growth (Chapters 6–13); Part 3 discusses market-pricing problems associated with the goal of economic efficiency in the allocation of resources (Chapters 14–19); Part 4 evaluates selected economic problems characteristic of the American economy in the 1970s (Chapters 20–24); and Part 5 introduces major problems in the international economy (Chapters 25–28).

Tabular data and diagrammatic illustrations are presented together with the hope that the combined use of such information will facilitate understanding. Two appendixes present further refinements in economic theory. This may be desired by some instructors.

Although understanding the fundamentals of economic theory is important, introductory economics can no more afford to pursue intellectual rigor indiscriminately than it can afford to become a wasteland of casual and inconclusive facts. In this book, care has been taken to present the basic principles of economic theory in as simplified a manner as possible. Where economic theory is unsettled, vague, or deficient, these realities have been presented openly to the student. Thus, the controversy over Monetarism and fine-tuning of the economy is given extensive treatment, the unemployment-inflation tradeoff relationship is discussed, a full critique of price theory is presented, the viewpoints of dissenting economists are aired, and the normative and social-science perspectives of economic problems are examined.

Among other features of the text, there is extensive use of the concept of a full-employment budget. Because welfare is another subject of increasing importance in the American economy, the welfare implications of market pricing are given full coverage. In this context, stress is placed upon the objective of economic efficiency and its narrow welfare implications through use of the competitive model of pricing. In the discussion of the operation of a price system, I have also made it a point to emphasize repeatedly that economic "models" are only models—not necessarily an accurate image of the American (or any other) economy. Throughout the text, current problems in economics such as discrimination, the role of economic power in markets, poverty, environmental debasement, the economics of war and peace, and the problem of public choice in government finance receive extensive treatment.

Economics is not a pure science, and economists can ill afford to hide behind the transparent claim that it is science alone. Where the issues and facts are clear, or where a measure of consensus exists among professional economists, judgments are set forth in this book without apology. What is at stake today is relevancy to real-world problems and policies, and if reality is to be improved upon, the inherent relevancy of subjects such as economic justice and equity cannot be treated superficially. There is much that is unsettling to today's generation about economic injustices, and in many instances the failures of economic policy are quite evident. Where such policy failures have occurred, I have made a conscious effort to tell it like it is just as the achievements of government policy are also made apparent to the reader.

## STUDY HINTS FOR THE STUDENT

Every student no doubt has his personalized style of learning from a text book. The reader will benefit, however, from realizing that there are certain characteristics unique to economics as a subject matter. For instance:

1. Economics is not a subject which can be memorized, nor can a text be read in a casual manner as one might read a novel. It is necessary to study economics, not simply read words; subject matter should be read for the purpose of understanding, and the temptation to memorize should be resisted at every turn.

2. The material in a beginning course in economics is often cumulative. An incomplete or faulty understanding of material covered at an earlier stage may lead to problems in a sequential and ultimately irreversible way. Consequently, it is important to follow two very basic guidelines: first, make every effort to understand new ideas in the sequence in which your instructor presents them; second, keep abreast of reading assignments as they are made. If reading assignments are postponed, much of the value of lectures and class discussions can be lost, and a backlog of new material builds up.

3. There are several useful study aids built into this text. Like many new subjects to which students are exposed, economics has its own vocabulary. Thus, the first time a new term or concept is used in a chapter, it is italicized and then identified in a special section at the end of each chapter. Problem and essay questions presented at the end of each chapter should be given careful consideration. The number of questions has been limited to encourage their use. Each question provides broad coverage of the *major* concepts in the chapter.

4. Before reading a chapter for the first time, it is worthwhile to read carefully the summary at the end of each chapter. It is also wise to spend a few moments examining the organizational structure of each chapter. This way you will have some idea of the sequence in which new material is being presented. This book has been organized around four different head and subhead levels, and knowing this is useful in maintaining a logical set of class notes and in providing an overall perspective of the contents of each chapter.

5. One final word of advice. Major concepts and the most important data pertaining to the specific subjects are illustrated in diagrammatic and tabular form throughout the text. These are learning aids designed to enrich your understanding of economic relationships, and you should devote special attention to illustrations before continuing to read in a chapter.

## SUPPLEMENTARY MATERIALS

Professor John McKean and I have prepared several teaching aids to accompany this book. *Readings in Introductory Economics* is a collection of essays on a variety of economic issues and problems. This collection serves to enrich and bring economics alive by presenting the views of many economists on day-to-day economic problems.

Students can also benefit a great deal from having an opportunity to work directly with economic principles and to analyze economic problems. The *Study Guide* accompanying this text offers this opportunity. As it develops a glossary of economic terms and concepts by chapter, it presents the student with self-test opportunities, using multiple-choice, true-false, and essay questions; and it provides practice in working with key economic principles and analyzing problems.

The *Instructor's Manual* is another supplement, containing objective questions for testing purposes. It has a limited number of one-page quiz problems which cover the most basic economic concepts and can be easily reproduced. My co-author on the *Manual*, John Whippen, and I have found these materials to be particularly useful as a periodic quiz- or a lab-session substitute for daily lectures. A set of outlines for lecture notes is also available to instructors upon request. While it is impossible to allow fully for the variety of styles and nuances each teacher incorporates into his course, these outlines are carefully organized to provide the structure and basic format for daily class lectures or discussions.

## COURSE ORGANIZATION

This book is designed for several alternative organizational patterns. Within the 28 chapters there are 94 topical subject units identified as major heads A, B, C, D, and E. Division by subject unit allows an instructor considerable opportunity to make organizational adjustments of his choosing. Microeconomics can precede or follow macroeconomics; an instructor can delete some subject units from a chapter, add selected subject units, or cover them in a different order (in most cases); and those who prefer to cover less material can omit selected chapters in each of the five parts of the book. This organizational flexibility makes the text especially suited for one-semester or nonmajor courses. In addition to the conventional division between macroeconomics (Chapters 1–13) and microeconomics (Chapters 14–28), two other suggested one-semester outlines are presented following the table of contents.

## ACKNOWLEDGMENTS

My indebtedness to others who have contributed to this effort in numerous ways is great. I am especially indebted to the economists who provided written reviews on portions or all of the manuscript: Paul W. Barkley of Washington State University, Sidney M. Blumner of California State Polytechnic College, Lester V. Chandler of Atlanta University, John A. Cochran of Arizona State University, William E. Gibson of the University of California, Los Angeles, George D. Green of the University of Minnesota, John H. Kareken of the University of Minnesota, the late Lewis F. Manly of Tufts University, Wallace L. Nelson of Wichita State University, Myron H. Ross of Western Michigan University, James A. Stephenson of Iowa State University, E. S. Wallace of the University of Nebraska, Harold R. Williams of Kent State University, and Pan A. Yotopoulos of Stanford University. Among my Colorado State University colleagues who so willingly assisted me at various points, special acknowledgment is due Professors Leslie Anderson, Huntley Biggs, L. S. Fan, Lee Gray, L. M. Hartman, Kenneth Nobe, Terry Ozawa, Rodney Peterson, Richard Walsh, and Robert Young.

I wish to express my gratitude to Miss Kay Kilburn whose tireless attention was instrumental to this effort. I must acknowledge my special indebtedness to my wife, Nancy, for the assistance and encouragement she provided.

*Ronald A. Wykstra*

# Contents

# PART 2 Macroeconomics: Employment, Prices, and Economic Stability

## PART 3 Microeconomics: Prices and the Allocation of Resources

## PART 4 Domestic Economic Issues

## PART 5 The International Economy

# Suggested One-Semester Survey Course in Economic Problems and Issues

*Optional Chapters or Parts Within Chapters.* There are 423 pages if all optional material is covered, and 362 pages if all optional material is omitted.

The optional material by chapter numbers are as follows: Chapter 19, Parts A and D; Chapter 20, entire chapter; and Chapter 23, entire chapter. The suggested outline for Chapters 7, 9, and 12 are meant to include only Part A of Chapter 7, Part C of Chapter 9, and Parts A and C of Chapter 12.

Greater emphasis may be placed upon microeconomic theory by including Chapters 15 and 16, for example. If an instructor wishes to cover macroeconomics more completely, various portions of Chapters 7–10 could also be included.

# Suggested One-Semester Course in Economic Principles

*Optional Chapters or Parts Within Chapters. There are 440 pages if all optional material is covered, and 310 pages if all optional material is omitted.

The optional material by chapter numbers are as follows: Chapter 9, entire chapter or Parts B and C; Chapter 12, Parts A and B; Chapter 13, Parts A and B; Chapter 18, entire chapter or Part D; and Chapter 20, entire chapter or Parts A and C.

Microeconomics can precede macroeconomics, and other chapter parts and appendixes A and B may be omitted or utilized, depending upon the instructor's preferences.

# PART 1

Individuals can be viewed as separate biological, chemical, psychological, or skeletal *systems*. Similarly, the organization of man into groups is usually studied in the context of social, political, cultural, or economic systems. The purpose of these introductory chapters is to explain in general the role of economic systems in coping with scarcity. Systems of economic organization are basic to an organized society, and the way in which economic choices and decisions are made affects every citizen. The first step toward a basic understanding of economics is to identify the economic problems faced by a society and explain the economic role of households, firms, and government.

# Fundamentals of Economic Systems

**1.**

**Introduction**
Economic issues and problems
of contemporary society

**2.**

**The Foundations of Economics**
Scarcity, resources, and
approaches to studying
economics

**3.**

**Overview of the Market Economy**
Economic organization and
characteristics of a
market economy

**4.**

**The Private Sector and the
Market Economy**
Facts and functions of business
firms and households;
economizing problems in a
market system

**5.**

**The Public Sector
and the Market Economy**
Facts and functions of
government in an economic
system

# CHAPTER 1
# Introduction

Economics was long ago defined by Adam Smith as an "inquiry into the nature and causes of the wealth of nations" and by Alfred Marshall as "a study of mankind in the ordinary business of life." More recently, John Maynard Keynes described economics in these words:

From the earliest time of which we have record—back, say, to two thousand years before Christ down to the beginning of the eighteenth century, there was no very great change in the standard of life of the average man living in the civilised centres of the earth. . . . The economic problem, the struggle for subsistence, always has been hitherto the primary, most pressing problem of the human race.[1]

The struggle for subsistence derives from the scarcity of resources, and scarcity is indeed a harsh reality for millions of people. Thus it is that of 100 infants born on the continent of Africa and 100 infants born in America, more Americans will still be living at 53 years of age than African infants of 1 year of age. Indeed, the typical American at age 31 has as many years of life expectancy remaining as does the average African at birth.

While Keynes recognized that the economic problem of scarcity is still with us, he was also aware of the fact that the economic problem has changed enormously and in unalterable ways in the last century or two. Today vast social systems with undreamed of affluence are capable of waging nuclear war, and while this planet might survive, it could also perish. Therefore, man must also decide how to "best" use nature's bounty.

As a body of knowledge, economics is a relatively new subject, having been around formally a scant two centuries, but subsistence, wealth, and the ordinary business of life are, as we all know, as old as mankind. Issues and problems concerned with economics have arisen since civilization began, and one need not stretch his imagination to visualize even Stone-Age man faced with the choice of using timber as weapons or as firewood. Indeed, when the ancient Egyptians built massive pyramids, they too had to forgo other uses for the resources devoted to those arrogant boasts of material achievement.

Much of the "progress" and the "advance" of civilization is economic in nature. Today, great abundance is available to many people and nations, but it has also eluded many more. Where greater levels of material well-being have increased living standards, the youth of today are able to spend many years in school. In contrast, less than a century ago children at the tender age of 8 or 10 typically worked 50, 60, or even 70 hours

---

[1]John Maynard Keynes, *Essays in Persuasion* (New York: Harcourt Brace Jovanovich, 1932), pp. 360, 366.

weekly—often under conditions too cruel to imagine. But while large segments of the American population share—even though unequally—in the abundance of life, there are also entire nations and millions of people who have experienced little or no economic progress beyond that known in the time of Christ. The achievement of material well-being and the wealth of nations surely is of economic interest, but so too are the problems encountered in the ordinary business of life. Indeed, very important economic problems exist in the most affluent as well as the poorest nations.

Problem-solving is both art and science. Identifying economic problems, for example, means that the relative importance of each must be weighed, and that factual information must be gathered. It is also necessary to delineate goals—to specify personal and social objectives—in attempting to solve economic problems. As a consequence, mankind must make value judgments and must recognize that expressed values may or may not be in harmony with the values of others in a society. Finally, remedying economic problems requires that different solutions be developed, assessed, and evaluated, for there often are several alternative means to desired ends. Although these are elementary problem-solving procedures, they are also very important steps because they help to separate facts from goals, values, and alternative solutions. In examining current economic issues one feature stands out: the ever-present need to redefine them. Since economics is a study of the ordinary in life, let us next glance about our world and examine some contemporary economic problems.

## Contemporary Economic Problems

In 1970, several hundred thousand professional workers—highly qualified engineers, chemists, and executives—were without work, and the number of such persons unemployed was increasing well into 1971. Indeed, on many campuses, new Ph.Ds in some fields remained as teaching and research assistants because they were unable to obtain jobs. Even larger numbers of students with undergraduate degrees had comparable difficulties in obtaining work. While many find it shocking to spend thousands of dollars for education only to be unemployed, for the millions of disadvantaged minorities and lesser-skilled workers who never had the opportunity to acquire a higher education unemployment is an everyday experience.

The paradox of unemployment is that, in a general context, human resources are relatively scarce because they are needed to satisfy man's wants by providing the material well-being and wealth spoken of earlier. Despite this need, however, involuntary unemployment was a hardship borne by nearly 5 million persons in the American labor force as 1971 began. This waste of manpower represents a multibillion dollar loss of potential output and results in personal disillusionment, despair, poverty, and urban-ghetto problems which are noneconomic costs imposed upon people and society at large.

Consider another contemporary problem—that of increases in the general price level from one year to another. This, too, is a relevant concern today, particularly for persons whose wages and incomes do not increase as rapidly as prices—which is true for most Americans. Because the prices of goods and services purchased by the typical consumer rose about 5 percent annually during the five-year period from 1966 to 1971, the dollar value of wage increases was completely eroded by inflation. After adjustments are made for price-level increases in this same period, the typical worker in manufacturing industries experienced *no* increase in average weekly earnings.[2]

Unemployment and inflation are interrelated in very disconcerting ways. In 1970, for example, the number of persons unemployed increased by some 1.5 million persons and the consumer price level increased by more than 5 percent. A problem of this sort in the American economy ultimately places political leaders in the uncomfortable position of having to choose either *more* unemployment or *greater* inflationary pressures—a "devil-or-deep-blue-sea" choice which economists have yet to resolve. Popular opinion aside, there really is no Santa Claus where economic issues such as unemployment, inflation, and economic growth and income are concerned.

Another class of economic problems in the pricing category includes questions such as: How does a nation decide what to produce in transforming resources into goods and services? How are resources such as capital and labor combined in production? Are resources used in the most productive or efficient way? It is important to everyone that an economy produce those goods which people do in fact want instead of a dangerous or pollution-causing transportation system, horse-drawn carriages, or antiquated kerosene lamps. When one considers the thousands of economic choices required in a nation each day, the organizational requirements of a modern economy are truly staggering. Such production decisions must make the "best" use of different methods of producing goods and services if consumers are to obtain as much as is possible from limited incomes. Analyzing these complex economic problems and issues usually requires consideration of the role of government. The public sector may (and does) become involved in the ordinary business of life where economic issues such as unemployment, inflation, economic growth, and the efficient use and allocation of resources are concerned.

In addition, government is interested in economic justice. May a major employer in a given locality pay workers laboring under hazardous conditions a pittance of a wage, or should government intervene to protect the worker? Is it desirable for dominant and large business firms with substantial economic power to impose economic ruin upon others by charging high and discriminatory prices as the railroad barons did not too many years ago? And what of the fact that the automotive transportation system is responsible for a few thousand dead and maimed Americans each week? What stake and attendant costs characterize the general public's interest in the quality of food and drug products or in false and misleading advertising—or does government intervention infringe upon freedom of producers? Another economic problem arises from chemical and steel producers dumping wastes into streams and in other ways polluting the environment. And remember, while these firms might be avoiding some rather obvious production costs, they can claim to provide jobs for thousands of workers while producing goods at relatively low costs for consumers.

[2]That is, the worker's standard of living did not increase in terms of the "purchasing-power" measure of earnings, which remained at an average of $99 per week.

Still another class of economic problems involves the distribution of goods and services. As we have seen, the typical American manufacturing worker's wage did not increase in terms of real purchasing power from 1966 to 1971. However, federal, state, and local government receipts and expenditures did increase in terms of purchasing power—about 40 percent, as a matter of fact. Whether government expenditures are really used to satisfy people's true wants and whether they do in fact enhance and secure economic justice are crucial economic questions. To assess them, it must be realized that government influences economic dimensions of life in ways which many people may not recognize.

Economic problems arise when United States government agencies allow the legally monopolized communications industry to increase rates, attempt to cope with the vast economic power of large corporations or labor unions, or use the law in effect to require a worker to join a union. The government also influences income distribution through taxation. The least-prosperous one-tenth of all American families receives less than 2 percent of all family income, whereas the most affluent one-tenth receives some 25 percent of all family income. Presently, one out of eight citizens of the United States is officially classified as living at or below the poverty level, and the average black male earns a lifetime income substantially below that of a white male with a like number of years of education. One-half of those living in poverty are children, while the majority of poverty-level adults are poor for reasons other than a refusal to work. It is also well known that government regulates the import of oil, shoes, textiles, autos, and hundreds of other goods, and such regulation amounts to a multibillion dollar tax paid by consumers in the form of higher prices. Finally, the United States government must take an interest in underdeveloped countries. The relative prosperity of the United States is a most *uncommon* experience for the majority of the nearly 4 billion people who inhabit the earth. This two-thirds of the world's population is growing at a rate such that it nearly doubles every 25 years, and these same people live under the very conditions of economic subsistence described in the earlier quote by Lord Keynes.

The involvement of government in domestic economic affairs also raises knotty financial and ethical questions. Running a political system is costly, and about one-third of the aggregate income received by all American citizens is used to finance all types of public goods and services. But just how much of the cost of government does each of us pay for, and in what measure should individuals from unequal economic stations in life be taxed? How fair and equitable is taxation when the laws allow millionaires to receive an unlimited income from tax-free bonds? The more than one-third of a trillion dollars government debt further complicates government finance and concerns many people.

Furthermore, it matters to everyone whether government spends more or less for national defense, allocates several billion dollars each year to subsidize middle-class college students, or trains disadvantaged citizens and the hard-core unemployed. We all have a stake in government decisions to provide subsidies to the most rather than to the least prosperous farmers, or decisions to construct freeways and national parks instead of revitalizing urban America. While government is costly, and while there is much room for disagreement among individuals concerning their proportionate share of taxes and benefits, there also are important needs for public goods and services. Certainly there is a need for judicial systems, transportation systems, public schools, fire and police protection, public sanitation and health facilities to control communicable diseases, as well as a need for national defense. But how much of a need is there in each of a dozen areas, and what are the public priorities for different programs?

These, then, are some of the many dimensions to that "ordinary business of life" called "economics." As contemporary issues they continue to perplex and rankle men as they have in the past.

## Whither the Future?

Our brief encounter with selected economic problems in America has demonstrated that economic subsistence is a problem for some people some of the time, but for the most part, modern times have preempted brute subsistence. In its place, there has arisen an array of difficult decisions about problems of economic welfare which all nations must confront. So, while the economic problem is always with us in relative terms, it is not invariant with the passage of time.

As John Maynard Keynes foresaw, the "strenuous, purposeful money-makers" have carried many people in economically developed nations to abundance which, to be enjoyed to its fullest, requires that man now practice the art of living. The contemporary economic problem of how to use abundance is the product of the ordinary process of living in a society which relies upon rules, customs, and conventions. These rules help to organize and arrange economic affairs and to buttress the values and socioeconomic institutions of civilizations today, and must change as economic problems change.

Some four decades ago, Lord Keynes eloquently spoke of the impact of the changing economic problem and the need for social change in describing a future day when:

We shall once more value ends above means and prefer the good to the useful.
We shall honour those who can teach us how to pluck the hour and the day virtuously and well, the delightful people who are capable of taking direct enjoyment in things, the lilies of the field who toil not neither do they spin.

But beware! The time for all this is not yet. For at least another hundred years we must pretend to ourselves and to every one that fair is foul and foul is fair; for foul is useful and fair is not. Avarice and usury and precaution must be our gods for a little longer still. For only they can lead us out of the tunnel of economic necessity into daylight. All kinds of social customs and economic practices affecting the distribution of wealth and of economic rewards and penalties, which we now maintain at all costs, however distasteful and unjust they may be themselves, ... we shall then be free, at last, to discard.[3]

Men and societies can err in important ways en route to realizing change, and not because they pursue change, for we need lots of people doing that each day. Where they err is in failing really to learn how an economic system works and in assuming that wand-waving is a substitute for constructive reform. These are very good reasons for studying eco-

[3]Keynes, *op. cit.*, pp. 372, 369–370.

nomics, and while you will not find it an easy task all of the time, learning something about economics—its history, facts, theory, statistics, and even the rules and customs that govern societies—is worthwhile because it will directly affect the rest of your life. You may have to pay the price of a little work to gain that knowledge.

## Questions to Answer

1. What did Alfred Marshall mean by "the ordinary business of life"? Do you think this quotation is applicable today?

2. What are the major procedures in economic problem-solving?

3. Why are increases in the general price level from one year to the next of major concern to most Americans?

4. What is the public sector? Identify some of the ways it plays a major role in America today.

5. How are unemployment and inflation related?

6. What interest does the United States have in international economic affairs?

7. Why are there economic problems in relatively affluent societies today when economic subsistence is not a problem for most people?

# CHAPTER 2
# The Foundations
# of Economics

Economics deals with many socioeconomic issues, most of which are of immediate concern to us. Although it is tempting to continue to discuss important economic problems, such a discussion would be premature. To form a reasoned opinion, it is necessary to analyze the issues carefully, a process which requires a meaningful, sequential exposure to economics. Let us begin by devoting our attention to the meaning of economics (Part A), economic resources (Part B), economic reasoning (Part C), and economic models and tools of analysis (Part D).

## A. THE MEANING OF ECONOMICS

Throughout history, man has exhibited an insatiable appetite to consume. Unfortunately, his unlimited wants are seldom if ever matched by society's ability to fulfill them because resources are limited. In *Conduct of Life*, Ralph Waldo Emerson aptly described the primary concern of economics as follows:

Want is a growing giant whom the coat of
Have was never large enough to cover.

As people have attempted to fulfill wants, they have been required to make choices among scarce resources. Intense rivalries for these resources have resulted. These rivalries have produced conflicts of enormous proportions on both domestic and international levels in every known civilization, including our own. Even the most casual observation of contemporary socioeconomic problems such as poverty, the urban crisis, or the environment reveals a vying for limited resources. The underdeveloped world, which embraces more than 2 billion persons in the early 1970s, furnishes another example of the universal nature of choice, scarcity, and potential conflict. The *good life* is a near-impossible dream, partly because wants are unlimited relative to the resources capable of producing goods and services to meet them.

### What Is Economics?

Although economics can be defined in a variety of ways, it broadly encompasses the behavior, institutions, and consequences associated with scarcity. More specifically, *economics* is defined as the study of the alternative ways mankind chooses to use scarce but productive resources to produce goods and services to satisfy wants. Note that this rather standard definition of economics implies several things. First of all, it requires a system of economic organization guided by rules within an institutional framework. Second, it states that mankind must choose among alternative uses for scarce resources. This raises such problems as how choices are made, who makes them, and how the decision-making process relates to a system of economic organization. Third, the definition implies an interest in getting as much satisfaction as possible from scarce resources. For all of these reasons, we must be concerned with the way an economic system accomplishes the production and exchange of goods and services. The study of economics centers upon questions like: Whose wants are satisfied? To what extent is satisfaction achieved? Can resources be used more fully or more efficiently to produce more output? In a general sense, economics is the study of the decision-making and choice necessitated by unlimited wants and scarce resources. Economics is a search for ways to expand our limited capability to fulfill our wants.

### Economics and Social Systems

Basically man is involved in at least four identifiable relationships: (a) man with himself, the general topic of psychology; (b) man with the universe, the study of the biological and physical sciences; (c) man with the unknown, covered in part by theology and philosophy; and (d) man in relation to other men, the general realm of the social sciences, of which economics is a part. It is hazardous to delineate these areas of inquiry explicitly. However, the social sciences are generally defined to include economics, sociology, political science, anthropology, and portions of both history and psychology. Economists use history, sociology, and various other fields such as statistics and mathematics as valuable adjuncts to their study.

The relationship between political science and economics is particularly strong. Alternative types of systems—social, political, and economic—differ from each other in certain unique ways. A political system is not the same as an economic or a social system. However, certain combinations of political, social, and economic systems are compatible with each other because of common characteristics and goals. Whenever any functional part of a society's system is out of order, some corrective action must be taken to restore harmony. The system—or "establishment," if you prefer—must use political power to develop policy and alter certain economic or social institutions to bring about the required change. For this obvious reason we must know something about economic systems and at the same time realize that an economic system cannot be studied in total isolation from its host—society at large.

The political system in the United States is a democracy, and the economic system is a *mixed market economy,* a system of economic organization under which producer and consumer decisions to buy and sell are made privately with some monitoring by government. In this combination of systems men are relatively free to govern themselves through chosen representatives, and they are also relatively free to conduct their economic affairs *within the rules and framework of the system.* Some degree of freedom and political control is necessary to sustain the rules and institutions which characterize the mixed market economy. Problems can and do arise when certain economic groups exercise control over income or prices; advantageous power positions then accrue to one group that may diminish the freedom of another. "Political economy" describes the use of such political control in economic affairs. When situations arise which are not in the best interest of society as a whole, political readjustment of rules and institutions must be made.

### The Scarcity-Choice Dilemma

A society is limited in what can be produced by its scarce resources. It must choose between producing cannons and cotton, highways and hairpins, national defense and nutrition. Furthermore, individuals must privately choose between shirts and shoes, boats and skis, and innumerable other goods. For many persons, a vastly improved wardrobe, a new GTO, and a better education are not real possibilities. Economic choice is an important dimension to systems of economic organization.

With a little reflection, it becomes quite apparent that constraints are imposed in fulfilling wants. While at first glance it may seem easy enough to produce the desired goods and services, the process is not that simple. Who will produce? What will be produced? For whom will it be produced? How much will be produced? Available resources are scarce enough to require that a price be paid by anyone desiring to use either resources or the goods and services they can produce. The four attributes of a scarcity-chain problem are interdependence, prices, conflict, and freedom.

#### INTERDEPENDENCE

In economics, as in many areas of life, man lives in cooperation with his fellow beings. To satisfy the simplest of wants, you and I are dependent on the efforts of thousands of persons throughout the nation and world. In a complex economy, simple products like table salt, soap, and shoe laces are produced and distributed through a vast economic network characterized by cooperative behavior. Yet, there is no omnipotent director of economic exchange to see that the right kinds and quantities of goods and resources move in and out of Seattle or Los Angeles. In many nations the organizing economic force centers around self-interest and prices. Prices and consumer choice help provide the direction an economic system needs.

#### PRICES

Unlimited wants and limited resources create a perpetual environment of choice and scarcity which generates a pricing need. *Prices* represent the value placed upon scarce items, usually identified by some common denominator used as a medium of exchange such as dollars, pounds, francs, or rubles. Producers and suppliers, in search of profits, are enticed into cooperation. Those who wish to participate in the economic process of acquiring something of value must have *both* the ability and the willingness to use money to meet established prices. This means that incomes—which men acquire to the extent that they own and supply scarce resources—must be made available through the pricing system.

But what happens if some people lack the ability to acquire goods and services? Other members of a society could pay part or all of the prices of certain goods for everyone, perhaps out of an enlightened attitude or the desire to share collectively or to "socialize" some goods or services. In some instances, moral or ethical considerations may persuade individuals to provide others with goods and services in the interest of public welfare. Finally, of course, persuasion and coercion may be used to induce a segment of society to relinquish its claims on limited goods (social security taxation is an example). Needless to say, hostilities may result when the means of satisfying wants are transferred to others in society. A nebulous line sometimes divides enlightened attitudes, morality, persuasion, and coercion. Indeed, what is persuasion and morality to one person may be coercion and immorality to another. Any system of economic organization must confront these problems of choice, interdependence, and prices. In addition, however, it must also deal with the conflicts that arise over these problems.

## CONFLICT

Scarcity and choice set the stage for economic conflict, and in contemporary societies this conflict can no more be ignored than can interdependence and cooperation. Individual decisions to buy and sell denote the use of private choice to resolve conflict; choice is a reflection of a prospective buyer's (or seller's) perception of value and wants. Conflict can arise over scarce resources, the distribution of income, the prices charged for products or resources, wage or job discrimination, the incidence and burden of taxes, or the distribution of government-sponsored goods and services. More difficult conflicts arise when private choice is replaced with a public decision.

When scarcity is theatening to encircle one interest group more than another, economic conflict may become a particularly acute problem. Taxation which one person considers "enlightened" may represent treason to another, and attitudes about poverty that are ethical and moral to some may seem just the opposite to others. Applied forcefully enough, power can be used to resolve such economic conflicts, but this solution is not altogether pleasant for the powerless. The important point about a mixed market economy is that prices serve to mediate economic conflict and choice, except, of course, when government authority is used to control the private sector of the economy.

## FREEDOM

Mankind is strongly oriented toward making economic choices on an individual basis. Nevertheless, society does levy taxes and make expenditures for the general good. By public decree, certain kinds of goods or services may or may not be produced or consumed. On many university campuses the student is subject to restriction if he chooses to use "pot," while very often he is required to purchase athletic tickets. In the first case, society has collectively chosen that its citizens shall not have "pot" at any price. In the second instance, it has decided that students shall support an athletic system by paying a fee, regardless of their desires. It is obvious from these rather mundane examples that freedom of choice is an important dimension of the economic problem of scarcity.

It is clear that scarcity and choice represent the general theme of economics—a subject which demands that a vast array of complexities be sorted out and approached as integrated, yet reasonably distinct, elements. Economics is important because freedom of choice and conflict, or the lack thereof, are of paramount interest to mankind. In addition, an understanding of the economic system is vital if citizens are to be well informed and able to make intelligent decisions affecting their economic lives. The rules and institutions of an economic system either restrain or enhance its effectiveness. Literally millions of economic decisions are made daily, and these require a form of economic organization, which in our society is supplied by the relatively informal, price-directed mixed market system. Economic knowledge can be of considerable practical value to consumers, business firms, and owners of resources. Those who understand the consequences and significance of the economics of pollution, unemployment, inflation, a balance-of-payments deficit, or poverty amid affluence are able to work toward the achievement of a fuller life.

## B. ECONOMIC RESOURCES: OVERCOMING SCARCITY

How does society go about filling unlimited wants? The activities and objects used to meet economic wants are *resources*. For this simple yet most pervasive reason, economics can be described as the study of: (a) the full and stable employment of all resources, (b) achievement of the efficient use of all resources, and (c) the arbitration of conflict that arises in a system of economic organization.

When used in the economic process, resources are *factors of production*. The four factors of production are entrepreneurial ability, labor, capital, and natural resources. The first two of these factors of production are *human resources*, and the latter are *property resources*. The technological methods of producing are an important determinant of how resources are used. We all know of instances in which technology has changed, affecting the use of scarce resources in different ways. Should automobiles become obsolete (or illegal), vast quantities of capital resources—machinery, plants, and the like—would have to be adapted and adjusted to other uses, just as the blacksmiths of the past were required to adjust to change. Situations arise in which scarce resources are unused because of technological change. While this is an important economic problem, such unemployment characterizes slippage in an economic system, rather than a refutation of the scarcity premise. In general, the four factors of production are scarce, and because they are, they all have alternative uses. When a natural resource such as land is used for a new golf course, society sacrifices space for an industrial park or a residential development. A capital resource such as a building might be used to produce clothing, to house a football team, or to produce cat food. Because they are scarce, human resources also have alternative uses. A recently matriculated student may join the military manpower pool, or he may become an engineer or a member of the medical profession. Every alternative use of scarce factors of production involves choice and pricing.

### Human Resources

*Labor* generally refers to human skills or manpower used directly in the production process. *Entrepreneurial ability* refers to the indirect use of human resources. Both the quantity and the quality of human resources are relevant to the problem of scarcity, and thus both concern the economist. The size of a population is an outer boundary or supply constraint to human resources as factors of production. Typically, however, the limit of productive human resources is considerably less than total population size because young, old, disabled, and poorly trained human resources do not fully participate in the production process.

FUNDAMENTALS OF ECONOMIC SYSTEMS

*Labor resources* are used directly to produce goods and services under the direction of other human resources. Because employed manpower resources are scarce and have alternative uses (including leisure) they command a price. The incomes earned by labor or manpower resources are *wages* and *salaries*. The extent to which manpower resources are employed is important because the income received by labor is a vital component of the spending stream in an economic system. In contrast to employed manpower, *entrepreneurial resources* organize the production processes, assume certain risks, and direct the combined use of the factors of production. *Profits* are the income payment to scarce entrepreneurial resources.

### HUMAN-RESOURCE SCARCITY?

Is it true that human resources are scarce? In general, the answer is yes, despite contemporary concern about overpopulation and unemployment. There must be adequate human resources relative to available property resources and their quality or level of skill must be sufficient in relation to the techniques used to produce goods and services. Between 1800 and 1970, for example, the estimated world population increased nearly fourfold, from 0.9 billion to 3.5 billion persons, and the population of the United States by the year 2000 is projected at one-third of a billion persons. Much of the increase has occurred in nations like India, Chile, and China where bare subsistence remains the norm. Thus, some nations do have excess human resources *in relation* to available property resources and technical modes of production. Many Asian, African, and South American nations remain on the brink of subsistence, partly because of vast differences between the quantities of their human and property resources. Indeed, some two-thirds of the world's people have experienced little economic progress for centuries for this very reason.[1] On the other hand, wealthier nations such as Germany and the United States have experienced rapid economic growth because increased property resources and improved technology have accompanied population expansion.

In advancing societies, considerable effort is put forth to train and develop human resources. This effort, of course, requires investment expenditures—the use of other human and property resources to provide educational and health facilities. Furthermore, those persons receiving training must often withdraw from the labor force while they are being educated. Needless to say, such investments in human resources require considerable national wealth. It also involves thousands of choices concerning such matters as the number and hours of work, the kind of manpower needed, and the ways that human resources can be utilized more fully and efficiently.

### Property Resources

The characteristic distinguishing human and property resources is the custom of a society regarding ownership. In most of the world today, ownership of human resources is vested in each individual; it is illegal to "own" other human factors of production. In contrast, many nations encourage private ownership of property resources. However, others minimize such

---

[1] See Chapter 27 for a further discussion of the less developed nations.

ownership, vesting much of it in the state. The United States and the Soviet Union illustrate these two approaches to ownership of property resources.[2]

## NATURAL RESOURCES

*Natural resources* such as land, mineral deposits, water, or timber are gifts of nature that contribute to the production process and economic progress. A timber stand as a natural resource has one type of value if allowed to remain a part of nature. Its value and utility as a resource are quite different if it is harvested and used to construct schools or factories, and other quite different social consequences may occur if the harvesting results in soil erosion and dangerous flood conditions. Water may be used for irrigation, hydroelectric power, or industrial waste disposal, and such uses dramatically affect its value as a natural resource.

The quality of natural resources is important, as anyone exposed to smog-fouled air will confirm. Consider land resources, where fertility, temperature, climatology, and topographical characteristics may vary widely. An acre of river-basin land, a gold mine, or a plot on the edge of a rapidly growing megalopolis may be a natural land resource, but the differences as a factor of production are very obvious. Adequate quantities or stocks of natural resources are important to economic progress, but some nations such as Japan, Switzerland, and Britain have achieved substantial economic gains without adequate natural resources of their own. On the other hand, nations such as those in Africa and South America may have abundant natural resources, but lack other resources such as capital or a trained labor force. Such nations may fail to utilize their natural resources fully and may thus continue to endure a serious level of scarcity.

Finally, natural resources are partially dependent on the state of technology or the art of production prevailing in a society. For example, if they are to be fully utilized, mineral or oil deposits require a technology beyond that available in a simple peasant society. Similarly, a web of inland rivers and abundant water supplies capable of providing hydroelectric power, transportation, and irrigation may be vastly underutilized in a technologically backward society. Indeed, natural resources are valued as a factor of production only insofar as a particular economic system can use them as an input to create some output which satisfies the needs of people. Uranium and crude oil are now regarded as natural resources, but earlier in mankind's history they were viewed as a blight upon what otherwise might have been tillable land. Like other resources, natural resources constitute a potential source of wealth to their owners; they have alternative uses, within prescribed limits; and both scarcity and choice characterize their use as factors of production.

## CAPITAL RESOURCES

*Capital resources* are all man-made factors of production used to produce goods and services. Capital resources include such things as buildings, railroad cars, dams, machinery and equipment, and inventories of materials and finished equipment. Note that this definition of capital resources is different

[2] It is important to note that even in the United States some property is held by the government (such as Yellowstone Park), and even in the Soviet Union some property is held by individuals (automobiles, for example).

from the usual one. To many people, "capital" denotes money, stocks, bonds, and other pecuniary paper forms of claims to wealth. Economics does not use this definition because in the final analysis money, stocks and bonds, or savings accounts are themselves unproductive, and represent only title to capital resources or other forms of wealth. One of the easiest ways to remember the meaning of capital as an economic resource is to realize that capital resources are real physical resources.

The acquisition of tools, machinery, or large factories is very important in overcoming scarcity. The process of acquiring capital resources requires that a society refrain from consuming all of its output; that is, nations must save and invest. Someone in society must allocate resources from present consumption to the production of capital resources. If you are contemplating opening a pizza shop, for example, it is obvious that several levels of capital equipment can be used, ranging from a small, open campfire oven to a highly automated production system. To acquire even the smallest amount of capital resources such as wood, pans, and the ingredients needed to produce pizza in a simple campfire oven requires saving instead of consuming or investing in other capital resources. Cutting back on present consumption to accumulate capital resources is not easy for a nation that is barely subsisting at its present level of production. Capital formation for increased future production and consumption is one of the great problems of the less developed nations of the world.

Capital resources are closely related to technology. Production technology changes through scientific research, inventions, and innovations. The wheel and the computer were both products of creative minds, and each "discovery" revolutionized its world. However, both the simple round wheel and the complex computer became useful in man's struggle with scarcity largely as they became capital resources. In other words, technology becomes *embodied* in capital resources. This is an important explanation of the vital role capital resources play in the economic process.

*Summing up:* The central problem in economics can be summarized as making choices about the alternative use of scarce resources, a process in which prices perform a key role. Societies need a system of economic organization to order economic affairs—to decide how resources should be used to produce goods and services, to choose between the production of goods X and Y, and so forth.

## C. ECONOMIC REASONING

Economic reasoning is based upon the use of empirical and statistical information combined with a logical (and sometimes abstract) way of viewing economic events, institutions, and relationships. Economic reasoning requires a sequential movement from factual information to policy, a need to distinguish between normative and positive economics, and consideration of the ways in which economic theory and reasoning relate to reality.

### Approach to Economic Reasoning

Basically the study of economics is approached in three broad but distinct steps: (a) assembling economic data and facts, (b) developing theoretical models and relationships about these economic facts, and (c) establishing economic policy, or courses of action designed to change economic events and facts to correspond to economic goals. The procedures followed in the study of economic problems are illustrated in Figure 1.

## FACTS

Scientific inquiry is based upon observation of facts, and economics, as a branch of the social sciences, utilizes historical information and empirical data in describing economic relationships and events. The economist is concerned with the behavior of individuals as consumers and as producers; the social role of such institutions as business firms, labor unions, and banks; and the empirical information related to government as it influences the production, exchange, and consumption of goods and services. Gathering such facts is an important task of economic analysis, but it is essential that the facts be relevant to the problem(s) at hand. Therefore, the key economic issues must also be identified. For example, in dealing with the problem of poverty, it is necessary to use economic statistics and other historical or quantitative data to discover the degree and incidence of poverty and the influence of institutions on poverty. Furthermore, to be useful, facts need to be systematically interpreted and arranged—a task of economic theory.

## THEORY

From facts, the economist can sometimes develop theories or generalizations about economic relationships. The terms *theory, model,* and *principle* all describe the same thing; namely, generalizations about reality in a simplified context. Theories serve as an organizing device and are merely generalized concepts based upon events and relationships in the real world. Theory formulation requires abstract reasoning or thinking about a problem in

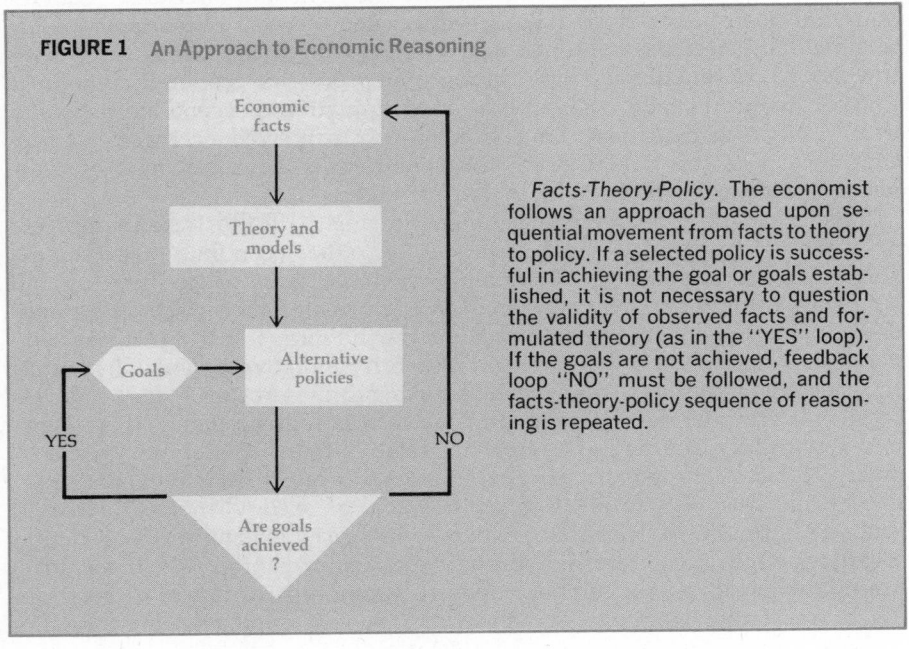

**FIGURE 1**   An Approach to Economic Reasoning

Economic facts

Theory and models

Goals → Alternative policies

YES                    NO

Are goals achieved?

*Facts-Theory-Policy.* The economist follows an approach based upon sequential movement from facts to theory to policy. If a selected policy is successful in achieving the goal or goals established, it is not necessary to question the validity of observed facts and formulated theory (as in the "YES" loop). If the goals are not achieved, feedback loop "NO" must be followed, and the facts-theory-policy sequence of reasoning is repeated.

order to sort out only the most basic relationships. Simplification is achieved by making assumptions that allow one to represent reality by an example or model that is easily understood and studied. The interrelationships between economic facts and theories (depicted by the arrow in Figure 1) is important because facts and theories must be compared and reexamined continually to verify the latter's reliability. Although theory is often useful, it is important that the assumptions and simplifications be evaluated carefully when it is applied to real-world problems.

## POLICY AND GOALS

The third step in economic reasoning, developed from observed facts and formulated theories of economic relationships, is to establish an economic policy capable of altering economic institutions and conditions. Such policies are influenced by the economic goals of society. Identification of these goals depends upon the society's values, prevailing economic conditions, economic institutions, and the position which the society historically has taken on economic issues and problems, as Chapter 1 implied. Three generally accepted economic goals are: (a) the full use of all resources, (b) the efficient use of resources, and (c) the resolution of economic conflict, problems, and issues. It is apparent that these general objectives embody ends like economic growth, price stability, economic freedom, control of unemployment, economic security, economic justice, and control of economic power.

Economic policy requires considering and selecting the best policy alternatives available to achieve various goals. Just as the student's goal of getting to a class may be achieved by walking, driving, or riding a bicycle, economic goals may be reached via alternative courses of action. Economic reasoning involves economic decisions, which must be made in terms of the question in Figure 1, "Are goals achieved?" If the answer to the decision question is "Yes," we simply move back to the economic goals and alternative courses of action open to society through feedback loop "Yes." If economic policy is not totally effective (which is nearly always the case), one is faced with the task of continually thinking through the process of economic reasoning. This procedure usually begins with a reexamination of economic facts and theory, because facts may have been poorly perceived or theories badly conceived. The reformulation of economic relationships that may be erroneous is shown by feedback loop "No" of Figure 1.

Examining the problem of high unemployment will illustrate the process of economic reasoning. The first task is to gather economic facts, for example, on the seriousness of unemployment in terms of its duration and incidence throughout the economy. On the basis of these facts one might develop the theory that unemployment can be mitigated by increased expenditures on the part of consumers, investors, and government. The theory is based upon the logic that increased expenditures result in higher levels of income and therefore more employment. In selecting a policy, it is important to consider alternative approaches relative to other economic goals. A policy of increasing government expenditures is one alternative, but it may not be the best way to achieve another goal of society, that of increased economic growth. Policies that encourage increased expenditures on capital resources might be a preferred alternative to achieve both goals. If the goals are not achieved, it is incumbent upon the economist to return to the process of reasoning from facts to theory to policy. Coping with conflicting goals and policies is a second important feature of economic reasoning. Attempts to reduce unemployment, for example, may conflict with the goal of price stability. When goals conflict with each other, economic theory and policy may not provide clear-cut answers. Thus, the judgment of a nation's leadership becomes important in setting goals and priorities for economic policy.

### Normative and Positive Economics

Economic issues embrace many controversial matters about which people often have strong feelings. To increase the visibility of value judgments and assess the validity of an economic issue, a distinction is made between positive and normative economic analysis. *Positive economics* is concerned with the existing situation, or "what is." *Normative economics* deals with what "should be" from the viewpoint of a person or group. One way in which a presumably objective economic position can be enhanced is to use a theory based upon observed facts—or "what is." Unfortunately, this does not assure that the economic position taken is necessarily a positive rather than a normative one, because the facts and problems that one *chooses* to examine in his theory may very well influence the theory developed and the policy prescribed from it. If one is personally involved with an issue, it may be difficult to remain detached. Moreover, true objectivity is also sometimes obscured by conflicting facts.

Positive economic statements can be supported by carefully examining the facts and logic behind them. "Should-be" statements about economic issues cannot be settled so easily because normative analysis is highly inter-related with values—the cultural, philosophical, political, and religious beliefs of people and institutions in society. It is obvious that considerable disagreement may arise over normative statements even when one appeals to positive factual information. Nevertheless, normative economic matters are important, and one of the purposes of education is to help individuals use their knowledge to support well-reasoned normative positions.

Let us consider an example illustrating the difference between normative and positive positions. The statement, "It is not now possible to cure cancer" is a positive statement (although it may be refuted in the near future). In contrast, the statement, "Society should develop a cure for cancer" is a normative one—an expression of a value judgment. Positive facts about personal health and shortened lives may help support the statement that "Society should cure cancer." Alternatively, positive statements about the population explosion may refute it. Everything really depends on one's preconceptions of good and bad at this level. It is most important to fully uncover all the positive matters that bear upon views of what should be. However, this does not mean that appealing to facts will always, or even usually, resolve disputes over normative issues.

The truth about normative economics is that *it depends*—it depends upon a value system and the related positive facts and consequences used to buttress or refute these values. In economics, it is very important to realize that when we think something should be, we are dealing with normative economics, whereas positive economics deals with what is. Also remember that one purpose of economics is to present as objective an appraisal as possible of *all* facts related to economic issues, problems, and theories. A doctor or an atomic scientist studying heart disease or nuclear weapons systems is not necessarily in favor of either simply because he studies them. Similarly, it is erroneous to presume that an economist who discusses weaknesses in the American economy necessarily supports a socialistic economic system.

### Theory and Reality

Economic theories or models are sometimes described in narrative, expository form and in other instances in the language of mathematics or geometry. No matter how they are presented, economic models are nothing more than simplified representations of the real world in which less important or complicating factors are held constant or assumed not to exist so that major points and relationships are clearly visible. The purposes of theory are to explain and predict observed phenomena—in our case, the economic behavior of men and societies. The value of economic theory is that it allows us to concentrate on a few important relationships. An economic model can be as valuable as a road map is to the traveler; both are theoretical abstractions from reality. Many bumps, curves, and side routes are not depicted on a map, but as a generalized portrayal of "what's out there," the map is valuable. So it is with economic theory.

Theories are *proposed* explanations or hypotheses; they are not immutable truths unless and until *all* available evidence has corroborated them. It is important to remember that economic theory may be correct or incorrect, depending upon factual validation. The steps taken in formulating economic theory are:

1. Observe relevant facts, relationships, and behavior.
2. Hypothesize certain cause-and-effect relationships or theories.
3. Derive the logical implications, conclusions, and predictions from theory.
4. See if the implications, conclusions, and predictions of theory correspond to the real world.
5. If they do, no further action is needed. If the theory does not fit reality, either reject or modify it.

Although, in an introductory course in economics, it is not possible to devote as much effort to testing economic theories as might be desirable, much of the existing evidence on the validity of economic theory will be reviewed as we proceed.

Not infrequently, students (and some professors) become disillusioned with the study of economics because when a theory is developed and simplifying assumptions are made, the subject seems to depart from the world of reality. One frequent objection centers on the contention that numerous important aberrations and exceptions to theory are ignored. In response to this criticism, it should be said that major aberrations can be and are considered; however, all aberrations cannot be completely identified without first understanding the theoretical system. To be useful, theory, including the theory of gravitation as well as economic theory, need not conform to all possible technical aberrations of the real world. Certainly the theory of gravitation is no less useful because Wilbur and Orville got off the ground. As a matter of fact, the theory is all the more valuable because of this exception!

A homely, but nevertheless relevant, illustration about how most people think of a closed door may demonstrate the significance and the importance of theory. The "general theory" is that if we walk up to a door and turn the handle, it will open. This is a useful although simplified theory that may prove to be reasonably accurate. At the same time, it could be disastrously inaccurate if applied to the door of a strange house, on an unfamiliar street, in a strange town at 3.00 A.M. on a dark evening. Because it is exceedingly simplified, there are many other circumstances in which the conventional "general theory" about opening a door is not realistic. The door may be locked, it may be nailed shut, it may be operated by an electric eye or it may lead a man to a powder room. For that matter, the door knob may be useless without a general understanding (another theory) that turning it will open the door—but this knowledge was also assumed, wasn't it? Probing the aberrations most likely to exist is a necessary exercise, but before granting the license to investigate assumptions and examine aberrations in economics, a basic understanding of economic theory is required.

A second criticism of economic theory is that for many reasons it cannot always be varified or refuted by controlled and explicit empirical testing. This circumstance simply has to be accepted by budding and antiquated scholars alike as the best of the rather poor alternatives that life offers. Unfortunately, much of human behavior, and as a consequence numerous areas of inquiry in the social sciences, are plagued by the inability to perform tightly controlled lab experiments. War, love, attitudes, environment, success, and intelligence are a modest sample of important matters that are difficult to analyze in terms of concrete facts and conclusions in controlled laboratory settings.

What conclusions and implications can we draw from this discussion? In the simple and forthright manner befitting any theory:

1. Man is a *model man*, living, acting, and reacting on the basis of thousands of theories. Many theories, such as our theory about doors, are so commonly accepted, simple, and irrelevant to contemporary problems that they receive little or no attention.

2. Economic theory, like any theory, is expressed as a model or road map—a simplified prototype of reality that requires testing and validation.

3. Often the most interesting and valuable aspects of economic models surface when we examine aberrations and exceptions to them. The policy prescription for a locked door, as one of several possible aberrations, is a key that fits (and a prayer that the door is not nailed shut). We will gain access to economic understanding in a similar fashion.

## Problems in Economic Reasoning

Errors in economic reasoning can lead to the wrong conclusions about the very economic events we are trying to understand. Several problems common to economic reasoning are: (*a*) economic jargon, (*b*) the fallacy of composition, (*c*) extremity of position, (*d*) cause-and-effect errors, (*e*) false analogies, and (*f*) preconceptions.

### ECONOMIC JARGON

Terminology is one of the most troublesome problems for beginning students of economics. As in most other subjects, the beginner in economics is inundated with unfamiliar terms and definitions. Some of these are unavoidable because scientists in any field often need more precise definitions than does the man in the street. For example, as noted previously, "capital" to the economist describes real or physical assets like machinery, while many people conceive of "capital" as money or corporate bonds. The use of dual terminology is another problem in economics. You already know that "factors of production" and "resources" are comparable. Similarly, the terms "theory" and "model" often are used in describing the process of simplifying or generalizing. Needless to say, the jargon dilemma is something we could well do without, yet there are instances in which it cannot be avoided. Much of the semantic problem can be overcome if the reader makes it a point to learn unfamiliar terms as they are encountered and if the writer avoids unnecessary confusion, a bargain the latter will keep.

## THE FALLACY OF COMPOSITION

The fallacy of composition describes the common mistake of reasoning that because a particular theory or conclusion is accurate for an individual, it necessarily applies to an entire group. As an example, assume that *everyone in a class* increases his study efforts by 20 percent under the theory that grades will rise. If only a few individuals devoted more effort to their studies, their grades should improve, but if the professor grades on a "curve," widespread additional effort may have little or no impact. Consider another example. One firm may be able to increase its profits by producing more yogi robes because consumers are demanding more of them. Can we conclude that all firms will be able to increase profits by producing more yogi robes? Not necessarily, since the action of the producing group may result in excess supplies of yogi robes which may drive prices down for all firms. In short, the fallacy of composition can trap the unwary who fail to consider carefully whether or not the sum of all parts does in fact constitute a whole. *In economics, what is true for the particular may not be true in general.*

## EXTREMITY OF POSITION

Quite often in discussing economic problems, extreme positions are assumed by parties whose opinions or values are in conflict. Consider, for example, the question of a guaranteed income that would provide all Americans with a minimum standard of living. On one hand, there is the notion that making minimum incomes available to all persons creates disincentives, and that persons now working but still living in poverty will stop working altogether. Thus, one could conclude that a guaranteed-income plan would create a need for increasing amounts of funds since it would subsidize people for being lazy. The opposite extreme on this issue is the theory that an adequate income will encourage people to upgrade their status, causing positive incentive effects. A similar misunderstanding is perpetuated by activist college students who classify the establishment as being in dire need of total overthrow and by conservative members of the establishment who classify all college students as unkempt long-hairs in need of the hickory switch. Both examples are oversimplified and encumbered by a very loose use of facts, theory, and policy. A good deal more factual information is required because the opposing theories are far too general, policy alternatives are underspecified, many relevant characteristics are ignored, and the entire process of thought is so heavily normative that the only likely result will be further argument.

## CAUSE AND EFFECT

A fourth common error in economic reasoning involves misuse of causation. Cause-and-effect relationships are important in economics, but causation must be carefully analyzed. It is hardly correct, for example, to conclude that since beagles howl in the evening, the din created causes the moon to rise. Similarly, it is quite inappropriate to conclude that a stock-market crash causes economic depression. Once again, we simply do not have enough information and have not taken enough facts into account to reach these conclusions. Just as more fundamental matters of physiology, environment, and astronomy cause beagles to howl and the moon to rise, more basic economic factors create stock-market crashes *and* economic depressions. When looking at cause-and-effect relationships, it is most important to look beyond the simple statistical properties of events. A theory of relationship is valued because of its logical and analytical soundness, not because of fortuitous circumstances.

## FALSE ANALOGIES

The false analogy is a fifth error in economic reasoning. A 4.0 grade-point record for one person is a rather weak basis for expecting that his brother will achieve the same. Similarly, it is incorrect to maintain that because the Irish and Polish immigrants who once settled in American slums were capable of rising from the poverty of that era the same can be expected today from the poor nonwhite. There are several significant differences between the two groups, not the least of which is the ability of the former to mask their ethnic origins and become assimilated into a relatively homogeneous white community. Like the errors in reasoning discussed above, the false analogy leads us nowhere at best.

## PRECONCEPTIONS

Many individuals have preconceived notions or biases on economic issues. A legitimate learning experience requires dissociation from any viewpoint that may be based upon normative preconceptions. Initiating an inquiry on an issue with a preconceived answer, and then attempting to develop supporting evidence for one's preconception is so bald a violation of objectivity that one can only hope it will remain unrecognized. Many examples of self-interest can be found in so-called "economic reasoning." In a typical AFL-CIO newsletter, strong cases are made for wage increases, a shorter workweek, or fewer legal restrictions upon unions. At the same time, a casual glance through the *Wall Street Journal* frequently will yield equally cogent arguments for lower wages, longer hours to increase production, and a need to strengthen public control of labor-union activities. Because controversies about economics often involve economic conflict, they may be imbued with layer upon layer of bias and preconceptions. Consequently, it is extremely important that objective information be obtained on economic issues, and that each individual *critically* evaluate *all* available information. Masking interest-group values as scientific inquiry is blatant deception.

Although individuals always like to feel that appealing to real-world experiences is valid, many pitfalls also prevail in such thinking. First of all, careful, systematic observations of many cases are needed to reach conclusions that may be valid. To generalize on the basis of a limited number of observations is extremely dangerous. Because you have observed one or two instances in which cats swim hardly provides a representative basis for reaching a general conclusion that all cats swim. Citing a small sample of factual evidence is a favorite defense mechanism to preserve preconceptions and it should be avoided in economics. In addition, it is important to recognize that two individuals can interpret facts in vastly different ways. Consider the case of a Sunday-school teacher who was trying to show her class how brave and faithful the early Christian martyrs were. She held up a picture of the Christians being thrown to the lions then asked her students for their thoughts. One especially sad-faced little boy said, "Look, teacher, this poor little lion doesn't have anyone!" Even facts must be handled with care, as most of us know.

### D. ECONOMIC MODELS AND TOOLS OF ANALYSIS

Models, as we have seen, are used to improve understanding in economics, and these models employ certain tools of analysis that are sometimes unfamiliar to beginning students. It is important to understand these analytical tools because their correct use can help to make economic theory less difficult.

### Graphs and Functional Relations

Economic relationships and models are presented in graphic form for many of the same reasons that engineers construct prototype models of airplanes and computers, physicians dissect cadavers, and football coaches construct model plays and formations. A graph is one convenient way of expressing the relationship between two economic measures, usually called *economic variables*. The visual basis for a graph, illustrated in Figure 2, is divided into quadrants (fourths) by a vertical and horizontal axis or line intersecting at 90° angles. A numerical scale is shown on each axis to measure the economic variables. At the intersection point, called the "origin" (point 0 in Figure 2), both variables have a value of zero. All numerical values above the horizontal axis have positive values that increase as one moves up the vertical axis, away from the origin. All values to the right of the vertical axis have positive values that increase as one moves to the right on the horizontal axis. For the most part economics uses the gold upper right-hand quadrant, because this quadrant is the only one of the four in which all values measured on both axes are positive.

As an example of the use of graphs, let us examine a student's level of performance in a class by proposing a crude relationship between grades and effort as represented by time spent studying. This model or theory is shown in Figure 2 as a series of dots connected by the broken line s associating the common numerical value for the two variables, percentage grade and study hours per week. The vertical axis is a numerical representation of percentage scores achieved on tests, and the horizontal axis numerically depicts hours of study. Line s is frequently referred to as a "schedule" or a

**FIGURE 2** Graphs and Functional Relations

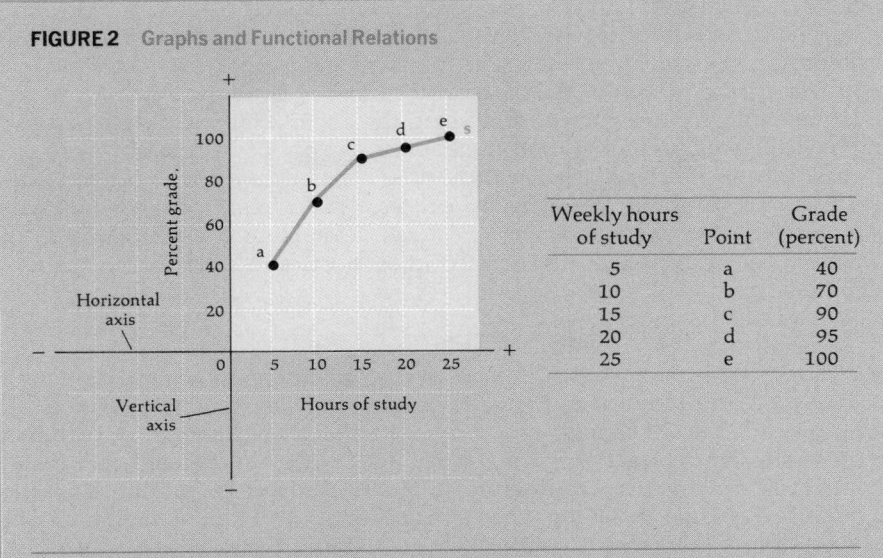

| Weekly hours of study | Point | Grade (percent) |
|---|---|---|
| 5 | a | 40 |
| 10 | b | 70 |
| 15 | c | 90 |
| 20 | d | 95 |
| 25 | e | 100 |

*Using a Graph.* The functional relationship between two variables can be plotted on a graph. The graph is based upon four quadrants established by two axes. The intersection of a vertical and horizontal axis is a zero-zero point, and the upper righthand quadrant depicts positive values for both variables. A schedule such as s is derived by plotting the values for hours of study and percent grade on their respective axes as one point and connecting those points.

"curve." The importance of schedule s is that it does reveal the existence of a functional relationship between study time and grades. Mathematicians describe a *functional relationship* as one in which the value of one variable depends upon another, where *f* denotes functional dependence. Thus, in this example we can write

Grades = function of study hours *or* grades = *f* (study hours)

In Figure 2 a grade of 40 percent is associated with 5 hours of study, a grade of 70 percent is associated with 10 hours of study, a grade of 80 percent is associated with 15 hours of study, and so forth. The association between grades and effort is a *direct* relationship because grades increase as study hours increase, and decrease as they decrease.

We can easily alter the facts examined in a graph by changing the variables. For example, if we are interested in the relationship between hours of study per week and hours spent dating per week, we might change the vertical axis from a numerical measure of grades to a numerical measure of dating hours. Note that the relationship which would then be depicted is *negative* or *inverse;* that is, *more* study hours imply *fewer* dating hours and fewer study hours imply more dating hours.

Graphs showing functional relationships between variables are a useful way to depict a theory, but it should be apparent that such a model can be based upon poorly specified theory. Oversimplification, incomplete or erroneous models, poor comprehension of a problem, bad predictions, and poor policies may result. For example, grades are related also to intelligence, quality and method of instruction, past achievement, and other variables. It is important to recognize that schedule s in our model is incomplete and deserves critical scrutiny. All factors not directly brought out by a model must be explicitly recognized, something the above example did not do. We might do this by assuming that intelligence, quality of instruction, and past grades do not affect the grade–study-time relationship, for example. Once we know more about the learning process, these restrictive assumptions can be released, and perhaps we can be more complete in our analysis. This is similar to the approach that is used in economics in establishing theories and models.

### Numerical Relationships: Marginal Values

*Marginal* means change or additional. When a change in one variable such as study hours produces a change in a related or dependent variable such as grades, the grade change is a *marginal value*. For example, if a student takes a ski trip, his action typically results in some marginal (additional) amount of satisfaction or pleasure. Similarly, a rise in income typically generates a change in saving; that is, additional or marginal saving. If one less ski trip is taken, satisfaction may be lost and there is a negative marginal value. Similarly, when income declines, marginal saving may be negative, as Figure 3 reveals.

Figure 3 portrays a hypothetical relationship between income and saving. This model reveals that as income changes by $5, the marginal amount of saving associated with the change is $1. In economics, we usually use Δ to denote change or a marginal value. Denoting income by $Y$ and saving by $S$, we can say: $\Delta S$ of $1 is associated with $\Delta Y$ of $5, as shown by the gold area of the figure. This is true whether we go from $Y = \$20$ to $Y = \$15$, or from $Y = \$15$ to $Y = \$20$. The only difference is that in the first instance $\Delta S = -\$1$ and in the latter $\Delta S = +\$1$. Accordingly, the functional relationship of Figure 3 is such that a $5 change in income produces a

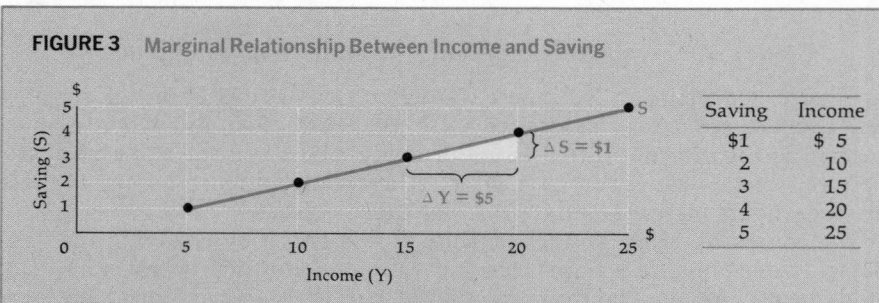

**FIGURE 3**   Marginal Relationship Between Income and Saving

| Saving | Income |
|--------|--------|
| $1 | $ 5 |
| 2 | 10 |
| 3 | 15 |
| 4 | 20 |
| 5 | 25 |

*Income and Saving.* The functional relationship between income (Y) and saving (S) is described by saving schedule S. As income (measured on the horizontal axis) changes in amounts of $5, saving (measured on the vertical axis) changes by $1. Marginal or additional amounts of saving (ΔS) and income (ΔY) are shown between any two points on saving schedule S. Note that the slope of schedule S is ΔS/ΔY, or 1/5 = .2, meaning that for every $1 increase (decrease) in income, saving will increase (decrease) by 20 cents.

change of $1 in saving. The saving–income relationship shown in Figure 3 can be expressed as follows:

$$\text{Saving} = \text{a function of income}$$
$$S = f(Y)$$
$$S = 0.2(Y)$$

If we simply specify alternative levels of income as $Y = \$5$, $\$10$, and $\$15$, the level of saving is computed as 0.2 or 20 percent of $Y$ (when $Y = \$10$, $S = 0.2Y$ or $\$2$).

Figure 3 is a very general model because we have not recognized the impact of expectations regarding prices, employment, or income on the saving-income relationship. When an economic theory ignores other relevant variables or fails to specify the relationship between two variables completely, the letter $u$ is used to designate these errors or omissions. More realistically, then, saving is a function of income and the error term, $u$:

$$S = f(Y, u)$$

Graphs and numerical relationships are not important in themselves, but you will find them to be very useful tools in economics. For that reason, a careful review of marginal values and the plotting of functional relationships is worthwhile.

## REVIEW

### Summary

1. Scarcity constitutes the economic problem in its most primitive form. Because of the scarcity of resources, goods are available in limited supplies, and we study the way mankind chooses to use goods and resources. Economics relies on several other fields in the social sciences such as history, sociology, and political science in describing the economy of a society.

2. Mankind's quest to overcome scarcity necessarily forces consideration of the prices of goods and resources, interdependence and cooperation, choice, conflict, and freedom—the immediate consequences of unlimited wants and a limited ability to fulfill wants.

3. Factors of production include those which are human—labor and entrepreneurial resources—and those which are property—natural and capital resources. A society utilizes resources and distributes the goods and services produced by scarce resources through a system of economic organization.

4. Economic reasoning relies upon observation of facts, development of theory, and application and evaluation of policy to economize in the use of scarce resources. For clarity of reasoning it is important to distinguish between normative (should-be) and positive (what-is) economics. Economic theory is drawn from and must relate to reality, but economic theory or models may appear to be unrealistic because theory is a simplified generalization of the real world.

5. It is not difficult to fall into pitfalls in thinking about economic matters. Among the more common traps are economic jargon, the fallacy of composition, extremity of position, questionable cause-and-effect relations, false analogies, preconceptions, and different perceptions of fact.

6. Economists use analytical tools to illustrate and clarify economic theory and relationships. Graphs are so frequently used that it is difficult for a student not familiar with them to fully comprehend a beginning course in economics. Numerical relationships are also important, as is the marginal concept. There is nothing difficult about marginal values if the reader will spend a little time in reviewing these tools, a task which will best economize a scarce resource of all students—time.

### Identify the Following Concepts and Terms

- economic goals
- prices and scarcity
- marginal values
- fallacy of composition
- capital resources
- factors of production
- schedule
- functional relationships
- normative and positive economics
- economic theory

### Questions to Answer

1. Suppose numerous individuals living in a large metropolitan center decide to seek remedies for air-pollution problems caused by high population densities, industry, and the many conveniences of contemporary life. Explain how political economy and scarcity relate to this problem. (Include consideration of prices, interdependence, choice, conflict, and freedom.)

2. The use of resources in producing goods and services depends heavily on technology. How are natural resources in part the product of technology? Is it possible that technology is dependent upon being "embodied" in capital, and if so, how?

3. Evaluate the statements:
   (a) "Economics is purely objective and positive."
   (b) "Economic theory is of no value because it is unrealistic."

4. Give several contrasting examples of positive and normative statements about economic issues and problems of which you are aware.

5. One frequently used economic model is the functional relationship between the *price* of goods and services such as lemonade or a college education and the amount or *quantity* consumers will demand. Can you guess whether the relationship is direct or inverse? (It is inverse.) Graph the inverse relationship below for price (tuition) and the number of students in college. In other words, if tuition were $10,000; $6,000; $2,000; and $1,000 per year, what approximate proportion or quantity of your graduating high-school classmates might be in college?

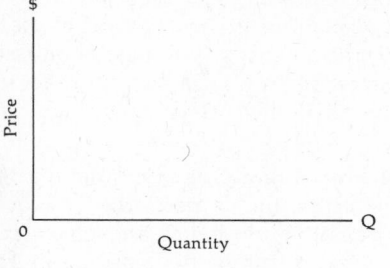

| Price | Quantity |
|---|---|
| $10,000 | _____ |
| 6,000 | _____ |
| 2,000 | _____ |
| 1,000 | _____ |

# CHAPTER 3
## Overview of the Market Economy

A broad overview of the entire economy is needed to understand how the activities of millions of diverse economic units merge together to form an operational economic system. This chapter explains the economic organization of a society and stresses the major features of a market economy, since this form of economic organization characterizes several major nations in the developed world. We first consider (in Part A) how scarcity leads to a need for economic organization and then trace the development of selected ideas in a political economy. The major operational features of a market economy are explored next (Part B), and with this background, a model of circular-income flows is introduced (Part C).

An *economic system* is the way in which a nation organizes its economic affairs in order to make decisions about the use of scarce resources. Were there no limits to the resources available and capable of fulfilling wants, the economic organization of a nation might not be very important. As it is, however, the production possibilities of any nation are limited, and in all known instances societies from the most primitive to the most advanced are characterized by a systematic way of organizing economic matters.

### Production Possibilities

Figure 1 is a model of our earlier discussion of scarcity in Chapter 2, indicating the general direction taken in studying economics. The production possibilities shown for a hypothetical economy describe the nature of the economic problem of scarcity. Assume that the model economy of Id produces only two products (food and weapons) by transforming a constant supply of resources into outputs in the production process. When all resources are employed as fully and efficiently as possible, total output of the two products in this economy can be any of the combinations indicated by a production-possibilities curve or "frontier" such as PF drawn from the tabular data shown in Figure 1. For example, all resources can be used to produce 1,000 units of food and zero weapons (point e), 1,000 weapons and zero units of food (point a), 900 weapons and 400 units of food (point b), and so forth. Now, what does this model economy reveal?

First, it is apparent that scarce resources can be used to produce alternative output (weapons or food in this simple example), *but there is a limit* to the amount that can be produced. The limit that can be produced is the production frontier labeled PF in Figure 1. It is not currently possible to

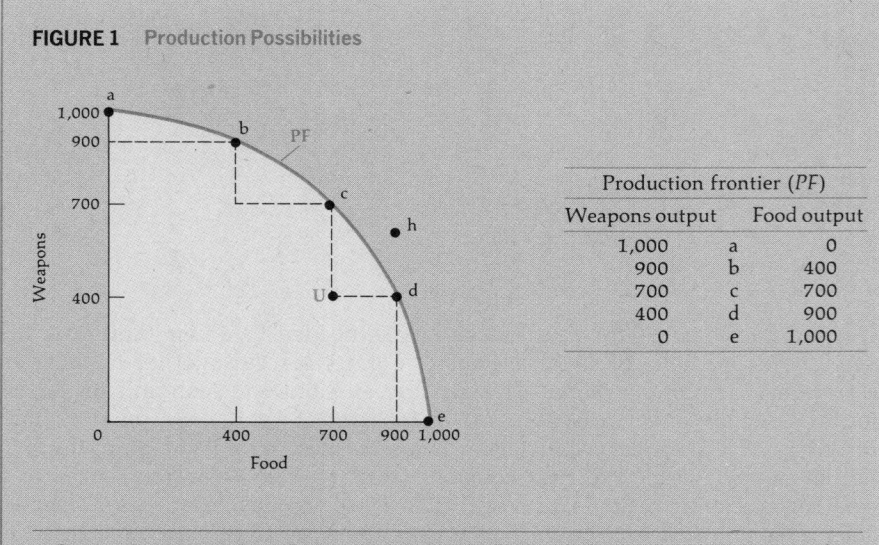

**FIGURE 1** Production Possibilities

| Production frontier (*PF*) | | |
| --- | --- | --- |
| Weapons output | | Food output |
| 1,000 | a | 0 |
| 900 | b | 400 |
| 700 | c | 700 |
| 400 | d | 900 |
| 0 | e | 1,000 |

*Production Alternatives.* An economy must decide how to use its resources to produce two alternative goods, such as weapons and food. Only by using resources fully and efficiently can the production-frontier levels of output be achieved at points *a, b, c, d,* or *e.* Somehow a decision must be made about how much of each good to produce, a choice required because production alternatives exist. As more food is produced, a greater amount of weapons output must be sacrificed because resources are not perfectly adaptable. Thus, the opportunity cost of a move from *a* to *b* is the 100 weapons sacrificed to produce 400 additional units of food. As the nation produces more food, increasing opportunity costs set in as 200, 300, and 400 units of weapons are sacrificed, and less and less food output is gained when a nation shifts its constant supply of resources from weapons to food production.

produce 600 weapons *and* 900 units of food at point *h* simply because there are not enough resources to do so. A nation could produce any combination of goods below the production frontier *PF,* such as that represented at point *U.* Needless to say, this is not as desirable as producing on the production frontier because the maximum possible output is not being produced with limited resources. Because less total output would be produced for any combination of goods below the production frontier (in the gold area of Figure 1), we presume for the moment that Id would not willingly select attainable output levels other than those on the production frontier.

Second, choice is inherent in economic affairs. If all resources are efficiently employed, the economy of Id can produce many different combinations of the two goods on the production frontier; for example, Id could produce at point *b* or at point *d.* Decisions must be made about how much of a good is produced, who does the producing, and for whom the model economy of Id produces—those wanting more food or those wanting more weapons.

Third, the presence of scarcity-enforced alternatives and choice in our model economy suggests the need for some measure of value or prices.

By moving from point *a* to *b*, 100 weapons are sacrificed for 400 units of food. This means that the per unit value of food (its price) is one-fourth as great as the value of weapons; otherwise, a society would not elect such a move.

Fourth, resources are imperfectly adaptable to the production of different goods. Note that the quantity of weapons output forgone to augment food output increases in moving from points *a* . . . *e* as more and more food is produced. The alternative output forgone in producing more of a good is termed *opportunity cost*. In other words, the opportunity cost of going from zero to 400 units of food is 100 weapons. Successive increases in food production from points *b* to *c* . . . *e* require the sacrifice of *more* and *more* weapons. For example, between points *d* and *e* food output increases from 900 to 1,000, or by 100 units, but 400 weapons must be sacrificed. Why does the opportunity cost of food increase? Simply because scarce resources are *imperfectly* adaptable to alternative uses. Plumbers (as a human resource) are poor substitutes for dentists, the Arizona desert is not as readily adaptable to growing wheat as are the flatlands of Kansas, and labor is a rather imperfect substitute for capital in the form of a complex computer system. As the production of food is increased, resources that are less productive in creating food output must be used. The increasing opportunity costs due to imperfections or inflexibilities in resource substitution explain why a production frontier is concave or bowed outward from the origin.

What have we learned about the economy of Id?

1. Scarce resources make it possible to produce only a certain combinations of goods and services as denoted by a production frontier.

2. It is necessary for a nation to choose among certain combinations of alternative outputs, which dictates some given pattern of resource allocation.

The need to choose between different goods leads to a pricing need. Some measure of value or worth—a price for food and for weapons—is required to help a society decide what and how much to produce with scarce resources. Money is a characteristic of the economic organization of societies, in part because it is needed to facilitate exchange and determine "value."

## Money

*Money* is anything that a society believes is money and it has value in relation to the available supply. Essentially, money functions as a medium of exchange and as a store and standard of value. Two conditions determine the usefulness of money in performing these tasks: (*a*) Money must be acceptable as a representation of value, and (*b*) the supply of money must be limited.

Money as a medium of exchange is far superior to simple barter. Barter is cumbersome because of the noncoincidence of wants and multiplicity of values it entails. A college coed might find it difficult to secure the services of a professor for a course in economics through the barter process. Assume that the professor needs three little red wagons and that the coed is willing to pay a price of 20 hours of labor (in addition to study and class time) to attend a course in economics. In the first place, the exchange would be difficult to complete because of the noncoincidence of wants. Access to the particular course the coed desires would be further complicated by university administrators, who might prefer scotch to red wagons. Barter requires a vast number of different value equivalents for products and resources. In our simple example, the three persons involved must determine that $X$ units of scotch = $Y$ units of red wagons = $Z$ units of coed labor. It is not at all difficult to see why barter is inferior to the use of some item that can serve as a medium of exchange.

## COMMODITY MONEY

*Commodity money* describes the use of a physical good as a common denominator or monetary unit to facilitate exchange. At one time or another in various societies furs, beads, slaves, wives, cattle, red-headed woodpecker scalps, and nails have been accepted monetary units. An edict declaring nails or gold to be a nation's monetary unit does simplify the barter process described above, but commodity monies present certain difficulties too. To exchange the nearly $1 trillion of output produced each year in the United States today for gold as a unit of exchange would be a hollow dream, if for no other reason than that the nation's supply of gold is only about $12 billion (and this is about one-fourth of the world's supply at that)! Commodity money also is awkward as a medium of exchange. Commodities such as leather, tobacco, or wives vary in the degree to which they represent a reasonable standard or store of value. For example, a wife may deteriorate with the passage of time; a commodity may be difficult to store, depending upon its bulk and consumption properties; and a commodity is not always easily divisible into the smaller units that are needed to exchange goods.

## NONCOMMODITY MONEY

Thus it is that as societies have become more sophisticated and complex, they have turned increasingly to *noncommodity money* as represented by paper bills or metal coins that serve as a conveniently divisible medium of exchange as well as a standard and store of value. Contemporary money such as the dollar is of no value in itself; rather, it is desired simply because it provides access to goods or services that satisfy wants. Contemporary monetary systems are a social convention, and money is accepted as money because everyone accepts the same monetary unit. Although money *may* be backed by hoards of gold, there is no *economic* reason to dig a hole in the ground to find gold and then turn around and bury it again for safe keeping. The real backing for money is its acceptability and relative scarcity in a society, not the fact that it has intrinsic commodity (gold) backing.

## Specialization

In a simple society, the specialized use of resources may be limited, since individuals tend to produce and fulfill most of their own immediate wants. Even the lowly ant, however, does practice specialization in a limited way; some ants function as warriors and others serve in a maternal capacity. Most primitive societies assign their members different responsibilities; depending upon their talents and prowess, individuals may hunt, fish, fight, or cook. Division of labor or specialization permits the best use of resources and may increase the total output of an economy because each participant can become more skilled in performing a limited number of tasks. Specialization is advantageous because: (a) it allows human resources to work more efficiently and rapidly on a few tasks, (b) there is less redundancy in using man-made capital resources as aids to production, and (c) more sophisticated capital resources may be utilized than would be possible otherwise. The advantage of specialization was aptly illustrated by Adam Smith some two centuries ago in his now-famous book, *The Wealth of Nations*. Smith observed that if one man attempted to make pins from start to finish, he could produce only a few each day, whereas several individuals, all of whom specialized in certain aspects of the production of pins, might be able to produce thousands of pins per day. Specialization becomes important to an economy which can produce only a limited amount of output.

### Economic Organization

Nations must organize economic affairs in some fashion because decisions must be made about the use and allocation of resources. Existing evidence indicates that some societies have succeeded in pushing back scarcity barriers in remarkable and very significant ways. Nevertheless, even the most affluent nations today have achieved only a partial solution to the scarcity problem. The dilemma of scarcity and choice is affected by the system of economic organization adopted by a society, as well as by the availability of resources to produce goods and services.

### THE MEANING OF ECONOMIC ORGANIZATION

Civilizations have used various organizational techniques to bring order to economic activity, which would otherwise be chaotic. It is nearly impossible to imagine the carrying out of millions of economic decisions in the absence of any type of economic organization. Too many firms constructing too many houses or shoes, or supplying too few beans, pencils, and lawn mowers could lead to economic disaster. The decisions of too many or too few to seek a quantity of goods or resources consistent with available supplies affect everyone in a society. The fact that man is intensely preoccupied with his own self-interest makes the achievement of economic cooperation and organization on a society-wide scale all the more astounding.

Several methods have been used to preserve order in this potentially chaotic state of economic affairs. One method has been custom, handed down by families or society. Authoritarianism or edicts by a supreme power (augmented by requisite enforcement) have also been used to shape the economic community. In the last few centuries still a third form of economic organization, the market system, has come to the fore in many parts of the world.

A *market system* is a form of economic organization in which individual decisions to produce and consume goods and services and to sell or purchase resources determine how resources are allocated—how "choice" problems are resolved. Consumers voice their feelings about the desirability of acquiring the output of scarce resources by bidding dollars, pounds, or francs for products, a process which helps establish a price. Producers respond to market prices as a reflection of consumer demand by purchasing resources, producing goods and services, and supplying their output in a system of product markets similar to that shown in Figure 2. Prices are thus established for products and, in addition, because producers demand resources as factors of production, resource-market prices are also established. The market system is an immensely complicated and closely knit pricing mechanism that reflects the decisions of the buyers and sellers of products as well as those of the buyers and sellers of scarce resources. The circular relationship in Figure 2 shows pricing in the market system to be an interactive process between *two* markets: Producer demand for factors of production in the *resource market* is caused by consumer demand for goods and services in the *product market*. Prices thus represent the key organizing tool through which resource-allocation choices are communicated, a matter which we shall say a good deal more about in a moment.

The need to reduce relative scarcity and the related ability of mankind to

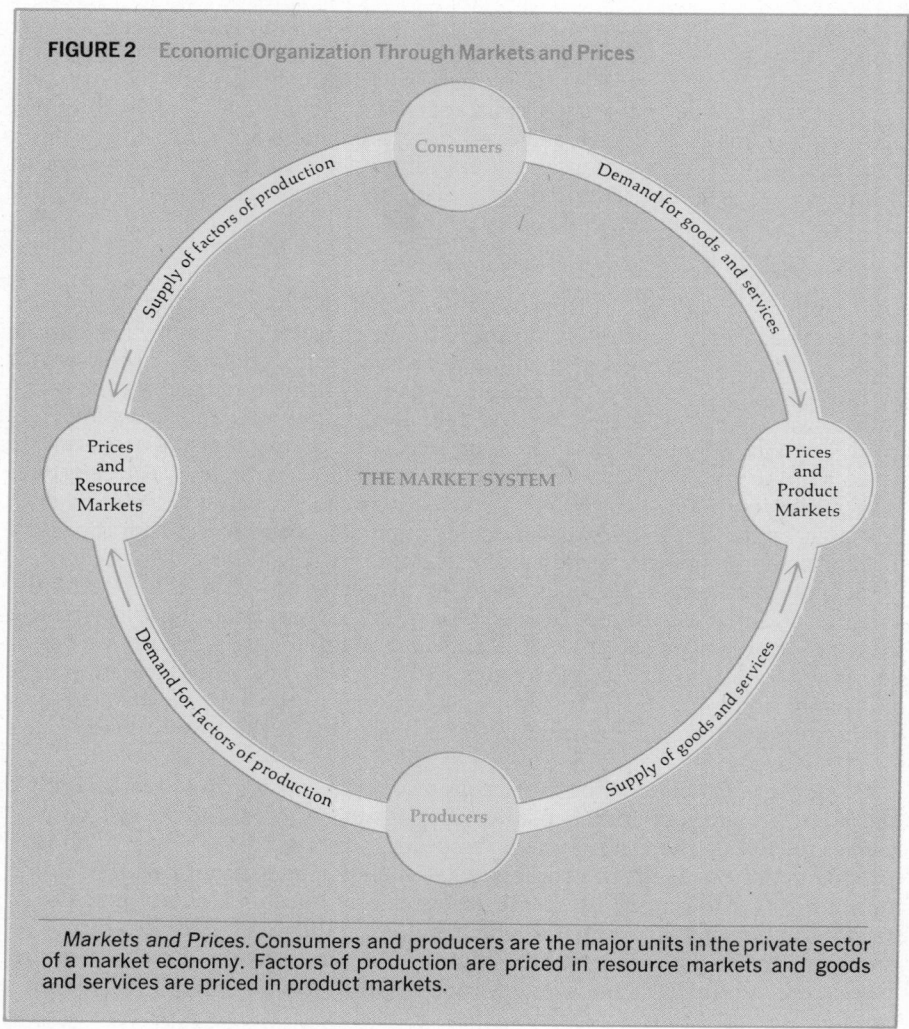

**FIGURE 2**  Economic Organization Through Markets and Prices

Consumers

Supply of factors of production

Demand for goods and services

Prices and Resource Markets

THE MARKET SYSTEM

Prices and Product Markets

Demand for factors of production

Supply of goods and services

Producers

*Markets and Prices.* Consumers and producers are the major units in the private sector of a market economy. Factors of production are priced in resource markets and goods and services are priced in product markets.

function in a formal society while managing his economic affairs has long intrigued renown thinkers. Although many philosophers have contributed significantly to the development of economic thought, consideration of the works of Adam Smith, Karl Marx, and John Maynard Keynes serves to capsulize many of the great ideas concerning economic organization.

## ADAM SMITH TELLS IT LIKE IT WAS

One of the foremost eighteenth-century philosophers to observe the birth of the Industrial Revolution and the market system was Adam Smith, a Scotsman who spent much of his life teaching moral philosophy at the University of Glasgow. Smith was interested in the economic order prevailing in the universe he knew, and he was heavily indebted to some of the great philosophers of his time, including Locke, Quesney, and Petty. His treatise, *The Wealth of Nations* (1776), vividly described eighteenth-century England and the emerging market economy. The English economy at that time was beset with numerous government restrictions on wages, prices, migration, and international trade. A central thesis of Smith's book was that the economic organization of society was best accomplished through a laissez faire policy—minimization of government control. According to Smith, the individual's pursuit of self-interest best served the economic needs of society because, in hopes of gaining a profit, individuals were motivated to produce goods and supply scarce resources that others would purchase.

Competition was the "regulator" in Smith's description of the market economy. When the profit motive prompted a few persons to produce and supply goods and resources in a free and mobile society, others would be similarly motivated. Competition would impose restraints on the participants, ultimately prohibiting any one individual from charging excessive prices to earn high profits. Accordingly, if firms produced and sold goods in a competitive environment in which no one party was powerful enough to affect prices, all would be forced to accept a competitively determined market price which limited profits.

Smith reasoned that when producers sought their own best interests in the form of individual profits, resources would be allocated in the most efficient way—in a manner directed by the preferences and tastes of consumers. Furthermore, competition for the scarce resources needed to produce the goods desired by society would result in the regulation of the incomes of resource owners according to a large and impersonal market. For example, when society decided there was a need for more bone buttons and fewer cloth-covered buttons, the market system would automatically adjust in the following way:

1. Firms producing bone buttons would be able to charge higher prices and earn greater profits, whereas producers of cloth-covered buttons would tend to experience lower prices and profits.

2. To produce more of the desired product, additional resources would be allocated to the bone-button producers, whereas fewer resources would be used to produce the less desired product because of declining prices and profits.

3. Upon learning that it was profitable to make bone buttons, new firms would enter the market and increase production. This would create down-

ward pressures on the prices and profits of other producers in these industries most favored by consumer demand.

In short, increases in the quantity of bone buttons supplied in a competitive market would provide a check upon excess profits and prices. Society's demand for a product ultimately would result in the allocation of additional scarce resources to those products most in demand. Moreover, resources capable of being used most effectively in more favored markets would ultimately move to those markets. In essence, Adam Smith's pure market economy, sometimes labeled "capitalism," was depicted as a self-regulating system in which the guardian of the economic welfare of society was a price-directed communications network guided by the profit motive and competitive markets. Scarce resources were economized (i.e., allocated efficiently) by the "invisible hand" of consumer votes being cast in the marketplace.

Adam Smith's laissez faire philosophy was tempered by his recognition of the economic problems and issues that could emerge in a market system. Although he emphasized self-interest, profits, and competition, he also spoke of the need for government regulation in certain instances to ensure competition and mediate conflict in an impersonal market economy that might or might not meet all needs of a society. Karl Marx, a later philosopher, constructed his theory of a political economy on certain conflicts and aberrations he believed to be inherent in Smith's description of the market system.

## KARL MARX: DISCONTENTS ARISE

Karl Marx was a German political refugee who spent most of his literary life in London. Marx is most famous for *Das Kapital*, which first appeared almost a century after *The Wealth of Nations*. Mid-nineteenth-century England was then enduring the agony of the Industrial Revolution, which had just begun during Adam Smith's time. The barbaric and deplorable working conditions of labor and the masses of people living in abject poverty in the emerging industrial environment aroused other writers as well as Marx (notably Charles Dickens).

Marx argued that capitalism was predicated upon the exploitation of labor. According to Marx, all value resulting from production was ultimately due to man's past and present labor. While labor was the source of all value, Marx argued that the common worker was exploited because a portion of the value of his output was absorbed in the form of profits by capitalistic owners of other resources. According to Marx, capitalism survived by exploiting labor value, part of which was embodied in capital resources. Marx believed that the situation could only deteriorate—the rich would become richer and poverty would become self-perpetuating. As capitalist business firms expanded markets in their search for profits, subsistence-level wages would continue. In addition, as firms employed more capital resources, less labor would be directly employed, and increasing numbers of workers would find it impossible to obtain the jobs they needed to subsist. Marx also believed that the profit orientation of a capitalistic society was reinforced by the private ownership of valuable resources and by increasingly severe economic depressions which resulted in hardening social class lines.

Capitalism thus created the seeds of its own destruction which would alter the existing system of economic organization. Hardening class lines and a large army of unemployed and exploited proletariats would set the stage for political revolution and overthrow of the market economy. Revolution was not only inevitable; it was a goal to be pursued according to Marx, who encouraged workers in *The Communist Manifesto* to unite, since ". . . you have nothing to lose but your chains." The only permanent solution to the problem of economic organization, in the Marxian view, was abolition of private property and adoption of a communist system of economic organization which produced for all people instead of for a profit. The new system would be a classless society in which people would not be distinguished by wealth. Ultimately, concentrated ownership of scarce resources and economic conflict would no longer prevail.

Marx's thesis has met with both refutation and confirmation. One of the major errors in the Marxian notion that capitalism would collapse is that Marx failed to take adequate account of the effect of technology and economic growth, which create new jobs rather than destroying them. In the United States capitalism evolved into a less structured socioeconomic system because the age-old class system of Europe never fully formed here. Changes in attitudes and value structures became a norm in the United States, which wrestled with a democratic resolution to economic problems and conflict. However, one cannot take the Marxian challenge to the market system lightly. Modern-day descendents of Marxian theory have led to the establishment of the democratic-socialist form of economic organization common in Britain and certain other Western European nations. Revolutionary communism is an even more direct descendent of Marxian economic theory. Today, Russia, China, and several other nations rely on a centrally directed form of economic organization which is an outgrowth of the Marxian ideal.

## THE WORLD OF JOHN MAYNARD KEYNES

Even a brief account of the major economic ideas of the last two centuries would be incomplete without mention of John Maynard Keynes, an English economist whose major contributions to economic thought uprooted conventional economic ideas during the Great Depression of the 1930s. In his essay *The General Theory of Employment, Interest and Money,* Keynes expounded upon the means by which recurrent economic booms and recessions, which have been prevalent in the market system, could be mitigated. The "Keynesian revolution," as it is sometimes called, was significant because it offered both an explanation of and a remedy for the unemployment, declining incomes, and diminution of economic welfare that accompany an economic depression. Moreover, the Keynesian remedy did not require the violent overthrow of the market economy envisioned by Marx and his followers.

Prosperity in the Western world early in the twentieth century provided an unprecedented reduction in economic scarcity. This affluence came crashing down in the 1930s when unemployment rose and incomes fell precipitously.[1] There was no economic explanation of why millions who wanted to work

---

[1] The American economy, for example, produced $104 billion of final goods and services in 1929 and $56 billion four years later in 1933. As many as one out of every four persons seeking work was unable to find a job in 1933.

were unable to do so. Although Keynes did not develop a full explanation of the operation of a market economy, his lucid analysis refuted the idea accepted among contemporary economists who argued that prolonged economic depressions were impossible. The depths of economic despair reached in the 1930s were shown by Keynes to be a natural outgrowth of a decentralized market system. His explanation of the process of economic decline and stagnation will be discussed in detail later, but it is important to recognize here that Keynes called for active government policies to monitor the market economy. Thus, Keynes can be placed between Adam Smith's laissez faire thesis and the Marxian theory of complete government ownership and control of markets. Keynes demonstrated that economic imbalance could be corrected by government influencing the level of expenditures in a market system. He did not argue that government should supplant private expenditures and decision-making in a market economy. Rather, he viewed government spending as a *supplement* to be invoked to prevent economic slippage and preserve the market system of economic organization.

*To summarize:* Since Smith and Marx developed their ideas on political economy, much has happened both to our understanding of economics and to the way in which economic activity is organized. Scarcity of resources and the need to economize still prevail, although for some nations they are admittedly less severe than in past decades. In the days of Adam Smith, laissez faire was a dominant philosophy (even though less of a reality). Since the time of Marx, however, the trend throughout the world has been toward a more pervasive role for government—along the lines envisioned by Keynes. In some nations the contemporary system of economic organization is a close parallel to the result foreseen by Marx: The state owns many scarce resources and directly controls the economic process of resource allocation. In contrast, the American economy is sometimes described as a "free-enterprise society." While it is an enterprise society, it has never been and probably never will be free in an absolute sense. Instead, the United States and a large number of other nations rely on a "modified" market form of economic organization—a fusion of individual economic choice and public determination of economic choice. The *modified* or *mixed market economy*, henceforth simply called the "market system," is an alternative form of economic organization that differs both from Adam Smith's laissez faire visions and from centrally directed systems of economic organization that have their genesis in the ideas of Karl Marx.

## B. HOW A MARKET SYSTEM WORKS

One of our first tasks in comprehending the market system is to examine its primary characteristics. The two main features of a market system of economic organization are individuality and market determination of prices.

### Individuality

The individuality of producers, resource suppliers, and consumers is a primary characteristic of the market system. Individual freedom is stressed—freedom to own scarce resources privately, to work in enterprises and activities of one's choice, and to exercise a certain amount of choice in making decisions to consume the output of an economy.

## PRIVATE PROPERTY

Individual ownership of private property as an expression of individuality has been sustained by inheritance laws, but today it is not an absolute, unlimited right. Property ownership in a contemporary market economy is constrained in many ways. Government is a property owner in many instances. In addition, the privilege of private-property ownership and use carries with it the responsibility of behaving within the confines of accepted institutions and values. Business firms must provide some economic security for employees in the form of retirement, disability, and unemployment compensation, and there are restrictions on employing child labor or maintaining hazardous working conditions. Increasingly, private ownership of natural resources does not carry with it unrestrained rights to abuse the environment, as is shown by laws against water pollution and strip mining. Government may regulate or even relieve a resource owner of property when such action enhances the general welfare of society, provided that appropriate compensation is paid to the owner.

## ENTERPRISE

Freedom of market choice is another expression of individuality closely related to the ownership of property. For the most part, the market system allows individuals to select the occupation, temporary job, or business venture that best suits their tastes. However, there are also restrictions in this area. Despite individual views, selling wood alcohol as a cure for ailments ranging from Saint Vitus's dance to appendicitis is not allowed. Nor is an enterprising person allowed to charge exorbitant interest rates in lending money. False advertising and blatant packaging deception are frowned upon, and it is not legally possible to set up a riot stand to sell Molotov cocktails to dissident students. Restrictions on the right to establish enterprises are intended to prevent abuses which might negatively affect the general welfare.

## CONSUMER CHOICE

The freedom of choice of consumers is a third dimension to individuality in a market system. This freedom is particularly strategic in the market system because by casting dollar votes for products, consumers signal approval or disapproval back to the producers who use scarce resources to supply goods, and thus set resource allocation changes in motion. Again, however, the right of consumer choice is not absolute. It is sometimes legally controlled, depending upon its impact upon others in society. Anyone doubting this can attempt to purchase home-brewed corn mash or acquire a hydrogen bomb. The broader restraints on consumer choice arise through government which restrains consumer choice on behalf of the general welfare of society.

Despite restraints upon property ownership, enterprise, and consumption, a market system is characterized by a relatively high degree of individuality. However, individuality is a restricted right governed by the values and institutional rules of a society—as firms accustomed to dumping industrial sewage in open streams are now learning.

### Markets and Prices

Earlier we described the market system as a pricing network that directs production and allocates resources. Market determination of prices is a second characteristic of the market system. Just how prices are established and resources are allocated deserves further attention.

## DEMAND, SUPPLY, AND PRICE

A *market* denotes organized exchange between buyers and sellers of both products and resources. Prices are established in markets that mirror millions of individual decisions to buy and sell—to exchange products and resources. There are three important economic ideas that describe the way in which markets work: (*a*) the principle of demand, (*b*) the principle of supply, and (*c*) equilibrium price.

*The Principle of Demand*   *Demand* describes the quantities of a good consumers are able and willing to buy at alternative prices. *Demand for resources* similarly describes the quantities of resources producers would buy at different prices. Many factors such as consumer incomes and buyer preferences influence demand for a product, but common sense tells us that the price of any product is also important in determining the quantity people demand. By assuming that everything other than product price is constant, the *principle of demand* says that *the lower the price of a product, the more of a product consumers will buy; the higher the price, the less that will be purchased.* Intuition offers some validation of the principle of demand. An inverse price-quantity relation would obviously generally apply to the demand for: (*a*) higher education (compare differences in the quantity demanded by students at a "price" of $10,000 vs. $100 per semester); (*b*) shoes ($100 vs. $1 each); and (*c*) the resources employed by a firm, such as labor (the quantity of waiters hired at $20 vs. $1 per hour).

Figure 3(a) depicts the *inverse* or *negative functional relationship* between product price and the quantity of shirts demanded. The general reason for this inverse price-quantity relationship is that consumers have limited incomes; therefore, price acts as a barrier to consumption. In an attempt to obtain as much satisfaction as possible, some consumers will elect not to purchase various products at higher prices, but they may purchase larger quantities of goods at lower prices.

*The Principle of Supply*   *Supply* describes the quantities of goods that producers will offer at different product prices. In very general terms, we know that *at higher prices, more of a product is produced and offered in the market; the lower the price, the lower the quantity supplied.* This definition of the principle of supply applies generally to products like shirts and corn (as long as other complicating factors are ignored).[2] In general terms, the principle of supply is also applicable to resources simply because they are scarce. The principle of supply is depicted as a direct functional relation between price and quantity supplied in Figure 3(b). The quantity of a product supplied increases as price rises because producers incur costs in employing resources to produce goods and services. Consequently, firms will use resources to produce more food and less weapons, for example, in the measure that product price is sufficient to induce the transfer of resources

[2] At this point our concern with markets and prices is restricted to the briefest possible explanation of demand and supply. Many other considerations are important, however—a matter deferred to Chapter 14.

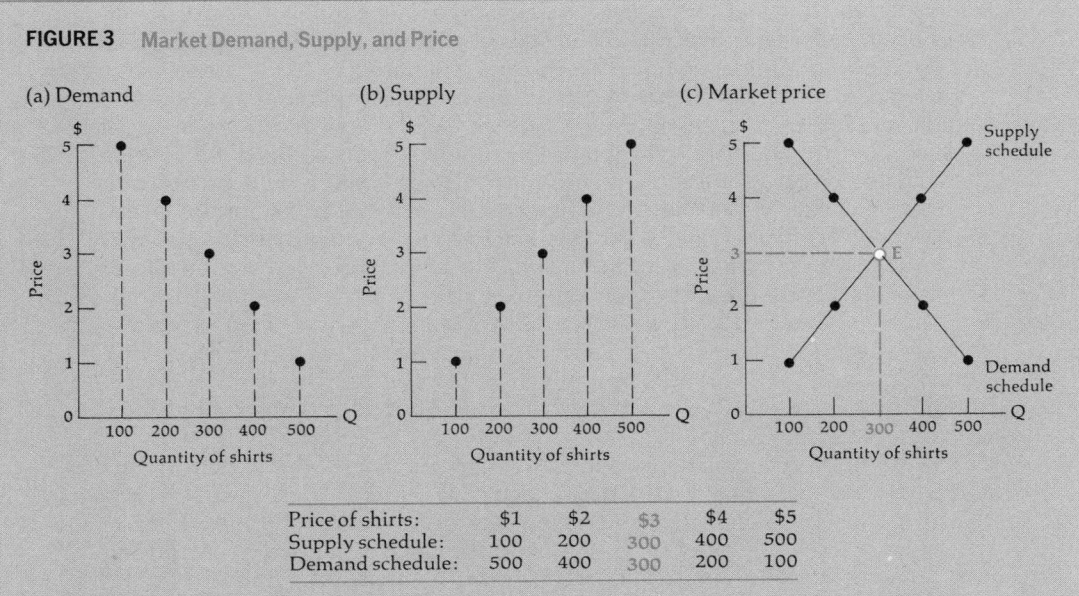

**FIGURE 3**   Market Demand, Supply, and Price

(a) Demand

(b) Supply

(c) Market price

| Price of shirts: | $1 | $2 | $3 | $4 | $5 |
|---|---|---|---|---|---|
| Supply schedule: | 100 | 200 | 300 | 400 | 500 |
| Demand schedule: | 500 | 400 | 300 | 200 | 100 |

*Principles of Demand, Supply, and Price.* Consumers purchase more of a product at lower prices than higher prices because product price is an obstacle to consumption. The quantity of a product producers supply increases as price increases and decreases as price decreases. This is because firms must hire scarce resources to increase output. The interaction of quantities supplied and demanded determine a market price. When supply = demand the market price is *stable* or in *equilibrium*. However, at a high price, excess quantities of a product are supplied and price falls. At low prices, a shortage exists and price rises until a stable price is achieved as shown in (c).

(remember, there are opportunity costs to using resources). At a lower product price the quantity of a product supplied is less, since fewer scarce resources can be employed at lower prices. Although we are ignoring many factors, the oversimplified model of the principle of supply shown in Figure 3(b) is adequate for the present. Simply remember that the supply decisions of all producers of a given product are "added up" into one market-supply quantity at each alternative price ($1, $2, and so on), as shown in the figure.

*Equilibrium Price*   Demand and supply measure prices and quantities for some product (or resource) and they interact to determine a market price. To keep our general understanding of price determination as uncluttered as possible, suppose we are talking about white shirts. Ignoring such factors as differences in quality, consumer incomes, and time, intuition once again explains how prices are set. Figure 3(c) develops a schedule (or curve) of demand and a schedule of supply by plotting the price-quantity relations for demand shown in 3(a) and supply shown in 3(b). The interaction of supply and demand determines market price at the point where the quantity pro-

43

ducers supply is equal to the quantity consumers demand. Thus, an *equilibrium* or *stable* market price of $3 is shown at point *E* in Figure 3(c) where the quantity supplied equals the quantity demanded (300 units). At a higher price, the quantity of shirts consumers demand is low, the quantity producers supply is large, and *market price will decline*. In Figure 3(c), for example, a price of $5 corresponds to market supply of 500, but market demand of only 100 units; thus, too much of the product will be supplied and market price will decline as some suppliers attempt to dispose of excess inventories. Conversely, at a price such as $1, the quantity demanded is large, quantity supplied is low, and *market price will rise* because of the shortage. In Figure 3(c), the quantity demanded at $1 is 500 units but producers supply only 100 units. Because the quantity demanded is greater than producers supply at a price of $1, consumers "bid up" prices; producers increase the quantity supplied as price rises; and at the higher equilibrium price of $3, the market is cleared of shirts because supply and demand are equal.

At this point in our discussion of the market system, there is no reason to become bogged down in the many technical features of demand, supply, and price. It is sufficient to keep in mind that demand and supply interact in a market system—as even young children know when they set up their first lemonade stand. At a very high price, demand for lemonade is not sufficient to clear market supply, whereas at low prices the problem of excess demand tends to prevail. The crucial point to remember is: Inequality between the quantities of a product demanded and supplied leads to price changes until some equilibrium (stable) price is reached where supply and demand quantities are equal.

## PRICE AS A RESOURCE-ALLOCATION DEVICE

A market price is established by the amount of a good supplied by producers in relation to consumer demand for that good. If consumers in a market economy decide they want more sandals, for example, this decision will normally cause the price of sandals to rise—an event which encourages producers to increase the quantity of sandals supplied. Product price signals information to the producer which suggests that his profit interests can be furthered by increasing the output of sandals. In contrast, if more sandals are offered than consumers desire, excess quantities of sandals accumulate in the market, ultimately causing price to fall. Declining prices then transmit a signal to the producing firms to cut back on the production of sandals and employ fewer resources. Accordingly, product prices play a crucial role in allocating scarce resources.

Of course, the market system of prices can be short-circuited. In a hypothetical dictatorship such as the kingdom of Id, the King can make these decisions. If the King of Id decrees that everyone must wear sandals (or go barefoot), markets and prices will be a good deal less important. The King of Id, as the central authority, can also manipulate the price signal. Had the King taken a course in economics at Harvard, he might decide to use markets to his advantage by not allowing others to produce or by supplying only a fraction of the sandals desired by his subjects. He might thus obtain a handsome price and perhaps a very large profit which he could use to finance a new war. On the other hand, he could end up with a revolt inspired by noblemen and peasants alike. Such a course of action by the King, however, would be a departure from use of the market system to organize economic activity.

The key link between resource utilization and goods produced is the price signal transmitted from the product market to the markets for factors of production. For example, if the number of persons entering the sandal-making profession increases when society really needs more plumbers, the price of plumbing services (and the wages of plumbers) will rise, while prices (and wages) will decline in sandal-making occupations. Prices perform an allocating function in this instance because they motivate resource-allocation decisions. Rising incomes for plumbers encourage more people to enter that occupation, whereas price (and wage) deterioration in the sandal industry discourages producers, faced with a shrinking market for sandals, from employing as many resources.

The signaling function of prices in a market system accomplishes several specific objectives. For one thing, prices act as a *measure of value* or an objective yardstick whereby, for example, a student can obtain a uniform estimate of the worth of a used book. Also, product prices perform a *coordinating role* by rationing available but limited output and allocating scarce resources. Because price is an obstacle to consumption, the limited number of goods that are available are rationed to those who are willing and able to buy them. Similarly, product prices ultimately help allocate scarce resources which have alternative uses and command a price when used to produce something. Only those business firms willing and able to pay the prices that the market establishes for resources can secure them, and firms unable or unwilling to cast a dollar vote will not secure needed resources. In this way, prices not only indicate to the producer what and how much to produce; they also influence how a product is produced. If people are willing to pay very high prices for yogi robes, a producer may use more and better resources, whereas if buyers desire an inexpensive garment, a less costly combination of resources may be used. Finally, prices help determine both how much income owners of resources will receive and to whom the limited output of a society will be made available. It is through the marketing of their resources that individuals receive incomes which in turn dictate how much of society's limited output they can consume.

Remember, though, that, depending on the goals of society, markets may not always ration goods and allocate resources in a "socially desirable" way. A market system may deprive large groups of essential commodities or it may allocate resources to producing gadgets and trinkets while ignoring polluted streams. Moreover, it is possible to rig markets, as most governments do in the case of the market supply of military manpower. The much simplified model of demand, supply, and market price shown in Figure 3 ignores such considerations. However, it is rather apparent that individuals do have a real stake in the way specific markets work.

**C.** ACTIVITY FLOWS IN A MARKET ECONOMY

Although some knowledge of the characteristics of a market system is useful, it is difficult to gain a meaningful understanding of the operation of an economic system from description alone. Carrying our analysis one step further requires that we examine profits and competition and then establish a simplified model of income flows in a market economy.

### Profits

Man, in pursuit of his own self-interest, is motivated partially by the prospect of economic gain, since higher incomes and profits improve one's economic status by relieving scarcity. The pecuniary motive is one feature of a market economy that may entice business firms to produce yogi robes rather than sandals, engineers to work for aircraft firms rather than a municipality, children to sell lemonade rather than play, and college students to study rather than ski. It is true that many other motives drive man to behave as he does, and we can all be grateful for that. Nonetheless, business firms which use resources to produce and supply goods and services consumers want are dependent in no small measure upon profits. Profits are a reward for assuming risks, for being innovative, and for carefully observing the needs and desires of a society bent upon consuming goods to fulfill wants. Depending upon the costs of transforming resources into products and the prices that goods command, it is more or less profitable to use resources to produce one product rather than another. The potential of increasing profits by selling more products may encourage a firm to hire more resources, to undertake additional risks, to develop new products, or to use new production methods. In short, profits act as an incentive which, in combination with prices and markets, lends flexibility to resource utilization in fulfilling consumer satisfaction. Market price and profits are the bedrock upon which a market economy is established.

### Competition

The pursuit of profit in a market system of economic organization cannot go unchecked. Adam Smith's description of the laissez faire economy stressed that competition served to control excess economic power in the marketplace. Competition between buyers and sellers acts as a control mechanism, assuring economic participants of some degree of equality in the distribution of market power and authority. If competition does not exist, however, market power and authority can become concentrated in the hands of whoever controls scarce resources or limited outputs—a situation akin to control by the King of Id.

*Pure competition* prevails in a market if there are a large number of independently acting buyers and sellers, none of whom can influence price because of competition with numerous other economic units. Under pure competition there is widespread diffusion of economic power among sellers and buyers in the marketplace. Under conditions of *imperfect competition*, individual buyers or sellers are able to influence product price (i.e., firms have some degree of market power). As a coordinating device, price then loses much of its resource-allocation influence. When the local bookstore is the only accessible market for used books, the owner can be described as a *monopolist*, meaning that he is free to exercise some degree of market power at will. As a seller of books, the bookstore may be able to earn a very large profit by charging high prices. As a buyer, it may profit handsomely by paying low prices for used college texts. The key problem of imperfect competition is that the allocation of additional resources to a product desired by society is influenced by the price-setting decisions of those possessing market power. In the absence of market competition, price and profit signals between consumer demand and the resource-allocation process are short-circuited and distorted.

## Circular-Income Flows

A circular-income-flow model of an economic system depicts the relationship that exists between product and resource markets and the private sector of a market economy—between business firms and households. Business firms produce goods that are exchanged in product markets for the expenditures of consuming households. These expenditures constitute income receipts for firms as shown in Figure 4. There is a flow of goods

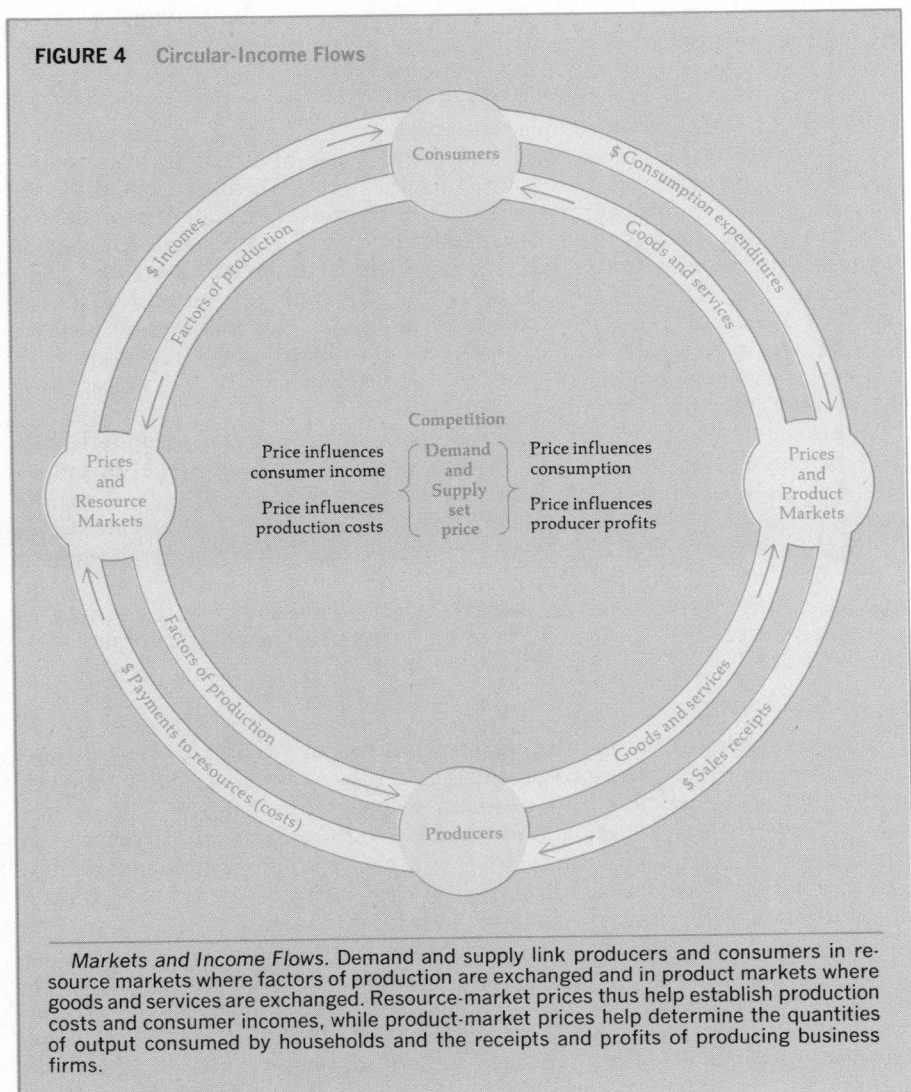

**FIGURE 4**   Circular-Income Flows

Consumers

$ Consumption expenditures

$ Incomes

Factors of production

Goods and services

Competition

Price influences consumer income

Price influences production costs

Demand and Supply set price

Price influences consumption

Price influences producer profits

Prices and Resource Markets

Prices and Product Markets

Factors of production

$ Payments to resources (costs)

Goods and services

$ Sales receipts

Producers

*Markets and Income Flows.* Demand and supply link producers and consumers in resource markets where factors of production are exchanged and in product markets where goods and services are exchanged. Resource-market prices thus help establish production costs and consumer incomes, while product-market prices help determine the quantities of output consumed by households and the receipts and profits of producing business firms.

from producers to consumers through product markets because of the ability and willingness of households to consume and the willingness of firms to produce for a profit. As we know, product demand and product supply interact to determine market price. Households are able to purchase and consume products because they own and supply resources purchased by profit-oriented business firms.

Competition acts as a control mechanism in *both* resource and product markets, where *resource-market prices determine consumer income and production costs* and *product-market prices influence consumption and profits earned by producing business firms*. To the extent that it exists, competitive demand and supply provide a check-and-balance system to concentrations of economic power, thereby monitoring prices, profits, incomes, and ultimately the allocation of resources in the private sector of an enterprise-oriented society.

### INTERDEPENDENCE OF CIRCULAR-INCOME FLOWS

Figure 4 quite properly abounds with circularity. The parts of an economy are interdependent because receipts from the sale of goods in the product market are a constraint to earning profits and acquiring productive resources. This fact implies that business firms must consider the consumption needs and desires of households; producing Edsels and chocolate-covered ants is one thing, but selling them is quite another, and very important matter. Note, too, that households must be attentive to the resource needs of producers in order to obtain the incomes needed to satisfy consumer wants. In recognition of this fact, human resources may become aerospace engineers instead of blacksmiths or computer programmers rather than accounting clerks.

Interdependence, however, sometimes complicates the task of understanding economic relationships. We cannot say that increasing the output of automobiles by 5 million units annually will increase total income in like proportions. To produce more automobiles, the output of steel and textile firms must increase, more labor and capital resources may be required, and so on. One relatively small change in the economy has a multiple impact on hundreds and even thousands of markets for goods and services as well as resources. Prices are continually being adjusted because of economic interdependence.

### LIMITATIONS TO THE CIRCULAR-INCOME-FLOW MODEL

The primary value of the circular-income-flow model is that it makes quite apparent the interdependence of product- and resource-market flows between households as consumers and business firms as producers in the private sector. Nevertheless, a circular-flow model is only a crude approximation of the economic relationships that exist in a society. Figure 4 does not indicate the output that business firms sell to each other. There is also a certain amount of activity among consuming households which exchange both products and resources. Another limitation of the model is that it shows nothing about the levels of total output, the determination of specific prices for both products and resources, or the impact of imperfect competition. The circular-flow relationship of Figure 4 also assumes that *all* income received by business firms and consumer household units is spent—an assumption that is not necessarily correct. Leakages from the income-expenditure stream shown in Figure 4 can create a considerable problem, as we shall see later. Finally, the model assumes that all economic transactions occur in the private sector. It ignores the public sector—government—completely. Thus, the circular-income-flow description of the way a market system works is as oversimplified as the illustration of price determination shown in Figure 3.

There is, however, a distinct difference between a market system and other forms of economic organization. Some economic systems are more closely allied than the market system to authoritarian societies that rely on central direction to monitor economic activity. The fundamental difference between a market system and a planned economy is one of decentralized vs. centralized decision-making about economic choices. A centrally planned economy like that of the Soviet Union does not normally establish prices on the basis of relatively independently cast dollar ballots that are tabulated in the markets for products and resources. Rather, central planning authorities determine the amount of a resource they wish to devote to the production of a given product. While price may act as a device to ration limited goods to consumers, it is not used to allocate resources in the manner of a market system. If we turn back to Figure 1 for a moment we will see the difference between a market system and a centrally directed economy. The choice between any combination of goods produced and consumed in a competitive market system, like weapons and food, is a decision to allocate scarce resources in a given fashion based on consumer demand, producer supply, and market price. In a command economy, in contrast, some higher authority makes the decision on what is produced and how resources are allocated.

## REVIEW

### Summary

1. A production frontier depicts the combination of alternative goods a nation can produce when all scarce resources are fully and effectively used. When a society operates on the production frontier, an economic choice must be made. This need for a decision, together with the prevalence of economic scarcity, requires any society to adopt some system of economic organization. Money, which is a characteristic of all types of advanced economic systems, is important as a medium of exchange, a standard of value, and a store of value. Specialization also is a characteristic of modern societies, largely because the specialized use of resources allows nations to achieve more output and experience less scarcity.

2. Economic organization can be accomplished by relying on tradition, authority, a market system of economic organization, or some combination of these three methods. Adam Smith's view was that a market system composed of competitive forces was best because it allows a society to squeeze the greatest possible output from scarce resources.

3. The market system described by Adam Smith has not gone unchallenged. Karl Marx argued that capitalism exploited workers and he demanded a more centralized form of economic organization in which the state owned resources. John Maynard Keynes addressed himself to solving the problem of unemployment, an inquiry that advocated using government as

a monitoring device capable of guiding a pure market system to enhance the welfare of the public in general.

4. Individuality is an important characteristic of a market system. It is expressed through private ownership of property, as well as freedom to produce and consume. Demand, supply, and prices help coordinate economic choices and decisions. The quantity of goods consumers demand is inversely related to product price, but the quantity of goods producers supply is directly related to product price. When market demand and supply are equal, price is stable or in equilibrium. The two crucial functions of price are the rationing of limited goods and the allocation of scarce resources.

5. Two other characteristics of a market system that are of particular importance are profits and competition. Profits act as a motivating factor which guide a market economy to a pattern of resource allocation consistent with consumer demand. Competition is necessary to maintain this consistency because it is a device for regulating a market system by controlling market power. In the absence of competition, some buyers or sellers in either the resource or product market may be able to exercise market power and possibly misallocate resources.

6. The interdependence between product markets and resource markets is illustrated by a circular-income-flow model which connects two important economic units—consuming households and producing business firms.

### Identify the Following Concepts and Terms

- the production frontier
- opportunity cost
- the principle of supply
- laissez faire
- the principle of demand
- Marxian "demise-of-capitalism" thesis
- product and resource markets
- the rationing function of price
- competition
- equilibrium price
- profit incentive
- the allocating function of prices

### Questions to Answer

1. Why is some system of economic organization necessary for a society? Contrast the views of Adam Smith and Karl Marx on economic systems.

2. Give a general explanation for a downward-sloping demand schedule and an upward-sloping supply schedule when you are: (a) consuming steak on a monthly basis, and (b) a rancher supplying the steak. Illustrate and explain where and how supply and demand result in an equilibrium market price.

3. "Prices, profits, and competition are three key ingredients in a market economy." Evaluate this statement and explain how it is true. What might happen to prices and profits if some central authority made the economic decisions for the society?

# CHAPTER 4
## The Private Sector and the Market Economy

Because markets do not always operate perfectly in organizing economic affairs, issues and problems arise that a market economy may not necessarily resolve in ways that further the welfare of society as a whole. For example, the effectiveness of a market system can be limited if firms rig prices and profits or if resource owners can avoid competitive pressures. Moreover, the market system is an impersonal mechanism, supplying yachts, liqueurs, and caviar while ignoring lifesaving vaccines or food for less favored households. Thus, one finds that the economic process centers upon the private sector (firms and consumers) *as well as* on governmental units that cope with economic issues and problems.

The purpose of this chapter is to provide a factual background on business firms as producers (Part A) and household units as consumers (Part B). In addition, three classes of economizing problems that arise in the private sector of a market economy are identified in Part C. Chapter 5 provides additional information on the public sector.

**A.** PRODUCTION IN THE PRIVATE SECTOR

Business firms and consuming household units are central to a market system of economic organization. Firms are fundamental elements of a market economy in that: (*a*) They produce most of the goods and services or "output" required to satisfy a society's unlimited wants, and (*b*) they are the primary users of scarce resources or "inputs." In short, business firms *supply* limited products and *demand* scarce resources. Household units are important because: (*a*) They consume the output of a society, and (*b*) they own most of a nation's resources. Very simply, households *demand* products and *supply* scarce resources. Consumption of goods and services is tallied in the marketplace, where the prices of products are established. Firms produce output and earn a profit by responding to consumer demand; that is, by shifting resources and production to those markets in which consumers bid prices up. Resource owners similarly respond to demand and prices for factors of production, thereby earning income that can be used to consume limited outputs. Taken together, producing firms and consuming households represent the basic source of authority in the market system of economic organization, as the circular-income-flow model in Chapter 3 suggested.

American business firms are a diverse and a vital component of the economy, producing some $1 trillion of finished goods and services each year and employing approximately four-fifths of the 85 million persons currently in the American labor force. Among the 12 million business firms in existence, there are three different forms of business organization.

1. The *proprietorship* is an unincorporated business owned and operated by an individual. Nearly three-fourths of all business firms are proprietorships.

2. The *partnership* is an unincorporated business firm normally managed and owned by two or more persons. Partnerships comprise less than 1 million business firms, or about 7 percent of the total.

3. *Corporations* are the third form of business organization. Although less numerous than proprietorships and partnerships, corporations produce most of the output of the private business sector.

American corporations own assets valued in excess of $2 trillion, most of which are property resources such as capital and land. There are nearly 4,000 corporations with assets in excess of $50 million each, and the largest 500 industrial corporations have a sales volume of approximately $500 billion. General Motors, Standard Oil of New Jersey, American Telephone and Telegraph, and Ford Motor Company are among the larger corporations. Each of them sells in excess of $10 billion of goods and services annually and usually earns over $1 billion in profit. Size has its advantages and disadvantages, but it is very clear it is impossible to finance the giant business firm often required by a modern technology through any means other than state ownership or the sale of corporate stock to investors scattered across the nation and the world.

The indebtedness or liabilities of business failures averaged over $1.2 billion annually in the United States during the 1960s—a sizable loss by most standards. During the last decade the number of proprietorships and partnerships declined slightly from the 10 million in existence in 1960. In contrast, corporations now number nearly 2 million, an increase of more than 50 percent since 1960. In recent years, new business corporations have been started at a rate of over 200,000 firms per year and 9,000 to 11,000 have failed each year. Nevertheless, there are still nearly seven times as many proprietorships as corporations.

One of the problems encountered in examining magnitudes like "billions of dollars" is the difficulty of comprehending such amounts. Just how big a billion dollars really is becomes clear once it is realized that if one started spending at the rate of $1,000 a day in 740 B.C., $1 billion would have been spent by the year 2000 A.D. With this background concerning the size, diversity, and fluidity of business firms in the private sector of the American economy, let us first consider the unincorporated forms of business organization and then examine the vastness of corporate enterprise.

UNINCORPORATED FIRMS

The slightly less than 10 million unincorporated business firms in the United States are either proprietorships or partnerships. Most of these firms are small; they were started by one or a few individuals from savings and small amounts of borrowed capital, and they are usually a source of employment for their owners and perhaps one or two additional employees.

There are several advantages to the unincorporated firm. One is the ease and simplicity of organization; little expense and few legal problems are entailed in establishing a proprietorship or partnership. Another advantage is the relatively high degree of autonomy and independence that characterizes such firms. A third advantage of the proprietorship or partnership is that all profits accrue to the owner(s). Finally, in the case of a partnership, a modest degree of specialization is possible, since partners can assume those functions that are most appropriate to their skills, training, and interest. This, of course, is not possible in the proprietorship.

Although it might appear at first glance that there are few significant disadvantages to the unincorporated business firm, this is not the case. In the first place, both the proprietorship and the partnership are limited in their ability to command financial resources. The unincorporated business firm's access to financing is usually restricted to the saving and personal borrowing power of the owner(s). Therefore, the growth potential of the unincorporated business firm is limited. A second major disadvantage of the unincorporated business firm is the problem of survival, since the life span of an unincorporated business is limited by that of the proprietor or the partners who own it. In some instances, a surviving partner may purchase and reestablish the firm as a proprietorship or acquire a new partner on the death of the original partner. This action, however, does not assure the continuity of the unincorporated business firm. The unincorporated firm is also exposed to the disadvantages of limited specialization. In a proprietorship or a small partnership, one or two persons generally make decisions concerning marketing, production, personnel management, technical matters, advertising, and so forth. However, the most significant disadvantage of the unincorporated business is that the owner(s) of the firm are subject to unlimited liability. Debts that are incurred by a proprietorship or partnership are legally viewed as personal debts of its owner(s). This means that not only does an owner stand to lose valuable business assets, such as inventory, cash, and physical property; he may also be subject to the loss of personal assets, including his home, furniture, and automobile. Because unincorporated business firms and their individual owners are regarded as one entity, bad judgment on the part of a proprietor or a partner can result in the loss of personal as well as business wealth.

## THE CORPORATION

An incorporated business firm is viewed as a legal entity, and as such, is able to own resources, to borrow, and to extend credit as a legal person. Because of this, a charter or license is required from the state, identifying the corporation's operation, the market it serves, and the general nature of its financing. The incorporated business firm is represented by registered officers of the firm who speak for it. Owners are distinctly recognized as simply owners and not managers or spokesmen for the firm.

There are several advantages to the incorporated business firm. Because the owners or stockholders of a corporation are not personally involved in the business of the firm, they are not subject to unlimited liability. Rather, the officers and management of the corporation are accountable to the stockholders for actions taken in the name of the corporation. Stockholders in a corporation risk only the amount of their stock purchase, regardless of the size of the indebtedness incurred by a firm. In a bankruptcy situation, creditors cannot sue the owners; rather, they are restricted to a dissolution or reorganization of the corporation. A second advantage of corporations is much easier access to financing. Financing a corporation may involve the sale of stocks, which represent ownership of a corporation, or the sale of bonds, which represent the indebtedness of the corporation. Incorporated business firms also often have easier access to short-term credit from the banking community. Still another advantage of the corporation is that it has an independent and virtually perpetual life, depending upon the profitability of its operation. Corporate ownership is transferred through the sale of securities, which does not disrupt the longevity and continuity of a corporation as an operating business firm. The death of a large stockholder or of the president of the firm does not necessarily have any impact upon the legal life and operation of the incorporated business enterprise. A fourth advantage of the corporation is that its larger size permits more specialization and division of labor than is possible in smaller, unincorporated firms. It is not usually necessary, for example, for one man to act as manager of sales, production, traffic, and accounting. Corporations can therefore acquire more efficient and highly specialized human and property resources.[1]

There are disadvantages as well as advantages to the corporate form of business organization. In the first place, it is a more difficult form of business enterprise to establish, both legally and financially, than the proprietorship or partnership. Second, incorporated business firms can present certain social and economic problems for society. For example, an unscrupulous financier may avoid personal liabilities by using the corporate form of business organization to sell near-worthless securities. Finally, although the interests of management and the stockholders generally revolve around the common goal of efficiency and profitability, the separation of ownership and control of the corporation is a disadvantage. In a theoretical sense, corporations are managed on a democratic basis, since shareholders vote the number of shares of stock they own. In a practical sense, however, a large and diverse ownership leaves a void between management and the stockholders of the corporation. Stockholders tend to be lethargic in voting, usually signing a stockholder proxy giving voting rights to the corporation's officers. In time of corporate difficulty, shareowners may question the decisions of management and band together to initiate needed changes. However, this alternative is expensive, time-consuming, and generally unsuccessful. Proxy fights by organized opponents may have an impact on management, but they are a most imperfect solution to the separation of ownership and control.

## PROFITS AND THE CORPORATION

In recent years incorporated business firms have earned profits approaching $100 billion annually before taxes. Figure 1 illustrates the change and distribution of corporate profits over the four-decade period, 1929 to 1970. During this 40-year period, net profits (gross profits less taxes) have in-

---

[1] It is sometimes suggested that the corporation has a tax advantage (or disadvantage) over the unincorporated business firm. In recent years, however, the Internal Revenue Service has relaxed regulations regarding the taxation of small proprietorships and partnerships. The consequence of these changes has been to give the small firm more flexibility in computing its tax liability. Insofar as large corporations are concerned, the corporate profit tax rate of 48 percent is more advantageous than the personal income tax rate that would prevail at high levels of earnings.

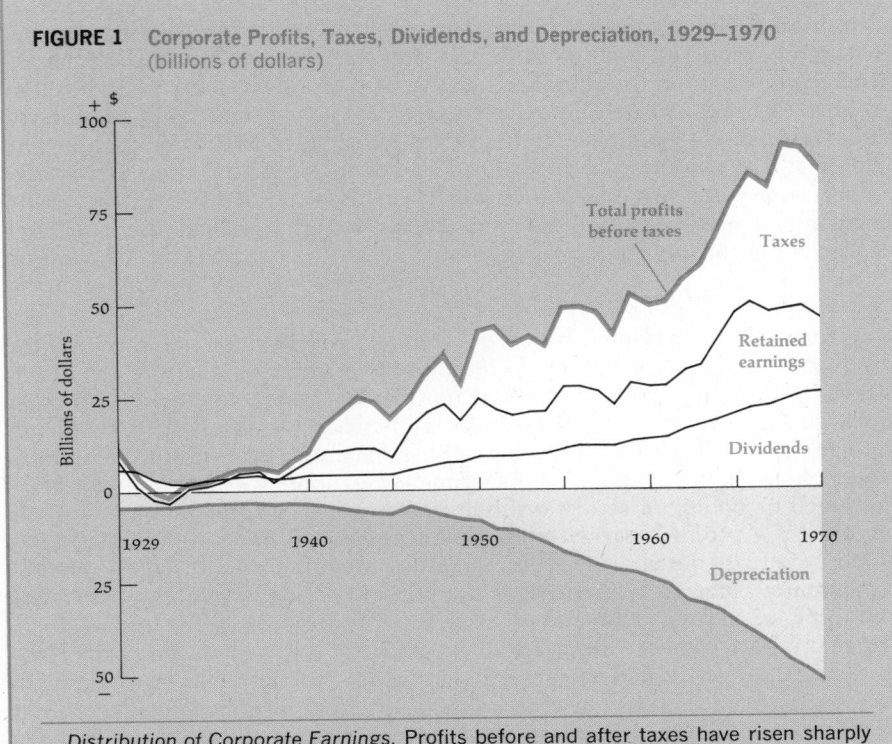

**FIGURE 1**  Corporate Profits, Taxes, Dividends, and Depreciation, 1929–1970
(billions of dollars)

*Distribution of Corporate Earnings.* Profits before and after taxes have risen sharply between 1929 and 1968 for American corporations, supplying dividends for stockholders, increased tax revenues for government, and funds for corporate expansion from retained earnings and depreciation.

SOURCE: *Economic Report of the President* and *Economic Indicators, 1970.*

creased irregularly, reaching over $50 billion at the end of the 1960s. In recent years, net profit has been almost equally divided between earnings retained by business firms and dividend payments to stockholders. *Depreciation,* the estimated dollar value of capital consumption, is nearly as large as net profit, as Figure 1 shows. Capital equipment used by producers usually has a productive life extending over several years. In the process of producing goods and services business firms use up or "consume" physical-capital resources such as buildings and machinery; consequently, it is not appropriate to charge the total cost of acquiring capital resources to the year in which firms purchase them. Instead, firms charge a portion of the cost of capital to each year of its use. (For example, a $16,000 truck estimated to have a productive life of eight years might be depreciated at $2,000 annually.)

## Financing Corporate Enterprise

Since corporations produce most of the output in the American economy, let us look carefully at their financing. Incorporated business firms are financed: (a) externally through the sale of corporate securities, and (b) with internal funds generated by retained earnings and depreciation allowed on capital resources such as buildings and machinery. Corporate business firms in nonfarm and nonfinancial enterprises alone have used $100 billion or more of funds annually in recent years. Of this amount, only about two-fifths is typically obtained from sources external to the firm, such as the sale of stocks or bonds or short-term borrowing. In the United States corporate enterprise has reached a level at which almost two-thirds of its financing is generated by the firm itself through retained earnings and depreciation allowances.

### EXTERNAL FINANCING

One form of security sold by corporations is *common stock*. In return for the money invested, a buyer of common stock receives a certificate which attests to his ownership of a given number of shares of stock. At annual stockholders' meetings, holders of common stock usually have the right to vote for a board of directors who will manage the corporation. Common stockholders stand to gain or lose depending upon whether the company does well or poorly; a return on their investment—a *dividend* payment—is possible *if* a profit is earned and *if* management declares a dividend. Dividend payments per share of common stock are not automatically limited to a maximum amount, but neither is a minimum dividend guaranteed. A second type of security sometimes sold by corporations is *preferred stock*. Persons who purchase preferred stock usually do not incur the same risks as a common stockholder, primarily because they enjoy a legal claim to dividends ahead of those of common stockholders. Preferred stocks do not guarantee dividends, but normally they do specify the amount (often a ceiling amount) to be paid before common-stock dividends can be declared. In most instances, preferred stocks do not carry voting privileges. *Bonds*, a third type of security, denote corporate indebtedness or a loan made to the corporation. Bonds carry the least amount of risk to an investor because they usually specify the interest payments due the bondholder, when payments will be made, and the maturity date of the bond (the date when the principal will be repaid). Interest payments due on bonds take precedence over all other securities issued by the corporation, including preferred-stock dividends. If a firm is unable to honor the payments due bondholders, the latter can force the company to change management or to liquidate all assets.

### SECURITY MARKETS

A few brief comments on the market for securities are in order here. Having elected to incorporate a firm, the owners file for a charter with state government authorities and sell securities. This sale of securities is accomplished with the assistance of investment-banking firms—financial middlemen who specialize in marketing new securities. Corporate stocks and bonds are traded among individuals and institutions (such as insurance companies) on a *stock exchange*.

The New York and American Stock Exchanges are the two largest markets for corporate securities. Both exchanges are regulated in certain respects by government through the Securities Exchange Commission. Once new securities have been issued, they are traded on these markets or on the "over-the-counter" market by brokers located in offices throughout the country who retail securities to the average citizen. The price of any given security can vary considerably, depending upon a firm's earnings, financial condition, growth record, and the economic conditions as well as psychological-speculative patterns governing the market at the time. In general, supply and demand for securities govern market prices. If the market is flooded with buy orders from a particular stock, prices rise, sometimes dramatically, but a reverse price movement is also a distinct possibility. There are countless examples of newly created rich men and paupers, and those playing the Wall Street game need an uncanny understanding of present and future trends in equilibrium prices.

The market for securities has experienced tremendous growth in recent years, rising from sales of $46.9 billion in 1960 to nearly $200 billion today. Nearly four-fifths of all transactions occur on the New York Stock Exchange, where some 3 billion shares and $150 billion in securities are exchanged annually. Funds invested in securities are attracted by the prospect of dividend and interest earnings. In addition, there may be a potential for increased market value, provided that business profits expand with the passage of time. Several measures or indexes of growth in the value of common stocks are available to guide a prospective investor. For example, the Standard and Poor's 500 Common Stock Price Index reveals that a $1,000 investment in 1942 would have appreciated to $1,840 by 1950, $5,585 by 1960, and more than $10,000 in early 1969. Although long-run growth of this sort does characterize the value of some common-stock investments, security prices fluctuate. The unwary investor who invested $1,000 in the typical mix of common stocks on the Standard and Poor's Index in January 1966, for example, would have held common stocks with a market value of less than $900 had the stocks been liquidated one year later. Similar difficulties occurred in 1969 and 1970, when stock prices as measured by the Dow-Jones Averages declined by one-third over a period of one and one-half years.

## Industrial Giants and Economic Power

The market economy envisioned by Adam Smith hardly describes conditions in much of the American economy today. Many observers like John Kenneth Galbraith, Adolph A. Berle, and Gardner Means have expressed concern about the potential danger of increasing amounts of economic power being concentrated in the hands of a few hundred corporate "monarchs." In his renowned treatise *Capitalism, Socialism and Democracy*, the late Joseph Schumpeter, a staunch proponent of the market economy, predicted the replacement of the entrepreneur with a managerial class, and an increasing concentration of production and power in the market economy. The importance of large corporations derives from the potential market power a few firms share—a power that can be used to fix prices. In industries like steel, aluminum, breakfast foods, soap, aircraft, computers, metal cans, photographic equipment, and automobiles, between three and six firms produce 50 percent or more of total output. The net profit of the ten largest industrial corporations annually exceeds the saving of *all* American households. One dean of the corporate Goliaths, General Motors, normally earns a net profit equal to one-fifth of total household saving and its sales exceed the total personal income of all eight states in the Mountain Region.

One factor contributing to the growth of some corporations has been the search for production efficiencies needed to serve mass markets. In addition, increase in size has been prompted by desires for prestige, power, security, and the survival of the firm. Although we cannot investigate fully the value of size so early in our study of economics, there are certain facts about big business that should be noted.

The concern is often expressed that the few very large firms that dominate some markets represent a threat to the effective operation of a competitive market system. This concern is not without cause, because when market competition breaks down, distortions in resource allocation can occur. Misallocation is possible if a few industrial giants are able to use economic power to control and raise industry prices. Firms that can pass arbitrary price increases on to consumers contribute to inflationary pressures by using market power to set prices. Furthermore, when firms have price-setting discretion, competition is no longer an effective constraint on supply-and-demand-determined prices and profits, and the market approach to the allocation of resources is blunted.

*In summary:* Private business firms are a vital anchor in the market economy. American corporations are large and very often markets are concentrated; that is, a few large firms account for a large share of economic activity in certain industries.

## B. HOUSEHOLDS AND THE PRIVATE SECTOR

Households are important because they supply firms with resources such as labor and because incomes earned are used to consume the bulk of a nation's output. Currently, there are approximately 60 million household units in the American economy, four-fifths of which are multiple-person family units. Because they are important, we will examine the major characteristics of American households as workers and then as consumers in the economy.

### Households as Workers

Figure 2 shows the distribution of the total population of the United States and of the working-age population (individuals over 16 years of age), indicating the total number in the labor force, the number employed in agricultural and nonagricultural jobs, and the number of persons unemployed for selected years since 1929. Out of a working-age population of approximately 166 million persons, 100 million persons over 16 years of age are expected to be in the labor force by 1980. Typically, 60 percent of the working-age population participates in the labor force in some capacity. Those persons *not* in the labor force include housewives and increasing numbers of persons who are either attending school or retired. Recently the number of persons unemployed has been rather small, numbering 3 to 5 million persons or 3.5 to more than 6 percent of the labor force. However, the proportion of the labor force unemployed does vary. Unemployment was the lot of nearly 6 percent of the labor force in 1949, as Figure 2 shows, but between 15 and 25 percent of the labor force (as many as 12.8 million workers) were unable to find jobs over the ten-year period during the Great Depression starting in 1930. The proportion of agricultural jobs to all labor-force opportunities has declined since 1929, as the figure also indicates. In 1929, for example, more than one-fifth of the labor force was employed in

**FIGURE 2**  United States Population and Labor-Force Distribution,
1929, 1949, 1968, Estimates for 1980
(millions of persons)

|  | 1929 | 1949 | 1969 | 1980 |
|---|---|---|---|---|
| Total U.S. population | 121.8 | 149.2 | 201.2 | 243.3 |
| Working-age population (16+ years) | 92.0 | 105.6 | 137.8 | 165.5 |
| Total labor force | 49.4 | 62.9 | 84.2 | 99.9 |
| Agriculture | 10.5 | 7.7 | 3.6 | 3.0 |
| Nonagriculture | 37.3 | 51.6 | 77.8 | 92.9 |
| Unemployed | 1.6 | 3.6 | 2.8 | 4.0 |
| Percent of labor force unemployed | 3.2 | 5.9 | 3.5 | 4.0 |

SOURCE: *Economic Report of the President,* 1969. Estimates for 1980 from the *Manpower Report of the President,* 1969.

agricultural jobs, whereas by 1980 only about 3 percent of all jobs are expected to be agricultural.

JOB OPPORTUNITIES

Over the years, not only have American workers increased in numbers, but there have been significant changes in the occupational distribution of employment. Figure 3 traces the distribution of the labor force by occupational category from 1950 through 1975. By 1975, for example, it is estimated that 87.2 million persons will be employed in the civilian labor force, an increase of approximately 33 percent of 22 million persons since 1960. It is anticipated that between 1965 and 1975, 16.5 million *new* jobs will be created, and another 22.3 million *additional* jobs will be available because of vacancies caused by retirement and death. Total new employment opportunities between 1965 and 1975, therefore, will number 38.8 million. It is also interesting to note that of the 16.5 million new jobs that are expected during the 1965–1975 decade, nearly one-fourth will be in highly skilled professional and technical occupations, and over two-thirds of all new jobs will fall within the professional-technical, clerical, and service occupations. Although 11 million individuals were employed as unskilled nonfarm and farm laborers in 1950, it is anticipated that only 6.8 million such jobs will be available by 1975. Change in occupational structure is decidedly in the direction of more highly skilled jobs.

EARNINGS AND PRODUCTIVITY

Between 1900 and 1930 the average workweek declined from 55 to 40 hours, and since that time the 40-hour workweek has remained relatively unchanged. However, in recent decades, the average number of weeks worked each year has declined. Thus, during this century the average hours worked per man-year has declined from something like 2,700 hours to 2,000. Average gross weekly earnings also have increased over these 70 years, tending to double every 20 years. The two reasons for increased earnings are increased productivity in the private sector of the American economy and increases in the general price level.

**FIGURE 3**   Distribution of Employment by Occupation, 1950–1975
(millions of persons)

| | 1950 | 1960 | 1965 | 1975 | 1965–1975 change | | |
| | | | | | New jobs | Vacancy | Total |
|---|---|---|---|---|---|---|---|
| Professional and technical workers | 4.5 | 7.5 | 8.8 | 12.9 | 4.0 | 2.5 | 6.5 |
| Managers, officials and proprietors | 6.4 | 7.1 | 7.3 | 9.0 | 1.9 | 2.0 | 3.9 |
| Clerical workers | 7.6 | 9.8 | 11.1 | 14.8 | 3.4 | 4.4 | 7.8 |
| Sales workers | 3.8 | 4.2 | 4.5 | 5.6 | 1.1 | 1.4 | 2.5 |
| Craftsmen and foremen | 7.7 | 8.7 | 9.2 | 11.4 | 2.2 | 1.8 | 4.0 |
| Operatives | 12.1 | 12.0 | 13.3 | 14.7 | 1.6 | 3.0 | 4.6 |
| Service workers | 6.4 | 8.0 | 8.9 | 12.0 | 3.3 | 4.6 | 7.9 |
| Laborers | 3.5 | 3.6 | 3.7 | 3.6 | —0.2 | 0.7 | 0.5 |
| Farmers and farm laborers | 7.5 | 5.2 | 4.1 | 3.2 | —0.8 | 1.8 | 1.0 |
| Total | 59.6 | 65.8 | 71.1 | 87.2 | 16.5 | 22.3 | 38.8 |

SOURCE: *Manpower Report of the President*, 1969. Data and estimates exclude military and unemployed persons. Data may not add due to rounding.

*Productivity* is measured as the quantity of output produced per manhour of labor input, or the ratio: *total output/manhours*. Increased productivity and earnings have allowed American households to enjoy both improved living standards and increased leisure due to reductions in the average number of hours of work per year.[2] For the time being, it is sufficient to note that productivity has grown at a rate of about 3 percent annually in recent years, allowing output per manhour to double every 25 years or so.

Prices of goods and services have also increased in recent decades and because the general price level has increased, a given income level buys less today than it would have ten years ago. One of the more common measures of price-level changes is the Consumer Price Index, which indicates how much a "package" of goods and services purchased in one year would cost at some later date. For example, to purchase $100 worth of consumer goods at 1947 price levels required $175 in 1970, since prices increased about 75 percent in this period. Needless to say, it is important to clarify whether or not income or earnings data have been adjusted for price changes. Economists describe earnings adjusted for price increases as *real* or *constant-dollar earnings*. In contrast, the terms *money* or *current-dollar earnings* are used to describe earnings that are not adjusted for price changes. Typically in recent decades, prices have increased about 2 percent and earnings have risen about 5 percent each year. Thus, if earnings increased 5 percent from $100 to $105 per week between 1971 and 1972, about $2 (2 percent) of the $5 increase in *money* earnings would be canceled by rising prices, leaving an increase in *real* earnings of $3—about equal to the average in-

[2] Several factors contribute to rising productivity and economic growth, as Chapter 13 indicates.

crease in productivity of 3 percent per year. While more will be said about measuring prices and inflation later, for now simply remember the distinction between real and money earnings.

### Sources and Consumption of Personal Income

Income received by households is *personal income*. After personal taxes are deducted from personal income, we have *disposable income*, which measures the net income received by households that is either *consumed* or *saved*. In 1970, the *money* personal income available to all American households was approximately $800 billion. About 15 percent of this represented personal taxes paid to the government, leaving a little less than $700 billion for consumption and saving. In normal times, households tend to save between 5 and 7 percent of disposable income. About $50 billion of disposable income was saved in 1970 and the remaining amount was consumed by household units.[3]

### SOURCES OF HOUSEHOLD INCOME

Households as income-receivers obtain their income from a variety of sources. Figure 4 illustrates the sources of personal income received by

[3] This level of saving does not always occur. Between 1942 and 1944, for example, household units saved between 23 and 25 percent of total disposable income because consumer goods were scarce and price controls existed. In contrast, during 1933, in the midst of the Great Depression, savings were —2 percent of disposable income.

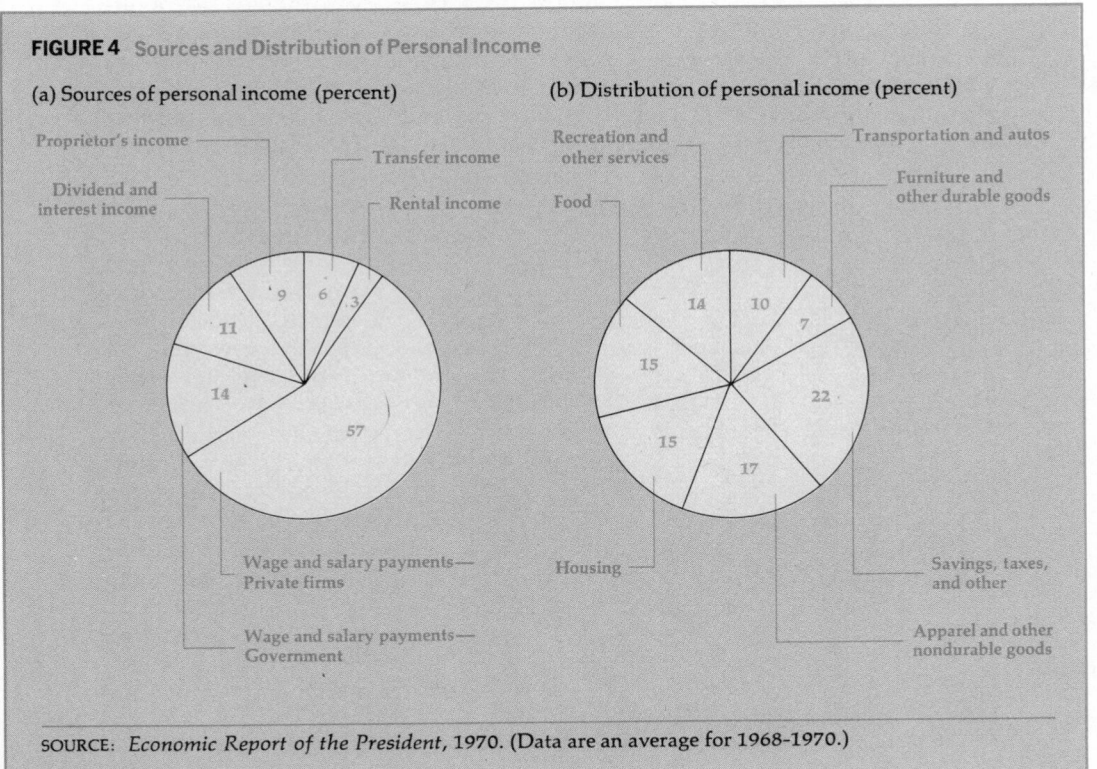

**FIGURE 4**  Sources and Distribution of Personal Income

(a) Sources of personal income (percent)

(b) Distribution of personal income (percent)

SOURCE: *Economic Report of the President*, 1970. (Data are an average for 1968-1970.)

households in recent years (the average from 1968 to 1970). Over two-thirds of all the income received came from wage and salary payments to households as workers. A growing and substantial portion of wage and salary payments originate in the public sector of the economy: Government accounts for one-fifth of personal income when transfer payments (such as public welfare, unemployment compensation, and social security payments) are added to government wages and salaries. Proprietor's income is about 10 percent of total personal income, and interest and dividend income accounts for slightly more than 10 percent.

HOW HOUSEHOLDS SPEND THEIR INCOMES

Figure 4 also shows the distribution of the personal income and consumption expenditures of households. Saving and personal taxes account for about one-fifth of personal income. The largest proportion of consumer expenditures are made for apparel and nondurable goods, recreation and other services, housing, and food. These four categories of expenditures together account for approximately two-thirds of total consumption. Transportation and automobile expenditures as well as furniture and household equipment purchases also loom large in the spending plans of consuming households.

ECONOMIC WELFARE

Figure 5 indicates how the standard of living and the consumption pattern of the average American have changed since 1929. Even though the population increased from 122 million to more than 200 million persons between 1929 and 1970, *real disposable per capita income* (income per person after adjustment for price changes and taxes) has doubled in 40 years. In 1970 each man, woman, and child averaged approximately $2,600 in *real* disposable income, in contrast to $1,236 in 1929. (Note also in Figure 5 that dur-

**FIGURE 5** Total Population and Real Per Capita Disposable Income and Consumption, 1929–1970

| Year | Millions of persons | Real per capita disposable income | Real per capita consumption |
|---|---|---|---|
| 1929 | 121.9 | $1,236 | $1,145 |
| 1935 | 127.4 | 1,035 | 985 |
| 1940 | 132.1 | 1,259 | 1,178 |
| 1945 | 139.9 | 1,642 | 1,308 |
| 1950 | 151.7 | 1,646 | 1,520 |
| 1955 | 165.3 | 1,795 | 1,659 |
| 1960 | 180.7 | 1,883 | 1,749 |
| 1965 | 194.6 | 2,235 | 2,044 |
| 1970 | 204 | 2,600 | 2,420 |

SOURCE: *Economic Report of the President,* 1970 and *Economic Indicators.* Adjusted to constant 1958 dollars.

ing the Depression of the 1930s, *real* disposable income per capita actually declined.) Today American household units consume more than $2,400 of goods and services per person, in contrast to an average of $1,145 in 1929. Thus, it is clear that consuming household units have benefited considerably in the aggregate because of the increased productivity and growth of the American market economy.

Although much can and will be said about the distribution of income, it is important to recognize that income data averaged by households or persons can be very misleading. The issue of who receives a nation's income and how much is distributed to different segments of the population is complex and many-sided. Even though average incomes have grown substantially during the last quarter of a century, household incomes are by no means distributed equally, and many Americans have not shared in the general prosperity. From those government agencies that collect data on the distribution of income and the economic welfare of select groups in society we find that:[4]

1. The poorest 20 percent of all households receive less than 6 percent of total personal income, including government transfer payments. In contrast, the wealthiest 20 percent of households receive more than 40 percent of total personal income.

2. Although poverty has declined significantly in recent years, about one out of eight Americans (or 25 million persons) live below the poverty-designated income level, which varies depending on family size, family composition, and geographic region.

3. Income-disadvantaged groups do not share fully in economic progress for a variety of reasons, including discrimination, unemployment, poor health, and inadequate training. Income discrimination and scarcity problems are most severe among nonwhites, females (particularly female family heads), undereducated and aged workers, and unskilled laborers. Many persons in these classes do not participate in the income and consumption process at anywhere near the average levels discussed earlier.

*To summarize:* Business firms and households, the two chief components in the private sector of the American economy, function alongside government. The issues of big business and market power and the problems of income distribution suggest that a variety of difficulties are encountered in a market economy. We shall examine three classes of economizing problems associated with the American market system and then, in Chapter 5, turn our attention to how the public sector deals with these problems.

## C. ECONOMIZING PROBLEMS

Like any system of economic organization, the market system encounters problems when it does not operate smoothly. A market economy both creates and solves economic problems because it functions imperfectly in a variety of ways and because it is impersonal with regard to the needs of complex societies. Competition is not fully operable in many product and

[4] Data are from the United States Departments of Commerce and Labor as well as the *Economic Report of the President*. Additional details and formal sources are discussed in Chapter 24.

resource markets because of the market power enjoyed by large corporations and unions, and some consuming households are constrained by income inequality and poverty. A market system left to its own devices may not reflect all costs of production fully; consumer, producer, and resource-owner knowledge about market conditions may be imperfect; and the need to devote resources to producing goods used collectively such as public health may not be fully and accurately reflected. Because the market system is imperfect and impersonal, economizing problems arise in three areas: (a) the full employment of all resources and achievement of economic growth, (b) the efficient allocation and use of resources, and (c) the resolution of a variety of economic problems and conflicts arising from different goals and values in a market system. Since discussion of these three classes of economizing problems will constitute the core of our inquiry into economics, a brief preview of where we are going in subsequent chapters is worthwhile.

### Macroeconomics: Full Employment and Growth

*Macroeconomics* considers problems and policy questions arising from the functioning of the economy as a whole—the aggregate economic system. One key question macroeconomics attempts to answer is: How much total output is produced relative to a nation's productive capacity? Macroeconomics focuses attention on how an economic system attempts to resolve problems such as unemployment, inflation, and inadequate economic growth.

An illustration of these three macroeconomic problems is given in Figure 6, which reproduces the production-possibilities data presented in Chapter 3. As before, the production frontier (*PF*) is an outer limit or boundary to the total output of two goods—consumer goods produced for present consumption and capital goods produced for the future. Increasing opportunity costs exist, as we know, because resources are not fully adaptable, and this causes the production frontier to be concave for the two hypothetical goods. (Remember that capital goods are productive resources themselves.)

### UNEMPLOYMENT

When for some reason an economy is unable to employ fully all its resources, it does not operate on the production frontier shown in Figure 6(a). This paradoxical situation is one of the chief problems faced by a decentralized market economy that emphasizes individuality and freedom of choice. Instead of producing on the production frontier at some point like A, a society with unemployed resources produces at some point such as U. Unemployed resources simply mean that a nation forgoes goods and services which otherwise could be used to satisfy consumer wants, as when 400 units of capital and 400 units of consumer goods are produced at point U in Figure 6(a).

### INFLATION

*Inflation*, loosely defined as an increase in the general level of prices, is another problem of macroeconomics. Suppose in Figure 6(a) that a combination of 400 units of capital goods and 900 units of consumer goods is produced by an economy on the production frontier at point A, and that this combination of output is sold for $100 billion. With inflation, the same

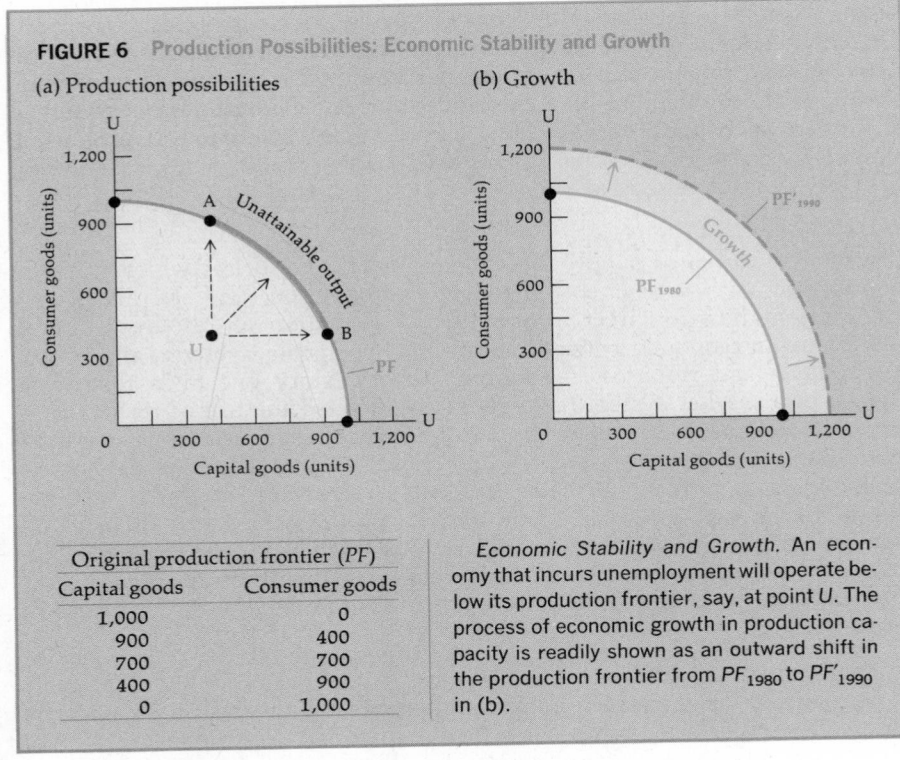

**FIGURE 6**  Production Possibilities: Economic Stability and Growth

| Original production frontier (PF) | |
|---|---|
| Capital goods | Consumer goods |
| 1,000 | 0 |
| 900 | 400 |
| 700 | 700 |
| 400 | 900 |
| 0 | 1,000 |

*Economic Stability and Growth.* An economy that incurs unemployment will operate below its production frontier, say, at point *U*. The process of economic growth in production capacity is readily shown as an outward shift in the production frontier from $PF_{1980}$ to $PF'_{1990}$ in (b).

fixed level of output (400 + 900 units) that sold for $100 billion in one year could sell for $150 billion a year later (or any other amount, for that matter). Even though money output is $150 billion due to a 50 percent increase in prices, *real* output has not changed.

## ECONOMIC GROWTH

A third matter of macroeconomic concern is economic growth from year to year. Like unemployment and inflation, the process of economic growth is much too complex to explain in detail here, but the growth problem is identified and illustrated in Figure 6. A nation which produces at point *B* rather than at point *A* in Figure 6(a) could expect a more rapid rate of growth, because the more resources a nation devotes to the production of capital resources, the greater the expansion of productive capacity. When the capacity to produce expands, the production frontier shifts outward from *PF* to higher levels of output, such as *PF'* in Figure 6(b). The significance of growth in the quantity of real output produced is clear as long as wants are unlimited. Furthermore, if a nation's population expands and its economy remains on a static production frontier like *PF*, it ends up with fewer goods to be spread among more people—a problem of many less developed nations in the world today.[5]

---

[5] The three macroeconomic problems of unemployment, inflation, and economic growth are taken up in Chapters 6–13.

## Microeconomics: Efficient Allocation of Resources

The chief concern of *microeconomics* is to examine the component parts of the economic system and to understand how resources are allocated efficiently in the production of goods and services. Microeconomics attempts to answer such questions as: How are resources combined in producing goods? Who produces? What is produced? How do prices affect the use of a society's scarce resources?

### PRICES AND RESOURCE-ALLOCATION ADJUSTMENTS

The market forces of supply and demand determine prices which work in conjunction with consumer preferences, competition, and the producers' profit orientation to direct informally the allocation of resources. Prices coordinate an economic system by transmitting signals to buyers and sellers of products and resources. Looking back in history one finds that price signals in a market system have generally directed the use of resources in response to consumer demand and technological changes. For example, at one time a considerable quantity of resources was allocated to horses, buggywhips, and the like. Later, resources were transferred increasingly into ship, railway, automobile, and air transportation systems. Transportation today is dominated by jets and by possible space travel. Supply, demand, prices, profits, and varying degrees of competition informally communicated these choices and influenced the resource-allocation process in these markets.

### MARKET IMPERFECTIONS

Participants in an imperfect market system can acquire and maintain market power. Imperfectly competitive firms capable of exerting market power can redistribute a nation's income and thereby alter the claims on its limited goods in their own favor. The market for manpower resources may also be imperfect, as is demonstrated by the bargaining strength of labor unions; certainly the resource market operates imperfectly where nonwhite and female labor are concerned. Such market imperfections result in the misallocation of resources and failure to attain the production frontier. That is, resources are not used as efficiently or as productively as is possible, and the economy operates at some point below the production frontier such as point $U$ in Figure 6(a).

### Economic Conflict

A variety of important economic problems arise because of the impersonal way the market system operates. Once a nation is operating on its production frontier, choice and conflict are inherent in the reallocation of resources. For example, if a nation is at point $A$ on the production frontier in Figure 6(a), movement to point $B$ is possible only if some amount of another good is forgone. Thus, between points $A$ and $B$ on the production frontier of Figure 6(a) denotes a "conflict range." The debate in the U.S. in the early 1970s over whether to use resources to produce output for war or for pollution abatement is a good example of this type of conflict. Moreover, the market system is completely oblivious to situations in which some proportion of the population may not have dollar votes to cast in the marketplace. Casual inspection of the conflict range $AB$ in Figure 6(a) indicates that it could just as readily depict conflict over whether to allocate society's resources to private or social goods.

*Social goods* such as national defense and public highways are those goods produced or consumed in the public sector, and it is likely that a market economy may not or will not meet the demand for these goods adequately. The opportunity cost associated with more social goods—the fewer goods that can be consumed privately—represents a source of potential conflict. Conflict is also possible because the market system can be insensitive to resource-ownership and resource-utilization problems. A market system in which 10 percent of the population owns 90 percent of all productive resources is quite different from one in which all of the citizens claim equal title to productive resources that generate incomes. In addition, a market system may allow (and even encourage) producers to avoid certain private production costs. This results in *social costs*—costs imposed on society (such as pollution) because the private sector uses resources in such a way as to avoid some private costs of production. An uncontrolled market system may well remain oblivious to the social costs of oil slicks or strip mining that destroy resources for other citizens.

## MARKET MODIFICATION BY GOVERNMENT

Thus, the imperfect and impersonal character of the market economy generates economic problems and conflicts which lend much relevance to the study of economics. Government performs a number of economic functions, many of which are oriented directly to strengthening and modifying the economic system. Modification of this kind involves a purposive short-circuiting of the price-directed market system—which itself creates a special set of economic problems. After all, once government enters the economic arena, consumer-determined prices neither ration goods nor allocate resources. The political process renders market decisions impotent.

Economic action or inaction on the part of government brings us face to face with the issue of changing values and institutions in a society. The economic establishment in not unchanging, but rules have a way of remaining rigid. Similarly, what economists regard as crucial problems worthy of their attention change slowly. Much of our knowledge about economics today is confined to conventional macroeconomic and microeconomic problems like full employment, economic growth, and efficient allocation of resources. However, environmental deterioration due to economic growth is not rendered unimportant by the emphasis on economic growth. On the contrary, both growth and the environment are all the more important because they are related. Special economic problems also arise for the public sector because decisions to allocate more or fewer resources to public health, for example, are guided only indirectly by contemporary values, institutions, and perceptions of demand and social need working through the political process. While business firms and consuming households are central features of a market economy, government also has a crucial role to fill, as we shall see next.

## REVIEW
### Summary

1. The private sector of a market system of economic organization revolves around households as consumers and resource suppliers and around business firms as producers. Consumers and firms are interrelated by

common resource- and product-market transactions. The organization of business firms varies, but their role is a cornerstone of the private sector. Unincorporated firms and corporations each have several unique advantages and disadvantages.

2. Total gross profits of U.S. corporations are approaching $100 billion annually, a level of profitability that exceeds the total national production of all but a few wealthy nations. Taxes, dividends, and retained earnings are the three claims on gross profits. Business firms are financed externally through loans and the sale of securities to the public, and internally by retained earnings and depreciation allowances.

3. Many U.S. corporations are big, and market power is concentrated in the hands of a few large producers in much of the manufacturing sector of the economy. While large size itself does not automatically lead to the undesirable use of market power, corporate giants have the potential to misallocate scarce resources by fixing market prices above a competitive market supply-and-demand level. Prices that are higher than the competitive market equilibrium restrict the quantities of goods consumers demand.

4. Households are important as consumers of output and as suppliers of factors of production, including human resources. While average real earnings and incomes of households have increased dramatically in recent years, the averages conceal problems of income distribution.

5. More than one-half of the total personal income of households is derived from wages and salaries paid by private business firms. The public sector furnishes another one-fifth of total personal income in the form of wages, salaries, and transfer payments. The remainder of personal income is derived from other business ventures.

6. American households consume well over $9 out of every $10 received, much of which is spent for food and housing. Other significant consumption expenditures include outlays for recreation and other services, automobiles and other forms of transportation, and apparel.

7. Economizing in the use of scarce resources is a central concept in the study of economics. In macroeconomics the economy is viewed as an aggregate, while in microeconomics the component parts of an economy are examined.

8. The private sector of a market system encounters three classes of economizing problems. Macroeconomic problems of unemployment, inflation, and economic growth are among the more important. Microeconomic problems are related to the process of resource allocation and the extent to which resources are utilized most effectively. The third category of problems consists of economic issues and conflict over matters such as the distribution of income or social goods and social costs.

9. When economic conflict does arise, it often requires difficult choices. Resolution of conflict frequently implies the allocation of more resources (and output) to one interest group at the expense of fewer resources (and less output) for other interest groups. A social good such as more buildings for higher education frequently implies fewer social goods for other

purposes such as national defense or fewer private goods. In addition, the resolution of economic conflict may require that government impose restrictions on certain sectors (firms or consumers polluting the air or water) to control social costs.

### Identify the Following Concepts and Terms

- disposable income
- private sector
- economic welfare
- three economizing problems
- social costs
- limited liability
- productivity
- real vs. money earnings or income

- labor force
- depreciation
- transfer payments
- proprietorship
- consumption
- macroeconomics
- microeconomics
- social goods

### Questions to Answer

1. What are the major differences in organizing unincorporated business firms and corporations? How is the American corporation of today financed? What impact can imperfectly competitive large corporations have on an economy?

2. Explain the relations between productivity, real earnings, and the economic welfare implications of changes in real per capita income for recent decades.

3. With the aid of a production frontier, evaluate the nature of macroeconomic problems. How might the macroeconomic goals of growth and employment stability relate to the "quantity" and "quality" of life?

4. "Microeconomic concerns for the efficient allocation of resources and related problems of economic conflict are not relevant to the study of economics today." Evaluate this statement and give some examples of how it is true or untrue.

# CHAPTER 5
# The Public Sector and the Market Economy

The public sector is a vital part of our economy. In this chapter we will study the extent to which the market economy of the United States is modified by government and the impact of the public sector on the market system.

Our study of the public sector starts in Part A with an overview of the way in which government influences a market economy. Part B considers the economic role of the public sector by identifying some of the most important functions of government as it modifies the market system. Part C presents selected economic facts about public-sector expenditures, and Part D is a survey of government taxation.

## A. CIRCULAR-INCOME FLOWS AND GOVERNMENT MODIFICATION OF THE MARKET SYSTEM

In view of the economizing problems and the generally imperfect and impersonal features of a market system, the circular-income-flow models presented earlier are not very realistic. The major omission which can and must be remedied is explicit recognition of the public sector as a major component of contemporary market systems.

### The Mixed Economy

An economy theoretically could cope with its problems by reliance on free markets at one extreme or complete authoritarian control at the other. However, neither extreme is pragmatic nor desirable. Economic organization in most contemporary societies is a mixture of public- and private-sector involvement, with somewhat vague "degrees" of public-sector control demarcating the popular but much abused terms, "capitalism," "socialism," and "communism."

Figure 1 summarizes the way the public sector relates to the circular-income flow that links product and resource markets to producing business firms and to households as consumers and ultimate owners of scarce resources. The tools that are used by government to alter the operation of a diffident market system are government expenditures, taxes, and direct regulation of a legal or quasi-legal character. The economic functions of government are numerous and varied, as Figure 1 shows. In a decentralized system of economic organization in which markets and prices ration goods and allocate resources, five public-sector functions are to implement: (a) policies intended to insure full employment and economic stability,

**FIGURE 1** Circular-Income Flows and Public-Sector Functions

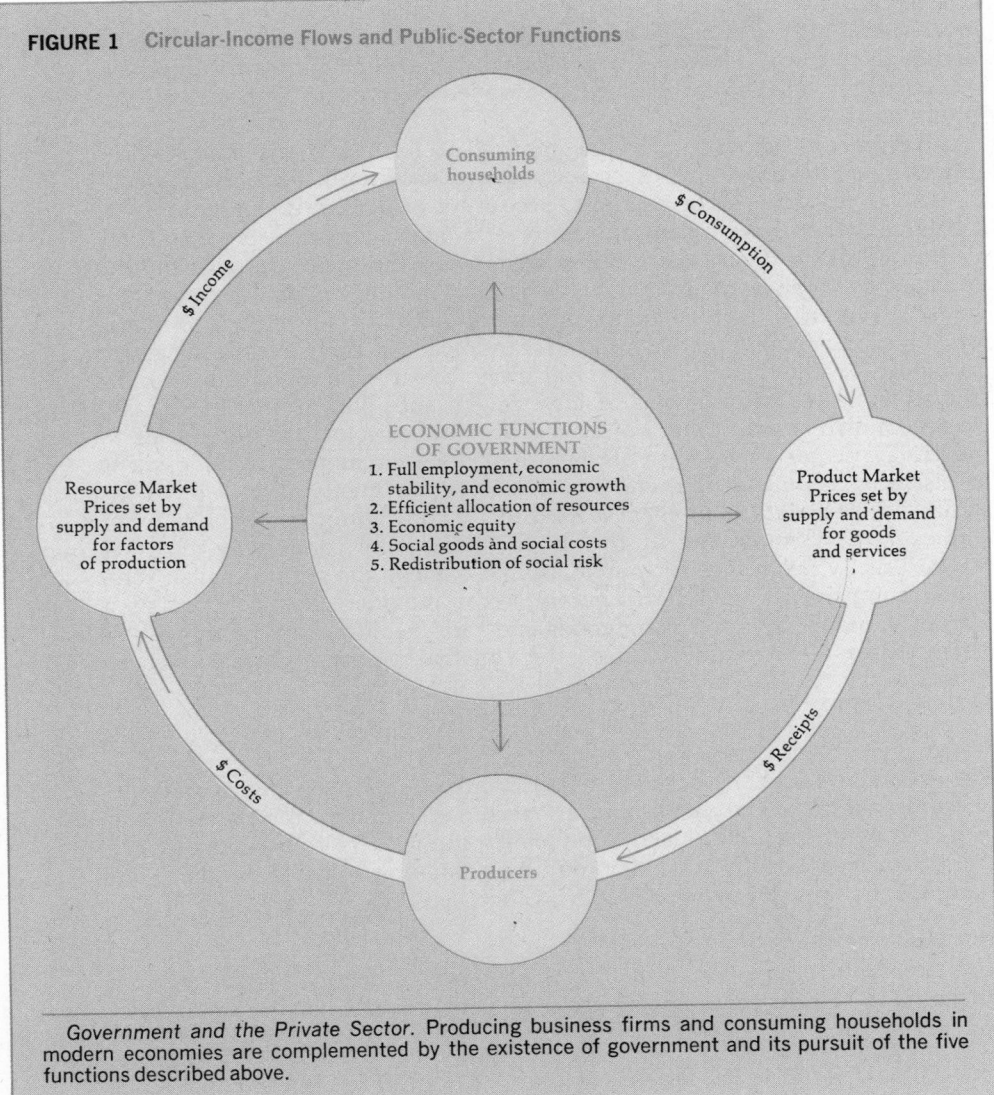

*Government and the Private Sector.* Producing business firms and consuming households in modern economies are complemented by the existence of government and its pursuit of the five functions described above.

(b) procedures intended to cope with problems of resource allocation and control of market power, (c) policies designed to enhance economic equity, (d) government control of social costs and social goods for the general welfare, and (e) policies intended to control and redistribute scarcity and risk. All things considered, the role of government complements the operation of the price-directed market system.

### Government: A Sentinel for the Public Welfare

The American economic system is a *mixed* (or market) economy because prices, profits, and competition are tempered by government modification.

It is tempting to open the Pandora's box related to the query, How much government modification is desired, and when, why, and where should modification occur? However, a good deal more specific information about the economic role of government is needed before we can answer this question.

Government can alter the consumption of limited goods and services and change the allocation of scarce resources through taxation, expenditures, and regulation. For example, producers of agricultural products are subsidized when government agrees to set a minimum price for some commodity. Other industries are subsidized by government controls on the purchase of foreign goods that help maintain higher domestic prices than would prevail if foreign competition were allowed. Tax incentives to investors in capital equipment, depreciation allowances for certain real estate investments, and capital gains tax rates on security transactions exemplify still other, less obvious forms of government subsidies or sharing of risk. To accomplish certain other objectives, the public sector transfers funds to the private sector in the form of welfare or relief payments, unemployment or disability compensation, and social security payments. In still other instances, government may enact laws directly controlling relations between employers and employees or the use of child labor, or it may even set prices directly, as it does for public utilities such as the natural-gas or telephone companies. Finally, the public sector modifies the operation of a market economy by purchasing goods and services directly as in the case of expenditures for national defense, the construction of highways, and so forth.

## B. THE ECONOMIC ROLE OF THE PUBLIC SECTOR

The economic functions of government identified in Figure 1 have one general purpose: to remedy a number of specific economic problems related to using economic resources and producing output. The role of the public sector can most readily be understood by examining some of the more important functions government performs today.

### What Government Does

The expenditure, taxation, and direct regulatory functions of government, as guardian of the economic welfare of society, are all aimed at the following goals.

#### FULL-EMPLOYMENT, ECONOMIC STABILITY, AND ECONOMIC GROWTH

Government policy is of primary importance in achieving full employment, relatively stable prices, and maximum attainable economic growth. Because scarcity is universal, it is important that both property and human resources be fully employed. This requires a stable economic environment; an economy alternating between high and low levels of output and employment does not fully use its scarce resources. Economic ups and downs have occurred repeatedly throughout the history of the United States, reaching unprecedented severity in the Great Depression. The same problem has plagued other nations, sometimes resulting in political revolt and always creating hardship. Economic instability results in vast personal losses and it can also result in a serious loss of output to society, whether it is characterized by unemployment or by inflation. Inflation is disruptive to a society, particularly those living on fixed incomes, persons who have accumulated savings, and creditors who are paid back in dollars that buy fewer goods and services.[1] Economic growth is required to satisfy the ever-increasing wants of a larger, more demanding, and aspiring populace. Most of us have come to expect more and better things in the future, and less scarcity on an individual and collective basis. Nations whose population increase equals or exceeds the rate of growth in output face a serious problem in trying to improve or even maintain their standard of living. If a population increases 25 percent over a decade, it is apparent that the total welfare of all people will decline unless the amount of goods and services produced also increases by at least 25 percent.

In recent years it has become evident that government can have a profound impact on unemployment, inflation, and the growth in output of an economy. Depending upon how and when they are used, government tax, expenditure, and monetary policies may either hinder or help a nation achieve full employment, price stability, and growth. Policies that stabilize the economy lessen the fluctuations that occur in the private sector. Economic growth requires a combination of policies aimed at using resources fully and more efficiently, obtaining larger quantities of human and property resources, or achieving technological improvements in the use of resources. In addition, economic growth may be aided by government policies that increase saving and investment in capital resources, or by policies such as public investment in education that lead to improvements in the quality of human resources. However, a government policy may also hinder the achievement of economic stability and growth. Thus, one must ask: To what extent, how, when, and where should government action be implemented in the name of the goals of full employment, price stability, and economic growth?

## EFFICIENT ALLOCATION OF RESOURCES

Resource suppliers and producing firms respond to consumer demand as tallied in the markets for goods and services, where competition and the search for economic gain function as an informal regulatory device. However, under conditions of imperfect competition, market power is stripped from the consumer and reverts to the privileged and powerful few. The local telephone and utility companies, mandatory residence in university dormitories, and the "Big Three" in the auto industry illustrate various degrees of imperfect competition in which sellers can acquire market power. On the other hand, if a few buyers operate in imperfectly competitive markets, their use of market power may conflict with the economic welfare of sellers. Government as a buyer of war equipment, large corporations employing unorganized labor, or the university as an employer in a small town are examples of buyers' market power. Control over labor skills such as those of attorneys, medical doctors, or auto workers similarly smacks of market power and imperfectly competitive markets. The public sector is

[1] As price levels increase, the purchasing power of dollars declines. Thus, persons living on pensions or savings, and individuals who have lent funds to others find that their fixed stock of dollars buys fewer real goods (see Chapter 4).

generally responsible for checking excess market power in economic affairs and preserving a socioeconomic framework that is conducive to the free and competitive interplay of markets.

Government has accepted direct responsibility for regulating the use of economic power in both product and resource markets. For example, during the early 1960s, economic and political pressure was put upon the steel, auto, and aluminum industries to restrict individual firms from announcing price increases. As a consequence of proven price-rigging by prominent electrical-equipment firms, individual fines were levied, brief vacations to Leavenworth were arranged for certain executives, and selected corporations paid several million dollars in penalties. Direct government controls have also been extended to the market for human resources; for example, a collective-bargaining system has been set up for both employer and employee representatives, requiring that set procedures be followed in negotiating labor conflicts. In the late 1960s and early 1970s the public sector voiced informal "concern" that the failure of participants in key labor disputes to settle their differences would lead to disruption of the aggregate economy.

These various government practices do not mean, of course, that uniform modification of the market system will occur. In the days of Adam Smith, for example, lawyers banded together in the "bar," but ordinary laborers were prosecuted by the legal profession for joining then illegal "workingmen's associations." Today we regulate bank mergers or companies selling telephone services to the consumer, but we ignore uncommonly uniform price hikes in the auto and steel industries and similar increases in medical fees. Needless to say, the task of government in regulating economic power and promoting the efficient allocation of resources is neither an easy nor a popular one. Moreover, failure to achieve an efficient pattern of resource allocation often leads to economic conflict over equity concerns.

## ECONOMIC EQUITY

The public sector is also concerned with economic equity, a more normative responsibility that deals with the minimization and resolution of economic conflicts over security, justice, and freedom.

A minimum level of economic security has been achieved through programs which stabilize and control the monetary system. The need to control the monetary system resulted from a long history of bank failures that imposed severe hardships on savers and short-circuited economic progress during numerous financial panics. Unemployment compensation is another avenue to economic security that exists in the United States and most advanced nations. Retirement, illness, and death benefits embodied in social security and medical insurance programs provide other illustrations of the nation's concern for economic security. Generally speaking, Americans have a real desire for security against some of life's economic uncertainties. Despite numerous government programs, however, the value structure of American society is such that total public sponsorship of economic security is not an accepted concept and, as a result, private insurance programs are also significant. Obviously, the amount and type of economic security to be provided by government is a hotly debated issue, because more security for individual A (who may not be able to pay for it), may increase the scarcity endured by individual B. Furthermore, greater economic security for A may also conflict with individual B's notions of economic freedom or justice—particularly if B's taxes support A.

The attainment of economic justice is closely related to economic equity, and it also is an individual and normative matter. Many people possess personal concepts of economic justice designed to buttress their own values. Nevertheless, the concept of economic justice has induced this country to establish minimum wages and poverty programs financed by taxes. Manpower training and development programs, welfare programs for the indigent, the policing of industry for false advertising, and making a subsidized college education available on a near equal-opportunity basis are still other examples of attempts to achieve economic justice. How much justice or injustice exists as a result of specific public-sector measures is quite another issue, however. Once again, the quantity of economic justice and its distribution among individuals and interest groups is a subject of heated debate, particularly because greater justice for one group may be perceived as unjust to another segment of society.

A third dimension to economic equity in contemporary societies centers upon economic freedom. As is true of economic security and justice, the extent to which economic freedom is or is not enlarged through government action is a subject of much debate. The automobile industry may very well interpret freedom as protecting its right to produce cars that are "unsafe at any speed," since they are what the consuming public purchases. On the other hand, critics may regard economic freedom as their right to be protected from numbering among the some 55,000 annual deaths associated with our contemporary transportation system. Or consider the lowly hot dog. Heated governmental debates and considerable lobbying pressures by the meat industry have surrounded the issue of government-prescribed contents for the hot dog. On one hand, hot-dog producers regard government controls as unnecessary intervention with their freedom. Others, however, feel that consumer protection is sadly lacking when current standards allow a hot dog to contain 3.5 percent cereal meal, 10 percent water, and 30 percent fat, among such optional meats as ". . . pork lips, snouts and stomachs, goat lungs, spleen, unskinned pork jowls, and tripe."[2] Absolute freedom is seldom permitted in economic matters. Government may outlaw or control certain kinds of markets, such as those for forced labor, draft deferments, usurious interest rates, spoiled food, and prostitution. In addition, market restrictions may be forced upon the citizen for a variety of reasons. National defense, space exploration, and compulsory education are examples of forced markets that may impinge on the economic freedom of some individuals.

Economic equity is a relative matter and attempts to achieve it are also a normative function of government. Security, justice, and freedom are not absolutes which any one individual or group of individuals can identify. Furthermore, individuals cannot pursue their concepts of equity without regard for the economic security, justice, and freedom of others. Convincing hot-dog manufacturers, pollution-prone steel and auto producers, or mammoth industrial firms and large labor unions of the validity of competing equity claims is no small task, as you can imagine.

[2] *U.S. Consumer*, Vol. III, No. 2 (April 2, 1969).

## SOCIAL GOODS AND SOCIAL COSTS

Government is charged with providing social goods (e.g., public education or national security) and is responsible for controlling social costs (e.g., environmental pollution). Three special characteristics of public-sector activity concerning social goods and social costs merit further consideration.

*Externalities* Many social goods provided collectively to society generate external economies, more simply termed "externalities." Externalities are generated by both the private and public sectors of an economy, and are the benefits that accrue to society at large which exceed those generated for one individual. Police protection or a community hospital are good examples of external economies derived from social goods. Each benefits an individual on the rare occasion he requires such services, but all persons in a community receive considerable favorable externalities because their neighbors have adequate safety and health protection. *External diseconomies* describes the *social costs* or unfavorable spillover effects, such as those created by polluted streams, unsafe drugs, lax sanitation standards for packaged foods, or failure-prone automobiles. The undesired external diseconomy effects of such products are currently attracting considerable attention.

*Indivisibility* Social goods and services are the responsibility of the public sector in part because they are indivisible (the benefits of police protection cannot be divided and sold competitively only to those members of society who want them). For that reason, social goods are not usually produced by the private sector; such production is neither feasible nor profitable.

*Diffused Benefits* Typically, the benefits of social goods are diffused and the pricing mechanism common to a market system often cannot establish a "user price." A private good or service allows consumers to be excluded from consumption simply by a decision to not purchase. In contrast, social goods such as national defense or a system of courts diffuse benefits to all persons; the so-called "exclusion principle" does not operate.

Many social goods are capable of generating significant external benefits to society at large. Without government modification of the economy, such goods would not be available through the private sector in the magnitude desired or needed. Social goods involve the reallocation of resources from private and individual want-satisfying output to public output. When firms avoid a portion of private production costs, with resultant external diseconomies, the consequence is overproduction, because product prices can be lower than they would be otherwise. Consequently, more resources are allocated to that good or service than would be possible if the full cost of production were absorbed. Government has a crucial function to perform in monitoring social goods and social costs.

## REDISTRIBUTION OF RISK AND INCOME

In recent decades the public sector has directed its attention increasingly to the less advantaged segments of society. Some welfare expenditures consist of the direct transfer of income from one group to another. The public sector may also subsidize one segment of the economy through various regulatory schemes, such as creating tax advantages, charging less than full cost for a government service, or subsidizing the price at which goods or resources must be sold. Since motives for redistribution vary widely, we can best understand this function by considering a few examples.

The public sector has underwritten a social insurance system whereby people receive minimum financial risk protection against retirement, old-age medical needs, and unemployment. Other government funds are used for the eradication of urban ghettos and improvement of slum living conditions. Nominal financial support is available for disadvantaged groups such as widows, orphans, and minorities who do not have the ability to participate fully in the labor force. The motives for programs such as these cannot be separated from other government goals such as furthering economic equity, but it is nonetheless clear that government does redistribute risk and incomes.

Subsidy payments to selected producers in the American economy are sometimes motivated by risk-sharing or "socialization." Throughout their history, for example, airlines have been subsidized to varying degrees by the public sector, as was the railroad industry when it paved the way for the commercial development of the American economy. The creation of larger oil reserves for the future is provided by the "infamous" oil-depletion allowance as another good example of public-sector socialization of risk. The public sector also subsidizes Wall Street financiers by taxing earnings from speculation in securities at a lower rate than those that would apply under current income tax laws. Many industries in the American economy are subsidized through both trade controls that limit foreign competition and the privilege of mailing at less than full cost. Agriculture is still another subsidized sector which has received aid for many decades. Even though landlords may loathe government rent controls and sponsorship of public housing projects, they rarely if ever complain about government regulations allowing depreciation of property, which lowers the taxes they pay.

The diversity, subtlety, and variety of contrivances that have been created to redistribute income and share or socialize risk clearly demonstrate both the ingenuity of man and the contemporary relevance of economics. The transfer of risk (and income) in society is nearly always controversial, particularly since it often involves the resolution of conflict over the distribution of economic scarcity. This problem reaffirms the validity of our earlier assertion that scarcity and choice are important, and it amply demonstrates the complex character of the operation of the public sector in achieving economic goals. In some instances, redistribution of scarcity and risk is prompted by noble social objectives such as furthering the progress and equity of contemporary life. In other instances, political pressures accumulate to retain or advance the economic welfare of one segment of society at the expense of a less powerful group. The paradox of public-sector efforts to redistribute scarcity is that so often those who complain about "creeping socialism" or the "welfare state" when public-relief or welfare programs as discussed are prone in the next breath to champion public-sector intervention in the market system that socializes risks or otherwise subsidizes their own economic interests.

## Economic Issues and the Public Sector

Evaluating the economic role of the public sector is no simple task. It is generally clear that government indeed has legitimate and meaningful economic roles. At the same time, the functions of government identified above are beset with a wide variety of problems including: (*a*) interdependence and conflict between various functions and goals, (*b*) the question of "balance" between private goods (consumer sovereignty) and social goods (public sovereignty), (*c*) the problem of efficiency in government, and (*d*) the normative character of public-sector functions. Although a good deal more attention will be devoted to these issues when specific economic problems are studied in detail, they are worthy of identification here before we examine public expenditures and taxes in what remains of this chapter.

## CONFLICT OF FUNCTIONS

There is a potential for conflict among the five functions of the public sector. Achieving economic stability, for example, may conflict with the objective of efficient allocation of resources as government attempts to slow down or speed up economic growth. By pursuing policies that stabilize prices and retard inflation, government may contribute to unemployment for millions. Rapid economic growth may conflict with the amelioration of pollution as a social cost, and the capital resources required for growth may interfere with the production of needed social goods. In sort, there are innumerable ways in which the many functions of government can and do work at cross-purposes.

## SOCIAL BALANCE

*Social balance* describes conflict over *both* the relative importance of social and private goods, and the distribution of social goods among the citizenry. The question of the relative quantities of social and private goods that a society should produce is a widely debated issue. Some observers contend that government is too big and that retrenchment is in order. Still others argue that the market system naturally discriminates against social goods and, in any event, there are too few social goods today. This problem is one familiar to us—conflict over the use of scarce resources because private goods may have to be sacrificed to acquire additional social goods. Once a nation does decide to increase its output of social goods, the problem encountered then is: For whom should social goods be provided? Will more weapons or more educational facilities be developed? Are recreational facilities to be supplied for the ghetto or in mountain parks normally frequented by the middle- and upper-income groups?

## EFFECTIVENESS AND THE "EXTRA-MARKET" ECONOMY

The public sector has no decentralized price mechanism to guide resource-allocation decisions. Government operates in an extra-market environment in which authoritative decisions rather than supply, demand, and price dictate whether more or fewer resources should be devoted to one function or another. By *extra-market* we mean that government has the power to consume output and allocate resources by dictate or direct control, and is not subject to the pricing mechanism of market demand and supply. Questions of efficiency and effectiveness may plague the public sector, creating a potential for tradition and custom, lobby pressures, and power relations to influence public decisions. As we shall see later, the public sector has attempted to measure the benefits and costs of government programs in recent years, but enormous measurement problems have been encountered.[3] You can readily appreciate the benefit-cost problem by considering a question like: What are the benefits of spending an additional $10 billion on higher education, national defense, or public welfare?

The basic rationale for using the public sector to monitor and strengthen "free" market transactions is that such action allegedly increases welfare. If a given course of action generates greater "compensation" benefits for some than are lost by others, welfare for society as a whole will have increased. Water- or air-purification programs, improved job training, and equal opportunities for the disadvantaged typify the logic of expanding aggregate freedom and economic welfare by restricting individual freedom. The *compensation principle* is universally agreed upon, but its implementation is often debated. Yippies advocate love or perhaps "pot," while a staunch establishment cries for short hair and shoes; conservatives demand less government and liberals a more viable poverty program; professors plead for more time for research and students for more time for teaching. Yet, all sides claim to pursue the "greatest good for the greatest number." There is little doubt that a benefit-cost measurement problem of scandalous proportions prevails. It is difficult to assess the value and effectiveness of public-sector activities simply because so many external and noneconomic benefits are generated in the "extra-market" environment that embraces the public sector.

## THE NORMATIVE CHARACTER OF PUBLIC-SECTOR FUNCTIONS

Is political economy that vague? Are matters that subjective? In a way the answer is no, and in another sense, it is yes. The normative is characteristic of a large part of the economic role of the public sector. Zoning regulations are intended to control the location of business and industrial activities in relation to suburbia, but "economic progress" and "urban blight and sprawl" are inexorably intertwined in the eyes of some viewers.

The normative character of economic matters sometimes cannot be avoided, but it must always be recognized. Even economists are sometimes prone to forget this fact. The propositions that full employment, economic growth, or efficient use of resources are worthwhile economic goals are nothing more than normative assertions predicated upon a preconceived notion of the validity and ubiquitous influence of scarcity—a premise of economics! You should remember that scarcity and certain goals are based upon value judgments commonly accepted in economics. There is little proof that a goal such as full employment is more (or less) important than more leisure or love, unless you are willing to elevate the scarcity premise to the level it enjoys in economics. The historical development of economics has emphasized such problems as scarcity and full employment, perhaps in no small measure because it is easier to be definitive about these matters than about leisure or love. Perhaps the advocates of greater economic justice are more nearly correct than those who advocate the conventional concern for full and efficient employment of resources. One thing is clear, however: The relevance of economics today exceeds anything known in the past.

*To summarize:* We can identify the generally accepted rules applying to

---

[3] Further consideration is given to benefit-cost analysis in Chapters 20 and 22.

government modification of the market system. First, public-sector modification of a market system is justified to the extent that it conforms to and advances economic welfare. Second, the policies selected should be designed to use scarce resources as efficiently as possible. Third, inaction in the public sector *is not* a neutral policy. The absence of public policies to cope with poverty is not neutral, and government modification, as a principle, is represented just as much by a low tax on capital gains or by an oil-depletion allowance as it is by a guaranteed income or a manpower-training program. *Whether one type of modification is more or less desired by the reader is his own normative hang-up. The economist is in a position to sort out, analyze, and explain positive economics: He is not endowed with supreme authority to decide what should be.* In a democracy, these matters are decided at the ballot box. Having little in the way of information or analytical tools to treat such a hornet's nest so early in our study of economics, let us extricate ourselves with three concluding admonitions:

1. Scarcity is one (and only one) fundamental attribute of contemporary life, creating a concern for such problems as full employment, price stability, economic growth, economic efficiency, the redistribution of income, and the resolution of economic conflict over matters related to economic equity.

2. The economic functions of the public sector, so critical to all our lives, are important in shaping the viability and direction of a market economy.

3. Even though public-sector functions at times embody normative matters, a considerable amount of factual information and theoretical knowledge can be assimilated and examined in order to better understand contemporary economic problems and policies. We shall start here by examining public-sector expenditure patterns.

## C. PUBLIC-SECTOR EXPENDITURES AND RECEIPTS

It should now be perfectly clear that because the public sector supplies society with social goods and services and also fulfills other functions, we live in a modified system of economic organization. Our examination of the details of federal, state, and local government operation will concentrate first on the public sector as an aggregate. We will then examine the expenditures and receipts of the federal government and briefly review similar economic facts concerning state and local governments.

### The Public Sector as an Aggregate

It is difficult to determine precisely how significant an influence the public sector is on the quantity and quality of American life. One crude indicator of the economic role of the public sector is the relationship of government expenditures to *gross national product* (GNP), which is defined as the total final output of goods and services produced in the economy of a nation. Figure 2 indicates that *total* government expenditures have increased dramatically in the last four decades, rising from $10 billion in 1929 to an estimate in excess of $300 billion in 1970. Large increases in government expenditures from 1940–1945 and 1965–1970 suggest that a considerable amount of public-sector spending is related to national security.

In recent years, approximately two-thirds of all government (federal, state, and local) expenditures have represented purchases of final output,

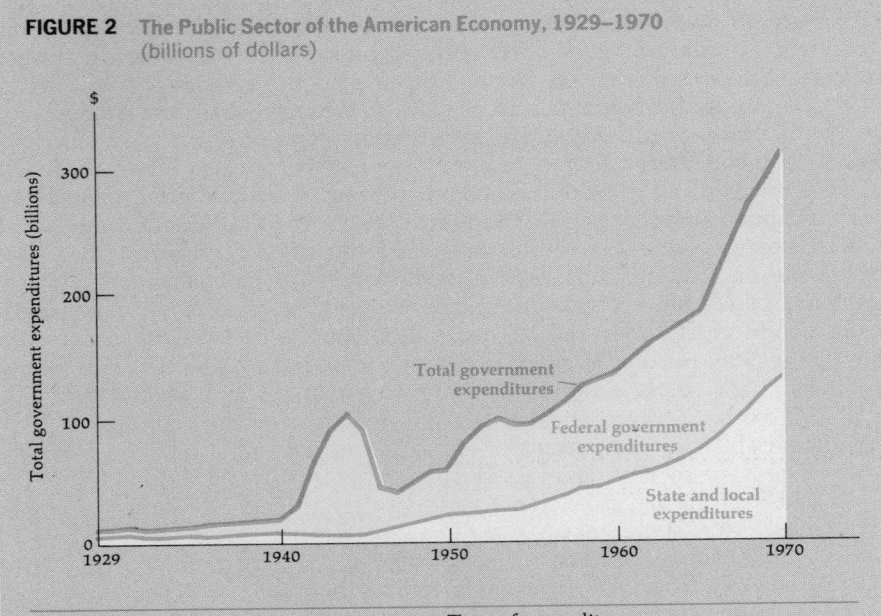

**FIGURE 2** The Public Sector of the American Economy, 1929–1970
(billions of dollars)

Total government expenditures

Federal government expenditures

State and local expenditures

| Calendar year | Total output (GNP) | Type of expenditure | | All government expenditures per capita |
|---|---|---|---|---|
| | | Goods and services | Transfers and subsidies | |
| 1929 | $103.1 | $ 8.5 | $ 1.8 | $ 85 |
| 1935 | 72.2 | 10.0 | 3.4 | 105 |
| 1940 | 99.7 | 14.0 | 4.4 | 139 |
| 1945 | 211.9 | 82.3 | 10.4 | 663 |
| 1950 | 284.8 | 37.9 | 22.9 | 399 |
| 1955 | 398.0 | 74.2 | 23.4 | 588 |
| 1960 | 503.7 | 99.6 | 36.5 | 753 |
| 1965 | 684.9 | 137.0 | 49.9 | 956 |
| 1970 | 980.0 | 218.0 | 95.0 | 1,495 |

*Public-Sector Expenditures.* Total expenditures by government level (federal or state and local) and by type (goods or transfers) have increased markedly since 1929. Increased demand for social goods helps explain why public-sector expenditures have increased rapidly.

SOURCE: *Economic Report of the President,* 1970. Estimates for 1970 derived by prorating and converting official 1971 fiscal-year budget estimates published by the Council of Economic Advisers. (Data may not add due to rounding errors, and state and local government expenditures include federal grants-in-aid.)

and one-third have been subsidy and transfer payments to the private sector of the American economy. Government purchases of goods and services include such expenditures as payments for constructing buildings, highways, or hiring employees. Transfer payments and subsidies, on the other hand, are not payments for goods and services, but rather a shifting of funds from one segment of society to another. As we have seen before, unemployment compensation, relief payments to the disadvantaged, and subsidies to selected industries or firms are direct or indirect transfers. It is important to distinguish between these two categories of expenditures because the purchase of goods and services represents government reallocating resources away from the production of private goods to the production of social goods. In contrast, transfer and subsidy payments rearrange consumption patterns and thereby change the incidence of scarcity by redistributing the income of society.

Two-thirds of all public-sector expenditures are federal government outlays, as shown in Figure 2. In the past 40 years, the total final output of the nation has not risen as rapidly as public-sector expenditures. It is also worth noting that expenditures on goods or services have declined *as a proportion of GNP* since 1945. Government expenditures on a per capita basis have also increased over the 40-year period shown. In 1929, the public sector spent $85 for every man, woman, and child in the United States, whereas public-sector expenditures now approximate $1,500 per capita.

The increasing importance of the public sector in the economy reflects significant shifts in the pattern of consumer needs and wants. An economically backward society tends to consume most of its output privately in the form of badly needed subsistence products produced by the private sector. After basic subsistence needs are filled, the demand for social goods rises rapidly because of the growing complexity and interdependence of an industrialized economy. The increasing role of the public sector in the United States is primarily associated with the government's roles as a source of transfer payments and as a supplier of social goods that for the most part do not compete directly with private-sector production. Unlike the system of economic organization that prevails under democratic socialism or communism, the public sector of the American economy does not own large amounts of scarce resources.

### Federal Government

Figure 3 shows the major sources of budgeted *federal* government receipts and expenditures anticipated for fiscal year 1971. Personal income taxes, for example, account for more than two-fifths of every tax dollar. Corporate profit taxes, payroll taxes, and excise duties or taxes on certain commodities (i.e., tobacco and liquor) are additional important sources of revenue for the federal government. Payroll taxes are separately maintained in government trust funds earmarked specifically for social security and unemployment-compensation programs.

Expenditures by the federal government are related significantly to national security. Between 1968 and 1970, for example, about $80 billion per year, or some 40 cents out of each tax dollar, has been allocated to national defense and veterans' benefits. Moreover, the bulk of the interest charged on the national debt (estimated at $18 billion for 1971) is primarily war-related. Health, education, manpower, and housing expenditures absorbed 14 cents, and another 25 cents of the federal government's expenditure dollar went to income-security programs. Most of this amount consists of social security and unemployment-compensation benefits specially provided for by taxes held in government trust funds. Finally, federal government expenditures for transportation, commerce and community development, and agriculture are identifiable outlays.

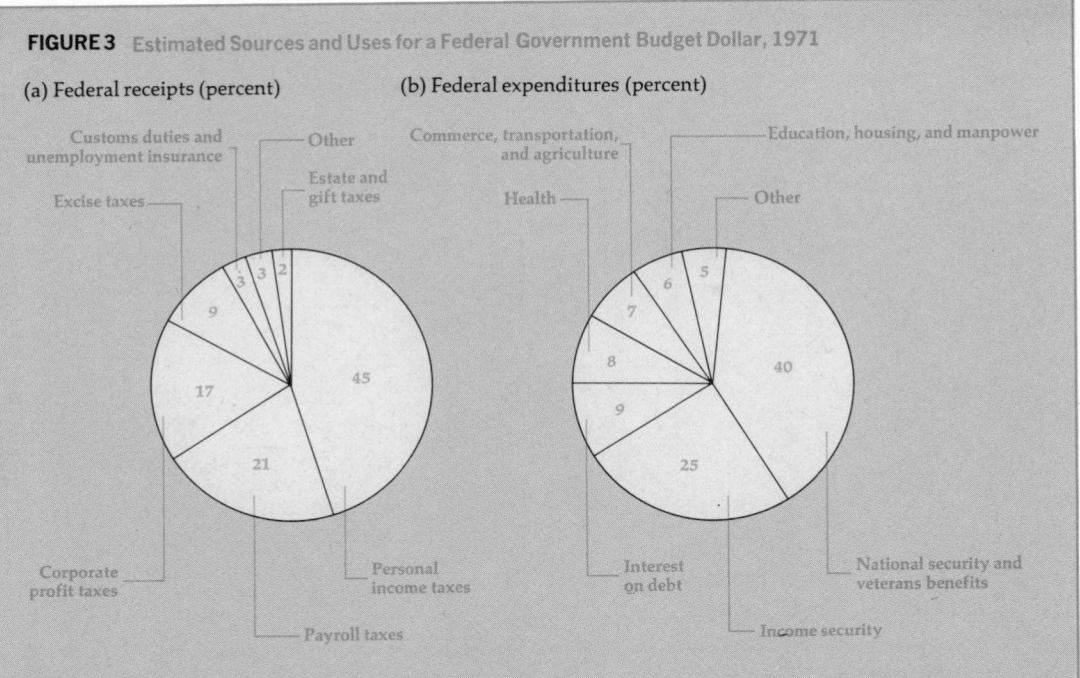

**FIGURE 3** Estimated Sources and Uses for a Federal Government Budget Dollar, 1971

(a) Federal receipts (percent)

(b) Federal expenditures (percent)

*Federal Receipts and Expenditures.* The federal government derives approximately two-thirds of its revenues from personal income and corporate profit taxes. About one-half of all federal funds are spent for national security and interest on the debt, much of which is war-related. The bulk of health, education, and welfare expenditures are Social Security payments, provided for by payroll taxes flowing into special government trust funds.

SOURCE: *Economic Report of the President,* 1970. (Data are based upon the Unified Federal Budget.)

### State and Local Governments

Figure 4 shows the breakdown of state and local government receipts and expenditures. State and local governments obtain about one-half of their total receipts from sales and property taxes. For the most part, local governments rely on property taxes, while state governments derive most of their revenues from sales taxes. At the present time, 17 cents of each state and local government tax dollar comes from a federal grant to state and local governments. Personal income taxes and social insurance taxes also account for identifiable portions of state and local government receipts.

Expenditures on the part of state and local governments are largely allocated to education, which accounts for about two-fifths of all state and local expenditures. Highway expenditures account for 14 cents of the total state and local tax dollar, and health and hospital expenditures, public welfare outlays, and costs associated with the administration of government each require about 10 percent of total expenditures.

**FIGURE 4** The Distribution of State and Local Government Receipts and Expenditures

(a) Receipts (percent)

(b) Expenditures (percent)

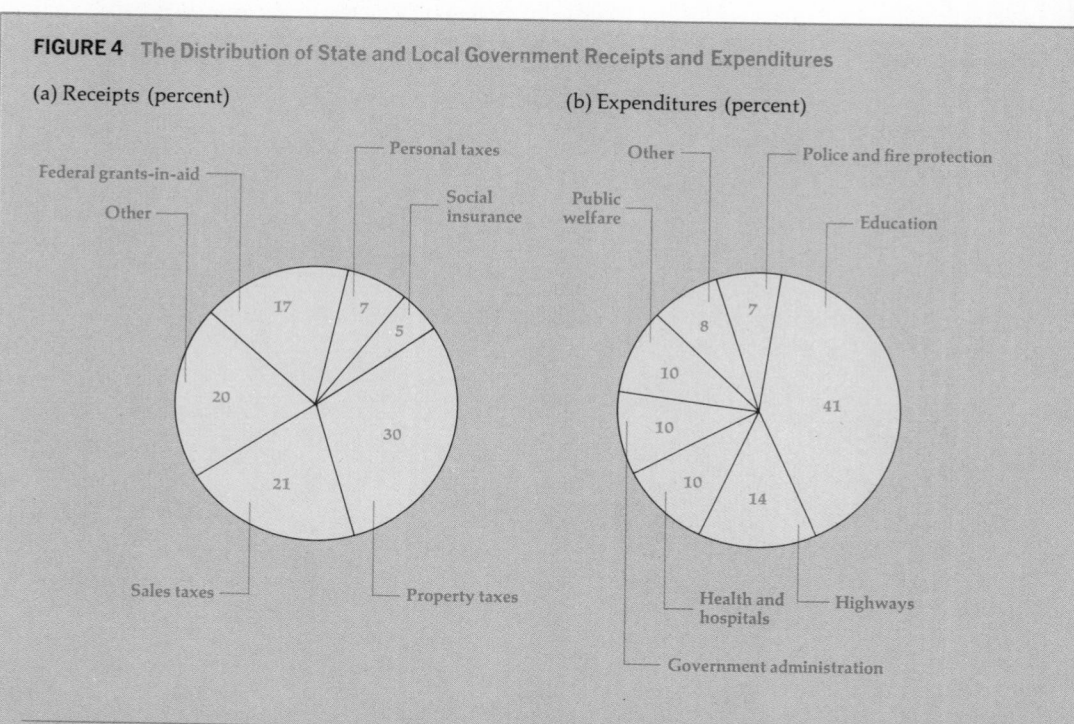

*State and Local Finance.* State and local governments receive most of their income from sales and property taxes respectively. In addition, federal revenues are increasingly being returned to state and local governments in the form of grants. Education and highway expenditures account for the largest proportion of outlays on state and local services.

SOURCE: United States Department of Commerce, *Survey of Current Business, July 1971.* (Data are the average for 1967-1969.)

## D. TAXATION AND THE PUBLIC SECTOR

Taxation and expenditures for social goods and services affect the distribution of income and thus the economic welfare of members of society. Therefore, when a society levies taxes to pay for social goods and services, it must decide "from whom" private funds will be taken as well as "for whom" the goods and services will be made available. In addition to the distribution of the tax burden, most citizens are also concerned about the aggregate level of taxes.

We have seen from Figure 3 that personal income taxes are the largest single source of revenue for the federal government, providing an estimated $91 billion in 1971. Suppose a single individual earns $25,000 in wages and takes the standard personal exemption and deductions to which he is entitled. Under these conditions his tax bill will be over $7,000. However, a comparable individual earning $25,000 from investments in municipal bonds would pay no taxes. Or consider the case of an affluent citizen in the 60 percent income bracket. Instead of paying the standard income tax rate of $6,000 on a long-term capital gain from the exchange of property sold at a profit of $10,000, he is required to pay only a 25 percent capital gains in 1971.[4] "Witchcraft" of this sort is legal. It is also confusing, it certainly keeps tax attorneys fully employed, and it has an impact upon the public sector as a procurer of social goods. Tax burdens, as a dimension to the transfer of scarcity and income accomplished through government, are apportioned in ways quite unlike those that appear on the surface, and different types of taxes have different impacts. We need not introduce further tax complications here, however. The critical facts are that the tax loopholes deny revenue to the public sector and the equity of taxation is distorted through such legal contrivances as the oil-depletion allowance and the capital gains tax. Although many authorities have questioned the legitimacy of tax privileges for individuals earning hundreds of thousands of dollars annually, as yet little has been done to remedy heavily used loopholes.

## Tax Burdens

What are the alternative philosophies of spreading the burden of taxation among members of a society?

If you and I are alike in terms of both *earning power* and *the benefits we receive* from utilizing social goods and services, we might argue that each should pay equally for those goods and services consumed. One individual should not incur a smaller tax burden because he weighs 200 rather than 225 pounds, any more than a politician's friend should pay more or less because of that friendship. The rationale that "like individuals should be taxed alike" appears to be a rather broadly accepted idea. If we agree with the principle that equals should be equally taxed, we can presume that unequal taxation is appropriate for unequal individuals. While all of this sounds easy enough in theory, matters are not that simple in practice.

### TAXATION PRINCIPLES: BENEFITS RECEIVED AND ABILITY TO PAY

First, there are two fundamentally different aspects to the equality-inequality principle. On the one hand, we might argue that fairness and equity require that people be equally taxed in relationship to the *benefits they receive* from the social goods and services provided through the public sector. In other words, individuals should pay for national defense, highways, education, welfare, fire and police protection, and economic-security programs *in proportion to their utilization* of these social goods. In situations where public-sector benefits clearly accrue to recognizable groups, the problem can be avoided by taxes associated with a "user price" for the social good provided. Taxes on gasoline or highways and toll-road fees

[4] There are a variety of other special privileges or "loopholes" in the current income tax structure. Consider what happens if the same individual, an unmarried engineer, has salary earnings plus a $25,000 investment in a limited partnership in the oil-exploration industry. He will have a tax deduction, when all legal oil-depletion allowances are taken, of approximately $18,000 against his earnings for that year. Thus, his taxable income will be less than the $7,000 tax bill he would have paid in the absence of such an investment (about $6,000 in taxes are legally "avoided"). The story need not end here, since the oil-company investment might be sold and reinvested in depreciable property such as cattle or donated to charity during a subsequent year, thereby furnishing even further tax deductions—again financed in part by government-established tax loopholes.

illustrate the application of a user-price basis for implementing the benefits-received tax principle. In most instances, however, the workability of this principle is limited because social goods, as noted before, are often indivisible and yield diffused external benefits which accrue to society as a whole. It is impossible to determine the precise extent to which you and I benefit from national defense, police protection, or space research. Moreover, it is difficult to tax an unemployed worker or welfare recipient for the unemployment-compensation or social-assistance benefits received. After all, the incidence of unemployment and poverty is largest among low-income groups, the disadvantaged, and the less skilled workers in a society, all of whom are least able to pay taxes.

## EQUITY AND TAXATION

Reality has demolished our equality-inequality theory. Or has it? Because benefits are hard to measure and some individuals cannot afford to pay for those they receive, it may be in the best interests of *all* members of society to underwrite government irrespective of benefits received. This competing tax philosophy is based upon the *ability-to-pay principle* of taxation, which holds that taxes should be levied in relation to a person's ability to bear the burden. The ability-to-pay dictum states that households or business firms enjoying larger incomes should pay larger taxes. If one household earns $15,000 per year and another earns $5,000 per year, adding $100 to the tax bill of the higher-earning household unit would cause it to sacrifice relatively less in priority needs than the household earning $5,000 per year would if its tax bill were raised by $100. The tax would be assessed equally against two parties who are unequal in terms of income level, a direct violation of the equality-inequality notion discussed above. Unfortunately, just what is an equal sacrifice for two households with very different income levels defies clear delineation.

The *ability-to-pay* taxation philosophy raises the thorny possibility that as incomes rise, the *relative* or percentage tax burden may either rise, fall, or remain constant. If ability to pay implies a larger percentage tax, one is suggesting that *relative* tax equality is not appropriate. Although it borders on a dilemma, there may be support for this idea. For example, a constant 20 percent tax on households earning $5,000 and $15,000 annually generates $250 and $750, respectively. If households earning $5,000 and $15,000 are each required to pay a tax equal to 20 percent of their income, it might be argued that the 20 percent reduction in private consumption benefits lost by the lower-income household is a greater sacrifice; and that the *tax rate* should therefore increase as incomes rise. This proposition assumes that a successively higher income generally is spent for less pressing needs.

Acceptance of the ability-to-pay and equal-sacrifice philosophy of taxation leads to the conclusion that the tax system could be "graduated" or "progressive," but no one can give an objective answer to the question of how progressive tax rates should be.

### Graduated Tax Burdens

Rates of taxation can be viewed as falling into one of three categories: proportional, regressive, or progressive. A *proportional tax* is a tax which imposes the same fraction or percentage tax burden upon high-income households that it does upon low-income households. A *regressive tax* is a tax which imposes a larger relative burden upon individuals with lower incomes. Finally, the burden of a *progressive tax* falls most heavily on those earning higher incomes.

Suppose family A earns $5,000 annually and family B earns $20,000. The proportional, regressive, and progressive tax concepts might then have the following effects:

A *Proportional Tax*   A constant tax rate of 10 percent would require family A to pay taxes of $500 (10% × $5,000) and family B to pay taxes of $2,000 (10% × $20,000).

A *Regressive Tax*   The tax rate on a $5,000 income household (say, 10 percent) is larger than the tax rate on a $20,000 income household (assume 8 percent). Now family A pays $500 and family B pays $1,600 in taxes.

A *Progressive Tax*   The tax rate rises as income increases. If a $5,000 income level is taxed at a 10 percent rate and $20,000 income is taxed at 20 percent, family A would pay $500 but family B's taxes would be $4,000. Note that in all three cases the dollar amount of the tax increases as incomes rise, although the percentage relationship varies in the cases of a regressive or progressive tax.

In determining whether or not a tax is regressive or progressive it is necessary to examine variations in both the tax rate *and* the base to which the tax applies. For example, many people view a sales tax as being proportional because every individual in society pays a proportionate amount of taxes on consumption expenditures—let us say 4 percent. The sales tax turns out to be regressive, however, if it is considered in relationship to income. A household earning $5,000 annually may spend nearly all of its income on goods subject to a 4 percent tax. Another household earning $15,000 annually but consuming only one-half of this amount pays a sales tax of 4 percent on $7,500, or an effective tax rate of 2 percent of total income. Or consider the property tax that provides most of the receipts for local government today. The property tax for an owner of rented apartments is typically shifted to those renting apartment units, which limits the proportionality characteristic of the tax. Moreover, the property tax tends to be proportional *only* if assessed values are equal in relationship to the market price of the homes and the incomes of their owners. If higher-value residences are not fully assessed in relationship to low-income housing, as is typical today, the property tax becomes mildly regressive.[5]

Personal income taxes, which constitute a major source of income for the federal government, are generally progressive in nature, although there are a number of loopholes that can be utilized to avoid this progressivity, as we have noted. Adjustments must be made for tax-free income from such sources as municipal bonds, expense accounts, depreciation and depletion allowances, and investment tax credits. Corporate profit taxes are proportional in nature, since the corporate profit tax rate is constant in the United States, except that incorporated firms earning less than $25,000 annually

[5] The property tax takes still another regressive twist when the owner of rental property deducts the tax from his income and thereby generates a lower personal income tax.

are taxed at a rate of 22 percent. However, corporate profits redistributed to stockholders as dividends generally are taxed in a progressive manner. Thus, distributed profits are taxed twice, once as profits and a second time as dividend income.

In short, the total impact of *all* federal, state, and local taxes is moderately regressive within an income range that includes four-fifths of all Americans. This means that lower-income households pay a greater proportion of their income as taxes than do higher-income households, largely because of generally regressive sales and property tax rates.

## THE INCOME TAX: PROGRESSIVITY AND THE "LOOPHOLES"

Personal income taxes and corporate profit taxes are less progressive and more involved than meets the eye because the income base to which tax rates apply varies with the source and type of income. Although it is not commonly known, preferential tax treatment allowed 21 millionaires to pay *no* taxes in 1967. Generally speaking, a variety of tax loopholes provides preferential tax treatment for persons with nonlabor incomes (incomes from royalties or property ownership). Had income from capital gains been taxed as ordinary income, for example, the United States Treasury has estimated that it would have received $8.5 billion in additional tax revenues in April 1970.

The data in Figure 5, taken from the 1969 *Treasury Department Tax Reform Studies,* compare actual and reported tax rates on two measures of personal income. *Taxable income* is gross income less deductions and exemptions as normally reported by most taxpayers, whereas *income amended* includes the impact of adjusting income for certain exclusions such as capital gains—the biggest factor in reducing tax rates for higher-income groups. The reported income tax rates implied by the forms that millions of households receive and read each year clearly overstate the extent to which income taxes are progressive. Once adjustments are made for tax loopholes other than capital gains (such as tax-exempt interest on state government bonds), and tax rates are computed as a percent of total gross income received, as shown in Figure 5 for the "super-rich," we find an average tax of 28 percent for persons earning more than $100,000 annually and slightly less than that (25 percent) for millionaires. While the federal income tax is progressive, it is clearly much less burdensome for the "super-rich" than is generally suspected. Corporate profit tax rates are equally misleading. The actual tax on corporate profits for all industries was estimated by the Treasury Department at 37.5 percent of total net income instead of the "book" rate of 48 percent, and petroleum industries were taxed at an average rate of only 21 percent.[6]

## TAX INCIDENCE

Finally, it is important to consider the *final* incidence of a tax. Just as a property owner may shift the property tax to renters, the incidence of a sales tax is shifted when merchants mark up prices by the amount of the tax. Excise taxes on goods and services such as cigarettes, liquor, cosmetics, and travel are also transferred to the consumer and tend to be regressive

[6] Data are from United States Congress, Committee on Ways and Means, *Tax Reform Studies and Proposals of the U.S. Treasury Department*, Parts I, II, and III, 1969.

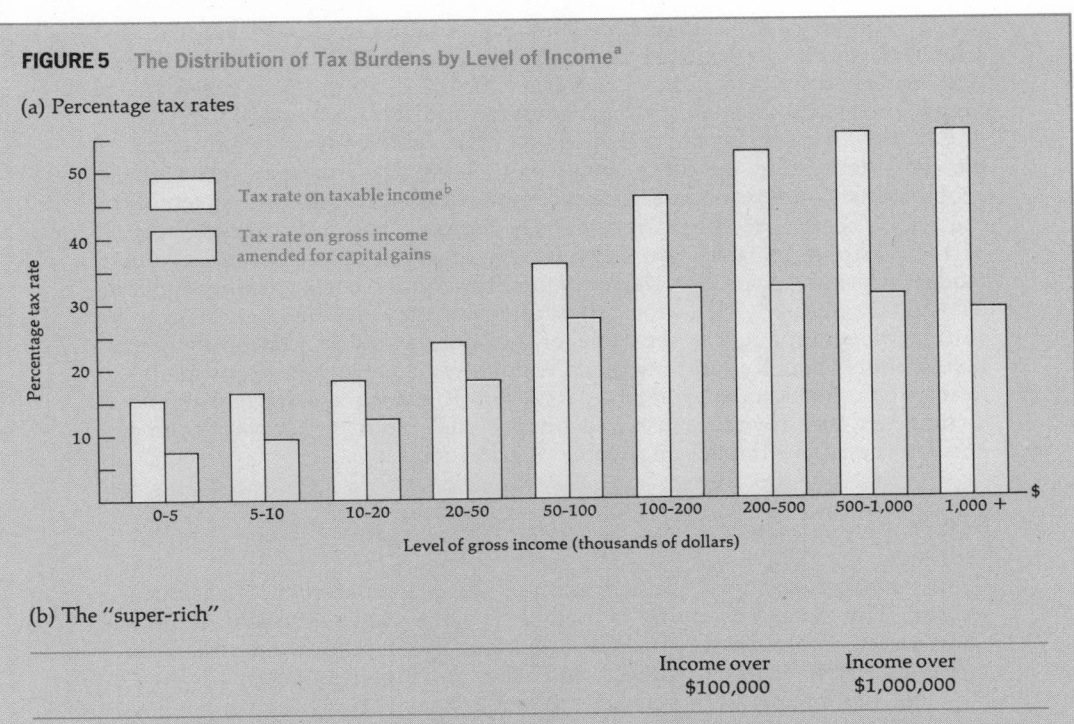

**FIGURE 5**  The Distribution of Tax Burdens by Level of Income[a]

(a) Percentage tax rates

Legend:
- Tax rate on taxable income[b]
- Tax rate on gross income amended for capital gains

Y-axis: Percentage tax rate (10, 20, 30, 40, 50)

X-axis: Level of gross income (thousands of dollars) — 0-5, 5-10, 10-20, 20-50, 50-100, 100-200, 200-500, 500-1,000, 1,000 +

(b) The "super-rich"

|  | Income over $100,000 | Income over $1,000,000 |
|---|---|---|
| Gross income received (millions) | $16,720 | $2,640 |
| Deductions (millions) | − $2,350 | − $290 |
| Excluded capital - gain income (millions) | − 3,775 | − 940 |
| Exempt interest income (millions) | − 440 | − 40 |
| Other "exempt" income (millions)[c] | − 285 | − 105 |
| Taxable gross income (millions) | $9,870 | $1,265 |
| Tax as percent of taxable income | 47.8 | 52.3 |
| Tax as percent of gross income received | 28.2 | 25.1 |

[a] Income from 1966 and 1967 federal tax returns.
[b] Gross income adjusted for exemptions and deductions.
[c] Includes excess charity deductions, farm "losses," and excess depletion allowances. Tax rates on gross income remain understated by omission of fringe benefits and stock options, accelerated depreciation, and so forth.

SOURCE: United States Congress, Committee on Ways and Means, *Tax Reform Studies and Proposals of the U. S. Treasury Department*, Part I, 1969.

for that reason. The ability to shift tax incidence depends on the uniformity of the taxes on products which may be good substitutes. A tax increase on airline travel is more difficult to shift to the consumer than a tax increase on tobacco, because although consumers may elect another means of travel, there are few good substitutes for tobacco products. In 1969–1970, telephone utilities in more than one state were granted permission to increase the price of their services to consumers because of the income surtax introduced in the late 1960s. This was possible because substitutes for telephone services are rather poor at best. If a business firm is capable of passing the corporate profit tax burden on to consumers in the form of higher prices, the incidence of a corporate profit tax also may be shifted.

*To recapitulate:* Over four-fifths of all Americans are burdened or blessed—depending on one's view—with a tax system that seems to be proportional to very moderately regressive when all sources of revenue for the public sector are considered. Hence, the poor pay a greater proportion of their income in taxes. On the average, the total tax structure regains a modestly progressive character only for those individuals earning upwards of $20,000 annually. The incidence of a tax may be direct or it may be shifted, depending upon the type of tax one considers. The principle of taxing equals equally (and unequals unequally) is not a significant reality in terms of proportionate ability to pay. Were it not for a progressive federal income tax, the revenues used to finance the public sector would have a decided regressive impact on income distribution.

## REVIEW

Summary

1. In a market economy, consideration of the private sector alone is unrealistic. The market economy is modified by the public sector in numerous ways and for a variety of purposes, and this modification affects both product and resource markets, as well as having an impact upon households and business firms in the private sector.

2. Public-sector modification is characterized by five general functions performed by government: (*a*) achievement of full-employment, economic stability, and economic growth; (*b*) efficient allocation of resources; (*c*) achievement of economic equity; (*d*) provision of social goods and control of social costs; and (*e*) redistribution of risk and income.

3. The functions of government are not achieved without duress and conflict. In some instances one goal conflicts with others; there are concerns about the "proper" balance between social and private goods; alleged government inefficiency is an omnipresent public-sector issue; and difficulties are encountered because government modification of the private sector often embraces normative matters.

4. Federal, state, and local governments constitute the public sector of the American economy. Total public-sector expenditures have increased rapidly in absolute terms since 1929. At the present time, the estimated level of public-sector expenditures is about $1,500 per capita and total government revenues used to support purchases plus transfer payments are the equivalent of one-third of GNP.

5. The federal government's budget alone exceeds $200 billion today, and state and local government expenditures add more than $100 billion annually. The bulk of federal government revenue is derived from personal income and corporate profit taxes. In contrast, state and local governmental units rely heavily on property and sales taxes and spend about $4 of every $10 on education, one of the largest "industries" in contemporary America.

6. The tax structure of the U.S. is vague in its incidence and replete with inconsistencies. "Benefits received" and "ability to pay" are different taxation philosophies. Taxes are classified as regressive, proportional, or progressive depending upon their impact on consuming households. Although personal income taxes are progressive, the total tax structure in the United States is moderately regressive for most families.

7. Tax loopholes, divergence between taxation theory and practice, and the shifting of the incidence of taxes contribute to the difficulties of evaluating the equity of tax burdens. Because of the variety of tax advantages extant today, many very high-income families pay little or no income tax.

### Identify the Following Concepts and Terms

- benefits received -
- regressive taxation -
- economic equity -
- market power
- shifting tax incidence
- proportional taxes -
- risk-sharing or "socialization"
- "extra-market" economy -
- ability to pay -
- the mixed economy -
- externalities -
- indivisible social goods -
- imperfect competition -
- compensation principle -

### Questions to Answer

1. As a United States Senator, different groups among your constituents have asked you to support legislation designed to: (a) control environmental pollution, (b) encourage industrial development in your state through the granting of tax advantages, and (c) both lower taxes and increase welfare payments to the poor. Just how might you use your knowledge about the economic role of government and concepts such as social goods, social costs, and externalities to explain your action (or inaction)?

2. Explain and evaluate how all levels of government use the tax funds they receive.

3. If you were the first ruler of a new nation setting out to tax the populace for the first time, what principles of taxation might you become concerned with and why?

# PART 2

We have seen that the economic organization of
society involves a private and a public sector
which share decisions about economic scarcity.
The objective of Part 2 is to acquire knowledge
about the full employment of resources and the
level of aggregate economic output. The next several chapters discuss employment, prices, and
economic stability—the subjects of *macroeconomics*. In studying questions related to macroeconomics, attention is focused on: (*a*) measuring
the aggregate output of a society, (*b*) determination of income and employment levels, (*c*) government action to regularize output, and (*d*)
macroeconomic issues in developed nations. The
purpose of this study is to decide what measures
an economy can take to achieve the goals of full
employment and stable prices.

# Macroeconomics: Employment, Prices, and Economic Stability

# CHAPTER 6
# Measuring Economic Activity

The purpose of the next several chapters is to examine how, in a stable and growing economy, resources can be fully employed at a point in time and over a period of time. Our concern is with broad or aggregate economic relations—*macroeconomics*. We shall rely heavily on two ideas as we proceed. The first is that producers pay persons owning scarce resources for their use, thus generating incomes for households as resource owners. This income flows back to the producers as consumer expenditures in a *circular flow of income*. Second is the idea that it is essentially spending by households and business firms that determines income and employment levels in an economy. As we proceed, it will become clear that the three major economic problems of full employment, price-level changes, and economic growth are important by-products of scarcity and choice in a market economy.

The immediate objective of this chapter is to understand fluctuation in levels of economic activity by showing how a nation's economic performance is measured and how economic activity varies from year to year. Following a brief introduction to three macroeconomic problems in Part A, methods of measuring a nation's income or output are discussed in Part B. Next, the record of historical variations in the level of economic activity is presented (Part C). With the data on factual measurement firmly in mind, we will proceed in subsequent chapters to examine theories and policies related to the achievement of full employment, stable price levels, and economic growth.

## A. A PREVIEW OF MACROECONOMIC INSTABILITY

It is often said that the one constant in economics is change. Change in the level of economic activity means that an economy vacillates from periods of rapid expansion, often characterized by price increases, to sluggish contraction, usually accompanied by higher levels of unemployment. There is nothing inherent in a market-oriented economy to prevent such fluctuations in economic activity.

Efforts to stabilize the economy have concentrated on managing the level of total spending for a nation's output. This approach is sometimes described as the "New Economics." Frequently, "Keynesian economics" is equated with the New Economics because much of macroeconomic theory and policy can be traced to the stirring contributions of the late Lord Keynes.[1] With very rare exceptions, modern economists generally accept

---

[1] The label "New Economics" is somewhat misleading, since the essential features of macroeconomic theory have existed for more than one-third of a century. Notions of newness are derived largely from the recent public acceptance of macroeconomic policy (for example, alteration of tax rates in the 1960s).

the economic relationships of Keynesian economics. However, points of disagreement and a variety of useful extensions of macroeconomic theory have been developed in recent decades, and these will be presented along with evidence on the validity of the New Economics as we proceed.

### The New Economics

Looking backward in history, it is apparent that developed nations have experienced a good deal of economic expansion that has enhanced the economic well-being of their citizenry. However, a considerable amount of unevenness has also characterized the economic growth of all nations, including the United States. The fundamental macroeconomic problem is this unevenness in growth. In some years as few as one-half million persons have been without work, whereas nearly 13 million individuals were unemployed in 1933 in the United States. Consumer prices have both decreased and increased as much as 7 percent annually. The aggregate economy has sometimes grown rapidly and at other times has actually declined.

The problems of unemployment, inflation, and retarded rates of economic growth are important for several reasons. Achieving maximum use of resources leads to higher incomes, which in turn reduces scarcity both at any one point in time (such as a year) and over a period of several years. But if an economy experiences periods of economic instability, the resultant uncertainty and economic insecurity interfere with the operation of a market economy. Thus, the maintenance of economic stability with full employment, stable prices, and capacity rates of economic growth is the goal of the New Economics. Does full employment mean everyone must be working? No. *Full employment* is typically defined as existing when 96 percent of the labor force (persons actually seeking work) are employed; that is, 4 percent unemployment is regarded as the capacity output level.

### Employment, Growth, and Prices

A brief preview of the factual evidence on the problem of economic instability readily demonstrates its importance. If we accept the notion that 4 percent unemployment is "normal," then in 1958, for example, when the unemployment rate was 6.8 percent, there were 2.8 percent (6.8%–4.0%), or some 1.8 million persons, needlessly without work. The personal and social cost of this level of unemployment is not insignificant in terms of joblessness and lost income. (Other examples of selected amounts and years of *excess* unemployment are shown below.)

|  | 1933 | 1949 | 1954 | 1958 | 1961 |
|---|---|---|---|---|---|
| Millions of unemployed persons above the 4 percent level | 10.8 | 1.2 | 1.0 | 1.8 | 1.9 |

SOURCE: *Economic Report of the President*, 1970.

Figure 1 illustrates the importance of economic growth and suggests why inflation is a macroeconomic concern by examining the paycheck of a hypo-

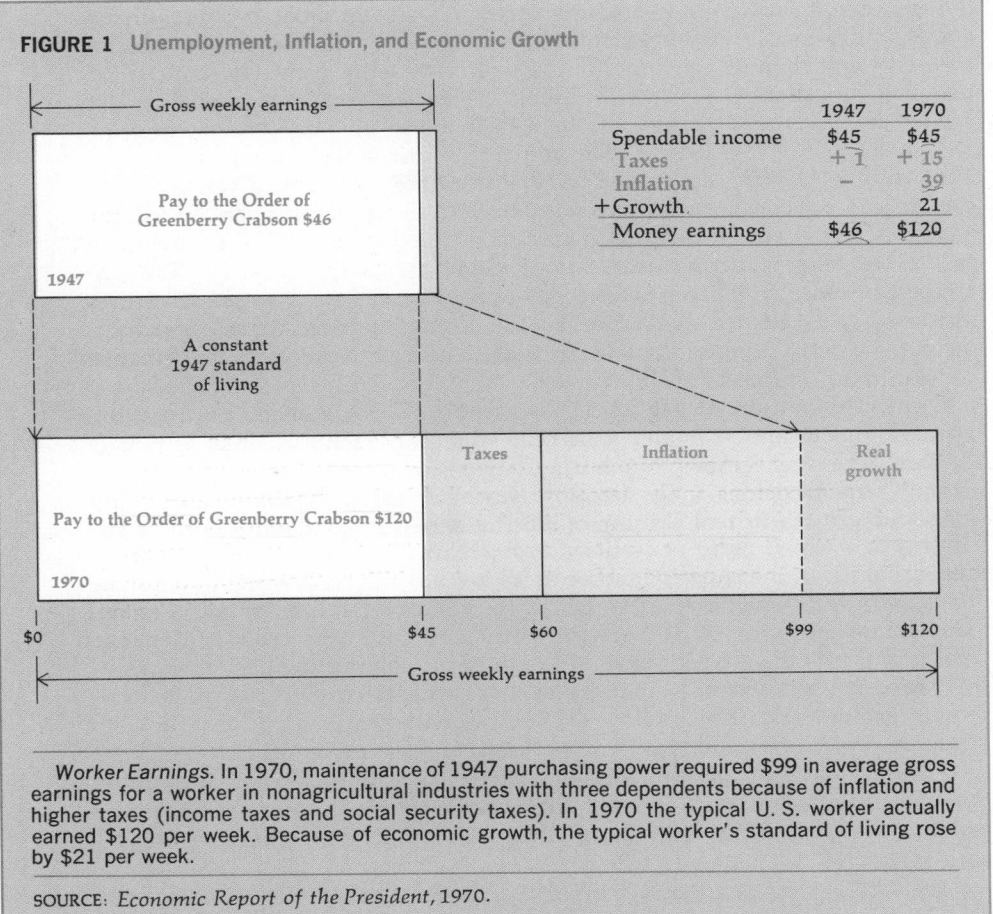

FIGURE 1  Unemployment, Inflation, and Economic Growth

|  | 1947 | 1970 |
|---|---|---|
| Spendable income | $45 | $45 |
| Taxes | +1 | +15 |
| Inflation | – | 39 |
| +Growth | | 21 |
| Money earnings | $46 | $120 |

*Worker Earnings.* In 1970, maintenance of 1947 purchasing power required $99 in average gross earnings for a worker in nonagricultural industries with three dependents because of inflation and higher taxes (income taxes and social security taxes). In 1970 the typical U. S. worker actually earned $120 per week. Because of economic growth, the typical worker's standard of living rose by $21 per week.

SOURCE: *Economic Report of the President,* 1970.

thetical, but nonetheless typical, worker in the private, nonagricultural sector of the economy. In 1947, earnings for workers in nonagricultural industries in the private sector of the American economy averaged nearly $46 weekly, all but $1 of which was spendable (take-home) earnings.[2] By 1970, on the average, the same typical worker's paycheck had grown to $120 of weekly earnings.

However, Figure 1 indicates that the $74 increase in earnings ($120–$46) was not fully available to improve the real economic welfare of our hypothetical worker. First of all, income taxes and social security taxes rose from an average of $1 to $15 to finance additional government goods and services. Therefore, a hypothetical worker with three dependents actually needed an additional $14 in gross weekly earnings, or a paycheck of $60 per week in 1970 just to maintain his 1947 standard of living as shown by his spendable income. *Note very carefully,* however, that the increase in taxes which lowered spendable income does not mean that standards of

[2] That is, gross earnings less income taxes and social security taxes.

living were lower by that amount. After all, government provides many goods and services which enhance the welfare for all. Second, prices increased more than 70 percent; that is, the purchasing power or value of $1 declined to about 58 cents between 1947 and 1970. Increased prices eroded a substantial portion of the $74 increase in *money earnings* from $46 to $120 for this period. The impact of price-level increases between 1947 and 1970 was such that the typical worker required a weekly addition to his paycheck of $39 to counter the effects of inflation. Thus, the paycheck required in 1970 to maintain a constant standard of living in spendable *money* income was $46 + $14 (increased taxes) + $39 (increased prices), or $99 per week. However, average gross weekly earnings increased to $120 per week. Because of economic growth, *real spendable* income was $21 higher than the private earnings required to maintain a constant 1947 standard of living.

From examination of Figure 1, the importance of controlling inflation, unemployment, and economic growth is apparent. Each can affect economic welfare. Inflation erodes purchasing power or real standards of living, unemployment denies a worker his paycheck for a period of time, and economic growth in real earnings (and the American economy) is the vehicle through which more real output is made available to consuming households. Bear in mind, however, that these are not the *only* worthy economic goals, nor are they necessarily indicative of a better life for all. Against gains in real income must be weighed other "costs" of economic change (pollution, urbanization, or several hours spent commuting each week).

Before we can examine matters such as unemployment, inflation, economic growth and the "quality of life," however, we must learn how to measure the performance record of an economy more accurately. Since business firms and households gauge their economic health by examining income and expenditure flows, we shall do the same thing for the aggregate economy by reviewing the national-income accounting system.

## B. THE MEASUREMENT OF AGGREGATE INCOME

The aggregate income of a society can be *estimated* by measuring either expenditures for goods and services or payments made by firms to factors of production. The first step in national-income measurement is to understand the income concept. Then we shall review the actual process of measurement and proceed to study alternative income accounts.

### The Income Concept

To estimate national income the exchange of resources and outputs must be measured by some common denominator. Adding up the oxen and asses, nuts and apples, and weapons and lovebeads produced gives no representative idea of the value of a nation's output. In the United States, dollar flows from firms to resources and from consumers to producers represent the standard of measurement.

### GROSS NATIONAL PRODUCT (GNP)

The broadest measure of a nation's total income is *gross national product* (GNP)—a measure of the market value of all final output produced over a period of time. It is generally agreed that GNP is a reasonable indicator of the health of an economy, although there are several shortcomings to this measure, as we shall see.

The *market value* of goods and services describes GNP because market prices most nearly represent the value of final output. Measurement of the market value of final output excludes some nonmarket transactions—such as the labor of a housewife or a husband's handyman services—from GNP. Note, too, that GNP is a measure of *final output* only. Secondhand sales are excluded because the resale of a home, automobile, or appliance represents final output which has already been counted. Purely financial transactions, such as the exchange of securities, are excluded from GNP because the exchange of title to assets represents no new output.[3] Finally, transfer payments from the public sector to firms or individuals are excluded from GNP on the grounds that these transfers merely denote "income switching."

### EXPENDITURES ≡ GNP ≡ INCOME PAYMENTS

It is possible to measure the value of a nation's gross output either as expenditures for output or as income payments to the four factors of production, as Figure 2 shows. In the expenditure context, GNP is made up largely of household consumption expenditures, business investment expenditures, and government purchases of goods and services. In the context of income payments, GNP is the sum of wages, salaries, and profits earned by human resources; rent and interest payments to property resources; and two types of nonincome payments—the value of capital resources used up or "consumed" in production, and indirect business taxes.

[3] The *value added* by services provided through a realtor, car dealer, or broker who sells secondhand goods and securities *is* included in GNP.

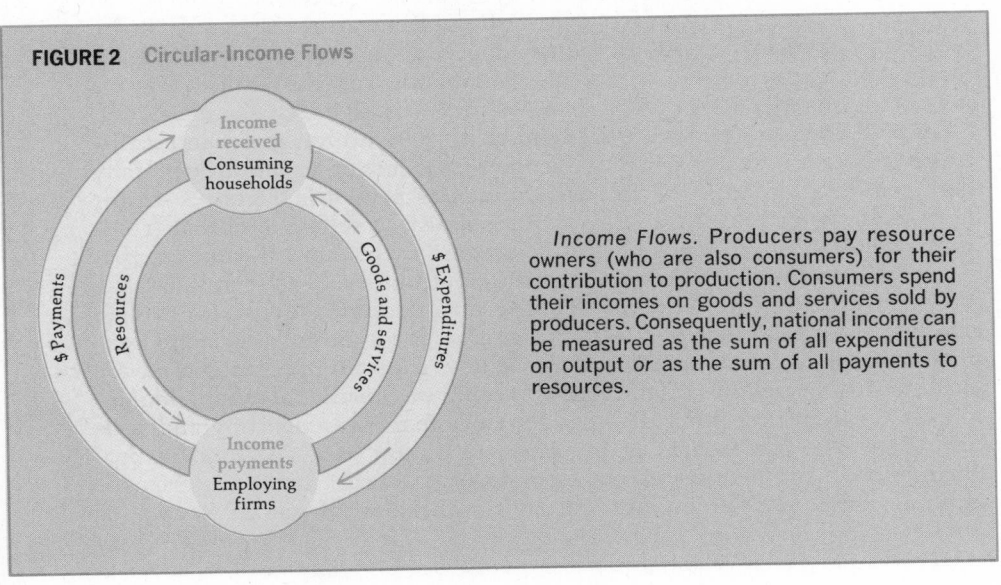

**FIGURE 2**   Circular-Income Flows

Income received
Consuming households

Income payments
Employing firms

$ Payments

Resources

Goods and services

$ Expenditures

*Income Flows.* Producers pay resource owners (who are also consumers) for their contribution to production. Consumers spend their incomes on goods and services sold by producers. Consequently, national income can be measured as the sum of all expenditures on output *or* as the sum of all payments to resources.

The dual nature of income receipts paid to resources and income expenditures for output is important. The circularity of income flows is illustrated in Figure 2 for a simplified economy consisting only of consumers and producers. (Actually, households, firms, government, and other nations are consumers of a sort, since they all purchase a nation's output.) Firms produce the bulk of all goods and services, although again, households, government, and other nations are also producers in certain contexts. Assuming the existence of only consumers and producers, Figure 2 demonstrates that *actual* income payments to resources must exactly match *actual* expenditures on output. Total income can be measured either way because we are talking about the same event—exchange between sellers and buyers of outputs and inputs. Everything spent for output represents income flowing back to producers that is later paid to resource owners. Any output produced and not sold is treated as if it were purchased by the producer who maintains an inventory of goods. Thus, the amount that firms receive as income represents the expenditures of consumers on a nation's current output. Similarly, the total of all payments made by producers to resource owners represents the value of a nation's output. Thus a second and equally valid alternative for measuring GNP is to total the payments made by producing firms to all productive resources.

*Conclusion:* Actual expenditures on output ≡ income payments to the factors of production, where ≡ indicates on identity or truism.

## GNP ≡ VALUE ADDED

An accurate measurement of GNP demands that the value of goods and services produced be measured only *once*, and not a number of times as goods pass through various stages of production. For example, it is inappropriate to add the total market transactions involved in production. Double counting appears in summing gross expenditures for corn to feed cattle plus expenditures for cattle hides sold to leather processors who sell to shoe manufacturers, and so forth. Instead, GNP measures the *value added* by making payments to resources in each production stage. Examination of a simplified input-output model of an economy[4] is the easiest way to understand the idea that *GNP* ≡ *value added.*

Suppose there are two industries producing agricultural and manufacturing goods. Both industries employ factors of production or inputs, generally identified as a "bundle" of resource inputs, as shown in Figure 3. In the figure both manufacturing and agriculture appear as sellers of output (reading by row) and purchasers of inputs (reading by column). Reading across by row shows that $120 of manufacturing output is sold to manufacturing for further processing, another $200 of manufacturing output is sold to agriculture, and ultimately $180 of manufacturing output is sold to consumers as final goods and services. These consumption purchases are financed by households that receive income payments for supplying resources to producing firms. The figure shows that manufacturing and agriculture are also purchasers of intermediate output of goods used in producing goods and services. Over a period of one year, manufacturing, for example, buys $120 of its own output, another $80 of output from agri-

[4] Harvard's Professor Wassily Leontief pioneered in the construction of input-output models.

**FIGURE 3** Input-Output Illustration of GNP ≡ Value Added
(billions of dollars)

| | Manufacturing purchases | Agriculture purchases | Final consumer demand | Gross sales of output |
|---|---|---|---|---|
| Manufacturing sales | $120 | $200 | $180 | $500 |
| Agriculture sales | $ 80 | $ 40 | $220 | $340 |
| Payments to resource inputs | $300 | $100 | $400 = GNP | |
| Gross purchases of input | $500 | $340 | | $840 |

*Final Output.* The final output of a nation excludes intermediate transactions as goods move through the production process. Therefore, gross sales (or purchases) are larger than GNP which is the value added in production, the sum of all payments to resources, and the sum of final consumer demand expenditures ($400 billion).

cultural firms, and $300 of resources used to produce goods. Similarly, agricultural firms buy $200 + $40 + $100 worth of inputs (read by column) and sell $80 + $40 + $220 worth of outputs (read by row). Now let us see what we can learn from this model.

First, *gross* sales and *gross* purchases are both $840. These total transactions are identical because the dollar amount exchanged between buyers and sellers is really like heads and tails on a coin. Second, the $840 in transactions is *not* the market value of final output, or GNP. Gross purchases and gross sales by the agricultural sector are $340, but the amount of *final output* produced and sold to consumers is valued at only $220. Why? Because agriculture sells $120 of its gross outputs for manufacturing inputs ($80) and agricultural inputs ($40). Including intermediate transactions needed to produce *final* output in measuring GNP clearly represents double-counting, an error that must be avoided, since only the value of final output is included in GNP. Including the many intermediate transactions required to produce shoes, bread, machinery, or just about any other product exaggerates the value of final output. Observe that GNP = $400 ($180 + $220) when it is measured as final consumer-demand expenditures on output in Figure 3. However, GNP can also be measured as income payments to all resources for the value added in production. As payments to resources, GNP is $300 + $100 = $400. This amount is the value added by resources, or what producers were required to pay factors of production to create the total output of $400. As before, GNP viewed as income payments is the equivalent of GNP viewed as expenditures on final output.

GNP can be estimated by summing either income payments to all resources or expenditures for final output. Either way, we are measuring only the current *final market value* of goods and services produced.

Having concluded that GNP is the sum of expenditures on final output or aggregate factor-income payments, let us examine the four main types of expenditures that comprise GNP: consumption (C), gross investment (I), government purchases of goods and services (G), and net exports (Ex). Final output or GNP is the sum of $C + I + G + Ex$, where each expenditure component is a composite of a variety of expenditures. Adding these expenditure categories, as is done in Figure 4, reveals that money GNP midway in 1970 was $971 billion:

$$GNP = C + I + G + Ex$$
$$\$971 = \$614 + \$134 + \$219 + \$4$$

## CONSUMPTION (C)

Consumption outlays are largely household expenditures for services (haircuts and attorney's fees), durable goods (automobiles and appliances), and nondurable goods (clothing and food). In measuring consumption expenditures, national-income accountants also include estimates of the value of food grown and consumed by farmers as well as the rental value of owner-occupied housing.

## GROSS INVESTMENT (I)

Although gross investment expenditures are not as large as consumption, they are an important expenditure component because investment varies

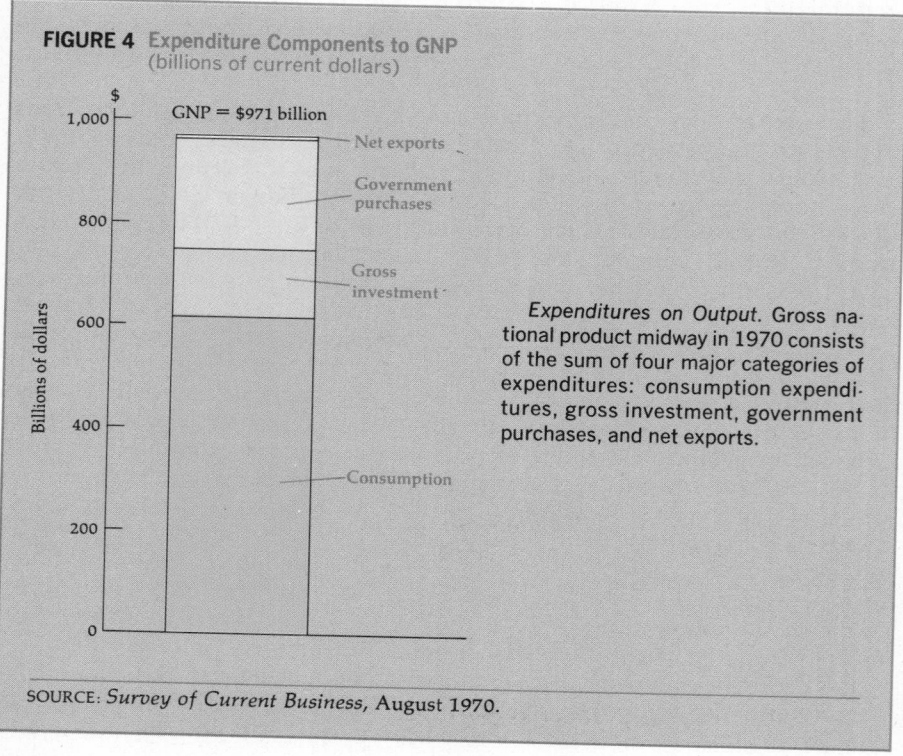

**FIGURE 4**  Expenditure Components to GNP
(billions of current dollars)

GNP = $971 billion

Net exports
Government purchases
Gross investment
Consumption

*Expenditures on Output.* Gross national product midway in 1970 consists of the sum of four major categories of expenditures: consumption expenditures, gross investment, government purchases, and net exports.

SOURCE: *Survey of Current Business*, August 1970.

considerably from one time to another. *Gross investment* consists of total expenditures for plants, production equipment, all types of construction, and changes in business inventories, which reflect additions to or deletions from prior inventory levels arising from the difference between sales and production for a given year. Since double-counting would be evident if total inventory stocks were used year after year, the *change* in inventory stocks is used. Inventory change is regarded as an investment because goods produced and not sold to consumers are accumulated and must be held by firms. The value of changes in inventory must be included in GNP to reflect output accurately for that year. When inventories are depleted (the change in inventory investment is negative), GNP is lowered by that amount because output created in some prior time has been sold. Construction, including residential construction, is regarded as an investment expenditure, but the sale of existing residential structures is excluded altogether from GNP because it is a transfer—no *new* final output is created. Also remember that the secondhand sale of capital equipment or the exchange of monetary assets (securities) is not regarded as investment because these transactions are not a reflection of investment in new capital resources.

### GOVERNMENT PURCHASES (G)

Expenditures for the goods and services purchased by government units are also included in GNP. However, interest on the government debt; transfer payments to households, such as unemployment compensation or social security payments; and business subsidy payments are excluded from GNP. National-income accountants are interested only in payments for *current* production. Pensions, relief payments, subsidies, or interest payments on government bonds are simply transferred between households and firms and do not represent expenditures for current production. Because government purchases include only the actual purchase of goods and services, the budget for all government expenditures will be larger than the *G* component in GNP by the amount of transfer and interest payments.

### NET EXPORTS (Ex)

Most nations trade goods and services with other nations. The portion of a nation's output sold to foreign countries is gross exports, whereas the purchases from other nations are gross imports. *Net exports* consist of gross exports *less* gross imports, and may, therefore, be negative or positive. If gross exports exceed gross imports, net exports are positive; but if gross imports exceed gross exports, net exports are negative, meaning that on balance a nation spent funds for output produced abroad.

### Five Income Accounts

Now that we have some knowledge about the procedure for estimating GNP as a measure of a nation's final output, we can briefly identify five income accounts commonly used to measure economic activity. These five income accounts are used for different purposes, as we shall see. Let us start with GNP and subtract or add the requisite items to each account as shown in Figure 5.

1. Gross national product (GNP). A nation's *market value of all final output* or income produced in a year, identified as GNP, is defined as the

## FIGURE 5 Five National Income Accounts
(billions of dollars)

| Income account definition | 1970 | Income account entries |
|---|---|---|
| 1. Gross income or output-created: GNP | $971 | Gross National Product $(C + I + G + Ex)$ |
| | − 84 | (less depreciation of capital stock) |
| 2. Net income or output-created: NNP | $887 | Net National Product |
| | − 89 | (less indirect business taxes) |
| 3. Net income earned by resources: $NI$ | $798 | National Income |
| | − 78 | (less corporate profits) |
| | − 55 | (less social security taxes) |
| | + 57 | (plus dividends and interest) |
| | + 79 | (plus transfer payments) |
| 4. Net income received: $PI$ | $801 | Personal Income[a] |
| | −117 | (less personal taxes) |
| 5. Disposable or spendable income: $DI$ | $684 | Disposable Income |
| | 632 | Consumption[a] |
| | 52 | Saving |

[a]Includes interest paid by consumers and government. Interest paid by consumers is also included in consumption expenditures.

SOURCE: U.S. Department of Commerce, *Survey of Current Business*, August 1970. (Data are second quarter, 1970.)

sum of expenditures for consumption, gross investment, government purchases, and net exports.

$$GNP = C + I + G + Ex$$

2. Net national product (NNP). NNP measures net income or output created, or gross output less depreciation (D) of capital resources. NNP differs from GNP because some investment expenditures replace the capital equipment depreciated in any given year. Buildings, machinery, and trucks do not have an infinite life and each year of use results in more wear and tear, or depreciation of capital resources. Another way to view NNP is to add *net, not gross, investment* to $C + G + Ex$. The difference in gross and net investment is *capital consumption* or *depreciation* for a year. As long as continued production uses up some portion of existing capital resources, future productive capacity is impaired. Therefore, NNP is a more accurate measure of a nation's net annual output than GNP.

$$NNP = GNP - D \quad (\text{or } G + I_{\text{net}} + G + Ex)$$

3. National income (NI). To measure *income earned* by all resources used in the production process, indirect taxes are subtracted from NNP. In short, national income measures the market costs of economic resources used in producing a year's output. We derive *NI* by subtracting indirect

business taxes (such as sales or excise taxes on tobacco, gasoline, or liquor) from NNP. Indirect taxes ($Ti$) represent a cost of doing business, but they are not regarded as a payment to a factor of production.

$$NI = NNP - Ti$$

4. Personal income ($PI$). Sometimes it is helpful to know the total *income received* by all persons, a measure denoted as $PI$. Personal income is derived by subtracting two items from $NI$: corporate profits ($P$), and social security taxes ($Ts$). None of these represents income received by persons. It is then necessary to *add* dividends and interest payments ($di$), plus all government transfer payments ($tr$) such as retirement benefits, unemployment compensation, welfare payments, and interest payments. Thus:

$$PI = NI - P - Ts + di + tr$$

5. Disposable income ($DI$). Finally, the amount of *income available* for spending is personal income less personal taxes ($Tp$), most of which are income and property taxes. Generally speaking, disposable income can be used in one of two ways. Recipients can either consume ($C$) or save ($S$) their income. This idea will be very important later when we look at consumer spending in more detail.

$$DI = PI - Tp \text{ or } C + S$$

*In summary:* The five national-income accounts are distinctive measures of income that are useful in different contexts. GNP measures *gross* income, NNP measures *net* income, NI measures income *earned*, PI measures income *received*, and DI measures *disposable* income received. For some general purposes, it does not make a great deal of difference which of the five income measures are used in discussing a nation's output. In other instances, such as consideration of the income available to households, it makes a great difference. For that reason, it is important to remember the composition of these income accounts.

PRICES: MONEY INCOME VS. REAL INCOME

Because of increases in the general price level or inflation, it is necessary to look more carefully at *money* or *current-dollar* GNP (data not adjusted for price-level changes) and *real* or *constant-dollar* GNP (measures of income adjusted for price-level changes). Unless otherwise qualified, references to income, earnings, or wages typically describe current-dollar values unadjusted for price-level changes—a convention to which we shall adhere.

GNP is the sum of all *physical* outputs multiplied by their prices. Since GNP = output × prices, an increase in income may reflect increased physical output, increased prices, or a *combination* of both rising output *and* rising prices. Suppose the prices of goods and services increased 25 percent between 1965 and 1975. Any dollar measure of GNP estimated in 1975 would also rise by 25 percent, even though physical output remained constant, because the dollar "yardstick" used is variable. A 25 percent increase in GNP due to rising prices does not leave a society better off; thus, it is appropriate to correct income measures for changes in the price level.

*Computing a Price Index*   What does it mean if the Consumer Price Index is 100 in 1958, or 136 in 1971? An index value of 136 means that in 1971 the general level of consumer prices was 36 percent higher than in 1958. An index of 100 for the arbitrarily selected base year 1958 simply means that in that year $1 = $1. An index value of 90 means prices are 10 percent lower than they were in 1958, the base year. Construction of a price index proceeds as follows:

1. Some period of time is selected as a base period, a period when prices are regarded as being 100 percent; that is, each $1 is equal to $1 in purchasing power. The base year selected could be any year, although the average price level for 1957–1959 is presently used.

2. The United States Bureau of Labor Statistics has defined some 400 items purchased by consumers as a "typical basket" of goods and services. The price and relative importance of each item as a proportion of total expenditures is measured from one time period to another. Using 1957–1959 as the base period, the Consumer Price Index (CPI) for that period is:

$$\text{CPI} = \frac{\text{price of basket 1957–1959}}{\text{price of basket 1957–1959}} \times 100 = 100 \text{ for the base period}$$

Suppose a basket of typical consumer purchases sold for $40 in 1957–1959 and $60 in 1975. The Consumer Price Index for 1975 would then be:

$$\text{CPI} = \frac{\text{price of basket 1975}}{\text{price of basket 1957–1959}} \quad \text{or} \quad \frac{\$60}{\$40} \times 100 = 150$$

Apparently, prices increased 50 percent over this period. In other words, the purchasing power or value of the 1957–1959 dollar declined, because it takes $1.50 to buy what $1 purchased earlier. The base period for a price index can be changed to another year, such as 1975. Then, the price index for 1957–1959 is:

$$\text{CPI} = \frac{\$40 \ (1957–1959)}{\$60 \ (1975)} \times 100 = 66.7$$

This figure simply shows that the same bundle of goods that costs $1 in 1975 could be purchased for 67 cents in 1957–1959. It really does not matter what year is used as a base, since a price rise from 67 cents to $1 also represents a 50 percent increase in prices. (One-half of 67 cents is 33 cents, the sum being $1.)

*Adjusting Money to Real Income*  To correct money GNP, wages, or any other current-dollar measure for price increases or decreases, simply divide money income for each year by the appropriate price index for that year:

$$\text{Real GNP} = \frac{\text{money GNP}}{\text{price index}}$$

Using 1958 as a base year in the example below, 1970 *money* GNP of $971 billion is *deflated* to $725 in *real* GNP by dividing by the price index for 1970 of 134.[5] Because the general price level was lower in 1948 than it

[5] The implicit price index for GNP reflects weighted indexes associated with several component parts of GNP. The 1970 GNP data are second quarter estimates on an annualized basis.

was in 1958, the $257.6 billion in *money* GNP for 1948 is *inflated* by dividing by the price index of 79.6, yielding real GNP of $323.7 billion.

| Year | (1) Money GNP | (2) Price index | (3) Real GNP (1) ÷ (2) |
|------|------|------|------|
| 1948 | $257.6 | 79.6 | $323.7 |
| 1958 | 447.3 | 100.0 | 447.3 |
| 1970 | 971.0 | 134.0 | 725.0 |

*In summary:* Changes in price levels are measured by: (*a*) comparing the percentage change in prices from one period to another, and (*b*) adjusting current-dollar income for price changes to obtain real income by dividing money income by the price index for a given year. In this manner, real or constant-dollar measures of income can be used to gauge changes in output. Had we not adjusted for price-level increases between 1948 and 1970, for example, GNP would be described as having increased almost twice as rapidly as it did in real terms.

LIMITATIONS TO NATIONAL-INCOME ACCOUNTING

There are many difficulties in measuring a nation's income. Some of the more important shortcomings encountered are described below.

*Quality*  Income accounts like gross national product or personal income represent the current market value of output. They do not normally reflect changes in the quality of output—or of life in general, for that matter. Advances in medical care, transportation, frozen foods, and no-iron clothing are a few of the many contemporary changes in the quality of output not reflected by GNP. Improvements in the quality of goods over the years imply that levels of living may exceed the dollar magnitudes represented by GNP. At the same time, GNP does not reflect the debasement of the environment due to smog or water pollution which reduces the quality of life.

*Leisure*  Gross national product is deficient as a measure of economic welfare also because it ignores increased leisure time. Certainly the movement from a 55- to a 40-hour workweek since the early 1900s denotes an increase in economic welfare, even though it is not reflected by income measures.

*Output Distribution and Composition*  It is difficult to determine the extent to which a nation is better off simply because its gross national product has increased. Both the *distribution* and the *composition* of increased output must be considered. Increases in GNP due to more weapons output may represent a deterioration in economic welfare rather than an improvement. If additional income is distributed to the wealthy but not to the poor, its implications for economic welfare again are unclear.

*Nonmarket Measurement Failures*  Gross national product excludes some output not passing through the marketplace. The classic example of output not included in GNP is the housewife's output, productive though she may be. Much academic research is similarly not included in GNP (questions of productivity aside). The treatment given to output produced or in process and not yet sold is still another problem area. Usually, inventories are valued as if sold, whereas goods in process are valued at their cost to the firm. In still other instances, as when a handyman paints his home, production and consumption occur that are not included in GNP.

*Social vs. Private Market Values*  Income accounts are deficient technically in that they measure only the private market value of output. It is possible that market values may differ substantially from social and psychic values. There are no unambiguous ways to measure social values, yet many would agree that private market values may overstate the value of such output as liquor, drugs, or tobacco, at least in those instances in which they lead to disease, crime, or death. Income estimates privately valued are not adjusted for polluted air, billboard-cluttered highways, or junkyards adjacent to otherwise attractive areas, all of which may have important social value. The real paradox, however, is that as GNP grows and pollution increases, GNP increases even more as the economy produces pollution-abatement equipment to overcome the effects of the initial growth in output.

In short, there are many hazards in trying to gauge the value of economic output, although these limitations can be minimized if measurement criteria are applied consistently. Even though there are shortcomings to national-income accounting, measures of gross national product, net national product, national income, personal income, and disposable income are useful and reasonably accurate, quite aside from being the best measures available at this time.

## C. FLUCTUATIONS IN ECONOMIC CONDITIONS

With some rudimentary ideas on measuring a nation's income in hand, it is now possible to examine more closely economic activity in the United States over a period of time. We will look at the record of instability in business activity and then review the three problems of unemployment, inflation, and uneven economic growth. The economy of the United States is in perpetual motion, exhibiting an approximately wavelike oscillation from expansions to slowdowns superimposed upon the upward growth trend in a nation's total output. Generally speaking, economic instability retards economic growth and sets the stage for unemployment and inflationary pressures.

### The Record of Economic Instability

A steady rate of economic growth that is free of unemployment or inflationary forces is as desired an ideal as it is atypical of economic performance in this (or any other) nation. Instead, history reveals that economic activity fluctuates, moving in rough oscillations often dubbed "business cycles." Patterns of expansion, contraction, and expansion appear again and again in a large number of economic indicators as Figure 6 shows. General economic declines, denoted as "peak" (*P*) to "trough" (*T*) periods, as identified by the

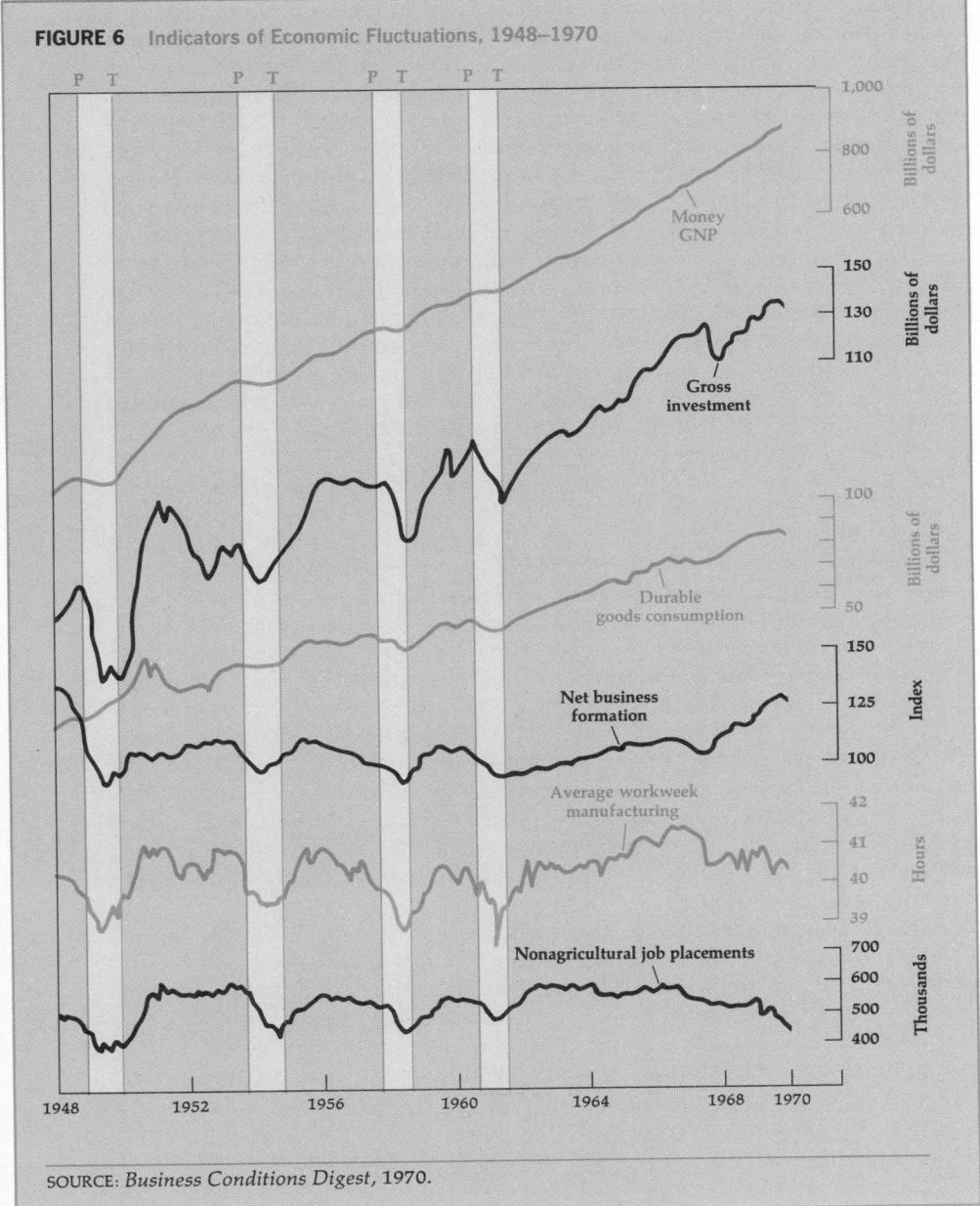

**FIGURE 6** Indicators of Economic Fluctuations, 1948–1970

SOURCE: *Business Conditions Digest*, 1970.

National Bureau of Economic Research, are indicated in the figure. Periods of economic decline, or recessions, in the post-World War II era are apparent during 1948–1949, 1953–1954, 1957–1958, and 1960–1961. Setbacks also occurred in 1966 and 1969–1970, periods labeled by some as "mini-recessions."

After studying data similar to that presented in Figure 6, observers have reached several tentative conclusions about economic instability. There is no regularity of time or amplitude characterizing business fluctuations, even though ups and downs seem to prevail. Some economic time series fluctuate markedly (such as the gross investment component of GNP), whereas others merely level out during recessions. Economic activity varies from one economic series to another and from time period to time period. Nevertheless, sensitive economic indicators like those shown in Figure 6 reveal common fluctuations in a given period of time. Economic data may reflect four distinct movements. A growth trend represented by rising economic activity over many years appears in some economic data like GNP or durable-goods consumption, shown in Figure 6. Economic fluctuations, a second distinct movement, are shown in the figure when an economic indicator declines from a peak to a trough. Seasonal and irregular movements also occur in many measures of economic activity. However, we are largely interested in growth and fluctuation movements because they are both more important and more controllable.

The value of knowing something about measuring an economy's output is clearly evidenced by the data shown in Figure 6. However, measuring economic fluctuations or highway deaths is quite a different matter from discovering causes and remedies for the problem. Both incantation and reason characterize the early history of research into causes and cures for economic instability. Not long ago, economists suspected that such influences as weather cycles, Wall Street, sunspots, and planetary movements might cause economic fluctuations. While such research was being pursued by W. S. Jevons and Henry Moore, still other observers started measuring the length of "cycles."[6] Clement Juglar, a French doctor of sorts, described historical swings in economic activity averaging 9–10 years in duration which were called "Juglar cycles." Some one-half century later, Joseph Kitchin observed a shorter 3–4-year cycle. Then Nikolai Kondratieff argued that long cyclical waves averaging some 50 years in duration also existed. Joseph Schumpeter combined these three movements into a three-stage pattern of fluctuations. More recently, special attention has been directed to recurrent swings in construction activity and inventory investment. At one time, economists argued that money imbalances, overinvestment, or underconsumption explained why economic conditions vary over time.[7] In short, economic instability and stop-and-go economic growth have concerned economists for a long time. Although until very recently little was done to modify wide swings in unemployment, income, and prices, early investigators established an important heritage in the form of empirical economic data. They also left a sometimes perplexing and almost amusing legacy of inquiry into the causes of economic instability.

[6] W. S. Jevons, *Investigations in Currency and Finance* (London: Macmillan, 1884); and Henry L. Moore, *Economic Cycles: Their Law and Cause* (New York: Macmillan, 1933).

[7] R. G. Hawtry, Knut Wicksell, Friedrich Hayek, D. H. Robertson, and W. H. Beveridge are among other prominent "cycle theorists." A good summary of cycle theory can be found in M. W. Lee, *Macroeconomics, Fluctuations, Growth, and Stability* (Homewood, Ill.: Richard D. Irwin, 1967), chs. 11 and 12.

Arthur Burns (now Chairman of the Federal Reserve) and the late Wesley Mitchell, while at the National Bureau of Economic Research, divided economic fluctuations into basic expansion-contraction stages marked by peak and trough turning points. Although by their very nature economic fluctuations are not consistent in timing and amplitude, the expansion-contraction distinction is a worthwhile one, oversimplified though it may be.

Recovery upwards from a trough or low recession stage, generally described as expansion, is illustrated in Figure 7(a). The economy tends to recover from high levels of unemployment in an expansion as underutilized industrial capacity is increasingly put back to work. Profits recover from their earlier lows, confidence in the future increases, and businessmen anticipate the need for additional investment as consumer spending and employment expand. Price levels typically remain relatively constant during early recovery, but, as expansion continues, inflationary pressures mount. With spending pressures mounting, shortages of resources and goods appear when previously unused capacity has been pressed into use. Peak levels of economic activity are characterized by intensified inflationary pressures because the demand for output exceeds capacity to produce as the economy approaches full employment. Figure 7(b) shows the general relation between real GNP and the price level where $GNP_{fe}$ represents full employment (no more than 4 percent of the labor force is unemployed). As

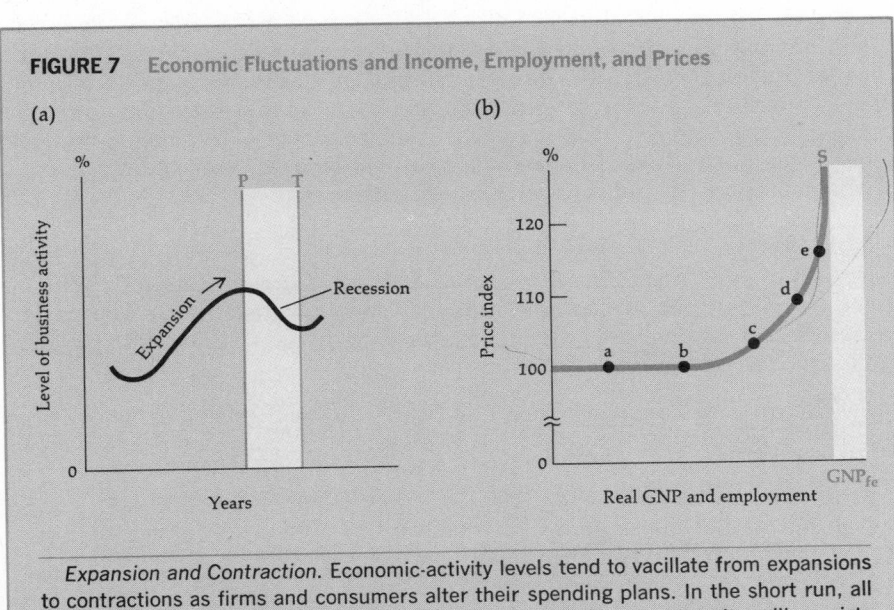

**FIGURE 7** Economic Fluctuations and Income, Employment, and Prices

(a)

(b)

*Expansion and Contraction.* Economic-activity levels tend to vacillate from expansions to contractions as firms and consumers alter their spending plans. In the short run, all economies can produce a limited amount of real output. Because a capacity ceiling exists at full employment, additional spending will only add to price-level increases once maximum output is reached. Typically, prices rise prior to reaching full employment.

the economy expands from low output levels to a higher level of GNP, spending pressures cause prices to rise more and more rapidly until full employment ($GNP_{fe}$) is reached. The total supply of output expands along schedule $S$ from points *a-b-c-d-e,* as shown in Figure 7(b), indicating that price levels rise with increasing intensity as peaks in economic activity and full employment are approached. Once capacity is reached, further spending causes prices and money GNP to rise, but real GNP remains unchanged.

Like a cumulative expansion, a downward contraction gradually gathers momentum on its own. Waves of pessimism accompany what appears to be an increasingly bleak outlook for sales, consumer demand, and profits. Prices begin to stabilize, but they tend to remain rigid at the higher level reached at the peak of an expansion. Unemployment rises and investment alternatives, once looked upon favorably, lose their appeal. Ultimately declines in spending, employment, and income reach a recessionary trough from which a new recovery and expansion period may be initiated, as Figure 7(a) reveals.

### CONTRIBUTING FACTORS IN CUMULATIVE EXPANSIONS AND CONTRACTIONS

There are a variety of factors which can influence economic activity. Wars, for example, often prompt expansion and inflationary conditions as nations speed production up to or beyond normal capacity levels. World Wars I and II as well as the Korean and Vietnam hostilities had this impact on the economy of the United States. Major technological innovations and discoveries, such as the birth of the railroad industry or the discovery of gold in the late nineteenth century, also induce rapid expansion. Historically, expansions in the United States have been followed by recessions and even financial crises, attributable in part to the optimistic and sometimes speculative fervor that prevailed earlier. While such external factors can influence economic events, our primary interest is in discovering and managing events internal to the economic process that may contribute to waves of expansion and decline. Attention to internal economic relations focuses on spending, particularly on investment and consumption expenditures.

### ANATOMY OF ECONOMIC INSTABILITY

Here and in subsequent chapters, it will be demonstrated that variations in spending on output are at the root of economic instability. The major cause-effect relationships influencing the level of GNP and its expansion or contraction over a period of time are:

1. The level of consumer spending, which is itself partly dependent on income—a reasonably sensible *a priori* assertion for one individual or society at large.

2. A nation's income depends in part on consumer expenditures, as we saw in our earlier discussion of the measurement of GNP. Thus, there is a two-way relation between $C$ and GNP, or $C \longleftrightarrow GNP$.

3. Consumer expenditures may accelerate or decelerate investment in inventories, buildings, and equipment as producers react to household decisions to consume or save. Thus, the relation $C \longrightarrow I$ is part of the anatomy of economic fluctuation.

4. Investment expenditures, also a component of GNP, influence the level of income; hence the relation $I \longrightarrow GNP$.

5. Developments in financial markets may also influence the tripartite income-consumption-investment relationship. The availability of credit to firms and households is dependent upon the supply of money, which influences expenditures and GNP.

Although it is always dangerous to simplify one aspect of a complex process, available evidence appears to confirm that investment spending is volatile and of unusual importance in determining the stability and level of GNP. For one thing, inventories are a "buffer" investment intended to facilitate sales or flows of output which may be unsteady. Investment in plant and equipment likewise is sensitive to consumer demand, and producers may expand or contract capacity, depending on current rates of capacity utilization. Investment expenditures for residential construction are particularly sensitive to the availability of financing and the money supply. Remember, too, that even though consumption expenditures are relatively stable, almost two-thirds of GNP consists of these expenditures. Because of the large absolute size of consumption spending, small variations may have a large impact on GNP. Let us now consider how consumption, investment, GNP, and monetary conditions interact to produce economic instability.

*The Expansion Phase*   As GNP and household incomes rise, consumer expenditures tend to increase, prompting business firms to accelerate investment in capital goods and inventories in anticipation of increased future profits. Construction activity, including residential housing, may also expand rapidly in the early stage of economic expansion. For example, the relatively prolonged expansion of the 1920s was aided by the backlog of demand for investment goods not available during World War I. In addition, new industries (e.g., electricity and communications), the advent of mass-production techniques, and a booming housing market contributed to the prosperity of the 1920s. Expenditures on consumer-durable goods may rise rather rapidly as income and employment prospects brighten (particularly if households earlier postponed such purchases due to a bleak economic outlook), adding even further to increased spending on output. The availability of credit on more favorable terms also contributes to increased consumer, and thus increased investment, spending. Finally, spending plans are sometimes stepped up by consumers and investors simply because they anticipate rising prices in the future.

Whatever the combination of internal and external expansionary factors, it is clear that production capacity cannot be expanded infinitely at one point in time. In the short run, capital and labor resources cannot be increased significantly, and as full-employment conditions are approached, prices tend to rise. If excess spending persists, it can only drive the prices of goods and resources upward. Throughout the 1940s, high levels of economic activity were maintained in the United States as war production was buttressed by rising consumer incomes. Later, wage and price controls were used as inflationary pressures mounted, and, in the postwar era, a war-induced backlog of consumer and investment spending pushed the economy into further inflationary expansion broken only briefly by mild recessions in 1946 and again in 1948–1949. The same general pattern of inflationary expansion characterized the American economy from 1967–1969 as Vietnam hostilities mounted. Inflationary increases in wages and prices associated with a boom may tend to erode profit margins and thereby contribute to a leveling off and gradual decline in economic activity that is as complex as an economic expansion.

*The Contraction Phase*  Cumulative expansion is checked and an economic decline is started in part by consumers saving more and spending less of their incomes as higher product prices meet increasing consumer resistance. Moreover, inflation tends to depreciate the purchasing power of past savings, worsening the economic status of households living on fixed incomes. Then too, consumer demand for durable goods may become satiated as peak levels of economic activity are reached. As fewer consumer dollars are passed around the circular-income stream, inventories may rise and some portion of the newly increased productive capacity may go unutilized. Business investment plans may be cut back in anticipation of lower sales and profits. At the peak of economic activity bankers may be either unable to lend all the funds borrowers demand or unwilling to accept risks, another factor acting as a potential ceiling to economic prosperity. As a matter of historical fact, in the American economy, many rapid expansions culminated in the virtual collapse of the banking system. As confidence in the future diminishes, cumulative declines in employment, income, and spending drive an economy into a recession. Consumers may cut back on expenditures even further, in part because of rising unemployment and in part because of uncertainties about the future. Business firms also may find that they need not replace worn-out capital equipment because of declining consumer demand. In any event, a profit squeeze and pessimistic attitudes about the future retard consumer and investment spending.

In late 1929, for example, the United States economy was devastated by the Great Depression—an event that halted economic progress in the nation for more than a decade. What happened is best revealed by real GNP, which declined some 30 percent between 1929 and 1933. Ten years later, in 1939, real GNP still remained very near the 1929 level of $203 billion. Per capita disposable income in real dollars was lower in 1939 than in 1929 as output and employment stagnated, pushing the nation close to disaster. Several thousand banks failed during this decade, and a variety of important social and economic reforms swept the country.[8] Another example of contraction is the United States economy as it experienced long-term growth throughout the 1950s. The post-Korean War recession that occurred in 1954 came as firms readjusted inventory and production plans back to a level consistent with prewar consumer spending. Still another recession occurred in 1958 as business investment again declined due to a decrease in consumer spending for durable goods. Later, in 1959, consumer credit eased up and both construction spending and government expenditures gradually increased, thus paving the way for a renewed expansion. However, unemployment remained unusually high during the 1958–1959 period, and it was not until after the recesssion of 1961 that the economy

[8] Although speculation on real estate and in security markets was a part of the 1929 collapse, note very carefully that the so-called stock-market "crash" is not considered causative. The stock-market crash was more a symptom of the Depression than a cause.

clearly broke into a full-fledged expansion characterized by prolonged prosperity. The 1960s were a unique period because of the prolonged expansion, which was partly due to the attention government devoted to maintaining a stable economic expansion—a subject to be examined further in later chapters.

Economic fluctuations are by no means as simple as described here. Variations occur in the timing, duration, and amplitude of the impact of changes in economic conditions on various industries and regions. Nevertheless, economic fluctuations in the aggregate economy generally include noticeable variations in spending, unemployment, and income. *The contemporary explanation of fluctuations in economic activity concentrates on planned spending as the causal factor,* where consumption, investment, government, and net exports comprise useful spending categories.

### PERMANENCY OF STAGNATION

Is it possible for recurrent periods of prosperity and recession in a market economy to continue unabated? The historical answer to this question is mixed, although, in principle, there is no reason why excessive expansionary surges and declines in economic activity cannot be ameliorated. The possibility for controlled expansion exists, but the probability of avoiding expansionary excesses is small unless government policies are properly used. If the economic havoc of the 1930s demonstrated anything, it was that a market economy oriented to the profit motive contains no automatic corrective device capable of restoring full employment. Indeed, economic relations in a market economy are characterized by some degree of overreaction and variability in spending, the critical determinant of expansions and contractions in economic activity.

### The Consequences of Instability

The primary consequences of economic instability are: (*a*) unemployment of labor and other resources, (*b*) general price-level increases (inflation), and (*c*) failure of the economy to achieve its potential rate of economic growth. There are costs associated with this triad of events which merit brief investigation.

### THE IMPACT OF UNEMPLOYMENT

There are personal, social, and economic costs associated with failure to achieve full employment. Earlier we stated that most authorities today regard 4 percent unemployment as "normal"; that is, when 96 percent of the labor force is employed, we are said to have full employment. The reason for using 4 percent as a full-employment norm is that some unemployment is unavoidable because of seasonal jobs, job attrition, changes in occupation or region, and new entrants to the labor force. Moreover, with the labor force in the United States numbering in excess of 80 million persons today, we can expect it to include some unemployable persons—those with poor health, inadequate training, or technologically outmoded work skills—seeking work. Although there is no definitive guide to the minimum amount of unemployment that can be achieved in the United States, Congressional and other research results suggest that between 2 and 4 percent unemployment is unavoidable.[9] Therefore, identification of 4 percent unemployment as full employment represents a reasonable (but maximum) boundary limit.

The extent to which full employment has been an elusive and rarely achieved goal is partially demonstrated by considering the decade of the 1930s, when more than 100 million man-years were wasted, or some two years of GNP were lost because of unemployment. Uncertainty, fear, and in many instances hunger and deprivation accompany unemployment, particularly during severe and prolonged depressions. Loss of self-respect and the will to improve one's economic lot travel with poverty among the unemployed. Even though the personal costs of unemployment are masked by statistics, such costs are no less real.

Unemployment statistics are inadequate on many counts. Aggregate data conceal the uneven impact of unemployment on different segments of the population. During the comparatively minor recessions of 1958 and 1960, for example, one out of every eight nonwhites was unemployed. Moreover, full-employment conditions (as during the prosperous 1960s) fail to reveal the realities of unemployment. Between the mid-1960s and early 1970, full employment was generally achieved in the aggregate, but the nonwhite unemployment rate was approximately *twice* that of whites, and unemployment rates for white teenagers ranged from 12 to 18 percent. Unemployment rates for nonwhite teenagers have remained alarmingly high. In 1968, for example, one-fourth of all nonwhites between 16 and 19 years of age were unemployed. The number of persons enumerated as officially unemployed is also biased downward because persons employed part-time are counted as fully employed. In addition, workers who withdraw from the labor force after searching fruitlessly for a job are not counted among the unemployed, since they are not actively seeking work. Although we do not have accurate estimates of "hidden unemployment" of this type, concealed joblessness may afflict millions—and might raise unemployment rates to 6 or 7 percent, rather than the reported 4 percent at full employment.[10]

### THE COSTS OF INFLATION

It is reasonably clear that maximum employment is desirable, but what is the significance of inflation? Inflation is important because apparent increases in income are partially eroded by price-level increases, and output and income can be capriciously redistributed through inflation. Savings and fixed-value assets decline in value, debtors are helped and creditors are hurt, and persons on fixed incomes are penalized when the general price level increases.

Inflation tends to redistribute income away from those who are owners of fixed-value assets. Consider the example of a newly married couple who purchase an insurance policy which will furnish $10,000 for their children's college education. If prices increase in the future as in the past, the purchasing power of $10,000 will have been halved within 24 years. At that rate of increase in prices, an insurance policy providing $100,000 in retirement income for an 18-year-old entering the labor force would be worth less than

[9] U.S. Congress, Joint Economic Committee, *The Extent and Nature of Frictional Unemployment*, 1959.

[10] R. A. Wykstra, "Some Additional Evidence on the Effects of Education on Labor Force Participation," *The Western Economic Journal* (Summer 1967), 288–293.

$30,000 when he reached age 65. The impact of inflation on savers and creditors, most of whom are middle-class Americans, also contributes to hostility toward inflation. Most middle-class Americans have checking and modest savings accounts, a pension fund to which they contribute current dollars of purchasing power, life insurance policies, and perhaps government bonds. To the extent that they are lenders instead of borrowers (as many are), inflation means that they will receive fewer *real* dollars back than they set aside to provide for the future. On the other hand, debtors (largely business firms) actually pay fewer *real* dollars back. Because inflation redistributes income away from persons living on fixed incomes, they also tend to be the unwilling recipients of more future scarcity than they anticipated. Retirees, persons depending on relief or other government transfer payments, and salaried persons unable to obtain short-term wage adjustments are among the penalized. The problem of inflation is that it tends to favor debtors and penalizes weaker consumers and the fixed-income groups least able to carry such a burden.

## INFLATION: "CREEP OR GALLOP"?

Rapid and intense inflation—dubbed "galloping inflation"—is regarded as undesirable by all. Historically, in this and other countries, rapid price movements usually have been associated with major wars or political turmoil. Mild or "creeping inflation" is another matter about which there is little agreement. Some observers argue that a mild inflation (1 to 3 percent annually) may stimulate an otherwise sluggish economy, leading to rising profits, increased investment expenditures, and full employment.

Still others warn that mild inflationary pressures tend to spiral and gain momentum—another important reality in some instances. Should prices increase rapidly, economic transactions among firms, investors, and consumers can be severely disrupted and real output may decline. Increased product prices spur labor to request higher wages, which reinforces the need for price increases, and so forth. Furthermore, anticipated price increases encourage buyers to buy more, adding fuel to the existing fire. In any event, income redistribution remains a problem with any type of inflation—including the creeping variety.

## ECONOMIC GROWTH: THE GNP GAP

The fundamental problem associated with unemployment and inflation as by-products of economic instability can be summarily described in terms of growth in real income and output. Nations, like individuals, desire an orderly economic process whereby they can squeeze the greatest amount of output possible from available resources. This is true for any given year, and it is an equally important goal over several years.

Rising productivity and increases in the quantity and quality of human and capital resources allow the productive capacity of a nation to expand over a period of years. Even though the aggregate capacity of a nation increases, an economy may fail to operate at full employment if spending is inadequate. The result of instability-induced unemployment can be expressed as a real *output gap,* or the difference between potential and actual GNP, as shown in Figure 8. *Potential GNP* is that level of aggregate output which could have been produced had the economy achieved full employment (4 percent unemployment) year after year. The output gap is the

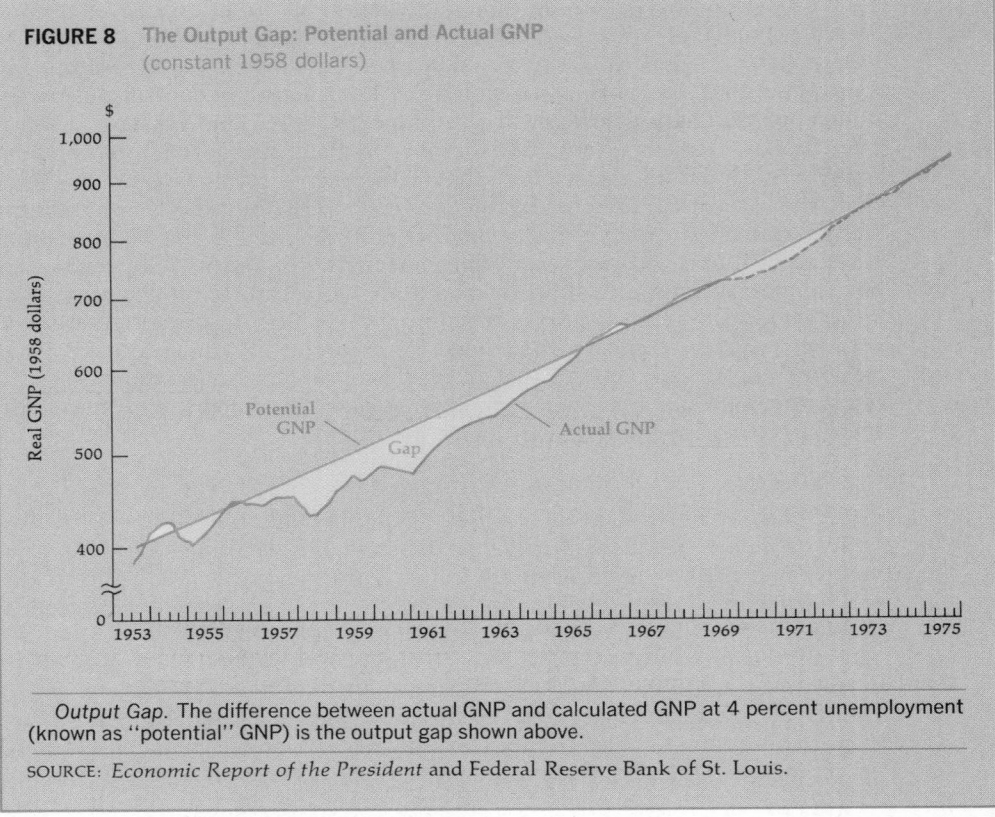

**FIGURE 8** The Output Gap: Potential and Actual GNP (constant 1958 dollars)

*Output Gap.* The difference between actual GNP and calculated GNP at 4 percent unemployment (known as "potential" GNP) is the output gap shown above.

SOURCE: *Economic Report of the President* and Federal Reserve Bank of St. Louis.

amount of real GNP *not* produced, or the shaded area in Figure 8 between *actual* and *potential* GNP. Failure to operate at full-employment capacity is reflected by a lower-than-potential GNP that cumulatively amounts to several hundreds of billions of dollars of lost output.

Since 1961, the output gap in real GNP has gradually closed, and inflationary output levels prevailed toward the end of the decade, as Figure 8 shows. The key to elimination of a GNP gap, and thus to achievement of capacity rates of economic growth that create new jobs for a growing population, is control over aggregate spending, a notion examined in the following chapter. As we shall see, the output gap which emerged again in the early 1970s is the result of both private- and public-sector expenditures.

## REVIEW
### Summary

1. The full employment of all resources is important to a society characterized by economic scarcity; yet, a market economy does not automatically use all resources fully. The New Economics is concerned with economic instability in aggregate income. Unemployment, inflation, and uneven economic growth typify the instability that characterizes a market system.

2. The amount of output or goods and services produced by a nation, typically described as aggregate income or gross national product (GNP), can be measured either as expenditures on output or as aggregate income payments to factors of production. In either event, GNP is the value added as goods and services move through the production process.

3. Gross national product, a measure of the *market value of final output*, is the sum of four expenditure streams: consumption (C), gross investment (I), government purchases (G), and net foreign exports (Ex).

4. Five income accounts commonly used in measuring a nation's income are GNP, *total* final income or output; net national product (NNP), *net* final income, or GNP adjusted for depreciation of capital resources; national income (NI), income *earned* by all resources; personal income (PI), income *received* by persons; and disposable income (DI), income *available* to persons after adjustment for personal taxes. Disposable income is either consumed or saved.

5. Changes in price levels are a major problem encountered in measuring a nation's income. A price index measuring the percentage change in prices from one point in time to another is computed as follows: Price index = prices of goods in year X ÷ prices of goods in year N, where N is the base year. Money or current-dollar GNP is aggregate income unadjusted for price changes. Money GNP is adjusted to real or constant-dollar GNP to remove the effect of price-level changes as follows: Real GNP = money GNP in year X ÷ price index in year X.

6. National-income accounting estimates are imperfect measures of a nation's production because the quality of output, leisure, the distribution of income, nonmarket production and consumption, and social values are not fully reflected in any of the five income accounts.

7. The historical record of economic activity in the United States is marred by economic fluctuations. The market economy has vacillated from expansion to contraction to expansion time and time again. Economic instability of this sort sometimes can be traced to factors external to the economic process, such as war. In other instances, internal factors related to business and consumer-household spending explain economic fluctuations. Consumption and investment expenditures as well as monetary conditions are key factors in explaining economic instability arising from elements internal to the operation of an economy.

8. Expansions are characterized by expenditure booms which gradually taper off as peak levels of economic activity are reached. Contractions are characterized by expenditure declines and the underutilization of productive capacity.

9. When an economy alternates between rapid expansion and economic contractions, three distinct problems arise. Unemployment tends to be excessive as some portion of potential GNP is not produced, inflation or increases in the general price level occur, and economic instability results in ragged and uneven economic growth. When resources are not fully employed, an "output or GNP gap"—the difference in actual and potential full-employment GNP—characterizes economic instability.

MACROECONOMICS: EMPLOYMENT, PRICES, AND ECONOMIC STABILITY

## Identify the Following Concepts and Terms

- macroeconomics
- potential GNP
- New Economics
- GNP
- net investment
- price index
- peaks and troughs
- input-output model

- expenditures ≡ income payments
- output or GNP gap
- value added
- creeping inflation
- net exports
- factors internal to fluctuations
- money- and real-income adjustments
- full employment

## Questions to Answer

1. Explain why an increase in pay from $120 to $150 per week between 1971 and 1975 may not result in a $30 increase in a real standing of living. Compute a price index and adjust the above data to show the change in real income when the price of a "basket" of consumer goods rises from $50 to $55 from 1971 to 1975.

2. Using the following data, explain and compute GNP, NNP, *NI*, *PI*, and *DI* (data are in billions).

| | | | |
|---|---|---|---|
| Consumption | $537 | Personal taxes | $ 97 |
| Depreciation of capital | 73 | Indirect business taxes | 74 |
| Net investment | 53 | Corporate profits | 80 |
| Gross exports | 46 | Social security taxes | 47 |
| Gross imports | 43 | Transfer payments | 84 |
| Government purchases | 200 | Dividend and interest payments | 24 |
| Saving | 41 | | |

3. Potential GNP at full employment and actual GNP may deviate from each other over the course of time. Explain how certain key factors contribute to this gap in real GNP. How does the gap relate to three consequences of economic instability?

# CHAPTER 7
# Income and
# Employment Theory

The description of economic conditions in the previous chapter indicated that full employment, stable prices, and potential levels of economic growth are not always achieved. The record indicates that sporadic, roller-coaster bursts of unemployment or inflation may be more characteristic of economic activity than is economic stability. This chapter explains the causes of unemployment and economic instability—a task continued in Chapter 8. Much of our attention in this chapter will be devoted to developing tools of analysis that are useful in studying economic instability. Part A begins with a review of the causes of instability using a circular-income-flow model of an economy. Indeed, we shall explain the determination of income and employment in two different ways (in Parts A and B). The verbal description of economic instability in Part A is necessary to set the stage for two new concepts: the *aggregate* demand for a nation's output and the *aggregate* supply of output provided by all producers. Part B develops three important tools of analysis needed to understand stable income and output levels at full employment, and Part C briefly examines the components of aggregate demand. Part D completes our survey of the macroeconomic problems of unemployment and inflation by describing in precise terms how government policies may be used to stabilize the economy.

## A. INSTABILITY IN THE CIRCULAR-INCOME FLOW

In our examination of national-income accounts in Chapter 6 we saw that many levels of aggregate income and output are possible. Furthermore, a given level of income is not necessarily one that fully employs all resources, a point illustrated by the existence of the GNP gap. What is it, then, that determines the levels of income, output, and employment? The deceptively simple answer to this question is: A nation's income is determined by total spending for output. Firms produce a level of output they anticipate being able to sell. Anticipated spending for output determines income, employment, and the extent to which a nation utilizes its productive capacity. Today, this is a widely accepted explanation of the determination of income and employment. However, not too long ago economists held quite different views about the determination of income and employment. These are worthy of passing notice.

### The Classical Theory

Classical economic theory argued that prolonged unemployment is not possible because all output will be purchased, a proposition sometimes termed "Say's Law" after J. B. Say, a French economist of the 1800s. Classical theory stated that temporary spending declines were accompanied by declining prices for goods and resources available in surplus amounts which, in turn, induced buyers to increase expenditures. For example, as the interest-rate "price" of funds used for capital investment declined, classical economics argued that the economy would put more such resources to work and thus augment total spending. Furthermore, declining wages would encourage firms to employ more labor and falling product prices would encourage households to demand more goods and services. Downward price adjustments due to unused *supply* ultimately would create *demand* sufficient to clear the market of output and maintain full employment. Therefore, *real* income and output could not remain in a depressed state, nor would unemployment be a serious problem, largely because of the flexibility of wages, prices, and interest rates. Thus, automatic supply and demand adjustments in a market economy were seen as capable of maintaining full employment.

All of this sounds plausible enough on the surface—or does it? First look at the facts presented in Chapter 6. If the classical view is correct, can you explain why some 100 million man-years of cumulative unemployment occurred in the 1930s? The classical economists could not; hence, their theory was abandoned, on three grounds.

First, the facts show that wages, prices, and interest rates are not quickly flexible in a *downward* direction. Firms, financial institutions, labor unions, and other institutions in the economic system resist downward adjustments in wages and prices. Second, if wages do fall, household incomes decline, an event that depresses the consumption component of total spending. Finally, Lord Keynes dispensed with the classical argument that over a long period price and wage adjustments would lead to full employment by reminding its proponents that ". . . in the long run we will all be dead." The stage was set for abandonment of the classical economic theory of employment and income, and the New Economics was born.

### Modern Macroeconomics

In debunking the ideas of classical economists, John Maynard Keynes coined two important ideas: aggregate demand and aggregate supply. *Aggregate demand (DD)* represents total planned expenditures for the output of a nation. Expenditures, as we have learned, can be categorized as consumption (C), investment (I), government purchases of goods and services (G), and net exports (Ex). *Aggregate supply* is the amount of total output firms produce in anticipation of some level of aggregate demand that can be produced and sold profitably. When producers anticipate that total expenditures will clear the market of $X billion of GNP, they produce that level of aggregate supply. The problem of economic instability begins when aggregate demand and aggregate supply are not equal at full employment.

Suppose that the aggregate supply of output remains unchanged and that total spending for output declines from a level achieved in 1970 that just happened to fully utilize all resources. The consequences of a reduction in total spending are: (*a*) Firms will not be able to produce profitably and sell as large a volume of goods and services as before; (*b*) inventories will rise as unsold goods accumulate and production and output will be cut back as a result; (c) fewer resources will be employed to produce the smaller output needed for a future time period (say, 1971); and (d) aggregate income and employment levels will decline. As income declines, the consumption and investment portions of total spending decline still further in later periods because of declining employment and the bleak business outlook, unless consumers and investors draw upon past savings, borrow, or otherwise buttress a contracting demand for output. Unfortunately, the contractionary process is reinforced once it starts, and declining levels of economic activity naturally tend to encourage consumers and business firms to save more and spend and borrow less. Failure to use productive capacity fully generates unemployment and retards economic growth. The culprits are reductions in consumption spending by households, business-firm investments, government expenditures, or net exports to other nations—the four expenditure components of aggregate demand.

Suppose now that the business community anticipates that consumption spending will rise and it does. As total spending for a nation's output expands, production rises because more goods and services can be sold profitably. Since firms may not immediately reach the production and inventory levels desired, they may be encouraged to invest in additional plant, equipment, and inventories. Cumulative expansionary forces are further reinforced if the investment component of total spending increases. More resources are employed, incomes received by factors of production increase, and consumption may rise even more, adding still further impetus to the upward spiral of expenditures and income in subsequent time periods. As long as *full-employment* capacity is not reached, real income and employment rise. As the capacity limit to production is *reached* because resources are fully employed, competition for limited goods and resources drives up the general price level.

### INCOME, OUTPUT, AND EMPLOYMENT LINKAGES

The linkage between spending for output, aggregate income, and employment levels constitutes a feedback system, as shown below. Two features of this summary of macroeconomic relationships are important. First, aggregate demand ultimately determines the level of aggregate output, employment, and income in a nation. Second, *future* expenditures are influenced by the income level, as shown by the upper feedback loop. That is, the level of GNP in 1971 partially determines consumption and investment spending in 1972. This is particularly true for consumption expenditures, since they depend in a large measure upon disposable income (*DI*). Moreover, the level of consumption may influence investment expenditures, since business firms

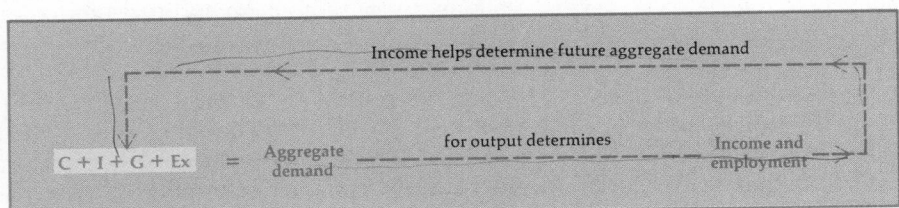

invest in plant and equipment in anticipation of consumer demand. Prosperity and rising income levels tend to intensify total spending pressures, whereas economic declines tend to dampen spending.

We can summarize the direction of income and employment changes in response to a change in $C + I + G + Ex$ viewed as planned expenditures as follows:

INCREASES IN $DD$ yield EXPANSION OF OUTPUT, EMPLOYMENT, AND INCOME
DECREASES IN $DD$ yield CONTRACTION OF OUTPUT, EMPLOYMENT, AND INCOME

These fundamental relationships of the unemployment-inflation problem will be examined in greater detail as we proceed. Before we do, let us reexamine the record of spending variability that is alleged to be responsible for variations in income and employment levels.

## VARIABILITY OF SPENDING

How valid is the argument that variability in spending determines a nation's income and employment levels? Although empirical data on an annual basis give only a crude comparison, we can get some idea of the validity of this assertion by reexamining the expenditure changes in selected recession periods discussed in Chapter 6. Gross investment and expenditures for consumer durable goods are among the more volatile spending components in GNP.

Furthermore, these expenditures comprise more than one-third of GNP, they are also important in an absolute sense. Gross investment expenditures increased from $34 billion to $72 billion between 1947 and 1961, for example, but marked contractions did occur during postwar recessions, as the data for selected recession years below show. Indeed, earlier data reveal that

| Billions of dollars | 1948–1949 | 1953–1954 | 1957–1958 | 1960–1961 |
|---|---|---|---|---|
| Change in gross investment | −$10 | −$1 | −$7 | −$3 |
| Change in consumer durables | +$ 2 | −$1 | −$3 | −$1 |

from 1929 to the depth of the Great Depression in 1933, gross investment expenditures declined from $16 billion to $1 billion. Variability in investment expenditures is not surprising, since firms base such expenditures upon the levels of income, profit, and production *expected* in the future. Consumer expenditures for durable goods (automobiles, furniture, appliances, etc.) are also somewhat volatile. Even though expenditures on consumer durables rose from $46 billion to $100 billion between 1947 and 1961, actual declines did occur during most of the post-World War II recession periods. Durable consumer-good expenditures can vary from year to year because households are able to postpone such purchases. (Items like automobiles and appliances can be repaired and allowed to deteriorate over a short period of time.) Thus, it turns out that the record does show that consumption and investment expenditures vary between expansions and contractions in economic activity.

## The Circular Flow and Income Determination

Income in an economy is a continuous flow of expenditures and receipts from one time period to another. Measurement of actual income at a point in time is static, just like a photographic snapshot that stops action or movement in contrast to a motion picture that reveals change. While our interest is in the dynamic changes an economy exhibits, we can learn a good deal about income and employment relationships by examining the circular flow of income.

### SPENDING-STREAM INFLOWS AND LEAKAGES

Figure 1 is a circular-income-flow model (discussed in earlier chapters) which emphasizes income flows from the perspective of national-income accounting. Income received by households, firms, or government can be either spent or saved. That portion saved by households is a *leakage* from the spending stream, as Figure 1 suggests, whereas consumption expenditures flow back to producers. Similarly, business firms may not pay out all of their receipts to households, but may instead save by retaining some portion of earnings. In a realistic model of income flows, two other leakages from the spending stream are identifiable: government taxes and imports of goods and services from foreign nations.

All leakages contract the income-expenditure stream flowing back to producers in the form of total spending. Any withdrawal from the income stream means that future GNP will be lower than would otherwise be the case. However, withdrawals from the spending stream may be offset by other spending-stream inflows, such as business investment outlays, gov-

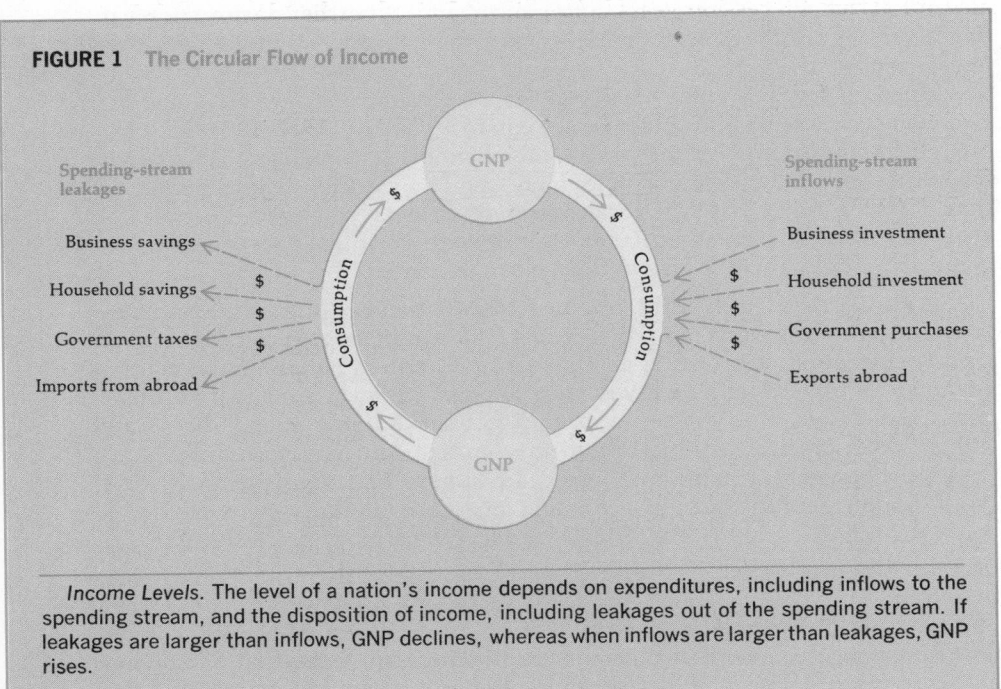

**FIGURE 1**   The Circular Flow of Income

Spending-stream leakages

GNP

Spending-stream inflows

Business savings

Household savings

Government taxes

Imports from abroad

Consumption

Consumption

Business investment

Household investment

Government purchases

Exports abroad

GNP

*Income Levels.* The level of a nation's income depends on expenditures, including inflows to the spending stream, and the disposition of income, including leakages out of the spending stream. If leakages are larger than inflows, GNP declines, whereas when inflows are larger than leakages, GNP rises.

ernment expenditures on goods and services, or income receipts from exports. Thus, the future income level may rise, fall, or remain unchanged, depending upon the stability or instability of consumption expenditures and the extent to which leakages and inflows in the spending stream offset each other. An example may help show why a stable income level requires that leakages from the spending stream must be offset by spending-stream inflows in a like amount (assuming consumption is unchanged).

Assume that in the city of Albuquerque $1 million in daily output is produced which entails income payments of a like amount to resources. Suppose now that, for one reason or another, spending-stream inflows of the investment variety decline by $50,000. Assuming no other changes in spending, this means that expenditures on output are going to decline initially by $50,000, and GNP will now be less than $1 million daily. Unfortunately, income instability does not necessarily end at this point, because the initial decline in spending will trigger further changes in the economy of Albuquerque. The important point to remember, however, is this: Provided that $1 million is respent as aggregate demand for output, the circular-income flow of $1 million continues unaltered indefinitely. This situation is defined as a *stable* or *equilibrium income condition*. Equilibrium is possible *only* if expenditures on output clear markets of total output. What this means for an economy is that a stable or equilibrium income level requires that inflows into the spending stream due to investment, government, or export expenditures *must* equal spending-stream leakages to saving, taxes, and imports from other economies.

In summary, the critical points are these three:

1. Leakages such as saving represent a withdrawal from the spending stream that depresses the circular flow of income, whereas consumption expenditures and inflows such as investment raise the level of total spending and income.

2. Income stability will prevail only if the total of leakages from and inflows into the circular-income flow are equal.

3. If leakages exceed inflows, total spending is smaller than output produced, and income and employment tend to decline over a period of time. On the other hand, if total spending exceeds aggregate output, the spending stream is enlarged; that is, inflows exceed leakages, causing income and employment to rise in the next time period.

We now have identified the primary role of spending in income and employment determination and the concept of equilibrium income levels. A circular-income-flow model is useful as a first approximation of the macroeconomic problems of unemployment and inflation, but many important characteristics of the income- and employment-determination process are hidden or imprecisely approximated in Figure 1. For that reason, the concepts of aggregate demand and aggregate supply must be developed more fully. Supplementary tools of economic analysis will allow us to develop a more definitive "second-generation" model to deal more precisely with the goals of full employment and price stability.

## B. A MODEL OF AGGREGATE DEMAND AND AGGREGATE SUPPLY

In examining changes in income and employment, an important distinction must be made between *actual* spending and *planned* spending which, once realized, contributes to changes in income and employment.

To those interested in accounting for a nation's *past* income, the sum of actual expenditures, or $C + I + G + Ex$, is identical to income received by all factors of production, as we learned in Chapter 6. Suppose that we ignore government and net foreign expenditures in national-income flows and simply consider the fact that firms and households either spend or save their incomes. This means that in measuring actual national income from the expenditure side, GNP = $C + I$. Because households and firms can either consume or save the incomes they receive, we can also say that GNP = $C + S$, where $S$ designates saving. Since $C$ is identical in either instance, *actual* $I \equiv S$, where $\equiv$ indicates an identity; that is, *actual* investment and *actual* saving are the same thing looked at two different ways. Actual income *not* consumed (or saving), is thus equivalent to investment expenditures, but only when we measure income for some *past* time period. The distinction between *planned* and *actual* levels of investment spending is important because, unlike the identity characteristic of $C + I \equiv C + S$ used to measure *actual* GNP, there is nothing that assures us that the amount of output producers *plan* to supply will equal the amount of income consumers and investors *intend* to spend.

Actual aggregate-demand and aggregate-supply relations are meaningless if we are talking about the forces causing income and employment to change. It is the intention to spend, and particularly *planned investment*, that produces changes in future output, income, and employment levels. This being the case, we shall understand all future references to $I$ to mean *intended* or *planned* magnitudes, not the actual magnitudes used in national-income accounting. Thus, while actual $I$ and $S$ must always be equal, some unintended investment may be included in $I$ and this can encourage firms to reduce future output. Alternatively, if intended investment is not realized because inventory *dis*investment occurs, firms will be encouraged to step up production, causing income and employment to rise.

A final clarification is needed of three assumptions made to simplify the explanation of the determination of income and employment which follows.

1. Technology and resources are constant, and money is viewed as having no impact on a nation's output level. Techniques of production are assumed not to change, and all resources, including labor, are held constant at some given level. This means that aggregate supply is fixed—economic growth is excluded from the analysis. In addition, we continue to presume that income and employment increase or decrease in some approximate but direct proportion to each other. Even though the full-employment level of output *does not* change, actual employment *can* rise up to the full-employment level.

2. Investment and income are net concepts. Instead of using GNP as a measure of a nation's output, we define income as NNP (GNP less depreciation of capital resources). Thus, investment expenditures refer to *net investment*—new additions to the stock of capital resources. In short, we are concerned with *net* additions to the spending stream in the form of intended investment expenditures above and beyond those required to cover depreciated capital equipment.

3. Government and foreign trade do not exist. By assuming government and foreign trade to be nonexistent, we can define expenditures on output or aggregate demand as simply $C + I$, even though we know that in reality

it is composed of $C + I + G + Ex$. Exports and imports henceforth can be regarded as buried in net investment. Government is ignored temporarily to allow study of the domestic sector of a market economy. By ignoring government, our concept of income is considerably simplified, since taxes account for the basic differences in various measures of income such as $NI$, $PI$, and $DI$. Thus, it is possible to designate income loosely, understanding it to identify any income account ranging from NNP to $DI$ as the context of our discussion is altered.

## Aggregate Supply and Aggregate Demand

Because the government and the foreign-trade sectors included earlier in our circular-income-flow model have been assumed away, we can simply regard the economy as consisting of producers (largely business firms) that supply and consumers (largely households) that demand a nation's aggregate output. Our point of departure will be delineation of an aggregate-supply schedule.

### THE AGGREGATE-SUPPLY SCHEDULE

Figure 2 illustrates a schedule of aggregate supply, measured on the horizontal axis and designated as NNP. Firms produce a level of NNP ranging from $600 billion to $900 billion, depending on expected $C + I$ spending, which is measured on the vertical axis of Figure 2(a). A 45° line like that

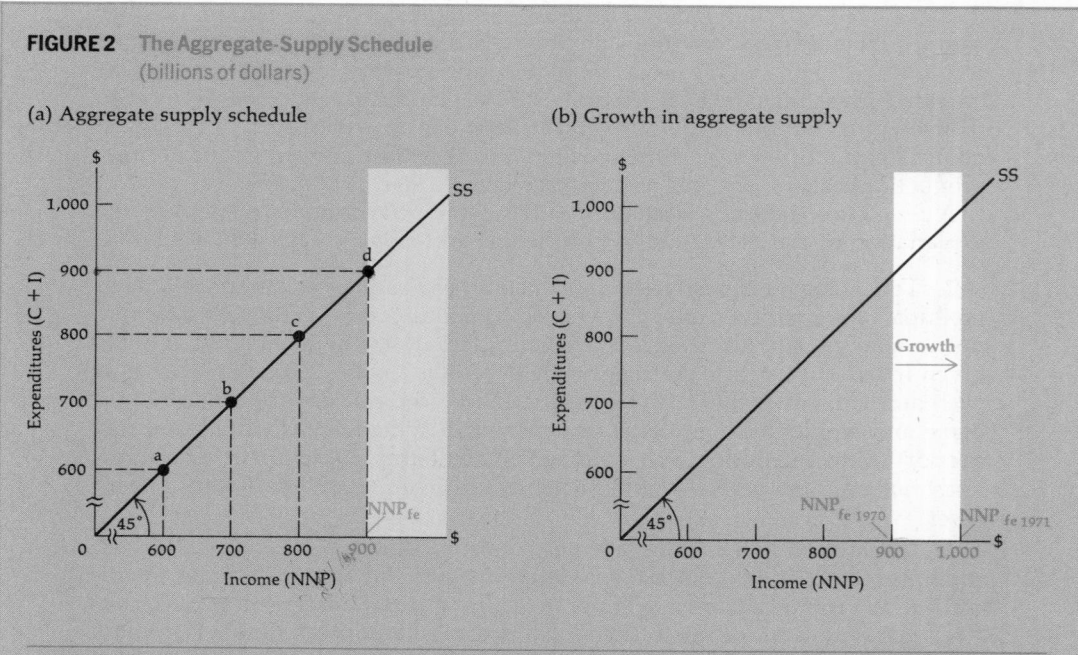

**FIGURE 2**  The Aggregate-Supply Schedule (billions of dollars)

(a) Aggregate supply schedule

(b) Growth in aggregate supply

*Aggregate Supply.* Firms produce that level of NNP demanded in a market economy (a). The schedule of aggregate supply produced is $600, $700, $800, and $900 billion, as shown by *SS provided that* aggregate demand is a comparable amount. As time passes and technology improves or more resources are made available, maximum capacity or full-employment levels of NNP expand, as shown in (b).

shown in Figure 2(a) is equidistant between the horizontal axis (NNP) and aggregate $C + I$ expenditures shown by the vertical axis. Any point on a 45° line thus indicates equal dollar amounts of NNP and $C + I$ spending. Schedule $SS$ depicts aggregate supply as different levels of output, where each point on $SS$ corresponds to an identical level of expected $C + I$ spending. At point $a$ in Figure 2(a), $600 billion in $C + I$ spending is expected, and producers can supply a level of income (and thus employment) warranted by that level of spending. _Conclusion:_ A 45° line equidistant between the vertical axis denoting total $C + I$ spending and the horizontal axis indicating levels of possible output (NNP) represents alternative levels of aggregate supply firms will offer.

While various levels of NNP can be produced, full-employment output ($NNP_{fe}$) is arbitrarily identified at $900 billion in Figure 2(a). _Money_ expenditures on output could be higher, but _real_ NNP cannot exceed the full-employment level. Note very carefully that the largest possible level of _real_ output in Figure 2(a) is $NNP_{fe}$ = $900 billion. Growth in _real_ NNP can occur as resources expand or become more productive. Then aggregate supply will shift to the right, as shown by the shift from $NNP_{fe\ 1970}$ to $NNP_{fe\ 1971}$ on schedule $SS$ of Figure 2(b). However, since we have momentarily ruled out economic growth by assuming that the supply of resources and technology are constant, $NNP_{fe}$ = $900 billion can be regarded as the maximum amount of _real_ output that is possible.

## THE AGGREGATE-DEMAND SCHEDULE

Aggregate demand ($DD$), defined as planned spending at each possible NNP level, is shown in tabular form in Figure 3, and a schedule of $DD$ is also plotted in Figure 3(a). Schedules of $DD$ reveal the investment ($I$) and consumption ($C$) spending intentions of households and business firms. (Remember, we assumed that government and international trade do not exist.) Thus, a schedule of $DD$ consists of the _sum of consumption (C) and intended investment (I) expenditures at each_ NNP _level._ The critical feature about schedule $DD$ in Figure 3(a) is that the planned expenditures measured on the vertical axis do not exhibit a one-to-one relationship to NNP, shown on the horizontal axis. In Figure 3(a), $DD$ rises by $50 billion when NNP increases by $100 billion (for reasons which will become fully apparent shortly).

## THE EQUILIBRIUM-INCOME LEVEL

Figure 3(b) combines the schedules of $DD$ and $SS$ shown earlier to illustrate why a stable- or equilibrium-level NNP must occur at an output level of $800 billion. At any lower level of output (such as NNP = $600 billion), aggregate demand exceeds aggregate supply; that is, inflows into the circular-income flow (shown earlier in the circular-income flow of Figure 1) exceed leakages (such as saving). Because expenditures exceed the supply of output, inventories are depleted, production is expanded, and income and employment rise to $800 billion—a higher equilibrium level shown in Figure 3(b).

Should producers in the private sector decide to supply NNP = $1,000 billion, income will decline because excess goods and services will be produced. Aggregate output supplied at NNP = $1,000 billion is not fully absorbed by $C + I$ spending of $800 billion, and surplus output accumu-

FIGURE 3 Aggregate Demand and Equilibrium Income
(billions of dollars)

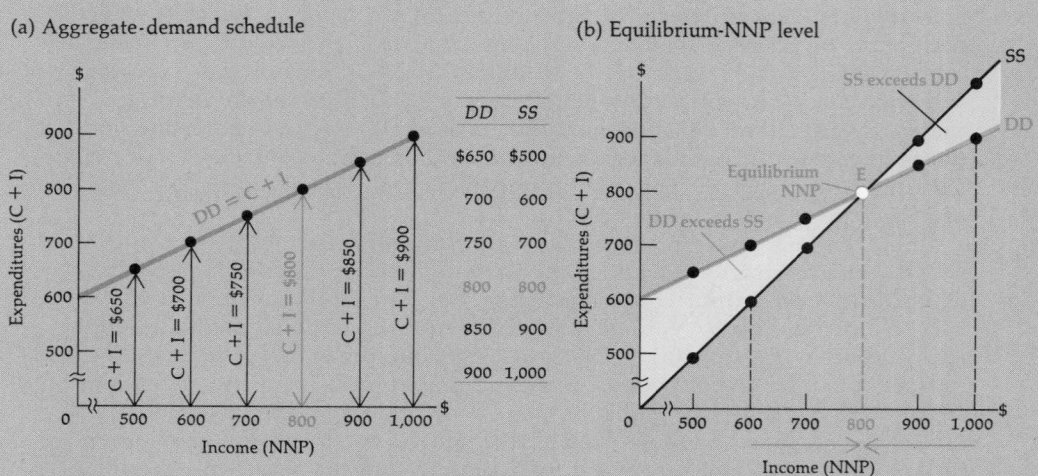

(a) Aggregate-demand schedule

(b) Equilibrium-NNP level

| DD | SS |
|----|----|
| $650 | $500 |
| 700 | 600 |
| 750 | 700 |
| 800 | 800 |
| 850 | 900 |
| 900 | 1,000 |

*Aggregate Demand.* The level of total spending planned at each possible NNP level is defined as aggregate demand, plotted as schedule *DD* in (a). If the public and foreign sectors are excluded from a model, *DD* consists of consumption (*C*) and investment (*I*) only.

*Equilibrium.* A stable income level exists only if *DD* = *SS*. Equilibrium occurs only where NNP = $800 billion in (b). At higher income levels, *SS* exceeds *DD* and net leakages from the income stream force the level of income to decline. In contrast, at income levels below NNP = $800 billion, *DD* exceeds *SS* and the level of income rises because of inflows into the spending stream.

lates until NNP declines. In terms of the circular-income flow of Figure 1, the income stream contracts. Therefore, inventories accumulate, producers are motivated to reduce output, income declines, and unemployment rises.

*Income and employment are forced to change in the direction of equilibrium where DD = SS because leakages from the spending stream do not equal inflows pumped back into the income stream at any other level of output.*

### INCOME EQUILIBRIUM AND FULL EMPLOYMENT

The macroeconomic problems of unemployment and inflation go beyond the annoying facts that income may be unstable and economic activity may fluctuate. The real problem is maintaining a relatively stable and growing income level *at full employment—the capacity limit to aggregate supply.* The troublesome issue of balancing income and employment levels at full employment reaches to the heart of macroeconomics. If full employment just happened to occur at NNP = $800 billion in Figure 3(b), the unique condition of *equilibrium and full-employment* NNP would be realized. While our objective is to understand how a nation achieves a stable or equilibrium income level at full employment, a "triple threat" to this happy state of affairs is possible.

1. Income can be stable at *any* level of income and employment—not just at full-employment NNP.

2. Even if a nation is at full employment to begin with, aggregate demand might increase due to imbalances between spending-stream leakages and inflows and thus lead to price-level increases.

3. When a nation is at full employment, it is also possible for $C + I$ spending to decline as spending-stream leakages increase or inflows decline. This will lead to lower levels of income and employment in the future and the economy will operate at less than full employment.

One of the chief contributions of Lord Keynes, and a major thesis of the New Economics, is that full employment and income stability are not reached automatically, nor are they uniformly related in a market economy. *Therefore, the basic problem is to understand how income equilibrium can be achieved at stable prices and full employment.*

## A RECAPITULATION

The essence of income and employment determination can be summarized in terms of four ideas:

*Income and Employment Rise*   Suppose a hypothetical economy is producing NNP = $600 billion currently as measured on the horizontal axis of Figure 3(b) and aggregate demand is $700 billion. The results are predictable: Shortages of goods appear because $C + I$ spending exceeds aggregate supply; production is expanded; and output, income, and employment rise.

*Income and Employment Fall*   Consider the reverse situation in which an economy is currently producing NNP = $1,000 billion and $C + I$ spending is $900 billion. Demand for output is not adequate to support the $1,000 billion level of output supplied. Leakages in the form of saving exceed investment inflows, or $SS$ exceeds $DD$. Inventories accumulate; firms reduce production; and output, income, and employment decline to the equilibrium level.

*Income Equilibrium*   The concept of equilibrium income describes the situation in which income is stable or at a level from which it will not change. We have just seen that equilibrium *is not* attained if $DD \neq SS$. Equilibrium income is achieved only when $DD = SS$ because only then are saving leakages and investment inflows equal. Such a point is identified in Figure 3(b) where producers offer and buyers purchase $800 billion of goods and services.

*Full Employment*   Even if income is stable at some level (such as NNP = $800 billion), this *does not necessarily* mean that full employment is achieved. If aggregate demand remains as shown in Figure 3(b) and full employment occurs at NNP = $900 billion it is obvious that aggregate demand is insufficient to achieve full employment.

Income and employment theory reaches one straightforward conclusion: Income equilibrium exists from time period to time period only if $C + I$ spending is equal to the quantity of total output supplied. When some level of aggregate demand *anticipated* by producers does not materialize and aggregate supply is excessive or deficient, income will increase or decrease to a new equilibrium level. Firms may invest more or less in inventories than is *intended* and the saving realized in an economy may deviate from the level *planned* by households and firms, all of which contribute to changes in NNP and employment in the future.

## C. COMPONENTS OF AGGREGATE DEMAND

Since expenditures for output are the crucial determinants of income and employment, it is appropriate to examine the consumption and investment components of aggregate demand in greater detail. The level of consumption expenditures (C) in an economy is influenced by many factors, the chief of which is income. In other words, consumption is a function of income, particularly disposable income (DI). Since disposable income can be either consumed or saved, saving is also influenced by the disposable income of consuming households.

### Consumption Demand and Disposable Income

The main determinant of consumption demand is the level of disposable income available to households. Disposable income and consumption expenditures rise or fall in a crudely parallel fashion over the years. Recent empirical evidence indicates, for example, that an average of 93 or 94 percent of disposable income is typically consumed.[1] On the other hand, examination of consumption data reveals that 102 percent of disposable income was consumed in 1933. That is, saving can be negative as consumption outlays exceed disposable income.

Another useful way to look at the direct relation between consumption and disposable income is by income level. Generally speaking, the lower the level of family income, the greater the proportion of income consumed. What we also find in looking at consumption by different income levels is that family units may consume more than their total income in any given year. Newly formed families, for example, may purchase appliances, furniture, or a home by borrowing and thereby absorb more of a nation's output then they produce and earn that year. Anticipated disposable-income increases often justify consumption patterns of this type. Consequently, any discussion of consumption as a component of aggregate demand must be in the context of consumption expenditures that can be, and are, influenced by factors other than disposable income.[2]

Although the disposable income-consumption relation depicted in Figure 4 is not precise, it does show that as disposable income rises, consumption expenditures also increase absolutely. The percentage of income consumed is *not* constant over the course of expansions and contractions in economic activity, however. Professor Milton Friedman of the University of Chicago and others have found that short-run variations in the disposable income–consumption relation sometimes correspond to the *permanent-income hypothesis.* This hypothesis states that people consume in accordance with the permanent income they anticipate over the long run. Temporary declines in

---

[1] Council of Economic Advisers, *Economic Report of the President*, 1969, p. 244.

[2] Many other factors also determine the amount of consumption expenditures, but we shall put aside other determinants for now and concentrate on the income relationship.

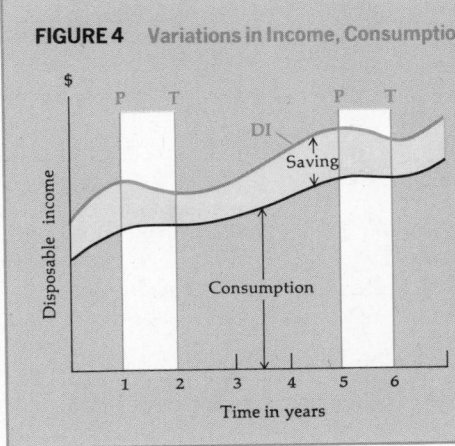

**FIGURE 4**   Variations in Income, Consumption, and Saving

*Consumption Demand.* As disposable income rises, consumption expenditures rise, but by a smaller amount. Similarly, as incomes decline, consumption declines, again in a smaller amount as consuming households draw on past savings in an attempt to maintain already-established living standards.

disposable income may not be matched by proportionate declines in consumption demand if the decline in income is conceived of as temporary. Other economists have suggested that as disposable income rises, the consumption pattern of some individuals bent on "keeping up with the Joneses" may be altered. Professors James Duesenberry and Franco Modigliani have suggested that if disposable income declines to some former level, consumption may not decline in the same proportion because households have acquired a permanent taste for higher levels of consumption.

Suppose we hypothesize that consumption expenditures rise as disposable income increases, but individuals consume only a portion of their increased income and save the remainder. This consumption hypothesis—also known as Keynes' *fundamental psychological law*—is what Figure 4 illustrates. Consumption demand varies directly with disposable income. As peaks of business activity are more nearly reached, the proportion of disposable income leaking into saving tends to rise. As disposable income declines in a contraction, consumption declines by a smaller absolute amount as consumers draw on past and present saving to maintain their customary standard of living.

### The Consumption Schedule

Since we need a schedule of *planned* (*or desired*) consumption-income relations, historical relations between aggregate consumption and disposable income are of limited use. The consumption relationship formalized by Keynes is shown in Figure 5, where a schedule of consumption is plotted as a function of disposable income. Note that income is measured on the horizontal axis and that consumption spending depicted by schedule C is measured on the vertical axis. When disposable income (*DI*) rises from $300 billion to $700 billion, both consumption and saving rise. Note, too, that Figure 5 shows negative saving below the break-even income level of *DI* = $500 billion, whereas saving is positive above that aggregate income level. The 45° line denotes points of equal values for C and *DI*. Thus, at low income levels C exceeds *DI* (dissaving) and at high-income levels C is greater than *DI*.

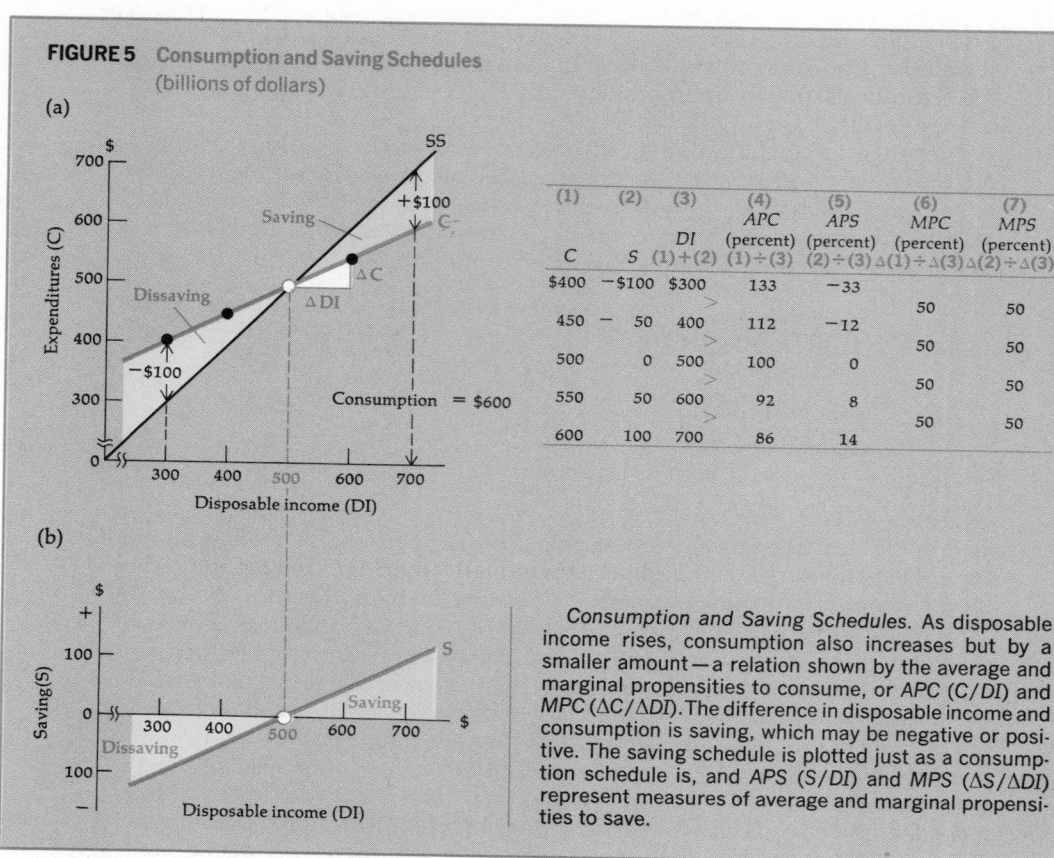

**FIGURE 5  Consumption and Saving Schedules**
(billions of dollars)

(a)

(b)

| (1) | (2) | (3) | (4) APC (percent) (1)÷(3) | (5) APS (percent) (2)÷(3) | (6) MPC (percent) Δ(1)÷Δ(3) | (7) MPS (percent) Δ(2)÷Δ(3) |
|---|---|---|---|---|---|---|
| C | S | DI (1)+(2) | | | | |
| $400 | −$100 | $300 | 133 | −33 | | |
| | | | | | 50 | 50 |
| 450 | − 50 | 400 | 112 | −12 | | |
| | | | | | 50 | 50 |
| 500 | 0 | 500 | 100 | 0 | | |
| | | | | | 50 | 50 |
| 550 | 50 | 600 | 92 | 8 | | |
| | | | | | 50 | 50 |
| 600 | 100 | 700 | 86 | 14 | | |

*Consumption and Saving Schedules.* As disposable income rises, consumption also increases but by a smaller amount—a relation shown by the average and marginal propensities to consume, or APC (C/DI) and MPC (ΔC/ΔDI). The difference in disposable income and consumption is saving, which may be negative or positive. The saving schedule is plotted just as a consumption schedule is, and APS (S/DI) and MPS (ΔS/ΔDI) represent measures of average and marginal propensities to save.

## Propensities to Consume and Save

With disposable income as the primary determinant of consumption expenditures, the portion or fraction of income consumed and saved is a useful way to identify the Keynesian notion that consumption does not increase or decrease as rapidly as disposable income. The proportions of income consumed and saved at any income level are called the *average propensity to consume (APC)* and the *average propensity to save (APS)*, respectively. To measure *APC* and *APS* at any level of disposable income, we need only compute

$$APC = \frac{\$consumption}{\$income} \quad \text{or} \quad \frac{C}{DI} \left( \text{e.g.,} \frac{\$550}{\$600} = 92\% \right)$$

and

$$APS = \frac{\$saving}{\$income} \quad \text{or} \quad \frac{S}{DI} \left( \text{e.g.,} \frac{\$50}{\$600} = 8\% \right)$$

For example, at NNP = $500 billion in Figure 5, APC = 100 percent and APS = 0 percent. At lower income levels, aggregate consumption is larger than income, and APC exceeds 100 percent as consumers draw upon past saving. As income rises, APC declines and APS rises. For example, at the

$700 billion income level $APC = 86$ percent and $APS = 14$ percent. Consequently, the consumption schedule shown in Figure 5 is consistent with the hypothesis that proportionately less is consumed at higher disposable income levels.

A change in consumption as disposable income changes is measured by the *marginal propensity to consume* (MPC), where marginal means "additional" or "change in." Similarly, the *marginal propensity to save* (MPS) reflects the change in saving as income changes, where a change is denoted by Δ. These ratios of a change in consumption and saving to a change in income are:

$$MPC = \frac{\text{change in consumption}}{\text{change in income}} \quad \text{or} \quad \frac{\Delta C}{\Delta DI} \left( e.g., \frac{\Delta\$50}{\Delta\$100} = 50\% \right)$$

$$MPS = \frac{\text{change in saving}}{\text{change in income}} \quad \text{or} \quad \frac{\Delta S}{\Delta DI} \left( e.g., \frac{\Delta\$50}{\Delta\$100} = 50\% \right)$$

Measurement of MPC and MPS is illustrated graphically in Figure 5 between the $500 billion and $600 billion income levels, where $MPC = 50$ percent or 0.5, revealing that one-half of every additional dollar in disposable income is spent for consumption. Diagrammatically, MPC relates the change in consumption (measured on the vertical axis as a "rise" or $\Delta C = \$50$ billion) to the increase in income (measured on the vertical axis as a "run" or $\Delta DI = \$100$ billion). As it turns out, MPC is a measure of the slope of a consumption schedule C [the slope is the vertical change ($\Delta C$) divided by the horizontal change ($\Delta DI$)]. The larger the proportion of a change in disposable income spent, the steeper the slope of a consumption schedule. Thus, if $\Delta C/\Delta DI = \$9/\$10$, we know that $MPC = 0.9$, which means simply that nine-tenths of each additional dollar of disposable income is consumed. If $MPC = \$2/\$10 = 0.2$, one-fifth of each additional dollar is consumed, and the consumption schedule would be a nearly horizontal line.

For some purposes it will be helpful to separate a schedule of saving from consumption as is done in the lower portion of Figure 5. This can be accomplished by measuring saving on the vertical axis and plotting values for saving at each disposable income level shown on the horizontal axis. Schedule S is plotted as saving of $-\$100$ billion at $DI = \$300$ billion, $0 at $DI = \$500$ billion, and $100 billion at $DI = \$700$ billion. The MPS is illustrated as $\Delta S/\Delta DI$ at a given income level, where the MPS also measures the slope of a saving schedule.

*To summarize:* Consumption and saving are represented as a function of disposable income, where it appears reasonable to accept the hypothesis that as disposable income rises, consumption rises by a smaller amount. Because consumption and saving comprise disposable income, $APC + APS = 1$ and $MPC + MPS = 1$. Marginal propensities to consume and save measure changes in C, S, and DI. For now, the MPC and MPS are regarded as constant at all income levels, in part because statistical evidence indicates this to be a reasonable approximation and also because our future analysis of income determination is thus simplified.

### Investment Demand

While consumption is determined primarily by income, there is no single unambiguous and dominant determinant of investment expenditures—the second key component of aggregate demand. Many factors influence intended investment, and the relationships of these factors to investment are not as firm as in the case of disposable income and consumption. Consequently, we must first explain how investment expenditures are related to anticipated profits and then examine investment in relation to the income level of a nation.

## INVESTMENT EXPENDITURES AND ANTICIPATED PROFITS

Business firms decide to invest in capital resources on the basis of the expected profitability or earnings of investment alternatives. The profitability of investment expenditures is usually expressed as a percentage rate of return, which is most simply identified as the earnings generated by capital resources divided by costs.

Suppose that a machine can be purchased at a cost of $300, its estimated earnings are $60 a year, and a firm decides it will not invest unless the rate of return is 20 percent. Under these circumstances an investment outlay would be made, since a 20 percent return on a $300 outlay is just equal to $60. If the firm had to pay a higher price for the capital equipment, or if anticipated earnings were less than $60 annually, the capital investment would not meet the "cutoff" return of 20 percent and the investment presumably would not be made. The rate of return on capital having both constant and permanent earnings can be expressed as:

$$\text{Rate of return} = \frac{\text{earnings}}{\text{cost}} \quad \text{or} \quad \frac{\$60}{\$300} = 20\% \text{ in our example.}$$

If both the desired percentage return and the cost of capital are known, a firm can also determine the absolute dollar earnings that must be achieved by capital resources:

$$\text{Earnings} = \text{rate of return} \times \text{cost of capital} \quad \text{or} \quad 20\% \times 300 = \$60$$

Similarly, the maximum cost of an investment in capital is:[3]

$$\text{Cost of capital} = \frac{\text{earnings}}{\text{rate of return}} \quad \text{or} \quad \frac{\$60}{20\%} = \$300$$

In general, the higher the rate of return on investment in capital, the greater the profitability of an investment expenditure, and the more likely it is that the expenditure will be made. In reality, firms tend to require a rate of return considerably in excess of the "price" of funds—the interest rate at which a firm can borrow to finance expenditures on capital resources. This tendency is partly due to the risk and uncertainty involved in committing funds to fixed capital resources, whose anticipated returns are influenced by factors such as product demand, expected business conditions, the cost of operating capital resources, the extent to which existing

[3] Suppose $r$ stands for rate of return, $K$ for capital costs, and $E$ for earnings. The rate-of-return relationship is $r = E/K$, where we solve for $E$ by multiplying both sides of the equation by $K/1$. Similarly, $K$ is derived by dividing each side of the expression $E = r \times K$ by $r$. Once finite periods of time are taken into account, the arithmetic of discounting and computing $r$, $E$, or $K$ is somewhat more complicated—a matter ignored for the time being.

capital resources are utilized, and so forth. All of this means that investment expenditures can vary widely at any given level of NNP, depending on the many factors bearing upon profit expectations. For this reason, such expenditures are often regarded as *autonomous investment* or expenditures that are independent of the level of income.

## INVESTMENT RETURNS AND INCOME-EMPLOYMENT LEVELS

The assumption that investment demand is largely determined by anticipated profits expressed as the rate of return on investment in capital adds further significance to our earlier emphasis on *intended* investment. Business firms *plan* their investment expenditures on the basis of profits *anticipated* in the future, which in turn are based upon expected sales and the levels of inventory investment anticipated to be necessary to do business. Suppose sales expectations are not realized because consumer demand is less than was anticipated; business firms will then be required to invest in the excess production which is not sold. Thus, total investment is larger than intended; sales and profits do not live up to expectations; and because more investment dollars in inventory are required to do business, the rate of return on investment is less than firms had anticipated. In other words, equilibrium income requires that saving ($S$) equal intended investment ($I$) but this condition is not attained. Instead, equilibrium is reached only as business firms absorb a positive amount of unintended investment:

$$S = I \text{ intended} + I \text{ unintended}$$
$$\$100 \text{ billion} = \$90 \text{ billion} + \$10 \text{ billion above planned inventory.}$$

Consequently, the production of goods and services (NNP) and employment decline in the future because the actual return to more investment dollars is less than was anticipated due to $10 billion of unintended investment. The exact opposite conditions prevail if intended investment exceeds saving when consumer demand is sufficiently strong to deplete inventories. Then, saving is less than intended investment:

$$S = I \text{ intended} - I \text{ unintended}$$
$$\$100 \text{ billion} = \$110 \text{ billion} - \$10 \text{ billion unintended inventory depletion.}$$

Because sales to consumers exceeded expectations, inventories are depleted and business firms earn greater profits and a higher rate of return on fewer investment dollars. Consequently, output, income, and employment are likely to expand in the future as firms step up production to meet the $C + I$ spending for aggregate output.

## D. DETERMINATION OF INCOME AND EMPLOYMENT: A RESTATEMENT OF THE PROBLEM AND THEORY

In the last several pages we have developed a model of aggregate output as a tool of analysis to explain how consumption, investment, and saving determine income and employment. The logic of equilibrium income can be developed more fully if we use some of the analytical tools inherent in schedules of consumption and investment as two components of aggregate demand. Moreover, these analytical tools are helpful in illustrating the impact of inflation and unemployment on an economy.

First, let us reassemble what we now know about equilibrium income and aggregate demand. Aggregate demand for output, shown as schedule $DD$ in Figure 6, is the sum of $C$ and $I$ expenditures at each level of NNP. As before, investment is autonomous or constant at $100 billion for all income levels. Each point on aggregate-supply schedule $SS$ represents a *potential* output level, but *the only equilibrium level of income is NNP = $700 billion* (point $E$). Why? Thinking back to our earlier discussion we know that income equilibrium exists when:

1. $DD = SS$ ($C + I$ purchases equal actual output).
2. $S = I$ (saving and intended investment are equal).

In short, a stable or equilibrium income level from one period of time to another occurs only when leakages from the income stream are exactly offset by inflows, where saving is the only leakage and investment the only inflow so long as we ignore government and international trade.

The crucial problem encountered in an economic system is achieving income equilibrium at full employment. Let us look at the two basic problems of unemployment and inflation in that order.

### The Unemployment Problem: A Deflationary Gap

Suppose that full-employment NNP occurs at $800 billion of aggregate output and that aggregate demand (the sum of $C + I$ expenditures) is represented by schedule $DD$ in Figure 6. If firms produce $800 billion of output in anticipation of selling that amount of aggregate supply, inventories will pile up, production will be cut back, and NNP will decline. A *deflationary gap* of $-$50 billion is shown in Figure 6 as the difference between spending on output and the actual level of output at full employment; $NNP_{fe} = $800 billion cannot be maintained given the illustrated level of $DD$. Deflationary pressures prevail to the extent that $C + I$ is insufficient to clear the market of $800 billion of output—the full-employment level of production. Full employment is not possible in this economy. Income will therefore decline to its equilibrium level and unemployment will rise. Unemployment and sluggish levels of economic activity will prevail until a higher level of aggregate demand is achieved. Figure 6 illustrates the deflationary gap in a second way by comparing autonomous investment demand, schedule $I$ ($= $100 billion) and spending-stream leakages to saving, represented by schedule $S$. Saving exceeds intended investment of $100 billion at $NNP_{fe} = $800. Since the aggregate supply of output exceeds aggregate demand, firms will be required to invest more than is intended in accumulated inventories and will cut back on production, causing NNP to decline to the lower equilibrium level of $700 billion. Note carefully that once equilibrium is achieved at NNP = $700 billion, and provided that aggregate demand remains unchanged, the economy will remain at this "stagnation" level of output; that is, unemployment will persist as long as $DD$ remains unchanged.

### The Problem of Inflationary Gaps

An inflationary gap occurs if households and business firms try to buy more output than can be produced. Under inflationary conditions, income equilibrium occurs at a level of *money* NNP in excess of the full-employment-

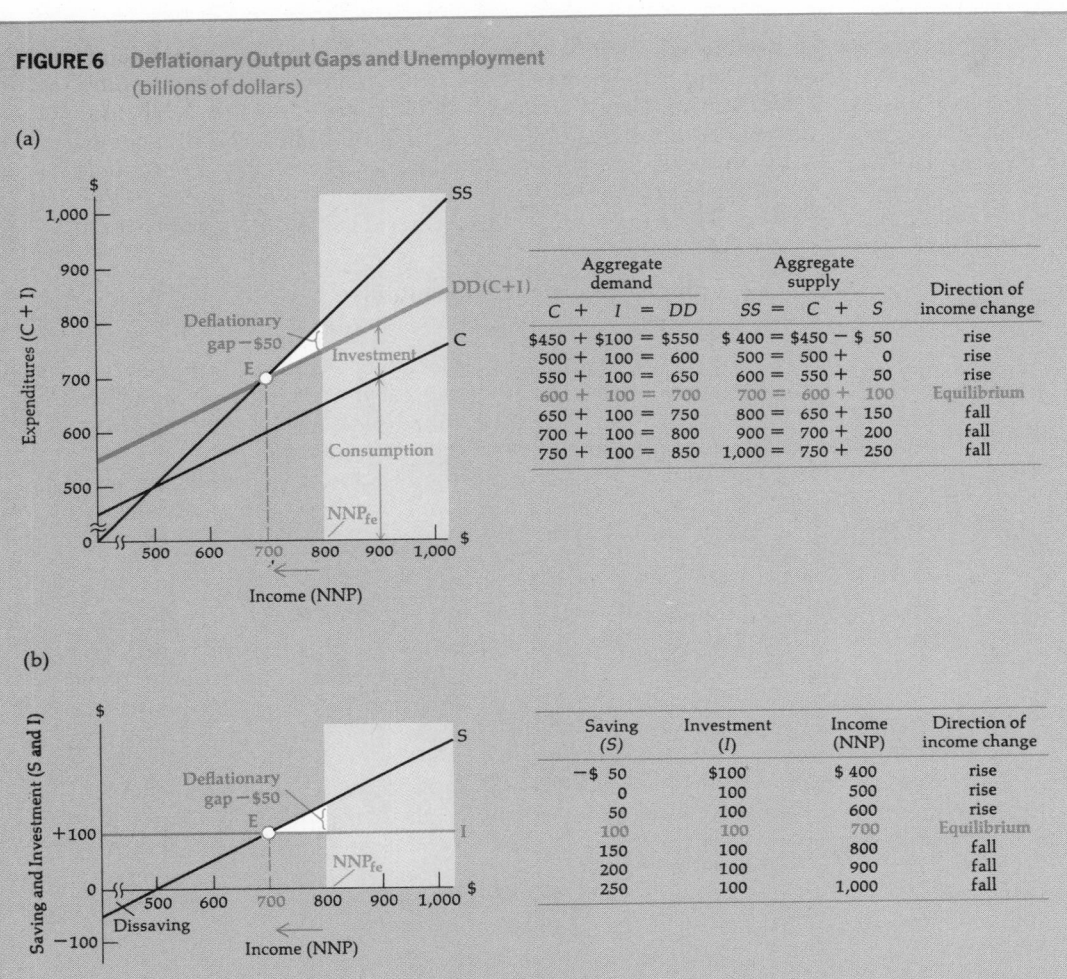

**FIGURE 6** Deflationary Output Gaps and Unemployment
(billions of dollars)

(a)

| Aggregate demand | | | Aggregate supply | | | Direction of income change |
|---|---|---|---|---|---|---|
| C | + I | = DD | SS = | C + | S | |
| $450 + | $100 = | $550 | $ 400 = | $450 − | $ 50 | rise |
| 500 + | 100 = | 600 | 500 = | 500 + | 0 | rise |
| 550 + | 100 = | 650 | 600 = | 550 + | 50 | rise |
| 600 + | 100 = | 700 | 700 = | 600 + | 100 | Equilibrium |
| 650 + | 100 = | 750 | 800 = | 650 + | 150 | fall |
| 700 + | 100 = | 800 | 900 = | 700 + | 200 | fall |
| 750 + | 100 = | 850 | 1,000 = | 750 + | 250 | fall |

(b)

| Saving (S) | Investment (I) | Income (NNP) | Direction of income change |
|---|---|---|---|
| −$ 50 | $100 | $ 400 | rise |
| 0 | 100 | 500 | rise |
| 50 | 100 | 600 | rise |
| 100 | 100 | 700 | Equilibrium |
| 150 | 100 | 800 | fall |
| 200 | 100 | 900 | fall |
| 250 | 100 | 1,000 | fall |

*Deflationary Gap.* Equilibrium NNP *does not* occur at full-employment NNP of $800 billion. Full-employment levels of output cannot be sustained as long as *DD* remains unchanged with the −$50 billion deflationary gap shown. At NNP$_{fe}$, *SS* exceeds *DD* and *S* exceeds *I*, causing income and employment to decline to the equilibrium level of $700 billion. Production and spending plans are in equilibrium only where *DD* = *SS*, which means that planned *I* = *S*.

capacity constraint, shown in Figure 7 as NNP$_{fe}$ = $600 billion. That is, *DD* exceeds *SS* or intended *I* exceeds *S* at full employment, driving prices, wages, and *money* income up to a higher equilibrium level.

Suppose the labor force is such that full employment (4 percent unemployment) occurs when 80 million persons are working at NNP$_{fe}$ = $600 billion. The inflationary gap of $50 billion depicted in Figure 7 reflects the reality of excess aggregate demand. Any level of *real* income greater than NNP$_{fe}$ = $600 billion is clearly unattainable, since at NNP$_{fe}$ resources are fully employed. The excess aggregate demand of $50 billion shown in

# FIGURE 7  Equilibrium Income and Inflationary Gaps
### (billions of dollars)

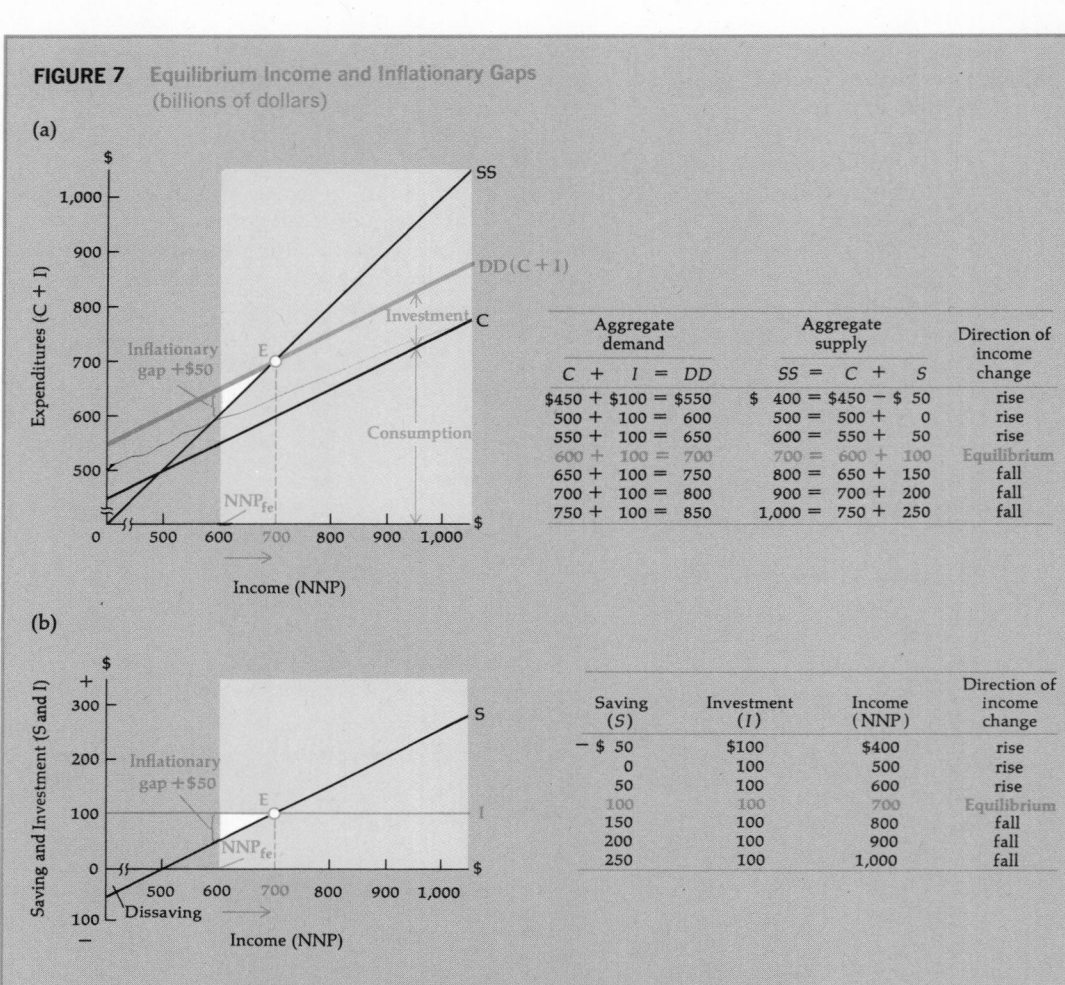

**(a)**

| Aggregate demand | | | Aggregate supply | | | Direction of income change |
|---|---|---|---|---|---|---|
| C + | I | = DD | SS = | C + | S | |
| $450 + | $100 | = $550 | $ 400 = | $450 − | $ 50 | rise |
| 500 + | 100 | = 600 | 500 = | 500 + | 0 | rise |
| 550 + | 100 | = 650 | 600 = | 550 + | 50 | rise |
| 600 + | 100 | = 700 | 700 = | 600 + | 100 | Equilibrium |
| 650 + | 100 | = 750 | 800 = | 650 + | 150 | fall |
| 700 + | 100 | = 800 | 900 = | 700 + | 200 | fall |
| 750 + | 100 | = 850 | 1,000 = | 750 + | 250 | fall |

**(b)**

| Saving (S) | Investment (I) | Income (NNP) | Direction of income change |
|---|---|---|---|
| − $ 50 | $100 | $400 | rise |
| 0 | 100 | 500 | rise |
| 50 | 100 | 600 | rise |
| 100 | 100 | 700 | Equilibrium |
| 150 | 100 | 800 | fall |
| 200 | 100 | 900 | fall |
| 250 | 100 | 1,000 | fall |

*Inflationary Gap.* Equilibrium NNP *does not* occur at full-employment NNP of $600 billion. So long as *DD* remains as shown, an inflationary gap of +$50 billion prevails. At NNP$_{fe}$, *DD* exceeds *SS* and *I* exceeds *S*, causing *money* NNP to rise to an inflationary equilibrium of $700 billion (real output does not increase). As before production and spending plans are in equilibrium only where *DD* = *SS*, which means that planned *I* = *S*.

Figure 7 represents an inflationary gap because producers cannot respond by increasing *real* output. As a result, there is an upward spiral in prices as consumers compete for a limited supply of output and bid prices up. Although the *money* level of NNP rises to $700 billion, *real* output cannot exceed $600 billion. The inflationary gap prevails until such time as aggregate *DD* contracts to a level consistent with the full-employment limit to capacity, or until such time as aggregate supply can be expanded through economic growth.

*To conclude:* A stable or equilibrium level of output occurs only when aggregate demand and aggregate supply are equal, a condition also described by equality between intended investment and saving. When $C + I$ expenditures exceed aggregate supply, NNP rises, and if $C + I$ expenditures are deficient relative to aggregate supply, NNP declines. Full employment may or may not prevail at equilibrium levels of output. If $SS$ exceeds $DD$ at full-employment NNP, a deflationary gap prevails and income equilibrium occurs while some resources are unemployed. In contrast, an inflationary gap exists as long as $DD$ exceeds $SS$ at full employment, in which case *money* NNP rises to a higher equilibrium but *real* income remains unchanged. Indeed, the odds are that different combinations of inflationary and deflationary gaps will occur. This being so, it is important to investigate ways in which aggregate demand can be stabilized at full employment. When income equilibrium does not correspond to full employment, either unemployment or inflation can present serious problems, and government must take steps to stabilize the economy.

## REVIEW
### Summary

1. Economic instability results in excessive unemployment at one extreme and increases in the general level of prices or inflation at the other extreme. Classical economists argued that because price, wage, and interest-rate adjustments occurred in product and resource markets, supply created its own demand and prolonged periods of unemployment or inflation were not possible. Keynes denied that price, wage, and interest-rate flexibility functioned in this fashion and pointed the way for the New Economics by suggesting that spending on a nation's output determines the level of income and employment.

2. According to the New Economics, unemployment and inflation problems arise when planned expenditures for output fall short of or exceed the aggregate supply of output made available by producers. In a market economy, aggregate demand (the sum of consumption, investment, government, and net foreign expenditures) is an important determinant of income and employment.

3. Income is stable from one period to another only when leakages from the spending stream equal spending inflows. Any level of income may be achieved, however, and stability need not occur at a level of output at which all resources are fully employed.

4. An economic model of aggregate demand ($DD$) and aggregate supply ($SS$) reveals how income is determined in a nation. By holding technology and resources constant, we can identify the full-employment level of aggregate output as one point on a schedule of aggregate supply. Consumption and investment are the two major components of an aggregate-demand schedule in the private sector. When scheduled aggregate demand exceeds aggregate supply, income rises; and if scheduled aggregate demand is less than aggregate supply, income falls. While past amounts of actual saving ($S$) and investment ($I$) are identical by definition, differences in intended or planned $I$ and $S$ explain why an economy moves toward income equilibrium.

5. Consumption expenditures (C) are influenced largely by disposable income (DI). The consumption-disposable income relationship is a direct one where C rises and falls as DI rises and falls. The average propensity to consume or save (the ratios C/DI and S/DI) reflect the fact that consumption tends to rise or fall by an amount smaller than changes in disposable income. Marginal propensities to consume (MPC) and save (MPS) measure the ratio of a change (Δ) in consumption and saving to a change in disposable income: $MPC = \Delta C/\Delta DI$ and $MPS = \Delta S/\Delta DI$.

6. Investment expenditures vary with the rate of return or profitability of investment in capital resources. Since expectations and uncertainty influence investment, it is not uncommon to regard investment demand as independent or autonomous of the level of income.

7. The problems of fully employing resources and maintaining price stability are summarily illustrated by examining two possible cases:
   (a) A deflationary gap depicts unemployment attributable to the fact that at full-employment NNP, aggregate demand is less than aggregate supply. The deflationary gap is measured as the difference between aggregate demand and aggregate supply at full employment.
   (b) An inflationary gap reflects rising *money* NNP but a constant level of *real* NNP. Once at full employment, *real* income cannot rise in the short run, but prices and wages rise to the extent that aggregate demand exceeds aggregate supply at full employment.

## Identify the Following Concepts and Terms

- aggregate demand and aggregate supply
- inflationary gap
- autonomous investment
- planned spending
- deflationary gap
- marginal propensities to consume and save (MPC and MPS)
- aggregate supply as a 45° line
- the full-employment constraint to NNP
- planned or intended $I = S$
- rate of return as an investment determinant
- average propensities to consume and save (APC and APS)
- equilibrium NNP
- Keynes' "fundamental psychological law"
- spending-stream inflows and leakages
- income and employment at full employment

## Questions to Answer

1. Construct a circular-income-flow model for a nation and explain how an increase of $10 billion in each of the spending-stream leakages affects GNP and employment. What might happen if exports to foreign nations or investment spending increases by $8 billion?

2. Using the data below, plot and label a consumption schedule. Also add $60 billion of autonomous investment (I) to consumption (C) spending and explain why the sum of $C + I = DD$. Be sure to label each axis. (*Hint:* see Figure 3)

| DI (billions of dollars) | (C) (billions of dollars) |
|---|---|
| $100 | $ 80 |
| 200 | 160 |
| 300 | 240 |
| 400 | 320 |
| 500 | 400 |

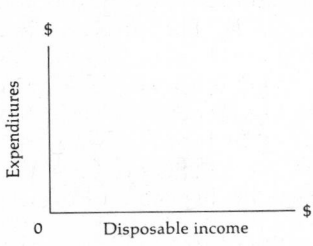

3. Using the same diagram developed in the previous question, identify and explain aggregate supply and equilibrium income. Why is it that, assuming there is no government, NNP and *DI* can be regarded simply as aggregate income or output?

4. Assuming that full employment in 1965 was $200 billion of NNP, explain and illustrate why an inflationary gap exists in the diagram used for the previous question. What conditions would prevail if full-employment NNP in 1975 happened to occur at NNP = $400 billion in this illustration?

5. Explain how the average propensity to consume (*APC*) and the marginal propensity to consume (*MPC*) illustrate a key relationship between consumption and income. Assuming that *DI* increases in increments of $100 billion up to $500 billion ($100 to $200 to $300 to $400 to $500) compute *APC* and *MPC* at each income level for the data given with the diagram above.

# CHAPTER 8
# Income-Employment Disequilibrium

Three distinct questions are studied in this chapter. What causes income disequilibrium or instability in output and employment? What is the net impact on NNP when consumption or investment expenditures rise or fall? Can anything be done to achieve full-employment NNP in a market economy?

In Part A, our knowledge about income and employment theory is used to study the common and interesting problem of income disequilibrium where NNP and employment change from one level to another. Part B explains why the magnitude by which income rises or falls is a multiple of the initial change in aggregate demand. In Part C, the model of income determination is expanded to include the public sector in order to study the ways in which government spending and taxation can be used to stabilize economic activity.

## A. DISEQUILIBRIUM CAUSED BY EXPENDITURE CHANGES

An explanation of the instability in NNP and employment requires investigation of changes in spending plans. The earlier concept of aggregate demand, represented as a schedule of consumption (C) and investment spending (I) is an oversimplification. Instability in consumption or investment expenditures moves or "shifts" a schedule of aggregate demand. Continuing our assumption that government and foreign trade are nonexistent, what, then, does aggregate demand really look like? Since aggregate demand is the sum of planned investment and consumption expenditures where any income not consumed is saved, we really want to know what the real-world schedules of C, I, and S look like.

### Shifts in Aggregate Demand

Figure 1 shows planned investment, consumption, and saving under real-world conditions, where the vertical axis represents total spending and the horizontal axis shows the level of NNP and employment. Each dot in Figure 1(b) represents *one* particular consumption-income relationship at a particular point in time. Similarly, specific values for S and I relative to the level of NNP are represented by dots in Figure 1(c). The schedules shown in Figure 1 *do not* represent the real world perfectly; instead, statistical techniques have been used to *estimate* schedules of C, S, I, and thus DD. Thus, point values for S (dots) and for I (x's) would allow various schedules of S and I to be drawn.

What the economist does when he hypothesizes the existence of schedule C, for example, is to generalize upon an imperfect, but nonetheless reason-

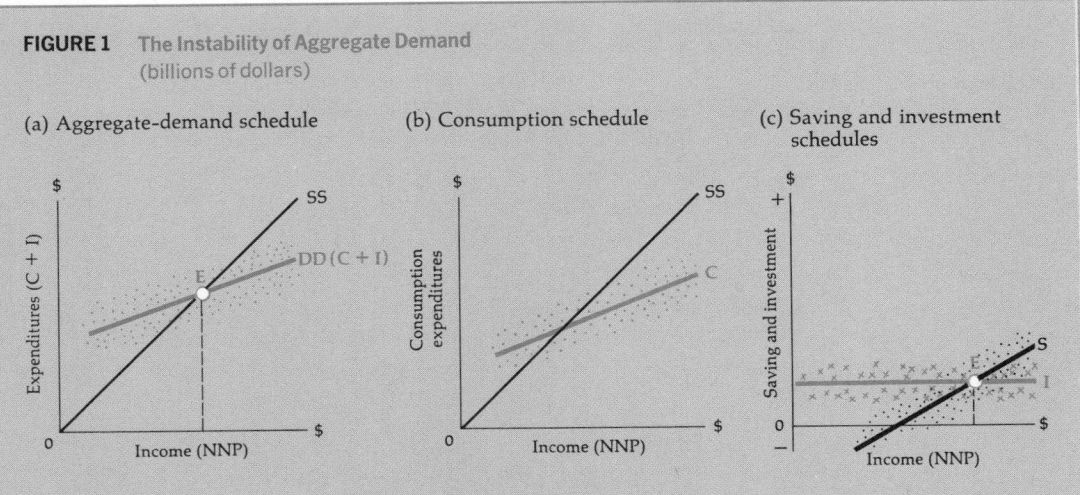

**FIGURE 1**  The Instability of Aggregate Demand
(billions of dollars)

(a) Aggregate-demand schedule

(b) Consumption schedule

(c) Saving and investment schedules

*Real-world DD, C, S, and I.* Any schedule of *C*, *S*, or *I* is an approximation of real-world values that assumes that consumption varies only as income varies and that all investment is autonomous or independent of the income level. In reality, many factors influence *C*, *S*, and *I* and several schedules of *DD*, *C*, *S*, or *I* could be derived. If scheduled *DD* were to change in (a), income equilibrium would be altered, as we know.

able relationship between consumption and income. Factors *other than income* that influence consumption demand are momentarily assumed away. By holding other things constant, we can study a manageable set of relationships that influence NNP and employment. Developing theory in this way is useful, but as we have said before, it is also important to release assumptions made in generalizing about the real world. Because we have not explained all the factors that influence the level of consumption or investment spending, the schedules of Figure 1 are imperfect representations of a generally valid relationship. For example, aggregate demand could be represented by a good many schedules other than the schedule *DD* shown in Figure 1(a). Since *income equilibrium is determined by DD = SS (or I = S), it would be different for any schedule of DD other than that shown at E in Figure 1.* This difference is the heart of the so-called "business cycle."

Because *DD* can shift, it is important to know more about real-world exceptions to the theoretical model of income determination. Changes in the the *quantity of output demanded* reflect how aggregate demand changes as NNP rises or falls. Changes in the quantity demanded are always depicted as movement along a schedule. Movement between any two points on schedule $DD_i$ of Figure 2(a) reveals an increase or decrease in the quantity demanded. A change in aggregate demand is always depicted as a change or *shift* in the entire schedule *DD*. In Figure 2(a), for example, an *increase in aggregate demand* is depicted as a change from $DD_d$ to $DD_i$.

INCREASES IN AGGREGATE DEMAND

Consider what happens to consumption expenditures if a large number of households become less thrifty. First, consumption rises at all levels of

145

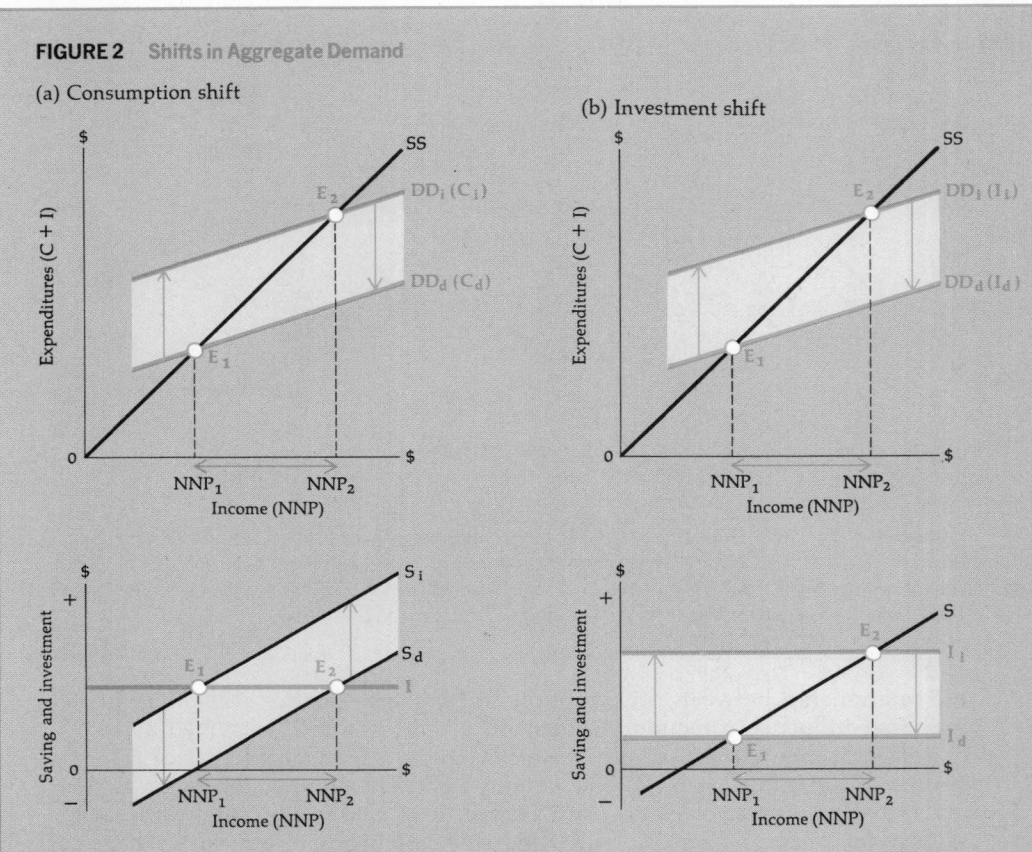

**FIGURE 2** Shifts in Aggregate Demand

(a) Consumption shift

(b) Investment shift

*Shifts in Consumption.* (a) If scheduled C (and hence S) increases or decreases, the level of NNP and employment changes because a new *DD* = *SS* equilibrium is achieved.

*Shifts in Investment.* (b) When the investment component of scheduled *DD* increases (to $I_i$) or decreases (to $I_d$) this results in a higher or lower equilibrium NNP. Any increase or decrease in scheduled C, I, S, and *DD* is depicted as a shift in the schedule.

NNP. Because more is consumed at all levels of NNP, the aggregate-demand schedule shifts upward at all income levels from $DD_d$ to $DD_i$ in Figure 2(a). Second, less is saved at each NNP level and saving decreases or shifts downward from $S_i$ to $S_d$. Schedules C and S move in opposite directions because income consumed is not saved.[1] Third, the increase in consumption and aggregate demand shown as an upward shift from $DD_d$ to $DD_i$ in Figure 2(a) results in a higher equilibrium income level. Because aggregate-demand schedule $DD_i$ exceeds aggregate supply at $NNP_1$, output increases to $NNP_2$ where $DD_i = SS$. A similar outcome is shown in Figure 2(a) for a decrease in saving from $S_i$ to $S_d$, which drives equilibrium income from $NNP_1$ to $NNP_2$. Less is saved at all income levels and the smaller leakages

[1] Remember, disposable income = consumption + saving.

to saving implied by larger consumption expenditures result in output rising until $S_d = I$ at $NNP_2$. Finally, note that an increase in investment spending also causes aggregate demand to shift upward, as is shown in Figure 2(b). Once again, increased aggregate demand results in a new equilibrium being established at $NNP_2$ where $DD_i = SS$ and the higher level of autonomous investment expenditures shown by $I_i$ are equal to $S$ in Figure 2(b).

## DECREASES IN AGGREGATE DEMAND

A decrease in consumption lowers aggregate demand from $DD_i$ to $DD_d$, causing income to decline until a new equilibrium is reached at $NNP_1$ in Figure 2(a). Figure 2(a) also reveals that as consumption declines ($DD$ shifts downward) scheduled saving rises from $S_d$ to $S_i$ and a new saving-investment equilibrium is reached at $NNP_1$. Figure 2(b) illustrates how a decrease in investment expenditures at each level of income results in a similar decline in equilibrium income. Thus, as investment spending declines to $I_d$, aggregate demand declines and equilibrium NNP declines to $NNP_1$.

*To summarize:* A change in aggregate demand is shown as a *shift* in the schedules of C, S, or I, whereas a *change in the quantity* consumed or saved is shown as *movement along* a schedule. Changes in either consumption or investment expenditures cause aggregate demand to shift. The result is that income equilibrium is disturbed and a new equilibrium level of NNP and employment will prevail. Thus, economic fluctuations caused by erratic bursts and declines in aggregate demand result in income and employment variations. Let us see next what might cause consumption and investment expenditures to change in this manner.

## Nonincome Determinants of Consumption

Shifts in consumption (and saving) are caused by several *non*income determinants of consumption, such as:

1. **Credit.** The extent to which consumers can borrow to finance purchases may change the level of consumption. The demand for durable goods like appliances and automobiles is particularly sensitive to the availability of credit because such goods involve sizable expenditures. A high level of debt may dampen consumer demand because repayment in the future will be necessary, making less funds available for current consumption. In addition, interest-rate levels, the maximum time period for repayment, downpayment requirements, and the ease of access to financial institutions may cause consumer spending for durable goods to increase or decrease.

2. **Income distribution.** Changes in the distribution of income may alter consumption demand if high-income households consume a smaller proportion of disposable income than do low-income households. If net income were redistributed toward low-income households having a larger propensity to consume, the community consumption schedule would rise, while a less equal redistribution of income would have the opposite effect for analogous reasons. The impact of income redistribution on consumption expenditures is not unambiguous, however. If higher-income groups spend a large portion of their income to "keep up with the Joneses," income redistribution in favor of low-income households will have an uncertain impact on the consumption schedule.

3. Liquid assets and wealth. Both the supply of liquid assets (money, securities, or bonds) and the wealth represented by existing quantities of durable goods may influence consumer expenditures.

Consider liquid assets first. Many observers contend that a greater stock of liquid assets enhances feelings of economic security and may thereby prompt greater consumption expenditures. Income and saving statistics compiled during and immediately after World War II lend some support to this hypothesis. The postwar consumption boom of the late 1940s reflected an increased willingness to consume due, in part, to postponed wartime consumption and the large quantities of liquid assets accumulated during World War II. To the extent that liquid assets are important determinants of consumer demand, changes in stock and bond prices may influence consumption, either encouraging or restraining it as households feel more or less wealthy.

The age and quantity of existing durable goods as another form of wealth also introduce uncertainty into the level of consumer expenditures. The possession by households of large quantities of relatively new durable goods can dampen current or future consumer demand, particularly if the economic outlook is bleak. This is because durable goods can be allowed to deteriorate or can be repaired. Generally, a downturn in economic activity involves postponed consumption, whereas the purchase of new durable goods occurs as economic expectations improve. The boom in durable-goods production and sales after World War II mirrored postponed purchases during the war which had left consumers with a small and relatively old stock of such goods.

4. Price and income changes. Price and income changes are still other factors that may lead to instability in the consumption schedule. If households expect prices or incomes to fall, current consumption demand may decline. The paradox of this situation is that by acting upon their anticipations, consumers contribute to spending declines. Such anticipations dampen aggregate demand and prices, and may lead to a lower equilibrium NNP. In contrast, the expectation of higher prices and incomes prompts more immediate purchasing, thereby lending reality to the expectation that prices and incomes will rise in the future.

There is some evidence to suggest that expected declines in income and employment may decrease consumption and aggregate demand. At the same time, however, it is also true that consumers are reluctant to return to lower consumption levels when income declines. The evidence on the impact of already-realized price changes upon consumption is also not altogether clear. The late Professor Irving Fisher pointed out that a "money illusion" may prevail, making consumers feel better off when prices and disposable incomes rise proportionately. Even though real income does not change, consumers afflicted with "money illusion" may increase the proportion of their incomes spent when money income rises. The so-called "Pigou effect," named after the English economist A. C. Pigou, notes that falling prices which increase the *real* value of fixed liquid assets such as bonds or retirement annuities increase consumption. The combination of money illusion, falling prices, and increases in the real value of a fixed asset may induce consumers to spend more or less. Although the impact of price changes on consumption may not be uniform, it is clear that either *expected* or *realized* price and income changes can lead to shifts in a consumption schedule.

## Changes in Investment Demand

The determinants of investment opportunities which are primarily responsible for shifts in the investment schedule work through expected profits. Several of the most important determinants of investment that merit consideration are:

1. Interest rates and the marginal efficiency of capital. The *marginal-efficiency-of-capital* schedule shown in Figure 3 generally describes how much investment is forthcoming at alternative rates of interest. At any given time, a wide variety of investment expenditures are available to business firms. Interest rates, as a cost of using funds to acquire capital resources, are negatively related to investment opportunities. At higher interest rates, such as $i_2$, firms will not invest in those capital goods least likely to yield a sufficient rate of return. Consequently, investment demand will be smaller at higher interest rates, but lower investment yields can be accepted when the cost of using funds is lower. Thus in Figure 3, a drop in interest rates from $i_2$ to $i_1$ expands investment demand from $I_1$ to $I_2$, which shifts aggregate demand upward and increases equilibrium NNP. The principle of the marginal efficiency of capital applies to funds generated internally in business firms as well as to borrowed financing. This is because a firm incurs an opportunity cost in using its own funds in the form of interest earnings sacrificed by choosing to purchase capital equipment.

2. Technology. Technological improvements in production methods are another important determinant of investment demand. Innovations leading

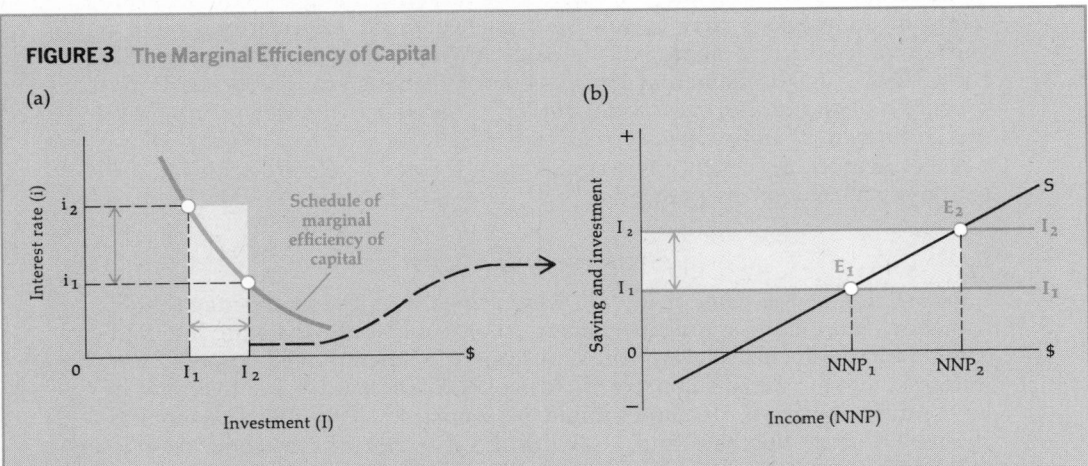

**FIGURE 3** The Marginal Efficiency of Capital

(a)

(b)

*Interest Rates and Investment.* The general relation between interest rates and investment demand is shown by the marginal-efficiency-of-capital schedule. Declining interest rates may prompt an increase in investment expenditures which will increase the equilibrium level of income, whereas less investment is forthcoming at higher rates of interest because fewer capital investment projects yield a sufficient rate of return.

to new products, markets, or modes of production encourage firms to expand investment outlays in search of profits that may be achieved through either increased sales or lower production costs. In many instances, technological advances can be achieved only by investment in new capital goods (the computer is an example).

3. Economic outlook. Optimistic business expectations also encourage investment expenditures for additional capital goods. In contrast, uncertainty and greater NNP risks tend to discourage firms from making commitments to capital resources that may not be needed to produce at a lower level of NNP.

4. Costs, durability, and stock of capital goods. Investment in capital goods is also influenced by the costs of acquiring, maintaining, and operating capital resources. Investment expenditures are discouraged when higher acquisition and operating costs of capital prevail; under such conditions, firms tend to substitute other factors of production for capital resources. To the extent that capital goods are durable, firms may repair them and even postpone new purchases when the economic outlook is bleak. Finally, the current stock of durable capital equipment on hand, as well as its age and condition, may influence decisions to postpone purchases or to make new investment expenditures.

*In summary:* Easy credit conditions, less frugality, more equal income distribution, greater wealth, anticipated future price increases, and an optimistic economic outlook tend to shift consumption and aggregate demand upward, raising equilibrium NNP. The reverse conditions for nonincome determinants of consumption (e.g., tight credit or the expectation that income will decline in the future) may lower a schedule of *DD* and cause equilibrium NNP to decline. For analogous reasons, changes in the determinants of investment that favorably influence profit expectations tend to shift investment and aggregate demand upward, thus increasing equilibrium NNP. The fundamental conclusion we reach is straightforward: *Aggregate demand is not necessarily stable in the short run. Therefore, NNP and employment may change from one month or year to the next.* Moreover, remember that even when equilibrium income levels are achieved, full employment may or may not exist.

### B. MAGNITUDE OF INCOME CHANGES: THE MULTIPLIER

Suppose that as the King of Id, you were armed with the knowledge that by somehow increasing aggregate demand, you could raise the kingdom's income (and your tax levies), thus putting the unemployed knaves, now loitering in your palace courtyard, to work. You would want to know by how much aggregate demand should be increased. Knowing that equilibrium NNP may fluctuate and knowing the *direction* that income changes will take when the aggregate-demand schedule shifts provides only partial knowledge about the problem of economic instability. After all, if aggregate demand increased rapidly, inflation could destroy the value of your horde of gold because the kingdom would be pushed beyond the full-employment NNP limit into an inflationary gap. By how much will NNP change when aggregate demand shifts up or down? The answer to this question is provided by the *multiplier*, which demonstrates that income changes by a multiple of the initial change in aggregate demand. Because this concept is one of the most important ideas in macroeconomics, the logic of magnified income changes will be explained before we formally analyze the multiplier.

### The Simple Logic of the Multiplier

To see how economic instability works, suppose we look at an isolated event in Wamsutter, Wyoming. We presume that for one reason or another aggregate demand rises autonomously, perhaps because consumers spend or firms invest an additional $100. Does Wamsutter's income rise by $100? Clearly it does not. Let us see why.

First of all, some of the $100 may be spent elsewhere to purchase materials or resources not available in the 300-person community of Wamsutter. If the $100 were spent entirely in another community, Wamsutter's level of output would remain unchanged. But what would happen if Wamsutter were a more self-sufficient or "closed" economy, more nearly like a nation that does relatively little or no trading with other countries? If the $100 were paid to local construction workers, to firms selling building materials, to rooming-house matrons, and so forth, the community would experience an increase in income larger than $100, because some portion of the additional incomes received by all of these individuals would be spent *again* for food, clothing, housing, new automobiles, and the like. The amount spent and saved in this circular-income-flow process depends on the marginal propensity to consume (*MPC*) and the marginal propensity to save (*MPS*). Whatever portion of the change in income is respent—the *MPC*—will flow through Wamsutter's economy again and again. Consequently, over a period of time, the banker, butcher, baker, and others supplying goods and services will receive and spend additional funds.

Suppose that in the aggregate the marginal propensity to save is 20 percent (*MPS* = $2/$10 = 20 percent), and 80 percent of all income is spent (*MPC* = $8/$10 = 80 percent). The initial $100 moves successively through Wamsutter's economy from one person and time period to others, creating additional income for a variety of economic units, each of which consumes and saves a portion of the income received. An additional $100 injected into Wamsutter's circular-income flow is multiplied into a larger aggregate amount of total income over a period of time (say, one year) as follows: Income rises by ($100 × 0.8 = $80) + ($80 × 0.8 = $64) + ($64 × 0.8 = $51), and so forth from one spending round to the next. In each spending round, 80 percent of all income received is consumed and 20 percent leaks out of the income flow into saving; thus, smaller and smaller fractions of the original $100 circulate through the Wamsutter economy as consumption expenditures. Nonetheless, the initial $100 is magnified or "multiplied" into a larger total change in income, just as the total amount of oil circulating through a motor in an hour may greatly exceed the few quarts of oil an engine holds.

### THE MULTIPLIER PROCESS

There are three important lessons to learn from this example. In the first place, because income recipients normally do not spend 100 percent of the additional income they receive, *less* and *less* income is passed on in successive spending rounds. The $100 in increased expenditures—which is comparable to a shift in *DD*—snowballs into a larger change in income and employment. By letting $m$ designate the size of the multiplier, we can see that one definition of the multiplier is the ratio of the change in income to the change in aggregate demand,

$$m = \frac{\text{final change in income}}{\text{initial change in aggregate demand}} = \frac{\Delta NNP}{\Delta DD}$$

Second, the size of the final equilibrium increase in Wamsutter's income depends in part on the extent to which funds are spent on output produced in our little megalopolis. Had all goods and services been imported from another local economy, there would have been no permanent increase in aggregate demand or income. Similarly, if the $100 all leaked out of the spending stream into saving after the initial expenditure, Wamsutter's income and employment would increase only by the initial $100, not by a multiple of the change in aggregate demand. Accordingly, the magnitude of rising income initiated by an upward shift in aggregate demand is dependent upon the amount of additional income spent, which is given as the *MPC* for the community.[2] Finally, it is worth noting that as Wamsutter residents experience income increases, rising consumption expenditures may induce additional investment expenditures because firms may find it necessary to expand their capacity to produce consumer goods. Thus, a further intensification or acceleration of changes in income may occur.

The size of the multiplier, defined earlier as $m = \Delta NNP/\Delta DD$, is determined by the portions of additional income spent and saved. The multiplier is simply the reciprocal of the marginal propensity to save. (A reciprocal is $1 \div$ another number, or the *MPS* in this case.[3])

$$\text{Multiplier} = \frac{1}{\substack{\text{marginal propensity} \\ \text{to save}}} \quad \text{or} \quad m = \frac{1}{MPS}$$

An initial increase in aggregate demand is magnified into a larger increase in income because, during a given period of time, an increase in expenditures circulates through an economy many times over. Consumption expenditures, and therefore the amount of income passed from one spending unit to others, decline according to the value of the marginal propensities to consume and save.

### CALCULATION OF MULTIPLIER VALUES

Suppose that one of every two additional dollars is consumed, and that *DD* rises by $10. We then know that 50 percent, or $5 of each increment of income, is respent ($MPC = 0.5$), and the remainder is saved ($MPS = 0.5$). Income initially rises by $10, of which $5 is consumed and, therefore, is income received in a second spending round. With an *MPC* of 0.5, still another $2.50 is consumed as expenditures move through the circular-income flow in a third round. Diminishing rounds of consumption expenditures and income payments flow through the economy as shown below.

[2] Remember, the *MPC* is a measure of the slope of the consumption schedule which cannot exceed 1 ($\Delta C/\Delta DI = \$10/\$10$), in which case any schedule $C$ is plotted as a 45° line.

[3] Because $MPC + MPS = 1$, it is also possible to view *MPS* as $1 - MPC$; therefore, the multiplier is also $1/ 1 - MPC$.

| Initial increase in income | 2nd round | 3rd round | 4th round | 5th round | 6th round ... | Income increase through all rounds |
|---|---|---|---|---|---|---|
| +$10 | +$5 | +$2.50 | +$1.25 | +$.675 | +$.33 | NNP = +$20 |

With an *MPS* of 0.5, the size of the multiplier is

$$m = \frac{1}{MPS} \quad \text{or} \quad \frac{1}{0.5} = 2$$

The cumulative spending chain of the multiplier process for an increase in aggregate demand of $100 million is illustrated in Figure 4. In Example I we assume an *MPC* of 0.8, whereas Example II uses a relatively low *MPC* of 0.2. Both examples illustrate the following properties of the multiplier:

1. The multiplier process depends on the fact that people respend a portion of each income increment received. A change of $100 million in aggregate demand would not produce second- and third-round increases in NNP if further consumption out of additional income did not occur.

2. The total change in income is the initial change in aggregate demand times the multiplier or $\Delta NNP = \Delta DD \times m$. If aggregate demand increases, income will increase by the sum of *all* incremental consumption expenditures reinjected into the circular-income flow, since each increment of con-

**FIGURE 4** The Multiplier at Work
(millions of dollars)

Example I: *MPC* = 0.8; *MPS* = 0.2; *m* = 5

| | 1st round | 2nd round | 3rd round | 4th round | 5th round | 6th round ... | All spending rounds |
|---|---|---|---|---|---|---|---|
| Income | +$100 | +$80 | +$64 | +$51 | +$41 | +$33 | +$500 in $\Delta$NNP |
| Consumption | 80 | 64 | 51 | 41 | 33 | 26 | 400 in $\Delta$C |
| Saving | 20 | 16 | 13 | 10 | 8 | 7 | 100 in $\Delta$S |

Example II: *MPC* = 0.2; *MPS* = 0.8; *m* = 1.25

| | 1st round | 2nd round | 3rd round | 4th round | 5th round | 6th round ... | All spending rounds |
|---|---|---|---|---|---|---|---|
| Income | +$100 | +$20 | +$4 | +$.8 | – | – | +$125 in $\Delta$NNP |
| Consumption | 20 | 4 | .8 | .16 | – | – | 25 in $\Delta$C |
| Saving | 80 | 16 | 3.2 | .64 | – | – | 100 in $\Delta$S |

*Multiplier Impact.* Aggregate demand increases initially by $100 million as firms increase investment expenditures and pay out this amount to other firms and workers as income, who in turn consume and save the above portions of their increase in income. (Data are rounded.)

sumer expenditures also represents an income payment to someone. When the *MPC* is large as it is in Example I, relatively large additional consumption expenditures and indirect income changes follow. A small *MPC* produces the smaller income multiplier shown in Example II because the bulk of a change in income leaks out of the spending stream as saving.

3. The size of a multiplier and the final change in NNP are inversely related to the *MPS*. In Example I of Figure 4, *MPS* is small (0.2) and the multiplier is large ($m = 1/0.2 = 5$). Example II depicts greater leakages to saving, and the multiplier and final change in income are smaller because leakages to saving are larger. The final changes in income computed below show the consequence of differences in the *MPS* and the multiplier. The relatively small *MPS* in Example I generates a large multiplier impact. The final change in NNP of $500 million is the result of 80 percent of all additional income being respent, whereas in Example II the multiplier is small because of a large *MPS* and the change in NNP is less—$125 million.

| Example I | Example II |
|---|---|
| $m = 1/MPS$ or $1/0.2 = 5$ | $m = 1/MPS$ or $1/0.8 = 1.25$ |
| $\Delta\text{NNP} = \Delta DD \times m$ | $\Delta\text{NNP} = \Delta DD \times m$ |
| $= \$100$ million $\times 5$ | $= \$100$ million $\times 1.25$ |
| $= \$500$ million | $= \$125$ million |

4. Equilibrium income is reestablished when $S$ equals $I$. The multiplier process leading to changes in income ends when a new equilibrium is reached where saving and investment expenditures are again equal. In Figure 4, equilibrium is reached when the $100 million of additional investment is just offset by an increase in saving of a like amount. This important property of the multiplier is illustrated in Figure 5.

Suppose that aggregate demand increases by $50 billion from *DD* to *DD'*, perhaps because planned investment increases. Figure 5 summarizes how the cumulative multiplier process moves an economy from one equilibrium income position to another when $3 of each additional $4 in income is consumed (*MPS* = .25). Equilibrium output increases from NNP = $600 billion to NNP = $800 billion, an increase of $200 billion, or an income change four times as large as the initial increase in aggregate demand of $50 billion shown in the figure. Why? Because of the multiplier. When 75 percent of additional income is spent, we know that $m = 4$ and, ultimately NNP will be larger by $\Delta DD \times m$ ($50 billion $\times 4 = $200 billion). It is no coincidence that income changes by $200 billion in Figure 5 when investment increases from $100 to $150 billion. Income *must rise* by an amount sufficient for saving to offset the new investment inflow of $50 billion. Income equilibrium prevails only when intended $I = S$ because only then is the amount businessmen want to invest equal to what people save! This can occur *only* if income rises by $200 billion as long as the proportion of income consumed remains unchanged. Then, and only then, does saving change by the requisite $50 billion (25 percent of $200 billion) needed to

**FIGURE 5** The Multiplier Impact on Equilibrium NNP
(billions of dollars)

(a)

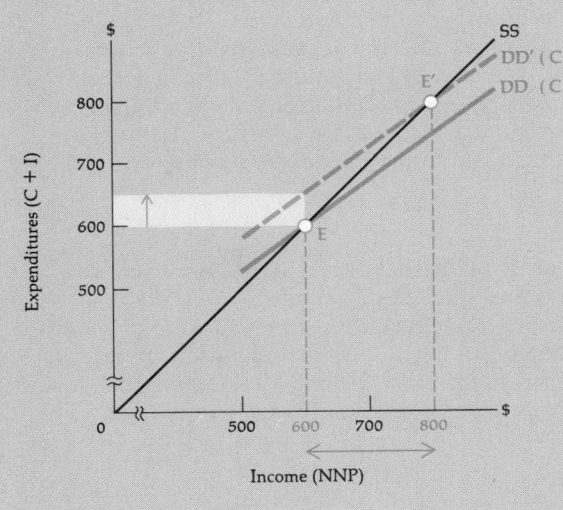

1. $\Delta DD$ due to $\Delta I = \$50$
2. Old equilibrium NNP $= \$600$
3. $MPC = .75$ so $MPS = .25$
4. $m = 1/MPS$ or $1/.25 = 4$
5. $\Delta NNP = \Delta DD \times m$
   $= \$50 \times 4$
   $= \$200$
6. $\Delta S = \Delta NNP \times MPS$
   $= \$200 \times .25$
   $= \$50$

(b)

| DD | SS | S | I |
|---|---|---|---|
| 575 | 500 | 75 | 150 |
| 650 | 600 | 100 | 150 |
| 725 | 700 | 125 | 150 |
| 800 = 800 | | 150 = 150 | |
| 875 | 900 | 175 | 150 |

*Multiplier-Generated Increases in NNP.* When aggregate demand increases, additional expenditures circulate through an economy several times over, causing NNP to rise by a multiple of the initial change in spending. The greater the *MPC*, the larger the final change in income. In the example above, the multiplier value is 4 ($1/MPS = 1/.25$) and NNP rises by $4 billion for every $1 billion increase in investment demand. For similar reasons reductions in aggregate demand lead to magnified declines in NNP.

offset the investment inflow of $50 billion. Income will continue to change until equality between investment inflows and saving leakages is achieved, thus stabilizing the circular-income flow.

Although the multiplier is discussed above in terms of increased expenditures, a *decline* in aggregate demand, say from *DD'* to *DD* in Figure 5, would also result in a multiplier impact—a reduction in equilibrium NNP.

Output would fall from $800 billion to $600 billion because aggregate spending decreased by $50 billion. Like a spending increase, a decline in aggregate demand is magnified into larger declines in income and output through the multiplier process, a condition that leads to rising levels of unemployment and lower NNP.

The multiplier would not be a very important phenomenon if the $C + I$ components of aggregate demand were stable. But because relatively small incremental changes in aggregate demand are magnified into larger increases or decreases in income and employment, fluctuations in spending can pose serious problems. This is particularly true where investment expenditures are concerned because they are characterized by a good deal of volatility and uncertainty.

### The Crucial Role of Investment

Equilibrium income cannot exist until planned $I = S$, as we now realize. Investment expenditures are crucial and likely to fluctuate widely because: (a) saving and investment decisions are made for different reasons by different economic groups, and anticipated profits are uncertain and variable; (b) inventory investments reflect business expectations that may or may not materialize; and (c) changes in consumption and income may accelerate or decelerate investment expenditures.

#### SAVING AND INVESTMENT DISCREPANCIES

If we exclude business depreciation of capital resources as a form of saving, over one-half of all saving originates with households.[4] While decisions to invest are generally made by business firms in relation to interest rates and expected profits, household decisions to save are related to decisions to consume and may be quite disassociated from the interest rate. The decision to save, as we have seen, is directly affected by consumption expenditures and income levels, the habit or custom of thrift, the cost and availability of credit, the desire to hold liquid assets, anticipated large purchases, and price and income changes. Business investment decisions, on the other hand, are motivated by the expected profitability of acquiring additional capital resources. Profit expectations are subjective, they can vary from one time to another, and they are necessarily plagued by uncertainty. Because of this uncertainty and because different groups make saving and investment decisions for different reasons, imbalance between saving and planned investment is very possible. The critical point to remember is that a market economy is susceptible to disequilibrium when the amount households intend to withdraw from the income stream as saving varies from the amount of investment firms plan to inject into the circular-income flow. Indeed, disequilibrium, where planned $I \neq S$, is a more likely event than equilibrium and income stability, where planned $I = S$.

#### INVENTORY INVESTMENT

Business investments in inventory depend on expected production and sales, and when sales expectations do not materialize, some unintended investment is forced, and aggregate demand falls short of aggregate supply.

---

[4] Since our interest is confined to net investment above and beyond capital replacement needs, no serious injustice is entailed in ignoring depreciation as a source of funds. In an important sense, it is not saving in any event.

Actual inventories will then accumulate beyond the level that firms desire, and this *unintended investment in inventories has a contractionary impact on the economy*. Producers will cut back on future production to reduce inventories, and output will decline. Firms may also abandon planned investment in plant expansion. In contrast, unintended *dis*investment in inventories occurs if firms underestimate aggregate demand and are unable to achieve the desired ratio of inventory to sales. Production, output, and employment will then rise in a multiplier-driven fashion.

## INDUCED INVESTMENT

Thus far, we have continued to assume that all investment is autonomous when, in fact, changes in income and consumption can induce investment expenditures. Induced investment is important because it accelerates bursts of expansion and contraction, thereby intensifying swings in economic activity.

Suppose that Blimey Ale, Ltd., has ten stills, each capable of producing 1,000 gallons of output per week, and that each year one still is worn out. Consequently, one unit of capital is replaced annually because of depreciation. Now if Blimey's board of directors expects income and consumption demand to increase by 10 percent (1,000 gallons weekly) in the next year, they will invest in not one but *two* stills. Demand for capital, and therefore investment expenditures will rise by *100* percent when anticipated income and consumption increase by only *10* percent. Suppose, on the other hand, that the board expects demand to decline by 10 percent, perhaps because of declining incomes and fewer available jobs for those consuming Blimey in the local pubs. Instead of acquiring the usual replacement unit, they may decide to invest no capital because nine stills provide adequate capacity when demand declines by 10 percent. Thus, a decline in income induces less investment than is normal. The effect of induced investment can be even more pronounced, given the uncertainty that surrounds investment decisions in the real world. After all, the board of directors could be wrong and anticipate a need for more capital when in fact demand might decline and less investment might be required.

Induced investment accelerates the change in income beyond the normal multiplier effect because any increase in C causing NNP to rise via the multiplier also causes I to rise in some proportion to the level of NNP or the change in NNP. Technically, it makes a great deal of difference whether investment is induced by the *level of income* or the *rate of change* in income.[5] For our purposes we need only recognize that both an initial change in aggregate demand and induced investment expenditures can contribute to changes in income. If we recognize that investment is dependent upon consumption and income to some extent, it can be shown that consumption-induced investment accentuates the magnitude of income changes even further. The combined effect of the multiplier applied to autonomous *and* consumption-induced investment is shown in Figure 6. In the figure, the investment-demand schedule slopes upward, denoting that some investment is induced. Every additional $100 in NNP is matched by an increase of $5 in additional induced investment.

[5] The example of the accelerated multiplier ignores this distinction, which is normally covered in more advanced courses.

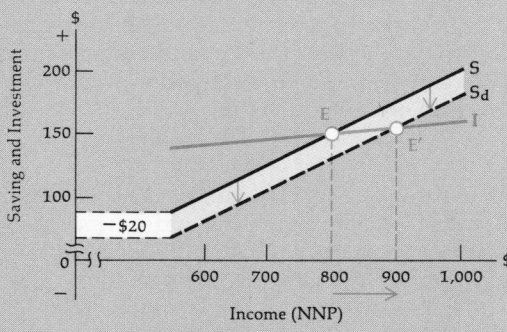

**FIGURE 6** Induced Investment and Equilibrium Income
(billions of dollars)

| NNP | $I$ | $S_d$ | = | $S + \Delta S$ |
|---|---|---|---|---|
| $ 600 | $140 | $ 80 | = | $100 (−$20) |
| 700 | 145 | 105 | = | 125 (− 20) |
| 800 | 150 | 130 | = | 150 (− 20) |
| 900 | 155 | 155 | = | 175 (− 20) |
| 1,000 | 160 | 180 | = | 200 (− 20) |

$$\Delta \text{NNP} = \Delta DD \times 1/MPS$$
$$= (\Delta C + \Delta I) \times 1/.25$$
$$= (+\$20 \text{ billion} + 5 \text{ billion}) \times 4$$
$$= +\$100 \text{ billion}$$

*Induced Investment.* If investment demand is positively related to NNP, an autonomous increase in consumption of $20 billion causes (*a*) saving to decline by $20 billion at all levels of NNP, and (*b*) as income rises additional investment is induced in the amount of $5 billion in this example. Consequently, $\Delta DD = C$ of $20 billion + $I$ (induced) of $5 billion and NNP rises by $100 billion since $\Delta$NNP $= \Delta DD \times m$, or $100 = $25 \times 4$.

If for some reason consumption expenditures increase by $20 billion, the chain reaction set in motion by this autonomous increase in aggregate demand of $20 billion is as follows: Increased *DD* causes scheduled saving to decline to $S_d$ at each level of income. Consequently, NNP and employment rise to a new and higher equilibrium level where planned $I = S_d$ at an NNP equilibrium of $900 billion. Note, however, that higher levels of C and NNP also induce investment to increase by $5 billion. Aggregate demand ultimately increases by $20 billion in autonomous consumption *plus* another $5 billion of investment induced by higher levels of consumption and income. Taking account of both $+ \Delta C$ and $+ \Delta I$ (induced) means that NNP ultimately will rise by $100 billion. The $\Delta DD$ of $20 billion in consumption plus $5 billion in induced investment is multiplied by a multiplier of 4 (since $MPS = 0.25$), resulting in $\Delta$NNP of $+ $100 billion.[6]

## Thrift: Vice or Virtue?

One paradoxical implication of income equilibrium is that saving may be a public vice even though it is a cherished private virtue. Attempts to *increase* saving by reducing consumption demand cause actual saving to

---

[6] The end result of induced investment impacts can be presented crudely by adjustment of the multiplier formula, $m = 1/MPS$. When investment inflows are induced, as they are in Figure 6, *net* leakages to saving in each spending round are smaller by that amount. An adjusted multiplier ($m^*$) can thus be expressed as the reciprocal of the marginal propensity to save *less* the proportion of investment induced by a change in income. In Figure 6, $MPS = \$25/100$ (0.25 so $m = 4$), and investment changes by $5 for every $100 change in NNP. The adjusted multiplier is $m^* = 1/MPS^*$ or $\dfrac{1}{0.25 - 0.05}$ $= \dfrac{1}{0.2} = 5$.

*decline.* To see why the pursuit of greater aggregate frugality leads to lower saving, aggregate income, and employment, visualize the consequences of attempts to increase saving in Figure 6. Increased saving of $20 billion at all income levels is represented as a shift from schedule $S_d$ to $S$, indicating that aggregate demand declines because consumption expenditures are reduced at all levels of income as saving increases. A new and lower level of equilibrium NNP is established at $800 billion where *actual saving* is lower than before. When a nation attempts to save $20 billion more at each level of output, and the saving schedule shifts from $S_d$ to $S$, the higher NNP cannot be sustained at $900 billion because saving exceeds planned investment, causing production, saving, and income to decline to a lower equilibrium at point $E$ in Figure 6.

The ironic conclusion that frugality may be detrimental to the aggregate economy is only partially correct, but it does furnish further insight into the causes of economic instability. Individual parsimony is not the culprit. Because increased aggregate saving causes aggregate demand to decline, the culprit is the *aggregate,* not individual, decision to save more and spend less. Thrift is a problem only if aggregate saving intentions rise when an economy is operating at or below full employment. The irony in the *thrift dilemma* is that attempts to save more can lead to actually saving less because of declining income and employment, as is illustrated in Figure 6. When firms and households anticipating an economic recession are inclined to reduce expenditures and increase saving, their actions intensify fluctuations in economic activity. Thus, anticipated declines in sales, profits, income, and employment encourage *less* aggregate demand (and more saving) when just the converse is needed to achieve full employment! When these initial declines in aggregate demand are magnified by the multiplier process, income and employment contractions may steamroll an economy into a recession.

### C. ACHIEVING FULL EMPLOYMENT THROUGH DISCRETIONARY FISCAL POLICY

Thus far in our study of income and employment determination, six major conclusions have been reached.

1. Expansionary and contractionary bursts of unemployment and inflation speed up and retard economic growth in an uneven manner. Moreover, economic activity *fluctuates around and does not necessarily remain at* full employment.

2. Investment inflows and saving leakages from a circular-income flow account for economic instability, when government and foreign trade are ignored. A stable or equilibrium income level is achieved when $DD = SS$, which means that planned $I = S$.

3. The key factors in economic instability are variations in spending relative to aggregate supply. The investment component of aggregate demand is particularly apt to generate instability.

4. Full employment of resources is not necessarily consistent with income equilibrium and, in any event, variations in aggregate demand readily result in the appearance of deflationary or inflationary gaps.

5. Consumption and, particularly, investment expenditures are volatile. When aggregate-demand shifts occur, the multiplier magnifies small changes in spending into even larger variations in income and employment. Multi-

plier effects are determined by the proportion of income remaining in the circular-income flow. Consequently, small leakages to saving give rise to larger changes in NNP and employment.

6. The extent to which NNP rises or declines can be estimated by multiplying a change in any autonomous component of aggregate demand (such as investment) by the multiplier. Multiplier effects are magnified *further* and accentuate swings in economic activity to the extent that investment demand is induced by income and consumption changes.

With this awareness of the facts of income and employment determination and the causes of unemployment and inflation in hand, let us next see what action can be taken to remedy economic instability.

### The Theory of Fiscal Policy

Shifts in the private-sector components of aggregate demand are amplified by multiplier effects that alter equilibrium NNP. The usual situation in a market economy is one of income instability and disequilibrium because aggregate demand is continually changing. As the elusive objective of full employment is pursued, either inflationary or unemployment pressures may prevail if private-sector consumption and investment spending vary from the full-employment level. Because nations cannot instantaneously adjust to a world in which diverse expectations, unknown intentions, and a generally uncertain environment influence aggregate demand, income disequilibrium is often the result.

Consequently, government must be brought into our understanding of income determination. Aggregate demand includes government purchases of output. Moreover, we must consider the expansive influence of transfer payments on aggregate demand and the contractionary influence that taxes have on investment and consumption.[7]

Macroeconomic management of the economy is directed to the related problems of reducing income instability and synchronizing equilibrium income at full employment. *Fiscal policy* is the explicit use of government spending or taxation to increase or decrease aggregate demand. Taxes ($T$) have a contractionary impact on NNP because higher taxes tend to lower the consumption and investment components of aggregate demand. Tax revenues are like saving, in that they are leakages, whereas government purchases are inflows into the circular-income flow. Government expenditures to purchase goods and services increase aggregate demand *directly*.

If the government component of aggregate demand (denoted by $G$) is included in an income-determination model, $DD = C + I + G$. Government transfer payments to households and firms *indirectly* alter aggregate demand because they alter disposable income and thus affect consumption or investment expenditures. Fiscal policy, then, alters income and employment by shifting aggregate demand which works through the multiplier process to magnify the initial change in spending into larger changes in NNP as shown at the top of page 161.

[7] Ignored for the moment are: (*a*) distinctions between NNP and *DI* resulting from government expenditures and taxes; (*b*) the possibility that government spending may influence *C* or *I*; (*c*) the effects of regressive, proportional, or progressive tax rates; (*d*) the difference in public-sector purchases of output compared to transfer payments; and (*e*) the effect of money and interest rates.

| Fiscal policy: | $\Delta G$ or $\Delta T$ ——————→ | $\Delta DD$ × m ——————→ | $\Delta NNP$ |

The appropriateness of a fiscal strategy depends upon whether an economy is experiencing a deflationary gap and unemployment, or rapid expansion and an inflationary gap. Although achievement of economic stability through fiscal policy is complicated by a variety of factors, the policies generally appropriate for closing a deflationary or inflationary gap are as follows: An inflationary gap, characterized by $DD$ in excess of full employment $SS$, can be corrected with fiscal policy by reducing $G$ or increasing $T$, both of which shift aggregate demand down. Since a deflationary gap is characterized by unemployment and inadequate aggregate demand at full employment, increases in $G$ or reductions in $T$ are useful expansionary fiscal measures. A convenient way to view expansionary or contractionary fiscal policy is to think in terms of government expenditures relative to tax revenues in the circular-income flow. .

### Government and Circular-Income Flows

Figure 7 describes the equilibrium condition in a circular-income-flow model in which investment expenditures *plus* government expenditures on output now comprise spending-stream inflows, and *both* saving and tax revenues constitute leakages from the spending stream. Expansionary fiscal policy will increase inflows if $G$ is increased or reduce leakages if $T$ is decreased. In contrast, contractionary fiscal policy increases $T$ leakages or

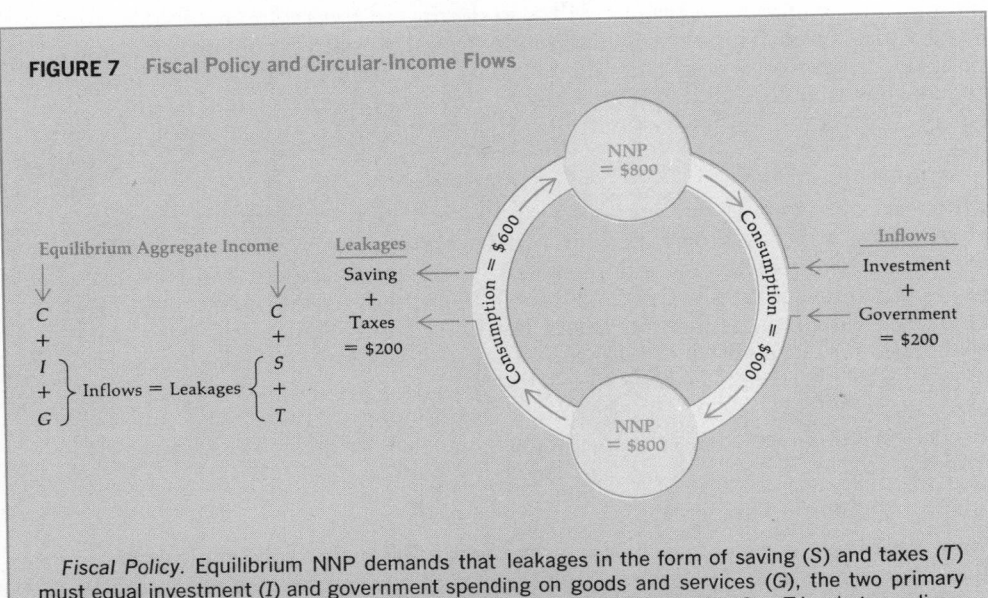

**FIGURE 7**   Fiscal Policy and Circular-Income Flows

*Fiscal Policy.* Equilibrium NNP demands that leakages in the form of saving (S) and taxes (T) must equal investment (I) and government spending on goods and services (G), the two primary spending-stream inflows. Fiscal policy may alter the level of NNP by varying G or T in whatever direction and combination that moves the economy toward full employment and price stability.

decreases $G$ inflows, thus altering the income level. In theory, expansionary fiscal policy would be employed to increase the equilibrium level of NNP under conditions of less than full employment. Contractionary fiscal policy —a deliberate reduction in aggregate demand—is useful under inflationary conditions. By deliberately shifting aggregate demand and creating income disequilibrium conditions, fiscal policy may be used to help achieve full employment.

### DEFLATIONARY GAPS

Suppose that (as in Figure 7) the equilibrium NNP of $800 billion is below the full-employment output level, assumed to be $NNP_{fe} = \$900$ billion. Under these circumstances, one fiscal-policy option is to increase $G$, thus raising $DD$ and output to the required $NNP_{fe}$ level. Alternatively, the $C$ or $I$ components of $DD$ could be increased by a tax cut in order to increase output to the required $NNP_{fe}$ level. The net effect of expansionary fiscal policy is a larger federal government budget deficit (or smaller budget surplus), which adds to aggregate demand, causing the income stream to expand to the desired NNP level. The budget balance is tax revenues ($T$) less government expenditures ($G$).

### INFLATIONARY GAPS

Now assume that the equilibrium NNP of $800 billion in Figure 7 is above the full-employment level of output and inflationary conditions prevail ($NNP_{fe} = \$700$ billion). Fiscal-policy options now include lowering the $G$ component of aggregate demand; thus, $DD$ declines and output and employment fall to the required full-employment level. By using taxes as a fiscal-policy weapon, a contraction in the $C + I$ components of $DD$ can be induced and equilibrium output will also decline to the required $NNP_{fe} = \$700$ billion level. On balance, contractionary fiscal policy results in a larger budget surplus (or a smaller budget deficit) than existed earlier. The consequence is that spending and incomes decline to a level consistent with the $NNP_{fe} = \$700$ billion level of output.

### Government Tax and Expenditure Policies Compared

When an economy is not operating at full employment, either increased government purchases or a tax cut will be expansionary, but not equally so. Figure 8(a) depicts a deflationary gap where aggregate demand initially is governed by schedule $DD = C + I + G$, and equilibrium output is $NNP_u$, less than the full-employment level of output. Figure 8(b) portrays an inflationary gap, since $DD$ exceeds $SS$ at full employment which causes *money* NNP to rise. Assuming that $2 of every $3 in disposable income is consumed ($MPS = 1/3$), all investment is autonomous, and that $T$ and $G$ effects on NNP are as given, the impact of fiscal policy can take several forms.

### DISCRETIONARY CHANGES IN GOVERNMENT SPENDING

First, aggregate demand can be increased from $DD$ to the full-employment level $DD_i$ shown in Figure 8(a) by increasing government *purchases* of goods and services in the amount of the deflationary gap ($10 billion), assuming that taxes remain unchanged. Increasing government expenditures by $10 billion for goods and services such as roads, construction of build-

**FIGURE 8** Fiscal Policy and Full Employment
(billions of dollars)

(a) Closing deflationary gaps: ↓$T$ or ↑$G$

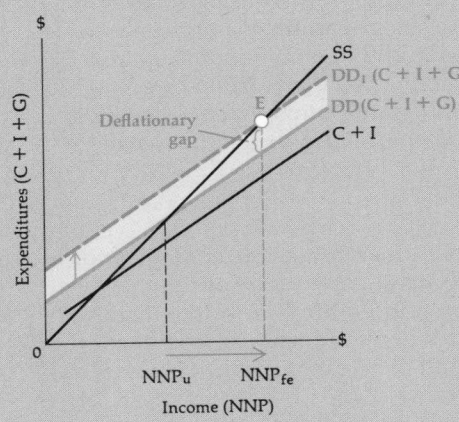

1. Problem: Unemployment
2. Assumptions: $MPS = 1/3$ so $m = 3$
3a. Policy: Increase $G$ + $10
$$\Delta NNP = \Delta DD \times m$$
$$+\$30 = +\$10 \times 3$$
  b. Policy: Lower $T = -\$15$
$$\Delta C = +\$10$$
$$\Delta S = +\$5$$

$$\Delta NNP = \Delta DD \times m$$
$$+\$30 = +\$10 \times 3$$

(b) Closing inflationary gaps: ↓$G$ or ↑$T$

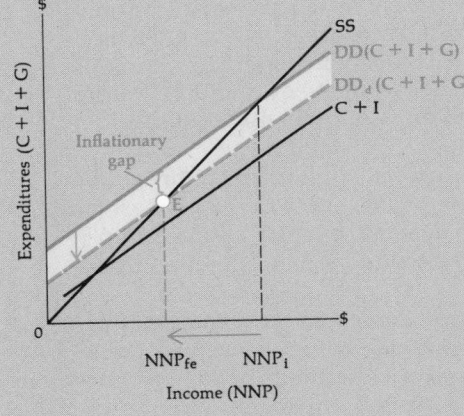

1. Problem: Inflation
2. Assumptions: $MPS = 1/3$ so $m = 3$
3a. Policy: Decrease $G = -\$10$
$$\Delta NNP = \Delta DD \times m$$
$$-\$30 = -\$10 \times 3$$
  b. Policy: Raise $T = +\$15$
$$\Delta C = -\$10$$
$$\Delta S = -\$5$$

$$\Delta NNP = \Delta DD \times m$$
$$-\$30 = -\$10 \times 3$$

*Deflationary and Inflationary Gaps.* Fiscal policy refers to the use of government expenditures and taxes to shift aggregate demand to a level consistent with full employment. Increasing $G$ and reducing $T$ closes a deflationary gap (a), while reducing $G$ and increasing $T$ closes an inflationary gap (b) through the multiplier process. Because some portion of a tax change alters saving as well as consumption demand, a tax cut is less expansive than an increase in government purchases, and a tax increase is less repressive than a reduction in government spending on goods and services for the same reason.

ings, national defense, or parks shifts aggregate demand upward and the full-employment NNP is attained. With a multiplier of 3, the full-employment output level is achieved once $\Delta NNP = \Delta DD \times 3 = \$30$ billion. Take very careful note of the fact that government *transfer payments* may not shift aggregate demand as much as direct purchases. When funds are transferred to the private sector, consumption may not increase by the total amount of the transfer. If saving increases as disposable income rises because of additional transfer payments, the changes in aggregate demand and in income will be *smaller* than an equal change linked to varying government purchases of goods and services. When government purchases are reduced, aggregate demand declines by $10 billion and mounting inflationary pressures can be ameliorated as shown in Figure 8(b). The magnitude of the decrease in spending and NNP (and employment) depends on the net change in aggregate demand and the multiplier relation, where $\Delta NNP = \Delta DD \times m$, as before.

## TAXES AS A FISCAL-POLICY TOOL

Second, the impact of a tax cut to counteract unemployment is similar to, but not precisely the same as, the effect of increased government purchases. Reducing taxes on personal incomes as shown in Figure 8(a) raises disposable income, thereby increasing both $C$ and $S$. Government tax and spending policies are different because some portion of the increase in disposable income generated by a tax cut leaks into saving. When $MPS = 1/3$, $1 of every $3 of additional disposable income will be saved. If taxes were reduced by $10 billion, consumption and aggregate demand would initially increase by $6.7 billion, or two-thirds of $10 billion. This is not a large enough increase in aggregate demand to close the deflationary gap and reach the $NNP_{fe}$ shown in Figure 8(a). A deflationary gap of $10 billion requires a $15 billion tax cut, given $MPS = 1/3$. By making $15 billion of additional disposable income available to households, $\Delta C$ (and therefore $\Delta DD$) $= +$10 billion and $\Delta S = +$5 billion. Consequently, equilibrium NNP rises by the required $30 billion.

The impact of increased taxes intended to reduce inflationary pressures is shown in Figure 8(b). Again, assuming that $MPS = 1/3$, a tax increase of $15 billion is needed to reduce aggregate demand by $10 billion, simply because higher taxes cause consumption to decline by $10 billion and saving by $5 billion.

*Conclusion:* Discretionary increases or decreases in government purchases of goods and services can be used as a stabilizing device because $G$ is an integral component of aggregate demand. Furthermore, as long as consumption and investment expenditures are responsive to tax cuts or increases, tax policies can also be used to alter aggregate demand. However, the tax arm of fiscal policy is not as powerful a weapon as variations in government spending on goods and services.

## THE BALANCED-BUDGET MULTIPLIER

Although it might appear intuitively that a balanced government budget (one with no surplus or deficit) has a neutral impact on NNP, this is not the case. A change in taxes affects *both* consumption and saving; hence, tax policies have a partial impact on aggregate demand. The differential effects of changes in $G$ and $T$ simply reflect differences in the $MPC$ between the public and private sectors of an economy. As long as government spends a larger proportion of its income than the private sector, tax policy is a less powerful fiscal device than government purchases of goods and services. The *balanced-budget multiplier* reveals that identical increases in $G$ and $T$ may be expansionary, whereas identical decreases in $G$ and $T$ are contractionary. Here is how it works.

Suppose that taxes and government purchases of goods and services are both increased by $1 billion, the $MPC = 2/3$, and the current budget is balanced; i.e., the difference between tax receipts and government outlays is zero ($T - G = 0$). With equal tax and expenditure increases of $1 billion, equilibrium NNP will rise by $1 billion, and the budget will remain in balance. This is shown in Example I below (all dollars are in billions):

Example I: Unemployment

$MPS = 1/3$ $\quad \Delta T = +\$1$ thus, $\Delta C = -\$.67$ $\quad$ $\Delta NNP = \Delta DD \times m$
$\quad m = 3$ $\qquad \Delta G = +\$1$ $\qquad\qquad\qquad\qquad$ $= \$.33 \times 3$
$\qquad\qquad$ Net $\Delta DD = +\$.33$ $\qquad\qquad\qquad\qquad\qquad$ $= \$1$

1. A tax increase of $1 billion reduces aggregate demand by $.67 billion.
2. Additional government purchases (but not transfer payments) increase aggregate demand by $1 billion.
3. Consequently, aggregate demand increases by $.33 billion, which means that with a multiplier of 3, NNP will rise by a maximum of $.33 billion $\times$ 3 = $1 billion.

Because the final impact of equal changes in spending and taxes on *DD* varies in relation to the marginal propensities to save and consume income in successive income rounds, the impact of the balanced-budget multiplier normally is no larger than the total change in government expenditures. This is shown by equal tax and expenditure cuts in Example II, where *MPC* is assumed to be 0.5 and the multiplier is 2. Here a reduction in taxes and government expenditures of $1 billion results in a decline of $.5 billion in aggregate demand and $-$$1 billion in NNP. When a nation's *MPC* (and *MPS*) are altered because of the effect of fiscal policy, the net change in spending and multiplier-magnified changes in NNP are something less than the one-for-one relationship in the balanced-budget example.

Example II: Inflation

$MPS = 1/2$ $\quad \Delta T = -\$1$ thus, $\Delta C = +\$.5$ $\quad$ $NNP = \Delta DD \times m$
$\quad m = 2$ $\qquad \Delta G = -\$1$ $\qquad\qquad\qquad\qquad$ $= -\$.5 \times 2$
$\qquad\qquad$ Net $\Delta DD = -\$.5$ $\qquad\qquad\qquad\qquad\qquad$ $= -\$1$

The most expansive fiscal policy is a tax cut that stimulates aggregate demand in the private sector ($C$ and $I$) *combined* with increased government purchases. Similarly, a tax increase and declining government expenditures on goods and services are the most powerful combination of fiscal tools to fight inflation. Our interim conclusions also recognize the idea that the public sector's budget can be both balanced and expansionary (or contractionary) as needed. When $G$ and $T$ are raised or lowered simultaneously, equal increases (or decreases) in $G$ and $T$ tend to increase (decrease) NNP, as the balanced-budget multiplier reveals. In addition, note carefully that a larger *absolute* amount of government expenditures on goods and services may be more expansive than a smaller level of expenditures. The balanced-budget multiplier is responsible for this absolute effect, assuming that the public spends all of an initial change in income, and the private sector of the economy spends a smaller portion of a change in income. If the propensities to consume in the private *and* the public sectors were equal, the balanced-budget multiplier would not exert any influence, nor would larger absolute government expenditures be expansive. Finally, remember that transfer payments *are not* subject to balanced-budget multiplier effects because they depend on the normally lower *MPC* in the private sector.

## CONCLUDING REMARKS ON FISCAL POLICY

Some light has now been shed on the use of public policy to counter the unemployment-inflation problem. The theory of income and employment determination suggests that discretionary fiscal-policy remedies are one possible way of achieving a stable and fully employed economy. There remain, however, a wide variety of problems and policy matters not yet touched upon. As yet, we have not examined the effectiveness of fiscal policy applied in a political world in which it may take time to implement tax or expenditure changes, nor have we examined the idea that some taxes and expenditure changes occur automatically as NNP changes. Although we have described the problems of unemployment and inflation as being due to variations in aggregate demand, there are other, more complicated causes. Discretionary changes in taxes and government spending are a deliberate and important fiscal arm of economic stabilization, but reality is not as cleverly manipulated as a theoretical model—as the next chapter reveals.

## REVIEW
### Summary

1. A change in the *quantity* of output demanded is shown as movement on schedule *DD* describing only how consumption and investment vary as *income* changes. The level of NNP fluctuates as aggregate demand (*DD*) changes due to shifts in consumption and investment demand. While a schedule of spending visually appears as one line, this is an oversimplification of the real world. Upward and downward shifts in scheduled *DD* denote *changes in aggregate demand* that cause NNP to rise and fall.

2. At all income levels, consumption (*C*) shifts may be caused by changes in the availability of credit, income distribution, the stock of and demand for liquid assets and durable goods as a form of wealth and anticipated or realized prices and incomes. Investment (*I*) expenditures respond to profits and are sensitive to interest rates; technology; the economic outlook; and the costs, durability, and supply of capital resources. Thus, the *C* + *I* components of *DD* may vary for many reasons.

3. When aggregate demand does shift, a new equilibrium level of NNP is established where *DD* = *SS* and planned *I* = *S*. An initial increase in *DD* is magnified into larger changes in NNP through the multiplier, which is determined by the marginal propensities to save (*MPS*) and consume (*MPC*). The multiplier, $m = 1/MPS$ [or $1/(1 - MPC)$], and income changes are related to aggregate demand as follows: $\Delta NNP = \Delta DD \times m$. A smaller *MPS* produces a larger multiplier because more income recirculates through the circular-income flow as expenditures,

whereas a larger *MPS* generates a smaller multiplier because larger proportions of the income received leak out of the spending stream into
saving.

4. Investment expenditures are of major significance to changes in NNP
   and employment. Investors and savers are motivated by different factors
   and are generally members of different economic groups; uncertainty
   and the failure to realize planned $I = S$ have an immediate impact on
   inventory investment, production, income, and employment. In addition, the multiplier impact is enlarged or accelerated by induced investment. Because changes in saving and consumption are negatively related, attempts to save more may lead to *less* actual saving.

5. Fiscal policy describes the influence of government expenditures (G)
   and taxes (T) on aggregate demand, NNP, and employment. An expansionary fiscal policy is one that increases aggregate demand and NNP
   by increased *G* or reduced *T*. In contrast, public-sector reductions in *G*
   or increased *T* reduce aggregate demand and NNP.

6. Government purchases of goods and services tend to change aggregate
   demand by greater amounts than either a change in taxes or transfer
   payments, as long as the *MPC* in the public sector is larger than in the
   private sector. Consequently, equal or balanced-budget increases in *G*
   and *T* are expansive, whereas reductions in *G* and *T* are contractionary.

### Identify the Following Concepts and Terms

- change in aggregate demand vs. change in the quantity demanded
- marginal efficiency of capital
- a shift in investment
- corrective budget balance for inflationary gaps
- $1/MPS$
- "thrift dilemma"

- decrease in aggregate demand
- "money illusion"
- balanced-budget multiplier
- fiscal policy
- induced investment and the multiplier
- decrease in aggregate demand

### Questions to Answer

1. Explain the conditions under which several nonincome determinants of
   consumption may contribute to shifts in: (*a*) a consumption and (*b*) a
   saving schedule. In the space provided below illustrate and explain how
   a decrease in consumption affects equilibrium income.

(a)

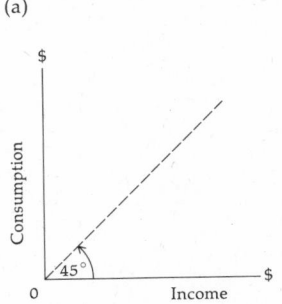

(b)

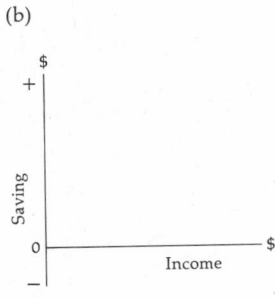

2. The Chamber of Commerce in Dayton, Ohio, announced in February 1971 that new industrial-development plans would result in an increase in investment expenditures of $350 million in the metropolitan area. Explain how the multiplier impact might affect income and employment in Dayton.

3. Suppose the *MPS* = 0.4 and investment changes as noted in the previous question. Assuming there are no leakages from Dayton's income stream to other economies, estimate the multiplier and the final change in income. What would happen to the level of income if consumer demand declined by $100 million due to a strike? Why?

4. Describe how fiscal policy (both government purchases and taxes) affects aggregate demand and income. Why are transfer payments and taxes likely to have a smaller net impact on *DD* than government purchases of goods and services?

5. Evaluate the statement, "If *G* and *T* are increased in equal amounts, income and employment will remain unchanged." Illustrate your answer with an example.

# CHAPTER 9
# Full Employment
# and Fiscal Policy

This chapter will expand upon our knowledge of the use of fiscal policy for economic stabilization. Part A examines automatic tax and expenditure adjustments that complement discretionary fiscal policy and discusses the primary limitations on the use of fiscal policy for stabilization purposes. Budget control from the perspective of fiscal stabilization is the topic of Part B, which stresses the notion of a potential full-employment budget surplus or deficit. Finally, facts and issues surrounding the national debt are discussed in Part C.

## A. THE SELECTION AND USE OF FISCAL TOOLS

*Discretionary fiscal policy* consists of explicit or overt decisions to change either taxes or government expenditures. The causal chain reaction between fiscal policy, aggregate demand, and NNP is such that once an expenditure component is autonomously altered, NNP changes. The influence of increases or decreases in a nation's income level are transmitted through the $C + I$ expenditure streams. Expansionary fiscal policy is required to remedy unemployment under deflationary-gap conditions, where increased government expenditures $(+ G)$ or tax reductions $(- T)$ increase aggregate demand, NNP, and employment. In contrast, inflationary levels of output are countered by some combination of $- G$ and $+ T$, thus reducing aggregate demand and income equilibrium.

Given a large and influential public sector that both levies taxes and makes expenditures for social goods, it is important to channel fiscal policy in a constructive direction that reduces rather than increases inflation or unemployment. The use of fiscal policy for economic stabilization demands that the policy be flexible as well as accurately timed. A decision to use discretionary fiscal policy to counter economic instability may be subject to a "recognition" time lag, an "administrative" time lag, or an "operational" time lag. The exact course of economic conditions is not readily seen in all instances (the recognition lag); the political administration of a change in taxes or government spending requires time (the administrative lag); and time is also needed before a change in aggregate demand has its full impact on NNP (the operational lag). Furthermore, only a small portion, perhaps as little as 5 percent, of total government expenditures are variable in the short run. For all of these reasons, *nondiscretionary fiscal policy* that automatically reacts to increases or decreases in NNP is needed. As a supplement to discretionary fiscal policies, automatic tax and expenditure stabilization measures merit our attention.

As we know, decisions to alter government expenditures or tax rates can be potent discretionary fiscal weapons. Most contemporary governments also have certain automatic or "built-in" fiscal stabilizers. In a situation of rising NNP, such expenditure and tax devices simultaneously generate a relative *reduction* in government expenditures and an *increase* in tax receipts to exert dampening pressures so that the expansion of aggregate demand and money income is partially restrained. On the other hand, when NNP declines, tax receipts fall more rapidly than NNP and federal government expenditures automatically rise to some extent. The most important of these automatic stabilizers are the income tax and various transfer payments, such as unemployment compensation and welfare payments.

## TAX STABILIZERS

Suppose that a nation currently has a balanced budget; that is, government expenditures ($G$) and tax revenues ($T$) are equal, or $T - G = 0$. As NNP rises during an expansion, tax receipts also rise. Progressive taxes such as the personal income tax result in tax revenues which rise somewhat more rapidly than the expanding NNP. Expansion of aggregate demand and income is thus partially restrained because of increasing tax leakages from the spending stream. Conversely, as NNP declines in a contraction, tax revenues fall more than proportionately, thus shoring up disposable income and consumption demand in the private sector. With government expenditures held constant at $200 billion, for example, and increased tax revenues as NNP rises, the budget balance is converted into a surplus which restrains aggregate demand. In contrast, if $G$ is fixed and NNP declines, $T$ will also decline and a balanced budget is converted into a deficit which stimulates aggregate demand.

## EXPENDITURE STABILIZERS

To some extent, government expenditures also vary automatically with short-run variations in income. As economic activity declines and unemployment rises, compensation payments amounting to about 35 percent of average earnings are available to qualified unemployed workers, usually for a maximum of 26 weeks. Various other welfare and relief payments such as social security payments also tend to stabilize aggregate demand. Furthermore, during a recession the prices of some farm commodities are automatically supported at higher-than-market prices by government subsidies administered through the agricultural price-support program. The rising government transfer payments that accompany a decline in NNP tend to strengthen disposable income and therefore consumption as the economy contracts. Conversely, during a boom, certain government expenditures taper off automatically as unemployment and welfare needs are dissipated, dampening the expansion of aggregate demand.

## THE NET IMPACT OF BUILT-IN STABILITY

Figure 1 illustrates the potential stabilizing influence of automatic expenditure and tax adjustments as NNP changes from $700 to $900 billion. Expenditure schedule $G_s$ in Figure 1(a) provides some built-in stability because government expenditures automatically decrease as NNP rises and increase as NNP declines. Schedule $G_d$ of Figure 1(a) is *de*stabilizing because gov-

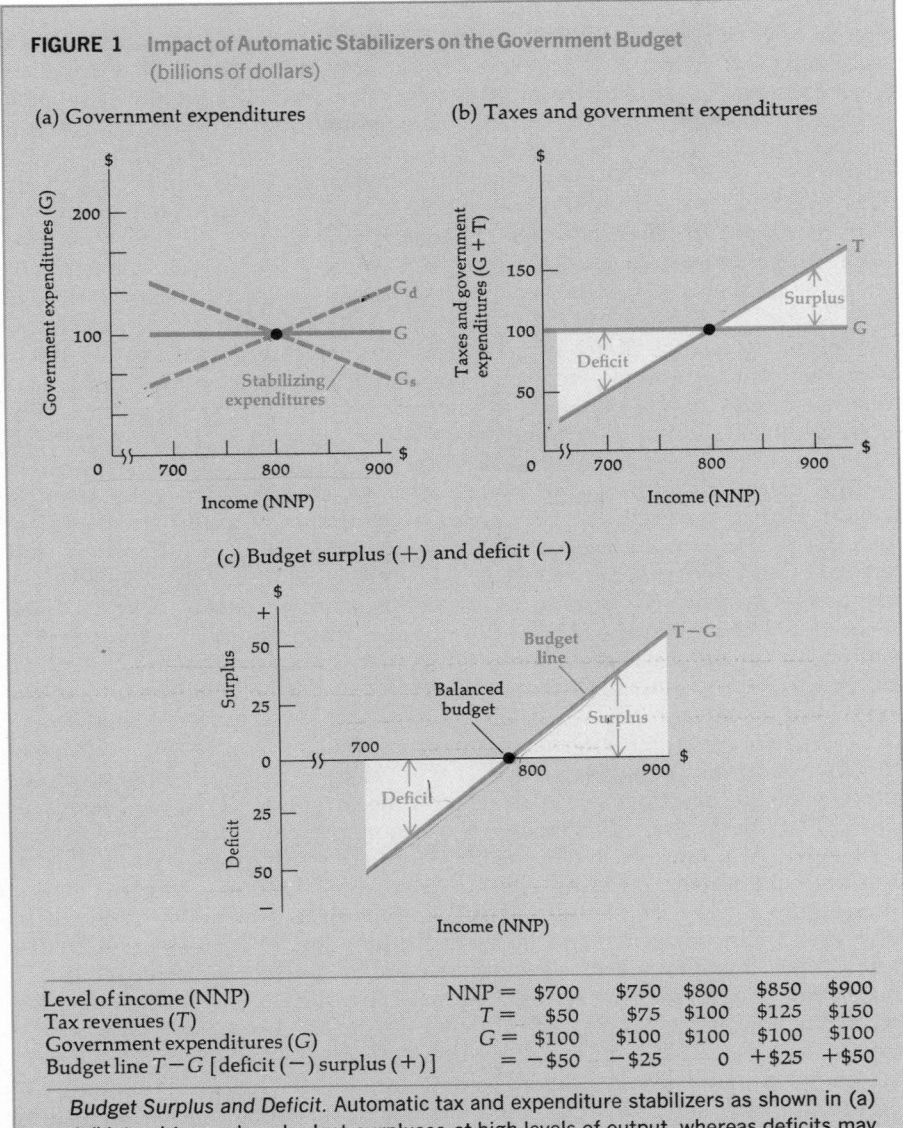

**FIGURE 1** Impact of Automatic Stabilizers on the Government Budget
(billions of dollars)

| Level of income (NNP) | NNP = | $700 | $750 | $800 | $850 | $900 |
|---|---|---|---|---|---|---|
| Tax revenues (T) | T = | $50 | $75 | $100 | $125 | $150 |
| Government expenditures (G) | G = | $100 | $100 | $100 | $100 | $100 |
| Budget line T−G [deficit (−) surplus (+)] | = | −$50 | −$25 | 0 | +$25 | +$50 |

*Budget Surplus and Deficit.* Automatic tax and expenditure stabilizers as shown in (a) and (b) tend to produce budget surpluses at high levels of output, whereas deficits may occur as output declines. The budget line shown in (c) illustrates deficits (below NNP = $800 billion) and surpluses (above NNP = $800 billion).

ernment expenditures and NNP rise and fall together. When NNP rises from $800 to $900 billion and government expenditures also rise, as in schedule $G_d$, more upward pressure is added to aggregate demand, intensifying expansion in the circular-income flow. Schedule $G$ is a constant or autonomous expenditure schedule, indicating that government expenditures remain at $100 billion whether NNP rises or falls.

If taxes are to stabilize swings in economic activity, tax revenues should rise as NNP increases and decline when NNP falls. Figure 1(b) illustrates a stabilizing tax schedule ($T$), where tax receipts rise and fall directly as income changes. Because tax receipts also increase as NNP rises during expansions, tax leakages from the circular-income flow rise, whereas tax receipts decline as NNP falls. The higher the tax rate, the steeper the slope of a tax schedule such as $T$. The illustrative tax rate shown as schedule $T$ in Figure 1(b) is 50 percent ($\Delta T/\Delta NNP = 25/50 = 0.5$), as the data in the lower part of Figure 1 reveal. Moreover, schedule $T$ shows a *proportional* tax because the tax rate ($\Delta T/\Delta NNP$) does not change.[1]

## THE BUDGET BALANCE

Although the actual slopes of schedules $G$ and $T$ are difficult to pin down in an empirical context, we do know that the combined expenditure-tax relation of the federal budget is influenced by automatic stabilizers. In general, as income rises, the public sector moves toward a budget surplus as tax receipts rise; and as income declines, the public-sector budget changes in the direction of a deficit as tax receipts decline. The gold areas in Figure 1(b) show how the difference between automatically stabilized expenditures and tax revenues produces a budget surplus or a deficit as output rises and declines, respectively. At NNP = $800 billion, $T - G = 0$; the budget is balanced. In contrast, at a higher output level of NNP = $900, $T - G$ is $150 billion − $100 billion, generating a budget surplus of $50 billion, using the illustrative data of Figure 1. In contrast, at NNP = $700 billion, $T - G$ denotes a budget deficit of $50 billion. The deficit–surplus relation derived from $T - G$, called the *budget line*, is plotted as schedule $T - G$ in Figure 1(c) at alternative levels of NNP.

The importance of budget line $T - G$ is that, in general terms, it reveals the repressive or expansive character of fiscal policy at various levels of NNP. Note very carefully that any tax or government-expenditure schedule such as $T - G$ shown in Figure 2(a), implies some given level of discretionary government spending and taxation which affects aggregate demand [see Figure 2(b)]. For example, if full employment prevails at output level $NNP_2$ and aggregate demand is given by schedule $DD$ in Figure 2(b), we know that unemployment will exist at equilibrium income level $NNP_1$. To reach full employment, expansionary fiscal policies are needed; that is, government must shift aggregate demand to $DD'$ by shifting the budget line to $T - G'$. As discretionary government expenditures increase or taxes are reduced at all levels of NNP, for example, the budget line shown in Figure 2(a) will shift down and to the right to schedule $T - G'$, indicating expansionary fiscal policies at various output levels. Similarly, when full employment is represented by $NNP_1$, and $DD'$ prevails, discretionary reductions in $G$ or increases in $T$ will shift the budget line upward from $T - G'$ to $T - G$, an appropriate tactic if there is a need to reduce aggregate demand to a lower level of full-employment output. Given some level of discretionary spending and taxes as implied in Figure 2, the *net* impact of

---

[1] A progressive or regressive tax schedule would be a curve rather than the linear schedule shown in Figure 1(b). Regressive tax structures are destabilizing because the ratio $T/NNP$ declines at higher income levels. Proportional and progressive tax structures tend to provide more stability in an economy.

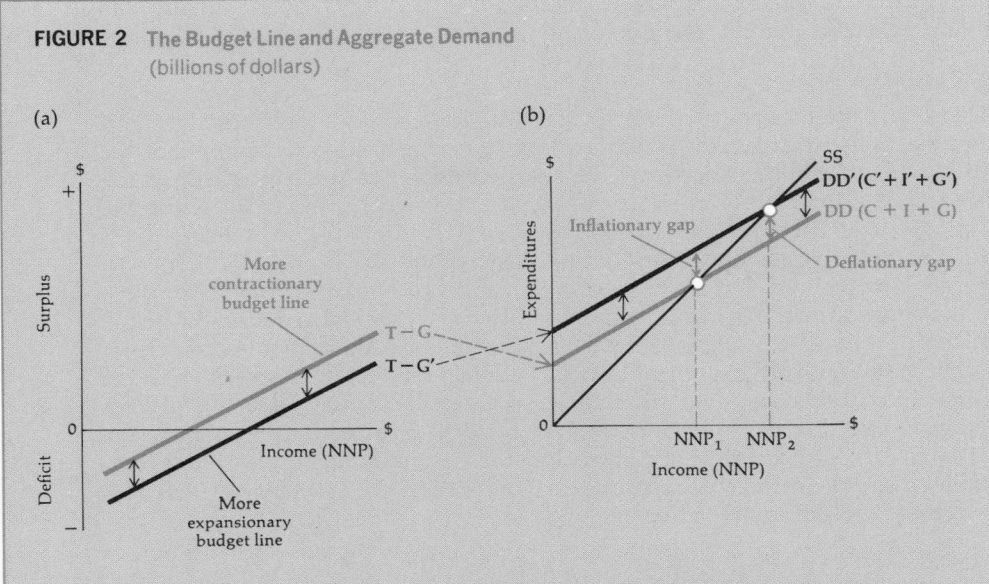

**FIGURE 2** The Budget Line and Aggregate Demand
(billions of dollars)

*Budgets, Aggregate Demand, and Full Employment.* When NNP$_2$ in (b) represents full employment and NNP$_1$ is the actual level of output, a shift to *T—G'* in (a) will increase aggregate demand to *DD'* and income and employment will rise. If an inflationary gap persists (assuming NNP$_1$ represents full employment and *DD'* indicates total spending), a reduction in aggregate demand to *DD* will be prompted by a shift to *T—G.*

the public-sector budget on aggregate demand and future income and employment is generally expansionary (positive) for a larger deficit or smaller surplus and contractionary (negative) for a smaller deficit or larger surplus. A budget deficit adds a net increment to aggregate demand, and a surplus prompts a net reduction in aggregate demand.

### THE IMPACT OF AUTOMATIC STABILIZERS

Automatic stabilizers reduce the magnitude of fluctuations in income and economic activity by about one-third, since government expenditures and taxes move in a counter-cyclical pattern. Typically, automatic stabilizers lessen declines in income by about one-half, as aggregate demand is shored up by lower taxes and larger transfer payments to the private sector.[2] During economic upswings, 30 to 40 percent of the expansion is automatically siphoned off by rising tax revenues and declining government expenditures. Automatic fiscal stabilizers tone down, but do not fully eliminate, erratic swings in aggregate demand and output. While changes in NNP and employment are lessened by the existence of automatic stabilizers, discretionary variations of *G* and *T* remain important tools of fiscal policy, as suggested in Figure 2. Most informed observers agree that discretionary fiscal

[2] M. O. Clemont, "The Quantitative Impact of Automatic Stabilizers," *The Review of Economics and Statistics* (February 1960), p. 60; and Peter Eilbott, "The Effectiveness of Automatic Stabilizers," *The American Economic Review* (June 1966), p. 463.

policy and automatic stabilizers remain the key tools in stabilizing the economy at full employment.

### Evaluation of Fiscal Policy

There are limitations to the use of fiscal policy. Both discretionary and automatic fiscal measures imperfectly reshape aggregate demand, income, employment, and the price level. The real world is not as easily manipulated for stabilization purposes as a model, and we would be remiss to ignore the limitations of fiscal policy.

There are five general shortcomings inherent in fiscal policy which complicate the achievement of price stability and full employment. These difficulties are: (*a*) timing lags, (*b*) inflexibility, (*c*) "political economy," (*d*) the uncertain impact of policy changes on income and employment, and (*e*) the implications of public-sector "control." The variety and pervasiveness of these limitations are such that observers readily admit that the perfect policy is yet to be found. However, history resoundingly confirms the validity of the theoretical structure and the policy implications of the New Economics. Nevertheless, attempts to "fine-tune" the economy at full employment are not easily achieved.

### TIMING

No small amount of the difficulty associated with stabilizing fiscal policy derives from imperfect awareness of the exact state of health of the economy. The effectiveness of discretionary fiscal policy depends on doing the right thing (which is generally conceded as known) *at the proper time*—the recognition lag spoken of earlier. Measurement of economic fluctuations—particularly the forecasting of near-term economic conditions—is far from perfect. Moreover, discretionary fiscal policy requires the approval of both the Chief Executive and Congress, creating an administrative lag. There is also a lag in implementation; that is, the impact of fiscal-policy decisions to alter expenditures or taxes is not felt at once. A tax increase or a reduction in expenditures needed to dampen economic activity, for example, may coincide poorly with the timing of an economic problem. Indeed, a perverse feedback is possible if a once-needed contractionary fiscal policy comes too late and its impact is felt during a recession. Although several authorities have suggested that it might be appropriate to grant government officials a wider range of discretionary choice to help overcome this problem, as of this writing a more rapid implementation of discretionary fiscal measures has not been adopted.

### INFLEXIBILITY

Government expenditures as one aspect of fiscal policy can be particularly inflexible and cumbersome. Opposition to letting or canceling contracts that affect particular Congressional districts can be cantankerous. In addition, many expenditure programs (construction of a building or bridge, for example) are difficult or impossible to alter once started. Discretionary spending also may entail long planning periods, rendering expenditure changes useless in countering short-run income- and employment-instability problems. Expenditures for military bases, highways, or welfare programs also may come to be regarded as long-term commitments as political pressures build up to retain or expand the programs. The problems of inflexibility associated with fiscal policy have led some critics to argue for greater reliance on automatic stabilization policies, while other observers, including Professor Milton Friedman of the University of Chicago, have concluded that fiscal policy just cannot do the job.

## POLITICAL ECONOMY

Discretionary tax and expenditure changes are difficult to implement simply because the decision to do so is made in the political arena. Tax increases, for example, may not be acceptable to a Congressman about to run for re-election. Even if reelection is not an issue, other relevant political questions arise. What expenditures will be cut or increased, and by how much? What regions of the country will be affected? Whose tax bill should be decreased or increased? In some cases, mixed readings of the state of the economy inject uncertainty. Politicians may be loath to act, simply because there may be one chance out of three that their action could turn a current inflation problem into a recession in a few months. The 1964 tax cut, for example, was not immediately accepted. In the latter part of 1962 the Council of Economic Advisers and others close to the late President Kennedy persuaded him that a tax reduction was in order; yet, it took well over a year to persuade the average citizen's Congressman that such action was appropriate. In 1964, Kennedy's successor, Lyndon Johnson, finally achieved approval. By 1966, some economists were suggesting the need for a tax increase, but the hard realities of politics retarded enaction of the surtax for well over a year, again in part because there was protracted debate about the alternative of reducing government expenditures to counter inflation. Later (in 1970) economic activity declined and government authorities championed expansionary policies.

## THE IMPACT OF POLICY CHANGES

Fiscal policy can have uneven and uncertain impacts in several different ways. First, remember that the impact of government purchases of goods on NNP tends to be greater than that of a tax change because the latter must be filtered through changes in disposable income, consumption, and saving. In addition, purchases of goods and services tend to promote larger multiplier effects than do government-transfer expenditures. As we have seen before, the latter, because of private saving, may increase aggregate demand in an amount less than the total dollars transferred. Use of the tax arm of fiscal policy has a reasonably predictable impact on the consumption component of aggregate demand, but a less predictable impact on business firms and investment expenditures. Even though the magnitude of fiscal change may be correctly selected, its expansive or contractionary effect can be excessive for some regions or industries. Still another dimension of the problem of uneven impact relates to state and local government expenditures, which currently comprise about two-fifths of total government outlays. Very often, state and local fiscal action accommodates or intensifies swings in economic activity. In addition, since built-in tax and expenditure changes do not totally iron out all variations in aggregate demand, automatic fiscal stabilizers may become increasingly repressive from year to year. Currently, a 4 percent increase in GNP creates some $10–$12 billion of additional tax revenues annually. If government expenditures do not rise to offset this growing budget surplus, the tax leakages from the income stream increasingly will retard income and employment expansion. Finally, the financing of the budget deficits and surpluses arising from a fiscal policy may have a variable impact on NNP.[3]

### THE ISSUE AND IMPLICATIONS OF "PUBLIC CONTROL"

Although there is no general agreement about the desirability of shrinking or enlarging the public sector, different combinations of fiscal policy either contract or expand government's role in economic affairs. An expansive fiscal policy of increased expenditures enlarges the public sector, whereas tax reductions emphasize private spending. In some instances, fiscal expenditures may conflict directly with private enterprise, as in the case of government-sponsored low-income housing or the construction of power plants.

Thus, one point of view opposes increased government expenditures as well as control by taxation as quasi-socialism. Tax increases are usually disliked and, in addition, some people are fearful of encouraging government expenditures that may become permanently embedded in future programs. The opposite viewpoint argues that one of the public sector's primary responsibilities to the populace is a stable and prosperous economy. Since the unadulterated market system does not provide the checks and balances needed for economic stability, the public sector must redress imbalance. Many informed observers, including Professor John Kenneth Galbraith of Harvard, also add that in some facets of our economic life there is too little government involvement. Inadequate supplies of social goods, ineffectual control of social costs such as air and water pollution, and the existence of underdeveloped regions in the United States are among the problems cited to buttress the latter position. Debate over the issue of the extent to which the public sector should become involved in the economy may hamper effective stabilization policy.

Using fiscal policy to achieve stabilization does present practical difficulties not easily overcome. Yet, on balance, it is clear that fiscal-policy choices must be made by government. A firm consensus of opinion exists about the desirability of coordinating fiscal decisions to achieve identified macroeconomic needs and goals such as full employment. Fiscal policy is a valuable tactic capable of ironing out some of the wrinkles that recur in economic activity, despite the existence of the limitations and difficulties discussed above.

### B. FULL EMPLOYMENT AND BUDGET CONTROL

We should not be led to conclude that government tax and expenditure policies are ineffective. The net impact of both discretionary and automatic fiscal policy on aggregate demand and NNP is most important, as we can clearly see by examining the budget of the federal government in greater detail.

### Management of Government Budgets

The use of fiscal policy for stabilization purposes carries the clear implication that something other than a balanced budget may be necessary to achieve full employment. Is this an acceptable approach to public finance?

[3] The relationship of fiscal policy to finance is discussed in Chapter 10.

The answer is yes. An annually balanced budget is one philosophy that a nation might adopt, but it is not the only one, and it does not necessarily represent an appropriate fiscal objective. Excessive concern over a budget deficit can accentuate instead of moderate ups and downs in economic activity. Before the 1930s the United States considered sacrosanct the idea of balancing the budget, only to abandon it irreverently in recent decades. While many casual observers of economic issues still revere the philosophy of a balanced budget, nearly all economists gave it up some years ago.

## BALANCED BUDGETS AND PUBLIC FINANCE

To see why a balanced budget may not be appropriate, consider the economic impact of the public sector's budget on aggregate demand, first under inflation and then in the context of recession. As money incomes rise during expansion, tax revenues increase absolutely. Consequently, to maintain a balanced budget taxes must be reduced or government expenditures must be increased—both actions which violate the objective of economic stability. Either measure would eliminate a budget surplus but it also would increase aggregate demand and could thus *intensify* potential inflationary pressures. Similarly, a contraction in NNP will result in a budget deficit as transfer payments rise and tax revenues automatically decline. Balancing the budget during recession would demand increased taxes or reduced government expenditures. Again, these are fiscal policies that could *intensify* the problem. Clearly, then, strict adherence to a balanced-budget concept is not a neutral policy, since such a policy may increase economic instability instead of moderating it.

## FUNCTIONAL FINANCE

*Functional finance* is the use of the government budget to provide noninflationary, full-employment levels of output. The so-called "prudent principles of budget and debt management" turn out to be most undesirable if economic stability at full employment is an announced policy goal. Recognition of the destabilizing features of a balanced-budget policy spawned the notion of a functional approach to public finance. If full employment and economic growth with relatively stable prices are to be achieved, the government budget should be used for these purposes. In short, functional finance demands that deficits or surpluses be accepted when needed, *irrespective* of what might intuitively appear to be a desirable level of public indebtedness (a quite different issue to be examined shortly).

Several concerns are often expressed about the legitimacy of functional finance. Some critics argue that deficits are inflationary. However, deficits need not lead to inflation and they will not, unless they are incurred when an economy is operating at full employment. Still others maintain that the budget should be balanced over the course of the expansion and contraction phases of the business cycle. This view is a good deal less meritorious than it seems, since it implies that budget deficits incurred in contractions are to be offset by surpluses during expansions. The fundamental problem with this idea is that expansions and contractions often differ in severity and duration. When a severe depression (like that of the 1930s) is followed by a short and modest expansion, it may not be possible to cover deficits incurred earlier. Premature attempts to force a budget surplus will further inhibit a return to prosperity and full employment. Moreover, it must be remembered that public finance serves other masters, such as the need for national defense or social goods, which cannot be brushed aside in the interest of a budget surplus.

Does this mean, then, that the budget should always be balanced at full employment? No. Whether a balanced, deficit, or surplus budget is required in using fiscal policy to achieve full employment depends entirely on the private sector ($C + I$ expenditures). If aggregate spending is insufficient to generate full-employment conditions, a larger deficit or smaller budget surplus is in order. In contrast, when inflationary conditions prevail, smaller deficits or larger surpluses are appropriate to decrease aggregate demand. The point of functional public finance is this: The government budget balance must be used to provide restraint or additional stimulus to aggregate demand. Remember, too, that: (*a*) multiplier-magnified changes in income accompany smaller changes in aggregate demand, and (*b*) even the balanced-budget multiplier can offset fluctuations in aggregate demand, income, and employment.

Accordingly, fiscal policy stresses economic stability, rather than the once-revered principles of debt-free public finance. Tax and expenditure changes leading to budget surpluses or deficits are controlled in part so as not to be unduly expansive or repressive at full employment. Given the goal of economic stability, this philosophy must govern budget management in the public sector.

### The Full-Employment Budget

Until now we have talked about *actual* or *realized* budget deficits or surpluses, but there are severe limitations to using the actual budget balance as a guide to the performance and impact of fiscal policy. This is because tax receipts, and thus the size of the budget deficit or surplus, vary at different levels of NNP.

The net impact of both discretionary and automatic fiscal policies on NNP is most clearly seen by examining the potential *full-employment budget deficit or surplus*—that level of tax revenues ($T$) and government expenditures ($G$) which *would* exist at full employment. The term "potential" deficit (or surplus) denotes concern for what *would* have happened at full employment, not the *actual* budget balance. In other words, the potential deficit or surplus is the calculated amount that would have prevailed at various levels of NNP, given selected and constant discretionary tax and expenditure policies.

Deficits or surpluses revealed by a budget line tend to raise or lower aggregate demand, respectively, as we saw in Figure 2. A given budget deficit may not provide enough stimulus to achieve full employment, nor is a given budget surplus necessarily adequate to maintain relative price stability. If an economy is well below the full-employment level of output because of sluggish aggregate demand in the private sector, the impact of automatic stabilizers may retard recovery. Similarly, badly needed decreases in money NNP may be dampened by the impact of automatically rising tax revenues, but the budget surplus may not be sufficient to reduce inflationary pressures.

These ideas about the potential budget balance at full employment and the impact of fiscal policy are illustrated in Figure 3. In Figure 3(b), the vertical axis denotes the budget surplus or deficit. Alternative levels of

NNP (and implied unemployment rates) are measured on the horizontal axis. The actual budget deficit for 1964 (about $3 billion) and a calculated full-employment surplus of about $5 billion is shown by budget line $T - G$. The budget line also shows the deficits and surpluses that would be incurred at alternative levels of NNP, given the existing automatic stabilizers and discretionary fiscal policy. Budget line $T - G$ in Figure 3(b) suggests that automatic stabilization does characterize fiscal policy. A budget schedule sloping upward and to the right means that as NNP rises, the budget gradually becomes more repressive as tax revenues automatically rise and expenditures automatically decline. Discretionary increases in $G$ or cuts in $T$ push a budget line down at all levels of NNP. Conversely, a budget line shifts upward at all levels as $T$ increases and $G$ declines. Figure 3(b) reveals that both the level of full-employment NNP and the budget balance must be coordinated to determine how repressive or expansive fiscal policy is.

The full-employment budget surplus of Figure 3(b) acts as a restraint on aggregate demand, thwarting increases in income up to $NNP_{fe}$. Also note that the *actual budget* deficit at the lower income level provides some thrust for the economy, but not enough to encourage expansion to full employment (i.e., aggregate demand is dampened). We can measure the repressive impact of the budget balance by comparing the actual and potential budget surpluses or deficits. Even though the *full-employment* budget surplus in Figure 3(b) is repressive whereas the *actual* budget deficit is expansive, the key problem is that the actual deficit is *not* large enough to move the economy toward full employment. This is because the $5 billion surplus at full employment is "dragging" aggregate demand down. In contrast, the actual $3 billion deficit is providing some, but not enough, upward thrust to aggregate demand.

The critical message of Figure 3(b) is simply that no one combination of expenditures and tax receipts generated by fiscal policy is necessarily consistent with full-employment NNP. The forces leading to income equilibrium and economic fluctuations in a market economy center heavily on changes in the $C + I$ components of aggregate demand. A full-employment stabilizing budget for one level of aggregate demand can generate unwanted stimulus or restraint if $C + I$ change for some reason, or for that matter, if full employment changes from year to year.

## FISCAL RESTRAINT AND ACTUAL BUDGET DEFICITS

The expenditure-tax combination that results in budget line $T - G$ in Figure 3(b) is important because it reveals that fiscal policy can be repressive even when an actual budget deficit occurs, as at the low level of NNP of 1964. This is possible because of the *full-employment surplus* of $5 billion. Is this surplus desirable? It depends on the strength of aggregate demand in the private sector, and in 1964 the full-employment surplus *was not* desirable because the economy was not operating at capacity. If the economy had been at a full-employment equilibrium NNP, perhaps a budget surplus would have been just what was needed. Selected full-employment surplus values for the federal budget are shown in Figure 3(a) for 1957 to 1970.

The President's Council of Economic Advisers has described the relations shown in Figure 3(a) as a ". . . particularly enlightening measure of fiscal

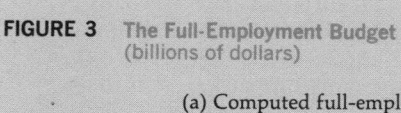

**FIGURE 3** The Full-Employment Budget
(billions of dollars)

(a) Computed full-employment budget, 1957–1970

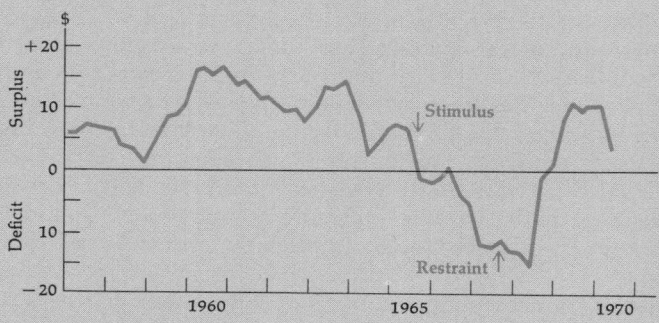

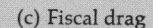

(b) Actual and full-employment budget balance

(c) Fiscal drag

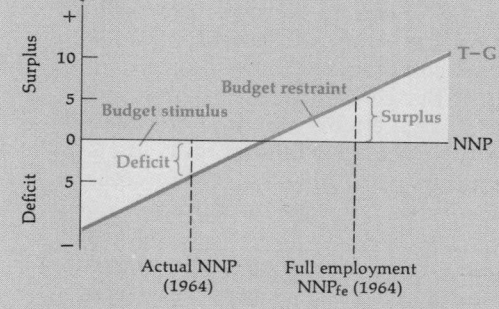

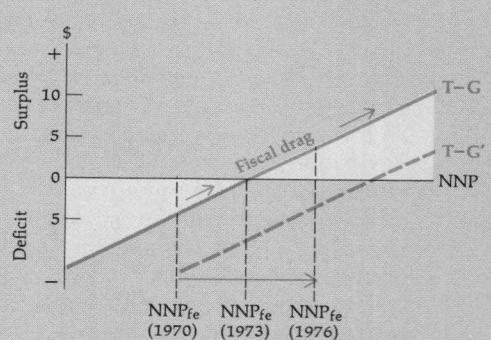

*Full Employment and the Budget.* Panel (b) shows how an actual budget deficit in 1964 was not large enough to restore full employment because of the *drag* or *restraint* of a full-employment surplus. The historical record of a repressive full-employment surplus from 1957 through mid-1965 is shown by panel (a). Starting in 1964, fiscal policy became decidedly expansionary, moving to an excessive full-employment deficit of $16 billion in 1968. The concept of fiscal drag is shown in (c) where continued economic growth is accompanied by movement to a larger and larger budget surplus over the years.

SOURCE: Federal Reserve Bank of St. Louis.

policy in the 1960s when the economy was far below its potential."[4] The potential full-employment budget surplus or deficit is worthy of careful attention because it summarizes fiscal policy in one overall context, as the following cases reveal.

At the historical levels of *actual* NNP for the seven-year period from 1958 through 1964, *actual* budget deficits averaged $3 billion per year. But the combination of discretionary and automatic fiscal policies was repressive when added to aggregate demand in the private sector because repressive *full-employment* budget surpluses averaged $9 billion for this

[4] Council of Economic Advisers, *Economic Report of the President,* 1969, p. 73.

period, as shown in Figure 3(a). In short, government policy along with sluggish $C + I$ expenditures inhibited the achievement of full employment. Remedial fiscal measures required a reduction in $T$ and an increase in $G$, or both. The full-employment budget had to be shifted down to higher deficits (or lower surpluses) at all levels of output. The actual $3 billion deficit for 1964, unintended though it was, was simply the product of inadequate aggregate demand further hampered by a repressive fiscal policy.

## BALANCED BUDGET AT FULL EMPLOYMENT

It might appear to be an agreeable situation if the full-employment level of NNP coincided with a balanced budget at $NNP_{fe}$ in Figure 3(b). At higher levels of output, automatic stabilizers would produce a repressive surplus. At less than full-employment NNP, expansionary deficits would be incurred. However, any given level of tax and expenditure programs may well not, and certainly *need* not, result in this seemingly idyllic situation, as we have said before. The need for a balanced full-employment budget is easily disturbed by a shift in the $C + I$ components of aggregate demand. Then, too, the expansionary balanced-budget multiplier may very well negate the desirability of a balanced budget at full employment, provided that the public sector spends a larger proportion of income than the private sector.

## FISCAL DRAG

A third important dimension to fiscal policy shown in Figure 3(c) is fiscal drag. The term *fiscal drag* denotes the increasingly severe restraint of public finance over a period of time. As an economy grows or the full-employment level of output increases as shown in Figure 3(c), the budget balance moves in the direction of smaller deficits or larger surpluses. As long as government expenditures remain unchanged, full-employment growth in output is accompanied by a *growing* full-employment budget surplus, sometimes termed a "fiscal dividend," that expands by $10–$12 billion annually.

That is, as the economy of the United States grows each year, increased full-employment capacity produces a "fiscal dividend" because of expanding public revenues. The fiscal dividend can either be used to provide additional social goods, or, alternatively, it can be returned to the private sector through tax reductions. To avoid an increasingly severe fiscal drag that grows more repressive each year, schedule $T - G$ must be shifted downward and to the right to $T - G'$ in Figure 3(c) by discretionary reductions in taxes, increases in government expenditures, or both.

A repressive fiscal drag did exist in conjunction with actual budget deficits during the 1930s, the latter years of the 1950s, and the early 1960s. During the 1930s, for example, *actual* budget deficits averaged approximately $2.5 billion annually for a decade. Rather than disproving the concept of functional finance, this information merely corroborates the severity of fiscal drag during that decade. The relatively modest budget deficits of that era grossly failed to increase aggregate demand sufficiently. Because of weak policy measures, income, output, and employment declined to unprecedented lows. Again, during the 1958–1959 recessionary period, the *full-employment budget surplus* averaged better than $6 billion annually, while an *actual* cumulative two-year deficit of over $11 billion accompanied an unemployment rate in excess of 6 percent. From 1961 through 1964, *actual* budget deficits were incurred again, yet unemployment ranged from 5.2 to 6.7 percent. During this same period the drag of the full-employment budget surplus varied from $5 billion to $14 billion. The severity of fiscal drag in the mid-1960s was demonstrated by the fact that even though social security payments and defense expenditures were increased in 1961, and investment tax credits and depreciation allowances were liberalized in 1962, a serious deflationary gap remained. In 1964 taxes were *cut* by some $11 billion in recognition of repressive fiscal drag. The Kennedy-Johnson tax cut prompted expansion of NNP, tax revenues rose, and unemployment declined to 4 percent by year-end as the deflationary gap was closed. Actual and potential output converged, and an actual 1965 budget surplus of $2 billion replaced the $1.4 billion deficit of 1964.

## TOO MUCH FISCAL PUSH

Now consider the reverse extreme of a full-employment budget deficit for an economy already at full employment. Assuming that full employment already exists, the expansive character of a budget deficit contributes to pushing the economy into an inflationary spiral. From 1966 to 1968, a full-employment deficit did push aggregate demand upward and, in conjunction with the income multiplier, increased the general price level and money NNP. Fiscal "push" due to a full-employment budget deficit may be appropriate, but only if a nation is producing below the full-employment output level. Clearly, the fiscal push shown in Figure 3(a) for the years 1967 and 1968 was inappropriate. Fiscal push snowballed the United States economy into inflation from early 1967 through 1970, largely because of unexpectedly large expenditures on the Vietnam War. Unemployment dropped below the 4 percent full-employment barrier, and prices rose as rapidly as 6 percent annually from mid-1968 to mid-1970, for example. A far too vigorous expansion ensued, in spite of the restraint provided by movement from a full-employment deficit to a modest budget surplus by 1969. Even though the tax increase proposed in 1967 was belatedly enacted in mid-1968, the pressures of the Vietnam War imposed severe inflation on the American citizen. Similar inflationary gaps have prevailed during other war periods, including the Korean conflict and World Wars I and II.

The amount of the drag and the push due to fiscal policy throughout the last decade, when the economy moved from a deflationary gap in 1960–1965 to a decidedly inflationary gap during the latter 1960s, is explainable in terms of the full-employment budget. Although the government budget did provide some fiscal push during the early half of the decade, it acted belatedly and hesitantly. Moreover, war-related expansionary action and mounting $C + I$ expenditures from 1967 through 1970 lead to consumer prices increasing rapidly enough to double every 12 years.

## THE EXPENDITURE-TAX MIX

Sometimes ignored budget implications arise from varying the expenditure-tax mix in using fiscal policy. This is true with respect to the impact of fiscal policy on the public debt and the relative size of the public and private sectors of the economy. To implement the functional-finance notion through fiscal policy, several combinations of expenditure and tax changes can be used. (See Figure 4.)

The choice of fiscal goals can influence the combination of tax and expenditure changes selected. One criterion might be that of a lower tax

## FIGURE 4 The Fiscal Expenditure-Tax Mix
### (billions of dollars)

| | (1) Government expenditures | (2) Tax receipts | (3) Budget surplus or deficit (1) − (2) | (4) Change in consumption, $MPC = 2/3$ (2) × MPC | (5) Shift in aggregate demand (1) + (4) | (6) Income change (5) × m |
|---|---|---|---|---|---|---|
| Policy A | +$20 | +$21 | +$ 1 | $\Delta C = -\$14$ | +$6 | +$18 |
| Policy B | + 18 | + 18 | 0 | $\Delta C = - 12$ | + 6 | + 18 |
| Policy C | + 6 | 0 | − 6 | $\Delta C = 0$ | + 6 | + 18 |
| Policy D | + 2 | − 6 | − 8 | $\Delta C = + 4$ | + 6 | + 18 |
| Policy E | 0 | − 9 | − 9 | $\Delta C = + 6$ | + 6 | + 18 |
| Policy F | − 6 | − 18 | − 12 | $\Delta C = + 12$ | + 6 | + 18 |

*Tax-Expenditure Impacts on the Budget.* The combined impact of expansive fiscal tax and expenditure policies on the budget deficit varies substantially. Tax and expenditure changes cause aggregate demand—government expenditures [column (1)] and consumption [column (4)]—to change as shown in column (5). As before, the final change in NNP is column (5) times the multiplier: $m = 1/MPS$, where $MPS = 1/3$. In general, larger budget deficits accompany fiscal policies associated with increasing the role of the private sector relative to government.

bill—an end popular with most consumers. Minimizing the absolute size of government expenditures represents a second possible criterion, since some observers suggest that the public sector is already too large relative to the private sector. Other observers hotly dispute this position, maintaining that a large backlog of unmet social needs still exists. Suppose we ignore the argument about the size of the public sector for now and accept the criterion of a lower budget deficit, in deference to those who look askance at the public debt. Although one finds reasonably widespread agreement over the idea that fiscal policy can be used to reduce or increase NNP and employment, paradoxical choices must be made concerning lower taxes, minimization of the government sector, and avoidance of budget deficits. Figure 4 illustrates how various fiscal policy measures affect the national budget.

Consider the following situation. The economy is operating below full employment, and fiscal measures designed to remove a deflationary gap of $6 billion at full-employment NNP are needed. Assume an $MPC$ of 2/3 [the multiplier $(m)$ is 3], and a currently balanced budget. For simplicity, also presume that the current level of government expenditures and tax revenues will remain unchanged as NNP rises. Figure 4 ranks six combinations of fiscal measures involving various government expenditure and tax policies, all of which are designed to close a deflationary gap of $6 billion and raise NNP by $18 billion while adhering to the deficit-minimization criterion. Policy A removes a $6 billion deflationary gap in $DD$ and produces $\Delta NNP = + \$18$ billion with a budget surplus designed to please even arch-conservatives. Unfortunately, however, taxes must be increased by $21 billion, resulting in a $14 billion decline in private-sector consumption, while government purchases of goods and services must rise by $20 billion. Thus, this policy requires the *largest* increase in the economic role of government of the six options shown in Figure 4. Government outlays increase by $20 billion, consumption expenditures decline by $14 billion, and saving declines by $7 billion ($MPS = 1/3$). The net change in aggregate demand is $+ $6$ billion ($+ $20$ billion less $14 billion), just enough to achieve full employment with a multiplier of 3. Observe carefully that it is important to know whether government expenditures are used to purchase goods directly or as transfer payments to the private sector. Suppose that instead of spending the additional $20 billion directly for goods and services, the government transferred the same amount to households and firms in an expansive fiscal move. As we know, transfer payments would not be as expansive as outright government purchases because some portion of income is saved. Consequently, the final increase in NNP would be less, because only a fraction of the income transfer would move into the spending stream.

Policy B also expands the relative role of the public sector to a large degree, but it does maintain a balanced budget while generating the required rise in NNP to full employment. Output increases because of the balanced-budget multiplier that applies to increased government expenditures of $18 billion financed by increased taxes of $18 billion which reduce consumption by $12 billion and savings by $6 billion. Thus, $\Delta DD = + $6$ billion and $\Delta NNP = $6$ billion $\times$ 3 = $18 billion. At the other extreme, Policy F, involving both expenditure and tax reductions, expands the economic role of government least, but it does create a budget deficit of $12 billion. Government's role in the economy is diminished (public expenditures decline by $6 billion) and increased private-sector purchases are possible with a tax cut of $18 billion. Aggregate demand increases by the required $6 billion as one-half of the $12 billion rise in consumption is offset by a $6 billion government expenditure decline. The comparisons of Figure 4 show that expansion of the public sector is inversely related to the size of the budget deficit. Needless to say, this situation poses a serious dilemma for those who want both a small budget deficit *and* a smaller government sector. This combination is not feasible unless, of course, more unemployment is accepted or other means of stabilizing the economy are found.[5] *Conclusion:* A smaller role for government requires a larger public debt, or less public debt is possible only at the tradeoff cost of expansion of the economic role of government.

## C. THE PROBLEM OF NATIONAL DEBT: MYTH OR REALITY?

Although there are a variety of objections to fiscal policy, the most frequently heard (and least valid) complaint is that a stabilizing fiscal policy leads to unbalanced budgets that increase the national (federal government) debt. Has the national debt grown "too" rapidly? Is debt a problem? If so, just how? Let us first look at the facts about the national debt and then study these questions.

### Facts About the National Debt

Although there is no one answer to how large the national debt can or should be, the oft-expressed opinion that it is too large is misleading and not neces-

---

[5] An enlightened conservative such as economist Milton Friedman has a rebuttal to the dilemma of more government or more debt: the use of monetary policy. More on these matters in Chapter 10.

sarily correct. The federal government's debt has grown rapidly to more than one-third of a trillion dollars. The national debt is nearly $1,800 per capita, and interest payments absorb approximately 7 percent of the federal government budget. Yet, the most important aspect of federal government indebtedness is the proper management of the debt to achieve a fully employed, stable, and growing economy.

## AGGREGATE DEBT

Before becoming alarmed at the size of the national debt we should study it in relation to the debt of the total economy. Currently, aggregate net indebtedness exceeds $1.5 trillion, slightly over two-thirds of which is the private debt of corporations, unincorporated firms, and individuals. As Figure 5 reveals, public indebtedness (including state, local, and federal debt) increased very rapidly—by nearly one-quarter of a trillion dollars—during World War II. Much of the growth in aggregate net debt is also due

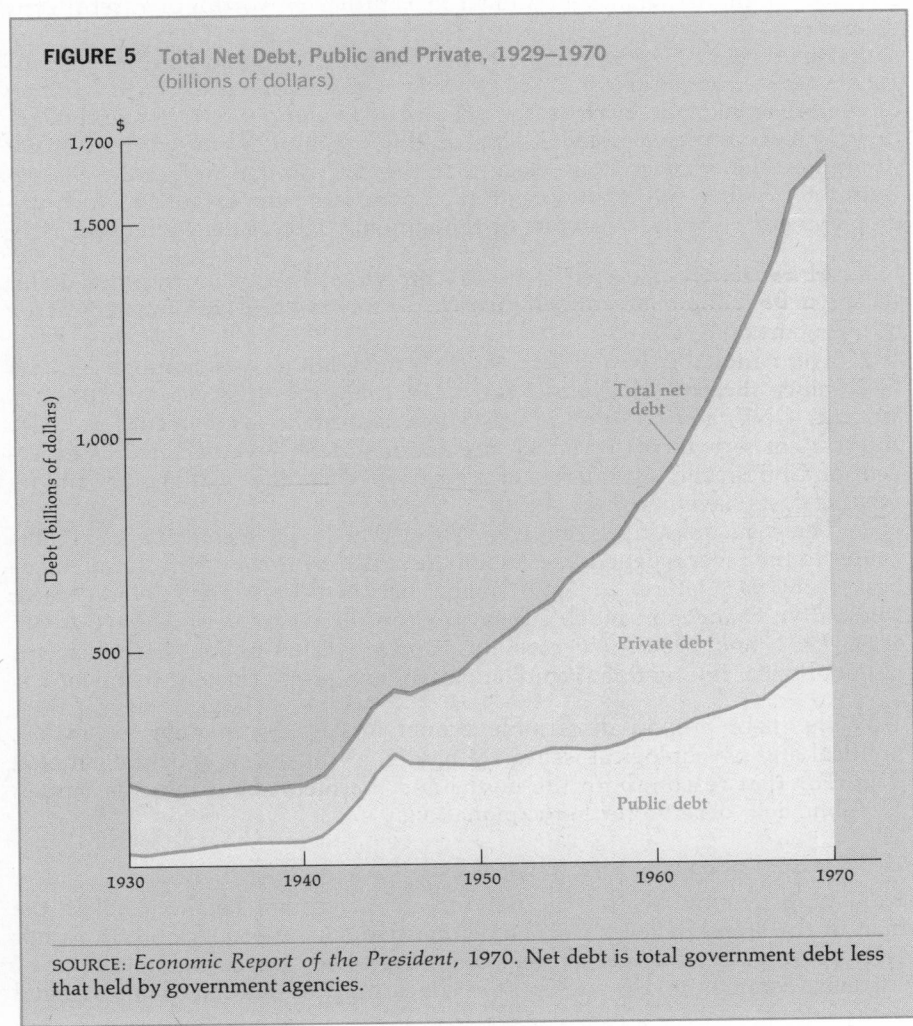

**FIGURE 5** Total Net Debt, Public and Private, 1929–1970 (billions of dollars)

SOURCE: *Economic Report of the President*, 1970. Net debt is total government debt less that held by government agencies.

to rapid debt expansion in the private sector of the economy since 1950. Those who persist in undue alarm about the national debt might more legitimately give further thought to the some 400 percent increase in private debt since 1950.

## THE NATIONAL DEBT

The observation that our national debt amounts to nearly $1,800 per capita is an overstatement as well as being of questionable relevance. First of all, one-fourth of the $372 billion debt of the federal government is held by federal agencies like the Federal Reserve Banking system. Interest payments on the government-owned portion of national indebtedness are merely bookkeeping transfers between government agencies. Second, and more important, the dimensions of the national debt must be compared to the productive wealth of the economy, much as corporate debt is often compared to the productive capacity of business firms. The absolute and relative size of the national debt shown in Figure 5 is worthy of careful consideration.

As the data in Figure 5 suggest, if GNP grows approximately 4 percent each year, a comparable rate of growth in the national debt ($14 billion annually) would not increase the *relative debt burden*. Of course, budget deficits and increased indebtedness of this magnitude are not necessarily desirable. Nonetheless, it is clear that the size of the budget deficits required to achieve full employment must depend on the extent to which unemployment prevails, questions of the national debt aside. Moreover:

1. Although the national debt has grown markedly in absolute dollar terms, neither the debt nor the interest payments on it are unusually large as a proportion of GNP.

2. The national debt and interest on it have not grown as rapidly as has GNP since the end of World War II. In 1945, the debt was 1.3 times as large as GNP, and by 1968 it was about two-fifths (44 percent) of GNP. Interest costs required to service the national debt have declined as a percent of GNP in the last quarter of a century. Thus, the relative debt and its relative costs have declined.

3. The costs of war (particularly World War II) have contributed significantly to the federal debt, a fact plainly revealed by the increase in indebtedness from $45 billion to $278 billion between 1940 and 1945. Indeed, cumulative changes in indebtedness for the three war periods 1940–1945, 1950–1953, and 1966–1970 account for nearly $300 billion of the current national debt. International conflict clearly is a costly form of behavior!

While there are no discernible economic barriers to debt expansion, political and psychological issues are hidden in the question of the national debt. For that reason, both the myths and the facts about the true burden of public debt deserve further explanation.

### Myths and Realities About the National Debt

Reasoning that the size of the national debt may not be the problem the man in the street believes it to be neither debunks improper objections nor fully accounts for the real burdens debt may entail. Let us examine some of the more common myths and realities concerning the burden of our national debt.

1. *The national debt is "bad" and must be limited because there are normal constraints to debt capacity.* Much of the contemporary fallacy condemning the national debt arises from the ill-conceived notion that financial constraints limiting the debt capability of individuals must also apply to the public sector. Individuals must repay debts, but an immortal government is under no compulsion to retire debt, any more than are corporate firms like General Motors or U.S. Steel. Whereas individuals must forgo consumption at some future date to repay debt incurred by earlier borrowing, an economic institution like a corporation or government need not do so, as long as it is able to obtain financing. In addition, most of the national debt is the citizen's indebtedness to himself; that is, the national debt is not repayable to another distinct unit as is private indebtedness. The public–private debt analogy is erroneous because the two-thirds of the national debt that is held by nongovernment units is, for the most part, the debt of the same people and institutions that own government bonds and receive interest payments. The government debt that is held internally by a nation's citizens is also owed to the citizenry; therefore, full repayment could be accomplished only by massive income transfers, taxing some taxpayers to pay other taxpayers who own the debt.

2. *Debt encourages income redistribution and inequality.* This point brings us to an important reality concerning debt—namely, that the national debt may increase income inequality. The interest earned on a large national debt redistributes income from the run-of-the-mill taxpayer to generally wealthier bondholders, particularly large financial institutions and corporations. The redistribution of some $17 billion in current interest cost is generally small in comparison to total income, but some income redistribution occurs nonetheless. Obviously, retirement of the entire national debt, quite aside from constituting a ridiculous policy, would contribute to a significant redistribution of income favoring the wealthy.

3. *Externally held debt imposes real costs.* Another important reality of the national debt is that the portion of the national debt owed to foreign nations or persons does constitute a real cost or burden. Although internally held debt poses the income-transfer problem noted earlier, payment requirements on externally held debt clearly represent a potential burden. Interest payments (as well as principal repayment) can be achieved only by giving other nations hard-dollar claims on domestic output. If $2 billion in interest is paid to the rest of the world annually, this figure represents their claims on our domestically produced output. Debt held by other nations constitutes a real burden on taxpayers, who ultimately are responsible for meeting the interest obligations of bonded indebtedness. Currently, about 5 percent of the national debt is externally held.

4. *Debt causes inflation.* Deficit financing, as we have seen, can be a useful expansionary tool. However, there is nothing *inherent* in public debt that causes inflation. When there is inflation, the culprit is not the debt, but rather, improper budget control—failure to raise taxes or lower government expenditures as required by conditions of full employment or inflationary levels of aggregate demand in the private sector. Inflation-prompted economic collapse is not likely when debt is related to a nation's growing productive capacity, its expanding stock of productive resources, and its ability to generate tax revenues. Productive capacity, and thus the debt capability of a country, depends on prudent fiscal decisions to achieve economic growth and operate at or near full employment.

Our conclusion, then, is that the national debt can contribute to inflation, but it need not, and probably will not, if stabilizing fiscal policies are followed.

5. *Debt may distort interest rates.* Government bonds worth billions of dollars mature and must be refinanced each month of the year. The United States Treasury prefers low interest rates for obvious reasons, yet during a rapid expansion, interest rates cannot be maintained at artificially low levels by monetary authorities without precipitating inflation. Holding interest rates down during periods of rapid expansion in the economy may encourage a further increase in expenditures when the converse is actually needed. Under the threat of an inflationary gap, monetary authorities should allow interest rates to rise, as the following two chapters will discuss. Accordingly, the United States Treasury's interest in minimizing debt-service costs may conflict with higher interest rates that are helpful in reducing excessive aggregate demand under inflationary conditions. This conflict need not lead to inflation, but it may, depending on which master is served—Treasury borrowing costs or economic stability.

6. *Debt alters incentives and investment.* It is also implied in some circles that a large public debt reduces investment expenditures and incentives to bear risk. It is unclear, however, whether tax revenues supporting interest charges on the national debt do in fact dampen incentives and investment in significant ways. Most informed observers think not. One would suspect it would be rare indeed for a firm to pass up an otherwise profitable investment opportunity because of a modest tax increase needed to cover the interest costs on the national debt. Business investments appear to be based much more on demand, profits, and existing capacity. However, expansion of the national debt can hamper future economic growth if government consumes output produced by resources that otherwise might have been *invested* in capital goods. When government consumption of goods and services replaces private investment expenditures, the stock of capital resources and future economic growth may be impaired. Government expenditures impose opportunity costs on the private sector in the form of forgone investment that might otherwise have occurred. Either less capital formation, which represents a real debt burden for future generations, or smaller private-sector consumption expenditures for the present generation result from expansion of the public sector in a fully employed economy.

*To summarize:* Much of the apprehension about the magnitude of the national debt is placed in proper perspective when it is related to a nation's capacity to carry debt. Existing evidence suggests that current levels of output and indebtedness are not unreasonable. The public debt *could* become unbearable *if* it rose mightily relative to a nation's output. However, this is a most unlikely event as long as the public sector adopts policies designed to maintain a fully employed economy. Under most circumstances, control of the budget is infinitely more important than control of the public debt. Although the evidence on the debt issue is mixed, it is clear that some oft-expressed concerns are myths, and that appropriate fiscal policy designed to control aggregate demand can help avoid most of the burdens of the national debt discussed above. Some objections to the national debt are given undue importance, but others cannot be ignored. It is evident that debt has a complex, often improperly understood, and sometimes unclear impact on a nation's economy.

### Is the National Debt a Future Burden?

But what about the argument that the national debt is a burden transferred to subsequent generations? In large measure, this is a false contention. There are no costs, only benefits associated with debt incurred to promote full employment. Resources that otherwise would be idle are employed, thus increasing employment, income, and the real output of consumer and capital goods. The burden of fiscal drag in the 1930s was *lost output* and *high levels of unemployment*, which were the result of a level of public indebtedness that was not large enough to create full-employment conditions. Most important, the Depression of the 1930s imposed a burden on future generations to the extent that capital formation was retarded throughout the decade. The paradox of the Great Depression is that the burden associated with the public debt incurred in that decade was due to *not enough debt* instead of too much.

There are, however, burdens associated with increasing the public sector's claim on a nation's output when it is experiencing *full-employment conditions*. When private consumption is restrained, as it was during the early 1940s when the national debt grew rapidly, citizens bear a debt burden—they consume less real output. Some of the real cost of World War II, therefore, was deferred consumption borne by that generation. The diversion of resources to war output was also financed in part by higher taxes as well as by the hidden tax of inflation related to borrowing some one-quarter of a trillion dollars.

In addition, a portion of the World War II debt burden was shifted to the future. As government expenditures increased when the economy was at full employment, resources were diverted from investment in capital goods to current consumption (tanks, planes, and ships in World War II). Any time something like this happens, a burden *is* imposed on future generations, because they inherit a smaller and inferior stock of capital resources, and future economic growth is impaired. During the five-year period from 1941 to 1945, for example, cumulative *net* investment was only $1 billion, compared to some $20 billion in 1946 alone. Capital formation did suffer because of the war, the vice being "consumption" by destruction. However, this capital depletion was somewhat offset by the technological improvements that occurred during the five years of World War II, and by the recovery from the stagnation of the 1930s brought on by the war. Also, the opportunity cost of losing the war, involving potential destruction of the existing stock of capital resources on a mass scale, might have constituted an even larger burden. A second way in which debt burdens are shifted to future generations arises from increases in foreign-held debt. Debts held by other nations must be repaid by a future generation sending domestic output abroad. Finally, a debt burden can be shifted forward if a generation feels wealthier and thus steps up consumption at the expense of investment because wealth (in the form of larger saving, for example) has increased. When a nation's population increases consumption at the expense of investment, less net capital formation occurs, as we have said before.

However, note very carefully that past indebtedness does not result in the transfer of financial debt burdens forward in time simply because interest payments must be made in the future. Interest payments due in 1980, 1990, and 2000 will be a simple transfer of income *at that time*. Either debt refunding or repayment in the year 2000 only transfers that generation's financial claims on output. If more of our public officials at the state and local levels clearly understood this fact, they might consider policies other than paying off the principal on school bonds, for example. While there may be important redistribution effects associated with the national debt, there are few real economic burdens to debt.

## REVIEW

### Summary

1. Fiscal policy has an expansionary or contractionary impact on aggregate demand and NNP depending on the budget balance. When government expenditures rise and tax revenues decline (deflationary-gap policy), fiscal action is expansionary; but if government expenditures decline while tax receipts rise, contractionary fiscal policies prevail. Expenditures and tax changes may be the result of discretionary action taken by Congress or the consequence of the working of automatic stabilizers.

2. Generally, automatic stabilizers such as income taxes change in greater proportions than NNP, thus dampening swings in economic activity. Some government expenditures (e.g., unemployment compensation) change in the opposite direction to a change in NNP and this lessens fluctuations in output. The combined impact of automatic tax-expenditure stabilizers results in larger budget surpluses as NNP rises and larger deficits as NNP declines. Studies indicate that the amplitudes of economic fluctuations are generally reduced by one-third to one-half because of the compensation generated by automatic stabilizers.

3. While fiscal policy is one useful way in which aggregate demand and NNP can be stabilized, this approach does not provide an entirely satisfactory answer to fluctuations in economic activity. Among the more important shortcomings to fiscal policy are: (*a*) timing problems and errors, (*b*) inflexibility, (*c*) political difficulties in implementing tax and expenditure changes, (*d*) the uneven and uncertain impact of policies, and (*e*) concerns about the size of the public sector relative to that of the private sector.

4. A government budget that is balanced annually may be dangerous because it prevents effective control of unemployment and inflation. Consequently, most observers recognize that a federal government budget surplus or deficit should be used to achieve full-employment and price stability—a notion termed "functional finance."

5. By computing the potential or full-employment budget surplus or deficit at various levels of NNP, fiscal authorities can gauge how repressive or expansive fiscal policy will be at full employment. When a full-employment budget surplus occurs along with an actual budget deficit (at less than full-employment NNP), a fiscal restraint prevails, and the economy is stagnating. Increasing restraint or fiscal drag accumulates over time, making achievement of full employment increasingly difficult.

If, on the other hand, actual NNP is at full employment and a budget deficit prevails, fiscal push is driving the economy into inflationary levels of output.

6. Different tax and expenditure combinations can be used to stabilize the economy. The smaller (larger) the budget deficit, the greater (smaller) the relative growth in the public sector in relation to the private sector.

7. There are a variety of misconceptions surrounding the national debt. In fact, the indebtedness of *all* government units is less than one-third of the $1.5 trillion of aggregate debt, one-third of the some $358 billion of the national (federal government) debt is internally held, the national debt and interest on this debt have declined as a proportion of GNP since World War II, and about 80 percent of the national debt is war-related.

8. It is incorrect to regard the national debt as dangerous just because personal debt is, because most of the public debt is internally held. Interest on the national debt does, to some extent, redistribute income from the less to the more affluent. The debt itself is not inflationary under normal conditions, but it may be inflationary if not responsibly controlled in relation to full employment. Concerns are sometimes also expressed about the influence of the national debt on interest rates, but again this need not represent a problem if correct stabilizing fiscal policies are followed.

9. For the most part, the national debt imposes a burden on society only to the extent that present consumption is altered and capital investment and future economic growth are distorted. As often as not, these "real" costs have arisen because the debt was not expanded rapidly enough in a recession to boost the economy to full employment or because of international conflict. Since interest on the debt is primarily an internal transfer of funds, it is not true that debt refunding will impose a burden on future Americans.

### Identify the Following Concepts and Terms

- cyclically balanced budget
- myths and the national debt
- fiscal drag
- the full-employment budget
- automatic or "built-in" stabilizers —
- shortcomings to fiscal policy

- budget line $(T - G)$
- fiscal push
- debt burdens
- functional finance —
- fiscal dividend

### Questions to Answer

1. How do automatic stabilizers work to lessen the severity of fluctuations in economic activity?

2. Why is a balanced budget not necessarily an appropriate fiscal policy? Explain how minimizing the national debt and reducing the economic role of the public sector may conflict.

3. Critically evaluate the statement: "The national debt has grown far too rapidly in recent years and now threatens to undermine the American

economy, quite aside from the significant burden it imposes on our children who must pay for our reckless spending."

4. Using the data given below, plot and explain how the concept of a *full-employment* budget surplus and an *actual* budget deficit can occur simultaneously. Assume the economy is operating at NNP = $800 billion and full employment occurs at $NNP_{fe}$ = $900 billion.

| NNP (billions) | T − G (billions) |
|---|---|
| 600 | $150–200 |
| 700 | 170–200 |
| 800 | 190–200 |
| 900 = $NNP_{fe}$ = | 210–200 |
| 1,000 | 230–200 |

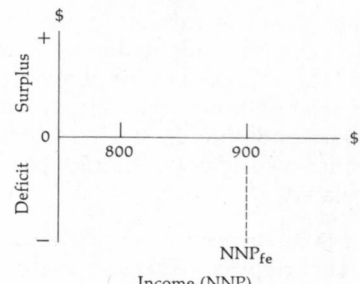

5. Under the conditions described in the previous question, what fiscal measures would be appropriate? Why? If the marginal propensity to consume were 90 percent and the C + I components of DD remained unchanged, by how much would T − G have to be shifted to achieve full-employment equilibrium $NNP_{fe}$ = $900 billion?

6. Explain why and how the following statement may be correct: "Even though the actual budget balance is a surplus, what we need is a larger full-employment budget surplus."

# CHAPTER 10
# The Monetary System

Thus far we have spoken of aggregate demand, investment, and income without direct reference to money when, in fact, economic transactions are normally expressed in terms of a common monetary denominator. No explanation of income, prices, and employment can be complete without considering the elusive but fascinating subject of money. The inflationary process is a monetary phenomenon in which the *value* of money declines. Moreover, many of the swings in economic activity in the United States have been closely allied to financial panics or crises. Thus, we cannot simply presume that fiscal policy is the only sure way to attain economic stability. As we shall see soon enough, it is possible to alter aggregate demand, NNP, and employment through regulation of the monetary system. Most economists feel that the supply of money is one factor that may help determine the level of economic activity; however, they are not in complete agreement about the *relative* importance of the quantity of money.

In this chapter we shall be concerned with demonstrating what money is and how it is created. (In Chapter 11 we will consider how the monetary system is "managed.") In Part A we shall discuss the meaning of money and the historical evolution of monetary systems. Part B introduces the key financial institutions in the American economy; and the way money is created is the topic of Part C.

## A. THE MEANING OF MONEY

The standard and most widely accepted measure of the *money supply* in the United States includes: (*a*) currency in circulation outside the banking system, and (*b*) demand deposits, which are bank checking accounts owned by the public—consumers, business firms, and government agencies. For convenience, "currency" describes both coins and paper money, and only currency *outside* the banking system is counted as part of the money supply.

### Characteristics of Money

Money is defined by its functions. Money used as a *medium of exchange* is a common denominator facilitating the exchange of goods and services. With a common monetary unit, societies can specialize in production and avoid the cumbersome barter process. Money also functions as a *standard of value,* or a yardstick by which the relative worth of present transactions can be gauged. Furthermore, money is a *store of value,* since it can be accumulated or stored and used for future transactions. Certain attributes of money determine how effectively it serves these three functions. It must be readily acceptable, it should be divisible into small and large units to accommodate small or large transactions, it should not deteriorate physically as time passes, and it must be scarce, since abundance can reduce or alter its value. Money is worth whatever it can buy in goods or services; that is, it is worth whatever it commands as a medium of exchange, standard of value, or store of value. Bearing these three characteristics of money in mind, it is easy to see why wives or mud pies do not serve efficiently as money.

At the most general level, items of economic value owned by a firm, household, or some other economic unit are *assets*. *Real assets* represent actual physical property such as a building or capital equipment, whereas *paper assets* represent a more generalized financial claim. A corporate or government bond, for example, is a paper debt of the issuer, but the same security is a paper asset to whomever owns it. Similarly, money is a generalized wealth claim on purchasing power—a *paper asset* to the holder and *paper debt* of the issuer (the government or governmental agency). Money—both currency and demand deposits—is thus both an asset and a liability or debt. Of course, many other kinds of outstanding liabilities—such as the promissory note you sign in borrowing funds from a bank, the bond issued by the federal government, or a corporate security—are paper assets to the owner and paper debts of the issuer. However, these forms of paper assets do not perform the three functions of money noted earlier.

### Historical Background of the U.S. Monetary System

Prior to the 1800s, anyone had the right to start a bank under the common law of the United States, and there are more than a few recorded instances of fictitious organizations renting space over a tailor's shop in Boston or Philadelphia; purchasing ink, paper, and a printing press; and printing paper bank notes to serve as currency. Later, banks were required to obtain a license or "charter," generally from the state government, although on two occasions before 1863, the federal government chartered national banks, in part for the purpose of monitoring monetary irregularities. State-chartered banks dominated United States banking throughout the 1800s.[1] During these years currency consisted of notes which were simply the circulating IOUs of hundreds of banks. As many as 1,600 private banks issued currency of different degrees of genuineness in the early 1860s, for example. Several firms existed only to maintain up-to-date lists of circulating bank notes that were fictitious, counterfeit, or irredeemable.

The chief problem of banking in those times was maintaining the convertibility of paper bank notes into gold, since in a pinch the public placed their confidence in the gold backing of bank notes. When the confidence of a currency was questioned, "runs" on banks started as the public clamored for gold in exchange for paper money. Frequently, banks failed because the large volume of bank notes they had issued could not be converted into gold. Even normally conservative and responsible banks were destroyed in financial panics, and holders of bank notes often ended up with worthless paper.

The typical replay of a bank run culminating in a financial crisis started with the public trying to convert bank notes into gold. Although you might

---

[1] In some states, charters were issued under reasonably stringent controls, but more often financial uncertainty and chaos either threatened or reigned.

think that banks could have sold paper assets (such as a local farmer's IOU), there is a limit to this process. Who would buy the bank's assets and with what? The public and the bank both wanted gold in a crisis, and when an entire nation started clamoring for quantities of gold no one on earth could supply, banks folded and entire economies collapsed. A failing bank cannot call in loans granted earlier because, in many cases, repayment cannot be made on short notice, and, in any event, repayment would probably be made in the form of paper money. Even when it was possible, repayment in paper money often meant that another bank lost gold as well as its capacity to maintain currency convertibility. If the Tucson Trust Bank demanded immediate repayment from an individual whose funds were deposited with Houston National Bank, and both banks were experiencing a panic, how eager do you suppose Houston's bank officers would be to lose gold to the Tucson Trust? Historically, large-scale bank runs were tenaciously matched by decreed "holidays" as bank after bank simply closed its doors. If you think gold is the answer to such problems, how would you propose paying off the some $400 billion in demand and savings deposits that exist today in the United States alone? The entire free world's monetary gold supply is slightly over $42 billion, and it required a great deal of futile work and expense to dig it out of the earth.

Break-the-bank syndromes start when people question their concept of money. The manner in which such feelings are expressed once a financial panic snowballs is something else again. Between 1834 and 1860, financial panics occurred on several occasions, and during the 1837–1843 crisis the total supply of bank notes and deposits declined as much as 60 percent. In prosperous times, in contrast, economic instability was intensified as banks rapidly expanded their currency and deposits. Thus, an inordinate degree of contraction in the money supply occurred during recessions, and excessive expansion prevailed in prosperity. This situation is exactly the opposite of the money-supply change required to stabilize economic activity, as we shall discover in a moment.

At one time, currency circulated as actual paper receipts for gold or silver. However, gold pieces and silver coins equal to the value of their gold or silver content as a commodity are extinct today as active money, although newly minted coins still contain a "token" portion of silver. When the United States raised the price of gold to $35 an ounce in 1933, paper-currency claims on gold were called in and Congress decreed that gold certificates would no longer be redeemed in gold. The move in the 1960s to reduce the silver content of coins was related to the rising price of silver. Had retirement not occurred in these and other instances, the gold- or silver-commodity content of these monies could have generated windfall profits, enticing the holders to melt coins down to acquire the higher-valued gold or silver.

Established in 1913 in the hopes of remedying the more severe banking problems, the Federal Reserve System proved to be an ultimate success in giving the federal government control over banking. Although it is not possible to describe the trauma of banking history experienced in the United States in a few words, it is noteworthy that this nation was outstanding among the developed countries for its high rates of bank failures in the early 1900s, even after the Federal Reserve System was established.

Nearly 13,000 banks failed between 1921 and 1933 alone. The personal hardships as well as the recurrent economic chaos brought about by financial panics leave little doubt about the importance of money and the need for viable monetary institutions.

### The Money Supply Today

There is an unsettling vagueness about any definition of the money supply, and if we think about money for a moment, it is clear that computerized plastic credit-card systems function as money in some contexts. Figure 1 provides some perspective on the definition of money and other paper assets.

### MONEY

Nearly all of the currency in circulation today consists of Federal Reserve Notes—paper IOUs which are liabilities of the Federal Reserve System, a banking agency operated under government authorization. Figure 1 shows that United States Treasury monetary debts (coins and a small amount of paper money) are the least important form of money. The bulk of the money supply consists of demand-deposit money—checking accounts held in commercial banks—as Figure 1 also shows. Demand deposits are included as part of the money supply because they are readily accepted as a medium of exchange and used as a standard and store of value. Although checking accounts are an asset, they are also a liability of some bank. When checks are written and given to another party, they are accepted in part because the check is honored as the bank's debt. Thus, money is a liability of one of three financial institutions: the United States Treasury, the Federal Reserve Banking System, or private commercial banks that serve the public.

---

**FIGURE 1**  Supply of Money and Near-Money
(billions of dollars)

| | | |
|---|---:|---:|
| Money supply: | | |
| Demand deposits | | $156.7 |
| Currency in circulation | | 47.9 |
| Paper money | $47.6 | |
| Coins | 6.1 | |
| Currency in banks | −5.8 | |
| Total | | $204.6 |
| Near-money supply: | | |
| Time deposits | | $202.1 |
| Savings and loan deposits | | 136.6 |
| Mutual-bank savings deposits | | 68.8 |
| Government securities (privately held, due in one year) | | 80.5 |
| Total | | $488.0 |

SOURCE: *Federal Reserve Bulletin* (July 1970), pp. A 16, A 17, A 18, and A 43. (As of June 1970.)

The public's stock of wealth also includes *near-money paper assets*. Near-money and money are distinguished by different degrees of liquidity. *Liquidity* is the risklessness and ease with which an asset can be transformed into money and serve as a medium of exchange. Currency and demand deposits are unique paper assets because they are highly liquid, whereas *near-money* must be converted into money before exchange can occur. *Time deposits* (savings accounts held in commercial banks), deposits or "shares" in savings and loan associations, savings accounts held by mutual savings banks, and short-term United States government securities are some types of near-monies. They are excluded from a formal definition of the money supply because near-monies do not technically serve as a medium of exchange or standard of value. Near-money may be superior to money as a store of value because holders of wealth claims such as government bonds normally earn interest on them. However, there are risks associated with holding a bond or security because its price may fall.

As economic affairs have become more complex, a wide variety of paper assets with near-money attributes have emerged to serve the lending and saving needs of society. Figure 1 gives only a few of the more important kinds of near-monies, which are highly liquid types of paper assets. Because the supply of money is important to economic activity, the supply of near-money paper assets is also important. Although the money supply is formally understood to include only currency in circulation outside banks and demand deposits, this *narrow definition* could be broadened to include other paper assets of the near-money variety that are easily transformed into currency or demand-deposit money. Conventionally defined, the money supply amounts to over $200 billion, but including just the few near-monies shown in Figure 1 boosts the money supply *broadly defined* to nearly $700 billion. There is no right or wrong definition of the money supply, nor is there any point in debating the definition of money further. Simply remember that a *very* vague line distinguishes money from near-money.

## Evolution of Monetary Systems

The history of money is, in a very meaningful sense, the history of the progress of mankind. Over the centuries, nations moved from primitive, barter societies to exchange systems in which commodities, including precious metals, were used as forms of money. Next, rare and durable commodities like gold and silver were minted into coins that served as a medium of exchange. The use of paper money followed. Paper currencies were initially regarded as money because governments and sovereigns held quantities of precious metals as backing for the paper debts issued. The next historical step involved removal of the commodity (gold) backing of money. This process is still going on throughout the world. Before we examine some of the key financial institutions in the United States today, we should clarify some additional features of monetary systems.

## DEBT AND FIAT MONEY

Suppose a primitive society of Merrymen decide to identify something as money and they select Friar Tuck as their banker since, being a man of the cloth, he is literate, honest, and can store money safely in the chapel. The

Merrymen could give the good Friar green paper and ink and authorize him to print "green-paper notes" to use as money. Green-paper notes printed by the Friar might be given to the Merrymen in exchange for gold, turkeys, or anything of value the Friar cared to hold. Suppose it is decided that the Friar will exchange $100 in green-paper notes for gold in some quantity, say, $1 for every pound of gold (the quantity does not really matter). The Friar's records of assets and liabilities or debts would appear as shown below. In short, the green-paper notes are now money (provided the Merry-

| Assets | Liabilities |
|---|---|
| Chapel owns 100 pounds of gold ($100) | Chapel owes $100 (the "green-paper notes" now owned by Merryman) |

men believe this hocus-pocus) *and* they are debts of the chapel—a measure of what the Friar owes the Merrymen who deposited gold with him.

The United States money supply (all currency in circulation plus demand deposits) is the paper indebtedness of its financial institutions, just as the "green-paper notes" are chapel debts. Figure 1 indicated that the currency in circulation in the United States today is the liability of the Federal Reserve Banking System and the United States Treasury, while demand deposits are the debts of private commercial banks. Money is nothing more than IOUs or debt. But who says green-paper notes are money? The answer is: Government has declared it so. Paper money is *fiat* money—that is, government-declared money—and *debt* money.

## VALUE OF MONEY

The value of money is determined by whatever it will buy in real goods and services. Paper money is exchanged for goods that satisfy wants as long as merchants know that others will accept whatever is offered as money. Confidence in money is based on both conventional acceptance and the fact that government has declared fiat money to be a legal form of payment. This does not mean, however, that the value of money cannot change.

Long ago, when money consisted of coins made of silver and gold, money was debased by scraping bits of the precious metal off a coin, a practice called "clipping." Ancient monarchs and governments minted facial expressions and rough edges on coins for the purpose of spotting "clipped" money. Another method of debasing commodity money was to mix copper or other more abundant metals with gold and silver—a practice sometimes followed by rulers in need of funds. Either clipping or content debasement produced a larger money supply. For example, if aggregate capacity is fixed and the King of Id mints coins on a one part copper to one part gold basis, a good deal more money is made available, but the actual full-employment capacity of Id does not necessarily increase. Money is no longer as scarce as before, and more money is chasing the same fixed quantity of output, with the result that the prices of goods and services rise. Therefore, *the value* or *the purchasing power of money declines*, and it takes more dollars, crowns, rubles, or what have you to purchase a fixed quantity of goods.

Enough, but not too much, money must be available to permit a volume of economic transactions that is consistent with reasonably stable prices. Firms and households accept money as a medium of exchange, standard of value, and store of value with the assumption (and hope) that its value will not change excessively. Money will be held as a store of value, but only if this value is relatively stable. If too much money is "created," inflation sets in and people lose confidence in money. As prices rise, the value of money falls, and people tend to get rid of monetary balances as rapidly as possible by spending, adding even more fuel to an inflationary spiral. If the situation is severe and persistent, populations revert to cigarettes, chocolate, or other commodities as units of exchange, as happened in several European nations after World War II.

## FRACTIONAL-RESERVE BANKING

In the example of Friar Tuck's green-paper notes, $1 of gold was held in "reserve" as backing for each $1 of green-paper notes used as money. Since each $1 note could have been converted into $1 worth of gold, we can say this is a 100 percent reserve system. *Fractional-reserve banking* describes holding reserves (like gold) equal to only a fraction or percentage of the total debt money issued. For example, a 10 percent fractional-reserve requirement against our hypothetical Friar Tuck would mean that each $1 of gold would support $10 of green-paper notes. Thus, if the Friar can run his bank on a fractional-reserve basis, his records might appear as shown below.

| Assets | Liabilities |
|---|---|
| Chapel owns 100 pounds of gold ($100) and $900 of loans | Chapel owes $1,000 in green-paper notes |

Of course, the Friar is not necessarily going to hand every Merryman $10 instead of $1 in green-paper notes for each pound of gold. Rather, it would be advantageous for him to purchase other assets, and he can purchase $900 worth if he needs to hold only a 10 percent reserve requirement. What he might well do is lend $900 to someone and charge interest on the loan; this is exactly what banks do today. However, if everyone demands gold at one time, the Friar has had it, since he can only convert $100 of green-paper notes into gold because he is a fractional-reserve banker. Like Friar Tuck's bank, contemporary monetary systems are based on banks holding fractional reserves against deposit liabilities; that is, demand-deposit money (the created debt of financial institutions) is fractionally backed by currency reserves in the United States today.

## GOLD AND MONEY

Today, a United States citizen cannot legally hold gold for monetary purposes. Moreover, currencies such as U.S. or Canadian dollars are backed by faith in the government and are not domestically convertible into gold. Before 1933 many nations were on a *gold monetary standard*, under which both coins and paper currency could be converted into gold. Britain abandoned the gold standard in 1931 and the United States followed suit two years later. At one time the Federal Reserve was required to hold gold certificates (title to physical stocks of gold) as backing for the paper money of the United States. In 1965, Congress eliminated the 25 percent gold "cover" required on bank reserves, and in 1968 it voided the gold "cover" for Federal Reserve Notes. Consequently, the primary role of gold in monetary affairs today is international, as it properly should be.[2]

Although domestic conversion is prohibited, many nations, such as the United States and Britain, remain on a limited international gold-reserve standard that allows *other nations* to convert the dollar (or pound) into gold. Nations like the United States cling to the legacy of money and gold internationally to the extent that other nations insist on this same fiction. The notion remains in international circles that a currency should be backed by gold, partly because nearly all nations have managed their monetary affairs poorly at one time or another.

Because gold could not be created as readily as paper money, a "gold standard" may once have served to restrain governments from irresponsibly tampering with the money supply. However, the rate of expansion in the money supply needed for a growing economy can also be restricted by the amount of gold available. The rapidity with which gold can be brought out of the bowels of Mother Earth is hardly a reasonable economic criterion for expanding or contracting a money supply that may be important to the level of economic activity. As long as government operates a paper monetary system responsibly there is no reason to use gold as a monetary standard any more than any other commodity. The need to control the money supply essentially returns to a need to maintain a stable, full-employment economy. Today the creation of debt money is a relatively orderly process, and nations are better off not having to depend upon getting just enough gold to provide the needed supply of money.

## B. CONTEMPORARY FINANCIAL INSTITUTIONS

Four types of institutions are important to the United States monetary system: (a) the United States Treasury; (b) the Federal Reserve System, a "central bank" that is a quasi-governmental agency charged with regulating monetary activities; (c) financial intermediaries—institutions such as life insurance companies and credit unions that deal with a wide variety of near-monies; and (d) private commercial banks. Commercial banks are unique financial institutions because they actually create demand-deposit money; however, all four financial institutions deal in debt and credit or

[2] For those who remain unconvinced about the nominal role of gold in a domestic economy, suppose that the government had decided during World War II, in fear of invasion, to bury all gold in the ocean off the Florida Keys. Unfortunately, the individual aware of the precise longitude and latitude dies without revealing the location. Would the loss really matter to the domestic economy? It certainly need not, as long as the existing currency is accepted by the populace. Their wages, education, homes, and other economic assets are no less valuable because the gold cannot be found.

function as intermediaries among savers and borrowers. Between them, more than $1.5 trillion of debt is financed today. Since these institutions are a part of an interrelated financial system and yet differ in critical ways, a brief examination of each is appropriate.

### United States Treasury

The Treasury is one of three financial institutions that issue money, which is largely in the form of coins. As the agent of the federal government, the United States Treasury has general authority over the financial affairs of the federal government, including the sale and redemption of government securities as well as the purchase and sale of gold. While this monetary institution does not purposively attempt to influence the money supply, Treasury actions can have an important influence on monetary conditions, as we shall see in Chapter 11.

### The Federal Reserve System: Central Banking

In 1913 the banking industry was centralized under one federal government agency, the Federal Reserve Banking System. Central banking in the United States is the responsibility of a seven-member Board of Governors appointed to 14-year terms by the President. The major task of the Federal Reserve that interests us is how it influences the total money supply by increasing or decreasing bank reserves. In addition, central-banking responsibilities include issuing paper currency, auditing commercial banks, and performing other regulatory functions designed to provide a stable monetary system. Because of its importance, the Federal Reserve will be studied in considerable detail in Chapter 11.

### Financial Intermediaries

Institutions that deal in paper assets of the near-money type are called financial intermediaries. Savings and loan associations, finance companies, and life insurance companies act as middlemen between borrowers and savers.

Intermediaries are unique in that they hold most of the more than $1.5 trillion of aggregate net indebtedness outstanding today. Financial intermediaries lend funds and create near-money paper assets like charge-account credit, savings and loan shares, or installment-loan credit. The effect of these near-monies is to enhance the lending capacity of financial firms by channeling funds from less to more active use than would be the case if individuals held monetary balances. When the public obtains a "share" in a savings and loan association or purchases a government bond, a newly created near-money is substituted for the protection and liquidity that money previously provided. Currently, financial intermediaries own approximately 80 percent of the $400 billion in mortgage debt outstanding and more than one-half of some $100 billion of consumer-installment debt. The assets of life insurance companies, savings and loan associations, and mutual savings banks alone amount to about $0.5 trillion. Even if the narrowly defined money supply (currency plus demand deposits) does not change, financial intermediaries affect the use of the supply of money and can have profound effects on income and employment. Consequently, they are important financial institutions.

The operational level of monetary activity is carried out by some 13,500 private commercial banks that hold the public's time (savings) and demand (checking) deposits. There are several different types of commercial banks. *Reserve-city banks*, for example, are typically large banks located in urban centers. *Country banks* are smaller banks and are usually situated in smaller communities or rural areas. *National banks* are those that receive an operating charter from the federal government, whereas *state banks* are chartered by state authorities. National banks are required by law to join the Federal Reserve System, and state banks may join the Federal Reserve if they choose to do so. Less than one-half of all commercial banks are members of the Federal Reserve System, and most "member" banks are nationally chartered. Although a large number of commercial banks do not belong to the Federal Reserve System, "nonmember" banks are comparatively small in size. More than four-fifths of all bank assets are controlled by member banks which are responsible for most of the nation's banking activity. Numerous nonmember banks maintain deposits, borrow, and rely on member banks to act as their correspondent or agent for check-clearing services and other benefits that can be derived only from the Federal Reserve System. Consequently, the regulatory aspect of central banking is significant even though only a small proportion of all banks are members of the Federal Reserve System.

### The Balance Sheet for Commercial Banking

Commercial banks are private institutions with one primary function of interest to us: creating money. The process works like this.

A loan granted to a household for furniture, education, or an automobile is a consumer debt; a loan granted to a firm or the corporate bond purchased by a bank is a debt of the firm; and the government bond or security purchased by a commercial bank is the debt of the United States Treasury. In exchange for consumer, investor, or government indebtedness, commercial banks turn around and give a borrower checking-account money—a commercial-bank liability or debt in the form of a demand deposit. The commercial bank gives borrowers credit, usually in the form of a demand deposit—a checking account *that is money*. When commercial banks accept the repayment obligations of borrowers, this IOU (sometimes backed by a borrower's pledging title to real assets) is a *paper asset* to the bank in the form of the public's legal promise to pay interest and the borrowed principal amount.

As long as checking accounts function as a medium of exchange, they are money just as silver coins, gold, or whale teeth have been used as money at one time or another. Thus, commercial banks are capable of taking our debts that are not money and creating their own debts that are demand-deposit money. Commercial banks are important because the money-creation function is unique to them. In certain ways, the need to regulate demand-deposit money is not very different from what it was when thousands of state banks printed up a wide variety of bank notes to be used as currency in the 1800s.

Before we can talk intelligently about the creation of demand-deposit money, it is necessary to know more about how commercial banks operate. Figure 2 summarizes commercial-bank operations in balance-sheet form.

A *balance sheet* identifies a firm's *assets* (things owned of economic value) and *liabilities* (all debts and ownership claims against the firm). The balance sheet or "t-account," as it is sometimes called, is important because it always balances; it must, since everything of economic value is always owned or claimed by someone. Let us first examine the debts and ownership claims of all commercial banks that are members of the Federal Reserve System.

## COMMERCIAL-BANK LIABILITIES

Deposit liabilities are important in several respects. In the first place, the operation of commercial banks is dependent upon time- and demand-deposit liabilities, and because of this dependence, commercial banks compete with each other and with financial intermediaries like savings and loan associations for customers. Note in Figure 2 that a large proportion of commercial-bank deposit liabilities are demand deposits; that is, monetary liabilities in the form of checking accounts payable on demand. Commercial bankers know that on any given day some (but by no means all) of their deposit liabilities may be withdrawn when the public writes checks or draws upon savings accounts. Moreover, bankers know that the public normally makes new deposits daily. Consequently, the amount of cash needed by the commercial-banking system for day-to-day operating purposes will be a small fraction of total deposit liabilities—about 1 to 2 percent under normal conditions. Note that the some $300 billion in demand- and time-deposit liabilities of member banks are several times larger than their reserves. Figure 2 also illustrates how vague the distinction between money and near-money really is. Because time deposits do not function as a medium of exchange, technically they are not defined as money. While commercial banks legally may insist on imposing a 30-day waiting period on time deposits, they do not normally do so. Depositors can go to a commercial bank without prior notice and transfer funds from a time to a demand deposit; that is, move out of near-money into money. The liability entry in Figure 2, capital

**FIGURE 2** Consolidated Balance Sheet for Member Commercial Banks (billions of dollars)

| Assets | | | Liabilities | |
|---|---|---|---|---|
| Reserves | | $ 27.9 | $153.5 | Demand deposits |
| Federal Reserve | | | 155.0 | Time deposits |
| deposits | $21.9 | | 32.8 | Capital accounts |
| Vault cash | 6.0 | | 78.5 | Other |
| Loans | | 238.9 | | |
| Securities | | 94.9 | | |
| Other | | 58.1 | | |
| Total | | $419.8 | $419.8 | Total |

SOURCE: *Federal Reserve Bulletin* (July 1970), pp. A 13, A 17, and A 19. (As of June 1970.) Consolidated for all commercial banks belonging to the Federal Reserve System.

accounts, represents the ownership claims or the net worth of all member commercial banks.

## COMMERCIAL-BANK ASSETS

The fact that commercial-bank reserves are only a fraction of deposit liabilities reflects the fractional-reserve characteristic of commercial banking. *Reserves,* a distinctive asset in the balance sheet of member commercial banks shown in Figure 2, are the sum of all commercial-bank currency held as vault cash for day-to-day operations plus deposits which commercial banks keep with the Federal Reserve System. The Federal Reserve System requires all member banks to hold reserves equal to a specified percentage of both time- and demand-deposit liabilities. The largest category of commercial-bank assets shown in Figure 2 consists of loans and securities—the debts of business firms, households, and government borrowers. Commercial banks acquire paper assets either by using funds to purchase securities or by granting loans. Securities and loans are acquired because repayment and interest earnings are expected. In short, banks are business institutions that earn a profit by dealing in the paper debts of customers. When a commercial bank grants an individual a loan, the interest charge it earns is intended to cover the risk incurred in accepting these IOU's, its operating expenses, and a profit, just as other business firms operate to earn a profit.

## FRACTIONAL RESERVES

Even though no more than 2 percent of cash reserves need be held by a prudent bank in a reasonably healthy economy, the Federal Reserve System imposes a much larger *legal-reserve requirement.* The amount of legal reserves held are governed by the *required-reserve ratio*—the fraction or percentage of deposit liabilities that banks must hold in reserve. Reserves are vault cash or commercial-bank deposits with the Federal Reserve System, as we know. The reason the central bank sets a legal-reserve requirement is *not* to provide security for depositors, although reserves do afford a modest amount of assurance for the public. *The chief purpose of the legal-reserve requirement is to control the amount of commercial-bank deposit liabilities.* Member commercial banks maintain reserve accounts in the Federal Reserve Bank just as you and I use a commercial bank for our checking accounts. The consolidated balance sheet of member commercial banks shown in Figure 2 lists more than $300 billion in time- and demand-deposit liabilities and less than $30 billion of reserves. If the Federal Reserve required the commercial-banking system to hold reserves equal to 10 percent of all deposit liabilities, all commercial banks shown in Figure 2 could hold *no more than* $10 of deposit liabilities for every $1 of reserves (10% of $10 = $1). Thus, the reserve requirement limits commercial-bank credit, particularly demand-deposit liabilities which comprise the bulk of the money supply.

The banking community invests funds entrusted to it in interest-earning loans and securities in hopes of earning profits. Even though deposits payable on demand are several times larger than reserves, all depositors do not normally make withdrawals simultaneously, as bankers discovered some time ago. Holding either excess vault cash or excess deposits in the Federal Reserve can be costly for a commercial bank that otherwise could lend these funds at interest to borrowers. On the other hand, bankers have to manage their investments in securities and loans wisely to avoid undue risk. More-over, nearly all commercial banks keep some highly liquid near-money assets on hand as secondary reserves in the event of unexpected withdraw-als. As a secondary reserve, commercial banks frequently maintain an inventory of government securities with short-term maturities that can be readily converted into currency.

## TOTAL, REQUIRED, AND EXCESS RESERVES

The required-reserve ratio established by the Federal Reserve is a percent-age amount of demand- and time-deposit liabilities which commercial banks must hold as vault cash or as deposits in the Federal Reserve System.

While *total reserves* are all commercial-bank deposits in the Federal Re-serve plus vault cash, *required reserves* are determined by the required-reserve ratio and the level of deposit liabilities:

$$\text{Required reserves} = \text{reserve ratio} \times \text{deposit liabilities}$$

or, for example,

$$\$10,000 = 20\% \times \$50,000$$

*Excess reserves* are the difference between total and required reserves. If the total reserves held by a commercial bank exceed required reserves, posi-tive excess reserves exist; excess reserves would be negative if total reserves were less than required reserves. Designating total reserves as $TR$, required reserves as $RR$, and excess reserves as $ER$, we have $ER = TR - RR$ or $0 in the above example if total reserves are \$10,000 $(TR = RR)$. Under fractional-reserve banking, commercial banks hold required reserves equal to a fraction of deposit liabilities. What is significant about this system is the amount of excess reserves that exists. If the required-reserve ratio were 20 percent and deposit liabilities were \$40 million for a bank, required re-serves would be \$8 million (20% of \$40 million). If the total reserves held by the bank were equal to \$10 million, excess reserves would be \$2 million.

The commercial-banking system normally maintains a relatively small margin of excess reserves simply because such funds are not earning assets. Negative excess reserves are not legal since all member banks *must* meet the required-reserve ratio set by the Federal Reserve System. We emphasize fractional-reserve banking and excess reserves for one important reason: The excess-reserve position of the commercial-banking system directly in-fluences how large deposit liabilities can be, and demand-deposit liabilities are an important component of the money supply.

## C. ORIGINS OF THE MONEY SUPPLY

To understand the demand-deposit component of the money supply, we first need to know where currency comes from and then find out what hap-pens when commercial banks grant loans or invest in government or corpo-rate securities. The simplest way to see how the banking system works is to examine changes in balance sheets.

### Paper Money

Currency is government-issued money manufactured by the United States Bureau of Engraving and Printing and the United States Mint. The bulk of currency today consists of liabilities of the Federal Reserve System, just as Friar Tuck's "green-paper notes" were debts of the chapel. As the central bank of the government, the Federal Reserve System supplies whatever amount of paper currency the public demands from commercial banks. Under normal conditions, the demand for currency is related in a relatively stable fashion to demand deposits (about $1 of currency has been required for every $4 to $5 of demand-deposit money in recent years). An additional amount of currency can be put into the hands of the public (in circulation outside the banking system) in one of several ways.

The most common way in which currency enters into circulation and becomes a part of the active money supply is by business firms and individuals cashing checks at their commercial banks. Once currency has been shipped to the Federal Reserve from government currency "factories," it becomes part of the money supply as follows:

1. The individual cashes a check, say for $100, at a bank, and obtains the currency he desires, perhaps five $20 bills.

2. The commercial-banking system loses $100 in reserves in the form of vault cash. In addition, demand deposits normally decline in the commercial-banking system. Thus, commercial-bank assets (A) and liabilities (L) shown earlier in Figure 2 decline by $100. The net effect of this transaction is to leave the money supply unchanged because the additional $100 of currency in circulation is offset by an equal reduction in demand deposits—also a part of the money supply.

While there are many other ways in which currency can be put into circulation and therefore become a part of the money supply, the essential point of this transaction is this: Currency is nothing more than a circulating IOU of government banking agencies. As the demand for paper money rises, commercial banks simply "retail it" to the public. Of course, commercial banks do lose reserves in the process; however, if they want more reserves they need only sell other assets, such as government bonds held as secondary reserves to the central bank. For example, if the Federal Reserve purchases $100 in securities from a commercial bank, *Federal Reserve* assets (A) increase as shown in the balance sheet below. Other balance-

| New Commercial-Bank Reserves | | | |
|---|---|---|---|
| Federal Reserve System | | Commercial-banking system | |
| A | L | A | L |
| Government securities +$100 | +$100 Reserves | Government securities −$100 Reserves +$100 | |

sheet changes that occur when the central bank buys $100 in securities from a commercial bank are:

1. The Federal Reserve increases its liabilities (L) in the form of commercial-bank reserves.

2. The commercial bank disposes of one type of paper asset (a government bond) and obtains either more currency to use as vault cash or a reserve deposit in the Federal Reserve System.

The distinctive feature of the purchase of securities in this instance is that *currency in circulation* outside the banking system (the money supply) *did not increase*. Nevertheless, commercial-bank reserves *did increase*, and these reserves are the basis for the creation of demand-deposit money.

### Demand-Deposit Money

The commercial-banking system is unique for two reasons. First, it is the only private financial institution capable of creating money in the form of demand deposits. Second, *all* commercial banks together can create much more in demand-deposit monetary liabilities than the reserves they hold. Multiple expansion of the money supply occurs as each commercial bank in the banking system generates demand-deposit money by lending out amounts equal to (but no greater than) its excess reserves. The way demand-deposit money is created by commercial banks is most readily seen by looking at one *loaned-up bank*—a bank which has *no* excess reserves.

### ONE LOANED-UP BANK

For the moment assume that: (*a*) The banking public does not take any deposits out of commercial banks in the form of currency, (*b*) the Federal Reserve System has established a 20 percent required-reserve ratio against deposit liabilities, and (*c*) the commercial bank selected, Wamsutter National, has no excess reserves. Case I below depicts a simplified balance sheet for Wamsutter National, a commercial bank with $100 million in demand deposits (*D*), $80 million of investments in paper assets that could be either loans (*L*) or securities (*S*), and $20 million of reserves (*R*).

The commercial bank in Case I has been able to acquire assets by accepting deposits. Thus, if $100,000 were deposited in Wamsutter National by a local businessman, the bank might simply use four-fifths of that amount to buy government securities. With many more such transactions, the balance sheet would appear as it does below. With demand-deposit liabilities of $100 million, *required reserves* are $20 million, an amount just equal to the bank's *total reserves*; there are no *excess reserves*.

---

**CASE I**    Wamsutter National: A Loaned-Up Commercial Bank
(millions of dollars)

| A | | L | |
|---|---|---|---|
| *R* | $20 | $100 *D* | |
| *L* and *S* | $80 | | |

Total reserves = $20
− Required reserves = 20% of *D*

Excess reserves = $ 0

---

Not being inclined to hold idle cash balances beyond prudent banking needs, commercial banks grant loans to borrowers and invest in interest-earning securities or bonds issued by corporations and the government. But where does the bank obtain funds to make such investments? They use the funds of depositors who are given bank accounts in return for their currency. Like all commercial banks, Wamsutter National long ago discovered that each day they lose and receive new deposits and, on the average, only a fraction of deposit liabilities need be kept on hand.

If you object to this procedure, your rebuffed banker's explanation might be as follows: "After all, I am in business to earn a profit, which means that I must invest in securities and loans. How do you expect me to provide you with nationwide checkbook money, grant you loans on a home or car, provide safekeeping services for your money, and pay you interest on your savings on top of everything else? As it is right now, I am a member of the Federal Reserve meeting the required-reserve ratio, and therefore I have a good deal more cash reserves on deposit in the central bank than I need. Moreover, your deposits are insured up to $20,000 with a government agency, the Federal Deposit Insurance Corporation; many of my investments are backed by valuable assets like your home; and a reasonable number of my investments, such as short-term government securities, can be sold this very moment if I need more cash. Of course I use the funds you deposit with me, and if you don't like it, take your silly money home and stuff it in your mattress."

## CREATING MONEY WITH EXCESS RESERVES

The basic principles of money creation are most readily explained by examining simplified balance-sheet transactions for a commercial bank that receives a new deposit of currency, perhaps from a depositor who has just sold a government security and received paper currency from the Federal Reserve. Case II below depicts this transaction in a commercial bank's balance sheet. We continue to assume a reserve ratio of 20 percent and a bank with no excess reserves initially. In the simplified balance-sheet form shown below in "t-account" A, $100 of currency initially in the hands of the public is deposited in a checking account. The money supply does not change because a $100 decline in Federal Reserve Notes (currency) in circulation outside the banking system was offset by a like amount of new demand-deposit money. Had the public deposited the $100 as a time deposit, the money supply *would have declined* and $100 of additional near-money would have been created.

**CASE II** Wamsutter National Creates Money Equal to Excess Reserves and Monetizes Debt

| A | | B | | C | | D | |
|---|---|---|---|---|---|---|---|
| $100 new deposit | | Money is created | | Check clears | | Ending balance sheet | |
| A | L | A | L | A | L | A | L |
| $R$ +$100 | +$100 $D$ | $L$ +$80 | +$80 $D$ | $R$ −$80 | −$80 $D$ | $R$ $20 | $100 $D$ |
| | | | | | | $L$ and $S$ $80 | |

Required reserves = +$20
Excess reserves = +$80

Required reserves = $20
Excess reserves = $0

Wamsutter National's demand-deposit liabilities rise by $100 with the new deposit, as t-account A shows. With a reserve ratio of 20 percent, *required reserves* increase by $20 and *excess reserves* are now $80. Our commercial bank can now grant a loan (or invest in a security) and create new demand-deposit money in the amount of $80, as shown in t-account B. Suppose that the bank grants an $80 loan to Jeremiah Jones, a trustworthy Wyoming sheepherder hitting the streets of Cheyenne for the first time in a year. Since demand-deposit liabilities increase by $80 when the bank grants this loan, money has been created! The commercial bank created $80 of new money by lending out an amount equal to its excess reserves. Now Jeremiah is an earthy soul, but not so simple-minded as to borrow money and leave it in the bank as an unused demand deposit. His perfectly logical intention is to write a check in the amount of the loan to purchase certain amenities. Since there are thousands of commercial banks, the likelihood is that when a check is written in the amount of the loan, it will be deposited in a different bank. Suppose this happens and Jeremiah's check clears against the Wamsutter National Bank. Demand-deposit liabilities *and* reserves decline by $80, as shown in t-account C. When the individual who sold goods to Jeremiah deposits the check in his bank, say Dillion Trust, that bank then receives the $80 in reserves.

The point of all this is straightforward enough: One commercial bank monetizes debt (Jeremiah's IOU) and lends an amount equal to its excess reserves to acquire an additional earning asset. After the bank lends an amount equal to its excess reserves, it is fully *loaned up* and just meeting its reserve requirement, as t-account D reveals. That is, Wamsutter National is again just meeting the reserve requirement of 20 percent against all demand-deposit liabilities. Observe very carefully that a larger loan cannot be made safely because of the threat of adverse clearings against a commercial bank once a check is written. Had a loan been granted for $100, Wamsutter National would not have been able to meet the required-reserve ratio once the check cleared.

*Conclusion:* A commercial bank creates demand-deposit money by granting loans or buying securities. One bank can safely lend an amount equal to (but no larger than) its excess reserves because checks may be cleared against the originating bank and deposited in another commercial bank.

## A MONOPOLY BANK

Even though one bank in a commercial-banking system can safely lend only an amount equal to its excess reserves, no such restriction applies to all commercial banks taken together. The commercial-banking system is like a monopoly bank in that it can create money by a multiple of excess reserves, as we illustrate next. The importance of the monopoly-bank example is that it shows what happens if reserves are not lost because of adverse check clearances.

Suppose that Wamsutter National again has no excess reserves, that it is the only (or monopoly) bank in an imaginary economy, and that it must meet a 20 percent reserve ratio. Under these circumstances, checks written by depositors and borrowers would simply be redeposited in the monopoly bank. With a new deposit of $100 and a reserve ratio of 20 percent, a monopoly bank's deposit liabilities can be *five times as large as its excess reserves*, as shown in Case III below. Using only balance-sheet changes again, initially new deposits and *total reserves* are $100 and *required reserves* are $20. As a monopoly bank, Wamsutter National can now have a maximum of $500 in additional demand-deposit liabilities and just meet the 20 percent reserve requirement. It can now create $400 in demand-deposit money by purchasing securities or granting loans for $400. Multiplying total-deposit liabilities of $500 by a 20 percent required-reserve

---

**CASE III**  A Monopoly Bank

| | | | | | | | | |
|---|---|---|---|---|---|---|---|---|
| R $100 | $100 D | L and S +$400 | +$400 D | L and S | R $100 | $100 D | | |
| | | | | | $400 | $400 D | | |
| | | | | | $500 | $500 | | |

Required reserves = $20  
Excess reserves  = $80

Required reserves = $100  
Excess reserves  = $0

---

ratio yields $100 in *required reserves*—the actual level of *total reserves* available to the monopoly bank. Accordingly, a monopoly bank (or an entire banking system) can lend by a multiple of its excess reserves. In Case III, with a reserve ratio of 20 percent, demand deposits can be five times as large as total reserves.

MULTIPLE CREATION OF MONEY IN THE BANKING SYSTEM

Our first clue to the possibility that money creation is not ended when one bank lends out its excess reserves is that a check can be, and usually is, deposited in another commercial bank. If we had looked further at the balance-sheet transactions associated with the transfer of funds between the Wamsutter and Dillion Banks in Case II, we would have found that Dillion's demand deposits and reserves increased when our sheepherder wrote the check on Wamsutter that was then deposited in *another* bank.

Because individuals normally pay someone who is likely to deposit the check in a bank, once excess reserves are activated and debt is monetized, a chain reaction is started that makes it possible for the total banking system to expand deposits by a multiple of the reserve ratio. Figure 3 illustrates balance-sheet changes for several banks in a commercial-banking system. Our conclusion that the entire banking system can lend and create demand-deposit money by a multiple of excess reserves even though one bank is limited to lending an amount equal to its excess reserves (*ER*) is explained as follows:

*Transaction 1:* Suppose $100 is deposited in Bank A; the banking system has no excess reserves to start with; the reserve ratio is 20 percent; and Bank A now has $80 of excess reserves.

*Transaction 2:* Bank A now lends an amount equal to its excess reserves to a customer. When the loan is granted, demand deposits increase by $80 and *new money has been created!*

*Transaction 3:* The customer now writes a check in the amount of the

**FIGURE 3** Creation of Money by the Banking System
(assume reserve ratio of 20 percent)

| | Initial balance sheet | | Change in balance sheet | | Ending balance sheet | |
|---|---|---|---|---|---|---|
| | A | L | A | L | A | L |
| A | $R$ \$100 | \$100 $D$ | $L$ and $S$ +\$80 <br> $R$ −\$80 | +\$80 $D$ <br> −\$80 $D$ | $R$ \$20 <br> $L$ and $S$ \$80 | \$100 $D$ |
| | $ER = \$80$ | | | | | |
| | A | L | A | L | A | L |
| B | $R$ +\$80 | +\$80 $D$ | $L$ and $S$ +\$64 <br> $R$ −\$64 | +\$64 $D$ <br> −\$64 $D$ | $R$ \$16 <br> $L$ and $S$ \$64 | \$80 $D$ |
| | $ER = \$64$ | | | | | |
| | A | L | A | L | A | L |
| C | $R$ +\$64 | +\$64 $D$ | $L$ and $S$ +\$51 <br> $R$ −\$51 | +\$51 $D$ <br> −\$51 $D$ | $R$ \$13 <br> $L$ and $S$ \$51 | \$64 $D$ |
| | $ER = \$51$ | | | | | |

| Bank | Additional deposits | Required reserves | Excess reserves | New deposits and loans |
|---|---|---|---|---|
| A | +\$100 | \$ 20 | \$ 80 | \$ 80 |
| B | + 80 | 16 | 64 | 64 |
| C | + 64 | 13 | 51 | 51 |
| D | + 51 | 10 | 41 | 41 |
| E | + 41 | 8 | 33 | 33 |
| F | + 33 | 7 | 26 | 26 |
| G | + 26 | 5 | 21 | 21 |
| H | + 21 | 4 | 17 | 17 |
| Others | + 84 | 17 | | 67 |
| Total banking system | +\$500 | \$100 | | \$400 |

*The Banking System.* Money is created in the commercial-banking system as each bank lends in an amount equal to its excess reserves. *All* commercial banks create new deposit money in an amount equal to a multiple of excess reserves in the banking system. Bank A, for example, can loan out \$80, which is deposited in Bank B, creating \$64 of excess reserves. In turn, Bank B creates new deposit money that increases excess reserves in Bank C (by \$51), and diminishing amounts of excess reserves are monetized in turn by Banks D, E, F, G, etc., throughout the entire banking system. Ultimately, new deposits are created in an amount equal to the "deposit-expansion factor" (1/reserve ratio) times the initial amount of excess reserves in the banking system.

\$80 loan for the purchase of household supplies from a firm that deposits the check in Bank B, where its account is maintained. Commercial Bank A loses \$80 in reserves and Bank B gains that same amount in reserves and demand deposits. As long as the check is redeposited in another commercial bank as a demand deposit, the money supply is larger by $80 and reserves stay in the banking system.

Bank B now has $64 in excess reserves (20 percent of the $80 represents required reserves) that might be used to purchase a government security or grant a loan in a second set of transactions. In paying a broker who sells government bonds, Bank B loses $64 in reserves and in deposit liabilities when the broker deposits his check in Bank C as shown in Figure 3. Now Bank C has $64 of additional demand-deposit liabilities and reserves, or $51 of excess reserves. Again new deposits can be created by Bank C through investments in earning assets—purchasing securities or granting a new loan.

Up to this point, look at what has happened. First, $100 of new deposits in Bank A generated $80 in excess reserves. By lending out amounts equal to excess reserves, *demand-deposit money* has been created in the amounts of $100 + $80 + $64 + $51 or $295. If the initial $100 in new deposits injected into Bank A came from a reduction in currency in circulation, the first $100 in demand deposits *is an offset to a reduction in currency in circulation and not a net increase in the money supply*. Expansion of loans or *net* increases in the demand-deposit money supply are +$80 +$64 +$51 +$41 +$33 +$26 and so forth. As long as deposits do not leave the banking system as cash withdrawals and as long as all banks lend out all excess reserves, money creation can continue with each bank lending an amount equal to its excess reserves.

How much new money is finally created? This question can be answered by appealing either to common sense or to arithmetic logic. Common sense tells us that if *total reserves* initially are $100 and the required-reserve ratio is 20 percent, the *maximum* amount of all demand-deposit liabilities in the banking system can be no more than five times the amount of total reserves: 5 × $100 = $500 of deposit liabilities. *Required reserves* will then be 20 percent of $500, exactly equal to *total reserves* of $100. Similarly, if excess reserves are $80 initially, as they were in Figure 3, five times that much or $400 of *new* demand-deposit money can be created.

Each bank creates new money as it lends out amounts equal to *excess reserves*. For every $1 increase in *total reserves*, new deposits can increase by 80 cents, since the bank retains 20 cents to meet *required reserves*. By passing excess reserves around a fractional-reserve banking system, however, *all* commercial banks together can support $5 of demand deposits for every $1 of excess reserves with a reserve ratio of 20 percent.

If excess reserves had been $200, the banking system could have created $1,000 of new demand-deposit money. Note, too, that a larger required-reserve ratio allows the banking system to expand deposit liabilities; but by a smaller multiple, whereas a smaller required-reserve ratio allows a larger expansion in deposits. If the required-reserve ratio were 50 percent, only $2 of new deposits could be supported by every additional $1 of excess reserves. Thus, the required-reserve ratio as well as the amount of excess reserves influence the money-creating potential of the banking system. This relationship is most readily seen by examining the arithmetic logic of the reserve ratio.

*The deposit-expansion factor* is defined as the multiple by which new reserves support new deposits. Arithmetically the deposit-expansion factor is the reciprocal of the reserve ratio, or $1/0.20 = 5$ for a reserve ratio of 20 percent. This should look familiar, since it is based on the same converging series discussed when we studied the NNP multiplier. The banking system can create deposit liabilities by a factor of ten times total reserves if the reserve ratio is 10 percent ($1/0.10 = 10$) or, if the reserve ratio is 50 percent, deposits could expand by a factor of two times total reserves ($1/0.50 = 2$). The important point to remember is that the demand-deposit money supported by the banking system cannot exceed total reserves × 1/reserve ratio. For example, $100 × 1/0.20 = $500 for Figure 3. Similarly *new* demand-deposit money created cannot exceed excess reserves × 1/reserve ratio.

*Conclusion:* Multiple-money creation is not possible for one individual bank, which can lend no more than its excess reserves. But it is possible for *all* banks to create new demand deposits by a multiple of excess reserves, because the banking system, like a monopoly bank, does not lose reserves. For that reason, demand deposits in the banking system can be as large as total reserves × 1/reserve ratio, and the change in the money supply (*new* demand deposits) in the banking system can be as large as excess reserves × 1/reserve ratio.

## CONTRACTION OF THE MONEY SUPPLY

Just as multiple expansion of the money supply is possible, so too is multiple contraction of demand-deposit money. If each additional $1 of excess reserves supports $5 of new deposits in a commercial-banking system subject to a reserve ratio of 20 percent, deposits must contract by the same multiple for a banking system not meeting the reserve requirement. That is, every $1 of deficit reserves requires a $5 contraction in demand-deposit liabilities.

Assume a loaned-up banking system with −$100 of "excess" reserves initially attributable to Bank A. In order to meet the legal-reserve ratio, Bank A now sells a $100 government bond to a businessman who writes a check on his commercial bank, Bank B, for that amount. Bank B now has a deficit reserve position because it has lost $100 in *total reserves* while *required reserves* declined by $20, or 20 percent of the decline in demand deposits. This leaves a reserve deficit of −$80 in Bank B, which must either sell $80 in securities or call in $80 of loans outstanding to meet the legal-reserve requirement. This in turn causes yet a third bank to lose $80 in deposits and reserves. Reserve deficits are passed around the banking system in amounts of −$80, −$64, −$51, −$41, and so on. Since subsequent commercial banks must call in loans or sell securities, the cumulative contraction process continues.

### Qualifications to the Money-Expansion Process

There are several qualifications to the creation and destruction of demand-deposit money as it has been described. Reserves are affected by currency flows in and out of the commercial-banking system, checks do not always clear against a commercial bank, and excess reserves are sometimes unused.

### CURRENCY FLOWS

Under normal conditions, empirical studies show that the demand for paper money tends to rise or fall in approximate proportions of $1 of currency to

$5 of demand deposits. Suppose that for every $5 rise in demand deposits, currency needs rise by $1. Currency *outflows* of this sort drain off or reduce reserves being passed from bank to bank in the commercial-banking system, thus lowering the total amount of demand-deposit money that can be created. Commercial banks expand demand-deposit liabilities by less than the banks' excess reserves, anticipating that the public will withdraw additional currency. Instead of $500 of new deposit money being created for every $100 of excess reserves in a banking system subject to a reserve ratio of 20 percent, less than that amount is created. If currency outflows leaking into circulation amount to $50 and excess reserves are $100 initially, only $250 of new deposit money may be created (the *net* amount of excess reserves × its deposit-expansion factor is $50 × 5). The commercial-banking system magnifies *only the amount of excess reserves it retains* into a larger change in the money supply. Similarly, if $1 of currency flows into the banking system for every $5 reduction in demand deposits, the contraction process is diminished because the deficit reserves passed around are smaller by the inflow of currency.

### THE CHECK-CLEARANCE PROCESS

The possibility of some checks clearing *within* a single bank rather than clearing *against* it enhances its ability to expand deposits. To the extent that a commercial bank does not lose reserves to another bank, it can expand its lending ability by more than the excess reserves it gains from transactions. In practice, commercial-bank reserves expand and contract rather uniformly for all banks in the system. Commercial banks receive checks drawn on other banks and therefore can count on positive offsets to their reserve losses from checks that clear adversely. No one bank will necessarily lose or gain reserves as long as checks deposited and paid out between banks cancel each other out. Only when one bank expands deposits more rapidly than others will it lose reserves to the banking system.

### MAINTENANCE OF EXCESS RESERVES

A potential deposit-expansion factor of 5, for example, may not be realized if banks maintain excess reserves. Excess reserves are maintained for one of two reasons: prudence and the unwillingness to lend and borrow.

1. Prudence. Bankers are encouraged to manage their investment portfolios carefully, for when reserves are needed, it may be costly to liquidate securities whose values may have declined. Commercial banks sometimes maintain a small margin of excess reserves as a hedge against unusual fluctuations in deposits. Fluctuations in reserves are also met today by one commercial bank lending another bank its excess reserves for a day or two in the Federal Funds Market, a market maintained by large banks that lend and borrow excess reserves within the commercial-banking system for very short periods of time. In other instances, a commercial bank may borrow from the Federal Reserve; however, the central bank can be miserly in granting such loans, for reasons that will be described in the following chapter.

2. Willingness to lend and borrow. Both bankers and the public must be willing, as well as able, to lend and borrow. If interest rates are very low and uncertain economic conditions prevail, banks may not want to lend or

borrowers may be unwilling to assume further debt, in which case some excess reserves may remain unused. Between 1929 and 1933, for example, commercial-bank loans declined from $38 billion to $16 billion. Even though excess reserves were rather large during the 1930s, it was almost two decades before loans reached their 1929 peak of $38 billion. As the economic outlook improves both parties tend to be increasingly inclined to put excess commercial-bank reserves to work, but there is nothing which forces people to borrow or bankers to lend against their will.

*In summary:* A bank can create new loans and new demand-deposit money equal to its excess reserves and the banking system can expand the money supply by a multiple of its excess reserves. However, expansion or contraction of the money supply is not an automatic process. The process depends on:

1. The level of demand-deposit liabilities and the amount of total reserves available to commercial banks.
2. The reserve ratio, which determines required and excess reserves and therefore the potential expansion of the money supply.
3. The extent to which currency flows and check clearances alter deposit expansion and contraction, and the extent to which the desires of commercial banks and the public to do business mesh.

A fractional-reserve banking system generates high-powered money and magnifies expansion and contraction of the money supply several times over. Changes in the required-reserve ratio *or* changes in the absolute dollar amount of total reserves alter excess reserves and may affect the money supply; therefore, the reserve ratio and the volume of total reserves represent ways to regulate the money supply. Such regulation is the topic of Chapter 11.

## REVIEW
### Summary

1. As one type of paper asset, money performs three functions: It is a medium of exchange, a standard of value, and a store of value. The money supply, defined as currency in circulation outside banks plus demand deposits, is a debt of either the Treasury, the Federal Reserve, or the commercial banks. Many other paper assets have some attributes of money and thus are termed "near-monies."

2. Throughout its history, the United States economy has been plagued by an unstable monetary system and repeated financial crises which culminated in thousands of bank failures. Loose regulations and loss of faith in paper money contributed to "break-the-bank" panics that intensified fluctuations in economic activity.

3. In most contemporary economies: (*a*) Money is the debt of financial institutions; (*b*) money is "fiat," or government-declared; (*c*) the value of money is revealed by what it will buy in goods and services; and (*d*) monetary systems are based upon fractional-reserve banking, under which commercial banks hold reserves equal to some fraction of total-deposit liabilities. Today the role of gold in the monetary system of the

United States is largely international, since citizens may not legally acquire gold other than for approved commercial purposes.

4. In the United States today, four financial institutions are of major importance in achieving stable monetary conditions: the United States Treasury, the Federal Reserve System, financial intermediaries, and commercial banks. The Treasury issues currency, the Federal Reserve is a central-government bank that regulates the monetary system, financial intermediaries deal in near-monies, and the more than 13,000 commercial banks create the bulk of the money supply—demand deposits.

5. Commercial banks monetize debt by lending amounts equal to their excess reserves to borrowers and by purchasing securities. *One* commercial bank can safely lend an amount equal only to its excess reserves because checks may clear against it. Because the banking system as a whole does not lose reserves, *all* commercial banks can support demand-deposit money by a multiple of total reserves, the multiple or deposit-expansion factor being the reciprocal of the reserve ratio (1/reserve ratio). When commercial banks lend funds, they often create new demand deposits—that is, increase the money supply. The amount of *new* deposit money created by a banking system can be as large as excess reserves × the deposit-expansion factor.

6. The fractional-reserve banking system provides the basis for the money-creating ability of commercial banks, which depends on the amount of excess reserves in the banking system. The volume of total reserves *less* required reserves equals excess reserves. Positive excess reserves allow expansion of the money supply, whereas negative excess reserves enforce contraction of the money supply. In short, changes in the demand-deposit component of the money supply can be generated by private banking institutions. If the money supply does influence economic activity, as many experts contend, it is clear that the monetary system may help account for economic instability.

7. There is nothing automatic about the multiple-expansion process. Cash inflows, offsetting check clearances, and decisions not to use excess reserves all tend to alter the magnitude of changes in the money supply emanating from excess reserves. In general, multiple money-supply changes are tempered by these factors, although it is still clear that very sizable changes in the money supply are generated by small changes in the commercial-banking system's reserve position under a fractional-reserve monetary system.

## Identify the Following Concepts and Terms

- near-money
- gold and money
- monetizing debt
- multiple expansion of the money supply
- bank "runs"
- Federal Funds Market

- the required-reserve ratio
- fiat money
- deposit-expansion factor
- financial intermediaries and near-monies
- required and excess reserves

## Questions to Answer

1. Explain the following statement: "Money is what a society thinks it is, money is what functions as money, and the value of money depends on what society thinks it is worth and how well it functions."

2. It is often said that money is a debt of one of three financial institutions in the United States. Explain how this is true for each of these institutions. Are near-monies debts? If so, whose debts are they?

3. If the required-reserve ratio is 10 percent and one single commercial bank has $4 million in excess reserves, by how much can this one bank expand deposit liabilities? Does the money supply automatically and necessarily change? Given the same reserve ratio and amount of excess reserves for a banking system, by how much might deposit liabilities increase? Explain and illustrate these processes with t-accounts.

4. If you deposit $1,000 of currency in circulation into a loaned-up banking system, does the money supply change? Why or why not? What happens to total, required, and excess reserves? (Assume a required-reserve ratio of 12.5 percent.) What is the size of the deposit-expansion factor?

# CHAPTER 11
# Monetary Policy

The way in which the central bank regulates the money supply—*monetary policy*—is the subject of this chapter. A central-banking system is necessary because unregulated commercial banking tends to accentuate swings in economic activity as private commercial banks contract or expand the money supply in response to variations in reserves and deposits. Today the Federal Reserve System, acting as the nation's central bank, uses monetary policy to influence economic activity. It should come as no surprise that the purpose of monetary policy is to stabilize the economy at full employment and noninflationary levels of production. Part A briefly sketches the historical and institutional characteristics of the Federal Reserve System. Part B shows how the money supply is managed. In Part C some complications connected with monetary policy are discussed.

## A. CENTRAL BANKING: THE FEDERAL RESERVE SYSTEM

Repeated experiences in the United States with financial panics and the excesses of a loosely operated banking system ultimately led to the establishment in 1913 of a meaningful central bank—the Federal Reserve System. Time and time again public runs on commercial banks had resulted in vast currency withdrawals by depositors, loss of commercial-bank reserves, and, not infrequently, widespread bank failures and economic depressions. At its inception, the central bank was not responsible primarily for managing the money supply, but rather was viewed as a general regulatory agency that would also act as a fiscal agent for the government. One of the key functions that the Federal Reserve was set up to perform was to hold commercial-bank reserves, a function common to the central banks of most developed countries today. Our first task is to see how reserves influence monetary conditions and economic activity.

### Money, Spending, and Income

Whenever a nation is at inflationary levels of output, Federal Reserve authorities can clamp down on credit and money-supply expansion to dampen aggregate demand, a move described as a *tight-money* policy. If aggregate spending is insufficient to achieve full employment, central-bank authorities may take steps to allow expansion of the money supply—to create *easy-money* conditions. Monetary policy can be quite involved, but most economists feel that the linkage between the money supply, denoted by $M$, and a nation's output can be summarized in the series of five relationships shown below, where $\Delta$ stands for a change in $M$, NNP, and so on.

1. The Federal Reserve System influences the money supply ($M$) by changing commercial-bank reserves, which leads to expansion or contraction of demand deposits.

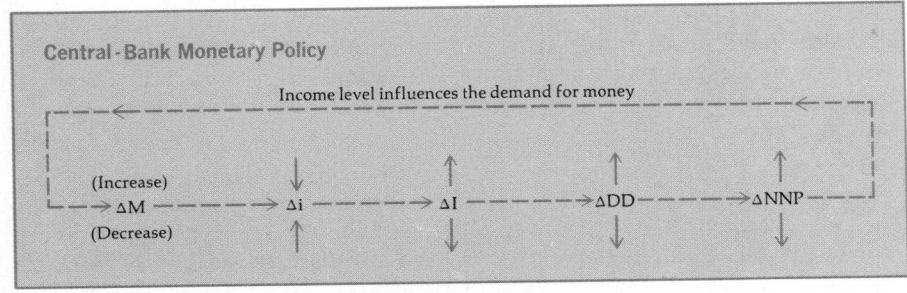

Central-Bank Monetary Policy

Income level influences the demand for money

(Increase)

ΔM ⟶ Δi ⟶ ΔI ⟶ ΔDD ⟶ ΔNNP

(Decrease)

2. Increased availability of credit expands the money supply and lowers interest rates (*i*). Conversely, contraction of the money supply restricts the availability of credit and leads to higher interest rates.

3. Lower interest rates and increased credit encourage spending, particularly investment demand (*I*), whereas higher interest rates tend to discourage investment spending.

4. Increases in investment spending alter aggregate demand (*DD*) and NNP as we have seen before, while decreases in spending dampen aggregate demand and depress expansion in NNP.

5. Finally, the level of output and changes in income and employment have a direct feedback effect on the demand for money because money is used for transaction purposes.

There are many complications and details ignored in this overview of the chain relationship between $\Delta M$, $\Delta i$, $\Delta I$, $\Delta DD$ and $\Delta NNP$ that we shall postpone considering for the moment. Nevertheless, these five relationships generally show why central banks are concerned with the monetary system in most developed nations.

## MONEY SUPPLY AND DEMAND

The key links between the money supply and income and employment hinge upon the supply and demand for money "balances." For the moment assume a narrowly defined money supply, where money is measured as currency in circulation outside the banking system and demand-deposit liabilities of commercial banks.

The supply of money is termed a "policy variable" because the Federal Reserve System can influence it, as this chapter will demonstrate. The demand for money, however, is largely determined by the amount of money business firms and households in the private sector wish to hold. The total demand for money balances is composed of a transaction demand and a paper-asset demand held for speculative and precautionary purposes.

1. The transaction demand for money varies directly with the income level. Since these money balances are needed for *exchange* or *transaction* purposes, it is reasonable to expect more demand for money balances at higher levels of NNP and a lower demand for money as NNP declines. Accordingly, the demand for money partially reflects the larger number of transactions needed to accommodate a higher level of income.

2. The paper-asset demand for money reflects the fact that individuals also hold money balances for purposes other than transactions. In some

instances, simple *precautionary* motives encourage people to hold money as a type of paper asset rather than to hold a near-money such as a security. Money balances may also be held for *speculative* reasons in anticipation of changes in prices and incomes, because of uncertainty about the economic future, and so forth.

The critical feature about the demand for money balances is simply that when people attempt to hold more money, expenditures on output tend to decline (given a fixed supply of money). Conversely, if the demand for money balances *diminishes*, people may rid themselves of their excess liquidity (money) by *stepping up expenditures*. The way the demand for money is related to interest rates and income can be illustrated in terms of an aggregate-demand model of economic activity (see Figure 1).

### MONEY, INTEREST RATES, AND INVESTMENT DEMAND

Since paper assets of the monetary type can be either held or used, we know in general that if the demand for money exceeds the supply of money, aggregate spending and NNP will decrease inasmuch as people acquire larger liquid-money balances by holding more money (spending less). On the other hand, when the demand for money is greater than some fixed money supply, individuals rid themselves of excess money balances by increasing spending, causing NNP to rise. The impact of discrepancies between the demand for money balances and the supply of money as a policy variable hinges on two important notions:

1. *Liquidity preference* describes an inverse relation between the interest rate and the demand for money, as shown in Figure 1(a) because there is an opportunity cost of forgone interest-earnings associated with holding

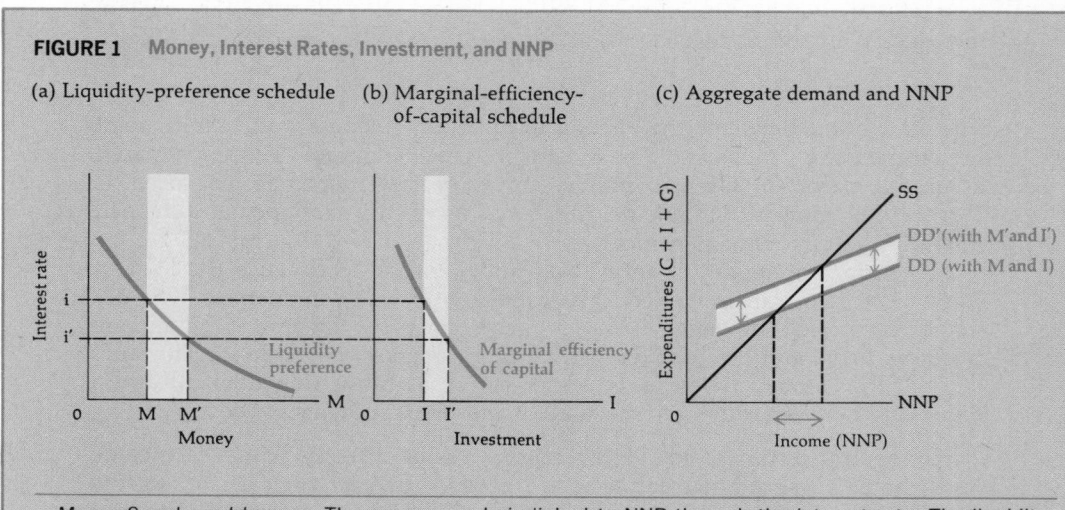

**FIGURE 1**  Money, Interest Rates, Investment, and NNP

(a) Liquidity-preference schedule  (b) Marginal-efficiency-of-capital schedule  (c) Aggregate demand and NNP

*Money Supply and Income.* The money supply is linked to NNP through the interest rate. The liquidity-preference schedule (a) shows the effect of an increase in the money supply from M to M' which lowers the interest rate to i'. The marginal efficiency of capital (b) reveals how a lower interest rate tends to increase investment demand from I to I' which increases NNP shown in (c).

liquid-money balances. Because interest is sacrificed to hold money, the quantity of money demanded declines as interest rates rise; i.e., earnings sacrificed per dollar of money balances held increase. At lower interest rates such as $i'$ in Figure 1(a), larger money balances may be held because interest-earnings forgone have decreased (the cost of holding money has declined). Thus, when the liquidity preference for a community remains as given by the schedule in Figure 1(a) and the money supply increases from $M$ to $M'$, there are two important consequences. First, an increase in the money supply causes the interest rate to decline from $i$ to $i'$. Second, although the lower interest rates may induce people to hold larger money balances, they also stimulate investment.

2. The *marginal-efficiency-of-capital* schedule [shown in Figure 1(b)] relates the yield on investment alternatives to the existing amount of investment demand. Firms may use more money at lower interest rates because they can invest in capital resources which produce lower yields, an action made possible by the lower interest rates. Although many factors affect investment demand, we know from our earlier discussion of the marginal efficiency of capital (Chapter 10) that investment depends in part on the cost of credit—the interest rate charged for using funds relative to the return earned by capital resources. In general, then, the demand for money and the level of investment is greater at lower interest rates, whereas higher interest rates discourage investment, as shown by Figure 1(b).

The rate of interest is important to both liquidity preferences and the marginal efficiency of capital, as shown in Figures 1(a) and 1(b), and interest rates are also the vehicle through which money indirectly alters NNP. Suppose for some reason that the money supply shown in Figure 1(a) does increase from $M$ and $M'$, and the demand for money balances reflected by the liquidity-preference schedule remains unchanged. With a larger money supply, excess money balances will encourage people to increase expenditures. Note too that as interest rates decline, larger money balances may be held, since the opportunity cost of holding money has declined. Most important, however, is the notion that declining interest rates may in turn increase investment demand [from $I$ to $I'$ in Figure 1(b)] because business firms find it increasingly profitable to invest in capital equipment. Consequently, aggregate demand increases, and NNP is driven upward by some multiple of the increase in aggregate demand, as shown in Figure 1(c).

The general chain of relations between money, interest rates, aggregate demand, and NNP described above applies in reverse when the demand for money balances is not satisfied by the existing supply of money. For example, when the money supply declines from $M'$ to $M$, interest rates rise, investment expenditures and aggregate demand diminish, and NNP declines as shown in Figure 1(c).

The *essential* feature of monetary policy is that reserves used by commercial banks as the basis for creating demand-deposit money can be altered by central-bank authorities. In general, Federal Reserve authorities encourage expansion or contraction in the money supply by: (*a*) altering the volume of total reserves, or (*b*) changing the required-reserve ratio. Before studying this all-important process further, let us see how the Federal Reserve is organized and examine its varied functions.

The most important organizational elements of the Federal Reserve System are: (*a*) the Board of Governors, (*b*) the 12 Federal Reserve Banks, and (*c*) the Open Market Committee. The President of the United States appoints seven members to the Board of Governors who are ultimately responsible for directing the central bank. Each appointee fills a staggered 14-year term on the Board, a term designed to encourage his political independence. Unlike central banks in some nations (Britain, for example), the Board may and often does make decisions on monetary affairs independent of the President's wishes. Because the Federal Reserve System regulates member commercial banks, the Board of Governors is primarily responsible for overseeing the United States monetary system.

The 12 Federal Reserve Banks which comprise the central bank are located in 12 separate geographic districts serving large commercial centers throughout the United States.[1] There are, in addition, 24 branch banks, over one-half of which are located in the more populous eastern United States to facilitate central-banking services in that region. As one might expect, some of the 12 Federal Reserve Banks are considerably more important than others. Indeed, over one-half of the Federal Reserve System's assets are held by the three Reserve Banks located in New York, Chicago, and San Francisco. Although the Federal Reserve System may earn a profit, its purpose is to supervise the nation's monetary system. If they do exceed the dividends the central bank pays to subscribing member commercial banks, the profits are channeled into the United States Treasury. Each commercial bank belonging to the Federal Reserve is required to buy central-bank stock equal to 3 percent of its capital account on which a 6 percent dividend is earned. Each of the 12 Reserve Banks has nine directors equally representing the public at large, commerce, and banking interests. Although owned by the slightly less than 6,000 member commercial banks, Federal Reserve Banks are quasi-public institutions under the direction of the Board of Governors.

Another important organizational aspect of the central bank is the Federal Open Market Committee. All Federal Reserve Banks elect five individuals for positions on the Federal Open Market Committee, which also includes the seven Governors of the Federal Reserve. The primary function of the 12-man Open Market Committee is to decide when to sell or buy government securities—a decision that alters the volume of total bank reserves.

### Functions of the Federal Reserve

The Federal Reserve System provides a variety of services to the government, member commercial banks, and the public at large. By far the most important function of the Federal Reserve is regulation of the money supply, particularly demand-deposit money created by the commercial-banking system. Before we see how management of the money supply is accomplished when the central bank alters the total volume of reserves or the amount of required reserves, a brief review of the more general functions of the Federal Reserve is in order.

[1] The cities are New York, Boston, Chicago, Minneapolis, Philadelphia, Atlanta, Cleveland, Richmond, St. Louis, Dallas, Kansas City, and San Francisco.

## BANK SUPERVISION

Member commercial banks are subject to special regulations and unannounced audits administered by the Federal Reserve System. Supervision of commercial banking is carried out under the general jurisdiction of the Board of Governors of the Federal Reserve as well as two other public agencies: the Comptroller of the Currency, responsible for all national banks; and the Federal Deposit Insurance Corporation, an agency responsible for insuring bank-deposit liabilities up to a maximum of $20,000 per depositor. Failure to comply with prudent financial practices and Federal Reserve regulations can result in suspension of a commercial bank's affiliation with the Federal Reserve System or forced changes in bank management. In addition, the Federal Reserve can limit the interest rates commercial banks may pay on time deposits, a power designed to curb competitive bidding-up of interest rates to the point where bank solvency is endangered.

## GOVERNMENT'S FISCAL AGENT

The Treasury uses the Federal Reserve as its fiscal agent. Being a large business in its own right, the federal government uses Federal Reserve Banks to sell and redeem government bonds or securities and maintain Treasury deposit accounts. The Treasury replenishes its funds and refinances the public debt by selling government securities to the public and to commercial banks through the Federal Reserve System. However, only a small portion of Treasury deposits are held in Federal Reserve Banks. Over two-thirds of all commercial banks in the United States maintain checking accounts for the Treasury, called *tax and loan accounts*. When the government needs additional funds, it simply notifies Federal Reserve authorities, who announce to each commercial bank the date and amount of funds the Treasury will "call" for its tax and loan account. As government's fiscal agent, the Federal Reserve also supplies currency. Most of the currency in circulation today consists of Federal Reserve Notes, paper debts of the Federal Reserve placed in circulation through the commercial-banking system.

## THE FEDERAL RESERVE AS A "BANKER'S BANK"

The three major services provided by the Federal Reserve to commercial banks are: (*a*) holding commercial-bank reserves on deposit, (*b*) clearing commercial-bank checks, and (*c*) granting occasional loans to the commercial-banking community.

Commercial banks are required by law to maintain reserves equal to a stipulated fraction or percent of *both* time- and demand-deposit liabilities. Reserves are held by the Federal Reserve System in the ratios specified on page 224 for different classes of banks. Because the Federal Reserve holds reserves for commercial banks, it can transfer funds from one bank to another to facilitate clearing checks. When a check for $100 is written against a Houston bank and is deposited in a commercial bank located in Detroit, the Federal Reserve simply:

1. Reduces the Houston bank's reserves by $100.
2. Increases the Detroit bank's reserves by $100.

Finally, on certain occasions central banks lend funds on a temporary and short-term basis to commercial banks in need of reserves.

| Class of bank | Demand-deposit reserve ratio (percent) | Time-deposit reserve ratio (percent) |
|---|---|---|
| Reserve-city banks | 17.5 | 3 |
| Country banks | 13.0 | 3 |

SOURCE: *Federal Reserve Bulletin* (October 1970). (As of October 1970 for banks with $5 million or more in demand deposits.)

## MONEY MANAGEMENT

By far the most important function of the Federal Reserve is control of the money supply, which it accomplishes through its control over bank reserves. The central bank can influence the amount of demand-deposit money created by commercial banks, thus affecting the interest rate, investment expenditures, and the level of economic activity. The commercial-banking system may alter the money supply by granting loans and creating deposits, as we know, *but only* if excess reserves exist. The Federal Reserve regulates the demand-deposit component of the money supply by altering the volume of total reserves *and* by changing the fraction of reserves commercial banks are required to hold against deposit liabilities.

### Operation of the Central Bank

The way in which the Federal Reserve System performs its four basic functions is most readily seen through examination of a consolidated balance sheet. Figure 2 is a summary balance sheet for the Federal Reserve System which relates Federal Reserve activities to the United States Treasury as well as to member commercial banks. Each year, more currency is placed in circulation to accommodate the needs of a growing economy. The amount of Federal Reserve Notes needed are printed by the Federal Reserve and circulate as the central bank's IOU. Figure 2 also shows that government securities are the single most important asset of the Federal Reserve System. The two most significant liabilities of the central bank shown in Figure 2 are Federal Reserve Notes (paper currency) and member-bank reserves. When less paper currency is needed by the public, as after the Christmas season, currency flows into commercial banks, increasing member-bank reserves, which are deposited in the central bank. Thus, circulating Federal Reserve Note liabilities decline. Federal Reserve Notes are placed in circulation when the central bank purchases a government security (or any other asset) from the public. If the buyer of a government security is a member commercial bank, however, its reserves increase, but paper currency in circulation *outside* the banking system (the money supply) remains unchanged.

Even though paper currency has not been domestically convertible into gold since 1933, the United States Treasury does buy and sell gold. The assets labeled "gold certificates" in Figure 2 are paper receipts for gold the Federal Reserve purchases from the Treasury. When the Federal Reserve

**FIGURE 2** Consolidated Balance Sheet, All Federal Reserve Banks
(billions of dollars)

| A | | L | |
|---|---|---|---|
| U.S. government securities | $57.7 | $47.7 | Federal Reserve Notes |
| Gold certificates | 11.0 | 23.0 | Member-bank reserves |
| Loans to member banks | .4 | 1.2 | Treasury deposits |
| Other | 11.8 | 9.0 | Other |
| Total | $80.9 | $80.9 | Total |

SOURCE: *Federal Reserve Bulletin* (July 1970), p. A 12. (As of June 1970.)

acquires more gold certificates, it simply increases the federal government's checking account (Treasury deposits). At one time, the Federal Reserve was required to hold $1 in gold certificates for every $4 in Federal Reserve Notes, as well as for every $4 of commercial-bank reserves.[2] While we shall have more to say about the monetary role of gold later, it is sufficient to note here that Treasury gold is held by the Federal Reserve in the form of gold certificates. Today, Federal Reserve liabilities are backed up by other central-bank assets, the most important being government securities.

Although reserve deposits are liabilities of the Federal Reserve, as Figure 2 illustrates, they are assets to a commercial bank, just as the funds in a checking account are assets to the depositor. Member banks draw on or add to their reserve account just as the public uses a checking account, except that commercial banks *must* maintain a required amount of reserves, as dictated by the required-reserve ratio. By holding reserve deposits, the central bank provides an orderly mechanism for settling demand-deposit claims against commercial banks throughout the nation. The acceptability of demand-deposit money is considerably enhanced through this check-clearing service, which is provided for member banks at no cost. The 12 Federal Reserve Banks coordinate check-clearing activities via the Inter-district Settlement Fund. Finally, note that assets entitled "loans to member banks" indicate, as we have said before, that the Federal Reserve does on occasion lend funds to commercial banks.

Figure 3 summarizes our discussion of the Federal Reserve in terms of its primary purpose of managing the money supply. Remember, increases in the money supply ease interest rates, encouraging investment spending and expansion in NNP and employment. In contrast, as the money supply contracts, interest rates rise and investment demand and NNP tend to contract. The money supply and credit available in the economy are determined by central-bank authorities through four tools of monetary policy.

1. The sale and purchase of securities on the open market by the Federal Reserve alter the *volume of total reserves* held by commercial banks; these are the base used to create more demand-deposit money.

[2] Both requirements have since been repealed, as indicated in Chapter 10.

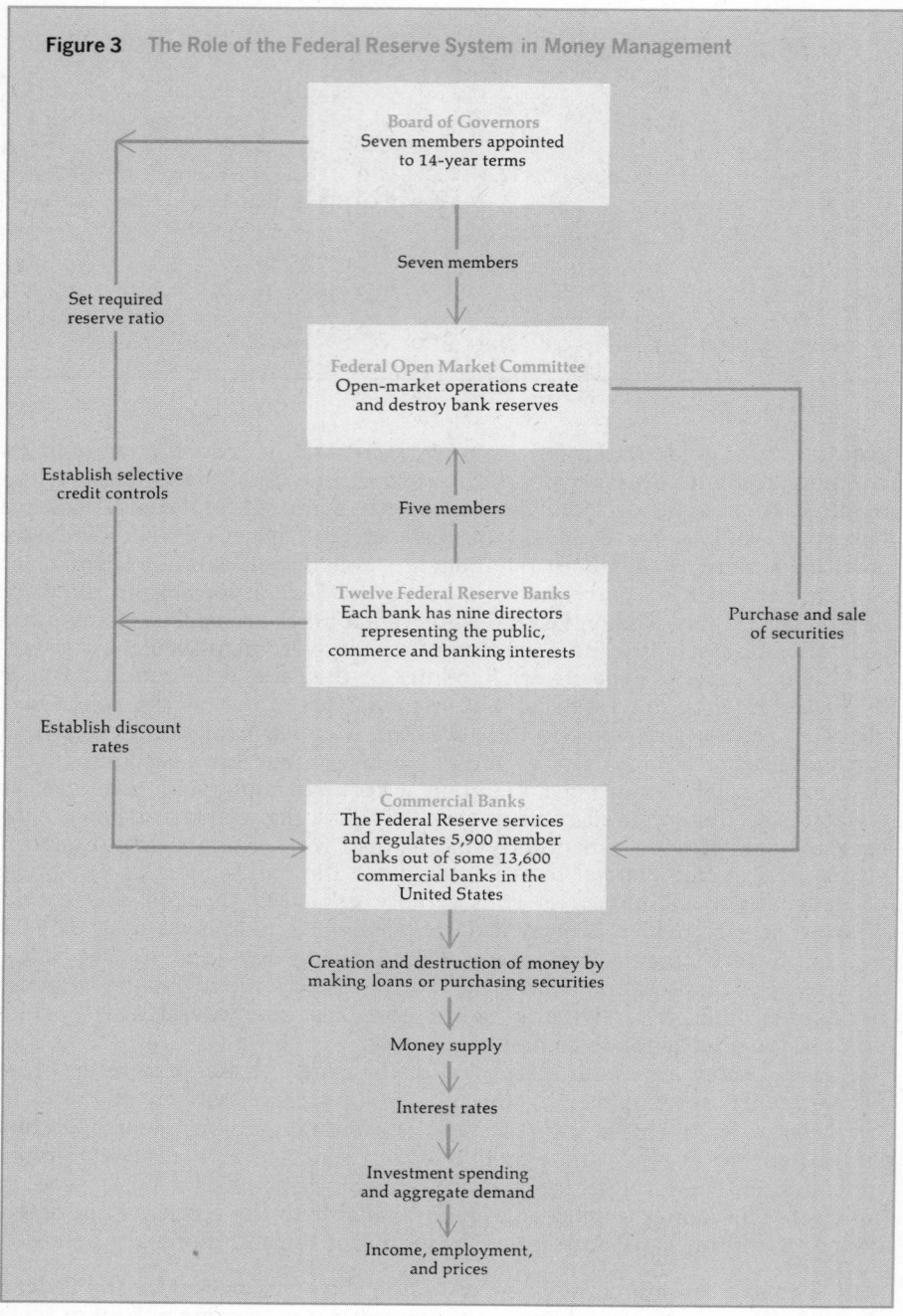

**Figure 3**  The Role of the Federal Reserve System in Money Management

Board of Governors
Seven members appointed
to 14-year terms

Set required
reserve ratio

Seven members

Federal Open Market Committee
Open-market operations create
and destroy bank reserves

Establish selective
credit controls

Five members

Twelve Federal Reserve Banks
Each bank has nine directors
representing the public,
commerce and banking interests

Purchase and sale
of securities

Establish discount
rates

Commercial Banks
The Federal Reserve services
and regulates 5,900 member
banks out of some 13,600
commercial banks in the
United States

Creation and destruction of money by
making loans or purchasing securities

Money supply

Interest rates

Investment spending
and aggregate demand

Income, employment,
and prices

2. The central bank also uses monetary policy by varying the required-reserve ratio, an act that alters *excess reserves* while leaving total reserves unchanged.

3. When short-term loans are granted to commercial banks, the central bank charges a *discount rate*. When the discount rate on loans granted member banks by the Federal Reserve is changed, commercial-bank credit terms are altered and the likelihood of commercial banks borrowing from the central bank also changes.

4. Finally, a variety of "selective" credit controls may be used to influence borrowing in specific sectors of the economy.

These "tools" of monetary policy are the primary weapons used by central-bank authorities to stabilize the economy. Our task is to see how monetary policy is implemented to achieve full employment, stable prices, and growth in income.

## B. THE TOOLS OF MONETARY POLICY

Today transactions in securities on the open market are the tool most frequently used by the Federal Reserve to implement monetary policy. We shall first discuss how open-market operations affect the volume of reserves and then examine the reserve ratio, the discount rate, and selective credit controls in that order.

### Open-Market Policy

Open-market policy influences *total* bank reserves and thus the money supply, interest rates, and income. Both commercial banks and the Federal Reserve own government securities. By selling or buying securities on the open market, the Federal Reserve allows commercial banks or the nonbank public to swap investments in government IOUs for more liquid currency assets. When the central bank wants to initiate an expansion of the money supply to create easy-money conditions, it *buys* government securities held by commercial banks, the total volume of commercial-bank reserves rises, interest rates soften, and a potential for multiple expansion of the money supply is created. When the Federal Reserve *sells* securities, the total volume of commercial-bank reserves declines, interest rates tend to rise, a basis is established for contraction of the money supply, and monetary policy is said to be repressive or tight.

### OPEN-MARKET POLICY AND INFLATION

Suppose Federal Reserve authorities sense that inflationary pressures are gaining a toehold (as occurred in 1968 and 1969), and they wish to restrict aggregate demand and increases in money NNP. The Federal Open Market Committee then *sells* securities on the open market either to commercial banks or to the public, both of whom can be induced to invest if yields on the investment are attractive. When the central bank sells large amounts of securities, the market price of these paper assets is driven down and the yield on government bonds rises. Consequently, interest rates in general tend to rise as bond yields rise. Moreover, the rise in interest rates heralds more intense competition for limited funds; that is, the availability of credit is restricted.

Representing total reserves by $R$, securities by $S$, loans by $L$, and deposit liabilities by $D$, the impact of the sale of government securities to commercial banks is shown by Balance Sheet I, below. The Federal Reserve's multi-billion-dollar inventory of government securities declines $(-S)$ as shown in t-account A. The loss of these paper assets is matched by an equal reduction in Federal Reserve liabilities to the commercial-banking system, which pays for securities by drawing down reserves $(-R)$. When a commercial

**BALANCE SHEET I** Restrictive Monetary Policy

| A | B | | C |
|---|---|---|---|
| Federal Reserve sells securities | Commercial banks buy securities | | Commercial-bank depositor buys securities |

| A | L | | A | L | | | A | L |
|---|---|---|---|---|---|---|---|---|
| $-S$ | $-R$ | | $-R$ $+S$ | | *but if the public buys securities from the Federal Reserve* | | $-R$ | $-D$ |

bank purchases government securities it gains an interest-earning bond $(+S)$ and loses reserves $(-R)$ used to pay for the newly acquired government securities, as shown in t-account B. Since the Federal Open Market Committee sells securities on the open market, the transaction may also involve the nonbank public, including such large financial firms as insurance companies. When the public pays for securities by check, commercial-bank demand deposits decline $(-D)$ and the bank loses reserves as the public's check is cleared against it, as shown in t-account C.

Open-market transactions with the public have an immediate impact on the money supply, whereas direct transactions with commercial banks affect reserves only. When the commercial-banking system buys $10 million of securities from the Federal Reserve, *both* total and excess reserves decline by $10 million. When the public buys securities, however, there is a smaller impact on excess reserves, but an immediate reduction in demand deposits (the money supply). Using an illustrative reserve ratio of 20 percent, *required reserves* would decline by 20 percent of the $10 million decline in deposit liabilities (or $2 million) when the public buys securities with its checkbook money, while total reserves would decline by $10 million. Therefore, excess reserves decline by $8 million. Although there is a difference between the impact of the sale of securities to the commercial-banking system compared to sales to the public, bear in mind that the similarities are even more important. The sale of securities to either group reduces bank reserves, thus contributing to a reduction in the money supply and higher interest rates which can help halt inflation.

*Conclusion:* By selling securities, central-bank authorities tighten up on monetary conditions and commercial-bank reserves decline, thus restricting the demand-deposit component of the money supply.

Federal Reserve purchases of securities increase commercial-bank reserves in a similar fashion. The generation of excess reserves may in turn increase the money supply and ease credit conditions. As the central bank expands the money supply by purchasing securities, the market prices of bonds rise, yields decline, and general interest rates soften. All of this stimulates economic activity by increasing aggregate demand. When the Federal Reserve purchases securities from the commercial-banking system, commercial-bank reserves increase and the central bank acquires additional securities, as shown below in t-accounts A and B in Balance Sheet II. If the Federal Reserve buys securities from the public, the money supply increases *directly* and demand deposits and commercial-bank reserves rise, as shown in t-account C.

---

**BALANCE SHEET II** Expansionary Monetary Policy

| A | B | | C |
|---|---|---|---|
| Federal Reserve buys securities | Commercial bank sells securities | | Commercial-bank depositor sells securities |

| A | L | A | L | | A | L |
|---|---|---|---|---|---|---|
| $+S$ | $+R$ | $+R$ $-S$ | | *but if the public sells securities to the Federal Reserve* | $+R$ | $+D$ |

---

One final point about open-market policy is worth noting. Tight monetary policy stemming from the sale of securities by the Federal Reserve generates a compulsory contraction in the money supply because commercial banks must reduce loans and deposit liabilities to meet the legally established reserve ratio. In contrast, although security purchases by the Federal Reserve expand commercial-bank reserves, the public is not compelled to borrow, nor are banks compelled to invest excess reserves. Since bankers do not like to hold large amounts of idle reserves which could otherwise earn interest, the inducements to lend are strong as excess reserves build up. The public likewise is encouraged to step up spending by obtaining additional credit because of the lower interest rates stemming from excess reserves. However, the policy is not foolproof. One major historical exception to the effectiveness of excess reserves in overcoming a deflationary gap occurred between 1934 and 1940, when excess reserves ranged from $1 billion to more than $6 billion.

### The Discount Rate

Discount-rate policy affects bank reserves and the money supply by raising or lowering the cost of borrowing from the central bank. When a commercial bank borrows from the Federal Reserve, it is charged an interest rate, just as the public is charged for the privilege of borrowing from a commercial bank. Usually commercial banks use their own holdings of government securities as collateral, although in years past banks frequently sold or "discounted" the loan obligations of customers to whom they had granted loans.

Suppose that the commercial-banking system is currently loaned up (excess reserves = 0), and the Federal Reserve wishes to expand the money supply to counteract unemployment and increase income. Lowering the discount rate may encourage commercial banks to borrow from the central bank as shown in t-account A of Balance Sheet III. The central bank regards a loan (denoted by $L$) granted to a commercial bank as an asset (a liability of a commercial bank), and commercial-bank reserves rise. Commercial-bank reserves decline in t-account B when the central bank raises the

**BALANCE SHEET III** Changes in the Discount Rate

|  | A | | | | B | | | |
|---|---|---|---|---|---|---|---|---|
|  | Lowering the discount rate to create easy money | | | | Raising the discount rate to create tight money | | | |
|  | Federal Reserve | | Commercial bank | | Federal Reserve | | Commercial bank | |
| | A | L | A | L | A | L | A | L |
| | +L | +R | +R | +L | −L | −R | −R | −L |

discount rate, because the commercial-banking system is less inclined to borrow. As the cost of borrowing increases, interest rates in general tend to rise simply because bankers cannot profitably operate if the interest rate they charge does not exceed the discount rate they are charged for borrowing reserves. Lowering the discount rate, then, has an expansionary impact on commercial-bank reserves and the money supply. Raising the discount rate encourages commercial banks to increase the interest rate they charge customers and discourages borrowing from the Federal Reserve, leading to a reduction in reserves, bank credit, and demand deposits.

Since central-bank loans to commercial banks amount to only between 1 and 4 percent of total bank reserves, discount policy is less important than open-market policy. As a matter of fact, central-bank authorities discourage commercial banks from borrowing on a long-term basis; they prefer to have commercial banks adjust their reserves through open-market security transactions. Discount policy is sometimes called a "passive" control device because altering the discount rate to change excess reserves is expansionary or contractionary *only if* commercial banks and the borrowing public respond to Federal Reserve policy. However, the announcement of a hike or drop in the discount rate usually has a psychological impact, tending to prompt a rise or decline in the interest rates charged on short-term loans by financial institutions. Tight conditions in the money market may also contribute to declines in stock and bond prices to bring yields on existing securities into line with current interest rates. Stock-market reactions of this sort typified the market declines of 1966 and 1969–1970, whereas announced reductions in the discount rate in 1967 and earlier in 1959 triggered stock-market booms.

In conclusion, *lowering the discount rate is expansionary* whereas *raising the discount rate is contractionary*. Discount-rate policy is important because it affects the willingness of member banks to borrow reserves from the Federal Reserve, and also because it is a general indicator of changes in short-term interest rates and the availability of credit.

## Required Reserves

A third power given to the Federal Reserve in 1935 allows it to change the commercial-banking system's excess reserves by altering the required-reserve ratio. A decrease in the reserve ratio from 20 percent to 10 percent, for example, tends to be expansionary in two ways. First, it generates excess reserves that may be used by commercial banks to expand loans and demand-deposit liabilities. In addition, a decrease in the reserve ratio increases the multiple by which the money supply expands. Remember, the deposit-expansion factor is a multiple defined as the reciprocal of the reserve ratio (1/reserve ratio).

Figure 4 shows how a *decrease* in the reserve ratio from 20 percent to 10 percent frees $2 billion in excess reserves and allows expansion of the potential money supply in the commercial-banking system by $20 billion, or the amount of excess reserves times a deposit-expansion factor of 10 (1/reserve ratio = 1/0.10 in this instance). Alternatively, an *increase* in the reserve requirement from 20 percent to 33 percent of deposit liabilities has a contractionary impact. If the commercial-banking system cannot meet required reserves because of an increase in the reserve ratio (that is, excess reserves are negative), a multiple contraction of the money supply is

**FIGURE 4** Changes in Reserve Requirements (billions of dollars)

| (1) Legal-reserve ratio (percent) | (2) Deposit-expansion factor | (3) Demand-deposit liabilities | (4) Total reserves | (5) Required reserves (1) × (3) | (6) Excess reserves (4) — (5) | (7) Potential change in the money supply (6) × (2) |
|---|---|---|---|---|---|---|
| 10 | 1/0.10 = 10 | $20 | $4 | $2 | +$2 | +$20 |
| 20 | 1/0.20 = 5 | 20 | 4 | 4 | 0 | 0 |
| 33 | 1/0.33 = 3 | 20 | 4 | 6⅔ | − 2⅔ | − 8 |

**Reserves and the Money Supply.** The Federal Reserve raises or lowers required reserves [column (5)] through changes in the reserve ratio [column (1)]. The potential change in the money supply is shown by excess reserves × the deposit-expansion factor.

forced and commercial banks are required to liquidate loans and investments. As before, money-supply contraction due to insufficient reserves is assured, but an expansion of the money supply and income level due to excess reserves depends on the willingness of banks, business firms, and households to lend and borrow.

### Selective Credit Controls

Open-market operations, the discount rate, and the reserve ratio are called *general credit controls* because they leave commercial banks free to determine how to allocate the available credit among different types of borrowers. *Selective credit controls* generally have a direct impact on specific sectors in the economy. Although they are not widely relied upon, selective credit controls can have an important temporary impact. Four significant selective credit controls are: (*a*) moral suasion, (*b*) margin requirements on stock purchases, (*c*) credit terms, and (*d*) interest-rate ceilings.

#### MORAL SUASION

Federal Reserve authorities sometimes subtly "suggest" that commercial banks restrict or ease up on lending policy. Although persuasion is not thought to be of great significance, it is reasonable to assume that commercial bankers do not completely ignore appeals made by Federal Reserve authorities, particularly since the latter conduct audits and are otherwise responsible for examination of commercial banks.

#### MARGIN REQUIREMENTS

The Board of Governors sets the *margin requirement*—the "downpayment" required on stock purchases. In recent years, individuals purchasing stocks on margin have been required to provide up to 90 percent of the purchase price as a cash downpayment. Margin requirements are lowered (as they were in the early Summer of 1970) to encourage economic expansion and are raised when tight-money conditions are desired. Although the margin requirement is designed to control such wild stock-market speculations as those of 1929—when one could purchase stocks on as little as 10 percent margin—it also is a monetary signal to the financial community similar to a change in the discount rate.

#### CREDIT TERMS

Federal Reserve authorities may also influence bank lending by altering downpayment requirements and the length of repayment time applicable to installment purchases of certain goods. During World War II and the Korean War, installment-credit terms were directly controlled for some consumer goods like automobiles and appliances through "Regulation W," and home mortgages were selectively controlled through "Regulation X." By 1952 the authority for these selective credit controls lapsed, although when severe inflation threatens, pressures for similar controls tend to mount. While selective control of credit terms can be an effective device in restraining or expanding credit, the money supply, and economic expansion, the very directness of such controls is bound to create hostility on the part of those interest groups adversely affected.

A fourth selective control invoked in recent years allows the Federal Reserve to set a maximum level for interest rates paid by commercial banks on time deposits. Commercial banks are prohibited from paying interest rates on demand deposits and are also limited by "Regulation Q" as to the rate that can be paid on time deposits. The importance of "Regulation Q" is that the variations in the interest rates on savings accounts that can be paid by regulated commercial banks and unregulated financial intermediaries may lead to a flow of funds between commercial banks and other financial institutions (e.g., savings and loan banks) that deal in near-monies.

In the 1950s competition for savings deposits broke out among financial institutions, particularly between savings and loan associations and commercial banks. Because of rising yields on government bonds and the ability of savings and loan associations to pay higher interest rates, commercial banks lost time deposits and total bank reserves declined. Federal Reserve authorities then raised the interest-rate ceiling that commercial banks could pay on time deposits, and thus channeled a flow of funds back to commercial banks. Still later, in 1969, central-bank authorities countered inflationary pressures by driving the general level of interest rates upwards without raising "Regulation Q" which allows commercial banks to pay higher interest rates on time deposits. Consequently, commercial-bank reserves were placed under additional pressures until 1970, when interest rates were allowed to increase under "Regulation Q". An uneasy and tenuous peace prevails between commercial banks and financial intermediaries concerning interest-rate regulations, and "Regulation Q" is now widely recognized as an instrument of monetary policy.

Aside from their limited effectiveness, the problem of selective credit controls stems from concerns about the equity of interfering with selected sectors within the economy. As funds flowed away from commercial banks to savings and loan associations in the late 1950s, for example, the housing-construction industry benefited, because financial intermediaries service that sector of the economy to a large extent. Imposing the cost of credit restraint selectively on some sectors of the economy is understandably challenged by those who bear the brunt of such a policy. For this reason, the Federal Reserve has relied heavily on general money-supply controls.

## C. MONEY MANAGEMENT IN ACTION

The extent to which monetary policy is tight or easy is not fully reflected by any one statistical measure. However, one of the more interesting indicators of monetary policy at work is the difference in excess reserves and the amount of funds commercial banks borrow from the Federal Reserve System. In addition, the overall character of monetary policy can be summarized conveniently by examining the reserve equation. Let us look at these two ideas further.

### Free Reserves

*Free reserves* are *excess reserves* less *borrowed reserves* (commercial-bank loans from the Federal Reserve System). If excess reserves are larger than borrowed reserves, free reserves are positive. In contrast, when excess reserves are smaller than borrowed reserves, free reserves are negative, as shown in Figure 5 for the period 1968–1970.

Although individual commercial banks attempt to hold excess reserves to a minimum, the entire banking system normally retains a modest margin of excess reserves which can amount to a rather sizable figure. In recent years, for example, excess reserves for all member banks have ranged from $200 to $500 million, as Figure 5 shows. Although the volume of total reserves has increased steadily in the last quarter of a century, Figure 5 clearly indicates that commercial banks avail themselves erratically of the discount privilege. Tight-money conditions required to dampen excess aggregate demand are characterized by declining excess reserves and rising borrowed reserves. In periods like the late 1960s, this combination generated negative free reserves as money conditions tightened. In contrast, easy-money conditions are characterized by positive free reserves, the result of rising excess reserves and declining borrowed reserves, as is seen in the figure for the period 1960–1965. After the recession of 1960–1961, Federal Reserve authorities eased up their monetary policy, as the substantial amount of positive free reserves for that period indicates.

Borrowed reserves may rise initially in an expansion if commercial banks need reserves to back up the expansion of credit, a trend that continues as long as the interest rates paid by the borrowing public can be increased to cover a higher discount rate. Increases in the discount rate during the latter 1960s tended to discourage more borrowing than that shown in Figure 5, but also pushed the general level of interest rates up. Normally, higher discount and interest rates serve to ration credit and ultimately to slow down the economy, provided that the precise timing and amplitude needed are gauged correctly—a difficult matter which we will discuss later. As negative

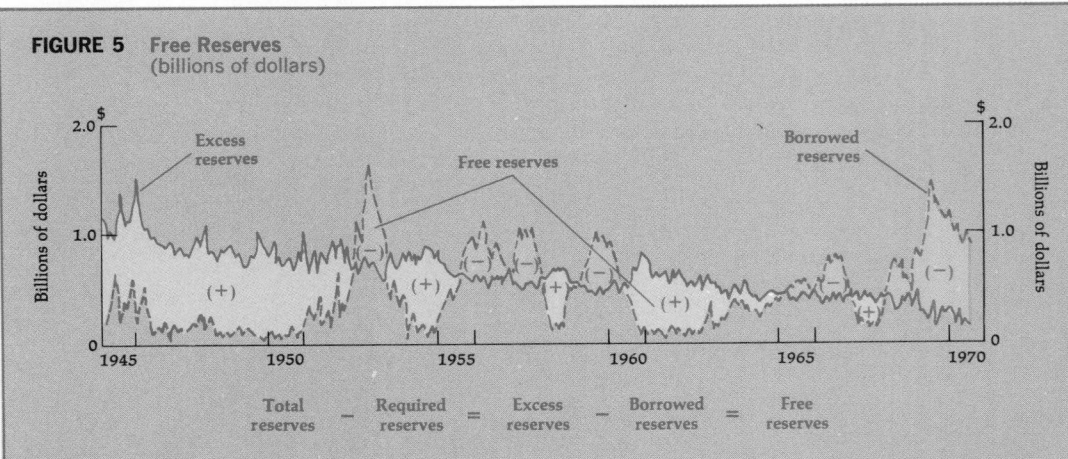

**FIGURE 5**  Free Reserves
(billions of dollars)

*Free Reserves in Member Banks.* Free reserves will be positive and indicative of easy money (as in 1961-1962 when borrowed reserves were much smaller than excess reserves). In contrast, free reserves are negative under tight-money conditions (e.g., 1968-early 1970). Free reserves are negative because reserves borrowed from the Federal Reserve System exceed all commercial-bank excess reserves.

SOURCE: *Federal Reserve Bulletin.*

free reserves appear, interest rates soar, the stock market may plunge, and industrial production and income gradually level out as they did in the latter part of 1966 and in 1970. By early 1967, for example, investment spending appeared to have slacked off and the Federal Reserve, fearing a more serious downturn, lowered the discount rate and began to expand total reserves within the commercial-banking system through open-market purchases of securities. Some critics of the Board of Governors felt that the Federal Reserve eased up too soon and argued that inflation was a paramount danger during 1966–1967, while other observers feared a recession. Easing up in 1967 proved to be premature, partly because rising defense expenditures and escalation of the Vietnam War resulted in expansive fiscal policy. By late 1968 it was clear that inflation was a problem, and despite the tight-money pressures revealed by the negative free reserves shown in Figure 5, the 1960s closed in the throes of severe inflationary pressures.

## The Reserve Equation

The simplest way to summarize the potential impact of Federal Reserve policy and related financial transactions on the money supply and level of economic activity is to compare all *sources* of commercial-bank reserves, sometimes called the "monetary base," to all *competing uses* for these reserves.[3] Using data compiled by the Federal Reserve on all sources and uses of potential commercial-bank reserves, we find that

$$\text{Reserve sources} - \text{reserve uses} = \text{total resources}$$

The commercial-banking system's supply of total reserves, consisting of deposits in the central bank plus vault cash, will increase provided that reserve sources rise or competing uses decline. Conversely, the volume of total reserves declines when sources of reserves decline or competing uses rise. Figure 6 is a partially consolidated balance sheet of the Treasury and Federal Reserve that identifies the primary sources of bank reserves, all of which could be used *entirely* for member-bank reserves if there were no competing nonbank uses.

### RESERVE SOURCES

The major source of commercial-bank reserves, described in Figure 6 as "Federal Reserve credit," consists of: (a) government securities held by the central bank, (b) loans extended to the commercial-banking system when it utilizes the discount privilege, and (c) a credit balance, termed "float" that the central bank extends to commercial banks in the check-clearing process. *Float* is credit extended by the central bank due to delay in reducing member-bank reserves when checks are cleared—credit somewhat comparable to short-term loans granted by the Federal Reserve System. Central-bank purchases of government securities or loans to the commercial-banking system cause total reserve sources to rise, while Federal Reserve sales on the open market are contractionary. The item shown in Figure 6 as "gold stock" represents the quantity of funds made available as the Treasury buys and sells gold, "Treasury currency" is the coin and paper

[3] A more complete and technically accurate description of the monetary base is presented in Jerry L. Jordan, "The Monetary Base—Explanation and Analytical Use," in Federal Reserve Bank of St. Louis, *Review* (August 1969), pp. 7–11.

| Sources | | Uses | | Total reserves |
|---|---|---|---|---|
| Federal Reserve credit (securities, loans, float) | $62.8 | Currency in circulation outside banking system | $54.1 | |
| Gold stock | 11.4 | Treasury cash and deposits (cash and Federal Reserve deposits) | 1.6 | |
| Treasury currency | 7.0 | | | |
| Vault cash | 4.9 | Foreign and other deposits (includes capital account) | 2.7 | |
| Total reserve sources | $86.1 less | Total reserve uses | $58.4 equals | $27.7 |

*Total Reserves.* The primary sources of bank reserves (consisting of Federal Reserve credit, gold stock, Treasury currency, and vault cash) less all uses, equal total reserves. Thus, if sources remain unchanged and uses (e.g., currency in circulation outside the banking system) rise, total reserves will decline.

SOURCE: *Federal Reserve Bulletin* (July 1970), p. A 5. (Data as of June 1970.)

currency issued by the Treasury, and "vault cash" is a reserve source of currency held in commercial banks for operating purposes. An increase in any of the four sources of the monetary base shown in Figure 6 is an expansionary policy move because it may cause commercial-bank reserves to rise.

RESERVE USES

Currency circulating outside commercial banks is the largest competing *use* for potential bank reserves. While it is in the hands of the public, currency is *not* within the commercial-banking system where it could be used as reserves, either in the form of vault cash or deposits in the Federal Reserve. When the central bank gives a wealthy Boston dowager $25,000 for government bonds, for example, commercial-bank reserves will increase *only if* these funds (usually Federal Reserve Notes) are deposited in a commercial bank. Commercial-bank reserves *will not* increase if the proceeds are kept as currency in circulation. Furthermore, when the Treasury holds cash, such funds are not available to the commercial-banking system. For that matter, any deposit the Federal Reserve holds for the Treasury or a foreign nation cannot be regarded as usable for reserves.

*In summary:* Subtracting competing uses from all sources of reserve credit leaves the amount of total reserves available to the commercial-banking system inclusive of vault cash. Any increase in sources or decrease in uses of reserves is expansionary, an appropriate policy when unemployment and a sluggish economy prevail. The converse policy is required for an overheated economy. Remember, though, that lowering or raising the reserve ratio, as well as selective credit controls, have an important role in monetary policy that is not shown in Figure 6. The reserve-source and use relationship shown in Figure 6 describes factors affecting the *volume of total reserves*, whereas the amount of free reserves depends on open-market operations, the reserve ratio, and the discount rate simultaneously.

Money is generally conceded to be an important determinant of income and employment, but opinion is divided on the relative importance of money and monetary policy. The case for monetary policy rests largely on the timely impact of monetary action. Unlike fiscal policy, Federal Reserve decisions to expand or contract commercial-bank reserves need not be characterized by long decision-making delays and the time-consuming procedure of obtaining Congressional approval. Although monetary policy is somewhat more adaptable than fiscal policy to changing economic conditions, it is also subject to certain built-in limitations that detract from its effectiveness.

GOLD FLOWS

Despite the fact that the gold standard was abandoned in 1933, gold flows stemming from international trade between nations can affect monetary policy. Although we shall have more to say about international trade later, it is important here to understand how gold flows and central-bank policies are related.

When a nation like the United States sells less abroad than it buys, other nations end up holding paper debts of the United States (e.g., currency) that can be readily converted into gold. Gold *outflows* reduce domestic bank reserves and, if there are no excess reserves, can force a contraction in the money supply. In contrast, when the U.S. sells more abroad than it buys, foreign nations in need of American dollars send foreign currency claims on gold to the United States. United States government agencies may acquire gold, paying exporters who normally deposit their funds in banks; thus, bank reserves increase. In short, gold *inflows* bring new reserves and money-creating potential to commercial banks. The simplest way to remember how gold flows increase or decrease bank reserves is to think in terms of the reserve equation shown in Figure 6, where gold represented a source of reserves.[4] Potential expansion or contraction in the domestic money supply due to international gold flows occurs outside the purview of the Federal Reserve, but can be neutralized by the central bank. For example, in a nation already at full employment, neutralization of the expansionary gold inflow requires simply that the Federal Reserve reduce its holdings of government securities (another source of reserves) through the sale of bonds on the open market.

---

[4] The way in which a gold flow affects commercial-bank reserves is as follows: Suppose a foreign central bank holds the check of an American auto dealer who has purchased foreign goods and services for $100. Commercial-bank deposits and reserves decline by $100, and if the foreign central bank desires gold (G) rather than Federal Reserve Notes, the Treasury draws upon its deposits (TD) and instructs the Federal Reserve to retire $100 of gold certificate (GC), which are liabilities of the Treasury and assets of the central bank. Thus, a direct decline of $100 occurs in the money supply, commercial-bank reserves, and gold.

| Treasury | | Federal Reserve | | Commercial bank | |
|---|---|---|---|---|---|
| A | L | A | L | A | L |
| −G | −GC | −GC | −TD | −R | −D |

A special problem may arise when the central bank maintains easy-money policies if unemployment and prolonged gold outflows occur simultaneously. In this instance, there is a conflict between a stabilizing monetary policy, which demands low interest rates, and maintaining a balance in international payments. The Federal Reserve could neutralize decreases in reserves due to a gold outflow by purchasing government securities, but buying securities may drive bond prices up and reduce U.S. interest rates relative to other nations. As a consequence, funds may flow abroad even more rapidly in search of higher interest returns in other nations, thus intensifying the gold drain. Since the early 1950s, the gold stock in the United States has declined from $25 billion to about $12 billion, partly for this reason. Even though the United States still has over one-fourth of the free world's supply of gold, it is possible that continued gold outflows could restrict the central bank's gold-neutralization capability and hamper the use of expansionary domestic monetary policies.

## CONFLICT WITH TREASURY OBJECTIVES

Sometimes the Federal Reserve's twofold task of acting as the government's banker and serving as manager of the money supply conflict. The United States Treasury is a very large debtor which cannot help but be interested in the costs of servicing its debt. Some one-third of a trillion dollars of outstanding bonds finance the national debt, and a 1 percent increase in interest rates costs the United States government something like $3 billion annually. During and after World War II the Federal Reserve openly accommodated Treasury financing needs by buying large quantities of government securities to maintain low interest rates.[5] This policy added to commercial-bank reserves and prompted easy-money conditions for the 1945–1953 period, as Figure 5 showed. Even though postwar inflationary pressures were severe, between 1946 and 1951 the Board of Governors chose not to sell government bonds as contractionary monetary policy demanded. In short, monetary policy for stabilization purposes was subordinated to cheap Treasury financing of government indebtedness. Many observers argued during the 1946–1951 period that the Federal Reserve should check inflation first and let government bond prices deteriorate and interest rates rise. The central bank finally broke with the Treasury and withdrew its support of bonds in an agreement the Treasury and the Federal Reserve hammered out in 1952.[6]

## THE PROBLEM OF TIMING IMPACTS

Even though central-bank authorities can generate sufficient pressures to contract the money supply in inflation and theoretically can induce an expansion of demand deposits by creating excess reserves under less than

---

[5] The money supply more than doubled from 1940 to 1945.

[6] The semiautonomous character of the Board of Governors, a unique feature of central banking in this nation, has repeatedly allowed the Federal Reserve to follow politically unpopular, but nonetheless stabilizing economic policies. During the late 1960s, for example, a tight-money policy was not in the best political interest of President Johnson nor of his successor, President Nixon. Without monetary brakes, however, the Vietnam inflation could have been much more serious, since government expenditures continued to fuel inflation in an already fully employed economy.

full-employment conditions, proper timing is crucial. The Board of Governors must assess both the current state of economic health and its future direction in terms of the full-employment goal. This is why economic indicators like free reserves, prices, unemployment, and investment are so important. Even with the wealth of data available today, however, determining with any degree of precision how close we are to a turning point in an inflationary boom or an economic downturn is neither an easy nor a comfortable task. How long will expansion last? Is it severe and rapid enough to require repressive pressures now or six months from now? How long will it be before the money supply reacts to monetary policies? What type of time lag exists before firms and households react to changes in the interest rate, or will they react at all? The consensus among many observers is that monetary policy has a decided but delayed impact on NNP, leading to changes in the economy some six to twelve months after action is first taken. Timing and forecasting the state of the economy are even more crucial for this reason, and it is very possible to err in prescribing monetary policy.

## DIFFERENTIAL AND UNCERTAIN IMPACTS

A fourth problem associated with monetary policy centers upon the uncertain and differential impact of changes in the money supply. In the first place, the mere creation of excess reserves by Federal Reserve authorities may not produce anticipated increases in the money supply, as we know. If commercial banks want excess liquidity or the public is not interested in borrowing, demand deposits and therefore spending may not respond, a dilemma that occurred in the late 1930s even though billions of dollars of excess reserves existed. In addition, changes in the demand for money balances may offset restrictive or expansive monetary policies.

Furthermore, the distributional impact of monetary policy is not uniform for all sectors served by the commercial-banking system. New, small, and less credit-worthy borrowers are the first to be squeezed when monetary conditions tighten. Well-established, large customers enjoy preferred treatment while the credit-rationing process restricts borrowers who are less secure. In addition, monetary policy tends to affect the construction industry, for example, more severely than many other sectors of the economy. This is what happened to residential construction in the "credit crunch" of 1966 and again in the 1968–1970 period.

## MONEY SUPPLY, INTEREST RATE, AND INVESTMENT RELATIONSHIPS

The link between monetary policy and income is the interest rate. It is hypothesized that tight money tends to raise interest rates and discourage investment demand, as the liquidity-preference and marginal-efficiency-of-capital schedules of Figure 1 showed. While economists generally agree that the money supply influences interest rates, which in turn influence investment demand, these relations are admittedly loose. If investment demand is not very sensitive to changes in interest rates, changes in the money supply may be of little value as a stabilization tool. The sensitivity of investment expenditures to interest rates is questioned by many observers and conceded to be variable by nearly all. We know, for example, that the expectation of unfavorable economic conditions may be an overriding consideration, in which case low interest rates may not be matched by increased investment demand under easy-money conditions. Conversely, in the face of technological advances and improved business expectations, increased interest rates may not reduce aggregate demand sufficiently to dampen inflationary pressures.

Another factor contributing to the loose money-supply and NNP relationship is that, in the face of contractionary monetary policy, commercial banks may liquidate some of their inventories of government securities held as "secondary reserves" in order to acquire reserves which will enable them to continue to grant more lucrative loans at higher interest rates. Commercial banks may also invest in securities and lower their reserves during recessions even though the central bank is attempting to ease up on monetary conditions. In short, government securities used as secondary reserves may complicate the impact of monetary policy. The ability of large corporations to finance their investment-expansion plans internally from retained earnings further qualifies the impact of monetary policy on NNP, particularly if firms also enjoy monopoly-sheltered market power that allows them to transfer the increased cost of borrowing to consumers by raising product prices.

### THE DEMAND FOR MONEY AND FINANCIAL INTERMEDIARIES

If the demand for money and spending were related in a constant fashion to the money supply, the lives of monetary policy-makers would be simple. We know from our earlier consideration of liquidity preferences that the demand for money may counteract monetary policies. Before the appropriate amount of a change in the money supply needed to support full-employment NNP can be identified, it is mandatory to determine how such a change will relate to the public's demand for money balances. Since people hold money balances for various reasons, the way in which demand for money responds to interest-rate changes is important. People tend to economize on money balances as the money supply contracts and interest rates rise, and this reduction in the quantity of money balances demanded may offset a restrictive monetary policy initiated by the central bank. Then, too, the expansionary impact of low interest rates generated by increasing the money supply may be offset by increases in the demand for the quantity of money held as a liquid asset. An unfavorable economic environment tends to discourage the public from committing its wealth to less liquid assets and strengthens the desire to hold larger money balances.

The rapidly expanding role of financial intermediaries is relevant to the problems of money demand. Savings and loan associations, credit unions, finance and insurance companies, mutual savings banks, and other financial firms aggressively mobilize the flow of funds from savers to spenders as money becomes tighter, thereby making a constant money supply turn over more rapidly. The public may turn increasingly to near-money substitutes in their optimism and eagerness to earn the interest returns that near-monies generate. Therefore, a constant quantity of money can serve more economic needs as money balances are economized through financial intermediaries. Because financial intermediaries can act as a buffer force that partially counteracts stabilizing monetary policy, some monetary authorities argue that intermediaries should also be regulated by the Board of Governors.

Most economists conclude that money and the use of monetary policy are important to a healthy economy. However, some authorities suggest that the variety of timing and impact problems that characterize monetary policy are so severe that we need *less*, not more, discretionary control over the money supply. In all respects, the real world is less easily manipulated than simplified economic theories suggest. There are limits to the effectiveness of monetary policy, just as there are to fiscal policy, but these limitations do not negate its usefulness.

## REVIEW

### Summary

1. The money supply and credit conditions in the United States are regulated by the Federal Reserve System, a quasi-public central bank which is responsible for monitoring economic conditions through changes in the money supply, credit availability, and interest rates. The Board of Governors of the Federal Reserve is generally responsible for the operation of the 12 Federal Reserve Banks. Major responsibility for control of the money supply lies in the hands of the Federal Open Market Committee.

2. The impact of the money supply on income operates through liquidity preferences and the marginal efficiency of capital, which link the money supply to a nation's output. Today, economists generally regard the money supply as being one factor that can influence economic activity, where $\Delta M \rightarrow \Delta i \rightarrow \Delta I \rightarrow \Delta DD \rightarrow \Delta NNP$. Both the money supply and the demand for money affect interest rates through the liquidity-preference schedule. As credit conditions are altered investment may be affected, which can result in a change in income. The relations between monetary variables and the level of income are admittedly loose, however.

3. The Federal Reserve System supervises commercial banking, acts as a bank for the federal government, and is a bank which holds commercial-bank reserves, lends to commercial banks, and facilitates the clearance of checks. The most important function of the Federal Reserve is management of the money supply, which is accomplished through open-market purchases and sales of securities, changes in the discount rate, variations in the reserve ratio, and manipulation of selective credit controls.

4. Open-market operations consist of the buying and selling of securities. Central-bank purchases of securities expand commercial-bank reserves, and the sale of securities contracts reserves. By changing the volume of total reserves in this way, excess reserves are altered and multiple expansion or contraction of the money supply occurs as described earlier (Chapter 10).

5. Increases in the discount rate make it more costly for commercial banks to borrow from the Federal Reserve and thus are contractionary. Lowering the discount rate encourages commercial banks to obtain reserves by borrowing from the Federal Reserve. An increase in the reserve ratio is a repressive monetary policy which reduces excess reserves, whereas easy-money conditions are generated by reducing the reserve ratio. Changes in the reserve ratio alter required and excess reserves, but do not affect total reserves.

6. Selective credit controls such as moral suasion, changing margin requirements, altering credit terms, and varying interest-rate ceilings on time deposits may also be used to influence economic activity. However, as with the discount rate and reserve ratio, selective credit controls play a comparatively minor role compared to open-market policy.

7. The degree of credit restraint is revealed in part by measuring *free reserves*—the difference between excess and borrowed reserves. It is a comparatively simple task to determine how changes in Federal Reserve credit, gold, and currency in circulation, for example, influence commercial-bank reserves by using the reserve equation, which shows the sources and uses for bank reserves. Anything that increases reserve sources (such as a gold inflow) or reduces uses (such as a reduction in Treasury cash), is expansionary. A reduction in reserve sources or an increase in reserve uses is repressive.

8. The effectiveness of monetary policy as a stabilization device is subject to several difficulties, largely because the relationship between the supply of money and NNP is loose and is neither constant nor uniform. Among the factors accounting for variability between management of the money supply and NNP levels are: (*a*) conflicts in goals, such as simultaneously stemming gold outflows and remedying domestic unemployment; (*b*) potential conflicts between monetary policy and Treasury concern for financing government debt; (*c*) the difficulty of accurately gauging the timing of monetary policy; (*d*) the uneven and differential impact of money-supply changes; (*e*) the loose relationship between money, interest rates, and investment; and (*f*) variations in the demand for money balances and the influence of financial intermediaries.

### Identify the Following Concepts and Terms

- tax and loan accounts
- required reserves
- free reserves
- discount rate
- liquidity preference
- borrowed reserves
- selective credit controls
- margin requirement
- open-market operations
- complications of monetary policy
- gold certificates
- "Regulation Q"
- reserve sources and uses

### Questions to Answer

1. What are the major limitations to monetary policy? How does each relate to Federal Reserve attempts to stabilize the economy through the money supply?

2. Suppose the required-reserve ratio is 20 percent and no excess resources exist in a commercial-banking system with $200 billion in demand-deposit liabilities. Trace the impact of a reduction in the required-reserve ratio from 20 percent to 15 percent. Will the money supply automatically increase? Why or why not?

3. Using the concepts of liquidity preference, the marginal efficiency of capital, and the NNP multiplier, explain how the money supply is linked to NNP.

4. Explain and illustrate with balance sheets how expansionary and contractionary open-market policies affect reserves in the commercial-banking system. Check the logic of your results by using the reserve equation. What differences arise when security transactions involve the public instead of a commercial bank?

# CHAPTER 12
# Macroeconomic Stabilization: Issues and Problems

We have seen that the central bank may use monetary policy to influence income, employment, and prices; in addition, we have seen that governmental fiscal actions—taxes and expenditures—have an important bearing on the level of economic activity. This chapter is a brief synthesis of fiscal and monetary policies. It is also a summary of the contemporary macroeconomic problem associated with the attempt to achieve full employment and price stability—the general theme of the last six chapters. The first task of Part A is to summarize economic-stabilization policy, an inquiry which brings out some critical issues and problems associated with coordinating fiscal and monetary policies. Part B reviews the lively debate of recent years over the comparative effectiveness of fiscal and monetary policies, and Part C investigates one of the most important problems of contemporary times: achieving *both* price stability and full employment.

## A. OVERVIEW OF INCOME THEORY AND PUBLIC POLICY

In general terms, we know that both fiscal and monetary policies can be used with varying degrees of success to monitor aggregate demand and the level of NNP. Figure 1 summarizes the problem and policy implications of variations in NNP. To the extent that levels of economic activity in a market economy fluctuate around the full-employment level of real output (shown in Figure 1 as a dashed line), discretionary and automatic fiscal and monetary policies may be used to diminish the severity of swings in business activity. As we know, stabilization policies generally rely upon variations in the money supply ($M$), government spending ($G$), and taxes ($T$), for periods of both inflation (year 1 in Figure 1) and unemployment (year 5 in the figure). For example, at the full-employment income level ($NNP_{fe}$) in year 1, aggregate demand (which now includes government expenditures) exceeds full-employment capacity to produce and, because of this inflationary gap, prices and money NNP rise. In contrast, in year 5, aggregate demand is less than full-employment capacity, contributing to a decline in income and employment.

### Stabilization Policy: The "Big Picture"

The way in which fiscal and monetary policies may alter income, employment, and the price level is summarized more precisely in Figure 2, which combines some of the major notions we have developed in the last several chapters. In this illustration, the income and monetary relations that determine NNP and employment are shown as a cybernetic system, where read-

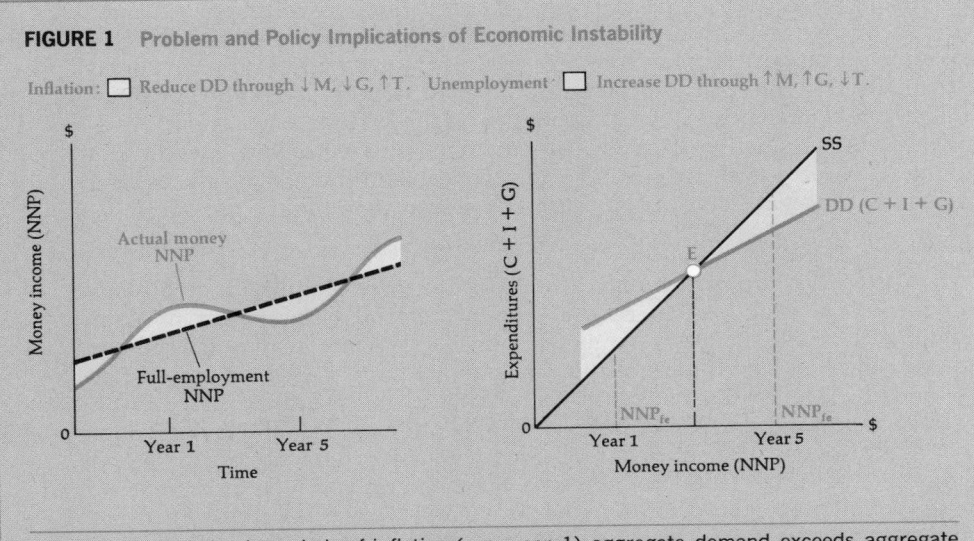

**FIGURE 1** Problem and Policy Implications of Economic Instability

Inflation: ☐ Reduce DD through ↓M, ↓G, ↑T.  Unemployment ☐ Increase DD through ↑M, ↑G, ↓T.

*Economic Stability.* In periods of inflation (e.g., year 1) aggregate demand exceeds aggregate supply at full employment while the reverse relation holds when unemployment appears (e.g., year 5). Government authorities attempt to manipulate aggregate demand through changing the money supply (*M*), government expenditures (*G*), and tax receipts (*T*), as shown above.

ing from right to left reveals that the primary question of interest to us is: Has income equilibrium with stable prices and full employment been achieved? If these goals are reached, the lower feedback loop reveals that no change in either fiscal or monetary policy is needed. In a market economy, however, adjustments are often needed, since aggregate demand (*DD*) may or may not correspond with full-employment NNP and price stability. In these instances, the upper feedback loop of Figure 2 indicates that policy changes are in order. Many of the more important concepts and ideas developed to explain the relation between economic policy, aggregate demand, and income equilibrium are also given in the figure as a reminder to the reader.

## STABILIZING FISCAL POLICY

As we have seen, the major expenditure components of aggregate demand may fluctuate from one time period to another. Consumption expenditures (*C*) may vary, although most observers agree that the consumption schedule is more stable than the investment schedule, which may shift erratically. Investment expenditures are the most volatile component of aggregate demand partially because of the uncertainty of expected demand and profits. Part of disposable income, the key determinant of consumption expenditures, is normally consumed and the remainder is saved, giving rise to the multiplier. As we know, there is an inverse relationship between the marginal propensity to save (*MPS*) and the multiplier ($m = 1/MPS$). Over a period of time, a change in aggregate demand is magnified into even larger changes in NNP as consumption expenditures circulate through the circular-income flow. The final change in income is determined by the multiplier, where $\Delta NNP = \Delta DD \times m$.

Several important concepts identified in the lower portion of Figure 2 remind us of the use of fiscal policy. By increasing government expenditures, reducing taxes, and moving in the direction of larger budget deficits, government authorities may counter deflationary gaps and excessive unemployment. The converse is a potentially viable fiscal prescription for inflationary problems once full employment is reached. Thus, when total spending exceeds productive capacity, a reduction in government spending, a tax increase, or movement toward larger government budget surpluses tend to reduce aggregate demand and thereby lessen inflationary pressures.

## MONETARY POLICY

Federal Reserve authorities may also influence price stability and full employment. The stabilization of the economy at full employment by contractionary or expansionary monetary policies depends heavily on the use of open-market operations to alter the money supply ($M$), interest rates ($i$), and the availability of credit, each of which have indirect impacts on aggregate demand and NNP. Thus under inflationary conditions, as monetary authorities restrict growth in the money supply, interest rates rise and a shortage of funds tends to dampen total spending and NNP. Conversely, under deflationary-gap conditions when unemployment is excessive, easing up on the money supply tends to lower interest rates and increase spending and NNP.

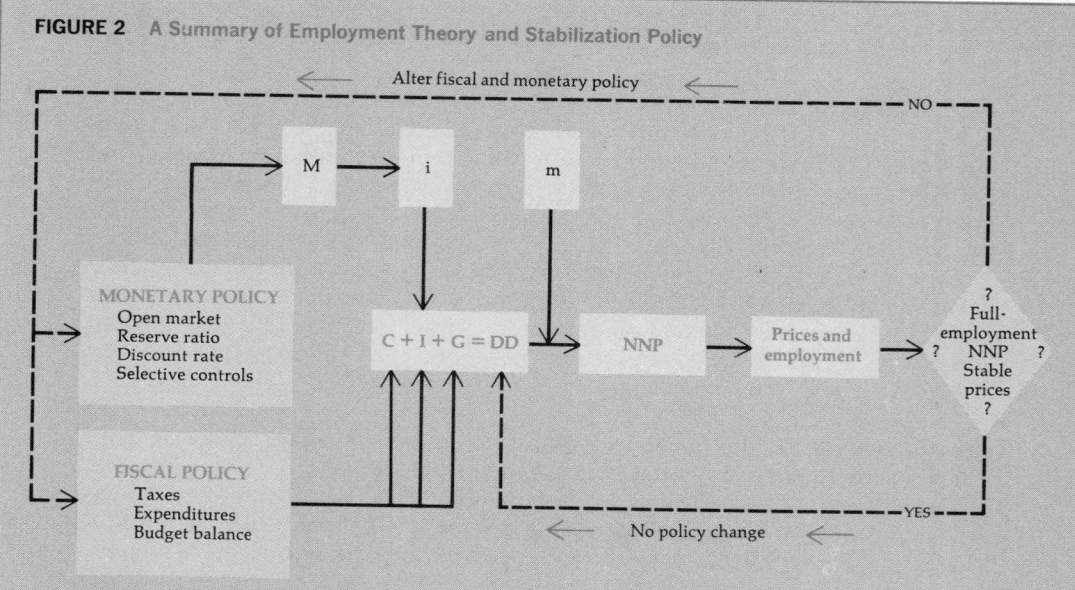

**FIGURE 2**  A Summary of Employment Theory and Stabilization Policy

*Income Theory and Policy.* The level of aggregate demand (*DD*) in relation to aggregate supply influences the level of NNP, through the multiplier (*m*), employment, and prices as shown above. When full employment and price stability are achieved, fiscal and monetary policy need not be altered for stabilization purposes as the lower feedback loop "Yes" shows. In order to achieve full employment some combination of fiscal and monetary policies may be selected. Stabilization policy works through several major variables, the most important being taxes, government expenditures, the money supply (*M*), interest rates (*i*), investment (*I*), and aggregate demand (*DD*).

The complexities of the real world cannot be represented fully in as simple a form as Figure 2, because the limitations to both monetary and fiscal policy are ignored. Both are plagued by timing problems as well as uncertain and uneven impacts. The extent to which investment demand responds to changes in the interest rate, the vague role of near-monies and financial intermediaries which complicate monetary policy, and the inflexibility that characterizes fiscal tax and expenditure programs are a few common limitations to stabilization policy. While we must remain aware of the complexities of income theory and policy, however, it is apparent that the theory and policy relations shown in Figure 2 do boil down to a reasonably coherent system.

## Coordination of Monetary and Fiscal Policies

What is the "best" mix of fiscal and monetary policy? Should government expenditures be reduced and taxes increased? Should the Federal Reserve reduce commercial-bank reserves, contract the money supply, and choke off the supply of credit while driving interest rates upward to counter inflationary pressures? Should a tax increase be imposed upon firms or on consumers? Are reductions in government expenditures for goods and services or smaller amounts of transfer payments in order? Questions like these are difficult to answer. The most effective policy combination depends upon the impact of stabilization efforts on the many related economic goals of society as well as on the efficacy of the various policies. It is clear, however, that fiscal and monetary policies are complementary economic weapons which must be coordinated to achieve full employment and price stability.

The mix of monetary and fiscal policies is important, and while both approaches are complementary in the general sense, they may cancel desired impacts on NNP if they are not properly coordinated. A few examples of possible stabilization policy and goal conflicts will illustrate the importance of policy coordination.

### CASE I: FISCAL AND MONETARY OFFSETS

First, the state of the government budget has an important impact on interest rates. For example, if an expansive budget deficit is financed by government borrowing and the money supply remains unchanged, the increased demand for funds arising out of a budget deficit tends to increase interest rates which, in turn, may *reduce* private-sector investment expenditures. The reduction in private-sector investment, however, may be offset in part or entirely by higher government expenditures and the hoped-for fiscal-policy stimulus may then materialize. Or consider the alternative of a larger budget surplus instituted to combat inflationary pressures while the monetary authorities leave the money supply unchanged. A budget surplus means that government increases the supply of loanable funds available to the private sector by borrowing less or retiring debt; therefore, declining interest rates and expansion of private-sector aggregate demand may tend to offset the fiscal restraint implied by a budget surplus.

The year 1964 provides a good example of the complementary use of fiscal and monetary policies, whereas the 1967–1970 era, particularly 1969, illustrates some degree of failure to coordinate policies. In the earlier period, the Kennedy-Johnson tax cut of $11 billion, belated though it was, represented a needed fiscal stimulus. The Federal Reserve complemented expansive fiscal pressures by enlarging bank reserves, thus allowing interest rates to remain relatively stable. In contrast, during the latter 1960s, stepped-up war expenditures added to expansive inflationary forces despite a tax increase and the Federal Reserve's policy of crunching down on the money market. For the better part of two years starting in 1968, the economy was caught in an inflationary crossfire which resulted in a downturn in 1970, even though interest rates rose to near all-time highs early in that year.

Timing and impact problems, as well as a variety of other difficulties, characterized the use of stabilization policy during the 1968–1970 period. Chief among the dilemmas faced by the Nixon administration were conflicting goals—economic stability vs. war expenditures as well as a vast demand for resources needed to cope with urban problems, poverty, and environmental pollution.

CASE II: DOMESTIC STABILIZATION AND THE BALANCE OF PAYMENTS

Potential conflicts between two or more economic objectives demand a careful and coordinated use of monetary tools and fiscal policy. Such a conflict can be seen in the economic goals of reducing domestic unemployment and lowering the balance-of-payments deficit. Suppose domestic expansion is required because of unemployment, while at the same time a nation experiences a deficit in its international balance of payments—the case in the early 1960s. The *balance-of-payments deficit* (due to gross payments made to foreign nations exceeding their payments to the United States) leads to financial outflows which most nations attempt to control, if not minimize. Expansionary monetary policy intended to counteract unemployment requires increases in the money supply to lower domestic interest rates and encourage additional investment spending. Unfortunately, lower interest rates may also drive funds abroad in search of higher yields, increasing the balance-of-payments deficit. To avoid a flight of financial capital and even larger balance-of-payments deficits, a tight monetary policy can be coordinated with an expansionary fiscal policy. Although tight-money conditions may restrict aggregate demand, expansive government expenditures or tax cuts are important fiscal complements that may allow the desired domestic expansion while monetary restraints stem the financial capital outflow and correct the balance-of-payments deficit.

Although economic problems and conflicting goals are not always so amenable to an integrated use of fiscal and monetary policies as these two examples suggest, it is important to use both policies in those combinations that best cope with the circumstances. This statement implies that as stabilization techniques, fiscal and monetary policies are equally important and equally effective—a misconception in the eyes of many, as is shown next.

**B.** ON THE IMPORTANCE OF FISCAL AND MONETARY POLICIES

The relative importance of fiscal policy compared to monetary policy, and the overall effectiveness of stabilization policy in general is a subject of debate in economics. For many years, conventional wisdom in macroeconomic theory has stressed the overriding importance of the Keynesian view of income determination. The basic explanation for the control of income and employment relies heavily on government expenditure and tax policies. The consequence of this viewpoint has been that fiscal policy has often been emphasized over monetary policy. However, some prominent authorities contend that money is more important than many fiscal-policy advocates admit, and further that the money supply should be increased steadily, say at 4 percent annually, regardless of mild swings in economic conditions. Led by Professor Milton Friedman of the University of Chicago, this school of thought concludes that government authorities are as apt to be wrong as right in forecasting and judging the timing and impact of discretionary monetary and fiscal policies. In fact, historical studies by "Monetarists" purport to show that the Federal Reserve has acted in such a way as to have a *destabilizing* effect on numerous occasions. The possibility of serious error and a destabilizing or procyclical policy is avoided by increasing the money supply at a constant rate. Even though a policy of constant growth in the money supply may not iron out minor ups and downs in economic activity, it will avoid Federal Reserve-prompted swings, according to Professor Friedman. While many are unwilling at the moment to apply Friedman's ideas, they are receiving increasing attention among academicians and in Washington and do merit consideration.

## The Theory of Monetary Policy

Although the general connection between monetary policy and NNP appears to be reasonably straightforward as shown by the cause-effect chain of Figure 2, there are a variety of factors that complicate monetary policy, not the least of which is the loose relationship between the money supply, interest rates, and investment. In order to examine the problems in implementing monetary policy it is helpful to understand the equation of exchange developed by Irving Fisher and more recently popularized by Professor Friedman as the "revised quantity theory."

### THE EQUATION OF EXCHANGE

The equation of exchange is a useful device to summarize the quantity theory of money, which identifies the direct importance of money. The *equation of exchange* states that spending on output equals income, a truistic statement which can be identified as follows:

$$\text{Money stock} \times \text{velocity or turnover} \equiv \text{price} \times \text{quantity}$$
$$M \times V \equiv P \times Q$$

M stands for the quantity or stock of money and V represents the *velocity* or turnover of money (that is, the average number of times a dollar is spent in a time period such as one year). P represents the price level (or average price per unit of output sold) and Q stands for the real volume of output in an economy.

Consider a simplified example where the total money supply = $200, each dollar turns over four times annually, and 400 units of goods are sold at an average price of $2. Aggregate output is then $800, since

$$MV \equiv PQ \qquad \text{or} \qquad \$200 \times 4 = \$2 \times 400$$

The equation of exchange is true by definition, being an identity. This is so simply because MV is the amount spent on output (the quantity of money multiplied by the number of times each dollar is used), and $PQ$ is the amount received for goods and services sold (the average price per unit multiplied by the physical amount of output). The two sides of the equation of exchange are different sides of the same coin: Spending on output $\equiv$ receipts from the sale of output.

## THE QUANTITY THEORY

The version of the quantity theory of money popularized by classical economists such as David Ricardo argued that both $V$ (the income velocity of money) and $Q$ (real output) were relatively fixed or constant. The classical version thus held that $M$ and $P$ are directly and proportionately related, so that "... if by any cause the quantity of money is greatly increased, its ultimate effect is to raise the price of commodities in proportion to the increased quantity of money."[1] Assuming $V$ is fixed at 4, $M$ rises from $200 billion to $300 billion, and real output ($Q$) remains at 400 billion, then average prices ($P$) rise by 50 percent from $2 to $3 in proportion to the change in $M$:

$$MV \equiv PQ \qquad \text{or} \qquad \$300 \times 4 \equiv \$3 \times 400$$

In summary, the classical version of the quantity theory embodies one dominant idea: If government increases $M$, inflation occurs as $P$ rises in proportion to changes in $M$.

The equation of exchange is a useful approach, even though it is a truism, furnishing several insights into the role and importance of money. However, economists long ago abandoned the "strict" quantity theory which says simply that as the quantity of money increases, prices rise in proportion. Today, modern quantity theorists recognize that $V$ is not a strict constant and that full-employment $Q$ is not assured.

## THE IMPORTANCE OF MONEY

First, the equation of exchange *directly* emphasizes money as an income-determining factor, a point which was de-emphasized in the Keynesian aggregate-demand (consumption-investment) explanation of NNP. Actually, the equation of exchange is harmonious with the consumption-investment approach because the quantity of money times the average number of times each dollar is spent ($MV$) is aggregate demand and $PQ$ is money NNP. While $MV \equiv PQ$ must be used with care because all four terms are variable and the relations between $M$, $V$, $P$, and $Q$ are loose, the severe post-World War I and II inflations in Germany and the recent rapid price increases in nations like Brazil certainly confirm the notion that very large increases in $M$ and $P$ are closely associated.

Second, the equation of exchange clearly highlights the stock of money. Even though an exceedingly simplified model of a complex world, the four terms in the equation of exchange conveniently and directly organize our thinking about money, income, and prices. For example, if we assume, as the classical economists did, that $V$ is constant, then we know that an increase in $M$ must lead to higher prices of goods ($P$), to more real output ($Q$), or to an increase in $PQ$ in which both real and money NNP rise.

---

[1] David Ricardo, *The Principles of Political Economy* (New York: E. P. Dutton, 1948), p. 198.

Third, the equation of exchange shows how the money supply as a policy variable determined by government can be directly related to full-employment NNP. Suppose the Federal Reserve takes steps to increase $M$ when real output is well below full employment. Much of the increase in output generated by larger spending is likely to be an increase in real output, or $Q$, because prices tend to remain relatively stable when an economy is operating well below full employment. On the other hand, if an economy is near or at full-employment output levels and $M$ is increased, real output or $Q$ cannot increase; thus, more $M$ drives up the $P$ variable in $PQ$; only money income rises as inflation sets in. This statement, of course, violates the classical assumption of a fixed full-employment level of real output, but we already know that the classical theory was wrong on that count from historical data and from our earlier discussion of income and employment theory.

Fourth, the equation of exchange clearly focuses attention on the importance of the demand for money. We know that there is an important paper-asset demand for money held for liquidity purposes. The demand for money is inversely related to the velocity of money. As people try to hold larger money balances out of a fixed money stock, dollars are detained in households and firms for a longer period of time—that is, velocity falls! Conversely, when the demand for money declines, each dollar turns over more rapidly. In essence, when the demand for money falls relative to the money supply, velocity rises. Thus, given a fixed money supply ($M$) and smaller velocity or turnover ($V$), aggregate spending declines. Conversely, if the demand for money declines, $V$ rises as individuals rid themselves of excess liquidity (aggregate spending increases). The notion that $V$ is not a strict constant flies squarely in the face of the classical economists' assumption of a fixed $V$, but history again lends credence to the idea that $V$ is not as stable as once was thought. By rearranging the equation of exchange ($MV \equiv PQ$) to solve for $V$ (the form is $V = PQ/M$) for select years, we find $V = 3.9$ in 1929, 2.2 in 1945, and 4.6 in 1969. The 20-year decline in $V$ between 1930 and 1950 was affected by the unusual events of a severe depression and a massive war. What happened during this period was that interest rates were extremely low and the preference to hold money was correspondingly high; holding money did not impose large opportunity costs in the form of interest earnings forgone. In addition, people held money longer because of uncertainty in the 1930s and shortages of goods in the 1940s. Although $V$ is roughly stable in the very long run when computed in relation to national income, variations do occur when people attempt to equalize their demand for money with the supply of money. Consequently, when $V$ changes and $M$ remains fixed, income levels are going to change (remember $MV \equiv PQ$). Accordingly, anything other than equality between the demand for and the supply of money balances will result in people changing the mix of assets they own. Aggregate demand may then shift unless changes in $M$—monetary policy—offset changes in $V$ that reflect the demand for money.

Fifth, since the $MV \equiv PQ$ relationship is loose, changes in $V$ may complicate the use and effectiveness of monetary policy. When people demand larger money balances in a recession, for example, declines in $V$ may help offset any increase in $M$ purposively pursued by monetary authorities. Conversely, as $M$ is restricted by monetary authorities under inflationary conditions, $V$ can rise and dilute the needed contractionary impact of monetary policy as the demand to hold money slackens.

Opinions differ on the relative importance of money and the usefulness of the "revised quantity theory" that takes into account the variability of the four components of the equation of exchange. Even though the equation of exchange does not necessarily identify rigid relationships between $M$, $V$, $P$, and $Q$, it is a useful framework in understanding how money and central-bank policy may affect income.

### Two Views on Money and Economic Activity

There are two different views on the impact of the money supply on NNP.

1. The view of money professed by the proponents of fiscal policy, is that the money supply influences credit availability, interest rates, investment, and output as shown earlier in Figure 2. However, liquidity preferences linking $M$ and $i$ and the marginal efficiency of capital linking $i$ and $I$ are commonly noted as loose relations that detract from the effectiveness of monetary policy.

2. An alternative view of money and economic activity professed by the "Monetarists" stresses the *direct* importance of $M$ as shown in the equation of exchange. The revised quantity theory depicted by the equation of exchange ($MV \equiv PQ$) emphasizes that both velocity and output may vary, but nonetheless $M$ is closely associated with money NNP (remember, $PQ$ is money NNP).

To some extent these two views have been polarized beyond what both the facts and their proponents intend. For example, the "naive" Keynesian view that *money does not matter* can be illustrated by regarding velocity in the equation of exchange as completely variable. Thus, in the relation $MV \equiv PQ$, any change in $M$ would be offset by subsequent and reverse changes in $V$. In contrast, the *money-is-all-important* thesis of the old quantity theory regards $V$ as a fixed and unchanging constant. Thus, changes in $M$ are transmitted fully to changes in $PQ$, and monetary policy can be regarded as completely effective.

Generally speaking, economists who emphasize fiscal policy and the *indirect* importance of $M$ contend that stabilization policy is flexible and agree that the Federal Reserve has been generally effective in moderating swings in economic activity. The Monetarist view suggests that fiscal and monetary policies are of limited effectiveness, and are uncertain enough to make discretionary policy changes in the money supply by the Federal Reserve neutral at best and probably harmful for the more minor swings in economic activity like those experienced in recent years. The notion that fiscal policy in and of itself is important is debunked by Professor Friedman, who claims that what is regarded as effective fiscal action in fact works through monetary policy. While research on this issue is not definitive and the debate continues, most observers are not inclined to either extreme. It is generally conceded that both fiscal and monetary policies are useful, but all recognize the shortcomings of stabilization policy.

Still, the policies implied by the disagreement over fiscal vs. monetary policy are at odds, and the fence-sitters are not in a comfortable position for that reason. Observers like Walter Heller concede that both monetary and fiscal policies are important while defending the use of stabilization policy.

In contrast, Professor Friedman contends that monetary and fiscal attempts to "fine-tune" the economy are in error.

### The Monetarist View of Stabilization Policy

The Monetarists generally argue that the money supply and the revised quantity theory are more important as a framework for understanding the economy than the aggregate-demand approach that masks the role of money in economic affairs. Unlike advocates of the "strict" quantity theory, Professor Friedman recognizes that $Q$ and $V$ in the equation of exchange are not strict constants. Money receives more emphasis in this framework because an increase in $M$ is seen as directly increasing money income ($PQ$), although not necessarily in direct proportion to a change in $M$, since $V$ and $Q$ do vary somewhat. While Friedman's concept of the revised quantity theory does not hold that $V$ is constant, he does contend that $V$ is reasonably stable and changes in $V$ are generally small and relatively predictable in comparison to the more variable income-multiplier impacts associated with fiscal policy. While all of this is an oversimplification of Friedman's ideas, it does lead naturally to debate about the relative importance of stabilization policies of any kind.

Let us examine more closely the particulars of the Monetarist view in order to gain a better appreciation of the character of this debate. The major ideas in capsule form are that:

1. Money matters very much, particularly as a determinant of prices and money NNP.

2. Historically, over any period of several years, there is a closeness between the stock of money, the level of prices, and the level of money NNP.

3. It is not possible to use any policy—monetary or fiscal—as a *precision* instrument to offset short-run forces causing economic instability, largely because, on the average, close connections between fiscal or monetary policy and NNP are quite variable in any given instance. Note that this conclusion applies to *either fiscal or monetary policy.*[2] However, fiscal policy is considered the weaker force compared to monetary policy.

Professor Friedman's notion that money is very important is clear when cast in the form of the revised quantity theory, $MV \equiv PQ$. He holds that, fiscal policy, by itself of no import, is being oversold; monetary policy is being oversold; and fine tuning is being oversold. Periods of rapid growth in the money supply encourage people to rid themselves of excess money balances, which are exchanged for real assets, causing aggregate demand to rise and tending to produce inflation under full-employment conditions. Sluggish or negative growth rates in the money supply similarly produce a direct decline in money NNP. Moreover, the money supply is seen as related more closely to NNP than fiscal-policy variables such as government expenditures, taxes, or the government budget, which are largely related

[2] Excerpts in U.S. Congress, Joint Economic Committee, *Hearings, Employment Growth, and Price Levels,* Testimony of May 25, 1959 (86th Congress, First Session) clarify Friedman's views. Also see Milton Friedman and Walter Heller, *Monetary vs. Fiscal Policy* (New York: W. W. Norton, 1969), p. 66.

to NNP via "... *a priori* reasoning" and not demonstrated effectiveness, according to Friedman.[3]

In conclusion, Professor Friedman argues that money does not receive adequate attention and that *both* monetary and fiscal policies have been oversold in the sense that we cannot rely as heavily as we have been on economic-stabilization devices that are apt to be wrong and belatedly timed. Friedman's reasoning is based on the loose relations between money, spending, and income which are also likely to be variable in unknown ways and subject to uncertain time lags. He acknowledges that money has a systematic influence on money NNP, but he also argues that this relation is subject to a good deal of variability. Instead of attempting to manipulate the money supply or to use fiscal policy to mitigate short-run variations in economic activity and run the risk of forecasting, time, and impact errors, he maintains that policy-makers should stabilize growth in the money supply by allowing it to expand at approximately the rate of growth in NNP. By arguing for stable expansion of the money supply over the long run, Professor Friedman is suggesting that expectations will stabilize and he is also implying that prices and wages in a quasi-competitive market will adjust and act as an automatic guidance device to direct economic activity.

Contemporary advocates of economic-stabilization policy have responded to Professor Friedman's views in part by admitting increasingly to the importance of money and the relevance of monetary policy. For example, the Council of Economic Advisers has stated that the "... relationships between movements in GNP and any of the money [supply] concepts *have been close enough* on the average ... to be difficult to pass off lightly."[4] Nevertheless, proponents of fiscal policy such as Walter Heller lovingly linger upon its efficacy by arguing that "... fiscal policy matters a great deal,"[5] a most discomforting conclusion to Professor Friedman. Although most economists agree that money is important, many are reluctant to de-emphasize fiscal policy to the extent that Friedman does, and even more observers are loath to abandon stabilization policy. That a large number of experts are by no means prepared to adopt the concept of fixed money-supply growth advocated by Friedman is confirmed by the Council of Economic Advisers, who reported in 1969 that "... any simple rigid rule related to the growth of the money supply (however defined) can unduly confine Federal Reserve policy."[6] Needless to say, confinement is precisely what Professor Friedman advocates.

The historical and statistical evidence on the issue of the relative importance of monetary and fiscal policies is by no means all in. Yet, there are indications that monetary policy may be more important than was once thought and may even be a more effective and timely device than fiscal policy.[7] While issues such as these require more definitive econometric re-

[3] Friedman and Heller, *op. cit.*, p. 53.

[4] Council of Economic Advisers, *Economic Report of the President*, 1969, p. 91.

[5] Friedman and Heller, *op. cit.*, p. 66.

[6] Council of Economic Advisers, *Economic Report of the President*, 1969, p. 92.

[7] Leonall C. Anderson and Jerry L. Jordan, "Monetary and Fiscal Actions: A Test of Their Relative Importance in Economic Stabilization," *Review*, Federal Reserve Bank of St. Louis (November 1968), pp. 11–23.

search before firm answers are forthcoming, the challenge posed by Professor Friedman is receiving increasing attention, as well it should.

## C. RELATIONS BETWEEN UNEMPLOYMENT AND THE PRICE LEVEL

One of the more troublesome policy dilemmas has been the difficulty of simultaneously achieving full employment and price stability, two macroeconomic goals that, at least in recent years, appear to be in conflict with each other in many Western European nations, as well as in the United States. As socioeconomic objectives, observers agree that price stability and full employment are desirable ends, but when they are confronted with choosing one goal over the other or identifying "acceptable" tolerance levels for unemployment and for inflation, their opinions differ significantly. Other examples of conflict between economic goals and policies will be evaluated in later chapters as the necessary analytical skills are acquired. However, the seeming incompatibility of full employment and price stability is outstanding for its tenacity and importance to a market economy.

### The Problem: An Unemployment-Inflation Tradeoff?

We know that excessive spending pressures raise the general price level, and that contractionary fiscal and monetary policies may help stabilize the general price level. However, unemployment is apt to rise when deflationary fiscal and monetary pressures are initiated. In short, fiscal and monetary policies may not be effective if inflation and unemployment are caused by factors other than inconsistencies between aggregate demand and full-employment levels of output.

The unemployment and price-level record of the recent past reveals that full employment and relatively stable prices have been achieved simultaneously only rarely in this and many other advanced nations. The problem is so severe that the Council of Economic Advisers has described it as "the nation's most important unsolved problem of overall economic performance."[8]

The problem of achieving *both* relative price stability and full employment is illustrated by Figure 3, which compares the unemployment rate and annual price-level increases for recent years. The relationship shown, dubbed the "Phillips curve" after its originator A. W. Phillips, is not a stable, precise, mechanical relation.[9] Still, the Phillips curve suggests that relative price stability generally corresponds to an unemployment rate of approximately 5 to 7 percent of the labor force. On the other hand, a full-employment level of output is associated with price increases on the order of 3 to 4 percent annually.

The unemployment rate reflects the demand for labor—a derived demand mirroring the demand for goods and services. Thus, unemployment may be viewed as a proxy for the demand for resources in the general sense. In a period of rising aggregate demand when a nation approaches capacity levels of output, firms attempt to attract labor and other resources from each

---

[8] Council of Economic Advisers, *Economic Report of the President*, 1969, p. 94.

[9] Professor A. W. Phillips first studied this problem for the United Kingdom in the late 1950s.

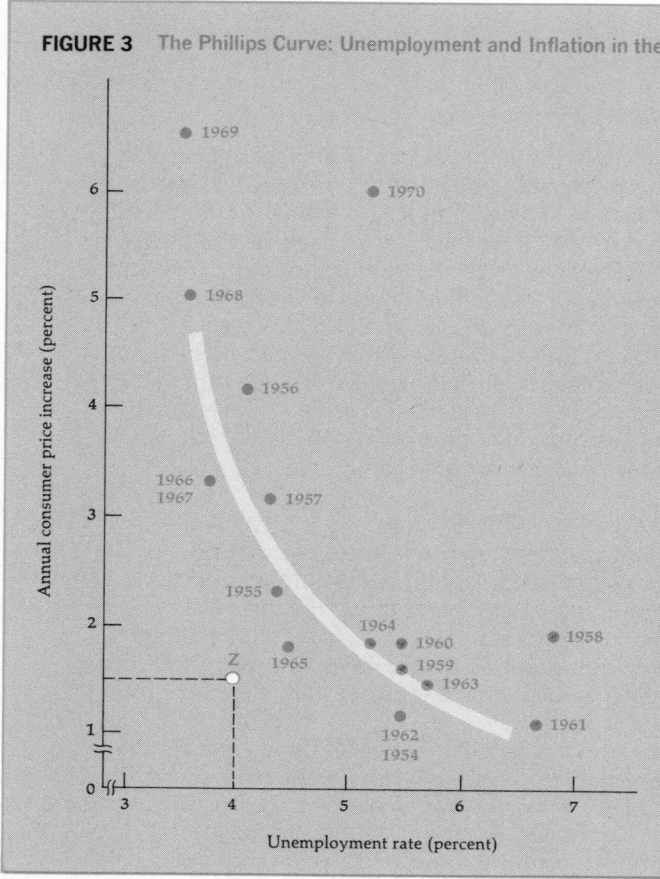

**FIGURE 3**  The Phillips Curve: Unemployment and Inflation in the United States

*Unemployment and Inflation.* The historical relationship between consumer price-level increases and unemployment is a negative one, where full employment is roughly associated with inflationary price increases. Price stability, on the other hand, tends to imply rather high levels of unemployment as the data in this figure show. The apparent conflict between the goals of full employment on the one hand, and price stability on the other, poses knotty problems for those concerned with economic policy. The usefulness of fiscal and monetary policy as stabilization tools is limited by the unemployment-inflation tradeoff. Relative price stability and full employment (say, point Z) has been an elusive objective since the early 1950s.

other by bidding up wages and prices. Upward price pressures mount when the tightness in the markets for resources and for goods and services intensifies as full employment is more nearly approximated. Scarcity of resources and limited supplies of output lead to successive rounds of price and wage increases that reinforce each other in product and resource markets. In contrast, during periods of falling demand for output and resources, a nation moves away from full employment, and prices may eventually stabilize while unemployment increases because pressures on resource and product markets are diminished. Apparently, the achievement of *both* full employment and price stability, a situation represented by point Z in Figure 3, is an elusive economic goal. And this is true regardless of how effective fiscal and monetary policies are in shifting aggregate demand to close inflationary or deflationary gaps in output. In other words, if an inflationary gap were effectively corrected by fiscal and monetary restraint, the tradeoff relations shown in Figure 3 imply that the "cost" of price stability is likely to be unemployment. In contrast, if expansionary stabilization measures are employed successfully to achieve full employment, rapidly rising prices are quite likely to occur. Ideally, of course, it would be desirable to operate at full employment with no increase in prices, but Figure 3 suggests that such an ideal condition has not been achieved. Let us see why.

### Factors Contributing to the Tradeoff Dilemma

Even though the tradeoff problem is an uncomfortable issue to many economists, the facts displayed in Figure 3 cannot be ignored because they suggest first, that an inflationary bias characterizes the American economy, and second, that stabilization policy aimed at controlling aggregate demand is not an entirely satisfactory solution to the problems of unemployment and inflation.

An inflationary bias is clearly revealed by the righthand portion of the Phillips curve, which depicts price changes and unemployment rates for the 1958–1964 period. Although unemployment exceeded 5 percent in each of these years, prices also increased by about 1.5 percent annually. Price rigidity or "stickiness" in the downward direction reflects in part the expectation of future inflation despite the existence of unemployment. In addition, powerful unions may step up wage demands, and monopolistic firms may plan price hikes regardless of the level of unemployment. What the Phillips curve reveals is that something other than excess aggregate demand contributes to inflation, reducing the effectiveness of fiscal and monetary policies. Furthermore, deficient aggregate demand apparently does not fully explain unemployment. Thus, policies may be required in addition to those that alter aggregate demand.

The major factors that limit the effectiveness of stabilizing fiscal and monetary policies and give rise to the tradeoff dilemma are: (a) structural unemployment, (b) market-power induced cost-push inflation, and (c) sectoral bottlenecks in resource and product markets. These three characteristics lead to rigidities in resource and product markets that maintain the rightward position of the Phillips curve that has not yet allowed consistent achievement of *both* full employment and price stability.

### STRUCTURAL UNEMPLOYMENT

Unemployment may be due to inadequate aggregate demand, in which case expansionary fiscal and monetary policies may be effective if used correctly. However, *structural unemployment* reflects joblessness due to such forces as technological change, inadequate education, or low skill levels. Structural labor-market problems are characterized by a mismatch between available labor supplies and the demand for manpower. Unemployment of this type is not evenly distributed throughout the economy by geographic area, occupation, industry, skill level, age group, race, or educational level. Untrained workers or persons whose skills are no longer demanded by modern technology are typical victims of structural unemployment. Individuals located in depressed geographic regions, those employed by declining industries, the poorly schooled or uneducated portion of a population, and nonwhite, aged, and very young workers also are frequent victims of structural unemployment. A few of the more obvious cases of structural disparity are revealed by unemployment-rate differentials by skill level, education, and geographic location. In general, the lower the skill level of workers, the greater the unemployment rate and the more likely it is that technological changes will displace workers.

Agreement on just what constitutes structural unemployment is as hard to come by as definitive estimates of the amount of structural unemployment. Nonetheless, it is recognized that unemployment can be attributed to structural imbalance between available manpower skills and the demand for labor, as well as to inadequate aggregate demand. Moreover, as the general level of unemployment rises, workers subject to structural disadvantages bear a disproportionate amount of joblessness.

Several economists suggested in the early 1960s that structural unemployment was becoming an increasingly severe problem, while others maintained that failure to employ available manpower fully during the late 1950s and early 1960s largely reflected deficient aggregate demand. The Council of Economic Advisers recognized that some unemployment was of the structural type but, along with the majority of economists, the Council maintained that inadequate aggregate demand was the primary culprit. Consequently, the Council argued that expansionary fiscal and monetary policies would help create employment opportunities for the structurally unemployed by increasing the demand for output and labor in general. Workers who otherwise might remain unemployed would be drawn back into the labor force as labor-market pressures intensified. At the same time, however, expansionary fiscal and monetary policies would lead to higher rates of increase in the price level implied by the Phillips curve of Figure 3. Expansionary fiscal and monetary policies were implemented in the mid-1960s, and in the latter part of the decade the economy did gradually move toward full employment. There remained significant areas of structural unemployment that required more direct public policies, such as job retraining.

Once we recognize the extent of structural unemployment, the tradeoff dilemma becomes more understandable. When pockets of unemployment prevail by skill level, by region, or because employment opportunities are unevenly distributed by race, labor-market imperfections and rigidities are seen as obvious contributors to the difficulty of achieving *both* full employment and stable prices. Placing enough aggregate-demand pressure on the economy lowers the aggregate rate of unemployment and may well absorb some of the structurally unemployed; however, the more nearly the 4 percent unemployment goal is achieved, the more intense are inflationary wage and price pressures.

## MARKET POWER: COST-PUSH INFLATION

*Cost-push inflation* is a second characteristic of the contemporary market economy that arises from imperfectly competitive markets and the use of market power. The term generally describes the administration of wages and prices by powerful monopoly groups who generate "cost-push" pressures in resource and product markets. In other words, large corporations and powerful unions, as sellers of goods and resources, administer price and wage increases that translate into cost-push forces which affect buyers of goods and resources. These in turn lead to even more general price-level increases throughout the economy. This type of inflation also weakens the effectiveness of fiscal and monetary policies because cost-push pressures are very different from the "demand-pull" inflation for which fiscal and monetary policies are designed. *Demand-pull inflation* is characterized by a rise in the aggregate demand for goods and services under full-employment conditions that creates excess aggregate spending in product and resource markets. Conventional fiscal and monetary policies can cope with demand-pull inflationary pressures by dampening excess demand, but they have less impact on inflationary pressures of the cost-push variety.

In the last two decades several nations, including the United States, have experienced inflationary pressures during periods of high or even rising unemployment when slackness in aggregate demand prevailed relative to capacity levels of output. For example, during 1956–1958, and again at the turn of the decade of the 1970s, price levels advanced while unemployment increased, overall industrial production declined, and many basic industries experienced noticeable declines in sales and profits as excess capacity built up. Clearly, neither demand-pull inflation nor structural unemployment fully explains these events. After Congressional hearings during the latter 1950s and appointment of a Cabinet Committee on Price Stability in 1969, many observers concluded that wage and price increases "pushed" the general price level upward.

Cost-push pressures may arise from the discretionary use of market power in the resource market—for example, when large labor unions or professional associations boost wages for their members even though aggregate unemployment exists. Discretionary power to demand higher wages *and* the discretionary power to grant wage increases lead to higher costs that are passed on to consumers in the form of higher product prices, lending an upward thrust to prices in general. Firms that are not participating in competitive markets also may increase prices in an attempt to protect their profit margins even in a sluggish economy. Market power of this sort can initiate a spiraling series of cost changes originating from either *wage-push* or *administered price-push* forces ultimately reflected in the general level of consumer prices.[10]

The wage-push and price-push characteristics of imperfectly competitive resource and product markets also help explain downward wage–price rigidities. Where market power prevails, and even in more competitive markets, wage and price reductions tend to be rigid or sticky. Powerful business firms contribute to this price rigidity, for example, by maintaining a normal markup price over cost, sometimes regardless of excess capacity in imperfectly operating product markets dominated by one or a few firms. Both powerful unions and corporations are usually eager to avoid wage and price cuts, and since they are capable of exerting market power, they normally avoid deflationary market pressures. Either way, wage- or price-push forces are transformed into cost pressures passed on to society at large, as the Phillips curve of Figure 3 implies. With large unions negotiating inflationary wage settlements, and powerful corporations that are capable of passing cost increases on to the consumer, erosion of the dual goals of full employment *and* price stability is even more understandable.

While available evidence does not clearly identify either corporate or union power as the sole or initial source of cost-push inflation, it is clear that both contribute to the tradeoff problem.

---

[10] Among the more recent evaluations of such circumstances see *Studies by the Staff of the Cabinet Committee on Price Stability*, (Washington, D.C.: U.S. Government Printing Office, 1969).

A third partial explanation for the unemployment-inflation tradeoff identifies *sectoral* or *structural* bottlenecks in markets as a possible cause of inflation, where demand-pull or cost-push forces, or both, may lead to price and unemployment problems. Sectoral inflation might result from uneven patterns of industry-by-industry growth, as spurts in demand occur in different resource and product markets at different times. Shortages may appear in some labor markets, or inadequate capacity may arise in some product markets even though aggregate demand is not excessive. Prices and wages increase in the expanding sectors and, in addition to the wage-price stickiness that exists throughout much of the economy not subject to excess demand, an upward price creep occurs—a bias that is most difficult to restrain. Cost-push forces in isolated sectors of the economy may also give rise to successive rounds of cost and price increases that are passed on throughout a structurally interdependent economy. Uneven expansion in economic sectors and market power create "spill-over" effects, as wage and price increases are both emulated and passed on to other markets, including those sectors of the economy experiencing contraction.

Changes in consumer tastes and technological change in the methods of producing are two key ingredients to sectoral bottlenecks. For example, in 1929 over one-fifth of the American labor force was employed in agriculture, but by 1970, 7 million fewer individuals, or less than 5 percent of all jobs, were in agriculture. Automation and the use of advancing technological modes of production have required the use of more costly and sophisticated capital equipment and less labor in automobile production, coal mining, oil refining, and many other industries. The economic fortunes of firms, industries, entire regions, and workers in a host of occupations are thus altered. New products and new industries are developed every year and such recent growth trends as those in the computer sciences, medical care, and pollution abatement dramatically alter the outputs and resources a dynamic economy demands. Rigidities, immobilities, and bottlenecks are a natural outcome of a changing economy because markets do not adjust instantly and uniformly while maintaining full employment. Then, too, markets are imperfect because information on job opportunities or profitability are not perfectly known. Prices may rise because of immediate supply scarcities in some sectors, whereas general underutilization of resources may prevail. The economic process of production and distribution continues to increase in complexity, specialization of resources continues to fragment, and bottlenecks in markets for resources and products are increasingly possible. After all, it does take time to switch from the production and use of coal, oil, and natural gas, to nuclear energy and perhaps ultimately to solar energy, all of which can lead to bottlenecks and structural imbalance.

Even though the unemployment-inflation argument is general and oversimplified, it is reasonably clear that structural unemployment, cost-push inflation, and sectoral or structural bottlenecks represent tentative explanations for the difficulty of achieving *both* full employment and relatively stable prices.

### Public Policy and the Unemployment-Inflation Tradeoff

A good deal more information and research are needed before we can cope fully with the unemployment-inflation tradeoff dilemma. However, certain policy steps that can be taken to deal with the tradeoff dilemma are shown in Figure 4. The current Phillips relationship (labeled *U-I*) implies a choice between point *a* (undesired inflationary levels) or point *b* (higher levels of unemployment). These are circumstances that appeal to no one. On the other hand, if structural unemployment, cost-push inflation, and market bottlenecks could be controlled, a leftward shift in the Phillips curve from *U-I* to *U-I'* might be possible.

Does the unemployment-inflation dilemma mean that fiscal and monetary policies are useless in waging war on unemployment and inflation? The definite answer to this question is no. In the case of inflation, for example, a key task of public policy is to avoid inflationary surges in aggregate demand through restrictive fiscal and monetary policies. Monetary restraint and the use of taxation and government expenditures were important tactics designed to return the economy to normalcy during the inflation of the latter 1960s, and properly so (questions of timing and impact aside). Fiscal and monetary policies can also be useful in dealing with structural unemployment, as was learned in the early 1960s; however, still more selective policies are required.

Essentially, what is needed to remedy the tradeoff problem is a shift to schedule *U-I'* in Figure 4. Given that imperfections and structural rigidities do characterize the market economy, a shift of the Phillips curve to the left might result from one or more of four policy measures: (*a*) wage-price controls, (*b*) strengthened control of market power, (*c*) human-resource development policies, and (*d*) moral suasion and voluntary restraint.

## WAGE-PRICE CONTROLS

Direct government intervention in markets to control wages and prices is one approach to the unemployment-inflation problem, but it is the least acceptable to many observers. Usually resorted to only in wartime, direct wage and price controls are difficult to deal with administratively and even less acceptable philosophically to most Americans. Control by government rule does alter the market economy, and distortions may arise because prices no longer ration output and allocate resources in the way envisioned

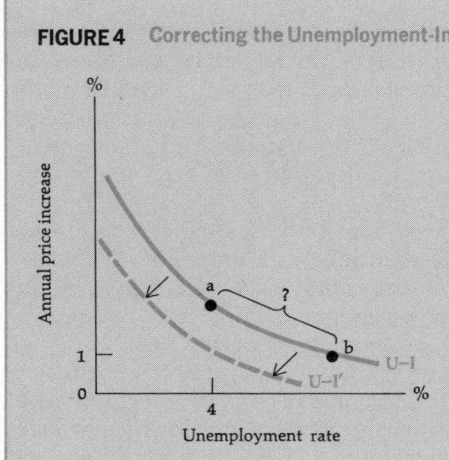

**FIGURE 4**  Correcting the Unemployment-Inflation Tradeoff

*Shifts in the Phillips Curve.* Remedies for the tradeoff relation between unemployment and inflation will shift the tradeoff curve from *U-I* to *U-I'* To accomplish this objective, however, cures must be found for cost-push inflation, structural unemployment, and other resource- and product-market rigidities and bottlenecks.

by proponents of the market system. Nevertheless, a number of informed observers whose ranks have increased in recent years support wage and price controls under severe inflationary conditions. Still other experts advocate lesser degrees of government intervention, such as establishing fact-finding boards, publicizing abuse of market power, or regulating to a limited degree those markets where control is most needed. Public attitudes toward direct control and involvement by the public sector range from tentative acceptance or skepticism to outright hostility, and the general opinion of economists is to avoid wage and price controls under all but the most serious conditions.

## REGULATING MARKET POWER

Control of imperfectly competitive markets to limit the use of market power may also be improved. Antitrust laws could be applied forcefully to those firms or labor organizations accommodating or generating cost-push pressures. Trust-busting is a messy and expensive business, however, quite aside from its unpopularity. Identification of violations and rational remedies for abusive use of wage- and price-setting power are difficult; therefore, the antitrust approach as yet has done little to remedy these specific problems in the United States. Although more will be said about market power and prices in later chapters, it is recognized that a solution spectrum ranging from outright wage and price controls to restriction of market power could be used to ameliorate the unemployment-inflation tradeoff problem depicted by the Phillips curve.

## HUMAN-RESOURCE DEVELOPMENT PROGRAMS

Fiscal and monetary policies remain the first line of defense for structural unemployment because correction of deficiencies in aggregate demand tends to draw some marginal and structurally displaced workers into the labor force. At the same time, we also know that boosting aggregate demand to capacity levels of output is not a final answer for structural unemployment characterized by the coexistence of skilled-job vacancies and high levels of unemployment for unskilled workers. Correcting the imbalance between the manpower skills needed and those available requires increasing labor mobility between occupations, industries, and geographic regions; improved knowledge about job opportunities; and manpower retraining and improved education for the unskilled portion of the labor force. Stepped-up efforts to reduce the number of educational dropouts and to lower or eliminate restrictive work barriers are also needed to reduce structural unemployment. If a society can deal effectively with structural unemployment, it can also reduce the severity of the apparent conflict between unemployment and inflation.

Technological advance and changes in consumer taste help determine changes in the education, training, and skill levels of the labor force. In a rapidly changing economy, hundreds of thousands of workers may be out of work or between jobs when consumer demand shifts and technology changes. Under these conditions, the accumulation of a "hard core" of disadvantaged workers is a real possibility. Many observers have expressed concern lest the process of automation accompanying the technological changes of the last few decades permanently displace increasing numbers of workers. Although automation processes do displace both blue- and white-collar workers, it is apparent that even more new jobs have been created by an advancing technology. Trends toward severe structural unemployment have not materialized because of qualitative improvements in human resources and increased mobility. By monitoring aggregate demand and developing human-resource policies directed at reducing structural unemployment, we should be able to continue to avoid the massive and permanent joblessness that some have predicted will soon be upon us.

## VOLUNTARY RESTRAINT: WAGE-PRICE GUIDEPOSTS

In 1962, the late President Kennedy invoked the *wage-price guideposts* to achieve price stability and full employment. The idea of the guideposts is to rely on voluntary restraint rather than on government control to keep average wage increases equal to average increases in productivity, measured as output per manhour. In addition to formal guideposts, public officials have also applied subtle forms of pressure, exhortation, or persuasion. President Kennedy, for example, "encouraged" the steel industry to renounce publicized price hikes in 1962. Again in 1965, President Johnson "encouraged" the aluminum industry to roll back price increases with a not too thinly veiled threat that the federal government might reduce its stockpile of aluminum if the price hike were not removed.

The way in which guideposts allegedly work is as follows: Suppose some hypothetical economy produced $100 of national income and experienced a 4 percent annual increase in productivity, and that wage and salary income amounted to $75, or three-fourths of national income. A noninflationary guidepost policy would allow wages and profits to rise by 4 percent per year, since 96 hours of labor could produce what 100 hours of labor had produced a year earlier. The guideposts suggest that $3 of the $4 increase in income should go to labor and $1 to profits, all the while leaving *per unit* production costs (and presumably prices) unchanged. Industries experiencing more rapid productivity increases than the national average are expected to *reduce* product prices, whereas price *increases* are permissible in those instances where industry productivity falls below the national average. Departure from guidepost wage increases is possible for firms in need of more or less labor, thus encouraging the resource mobility required in a market economy. Neither labor nor business gains at the expense of the other party and both participate in the rising productivity of the economy under the guideposts.

In reality, both labor and management were displeased with the guidepost policy, but there is some evidence to suggest that wages and prices did rise somewhat less rapidly in the 1961–1965 expansion than they otherwise might have. As the decade of the 1960s drew to a close, however, monetary expansion and stepped-up Vietnam expenditures contributed to inflation and ultimate abandonment of the guideposts.

While some reputable economists have questioned the effectiveness of guideposts, still others defend this approach and point to the modest evidence that wages and prices may not have risen as rapidly as they otherwise might have during 1961–1965. However, the Nixon administration was ambivalent about jawboning during the inflation of the late 1960s. Many nations of Western Europe, including Britain, the Netherlands, and certain Scandinavian countries, have used various forms of voluntary restraint in recent years and have experienced comparably qualified successes or failures. Different forms of voluntarism or persuasion have been used with varying degrees of success, and in most instances about the only clear conclusion one can reach is that moral pleas such as guideposts at best serve as a modest check on inflationary pressures and help direct attention to the general public's stake in price and wage decisions. Although voluntary exhortation has not been an entirely successful solution, it could be the least costly approach to problems that threaten to disrupt a stable and prosperous economy, provided that compliance is forthcoming.

Efforts such as those discussed above can enhance the likelihood of controlling inflation and unemployment when used with fiscal and monetary policies in pursuit of price stability and full employment. Still, there is little on the horizon to suggest that this nation has as yet fully come to grips with the problem of achieving both full employment and price stability. Should either the specific or the general stabilization policies required be ignored, the unemployment-inflation tradeoff dilemma could well loom as the Loch Ness monster of the 1970s.

## REVIEW

### Summary

1. Fiscal and monetary policies provide a means whereby nations can control inflation and unemployment in some measure. Because of the many limitations to stabilization policies, however, it is important to use both fiscal and monetary measures in a coordinated attack on the problems at hand.

2. Opinion varies on the issues of: (a) how effective fiscal policy is compared to monetary policy, and (b) whether or not it is desirable to use stabilization policies of any kind to moderate mild swings in economic activity. The pro-Keynesian view of these matters argues that money may be of some importance, but only through its impact on interest rates, credit availability, and investment spending. The Keynesian view concludes that fiscal policy is *very* important and that we should monitor the economic system in order to achieve a stable and growing economy.

3. The Monetarists, led by Milton Friedman, see the determination of income and employment quite differently. Money is accorded a primary role, and income levels are seen as being directly affected by expansion and contraction of the money supply. Moreover, the Monetarists view fiscal policy as being very weak, if not totally ineffective, *unless* accompanied by changes in the monetary variable. Finally, the Monetarists conclude that discretionary and variable changes in taxes, government spending, and the money supply should be abandoned because such policies do more harm than good for all but the most volatile swings in economic activity.

4. Even when one ignores the many built-in limitations to stabilization policies (such as timing problems and variable impact), the experience of recent years reveals a very serious policy limitation: namely, conflict between the goals of full employment and price stability. The so-called "tradeoff" problem results from the fact that nations at full employment have experienced increases in the price level of between 3 and 4 percent

per year, and when relative price stability has been achieved, between 5 and 7 percent of the labor force has been unemployed.

5. Three factors contributing to the unemployment-inflation tradeoff relationships expressed by the Phillips curve are: (*a*) structural unemployment, characterized by mismatching of the skills required for job openings and those possessed by the unemployed; (*b*) the existence of cost-push inflation, under which monopoly power in either resource or product markets creates inflationary pressures; and (*c*) structural bottlenecks and rigidities in markets for goods and resources—a somewhat natural outgrowth of a dynamic and growing economy.

6. Many nations have had only nominal success in coping with the tradeoff problem. Among the tactics that might be used to remedy this problem, direct wage and price controls and even persuasive guideposts have been used sparingly and with little success in the United States. Emphasis has been put upon manpower-development programs and the monitoring of powerful monopolized markets. This strategy has not remedied the problem by any means. In short, the United States and the developed nations in Western Europe simply have not yet found a solution to the tradeoff dilemma.

## Identify the Following Concepts and Terms

- cost-push inflation
- revised quantity theory
- unemployment-inflation tradeoff
- structural bottlenecks and inflation
- demand-pull inflation
- guideposts
- the Monetarists' view of the importance of money
- equation of exchange

## Questions to Answer

1. Briefly explain how monetary and fiscal policies affect aggregate demand, income, employment, and prices. Why is it important to coordinate both approaches to stabilization policy?

2. The equation of exchange is used to express the "quantity theory." Momentarily ignoring the differences between the classical economists and contemporary Monetarists, explain how the quantity theory provides useful insights on the importance of money.

3. Explain and evaluate the Monetarists' views on stabilization policy. In your opinion, is it possible to say that fiscal or monetary policy is more important? Why do you hold this position?

4. The unemployment-inflation tradeoff problem arises from several fundamental forces at work in the American economy. What are they? What policy steps are required to remedy this goal-conflict problem?

# CHAPTER 13
# Economic Growth: Problems and Policy

The purpose of this chapter is to examine economic growth in the industrialized nations of the world. Modern income and employment theory and policy explain unemployment and inflation for an economy, given a fixed amount of resources and a constant technology which set a productive capacity ceiling at one point in time (e.g., 1971). This is a short-run view of a static economic system capable of producing some maximum amount of output at one point in time, where concern is restricted to achieving full employment and price stability. In contrast, *economic growth* is a long-run perspective concentrating on income changes—increased productive capacity and the extent to which a nation utilizes its capacity. Net investment expenditures are a focal point of economic growth because net investment (*a*) increases the productive capacity of a nation, and (*b*) helps determine the utilization of growing capacity. Investment is usually thought of as the commitment of resources to the production of machinery, tools, and plants —*physical capital*—but it will become clear as we proceed that investment expenditures in the more general sense also alter the quality and quantity of other growth ingredients.

Economic growth over a period of time is of vital concern to both advanced and underdeveloped nations. Because nations differ in their economic development, economists have found it useful to distinguish between growth in developed nations and that in poorer or underdeveloped nations. In this chapter, however, we will focus our attention on those nations in the more advanced stages of economic development, which encompass about one-third of the world's population. (The economically underdeveloped countries, which include the bulk of the world's population, are a special problem which we will treat separately in Chapter 27.) We first discuss the meaning and facts of economic growth (Part A). Some important elements in the growth of productive capacity in developed nations are discussed in Part B. Part C then examines the theory of economic growth.

## A. THE MEANING AND MEASUREMENT OF ECONOMIC GROWTH

The term "economic growth" is both meaningful and meaningless. American citizens have a per capita income considerably more than 20 times as large as per capita income in India. Indeed, some two-thirds of the rapidly growing population of the world (which will reach 4 billion persons in the 1970s) live in nations in which per capita income is below one-tenth the average in this country. Internationally, some four out of ten persons are illiterate; world-wide life expectancy averages 18 years *less* than in the

United States; and infant mortality in the United States is one-fourth the world average. Thus, one might argue that nations similar to the United States, such as Canada and Great Britain, have "grown" more rapidly than some other nations; indeed, the differences in levels of living among nations are enormous, and, in that sense, economic growth cannot help but be a meaningful concept.

*A Warning About the Costs of Growth* Economic growth is a subject of both importance and controversy. Many authorities contend that nations can and must strive to enlarge their rate of growth in income by cultivating forces contributing to increased quantities of output and by stabilizing growth in total spending. Yet, more than one critic of "growthmanship" has remarked that billions of dollars in additional GNP are created by producing pollution-abatement equipment, and that upping the automobile death rate from 55,000 to 70,000 persons per year would likewise cause GNP to "grow." Certainly growth advantages such as a rising income and consumption level, expanded government ability to provide needed services, full employment of labor resources, and international economic viability are not to be taken lightly. At the same time, however, an interpretation of economic growth solely in terms of the quantity of output is questioned increasingly today because such progress has not been without cost. In short, assessment of the "progress" inherent in modern measures of economic growth is not an easy task. Stressing the rate of economic growth in certain respects emphasizes the quantity instead of the quality of life at a time when more, not less, emphasis needs to be placed on such factors as a desirable environment. In addition, emphasis on economic growth borders on an inflationary bias, since maximum potential growth requires full employment. Moreover, serious structural-resource adjustment may be required in a changing economy, although there is no evidence to date that permanent technological unemployment is a serious problem. Growth in GNP also requires investment—postponed consumption—and this represents another cost of growth.

Such arguments are not easily resolved one way or another, as you can well imagine. While our present task is to learn something about economic growth, it should be realized that a complete discussion of the pros and cons of growth requires more information than can be presented in a few pages. Each citizen must weigh the benefits and costs of growth, and to properly evaluate them, he must know about environmental economics, public finance, and other matters we will cover in later chapters. Thus, the first thing that must be recognized is that economic growth is not easily defined, and that growth is a *means to the end* of improving the welfare of man, *not an end itself.*

## Tradition and Change

In its formative years, the United States experienced vast changes in productive capacity, but today more emphasis is put on the growth in the demand for output. Economic growth centers upon one central ingredient: change, and this means change in areas which sometimes extend far beyond economic concerns. Poorer countries are faced with vast capital-accumulation needs, but even more basic changes in social, political, and cultural structures are required to increase productive capacity. There is a difference between economic development and economic growth, and part of that difference is that nations which are not heavily industrialized require relatively significant structural changes. In such nations, the structure of production must change from reliance on primary sectors of the economy (e.g., agriculture) to the creation and development of secondary and tertiary sectors (e.g., manufacturing and service industries). This process is just what occurred in developed nations years ago.

## EARLY AMERICAN GROWTH AND DEVELOPMENT

The American economy has undergone a variety of changes in the last two centuries. Economic growth and development have been characterized by several elements of change, the more important of which were:

1. Growth in factory industries and mass-production techniques during the Industrial Revolution.

2. Settlement and development of a vast wilderness area possessing abundant natural resources.

3. Emergence of broadened national markets through investment in *social-overhead capital;* that is, public-sector investment in power facilities, schools, highways, railway networks, and government itself.

4. Mass immigration which pushed the growth rate in human resources up to and even above 2 percent per year until the second decade of the twentieth century.

5. Technological and scientific advance in a wide variety of industrial markets (including the energy and fuel industries, oil processing, air transportation, and so on).

6. Rapid rates of private capital formation during the nineteenth century due to heavy investment inflows from Western European nations, particularly Great Britain. For nearly a century starting in the early 1800s, high rates of domestic investment augmented European investments, allowing the American economy to develop a massive stock of capital resources.

Many other elements helped create a social, political, and economic environment favorable to the development process, and very early in the twentieth century the economy of the United States had given firm evidence of its strength. By 1900, the per capita income level in the United States exceeded that of the United Kingdom, Germany, and France and was growing more rapidly than in the leading nations of continental Europe.

## CHANGE IN THE MARKET INSTRUMENT

When the historical record of economic growth and change in recent decades is reviewed, one startling conclusion emerges: The once-dominant market system of economic organization which was first given life in Europe (particularly England) has retained neither its dominance nor its original form. Systems of economic organization have changed as nations and people have, and today many countries rely on various degrees of government control and planning in conjunction with a market system. The political-economic system of unfettered markets has been altered and even replaced by the mixed market economy. Accordingly, with the passage of time, change and diversity have characterized the trajectory of economic systems.

An already developed or advanced economy such as that of the United

States typically is one which has, at some point in its past, avoided tradition-bound behavior. As economic growth has occurred in these advanced economies, certain common patterns have been repeated. For example, in recent decades economic change has involved an enlarged urban environment, heavy industrial development, and large corporations. The more developed, market-oriented economies are also typified by an expanding public sector charged with guiding the evolving economy. In contrast, poorer nations typically remain bound by custom, institutions, rules, and behavior which have been preserved for decades or even centuries. Modernization leading to growth in output requires political, social, cultural, religious, and even intellectual changes as well as economic ones, and these also remain important to developed countries interested in further economic growth.[1]

### The Growth Experience

Increases in GNP, NNP, or other income measures are fallible indications of economic growth, if for no other reason than that there are hidden assumptions and statistical shortcomings implicit in the measurement of national income. Some of the more common sources of confusion about the measurement of economic growth are worthy of brief attention.

### ASSESSING ECONOMIC GROWTH

Any one of several income measures such as GNP are generally used to measure growth in levels of output. One source of confusion in using GNP or any other income account to measure economic growth is changes in price levels, and this is the reason a distinction is made between *real* and *money* output. If a nation's total output rises from $400 billion to $800 billion during a period when prices also double, real output has not increased, even though the value of output in money terms has risen twofold. When we are concerned with economic growth, the context will always be that of *real* output unless otherwise stated.

For measuring changes in the *aggregate* productive capacity of a nation, total GNP may be the preferred gauge of economic growth. However, the rate of growth in per capita income is perhaps the most common measure. Measuring per capita income (the ratio of income/population) may be more accurate because it reflects increases in the standard of living of a populace. The percentage change in total GNP and growth in the population determine percentage increases in per capita GNP:

$$\text{Percentage change in per capita GNP} = \text{percentage change in total GNP} - \text{percentage change in population}$$

Thus, if population and GNP increase by 5 percent, per capita output remains unchanged.

In still other instances, it is sometimes helpful to gauge economic growth by measuring the ratio of total output/resource input. Thus, it is often said that the ratio *output/manhours of labor* reflects labor productivity. This

---

[1] Change in an underdeveloped environment is extraordinarily difficult to achieve, and some experts are convinced that authoritarian political-economic systems may be required to accelerate the pace of growth and development. See, for example, Robert Heilbroner, *The Great Ascent* (New York: Harper & Row, 1963).

measure of output per manhour is a useful index because it reflects the extent to which one manhour of labor can produce more output with the passage of time. Another commonly used measure of economic growth is the ratio *output/capital*, which reveals the amount of GNP created per dollar of capital resources. In both cases, however, "productivity" changes are a broad reflection of many other elements in the growth process. For example, the ratio GNP/capital shows the "productivity" of capital only in a limited sense because all other factors which also contribute to a larger output level (e.g., increases in the labor supply) are ignored. Furthermore, GNP does not reflect qualitative improvements in goods and services, it fails to account for nonmarket transactions, the changes in the quality of life due to increased leisure time, or the debasement of the environment. In short, there simply is no one completely accurate and best measure of economic growth—different measures are useful and necessary, depending upon the circumstances one is investigating.

## GROWTH IN DEVELOPED NATIONS

An economy does not grow without experiencing vast changes, but it is possible for nations to *not* grow, and such an event in no small measure reflects resistance to change. We can gain some insights into economic growth by examining its attributes in several industrialized nations, which are interesting subjects in their own right.

*Comparative Rates of Growth*   Little information is available concerning economic growth in developed nations during the nineteenth century. What information we do have suggests, for example, that the American economy did not experience as rapid a rate of growth in the early decades of its existence as has occurred more recently. After the Civil War economic growth began to accelerate, and for something like a century total GNP expanded at the rate of 3.5 percent annually while per capita GNP grew nearly 2 percent each year. Since the 1950s, total and per capita output have grown even more rapidly in this nation as well as in other industrialized nations such as France, Canada, Germany, and Japan.

Figure 1 illustrates the recent growth in real output for several of the more developed nations of the world. Real GNP has grown at the remarkable rate of more than 10 percent in Japan for nearly two decades, and four other European nations have grown at more than 5 percent each year. As is true for the United States, these rates of growth exceed the annual average for over a century of 3 to 4 percent per year.[2] Figure 1 overstates the average rate of growth in per capita GNP in the amount of the annual percentage increase in population, which has averaged approximately 1 percent per year (or less) for these nations. Thus, per capita GNP has grown approximately 9 percent annually in Japan and 2.5 percent annually in the United States since the early 1950s.

Currently, the economy of the United States, with something like one-twentieth of the world's population, produces approximately one-third of the world's total output measured in terms of gross national product. Per

[2] The long-term growth record of several nations is carefully analyzed in United States Department of Commerce, *Long-Term Economic Growth: 1860–1965* (Washington, D.C.: U.S. Government Printing Office, 1966).

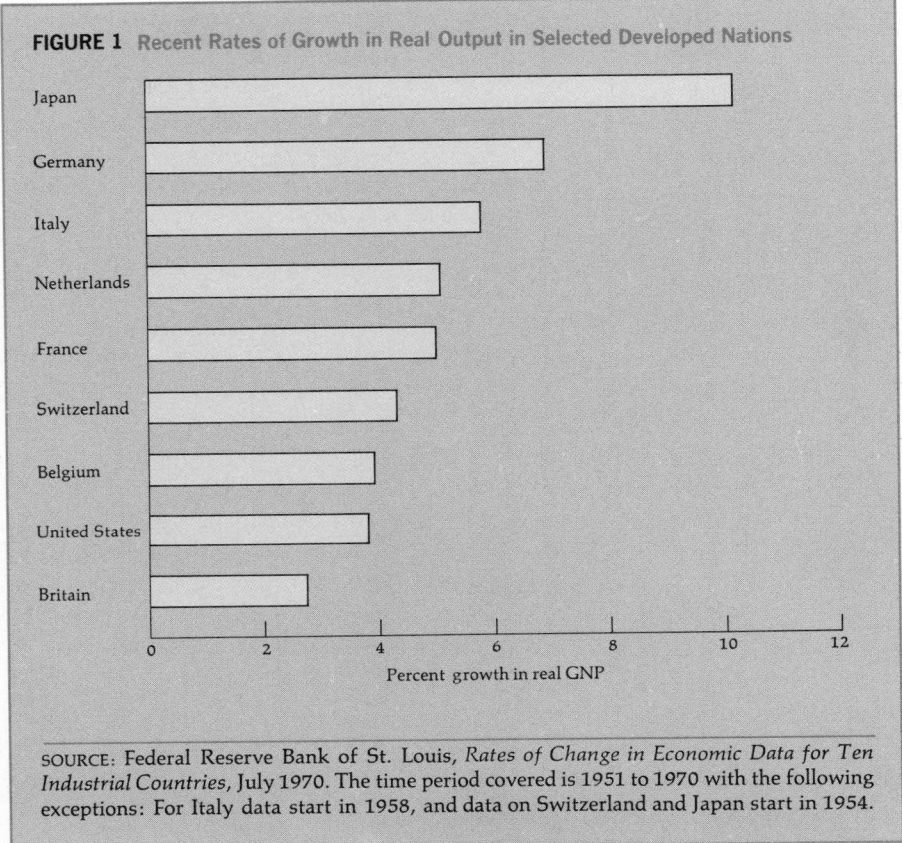

**FIGURE 1** Recent Rates of Growth in Real Output in Selected Developed Nations

Percent growth in real GNP

SOURCE: Federal Reserve Bank of St. Louis, *Rates of Change in Economic Data for Ten Industrial Countries*, July 1970. The time period covered is 1951 to 1970 with the following exceptions: For Italy data start in 1958, and data on Switzerland and Japan start in 1954.

capita *money* GNP in the United States is approaching $5,000 annually, and the total output of the state of California alone is larger than the total GNP of all but some half-dozen nations. If the impressive growth rates in real GNP of such nations as Japan, Germany, Canada, the United States, and France are matched in the future, total output will double every seven to twenty years. Impressive as these figures may be, however, there is a great deal of variation in growth from one time to another and one nation to another, with the result that the measurement and meaning of economic growth changes from time to time.

*The Growth Record of the United States*  Figure 2 summarizes the record of growth in the United States and includes estimates of trends for total and per capita GNP to the year 2000.[3] Even though growth has not occurred in

[3] Growth measures in Figure 2 are presented on a ratio or logarithmic scale. Equal distances on a ratio scale (e.g., from $200 billion to $400 billion and from $400 billion to $800 billion) represent equal percentage changes in GNP. Thus, if GNP is growing at a relatively steady *percentage* rate, it will graph as a straight line on a ratio scale as that shown in Figure 2.

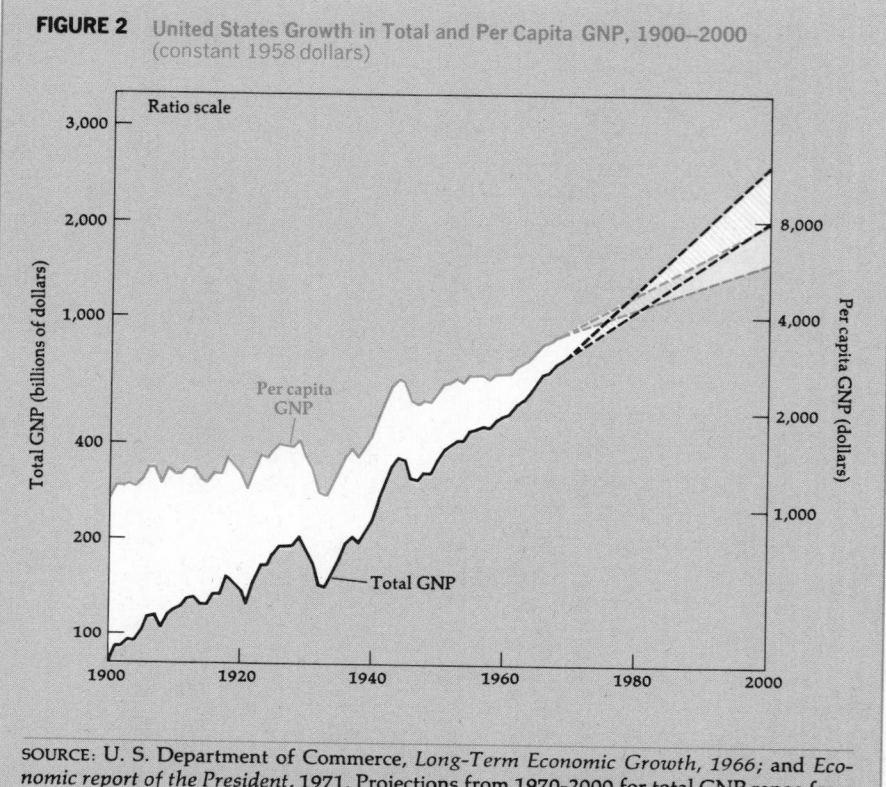

**FIGURE 2** United States Growth in Total and Per Capita GNP, 1900–2000 (constant 1958 dollars)

SOURCE: U. S. Department of Commerce, *Long-Term Economic Growth, 1966;* and *Economic report of the President,* 1971. Projections from 1970-2000 for total GNP range from a high of 4 to a low of 3.2 percent per year, and per capita GNP estimates are based on 2.7 and 1.7 percent per year respectively.

a perfectly steady pattern, real output has increased almost tenfold and per capita output has more than tripled in the last 70 years. Most authorities expect economic growth to continue at or slightly above the rates shown in Figure 2 for the three decades remaining in this century. If these observations are relatively accurate, the economy of the United States will hit the $2 trillion mark before the year 2000.[4]

## SIGNIFICANCE OF ECONOMIC GROWTH

It is clear from Figure 2 that whether or not a nation grows in the future is important. If the growth rate in GNP can be increased to a steady 4 percent per year, GNP will approximate $2.5 trillion by the year 2000, representing

---

[4] Economic growth has not proceeded at a steady rate from year to year. Indeed, if we were to examine GNP data carefully in different time periods, rather sharp year-to-year changes could be discerned. During the first two-thirds of this century, for example, growth in GNP ranged between +16 and —15 percent on a year-to-year basis. Because of the irregularity of growth revealed in Figure 2, it is hazardous to reach firm conclusions about growth trends based on data covering one or a few years.

some 25 percent or one-half trillion dollars more of real output than a growth rate of 3.2 percent would produce. Figure 2 also illustrates the result of combining a more rapid rate of growth in total GNP with the lower rate of growth in population typical of recent years. If the rate of growth in per capita GNP were held at 2.7 percent annually, real per capita GNP would double its 1970 level, rising to $8,300 by the year 2000.

A growing national income like that shown in Figure 2 eases the burden of devoting resources to social goods such as schools and urban renewal. Economic growth may also have an important potential impact on national security and international prestige. As long as additional tax revenues accompany economic growth, they will enable a growing economy to fill its backlog of unmet needs more readily. Economic growth may also ease the problems of the poor to the extent that their disposable incomes grow along with those of the more affluent.

Since the poor countries of the world have become aware of the advantages of developed nations, the political and social consequences of their frustrations are also part of the "growthmanship" stakes today. These countries have experienced a "revolution of rising expectations" which, in the absence of economic growth in the coming decades, may result in a political revolution grounded in frustration. Indeed, stability and freedom throughout the world may be influenced by the success or failure of the political-economic systems of the U.S. and the Soviet Union, for both are closely watched by ideologically uncommitted nations still in the throes of development.

## TWO DIMENSIONS TO ECONOMIC GROWTH

One further point about economic growth is necessary. The expansion of productive capacity—the potential supply of output—is a dimension of economic growth that is quite distinct from growth in the demand for output. Examination of growth in an economy's potential supply of output concentrates on those elements which expand productive capacity, such as labor and capital resources. In contrast, the "demand" side of economic growth concentrates on what happens when aggregate demand does not grow at a rate that matches growth in the potential supply of output. A major problem facing developed nations such as the United States is that of maintaining a rate of growth in the demand for output equal to the expansion of productive capacity.

Figure 3 distinguishes between these two growth perspectives by recalling the production possibilities for a model economy producing two hypothetical goods with a bundle of generally defined resources. The production frontier of Figure 3 portrays the combinations of two products that can be produced with a fixed supply of resources and fixed production techniques.

*Growth in Supply* Productive capacity or the potential supply of output changes from one year to the next as the basic elements of growth are expanded. Thus, if technological advances occur or if the quantity of a nation's natural, human, or capital resources expands, the production frontier shifts outward, from $PF_{1971}$ to $PF_{1972}$ as illustrated in Figure 3. Increases in the potential supply of output simply represent changes in the capacity to produce and *do not* reflect growth in the actual demand for output, which may or may not occur.

**FIGURE 3**   The Supply and Demand Sides to Growth

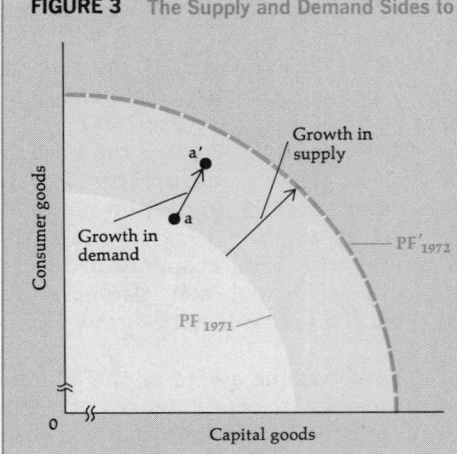

*Economic Growth.* Supply or capacity growth shifts a production frontier outward, allowing the production of more output. Just because potential capacity increases, actual income and output do not necessarily increase in an equal amount. Failure to use resources fully and in the most productive fashion known may cause an economy to grow less rapidly than its maximum potential. Consequently, a nation may end up at point a' in 1972 instead of on the production frontier $PF'_{1972}$.

*Growth in Demand*   Actual GNP is a demand measure of economic growth that reflects the utilization of productive capacity as time passes. Figure 3 illustrates how an economy might experience an insufficient rate of growth in the demand for output. Even though the *potential supply* of output expands to $PF_{1972}$ in Figure 3, it is possible for demand to grow by a smaller amount, say from point *a* on the 1971 production frontier to point *a'*, which is below the 1972 level of productive capacity. If this situation does occur, a nation fails to utilize fully its existing stock of resources; that is, the familiar GNP "gap" discussed in earlier chapters occurs.

### B. ELEMENTS TO GROWTH IN POTENTIAL SUPPLY

Information on the factors that contribute to increased productive capacity is rather meager; yet, there is general agreement that three important ingredients tend to cooperate in ways that are imperfectly and only vaguely understood. These three interrelated factors are: the resource base, the institutional environment, and technological change.

### The Resource Base

The quantity and quality of natural, human, and physical-capital resources are the factors of production termed the *resource base*. Either larger *quantities* of such resources or improvements in the *quality* of the resource base expand productive capacity. There are crucial differences between the three categories of resources, and even though they cooperate in stimulating economic growth, it is more useful to consider each separately.

### NATURAL RESOURCES

The quantity and quality of land, climate, minerals, water, and topography are part of the natural-resource base. Many natural resources (such as minerals and land area) are relatively fixed in supply, while others (e.g., climate) are unalterable in quality. However, a nation's natural-resource base is not fixed forever, because the application of an advancing technology and the use of changing human and capital resources continually redefine its known and useful properties. The supply of usable land has been expanded through irrigation and conservation techniques, and metropolitan centers such as Tucson have sprung up in desert regions once thought incapable of comfortably supporting all but the most hardy forms of human life. As time goes on, the unearthing of new supplies of known natural resources, the discovery of new ways to use them, and the uncovering of new types of natural resources accompany technological change and add to the nation's natural-resource base.[5]

The lack or the existence of abundant natural resources alone neither causes nor prohibits economic growth, but, other things being equal, an abundant natural-resource base does place nations in a better growth position. This observation simply drives home the fact that it is the *interplay* of such growth elements as institutions, technology, and resources (natural, human, and capital) that generates economic growth.

## HUMAN RESOURCES

A second basic resource is a nation's human resources. The *quantity* and *quality* of these resources comprise a factor of production that contributes significantly to economic growth. From the viewpoint of manpower supply, the underdeveloped nations of the world make one lesson abundantly clear: Enough, but not too many, human resources are needed. Many of the two-thirds of the world's population living in poverty reside in countries plagued by excess population relative to the other growth elements. In recent years, the combination of rising birth rates and falling death rates has pushed population growth rates upward and, when combined with modest rates of growth in total GNP, has resulted in near-constant per capita incomes in many nations of the world.

Little can be said with any authority about the optimal size of a population. However, it is clear that the quality of human resources is a key dimension to economic growth. Improved health, increased levels of education, enhanced manpower skills, a healthy attitude toward work, and greater labor mobility characterize the more rapidly growing and relatively affluent nations of the world such as Canada and the United States. Because the quality of human resources is so important, nations have increasingly recognized that investment in these resources represents a form of human "capital" which is vital to economic growth.

## CAPITAL RESOURCES AND INVESTMENT

Economic growth requires that ample natural and human resources be accompanied by the physical-capital component—the "tools" used to develop and utilize these other resources. The contemporary economic process of producing and exchanging goods and services is highly specialized and

[5] Heavy reliance on extractive industries in underdeveloped nations such as Chile places a time limit on resources, and even in the United States near-term depletion of certain metals represents a potential problem. Many other nations, some of which have experienced rapid rates of growth, have a relatively inferior supply of natural resources, although in several underdeveloped countries in Africa and South America, natural resources are vastly underutilized.

circular, and numerous production stages and large amounts of capital resources are involved in the most effective technological methods of converting resources into outputs. The historical record in developed nations provides a clear indication that there is a positive relationship between a
nation's stock of capital goods and its economic growth. Gross investment
in physical-capital resources in the United States today, for example,
amounts to about 15 percent of GNP annually, and physical-capital resources in the American economy are approaching a total value of $3
trillion. On the *average*, American workers are supplied with some $35,000
of capital equipment in the United States, a fact which helps explain the
economic strength of this nation.

Not too long ago some economists emphasized investment in such physical capital as tools, machinery, and buildings to the exclusion of investment in the many other vital and closely related sources of economic
growth. A literal interpretation of capital formation to mean physical-
capital assets alone is much too narrow a view of the process of economic
growth. However, saving and investment for all "capital" purposes, when
broadly viewed, is without question a most vital growth component. Technological advance often requires investment in new equipment and machines. In addition, investment in research and development often represents the technology and capital formation of tomorrow. The education of
human resources is, in part, an investment process in which unskilled and
relatively untrained labor is transformed into human capital, and the
natural-resource base also depends heavily upon investment for acquisition
and discovery, as we noted earlier. Thus, the capital-formation process is a
multi-faceted dimension to economic growth and one that facilitates the use
and development of all aspects of mankind's environment.

### The Social and Institutional Environment

Most economists agree that institutional characteristics and behavior—the
social, cultural, political, and economic environment—are also crucial to
economic growth.

#### THE INSTITUTIONAL SETTING

A great many observers feel that, as economic growth occurs, it is important
that the behavior patterns of a society lean in the direction of flexibility and
adaptation to change, instead of toward the preservation of the ceremonial
fetishes and rigidities that often encumber primitive nations. For example,
in the United States, economic institutions such as financial markets and
manufacturing firms have adapted to changing needs. Risk-taking has been
encouraged and the savings of millions of individuals has been mobilized
quickly for investment purposes. In the advanced and more rapidly growing nations of the world, political flexibility and social mobility seem to be
combined in a fashion that encourages individual initiative and personal
effort. The American government has been a key institutional force in the
growth process, promoting an environment sympathetic to private enterprise and the preservation of an orderly legal process. Many necessary
social goods such as transportation networks, education, and energy facilities are also outgrowths of the institution of government. The American
people, as well as those in many other developed nations, are not severely

burdened with social or cultural inhibitions about work, and they seem to possess relatively few cultural "sacred cows" that are at odds with economic growth.

Clearly, many qualifications to this simplified description of the social and institutional environment are in order. The American institutional scene is not a primrose path to economic growth and prosperity—many other nations (e.g., the Soviet Union and Japan) have grown startlingly with an entirely different mix of social, political, cultural, and economic characteristics.

## PRICES, MARKETS, AND RESOURCE ALLOCATION

The economies of nations like the United States and Canada are characterized by heavy reliance on markets in which supply, demand, prices, and profits lead to resource-allocation decisions. Prices and profits perform "organizing" functions, determining how limited goods are rationed to a consuming populace, how scarce resources are allocated to producers willing and able to use factors of production, and how smoothly and quickly the system responds to the changing needs of a dynamic economy. The market system determines *what* a nation produces and *how* efficiently it uses resources.

Maximum growth in output requires a smoothly functioning economic process that transfers resources from declining or less rapidly expanding segments of the economy to more rapidly expanding ones. When such changes do not occur completely and with reasonable speed, a nation fails to develop its productive capacity fully. Structural unemployment, monopoly power leading to the administration of wages and prices, and make-work practices are only a few examples of how contemporary economic systems may use resources in an inefficient way. Obviously, solutions to such problems are not easy to come by.

While the record is somewhat ambivalent on the matter of how efficient a price-directed market economy is in allocating resources, there are some indications that it has worked reasonably well. Many nations depend more heavily on centrally directed planning in allocating resources, however, and some of them (e.g., the Soviet Union) have made remarkable progress with modest reliance on the market institution.

### Technological Change

The term "technological change" is sometimes confused with the term "productivity," which is that portion of growth in output that cannot be explained by or attributed to changes in the quantity of resources such as labor or capital. To avoid ambiguity we shall regard *technological change* as the organized application of scientific knowledge, a process involving inventions and innovations which enhance economic growth in concrete ways. New products and industries such as plastics, computers, television communications, and space systems appear with startling frequency as a reflection of the advancing technical knowledge of man. Better strains of fertilizer and seed, automated factories, improved knowledge about irrigation and weather modification, and the development of jet propulsion, solar energy, and factory-assembled homes similarly reflect innovations that allow more output to be produced for each manhour of labor. Technology adds to both the quantity and quality of life, although it assures neither—as air and water pollution demonstrate.

Three attributes of changing technology merit brief comment.

### RESEARCH AND DEVELOPMENT

One-third of a century ago the United States was spending under $1 billion, or about one-half of 1 percent of real GNP on research annually. Throughout the 1960s research and development expenditures ranged between $20 and $30 billion per year—some 3 percent of GNP. More and more, such expenditures are the result of highly organized efforts by large corporations, government agencies, and universities, although the era of the one-man invention is not over. Even though these are only crude indications of the investment commitment to technology, it is clear that many surprises in areas ranging from genetics to space systems await this generation as the fruits of current basic and applied research mature.

### EMBODIED TECHNOLOGY

Often the innovations that symbolize technological advance can be embodied in the economic process only by investment in physical-capital equipment (computer and space communication systems are typical examples). Investment is thus an important component of technological advances that allow more output to be produced per unit of input. Technological change is also embodied in other sources of economic growth. A nation's institutional environment is related to technological change, and if behavior patterns, institutions, and people are rigid and custom-tied, changes in technology are less likely to arise and be accepted. Technology is also clearly an outgrowth of the quality of human resources in two ways. First, increased education expands knowledge and thus contributes to man's ability to control and use his environment. Second, changes in technology demand higher skill levels from human resources. A changing technology can also alter natural resources in dramatic ways, as will become apparent once nuclear and solar energy are transformed into commercial power.

### TECHNOLOGY AND SPECIALIZATION

Technological change is characterized by increasing specialization, mass production, and the development of large-scale markets—elements that are frequently lacking in underdeveloped nations. Specialization and an enlarged scale of producing and marketing represent the achievement of *economies of scale* or size. That is, increased specialization and an advancing technology have allowed firms to use resources more efficiently, and this factor has been important in lowering costs and complementing domestic economic development. Technological change and economies of scale have also been enhanced by the expansion of markets made possible through the growth of international trade. Specialization conducted on a worldwide level often carries with it other significant advantages, including the transfer of technological know-how.

### The Domains of Knowledge and Ignorance About Growth

The factors that contribute to growth in the capacity to produce cooperate in poorly understood ways. Because these growth elements are distinct in one sense and yet very interdependent, there is scanty evidence to allow us to isolate a single cause of growth, and little merit in doing so. Nonetheless, it is apparent that stocks of natural, human, and capital resources; the institutional environment of a society; and technological advances are supply-oriented growth elements that depend on investment and capital formation in very important ways. While we need not and do not contend that physical-capital resources are necessarily more or less important than the other supply factors mentioned, a society's ability and willingness to postpone present consumption to invest in the future clearly enhances the prospects for economic growth. After a brief review of the knowledge about measures that enhance growth in the potential supply of output, we shall comment on our growth ignorance.

## STEPS TO COMPLEMENT GROWTH IN PRODUCTIVE CAPACITY

For the most part, the economic policies that enhance future economic growth in the potential supply of output are recognizable as they affect the elements of growth in the potential supply of output described earlier.

*Resource-Development Policies*  Investment in physical and human-capital resources can be intensified through incentives in the form of investment tax credits, depreciation allowances, and public-sector support of manpower training and education. Investment opportunities have appeared regularly throughout America's past, and a stable economic environment in the future will do much to maintain growth in the resource base. Studies have repeatedly shown, for example, that returns on investment in education range between 10 and 18 percent per year, and that for nearly a century in the United States the rate at which investment in education has grown has exceeded the growth in investment in nonhuman capital resources. The quality of the physical-capital resources which are accumulated is also important. When $1 of investment in capital resources today does the work of $2 of investment 25 years ago, the age or "vintage" of the current stock of capital is of obvious importance. Other things being equal, the less the average age of a nation's stock of capital, the greater its productive capabilities. The maintenance and improvement of natural resources as well as investment in social-overhead capital also turn out to be a vital feature of economic growth. The resource base of a nation *can be* made more productive in a qualitative context through appropriate government policies.

*Institutional Environment*  Many observers feel that a cultural framework which stresses an orderly business environment, enterprise, work, competition, thrift, and individualism, must be preserved and strengthened to accommodate continued growth in output. Similarly, they feel that it is important that steps be taken to control impediments to growth such as social and institutional barriers that impede the resource-allocation function of markets. Policies designed to enhance the efficient use and the mobility of scarce resources are important to continued growth in productive capacity.

*Technology and Research*  Research and development require continuing support from the public and private sectors. These efforts often lead to a more productive and efficient technology. Moreover, they frequently generate "spillover benefits," allowing society at large to benefit from research investments. The research done many years ago has materialized in synthetics that are used for such things as throw-away beer bottles and plastic heart valves, while returns to space exploration, medical research, and the like promise to be equally startling. The results of research contribute significantly to increased growth.

### THE RESIDUAL OF IGNORANCE

In recent years, several economists have attempted to account for growth in a nation's output by measuring the contribution of the different elements of growth. Because the way in which these elements interact is poorly understood, observers have simplified growth theory by stressing the *quantities* of labor and physical capital. Measuring labor and capital formation is a reasonably simple task and, in addition, these magnitudes fit conveniently into economic analysis. Capital formation through investment has received particular emphasis because it is known that the quality and quantity of other growth-inducing elements (human and natural resources, as well as technological change) often require investment. If certain simplifying assumptions are made about the character of investment and capital formation, several important aspects of the economic growth process can be identified in the general framework of an aggregate production function.

*The Aggregate Production Function* An aggregate production function relating income or output to increases in resources such as capital and labor describes income as depending upon growth elements such as labor ($L$), capital ($K$), and a productivity residual ($R$), or

$$\text{GNP} = \text{function of } (L, K, R)$$

Several simplifying assumptions are made in using an aggregate production function.[6] First, investment is regarded as expenditures for physical-capital resources alone. Even though other important forms of investment occur, it is difficult if not impossible to measure their impact on technological change, human resources, or institutions with any accuracy. Second, natural-resource supplies are typically regarded as fixed and are therefore ignored. Of course, the productive character of the natural-resource base does change as technological change and investment occur, but this again is an unmeasurable growth ingredient. Third, stocks or quantities of labor and capital resources used as inputs (denoted by the terms $L$ and $K$) are adjusted to reflect the *relative* importance of each factor. Most often, the share of income going to labor and capital is used to weight each resource in terms of its relative importance in producing output. Fourth, other elements contributing to economic growth that increase productivity are denoted by $R$—a "rag-bag" collection of growth-inducing forces sometimes called the *residual of ignorance*. The vaguely understood elements in $R$ represent everything except changes in the quantities of capital and labor. Finally, the aggregate production function can be adjusted to reflect growth in income and in capital and labor resources.

---

[6] A more complete treatment of the technical properties and assumptions of the production function can be found in T. F. Dernburg and D. M. McDougall, *Macro-Economics*, 3rd ed. (New York: McGraw-Hill, 1968), pp. 277–296.

While it is distressing to resort to such loose generalities about economic growth, it must be remembered that growth is influenced by many non-economic and qualitative considerations, including the institutional, cultural, and behavioral characteristics of a society. Although these are important matters, they are also very much out of the purview of an introductory course in economics. Despite its limitations, the production function provides an instructive framework for studying productive capacity.

*The Meaning of the "Residual"* Several recent observers have attempted to account for growth in output by measuring the contributions of the different sources of growth identified in the production function. What scholars like Robert Solow, Simon Kuznets, and Edward Denison have found is that the growth contribution of *quantities* of capital and labor resources typically explain only about one-fourth to one-half of the rate of growth in GNP for developed countries. Thus, these investigators have shown that for a reasonably typical rate of growth in real output of $GNP_g$ = 3.3 percent per year, growth in the relative quantity of labor accounts for about one-third of increased output per year, growth in the quantity of capital accounts for about one-seventh, and the "residual" factors (such things as the quality of resources and technological change) explain the remainder of the total growth in output. Thus, if $GNP_g$ denotes the percentage rate of growth in output:[7]

$$\text{Income growth} = \text{labor growth} + \text{capital growth} + \text{residual}$$
$$GNP_g = 1\% + 0.5\% + 1.8\%$$

*A Note on Growth Sources* The important point concerning the residual $R$ is that authorities simply cannot fully answer the question, What causes an economy to grow? One of the reasons that the residual factor as a measure of ignorance about economic growth is considerably more significant than changes in the stocks of capital and labor resources is that the quality of human resources and technological change embodied in capital are not readily measured. Empirical attempts to identify the sources of economic growth have not been altogether impressive for this reason.[8]

Edward Denison's study for the Committee on Economic Development represents one of the more useful attempts to reduce the residual of ignorance by identifying certain sources of growth that are sometimes ignored. Although there are many hidden assumptions in his work, Figure 4 does give a crude perspective on the sources of growth for the United States during the course of this century as well as rough estimates for the future. The figure shows, for example, that some 29 percent of the full-employment growth rate established at 3.3 percent per year by Denison for 1960 to

[7] This formulation of output growth is that of Edward Denison's "time-series" approach to measuring changes in output and weighted resource inputs (weights are income shares, as noted earlier).

[8] Bear in mind that as a model of the growth process, an aggregate production function is oversimplified because we really do not know much about how the elements of growth interact. Although $R$ is a residual of ignorance, it accounts for a considerable amount of growth in income; indeed, it is largely because of the productivity residual that nations have experienced increases in per capita output.

**FIGURE 4**  Sources of Economic Growth in the United States

| Estimated growth sources | 1909–1929 (percent) | 1929–1957 (percent) | 1960–1980 (percent) |
|---|---|---|---|
| Increased quantity of labor | 39 | 27 | 29 |
| Increased quantity of capital | 26 | 15 | 15 |
| Increased quality of labor | 13 | 27 | 22 |
| Technological improvements | 12 | 20 | 24 |
| Economies of scale | 10 | 11 | 10 |
| Total accounted for | 100 | 100 | 100 |

SOURCE: E. F. Denison, *The Sources of Economic Growth in the United States* (New York: Committee for Economic Development, 1962).

1980 can be attributed to growth in the *quantity* of labor. While Denison's projections to 1980 are very tentative, it is noteworthy that in his analysis the quality of labor is of considerable importance.[9] Moreover, technological change (in much simplified form, a "quality" improvement embodied in capital resources) is also seen as an increasingly important source of future economic growth. Unfortunately, the assumptions and measurement problems encountered in such work limit the reliability of the data, and the residual of ignorance in identifying the sources of economic growth in many ways remains.[10]

## C. SOME OBSERVATIONS ON THE THEORY OF ECONOMIC GROWTH

Throughout the last two centuries, philosophers and economists have repeatedly studied the question, What makes an economy grow? In looking for answers, they identified the elements of growth which we have just discussed, and while they viewed the matter differently, they did develop some general economic principles that are useful in examining the growth experience of developed nations.

Adam Smith, that now-famous Scotsman of the eighteenth century, was concerned chiefly with economic progress or growth, as the title of his treatise—*An Inquiry into the Nature and Causes of the Wealth of Nations*—suggests. His was an optimistic view of a future that would provide increasing abundance. Smith stressed the specialization of labor along with competition and free markets which establish prices to guide the econ-

[9] One of the striking differences between economic growth in the periods before and after 1929 is the greater relative importance of the *quantity* of labor and capital in the 1909–1929 era. In the 1929–1957 period, improvements in technology and the quality of human resources (much of which is attributed to improved education in Denison's work) appear to be of increasing significance as sources of economic growth.

[10] Some observers have suggested that investment in replacement capital, which embodies new technology in newer-"vintage" stocks of capital may reduce the residual of ignorance by about one-half of the 1.9 percent shown earlier. See Barry N. Siegel, *Aggregate Economics and Public Policy* (Homewood, Ill.: Richard D. Irwin, 1970), pp. 290–292.

omy in the allocation of resources. If men were allowed to pursue their self-interest, he felt, those goods most desired would be produced in the quantities required, and resources would be best allocated through the "invisible hand" of competitive markets that furthered the welfare of everyone. Market prices, the search for profits, and thrift were cohabitants in Smith's wonderful world. Rising output and prosperity were spurred on by the accumulation of even more physical-capital resources, and as the tools required to complement the division of labor grew, income would continue to expand. If left to its own ends and not chained to the commands of feudal lords, kings, or dictatorial rule, the market form of economic organization would prosper.

What Smith saw was *economies of scale* or, what is loosely the same, increasing resource productivity—a condition in which doubling *all* inputs to production generates more than a doubling of output. *Constant returns to scale*, on the other hand, describe a condition in which doubling all labor and capital inputs, for example, results in a twofold increase in output. By virtue of a larger scale of operation and increased specialization, a more efficient use of resources allows economies of scale leading to increased productivity. Accordingly, when viewed in an aggregate production function, economies of scale are masked by the residual $R$.

All in all, Adam Smith saw an orderly world of progress, but at the same time he also wrote extensively on several problems common to economic systems. His was a somewhat ambivalent explanation of just how rising national output, poverty, and population growth were related. This void was quickly filled in a depressing way by Thomas Malthus, a clergyman, and David Ricardo, an English businessman and philosopher.

Malthus foresaw misery and bare subsistence along with the ubiquitous spectre of periodic starvation. In his famous *Essay on the Principle of Population*, he explained the dire poverty of his time by arguing that the population of a nation expands more rapidly than its capacity to produce. The output of food, according to Malthus, increases arithmetically (1, 2, 3, 4, 5, . . . ) but population expands geometrically (1, 2, 4, 8, 16, . . .), approximately doubling each generation. Ultimately the population grows more rapidly than available food supplies, resulting in less food per capita unless population growth is checked by war, pestilence, famine, or "moral restraint." Malthus observed that, in the absence of such checks, any increase in the wealth of a nation simply leads to increased population sufficient to fully absorb the additional output created. Consequently, per capita output is continually driven to and held at a bare subsistence level.

### The Principle of Diminishing Returns

The "Malthusian misery" prognostication received additional refinement at the hands of David Ricardo, who combined the idea of geometric population growth with the principle of diminishing returns to explain how economic stagnation could occur. The *principle of diminishing returns* says generally that smaller and smaller increases in output occur as increasing amounts of one resource, such as labor, are combined with fixed supplies of other resources, such as land. What Malthus and Ricardo foresaw was diminishing additions to total output because of an expanding population (and labor force) combined with a relatively fixed supply of natural land resources, an important basis for production in the eighteenth-century agrarian economy of Britain. As more and more laborers were put to work on fixed amounts of less productive land, total food *output* sooner or later would increase less rapidly than labor *inputs*. Continued population expansion would ultimately reinforce bare subsistence living conditions.

If innumerable laborers are working on a small plot of ground, it is reasonable to expect diminishing returns in the production process. Were this not so, the world's supply of cloth could be produced in one small textile mill. Although this example is ludicrous, it does show that the principle of diminishing returns is of crucial importance in production. To Ricardo, diminishing returns meant that the ratio of food output/labor input would ultimately decline, and with it the per capita standard of living (the ratio of output/population).

The implications of diminishing returns for economic growth as proposed in the tradition of Malthus and Ricardo assumed that land resources were fixed which, in the framework of aggregate production, suggests that income depends upon labor and capital. Since growth in income depends upon a growing labor supply, a growing supply of capital resources, and fixed land resources, three consequences follow:

1. The ratio of labor/land rises. Growth in the population (and labor force) relative to a fixed supply of land resources generates smaller and smaller increases in total output due to diminishing returns as more of the variable quantities of labor are employed.

2. Capital growth declines. Although physical-capital resources grow initially, the use of more and more of them with a fixed land supply also generates diminishing returns. Profit rates on capital decline, and investment must ultimately dry up because of lower returns on investment.[11]

3. Per capita income, or the output/labor ratio, declines to and remains constant at subsistence levels. Ultimately, diminishing returns and the disappearance of profits lead to declining investment, growth in total income ceases, the total supply of labor reaches a biological maximum at bare subsistence, and a static economy prevails.

For several reasons, events since the times of Malthus and Ricardo have not borne out their dismal prophecy for all nations. We cannot dismiss it lightly, nevertheless. The reality of abject poverty still haunts most nations and peoples in our world. However, Malthus and Ricardo did not foresee the progress known to developed nations today. Division of labor and specialization along with expanding markets have created higher, not lower levels of living for some nations. Today increased output can result from institutional changes, advancing technology, or improvements in the quality of natural, human, or capital resources. In other words, diminishing returns may be "short-circuited" by other elements in the growth process. Even when one resource such as land is fixed, economic growth is possible if there are offsets to diminishing returns. While these two classical economists failed to foresee modern progress, their theories furnish valuable insights that still bear heavily on economic growth. To see how, we must dig deeper into the subject of production.

[11] Returns to landowners will rise, however, since land becomes an increasingly scarce resource. Because of the relative scarcity of land, poorer and poorer land will be brought into production, even though it is less and less productive.

Productivity and Economic Growth

Neither scale economies nor residual growth elements imply that the principle of diminishing returns is invalid; rather, they suggest that it is not irrevocable because other elements in the growth process can temporarily offset it. Because of increased productivity, diminishing returns need not lead to economic stagnation.

The consequences of diminishing returns are contrasted to rising per capita income in more precise form in Figure 5. Figure 5(a) illustrates the principle of diminishing returns, where it is again assumed that one resource such as land is fixed in supply and increasing amounts of other resources such as labor (shown horizontally) are used in conjunction with fixed resources.

Diminishing returns are shown by the schedule of total product (TP) or output measured on the vertical axis of Figure 5(a). For example, as labor inputs are increased from 100 to 500 units in increments of 100, the quantity of total product increases, but at a decreasing rate. Diminishing returns result in output changing from 350 to 700 units (+350 TP), 700 to 850 units (+150 TP), and 850 to 900 units (+50 TP). Finally, total product may level out or even decline. Note that in this illustration *output per unit of labor* declines while the quantity of total product rises. The economy envisioned by Malthus and Ricardo faced such a dilemma in which per capita output declined, ultimately reaching subsistence levels, where it remained.

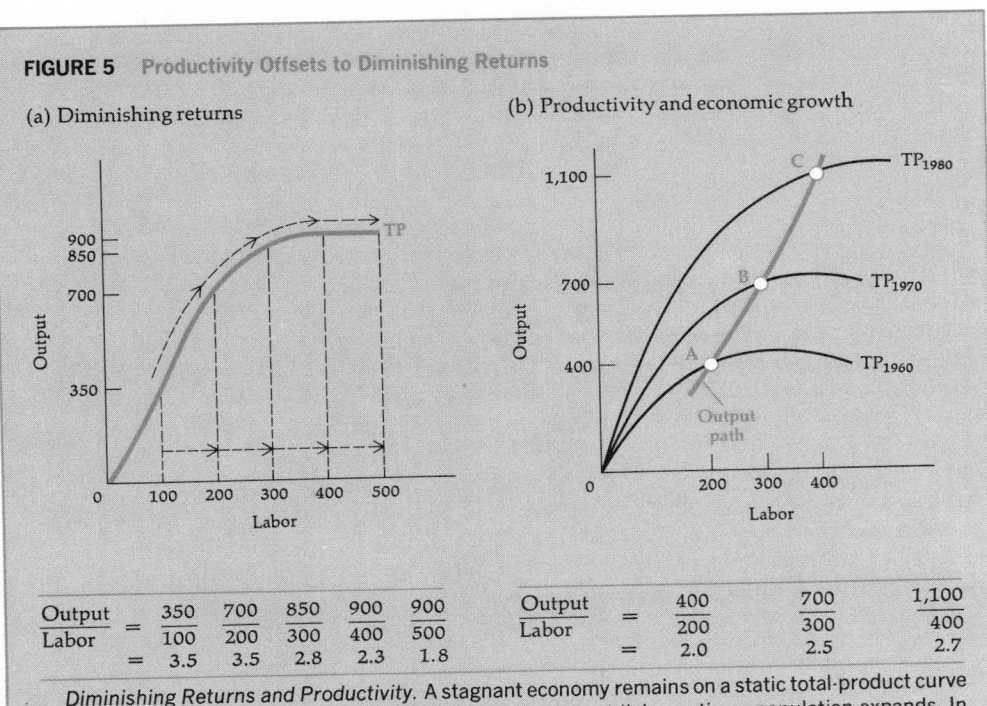

**FIGURE 5    Productivity Offsets to Diminishing Returns**

(a) Diminishing returns

(b) Productivity and economic growth

| Output | | 350 | 700 | 850 | 900 | 900 |
|---|---|---|---|---|---|---|
| Labor | = | 100 | 200 | 300 | 400 | 500 |
| | = | 3.5 | 3.5 | 2.8 | 2.3 | 1.8 |

| Output | | 400 | 700 | 1,100 |
|---|---|---|---|---|
| Labor | = | 200 | 300 | 400 |
| | = | 2.0 | 2.5 | 2.7 |

*Diminishing Returns and Productivity.* A stagnant economy remains on a static total-product curve such as TP in (a), the consequence being a declining output/labor ratio as population expands. In contrast, rising productivity may offset diminishing returns—the case shown in (b) when a nation grows along output path ABC.

The reason? Diminishing returns and geometric population growth ruled in a heavy-handed way.

Now compare the declining economy shown in Figure 5(a) to one experiencing rising productivity [Figure 5(b)]. The output path for a declining economy subject to the principle of diminishing returns is approximated by a fixed total-product schedule like $TP$ in Figure 5(a). In such a situation, per capita output falls as the population and labor force grow. In contrast, a *growing economy* with the same fixed resources—land, for example—avoids stagnation by expanding along growing output path $ABC$, moving to successively higher total-product levels such as $TP_{1970}$ and $TP_{1980}$. Even though the principle of diminishing returns still applies to aggregate production in a growing economy, new and higher levels of output are possible. This is precisely what has happened in the more advanced nations of the world such as Britain, the United States, Russia, and Japan. The one force (the principle of diminishing returns) that could lead to declining levels of per capita output has been offset by *rising productivity*—each unit of labor produces *more* output in subsequent periods of time, or the ratio of output/labor rises. The explanation of such increased productivity goes directly back to the supply sources of growth considered earlier: qualitative improvements in human and capital resources, technological change, and so forth.[12]

Malthus and Ricardo failed to fully appreciate the fact that new investment opportunities could continually arise, resulting in improvements in a nation's resource base, institutions, and technological know-how, causing a total-product schedule to *shift* upward and outward year by year. All of the factors previously noted as contributing to growth interact in producing rising levels of per capita output, but two characteristics of growing economies deserve special attention.

## THE DEEPENING OF CAPITAL

When capital resources ($K$) grow more rapidly than the labor supply ($L$), as has happened in developed nations, the ratio $K/L$ rises and capital deepening is said to occur—that is, each unit of labor works with more and more capital resources.[13]

But what are the consequences of the deepening of capital? After all, capital deepening (a rising ratio of $K/L$) is akin to Ricardo's observation of diminishing returns to the use of increased amounts of labor applied to relatively fixed supplies of land. Does not capital deepening lead to diminishing returns to capital resources? The answer is yes and no. Capital deepening does lead to diminishing returns, *but* diminishing returns to capital can be (and are) offset.

Under capital-deepening growth conditions, a relatively fixed labor factor cooperates in production with larger and larger amounts of capital which are subject to diminishing returns. And do not forget the very important

[12] While we are oversimplifying again, the underdeveloped nations of the world have not prospered because increased productivity has failed to cancel out diminishing returns. In many nations a growing population does press upon available food supplies, as Malthus and Ricardo envisioned. The needed improvements in institutions, technology, and the quality and quantity of natural, human, and capital resources have not been forthcoming in these countries.

[13] The stock of physical capital has increased about 2 percent annually in recent decades in the United States, and the labor supply has grown about 1 percent per year.

consequence that the return to investment in capital resources will tend to fall if additional capital investments are successively less productive as diminishing returns occur. Capital deepening accompanied by diminishing returns means that each additional dollar of capital produces less and less additional output. Investment would then decline and ultimately dry up because it would be increasingly unprofitable to invest. If population continues to expand, deepening of capital would lead to real output per person ultimately falling to subsistence levels, while profits and investment in physical capital would disappear just as Ricardo predicted. The facts, however, do not confirm the circumstances of a static Ricardian economic condition, for reasons described next.

## CONSTANT PRODUCTIVITY OF CAPITAL

It appears that diminishing returns should accompany the deepening of capital and lead to less output per dollar of capital (a declining average output/capital ratio, or falling $NNP/K$). However, the ratio $NNP/K$ as a crude reflection of the average productivity of capital in the United States has remained constant at about 1/3. That is, $3 of capital investment on the average has produced about $1 of additional income. Even though capital deepening (rising $K/L$) has occurred, the productivity of capital ($NNP/K$) has remained constant at about 1/3 and the rate of return on capital investment as well as the share of income going to capital has remained steady.

Speaking generally again, the reason for this situation is simply that in developed nations other growth elements have intervened and offset diminishing returns. Some combination of larger quantities and improvements in the quality of *all* resources, more efficient use and allocation of resources, technological and institutional changes, and the like have helped forestall diminishing returns to capital. If these residual factors *did not* intervene in the economic growth process: (*a*) A nation would be combining increasing amounts of capital with other relatively fixed resources like land or labor, (*b*) diminishing returns would ultimately lead to declining output per unit of labor and capital, and (*c*) incomes could be pushed to the subsistence level—the static condition envisioned by Malthus and Ricardo. Instead, we find that over several decades in advanced nations such as the United States, each unit of labor has produced about 3 percent more output per year on the average. Advancing productivity allowed 97 manhours in 1971 to produce the same output as 100 manhours did a year earlier, and *it is this force that offsets diminishing returns. Thus, capital deepening along with the modern technological, educational, institutional, and scientific revolution has offset diminishing returns and allowed per capita output to rise year after year.*

### Monitoring Growth in Full-Employment Demand

Increasing productive capacity is only a partial answer to the problem of economic growth in developed nations. The demand for output must also grow sufficiently to utilize productive capacity fully. The essence of the "demand" dimension to economic growth is this: as net investment in capital generates growth in the potential supply of output from year to year, aggregate demand for output requires continual monitoring to avoid a secular deflationary gap due to deficient demand on one hand or inflationary pressures on the other.

The significance of maintaining full-employment growth centers upon three basic ideas. First, net investment expenditures increase a nation's stock of capital resources. As net capital formation occurs, the potential level of output that can be produced—the productive capacity of a nation—expands from year to year. In short, the net investment of one year is the new capital formation of the next year, generating growth in the potential supply of output. Second, net investment expenditures are a component of the aggregate demand for output, as earlier chapters demonstrated. Therefore, changes in net investment also produce changes in aggregate demand and help determine the actual level of income realized in any given year. The third point that follows is: Net investment is a link between the creation of productive capacity (growth in the potential supply of NNP) and the demand for output (growth in the actual NNP level). *Thus, net investment is two-edged—it is a capacity-creating growth element as well as a component of aggregate demand which helps determine actual levels of output.*

The earliest attempts to explain how investment acts as an agent causing growth in productive capacity and also contributes to growth in the demand for output were made by Sir Roy Harrod and Evsey D. Domar.[14] In much simplified terms, the Harrod-Domar approach reduces an economy to a simple model in which growth is dependent upon two factors: (*a*) net investment, which causes a change in the stock of capital; and (*b*) the productivity of capital formed through net investment. In these terms, a distinction between growth in productive capacity resulting from net investment in capital (the "supply" view) vs. growth in the spending on output leading to some actual level of NNP (the "demand" view) is of crucial importance.

New capital resources are formed in 1972 because of the net investment of an earlier period, say 1971. A nation's productive capacity increases between 1971 and 1972 and it is therefore necessary for investment expenditures to grow also. The significance of these circumstances is best illustrated by considering an example.

## THE PRODUCTIVITY OF CAPITAL

We have seen that the so-called *"productivity of capital"*—the dollars of NNP capacity created by a nation's stock of capital—is the output/capital ratio, NNP/$K$. Thus, if NNP = \$300 billion and the stock of capital is \$900 billion, the productivity of capital shown by the output/capital ratio is NNP/$K$ = \$300 billion/\$900 billion, or 1/3. An output/capital ratio of 1/3 simply shows that, on the average, \$3 of capital can create \$1 of additional output. If we assume that the average and marginal productivities of capital are the same, any net investment ($I$) which adds to or changes the stock of capital ($\Delta K$) will create new output capacity in the amount of a \$1 billion increase in NNP for every \$3 billion of net investment.[15] Consequently, \$12

---

[14] The theory of economic growth based on the works of Harrod and Domar (the "Harrod-Domar model) is explained in greater detail in the appendix following this chapter.

[15] The discussion which follows ignores government and foreign trade and further assumes that there is a constant marginal propensity to save and the marginal and average productivity of capital are equal and unchanged. Furthermore, no adjustment lags beyond a one-year period are considered, and resource substitution is ignored initially.

billion of net investment in 1971, for example, will increase the stock of capital by that amount ($I = \Delta K$), and productive capacity will increase by $4 billion. The "supply" side of economic growth is:

Change in potential output $=$ net investment $\times$ productivity of capital
$$\Delta NNP_{1972} = I_{1971} \qquad \times \text{ output/capital ratio}$$
$$\$4 \text{ billion} = \$12 \text{ billion} \quad \times \text{ } 1/3$$

One point concerning the output/capital ratio merits careful attention: As a measure of the productivity of net investment in capital resources, the output/capital ratio reflects *all* of the growth elements considered earlier. More efficient or better-quality human and capital resources, technological advances, the vintage and longevity of capital, and even differences in the productivity of one type of investment compared to others (e.g., factories vs. computers) are all buried in an aggregate output/capital ratio.[16]

Suppose in 1971 an economy invests $150 billion. Since NNP $=$ $300 billion and $K$ $=$ $900 billion, the productivity of capital shown by the output/capital ratio is 1/3. The $150 billion of net investment in 1971 increases the capital stock by a like amount in 1972 and, given an output/capital ratio of 1/3, potential output ($\Delta NNP$) for 1972 will thus *increase* in the amount of $50 billion.

$$\Delta NNP_{1972} = I_{1971} \times NNP/K$$
$$\$50 \text{ billion} = \$150 \text{ billion} \times 1/3$$

*Therefore, capacity* NNP$_{1972}$ *increases from $300 billion to $350 billion.* Why? Because of net investment in 1971 which, in conjunction with the output/capital ratio, makes a larger NNP possible in the future. Three important characteristics of economic growth can be gleaned from this example.

1. Growth in productive capacity from 1971 to 1972 initiated by net investment and new capital formation increases the "required" equilibrium level of income. Figure 6 illustrates how $I = $150 billion in 1971 raises capacity NNP for 1972 and changes capacity from $E$ to $E'$. That is, in 1972 $DD$ and $SS$ must intersect at $E'$ to utilize capacity NNP$_{1972}$. The demand for output must grow at a rate comparable to the growth in capacity if the economy is to utilize its larger capacity level of output fully. Total spending, which includes investment, is "required" to grow to $350 billion if an equilibrium level of NNP which fully utilizes potential supply is to be achieved. If this does not occur, businessmen may not regard further investment in 1972 as "warranted," and the familar output gap will appear.

2. Net investment must continually increase. In the above example, the marginal propensity to save is 0.5, equilibrium saving and investment in 1971 is $150 billion, and saving increases by 50 percent of the $50 billion change in income from 1971 to 1972 to a new level of $175 billion. Hence, "required" investment in 1972 is also $175 billion, and if the data in this example are extended further to 1973 and 1974, it is clear that investment must rise to larger and larger amounts in each subsequent time period as NNP capacity expands. The economy must, in effect, run faster in the future

[16] Needless to say, aggregate output/capital ratios assume away the more interesting and important characteristics of the economic growth process. Still, several important characteristics of economic growth can be shown in even a terse description like that given above, which is sufficient for our present purpose.

290

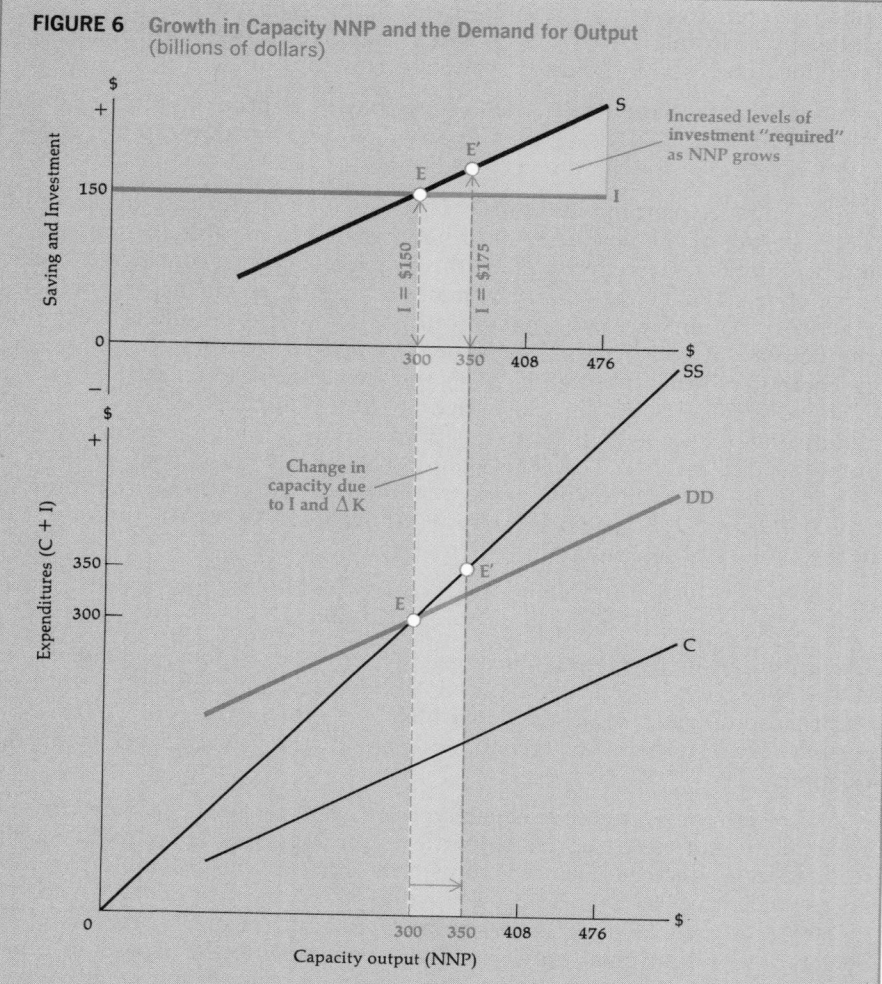

**FIGURE 6** Growth in Capacity NNP and the Demand for Output
(billions of dollars)

| Year | Capital stock (K) | Capacity output (NNP) | Saving and net investment (I and ΔK) | Change in capacity NNP (ΔNNP = I × NNP/K) |
|---|---|---|---|---|
| 1971 | $900 billion | $300 billion | $150 billion | |
| 1972 | 1,050 billion | 350 billion | 175 billion | + $50 billion |
| 1973 | 1,225 billion | 408 billion | 204 billion | + 58 billion |
| 1974 | 1,429 billion | 476 billion | 238 billion | + 68 billion |

(all data are rounded)

*"Required" Growth.* Assume 50 percent of income is saved, and the output/capital ratio is ⅓. The $150 billion of investment in 1971 increases productive capacity by $50 billion by 1972, and "requires" even larger amounts of investment to offset higher saving in subsequent years to reach full-capacity levels of output. This means schedule *I* in the upper diagram (*DD* in the lower diagram) must rise to higher levels each year (presuming *C* remains steady at 50 percent of income).

just to stand still, since investment must grow to maintain equilibrium between saving and investment.

3. The productivity of capital and the rate of investment (and saving) will determine how fast the economy grows. When investment (and saving) are 50 percent of NNP and each $3 of net investment generates $1 of capacity NNP, the *rate of growth in aggregate demand required is the proportion of income saved (and invested) × the output/capital ratio:*

$$\begin{array}{ccc} \text{Required percentage} \\ \text{growth in NNP} \end{array} = \begin{array}{c} \text{marginal propensity} \\ \text{to save} \end{array} \times \begin{array}{c} \text{output/capital} \\ \text{ratio} \end{array}$$
$$16.7\% = 50\% \times 1/3$$

Alternatively, if investment and saving equal 9 percent of a base income level of $100 billion, the growth in demand "required" to absorb new capacity would be 3 percent (9 percent or $9 billion/$100 billion × 1/3).[17]

*To summarize:* Equal rates of growth in capacity and demand are "required" because net investment performs two functions: It increases capacity and it is also a component of aggregate demand. Investment must continue to increase to offset additional saving if full-capacity growth in NNP is to be maintained. The rate of growth in output depends upon the productivity of capital and the portion of income saved and invested.

## THE PROBLEM OF IRREGULAR GROWTH[18]

Economic growth theory teaches us that it is not enough to have a constant level of investment because potential output is continually growing. Failure to achieve the "required" growth in planned investment and saving (i.e., aggregate spending and potential output) leads to stagnation or inflationary expansion. It is crucial, therefore, that fiscal and monetary policies be used as agents of economic growth policy. Economic growth that fully utilizes *all* resources is a precarious balance requiring continual growth in spending.

Moreover, even if output expands at the required rate to a new equilibrium, this level may or may not represent full employment. There are two different rates of growth in income levels. One is *full-capacity* growth—a growth rate that fully utilizes the new capacity created by net investment in capital—the subject of our recent discussion. The second is a *full-employment* rate of growth—changes in NNP sufficient to fully employ labor resources. The basic dilemma is that a rate of growth in spending capable of increasing aggregate demand enough to fully utilize a higher level of productive capacity created by net capital formation need not and often will not be comparable to growth necessary to fully employ an expanding labor force.[19] While many of the discrepancies between full-capacity NNP and

[17] Notice, "required" rate of equilibrium growth in output and investment is one which maintains an equal change between the potential supply of output [which is $I$ (or $\Delta K$) × NNP/K] and changes in the demand for output, which rely on the multiplier and autonomous net investment ($\Delta I$ × 1/MPS). Thus, $I$ × NNP/K = $\Delta I$ × 1/MPS, or growth in income and investment must be equal to $\Delta I/I$ = NNP/K × MPS (see the following appendix for more details).

[18] This section may be omitted at the instructor's option.

[19] If labor and capital substitution can occur and resource-market rigidities are minimal, this problem may be partially corrected as the relative prices of underemployed resources decline. Indeed, resource substitution is assumed to be impossible in the Harrod-Domar growth model, an assumption that makes the equilibrium growth rate appear more rigid than it is.

full-employment NNP can be left to more advanced courses, this sort of imbalance helps explain why economic instability is inherent in a market economy.

*Stagnation*    Total spending on output may not increase rapidly enough to achieve *full-capacity growth,* perhaps because firms overestimate consumer demand. Prior investments in capital facilities then ultimately generate excess capacity. Business firms are not likely to regard any further additions to capacity as desirable and may fail to increase investment. Even though full employment of labor may occur for a short period, potential supply ultimately outstrips total spending and, as unused capacity appears and inventories pile up, failure to utilize production capacity in one year further impairs investment incentives and net capital formation stalls. Consequently, future growth in the potential supply of output may be "demand retarded." That is, producers may feel that future investments in capital are undesirable. The problem here is simply that producer investment expands capacity too rapidly. Ultimately excess capacity appears in relation to slower rates of growth in the labor force and total spending tails off, leading to unemployment, stagnation, and a recession.

*Secular Exhilaration*    A second possibility is that growth in productive capacity may not be sufficient to meet a rapid increase in spending. The short-run consequences of this situation are price-level pressures, as we have seen on other occasions, because total spending exceeds *full-capacity* levels of production. While equilibrium *money* NNP rises, growth in productive capacity is not sufficient to accommodate the rapid rate of growth in the demand for output. Moreover, unemployment may accompany price-level pressures if full-employment growth in the labor force is more rapid than the full-capacity growth in NNP generated by new capital resources. Chronic unemployment of labor can thus occur, although some substitution of labor for capital may be induced if wages decline because of the abundant labor supplies.

Therefore, it is important to realize that *full-capacity growth* (equal growth in the potential supply of output created by capital and in the demand for output) may or may not coincide *with full-employment* growth for the labor force. This is what economic instability is all about, why it is so pervasive a problem, and why monetary and fiscal policies are important. Output can grow too fast, leading to ultimate stagnation and unemployment as the growth ceiling represented by the rate of growth in labor productivity is finally reached. In addition, full-capacity growth may lag behind full-employment growth, the consequence being chronic unemployment and perhaps price-level pressures because of a shortage of capacity.

## REVIEW

### Summary

1. Growth in income or output conveys the rather obvious advantages of increased income, but it also imposes costs on a society. A growing economy is an ever-changing one, as was the United States in its years of economic development. Output growth averages 3.5 percent each year in the United States and has resulted in vast changes over the decades.

There are two distinct perspectives to economic growth: (a) expansion in production capacity, or increases in the potential supply of output; and (b) growth in total spending on output. Starting from a particular point *on* a production frontier demonstrates that growth in the supply and the demand for output must be equal if full utilization of resources is to occur.

2. The resource base is one focal point in explaining how growth in the potential supply of a nation's output is possible. Changes in the quantity and quality of natural, human, and capital resources constitute improvements in the supply of factors of production used as inputs to produce goods and services.

3. Institutional characteristics—the social, political, cultural, and economic environment of a nation—can hinder or promote economic growth. A market approach to economic organization prevails in many developed nations, but there are several (e.g., Japan or Russia) which have grown rapidly under an entirely different institutional setting.

4. Technological change is one manifestation of flexible institutions in a society. Technology depends in part upon research and development and is closely related to the transformation and utilization of a nation's resource base. While technological change has varied and uneven impacts on different sectors of an economy, modern technology is often embodied in capital resources and frequently accompanies specialization.

5. An aggregate production function shows how output is related to quantities of labor and capital and clearly demonstrates the significance in the growth process of residual factors—that is, qualitative, institutional, and technological changes.

6. The principle of diminishing returns describes total output increasing at a decreasing rate when one resource is varied and another is fixed. In the absence of increases in productivity, diminishing returns leads to economic stagnation. Industrialized nations, however, have avoided diminishing returns, in spite of capital deepening. Increased productivity has offset diminishing returns and held the output/capital ratio constant. Much of the explanation of economic growth is buried in the residual of ignorance ($R$) which accounts for more than one-half of the growth in output in developed nations such as the United States.

7. Economic growth policy has two distinct dimensions: (a) measures to influence changes in the potential supply of output, and (b) steps to see that the demand for output increases in line with changes in capacity. Equilibrium or "required" growth-rate conditions involve the achievement of balanced growth utilizing full-capacity output levels from year to year.

8. There are a variety of difficulties associated with stabilizing economic growth. The chief problem is maintaining a balance between growth in supply and growth in demand. Another source of difficulty may be differences in full-capacity growth arising from additions to the stock of productive resources and full-employment growth of the labor force. If producers expand capacity too rapidly relative to the growth in labor,

stagnation and recession occur, and if full-capacity growth is sluggish relative to full-employment growth, chronic unemployment may arise.

## Identify the Following Concepts and Terms

- the resource base
- embodied technology
- output/capital ratio
- GNP = $f(L, K, R)$
- "Malthusian misery"
- the vintage of capital
- potential supply

- social-overhead capital
- principle of diminishing returns
- economies of scale
- capital deepening
- growth elements
- residual of ignorance
- the costs of growth

## Questions to Answer

1. Explain and critically evaluate the statement: "Investment in physical capital is a much too narrow view of investment in explaining economic growth, particularly if one views the output/capital ratio as a strict measure of capital productivity." How have institutions such as the market system aided economic growth in some nations? How is growth in per capita income related to growth in the population and total income?

2. What distinguishes diminishing returns from scale economies? How is this distinction important? What are the three key attributes of technology that relate to economic growth? How does each attribute affect economic growth in an economy?

3. Using an aggregate production function as a conceptual framework, explain how the "residual" affects increases in income. How are the ratios $K/L$ and $NNP/K$ related to trends in economic growth?

4. Suppose you are a member of Parliament in the nation of Zubarvia, where attention is currently being devoted to the following issues raised by an economist:

   (a) "Yes, it is true that deepening of capital has occurred, but we can take certain steps to see that the output/capital ratio remains constant as it has in recent years." Analyze and explain this statement.

   (b) "The great immediate danger to Zubarvia is that the demand for output is not growing rapidly enough. At the present time, for example, actual NNP = $90 billion, the output/capital ratio is 1/5, $K$ = $600 billion, current $I$ = $3 billion, and the economy is in a recession." Estimate the productive capacity of Zubarvia and explain the meaning of the relationships you used. Can you explain what fiscal and monetary policies will help remedy Zubarvia's problems and by how much will potential output increase next year? Can you add any further recommendations with respect to inflation and unemployment?

# APPENDIX A
# Macroeconomic Theory

While prior chapters have summarized the basic features of the income and employment problem, many real-world complications have been avoided in the interests of simplifying the explanation of economic instability and growth. Our purpose here is to further develop selected features of the income-determination process previously ignored. The topics covered in order are (a) consumption, taxes, and the multiplier; (b) multiplier values in the real world; (c) the output gap; and (d) economic growth.

## CONSUMPTION, TAXES, AND THE MULTIPLIER

The equilibrium-income condition has been defined as one where the aggregate supply of income or output ($Y$) intersects aggregate demand, consisting of consumption ($C$), investment ($I$), and government expenditures ($G$). Alternatively, equilibrium exists if withdrawals such as saving ($S$) and taxes ($T$) from the spending stream equal inflows such as $I$ and $G$ into the circular-income flow. Thus, aggregate output=aggregate spending, or in looking at *changes* in income (and ignoring foreign expenditures) equilibrium exists if:

$$\Delta Y = \Delta C + \Delta I + \Delta G \qquad \text{or} \qquad \Delta S + \Delta T = \Delta I + \Delta G \qquad (1)$$

Changes in aggregate demand ($\Delta DD$) induced by government-stabilization policy directed at $C + I + G$ spending and the multiplier impact of these changes on a nation's level of output are not quite as uncomplicated as suggested earlier. For purposes of keeping the exposition as simple as possible, it has been assumed for the most part that the multiplier is the result only of the fraction of *disposable income* ($Y_d$) consumed or the marginal propensity to consume ($c$) and the marginal propensity to save ($s$), where $\Delta C = c\Delta Y_d$, $\Delta S = s\Delta Y_d$, and $c + s = 1$. Thus, $c = \Delta C/\Delta Y_d$ and the multiplier (denoted by $m$) is attributable to the proportion of $Y_d$ consumed and not a $\Delta S$ leakage. Consequently, $m$ is the reciprocal of $1 - c$ and the change in *aggregate income* ($\Delta Y$) is the autonomous change in aggregate demand times the multiplier:

$$m = \frac{1}{1-c} \qquad (2)$$

which is

$$m = \frac{1}{s}$$

and

$$\Delta Y = \Delta DD \times m$$

However, the value of the multiplier depends on *all* inflows and leakages affecting the income stream, not just the consumption and saving out of changes in disposable income. Therefore, a multiplier which more accurately reflects changes in aggregate income relative to an autonomous change in aggregate demand must be adjusted to reflect the marginal propensity to spend. That is, the real-world multiplier, henceforth denoted by $m^*$, is the reciprocal of 1 *less* all induced spending changes in the circular-income flow. Thus:

$$m^* = \frac{1}{1 - \substack{\text{change in all spending} \\ \text{as a fraction of } \Delta Y}} \quad \text{or} \quad \frac{1}{\substack{\text{change in all leakages} \\ \text{as a fraction of } \Delta Y}} \quad (3)$$

and $\Delta Y = \Delta DD \times m^*$

While it is impossible to make all of the changes required in deriving a realistic consumption-expenditure multiplier, we can get some idea of the importance of major spending-stream adjustments leading to the use of $m^*$.[1]

First, consider the impact of autonomous changes in tax receipts and government transfer payments. Changes in tax receipts or transfer payments indirectly work through disposable income and lead to changes in aggregate demand, but they differ from changes in consumption, investment, and government purchases which are direct components of aggregate spending. A reduction in tax receipts (or an increase in government transfer payments) raises consumption by an amount *less* than the full tax change, depending upon the marginal propensity to consume. The change in consumption due, for example, to a tax change ($\Delta T$) is given by $\Delta C = -c\Delta T$. Given a change in taxes, and thus the consumption component of aggregate demand, the change in aggregate income is:

$$\Delta Y = -c\Delta T \frac{1}{1-c} = -\frac{c}{1-c}\Delta T \quad (4)$$

and the tax multiplier is $\quad \dfrac{\Delta Y}{\Delta T} = -\dfrac{c}{1-c}$

Thus, the multiplier is adjusted downward for reduced government taxes which raise consumption demand by a fraction of the decrease in tax receipts. In the case of transfer payments, the multiplier has the opposite sign because transfers are positively instead of negatively related to aggregate demand. The multiplier is smaller for taxes and government transfer payments than it is for direct government purchases or investment because some portion of the change in disposable income represents a leakage out of the spending stream to saving.[2]

As long as tax receipts and transfer payments are independent of changes

---

[1] Among the many intermediate texts that may be consulted in further pursuit of this subject, see Warren L. Smith, *Macroeconomics* (Homewood, Ill.: Richard D. Irwin, 1970), Chapters 6, 7, 9, 13, and 14.

[2] If $c = 2/3$, the transfer-payment multiplier is $\dfrac{c}{1-c} = \dfrac{2/3}{1/3} = 2$. Given $c$, the normal-expenditure multiplier is $\dfrac{1}{1/3} = 3$ which applies, for example, to autonomous changes in aggregate demand due to an increase in government purchases.

in aggregate income, it can also be shown that the balanced-budget multiplier is unity or less. Presuming that $c$ is constant at $\frac{2}{3}$, the balanced-budget multiplier applicable to a simultaneous \$4 billion increase in government purchases and tax receipts is the sum of the multiplier for government purchases, $1/(1 - c)$, and the multiplier for taxes, $-c/(1 - c)$:

$$\text{Balanced-budget multiplier} = \frac{\Delta Y}{\Delta G} + \frac{\Delta Y}{\Delta T}$$

$$= \frac{1}{1 - c} - \frac{c}{1 - c} = \frac{1 - c}{1 - c} = 1 \qquad (5)$$

That is, the net change in aggregate income is no larger than \$4 billion, since an increase in aggregate demand due to $G = +$ \$4 billion generates \$12 billion in aggregate income or \$4 billion $\times 1/(1 - \frac{2}{3})$ and the change in aggregate income due to $T = +$ \$4 billion is $-$ \$8 billion or \$4 billion $\times -\frac{2}{3}/(1 - \frac{2}{3})$. *Conclusion:* It is the proportion of aggregate income passed around in the spending stream—i.e., the fraction leaking out to saving $(1 - c$ or $s)$—which determines the multiplier and the final change in aggregate income.

## MULTIPLIER VALUES IN THE REAL WORLD

While an autonomous change in taxes or transfer payments is complicated by the fact that the change in spending is typically less than the fiscal action, there are even more important *induced* changes in spending. For example, tax receipts rise as aggregate income rises and fall as aggregate income falls, government transfer expenditures (e.g., unemployment compensation) increase as aggregate income declines and rise as aggregate income falls, and gross business saving rises and declines directly with changes in aggregate income. In addition, investment expenditures may increase as consumption and disposable income rise (or fall as they decline), and net foreign investment (net imports) may also vary inversely with changes in disposable income.[3] For instances in which increases in aggregate income induce added leakages from the spending stream (additional taxes) or reductions in inflows (declines in government transfer payments), the real-world multiplier is smaller than the simple expenditure multiplier examined earlier. Let us see why.

With an autonomous change in aggregate demand, disposable income will not rise (or fall) by as much as aggregate income because of other induced changes in the income stream. Equation (6) simply states that because the fractions $t$, $f$, and $p$ of income are induced, a change in disposable income will be some fraction or percent of a change in aggregate income. Thus, a change in disposable income, $\Delta Y_d$, is the change in aggregate income, $\Delta Y$, less leakages from $\Delta Y$ due to induced changes in taxes $(t = \Delta T/\Delta Y)$, transfer payments $(f = -\Delta F/\Delta Y)$, and business saving $(p = \Delta P/\Delta Y)$. Aggregate and disposable income are different by the amount of these induced changes.

---

[3] Depreciation allowances are ignored in what follows because they are more directly linked to the size of the capital stock than to aggregate income. Net foreign investment or net imports (exports — imports) may be further complicated by international trade and balance-of-payments problems also ignored here.

$$\Delta Y_d = \Delta Y - t\Delta Y - f\Delta Y - p\Delta Y$$

or

$$\Delta Y_d = \Delta Y (1 - t - f - p) \tag{6}$$

Thus, if government purchases and investment are ignored momentarily, and a change in consumption is a function of a change in disposable income, it is also a function of aggregate income.

$$\Delta C = c\Delta Y_d = c\Delta Y (1 - t - f - p) \tag{7}$$

The fraction of additional consumption out of a change in *aggregate* income is then $\Delta C/\Delta Y = c (1 - t - f - p)$.

Since the marginal propensity to consume out of aggregate income, $\Delta Y$, is smaller than out of disposable income, $\Delta Y_d$, we can show that the multiplier for aggregate income is reduced. Suppose $t$ percent of an increase in aggregate income leaks out to taxes, for example. Then only $1 - t$ percent of $\Delta Y$ remains in the disposable-income stream and $c (1 - t)$ is the fraction of aggregate income consumed. In considering leakages from $\Delta Y$ to business saving as well as tax receipts and transfer payment inflows which rise and fall as $\Delta Y$ decreases or increases, the multiplier adjusted for the differences in aggregate and disposable income applicable to an autonomous increase in consumption or government purchases is:

$$\text{Adjusted multiplier} = \frac{\Delta Y}{\Delta C} = \frac{1}{1 - c (1 - t - f - p)} \tag{8}$$

Suppose, for example $c = 80$ percent of the change in disposable income. The simple expenditure multiplier is then $1/(1 - c) = 1/.2 = 5$, indicating that a \$4 billion increase in government purchases would increase output by \$20 billion. However, the fraction of aggregate income remaining in the disposable-income stream shown by equation (8) is only $c$ percent of $(1 - t - f - p)$. The adjusted multiplier will increase aggregate income by a smaller amount than the simple expenditure multiplier because of $t$ and $p$ leakages and a reduction in $f$. If $t = .2$, $f = .1$, and $p = .08$, the aggregate income or GNP multiplier computed from equation (8) is:

$$\text{Adjusted multiplier} = \frac{1}{1 - .8 (1 - .2 - .1 - .08)}$$

$$= \frac{1}{1 - .8 (1 - .38)} = \frac{1}{1 - .5} = 2$$

Now let us assume that some investment is induced in relation to the *level* of disposable income, or $\Delta I_i = i\Delta Y_d$ in a static relationship.[4] Under these circumstances there is an inflow into the spending stream—the fraction of a change in disposable income spent as investment changes where $i = \Delta I_i/\Delta Y_d$. Finally, also presume that as disposable income rises, some additional amount is spent for imports from foreign nations, causing net foreign expenditures ($Ex = $ exports $-$ imports) to decline, or $Ex = - xY_d$. Accordingly, by sub-

---

[4] Notice that $\Delta I_i$ is viewed in static terms as a function of $\Delta Y_d$ and is not dependent upon the rate of change in income. As with the marginal propensity to consume, $c$, the marginal propensity to invest, $i$, is a fraction of disposable income or $i = \Delta I_i/\Delta Y_d$.

stitution in equation (1), induced changes in aggregate income now cognizant of induced investment and imports can be expressed as follows:

$$\Delta Y = \Delta C + \Delta I + \Delta Ex + \Delta G$$
$$= c\Delta Y_d + i\Delta Y_d - x\Delta Y_d + \Delta G$$
$$= (c + i - x)\,\Delta Y_d + \Delta G$$

and since
$$\Delta Y_d = \Delta Y\,(1 - t - f - p)$$
$$\Delta Y = (c + i - x)\,\Delta Y\,(1 - t - f - p) + \Delta G \tag{9}$$

The first bracketed term $(c + i - x)$ represents the net propensity to spend out of disposable income where induced consumption and investment increase the spending-stream flows (and the multiplier), while imports are a leakage which reduces the spending-stream flows (and the multiplier). Net leakages from disposable income are thus $1 - (c + i - x)$. The second term $(1 - t - f - p)$ represents the fraction of a change in aggregate income that is disposable income, and $\Delta G$ represents autonomous government expenditures as before. The aggregate-income multiplier $m^*$ in this case is the reciprocal of 1 − the marginal propensity to spend out of a change in aggregate income $(\Delta Y)$.[5] Thus, for a change in aggregate demand due to an increase in autonomous government purchases, for example, the multiplier from equation (9) is given as follows:

$$m^* = \frac{\Delta Y}{\Delta G} = \frac{1}{1 - (c + i - x)(1 - t - f - p)} \tag{10}$$

and
$$\Delta Y = \Delta G \times m^*$$

For example, if $c = .8$, $i = .2$, $-x = .1$, while $t = .2$, $f = .1$, and $p = .08$ as before, equation (10) shows that the adjusted GNP multiplier value is:

$$m^* = \frac{1}{1 - (.8 + .2 - .1)(1 - .2 - .1 - .08)}$$

or
$$= \frac{1}{1 - .9\,(1 - .38)} = \frac{1}{.44} = 2.3$$

Thus, for every $10 increase in direct spending (e.g., autonomous investment expenditures or government purchases) GNP increases by $23.

In summary, part of the reason for the much reduced multiplier $m^*$ compared to $m$ is that business saving $(p)$ and tax leakage $(t)$ increase as aggregate income rises. Also, when aggregate income rises, government inflows in the form of transfer payments $(f)$ are reduced. Thus, a change in disposable income is only 62 percent of the change in aggregate income. In addition, the leakages to saving $(1 - c)$ and foreign imports $(-x)$ are partially offset by induced investment $(i)$ at various income levels, where the sum $(c + i - x)$ is a spending-stream flow representing a net marginal pro-

[5] The multiplier for an autonomous change in tax receipts (only part of which flow into the spending stream) is $m^* = \dfrac{-(c + i - x)}{1 - (c + i - x)(1 - t - f - p)}$. The opposite sign in the numerator would produce a multiplier for changes in government transfer payments.

pensity to spend on consumption, investment, and imports out of disposable income.[6] While more fully refined studies are capable of greater accuracy in estimating multiplier effects, what we have done is sufficient to illustrate how such adjustments are made. Let us see next how such information is used.

## THE OUTPUT GAP

As a member of the Council of Economic Advisers in 1961, Arthur Okun developed a means of estimating capacity output levels based upon past trends in real income and unemployment. Potential or capacity output at full employment $(Y_c)$, defined as 4 percent unemployment is a normative target or goal relative to the inflationary pressures generated at greater capacity levels of production. Although historical relations in the past may be more or less accurate in the future, an estimate of capacity output based upon what is sometimes known as Okun's law is:

$$Y_c = Y[1 + .032 (U - 4)] \tag{11}$$

Capacity income based upon 4 percent unemployment is $Y_c$; $Y$ is the expenditures for actual output, and $U$ is the actual unemployment rate. Thus, if $U = 4$, the bracketed terms in equation (11) are unity ($U - 4$ is zero) and potential and actual income are identical ($Y_c = Y$). If $U = 5$ percent initially and declines to the 4 percent target, Okun's law shows that $Y_c$ will rise by 3.2 percent of $Y$. On the other hand if $U$ remains at 6 percent and $Y = \$900$ billion, then $Y_c = \$900$ billion $[1 + .032 (6 - 4)]$ or $900 billion (1.064) = \$958$ billion. While estimates from Okun's equation are accurate only with a range of $10–$15 billion, they do identify some important relationships.

The absolute and relative size of the output gap is the difference in capacity and actual income:

$$Y_{gap} = Y_c - Y$$

and (in percentage terms)  $\dfrac{Y_c - Y}{Y} = .032 (U - 4) \tag{12}$

In terms of our earlier example where $U = 6$ percent and $Y = \$900$ billion,

---

[6] Another refinement sometimes added to the multiplier reflects the demand for money balances $(lk)$ relative to the money supply $(M)$. Thus, if $M$ is held constant and autonomous government expenditures increase, the rise in $Y$ will increase the transactions demand for money $(lk)$ which will cause interest rates to rise and may reduce investment demand, thereby reducing the net change in aggregate demand. The point of this adjustment is that the above multiplier analysis is couched in terms of fiscal policy and ignores monetary variables, when, in fact, monetary policy may have an effect upon aggregate demand, the multiplier, and GNP. Indeed, there are Monetarists who see fiscal action as working through monetary policy alone. The clearest case for the interdependent relationships between fiscal and monetary policy is one in which a government deficit, due let us say to additional government spending, is accompanied by no increase in the money supply. Under these conditions fiscal borrowing may "crowd out" of the market some volume of added borrowing that would have financed additional private spending. In the measure that "crowding out" does occur, the multiplier is reduced and conceivably could be negative if added government spending results in an even greater reduction in private spending. See Roger W. Spencer, and William P. Yoke, "The 'Crowding Out' of Private Expenditures by Fiscal Policy Actions," *Review*, Federal Reserve Bank of St. Louis, October 1970, pp. 12–24.

the output gap is $58 billion less than full-employment output, or 6.4 percent of actual income.

The gap between potential and actual output represents the change in aggregate income needed to reach full-employment levels of output. Thus, we can use measures of the real-world multiplier, $m^*$, to estimate the size of the aggregate-demand gap at full employment. In addition to using the multiplier appropriate to an autonomous change in government purchases, expenditures, or tax receipts, the increase in aggregate demand required is derived from the relationship $Y_{gap} = \Delta DD \times m^*$, where if $m^* = 2.3$ the needed increase in aggregate demand to attain full employment is:

$$\Delta DD = \frac{Y_{gap}}{m^*} \tag{13}$$

or
$$\$25.2 \text{ billion} = \frac{\$58 \text{ billion}}{2.3}$$

While there is much about Okun's law which is approximate, other studies have confirmed the relative accuracy of equation (11).[7] The crucial point to recognize, however, is that a small reduction of, say 1 percent in the unemployment rate increases real output by an estimated 3.2 percent. But why is it that reductions in unemployment and real output are not proportional (i.e., a decline of 1 percent in $U$ raises $Y$ by 1 percent)? For one thing, at high levels of unemployment some workers withdraw from the labor force because of discouragement and are not counted among the unemployed. Conversely, when $U$ falls, the "discouraged worker" is drawn back into the labor force. Second, as the unemployment rate declines, say from 6 percent to 4 percent, output per manhour or average productivity rises. Much of the explanation for this event reflects the fact that firms do not reduce employment in proportion to the decline in production and sales because of training costs, shortages of certain types of skilled labor, and so forth. Finally, average hours worked per man increase as unemployment declines and income increases. Similarly, as unemployment rises, the workweek is shortened. While these and related economic and statistical difficulties complicate the use of fiscal and monetary policy, estimating the multiplier and the magnitude of spending changes needed to achieve price stability and full employment are important, as we know.

ECONOMIC GROWTH

Difficult problems are encountered, however, in maintaining equilibrium growth in income at full employment over a period of time. The basic problem of equilibrium growth can be introduced by examination of the Harrod-Domar growth model.[8] Suppose initial conditions of full employment exist along with a given and constant marginal propensity to save ($s$). Also assume that the output/capital ratio is fixed, in which case the average and marginal productivity of capital ($\sigma = Y_c/K$) are equal, where

[7] See, for example, R. M. Solow, "Technical Progress, Capital Formation, and Economic Growth," *American Economic Review*, May 1962, pp. 76–86.

[8] The simplified approach here follows the initial work of Evsey Domar, "Expansion and Employment," *American Economic Review*, March 1947, pp. 34–55, and R. F. Harrod, *Toward Dynamic Economics* (London: Macmillan & Co., 1948), pp. 63–100.

$K$ represents the capital stock and $Y_c$ is output capacity. If $I$ represents net investment, it is also the change in capital $\Delta K$ from one time period to another, and the capacity change in output (aggregate supply) is the number of dollars invested multiplied by the output/capital ratio ($\sigma$):

$$\Delta Y_c = I\sigma$$

and in dividing by $Y_c$ the growth rate is

$$\frac{\Delta Y_c}{Y_c} = \frac{I\sigma}{Y_c} = g \text{ percent} \tag{14}$$

Equilibrium income exists when net investment and saving are equal, or $I = sY$—the amount of actual income saved. If capacity is fully utilized, it is also true that $I = sY_c$. By substituting $sY_c$ for $I$ in equation (14), the equilibrium rate of growth in output can be seen to be the product of the productivity of capital times the marginal propensity to save:

$$\frac{\Delta Y_c}{Y_c} = \frac{I\sigma}{Y_c}$$

$$= \frac{sY_c\sigma}{Y_c} = \sigma s = g \text{ percent} \tag{15}$$

If the new capacity output is to be fully utilized, aggregate expenditures on actual income must grow at the same rate as capacity income. Because only a fixed portion of a change in actual income, $\Delta Y$, is absorbed by consumption ($\Delta C = c\Delta Y$), the remaining expenditures must come from *increased* investment spending ($\Delta I$). Using the simple multiplier theory developed earlier, we know that if consumption is given, a change in actual income is the change in investment spending times the multiplier:

$$\Delta Y = \Delta I \frac{1}{s} \tag{16}$$

By comparing equations (14) and (16), the equilibrium change in capacity income and actual income which continues to fully utilize capacity occurs if investment grows as follows:

$$\Delta Y_c = \Delta Y$$

which is

$$I\sigma = \Delta I \frac{1}{s}$$

and thus

$$\frac{\Delta I}{I} = \sigma s \tag{17}$$

In short, if capacity output is to remain fully utilized over time, investment (from equation 17) and income (from equation 14) must grow at the same rate of $g = \sigma s$ percent, in which case $\Delta Y = \Delta Y_c$. Ignoring government and international trade and assuming no changes in $\sigma$ or shifts in consumption, investment expenditures in the future must continually grow to utilize added capacity created by the investment of earlier periods. Thus, if $1 - c$, or the marginal propensity to save is 10 percent, and $\sigma = 1/3$, investment must grow by $\sigma s = 3.3$ percent each year. Larger and larger *absolute* amounts of investment spending are required to maintain equality between changes in the potential supply of output ($\Delta Y_c$) and changes in the demand for output ($\Delta Y$).

Suppose, for example, that in year 1: $Y_c = Y$ at \$750, $I = S$ ($= sY$ or .1Y) is \$75, and $\sigma$ ($= Y/K$) is 1/3. The absolute change in productive capacity from year 1 to year 2 due to $I = \$75$ in the earlier period is $\Delta Y_c$ of \$25 ($I\sigma = \$75 \times 1/3$) while the rate of capacity growth $g$ is 3.3 percent ($\Delta Y_c/Y_c = \sigma s = 1/3 \times .10$, or \$25/\$750). Assume next that net investment grows less rapidly than the 3.3 percent increase in capacity income, say at the rate $\Delta I/I = \$1.5/\$75 = 2$ percent per year. The absolute change in actual income between year 1 and 2 is then the change in net investment expenditures times the multiplier, or $\Delta Y$ of \$15 ($\Delta I\frac{1}{s} = \$1.5 \times 10$). Since $\Delta Y_c$ of \$25 exceeds $\Delta Y$ of \$15, it is also true that $Y_c$ exceeds $Y$ in year 2— a deflationary gap arises and capacity is underutilized. At the new capacity level of production aggregate demand is deficient (saving exceeds investment). Because of excess capacity it appears to producers that investment is excessive when, in fact, investment expenditures are not growing rapidly enough. On the other hand, inflation occurs if investment grows more rapidly than the equilibrium 3.3 percent increase in capacity, say at $\Delta I/I = \$4.5/\$75 = 6$ percent per year. Then the change in actual income is $\Delta Y$ of \$45 ($\Delta I\frac{1}{s} = \$4.5 \times 10$), whereas $\Delta Y_c$ is \$25 as before. A change in capacity output of $\Delta Y_c$ of \$25 (i.e., the change in potential supply) is less than a change in money expenditures on actual income of $\Delta Y = \$45$ (i.e., the change in effective aggregate demand), and an inflationary gap occurs. Investment is growing too rapidly and disequilibrium arises. Based upon rather restrictive assumptions, the Harrod-Domar growth model shows that output and investment must grow at the same rate $g = \sigma s$ *if price stability and full-employment capacity are to be maintained.* As long as $s$, $\sigma$, and technological change are constant, equilibrium growth is a precarious razor's edge.

This simple model teaches one important lesson: *Both income and investment—the potential supply of output and the demand for output—must grow at the same rate if an output gap* ($\Delta Y_c \neq \Delta Y$) *is to be avoided.* Thus, $g = \sigma s$ percent is a *warranted rate of growth* in the sense that past expectations of the rate of growth in output and investment are satisfied; that is, equality between saving and investment is maintained. If firms do not just happen to reach this growth rate, net investment in future time periods will be adversely affected. When investment growth is sluggish ($\Delta Y_c > \Delta Y$), excess capacity arises, it *appears* to the individual firm that too much has been invested, and firms may reduce investment spending when, in fact, aggregate-investment spending is too small to begin with. In contrast, when investment spending is excessive ($\Delta Y > \Delta Y_c$) inflation occurs, investment *appears* to the individual firm to be inadequate, and firms may step up investment spending when, in fact, aggregate-investment spending is excessive at the outset.

Furthermore, there is some "natural" full-employment rate of growth, as Sir Roy Harrod has noted, which reflects the limit at which an economy can grow with increases in human resources and technological improvements.

Suppose for example, an economy initially is experiencing unemployment and the warranted growth in productive capacity of the economy is more rapid than the natural full-employment rate of growth. The growth in productive capacity soon puts unemployed labor resources back to work at the higher warranted growth rate, but ultimately capacity growth hits and "bounces off" the natural full-employment growth ceiling. A situation in which the natural growth rate is 3 percent, and equilibrium growth in productive capacity occurs at a warranted rate of 5 percent is possible only in the short run for an economy initially operating below full employment. Since an output ceiling is set by the natural full-employment rate of growth, excess productive capacity ultimately will arise and discourage additional investment. Persistent underutilization of this capital-created capacity can stall and even cause investment to decline as labor shortages prevent the economy from growing at its warranted capacity rate, ultimately leading to recession and unemployment.

The reverse situation is no idyllic condition either. Under these circumstances, warranted *full-capacity growth* is assured, and the persistent shortage of capital may lead to inflationary pressures. Moreover, the more rapid natural full-employment growth in labor can lead to chronic unemployment; that is, full employment is not achieved even though full capacity (and perhaps inflation due to shortages of capital-created capacity) occurs. In this instance, chronic unemployment can appear along with price-level pressures because the natural growth rate in the labor force is running ahead of the warranted growth in capital-created capacity.

This simplified model is very useful for pedagogical purposes, but less applicable to the real world because of the restrictive assumptions it embodies. The precarious economic growth balance between $\Delta Y_c$ and $\Delta Y$ and differences between productive capacity and full-employment growth raises disturbing, but not totally hopeless, problems. For example, growth disequilibrium may encourage changes in $\sigma$ and $s$. Under chronic unemployment conditions, labor may be substituted for capital which may help increase $\sigma$ as relatively scarce capital resources are used for the most productive purposes. Moreover, $s$ may also increase—particularly if consumers save less than producers at the margin. Therefore, the warranted growth rate may rise to the natural full-employment rate. The reverse adjustments may also occur. Indeed, fluctuating levels of economic activity in the past suggest that while there are numerous obstacles to equilibrium growth, technological change is also of great importance to the growth process.

Consider the recent failure of the American economy to achieve a more nearly stable full-employment growth rate. This has been damaging on many counts, including the wasteful GNP gap entailed when a nation produces at some point below its production frontier. Even fiscal and monetary action can have strange stabilization effects, however, and policy may go astray as in the 1969–1971 period. The burst of inflation of the latter 1960s began to subside in 1970 as restrictive monetary policy and fiscal action began to be felt. In its *Annual Report* for 1970, the Council of Economic Advisers estimated that productive capacity would grow 4.3 percent per year, but the demand for output would grow at a lesser rate because of the emphasis placed upon restrictive economic policies aimed at de-escalating price-level increases. Because of this deflationary pressure, a GNP gap in excess of

$80 billion is expected between the potential supply of output and actual output between 1970 and 1972. The remedy for such problems is more evenly applied fiscal and monetary policies along with efforts to control the unemployment-inflation tradeoff. Providing for adequate and stable levels of aggregate demand sufficient to utilize productive capacity at full employment is both an important and difficult goal to achieve.

# PART 3

Efficient resource utilization, like full employment and economic growth, also impinges upon scarcity and augments economic welfare. Transformation of resources into outputs capable of satisfying the needs of a populace requires organization just as societies must coordinate political, military, and legal affairs. Economic organization may be dictated by a controlling authority, it may be governed by tradition and habit, or it may be loosely arranged in a market environment. One of the great questions facing civilizations of this century centers upon the optimal mix of these three coordinating tactics—a subject which is explored here by developing methods of analysis which are useful in the study of economic efficiency in the allocation of resources in the market system.

# Microeconomics: Prices and the Allocation of Resources

# CHAPTER 14
# Supply, Demand,
# and Prices

In the next several chapters we will study the efficient allocation of resources as one goal of an economic system. *Efficient resource allocation* is the use and allocation of resources in such a way as to produce, at the least possible cost, those goods that are wanted most to meet consumer priorities with the least sacrifice of scarce resources. The first step toward understanding the efficient allocation of resources is to learn how supply, demand, and prices ration output and allocate resources.

There are, however, two very important qualifications to the study of supply and demand:

1. Our definition of economic efficiency *does not* mean that maximum welfare is necessarily achieved in an efficient society except in a very limited technical sense. Economic efficiency is a limited concept for many reasons (e.g., the unequal distribution of income); therefore, "efficiency" is not to be confused with "welfare."

2. The forces of demand and supply examined here and in the following four chapters concern resource allocation in *only part* of the economy— the private sector.[1]

We first discussed how prices allocate scarce resources and ration limited output in a market economy in Chapter 3. To expand on this idea, we must next examine certain analytical tools which are used frequently in the study of economic problems. Part A introduces several basic concepts and tools which will be used in this and subsequent chapters, and Parts B and C develop formal theories of supply and demand, respectively. The meaning of equilibrium price is explained in Part D, and the topic of Part E is elasticity —the measure of quantity responsiveness to price changes.

## A. FUNDAMENTAL CONCEPTS AND PRINCIPLES

Beginning students in economics very often misunderstand the importance of supply, demand, and price determination. The simple and extremely important reason for studying price determination is that prices mediate the choice process in a market economy. Prices: (*a*) distribute limited goods and services to consumers, and (*b*) determine the allocation of resources. In short, prices are an organizing device that guide the market economy in deciding how to use and distribute scarce resources which are transformed into goods and services.

---

[1] Resource allocation and welfare issues, as well as government, are considered explicitly in Chapters 19 and 20.

*Microeconomics* describes the way prices are formed in individual producer and consumer markets. Supply and demand are important because they cooperate in determining the prices of products and resources. In order to examine these relationships and derive tentative conclusions about resource allocation, we will construct a model of an imaginary producer assumed to represent all producing firms in an economic system. This model firm and economy is a perfectly functioning institution in an equally perfect (and unrealistic) world. We assume that everything associated with production is known, mobile, and perfect.

In developing a model of a competitive firm, our primary interest is *not* the "proper" management of a business firm; rather, it is the economic efficiency of the allocation of resources throughout the entire economy. The two-part meaning of economic efficiency (the *least costly* combination of resources to provide *maximum satisfaction*) is a limited, but nonetheless very useful, idea in a society in which wants exceed the productive capacity of resources.

There are several reasons for beginning our study with a model:

1. To furnish a clear understanding of the meaning or to define the significance of economic efficiency in the allocation of scarce resources.

2. To provide a concept of how resources would be allocated in a model economy.

3. To establish a rational base from which we can then depart to examine discrepancies between the model world and reality. Such differences are due largely to economic imperfections and market power—the manipulation or control of prices.

It must be clearly understood that the theory of the firm developed in the next several chapters is a first approximation, similar to a plastic model of the bone structure of the human anatomy. Further identification of relevant facts and more realistic assumptions concerning human beings lead to an improved understanding of how the body functions. Similarly, we can develop increasingly useful knowledge about the economics of resource allocation as we move from simple to complex models. If our facts and theories generally coincide, undue distress over the lack of realism in a simplified model is unwarranted. After all, a plastic skeleton is not very realistic, but such models are still useful. We are obliged, of course, to examine the correspondence between facts, theory, and reality—a task which we can and will do once the necessary analytical equipment is mastered. However, we must have a general theory with which to start.

Figure 1 is a summary of the relationship of markets and prices drawn from the discussion of Chapter 3. The figure shows how supply and demand interact to determine price and also shows the general consequence of price changes. At a superficial level, it is generally apparent from the figure that supply and demand determine some particular price, which in turn influences profits and the allocation of resources. Figure 1 thus indicates in a very general way how resource markets are related to supply, demand, and prices in product markets. If the quantity of a product consumers wish to purchase exceeds the quantity producing firms offer, rising prices and profits tend to allocate more scarce resources to such product markets (e.g., the health-care industry today). Conversely, when market prices are gen-

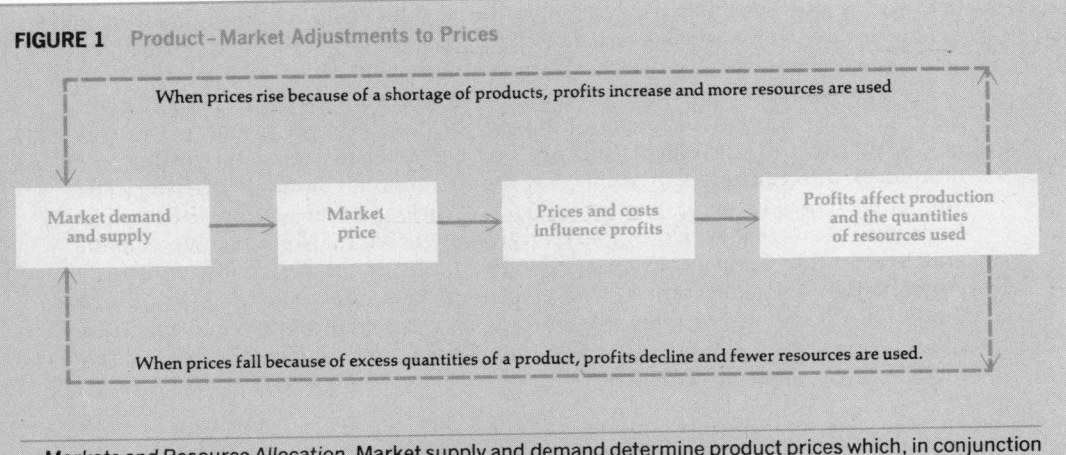

**FIGURE 1** Product–Market Adjustments to Prices

When prices rise because of a shortage of products, profits increase and more resources are used

| Market demand and supply | → | Market price | → | Prices and costs influence profits | → | Profits affect production and the quantities of resources used |

When prices fall because of excess quantities of a product, profits decline and fewer resources are used.

*Markets and Resource Allocation.* Market supply and demand determine product prices which, in conjunction with production costs, determine profits earned by firms. Firms employ more or fewer resources to produce, depending upon the profitability of such decisions. Prices and profits tend to rise when products are in short supply, whereas prices and profits fall if excess quantities of a good exist as the dashed feedback loops of the figure suggest.

erally contracting, fewer resources are used (as is the case of coal used for residential heating today). On the basis of this logic, product prices and the profits earned by firms allegedly organize an economy by allocating resources. More definitive tools of analysis are needed, however, to better explain how resources are allocated.

### Types of Markets

Individual producers in an economy are *firms*. Several firms related to the same market, such as all firms producing breakfast foods, steel, or guns, are *industries*. The market system tabulates and organizes innumerable individual economic decisions through the price mechanism. In this market environment, firms decide to produce liver pills, high-school graduates elect to become dental technicians, and housewives choose to buy new coats rather than new golf clubs for their husbands. If utter chaos is to be avoided, the variety and repetitiveness of such economic decisions require organization by a force or some set of forces. The market, an informal institutional arrangement for the sale and exchange of products and resources, is such a force.

### MARKET COMPETITION

It is important to distinguish between markets that are purely competitive and those that are imperfectly competitive.[2] A *purely competitive market* is characterized by price rivalry, ultimately resulting in only one market-, established price. Three conditions characterize a purely competitive product market: (a) Entry into and exit from the market by individual firms is easy, (b) all firms in the industry sell a uniform or a standardized prod-

---

[2] We will return to more formal distinctions between competitive and imperfectly competitive markets in Chapters 16 and 17.

uct, and (c) the number of firms is so large that no individual producer is able to influence the market price of the product.

If a firm has the ability to influence the market price of a product, an *imperfectly competitive market* condition is said to prevail. Imperfect competition or price control is characterized by: (a) barriers to entry and exit in the market; (b) products that are not perfectly identical but rather are unique or differentiated in some way; or (c) a small number of firms, enabling each producer to influence product price. Because this situation is common in the real world, imperfectly competitive markets receive considerable attention from economists. For the moment, however, we will postpone further consideration of imperfect markets and develop a simplified model of a competitive market economy. In later chapters we can relax the assumption of pure competition adopted here and develop more realistic models of the market economy.

## RESOURCE AND PRODUCT MARKETS

To understand the efficient allocation of resources in either a theoretical or a real economy, it is necessary to distinguish between product and resource markets. Generally speaking, the prices of both resources and products are shaped by supply and demand. Markets which serve as a clearing mechanism for goods and services are *product markets*. The product markets for breakfast food and fingernail polish establish a price in a monetary unit by tabulating innumerable consumer decisions to buy (demand) and producer decisions to sell (supply). Markets also exist for resources; that is, for all property resources (land and capital goods) and human resources (labor and entrepreneurs) used as factors of production. The purchase and hire of resources such as shovels, assembly-line workers, business managers, and bubble dancers are resource-market transactions for labor. Capital resources are also sold and bought in the resource market, which includes transactions involving physical capital such as machinery, inventory, and buildings. The price of capital is the *interest rate,* a rate of return on the money invested in physical capital, while the price of land resources is known as *rent.* The price of manpower or labor is a *wage* or *salary,* and entrepreneurial resources receive payment in the form of a *profit.*

To simplify our study of pricing, we will, for the moment, ignore the resource market and focus attention on product markets. What is important to remember is that the price established by supply and demand for a product will be related to the quantity supplied and thus will influence the quantity of resources used in production. If fingernail polish were somehow to increase in price from $1 to $1,000 for a one-half ounce bottle, and consumer tastes remained unchanged, it is readily apparent that society would devote fewer resources to this product simply because consumers would buy smaller quantities (given their incomes). It is in this way that product markets are related to resource markets.

While identifiable physical markets do exist in some areas (the village square in remote Vermont or the bazaar in the hinterlands of Mexico), markets in most economies are not physical. In reality, a market occurs when buyers and sellers synchronize their individual plans by conducting business at mutually agreed upon prices. However, freedom to participate in a market system is not absolute. As noted in earlier chapters, certain kinds of markets (e.g., the market for draft deferments) are not permitted. Nevertheless, the dollar-balloting process conducted in markets generally renders the ultimate decision on what will be produced, who will produce, how production will occur, and who will consume the produced output of society. This process is accomplished through the establishment of a system of prices determined by the individual decisions to buy and to sell which make up the forces of demand and supply. While it is true that supply and demand determine the prices of goods and of resources, the simplicity of such a statement masks the enormity of the problem that must be analyzed.

## B. PRODUCER AND MARKET SUPPLY

The *principle of supply* postulates that supply is positively or directly related to product price; for example, as price increases the quantity supplied increases, and as price decreases the quantity supplied decreases. Firms typically are encouraged to supply larger quantities of shirts, for example, at higher prices because they may be able to earn larger profits, and also because higher production costs can be covered if necessary. On the other hand, fewer shirts are offered at lower prices because production becomes less profitable as the price of shirts declines.

### The Supply Schedule

A schedule of supply is shown in Figure 2 to illustrate this direct price-quantity relationship. Six units of a hypothetical product are supplied at a price of $4 (point *b*), whereas 18 units are supplied at a higher price of $7 (point *e*). Such a schedule of supply is derived by plotting the price and quantity coordinates, also shown in tabular form in Figure 2. Supply schedule *s* in Figure 2 is consistent with our hypothesis that the price of a product and the quantity which firms are willing and able to produce and offer for sale are *directly related*.

Supply schedules for individual firms (such as *s* in Figure 2) can be converted into *market* supply schedules. To find a market supply curve one simply adds up the quantity supplied by each firm at a given price. By repeating this process for all firms at each price, a schedule of market supply can be developed. For example, if the one firm depicted in Figure 2 is precisely like 999 other firms in the industry, *market* supply can be illustrated as 6,000 units at $4, 11,000 units at $5, and so forth.[3]

### PRICES AND MARKET SUPPLY

The principle of supply is a common-sense notion that can be supported intuitively. From the viewpoint of a firm, product price is an incentive to produce. The higher the price, the greater the incentive to the firm to supply the product, other things being equal. The direct price-quantity relationship embodied in a supply schedule can be more fully explained by recognizing product substitution as a possible option open to a firm. If consumers are willing and able to pay higher prices for shirts, firms producing then will alter their pattern of production to produce more shirts. A higher mar-

---

[3] Actually, the derivation of market supply is not necessarily this simple because the decisions of firms to increase the quantity supplied may affect resource price. Nevertheless, we can regard market supply as a reflection of the principle of supply for a firm (a positively sloped schedule) and leave refinements for more advanced courses.

MICROECONOMICS: PRICES AND THE ALLOCATION OF RESOURCES

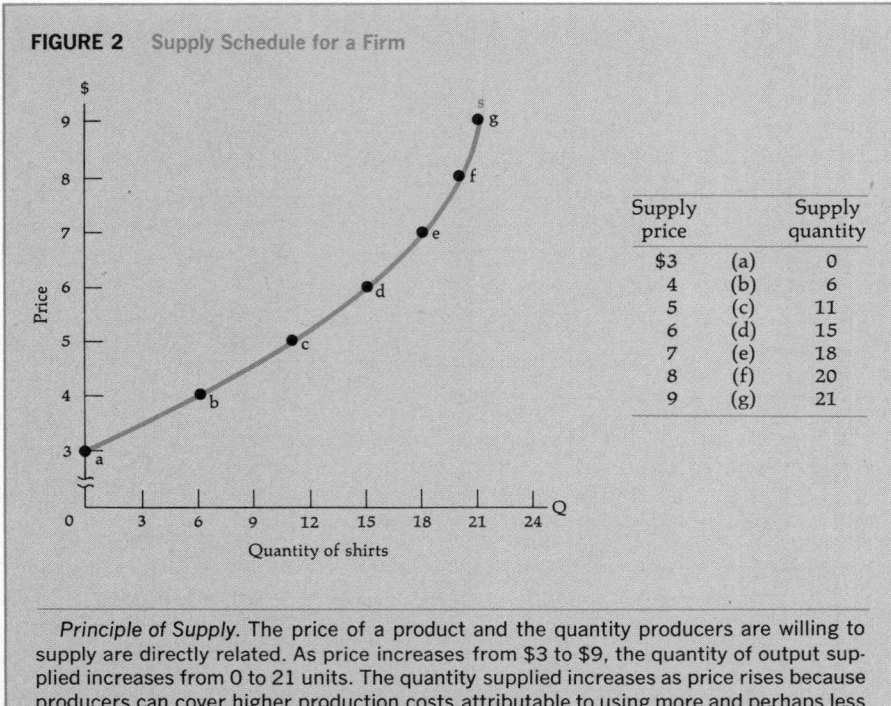

**FIGURE 2** Supply Schedule for a Firm

| Supply price | | Supply quantity |
|---|---|---|
| $3 | (a) | 0 |
| 4 | (b) | 6 |
| 5 | (c) | 11 |
| 6 | (d) | 15 |
| 7 | (e) | 18 |
| 8 | (f) | 20 |
| 9 | (g) | 21 |

*Principle of Supply.* The price of a product and the quantity producers are willing to supply are directly related. As price increases from $3 to $9, the quantity of output supplied increases from 0 to 21 units. The quantity supplied increases as price rises because producers can cover higher production costs attributable to using more and perhaps less productive resources. Similarly, the quantity supplied declines at successively lower prices.

ket price for shirts relative to jackets induces firms, in their search for greater profits, to use more resources to produce shirts and fewer resources to produce jackets. Accordingly, the profit advantage implied by a higher relative price is an organizing force in a market economy.

It may be impossible for a firm to increase output without an increase in costs, since to do so it may have to use more resources and perhaps less productive ones. Higher product prices may, however, entice firms to acquire more resources or to shift resources from one use to another. Although the substitution of resources is a good deal more complex than indicated here, it is apparent that rising product prices encourage firms to increase the quantity of output they will produce and offer on the market. Indeed, higher product prices may be necessary to entice firms to reallocate resources away from one product to the production of another.

OPPORTUNITY COSTS AND SUPPLY

These seemingly logical propositions are clearly revealed by Figure 3(a), which is a production-possibilities curve for a theoretical economy producing two goods—food and machines. To increase the output of food in constant amounts, more and more output of machines must be sacrificed, as Figure 3(a) indicates. In other words, we can see that the *opportunity cost* (the output sacrificed in using resources for a given purpose) of producing successive units of food rises as the output of food increases. The reason

FIGURE 3   Supply and Opportunity Costs

(a) The production frontier

(b) Opportunity costs

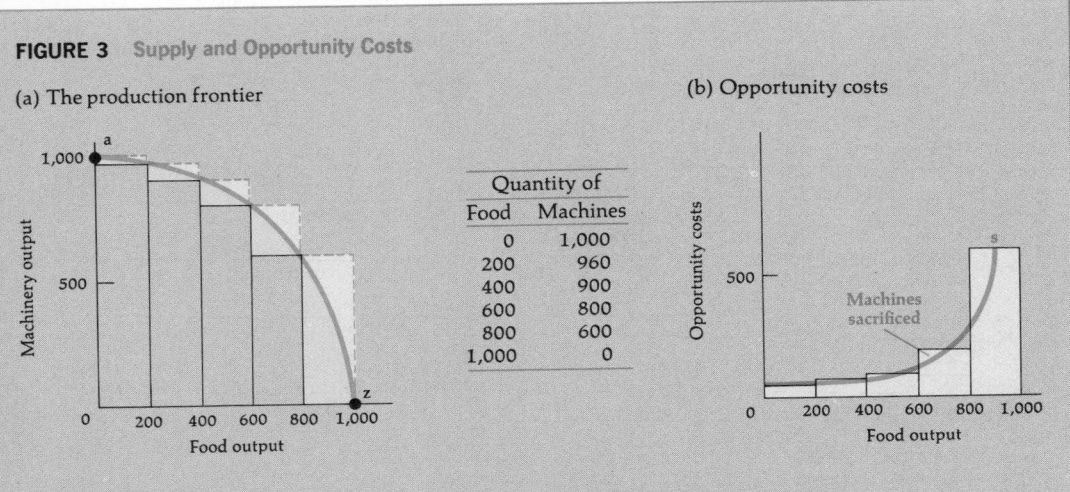

| Quantity of | |
| --- | --- |
| Food | Machines |
| 0 | 1,000 |
| 200 | 960 |
| 400 | 900 |
| 600 | 800 |
| 800 | 600 |
| 1,000 | 0 |

*Supply and Opportunity Costs.* The upward-sloping supply curve depicting a positive price-quantity relationship is approximated by the production possibilities for a two-commodity economy, where the costs of producing additional food output is the sacrifice of machinery output. Opportunity cost (the additional sacrifice of machinery output) rises with successive units of food output because resources are increasingly less productive as specialization in one product occurs. The machinery output sacrificed as food output increases from 0 to 1,000 units is represented by the shaded portions.

is the now-familiar principle of imperfect substitution of resources in producing a product.[4] Actually, the opportunity cost of food can be plotted separately [see Figure 3(b)] as increases in the quantity of machines sacrificed in moving from point *a* to point *z* on the production frontier. Note that the sacrificed output, or "machine costs of additional food output," resembles the supply curve shown earlier in Figure 2. An illustration of this sort demonstrates the relevance of the *increasing* opportunity cost a society incurs in making choices about the production of one good over others.

Resource-allocation choices are extremely important to everyone, as you would readily recognize if for some reason a society did not allocate resources to the production of mundane products like salt, shoes, or schools. Product prices are important for analogous reasons, since they ultimately help to determine in just what degree machines are sacrificed for food or the measure in which shirts are produced vs. shoes. Resource-allocation considerations, therefore, occupy a most legitimate and eminent role in economics.

### Supply Determinants

The proper way to read supply schedule *s* of Figure 2 is to observe that the quantity supplied varies directly with the price of the product. A given supply schedule describes one unique set of price-quantity relationships.

---

[4] Discussed in Chapter 3. We ignore here one additional explanation for a rising supply schedule; namely, the declining productivity of resources due to diminishing returns (see Chapter 15).

*Changes in the quantity supplied* describe movement along supply schedules from points *a* to *g* in Figure 4. The implication that the quantity supplied is a function solely of product price is not complete, however. Automobiles, for example, are not supplied in the relationship of six units at a price of $4 or twenty units at $8, nor are safety pins.

Supply is determined mainly by five factors in addition to product price. They are: (*a*) production technology, (*b*) the objectives of the firm, (*c*) the costs of productive resources which are transformed into output, (*d*) the prices of other products, and (*e*) the number of sellers in a market. Each of these five determinants of supply accounts for the location of a supply schedule. That is, *supply determinants locate the precise price-quantity relationships of a supply schedule.* A change in one of the five determinants of supply will shift the supply schedule, as shown in Figure 4. This is called a *change* or *shift in supply* and is different from a change in quantity supplied. *Supply changes* reflect a shift in the supply schedule from *s* to *s_d* or from *s* to *s_i*, whereas *changes in the quantity supplied* describe movement along a supply schedule, as noted above.

A supply *increase* is depicted by a rightward shift in the supply function from *s* to *s_i*, while a supply *decrease* is depicted by a leftward shift in the supply function from *s* to *s_d*. The supply increase (from *s* to *s_i*) means that firms are willing to supply larger quantities of a product at *each and every possible price*. Because supply changes are due to a change in one of the five determinants of supply, it is important to discover how each of these determinants can affect the supply schedule.

First, the effects of changing technology influence the firm's supply function by altering the costs of production. The use of more efficient and automated capital equipment may lower costs, thus permitting a firm to supply a larger amount of output at each possible price (the supply function shifts rightward, or supply increases from *s* to *s_i* in Figure 4). This has happened in the nuclear-energy and computer industries in recent years. Second, in some instances, a firm may be interested in objectives other

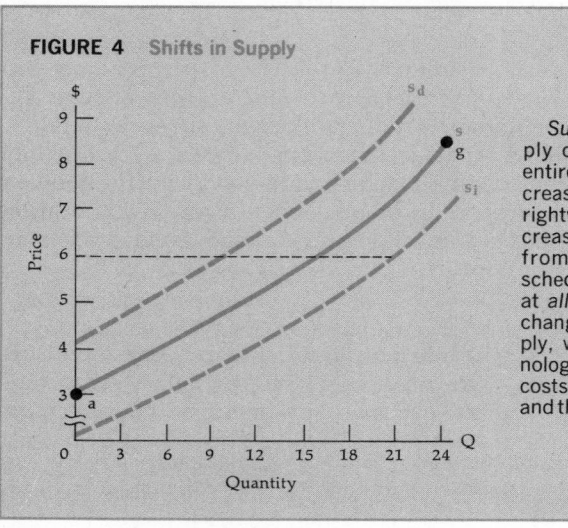

**FIGURE 4**   Shifts in Supply

*Supply Changes or Shifts.* A supply change is a movement in the entire supply schedule. If supply increases, the supply function shifts rightward from *s* to *s_i*. A supply decrease is denoted by a leftward shift from *s* to *s_d*. Shifts in the supply schedule change the quantity offered at *all* prices. A supply shift reflects changes in the determinants of supply, which include production technology, firm objectives, production costs, the price of related products, and the number of sellers in a market.

than selling at a profitable price. For example, assuming that other determinants of supply remain unchanged, a supply increase (a rightward shift from $s$ to $s_i$) may occur if the firm is interested in gaining entry to a new market. Third, the prices of resources used as factors of production (e.g., labor, capital, or land) also influence the location of the supply schedule. If the only change in supply determinants is a rise in wages that increases labor costs, supply tends to decrease (shifting leftward from $s$ to $s_d$). Fourth, the price of a related product may influence the supply of other goods. For example, a decline in the market-established price of wheat may prompt farmers to increase their production of beef or oats; thus, the supply of beef or oats would increase from $s$ to $s_i$. Fifth, the number of suppliers also has an impact on market supply. Generally, a reduction in the number of firms in an industry will decrease market supply. Conversely, as additional firms enter the industry, market supply will shift to the right.

The conclusions to be drawn from these facts are: (*a*) product price and the quantity supplied are directly related, (*b*) changes in the quantity supplied reflect movement along one supply schedule, (*c*) supply changes as the determinants of supply change, and (*d*) supply increases are shown as rightward shifts in the supply schedule (from $s$ to $s_i$), while supply decreases are shown as leftward shifts (from $s$ to $s_d$) in Figure 4.

## C. CONSUMER AND MARKET DEMAND

### Theory of Demand

The demand for a product is the schedule of quantities of a product consumers are willing and able to buy at different prices at a particular point in time. The *principle of demand* postulates an inverse or negative relationship between the price of a product and the quantity demanded. At higher prices, the quantity of a product demanded is less, and at lower prices the quantity demanded is greater, as is shown in Figure 5. Movement along demand schedule *d* of Figure 5 describes a *change in quantity demanded* as a result of a change in price. For example, the quantity demanded at a price of $8 is one unit (point *b*), the quantity demanded at $7 is three units (point *c*), and twenty-one units are demanded at a price of $3 (point *g*).

The negative or inverse price-quantity relationship characteristic of demand is validated by casual observation of consumer behavior. Product price acts as a deterrent that must be overcome if consumption is to take place; the lower the price obstacle, the greater the inclination of the consumer to purchase a given product, other things being equal. A second fundamental reason for the inverse price-quantity relationship is the diminishing satisfaction that accompanies consumption of increased quantities of a product.

#### DIMINISHING MARGINAL UTILITY

A considerable amount of evidence backs up our common-sense support for the shape of a demand schedule. The amount of satisfaction consumers receive from a product has been dubbed *utility*. Consumption of one additional unit of most products is said to yield *diminishing marginal utility*, where "marginal" means additional. Thus, diminishing marginal utility refers to continually declining amounts of additional satisfaction derived from consuming another unit of a product. The marginal utility of a first

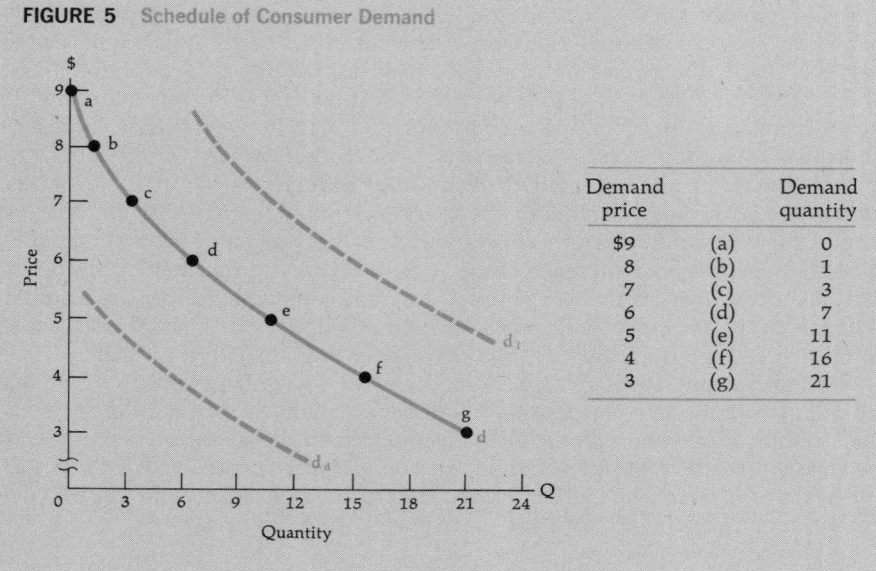

**FIGURE 5**   Schedule of Consumer Demand

| Demand price | | Demand quantity |
|---|---|---|
| $9 | (a) | 0 |
| 8 | (b) | 1 |
| 7 | (c) | 3 |
| 6 | (d) | 7 |
| 5 | (e) | 11 |
| 4 | (f) | 16 |
| 3 | (g) | 21 |

*Principle of Demand.* The price of a product and the quantity demanded are inversely related. As price declines from $9 to $3, new buyers are enticed into the market. People tend to buy more of a product at lower prices and less at higher prices because: (*a*) diminishing satisfaction accompanies the consumption of additional quantities of a product, and (*b*) there may be substitute goods competing for scarce dollars. A demand decrease is depicted as a leftward shift in the demand schedule (*d* to *d*$_d$), and a demand increase is portrayed as a rightward shift in the demand schedule (*d* to *d*$_i$). Demand changes or shifts are the result of a change in one of the determinants of demand, which include the level and the distribution of income, changes in the price of related goods, changes in consumer tastes, and the number of buyers in a market.

pair of shoes may be great, but succeeding purchases typically result in less and less marginal utility. If this is so, it follows in most cases that lower prices will be needed to entice a consumer to buy more of one product, which is what a demand schedule shows. Because of diminishing marginal utility, consumers value additional units of a product less and less, and generally are willing to purchase them only at lower prices for that reason.[5]

## PRODUCT SUBSTITUTION AND DEMAND SCHEDULES

Added support for the diminishing-marginal-utility argument in defense of a downward-sloping demand curve is furnished by the inclination of consumers to substitute one product for another. Substitution buttresses the inverse price-quantity relationships illustrated by the downward-sloping demand schedule *d* of Figure 5 because consumers typically have limited incomes. A decrease in the price of tea relative to the price of a substitute good such as coffee, for example, may encourage some consumers to sub-

[5] The concept of "utility" is considerably more important than this terse description suggests and will be developed further in Chapter 20.

stitute tea for coffee. Substitution, of course, depends on individual preferences and the products one considers. In a sense, all products may be regarded as very crude substitutes for each other in the long run, since the disposition of a limited income embodies numerous alternative choices made by consumers. The extent of substitutability varies greatly depending on the needs that different products satisfy—a new color television set is a more general and less direct substitute for a refrigerator than tea is for coffee.

The schedule of an individual's demand for a given product can be translated into a market demand curve. Market demand is obtained by horizontally adding the quantity demanded by individual consumers at each possible price. Suppose that every one of 1,000 college students' demands for residence-hall meals is represented by demand schedule d of Figure 5. Then, 3,000 meals might be purchased at a price of $7 per meal, 7,000 meals might be bought at a price of $6 for each meal, and so forth. This yields a *market* demand schedule similar to the down-sloping demand curve depicted in Figure 5, except that the quantities shown on the horizontal axis would be a multiple of those now shown.

### Demand Determinants

A *change in the quantity demanded* reflects movement along one demand schedule relative to changes in product price, just as a change in the quantity supplied represented a response of the quantity of goods supplied to price. A *demand shift or change* denotes a change in the location of the demand schedule shown in Figure 5. A *demand increase* is reflected by a rightward shift of the demand schedule (the shift from d to $d_i$), which reveals that consumers are willing and able to purchase more of a good at *each* price (or pay a higher price for the same quantity). While 11 units are demanded at a price of $5 on schedule d, for example, more units are demanded at $5 if schedule $d_i$ prevails. In contrast, a *decrease* in demand is shown as a leftward shift in the demand schedule (from d to $d_d$ in Figure 5).

Every demand curve is related to some given combination of the nonprice determinants of demand. They are: (a) the level and distribution of income, (b) changes in the price and availability of other products, (c) changes in consumer preferences or tastes, and (d) the number of buyers. Demand changes or shifts are a result of a change in one or more of the determinants of demand—the factors responsible for the precise location of a demand schedule.

For example, demand may increase (from d to $d_i$) or decrease (from d to $d_d$) as shown in Figure 5 as a result of the level of income available to consumers. Income increases will result in a demand increase only for *superior* products such as color television sets, skiing vacations, or graduate education. An increase in income may also result in a demand increase for butter and steak, which are superior goods relative to margarine and hamburger. An income increase may also result in a demand decrease (from d to $d_d$) for *inferior* goods. Demand for such goods as margarine and hamburger may decline as incomes rise and consumers opt for superior products. Changes in the distribution of income can also shift the demand schedule. In all likelihood, if income were to be more equally distributed, the demand for vacations to Bermuda would decline.

Furthermore, a demand schedule is also influenced by the price and availability of substitute and complementary goods. Coffee and tea are *substitute goods*, as are coal and natural gas for heating. Not many years ago coal was a primary source of heat for residential homes, but today natural gas is increasingly being substituted for coal. With the passage of time, the demand for coal decreased from $d$ to $d_d$ in Figure 5 as the availability of natural gas increased and its relative price declined. Another good example of product substitution is the increasing competition for steel products posed by the aluminum industry. In the case of *complementary goods*, a decrease in the price of one product, such as stereo tape recorders, may result in a demand increase (from $d$ to $d_i$) for another, such as for stereo tapes, because tapes are complementary to stereo units. Similarly, if the price of gasoline rises markedly, the demand schedule for tires may shift leftward from $d$ to $d_d$ because automobile tires are complementary goods to gasoline. The location of a demand schedule also reflects the relative preferences of consumers. In recent years, the demand for six-guns has decreased (a leftward shift from $d$ to $d_d$ in Figure 5) in deference to an array of space-age weaponry. Finally, demand reflects the number of buyers in a market. As the population and thus the number of prospective buyers of homes, automobiles, and clothing have increased, the demand schedules for these products have shifted rightward.

Our conclusions about the demand for products are similar to those we drew about supply. It is important to distinguish between a change in the quantity demanded and changes in demand—shifts in a demand schedule due to a fundamental change in nonprice determinants of demand such as consumer tastes. Keeping such distinctions clearly in mind will be very helpful in understanding how supply and demand cooperate in determining equilibrium prices—our next task.

## D. PRICE DETERMINATION BY SUPPLY AND DEMAND

The principle of supply specifying a direct relationship between price and quantity and the principle of demand specifying an inverse relationship between price and quantity can be integrated to develop a theory of equilibrium price. As we learned in Chapter 3, *equilibrium price* means a stable price—that is, a situation in which the quantity of a product supplied and the quantity demanded are equal. In such a case there is no market force leading to a price change unless one or more of the determinants of supply demand are altered.

### Equilibrium Price

A large number of prices exist at which consumers will buy and producers will supply varying amounts of a product, but there is only one equilibrium price. This equilibrium price synchronizes conflict between sellers who desire higher prices and buyers who desire lower prices, other things being equal. An equilibrium price is one at which the quantity decisions of buying consumers and producing suppliers exactly satisfy each other. As shown in Figure 6, for example, an equilibrium price and quantity is established at $5 and 11,000 units, where demand and supply are understood to mean the schedule of *market* supply and the schedule of *market* demand. Equilibrium is that point at which the demand schedule ($d$) intersects the supply

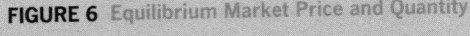

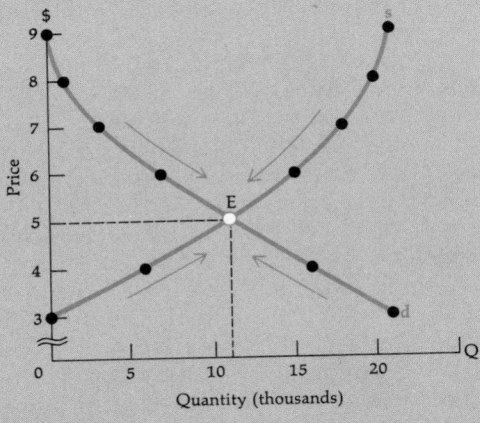

**FIGURE 6** Equilibrium Market Price and Quantity

| Demand quantity | Price | Supply quantity |
|---|---|---|
| 21,000 | $3 | 0 |
| 16,000 | 4 | 6,000 |
| 11,000 | 5 | 11,000 |
| 7,000 | 6 | 15,000 |
| 3,000 | 7 | 18,000 |
| 1,000 | 8 | 20,000 |
| 0 | 0 | 21,000 |

*Determination of Equilibrium Market Price.* The equilibrium market price of $5 and 11,000 units is determined by the intersection of supply (s) and demand (d). At a higher price such as $7, the quantity supplied as shown by schedule s exceeds the quantity consumers demand as shown by schedule d. The surplus drives price down toward the equilibrium level where the amount supplied in the market is equal to the amount consumers demand. At a price lower than the $5 equilibrium, the quantity demanded exceeds the quantity producers supply. At $4, for example, there is a scarcity of output forcing price up to the equilibrium level where the amount supplied is equal to the amount consumers demand.

schedule (s). It becomes more obvious why $5 is an equilibrium price by looking at alternative price-quantity combinations.

Consider first a price of $7, at which all firms in the industry are willing to supply 18,000 units and total consumer purchases would be 3,000 units. The quantity offered by firms exceeds the quantity that buyers would purchase by 15,000 units. Alternatively, at a lower price of $4, consumers will purchase 16,000 units and 6,000 units are offered. Both of these situations are unstable: The quantity offered is greater than the quantity purchased by 15,000 units at a price of $7, and at a price of $4 consumers are willing and able to purchase 10,000 units more than firms are willing to supply.

Where the quantity supplied exceeds the quantity demanded, equilibrium does not exist because the quantity and price expectations of buyers and sellers are not equal. Unsold quantities will accumulate in the market, ultimately causing the price of the product to decline because some producers will be left without buyers for their product. Surpluses accumulate, inducing competitive firms to reduce product price in hopes of increasing sales in a competitive market economy where all firms must accept a market-determined price. As a consequence of falling product price, the quantity purchased will increase along demand schedule d of Figure 6, and firms will gradually reduce production along supply schedule s. Thus, the price mechanism performs a "rationing function" as consumers purchase more of the product. Similarly, prices perform a "resource-allocating" function because fewer resources will be used to produce smaller quantities at lower prices. Price and quantity adjustments will continue until the equilibrium price ($5 in Figure 6) is reached.

Now consider what happens at a price of $4, at which 16,000 units will be purchased and the quantity offered by firms will be 6,000. An initial product price of $4 in Figure 6 means that there will be a shortage of 10,000 units. Consumers will bid against each other for the limited supply of a product, driving up product price. As product price increases, producers move along supply schedule s (additional resources are allocated to the production of the product), and the quantity purchased declines along demand schedule d (products are rationed to consumers). Only at a price of $5 and a quantity of 11,000 units is there an equilibrium at which there is neither a shortage nor an excess amount of the product on the market. Barring any supply or demand shifts, equilibrium exists at $5, where the supply decisions of firms and the demand decisions of consumers satisfy both parties.

At the equilibrium market price there is no excess or shortage of output, and prices apparently are sufficient to reward producers for their efforts. Throughout the price-determination process, the market dictates which firms should produce, as well as what and how much should be produced. Ideally, only those firms capable of profitably meeting the test of the competitive market are permitted to transform scarce resources into products, and ultimately only those products desired by consumers will be produced and supplied—all in the right quantities! Discrepancies in market supply and demand lead to price and quantity adjustments for products which implicitly direct a society's use of its scarce resources. The price system rations the final output in the model economy to those consumers willing and able to pay the price, just as it allocates scarce resources only to those firms efficient and wise enough to supply the products desired by society on a profitable basis. If a product becomes increasingly scarce, product price is bid up and profits rise, enticing firms to use additional resources to increase output and perhaps even encouraging other firms to enter the market. In contrast, firms producing products in markets in which surpluses exist are subject to a declining market price and unfavorable earnings, indicating the need for less output and fewer productive resources.

*Warning:* Although the trip we just took was through a model world, it is important to realize that it can give us new insights into old problems. Also bear in mind that the market equilibrium price is by no means immutable. An equilibrium price can be disturbed by many forces, including supply or demand changes, government or other external action, and the existence of firms and markets that are not purely competitive. We will examine the effects of changes in supply and demand and introduce government modification next. Because of our interest in consumer choice and the efficient use of resources, it is also important to look at market imperfections—a task we will reserve for later chapters because of its magnitude.

### Equilibrium Price and Shifts in Supply and Demand

Equilibrium may be altered by either a shift in supply or a shift in demand. Figure 7(a) depicts a supply shift with demand constant, and Figure 7(b) shows a demand shift with supply constant. Obviously, it is possible to construct a variety of other combinations of supply and demand changes

**FIGURE 7** Shifts in Market Supply and Demand

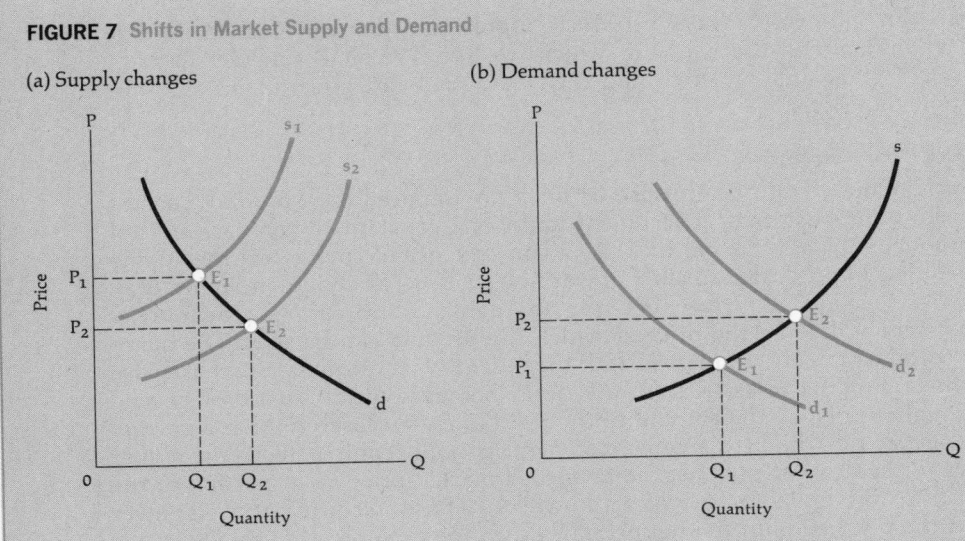

(a) Supply changes

(b) Demand changes

*Shifts in Supply and Demand.* In (a), a rightward shift in supply represents an increase, whereas a leftward shift in supply represents a decrease. If the quantity supplied at all prices increases (shifts rightward) from $s_1$ to $s_2$, the new equilibrium $E_2$, is at a lower price and larger quantity ($P_2$ and $Q_2$). If supply (decreases) shifts leftward from $s_2$ to $s_1$, the new equilibrium is $E_1$, a higher price and lower quantity ($P_1$ and $Q_1$). Shifts in demand are depicted in (b) where a demand increase ($d_1$ to $d_2$) raises equilibrium to price $P_2$ and quantity $Q_2$ at point $E_2$. A leftward shift in demand from $d_2$ to $d_1$ represents a demand decrease, where the new equilibrium is at $E_1$, a lower price ($P_1$) and quantity ($Q_1$).

which may result in an increase or decrease in equilibrium price and quantity, depending upon the direction and magnitude of the changes. A supply increase from $s_1$ to $s_2$ is depicted in Figure 7(a), resulting in a new equilibrium being established at $E_2$, at which $Q_2$ units are sold at price $P_2$. In contrast, a supply decrease alters equilibrium from $E_2$ to $E_1$, at which $Q_1$ units are sold at the higher price $P_1$. The shifts in the supply schedules depicted in Figure 7(a) are caused by changes in the determinants of supply, as we observed earlier. *Assuming that demand is constant, increases in supply lower equilibrium price and increase the quantity sold, but decreases in supply raise equilibrium price and reduce the quantity sold.*

Shifts in the demand schedule have a different effect on equilibrium price. Assuming supply schedule $s$ is constant, Figure 7(b) portrays a demand increase from $d_1$ to $d_2$ which is attributable to changes in the determinants of demand (e.g., a change in consumer preferences). The demand increase results in equilibrium moving from $E_1$ to $E_2$, at which, $Q_2$ units of output are sold at the higher price $P_2$. Conversely, a demand decrease is depicted by a leftward shift to schedule $d_1$, driving equilibrium from $E_2$ to $E_1$, at which $Q_1$ units are sold at the lower price $P_1$. It can be concluded, then, that *demand decreases lower equilibrium price and quantity, whereas demand increases raise equilibrium price and quantity, as long as the supply schedule remains unchanged.*

There are numerous ways in which supply and demand can be used to better understand the world in which we live. We shall consider first the effect of taxes and subsidies and then examine overt government administration of prices.

## TAXES AND SUBSIDIES

Consider the effect of an excise or sales tax imposed on a product such as whiskey. Suppose that government imposes a constant tax on each unit of a product sold, say, $1 per unit. As a consequence of such a tax, the supply schedule can be shown to shift upward by $1 to $s_d$, as shown in Figure 8(a). A price "wedge" is driven between the demand and supply schedules as producers add $1 to the price at which the product can be sold. The quantity producers sell decreases, and the quantity consumers purchase also declines. Product price rises from $P_2$ to $P_1$ because output must now be sold at a higher price by the amount of the tax. Note very carefully that a portion of the tax falls upon the consumer, who is now required to pay a higher price, $P_1$, instead of the lower undisturbed market price $P_2$. A portion of the tax also falls upon the producer, however, whose *net* price of $P_3$ is lower than the prior equilibrium net price of $P_2$. In the example of Figure 8(a), the tax revenue realized by government is the lightly shaded vertical distance between $P_1$ and $P_3$—the tax equivalent of quantity $Q_t \times$ $1 per unit. Also note that a tax of this sort lowers equilibrium output to $Q_t$ units, which means that *fewer resources are allocated* to the product subject to an excise tax. On the other hand, a constant government subsidy of $1 per unit of output has just the opposite effect, encouraging firms to supply $Q_s$ units which are sold to consumers at price $P_3$. The constant $1 subsidy per unit of output shifts supply downward to $s_i$, which lowers product price to consumers, increases equilibrium quantity, and therefore tends to allocate *more resources* to the market in question.[6] The total government subsidy cost is $1 $\times$ $Q_s$ units in Figure 8(a).

*In summary:* In Figure 8(a), an excise tax allocates resources away from the good in question. A portion of the tax is borne by the consumer and a portion by the producer. Government revenues are the $1 tax (the difference in $P_1$ and $P_3$) times the quantity sold, $Q_t$ units. On the other hand, a subsidy lowers consumer price and increases the quantity sold as equilibrium prices are bid up to higher levels. Federal aid to education and transportation, as well as favorable tax laws on oil exploration, represent subsidies which encourage the use of more resources than would otherwise be allocated to such efforts. Similarly, government influences the supply of medical care by subsidizing hospitals and educational facilities that produce medical specialists, thereby altering the quantity of output and the allocation of resources. Government involvement in markets in part reflects the notion—however "proper or improper" it may be—that unbridled market forces operate in an imperfect, impersonal way that ignores public welfare.

There are numerous other examples of the way in which the tools of

---

[6] Note that the illustrative $1 subsidy also looks like a "wedge" between demand and supply. The subsidy lowers the price to the consumer, who buys larger quantities moving down demand schedule $d$, and raises the net price to producers.

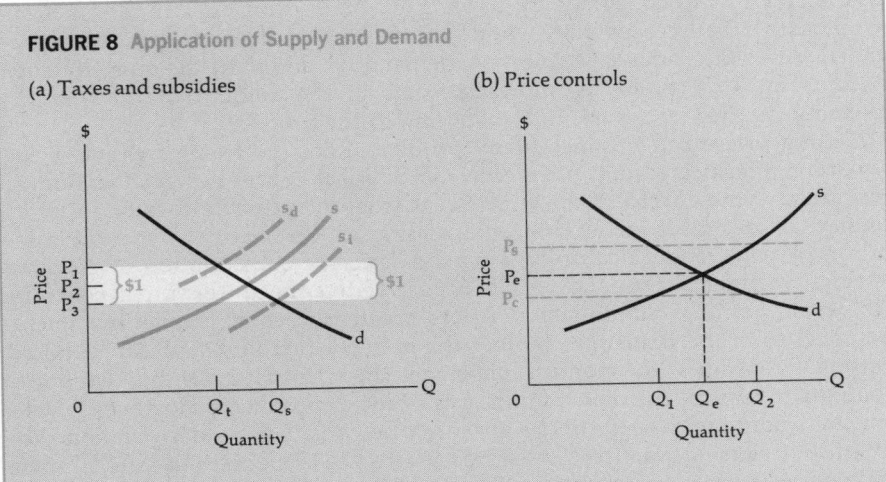

**FIGURE 8** Application of Supply and Demand

(a) Taxes and subsidies

(b) Price controls

*Taxes and Subsidies Per Unit.* In (a) a $1 tax per unit decreases supply from s to $s_d$ in the amount of $1, causing price to rise to the consumer and decline to the firm, while fewer resources are used to produce. A subsidy works in the reverse fashion, causing supply to increase from s to $s_i$ and encouraging the use of more resources.

*Ceiling and Support Prices.* In (b) a price support such as $P_s$ is a higher than equilibrium price ($P_e$) which causes more resources to be allocated to the product than would occur in the absence of a price support or "floor." In contrast, a price ceiling (e.g., $P_c$) under-allocates resources to a product, causing a shortage of $Q_1$ to $Q_2$ units.

supply and demand generally describe everyday events.[7] It should now be apparent that such issues of political economy are of no small consequence to a society, a contention that will be increasingly obvious as we proceed.

## DIRECT GOVERNMENT ADMINISTRATION OF PRICES

In addition to taxes and subsidies designed to reallocate resources, direct price controls may also be used by government. In such a case, a market-established price is "short-circuited" by establishing price ceilings or price supports.

*Price Ceilings*   Although interference with the price mechanism is held to a minimum in the United States, price ceilings can be established when government deems the true market equilibrium price to be higher than is desirable. The effects of a price ceiling are illustrated in Figure 8(b), in which the unrestrained market equilibrium is at price $P_e$ and quantity $Q_e$. When a price ceiling is established at price $P_c$, markets do not fully ration output and allocate resources. The ceiling price neither allows consumers to

---

[7] Many real-world supply and demand problems also arise out of imperfectly competitive markets—markets in which firms supply less than competitive quantities which result in consumers moving up a demand schedule and paying a higher price. Many authorities have pointed out that business firms may also "manage" consumer demand. (These subjects are discussed in Chapters 19 and 20.)

decide freely who consumes by bidding up prices, nor does it permit firms to allocate resources as they would if an unrestrained market price prevailed. At ceiling price $P_c$ consumers demand $Q_2$ units but the quantity supplied is only $Q_1$ units: A shortage exists in the amount of $Q_1Q_2$ units, meaning that resources are *underallocated* to the product.

Ceiling prices can produce many problems, not the least of which is the apparent official blessing given to some political concept of reallocation of resources. Note carefully, however, that it is not possible to judge a price ceiling as desirable or undesirable solely on the basis of market allocation of resources. Price ceilings on the domestic consumption of gasoline during wartime are one example of a positive need for price controls. However, publicly administered prices create a second problem, namely, the need for a mechanism to replace the price system in distributing limited output.[8] Attempts to monitor shortages may involve issuing rationing coupons to control the distribution of the output produced. However, black-market trading may occur in the absence of strictly enforced legislation prohibiting it. During wartime the United States has sometimes used legal price ceilings to control consumption. For the most part, however, the American people have exhibited considerable distaste for this approach to modifying the economic system.

*Price Supports* On some occasions, price supports may be established, again for the alleged purpose of enlarging economic welfare. *Supported prices* are prices set above the equilibrium market price, such as price $P_s$ of Figure 8(b). At these prices, suppliers are willing to produce $Q_2$ units, whereas consumers are willing to purchase only $Q_1$ units. Price-support systems exist in the United States today for selected agricultural products, such as cotton and some grains. Another subtle form of price support is the minimum wage, which represents, in this instance, a "floor" on the price of manpower resources. The rationale for such a program is usually the existence of deflation or depression in some sector of the economy. With price supports, producers are encouraged to supply more than buyers will purchase, creating a persistent surplus of the product. The "surplus" is a surplus only at the supported price, however, and *not* in the sense that more of the product is supplied than people want or need. A price-support "surplus" of food can exist while people are dying of starvation or suffering from malnutrition if they lack adequate incomes.

Just as price ceilings create regulatory problems, so do price supports. The government may be required to store or dispose of the surplus production [$Q_1Q_2$ units in Figure 8(b)] which is encouraged by price supports. An alternative way to handle the surplus is to sell it. Unfortunately, this is a messy business, because when the excess is dumped on markets, it tends to depress domestic and world prices even further. To avoid a persistent excess supply and constant overallocation of resources to a product, long-term

[8] The maximum rental rates set as a price ceiling on apartments in New York City nicely illustrate the distortion that is possible. Such rent ceilings are often low enough to negate the rationing function price $P$ performs. Thus, suave New Yorkers scramble for rent-controlled housing like little boys during a midnight raid on a watermelon patch.

remedies need to be developed to correct the circumstances that lead to a market equilibrium price below the "desired" price-support level.

*The Status of Price Intervention*   Today legally administered prices are supplemented by other policies in recognition of the occasional inability of the price mechanism to perform its product-rationing and resource-allocating functions in accord with what society thinks it should do. In recent years, complementary programs (such as acreage allotments to restrict excess supplies of farm products) have been used in agriculture.[9] Attempts to discover new markets and stepped-up research and development efforts to find new uses for farm products have also been undertaken to increase demand, and government has become a supplier in markets in which there are shortages (such as low-income housing).

Many people are not enthusiastic about using legally established prices as a control device, even though the absence of government control is not necessarily the best of all possible worlds. A good many problems arise when outside forces alter markets. Although it does not follow that we should allow unrestricted markets in graft or armed robbery, we should recognize that regulation does require a normative or "should-be" decision. Interestingly enough, government taxes, subsidies, and expenditure programs are frequently used in place of directly administered prices, partly because this type of subtle price manipulation is less visible to the public. It may be a long time before the typical citizen fully realizes the extent to which the doctor and professor are subsidized by laws which allow tax-sheltered annuities, or that the attorney and businessman can opt legally for tax-subsidized oil or real estate investments. The *general principles of supply and demand are useful aids in understanding such situations more fully.* Excise taxes and subsidies, or price ceilings and price supports, demonstrate how useful even such simple economic tools of analysis can be in understanding economic problems and issues.

### E. ELASTICITY: MEASURES OF QUANTITY RESPONSE TO PRICE CHANGES

Common-sense observation as well as our study of supply and demand reveal two fundamental ideas:

1. If supply is unchanged and demand *increases*, equilibrium price and quantity rise, but if supply is unchanged and demand *decreases*, equilibrium price and quantity fall.

2. If demand is unchanged and supply *increases*, equilibrium price falls and quantity rises, but if demand is unchanged and supply *decreases*, equilibrium price rises and quantity falls.

Consideration of the *direction* of change, however, ignores the magnitude of quantity changes in response to changes in product price. Moreover, we have skirted still another important matter: the effect of price changes on total income or the revenues received by a firm. Total revenue ($TR$) is derived by multiplying price ($P$) by quantity ($Q$) (i.e., $TR = P \times Q$). The

[9] Unfortunately, this program has encouraged the production of more output on limited acreage. (See Chapter 21.)

responsiveness of a change in quantity to price changes is shown by a measure commonly called *elasticity*, which also indicates the extent to which total revenue changes when price and quantity change.

### Demand Elasticity

The quantity of most products demanded varies in response to a price change. In some cases, a small reduction in product price evokes a large increase in the quantity demanded by consumers, while in other instances quantity is relatively unreponsive to a price change. Elasticity of demand describes these differences. Although measures of demand elasticity are usually given more attention in economics than measures of supply elasticity, comparable measures can be developed for changes in the quantity supplied.

Changes in the quantity of a good demanded in response to a price change are shown by the demand elasticity coefficient, $E_d$, which is:

$$E_d = \frac{\% \text{ change in quantity}}{\% \text{ change in price}} \quad \text{or} \quad \frac{\%\Delta Q}{\%\Delta P}$$

Remember, when price declines, the quantity of a product demanded increases along the typical downward-sloping demand curve.[10] The extent to which $Q$ increases, however, will determine whether the producing firm's total revenues rise, fall, or remain unchanged, because it is $P \times Q$ that determines total revenues. Because a $-P$ is somewhat offset by a $+Q$, there are two counterbalancing effects at work: The lower $P$ applied to all quantities sold has a revenue-reducing impact, but the higher $Q$ sold tends to increase the total revenue received by a firm. Without becoming involved in numerical examples, we can isolate three cases.

1. *Elastic demand:* When the $\%\Delta Q$ exceeds $\%\Delta P$, quantity is responsive to price changes and $E_d$ ($\%\Delta Q \div \%\Delta P$) is greater than 1.
2. *Inelastic demand:* If $\%\Delta Q$ is less than $\%\Delta P$, then quantity is unresponsive and $E_d$ is less than 1.
3. *Unitary elastic demand:* Equal $\%\Delta Q$ and $\%\Delta P$ exist, and $E_d = 1$.

Elastic demand reveals that the quantity response of consumers to small changes in price is relatively strong, whereas inelastic demand is indicative of relative quantity insensitivity to changes in product price. When the elasticity coefficient is 1, we know that the percentage change in quantity is equal to the percentage change in price.

Let us examine a typical problem in demand elasticity. Suppose the Board of Regents is contemplating lowering residence-hall fees, which are priced on a semester basis. Also assume a typical downward-sloping demand curve, where price and quantity are inversely related. The negative relationship between price and quantity simply reflects the probability that more students will find private housing accommodations (or leave school), the higher the residence-hall fee. Also assume that the student-housing market is competitive; that is, no one is forced to live in university

---

[10] The $E_d$ coefficient always has a negative sign which has no operational significance for our purposes. This is because price and quantity demanded are inversely related: Quantity demanded rises if price falls and quantity falls if price rises.

residence halls. From a mechanical point of view, lowering the price from $600 to $500 per semester is a $100 price reduction. Using the midpoint price of $550 to compute the percentage change in $P$ produces a $100/$550 = 18 percent reduction in price. Now assume 16,000 rental units instead of 12,000 are demanded at a lower price of $500. Thus, the percentage increase in quantity is 4,000/14,000, or 29 percent. The coefficient measuring demand elasticity is then 1.6.

$$E_d = \frac{\%\Delta\text{quantity}}{\%\Delta\text{price}} \quad \text{or} \quad \frac{4,000 \div 14,000}{\$100 \div \$550}$$

$$= \frac{28.6\%}{18.2\%} \quad \text{or} \quad \underline{\underline{1.6}} \text{ (elasticity coefficient)}$$

The coefficient for $E_d$ means that: (a) Demand is elastic, and (b) on the average, each 1 percent *reduction in price* is offset by a 1.6 percent *increase in quantity demanded* over the price range $600 to $500 and the quantity range 12,000 to 16,000 rental units. Now, suppose our friends on the Board of Regents were contemplating increasing fees from $500 to $600 and the same quantities applied. Each 1 percent *increase* in price now results in a 1.6 percent *decrease* in the quantity of rooms demanded.

But what is the point of calculating demand elasticities? For one thing, the elasticity coefficient indicates the effect of a change in price on total revenue, and in this example such knowledge could alter the pricing decision made by the Board of Regents—or it could even lead to a student strike! To trace through these implications we have constructed a hypothetical demand schedule for student residence-hall rooms in Figure 9. The demand schedule is the usual inverse one in which quantity rises as price falls. Figure 9 also depicts total revenue to the university, which is simply price times quantity for any combination of points on the demand schedule. Now reconsider the implications of elastic demand.

TOTAL REVENUE AND ELASTIC DEMAND

Elastic demand means $\%\Delta Q$ is greater than $\%\Delta P$. With elastic demand, a price decrease results in rising total revenue, and a price increase results in declining total revenue. The tabular data of Figure 9 indicate that a price decrease from $1,100 to $1,000 . . . $500 results in total revenue rising. This is because the positive influence of increased quantity on total revenue more than offsets the negative influence of a decline in price. Proof of this relationship is revealed by computing the elasticity coefficients, which exceed 1 for that portion of demand schedule $d$ above a price of $500.

Suppose demand is elastic ($E_d > 1$), and the Board of Regents *lowers* "product" price. Instead of selling 12,000 units at $600, for example, 16,000 units might be sold at $500 each, increasing total revenue from $7.2 million to $8.0 million. The total revenue schedule of Figure 9(b) rises because the increase in quantity demanded more than offsets relatively lower prices. But what happens if the Board of Regents *increases* price and demand is elastic? As price is increased from $500 to $600 . . . $1,100, the quantity demanded declines, and total revenue declines as we move up the elastic portion of demand schedule $d$ of Figure 9(a). For example, if the Board of Regents raises the price of a residence hall per semester from $500 to $600, the quantity demanded will decline from 16,000 to 12,000 units. The elas-

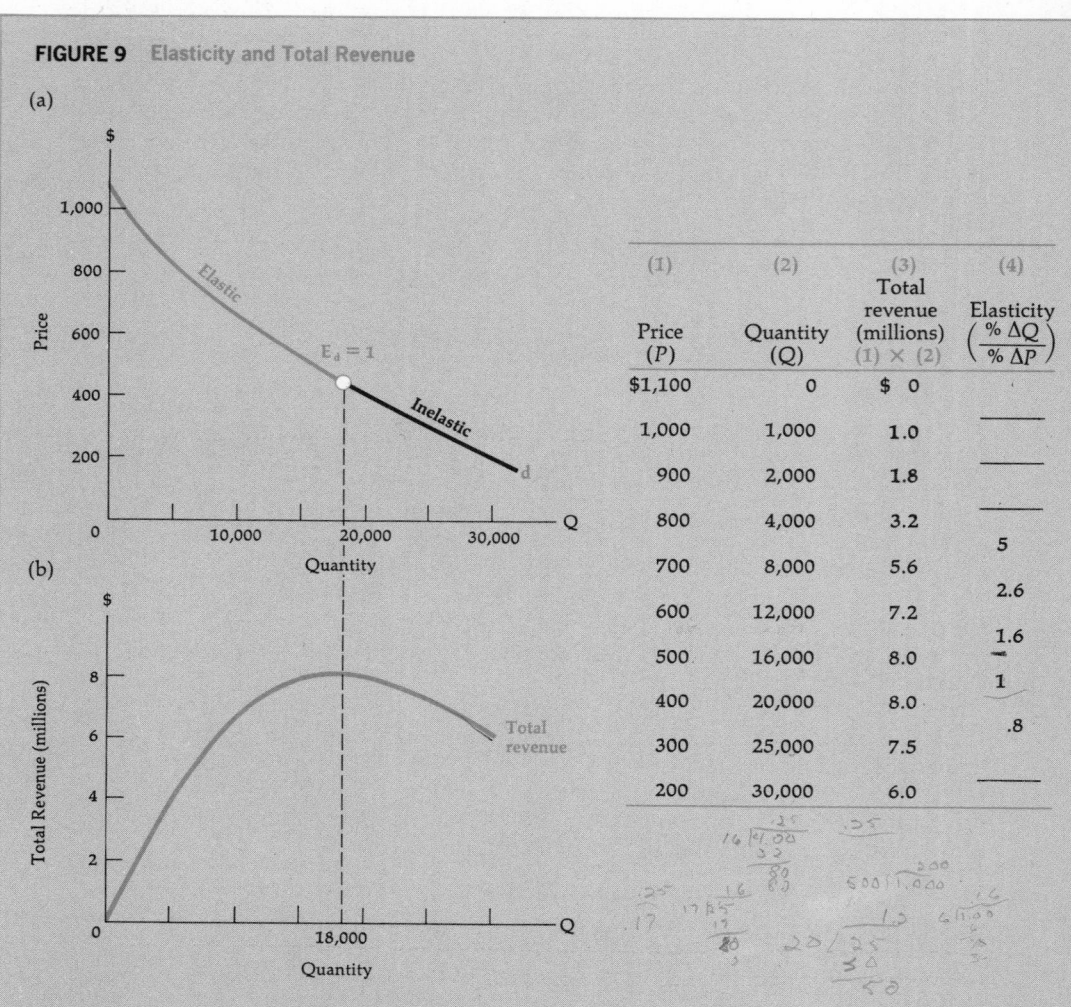

**FIGURE 9** Elasticity and Total Revenue

(a)

(b)

| Price (P) | Quantity (Q) | Total revenue (millions) (1) × (2) | Elasticity ($\frac{\% \Delta Q}{\% \Delta P}$) |
|---|---|---|---|
| $1,100 | 0 | $ 0 | |
| 1,000 | 1,000 | 1.0 | _____ |
| 900 | 2,000 | 1.8 | _____ |
| 800 | 4,000 | 3.2 | _____ |
| 700 | 8,000 | 5.6 | 5 |
| 600 | 12,000 | 7.2 | 2.6 |
| 500 | 16,000 | 8.0 | 1.6 |
| 400 | 20,000 | 8.0 | 1 |
| 300 | 25,000 | 7.5 | .8 |
| 200 | 30,000 | 6.0 | _____ |

*Demand Elasticity.* Demand is *elastic* if the percentage change in quantity exceeds the percentage change in price. If the percentage change in quantity is less than percentage change in price, demand is said to be *inelastic*. If both price and quantity change in equal relative amounts, *unitary elasticity* prevails and total revenue is at a maximum. This is so because with $E_d > 1$, a decline in price increases total revenue. In contrast, when demand is inelastic, further price declines reduce total revenue. Compute elasticity coefficients for the blanks in the table.

ticity of demand for this range of the demand schedule is $E_d = 1.6$, meaning that a 1 percent price *increase* is matched by a 1.6 percent *decline* in quantity. Those students who remain in the market for university housing are now paying a higher price, but university revenues decline (from $8 million to $7.2 million).

Whether this outcome is desired or not depends, of course, on many factors we have not mentioned, such as capacity, operating costs, and so

330

forth. Still, such information is of obvious usefulness to those involved in making decisions. If the Regents raise the price in hopes of increasing total revenues to cover higher costs, they may be surprised if demand is elastic. It may be, too, that this relationship helps explain why some universities do not allow market forces to operate, but instead insist that certain categories of students live in dormitories. Since maximum student or consumer freedom is a competing goal in society today, we will not speculate about the outcome of such a policy. Note, however, that demand elasticity is useful in evaluating the problem.

## TOTAL REVENUE AND INELASTIC DEMAND

Demand is inelastic when the percentage change in price exceeds the percentage change in quantity ($E_d < 1$). A price reduction lowers total revenue and a price increase raises total revenue if demand is inelastic. A price decrease from $400 to $300 in Figure 9, for example, results in falling total revenue, since the coefficient of elasticity is less than 1. On the other hand, if price *increases* from $300 to $400 when demand is inelastic, total revenue rises. This is because the percentage increase in price exceeds the percentage decrease in quantity. (Compute $E_d$ values for the blanks in Figure 9, being sure to use price and quantity midpoints.)[11]

These elasticity relationships are summarized in Figure 9, where elasticity varies throughout the demand curve. Between 0 and 18,000 units of output, demand is elastic and total revenue ($P \times Q$) increases as price is reduced. We move down the elastic portion of demand schedule $d$ to the point of unitary elasticity ($E_d = 1$ because $\%\Delta Q$ and $\%\Delta P$ are equal) at a quantity of 18,000 and a price of $450. At $E_d = 1$, total revenue is a maximum, as shown in Figure 9(b).[12]

## DETERMINANTS AND SIGNIFICANCE OF DEMAND ELASTICITY

Demand inelasticity is greater the smaller the number of good substitutes available, the less a product is regarded as a luxury good, and the smaller the product price relative to consumer budgets. There are few good substitutes for sugar, which is neither a luxury good nor an expensive item; thus, the demand for sugar tends to be inelastic. Mink coats are another matter, however, and elasticity, or quantity responsiveness to price changes for mink coats is large in comparison to that for sugar.

The importance of demand elasticity to firms contemplating price changes should be obvious. Producers considering a Spring sale of ski equipment, a proposed price reduction on Polaroid cameras, or an increase in the price of

[11] Midpoints or "averages" are used to approximate the percentage change in $P$ and $Q$ over a finite range. Elasticity of demand can be shown in more precise terms that are continuous through the first derivation of calculus, for those familiar with mathematics. If demand is the function $Q = f(P)$, the elasticity of demand is $E_d = dQ/dP \times P/Q$ at any point on the continuous demand schedule $d$ of Figure 9.

[12] Following footnote 11, the use of finite $100 price (and quantity) intervals serves to mask the point of precise unitary elasticity ($P = $450 and $Q = 18,000 at $8.1 million in total revenue) in Figure 9. There is only one point of unitary elasticity on schedule $d$, or on any demand schedule for that matter, except the function known as a rectangular hyperbola.

steel hinges in part on their knowledge about demand elasticities. This is so because a firm's total revenue is affected by $P \times Q$. When a Board of Regents argues that the increased costs of supplying residence halls must be covered, the university may very well be successful in raising more income through a price hike, depending on demand inelasticity. Of course, the Regents (or a powerful firm) may also obviate the free market by using some form of market control over students (or consumers) to remedy their dilemma.

## Supply Elasticity

Although the concept of elasticity of supply is useful in some areas, it is sufficient to note that the response of quantity supplied to a price change is determined largely by production conditions and costs as well as by the amount of time a firm has to adjust to a changing market. If the quantity supplied changes by 50 percent when price changes by 10 percent, the measure of supply elasticity is 5, indicating that, on the average, a 1 percent increase (or decrease) in price elicits a 5 percent increase (or decrease) in quantity, perhaps because production costs rise slowly as output increases. Thus, supply elasticity reveals the extent to which firms are stimulated to expand or contract output as price changes.

If storage or perishability problems prevail, or if production costs rise rather rapidly as output increases, incentives to increase quantity in response to a price increase are restrained, and the elasticity of supply ($\%\Delta Q$ supplied $\div$ $\%\Delta P$) tends to be small—perhaps even less than 1. Time is also an important determinant of supply elasticity, simply because producers cannot always switch resources quickly from one product to another. In a very short-run period (a few days or weeks), a farmer or boat manufacturer cannot respond significantly to price changes. Therefore, his quantity response to a large price increase will be small. Over the long run—say, a growing season for the farmer or a year for the boat manufacturer—resources can be shifted more readily and supply elasticity will be larger.

*Summing up:* Our discussion of elasticity can be more precise if we keep in mind the classifications noted earlier. *Inelasticity* of either supply or demand describes unresponsive $\%\Delta Q$ to $\%\Delta P$, *elasticity* depicts a responsive $\%\Delta Q$ to $\%\Delta P$, and *unitary elasticity* is the special case of equal percentage changes in quantity and price. The extremes of these conditions are illustrated in Figure 10(a) for supply and Figure 10(b) for demand. Note that the highly inelastic supply curve $s_i$ is nearly vertical, whereas the unitary and elastic supply schedules $s_u$ and $s_e$ tend to become more horizontal as a reflection of greater quantity responsiveness. At point $x$ in Figure 10(a) supply elasticity is 1 for all three schedules of supply. Demand may range toward inelasticity, as in vertical schedule $d_i$, or toward elasticity, as in schedule $d_e$.[13]

---

[13] A unitary demand schedule $d_u$ is a curve that maintains equal percentage changes in $P$ and $Q$ and not a straight-line demand curve with a constant $P$ and $Q$ slope in absolute terms. Any nearly linear demand schedule such as $d$ in Figure 9(a) exhibits varying elasticity throughout. While elasticity is a percentage $P$ and $Q$ relation, it is sometimes illustrative to depict inelastic demand as a near-vertical curve and elastic demand as a near-horizontal curve, as we shall do on occasions.

**FIGURE 10** Different Supply and Demand Elasticities

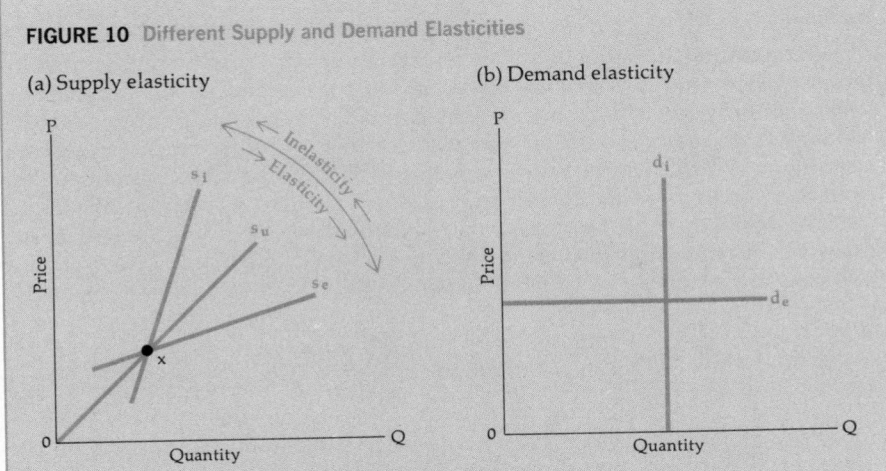

(a) Supply elasticity        (b) Demand elasticity

*Variations in Elasticity.* Elastic supply is shown in (a) by supply schedule $s_e$ which depicts a relatively large quantity response to small price changes. Equal relative $P$ and $Q$ changes are shown by unitary supply elasticity for schedule $s_u$. Inelastic supply is more nearly approached as the slope of the supply schedule increases toward $s_i$. Demand elasticity ranges from the extreme of perfect elasticity as shown in (b) by schedule $d_e$ to perfectly inelastic demand shown by schedule $d_i$. With perfectly elastic demand a small change in $P$ induces an infinite change in $Q$, but $Q$ does not respond at all if demand is perfectly inelastic.

*One last point:* Changes in total revenue are very different when we compare supply vs. demand elasticities. When we consider supply, total revenue always rises and falls directly with price changes because price and quantity are directly related. This is not the case with changes in total revenue relative to varying demand elasticity, as we saw earlier. Be sure that you understand each of the following three points about demand elasticity.[14]

1. Demand is *elastic* when price decreases result in total revenue increases and price increases result in total revenue decreases.

2. Demand is *inelastic* when price decreases result in total revenue decreases and price increases result in total revenue increases.

3. At *unitary elasticity* of demand, price changes leave total revenue unchanged, because the loss in total revenue due to a price increase ($\%\Delta P$) is precisely offset by the change in total revenue attributable to selling a larger quantity ($\%\Delta Q$).

[14] Elasticity is also important in determining who bears the incidence of a tax—consumers or producers—and just how market quantities and resource allocation are affected, as discussed earlier in this chapter. The more inelastic the demand and the more elastic the supply, the greater the portion of an excise tax shouldered by consumers, who pay a higher price. Larger quantity and resource-allocation adjustments are also associated with more elastic demand and supply schedules.

MICROECONOMICS: PRICES AND THE ALLOCATION OF RESOURCES

## REVIEW

### Summary

1. Understanding the allocation of resources requires an awareness of how supply, demand, and market prices ration output and allocate resources. An economy such as the one just described relies on supply and demand. It is understood that we mean by this a "pure" market economy analogous to the simple model developed in this chapter. Even in such a model economy we have seen that the synchronizing function of supply and demand can be tampered with—a topic we will continue to move toward because such tinkering fits the real world so much better than a simple model does.

2. In pursuing the study of economic choice and efficiency in resource allocation, it is important to recognize the significance of the various degrees of competition in markets. Our analysis of supply and demand is predicated upon the condition of pure competition, where the actions of *all* firms and *all* buyers result in one price continually monitored by the market consisting of competing firms. Imperfect competition exists when some firms are capable of influencing product price. Entry barriers, product differentiation, and price-setting power distinguish pure and imperfect competition.

3. Quantity supplied and product price are directly related, a relation which allows the derivation of an upward-sloping supply schedule. This schedule reflects the fact that higher prices entice firms to produce more output and use more resources. Supply shifts or changes are caused by changes in five supply determinants: production technology, firm objectives, resource costs, prices of related products, and the number of sellers in a market.

4. Quantity demanded and product price are inversely related, partially because higher prices act as a deterrent to consumption. This inverse price–quantity relationship reflects diminishing marginal utility as well as product substitution. Shifts in demand change the location of a demand schedule. This change is the result of changes in income levels and income distribution, the prices of related products, consumer tastes, or the number of buyers in a market.

5. The intersection of schedules of supply ($s$) and demand ($d$) depicts the equilibrium market price. Prices decrease if the quantity producers supply exceeds the quantity consumers demand, whereas prices tend to rise to a higher equilibrium level when less is offered than consumers wish to purchase. Equilibrium price is significant as a device for clearing markets and coordinating producer and consumer decisions. Prices ($a$) reflect supply and demand in markets, ($b$) ration scarce goods and services, and ($c$) allocate scarce resources to firms. Firms tend to adjust to market forces by comparing prices to costs, their motive being the profitability of producing.

6. Shifts in supply and demand will produce new equilibrium prices and quantities as the market-clearing process takes place. If supply remains unchanged, equilibrium price and quantity rise if demand increases and fall if demand decreases. If demand is constant and supply de-

creases, equilibrium price rises and quantity falls; but if supply increases, equilibrium price falls and quantity rises.

7. External forces may mute or distort a market equilibrium. Although distortion may be the result of any observed force with sufficient power, government taxes and subsidies as well as the administration of price ceilings and price supports are easily observed events that may change an equilibrium position. Taxes and subsidies have the effect of changing the allocation of resources and altering the prices paid by consumers and the "net" price received by firms. Price ceilings and price supports result in insufficient and excess output, respectively; that is, underallocation of resources for ceiling prices and overallocation of resources for supported prices.

8. Elasticity is the quantity response to a price change, defined as the ratio of a percentage change in quantity to a percentage change in price ($\%\Delta Q \div \%\Delta P$). If inelastic demand prevails ($E_d < 1$), total revenue increases as price rises and falls as price declines. With elastic demand ($E_d > 1$), a price increase reduces total revenue, and a price decrease raises total revenue. At unitary elasticity of demand, $\%\Delta Q \div \%\Delta P = 1$ and total revenue is a maximum. Total revenue always rises and falls in direct relationship to price changes along a supply curve, regardless of the elasticity of supply. Price and quantity changes are *both* positive (if price rises) and negative (if price declines).

### Identify the Following Concepts and Terms

- change in quantity demanded vs. change in demand
- principles of supply and demand
- inverse price-quantity relationships
- market demand
- inferior and superior goods
- price ceilings and price supports
- elasticity coefficient
- change in quantity supplied vs. change in supply
- determinants of supply and demand
- diminishing marginal utility
- substitute and complementary goods
- inelastic vs. elastic demand
- demand elasticity and total revenue
- equilibrium

### Questions to Answer

1. Using the data given below, plot and label demand and supply schedules, indicating equilibrium price and quantity. What explains why price and quantity are directly related for supply and inversely related for demand?

| Demand | Price | Supply |
|--------|-------|--------|
| 40 | $1 | 10 |
| 30 | 2 | 20 |
| 20 | 3 | 30 |
| 10 | 4 | 40 |

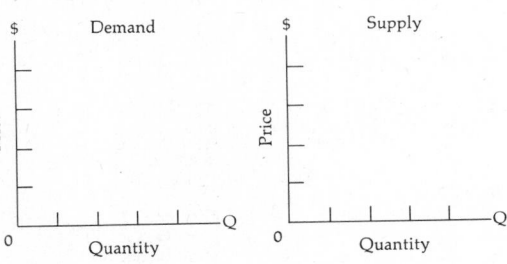

2. Compute demand elasticities using the data from the previous question. Why does total revenue rise (fall) as price is increased for an inelastic (elastic) demand schedule?

3. How is it possible to say that "elasticity of demand reflects changes in the quantity demanded and not a change (shift) in demand"? What might cause demand and supply shifts?

4. Suppose you are charged with evaluating the desirability of changing equilibrium for two products, A and Z. How might per unit subsidies and price ceilings affect good A? How might a per unit tax and price support affect good Z? Carefully evaluate the resource-allocation implications of such attempts to manipulate the market.

# CHAPTER 15
# Supply and Production Costs

Supply and demand as discussed in the preceding chapter are important forces in determining price, but we have barely begun to analyze price determination. Understanding the relation of price to economic efficiency in the allocation of resources requires an explanation of supply and production costs—the topic of this chapter. We will continue to consider the model world in order to develop a solid theoretical basis for our later analysis of efficiency in resource allocation. The discussion begins in Part A with the definition of important cost concepts and an explanation of the principle of diminishing returns. Parts B and C analyze costs in the short and long run, respectively.

## A. PRODUCTION COSTS AND DIMINISHING RETURNS

Unfortunately for the student of economics, the term "cost" can mean many different things. Therefore, it is imperative that the various cost concepts used frequently in economics be identified clearly at the outset. After these are defined and classified, it will be possible to analyze the cost structure of a hypothetical firm.

### Private Costs of Production

Production costs denote the opportunity costs associated with producing output. As we indicated in Chapter 14, the term "opportunity cost" denotes the output sacrificed or forgone when a society uses resources for one product rather than another. For purposes of clarity, we can say that the cost to society of transforming scarce resources into output are as follows:

| OPPORTUNITY COSTS OF USING RESOURCES *are* | EXPLICIT AND IMPLICIT COSTS OF PRODUCTION *paid as* | WAGES, RENT, INTEREST, AND NORMAL PROFITS |
|---|---|---|

Sometimes, however, the true opportunity costs to society are not fully borne by producing firms. In such instances the "private costs" of production are understated; that is, firms do not absorb all costs. These cost distinctions are more clearly identified below.

### EXPLICIT AND IMPLICIT OPPORTUNITY COSTS

Production costs include all payments explicitly and implicitly required to retain resources for a given use. The minimum payment to resource owners is that amount which will be just adequate to encourage those owners to supply resources to a particular line of production. *Explicit costs* are directly or explicitly recognized through monetary payments made by the user to owners of resources. Explicit costs, however, are only one type of opportunity costs.

The value of resources that may not receive explicit monetary payment is an *implicit cost* of production; that is, there are "implied" opportunity costs associated with using resources because they have alternative uses— if a resource were not used in producing product X, it could be used to produce product Y. Thus, the first important point about production costs is simply that they include *all* costs—explicit and implicit—which is why economists stress the idea of opportunity costs.

An owner-proprietor's operation of a corner drugstore can be used to illustrate the distinction between explicit and implicit costs. Certain explicit costs are incurred in operating the drugstore (supplies and clerical help are needed), and the proprietor may also assume some risk and contribute his own building, time, talent, and energies. Even though the proprietor may not pay himself a rent or a wage, these implicit or implied costs are bound up in sacrificed opportunities attached to the use of capital and labor. If the proprietor were not supplying these resources for the purpose of operating his own store, he would be able to earn a return by loaning funds, renting a building, or supplying labor to another firm. Thus, a firm that uses its own resources incurs implicit opportunity costs equal to the amount it could obtain by making these resources available to other users. The implicit opportunity costs to society of using resources for a war in Asia might be viewed as its inability to allocate resources to the eradication of slum housing or any one of numerous other alternative undertakings. For the student reading an economics text, implicit opportunity costs may be a forgone afternoon beer bust, whereas *not* reading could eventually mean an unsettling examination experience.

## NORMAL AND ECONOMIC PROFITS

The minimum cost required to secure the use of entrepreneurial resources that have opportunity costs is a *normal profit* in the sense that "normal" describes an amount just adequate to retain the services of the entrepreneur, and no more. In addition, land resources receive a "rent," capital-resource costs are called "interest earnings," and labor resources are paid a "wage." The sum of these four costs represents the costs of production. Consequently, to the economist, costs mean *all production costs*, including a normal profit! Normal profit is included as an element of production costs because it represents the opportunity cost of using the entrepreneur as one of four resources. Clearly, conventional definitions of the terms "costs" and "profits" differ from those used by economists. Since production costs already include a normal profit as the term is used in economics, any payment to the entrepreneur in *excess* of a normal profit is defined as an *economic profit*. That is, any difference between total income and production costs is an economic profit earned by a firm—a premium in excess of the minimum amount required to cover all economic costs of production:

$$\text{Total income} - \text{production costs} = \text{economic profit}$$

The distinction between a normal and an economic profit is important because of the implication that these two types of "profit" have for patterns of resource allocation. If the income received by some firms in a certain industry does not fully cover production costs, the opportunity costs of using resources are not fully covered and a normal profit is not being earned. Consequently, the firm will be induced to shift factors of production into some other market that has better alternative uses for the resources. On the other hand, suppose that total receipts exceed production costs, or an economic profit is earned. This situation is a signal to other resource owners to shift scarce resources into the preferred market where earnings are higher. Thus, less than a normal profit moves resources out of a given market, whereas a greater-than-normal profit attracts additional resources.

## Social Costs

*Social costs* are the "true" or full opportunity costs of transforming resources into output. Social costs consist of private costs *plus* whatever other costs may be imposed on other people or society at large (e.g., pollution). Whenever the total social costs of production are not fully absorbed by private producers, a portion of those costs are imposed upon society.

Often the process of producing and consuming goods and services generates *external* or "by-product" effects that are, in one way or another, significant to some individuals or to society. Firms dumping waste materials into streams are avoiding a private cost and imposing a cost on society. Consumers and producers contribute to air pollution by emitting residue and fumes that are transmitted into the atmosphere. Such pollution represents a social cost that exists because the private costs of consumption and production are lower than true social costs. Or consider the lumbering firm that values a timber stand at $1,000 per acre in terms of private costs. This private value may be less than the value society attaches to the forest for lumber, recreation, or conservation purposes, in which case, modification of private market decisions may be necessary. Without such modification, the firm may harvest the timber stand, forcing society to bear some social costs.

### MODIFICATION FOR SOCIAL COSTS

Correcting disparities between social costs and private costs is the responsibility of government. Forcing producers or consumers to pay for full social costs may not be popular, although various social costs are being recognized increasingly throughout the United States today. The critical question for economic policy is to determine the character and scope of social costs.

Recently, self-service retail stores have multiplied prodigiously. These firms have lowered private production costs, whereas the shopper now bears a greater burden in finding and selecting merchandise. We do not regard this as a social cost, however, unless the value of the time lost by shoppers has not been fully compensated for by lower prices, changes in the quality and quantity of goods consumed, or both. However, if hazardous working conditions attributable to coal dust or unsafe equipment shorten miners' lives, certain costs of production are being avoided and some social costs are being imposed on the miners. Unsafe automotive equipment or misleading advertising concerning the medicinal value of drugs may also represent social costs. The events of the 1960s surrounding automobile call-backs and thalidomide illustrate social costs as well as public reaction to certain obvious infringements imposed by producers on society.

Efficiency in the allocation of resources is achieved by a competitive price system only if *all* costs are privately absorbed; that is, if no social costs are pushed onto society. Differences between private- and social-cost valuations are important because they are a signal of inefficiency in the use of scarce resources and because they can occur in markets that otherwise appear to meet the idyllic conditions of pure competition. The crucial problems associated with social costs are recognition, factual measurement, and development of a remedial policy. Recognition is partially dependent upon personal perception, which varies widely among individuals. Air transportation firms may argue that the sonic boom accompanying the large commercial jet is a mark of progress, but housewives may very well regard it as a social cost. A corporation executive may argue that waste pollution is compensated for by other benefits such as the creation of jobs and economic growth in a region, while avid fishermen or those afflicted with sinus problems may have quite a different view of the matter. Resolution of such conflict over the existence and composition of social costs may require government involvement in the market system. At the same time, it must be recognized that some people are willing to pay a price (like living with smog) to avoid government modification of economic affairs. For now, simply bear in mind that social costs of various types are important in a contemporary economy and that we are presuming that private production costs associated with the use of scarce resources are equal to full social costs.

### Measuring the Costs of Production

Because time is sometimes needed to vary quantities of alternative resources used in the production process, it is necessary in economics to make a distinction between short-run vs. long-run time periods and fixed vs. variable costs. In measuring production costs there are four distinct cost concepts to recognize.

#### SHORT-RUN AND LONG-RUN COSTS

The "short run" is a period of time in which some resources are utilized in fixed amounts, but other resources can be employed in variable quantities. *Short-run costs* are those that apply to the short-run time period in which the quantities of *some* resources can be varied and other resources are employed in constant or fixed amounts. The physical capacity of a manufacturing plant and some of the larger pieces of complex capital equipment are examples of fixed resources in a short-run period of a few days, weeks, months, or even years, depending upon their physical properties. Labor and raw materials are examples of variable resources in the short run. Short-run costs may vary, depending on the quantities of variable resources employed.

*Long-run costs* occur in the long-run time period—a period long enough to allow producing firms to change the quantities of *all* resources employed, including physical plant and capital equipment. The long run is adequate time for: (*a*) existing firms to add additional producing units, (*b*) new firms to be created and enter the industry, and (*c*) existing firms to leave the industry. Long-run costs reflect the costs of varying *all* resources simultaneously—including those that are fixed in the short run. Although the distinction between the long and short run is somewhat arbitrary, it is a useful one that will be relied upon later.

## FIXED AND VARIABLE COSTS

Since by definition the long run is described as a period of time during which all resources can be varied, all production costs are variable costs in the long run. In the short run, total production costs can be broken down into two categories: (a) *fixed costs,* which do not vary with the quantity of output; and (b) *variable costs*, which change as output changes. In the short run, business firms normally incur both fixed and variable costs because both fixed and variable resources are used.

Consider the example of a firm which has funds to buy capital equipment and owns or leases property on which rental fees or taxes must be paid. These are fixed costs in the short run because depreciation, interest, rental payments, and taxes must be paid to cover the costs of such resources regardless of the level of production. The importance of fixed costs is that they must be paid even if physically fixed resources are not operated in the short run. In contrast, variable costs such as labor and materials are the costs of variable resources and are incurred only if those variable resources are employed to operate fixed resources. Once fixed resources are committed, the quantity of variable resources used can be changed in some direct proportion to the level of output. By definition, no such decision is possible for fixed resources in the short run because they are immobile.

## TOTAL COST AND AVERAGE COST

Costs can be measured on a total and on an average or per unit basis. *Total cost* includes all kinds of production costs incurred by firms. The total cost of producing 1,000 kegs of Blimey Ale may be $3,000, whereas the total cost of producing 4,000 kegs may be $8,000. The per unit or *average total cost (ATC)* is equal to total cost (TC) divided by total output (Q):

$$ATC = TC/Q \quad \text{or} \quad \$3,000/1,000 = \$3 \text{ at 1,000 units of output}$$

In the second case,

$$ATC = TC/Q \quad \text{or} \quad \$8,000/4,000 = \$2 \text{ at 4,000 units of output}$$

## MARGINAL COST

The term "marginal" means additional or extra, as has been noted earlier. Thus, the additional cost of increasing output by one unit is *marginal cost (MC)*. In the short run, total cost changes because more or fewer variable resources are employed by a firm. Therefore, marginal cost in the short run reflects a change in production costs associated with using more or fewer variable resources. Consider an example: Suppose production of 1,000 units of output (kegs of Blimey) per week results in a total cost of $3,000, while an output level of 1,001 units generates a total cost of $3,002. As output increases from 1,000 to 1,001 units, total cost increases by $2 (from $3,000 to $3,002)—the marginal cost of the increase in output is $2. *Note carefully* that all of this increase in total cost is due to a change in the use of variable resources because fixed resources are just that—fixed or constant in the short run.

*The significance of marginal cost is that it represents the value placed upon the final amounts of variable resources used to produce one more unit of output.* If this value fully reflects *all* costs of production, marginal cost is a proxy for the "social worth" of whatever scarce resources are transformed into output through production.

Now let us turn to analyzing the production process and see how these cost measures are used.

### The Principle of Diminishing Returns

Since we have some idea of the types of cost measures, it is now appropriate to look at the major influence upon the cost structure of a firm in the short run. This is diminishing returns due to using variable resources which can be added to fixed resources to change output levels. Later in the chapter, the long-run cost structure of a firm and the implications of a changing technology will be analyzed.

In the short run, a firm can vary its level of output, but only by adding variable resources to a constant amount of fixed resources. How does the addition of progressively more variable resources affect the level of output? The answer to this question is provided by the *principle of diminishing returns*, a common-sense observation which reasons that continued use of additional variable resources (labor) added to fixed resources (capital) results in total output increasing at a decreasing rate.

As the first few units of a variable resource are employed in conjunction with fixed resources, the total amount of physical output or total product may increase. This increase in output is the result of the division of labor and specialization—the complementary use of variable labor resources and raw materials with fixed capital resources. At low levels of production increasing short-run returns are experienced. With the continued addition of variable resources, however, increases in total product will become smaller and smaller as diminishing returns are encountered. Output does *not* rise in linear proportion to the increase in variable labor inputs used.

### DECLINING MARGINAL PRODUCT

The principle of diminishing returns is illustrated in Figure 1. The first column denotes the quantity of variable labor resources used; the second column denotes *total product* (TP) produced as variable labor inputs are added; and the third column depicts the change in total product, or *marginal product* (MP), that occurs as more labor is employed in increments of one unit. It can be seen that total product ultimately does increase at a decreasing rate, and that *marginal product* (the addition to total product) rises initially, but then falls and, in this example, actually becomes negative with the use of the fifth unit of variable (labor) resources. Thus, employment of more than four units of labor results in a *smaller* amount of total output. Output is at a maximum when marginal product is zero, because when marginal product is zero, total product remains unchanged. As long as the change in total output is positive when additional variable resources are employed, marginal product is also positive and total product *must* therefore increase. On the other hand, if marginal product is less than zero, a negative increment is added to total product, causing total product to decline. So long as the method or techniques of producing remain fixed, declining MP characterizes diminishing returns.

**FIGURE 1**  Diminishing Returns and Costs

| (1)<br>Units of<br>labor | (2)<br>Total<br>product | (3)<br>Marginal<br>product<br>(Δ2) | (4)<br>Average<br>labor<br>productivity<br>(2) ÷ (1) | (5)<br>Total<br>labor<br>costs<br>(1) × $10 | (6)<br>Unit labor<br>costs of<br>product<br>(5) ÷ (2) |
|---|---|---|---|---|---|
| 0 | 0 | | $ — | $ 0 | $ — |
| | | > 12 | | | |
| 1 | 12 | | 12 | 10 | .83 |
| | | > 14 | | | |
| 2 | 26 | | 13 | 20 | .77 |
| | | > 9 | | | |
| 3 | 35 | | 11⅔ | 30 | .86 |
| | | > 5 | | | |
| 4 | 40 | | 10 | 40 | 1.00 |
| | | > −1 | | | |
| 5 | 39 | | 7⅘ | 50 | 1.28 |
| | | > −4 | | | |
| 6 | 35 | | 5⅚ | 60 | 1.71 |

*Diminishing Returns.* As more variable labor resources are employed with fixed resources, marginal product (the change in total product) ultimately declines. The average productivity of variable labor declines because of diminishing returns, which also causes unit labor costs to rise; thus, declining marginal product causes costs to rise.

An example may clarify the operation and relevance of this principle. Assume that an enterprising college student decides to open a hot-dog stand near the local stadium and obtains fixed resources in the form of physical capacity equal to 100 square feet. Perhaps the first, second, and third students employed as variable labor resources will result in output rising at an increasing rate. As additional units of labor are employed and the stand becomes too crowded with workers, however, output or total product will change in different proportions to increases in the use of variable labor resources as the principle of diminishing returns sets in. Indeed, if variable labor inputs are added without reasonable discretion, a saturation point is reached and output may decline—an obvious result if the proprietor employs 50 persons in a 100-square foot hot-dog stand.

## DIMINISHING PRODUCTIVITY AND RISING AVERAGE COSTS

Consider for a moment the declining marginal product developed in Figure 1 as a reflection of diminishing returns. Declining resource productivity in the short run suggests that the costs per unit of output may rise because less and less additional output is generated by each additional unit of labor.

Diminishing returns is a technical physical relationship between the quantities of fixed and variable resources, and not the result of employing additional variable resources which are inherently less productive or "inferior." With some constant quantity of fixed resources, the average productivity of resources declines as shown in Figure 1 (assuming technology is unchanged). Thus, if 2 units of labor are used to produce 26 units of output in Figure 1, the *average* productivity of labor is 13 units (26 units of total product ÷ 2 units of labor). Employment of additional labor as a variable resource results in declining average productivity (11⅔, ... 5⅝ units of product are produced per average unit of labor), as column (4) of Figure 1 illustrates. Figure 1 also shows how the principle of diminishing returns relates to production costs. To simplify this relationship, we ignore other resources and assume the cost of each unit of labor is $10. The per unit (labor) cost is simply total labor costs [column (5)] divided by total product [column (2)]. As column (6) reveals, the per unit or average cost of output rises to $1.71 per unit as a reflection of declining marginal product. Diminishing returns thus have a major influence on the costs of production, ultimately causing average or per unit costs of output to rise.

The precise significance of the principle of diminishing returns for us at this point is that it helps explain why the average cost of a unit of output increases in the short run. We say "helps explain" because in the example above we assumed that there were no fixed costs of production, and that unit labor costs were therefore synonymous with total costs.[1] Despite this oversimplification, it should be clear that diminishing returns to variable resources as revealed by declining marginal product are an important influence on production costs in the short run.

## B. SHORT-RUN COST STRUCTURE FOR A FIRM

The principle of diminishing returns just described explains the declining marginal productivity of variable resources in the short run where the total cost of producing is the sum of costs attributable to employing both fixed and variable resources. Our next task is to examine more fully the relationships among total, fixed, and variable costs in order to see how a firm makes decisions about using resources for production.

### Cost Schedules for a Firm

As a first step toward understanding the costs of production in the short run, consider the tabular data shown in Figure 2, which represent a hypothetical firm producing a product such as boats in a market economy. The nature and derivation of total cost is as follows.

### TOTAL COST

Total cost (TC) is the sum of total variable cost (TVC) *plus* total fixed cost (TFC), as shown in columns (2), (3), and (4) of Figure 2. Total fixed cost does not change in the short run because such costs as interest payments, depreciation of capital equipment, and rental payments are not varied. Consequently, in Figure 2, fixed costs of $1,000 are incurred at all levels of output ranging from zero to eight units. Total variable cost represents the costs of all variable resources, such as labor or raw materials. Figure 2 clearly shows that the variable costs of production are not constant as out-

[1] Had some fixed cost been included, these relations would have become more complicated, as is shown later; however, the inverse relationship between marginal product and variable labor cost would still prevail.

# FIGURE 2  Short-Run Cost Structure of a Firm

| (1)<br>Quantity<br>of<br>output | (2)<br>Total<br>fixed<br>cost | (3)<br>Total<br>variable<br>cost | (4)<br>Total<br>cost<br>(2) + (3) | (5)<br>Marginal<br>cost<br>($\Delta$4) | (6)<br>Average<br>fixed<br>cost<br>(2) ÷ (1) | (7)<br>Average<br>variable<br>cost<br>(3) ÷ (1) | (8)<br>Average<br>total<br>cost<br>(4) ÷ (1) |
|---|---|---|---|---|---|---|---|
| 0 | $1,000 | $ 0 | $1,000 | | $ — | $ 0 | $ — |
| | | | | > $500 | | | |
| 1 | 1,000 | 500 | 1,500 | | 1,000 | 500 | 1,500 |
| | | | | > 375 | | | |
| 2 | 1,000 | 875 | 1,875 | | 500 | 438 | 938 |
| | | | | > 75 | | | |
| 3 | 1,000 | 950 | 1,950 | | 333 | 317 | 650 |
| | | | | > 150 | | | |
| 4 | 1,000 | 1,100 | 2,100 | | 250 | 275 | 525 |
| | | | | > 300 | | | |
| 5 | 1,000 | 1,400 | 2,400 | | 200 | 280 | 480 |
| | | | | > 450 | | | |
| 6 | 1,000 | 1,850 | 2,850 | | 167 | 308 | 475 |
| | | | | > 600 | | | |
| 7 | 1,000 | 2,450 | 3,450 | | 143 | 350 | 493 |
| | | | | > 750 | | | |
| 8 | 1,000 | 3,200 | 4,200 | | 125 | 400 | 525 |

*Short-Run Cost Structure of a Firm.* Even at zero output, some fixed costs are incurred. Average fixed cost declines as output increases. Variable costs reflect the use of variable resources and the law of diminishing returns. Total variable cost rises slowly at first and then more rapidly as diminishing returns are encountered. Average variable cost reflects this same influence, falling initially and then rising. Total cost is the sum of fixed and variable costs, and average total cost is the sum of average fixed cost and average variable cost at each output level. Marginal cost is the change in total cost (or total variable cost) due to increasing output by one unit.

put is increased. Total variable cost ultimately increases as output is expanded because of diminishing returns; that is, more and more variable resources are required to obtain one additional unit of output. In other words, marginal product is declining.

## AVERAGE OR PER UNIT COSTS

Figure 2 illustrates the nature and derivation of average costs as output is increased for a firm experiencing diminishing returns. The four important cost measures are:

*Average Fixed Cost (AFC)*  A fixed cost of $1,000 is incurred regardless of the level of output because some fixed resources (such as land) are used. Column (6) of Figure 2 depicts *AFC* where:

$$\text{Average fixed cost} = \frac{\text{total fixed cost}}{\text{quantity of output}} \quad \text{or} \quad AFC = \frac{TFC}{Q}$$

345

At low levels of output, *AFC* declines rapidly and then levels out because the costs of fixed resources ($1,000) are being spread over a larger and larger amount of output. For example, at two units of output, $AFC = \$500$, but if five units are produced, $AFC = \$200$. In short, *AFC* declines less rapidly as output is increased.

*Average Variable Cost (AVC)*   Average variable cost is computed by dividing total variable cost by the level of output:

$$\text{Average variable cost} = \frac{\text{total variable cost}}{\text{quantity of output}} \quad \text{or} \quad AVC = \frac{TVC}{Q}$$

We know that total variable cost represents the cost of variable resources and thus reflects diminishing returns. Consequently, average variable cost will also reflect the principle of diminishing returns, as column (7) of Figure 2 indicates. *Initially*, average variable cost declines due to increasing returns to variable resources, reaching a minimum in this example at four units of output ($AVC = \$275$). Beyond this point, however, average variable cost rises as diminishing returns are incurred—it takes more and more variable resources to produce each additional unit of output. As a consequence, average variable cost ultimately rises.

*Average Total Cost (ATC)*   Average total cost [column (8)] is derived by dividing total cost by the level of output shown in column (1):

$$\text{Average total cost} = \frac{\text{total cost}}{\text{quantity of output}} \quad \text{or} \quad ATC = \frac{TC}{Q}$$

Alternatively, $ATC = AFC + AVC$ at each level of output because $TC = TFC + TVC$. Average total cost will decline over the lower levels of output because of rapidly falling average fixed cost and declining average variable cost as increasing returns to variable resources occur. At higher levels of output, average total cost begins to rise because of diminishing returns.

Even though average fixed cost continues to decline as output increases, average variable cost ultimately begins to rise and offset the declines in average fixed cost. When *increases* in average variable cost exceed *decreases* in average fixed cost as output rises, average total cost rises. In Figure 2, this is evidenced by the fact that average variable cost reaches a minimum at four units of output ($AVC = \$275$), whereas average total cost reaches a minimum at six units of output ($ATC = \$475$). Beyond six units of output, average variable cost rises more rapidly than average fixed cost falls; therefore, average total cost must rise. For example, between six and seven units of output, average variable cost *increases* by $42 (from $AVC = \$308$ to $350), whereas average fixed cost declines by $24 (from $AFC = \$167$ to $143). Average total cost thus increases by $18 (from $ATC = \$475$ to $493 or $42 - \$24 = \$18$).

*Marginal Cost (MC) Revisited*   Column (5) of Figure 2 denotes the marginal cost of producing one more unit of output. As noted earlier, marginal cost is derived by comparing either the change in total cost *or* the change in total variable cost as output is increased by one unit. Total fixed cost does not change as output increases; therefore, marginal cost reflects *only* the change in total variable cost, which in turn reflects diminishing returns.

For example, consider the change in total cost [column (4)] and the change in total variable cost [column (3)] incurred by producing six in contrast to five units of output in Figure 2. Marginal cost is $450, since total cost is $2,400 for five units and $2,850 for six units of output, and marginal cost of $450 is also the change in total variable cost ($1,850 − $1,400) for the firm, as Figure 2 shows.

Note, too, that marginal cost rises after three units are produced because of diminishing returns. As long as variable resources can be hired at a constant price, *the only reason marginal cost rises as output increases is that each variable resource is successively less productive* when used in conjunction with fixed resources. Costs and output at the margin move in opposite directions—marginal product declines while marginal cost rises, as we have seen before.

### Short-Run Cost Relationships

Figure 3 is a graphic representation of the total and the average cost measures discussed in Figure 2. Several crucial cost relationships are highlighted in the figure.

First, note in Figure 3(a) that the total fixed cost of production ($TFC$ = $1,000) does not change as output varies. Variable and total costs do change as output increases (remember $TC = TFC + TVC$), depending on the cost and marginal productivity of variable resources.

Second, when average fixed cost declines as output increases, average total cost changes. This is shown in Figure 3(b), which gives schedules of

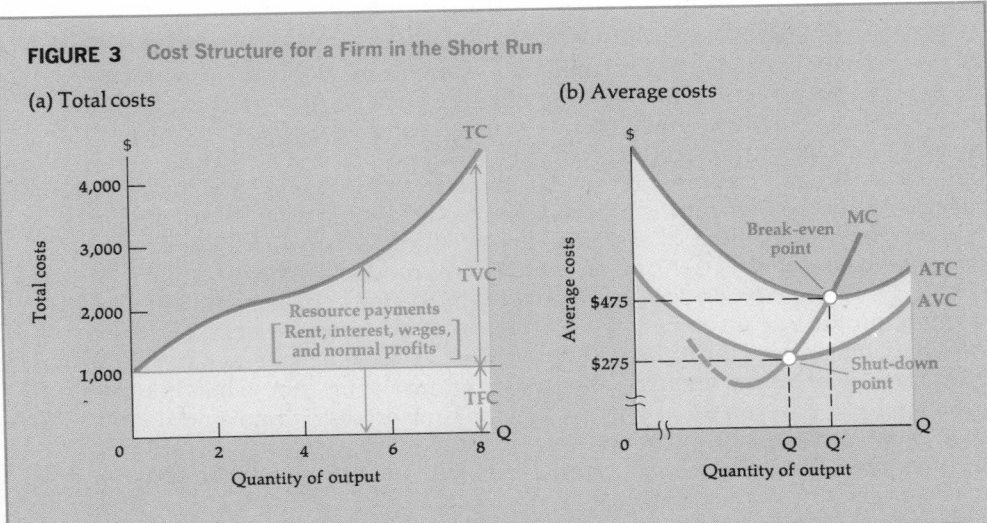

**FIGURE 3** Cost Structure for a Firm in the Short Run

(a) Total costs

(b) Average costs

*Cost Structure.* In part (a) total cost (*TC*) is the sum of total fixed cost (*TFC*) and total variable cost (*TVC*) at all levels of output. In (b) the difference in average total cost (*ATC*) and average variable cost (*AVC*) is average fixed cost (*AFC*). Marginal cost (*MC*) intersects *AVC* and *ATC* at their lowest points. The intersection of *MC* and *ATC* denotes minimum costs per unit of output where there is no economic profit. The intersection of *MC* and *AVC* denotes the origin of a firm's supply curve in the short run. As long as a firm cannot obtain a market price which covers *AVC*, the rational firm will not produce.

costs per unit of output. Cost schedules $ATC$ and $AVC$ move closer together as output increases because $AFC$ is declining where *the difference between $ATC$ and $AVC$ is $AFC$*. At lower levels of output, where $AFC$ is high, the difference between $AVC$ and $ATC$ will be large, but at higher levels of output the difference between $ATC$ and $AVC$ is small because $AFC$ is less. The influence of $AFC$ is also apparent in the data of Figure 2 where $ATC =$ \$525 and $AVC =$ \$400 at eight units of output but at two units of output $ATC =$ \$938 and $AVC =$ \$438.

Careful observation of Figure 3(b) reveals a third important characteristic of cost curves: $MC$ intersects $AVC$ and $ATC$ at their lowest points. Note, too, that $ATC$ and $AVC$ do not rise until $MC$ has intersected these two average cost curves. Figure 3(b) shows that when $MC$ is less than $AVC$ (between zero and $Q$ units), $AVC$ declines. When output increases beyond $Q$ units, $AVC$ rises because $MC$ exceeds the minimum $AVC$ of \$275. The reason average costs are directly influenced by $MC$ as output changes is quite simple. As long as the additional cost ($MC$) of one unit of output is less than the average, a new average will continue to decline. Most students are very much aware of this fact at examination time. Consider a student in economics with an average grade of 80 percent for four exams. If he scores 60 percent on the fifth exam (a "marginal" or additional observation), his *new* average grade falls. Conversely, if he scores 100 percent on one additional exam, his new average for all exams is higher than his previous average. By analogous reasoning, $AVC$ declines until $MC$ intersects it, and rises once $MC$ exceeds $AVC$. A schedule of $ATC$ also continues to decline as long as $MC$ is smaller than $ATC$ and rises thereafter, as shown in Figure 3(b).

Fourth, the lowest point on $ATC$ in Figure 3(b) (\$475 at a quantity of $Q'$) represents an important relationship. The intersection of $MC$ at minimum $ATC$ indicates a technologically efficient point of operation for a firm in the short run when fixed resources are already committed, because at this level of output, the firm is producing at lowest per unit cost. Therefore, this technological combination of fixed and variable resources used as factors of production results in the least costly combination of resources. It is possible (and quite likely) that the $ATC$ curve for one firm may be above or below the $ATC$ curve of another firm producing the same item. A lower $ATC$ could be caused, for example, by better management, the use of more productive resources, or a lower cost of acquiring resources. Under such circumstances, the firm with the lower $ATC$ will have a temporary advantage which may very well be translated into short-run gains. If I can produce Ripe Ale for \$1 a keg while your firm produces Blimey Ale at a cost of \$2 per keg, and both products are sold at \$2 as perfect substitutes to consumers, I will earn larger profits than you will. If we are competitors in a market economy, you could expect to lose customers to my firm as I reduce prices, and in order to stay in business, you will have to make your firm more efficient.

Fifth, the low point on the $AVC$ curve [$Q$ units at \$275 in Figure 3(b)] is also important because the intersection of $MC$ with $AVC$ denotes a *shutdown point of operation for a firm in the short run*. As long as a firm can produce and sell its product at a price in excess of out-of-pocket variable costs, it is preferable to do so in the short run even though a loss is incurred. Because the firm can choose to hire or not hire variable resources, variable-cost decisions to produce at a loss can be made in the short run, and this notion deserves careful consideration.

## "SHUT-DOWN" COST LEVEL

Consider the example of Figure 3, and assume that quantity $Q = 4$ units are produced at an $ATC$ of $525 and are sold for $300 each. What should the firm do? In the short run it should sell 4 units! A price ($P$) of $299 covers minimum $AVC$ of $275 and also helps cover $25 of fixed cost for each of the 4 units of output. If $Q = 4$ units are produced, total losses are: per unit loss × quantity, or ($P - ATC$) × $Q$, which is ($299 − $525) × 4 = a $904 loss. Notice carefully that this loss is *less* than the loss of $1,000 which would be incurred by not producing at all in the short run; therefore, producing 4 units of output *is* the most economical decision for a firm even though price is not sufficient to generate enough income to cover total production costs. Of course, as soon as fixed resources can be altered or disposed of, it is preferable to shut down entirely because the firm is not earning a normal profit! This action cannot be taken in the short run simply because we define this time period as one during which some resources are committed and cannot be taken out of production.

If product price were less than $AVC$, the firm would sustain losses equal to all fixed costs *plus* additional losses on a portion of variable costs. A firm unable to cover $AVC$ will be better off not producing and incurring the smaller loss of its fixed-cost investment. This is true at a price of $250 in Figure 3, for example, because this price does not cover $AVC$ of $275 for any quantity of production.

To drive the significance of the minimum $AVC$ home, assume that the data below (taken from Figure 2) represent your firm and you are hiring variable resources to produce a product. You already have $1,000 in "sunk" costs—your fixed cost outlay for a 10′ × 10′ office and equipment. If consumers will pay $250 per unit of output, how much would you produce under the conditions just described? If you produce nothing you lose your

| Output | 0 | 1 | 2 | 3 | 4 | 5 | 6 | 7 | 8 |
|--------|---|-----|------|------|------|------|------|------|------|
| AVC | 0 | $500 | $438 | $317 | $275 | $280 | $308 | $350 | $400 |

fixed-cost investment of $1,000 in the short run. Can you do any better than that to "minimize" losses? Not as long as the market price for your product is less than minimum $AVC$ of $275. This is true because at a lower price you can never cover the $AVC$ attributed to hiring any number of resources to produce any output level. If you are silly enough to produce 4 units that can be sold for $250 each, your total variable costs will be $275 × 4 = $1,100; total costs will be $2,100 ($1,100 + $1,000 in fixed costs); and total income will be $250 × 4 = $1,000. Your $1,100 loss is $100 *greater* than it would be if you produced nothing because your minimum $AVC$ of $275 *exceeds* product price by $25 per unit. If prices do not rise, you had better cut salaries, hire other more productive resources, or simply close up your business and absorb the $1,000 fixed-cost loss.

The importance of examining cost curves for a typical firm producing in the short run can be summarized without much fanfare. In addition to understanding the mechanical relationships involved in the different average cost curves, we have established the basis for two important conclusions.

*Minimum ATC Is a "Break-Even" Price and Output Level Where a Normal Profit Is Just Earned*    In the short run with a constant technology and utilization of certain fixed resources, minimum *ATC* is also the least costly level of output at which a firm can produce. Per unit price may equal per unit cost, and economic profits are zero at minimum *ATC*.

*Minimum AVC Depicts a Shut-Down Point*    A firm will be better off supplying zero output unless each unit can be sold at a market price that is *at least* sufficient to pay the costs of hiring variable resources. Zero units of output will be supplied, and the firm will absorb a loss equal to its fixed cost of investment in the short run if *AVC* cannot be covered. If the price of a given level of output is sufficient to more than cover minimum *AVC* but is not sufficient to cover *ATC*, the firm can produce and incur a short-run loss smaller than that which would prevail if it produced nothing and absorbed its fixed-cost loss.

## C. LONG-RUN AVERAGE COST

In the long run all resources are variable, firms can alter plant capacity, and other firms can enter or leave the industry. Since all resources are variable in the long run, all costs are also variable, and the previous distinction between fixed and variable cost is not necessary. In considering the cost curves for a firm producing in the short run we discovered that *ATC* and *AVC* declined and then rose again because of the influence of diminishing returns. However, the principle of diminishing returns is not applicable to long-run average cost because the firm can vary all resources, i.e., it is able to build different plant sizes.

### The Shape of Costs in the Long Run

When the firm is able to vary the quantities of *all* resources in the long run, its long-run average cost curve can be depicted as various short-run cost curves reflecting different plant sizes. The question that needs to be answered is, What happens to long-run average costs for a firm as expansion takes place?

Initially, as the producer moves from smaller to successively larger plant sizes, long-run average costs tend to decline. At some point, however, long-run average cost tends to rise with increasing plant size. These circumstances are shown in Figure 4. Each short-run *ATC* curve denotes one specific short-run plant size; that is, a given quantity of fixed resources (such as land, buildings, and machinery) employed in conjunction with different amounts of variable resources. Although only a limited number of alternative short-run plant sizes are presented in Figure 4, we could easily conceive of more. The critical point is that the construction of a larger plant results in a declining long-run average cost curve (*LRAC*) up to a plant

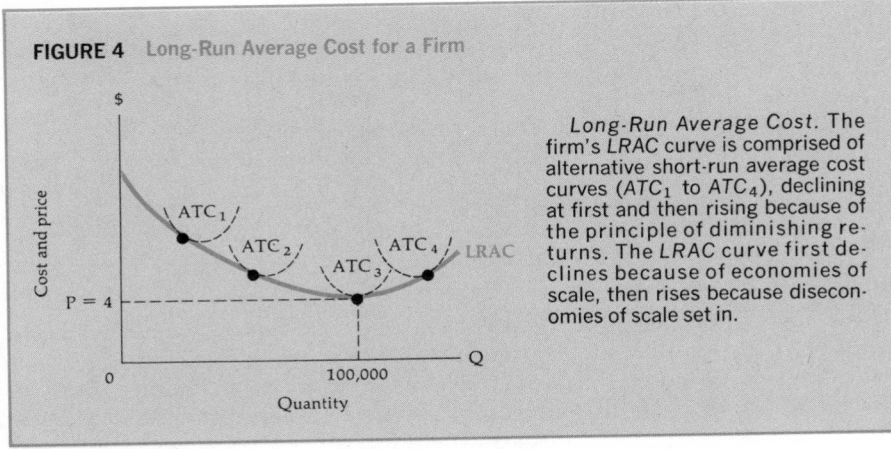

**FIGURE 4** Long-Run Average Cost for a Firm

*Long-Run Average Cost.* The firm's *LRAC* curve is comprised of alternative short-run average cost curves ($ATC_1$ to $ATC_4$), declining at first and then rising because of the principle of diminishing returns. The *LRAC* curve first declines because of economies of scale, then rises because diseconomies of scale set in.

size denoted by $ATC_3$. Beyond that point, however, a larger plant implies higher *LRAC*.

The *LRAC* curve reveals a scale of operation which generates minimum per unit cost *after* a firm has had adequate time to make long-run adjustments in the use of *all* resources. In planning the quantity it intends to produce and sell, each firm can select some short-run plant size that gives it lowest costs for a specified output level in the long run. Operating at the lowest point on the *LRAC* curve at plant size $ATC_3$ in Figure 4 may require expansion for some firms in an industry and reduction in plant size for others. This means that firms must alter the use of fixed resources over a period of time (remember, in the long run there are no fixed resources).

THE SIGNIFICANCE OF LONG-RUN COSTS

Operating at the lowest point on a *LRAC* curve may or may not be of any significance to the firm itself, but it is an important point of operation from the viewpoint of society. Minimum *LRAC* is significant to society simply because if all firms produce a level of output consistent with minimum *LRAC* we know that *all* resources (both those that are fixed and those that are variable in the short run) are used in the most efficient (i.e., lowest-cost) manner, given some level of technology. Moreover, minimum *LRAC* represents a break-even point of operation for a firm if price $(P) = $ minimum *LRAC* (e.g., *P* and *LRAC* = \$4 in Figure 4). In other words, firms are earning *normal profits only* as long as prices are equal to minimum *LRAC*. Intuitively this appears to be a desirable state of affairs from the consumer's point of view, since a normal profit is sufficient to attract the resources needed to produce those goods and services desired by society. However, achieving minimum *LRAC* is important to the firm only if all firms are somehow forced to sell a product at a price such as *P* in Figure 4. If competition between firms were sufficient to drive product price to this level, any producer not operating at the minimum point on *LRAC* in Figure 4 would fail to earn a normal profit.[2] However, the business firm is pri-

[2] Subsequent chapters will clarify the way in which a competitive economy forces all firms to operate at minimum *LRAC*.

marily interested in earning profits, not in minimizing costs for the consumer, and, as we shall see later, a firm's cost and output level may or may not be consistent with the 100,000 units of output denoted by minimum *LRAC* in Figure 4.

Up to this point, the contention that costs decline in the long run and then rise has been accepted at face value. However, is this really the case, and if so, why? The U-shaped *LRAC* curve of Figure 4 is explained by economies and diseconomies of scale in the long run when no resources are fixed.

### ECONOMIES OF SCALE

There are a variety of production efficiencies know as *internal economies of scale* associated with specialization, expansion of plant size, and large markets. Internal economies of scale explain the downward-sloping portion of the *LRAC* curve in Figure 4 for output levels between 0 and 100,000 units. As plant size increases, increased specialization of resources, the use of more efficient resources, and more effective utilization of by-products produce internal production efficiencies and lower the average costs of production in the long run.

For example, given a larger market, it may be possible to achieve internal economies of scale in a firm's use of resources because increased specialization of the labor force is possible. Rather than performing five or six distinctly different tasks, labor may be combined in such a way as to become more proficient in a limited number of skills. Thus, a skilled machinist can spend more of his time doing highly skilled work, and a controller can function primarily in the capacity of controllership. In other instances, economies of scale derive from the utilization of highly complex and more efficient capital resources that require an expanded market and a larger scale of operation. A firm may have to achieve a certain size because only a large market and a high volume of production will make utilization of certain capital resources economical. In the automobile and steel industries, for example, a technology involving assembly-line methods and elaborate capital equipment requires some degree of mass production to achieve efficiency and avoid a more costly manual operation. In addition, by-products of raw materials that might be wasted in a smaller operation may be utilized in certain large-scale operations. Economies of scale may also be realized by purchasing inputs in larger quantities or by achieving lower transportation costs, better access to financial capital markets, or improved distribution outlets.

### DISECONOMIES OF SCALE

The upward-sloping portion of the *LRAC* curve in Figure 4 reflects diseconomies of scale. *Scale diseconomies* are the result largely of internal inefficiencies related to problems of managerial coordination. Decision-making and efficient operation are endangered in an extremely large firm by a breakdown in communications and problems in coordinating human and property resources. Upper echelons of management may become increasingly remote from the actual business of producing, controlling, and selling as plant size increases and authority is delegated to innumerable subordinates. Management bureaucracy related to large size can result in diseconomies of scale overcoming whatever economies of scale might have once existed (a condition suspected to prevail in the automobile industry, for example). Consequently, *LRAC* rises as diseconomies of scale are encountered beyond the optimal level of operation.

### Competition and Long-Run Costs

We have just seen how internal scale economies and diseconomies are directly significant to society and the firm. The nature of *LRAC* curves for all firms is also important because of its influence on the competitive structure of markets and industries.

### MARKET STRUCTURE

The hypothetical firm shown in Figure 4 may not reach minimum *LRAC* if there is some restriction on plant size, perhaps because one or a few firms control vital resources or have monopoly access to a technological improvement protected by a patent. Expansion of markets might also be blocked by large capital requirements or by the dominant influence of a few large producers in the industry, in which case other firms in the industry may be unable to achieve scale economies. There may also be an excessive number of firms in an industry sharing a market, in which case all firms will operate at some point to the left of the minimum point on the *LRAC* curve. This situation may be a result of changes in consumer tastes or perhaps of inadequate growth in the demand for output in relation to technological improvements that permit greater scale economies than were previously possible. Under circumstances such as these, society may be penalized, since costs will be greater than they would be if internal scale economies could be achieved.

Internal scale economies and diseconomies also help determine the competitive structure of the industry in which the firm operates. Under circumstances in which economies of scale are likely and diseconomies are unlikely, a firm's *LRAC* curve will decline over a large range of output; hence, there are incentives for firms to become very large relative to the total market for a product. In the absence of adequate demand, only a few firms may be able to exist in the industry and achieve internal scale economies. Thus, competition may decline. Because of slowly exhausted scale economies relative to market size, there are industries in every economy that flourish with just a few firms, possibly as few as three—as in the American automobile industry today.

Figure 5(a) depicts declining *LRAC* over a relatively large range of output where economies of scale are protracted. A breakdown in competition is a possible and somewhat natural result in this situation, because it is possible for one or a few firms to expand output at lower costs and lower prices and ultimately to capture a large portion of the market, thereby squeezing out competitors. Lower unit costs are a *potential* advantage to society, but they will be realized only if the few surviving producers lower prices to the consumer after competition has been diminished. Unfortunately, the market provides no assurance that when competition breaks down, the remaining dominant firm(s) will behave in this way. As a matter of fact, there is some evidence to suggest that market power may be used by the remaining firms for their own advantages, as we shall see in Chapter 17. Figure 5(b) depicts the rapid exploitation of scale economies and the relatively early incidence of scale diseconomies, a condition depicted by *LRAC* increasing quickly. In this instance, minimum costs can be achieved

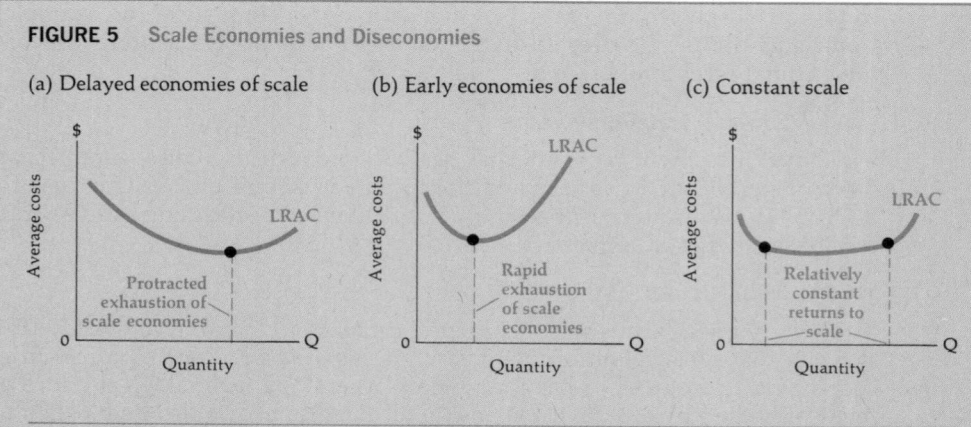

**FIGURE 5**   Scale Economies and Diseconomies

(a) Delayed economies of scale    (b) Early economies of scale    (c) Constant scale

*Scale.* If scale economies are delayed as in (a), only a few firms may survive in the industry, but if scale economies are exhausted rapidly relative to demand as in (b), the danger of a breakdown in competition is lessened. In (c) relatively constant returns to scale are illustrated.

by a large number of firms in the long run, as is the case of restaurants today. Figure 5(c) illustrates a third possible situation, where costs are relatively constant over a large range of possible output in the long run. Many economists believe that relatively constant *LRAC* is fairly common in many industries today.

Simultaneous achievement of market competition *and* the most efficient production techniques at minimum *LRAC* may not be possible in the steel, automotive, petroleum, or aircraft-manufacturing industries, for example, because internal scale economies relate to market size. This, of course, does not mean that Standard Oil or General Motors are in fact achieving an optimal long-run scale of operation at minimum *LRAC*; indeed, what evidence we have suggests otherwise. Diseconomies of scale may well characterize the sprawling industrial giants even though multiplant operations and corporate decentralization are sometimes used to avoid this dilemma. Firms such as General Motors and General Electric have subdivided into several operating divisional units to overcome managerial coordination problems leading to scale diseconomies. Each division can be managed on a semiautonomous basis, and, in some cases, one division may compete with other divisions in the corporation, as well as with other firms within the industry.

This situation has serious implications for an economy because the few firms capable of achieving delayed economies of scale retain the market power which accompanies diminished competition. Thus, a handful of firms and individuals can control vast portions of the economy. Furthermore, future technological change may promote even larger production units and further enhance the concentration of market power.

## INDUSTRY COSTS AND LONG-RUN SUPPLY

Internal economies and diseconomies of scale are concepts that pertain to the *LRAC* schedule for *one firm*. The nature of cost changes over time for an entire *industry* may be influenced by *external* economies or disecon- omies. The three possibilities that exist for industry cost and, therefore, industry supply curves over time are shown in Figure 6 as constant, in- creasing, and decreasing cost conditions. The prices paid for resources are an important determinant of industry costs and supply in the long run.

*Constant Costs and Industry Supply*   Constant costs occur as long as an industry can expand output over time without driving up the prices of whatever resources it employs. A constant-cost industry is shown in Figure 6 as horizontal supply curve *s*. If resources become more or less expensive or more or less productive, increasing or decreasing cost conditions will characterize industry supply.

*Increasing Costs and Industry Supply*   Suppose that an industry expands rapidly over time and, in addition, that it represents a major employer of highly specialized resources. In this situation, increasing cost conditions may occur (see $s_2$ of Figure 6) as additional resources are supplied at higher prices. Similarly, if factors of production become less productive, perhaps because of inferior resource quality, increasing costs may prevail—the case among certain firms which rely on mineral, timber, water, and land re- sources.[3]

*Decreasing Costs and Industry Supply*   A third possibility is decreasing costs due to *external* economies in production which may arise as the result of technological changes and increased specialization in related parts of the economy. External economies can be generated by a startling innovation, the rise of a new specialized industry, or the emergence of new markets which allow satellite firms to develop, thereby achieving lower unit costs as depicted by $s_1$ of Figure 6.

Consider what happened when motels first caught on a few decades ago. There were few trained motel managers and many firms which now spe-

[3] Diminishing "aggregate" returns may also enter in the case of increasing costs. If certain resource supplies are fully employed in a fixed amount and other variable re- sources are used more and more intensively as may be the case of land relative to the population "explosion," additional variable resource(s) may contribute smaller and smaller output increments.

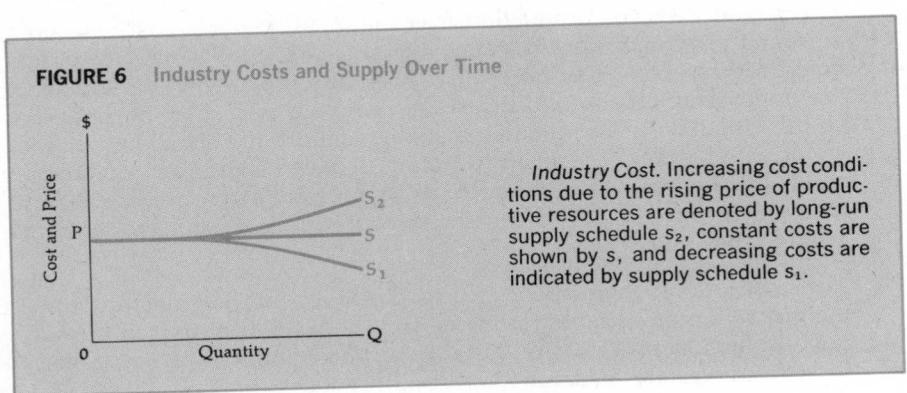

**FIGURE 6**   Industry Costs and Supply Over Time

*Industry Cost.* Increasing cost condi- tions due to the rising price of produc- tive resources are denoted by long-run supply schedule $s_2$, constant costs are shown by *s*, and decreasing costs are indicated by supply schedule $s_1$.

cialize in servicing the motel industry were nonexistent. Today motel managers and motel service industries are plentiful. The consequences are external economies of scale for the motel industry, which now operates more efficiently. With the passage of time the computer and space industries may experience similar external economies capable of leading to *decreasing costs*.

Without the external economies common to contemporary advances in technology and improved production processes, mankind would be a primitive being eking out a meager existence. Farmers rely on the farm-equipment industry, as well as on seed, fertilizer, and water resources they simply could not provide individually. Roads, schools, and communications systems provide massive external economies to business firms. Indeed, over the years, manufacturing firms have fragmented into innumerable "specialty" operations. The significance of external economies and decreasing industry costs lies in potentially lower consumer prices and the possible fragmentation of increasingly specialized markets among several firms that may check each other's market power. This has occurred in some measure between automotive and tire-manufacturing firms. Of course, if economic power pyramids in the hands of a few firms who integrate markets to achieve a larger market and lower costs, competition tends to break down as economies of scale are internalized and one or a few firms expand capacity and dominate the market.

*In summary:* By constructing a simplified model of a competitive firm, the relationship between resource costs and production has been identified in the short run and the long run. The achievement of least-cost efficiency for such a firm in the short run is at a level of output where $ATC$ is a minimum or at that quantity where $MC$ and $ATC$ intersect. When all resources can be varied in the long run, minimum unit cost is shown by the low point on $LRAC$, a level of operation which takes into account such things as economies and diseconomies of scale. These are important cost and output levels which will be discussed in the following chapter as being indicative of efficient use of resources and production from the vantage point of society at large.

## REVIEW

### Summary

1. The private costs of production may equal all resource costs, including a normal profit sufficient to retain the entrepreneurial factor of production. Production costs of both the explicit and the implicit variety denote the opportunity costs of using resources for a particular purpose. Several distinctions in production costs are important, including (*a*) social vs. private costs; (*b*) a time distinction between short-run and long-run costs; (*c*) distinctions between fixed and variable resources, which are reflected in fixed and variable costs; and (*d*) the meaning of total and average (per unit) costs.

2. The principle of diminishing returns describes the relationship between the utilization of variable resources and the level of output in the short-run production process. As variable resource inputs are increased and fixed resources are held constant, total product ultimately increases at a

decreasing rate. Marginal product (*MP*), or the change in total output as one more variable resource is employed, declines as a reflection of the principle of diminishing returns. When *MP* declines as a reflection of the diminishing productivity of resources, unit costs tend to rise.

3. Average total cost is the sum of average variable cost and average fixed cost (*ATC* = *AVC* + *AFC*). Marginal cost (*MC*), the change in total cost as output is increased by one unit, falls initially because of increasing returns. However, *MC* ultimately rises due to diminishing returns and intersects the *AVC* and *ATC* curves at their lowest points. At that point where *MC* intersects *ATC*, firms are operating efficiently in the short run. The *MC* and *AVC* intersection denotes the "shut-down" level of operation for a firm in the short run simply because product price must *at least* cover average variable cost if the firm is to produce anything at all!

4. Long-run average costs (*LRAC*) occur in a period of time long enough to vary *all* resources. The U-shape of *LRAC* for a firm is due to internal economies and diseconomies of scale. Long-run costs may also be viewed from an *industry* point of view, where constant, increasing, or decreasing cost conditions reflect changes in the costs of hiring resources over time as well as *external* economies or diseconomies. The low point of the *LRAC* curve reflects the optimum technological combination of all resources for a firm in the long run.

## Identify the Following Concepts and Terms

- explicit vs. implicit costs
- *ATC* = *AVC* + *AFC*
- normal and economic profits
- *LRAC*
- decreasing industry costs
- economic profits
- marginal product
- social costs
- economies and diseconomies of scale
- variable and fixed resources
- opportunity costs
- *MC* = *AVC* and *MC* = *ATC*

## Questions to Answer

1. In economics why do production costs include a normal profit? How do a normal *and* an economic profit relate to implicit opportunity costs?

2. Critically evaluate the following statement: "The marginal cost of production reflects the value or worth society attaches to resources, which may not be accurate if some social costs are excluded from the private costs incurred in producing a good." Give an example of your answer.

3. How are marginal cost and the principle of diminishing returns related? How is marginal product related to average total and average variable costs in the short run? Why is marginal product not related to the shape of a long-run average cost curve or to average fixed cost?

4. How do *MC* and minimum *ATC* as well as *MC* and minimum *AVC* relate to profit and to decisions to produce or not produce?

5. In the long run, internal scale economies and diseconomies are important in explaining the shape of a firm's cost curve. How is this so? Why are slowly exhausted scale economies important to competitive markets in which no one firm can influence market price?

# CHAPTER 16
# The Market System and
# Pure Competition

Chapter 14 briefly explained competitive markets and showed how supply and demand determine an equilibrium price which rations limited outputs and allocates scarce resources in a market system. Chapter 15 discussed the way in which a firm's cost structure is influenced by diminishing returns in the short run and also explained how firms can produce at minimum cost in the long run when resources can be employed in variable amounts. The purpose of this chapter is to explain how and why efficient resource allocation is achieved by producing firms operating in a purely competitive market economy.

Competitive firms in a market economy are forced, through the pressures of other sellers, to produce a level of output such that: (a) no economic profits are earned, (b) minimum average costs must be achieved, and (c) equal values are placed on additional inputs (resources used up in production) and outputs (products produced). Our discussion will be devoted largely to a purely competitive firm in a model world, in which we shall assume that technology is constant. Moreover, our interest in economic efficiency will be confined initially to efficiency in production. Very shortly, however, we shall abandon these crutches, which serve to explain the simplest model of markets as a decision-making instrument. Pure competition is not a reality of any significance, nor is it the "best" of all possible worlds for everyone. It is only efficient, and efficiency is "best" only in the measure that individuals and societies value it as a goal.

Part A describes the meaning of pure competition and, assuming that competition prevails everywhere, introduces three fundamental indicators of economic efficiency for a firm which is representative of all producers in an economy. Given our assumptions, the three indicators of efficiency are shown to be peculiar to a competitive market environment. Part B examines the nature and significance of market adjustments in the short run, and Part C examines resource allocation in the long run. Finally, a preliminary evaluation of the competitive model of a market system is presented in Part D. Before we begin our analysis, it is worthwhile to repeat one oft-stated warning: Economic models are just that, and like any theory about man's relationship to his world, they are incomplete, oversimplified, and sometimes unrealistic, but usually very valuable.

## A. THE THEORY OF PURE COMPETITION

The degree of competition that exists in an industry may be viewed as a continuum ranging from one extreme of pure competition to the other extreme of pure monopoly, as shown below. A single firm operating under *purely competitive* conditions is so unimportant in the whole market that it is a price "taker,"—it must accept a market-determined price. In contrast, a

---

**Four Market Structures**

| Pure competition | Monopolistic competition | Oligopoly | Monopoly |

---

*monopolist* determines product price because it is the only firm producing a unique product. A monopolistic firm may have substantial influence even though it is not an industrial giant. Between these two extremes, there are two additional degrees of competitiveness: *monopolistic competition*—competition among many producers, and *oligopoly*—competition among a few producers. Monopolistic competition is closer to competition than to monopoly, and oligopoly is closer to monopoly than to pure competition.

## The Competitive Conditions

In a market economy, three basic requirements have to be met under purely competitive conditions:[1]

1. Pure competition requires a large number of independent sellers and buyers in a market. In such a circumstance, all firms sell their product at the same price, which is set by market supply and demand. No individual firm supplies enough of the product to influence its price.

2. All firms in an industry offer a standardized product. This situation ensures that the product of one firm is a perfect substitute for the product of any other, and that *nonprice* competition (such as advertising) cannot effectively act as a substitute for price competition.

3. There are no barriers that prevent firms from entering or leaving the industry. This characteristic allows a sufficient number of firms to operate competitively by moving in and out of the industry and thereby shifting market supply.

Pure competition also requires all producing firms, all consumers, and all resources that are employed to be mobile and fully informed. The functioning of the profit motive is thus assured, because participants in the economic system are aware of and able to exploit all alternatives. The firm operating in a competitive market does not have a price policy as such. Rather, all producers simply adjust their short-run levels of output to the market price. No specific number of firms is required to make the number of independent sellers "large enough" to be forced to accept the market

---

[1] These conditions, first mentioned in the introductory chapters, are *assumptions* which we make in the model world—and should not be interpreted as descriptions of the real world. By making such assumptions, it is possible to reach certain conclusions regarding economic efficiency.

price. It is necessary only that the number of sellers involved be large enough to force the single producer to be a price taker and not a price setter. Finally, note that firms must maximize profits to survive in a competitive market. The profit-maximization condition permits us to form useful conclusions about economic efficiency in the allocation of resources even though it does not conform to reality on all counts.

Our analysis of market pricing, based as it is upon the condition that firms are guided by the profit motive, may be suspect if producers are not so motivated. The profit-maximizing condition, like the characteristics of pure competition listed above, is a simplification of reality which will be relaxed in later chapters because producers are interested in many objectives, only one of which may be maximization of profit. It should be apparent to even a casual observer that the conditions of pure competition are not likely to be met. Complete mobility, for example, is not common for firms or resource inputs (e.g., labor) in an industry. Freedom of entry into an industry or occupation may also be a divergence from reality in the market system. Furthermore, products are not completely standardized.

Even though pure competition is rare in practice, the merit of analyzing the purely competitive market is not negated, since this type of market provides a simple case by which market decisions in real-world economic systems can be illustrated. Also bear in mind that there are several reputable economists who contend that, when time horizons are extended, the competitive model of markets provides a substantially accurate approximation of the way the American economy operates. Many authorities remain relatively unconcerned about its stringent assumptions, as long as the competitive model yields realistic results. For now we can abandon such quibbling and get on with our task.

### Introduction to Indicators of Economic Efficiency

Perhaps the hardest problem encountered by students of economics is that of reasoning through three basic ideas about economic efficiency in the allocation of resources, a difficulty sometimes compounded by combining arithmetic and economic proofs into a hopelessly confusing array of numbers. Here we are going to introduce three indicators of economic efficiency without resorting to proofs. In Part B we will use the analytical tools we have developed in previous chapters to back up our contentions.

Efficiency of resource allocation, as we have said, means that wants are most nearly satisfied at least cost with the available supply of scarce resources. The term "efficiency," however, may accommodate a large number of conceptual definitions, depending upon the standard one seeks, economic efficiency being only one of these. An automobile might be regarded as efficient from the point of view of safety, but it might look and operate like a Sherman tank; if speed is the criterion for efficiency, something quite different is required; and esthetic values, minimum gasoline consumption, or absence of pollution would demand still other criteria. Because of these differences, the concept and the criteria for economic efficiency in using resources must be thoroughly developed. This will be done by first reiterating the influence of supply and demand on resource allocation. We shall then examine three indicators of economic efficiency in producing: (a) normal profits, (b) product price = minimum average cost, and (c) the meaning of equally valued resources and products.

Assuming that pure competition does exist, if consumers decide they want more hats and fewer shoes, the price of hats will be bid up and the price of shoes will fall. This event will encourage more firms to produce hats and ultimately some shoe-producing firms (particularly those with a higher average total cost than is typical of the industry) will become discouraged and leave the industry. Some consumers may not be able or willing to pay the new higher price for hats, and in this sense, a price-directed market system *rations* output and aids consumer choice.

Equally as important for the task at hand, however, is the idea that a rise in the price of hats also results in more resources being *allocated* to the production of this good; producers of hats are in a position to bid resources away from other users (firms producing shoes, for example). Indirectly, then, resources are allocated according to consumer demand as consumers express their desires in the market system. In order to survive in competitive markets, firms respond to changes in consumer sentiment. Because profits are sensitive to changes in demand, and because equilibrium price influences a firm's profits, profits are our first indication that resources are allocated efficiently.

## INDICATOR I: NORMAL PROFITS

A normal profit is one indicator of the efficiency of a theoretical firm, which we assume is a perfect replica of all firms operating in a purely competitive economy at *one* market-established price. A *normal profit*, as noted earlier, consists of a level of earnings just adequate to retain entrepreneurs as factors of production in an industry. The relationship between the production costs incurred in using scarce resources and the rising or falling prices obtained from selling the goods demanded by society shapes the profit earned by a firm, and thus firms respond to price changes.

As long as we talk in general terms about prices and costs, is it possible to say much about profits? At the moment, given the existence of competitive conditions, we can say this much: The competitive outcome in an economy is a situation in which prices are in equilibrium and profits are normal. Products are produced as long as total sales income just covers the total costs of acquiring productive resources, including a normal profit paid to entrepreneurial resources for risk-taking, managerial ability, and the like.

Just why is a normal profit efficient—why should profits not be less than normal or even larger? Suppose demand for a product decreases in a competitive economy. Prices decline, inefficient producers do not earn a normal profit, and ultimately they leave the industry. As firms leave the industry, market supply contracts, market prices tend to rise, and ultimately profits are restored to a normal level. In contrast, if profits in an industry are above the normal level because of a rapid increase in demand, new firms will be attracted to the industry, market supply will increase, product prices will fall, and profits will tend to decline to normal levels.

Thus, a normal profit—a return to firms that is "just adequate"—suggests that resources *may be* allocated efficiently.[2] In contrast, a profit that is larger than normal (an economic profit) encourages the entry of competi-

---

[2] Notice the emphasis on "may be." A normal profit is a necessary but not a sufficient condition of efficient resource allocation.

tors, while less-than-normal profits encourage the least efficient firms to leave the industry. The search for profits by individual suppliers is guided by market supply, demand, and price adjustments until an equilibrium price and a normal-profit level of operations is achieved. Microeconomic theory reaches the conclusion that resources are allocated efficiently because of this perpetual search for profits on the part of innumerable competitive buyers and sellers of resources and products—a search that finally forces all competitors to operate at normal profits.

### INDICATOR II: PRICE = MINIMUM AVERAGE TOTAL COST

Our search for a definition of efficient resource allocation is still dealing with a theoretical firm which is a perfect replica of all firms in a competitive economy in which resources and methods of production are fixed. The prevalence of normal profits in a perfect and competitive world is buttressed by a second indicator of efficiency: *Product price per unit (P) must equal the lowest possible unit or average total cost of production (ATC)*. (We will momentarily ignore the distinction between short- and long-run costs.) Why is this situation a significant indicator of efficiency?

For one thing, when price per unit just equals minimum cost per unit for a product, only normal profits are earned. Remember, per unit price covers all resource costs, including a profit which is just sufficient to allocate management resources to a given endeavor. Now, if the quantity $(Q)$ of a good produced is multiplied by unit price $(P)$ and by unit cost $(ATC)$, we can obtain total revenue and total cost, and thus determine if profits are above or below the normal level. Suppose that $P$ and $ATC$ = \$6, and $Q$ = 100:

$$P \times Q = \text{total revenue}$$
$$\$6 \times 100 = \$600$$

$$ATC \times Q = \text{total cost}$$
$$\$6 \times 100 = \$600$$

$$\text{Total revenue} - \text{total cost} = \text{profit}$$
$$\$600 - \$600 = 0$$

But what evidence do we have that $ATC$ is the minimum attainable unit cost? Assume that one of a large number of theoretical firms (Blimey, Inc.) has a higher unit cost (say, $ATC$ = \$8) than all other firms in the same competitive industry $(ATC$ = \$6). Competition among firms will force market price to \$6. This being so, Blimey will be in trouble! Unless a more efficient mode of production is introduced, the firm's output will have to be sold at a loss of \$2 per unit. If $Q$ = 100 again, losses will be \$2 per unit or total revenue − total cost = −\$200. Ultimately (that is, in the long run), the firm will leave the industry because it will not earn a normal profit. Those firms least efficient in producing and utilizing resources must either leave the industry or ultimately adopt a more efficient mode of production. New firms may be attracted to the industry if they can operate efficiently at the market price of \$6. Thus, firms unwilling or unable to adjust to the most efficient use of resources in the cost sense will be forced to leave the industry as competition intensifies among an increasing number of efficient firms. We can conclude that in pure competition efficient allocation of resources occurs when

1. Normal profits prevail *and*
2. Price (P) = minimum unit costs (*ATC* minimum).

The final indicator of efficient allocation of resources for a producing firm says that the value of a product must just equal the value or cost of using those resources needed to produce the last unit of that product. The value society places upon the last unit of output being produced is measured by the product price consumers are willing to pay. The value society places on the resources used to produce the last vat of Blimey Ale, for example, is the marginal cost (*MC*) of the last unit of output. In other words, *MC* represents the value of the resources used to produce the last unit of product. Our third indicator of efficiency in competition thus states that:

$$\text{Value of last unit of output} = \begin{array}{l}\text{value of resources used to produce} \\ \text{last unit of output}\end{array}$$

$$P = MC$$

If $P = ATC$ minimum and also $P = MC$, then it must be true that $MC = ATC$ at its minimum. Is this correct in other than a logical sense? Yes! Remember, we already concluded that marginal cost intersects an average cost curve at its lowest point. In terms of our third indicator of efficiency, *MC* must intersect *ATC* at its lowest point. In short, $P = ATC$ minimum assures us that profits are normal, and $P = MC$ assures us that consumer valuation of products is equal to the value of the resources used by producing firms—resources are thus used efficiently in the technical sense.

The concept of equally valued products and resources of Indicator III is most appealing logic. After all, if *P* is *in excess* of the value of the resources used up in production as shown by *MC*, this simply means that *more output is wanted*; society is placing a higher value on output than on the resources used in producing. Conversely, if *P* is less than *MC*, society is collectively signaling the economic system that *less of that product is wanted*.

How can we be assured that a competitive firm will in fact obey the three indicators of efficient allocation of resources which reduce down to $P = MC = ATC$ minimum at normal profits? At this point, only a partial and intuitive answer to this question can be provided, because we have not fully analyzed the nature of competitive firms. This analysis is the task of the remainder of this chapter. Remember, though, that competitive market supply and demand, and *not* a single firm, set *P* where normal profits exist once $P = ATC$ minimum. Because *MC* does in fact intersect *ATC* at its lowest point, the competitive producer cannot avoid the $P = MC$ rule.

*In summary:* Our three indicators of economic efficiency in allocating resources are:

I. A normal profit: $P - ATC$ minimum = 0 ($6 − $6 = 0).
II. Unit cost is a minimum: $P = ATC$ minimum ($6 = $6).
III. Products and resources are equally valued: $P = MC$ ($6 = $6).

The price-directed and profit-oriented market system tells firms to produce or not produce and further indicates how much should be produced, all the while allocating resources to those producers capable of operating efficiently. In a moment we shall see more clearly that as each firm pursues its own best interest (maximum profits), a competitive market system also allocates scarce resources in society's best interest—the most efficient way in terms of the three crucial economic indicators.

### In Deference to Reality

Does competition really exist in the automobile industry? Is it true that AT&T and all other firms maximize profits? Does $P$ really represent society's valuation of Crud wieners if 30 percent of their content is meal and animal intestines? Does $MC$ really represent the value or worth society attaches to the resources used if Crud, Inc., dumps blood in our rivers or refuses to hire Swedes? How do we know that any particular average total cost really is as low as it could be when gadgets and obsolescence are planned by automobile-manufacturing firms which at the same time may build a faulty steering column that could kill thousands of people? What does our economic system do if little old ladies cannot buy even Crud wieners because prices are too high and their incomes are too low because they have no resources to sell to producers? Will this type of economic system based upon a price–profit mechanism provide 125,000 educational institutions for some 60 million youth, the protection and justice related to 3.5 million crimes annually, or 491 million acres of public recreation areas? For that matter, what is so great about economic efficiency if people are jammed on top of each other in smog-polluted Chicago, New York, Los Angeles, and Pittsburgh while the colorful Colorado, Arkansas, and Vermont mountains and countryside are unpopulated wastelands? Why not use child labor in mines and factories for efficiency's sake?

Are the above really economic issues? In most cases, yes! To fully recognize such problems, to assimilate relevant facts properly, and to evaluate policy alternatives, we must know more about the model world of economic theory. We shall begin to acquire the knowledge needed to cope with such issues by careful analysis of the way a purely competitive firm reacts to a market environment. This process is not always comfortable for either student or teacher, but it is important to examine what is known, accepted, and disputed. In order to provide the tools of economic analysis required to study real-world problems such as those raised above, the remainder of the chapter will restate the conditions for efficiency in more formal terms, using the earlier-developed concepts of supply, demand, and price.

### B. OPTIMUM OUTPUT FOR THE COMPETITIVE FIRM IN THE SHORT RUN

Our first task is to show more fully how a competitive firm maximizes its own profits and at the same time ends up producing in such a fashion as to meet our efficiency criterion $P = MC = ATC$ minimum at normal profits. A second important task will be to identify the supply curve for a competitive firm.

The profit-maximizing level of output for a firm in the short run can be demonstrated by two approaches: (a) comparing total cost and total revenue, or (b) comparing marginal cost ($MC$) and marginal revenue ($MR$). *Marginal revenue* is defined as the additional revenue generated by producing one more unit of output.

## Total Revenue-Total Cost

Consider a firm producing boats in a competitive market. Total cost is the sum of total fixed cost and total variable cost. Since we are talking about the short run, the principle of diminishing returns explained in Chapter 15 will influence production costs. Total cost as shown in Figure 1 ultimately will rise at an increasing rate once diminishing returns set in. Moreover, since we can see that total cost = $1,000 at zero output, we know that there are $1,000 in fixed costs. Assuming that each firm faces one constant competitive product price ($P$) of $550 per unit, total revenue increases by increments of $550 as output is increased by increments of one unit, where these additions to total revenue represent marginal revenue. Figure 1 indicates: (a) that the firm should produce to make a profit, since a "break-even point" is reached beyond three units of output (point B); and (b) that the profit-maximizing level of output occurs at six units, where total revenue exceeds total cost by $450. Producing less than six units of output yields a smaller profit, and if more than six units are produced, total profits are also less than the $450 maximum.

Of course, this is only an example, but it is sufficient to illustrate the important points which we must explore further. The comparison of Figure 1 is adequate if the only thing of interest is telling a firm how to maximize profits. This, of course, is *not* our interest. Remember, the task set forth earlier was to demonstrate: (a) that price and marginal cost must be equal under competitive conditions, *and* (b) that profit maximization serves to merge society's interest in efficient resource allocation and the firm's profit interest. Moreover, we used the phrase "a constant competitive price." Just why price remains constant at $550 per boat deserves further attention.

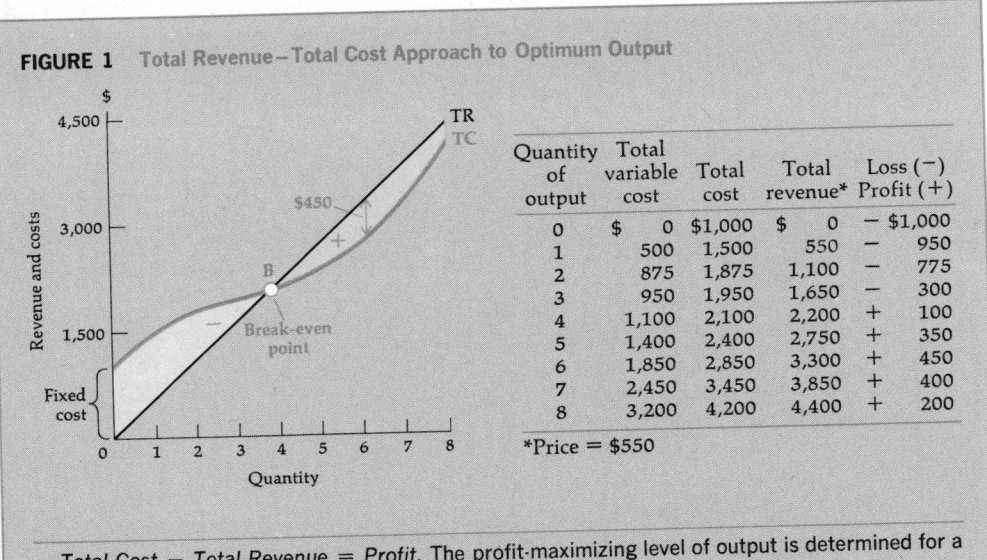

**FIGURE 1**  Total Revenue–Total Cost Approach to Optimum Output

| Quantity of output | Total variable cost | Total cost | Total revenue* | Loss (−) Profit (+) |
|---|---|---|---|---|
| 0 | $    0 | $1,000 | $    0 | − $1,000 |
| 1 | 500 | 1,500 | 550 | −    950 |
| 2 | 875 | 1,875 | 1,100 | −    775 |
| 3 | 950 | 1,950 | 1,650 | −    300 |
| 4 | 1,100 | 2,100 | 2,200 | +    100 |
| 5 | 1,400 | 2,400 | 2,750 | +    350 |
| 6 | 1,850 | 2,850 | 3,300 | +    450 |
| 7 | 2,450 | 3,450 | 3,850 | +    400 |
| 8 | 3,200 | 4,200 | 4,400 | +    200 |

*Price = $550

*Total Cost − Total Revenue = Profit*. The profit-maximizing level of output is determined for a firm by comparing total cost and total revenue.

Determining the most profitable level of output can be demonstrated by using what we shall term the *equimarginal rule*, which states that profit is at a maximum at the level of output at which additions to total revenue and additions to total cost, or marginal revenue (*MR*) and marginal cost (*MC*), are equal:

$$\text{Maximum profit is where } MR = MC$$

Our first step in understanding why profits are at a maximum where $MR = MC$ requires brief consideration of the demand schedule facing a competitive firm.

### DEMAND TO THE FIRM AND MARKET DEMAND COMPARED

The demand curve facing one competitive firm is perfectly elastic as shown in Figure 2(a). This is because the market determines some price $P$ for the competitive firm, which is defined as being so small in relation to total market supply that it cannot influence price. Thus, the only decision made by the competitive firm is how much output to produce. Moreover, Figure 2(a) also shows that the market-determined $P$ is equal to $MR$.

In other words, if a firm can sell any number of units at $550, the sale of one unit produces $550 in total revenue, two units produce $1,100 in total revenue, and three units produce $1,650 in total revenue. In each case, the *change in total revenue*, or *marginal revenue, is equal to $550*. In short, if $P = \$550$, then $MR = \$550$, as shown in Figure 2(a). Is the reasoning on this point consistent with the inverse price-quantity relationship of the market demand curve for *all* firms in the industry? The answer is, yes.

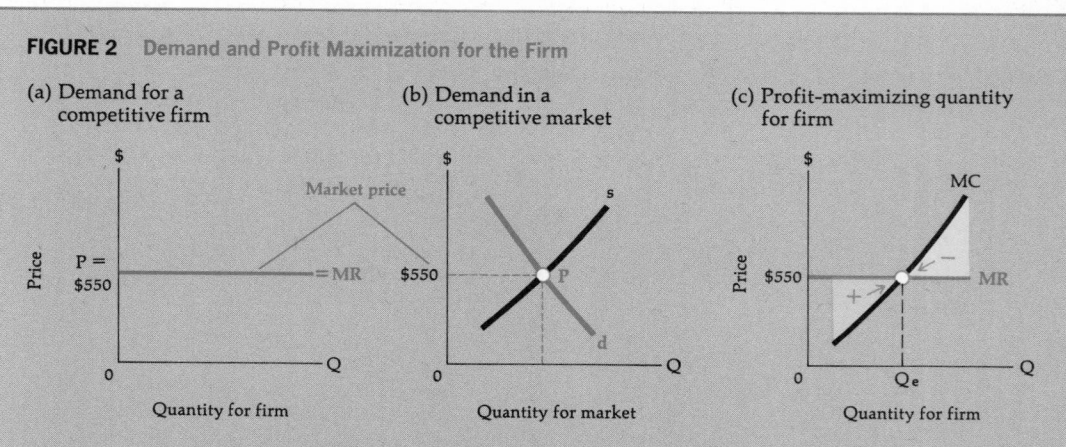

**FIGURE 2**   Demand and Profit Maximization for the Firm

(a) Demand for a
    competitive firm

(b) Demand in a
    competitive market

(c) Profit-maximizing quantity
    for firm

*Demand and Marginal Revenue.* A competitive firm is unable to influence product price (*P*). Even though industry demand is downward-sloping as shown in (b), the demand curve to competitive firms in an industry made up, for example, of 10,000 firms, is perfectly elastic and $P = MR$ at the going market price shown in (a). Only a quantity decision is made by the firm, and the profit-maximizing quantity of output to produce is where $MR = MC$. Expanding production up to that point adds positive increments to profits, but producing output beyond $Q_e$ in (c) reduces total profits.

Supply and demand viewed from the vantage point of the total market and all consumers identify one equilibrium price—one point such as $P$ on the down-sloping demand curve $d$ shown in Figure 2(b). The total industry demand schedule is downward-sloping because consumers will buy more of the product only at lower prices. This is a very different perspective of demand than that which applies to a competitive firm that must accept one market-determined price. Thus, a competitive firm is faced with a perfectly elastic demand curve such that $P = MR$ throughout, as shown in Figure 2(a).

### EQUATING MR AND MC

Figure 2(c) illustrates why a firm can increase profits by expanding output as long as $MR$ exceeds $MC$ and up to that quantity at which $MR = MC$ ($Q_e$ units). Each unit of output between zero and $Q_e$ in Figure 2(c) adds some net increment to profits by adding more to total revenue than to total cost ($MR > MC$). Producing beyond the point at which $MR = MC$ is not profitable, however, because after that point additional costs exceed additional revenues. The data from Figure 1 (repeated below) prove that the $MR = MC$ rule gives the same answer as was obtained by comparing total costs and revenues.

Note in the data below that $MC$ declines initially and then begins to rise after three units of output because of diminishing returns. A price of \$550

| Change in quantity | 0–1 | 1–2 | 2–3 | 3–4 | 4–5 | 5–6 | 6–7 | 7–8 |
|---|---|---|---|---|---|---|---|---|
| Price (MR) | \$550 | 550 | 550 | 550 | 550 | 550 | 550 | 550 |
| Marginal cost (MC) | \$500 | 375 | 75 | 150 | 300 | 450 | 600 | 750 |

produces a constant change in total revenue of $MR = \$550$, reflecting the fact that the firm can sell as much as it wishes to produce at this competitive market price. The profit-maximizing condition shown by $MR = MC$ is most nearly attained at six units of output, just as the total revenue–total cost comparison of Figure 1 revealed that profit is at a maximum of \$450 at six units. Producing five units clearly is incompatible with the desire to maximize profit because additional output will generate a larger change in revenue ($MR = +\$550$) than in cost ($MC = +\$450$); profit will rise by the difference of \$100. On the other hand, a level of output greater than six units is not profit-maximizing because marginal cost rises by \$600 (\$50 more than marginal revenue). *By most nearly equating MR and MC, each competitive firm maximizes profits and answers the question, How much should be produced?*

### Competitive Markets and the Firm in the Short Run

The above comparisons demonstrate that profits are maximized by expanding output as long as $MR$ is greater than $MC$, where $P$ and $MR$ are understood to be equal for a competitive firm. Now let us see how a firm adjusts production as the market price changes.

Consider how competitive firms react if market price varies in the short run. Since the firm makes decisions about quantity but *not* about price, it responds by changing the level of utilization of its variable resources. In this way, the firm can vary its output levels, which means that price and marginal cost (and thus diminishing returns) are determining factors in deciding how much a competitive firm will produce. To see this more clearly, consider the alternative situations, in which a firm produces: (a) a quantity to maximize economic profits, (b) a loss-minimizing quantity, and (c) a break-even quantity at which only a normal profit is earned.

Suppose the price of boats is $601 for a firm with the cost data shown in Figure 3. What quantity should such a competitive firm produce? The answer is: Expand output as long as MR is greater than MC, but do not go beyond that point at which MR = MC. The firm would not produce less than seven units of output, because MR exceeds MC up to that level of output. At lower levels of output, additions to total revenue exceed additions to total costs; thus, economic profits can be increased by producing up to seven units of output. The firm should produce the sixth unit, since it will add $151 to profits, and the seventh unit, which will also increase profits by $1. On the other hand, as long as the perfectly elastic demand curve facing a competitive firm remains at $P = MR = \$601$, the firm should

**FIGURE 3** Alternative Levels of Output and Profit for a Firm

| Quantity of output (Q) | Average total cost (ATC)[a] | Average variable cost (AVC) | Total cost (TC) | Marginal cost (MC) | Profit maximization P = MR = $601 | | Loss minimization P = MR = $301 | | Normal profit P = MR = $475 | |
|---|---|---|---|---|---|---|---|---|---|---|
| | | | | | Total revenue | Loss (—) Profit (+) | Total revenue | Loss (—) Profit (+) | Total revenue | Loss (—) Profit (+) |
| 1 | $1,500 | $500 | $1,500 | | $ 601 | —$899 | $ 301 | —$1,199 | $ 475 | —$1,025 |
| | | | | > $375 | | | | | | |
| 2 | 938 | 438 | 1,875 | | 1,202 | — 673 | 602 | — 1,273 | 950 | — 925 |
| | | | | > 75 | | | | | | |
| 3 | 650 | 317 | 1,950 | | 1,803 | — 147 | 903 | — 1,047 | 1,425 | — 525 |
| | | | | > 150 | | | | | | |
| 4 | 525 | 275 | 2,100 | | 2,404 | 304 | 1,204 | — 896 | 1,900 | — 200 |
| | | | | > 300 | | | | | | |
| 5 | 480 | 280 | 2,400 | | 3,005 | 605 | 1,505 | — 895 | 2,375 | — 25 |
| | | | | > 450 | | | | | | |
| 6 | 475 | 308 | 2,850 | | 3,606 | 756 | 1,806 | — 1,044 | 2,850 | 0 |
| | | | | > 600 | | | | | | |
| 7 | 493 | 350 | 3,450 | | 4,207 | 757 | 2,107 | — 1,343 | 3,325 | — 125 |
| | | | | > 750 | | | | | | |
| 8 | 525 | 400 | 4,200 | | 4,808 | 608 | 2,408 | — 1,792 | 3,800 | — 400 |

I. *Price is $601:* Profit is maximized at seven units of output when MR ($601) and MC ($600) are most nearly equal and an economic profit of $757 is earned.

II. *Price is $301:* The firm minimizes losses by producing five units of output when MR ($301) and MC ($300) are most nearly equal.

III. *Price is $475:* Maximum (and normal) profits are earned at six units of output when MR ($475) and MC ($475) are most nearly equal.

[a] ATC is rounded to the nearest dollar.

not produce beyond seven units of output because the marginal cost of the eighth unit is $800. Consider next what happens if product price declines to $301 in Figure 3. In this instance, the firm can minimize losses by producing a quantity such that $P$ and $MR = MC$, a condition most nearly met at five units of output. Observe carefully that a rather substantial loss of $895 is incurred at this level, but it is the smallest possible loss in the short run when the market price is $301 and it remains a preferable alternative to not producing at all, which imposes a $1,000 fixed-cost loss on the firm. Now suppose that the equilibrium market price increases to $P = $475$. Under these circumstances, the firm will produce six units of output. Observe that $P = MC = ATC$ minimum at $475 and no economic profit is earned ($P - ATC = 0$). Since a normal profit is part of the firm's costs, we know that normal profits are earned by producing six units of output. Production beyond six units is not advisable, since $MR$ is less than $MC$ at higher output levels, given a market price of $475. On the other hand, there is no point in producing less than six units either, because $MR$ exceeds $MC$ at lower output levels and the firm would incur a loss at these levels. (*Proof:* compare total revenue and total costs.)

## PROFIT-MAXIMIZING QUANTITY

We have just defined the supply curve for a competitive firm in the short run and we have also illustrated achievement of the three conditions of economic efficiency which were discussed earlier. This becomes more apparent by closer examination of the average- and marginal-cost relationships shown in Figure 3. Let us restate these conclusions momentarily using Figure 4, which illustrates the relationships presented in Figure 3.

If the market supply and demand shown in Figure 4(a) establish a market price of $601, the competitive firm's $P$ and $MR$ are also $601. At seven units of output, $MR = MC$, and the firm earns an economic profit of $zz'$ per unit for $Q = 7$ units. Total profits are per unit profits times the quantity of output sold, as shown by the gold area in Figure 4(a).

## LOSS-MINIMIZING QUANTITY

If a firm like that described in Figure 4(a) is earning a normal profit *and* an economic profit as well, other producers who observe these excess rewards will enter the industry, thereby increasing market supply from $s$ to $s_i$, as shown in Figure 4(b). Assuming market demand is constant, increased supply can drive price and marginal revenue down to $301 per unit. Losses will now be minimized by producing five units of output, because at $P = $301$, $MR$ and $MC$ are most nearly equal. The firm is *not* earning a normal profit, since average total cost exceeds price per unit of output. The loss incurred by producing five units is equal to the gold area in Figure 4(b)—the difference in $ATC$ and $P$ of $xx'$ per unit. Observe, however, that losses are less than the fixed-cost loss which would be incurred if the firm decided not to produce, because some of average fixed cost is covered. The difference between $ATC$ and $AVC$ at five units of output is the fixed cost per unit or $AFC$, and, as Figure 4(b) indicates, a modest contribution is made to the fixed cost of operating in the short run. The out-of-pocket or variable costs of producing are indicated by the area under the $AVC$ curve, and all of $AVC$ is covered at five units of output, as Figure 4(b) reveals. The loss-

**FIGURE 4**   Optimum Output and the Competitive Firm

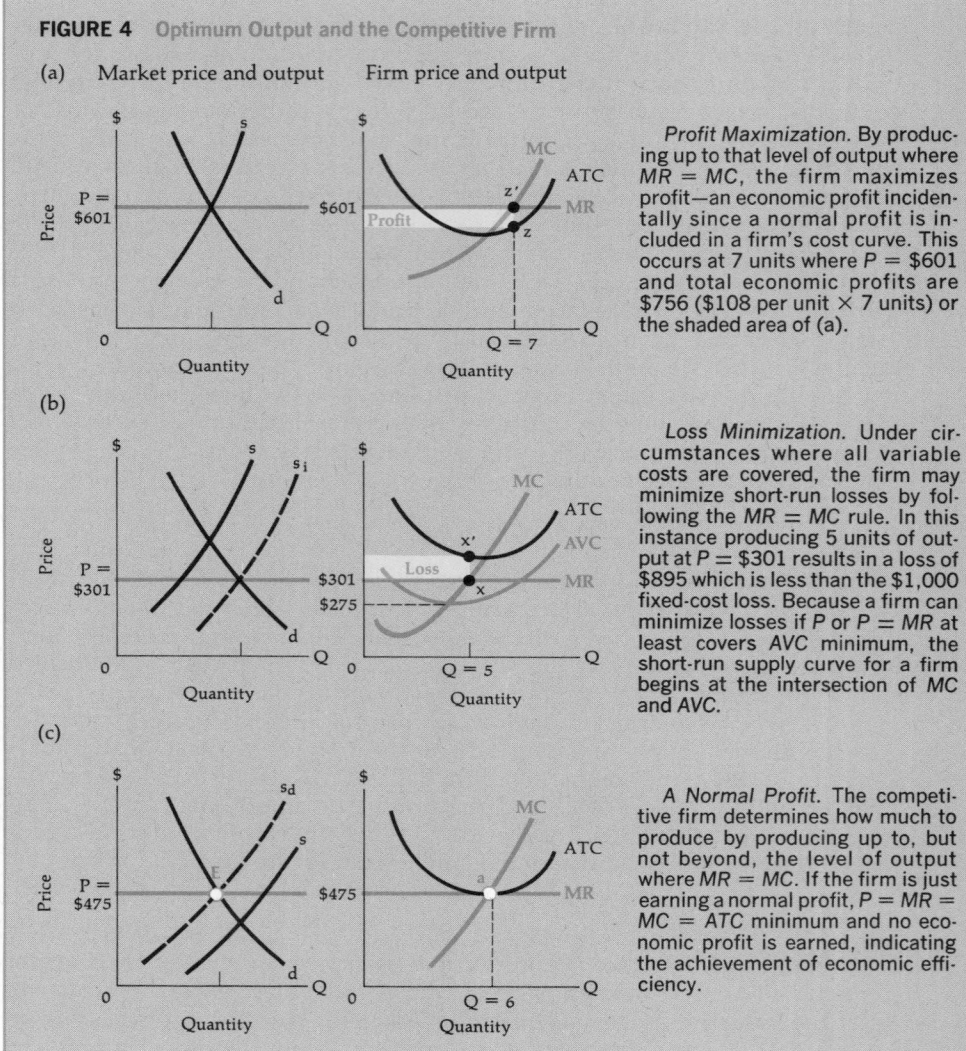

(a)   Market price and output    Firm price and output

*Profit Maximization.* By producing up to that level of output where $MR = MC$, the firm maximizes profit—an economic profit incidentally since a normal profit is included in a firm's cost curve. This occurs at 7 units where $P = \$601$ and total economic profits are $756 ($108 per unit × 7 units) or the shaded area of (a).

(b)

*Loss Minimization.* Under circumstances where all variable costs are covered, the firm may minimize short-run losses by following the $MR = MC$ rule. In this instance producing 5 units of output at $P = \$301$ results in a loss of $895 which is less than the $1,000 fixed-cost loss. Because a firm can minimize losses if $P$ or $P = MR$ at least covers AVC minimum, the short-run supply curve for a firm begins at the intersection of MC and AVC.

(c)

*A Normal Profit.* The competitive firm determines how much to produce by producing up to, but not beyond, the level of output where $MR = MC$. If the firm is just earning a normal profit, $P = MR = MC = ATC$ minimum and no economic profit is earned, indicating the achievement of economic efficiency.

minimizing firm therefore produces five units at $P = \$301$ in the short run by following the $MR = MC$ rule.

It is possible now to recognize that the portion of marginal cost above AVC is a short-run supply curve for the competitive firm. If $P$ or $MR$ does not cover AVC at its minimum of $275, the firm will close down and absorb the smaller fixed-cost loss. For example, if price and marginal revenue were smaller than the minimum $AVC = \$275$ indicated in Figure 4(b), the firm would be unable to minimize its losses because it could not cover variable production costs. A firm can minimize losses in the short run by producing a level of output at which $MR = MC$, but *only if* some portion of fixed cost can be covered. We can then conclude that schedule MC in

Figure 4(b) *is the firm's short-run supply curve at all levels of output greater than that point at which MC intersects AVC at its lowest level.*

A student selling hot dogs at a price of 10 cents each with a minimum AVC of 12 cents encounters a similar problem. The hot-dog stand should be closed down even if $MR = MC$ at 10 cents. Why? Because $P$ and $MR$ (10 cents) are less than AVC (12 cents) for each unit. Ignoring the fixed costs of production, the student would lose 2 cents in variable costs per unit sold—a loss that could be avoided by producing nothing at all! If product price is not adequate to cover minimum AVC, no production is preferable because it entails only the fixed-cost loss.

Another more realistic example of loss minimization may help demonstrate the validity of our contentions. Suppose you are an unfortunate fisherman working the Puget Sound area. Much of the cost of your operation is represented by fixed costs attributable to immobile capital resources (a large boat, nets, and the like). Lacking an alternative profession and the ability to otherwise use these specialized capital resources in the short run, you would attempt to minimize losses, especially since there are apt to be few immediate buyers for your boat and other fixed resources. Given enough time, of course, your resources can be reallocated, but it is not unreasonable to expect that you will operate only to reduce losses to something less than the total fixed-cost loss that you would absorb if you stopped fishing entirely.

*In summary:* Profit is maximized (and loss is minimized) by producing that level of output at which $P$(and $MR$) $= MC$, subject to the loss-minimization qualification that $MR$ must exceed minimum AVC. Most important, the segment of an MC schedule above minimum AVC is the short-run supply curve for a firm in pure competition, since it describes levels of operation which are preferable to closing down and absorbing a fixed-cost loss.

## A NORMAL PROFIT: EFFICIENT RESOURCE ALLOCATION

The situations described thus far are not representative of the competitive equilibrium outcome in a market economy because a normal profit is not earned. These conditions are shown in Figure 4(c), in which an equilibrium price of $475 is dictated by a decrease in market supply from $s$ to $s_d$. As before, if the firm wishes to maximize profits, it must produce that level of output at which $MR = MC$ [point $a$ in Figure 4(c)].

This is an important point of operation for each of a very large number of firms in pure competition. By producing this profit-maximizing level of output ($Q$ = six units) the firm earns a normal profit, and also produces at $P = MC = ATC$ minimum. The conditions of economic efficiency in using resources are met! In the first place, no economic profit is earned and no loss is incurred at the market-determined price of $475, which is just adequate to cover total cost for this firm (including a normal profit). Second, minimum ATC is achieved. Third, the value society attaches to resources ($MC = $475$) is equal to the worth that society attaches to the firm's product ($P = $475$) at this minimum unit-cost level of operation. In the simplest of terms, this situation suggests that resources are efficiently allocated by producing firms. Of course, if demand increased or decreased or something caused costs to change, the *efficiency equilibrium* would also be changed.

There are many factors which can cause a market economy to deviate from this ideal solution in which the best interests of producers (maximum profits) are perfectly compatible with technical efficiency in society ($P = ATC$ minimum, $P = MC$ and a normal profit is earned). Before we tackle such problems, however, let us see just how a competitive market economy adjusts to reach point $a$ described in Figure 4(c).

## c. COMPETITIVE MARKETS IN THE LONG RUN

Figures 3 and 4 showed that the special condition of efficient allocation of resources among producing business firms is only one of many possible levels at which firms may operate. The *coup de grâce* of our theory of the purely competitive firm is provided by the fact that by vying for consumer demand, firms are ultimately *forced* to operate at that level of output at which normal profits, minimum unit costs, and equally valued products and resources exist. But what guarantees the outcome? The answer is provided by competitive market supply and demand.

An economic profit under pure competition serves to attract new firms into the industry, causing supply to increase or shift rightward. An economic loss (less than a normal profit) encourages firms to leave the industry in hopes of earning a normal profit elsewhere. Under pure competition, the opportunity costs of using resources for any given endeavor set in motion market forces that bring about price and quantity adjustments leading to the optimum allocation of resources at normal profits and minimum unit cost, where the value of products and resources are equal. Under these conditions we can say that the economic system truly does operate efficiently. Let us see why.

### Industry Entry

Competitive industry and firm adjustments are illustrated in Figure 5, where we assume that the firm is initially in long-run equilibrium in a constant-cost industry.[3] An initial market price of $P$ is indicated by market supply schedule $s$ and market demand schedule $d$ in Figure 5(a). This equilibrium market price prevails for a hypothetical firm which is one of a large number of purely competitive producers. Figure 5(b) also depicts the cost structure for a firm, whose profit is maximized by producing $Q$ units at point $x$ where $MR = MC$. Given market price $P$, we can see that the firm in Figure 5(b) is earning a normal profit where $P = MC = ATC$ minimum.

Now assume that consumers decide for some reason that they prefer the product shown over some other good. A change in consumer taste results in market demand shifting rightward or upward from $d$ to $d_1$ in Figure 5(a), and a new equilibrium market price of $P_1$ is established. The new profit-maximizing quantity for the firm to produce at price $P_1$ is $Q_1$ units, denoted by $MR_1 = MC$ [point $y$ in Figure 5(b)]. The $ATC$ of producing $Q_1$ units is $z$, whereas price per unit is $y$. This amounts to an economic profit of $zy$ per

---

[3] These assumptions allow us to use the short-run supply and cost curves shown in Figure 5, where minimum long-run average cost remains at point $x$ in Figure 5(b). All firms are operating at optimal scale and constant costs are assured, since increased industry supply (from $s$ to $s_1$) does not affect resource prices and $ATC$ for a representative firm.

**FIGURE 5**  Pure Competition: Industry and Firm Adjustments to Demand Increase

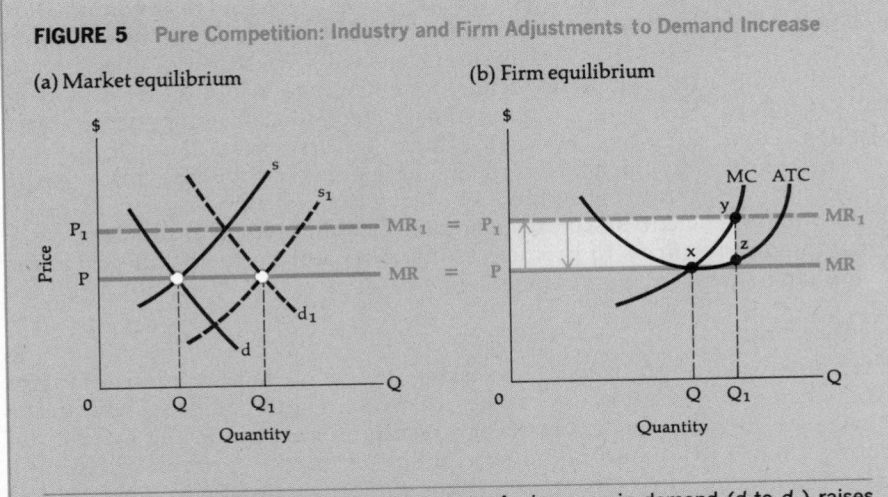

(a) Market equilibrium                    (b) Firm equilibrium

*Competitive Industry and Firm Adjustments.* An increase in demand ($d$ to $d_1$) raises equilibrium price from $P$ to $P_1$, and the firm earns an economic profit of $zy$ per unit as shown in (b). This encourages new entrants and an increase in supply ($s$ to $s_1$), which restores equilibrium price to $P$ at zero economic profit where $P = MC = ATC$ minimum.

unit, and the total economic profit is $zy$ times the output produced ($Q_1$ units). In short, a change in consumer taste results in increased demand for the product, the market-determined price increases, and an economic profit can now be earned by firms.

Unfortunately for the firm, life is not this easy in a purely competitive economy. Because of the new economic profit, some firms may expand plant capacity[4] and new entrants may be attracted to the industry. Entry into the industry is reflected by the shift in market supply from $s$ to $s_1$ which drives equilibrium market price down to $P$ once again [Figure 5(b)]. The firm finds its $MR = MC$ equilibrium reestablished at point $x$ and must follow the profit-maximizing rule of producing $Q$ units, in which case only a normal profit is earned. Each firm in the industry ends up once again producing at a point where $P = MC = ATC$ minimum, earning only a normal profit *in the long run*. This is the *best* the firm can do; producing firms *have* responded to the dictates of consumer demand; and, in a purely competitive economic system, this is also the point of *optimum efficiency*. We know this is true because the product ($P$) and the resources used to produce it ($MC$) are equally valued. It is obvious from examining Figure 5 that as long as the quest for profit functions spontaneously, the process of adjustment requires no external interference other than preservation of free entry into the competitive industry.

The cost structure of all firms in a purely competitive market need not be precisely like the firm depicted in Figure 5(b) at any given point in time. Suppose some firms have an $ATC$ curve which is higher (or lower) than

[4] Expanding firms are presumed to continue to operate on a horizontal portion of the long-run average cost curve equivalent to point $x$ in Figure 5(b).

others, perhaps because of a poorer (or better) technological combination of resources. Whatever the reason, firms that are most efficient have a profit advantage while firms that are least efficient will earn something less than a normal profit. This situation tends to encourage adoption of the most efficient known technology. The market system allocates more of its scarce resources to those firms which are more efficient (and these firms earn economic profits in the short run), while it denies productive resources to inefficient producers which ultimately leave the industry because of losses. Accordingly, efficient use of resources in combination with industry entry force competitive firms to produce at the low point on their unit-cost curve in the long run.

### Industry Exit

The same type of adjustment processes are set in motion in an industry experiencing a reduction in market demand. Figure 6 also illustrates a change in consumer taste, one which results in demand in the market declining from $d$ to $d_2$ and the initial equilibrium market price of $P$ declining to $P_2$. The firm now finds that *losses are minimized* by producing where $MR = MC$ at $Q_2$ units of output rather than at $Q$ units. Production of $Q_2$ units of output allows the firm to cover total variable cost and a small portion of total fixed cost. The firm experiences a loss of $zy$ per unit [the total loss is the gold area of Figure 6(b)]. This is a smaller loss by about one-half than the fixed-cost loss at $Q_2$ units of output. While $P_2$ is inadequate to cover all costs, the loss is minimized in the short run by producing, even though the firm cannot sustain this loss in the long run. Losses are not a viable set of circumstances for a firm in a competitive market system, be-

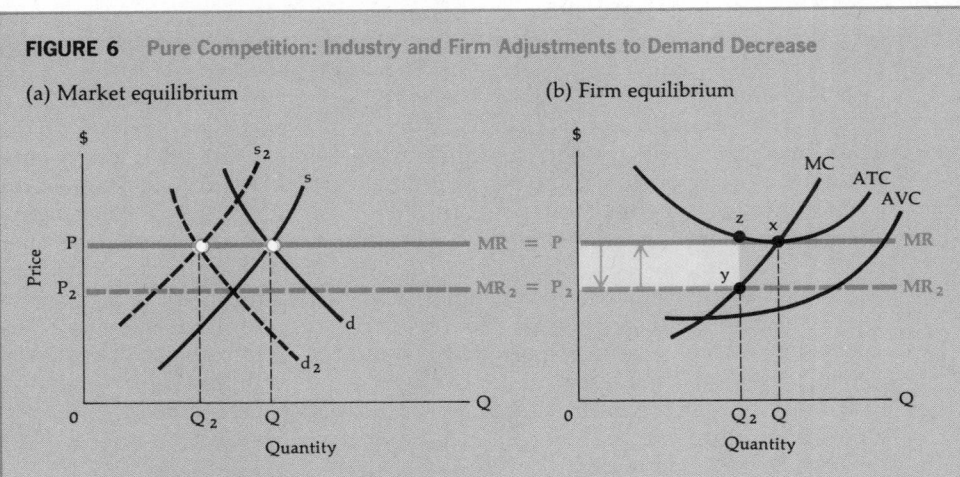

**FIGURE 6**   Pure Competition: Industry and Firm Adjustments to Demand Decrease

*Competitive Industry and Firm Adjustments.* Following a decline in demand from $d$ to $d_2$, price falls to $P_2$ and firms earn less than a normal profit as shown in (b). The per unit loss is $zy$ which encourages the least efficient firms to leave the industry. Market supply declines from $s$ to $s_2$, and price rises again to $P$, restoring a normal profit to firms remaining in the industry, each of which maximizes profit by producing $Q$ units at a price of $P = MC = ATC$ minimum in (b).

cause less than a normal profit is being earned and the opportunity cost of a sustained loss will force the financially less able, the weaker, and the least efficient firms to leave the industry. As a result, market supply will shift leftward or decline from $s$ to $s_2$, establishing a new equilibrium market price of $P$. Those firms capable of withstanding short-run adversity will once again earn a normal and maximum profit at point $x$ where $P = MC = ATC$ minimum and thus will earn a normal profit *in the long run.*

## The Breakdown of Competition

In short, the firm in pure competition produces at the most efficient cost level for society ($P = MC$) at the same time that it maximizes its own profit (or minimizes a loss) at $P$(and $MR$) $= MC$. The price-directed market system under competitive conditions responds to consumer demand, allocates resources efficiently in production, and achieves an equilibrium position at which a normal profit is earned by all firms as each producer pursues his own profit objectives. Generally speaking, the purely competitive market system rewards and penalizes firms for efficiency and inefficiency. Even though producers and consumers pursue their individual profit interest, the wizardry of the competitive market system is that it *organizes the private interests of all economic participants in a manner that uses resources efficiently from a social point of view.*

Under certain circumstances, prevailing cost conditions in the long run may be incompatible with a competitive market structure. If firms in an industry experience decreasing long-run average costs because of internal economies of scale when all resources are variable, the level of demand in a market may be insufficient to support the "large number" of firms competitive markets require. When decreasing cost curves prevail, there is no long-run competitive equilibrium level of output, since there is no minimum point on the long-run average cost curve consistent with competitive markets. Those firms in the best position to first achieve the economies of scale leading to decreasing costs expand their output knowing that their costs will decline, and ultimately competition in the industry diminishes. One, a few, or several firms are thus able to drive other competitors out of the industry and gradually the market turns into an imperfectly competitive one in which the remaining firms are capable of exerting control over product price. In many American industries, falling long-run cost curves do prevail for the relevant size range of firms, and competitive markets cannot survive, as indeed they have failed to do in the steel, automobile, and computer industries. The existence of dominant firms in some industries suggests that competition either has not been maintained or never developed for one reason or another—a subject we will return to in Chapter 17.

## D. INTERIM REVIEW OF THE COMPETITIVE MODEL OF AN ECONOMIC SYSTEM

We should pause here for a preliminary review of what we have accomplished by studying pure competition. We have tarried long in the model world analyzing supply, demand, prices, costs, and resource allocation for a theoretical firm which on no count is found in the real world. We have done this for the purpose of understanding important economic relationships that do exist in the real world. At present our model serves one purpose: It is a theoretical anchor—a road map which is just beginning to assume a form that can direct us, provided we continue to recognize pure competition as a model and not as a description of reality.

Generally speaking, economists agree that a purely competitive economic system leads to the technically efficient allocation of resources, although there are several notable qualifications attached to this conclusion (e.g., the maldistribution of income). *Moreover, the competitive model is predicated upon the normative presumption that least-cost efficiency is a worthy goal.* Thus, it is appropriate here to summarize the strengths and identify the limitations of a price-directed market system.

## Strengths of a Competitive Market

The chief strength of pure competition is the efficient allocation of resources, including its ability to adjust to market changes in an environment that preserves and encourages producer freedom and consumer sovereignty.

The goods and services produced in a competitive system are governed by market demand in relation to production costs and supply. Supply and demand determine an equilibrium price for goods and for resources. In the purely competitive system, output is rationed according to the willingness and ability of consumers to divert wealth claims (e.g., dollars) to output, and thereby to utilize productive and scarce resources. Consumers obtain wealth claims by selling scarce resources in this same competitive market. Firms produce those products that consumers want in quantities that yield a maximum (yet normal) profit. This situation *appears* to be consistent with the desires of consumers, producers, and society at large.

Price competition between firms and free industry entry and exit assure society of the elimination of any economic profit in the long run—again a desirable state of affairs from the point of view of "least-cost" efficiency. Use of the most efficient known technology results in utilizing a combination of resources and adopting a scale of operation that guides firms to minimum unit costs. Firms that fail to attain lowest possible unit costs are at a profit disadvantage that must be remedied in the long run either by leaving that market or by adopting the most efficient technology known. Moreover, the competitive market system is a form of economic organization that is responsive to a dynamic economy. The combined forces of changing consumer tastes and technology resulted in the declining use of coal as a household fuel. Hula hoops, the Hudson Hornet, and spats have also fallen victim to the market.

Price and marginal-cost inequality cannot be sustained in the long run as long as pure competition operates. The producer, the supplier, and the consumer are all encouraged to further their own self-interests so that *a competitive equilibrium* prevails, where society's value of the product ($P$) is precisely equal to its value of the resources used in production ($MC$). If producers stop short of this profit-maximizing level of output (e.g., if $P$ is greater than $MC$), a scarcity of output will exist because society places a higher value on the output than on the inputs used to produce the last unit of output. Output will then expand and more resources will be allocated to the product. On the other hand, if firms produce at a level such that $MC$ is greater than $P$, an excess quantity of the product will be produced, resources will be overallocated to it, and contractionary market adjustments will drive $P$ down. Were it not for several rather serious omissions in these conclusions, Nirvana could be said to exist.

## Limitations of the "Model" Market System

There are a variety of limitations to the above description of a competitive economic system, each of which deserves a much more thorough analysis than is possible here. We can, however, briefly identify these problem areas and give some examples which will be followed up in later chapters. Any final assessment of the competitive system of economic organization in a real-world context must weigh these limitations against the advantages of consumer sovereignty and producer efficiency allegedly inherent in an unbridled market system—a task we shall also concern ourselves with in subsequent chapters. Let us next consider the limitations to our efficiency conclusions.

### CONSTRAINED TECHNOLOGY AND SCALE

The purely competitive market system may not entail using the most efficient production techniques. Even though we have just argued that firms operate with the most efficient combination of resources at the minimum point on their unit-cost curve, this may or may not be true. The *most* efficient technological combination of resources may require only a few very large producers, if potential internal economies of scale are to be realized, and this situation could be inconsistent with a large number of firms operating in a purely competitive market. As an obvious illustration, consider the economies of scale potentially available to the telephone companies or other public utility corporations. Pure competition is simply not feasible in relation to the scale, technology, and capital-resource requirements in the industry. If pure competition did exist, all firms would be operating at a point well above minimum $LRAC$, each producer being much too small to realize inherent scale economies. Moreover, the chaos of several competing telephone and electrical lines in one city could be highly undesirable.

One further point: The late Joseph A. Schumpeter, an astute observer of the American economy, believed that big business and the concentration of a few firms operating under conditions vastly different from those of pure competition may have contributed in very significant ways to modern standards of living by generating innovations and technological changes, some of which are revealed by the achievement of scale economies. Schumpeter alleged that *imperfectly* competitive business firms have contributed to technological advances and economic growth in ways that very probably would not have occurred under pure competition. While many dispute his assessment, it is important to recognize that the claim of efficient technology under competitive market conditions is by no means a settled issue.

A competitive economic system may not entail the most efficient techniques of production if cost-saving technological changes are discouraged because an economic profit cannot be sustained in the long run under pure competition. If the rewards of an economic profit are not available, inventions requiring heavy research and development expenditures or large capital outlays could be retarded. Consequently, the notion that a purely competitive market system may retard technological advances and economic growth while resulting in higher unit costs than might otherwise exist cannot be completely discarded. We simply do not have enough solid information at present to evaluate these issues.

## STANDARDIZED PRODUCTS

Another characteristic of the purely competitive market system which may be questionable is the requirement (and vagueness) of the concept of standardized products. It may be just as well that the assumption of identical goods in pure competition is rarely encountered. Even when this condition is approximated (as in the case of aspirin), the producer (or consumer) may perceive real or imaginary differences in the product. In short, it is virtually impossible to identify a standardized product and define distinct markets. If consumer choices were seriously limited, most coeds would find a purely competitive market environment rather dull and unimaginative. What some regard as creative designs and improvements in existing products might well be stifled. Remember, however, that in a price system, product differentiation comes at a "price" of something other than pure competition.

## THE "LONG" LONG RUN

In a purely competitive market system, the long run may be too long and onerous because economic adjustments do not necessarily occur easily or quickly. Underemployed farmers and unemployed Appalachian coal miners are symptomatic of the possible destructive effects of competition. Structural unemployment due to technological displacement may be a costly and capricious solution to the efficient allocation of resources and may be as undesirable as union featherbedding or policies that restrict entry into the medical profession. Adjustments to declining demand entail the reallocation of resources; yet, resources are not as fully informed, mobile, and receptive to change as economic theory assumes. The cost of reversing occupational decisions may be great to participants in a dynamic and sometimes frivolous market system. The havoc that competitive reallocation can create for numerous interest groups may or may not be dealt with in a manner deemed "appropriate" under pure competition. While equitable solutions to these types of problems are not easy to identify, they are needed if the full economic benefits of a market economy are to be realized.

## COMPETITION BREEDS IMPERFECTION

In one sense, the competitive market system tends to sow the seeds of its own destruction. Man, being both imaginative and reasonably selfish, will seek alternatives to the rigorous normal-profit-only doctrine that would prevail under the competitive market system. The search for profit may well revert to a quest that limits competition and thus restricts the economic choice and freedom of others. Even the most unimaginative economic participant recognizes that one way of sustaining economic profits is to accumulate economic power and to use it to limit competition in the marketplace. Corporations, labor unions, professional associations, and even government agencies use institutional power tactics to protect themselves—in many instances from competition itself. In short, the competitive market system is "Darwinian" in nature in that survival of the fittest does prevail, and those threatened by such a system may well decide to achieve better control of their environmental discomfort. Generally speaking, such behavior is viewed as unacceptable, as existing antitrust laws and labor legislation suggest. Unfortunately, many forms and excesses of institutionalized economic power are seldom brought to the full attention of the public, and very often restriction of such power is uneven, depending upon the interest groups involved.

## THE REALITY OF IMPERFECTIONS

The real world is imperfect. Because the assumptions and characteristics of pure competition are unrealized on many counts, it is not possible to conclude without reservation that a market economy is the best way to allocate resources. Competition is fine as far as a model goes, but we do have to start releasing some assumptions. The basic theoretical apparatus of supply and demand allocating resources efficiently crumbles *if* such assumptions as maximization or mobility are in error. Knowledge is incomplete, imperfect, and uncertain for producers, firms, consumers, and resource owners. Mankind has created vestiges of authority and power, particularly where the distributive burden of economic scarcity is concerned. Farmers, union members, corporations, universities, and innumerable other groups *want*— and collectively band together to acquire—the requisite power to achieve their perceived wants.

## IMPERSONAL MARKETS: DISTRIBUTION AND SOCIAL GOODS

A competitive market system is impersonal in the distribution of income and may not accurately reflect the welfare of all consumers. Because the market system is price-directed and profit-oriented, it responds only to those needs and changes that are backed up by wealth—by dollar votes cast by persons who can purchase goods and services by virtue of having adequate incomes. Personal resources may be insufficient to allow adequate participation in the education of disadvantaged children or the construction of ghetto recreation facilities. These needs may require recognition, just as a college education and vast national parks were made available to middle-class Americans. Other people may not have enough funds to acquire proper medical assistance and services. Imperfect consumer knowledge may result in the use of substandard meats or poisonous chemicals, or in accepting deceptive and exorbitant interest-rate charges. Other segments of society (e.g., the mentally ill) may be incapable of making decisions in their own best interest and may require protection. Moreover, certain social goods used by all participants in an economic system (such as schools, roads, and public hospitals) may be very desirable and yet may not be adequately supplied by private enterprise in a competitive environment—or in the real world, for that matter. National defense and polio or smallpox vaccines represent valuable social goods that the purely competitive market system does not supply in adequate quantities. The impersonal characteristics of the price-directed market system: (a) may result in a maldistribution of both income and economic opportunity (given some concept of justice and equity), and (b) may also distort the need for social goods which are often ignored or simply undervalued in a competitive market environment.

The real-world economic system may not fully reflect all costs of production. The forces of a competitive environment require that producers assume only those costs that they must cover, and these costs may not fully reflect the full social costs of resource utilization. If a productive enterprise does avoid costs that it imposes on society, an otherwise competitive environment misallocates resources. Some current unaccounted for social costs—such as waste materials dumped into streams, air pollution, poorly planned and uncontrolled urban development, and stripped timber and mineral lands—are not fully represented in private marginal-cost curves. Indeed, the price-directed market system may *encourage* social costs—especially when a cutthroat competitive environment is imposed upon producers. If marginal cost fails to reflect full social costs, misallocation of resources occurs just as if supply, demand, and prices fail to reflect the true social benefits attached to social goods.

## THE PLURALITY OF ECONOMIC WELFARE

In summary, as was noted in the introductory chapters of this book, the welfare of a society in economic terms may extend far beyond the single objective of efficiency in using resources.

Economic efficiency, yes, but the competing objectives that cannot be ignored are: the distribution of income; adequate social goods (schools, parks, and hospitals); economic security, justice, and freedom; balanced economic power and democratic resolution of economic conflict; and economic growth and stability. Indeed, some of the most pervasive and difficult questions arising in economics are, What are our goal priorities and what "should be" society's goals and values?

Ultimately, one question must be confronted when we have recognized both the strengths and the limitations of the market system, namely: How much and what kind of modification of private markets is desirable? This, of course, is a question that most certainly demands a careful analysis—not the all-too-brief summary of virtues and limitations that we have presented here. It should be apparent that more must be known if we are to deal effectively with this kind of economic issue.

## REVIEW

### Summary

1. In an enterprise economy, pure competition as *one* possible form of market is characterized by a large number of sellers; a standardized product; freedom to enter or leave the industry; and mobile, informed resources and entrepreneurs. Pure competition means that each firm is a price taker facing a perfectly elastic demand curve. It is a theoretical model which is useful in studying many economic issues related to the efficient allocation of resources. Three indicators of economic efficiency in the use of resources are: (a) a normal profit, (b) price = lowest possible unit cost, and (c) price = the value of resources used in production.

2. The firm in pure competition determines how much output to produce by maximizing profit. Maximum profit is achieved by producing that level of output at which the difference between total revenue and cost is

largest, a level of output also determined by producing up to that quantity of output at which marginal revenue ($MR$) = marginal cost ($MC$).

3. A competitive firm may earn an economic profit in the short run by producing a level of output at which $MR = MC$. An economic profit, however, attracts competition, increases market supply, lowers product price ($P$), and restores normal profit conditions in the *long run* at an equilibrium output at which $P$(and $MR$) = $MC$ = $ATC$ minimum.

4. Firms that do not earn at least a normal short-run profit leave the industry. Market supply contracts, price rises, and a normal profit is restored to firms remaining in the industry in the long run where producers end up operating at $P$(and $MR$) = $MC$ = $ATC$ minimum.

5. In the long run, competitive firms are forced to a level of output at which costs per unit are at a minimum. This process is the result of profit-maximizing behavior. Competitive firms seek to obtain the most efficient technological combination of all resources, as they must because of competitive market pressures. At this efficient level of output, society's value of outputs (as measured by $P$) is equal to the value of the last inputs used (as measured by $MC$).

6. The strengths of the competitive market system are the efficient use of limited resources and the preservation of a high degree of consumer and producer freedom. Competition results in the maximum output being produced in a society in which wants are unlimited and resources are scarce.

7. The limitations of the competitive market system are: (*a*) possible constrained growth and technological advance, (*b*) some limits to consumer choice because of standardized products, (*c*) ruinous long-run competitive adjustments, (*d*) the natural tendency toward imperfectly competitive behavior, (*e*) the impersonality of the price system and inadequate recognition of social goods, (*f*) the failure of private markets to account for social costs, and (*g*) the plurality of economic welfare goals, only one of which is economic efficiency.

## Identify the Following Concepts and Terms

- four market structures
- $P = MC$
- normal profits
- competitive demand for the firm compared to market demand
- efficient resource allocation
- $MR = MC$ rule
- $P = ATC$ minimum
- loss minimization
- firm adjustments to short-run loss minimization
- $MC$ at and above minimum $AVC$

## Questions to Answer

1. In the graph on page 382: (*a*) Draw total revenue for a firm selling 1–10 units of output at a price of $55 each. Why is the demand curve in this problem that of a purely competitive firm? (*b*) Draw a short-run cost curve that reflects $100 of fixed cost, some economic profit, and diminishing returns.

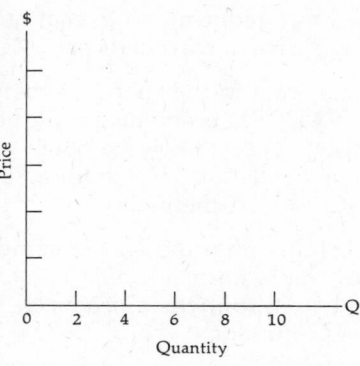

2. The illustration below shows three alternative prices all of which exceed minimum average variable cost *except* $P_1$. Explain: (a) how and why a firm adjusts output to each price in the short run, and (b) what industry or market adjustments prevail in the long run at $P_1$, $P_2$, and $P_3$.

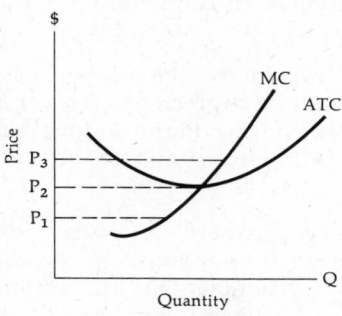

3. Critically evaluate the statement: "No authority or force 'should' intervene in the American market economy because competition assures society of the best possible allocation of resources."

# CHAPTER 17
# Imperfect
# Competition

In the model market economy developed in Chapter 16 we saw that scarce resources were most efficiently utilized by purely competitive firms that were forced to be price takers. This economic Garden of Eden furnishes a static standard to which other market structures can be compared in studying the achievement of economic efficiency in the allocation of resources. Our model of pure competition is just that—a model which needs to be modified because imperfections are always present in real-world economies. This chapter is concerned with the use of market power, and the impact of monopoly on the efficient allocation of resources in product markets.

The term "imperfect competition" is used generally to describe all degrees of imperfections in a market. Imperfect market structures arise from the existence of firms which have some ability to influence market price, and it is useful to make a distinction among three types of such markets: (a) monopoly, (b) monopolistic competition, and (c) oligopoly. Part A introduces imperfect competition, and pricing and resource allocation are discussed under monopoly (Part B), monopolistic competition (Part C), and oligopoly (Part D). A brief introduction to the public-policy implications of the theory of imperfect competition (Part E) concludes this chapter.

## A. THE NATURE OF IMPERFECT COMPETITION

The simplistic grandeur of the competitive-market model can be helpful as well as misleading. The competitive model of markets is helpful in two ways: It establishes an explanatory framework for an economic system which is loosely competitive in certain respects, and it provides a useful basis for identifying resource misallocation. However, this model can be dangerous if the ways in which it diverges from reality are not fully appreciated. Whether reputable economists ever thought pure competition was a full explanation of the economic organization of any society is doubtful. The fact is, today pure competition does not correspond to the real world, even though the competitive model has influenced the way many citizens view the American economic system. Clinging to antiquated concepts of competition and freedom from government intervention when time, technology, and economic power have altered the old order is as patently in error as is a blind demand for total government control resulting from a modest breakdown in the economic system. Comparison of the real and model worlds reveals that:

1. Most of the American economy relies on the market system as a

general form of economic organization, but in a partial and imperfect context.

2. A meaningful portion of economic activity in the United States can be compared to the competitive model in approximate terms, even though there is no one industry or market which meets the strict conditions and assumptions specified in the model of a perfectly competitive market.

3. The tools of analysis we have developed, as well as the theoretical framework of pure competition, are necessary to evaluate economic imperfections and problems in the real world.

*Monopoly* consists of only one producer who has no direct rivals whatsoever, an extreme as rare as pure competition. Because there is only one firm, the monopolist cannot be deprived of customers because someone else offers a similar product at a lower price. Moreover, in such a market, where the monopolist is the sole producer of a product for which there is no close substitute, entry barriers also exist. Outside of markets in which government has established legal monopolies (as in communications), pure monopoly is rarely encountered. However, as in the case of pure competition, certain markets approximate this extreme, and the analytical apparatus of monopoly is useful for identifying resource-allocation problems which we will have more to say about later.

Even though monopoly is a rarity, other forms of imperfect competition approaching this extreme are common. Both monopolistic competition and oligopoly are forms of imperfect product markets that are quite typical of firms in the American economy. Examples of imperfectly competitive markets in the American economy are the aluminum industry, railroad transportation, automobile manufacturing, petroleum, and steel production. In markets characterized by *monopolistic competition* a large number of firms exist, and no firm can fully control price. Monopolistic competition is typically characterized by differentiated products, relatively easy entry into the industry, and absence of collusion between producers. On the other hand, *oligopolistic markets* are those dominated by a few firms supplying all or nearly all of the output in an industry. Oligopolistic firms are dependent upon the acts and decisions of other oligopolists and may, therefore, behave in such a way as to anticipate the actions of their rivals. Oligopolistic markets may be characterized by either uniform or differentiated products, but entry into the industry is restricted. Barriers to entry sometimes arise, for example, when a firm acquires a technological advantage. Oligopolistic firms often engage in collusion by setting a common price, as well as by dividing up markets.

Concern over imperfect competition results from the ease with which imperfectly competitive firms may avoid the controlling forces of competition that lead to the efficient allocation of limited economic resources. The absence of rivalry among producers results in less output than the maximum possible with a given stock of resources and technology, a situation which causes society to endure unnecessary scarcity. Imperfections in product markets can also lead to a different composition of output from that which might be desired by society. Furthermore, imperfect competition may result in raising existing entry barriers into an industry. In comparison to pure competition, imperfectly competitive firms generally charge higher prices and earn economic profits, while producing less output—although these outcomes are not guaranteed by any means. Finally, and perhaps most important, imperfect competition grants power to favored firms, and this sheltered position may be used benevolently or it may be used to redistribute income to those enjoying market power. The very existence of market power distorts the forces of supply and demand and is inconsistent with the notion that consumer sovereignty is a basis of the market-oriented economic system.

## Market Power in Imperfect Competition

The root of the problem of market power is twofold: First, market power in product (or resource) markets may be wasteful and, if inefficient use of resources exists, a society produces less output than it could. Second, placing the privileges of market power in the hands of a few firms lacks legitimacy. Power to control the economic destiny of others should have some positive basis for existing in a free society, as it does in certain instances involving elected governments.

Under monopoly, market power is technically complete, whereas firms producing under oligopoly or monopolistic competition may enjoy some degree of market power because of their ability to control a portion of the product market. Even though a firm may be the only producer of a product (a pure monopolist), nearly all products have some substitute. Water is not a very good substitute for beer, and horse-drawn carriages are not good substitutes for automobiles, but if hypothetical producers of beer and cars set prices too high, some consumers may opt for these "poor" substitute goods or they may just save and not spend. Parking on many college campuses is sometimes "controlled" through a form of market power and, as the annual fee is increased, students substitute bicycles or simply "leg it" in deference to the price of parking. Of course, if a political dictatorship is strictly enforced, the absolute in economic power is possible. The King of Id could order consumers to buy the ale and spears produced in his brewery and munitions plant, just as a university could order all students to pay the athletic fee or live in campus housing—usually at the "calculated" risk of a revolt in Id as well as in academia. Realistically, market power is usually not an absolute; rather it is a relative matter describing the *degree* to which a seller is insulated from market competition.

Market power may exist on the buyer or the supplier side of a market. The term *monopoly* denotes a seller's market power, whereas *monopsony* refers to a buyer's market power. Automotive manufacturers in the United States, for example, have monopoly market power in the sale of automobiles, since there are only three major domestic firms. On the other hand, in many small university or college towns, if the university is a large employer of the area labor force, it can have monopsony market power in hiring manpower or in buying other goods and services.

Another important distinction to recognize with regard to market power is that it may exist in either product *or* resource markets. The electrical equipment and automotive industries as well as the Teamsters' Union and the American Medical Association illustrate market power in product markets and resource markets, respectively. Market power can assume the forms shown below. The matrix of market-power possibilities is expanded even further once we separate imperfect competition into the three specific market structures of monopoly, oligopoly, and monopolistic competition.

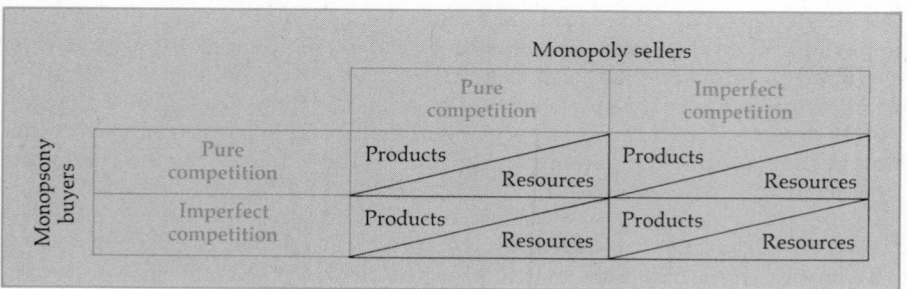

While we shall have a good deal more to say about the development of market power in the American economy later, in this chapter we will focus on the resource-allocation impact of market power in a model economy.

### Characteristics of Imperfect Competition

There are four general characteristics of imperfect competition: product differentiation, product promotion, entry and exit barriers, and price control by firms.

1. Product differentiation. One characteristic of imperfect competition is the existence of a differentiated product. Sometimes the differentiation is real and at others it is contrived in the eyes of the buyer. *Differentiation of products* means that producers distinguish the brand, quality, or ingredients of their products. Product differentiation correctly implies that the product or service of each firm is unique in certain ways, and that the products of other firms are not perfect substitutes. Differentiation thus allows producers to have an individual price policy. Consequently, the firm may be in a position to make either a price or a quantity decision—not just the latter, as was true in the purely competitive model.

2. Product promotion. Firms in an imperfect market also distinguish their output in part through promotional expenditures on qualitative differences. Depending upon the degree and character of the imperfect market, producers engage in advertising to promote alleged and real qualitative differences in hopes of convincing consumers that their product is unique from and superior in one way or another to the products of other firms. If it is successful, product promotion tends to make the demand curve *for each firm* become more inelastic and increase or shift rightward. That is, a higher price can be charged for *each* possible quantity depicted for an imperfectly competitive firm.

3. Entry barriers. Imperfect competition also may be typified by the existence of barriers which make it difficult or impossible for other firms to enter the industry. Large financial requirements, highly technical capital resources, patent laws, and exclusive ownership or control of limited supplies of raw materials are different types of entry barriers. When they are combined with product differentiation and product promotion, entry barriers help insulate an imperfectly competitive firm from competition. The tendency to advertise and differentiate products and the existence of entry barriers are characteristic of a large portion of the American economy. Thus, much of the economy is typified by monopoly market power and is quite forcefully distinguished from a system of pure competition.

4. Price control. The above three characteristics of imperfect competition are complemented by and often lead to the existence of limited numbers of firms in relation to market size. Although the differences between one firm (monopoly), a "few" firms (oligopoly), and many firms (monopolistic competition) are important, there are common characteristics here also. The important feature of imperfect competition is not the absolute number of firms, but rather the *extent* or degree to which firms can control or influence market price through their decisions. A small, localized market serviced by four or five medium-sized grocery stores, for example, may not appear to be a form of imperfect competition, but such firms may very well behave in ways comparable to the few large steel or automobile corporations. In pure competition, firms are so numerous that one firm *cannot* affect the market price, whereas in monopoly the firm has perfect control over price, since it is the only supplier for the market. Oligopoly and monopolistic competition involve less price control by the firm. The crucial consequence of imperfect competition as a general form of market structure is price control—demand is not perfectly elastic to such firms, as it is in pure competition. This fact has several important implications.

### Demand Under Imperfect Competition

Demand in pure competition is compared to demand in imperfect competition in Figure 1 to illustrate how imperfectly competitive firms fail to allocate resources efficiently. The figure shows price as well as total revenue and marginal revenue for a competitive and for an imperfectly competitive firm operating as a monopolist. Unlike the horizontal demand curve discussed in Chapter 16 and repeated again in Figure 1(a) for a competitive firm, the monopolist has a down-sloping demand curve shown as schedule *d* in Figure 1(b). The consequences of market imperfections—less output than would prevail under competitive conditions and a higher product price —can be traced to the nature of marginal revenue under imperfect competition.

Under conditions of monopoly, the firm's demand curve is down-sloping, as the data of Figure 1(b) show, because the firm *is the industry*. The monopolist can increase sales only by decreasing prices to all buyers, which is what the usual market demand schedule for a product indicates.[1] Consequently, imperfectly competitive firms have a price-setting ability. Second, and also very important, when the imperfectly competitive firm attempts to make more output available, product price is depressed along the market (and firm) demand schedule *d* in Figure 1(b). As we shall see, marginal revenue is thus less than product price, since the monopolist sells *all* units of output offered in the market at successively lower prices.

### COMPETITIVE DEMAND, PRICE, AND QUANTITY

Purely competitive firms are forced to charge a price of $P_c = \$5$, also equal to the marginal revenue (MR) for the firm denoted by Figure 1(a). Profits are maximized by equating marginal revenue and marginal cost (MR =

---

[1] Ignored for the moment is the special case of discriminatory pricing. The extreme case of perfect price discrimination depends upon the seller being able to charge *each* buyer the particular price he would be willing to pay, in which case the entire area under a demand schedule represents total receipts for the seller.

**FIGURE 1**   Demand and Output for the Firm: Pure and Imperfect Competition

(a) Demand for one competitive firm

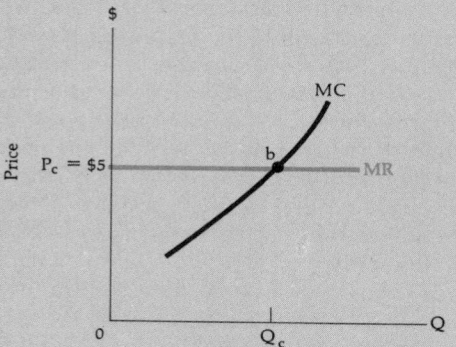

(b) Demand under imperfect competition

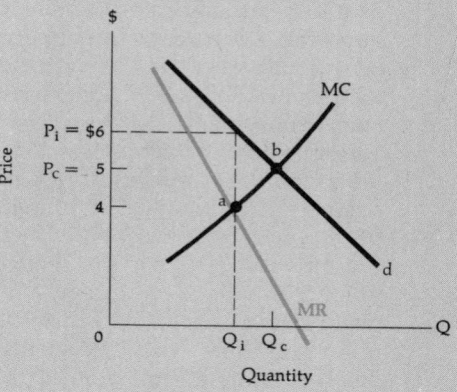

| Competitive firm |  |  |  |
|---|---|---|---|
| Price (P) | Quantity (Q) | Total revenue (TR) | Marginal revenue (MR) |
| $5 | 1 | $ 5 | |
| | | | + $5 |
| 5 | 2 | 10 | |
| | | | + 5 |
| 5 | 3 | 15 | |
| | | | + 5 |
| 5 | 4 | 20 | |
| | | | + 5 |
| 5 | 5 | 25 | |
| | | | + 5 |
| 5 | 6 | 30 | |

| Imperfectly competitive firm |  |  |  |
|---|---|---|---|
| Price (P) | Quantity (Q) | Total revenue (TR) | Marginal revenue (MR) |
| $8 | 1 | $ 8 | |
| | | | + $6 |
| 7 | 2 | 14 | |
| | | | + 4 |
| 6 | 3 | 18 | |
| | | | + 2 |
| 5 | 4 | 20 | |
| | | | 0 |
| 4 | 5 | 20 | |
| | | | − 2 |
| 3 | 6 | 18 | |

*Competitive and Imperfectly Competitive Demand.* Maximum-profit production occurs where $MR = MC$ no matter what market structure is involved. In competition (a), the entire market determines $P_c$, and the firm's demand curve is perfectly elastic where $P_c = MR$. In imperfect competition (b), the firm's demand curve is down-sloping because the firm's output *can* affect product price. Thus, $MR$ is below $d$. Producing at $MR = MC$ ($Q_i$ units) results in a product price of $P_i$ which is higher than $MC$.

$MC$, or each firm produces $Q_c$ units). The examples of the preceding chapter showed that a purely competitive firm's price is governed by market demand and supply, which set one market price ($5) for all firms. Now let us see what happens if this same market is monopolized, assuming that the newly created monopolist maximizes profits and experiences no change in costs.

### PRICE AND OUTPUT UNDER IMPERFECT COMPETITION

If costs remain unchanged, schedule $MC$ now pertains to a monopolist producer. Down-sloping demand curve $d$ in Figure 1(b) now becomes the imperfectly competitive firm's demand schedule, implying that the firm can make a price decision in selling a quantity previously sold by *all* competitive firms.

First, notice that the *MR* curve under imperfect competition lies to the left and below the firm's demand curve as shown in Figure 1(b) because the firm must charge less to sell more. Marginal revenue is equal to price in pure competition because the firm need not cut its price to sell more output. Selling one more unit of output adds an amount to total revenue just equal to price in Figure 1(a), which is what the elastic demand curve shows, and profit is maximized where *MR* (which is *P*) = *MC*. Under imperfect market conditions *P* and *MR* are not equal, however. Even though selling one more unit—a third—adds to total revenue, a lower price on the previous two units takes a little away from total revenue. Since *MR* is the sum of *two* effects, it will be less than price. Consider what happens if the imperfectly competitive firm lowers price from $6 (where it sells three units of output) to a price of $5 (the sale of four units) in Figure 1(b). As price is lowered, the change in total revenue or *MR* is $2 ($5 × 4 = $20 *less* $6 × 3 = $18). Even though the new price is $5 as shown in Figure 1(b), the addition to total revenue of *MR* = $2 is smaller than product price. To sell more output, the monopolist moves down a demand curve and gets a lower price *on all* units sold. This must be done according to demand schedule *d*, which indicates that consumers will purchase four units at a price of $5 per unit. Thus, in lowering price to sell more output, a lower price is charged for all quantities sold and marginal revenue declines more rapidly than price.

Second, note that *MR* = 0 at some point in Figure 1(b). Why? Because elasticity of demand = 1. Total revenue rises as price declines in the elastic range of a demand schedule, as Chapter 14 explained. At the point of unitary elasticity, total revenue is a maximum and *MR* is zero since the revenue-increasing effect of a positive percentage change in quantity is just offset by the revenue-reducing effect of a negative percentage change in price. Any further reduction in price beyond the point of unitary elasticity will result in *less* total revenue. *MR* becomes negative, as Figure 1(b) illustrates, because demand turns inelastic at that point at which *MR* is zero.

Finally, the divergence of price and marginal revenue in imperfect competition is of substantial importance to resource allocation. Essentially, the profit-maximizing firm shown in Figure 1(b) does not make price–quantity decisions that result in resources being allocated in an efficient manner. Unlike the competitive firm, *P* and *MR* are not equal for an imperfectly competitive firm. Because *MC* intersects *MR* from below, the profit-maximizing firm facing a downward-sloping demand curve *will always* produce a level of output at which *P* exceeds *MC*. To maximize profit, the imperfectly competitive firm of Figure 1(b) determines equilibrium output and price by setting *MR* = *MC* at point *a* in Figure 1(b) and charging a price of $P_i$ = $6. All competitive firms equate *MR* and *MC* [point *b* in Figure 1(b)] at the going market price, $P_c$. In short, when only $Q_i$ units are produced, society places greater value on the product (measured by $P_i$ = $6) than on the resources used in production (measured by *MC* = $4 at point *a*) and a scarcity of output prevails in society in comparison to the competitive quantity $Q_c$. Moreover, the monopolist also charges a higher price than would prevail under pure competition.

There are numerous causes of imperfect competition. First, many product markets are less than purely competitive because of location and transportation factors. The housewife typically does not travel from Ohio to Iowa for less costly hardware items, groceries, or clothing. Indeed, locational advantages often prevail within relatively confined geographic areas. The "corner" drugstore, a service station on the interstate highway, or the pizza shop immediately adjacent to campus reflect imperfections of the locational variety. Second, many consumers lack full knowledge of price and product characteristics—another factor which contributes to imperfect markets. Third, differing degrees of market power may persist because market rigidities and uncertainties abound in the real world. Resources are not perfectly mobile because it requires time and sometimes expense to adjust to a dynamic market characterized by risk and uncertainty. Firms may therefore advertise and otherwise promote their products to achieve "insulation" from whimsical changes in consumer tastes.

Many experts regard barriers to entry into an industry as a major reason for the existence of market power in an economy. Monopoly requires complete barriers to entry, and partial entry barriers can lead to varying degrees of partial monopoly as found in monopolistic competition or oligopoly.

In some instances barriers to entry to an industry are the result of scale economies. Where technology is conducive to large size relative to total market demand, a firm's long-run average cost schedule declines over a wide range of output, as we know. If firms are to achieve lower unit costs, they must be large-scale producers. New small firms that attempt to enter such an industry are not likely to survive unless they can achieve the size and market needed to allow scale economies in production. Survival and achieving a given size also will be more difficult if financial requirements are prohibitive. The automobile, steel, aluminum, and electronic computer industries all typify situations in which high financial requirements, large size, and scale economies are important; thus, it is not surprising that a few firms dominate these markets. Barriers to entry into an industry may also result from patent rights being granted inventors for exclusive processes. Under American patent laws, exclusive rights are granted for a period of 17 years in order to protect firms and individuals who contribute to technological advances. Two of the many companies that have benefited from patent rights include Polaroid and General Motors. Patent laws are designed to encourage research and development, but they also have the effect of creating a potential barrier to entry that can lead to monopoly power. Another type of entry barrier may result from control of essential raw materials. Initially control of this kind was significant in the development of the aluminum and copper industries. In order to discourage entry, existing firms in an industry may also follow cutthroat competitive policies in the short run. Policies of this type represent an entry barrier that can discourage potential competitors and drive existing firms out of the industry as well. Finally, there are economic benefits derived from being in the industry which may strengthen entry barriers. Superior access to capital markets can be important, and large and more secure firms often possess this advantage. Another benefit of being in the industry is superior access to market distribution, a characteristic that helps to explain why a few firms dominate the packaged food industry.

On the one hand, the preservation and use of market power by imperfectly competitive producers constitutes a very real threat to the efficient use of resources in an economy. However, in those instances in which economies of scale can be achieved only by monopolistic firms, monopoly may not be undesirable. We shall return to the potentially desirable effects of imperfect competition later; for the moment, let us examine the extreme of monopoly to illustrate more fully the nature of the threat posed by imperfect competition.

## B. MONOPOLY

Because monopoly is a market served by one producer, the demand curve for the monopolist, by definition, is the industry demand curve, as Figure 1(b) revealed. This demand curve is down-sloping since price must be reduced to sell additional output to consumers, and the monopolist's *MR* curve is less than the price charged consumers at every level of output. Now let us consider an example of a monopolistic firm which has the power to determine the price it will charge.

### Optimum Monopoly Output and Price

The chief difference between pure competition and monopoly is that total revenue increases by a constant increment equal to product price under pure competition, but under monopoly total revenue increases less and less (*MR* declines) as an additional unit of output is sold because the monopolist lowers price to sell more output. In the example below, we can see that total revenue [$P \times Q$ from the data of Figure 1(b)] reaches a maximum at $20 and then declines (the change in total revenue or *MR* is zero and becomes negative thereafter).[2] Notice that profit is at a maximum of $2 at three units of output (total revenue of $18 *less* total cost of $16). The *MR* from

| Quantity | 1 | 2 | 3 | 4 | 5 | 6 |
|---|---|---|---|---|---|---|
| Total revenue | $ 8 | $14 | $18 | $20 | $20 | $18 |
| Total cost | $11 | $13 | $16 | $20 | $25 | $31 |

the sale of a third unit is $4 ($18 − $14), whereas the *MC* of producing is $3. The firm can profitably produce three units, since *MR* exceeds *MC* by $1, but it will not produce beyond that level (say, the fourth unit) because *MR* ($2) is less than *MC* ($4) and total profits decline from the $2 maximum.

[2] Remember that, as explained earlier, $MR = 0$ at the point at which unitary elasticity of demand occurs (between four and five units). Further price reductions produce negative *MR* and declining total revenue.

**FIGURE 2**   Monopoly Output and Price

(a) Monopoly profit

(b) Monopoly loss

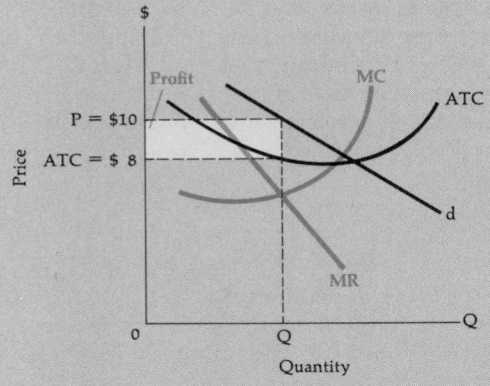

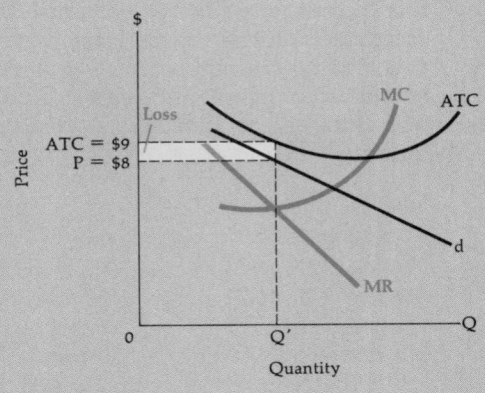

*Optimum Monopoly Output and Price.* The monopolist will attempt to maximize profit by equating *MC* and *MR*. Depending upon relative costs and the strength of demand, this may result in an economic profit of $2 per unit, as in (a), or a loss of $1, as in (b). Resources are misallocated in any event, since it is not possible for *P*=*MC* = *ATC* minimum in monopoly due to declining demand and *MR* curves for the firm.

Figure 2 illustrates profit-maximizing and loss-minimizing levels of output for a theoretical firm operating as a monopolist. The monopolist will expand output as long as marginal revenue exceeds marginal cost and will maximize profit by producing up to that quantity at which $MR = MC$, as just explained. The equal $MR$ and $MC$ rule for maximizing profit applies generally to all producers. In monopoly, however, the firm's $MR$ curve lies below the demand schedule, as we observed earlier. In Figure 2(a) maximimum total economic profits are earned by producing $Q$ units. The economic profit earned on each unit sold is the difference between unit cost ($ATC = \$8$) and price ($P = \$10$) at $Q$ units of output, or $2 per unit. Total economic profit is $\$2 \times Q$, indicated by the gold area of Figure 2(a). Assuming that the monopolist is able to maintain entry barriers, costs and technology are constant, and demand does not change, a monopolist can earn this economic profit forever. The firm could produce levels of output other than $Q$ in Figure 2(a) and still earn an economic profit, but this profit would be smaller than that achieved at $Q$ units of output.[3]

The monopolistic firm is not guaranteed an economic profit, as is shown in Figure 2(b), which illustrates a monopolist who is not earning a normal profit because of weak demand relative to production costs. Once again, the firm determines the optimum level of output by following the rule: Produce a quantity up to that level of output at which $MR = MC$.

[3] Figure 2(a) reveals that this monopolist could produce up to that level of output at which demand schedule $d$ and $ATC$ intersect and still earn a normal profit. If the quantity produced were to extend beyond that point, however, price would be less than $ATC$ and a loss would be incurred.

This requires the production of $Q'$ units of output, each of which can be sold at a price of $8. Losses are minimized at $Q'$ units of output even though the firm fails to earn a normal profit, provided, of course, that minimum $AVC$ is covered. Because $ATC$ is greater than $P$ by $1, the firm incurs a loss equal to $1 $\times$ $Q'$—the gold area of Figure 2(b). This loss is the smallest loss that the monopolist can incur, given the existing technology, the cost structure, and product demand. A larger loss would be incurred by producing something other than the $Q'$ units of output found by the $MR = MC$ rule—a situation which presumably would not be elected by a rational monopolist operating in the short run.

### Resource Allocation and Monopoly

The resource-efficiency implications of monopoly in comparison to pure competition are worth carefully noting again. The profit-maximizing monopolist in Figure 2(a) forces a scarcity of output on society by producing where $MR = MC$. He may earn a long-run economic profit; he charges a higher-than-competitive price that exceeds marginal cost; and he produces less output than would be produced under pure competition. Moreover, the monopolist that maximizes a profit or minimizes a loss is very unlikely to produce a quantity of output consistent with minimum $ATC$ as the competitive firm is forced to do.[4]

### INEFFICIENT USE OF RESOURCES

These indicators of *in*efficient resource allocation in monopoly are diagrammed in Figure 3, where we momentarily visualize a purely competitive market which would produce $Q_c$ units at the competitive price $P_c$ at the point at which $P$(and $MR$) $= MC = ATC$ minimum. Suppose the market becomes a monopoly. The competitive *industry demand* curve thus becomes the demand curve for the *one* monopolistic firm in the industry. Assuming that costs are unaffected by this change ($ATC$ and $MC$ remain unchanged, as shown in Figure 3), the monopolist maximizes profit by charging a price of $P_m$ and producing $Q_m$ units of output where $MR = MC$. Note the following three comparisons under monopoly:

1. Consumers are willing to pay a price of $P_m$ for $Q_m$ units of output, as is revealed by demand curve $d$ of Figure 3. At $Q_m$ units of output, the price $P_m$ charged consumers exceeds $MC$. Consumers value the product more than the resources used to produce the last unit of output, or $P_m$ is greater than $MC$.

2. In maximizing profit at $MR = MC$, the monopolist produces above the low point on $ATC$. Under conditions of pure competition, all firms would have produced at minimum $ATC$, but this situation does not occur under monopoly. All competitive firms would have produced $Q_c$ units by equating $MR$ to $MC$ at minimum $ATC$ because marginal revenue would have been the same as $P_c$ for each competitive producer.

3. Furthermore, under pure competition, the product would have been sold at the lower price $P_c$ rather than at the higher monopoly price $P_m$. The higher monopoly price allows the firm to earn an *economic profit*. The

---

[4] Only if $MR$ happened to intersect $MC$ at the minimum point on $ATC$ would the monopolist operate at lowest unit cost. Even then, however, price would exceed marginal cost.

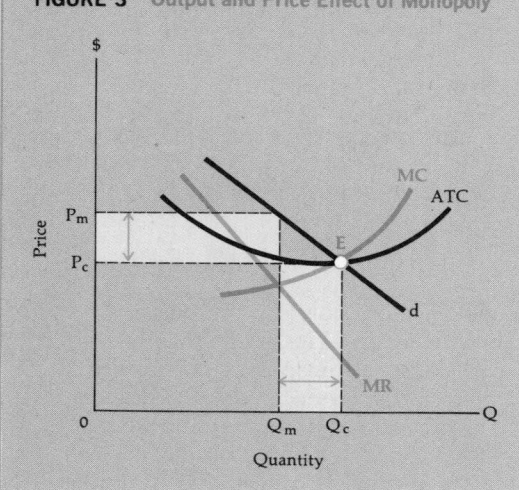

**FIGURE 3** Output and Price Effect of Monopoly

*Competition vs. Monopoly.* The effect of monopoly is a higher price ($P_m$) and lower output ($Q_m$) than is obtained in pure competition. The monopolist is faced with a declining demand curve and sets $MR = MC$ to determine output and price. A lower competitive price ($P_c$) at a higher level of output ($Q_c$) would result if each competitive firm were faced with an elastic demand curve at market price $P_c$ where each competitive producer would be obliged to maximize at $P$ (and $MR$) $= MC = ATC$ minimum at a normal profit level of operation.

monopolist charges a higher-than-competitive price that generates revenues above costs and produces a lower level of output than would have been obtained under pure competition.

Observe that the monopolist cannot simultaneously produce at minimum *ATC and* maximize profits because *MR* and *MC* are equal at a *lower level* of output. This situation is due to the declining *MR* curve facing the monopolistic firm. If the monopolist did produce $Q_c$ units of output at minimum *ATC*, his economic profit would disappear because price and unit cost would be equal. Thus, the monopolist does not meet our earlier-stated efficiency indicators of producing that quantity at which $P = MC = ATC$ minimum at zero economic profit.[5]

Monopoly power and the maintenance of economic profits may strengthen the financial position of the firm, which could raise barriers to entry into the industry. At the same time, the monopolist's economic profit may attract rival producers. (This happened when ballpoint pens and computers were first introduced and sold at prices considerably higher than those prevailing today.) *Complete* absence of competition or absolute monopoly power is hard to achieve, as is demonstrated by the industry competition

[5] Suppose a Congressman became chagrined at these circumstances and persuaded his colleagues to tax our monopolist and thus eliminate the economic profit of Figure 3. The firm would still be inefficient because $P$ is greater than $MC$ at $Q_m$ units. A more appropriate policy under the conditions of Figure 3 might be to regulate prices at price $P_c$ and force $Q_c$ units to be sold. However, Figure 3 is specially drawn to make the efficiency condition a possibility because $d$ intersects $ATC$ and $MC$. More likely than not, product price would not equal minimum $ATC$, in which case lowest unit cost would not be achieved and a tax or subsidy would be called for. It would then be necessary to find some way of rationing the product other than through the price system, however, because at a price of $P_c$, demand would exceed $Q_c$. (More on these matters in Chapter 21.) In addition, those individuals consuming the monopolist's product could still end up paying a $P$ greater than $MC$ unless Congress returned the tax receipts to the consumers of the specific product.

between natural gas and electricity, or steel and aluminum. Still, the monopolist is insulated from competition to some degree and the likelihood of earning an economic profit is therefore much improved. In addition, resource misallocation is clearly implied by monopoly power; the firm *underallocates* resources to the product produced ($P$ exceeds $MC$).

## ASSESSMENT OF MONOPOLY

Some potentially favorable effects may derive from monopoly, however. Some economists feel that, under some circumstances, monopoly may lead to lower unit costs than are attainable in pure competition because of scale economies or because an incentive for innovation and invention is protected by the long-run economic profit that is possible in monopoly. Adequate financial resources and motivation for technological change may be lacking in pure competition. However, because a monopoly firm avoids rivalry and enjoys a sheltered market position, there may also be *less* incentive to innovate than there would be in pure competition. Thus, some economists view monopoly power as an evil, as we suggested earlier in our evaluation of competitive markets.

Although our theory and knowledge simply are not sufficient to assess monopolized markets unambiguously, there is a general consensus among economists that monopoly is most likely to produce undesired effects. This attitude stems from numerous individual observations of the abuse of monopoly power in the American economy, as well as from recognition of the fact that, under monopoly, inefficient resource allocation does occur. Moreover, even if a society does benefit from scale economies exploited by a monopolist who is able to achieve lower long-run costs, price reductions are by no means guaranteed. The generally observed close relation between industry profit rates and the proportion of a market held by a firm lends further credence to a skeptical view of monopoly. Because a monopoly firm can erect barriers to entry that shelter the market, it may just as easily use its position to exploit the consumer. Economic profits used to finance research and rights to new patents allow the monopolist either to lower price or to raise existing barriers to entry and protect its sheltered status.

Sometimes government knowingly sanctions a "natural" monopoly such as a public utility company. Natural monopolies may be necessary, as is obvious if you envision even three or four firms providing telephones, electricity, gas, or public transportation in a small city. Such a situation would result in a costly product or service and create considerable havoc. Natural monopolies are therefore encouraged when they can offer cost, price, and service advantages because of scale economies. In return for their exclusive franchise, natural monopolies are subject to controls to prevent abuse of market power; indeed, the social desirability of a natural monopoly depends upon proper regulation.

Negative conclusions about monopoly power are by no means overwhelming and it is quite appropriate to keep a reasonably open mind on this issue for the moment. Certainly, regulated natural monopolies such as public utilities that can capture significant economies of scale represent an exception to premature negative conclusions one might otherwise reach.

### Mythology and Monopoly Pricing

There are six basic misconceptions about monopoly pricing that deserve clarification. These misconceptions are that the firm: (*a*) is assured of an economic profit, (b) charges the highest possible price, (c) maximizes profits where the difference between $P$ and $ATC$ is largest, (d) usually produces at lowest unit cost, (e) always maximizes profits, and (f) makes *both* a quantity and a price decision. Let us briefly consider each of these "myths."

### MYTH 1: GUARANTEED ECONOMIC PROFITS

There is no guarantee that a monopolist will automatically earn an economic profit. It is true that the likelihood of economic profit is greater under monopoly than under pure competition because the competitive firm is "doomed" to a normal profit through price and entry competition in the long run. If the cost and demand circumstances are unfavorable, however, a monopolist may earn less than a normal profit or even sustain a loss. In the long run, a monopolist cannot continue to sustain a less-than-normal profit any more than the competitive firm can. If a normal profit is not earned, there must be a cost-reducing technological change or an increase in demand, or the monopolist will be forced to leave the industry.

### MYTH 2: CHARGING THE HIGHEST PRICE

The monopolist *does not* charge as high a price as can be obtained. The demand curve of Figure 3 indicates that the monopolist could charge more than $P_m$, but that a higher price would lead to a *smaller* profit. The profit-oriented monopolist maximizes the difference between total cost and total revenue by producing a level of output up to the point at which $MR = MC$.

### MYTH 3: MAXIMUM UNIT PROFIT

The monopolist *does not* maximize a profit by producing that level of output at which profit per unit—the difference in $P$ and $ATC$—is greatest. After all, the sale of ten units at an economic profit of $10 per unit is preferable to the sale of nine units at a larger profit of $11 on each unit. Maximization of *total* profit is not necessarily consistent with the largest profit *per unit sold*. As long as additional sales compensate for a lower per unit profit, the monopoly firm will produce the larger quantity to maximize total profit (or to minimize a loss) at $MR = MC$.

### MYTH 4: OPERATING AT LOWEST UNIT COST

The monopolist typically does not produce at that point where $ATC$ is at a minimum. Profit is maximized for the monopolist where $MR = MC$, and this *is not* at all likely to be at lowest $ATC$, and even if it were, an economic profit would be earned because $P$ would exceed $MR$ at the intersection of $MR$, $MC$, and minimum $ATC$. In the long run, the purely competitive firm is forced to a minimum unit-cost level of output at which $MR = MC$ only because of price and entry competition. Remember, one major difference between competition and monopoly is that there is only one producer in monopoly, and as a consequence, there is no price or entry competition that forces the firm to its minimum on either a short-run or a long-run unit-cost curve ($ATC$ or $LRAC$).

### MYTH 5: A MONOPOLIST ALWAYS MAXIMIZES PROFIT

The monopolist may not follow the equimarginal principle and maximize profit. In actuality, the firm does not know the exact nature of demand, $MR$, or $MC$ and it may unintentionally charge too high or too low a price. Also, a monopolist may think in terms of maximizing profit in the long run. The firm may exercise restraint and purposely charge a lower price and produce a greater amount of output than is consistent with the greatest total short-run profit that can be earned. Oftentimes, monopoly firms have a great deal of public visibility and, as a result, may be sensitive to criticism. Earning a large economic profit could precipitate government intervention and regulation. In addition, the monopolist may limit profit to avoid attracting other firms contemplating entering the industry or offering a substitute product. Thus, voluntary restraints may be a real fact of life for a firm under monopoly.

### MYTH 6: A PRICE AND QUANTITY DECISION

The idea that a monopolist can control *both* price and quantity at the same time is not quite correct. The monopolist can make a quantity decision, in which case market demand determines price, or he can make a price decision, in which case the demand schedule determines how much output can be sold. The monopolist's real advantage lies in his ability to restrict the quantity of output offered in order to set price at the most profitable level.

### C. MONOPOLISTIC COMPETITION

Most of American industry is characterized by some degree of monopoly power, but not the degree implied in our analysis of monopoly. Pure monopoly is as improbable in the real world as pure competition. We shall next examine monopolistic competition, a relatively common market structure requiring the existence of *many* firms in an industry, but not the "large" number found in pure competition.

### Characteristics of Monopolistic Competition

Monopolistic competition is a market structure in which firms have some control over product price because each firm's product is differentiated from the output of rival firms, although not to an extreme degree. Because of differentiation, a monopolistically competitive firm may engage heavily in nonprice competition (advertising, for example), thereby achieving some degree of price control. In this way, a firm operating in monopolistically competitive markets may be able to convince consumers to use its brand rather than a rival's. The monopolistically competitive firm faces a *downward-sloping demand curve*, as shown in Figure 4. Whereas demand is perfectly elastic for a purely competitive firm, successful differentiation of a product tilts the demand curve downward in the direction of less elasticity. While the number of firms in monopolistic competition is large enough to make price-fixing or market-sharing collusion unlikely, nonprice competition is widely used by firms to differentiate their product to achieve something other than perfectly elastic demand conditions.

Product differentiation under monopolistic competition allows the firm to attract customers on a basis other than the market-established price charged for homogeneous goods. In short, the firm is a quasi-monopolist because of some unique element associated with its products or with the market it serves. The numerous small clothing stores in a typical city are one example of monopolistic competition. Gasoline stations, barber shops, and grocery stores are often other good examples. Some firms differentiate their output

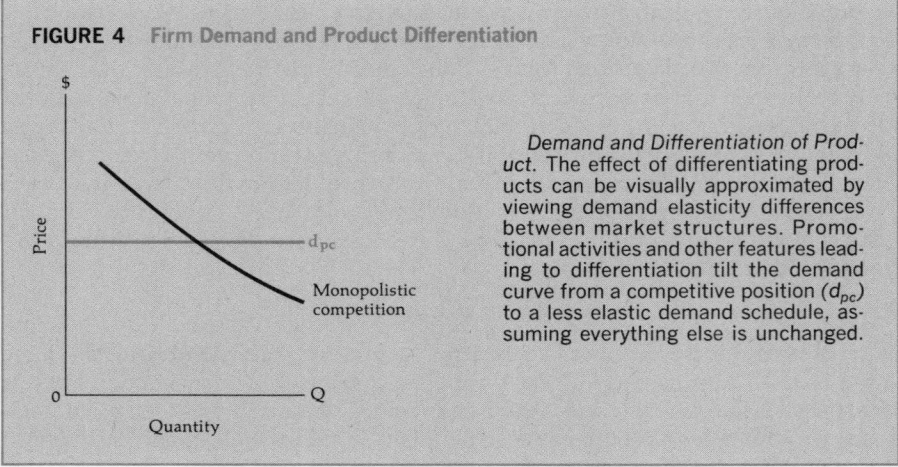

**FIGURE 4**  Firm Demand and Product Differentiation

*Demand and Differentiation of Product.* The effect of differentiating products can be visually approximated by viewing demand elasticity differences between market structures. Promotional activities and other features leading to differentiation tilt the demand curve from a competitive position ($d_{pc}$) to a less elastic demand schedule, assuming everything else is unchanged.

by producing a better-quality product; others may be more effective or courteous in providing service or may offer better credit terms. Still others may have locational advantages, being situated near a highway cloverleaf or in a major shopping center.

The firm in monopolistic competition is aware of a "going price" but it also operates to some extent in a personalized market. Another common characteristic of monopolistic competition is that a relatively small amount of capital resources is required to enter the market and other entry barriers are modest. As a result, monopolistically competitive markets are prone to overexpansion, which often leads to small profit margins. Economists generally conclude that monopolistically competitive firms use too many resources because each firm operates short of optimum capacity at minimum costs. Almost everyone has observed empty beauty shops or dozens of service stations located on busy streets, each servicing a few customers. The small profit margins which often prevail in such firms might be overcome by lowering costs or increasing volume. If little can be done about costs, the firm will attempt to differentiate its product by promotional policies designed to increase demand. An illustration of the output-price implications of monopolistic competition will clarify the significance of this type of market.

### Output and Price Under Monopolistic Competition

Like competitive and monopolistic firms, the firm operating under monopolistic competition may earn an economic profit or it may incur a loss in the short run. The theory of monopolistic competition applies primarily to the long run when all resources can be varied, and its implications for resource allocation are best observed in this context.

In the long run, firms in monopolistic competition tend to earn a normal profit. Figure 5 illustrates cost and demand relationships for a hypothetical firm in monopolistic competition in the long run. The demand curve for the firm is downward-sloping and, as a consequence, *MR* lies below demand. Equilibrium price and quantity in monopolistic competition are determined at that point at which $MR = MC$ and $Q_{mc}$ units are produced at a price of $P_{mc}$. This long-run equilibrium in monopolistic competition is the result of two basic forces: price competition and entry into the industry.

Because there are many firms, a common price is not set through collusion and there may be some modest tendency to practice price competition. Price competition involves movement down one demand curve. Because firms can enter monopolistically competitive markets easily, the demand schedule of existing firms decreases or shifts leftward as each new firm enters the market.

Entry is an important feature of monopolistic competition. Each firm's demand curve shifts leftward until $d'$ is tangent to long-run average cost (which includes a normal profit) at point $a$ on $LRAC$ in Figure 5. New entrants into the market cause each firm's demand to shift leftward until a zero economic profit is attained, as is illustrated by the shift from $d$ to $d'$. If an economic profit is earned in monopolistic competition in the short run, it only induces new firms to enter the industry. For example, if Shell and Texaco build service stations on a busy corner to compete with Standard Oil, economic profits are competed away as more firms share what amounts to a smaller market for each producer. On the other hand, losses that might be incurred in the short run will result in some firms leaving the industry until a normal profit condition is restored, again at point $a$ in Figure 5. Thus, a long-run equilibrium price and quantity is established at $P_{mc}$ and $Q_{mc}$ where firms tend to earn a normal profit.

### Efficiency Implications of Monopolistic Competition

Even though economic profits tend to be competed away via entry into the industry in monopolistic competition, resource misallocation is alleged to occur in this market structure. We say "alleged" because the inefficiency of monopolistic competition is not agreed upon even among well-known economists.[6]

[6] Edward H. Chamberlin was one of the first economists to evaluate monopolistic competition, and was long embroiled in the dialogue concerning the efficiency of this form of market structure.

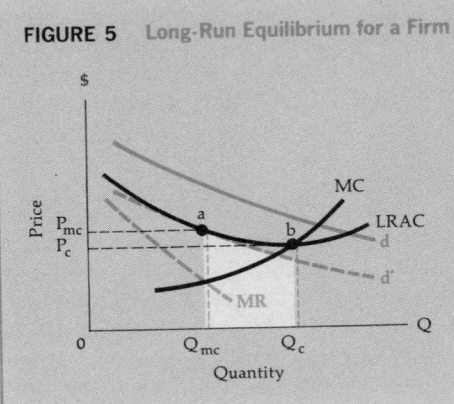

**FIGURE 5**   Long-Run Equilibrium for a Firm in Monopolistic Competition

*Equilibrium Price and Output in Monopolistic Competition.* Each firm has a small degree of monopoly power in monopolistic competition. All such firms tend to earn only a normal profit in the long run at point $a$, because demand shifts from $d$ to $d'$, but equilibrium output occurs where $P$ exceeds $MC$ which is not minimum $LRAC$. Each firm has excess capacity ($Q_c$ to $Q_{mc}$) and charges a price ($P_{mc}$) higher than the competitive price ($P_c$).

The equilibrium quantity produced by each firm in monopolistic competition is *not* a quantity at which per unit cost is minimized, a condition which is forced upon a competitive firm that maximizes and earns a normal profit by producing $Q_c$ units in Figure 5. In monopolistic competition, there are too many firms, all of which are operating short of minimum *LRAC*, a condition that suggests that existing resources are underutilized by each firm. Moreover, the equilibrium price ($P_{mc}$ in Figure 5) tends to be somewhat higher than that which would prevail under perfect competition ($P_c$), other things being equal. In addition, price exceeds marginal cost; once again, consumers are paying more for the product than the marginal cost of producing the last unit of output.

Suppose all monopolistically competitive barber shops in Wamsutter, Wyoming, have cost and revenue curves as shown in Figure 5. Each firm might then be described as having some unused or "excess" capacity in the amount of $Q_cQ_{mc}$ (the empty barber chairs that everyone has observed at certain hours). In monopolistic competition, therefore, consumers do not obtain the product at the lowest possible price consistent with minimum unit cost. Even more important, $P$ and $MC$ diverge as excess numbers of firms produce at less than optimal capacity—a condition "financed" by consumers paying a higher than purely competitive price.

## THE "VALUE" OF PRODUCT DIFFERENTIATION

There may be certain relative advantages to monopolistic competition, potential wastes aside. The demand curve for the monopolistically competitive producer tends to be more elastic than demand in monopoly, and an economic profit is unlikely to be maintained in the long run in this market structure. Moreover, differentiated products allow a wider array of consumer choice, and some product differentiation may be of real "value" to consumers. The improvements in a product or the satellite services provided by a firm that are sparked by a need to differentiate products may enlarge consumer satisfaction. Edward H. Chamberlin, who contributed much to the theory of monopolistic competition, suggested that its so-called "inefficiencies" partially represent quality competition. The "price" society willingly pays for such differentiation could be regarded as "excess capacity" or the quantity difference $Q_cQ_{mc}$ in Figure 5, which induces a price difference of $P_cP_{mc}$ per unit. At the same time, it is important to recognize that product differentiation may be illusionary (as in the case of aspirin, knockless gas, and the like) and thus may generate uncompensated allocative inefficiencies for society.

## PRODUCT PROMOTION: ADVERTISING WASTES?

Advertising for purposes of product differentiation may be designed to create imaginary differences in the minds of consumers. Trading stamps offered by stores and "gifts" proffered by the banking industry are good illustrations of product promotion and nonprice competition. Promoting superficial or nonexistent differences in product (the dried-up post-nasal drip which "Frost" accomplishes best) may waste valued resources, confuse consumer choice, and result in a higher product price by *raising unit cost* (*LRAC*) *at all levels of output*. This is a definite likelihood for firms that engage in promotional fanfare to counter the actions of rivals who may have increased their market share in a like fashion. Planned obsolescence is another technique used to differentiate products, and the American automobile, clothing, and shoe industries all illustrate this form of nonprice competition. Promotional activity in the name of product differentiation designed to persuade consumers of imaginary differences results in a misallocation of resources. These effects are not easily evaluated, however, particularly if housewives really feel that "little blue devils" do make white whiter.

The product-differentiation characteristic of monopolistic competition also may perform a positive role. Advertising may improve consumer satisfaction by conveying information, improving service, permitting wider choice, and encouraging more rational consumer decisions. Advertising could also generate more demand for a product, thereby allowing the firm to achieve economies of scale that otherwise might be impossible (an event that could also increase monopoly concentration in the market).

Although advertising can lead to economies of scale, there may be instances in which a higher volume of output produces *dis*economies of scale. A plant large enough for effective sales promotion may exceed the optimal size determined by technological factors alone. Promotional and advertising expenditures can be regarded as wasteful, if they lead to increases in unit costs, assuming product promotion lacks other redeeming advantages. With higher unit costs, higher prices are required than would occur in the absence of advertising. Finally, successful differentiation via advertising in monopolistic competition may generate increasing imperfections and raise entry barriers, leading, over the years, to accumulated monopoly power which fosters markets that are controlled increasingly by a few firms.

## A Final Comment on Monopolistic Competition

Estimates vary, but several observers have speculated that up to one-half of the aggregate output of the private sector of the American economy flows through markets that are characterized by monopolistic competition, where there are many firms engaged in nonprice competition selling differentiated products with some degree of discretionary price control. Monopolistic competition may best represent markets such as those for the services of lawyers, barbers, plumbers, and television repairmen; wholesale and retail trade activities including gas stations, grocery stores, and department stores; and much construction and small manufacturing activity. Because monopolistically competitive firms produce differentiated products, most of them practice nonprice competition. A significant portion of the output of the private sector of the American economy is also concentrated in markets that are dominated by a few large firms, and a brief examination of this type of imperfect market is in order.

## D. OLIGOPOLY

One of the major theoretical outgrowths of Chamberlin's theory of monopolistic competition was its emphasis on the interdependence among rival firms. Under oligopoly, product-price manipulation is dangerous, but producers do practice nonprice competition, such as advertising or selling cases of a product on "specials." Interdependence is an integral part of the theory of oligopoly.

## Characteristics of Oligopoly

Many industries in the American economy are characterized by the presence of a *few* dominant producers, rather high entry barriers, seemingly rigid price policies, and occasional price-fixing behavior or other forms of market collusion. One of the most important factors under oligopoly is the difficulty of entry into the market. Entry barriers resulting from mergers, ownership or control of key factors of production, and the existence of scale economies related to the "advantages of being established" are significant elements in creating and maintaining the dominance of a few firms in an oligopolistic market. Oligopoly tends to appear most frequently in technologically advanced and capital-intensive industries where high financial cost may be an important initial barrier to entry. The production of automobiles, steel, heavy electrical equipment, and aluminum are examples of capital-intensive and oligopolistic markets.

Even though a few firms generally control a significant portion of oligopolistic markets, they are not necessarily large in the absolute sense—the few oligopolistic barber shops or funeral parlors in Hazard, Kentucky, certainly suggest otherwise. A few producers does mean, however, that interdependence exists, since the action of one firm is likely to lead to a reaction by a rival oligopolist. In some cases (e.g., automobiles), products are differentiated, while in others (rolled aluminum or steel), little or no differentiation exists. Oligopoly and interdependence among firms concerning pricing breed their own peculiar disadvantages: rigid prices and collusion.

### Rigidity in Pricing and Collusion

There are two fundamental explanations for price rigidity. In some instances, firms establish a virtual monopoly by agreeing upon one common, uniform price in the marketplace—a quite illegal practice termed *collusion*. If firms do not formally agree to set one price or otherwise to refrain from competing, the same result may be obtained by "understood" informal collusion. Some industries appear to develop price policies based upon a "follow-the-leader" philosophy—one dominant firm acts as the standard-bearer for the industry in initiating a price change. Collusive pricing practices tend to be more prevalent the fewer the number of sellers, the more nearly identical their costs of production, and the more certain firms can be that their rivals will adhere to the agreed-upon tactic of avoiding price competition. Price collusion tends to intensify nonprice competition, since firms attempt to protect their market share via advertising and other forms of product and service promotion. Since collusive pricing is a subject we shall return to later because of its illegality, let us next consider a more subtle explanation of price rigidity.

Even in the absence of collusion of either the overt or the more subtle variety, there is resistance to price changes among oligopolists because as price rigidity is based on reactions of rival oligopolistic firms to a price change. Since there are only a few producers, any given oligopolist is unlikely to lower product price even though the action might be warranted (perhaps because of cost-saving technological changes). Suppose one oligopolist lowers product price in order to pirate a portion of a rival's market. The firm can generally expect its rivals to follow suit in an attempt to maintain their share of the market. Thus, prices fall and profits decline for everyone. There is not much incentive for an oligopolist to reduce product price for this reason. It is also unlikely that "noncollusive" oligopolists will increase product price because, if they do so, they may lose a considerable share of the market unless rival producers also increase their prices. Because pricing interdependence does characterize the few firms comprising an oligopolistic market, the demand curve facing such firms may be depicted as a *kinked schedule of demand*.

## KINKED DEMAND

Oligopoly demand and price rigidity are illustrated in Figure 6(a) for a firm that is not openly engaged in price-fixing activities.[7] The heavily drawn demand curve $d_1d_2$ in Figure 6(a) is constructed around the going price $P_0 = \$6$.[8] This demand curve is the consequence of two different demand schedules: the relatively elastic demand schedule $d_1$, which prevails for *price increases only*; and schedule $d_2$, which applies only to the *price decreases* contemplated by an oligopolist. Suppose an oligopolist considers reducing price by $1, anticipating that such action will allow the firm to

[7] There are a variety of models which depict price interdependence and which give further insight into producer behavior under conditions of interdependence, including the theory of games and conflict-resolution theory. (See Appendix B following Chapter 19.)

[8] Notice that we say "going" price. One of the shortcomings of the theory of oligopoly is that economists have difficulty explaining in an unambiguous fashion how the price of $6 is obtained.

**FIGURE 6**   Kinked Demand and Price Rigidity

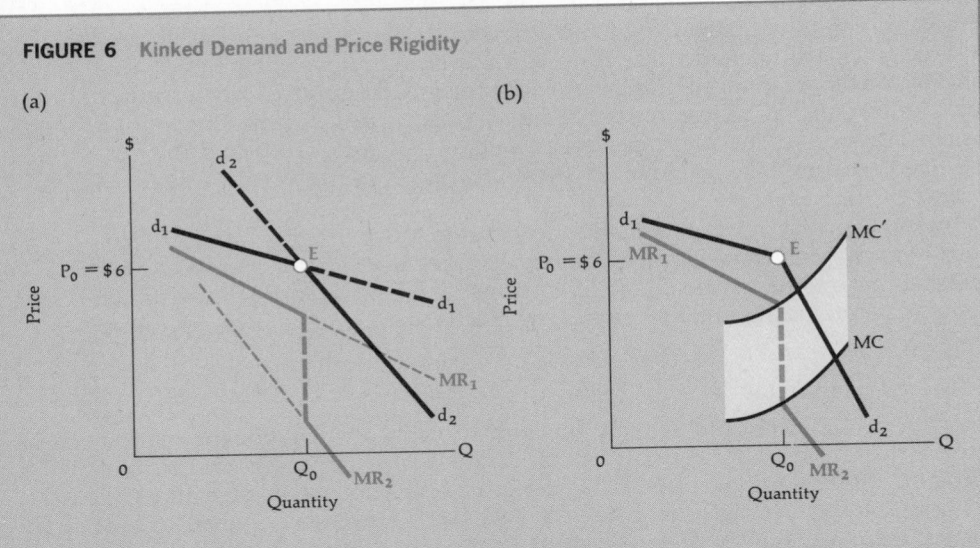

*Oligopoly Demand.* The demand curve facing oligopolistic producers is sometimes depicted as being kinked at the going price $P_0$ in (a), where price increases or decreases result in a firm losing revenues because of the reaction of rivals to a price change. In addition, the kinked demand curve produces a discontinuous *MR* curve as shown in (b). A maximizing oligopolist can thus maximize profit by equating *MR* and *MC* and avoid price changes over a wide range of changes in costs (e.g., shifts between *MC* and *MC'*).

increase total revenues along the dashed portion of demand curve $d_1$. If rival oligopolists follow suit and also reduce prices to maintain their share of the market, the firm may instead find itself moving downward on the less elastic demand curve $d_2$. Thus, very little additional revenue will be gained via the price cut and the market share of rival oligopolists will not change appreciably. Total revenue might well decline if the relevant portion of the oligopolist's true demand curve ($d_1d_2$) for a price decrease is inelastic as price falls. The firm, as well as its rival oligopolists, will have learned a good lesson: Do not engage in price wars because everyone suffers except the consumer.

On the other hand, if an oligopolist decides to increase price, the elastic portion of demand curve $d_1$ will prevail. Rivals *may not* follow the price increase initiated by the firm, in order to capture some of its market. Instead of moving up the dashed portion of demand schedule $d_2$, the firm ends up moving upward on the more elastic and heavily drawn portion of demand schedule $d_1$. The price increase thus results in a large reduction in quantity and total revenue may fall if rivals do not follow suit. In short, interdependent oligopolists not engaged in collusion are faced with: (*a*) a highly elastic demand schedule ($d_1$) if price is increased (total revenue may fall), and (*b*) relatively inelastic demand ($d_2$) if price is reduced (total revenue again may fall).

The implication of a kinked demand schedule for the price-rigidity hypothesis is clear if we examine the discontinuity of marginal revenue for a firm faced with such a curve. Suppose that the kinked demand curve $d_1d_2$ of Figure 6(b) prevails and that firms do not collude on prices. A profit-maximizing oligopolist equates $MR$ and $MC$ by producing $Q_0$ units, as is shown in the figure. Because of the different demand elasticities associated with segmented demand curve $d_1d_2$, $MR$ is discontinuous. This means that profits can be maximized at $MR = MC$ over a wide range of cost changes, such as $MC$ to $MC'$. Despite cost changes, then, firms are reluctant to alter prices because of the interdependence among their few rivals and the possibility that competing oligopolists will not follow a price increase, but will follow a price decrease.

Interdependent pricing behavior leading to price rigidity tends to encourage price collusion—which frequently takes the form of informal price leadership—among rival oligopolistic firms. As long as price changes are followed by less dominant firms, imperfectly competitive price rigidities prevail.

### ECONOMIC CONSEQUENCES OF OLIGOPOLY

Because of collusion and kinked demand, firms in an oligopolistic market are characterized by rigid prices which denote fear of a rival's reaction and leads to discontinuities in $MR$. As long as firms do not engage in price competition for fear of subsequent price wars or because of tacit agreements, whatever rivalry they elect must be pursued through advertising and product promotion.

Nonprice competition may strengthen barriers to entry and, because well-established firms promote brand-name products heavily to protect their market, potential competition is made a more hazardous undertaking. Oligopolistic firms often proliferate brands. The markets for soap, appliances, and medicine are a good deal more concentrated than the dozens of brand-name products would suggest. Oligopoly includes many easily recognized stalwarts of American industry—among them, General Electric, General Foods, General Motors, IBM, U.S. Steel, and Standard Oil.

Price rigidity and collusion among oligopolists may prompt an *inefficient* allocation of resources, particularly if cost-reducing technological changes are not passed on to consumers or if scale diseconomies are incurred. Moreover, oligopolists are less likely to be regulated by government than are monopolists, and large sums of money may be devoted to advertising designed to help firms burnish their image and convince consumers of the benefits of their particular product.

Successful price collusion may result in an outcome analogous to that characterizing monopoly if the cost and demand conditions facing each individual firm are comparable. In such a case, oligopolistic firms will find it in their interest to agree to charge one monopoly price together. As long as all firms stay with the agreed-upon price, all may maximize profits jointly (just as the monopolist does) at the "going" oligopoly price. In short, firms can maximize "joint" profits in the industry by collusive agreements to set or administer prices together. However, collusion itself is an imperfect process which depends in part on the number of firms which are required not to cheat on the agreed pricing practices. The fewer the number of firms, the less difficult it is to reach explicit or implicit agreements that are apt not to be violated. Many industrial sectors in the American economy are made up of a very few large firms and a larger number of smaller producers. These latter small firms may feel that a more aggressive pricing posture will allow them to grow and expand their market share so that they can move into the "big leagues." Price competition by smaller firms may also be viewed as a way to overcome the scale economies as well as the other nonprice competitive practices in which the industrial giants engage.

The great danger to smaller firms is that they may not have the financial "staying power" to war with their larger rivals for extended periods. Another feature worth noticing is that collusive pricing is sometimes short-circuited by disguised price-cutting practices. If one oligopolist can grant secret price concessions without being discovered by its rivals, it may be able to add to its market strength and profits. Of course, an all-out price war may develop if such secret pricing practices are discovered. If this occurs, the firm instigating the price war will not realize the gains it set out to achieve, but rather will be worse off, as will the other firms in the industry.

The general effects of oligopoly are difficult to predict because behavior in this market structure takes on many forms. Price and output levels are dependent upon the pricing strategies of one or more firms in the industry and whatever "understanding" they may or may not arrive at. However, it is unlikely that oligopolistic market structures operate according to the efficiency criterion of $P = MC = ATC$ minimum, where a normal profit is earned. Oligopoly is possible because there are only a few producers, and price rigidities and nonprice competition are widespread because these producers recognize their interdependence. Furthermore, barriers to entry tend to be maintained and strengthened under oligopoly. In the absence of such barriers, new firms might enter the industry, and an oligopolistic market would become increasingly competitive (assuming continued growth in demand). Even when hard times and large amounts of excess capacity prevail in oligopoly, prices tend to remain rigid while firms intensify non-price competition in the hopes of convincing consumers of the advantages of their particular products.

Modern production processes for steel products, computer equipment, transportation equipment, and a host of other markets require many billions of dollars of capital if known economies of scale are to be achieved. This is one reason that the large number of firms characteristic of pure competition are frequently nonexistent. Oligopolists may engage heavily in technological research and development as one of several forms of nonprice competition. There may be significant advantages to these research and development activities if future economies of scale benefit the consuming public.

At the same time, it is necessary to remember that oligopolists maintain their sheltered market positions by keeping entry barriers high and im-proving technological processes which may or may not produce lower product prices as costs fall. Consequently, oligopoly may be confining in the sense that the market power of a few producers can be easily abused.

Beyond this assessment of *possible* outcomes, the social desirability of oligopoly and the efficiency of resource allocation under this form of market structure are not easy to determine. One reason for this difficulty is that oligopolistic markets may progress toward technological change more rapidly than would purely competitive markets. This can result in lower unit costs in the long run as scale economies are achieved, but if prices are not reduced, it can also result in the misallocation of resources and larger economic profits.

Much of the technological progress experienced in the American economy has *not* been generated by large oligopolistic firms. We also have noted that there are instances on record of oligopolistic firms using their market power abusively by administering prices through subtle forms of collusion or out-right price agreements. The meager evidence that does exist suggests that such firms tend to be relatively prosperous. Parallel pricing achieved through tacit agreements or patterns of price leadership nurtured by dom-inant firms are not uncommon, but it is very difficult to remedy these methods of manipulating the market. Accordingly, suspicion cast over oli-gopolistic markets is due both to the concentration of power they allow and to the repeated use of such power.

### E. IMPERFECT COMPETITION IN RETROSPECT

The potential burden of concentrated economic power in imperfect product markets and the policy implications of these various market structures merit brief review.

#### The Burden of Inefficiency in Resource Allocation

The net burden of imperfectly competitive product markets is resource mis-allocation stemming from the contrived and unnecessary scarcity monopoly power causes a society to endure. This loss in net output is depicted in Figure 7, in which the economy is operating below its potential production-possibilities frontier at point $a$, instead of on the frontier at some point like $p'$. The loss of potential output may be presumed to be less of product X or of product Y. For simplicity, Figure 7 assumes that all output of product Y is produced under competitive conditions and the output of product X is

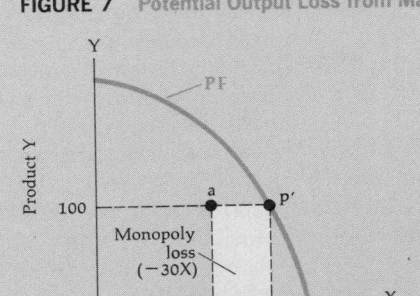

**FIGURE 7** Potential Output Loss from Market Power in Product Markets

*Monopoly Burden.* The loss of output due to market imperfections is generally represented by 30 units of X (as one possibility). An output loss (the shaded area of the figure) is a result of inefficient use of resources. Imperfectly competitive firms operate where P exceeds MC when resources are allocated inefficiently. Therefore, society does not achieve a desired output level such as p' on the production frontier, but rather operates below the frontier (e.g., point a).

produced under some form of imperfect competition. In the absence of imperfect competition, the hypothetical economy of Figure 7 could obtain, for example, 150 units of X and 100 units of Y. However, market imperfections restrict output to a lower and inefficient level of production.

The critical evidence that suggests that such a loss may occur in imperfect markets is that price exceeds marginal cost. Under such circumstances, a society could obtain greater consumer satisfaction from reallocating resources in a different manner. When other considerations are added (e.g., the wasted resources not fully utilized in monopolistic competition or the oligopolist's tendency to fix prices), it is clear that there are lost output burdens associated with market imperfections. In addition, market imperfections mean that minimum unit costs are not achieved and economic profits can be earned. Entry barriers, product differentiation, nonprice competition, and concentration of economic power all contribute to these inefficiencies.

*Summing up:* With imperfect competition prevailing in the magnitude that it does in the American economy, the hallowed Invisible Hand popularized by Adam Smith cannot convert the best interests of individuals into the best interests of a market system of economic organization, often labeled a capitalistic society. It must be remembered, however, that the theoretical conclusions which suggest a misallocation of resources do not fully confront the issue of "good and evil" concerning monopoly power. As we said in Chapter 16, the late Joseph Schumpeter went so far as to suggest that pure competition is "inferior" as a market structure because technological advances, scale economies, and lower unit costs are most likely to arise under imperfect competition. The case against monopoly power is weakened by this possibility, and empirical research on the question of how various market structures influence unit costs is receiving a good deal of attention for that reason. Some experts (the chief spokesman being John Kenneth Galbraith), have argued that the market power of imperfect competitors on occasion may be neutralized by "countervailing-power" forces on the other side of the market. In other words, the advantages of an imperfectly competitive seller, such as U.S. Steel, may be neutralized by the power of a monopsonistic buyer with comparable market power, such as General Motors. Power forces may also be diluted if competition between industries such as steel and aluminum produces what has been labeled "workable competition"—interindustry conditions that approximate the ideal world of pure competition. Thus, the case against product-market power and imperfections in a capitalistic economy is not completely one-sided, although it tends to lean toward disapproval.

Much has now been learned about product markets and problems of imperfect competition among producers. Our next task is to extend our study to resource markets and then, in later chapters, to examine public policy concerning resource-allocation problems.

## REVIEW

### Summary

1. Imperfect market structures typically recognized by economists include monopoly, monopolistic competition, and oligopoly. Imperfect competition among firms may result in misallocation of resources, higher-than-competitive prices and profits, and less than a competitive quantity of output. Market power accrues to firms producing in imperfect markets, thus raising the issue of the legitimacy of economic power and its use. Such market power can exist on both the supplier's and the buyer's side of the markets for both resources and products.

2. The chief characteristics of imperfect competition are product differentiation, advertising and product promotion, price determination by firms rather than by the market in general, and barriers to entering an industry. The imperfectly competitive firm is faced with down-sloping demand and marginal revenue curves in recognition of these characteristics, and consequently tends to produce less and charge a higher price than firms in pure competition.

3. Entry barriers, as a cause of imperfect competition, tend to reflect mass production and economies of scale, patent laws, control of essential raw materials or markets, and the advantages of already being in the industry. The imperfectly competitive firm maximizes profit by equating MR and MC. This results in an underallocation of resources and a scarcity of output because price exceeds marginal cost, minimum unit cost is not achieved, and it is possible (but not certain) that the monopolist will earn a long-run economic profit.

4. The monopolistic firm contributes to the inefficient allocation of resources by forcing a scarcity on society; however, natural monopolies sanctioned and regulated by government can be quite desirable under certain conditions. Under monopoly, a firm does not: (a) necessarily earn an economic profit, (b) charge the highest possible price, (c) produce at the greatest profit per unit, (d) produce at minimum unit cost, (e) necessarily maximize total profit, or (f) make both quantity *and* price decisions.

5. Monopolistic competition may result in the misallocation of resources, primarily because there are too many firms in the industry, all of which are producing with excess capacity short of minimum unit cost. Such firms frequently practice product differentiation and tend to earn a normal profit in the long run because of the entry of other firms and both

price and nonprice competition. However, excess capacity in this market structure may also be viewed as the price consumers willingly pay to avoid homogeneous goods.

6. Oligopolistic firms also may be socially undesirable, particularly because they may reach price-setting agreements to perpetuate economic profits. At the same time, this type of imperfect competition may be advantageous to society, particularly if it allows achievement of economies of scale and a more rapid rate of technological change than would occur under competitive conditions. Moreover, advertising may be partially desirable for informative reasons, or if it allows firms to achieve scale economies.

7. Countervailing market power may help mitigate the undesired consequences of imperfect markets. Sustained progress in the American economy may also be achieved through the maintenance of a "workable" form of competition achieved through a reasonable degree of rivalry among firms. As with imperfect competition in the general case, the possible advantages of oligopoly may partially offset the resource misallocation practices inherent in oligopolistic markets.

## Identify the Following Concepts and Terms

- market power
- oligopoly
- characteristics of imperfect competition
- natural monopoly
- myths of monopoly pricing
- monopsony vs. monopoly
- "price leadership"

- entry barriers
- divergence of $MC$ and $P$ at optimum monopoly output
- disadvantages of monopoly
- rigid oligopoly prices
- kinked demand
- product differentiation in monopolistic competition

## Questions to Answer

1. What causes imperfect competition? What are its characteristics? What are the different characteristics of the four major market structures—pure competition, monopolistic competition, oligopoly, and monopoly? How are they significant?

2. What are the characteristic problems of resource misallocation resulting from monopoly? (Illustrate your answer on the graph below.)

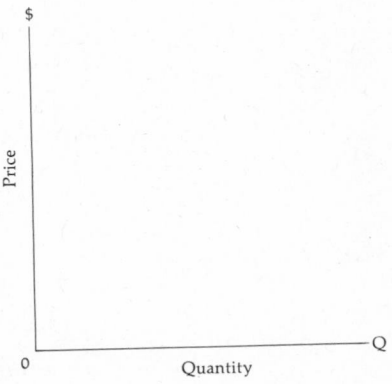

3. Critically evaluate the following statements:
    (*a*) "The absolute number of firms in an industry reveals the degree of competition or market structure."
    (*b*) "By regulating a natural monopoly, government can very easily achieve the efficient allocation of resources."

4. What potential gains may arise under monopoly? How is it possible that monopolists *do not* always maximize profits, earn an economic profit, charge the highest possible price, or operate at lowest unit costs and maximum per unit profits?

5. "Under monopolistic competition, product differentiation may compensate for production at less than 'optimal capacity.' Moreover, there are certain possible redeeming features (as well as wastes) associated with product-promotion tactics." Explain and evaluate these statements.

6. Price rigidity and collusion are two possibilities in oligopoly. Explain how each is related to a "kinked" demand schedule.

# CHAPTER 18
# Resource Markets and Prices

Recent chapters have demonstrated that imperfect competition in *product* markets results in the inefficient allocation of resources because impersonal markets do not inform firms of what and how much they should produce in an efficient, least-cost way that accords with the best interests of society. Because firms use scarce resources as factors of production, competition in *resource* markets is also important to resource allocation.

When factors of production are neither mobile nor competitive, the price signals generated in product markets *are not* accurately transmitted back to resource markets, where resource reallocation takes place. If somehow you could arrange to be the only high-school teacher, engineer, or Joe Namath graduating in 1975, the price for your services would be quite different from what it will in fact be. Resource-market pricing also has important implications for income distribution. Since income to any factor of production is a price-quantity relationship, individuals have two ways of increasing their personal affluence: They can influence either the price or the quantity of the resources they own.

Like product markets, markets for the four factors of production (land, capital, labor, and entrepreneurial resources) can be evaluated in a supply and demand context. For the most part, differences among the four factors of production are ignored in this chapter, but not because these differences are unimportant. Our interest here is in developing a general theory of resource-market pricing which will improve our understanding of resource allocation and will also be useful in later discussions of income distribution to human resources, environmental economics, poverty, and other contemporary issues.

Parts A and B explain resource demand and supply in that order, while Part C completes the discussion of the marginal-productivity theory of resource-market pricing under competitive and imperfectly competitive conditions. Finally, some special features of pricing in specific resource markets are briefly introduced in Part D.

## A. THE MARGINAL-PRODUCTIVITY THEORY OF RESOURCE DEMAND

Resource-market pricing poses unique problems which vary with the specific factor of production one considers. However, resource-price theory is generally analogous to the theory of product price.

### Why Study Resource Markets?

The price of the services furnished by factors of production is set by the supply and demand for those services. Moreover, the demand for factors of production partially reflects the value of the goods the resources produce; that is, *resource demand is derived* from the demand for products. The greater (less) the demand for a product, the greater (less) the derived demand for the resources used to produce that product. Today resources are not devoted to the production of attire for mass transit to the moon because there is no demand for such a product, although it seems reasonably safe to assume that there will be by the year 2000. In contrast, the demand for automobiles is strong, and therefore the derived demand for factors of production that produce cars, oil, and tires is also strong.

Resource-market pricing is important for several reasons. Resource prices ration scarce resource inputs among competing uses, just as product prices ration limited outputs to consumers. In view of the fact that demand for the output of an economic system changes (e.g., to space suits and the like), the reallocation of resources with the passage of time is important. (It would be unfortunate indeed if large quantities of resources were still used to produce buggy whips.) A second reason resource-market pricing is important is that economic efficiency in production demands the least costly combination of resources, and there are several ways in which resource-market imperfections subvert and distort the "least-cost" allocation of resources. A third reason for examining resource prices is that they influence the distribution of income. Because income to a factor of production is a price–quantity relationship, resource prices serve to distribute claims on the output of society to owners of scarce resources.[1]

### The Demand for Resources

Our examination of resource pricing begins with a discussion of the demand for resources under competitive conditions. The assumption of competition means that: (*a*) each firm sells products at one given market price which cannot be influenced by any one producer, and (*b*) each firm also is hiring a supply of resources at one competitive market price.

Price is influenced by the supply and demand for factors of production in much the same way that it is in product markets. The demand curve for resources is the typical down-sloping curve which indicates that, as the price of a factor of production declines, the quantity demanded rises. Declining resource demand curves can be traced back to the principle of diminishing returns, i.e., declining marginal product in purely competitive product markets.

### MARGINAL PRODUCTIVITY AND DERIVED RESOURCE DEMAND

The character of derived demand can be clarified by recalling how resources are related to production techniques. We know that there are numerous

[1] In a market economy, you either have resources or you do not, and if you do not, an income and consumption problem is imminent. Unemployed laborers consume greater amounts of hamburger than does the corporate executive, and this is no accident. The latter earns a larger income because he has either a larger "bundle" of resources which are ultimately laid at the feet of producers and consumers, or a greater ability to obtain a higher price for his services. When resource markets are viewed in these terms, it becomes apparent that the subject is an important one. Resource pricing in a market system is amoral, although in some instances resource buyers or suppliers may exert market power which may be regarded as undesirable. Chapters 22 and 24 consider the subject of income distribution in considerably more detail.

ways to employ variable quantities of all resources to produce a given amount of output. A dam could be constructed by millions of laborers working with teaspoons, hundreds of thousands of men working with shovels, or a few thousand men using modern capital equipment. The principle of diminishing returns (encountered earlier in Chapter 15) reminds us, however, that as more of *one variable* resource is employed along with other factors of production supplied in *fixed* quantities, total product increases at a decreasing rate. Diminishing returns occur as additional units of labor, for example, are employed with fixed capital and land resources. Labor's productivity is reflected by smaller and smaller amounts of extra output, or *declining marginal product*, as additional units are employed. If marginal product declines as more and more labor is employed, we can intuitively see part of the logic for a declining resource demand curve; using a greater quantity of one resource in conjunction with other fixed resources produces less and less additional output.

Resource demand also depends on the demand for what a resource produces. Firms demand factors of production because they are capable of producing goods and services consumers are willing to buy. Machinists are in demand in part because of what they produce, shovels are in demand because they are valuable in creating output, and if nobody wants a dam it does not really matter how productive dam-building resources are.

Suppose capital is efficient (productive) in the manufacture of Tom Mix six-guns. Does this mean that a lot of capital will be allocated to the production of scads of these guns? Not necessarily, for if a product has little value, it will not be produced. Furthermore, even when a product is highly valued, certain resources may not be employed because of their low productivity relative to their price.[2] We can thus conclude that product price also influences the demand for factors of production. *Resource demand reflects diminishing marginal productivity as well as the value of the products produced by resources.*

*Marginal Revenue Product* Figure 1 illustrates one firm's demand curve for a factor of production (let us say, capital) in order to bring the productivity and product-price determinants of resource demand into clearer focus. Assuming that all resources other than capital are supplied in fixed quantities, total product will increase at a decreasing rate because of diminishing returns—the additional output or marginal product of capital will decline, as the data in Figure 1 show. The monetary value of total product—*total revenue product*—is obtained by multiplying product price times total product. The monetary value of marginal product, which is called *marginal revenue product* (MRP), can be computed as the change in total revenue product. Thus, the change in total revenue product as one additional unit of a resource such as capital is employed is capital's *MRP*:

$$\text{Marginal revenue product} = \frac{\text{change in total revenue product as}}{\text{one more unit of a resource is used}}$$

$$MRP = \Delta TRP$$

[2] One rarely encounters economists performing tonsillectomies, electricians teaching chemistry, or lawnmowers operated by airplane engines for this intuitively obvious reason.

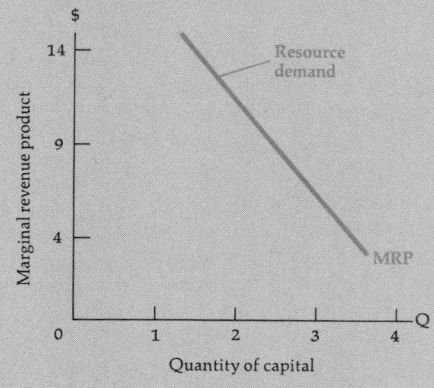

**FIGURE 1**   A Firm's Derived Resource Demand

| Quantity of capital resources | Total product (*TP*) | Marginal product (*MP*) | Total revenue product (*TP* × *P* of $1) | Marginal revenue product (*MP* × *P* of $1) |
|---|---|---|---|---|
| 1 | 12 | | $12 | |
| | | 14 | | $14 |
| 2 | 26 | | 26 | |
| | | 9 | | 9 |
| 3 | 35 | | 35 | |
| | | 4 | | 4 |
| 4 | 39 | | 39 | |

*Resource Demand.* The demand for a factor of production is the consequence of diminishing marginal product and the price of the product produced as reflected by *MRP*. Thus, *MRP* = Δ*TRP* or *MP* × product price (and marginal revenue) of $1 as set by a competitive product market. Resource demand declines as additional units of a resource are employed because of diminishing returns *only* since a competitive firm cannot influence the constant market price for a product.

As a matter of fact, *MRP* can also be found by directly obtaining the value of the marginal product produced in employing one more unit of capital. That is, *MRP* is the result of multiplying marginal product (*MP*) by marginal revenue (where in Figure 1, product price and marginal revenue = $1, for example).[3]

The demand for a resource is the schedule of marginal revenue product (such as that shown in Figure 1) because *MRP* denotes both the productivity and the monetary value of capital's extra output. Accordingly, marginal revenue product simply reflects the additional revenue generated by using one more unit of a resource. As the demand schedule for a resource, schedule *MRP* is a reflection of the producer's interest in generating the additional revenue contributed by hiring one additional factor of production. In Figure 1, the first unit of capital adds a marginal revenue product of $12, the second adds $14, the third $9, the fourth $4, and so forth. However, bear in mind that *it is all units* of capital, working together with other fixed quantities of resources, which create a given amount of revenue.

*The Profit-Maximizing Use of Resources*   Our earlier study of the firm revealed that profit maximization occurs when the last unit of output adds as much to total revenue as to total cost—i.e., profit is maximized in producing a product when the marginal revenue and marginal cost of *output* are equal.

---

[3] Remember, competitive product markets establish a constant product price (a perfectly elastic demand curve) for each firm, and for this reason *product* price (*P*) and marginal revenue (*MR*) are equal at $1 in Figure 1. Figure 1 ignores the possibility of rising marginal product for purposes of simplicity (see Chapter 15).

Thus, because a resource demand schedule indicates the additional revenue generated by employing one more resource, we can determine how much of a resource a firm should employ to maximize profits.

A firm using one resource can maximize profits by hiring resources up to that quantity at which the marginal revenue and the additional cost of the last resource hired are equal. The marginal revenue of a resource is its marginal revenue product, as shown in Figure 2, and marginal resource cost (MRC) is the additional cost of hiring one more unit of a resource. One important point: Observe that the price of a resource hired in a competitive market by one firm is equal to marginal resource cost, as shown in Figure 2. If labor's wage ($w$) is $10 per day, one competitive firm unable to influence the price of labor can hire as many mandays of labor as it wants at $10. Each additional manday employed then increases total cost by $10, an amount equal to the price of labor. Therefore, $w = MRC$.

In Figure 2(a) the profit-maximizing firm will hire $Q$ units of labor because this quantity maximizes profits;

$$\text{Marginal revenue product} = \text{marginal resource cost}$$

$$MRP = MRC$$

If labor's $MRP = \$9$ and $MRC = \$7$, the firm can profitably employ one more unit of labor. If an additional unit is employed, profits will rise, since revenues will increase by $2 more than costs ($MRP$ of $9 less $MRC$ of $7). Of course, if $MRP = \$9$ and $MRC = \$10$, another unit of labor adds more

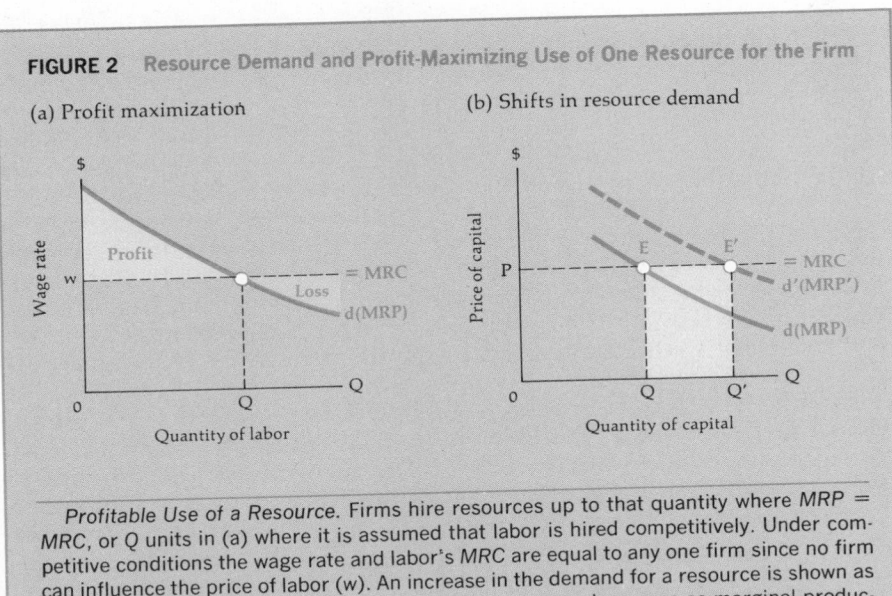

**FIGURE 2**  Resource Demand and Profit-Maximizing Use of One Resource for the Firm

(a) Profit maximization

(b) Shifts in resource demand

*Profitable Use of a Resource.* Firms hire resources up to that quantity where $MRP = MRC$, or $Q$ units in (a) where it is assumed that labor is hired competitively. Under competitive conditions the wage rate and labor's $MRC$ are equal to any one firm since no firm can influence the price of labor ($w$). An increase in the demand for a resource is shown as a shift from $d$ to $d'$ in (b). Resource demand increases or decreases as marginal productivity and product price change—an event that leads to changes in the equilibrium employment of a resource.

to total costs than to total revenue and, since the last resource employed provides no net "pay-off," a profit-maximizing firm will elect not to hire the last unit. In summary, then, the profit-maximizing equilibrium use of one factor of production is given by $MRP = MRC$, where marginal resource cost and the wage rate are the same.[4] Or, to maximize profits, one factor of production is employed until the ratio $MRP/MRC = 1$.

It is simply by mere extension of this same principle that a firm decides how much of two or more resources to employ. For example, in using capital *and* labor resources, each can be profitably employed up to that level where capital's $MRP/MRC =$ labor's $MRP/MRC = 1$. That is, the $MRP$ of *both* capital and labor are equal per dollar of resource cost.

### SHIFTS IN RESOURCE DEMAND

Changes in product price and increases or decreases in marginal productivity are the major reasons that the demand schedule for a resource increases or decreases. If the demand for a product increases and equilibrium product price rises from $1 to $3 per unit, for example, the demand for capital as a factor of production will shift upward or to the right to $d'$ ($MRP'$), as is shown in Figure 2(b). The derived demand for capital increases (or decreases) as consumers are willing to pay a higher (or lower) price for the product. Because resource demand increases to $d'$, $Q'$ units can be hired at the new profit-maximizing equilibrium of $E'$ in Figure 2(b). Individual firms hire more or less capital as $MRP$ increases or decreases, presuming that resource price remains unchanged in Figure 2(b).[5]

Because consumer demand has been strong, the derived demand for resources used in the production of computers and modular housing has increased in recent years. In contrast, declining product demand and decreased resource demand have affected factors of production engaged in producing black-and-white television sets. One important reason for rising employment and increased wages in recent decades is that the productivity of American labor has been rising, a trend triggered by technological changes, the increased skills and improved health of human resources, and the combination of more and improved capital and managerial resources with labor. In the absence of increased productivity, larger quantities of labor might have found employment only at lower wage levels. Because more and more capital is employed per unit of labor each year, labor's $MRP$ curve has gradually shifted rightward as productivity has increased. The process which otherwise would have required movement *down* labor's demand ($MRP$) schedule in Figure 2(a) to successively lower wages has thus been "short-circuited."

Has the use of more capital per unit of labor meant that the price of capital has fallen—that the economy has moved down a capital demand curve like that shown in Figure 2(b)? The answer is, no. Diminishing returns to capital have also been offset as the productivity of capital has in-

---

[4] We postpone for the moment discussing the consequences of market buying power (monopsony) on the part of an employer, which causes $MRC$ and $w$ to diverge. (See Chapter 23.)

[5] Of course, if *total* market demand for a resource increases, each firm may have to pay a higher resource price because of the increasing scarcity of resources, as explained in Part C of this chapter.

creased; that is, capital's *MRP* schedule has also increased throughout the twentieth century, as we saw earlier in our study of economic growth.[6]

## INTERDEPENDENCE AND THE DEMAND FOR RESOURCES

Production entails the use of a variety of resources, all of which cooperate to increase additional output. Therefore, the demand for one resource is dependent upon the use and prices of all resources. Two different effects influence the interdependence of resource demand—the output effect and the substitution effect. The *output effect* describes how a changing price for one resource leads to changes in production costs and product price which may increase or decrease the demand for other resources. The *substitution effect* describes how one resource replaces another.

First, consider the output effect. We will presume that the price of the capital resources used in the production of computers declines, allowing product price to decline and the quantity of computers demanded to increase. As more computers are sold, additional resources in the form of keypunch operators and programmers are needed to prepare and process input data. The output effect associated with the declining price of capital results in an increase in the demand for other resources such as labor. Now suppose that the price of the capital resources required in the production of computers increases. This event may reduce the quantity of computers demanded because higher product prices now prevail, and as business firms computerize less of their operations, the output effect leads to a reduction in the demand for other resources. Thus, a change in the price of one resource affects product price and demand, leading to more or less output and more or less demand for other resources. A contrary type of interdependence—the substitution effect—may also prevail. Consider the plight of computer keypunch operators when the price of the capital resources used to prepare input data declines. The price of labor relative to capital rises due to the technological advances in preparing input data, and the demand for labor declines—capital resources are substituted for labor.

Accordingly, the downward-sloping resource demand schedule (*MRP*) is influenced by the availability, technical capability, and prices of other resources. The precise interdependence in resource markets depends upon the magnitude of the output effect and the substitution effect, both of which may be at work simultaneously. Thus, labor resources have been replaced by capital (the substitution effect) in the automobile and meat-packing industries in recent decades, but greater production efficiencies have held product price increases down, and today families consume much larger quantities of beef and many families have two cars (the output effect). Converse events have decreased the demand for other resources over the years (the use of labor in delivering coal is an example). But what determines the *magnitude* of substitution and output effects on the demand for resources? The answer to this question brings us to another important topic—the elasticity of demand for resources.

## ELASTICITY OF RESOURCE DEMAND

*Elasticity of resource demand* is the percentage change in the quantity of a resource demanded relative to the percentage change in price of a resource,

---

[6] See Chapter 13.

and it is comparable to demand elasticity for a product.[7] There are four primary determinants of resource demand elasticity as a measure of the quantity response of employing firms to changes in resource prices: (a) the elasticity of product demand, (b) the relative importance of the cost of a resource compared to total cost, (c) the rate at which marginal product declines, and (d) the magnitude of possible resource substitution, which is influenced by such factors as resource mobility, production technology, and so forth.

First, demand elasticities for products and for resources are directly related; greater product demand elasticity implies more resource demand elasticity. Suppose that product demand is relatively elastic and the price of a product rises. Because product demand is elastic, the quantity demanded falls rapidly; therefore, the quantity of resources demanded also declines rapidly. The reverse situation prevails if product demand is highly inelastic. In such a case, product price increases are matched by modest declines in the quantity of a product demanded, and the quantity of resources used also declines modestly. Second, the less important the cost of a resource in relation to total production cost, the more inelastic or insensitive is the demand for that resource to increased *resource* prices. When labor costs rise, but constitute a very small percentage of the total cost of producing, total cost and product price will increase modestly and the demand for labor will be relatively inelastic (i.e., insensitive) to an increase in the price of labor. On the other hand, if capital resources constitute 90 percent of total cost, and the price of capital increases, (a) total cost increases markedly, (b) the reduction in the quantity of the product demanded may be relatively large because of the large increase in product price, and (c) the quantity of capital resources used declines significantly because producers *are* sensitive to resource-price changes. Third, if the marginal product of unskilled labor declines sharply as more labor is employed, the influence on the elasticity of resource demand is obvious. The greater the rate of decline in marginal product, the more inelastic is the demand for a resource (remember, $MRP = MP \times P$). Finally, the technological ease with which one resource can be substituted for another determines the elasticity of demand for resources. The more feasible is resource substitution, the more elastic is resource demand. If it is technologically impossible to substitute capital resources such as teaching machines or televised instruction, demand for professorial resources is highly inelastic or insensitive to large increases in salaries. In contrast, if it is technologically feasible to substitute computers for bookkeepers, highly elastic resource demand prevails for bookkeepers, and a wage increase will be matched by relatively large reductions in the quantity of labor demanded.

*Summing up:* The marginal-productivity theory of resource pricing rests on one basic assumption: Firms maximize profits by hiring one more resource up to the quantity at which resource demand given by *MRP* is equal to *MRC*. Within rather wide limits, the competitive theory of resource pricing helps explain how resource-market adjustments work. As-

---

[7] If wages decline from $10.50 to $9.50 per day and the quantity of labor demanded increases from 180 to 220, the elasticity of demand for labor is:

$$\frac{\%\Delta Q}{\%\Delta P} = \frac{40 \div 200}{\$1 \div \$10} \quad \text{or} \quad \frac{0.20}{0.10} = 2$$

suming the goal of profit maximization is sufficiently strong among resource buyers, we can see that there *are* incentives at work that will lead to the reallocation of resources required in a dynamic economy. If the price (*MRC*) of labor rises to a firm and *MRP* is unchanged, other resources may be substituted for labor. Thus, over the years, traffic-signal systems have been substituted for traffic-directing policemen. Similarly, computer systems now process and register students at most colleges and universities, whereas not many years ago, professors labored for hours and even days at such tasks. As resource productivity (shown by *MRP*) and costs (depicted by *MRC*) have changed, the utilization of different types of factors of production has been altered. There are, however, a variety of market conditions which bear heavily upon the allocation of resources, and understanding the supply of resources is a first requirement to filling out the competitive marginal-productivity theory of resource-market prices.

## B. RESOURCE SUPPLY

Our earlier analysis of product markets revealed that supply as well as demand was needed to study price determination, and so it is with resource-market prices. What does a resource supply curve look like? How does it change over time? How elastic or inelastic is resource supply, and why? Is there a supply shortage of recreational resources, clean water, or highly skilled human resources, and if so what are the implications of these circumstances?

There are hazards implicit in discussing market supply in general because again different factors of production exhibit unique characteristics. The market supply of rather mobile space engineers, for example, is markedly different from the supply of immobile farm land. The supply differences between human and property resources are particularly striking. A man and a drill press respond differently to noneconomic elements of the work environment such as hours or hazardous working conditions. Also, the supply of factors of production is not a fixed or constant quantity, although natural (land) resources do border on this extreme. However, even natural resources vary as technology changes. The application of other resources and much effort have reclaimed land from the sea and remedied soil erosion. Nevertheless, generalizations about resource supply can be very useful, even when confined to the bare essentials. Many of the differences that need to be pinpointed can be identified as we go along.

### Competitive Market Supply

One competitive firm encounters a perfectly elastic resource supply curve. However, the *market* supply schedule in Figure 3 slopes upward, reflecting the fact that larger quantities of a resource will be supplied at a higher price. To obtain more of a resource, firms must "bid" resources away from other industries and uses (e.g., leisure for labor). The equilibrium price illustrated for the labor market in Figure 3 is the price at which market demand (the *MRP* of labor in all uses) equals market supply at a wage of $10 per day. Notice that total wage income is shown by the gold area of Figure 3, which is price *w* times quantity *Q*.

There are opportunity costs associated with using resources which are generally scarce and can, for that reason, transfer or be allocated to alterna-

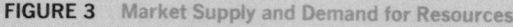

**FIGURE 3** Market Supply and Demand for Resources

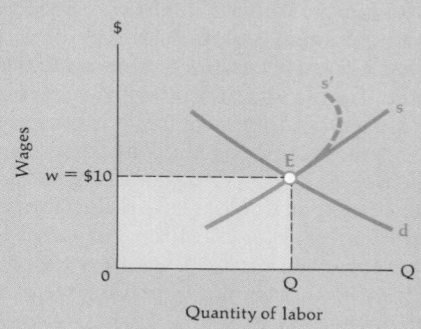

*Resource Pricing.* Market supply and demand determine the price of labor (and other resources). Total income to a resource is $w \times Q$, the shaded area shown in the figure. Under certain conditions, labor supply may be backward-bending as for $s'$, indicating that at higher wages, labor resources opt for more leisure and less work.

tive uses. Human resources, for example, can be induced to become plumbers, doctors, or undertakers, depending in part upon the wage rate, which is a crude reflection of other opportunity options. We say "in part" for very good reasons, since many things other than price influence the quantity of resources supplied. The market supply of undertakers can vary markedly from the supply of teachers because of certain nonprice amenities associated with processing the departed. Or stockbrokers, for example, may band together and set up standards restricting entry into their profession.

Resource owners supply factors of production to those end uses which generate the greatest net gain or benefit to the owner in relation to other alternatives. However, other alternatives may be particularly important to the supply curve for certain types of labor resources, which may exhibit the "backward-bending" characteristic shown for schedule $s'$ in Figure 3. The backward-bending shape of $s'$ simply reflects the possibility that individuals may prefer less instead of more work at a higher wage in a given time period—that is, beyond some wage, labor may prefer leisure to work. Human resources substitute leisure for work because the net benefits from additional work at a higher wage are less than the net satisfaction garnered from additional leisure time.

Resource prices are one important element in coaxing factors of production to move into various uses, but there are numerous and quite obvious difficulties bound up in empirical examination of resource supply. What is the nonmonetary "worth" of being a garbage collector, of entering a risky business venture, or of leasing land to your worst enemy? Are you better off implicitly renting your property to yourself to preserve a view rather than using the land to raise hogs? Each person may view such matters differently and may alter his views as events change. Still, it is clear that resources generally will be transferred to some alternative use if sufficient returns are not forthcoming.

## Economic Rent and Transfer Earnings

Rent is traditionally defined as a payment to property resources. *Economic rent* is used by economists to describe a payment to a factor of production that is attributable to its scarcity and is not needed to transfer the resource from different production efforts. That is, economic rent is a surplus payment above and beyond the payment needed to transfer resources from one use to another. When immobility, scarcity, and other problems result in an inelastic resource supply curve, an economic rent is paid to resources because that same market supply could be offered at lower prices.[8] In contrast, *transfer earnings* are payments that overcome a resource's opportunity costs—they are expenditures required to coax resource owners into supplying factors of production for a particular use.

Figure 4(a) distinguishes between economic rent and transfer earnings. The total payment to labor is the rectangular area of Figure 4(a), $10 per unit times the quantity of labor hired. The shaded areas of Figure 4(a) distinguish between transfer earnings and the residual, which is the economic rent or surplus earned by labor. Market supply curve s indicates the alternative wage levels necessary to entice owners of labor resources to offer varying quantities of their services, and it thus identifies minimum transfer earnings. Given an upward-sloping supply curve, some quantity of labor is offered at a wage less than $10, but hiring $Q$ units requires that employers pay the market price of $w = \$10$ to each unit of labor. The re-

[8] The term "economic rent" is unfortunately ambiguous, but it has interesting origins which go back to English classical economics at a time when controversy raged over the high price of grain. David Ricardo and other economists maintained that the price of grain products was high because of the scarcity of these commodities, a situation that caused farmers to pay high surplus "rents" to obtain more land resources to grow grain. According to Ricardo and certain other economists of that era, it was necessary to lower tariffs on imports and purchase more grain commodities from other nations—a policy disliked by landowners, as you can imagine.

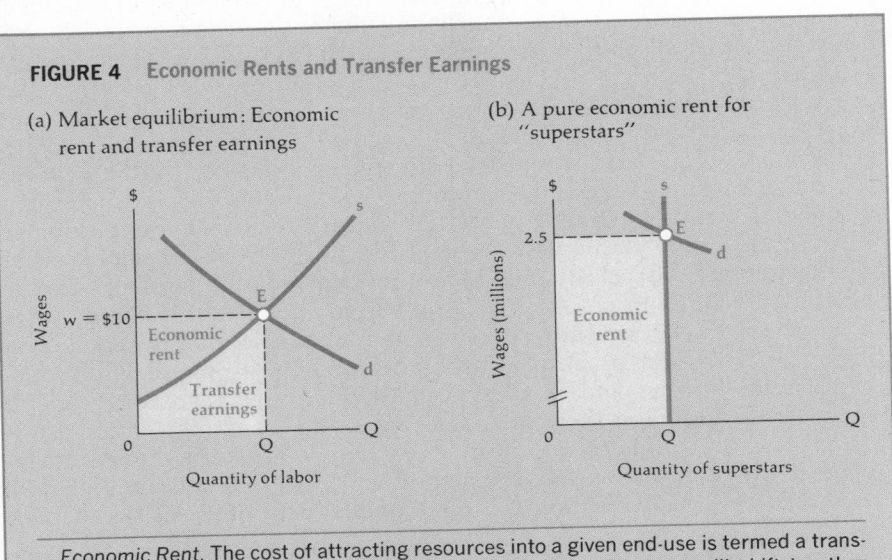

**FIGURE 4   Economic Rents and Transfer Earnings**

(a) Market equilibrium: Economic rent and transfer earnings

(b) A pure economic rent for "superstars"

*Economic Rent.* The cost of attracting resources into a given end-use is termed a transfer payment as shown in (a) since at a lower price some resources will shift to other industries. Economic rent is a surplus paid in excess of what each resource singularly would demand as shown by a supply schedule. The case of a "pure" economic rent shown in (b) illustrates what happens when a resource is extremely scarce and inelastically supplied.

sources offered at a lower wage are said to receive an economic rent. Any competitive firm desirous of hiring labor must pay the market wage, which consists entirely of transfer earnings for only the *last* unit of a resource hired. This wage must be paid to all other units of labor, and at any lower wage, the last worker hired will move to some alternative use where a wage of $w = \$10$ [as in Figure 4(a)] can be earned. Even though only the last unit of a resource receives pure transfer earnings, this is not the case for the labor supply between zero and $Q$ units. Hence, labor earns the economic rent shown in Figure 4(a).

### SIGNIFICANCE OF ECONOMIC RENT

Economic rent is implied by a supply schedule. When supply is perfectly elastic or horizontal, as it was in Figure 2, all resource earnings appear as transfer earnings alone to a competitive firm. Very often, what seems to a buyer of a resource to be a transfer payment is not a transfer cost to society at all, but simply an economic rent. The football team that hires superstar Karol Dullman regards a $2.5 million contract as a transfer cost that gives them a much desired resource and also denies another competitor Dullman's talent. From society's point of view, however, most of this payment is an economic rent, since Dullman's transfer price out of football and into another job is much less than this amount. In short, the scarcity of superstars is responsible for much of the $2.5 million payment. If we need more Dullmans in society, it is often less costly to create them by increasing their supply, rather than continue to pay outrageous economic rents. This is done in football, for example, by maintaining farm clubs in universities, just as the army breeds its generals. Economic rents are the pleasurable lot of owners of any scarce resource, including the only orthodontist in a small community as well as the firm supplying a unique product (e.g., Polaroid cameras).

The extreme case in which only pure economic rent is earned if supply is perfectly inelastic is shown in Figure 4(b)—an approximation of the rather enviable position enjoyed by superstar athletes or by the Beatles a few years back. In such a case, resources can receive large incomes even though the transfer earnings needed to allocate or attract scarce resources into use are small. Resource-market prices still perform an important rationing function in this situation. Any firm demanding a football superstar which is unwilling to pay, say, $2.5 million in Figure 4(b) is simply priced out of the market. This statement presumes, of course, that the equilibrium price of $2.5 million is not in excess of demand ($MRP$) for such a resource to potential buyers, and it also assumes that buyers do not "rig" the market by banding together. Of course, buyers do exactly this in the market for professional athletes, as most of us know. When all buyers do get together they can monopolize the market and substitute a draft system for price bidding, thus reducing the large economic rent otherwise available to superstars.

While it is a scarcity-enforced premium payment, economic rent provides important insights into the rationing of scarce resources and the income-distribution implications of resource markets. Failure to charge a high enough price helps account for congested rush-hour freeways, smog and water pollution, retarded rates of weekend play on most golf courses, and lecture classes of over 300 students, which impose their own noneconomic costs in the lives of most of us today. In these instances, a market-clearing price (that might yield an economic rent) is not charged for utilization of resources.[9] The income-distribution implications of economic rents need little further elaboration. They do help explain why professional football and basketball superstars receive contractual incomes now quoted in the millions. Rents are also attached to the names of some generals, Senators, and Congressmen in the military-industrial complex or in Washington's core of lobbying, legal, and regulatory groups. Similarly, the owners of downtown land or posh townhouses in bustling urban centers command high economic rents and incomes. In such instances, economic rents could be eliminated without affecting production efficiency, a fact which has led some economists to certain policy conclusions.

## PUBLIC POLICY AND ECONOMIC RENTS

If economic rents are unnecessary payments in the sense that they do not transfer more resources for specific purposes, why not eliminate them through price controls or taxation?

A ceiling price could be placed on resources earning an economic rent, but it would be unworkable because market-determined prices would no longer ration scarce resources and some mechanism other than markets would be needed for allocation purposes. Unfortunately, there are serious difficulties inherent in taxation too, as social critic Henry George discovered nearly a century ago. George argued that men arrive and depart as "guests at a banquet" with equal claim to all the land of a nation, and he thus proposed taxing away economic rents on land resources. Economic rents can be removed through taxation, but only to the extent that the *original* owner of a "rent-blessed" factor of production can be taxed. Anyone who disposes of resources capable of earning a rent (say, scarce midtown land in New York City, which has increased in value as the metropolitan area has expanded) builds a rental premium into the selling price paid by the second owner, who no longer captures the original economic rent. In addition, it is extremely difficult or impossible to quantify economic rents. Many property resources have been augmented by capital investments and use over the years (e.g., a prize vineyard), and human resources earning economic rents (e.g., a concert pianist or champion prize fighter) often have been the object of a considerable investment of time, forgone opportunities, and even money. Finally, insurmountable practical problems arise when the possibility of taxing economic rents earned from inherited property wealth is raised. These difficulties have discouraged the use of price controls and taxes as methods of eliminating economic rents.

## INELASTICITY, TIME, AND IMMOBILITY OF SUPPLY

The ultimate source of scarcity-enforced economic rents is the relative scarcity and inelasticity of supply, which is determined largely by time and

[9] Clean air, long regarded as a "free good" in downtown Los Angeles, has not been priced, and both producers and consumers have destroyed a portion of their environment by depleting the resource in question (temporarily, at least). In fact, you *cannot* buy clean air in many cities, except perhaps in antiseptic office buildings.

resource immobility. The supply of a resource tends to be more elastic the longer the period of time under consideration. The shorter the time period, the greater the likelihood that supply will be relatively inelastic. At one point in time, say a day or week, the supply of butchers, blast furnaces, doctors, or iron ore may be very inelastic, but this fixity of supply in the short run can be somewhat obviated in the long run. Over a longer period of time, more men can become butchers, methods of processing lower-grade ore may improve, and the number of physicians can be substantially increased. Indeed, time, technology, and the use of complementary resources have even allowed the Dutch to increase modestly the available supply of land, some of which was once claimed by the ocean.

The time dimension is significant for economic rents because some resource mobility is possible, given enough time. However, the innate immobility of factors of production is also important. Once a piece of land has a specialized building constructed upon it, both the land and the capital component are immobile for many purposes and for a relatively long time period. In such a case, resource supply tends to be inelastic and unresponsive to price increases (as is true of urban land), allowing owners to earn large economic rents if demand for the resource is sufficiently strong. Geography is also of particular importance to resource mobility: The physical relocation of empty space in upstate New York to remedy the scarcity of land in Times Square is not feasible. Occupational immobilities are particularly significant to labor resources. The willing payment of economic rents to a surgeon is understandable when one considers substituting a barber or the proprietor of a butcher shop. Anything that detracts from resource mobility, including the use of market power, acts as a fortress to provide and protect economic rents garnered by resource owners.

## C. THE MEANING OF MARGINAL-PRODUCTIVITY THEORY AND RESOURCE-MARKET PRICING

The subjects of resource supply and economic rents correctly suggest that resource-market pricing is an imperfect process as resources can be misallocated and income may be unequally distributed. Our remaining task is to tie resource demand and supply together in order to lay bare the resource-allocation and income-distribution implications of resource-market pricing. We shall first review the theoretical extreme of purely competitive firms and then force some realism into our views of resource pricing by considering market imperfections.

### A Summary of Pricing in Competitive Resource Markets

The demand for resources is a derived demand that has been identified as the marginal revenue product of a factor of production. Because a MRP schedule displays the marginal revenue added by one extra unit of a resource, we know that one profit-maximizing firm will employ resources until the additional revenue (MRP) and cost (MRC) of one more unit of a resource are equal. A competitive firm is faced with a perfectly elastic resource supply curve because the firm cannot influence market price. However, market supply is upward-sloping because, as numerous buyers compete for resources, they may bid prices up.[10] The upward-sloping market supply schedule indicates that more resources can be coaxed into use only as resource prices rise sufficiently to overcome other competing opportunities and uses for resources. There are three points about hiring resources to remember.

First, income (price × quantity) is distributed to factors of production according to their contribution to production as shown by *MRP*. Second, assuming that producers strive to maximize profits, one firm hires resources until diminishing *MRP* equals *MRC*. Of course, the *market* price of a resource may increase if a large number of firms are desirous of employing that resource; therefore, *prices ration resources via the market mechanism*. Third, since all competitive firms must operate at least cost, all resources used by a firm are combined in the most efficient way when *MRP* per dollar of cost is equal for all resources (as is necessary in pure competition). Just as using the most profitable amount of *one* resource such as labor is shown at *MRP*/*MRC* = 1, the same principle applies to employing *all* resources in the profit-maximizing *and* the least-cost quantities. That is, the least-cost use of all resources is indicated by equal marginal revenue product/marginal resource cost ratios for all factors of production.[11]

Resource substitution is still another important lesson learned from our study of pricing in competitive resource markets. When the price of one resource rises, for example, less of it tends to be used by some firms in their search for "best profits" and "least costs." Or, if labor resources become more productive than formerly (*MRP* increases), more labor is hired by competitive firms as demand shifts to the right. Hiring more of a resource may cause market price to drift upward and firms will stop using more labor when *MRP*/*MRC* = 1. Finally, resources are reallocated from lesser to more efficient uses in the model economy of pure competition. Competitive bidding among buyers sees to it that the *MRP* of any one resource is equal to resource price (and *MRC*) for a resource in different uses. For each resource used among *all* industries, the ratio *MRP*/*MRC* is equalized.[12]

---

[10] There are important implications associated with the resource supply schedule a monopsonist faces, deriving largely from the fact that an employer with monopsony power can depress wages, for example, by virtue of the fact that the firm is the only employer. (More on this subject in Chapter 23.)

[11] That is:

$$\frac{MRP \text{ labor}}{MRC \text{ labor}} = \frac{MRP \text{ capital}}{MRC \text{ capital}} \cdots = \frac{MRP \text{ other factors}}{MRC \text{ other factors}}$$

A firm would hire an eighth unit of labor if labor's *MRP* were \$20 while the wage and *MRC* were \$12, and it would not hire the twentieth unit of capital if *MRP* = \$60 and *MRC* = \$70. Why? Because labor's *MRP* (\$20) is greater than *MRC* (\$12), and more of this factor can be profitably employed, while capital's *MRP* (\$60) is less than its *MRC* (\$70). Therefore, less capital would be hired. *To use all resources at lowest cost, firms equalize additional revenues generated per dollar spent on each resource.*

[12] Thus, for labor in a competitive and fully mobile economy in which firms are maximizing profits we have:

$$\frac{MRP \text{ firm A}}{MRC \text{ firm A}} = \frac{MRP \text{ firm B}}{MRC \text{ firm B}} \cdots = \frac{MRP \text{ all firms}}{MRC \text{ all firms}}$$

Together, adjustments *within* the firm to operate at least cost and resource movements *between* firms result in the distribution of income to resources according to the value of their marginal revenue product.

From our study of resource pricing we can perceive a remarkable amount about the workings of a market system and better understand its shortcomings as well. The marginal-productivity theory of resource pricing shows that resource demand depends in part on production technology and marginal productivity as well as on the demand for products. The marginal-productivity theory also helps explain resource allocation and the substitution of one resource for others both *within* and *between* firms. Adjustments to resource productivity and prices are crucial to resource owners and to employers, both of whom respond to price differentials. In addition, we can see that efficient allocation is as important in resource markets as it is in product markets.

### Some Perspective on Resource Prices

The general economic relations explained by the marginal-productivity theory are useful, but it is also very important to realize that resource markets are quite imperfect in the way they operate—a not-too-surprising conclusion in view of what has already been explained about economic rent. Resource-market pricing is a pervasive albeit a partial influence in an economy, and total abandonment of the marginal-productivity framework of resource-market pricing would be out of order. At the same time that this theory is helpful, however, extreme care is necessary lest more be attributed to its explanatory characteristics than is justified. Resource demand and supply respond to numerous noneconomic influences, and the assumptions that employers maximize profits and resource owners are fully aware of competitive opportunities is a vast oversimplification of a complicated process. The effect of imperfect competition on resource markets and the errors of reasoning associated with the equity of income distribution deserve further clarification.

### RESOURCE DEMAND AND MONOPOLY IN THE SALE OF OUTPUT

Demand for a resource is distorted when a firm is selling in an imperfectly competitive product market because: (*a*) resources receive less than the full value of their marginal contribution to output, and (*b*) fewer resources are employed than under competitive conditions. These two consequences derive from the one central fact that, in selling goods and services, imperfectly competitive firms face a downward-sloping demand curve in the product market, and thus product price and marginal revenue diverge. Since our earlier evaluation of product markets already stated that pure competition is very rarely encountered, it is crucial to examine the effect of imperfect competition in product markets on resource markets.

Resource demand for a monopolistic seller of goods and services is illustrated in Figure 5. Like counterpart firms in a competitive market, a monopolistic employer will maximize profits by hiring resources up to the level at which *MRP* and *MRC* are equal. In the case of product-market monopoly, however, the resource demand schedule is depressed relative to a competitive firm's demand for resources. Under competitive product-market conditions, resource demand declines because of diminishing returns *alone,* but when a firm is an imperfectly competitive seller of output, the derived de-

**FIGURE 5** Resource Demand for Firms Selling in Imperfect Competition

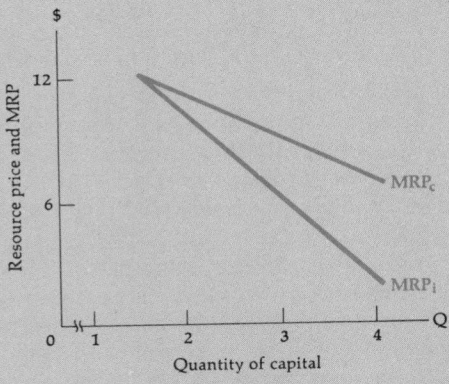

| (1) | (2) | (3) | (4) | (5) | (6) | (7) | (8) |
|---|---|---|---|---|---|---|---|
| | | | | Pure competition | | Imperfect competition | |
| Quantity of capital | Total product | Competitive product price | Imperfectly competitive product price | Total revenue product $(2) \times (3)$ | Marginal revenue product ($MRP_c$) $\Delta(5)$ | Total revenue product $(2) \times (4)$ | Marginal revenue product ($MRP_i$) $\Delta(7)$ |
| 1 | 12 | $2.00 | $3.00 | $24 | | $36 | |
| | | | | | $12 | | $12 |
| 2 | 18 | 2.00 | 2.66 | 36 | | 48 | |
| | | | | | 10 | | 8 |
| 3 | 23 | 2.00 | 2.43 | 46 | | 56 | |
| | | | | | 8 | | 4 |
| 4 | 27 | 2.00 | 2.22 | 54 | | 60 | |

*Imperfect Competition and MRP.* The demand for labor declines relatively more rapidly when firms sell their output in imperfectly competitive markets because of *both* declining marginal product *and* declining product price. Thus resources do not receive a wage equal to the value of their marginal product, and fewer resources are employed.

mand schedule for a factor of production (or *MRP*) declines because of: (*a*) diminishing returns and (*b*) *declining product price and marginal revenue.*

This is more clearly seen in Figure 5. Under competitive product-market conditions, product price *and* marginal revenue are equal at all levels of output because each firm is unable to influence the market price of the product sold. In employing one, two, three, or four units of capital, for example, the declining competitive resource demand schedule *MRP_c* reflects only diminishing returns because the firm's marginal revenue [and product price in column (3) of Figure 5] on each additional unit of output sold is always a constant amount of $2. The firm's demand for capital resources under competitive conditions declines only because of diminishing returns. Now compare competition in product markets to imperfect competition, under which price declines as the quantity of output offered in the market increases [as shown by column (4) of Figure 5]. Total revenue product is now influenced by declining product price as well as by diminishing returns. Marginal revenue product for an imperfectly competitive seller of output, shown by resource demand curve $MRP_i$, declines more rapidly than it does under competitive conditions. In short, demand is lower for all quantities of a resource employed by a firm selling under imperfect competition because product price declines as more output is sold.[13]

The implications of a monopolist's demand for resources are twofold:

1. Product-market imperfections result in the employment of fewer resources. When each additional unit of capital can be purchased at a price of $9, the competitive firm can profitably employ a third unit with $MRP_c$ of $10; but by comparison, the imperfectly competitive firm would not hire a third unit because $9 in MRC exceeds $MRP_i$ of $8, which would lower profits by $1.

2. Resources do not receive the full value of their marginal contribution to output, and for this reason imperfectly competitive firms distort income distribution and the movement of resources into their most valuable uses. If the imperfectly competitive firm of Figure 5 were to sell either 18 or 23 units of a product at a constant price of $2, $3, $4, or more, then the value of output produced by the third unit of capital, as shown by marginal revenue product, would exceed $9, and that third unit of capital would be employed. Resources are not paid a price equal to the full "value" of marginal product because product prices decline for the imperfectly competitive firm.

The point about imperfect competition in product markets is that resource demand is distorted. Under imperfect competition, MRP does not reflect the full value of a resource's marginal product because it is artificially lowered via declining product prices. Thus, resources such as capital or labor are paid prices and incomes below their competitive contribution to output. Moreover, when a monopolist maximizes returns for resources by hiring until $MRP/MRC = 1$, fewer resources are employed than would be in a competitive market—a situation that is a mirror image of Chapter 17's conclusion that imperfectly competitive producers restrict output.

## RESOURCE PRICING AND JUSTICE

Writers since the days of Aristotle and even earlier have debated issues of equity and justice concerning the way a society distributes income, and the marginal-productivity theory we have considered has been abused on this count. The market system as one possible way of organizing economic activity is sometimes defended on the grounds that the market's marginal-

[13] Suppose 1, 2, 3, and 4 units of capital produce a total product of 12, 18, 23, and 27 units of output, all of which can be sold at a constant product price and marginal revenue of $2 per unit by a competitive firm. Under pure competition in Figure 5, the marginal product of a third unit of capital is 5 units (the change from 18 to 23 units of total product). The marginal revenue product of a third unit of capital [column (6)] is the change in total revenue product of $10, or $MRP = MP \times P$, which is 5 × $2. Now consider the monopolistic seller of output that must lower product price from $2.66 per unit to $2.43 in order to sell the 23 units of total product that can be produced with 3 units of capital. Selling 18 units of output at $2.66 each creates total revenue product of $48, whereas selling the larger quantity of 23 units of a product at $2.43 per unit yields $56 in total revenue product. The marginal revenue product of a third unit of capital is $8 in the case of the imperfectly competitive seller in Figure 5. In short, $MRP_c = $10 for the third unit of capital for a competitive firm, whereas $MRP_i = $8 for the monopolistic firm.

productivity solution to the problems of resource pricing and income distribution metes out "justice." If man A is one-half as productive as man B, then A "should" receive one-half the income of the latter, according to the marginal-productivity doctrine. This argument is in error on three different counts.

In the first place, even under the highly unlikely conditions of pure competition, each of several units of labor, for example, *does not* receive a wage equal to the value of its specific marginal revenue product. Rather, *all* labor receives a wage equal to the marginal revenue product of the *last* unit employed. The wage paid to labor (or any resource) is less than marginal revenue product *except* for the last unit hired [see Figure 2(a)]. Curiously enough, in advocating that men should receive a wage equal to the value of their marginal product, proponents of the "marginal-productivity-is-justice" doctrine are bantering about a version of equity long held by such famed social reformers as Oskar Lange and Henry George.[14] Lange contended that labor is "exploited" because it does not receive the total of its product; that is, all of its total revenue product. To do so would require that *each* individual unit of labor receive a wage equal to his individual marginal revenue product. Henry George argued similarly with respect to property owners, who were alleged to appropriate the product of labor as the price of granting workers the privilege of working with land resources —the landowner receiving without producing and labor producing without receiving its full share.

There is a second explanation of why equity or justice is not synonymous with marginal productivity as a basis for resource pricing. Imperfectly competitive product markets do not price a factor of production according to its full worth, as we have seen. Moreover, resource immobilities, wage rigidities, monopoly power in the hands of sellers or buyers of factors of production, unequal access to education, discrimination, inherited wealth, and many other barriers impair the charming income-distribution solution illustrated by the competitive marginal-productivity doctrine. The truth is that throughout history, mankind has contrived a wide variety of self-enrichment schemes. Both the prices of resources and existing patterns of resource ownership have long depended on the rules, customs, and institutional fabric of society, as John Stuart Mill observed long ago, and it is the elite who are in the best position to make rules, enshrine customs, and control institutions. It is impossible to defend resource prices and income distribution in the real world on the basis of the perfectly competitive case, because this idyllic market does not exist.

Third, even if all resources were paid according to their marginal productivity, this is no mark of justice or equity. The market system would then work toward efficiently allocating factors of production and setting resource prices, of course, but this purpose is quite devoid of any moral merit. If one *assumes* that justice is the image of a resource's marginal revenue product, it then follows that justice is what "thou shalt receive." Nations raked with aggregate poverty (e.g., India) may be forced to equate efficiency and justice more nearly, but affluent societies facing less brute need may accord a

[14] See Oskar Lange, *Political Economy* (Warsaw: Polish Scientific Publishers, 1963); and Henry George, *Progress and Poverty* (New York: Robert Schalkenback Foundation, 1966).

higher place to other definitions of justice. It is a normative consideration whether or not efficiency is worth whatever "justice or injustice" markets mete out. Concepts of justice and equity are value judgments, differing dramatically depending upon who is currently licensed to write the rules in a society.[15]

## D. A NOTE ON PRICING IN FOUR RESOURCE MARKETS

When we look carefully at the complexities of resource markets in everyday life and compare what is "out there" to the general survey of resource markets developed above, the oversimplifications of the marginal-productivity theory are striking. Were real-world events to correspond fully to the theory and predictions of resource-market pricing, markets would have to be void of poor information, uncertainty, immobility, and any number of imperfections. Structural perfection demands uncompromised resource mobility and substitutability, perfect knowledge, and exclusive worship of the maximization "god" on the part of all those participating in resource markets. Income distribution arising from resource markets that generate profit payments to entrepreneurs, wage and salary payments to labor, rental (*not* economic) payments to owners of land and natural resources, and the rate of return as a payment to capital resources are much too complex to be fully explained by a simplified view of marginal-productivity theory alone. Remember, however, that every theory abstracts from cumbersome details and is based upon limiting assumptions, and this does not necessarily mean that theory is invalid. It is possible to incorporate more detailed facts, assumptions, and premises in our theory, but doing so requires an advance in the logical and mathematical properties of economic theory better left to later courses.

### Resource-Market Differentiation

One very important feature of resource markets is that they differ, depending upon the general category of resources being considered (e.g., capital vs. labor markets). Markets for resources are also differentiated in that any one resource market can be subdivided into a nearly infinite number of distinct markets.

We can, and in many instances must, examine resources in much greater detail than simply in terms of the four aggregate factors of production. In one sense, *human* and *property* resources can be conceived of as unique, since people are distinct from objects. Furthermore, the bricklayer and winemaker cannot be regarded as comparable units of labor, as any wine connoisseur will verify. Arizona desert and Mississippi delta land are noncomparable land resources, just as a tractor and a gyroscope are quite different forms of capital resources. Human resources of the entrepreneurial variety perform important coordination, innovation, and risk-bearing functions and earn a profit that can be distinguished conceptually from the wages and salaries paid hired manpower, which is more directly concerned with the tasks entailed in the physical process of production. Property resources such as natural land resources are distinct from capital resources,

[15] The issue of equity and justice in the distribution of income is more fully developed in later chapters.

although natural resources are dependent in a large measure on technology, which in turn interacts with capital.[16] As property, natural resources also differ from capital in that the former are gifts of nature, while the latter are directly created by mankind's decision to postpone consumption. Then, too, the supply of capital resources is more elastic because capital can be produced, whereas natural limits (whatever "natural" means) tend to constrain the supply of known natural resources.

It is important to realize that we cannot examine an entire economy and ascertain how much of the earnings of a bricklayer, entrepreneur, or schoolteacher is a return to the capital with which labor works, or to the "labor" inherent in man compared to the "investment" in education and training. Vagueness in distinguishing among resources cannot be helped, but it does pose a serious dilemma in studying resource pricing and income distribution in the real world. The marginal-productivity theory does not provide a fully realistic explanation for the distribution of income because it abstracts from so many important factors influencing the share of income going to capital, labor, and other resources. Economists need more detailed knowledge about specific markets than a simplified theory provides to explain resource prices and the distribution of income.

## Markets and the Four Factors of Production

Despite limited knowledge, resource pricing and the distribution of society's output are central to many economic issues today.[17] It is fitting, therefore, in what remains of this chapter, to very briefly introduce the pricing problems associated with each of the four factors of production.

### NATURAL (LAND) RESOURCES

Natural-resource markets are unique chiefly because of relatively fixed supplies and a high degree of resource immobility due to constraints of physical endowment and geography. Because of highly inelastic supply conditions, changes in demand dominate price determination in markets for natural resources. Increased market prices and economic rents often do not call forth more natural resources, and transfer earnings may be a negligible portion of income payments. Bear in mind, however, that economic rents often do represent a cost of production to firms, and that they also ration limited supplies of natural resources, even though the final value that any natural resource attracts from a covetous market system varies markedly according to mobility, geography, and similar factors.

Depending upon its climate, minerals, and fertility, land may be used for a variety of purposes. Natural resources such as parks and recreational facilities are "worth" quite different amounts and benefit very different groups if they are located in a ghetto, urbanized New York State, or rural

[16] Mountains of pure coal or lakes of oil seeping out of the ground might well be regarded as a blight and not a valuable natural resource by an agrarian tribal society. And it is possible literally to create productive land by the application of fertilizer or irrigation water (capital resources).

[17] Indeed, several subsequent chapters are devoted to the more vital resource problems. Government's public-welfare role is the topic of Chapter 20; the corporate system and entrepreneurial resources are covered in Chapter 21; natural- and environmental-resource pricing and returns are the subject of Chapter 22; and returns to human resources are discussed in Chapters 23 and 24.

Utah. As determinants of the environment, natural resources pose unique pricing problems. The supply, demand, and price characteristics of some natural resources (e.g., air, timber, parks, and water) vary widely, but they do constitute a vulnerable environmental base. We know that natural-resource debasement or depletion is a serious problem in many instances because such resources often are not priced. Clean air and water, for example, are often abused by a market economy centered upon the profit motive and maximizing personal gains. No doubt residents of Los Angeles, Pittsburgh, or Gary would pay dearly for clean air and water, as well as reasonably convenient recreational resources; yet, many such amenities are not available in adequate supplies *at any price!* In many instances, barring highly unusual changes in the values of society, natural-resource pricing is not a problem which the private sector of the economy will resolve. Strip mining, congested ground and air traffic, floods, and air and water pollution are problems of natural-resource pricing and allocation which are amenable to resolution only if the public sector enters the lives of all of us in greater measure. Environmental pollution is of great import to social and economic welfare today, and the accidents of past custom, enshrined values, and entrenched power positions must be remedied to alleviate the situation.

## CAPITAL RESOURCES

Capital resources such as machinery, buildings, and equipment are in demand because they are used widely in the roundabout production process characteristic of contemporary technology.[18] Once an investment in capital goods is made it tends to be relatively immobile; however, there is a significant degree of aggregate mobility to capital. Capital resources depreciate with use, and the stock of capital grows each year; therefore, net investment and depreciation reserves can be used to acquire more productive capital or capital can be mobilized into alternative uses. In this sense, pricing in capital markets can be effective in allocating resources.

The formation of capital resources through investment effectively requires a society to postpone using resources for present consumption. As we know, a society saves and invests by using the productive capabilities of resources to produce capital goods that are only *indirectly* capable of satisfying present consumption needs. Capital resources are productive man-made assets which yield a rate of return (an interest rate) that ultimately helps determine the "price" of capital goods, and it is this relationship which merits more attention here.

Individuals owning capital resources receive an income stream over some future time period, depending upon the productivity of capital and its useful life. The yield or rate of return to capital is a measure of net earnings relative to the costs of capital resources (see Chapter 7). If some selected capital asset costs $\$C$ and earns a net return of $\$E$ for each year in the future, the rate of return is $\$E/\$C$ (e.g., if $E = \$10$ and $C = \$100$, the interest returned is $\$10/\$100$ or 10 percent).[19] The *market price* of capital

[18] The term "roundabout" describes the many different stages of manufacturing and processing which typify the creation of final output in a complex economy.

[19] It is sometimes useful to distinguish between *money* and *real* returns to capital. Under the inflationary conditions Americans experienced in 1967–1970, the money interest rate in capital markets was driven to 9 percent (and even higher), but the *real* interest rate (approximately equal to the money interest rate *less* the percentage change in prices) remained quite steady at its historic average of 3–4 percent.

resources is the capitalized value of assets, and the interest rate is an important determinant of capital-market prices. In general, the lower the interest rate, the greater the market value of capital or other forms of assets, such as bonds. For example, the capitalized value of a capital investment creating a $10 perpetual income stream when the going market interest rate is 10 percent is:

$$\text{Capitalized market value} = \frac{\$\text{earnings}}{\text{interest rate}} \quad \text{or} \quad \frac{\$10}{0.10} = \$100$$

At a lower interest rate of 5 percent on investments in comparable capital resources, the market value would be $200 ($10/0.05), and if a higher interest rate of 20 percent prevailed, the market value of $10 in permanent income would be $50 ($10/0.20). Capitalizing the value of earnings generated by capital resources is thus nothing more than evaluating the present value of *future* earnings, which means that the market price of capital is viewed in terms of the *present discounted value* of capital assets yielding some fixed dollar payment in the future. Remember, too, that the further away in the future a dollar of earnings is, the less its present value.[20]

The general rate of interest performs the function of rationing and allocating limited supplies of loanable funds to different prospective projects and users, just as other resources are allocated via their prices. Economic expectations, risk and uncertainty, and existing economic conditions all alter the anticipated return to capital resources and therefore influence the capitalized market value of capital resources. Then, too, the "price" of liquid-money balances—the interest rate—is determined by the demand and supply for funds, which is subject to government monitoring via banking institutions such as the Federal Reserve System. If yields on one type of capital asset exceed the interest rate, additional capital investment is profitable, but if yields are less than the marginal return to capital as shown by the rate of return, firms tend to forgo additional investment. Consequently, a firm can invest profitably in fewer types of capital resources at relatively high interest rates than it can at lower interest rates, and in this sense, scarce capital is rationed among competing uses according to its relative productivity.

It is important to recognize that capital markets are diverse and imperfect just as are markets for other resources. In the first place, government does influence interest rates; moreover, banks may also ration limited funds by gauging the "credit-worthiness" of a borrower. Internal financing by large corporations as well as considerable concentration of wealth in the hands

---

[20] In Chapter 7 it was noted that you would be foolish to give me $100 today for a capital resource of some sort that would return $100 to you 12 months from today because your liquid-wealth claim of $100 can receive a positive interest rate. [You can set aside $93.46, and within a year it will grow to $100 at 7 percent interest; thus, the present value of $100 payable in a year is $93.46 (at 7 percent).] Similarly, the market price of capital assets producing any amount of earnings for a future period of *several* years is discounted to its present value because there is a positive interest rate. Thus, the present discounted value for *each* dollar invested in capital assets payable in two years is 87.3 cents today because a 7 percent annual return can be earned for two years. Discounting to present values is shown by a table of compound interest rates, where one need only divide the principal amount by 1 plus the compound interest rate. At 7 percent, a principal amount of $1 compounds at the rate: $ Principal $\times (1 + 0.07)^n$ and discounting to present value is simply $ Principal $\div (1 + 0.07)^n$, where $n$ denotes the number of years before payment is made.

of a few sizable financial institutions are also important to capital-resource markets. Moreover, technological changes can have a marked influence on capital yields, and uncertainty is an ever-present companion to investors. Capital-market pricing also is subject to important adjustments for risk, liquidity, taxes, and so on. Consequently, there is not one interest rate, but rather a complex structure of rates that relate to a wide array of capital resources. All in all, however, the interest rate and rate of return function as rough guidelines to allocate scarce capital resources.

### THE ENTREPRENEUR AND PROFITS

The entrepreneur functions in several distinct capacities: He is an assumer of known risks, a willing victim of economic uncertainty, a coordinator of the production process, and an innovator who must remain oriented to change. Normally, the entrepreneurial factor of production earns a profit for acting in these capacities. As an organizing element, short-run economic profits or losses "signal" the need for resource adjustments. Profits are a crucial motivational force in the market because they represent the return for performing the functions of directing resources to those uses most consistent with consumer demand. Normal profits are a legitimate payment to a resource because they "organize" producer response under competitive conditions in a market economy. Notice, however, that the importance of profits does not mean that they should be "high" or "low," nor does it imply that the profit motive smoothly and perfectly performs its role as an organizing force leading to the greatest good for the greatest number.

One sometimes overlooked feature of the profit return is that profits *include* a return to all implicit costs. Thus, the profit return may represent implicit rent, wage, and interest payments for the use of land, labor, and capital which must be managed and rewarded because opportunity costs are incurred in using scarce resources. The payment of profits is also a reward for the assumption of identifiable business risks as well as other economic uncertainties. The prospect of feast or famine—success or failure—imposes a cost which most men prefer to avoid and typically will avoid unless they receive a payment for accepting such uncertainty. Profits and risk also are integral parts of the urge to innovate, a process requiring that entrepreneurs make investment commitments to a course of events from which retraction may be extremely costly. Once these characteristics of the profit function are given their due, it is apparent that profits perform a vital function in society.

Preaching about profit legitimacy is one thing, but it is quite crucial to remember that competition is necessary to maintain checks and balances against excess profits. Competitive markets serve to fragment economic power, and without this check some of the return to entrepreneurial factors of production may revert to scarcity-induced economic profits—payments which exceed the transfer costs of the entrepreneurial factor of production. We have already seen in our discussion of product-market imperfections that monopoly tends to result in economic profits above and beyond implicit opportunity costs. The "normal" return is a legitimate reward for functions performed, just as an economic profit is an unnecessary premium accruing to selected power groups. Most economists contend that economic profits blunt resource mobility and producer response to consumer demand and thus are a tax which society can well do without.

Monopoly power represents an insurance policy against the whimsical changes of a competitive market, and for that reason market power is often acquired with some zeal in the business sector of an economy—a matter we shall return to in examining the business enterprise and public policy in Chapter 21.

## RESOURCE MARKETS FOR LABOR

Like other resource markets, labor markets are characterized by heterogeneity, imperfections, and institutional influences that have a profound impact on human-resource pricing and income distribution. Simplifying the complexities of real-world markets for labor through marginal-productivity theory is helpful, but a host of other matters render reliance upon a general theory of labor pricing very hazardous indeed. Two special features of labor-market pricing are the way in which immobility and market imperfections affect wages, and the manner in which labor prices and income distribution relate to contemporary social problems such as poverty and discrimination.

The simplest and least satisfactory explanation of wage determination is that differences in labor productivity cause wages to vary from market to market. On the one hand, evidence does suggest that over the long run and in the very general case, the marginal-productivity theory of wage determination is partially correct. But it also is very clear that economic theory leaves a great many questions about wage determination unanswered. The economic welfare of the vast majority of people is almost completely reliant upon the sale of their labor services, and for that reason monopoly power, geographic immobility, poverty, and economic inequality are among the many special dimensions to the pricing of labor resources. The structure of thousands of distinct labor markets differentiated by regional, occupational, and industrial characteristics also is a most important determinant of wages and income payments to labor. Much of the labor market operates imperfectly because it is fragmented by worker immobility; wages also vary in part because of differences in ability and quality among human resources; economic institutions such as labor unions and professional associations may affect wages; and some wage differentials also reflect an equalization payment for unpleasant or hazardous work conditions. Poverty and income inequality are related to education and age, customs, the law, the distribution of wealth, and the health of labor. Imperfect knowledge on the part of workers also acts as a differentiating barrier in labor markets, as does racial discrimination.

Unemployed Appalachian workers are not readily transported to job openings in Chicago any more than watchmakers are easily moved into ship-building. Noncompeting labor markets (e.g., butchers and surgeons) may promote income inequality, and some labor markets are characterized by supply restrictions due to entry barriers and licensing procedures (the case among plumbers or lawyers). In still other instances, an entire work force may be organized, as in the case of automobile production. Another interesting feature of labor markets is that millions of young, old, and female workers move in and out of the labor force in any given year, and this mobility influences supply, prices, and income distribution. Where labor resources are concerned, the magnitude and incidence of unemployment are also given special attention, as are manpower retraining and investment in education—all of which are related in crucial ways to the economic welfare of man. Finally, government has a special influence on wage determination and income distribution, as income taxes, collective-bargaining legislation, and minimum wages suggest.

*Summing up:* At the present time, the marginal-productivity theory of resource pricing remains a highly general and incomplete, yet nonetheless useful, explanation of resource-price determination that is capable of explaining some portion of the real world. Such a general level of analysis of the markets for factors of production is inadequate on many counts, however. Numerous other influences help determine prices and incomes for resources—and we will have to spend much more time on more specific details to better understand resource prices.

## REVIEW
### Summary

1. Resource markets are important because resource prices: (*a*) ration scarce factors of production to employers, (*b*) help determine how resources are comingled to produce efficiently, and (*c*) are one of several elements that determine the distribution of income. The demand for resources is derived from product demand—resources are used to produce in the measure that goods and services are in demand.

2. The two major influences on the demand for resources are marginal productivity (the additional output of one more unit of a variable resource) and the price (*P*) and marginal revenue (*MR*) of a product. When product markets are competitive, *P* and *MR* are equal, and the demand for resources declines only because of declining marginal product (*MP*). The demand schedule for a resource is defined as marginal revenue product (*MRP*), which is the change in total revenue product which results from employing one more unit of a variable resource, or the product of multiplying marginal product and competitive product price ($MRP = MP \times P$).

3. Firms employ the profit-maximizing quantity of resources by hiring up to that quantity at which additional revenue (*MRP*) is equal to the additional cost of a factor of production, which is termed *marginal resource cost* (*MRC*). Thus, if *MRP* is less than *MRC*, such a unit of a resource cannot be hired profitably, but if *MRP* exceeds *MRC*, it is profitable to hire another unit. The demand curve for a resource shifts when product price and productivity change. When resource demand as given by a *MRP* schedule increases, more of that resource tends to be hired by a firm; the converse is also true, as the $MRP = MRC$ rule for profitably using resources suggests. Both the output effect (the influence of changes in total output on resource demand) and the substitution effect (the technical substitution of resources) show interdependence at work in resource markets, and the elasticity of resource demand shows the quantity response to a price change for resources.

4. The market supply schedule for resources is upward-sloping because opportunities are sacrificed in using resources for any one purpose. Market equilibrium price is that point at which supply and demand for a factor of production are equal. Economic rents are a scarcity-enforced surplus payment in the sense that they are not transfer earnings that serve to allocate more or fewer scarce resources to given uses, but eco-

nomic rents do perform a rationing function. Remedying the scarcity and the inelastic supply characteristic of resource markets appears to be a more likely way of reducing economic rents than taxes or price ceilings. The greater the degree of supply inelasticity due to resource immobility, the more likely it is that economic rents will be a larger proportion of the total income payment to resources.

5. Resource pricing guides firms in their search for least cost, and competition between firms for factors of production encourages the employment of all resources up to that point of production at which equal MRP/MRC ratios prevail for *all* firms hiring *any* resource. Imperfect competition due to the existence of monopoly power on the part of a firm in selling a product distorts resource markets. The demand for resources is diminished because MRP is lowered via declining product price and marginal revenue as well as through diminishing returns. Finally, remember that even under competitive conditions, there is no special equity attribute to marginal-productivity theory. Illusions about justice prevailing when resource prices are equivalent to resource productivity are just that—illusions!

6. The convenient classification of resources into four factors of production can be misleading, because there are vast differences between types of labor and capital, for example. Each of the four factors of production presents different and unique pricing problems; however, the general approach embodied in the marginal-productivity theory can be helpful in understanding resource pricing *if* the distinctive features of the literally thousands of different resource markets are recognized.

## Identify the Following Concepts and Terms

- marginal revenue product
- marginal resource cost
- MRP = MRC
- substitution effect
- economic rent
- monopolistic MRP
- four resource markets
- derived demand
- output effect
- backward-bending supply
- transfer earnings

## Questions to Answer

1. Assume that the marginal product of labor and capital are as given below in the production of tons of grapes, which sell in a competitive market for $200 per ton. Compute and diagram the demand (MRP) curve for both resources. Assuming that labor for picking grapes can be hired competitively for $1,200 per unit for the season and capital can be hired at $3,700 per unit, how many units of each would be hired? Why?

| Labor | Marginal product | Capital | Marginal product |
|-------|------------------|---------|------------------|
| 1 | | 1 | |
| | 12 | | 30 |
| 2 | | 2 | |
| | 8 | | 24 |
| 3 | | 3 | |
| | 4 | | 18 |
| 4 | | 4 | |

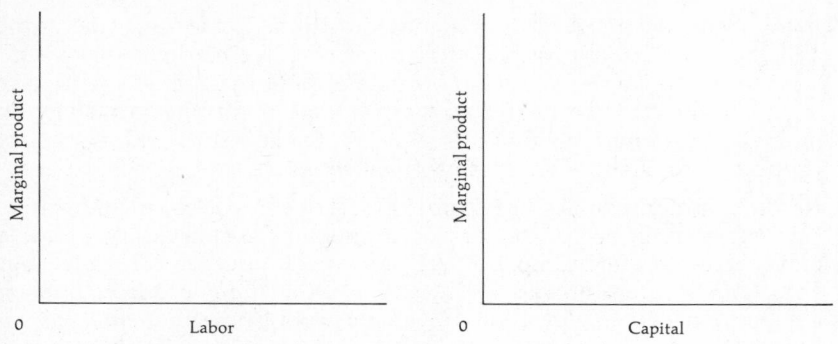

2. What pattern of resource reallocation would occur if the price of grapes fell to $110 per ton? Why? If the price of capital declined to $3,000 and the price of labor increased to $1,700, what changes would occur?

3. Explain what influences the elasticity of demand for a resource. How are the output and substitution effects different? How might they be related, if at all? If some resource earns an economic rent, what policies might be adopted to remedy the situation? Why might this be a desirable objective? What would it ignore?

4. Evaluate the following statements:
   (a) "Economists have demonstrated that the market economy functions perfectly in allocating resources to their most efficient uses with no distortions."
   (b) "Economic theory proves that the price of all resources such as labor should be equal to labor's productivity or *MRP*, and this is a just wage."

# CHAPTER 19
# Microeconomics in Retrospect

Our analysis of microeconomics has shown how markets and prices organize economic affairs and help allocate resources by determining *what* is produced, *how* resources are combined in production, and *to whom* the output and income of a nation are distributed. In this chapter we will review these ideas, stripping them of certain details in order to develop a basis for a microeconomic evaluation of market prices and resource allocation.

The four parts of the chapter summarize microeconomics at different, but incisive levels of analysis. In Part A the nature of consumer satisfaction is explained, while in Part B the relationships among thousands of individual but interdependent product and resource markets are discussed. In Part C we will consider economic efficiency as a dimension of social and economic welfare, and in Part D we will critically evaluate the theory of business firms and prices with which we have tarried so long. Attention in this chapter is confined largely to a review of the basic premises and tools of price theory in anticipation of considering current challenges and issues of political economy in a market system in subsequent chapters.

## A. CONSUMER SATISFACTION AND MARKETS

Thus far in our discussion, the notion of consumer satisfaction has been ignored, a shortcoming which needs to be remedied if we are to evaluate the market process. Knowledge about consumer satisfaction permits us to examine the market as a whole, to spell out the welfare implications of a price system, and to evaluate microeconomics.

### The Theory of Marginal Utility[1]

The general nature of consumer satisfaction must be clarified in order to fully develop the theory of competitive pricing and set the stage for the examination of selected welfare problems in later chapters. *Marginal utility* —the additional satisfaction gained from consuming one more unit of a product—helps explain an important aspect of economic efficiency and pricing. The principle of *diminishing marginal utility* describes how the consumption of increasing quantities of a good results in diminishing levels of consumer satisfaction or utility.[2]

Suppose that a typical consumer wishes to purchase and consume a

---

[1] This section may be omitted at the instructor's option without loss of continuity.

[2] Marginal utility, explained earlier in Chapter 14, is further developed in the appendix following this chapter.

product—let us say, bars of soap—in some defined time period. *Total utility* (satisfaction) from consuming the first few units may be rather high, but beyond some level of consumption, successive units of soap add less and less additional or marginal utility (assuming that we ignore variations in time, sanitary conditions, and so forth). Total utility increases at a decreasing rate as more and more of a single good is consumed. Figure 1(a) depicts the *total* utility of soap as five, eight, and nine units of satisfaction from consuming one, two, and three bars of soap. Notice in Figure 1(b) that the marginal utility (the change in total utility) of each additional bar of soap is five, three, and one units of satisfaction as the first, second, and third bars of soap are acquired. The additions to total utility as consumption of soap rises constitute the marginal-utility (*MU*) schedule drawn in Figure 1(b). Schedule *MU* of Figure 1(b) represents the subjectively valued satisfaction that is generated by consumption of greater quantities of a good.

The concept of diminishing marginal utility is useful because marginal utility represents the theoretical justification behind a typical downward-sloping consumer demand curve, as explained in Chapter 14. Notice too that Figure 1(b) shows that zero and even negative marginal utility (called "disutility") can occur. The zero marginal-utility point illustrated in Figure 1(b) occurs where total utility reaches a maximum of nine "utils" when three bars of soap are consumed. Consumption of more than three bars of soap actually reduces total satisfaction in this example, and thus marginal utility becomes negative. Several dozen refrigerators per home, hundreds of bars of soap per week, or several gallons of Blimey Ale consumed in a day could very well produce such marginal disutility.

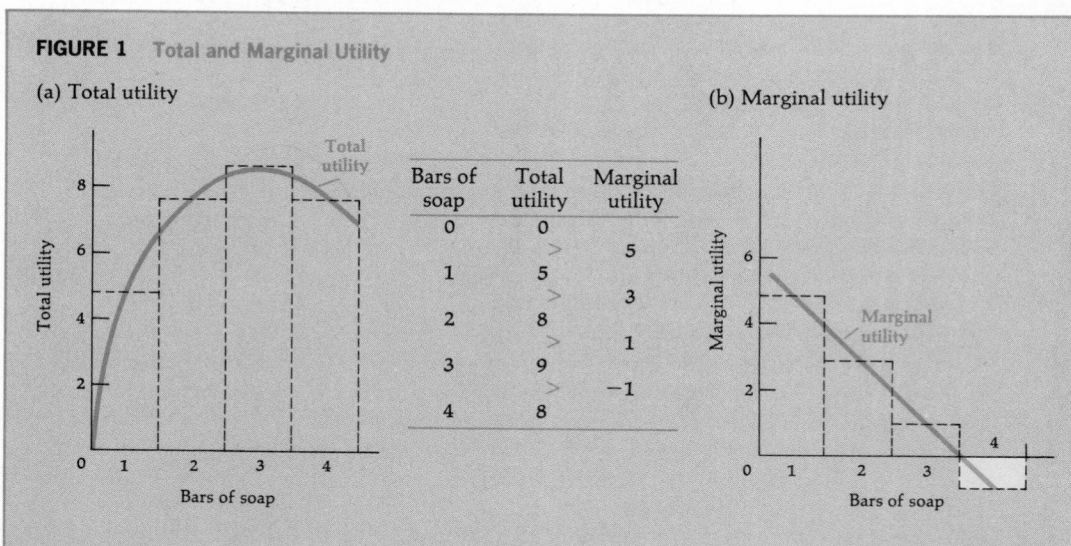

**FIGURE 1**  Total and Marginal Utility

(a) Total utility

(b) Marginal utility

| Bars of soap | Total utility | Marginal utility |
|---|---|---|
| 0 | 0 | |
| | | 5 |
| 1 | 5 | |
| | | 3 |
| 2 | 8 | |
| | | 1 |
| 3 | 9 | |
| | | −1 |
| 4 | 8 | |

*Diminishing Marginal Utility.* Satisfaction or total utility increases at a decreasing rate in (a) as consumption of one good increases. Therefore, a schedule of marginal utility is a downward-sloping curve and, like a demand schedule, may be regarded as the generalized value consumers place on additional items of a good. Total utility reaches a maximum at zero marginal utility, or three bars of soap in this example.

MARGINAL UTILITY AND PRICE

In economics a direct relationship is postulated between the price of a good and the marginal utility of that good to consumers. The declining marginal-utility curve is thus a conceptual explanation or representation of empirically derived demand curves. Lower marginal utility explains a lower product price, where price represents the consumer's sacrifice of forgone opportunities, since the consumer's limited income commands title to other goods.[3] In parting with scarce dollars that command goods and services to fulfill unlimited wants, consumers forgo meeting some wants to satisfy others; thus, the lower the marginal utility of a good, the less the consumer values that good in relative price terms.

Consider this dilemma. Why is the price of diamonds higher than the price of water, or why does a sports car like the Jaguar command a higher price than soap? Is it not true that the total utility of water exceeds the total utility of diamonds? It is, and the total utility of soap no doubt exceeds the total utility of Jaguars. The dilemma is solved once we realize that satisfaction from the *last* unit of a good consumed—a good's marginal utility and not its total utility—influences the price people can be induced to pay for it. Goods which require the use of vast quantities of costly scarce resources (e.g., Jaguars) are more likely to be limited in supply; therefore, they may yield greater marginal utility at some higher equilibrium market price. The equilibrium price determined by market supply and demand reflects both resource scarcity and marginal utility. Therefore, water, soap, and air are cheap, whereas diamonds, bathtubs, and Jaguars are dear in relative price terms.

Diminishing marginal utility does not mean that all goods will be consumed until zero marginal utility is reached because goods usually are not free. Unless goods are free goods which command no price, it is impossible to maximize their total utility (i.e., reach zero marginal utility) because consumer incomes are limited and price is an obstacle to consumption. Many products are not free goods; hence prices perform the vital rationing function noted often before.

MAXIMIZING UTILITY

A second feature of the theory of marginal utility is that because incomes and goods are limited, consumers must make choices. Economists typically assume that individual consumers make *maximizing* choices that provide the greatest possible consumer satisfaction from limited incomes. Faced with limited budgets and innumerable choices, a satisfaction-maximizing household must equalize marginal utilities per dollar spent for *all* goods. One consumer thus allocates his expenditures so that the marginal utility ($MU$) derived from the last unit of all the goods he consumes is proportional to product price ($P$). Thus, in choosing to purchase tea and beans, a maximizing consumer allocates his total expenditures so that the last unit of each product consumed yields like units of satisfaction per dollar of expenditure.

[3] Recall from Chapter 14 that both demand and supply determine the equilibrium price. The point about $MU$ and price is that the product-demand schedule is a proxy for additional consumer satisfaction, as shown conceptually by a schedule of $MU$.

$$\frac{MU_{tea}}{P_{tea}} = \frac{MU_{beans}}{P_{beans}} \quad \text{or} \quad \frac{100}{\$10} = \frac{50}{\$5} \quad \text{which is} \quad \frac{10}{\$1}$$

If the $MU$ or the $P$ of one product rises or falls relative to the other, consumers can increase total satisfaction by purchasing more of the high-utility-per-dollar good and less of the low-utility-per-dollar good.

Or consider alternative choices over dates with Jane Dour, Myrtle Fizz, and Gina Go-Go. A maximizing male would "invest" in date expenditures until marginal utility was proportional to price. The easiest way to prove this is to consider a disequilibrium situation. Suppose the choice involves one more date with either Miss Fizz or Miss Go-Go (we arbitrarily rule out Jane Dour), and the additional satisfaction is as follows:

$$\frac{MU_{Go-Go}}{P_{Go-Go}} = \frac{60}{\$10} \quad \text{and} \quad \frac{MU_{Fizz}}{P_{Fizz}} = \frac{10}{\$5}$$

Marginal utility per dollar is 6:1 for Gina and 2:1 for Myrtle; thus, a rational (maximizing) consumer would opt for spending more of his limited income on Gina and less on Myrtle.[4] Only when equal marginal utility/price ratios prevail is the consumer in "equilibrium," and as long as this condition is not met, he benefits by switching expenditures from low to high $MU/P$ goods. Accordingly, consumer satisfaction is maximized when $MU/P$ for one good is equal to $MU/P$ for other goods for one consumer.

Of course, \$1 may represent a quite different marginal sacrifice to a low-income migrant laborer compared to a wealthy corporate executive. Or a struggling student may well place a higher "marginal utility" value on another dollar of expenditure than does a professor, simply because the latter's income is usually several times larger. Lack of funds may ration the student out of some goods and give the professor and others in the affluent set clear access to them. Because the distribution of income and the marginal utility of money vary, an economy cannot be said to be organized to bring about the "greatest good for the greatest number," even though individual consumers maximize utility—a reality which the poor recognize in comparing their income to that of the Rockefeller brothers. After all, the consumers in a society could be maximizing individual utility, and at the same time, 90 percent of the population could starve to death for lack of income. Under such conditions, one could hardly conclude that social welfare is maximized. Maximum social welfare and the maximum satisfaction of individual consumers are not synonymous as long as the distribution of income is ignored. Also bear in mind that the marginal utility of a service or a good varies according to an individual's subjective preference. Relative preferences for books about economics and biology vary in predictably different ways among university professors in economics and in biology. For the most part, economists are in the dark when it comes to coping

---

[4] However, if time and events lead to that state called "love," $MU$ may rise for one lady or the other, and for that matter $P$ may become a rather unimportant consideration. Were Gina to become increasingly attractive in the state of love, this change would be depicted as an increase—a rightward shift—in the $MU$ schedule shown in Figure 1(b).

definitively with subjective preferences in real life and adjusting the consideration of utility for income distribution.[5]

*To recapitulate:* The theory of marginal utility is a highly oversimplified, but nonetheless instructive way of illustrating consumer satisfaction in very general terms. An individual consumer maximizes satisfaction or utility by purchasing products, $a, b, \ldots n$ until equal $MU/P$ ratios prevail for all goods consumed. Because it is difficult to specify an optimal distribution of income, it is impossible to determine maximum social welfare in measurable terms. However, if *all* consumers in a society are to maximize satisfaction, the marginal-utility ratios for all goods consumed must be proportional for *all* consumers who pay like product prices ($MU_a/MU_b$ must be equal for Brown, Smith, *et al.*).[6]

## B. A GENERAL EQUILIBRIUM VIEW OF MARKETS

So far our consideration of markets and prices has been partial in that we have looked at ideas one at a time, including the profit-maximizing operation of producing firms; the least-cost, efficient use of resources; and, most recently, maximization of a consumer's utility. Moreover, our attention has focused on one isolated market at a time, largely ignoring interactions among innumerable product and resource markets. Partial equilibrium analysis of this sort is useful in providing a bird's-eye view of prices and output in one market, for example, but it does make the unrealistic assumption that all other sectors of an economy are constant and unchanging. Even though such partial analysis is perfectly appropriate for some purposes, the larger dimensions of market and price interrelationships— *general equilibrium analysis*—deserve brief attention. General equilibrium analysis concentrates on the interaction of innumerable product and resource markets.

General equilibrium analysis typically begins with a consideration of households representing a population that consumes goods and services supplied in product markets. Conventional economic theory assumes that, in purely competitive markets, individuals pay the same price for identical products and use whatever limited incomes they have in a rational fashion; that is, they maximize their satisfaction or utility by rationally selecting from available goods.

### Circular-Income Flows and Markets

Figure 2 summarizes the key relationships among resource and product markets. Individuals demand goods and services, as we illustrate in the product-market portion of Figure 2, but these same consuming household units also own and supply scarce factors of production. Producing business

---

[5] We ignore recent research advances in utility theory involving simulation and other esoteric methods, which are better left to advanced courses. Interesting distinctions can be made between cardinal and ordinal utility, and entertaining exercises can be constructed using indifference-curve theory. Those interested in such mental ping-pong should consult the appendix following this chapter.

[6] If the $MU/P$ ratio is equal for all goods ($MU_{milk}/P_{milk} = MU_{beans}/P_{beans}$), we can also see that the marginal-utility ratios of two products (e.g., $MU_{milk}/MU_{beans}$) are equal to the price ratios for the products ($P_{milk}/P_{beans}$).

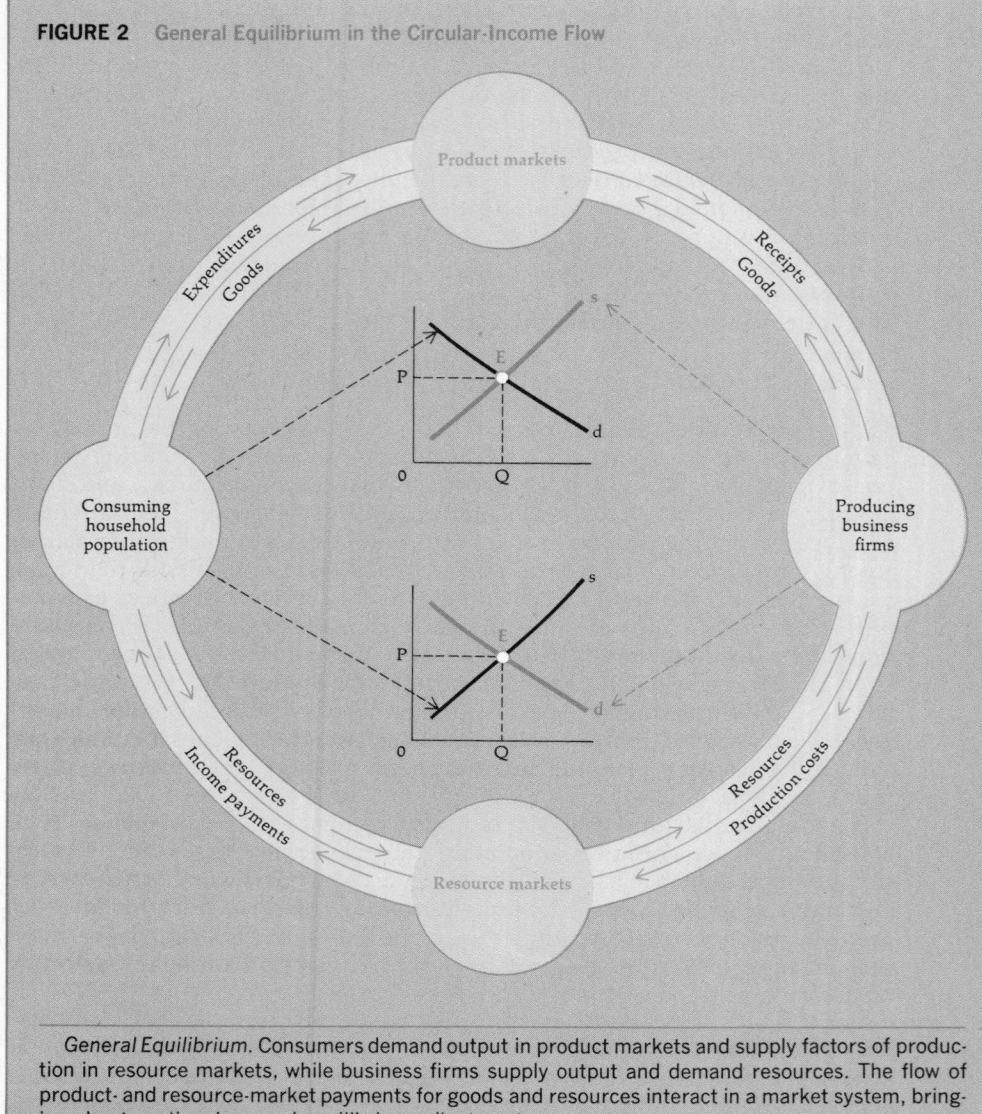

**FIGURE 2**    General Equilibrium in the Circular-Income Flow

*General Equilibrium.* Consumers demand output in product markets and supply factors of production in resource markets, while business firms supply output and demand resources. The flow of product- and resource-market payments for goods and resources interact in a market system, bringing about continual general-equilibrium adjustments.

firms supply output in product markets and demand resources, as Figure 2 also shows. As long as resources are scarce relative to the wants of consuming households, the income flows to households and to firms are limited. Consumers must make choices about their expenditures for society's limited output and firms must make choices about employing scarce resources. Prices act as a "mediating" device in: (*a*) rationing limited outputs, and (*b*) allocating scarce factors of production. Product-market prices serve to entice or dissuade consumption relative to the marginal utility of different goods, while resource-market prices induce or discourage firms from using factors of production relative to the productivity of resources.

Consumer demand for products responds to price signals established by supply and demand, where all households together help determine product price by forming total market demand for goods and services. In addition, these same product prices communicate consumer choices to business firms which supply goods and services. With a given production technology and resource cost, firms respond to consumer demand and decide what goods to supply in product markets, how much of a product to produce, and just how many of different types of resources to use as factors of production to meet consumer demand. Notice also in Figure 2 that the circular-income flow links product-market price signals to resource markets because the demand for factors of production is derived from the demand for goods and services. Accordingly, the quantities of resources demanded by firms are an image of consumer demand for products. Finally, remember that as resource demand and supply establish resource prices, the general distribution of income to capital, labor, and other resources is determined.[7]

The combinations of resources that are in fact used by firms are influenced by the firms' desire to maximize profits—a necessity in a competitive market if firms are to earn a normal profit under competition. It is important to recognize that, like the consumer's maximization of utility, profit maximization by the firm is an *assumption* upon which the theory of how competitive prices allocate scarce resources is based. Economists also invoke the maximizing doctrine to help explain the operation of a market economy by assuming that the supply of resources depends upon resource owners striving to achieve maximum returns from selling productive services. The assumption is that individuals owning scarce resources both influence and respond to resource-market price signals and, depending upon resource prices, supply fewer or more scarce factors of production in resource markets in exchange for income payments.

In short, *market prices for both products and factors of production organize society's use of resources.* Since individuals receive incomes for the use of productive resources, these payments are a key element in shaping product demand. As Figure 2 shows, we have completed a full round in the "microeconomic view" of *circular-income flows* that link product and resource markets. A nation's output and its resources move constantly through product and resource markets, and prices likewise are subject to perpetual adjustments. The process of resource reallocation is a continual one ultimately moving toward some new "general equilibrium" in *all* markets where supply and demand determine equilibrium prices. General equilibrium adjustments to a price change in one market also influence other firms and industries because product and resource markets are inexorably linked together. Indeed, the temptation to oversimplify in describing general equilibrium must be resisted. There are hundreds and even thousands of general equilibrium "feedback" adjustments generated by an initial market change, and it is very difficult to trace such effects throughout an economy.

[7] As noted in Chapter 18 and explained in Chapters 23 and 24, the distribution of income is a good deal more complex than such a generalized view of supply and demand indicates.

The general equilibrium just described depends upon competitive-market adjustments which are known to work imperfectly in the real world. Probably the best way to summarize what competitive markets mean and do not mean, is to consider a case study.

Suppose that you, as the King of Id, were responsible for organizing economic activity and allocating resources in an economy. Your tasks would include deciding what and how much of hundreds of thousands of goods and services should be produced, as well as what and how much individuals should consume. Firms would have to be told how much and what to produce, producers would need access to various resources at some price, and resource owners would have to offer the services of factors of production at the bidding of some force which also would determine just how much income individuals would have. These are not easy issues to deal with, as you no doubt suspect. As a matter of fact, if you err in deciding how much income different people "should" get, for example, it is possible that your very life might be lost. Even though the enormity of the data and calculations needed to make these decisions truly defies description, there are certain principles of resource allocation that could be followed to show how markets operate. However, it is one thing to specify how market prices work in a general equilibrium context, and quite another to judge how "well" market prices perform their task. Therefore, the first principle that must be at your disposal is some knowledge about what objective or goal you have in mind in allocating resources.

## ECONOMIC WELFARE: THE "NARROW" VIEW

To make judgments about the allocation of resources, you must have in mind some standard or criterion which you believe to be a "good" or desirable goal. The fundamental criterion of microeconomics is economic efficiency in the allocation of resources. Economic efficiency is defined, as we know, as the least-cost use of resources so as to maximize consumer satisfaction or utility.

It is important to recognize that providing maximum satisfaction for an insatiable consumer appetite is a narrow definition of economic welfare that is not unambiguous. Economic efficiency in using resources is only one limited concept of economic welfare—numerous other criteria might also be used to gauge how well an economic system operates. Full employment of resources, speedy economic growth, justice or equity in the distribution of income, and efficiency in the use of resources might all be used as *alternative standards* in gauging the economic welfare of society.

Efficiency, then, is economic welfare only as it is most narrowly (and partially) defined. There are, however, profound implications to the concept of the efficient allocation of resources that are relevant to many important contemporary economic issues and problems. Therefore, microeconomics is not necessarily confined to a quest for efficiency alone, but rather directs attention toward such issues as: Efficiency for whom and at what price? Should society allocate more or fewer resources to the production of hospitals or satellites, and in what manner should output (income) be distributed to the wealthy or the poor?[8]

---

[8] There are several reasons for what may appear to the reader to be an excessively dogged pursuit of the topic of efficiency in resource allocation. First, it is necessary to

Now back to our fable in which you, as the King of Id, have chosen to pursue the goal of economic efficiency and must organize the kingdom in some fashion to achieve that goal. Since we have some general ideas about how prices work, we shall assume that you choose to organize Id's economic affairs through the market system. Whether this decision is made out of ignorance or derives from an enlightened motive of altruism does not matter. Further, you decide to use neither your army to enforce the new economic organization nor computers and underemployed professors to serve as economic planners. Rather, by royal decree, markets and prices are "ordered" to serve as the mechanism for organizing economic affairs in Id by virtue of the following proclamation:

—BE IT KNOWN THAT—

Henceforth, Id's economy shall be nurtured by free competitive markets wherein all buyers and sellers are ordered to be fully informed, mobile, and knowledgeable, and all must pursue the object of their best interests. Thou shalt not consort together on prices and markets in any form under penalty of lifetime bondage to the King, and thou shalt maximize thine own satisfaction, incomes, and profits as consumers, as resource owners, and as entrepreneurs.

There is a moral to this proclamation, for as the King you *know* that once you have selected the market system, and if all your subjects adhere to your decree, economic efficiency will be achieved as follows.

*Efficiency in Production*    Producing firms must decide what to produce, how much to produce, and how to combine resources in production—resource-allocation decisions that are made through the decreed environment of pure competition. First, it is profitable for all firms to hire one more unit of a resource as long as the last unit of the resource hired creates an amount of additional revenue no less than additional cost. As long as one more unit of a resource adds more dollars to a firm's revenue than it adds to its costs, profits increase. Second, least-cost (economically efficient) production occurs since competitive firms will employ resources until the least possible production cost is achieved by each firm, where *all* firms pay an identical price for the same resources in competitive markets. If one resource is more productive than another for one producer, more of the most efficient resource will be employed by that firm. Thus, minimum per unit costs are

---

reveal fully how highly improbable achievement of efficiency is in real-world economic systems. Second, it is important to indicate the pervasive character of economic conflict and the normative questions often inherent in economics, particularly concerning government involvement in socioeconomic issues such as pollution, poverty, the farm problem, or discrimination. The goal of "efficiency" itself is a normative proclamation of what economists regard as important. Then, too, many myths about efficient resource allocation prevail, and it is important to recognize that economic welfare means much more than just efficiency in producing physical output, which may make habitation of the earth impossible.

achieved when a firm hires all resources until equal dollars of additional revenue (termed *marginal revenue product*) are generated per dollar of additional cost (termed *marginal resource cost*).[9]

But what prompts a firm to relentlessly pursue least cost? The answer (again by royal decree) is that *competition forces all firms to operate at least cost*, else they will be driven from the industry. Indeed, firms *must* operate at minimum cost at the convenient level of a "normal" profit—a profit just barely large enough to keep them in business. If any firm earns an above-normal or economic profit, perhaps by momentarily producing more efficiently than its competitors or by meeting a new consumer demand, other firms will be lured by these profits to enter that market. Conversely, firms (and resources) will move from markets in which profits are below the "normal" level. As business firms adjust to consumer tastes and maximize profits, competition and the entry or exit of firms cause more or fewer resources to be allocated to products demanded or rejected by consumers. Ultimately, product-market supply and demand changes are translated into market-price changes which allocate resources and tend to stabilize profits at a normal level.

*Equally Valued Resources and Products*    In a hypothetical kingdom governed by pure competition, each competitive firm earns its best possible competitive and normal profit and operates at minimum per unit cost when price ($P$) and marginal cost ($MC$) are equal, as stated earlier in Chapter 16.[10]

$$\begin{matrix} \text{Market valuation} \\ \text{of additional} \\ \text{output} \\ \text{(Price)} \end{matrix} = \begin{matrix} \text{Market valuation} \\ \text{of additional} \\ \text{resources} \\ \text{(Marginal cost)} \end{matrix} \quad \text{or} \quad P = MC$$

The reason that economic efficiency in production exists if $P = MC$ is intuitively clear under certain simplifying conditions. $P$ represents the consumers' valuation of a good—the positive gain or marginal utility of a product. In contrast, $MC$ represents the social valuation of resources—the forgone opportunities (or disutility) associated with using up scarce resources. Thus, economic efficiency is a combination of ($a$) efficiency in production (which depends upon the competitive maximization of normal profits), and ($b$) efficiency in consumption (individual consumer's maximization of satisfaction or utility).[11] For all goods produced by all firms

[9] This is the now-familiar least-cost rule described in Chapter 18, which defines the minimum-cost condition as prevailing where marginal revenue product/marginal resource cost ratios are equal for all resources employed.

[10] Bear in mind the lessons of Chapter 16, which demonstrated that under competitive product-market conditions, the price of a product is equal to marginal revenue as output increases by one more unit. Therefore, $P = MC$ at $ATC$ minimum where $ATC$ stands for the average total cost of a unit of output.

[11] Recall that all consumers paying identical prices for the same products in competitive markets must achieve maximum satisfaction from limited incomes in order to reach this state of efficiency. This being the case, no consumer can exchange goods with someone else and improve his satisfaction. If $1 spent on more beans adds more satisfaction or *marginal utility* than $1 spent on more milk, it is assumed that more beans and less milk will be bought to maximize satisfaction. This is the rule for maximizing consumer satisfaction discussed in Part A of this chapter.

and all goods bought by consumers, the utopian condition of efficiency in production and consumption dictates that the market value placed on a product (its price) equals both the value of the resources used by firms to produce another unit of the product (its marginal cost), *and* the value consumers place upon another unit of the product (its marginal utility).

As a matter of fact, the concept of a market demand schedule is, as we know, an image of marginal utility. Thus, a market supply- and demand-determined price ($P$) reflects marginal utility. If we ignore certain bothersome technical complications concerning interdependent utilities and interpersonal comparisons of marginal utilities, the typical supply and demand diagram of earlier chapters can be used to approximate the market's efficiency solution (see Figure 3).[12]

If we assume that different goods yield independent marginal utilities and that interpersonal comparisons of utilities among consumers are appropriate, we can add individual consumer demand curves for a product to obtain a market demand schedule ($d$ of Figure 3), which is a reflection of consumer valuation of a product. Similarly, the marginal cost schedules of all individual producers can be added to obtain a market supply schedule ($s$) as a reflection of forgone opportunities, where equilibrium price and quantity are shown at $E$.

The character of equilibrium price ($E$) is that it maximizes economic efficiency by bringing about a balance between supply (as a reflection of marginal cost) and demand (as a reflection of marginal utility). Thus, the competitive market of our fable achieves an efficient allocation of resources where $P$ equals $MC$ and $P$ also reflects $MU$. Markets equate the total

---

[12] By assuming that the utilities of goods are independent (i.e., consumer satisfaction and demand for milk and cereal are unrelated) and that your utility is comparable to mine, and by ignoring the fact that resources are not transferable at some constant opportunity cost, we are blatantly oversimplifying the subject of economic welfare.

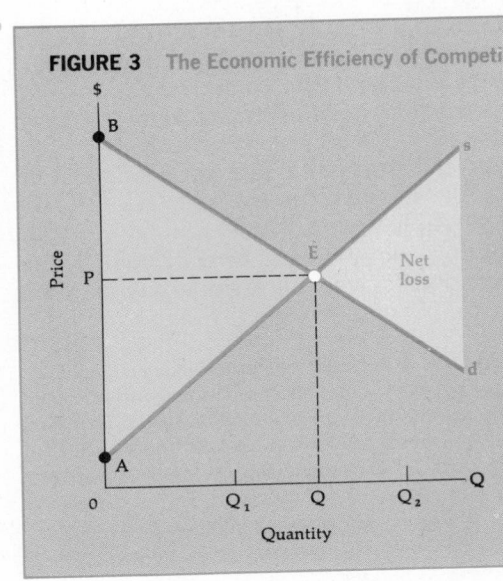

**FIGURE 3**   The Economic Efficiency of Competitive Markets

*Efficiency in Pricing.* Marginal utility is the basis for market demand schedule *d* and marginal cost represents forgone opportunities of using resources as a basis for market supply. Therefore, when equilibrium is established at *E*, product price *(P)* and quantity *(Q)* are efficient; that is, *P = MC* as the market coordinates minimum marginal costs represented by schedule *s* with marginal utility represented by schedule *d*. The triangular area of positive net gain *(ABE)* is maximized.

cost of producing (the entire area under schedule *s*) with the satisfaction of society (the entire area under curve *d*). Provided that monetary measures accurately reflect utilities and costs, price *P* and quantity *Q* of Figure 3 are efficient—a condition achieved only at *E* because the net excess of utilities over costs (the triangular area *ABE*) is as large as it can be only at price (*P*) and quantity (*Q*). At any smaller quantity (*Q₁*) some net satisfaction that could be gained is forgone, and at a larger quantity (*Q₂*) there is a loss of net satisfaction. As long as market supply fully reflects the marginal cost of resources, very real concerns for the "desired" distribution of income are ignored, and as long as market demand fully reflects the marginal utility of goods, economic efficiency is at equilibrium, as in Figure 3.[13]

## NIRVANA?

Each consumer maximizes satisfaction, producers are earning normal profits, and resources are being used efficiently. What more could a benevolent King desire? Everyone has the best of all possible worlds in the perfect allocation of resources! Of course, in Id, the King and his men may well be seated before a dram of brandy at the round table with fellow members in the Society of Zeus who have arranged to provide optimal satisfaction for everyone in the most efficient way. And if part of the tribal ritual consists of praising the model system of economic organization while ignoring the miasmal realities of economic life, inmanship will dictate that the membership of the Society sing each other's praises nightly. With such comforting knowledge about efficiency and consumer satisfaction under Id's market system of economic organization, it would not be surprising if the good King and his men were rather complacent, provided they believe in "Alice in Wonderland" economics.[14] We say this because the competitive general equilibrium model is by no means a full description of the real world. Market imperfections and slippage abound, and this is one reason for discussing economic efficiency as a fable. Pure competition itself is a myth; producers and consumers do not necessarily maximize in a perfect, certain, all-knowing, and mobile world. In fact, it makes no difference whatsoever that the remarkable Invisible Hand has comfortingly assured everyone in Id that economic efficiency has been achieved, for Id is only a model world.

As it turns out, however, Id University is populated by a number of dissident, unemployed intellectuals like Craven Grimes who ask embarrassing questions about this "best possible" world. Indeed, Craven *et al.* spend much of their time reexamining the standard fare of knowledge delivered each year to budding economists who may some day become members in the Society.

---

[13] The appendix following this chapter discusses a technical economic-efficiency definition of pure competition known as a *Pareto optima*, named after the nineteenth-century economist Vilfredo Pareto. In Figure 3, the area termed "net gain" consists of revenues paid firms factors (area *APQ*) plus a "consumer surplus" (area *PBE*) which distinguishes between actual payments for a good and consumer willingness to pay shown by the entire schedule *d*.

[14] The author's indebtedness to Martin Shubik, "A Curmudgeon's Guide to Microeconomics," *Journal of Economic Literature* (June 1970), pp. 405–429 is rather obvious here and in portions of Chapter 20.

Were the likes of Cravens' crowd ever admitted to Court, they would challenge the King and his retinue with questions like: "Perfect competition is imaginary, not real, so how can you speak of a 'consumer maximizing satisfaction'? For that matter, you cannot deal effectively with interdependent utilities at all, and making interpersonal comparisons of utility is really absurd because the satisfaction Mrs. Jones gets from another bottle of milk cannot be compared to Mrs. Brown's or Mr. Jones' satisfaction. Furthermore, we know markets operate imperfectly; that is, resources are not fully informed and mobile, uncertainty exists, some firms do have market power, and profit maximization itself is a *vast* oversimplification of what motivates business firms." Finally, the King's men would no doubt be asked about the way in which income and wealth are distributed. Does the King keep title to all of the nation's wealth, or is it given to his Barons or to the peasants, and in what proportion is income distributed? (Remember, that if 90 percent of the peasants are paupers the meaning of "economic efficiency" as a dimension to the welfare of the society is questionable.)

Although the dissidents at Id University are critical of competition as a description of the real world, it is clear that the price mechanism does act more or less as a signal-transmitting device to organize economic activity, imperfect though the process may be, and the competitive model of microeconomic theory is important to understanding the resource-allocation process. There are three useful features of the competitive model:

1. The conditions of competition show certain technical relations that must prevail if a society is to achieve a rigidly defined type of maximum satisfaction from limited resources.

2. Competition is the simplest view of a market system that can be presented, and its resource-allocation implications are valid for all systems of political economy—capitalism, socialism, communism, or communal anarchy—provided that a society is interested in the goal of technical economic efficiency.

3. Finally, the competitive model provides tools of analysis that can be used to study numerous economic issues and problems that arise as a society makes decisions about the allocation of resources. For example, limited resources demand that social choices be made between more hospitals or more satellites and the distribution of income to the poor vs. the rich, or the blacks vs. the whites.

Imperfect competition is prevalent in both product markets and resource markets. Prices are frequently rigid and administered by firms possessing various degrees of market power, while resource-market pricing is fraught with immobilities and complex institutional imperfections. These are hard realities, and Craven Grimes' warnings about microeconomic theory merit careful study.

## C. AN EVALUATION OF THE MARKET AS A PRICING INSTRUMENT

Enlargement of social and economic welfare is a universal objective of societies and individuals, but, as we have said, just what truly constitutes "welfare" eludes clear identification. Market pricing and economic efficiency presuppose the heroic conditions of maximizing behavior and pure competition—conditions which are not fully met by any existing system of political economy. Therefore, microeconomics requires critical evaluation at the level of the market as an organizing device.

## The Meaning of Economic Efficiency

The simplified and seemingly elegant model of economic efficiency is an ideal economic organization *only* in the measure that economic efficiency is a worthy goal. Greater efficiency in producing and distributing output is one way to reduce the relative scarcity borne by a society, and for that reason the efficient use of resources can be regarded as one important social goal. What a competitive general equilibrium solution to economic organization means is that nothing can improve upon society's allocation of resources provided that: (*a*) the unbridled force of competition is present everywhere; (*b*) the desire to maximize does in fact motivate consumers, firms, and resource owners; (*c*) the existing distribution of income is acceptable; and (*d*) all benefits and costs associated with economic activity are represented fully by transactions in the private sector of the economy.

With the price mechanism functioning as a guiding beacon, the profit motive and the maximizing interests of economic participants signal firms to hire more or fewer resources, allowing the achievement of economic efficiency through competition. Since lowest possible unit costs are required in competitive product markets, firms unattentive to consumer demand and those producing inefficiently cannot earn a normal profit. Some producers may be inefficient some of the time, but ultimately those not using resources both efficiently and in accord with society's consumption interests fail to earn the normal profit required to keep them in the industry. Ultimately, inefficiently used resources move into other, more opportune uses.

### WHAT EFFICIENCY DOES NOT MEAN

Of course, the competitive explanation of the market as a resource-allocation instrument is only a model, and thus tells an incomplete but nonetheless worthwhile story.

For example, there are many ways in which the King of Id and his subjects can fiddle with the system. Suppose that the King declares war and places a tax of $1 per loaf on bread. Less bread might then be consumed by each consumer because of the increase in price. If the principles of supply and demand generally hold (see Chapter 14), a smaller quantity of bread will be purchased at the higher price consumers must now pay, and producers will receive a lower after-tax price.[15] Accordingly, resources formerly allocated to the production of bread will be shifted to the production of other goods (e.g., weapons—which may be the general result that the King wants in the first place.)[16] Alternatively, those in charge of organizing economic affairs may subsidize the production of certain goods and

[15] We ignore here very, very inferior goods of the type involved in the rather special case called the "Giffen paradox," in which consumers conceivably would end up using more of the higher-priced, but very inferior good as their effective incomes declined. Giffen's paradox relies on reductions in effective incomes which become so low that expenditures on other less necessary products are substantially reduced and, as the consumer strives to subsist, *more* of the very inferior good is consumed.

[16] Many other matters are overlooked here, but the broad generalizations point us in the right direction.

services (oil exploration, nuclear research, or education are contemporary illustrations), thereby influencing consumer choice via lower prices and "directing" the allocation of resources to subsidized products. Then, too, producers may be capable, by virtue of their monopoly power, of manipulating prices and protecting their sheltered market through lobbyists, again causing resources to be misallocated and allowing the powerful few to enlarge their own incomes. The law (tax loopholes) and the growth of institutional power can also help certain groups receive larger incomes. The reverse circumstances might also prevail, of course. If word has it that persons named "Jane" customarily are "less desirable employees," the informal but rather effective institution of discrimination can be used to restrict job opportunities and equal wage payments to all Janes.

A good deal of insight into such economic tinkering can be gained through the rather simplified, abstract, and unrealistic model that concentrates attention on questions of resource allocation. What competitive economic efficiency does *not* mean thus becomes more important than what it does mean. After all, there is a good deal more to the welfare of a society than efficiently producing as much physical output as possible with scarce resources.

Even if idyllic competitive conditions were achieved, no one (perhaps least of all economists) could claim to have proven that the purely competitive society revealed by Adam Smith's laissez faire vision is best. Extended consideration of economic efficiency in the allocation of resources has by no means *proven* that American capitalism provides a maximum of economic satisfaction or welfare to all people. Nor has anyone argued that American capitalism in the 1970s is a purely competitive system of economic organization—for it most certainly does not meet the many stringent competitive criteria. Competitive efficiency does not mean that everyone in a real-world setting has the best of all possible worlds for many reasons —not the least of which is the value judgment required in prescribing the "best" distribution of income. If certain groups of consumers are lacking in income, they do not have an equal ability to pay the prices required to achieve satisfaction from consumption of a good. In short, it is possible for a competitive society to end up with urban slums along with sleek limousines and jets, and vast sums might also be spent on tobacco or electric pencil sharpeners even though water and air could be unfit for human use. A society's economic resources and output should produce optimal satisfaction to that society as an aggregate entity—and that is a subject which has confounded measurement and meaningful, positive identification for centuries. The tools of orthodox economic analysis can be useful in sharpening our understanding of these and related issues, but price or resource-allocation theory is not proffered as a *final* answer.

## THE EXCEPTIONS TO COMPETITIVE EFFICIENCY

Three limitations to the market system deserve consideration here. As a resource-allocation device, the private sector of the market system operates imperfectly. Moreover, the market is oblivious to equity issues, and private markets may not fully reflect social costs and benefits.

*Imperfections and Market Power*   First, as we already know, an economic system does not function in the all-knowing, perfect fashion conveniently assumed in economic theory. Market imperfections encumber attainment of utopian efficiency in the allocation of resources. Such imperfections are basic to the existence and use of market power. Large and powerful organizations strive to organize the very product markets which in economic theory they allegedly serve. Concentrations of market power representing capital and labor resources influence the social, political, and economic values and behavior of a society, and in addition, such power permits resource owners to earn larger incomes than would otherwise be forthcoming. Indeed, it may well be misleading to talk at all about consumers maximizing satisfaction and markets allocating resources efficiently. When the economic system is distorted so as to lead consumers to believe that their satisfaction can be increased by adhering to transportation systems which cause smog and several thousand deaths each month, serious questions can be raised about the meaning of efficiency and consumer satisfaction.

The increasingly complex basis of modern economies gives rise to the institutionalization of power in the hands of business, labor, and government. As long as the technological momentum of the recent past continues to prevail—and nothing yet suggests diminution of this trend—organized power can dominate markets. When organized power is capable of influencing prices, the allocation of resources via the market instrument is called into question.

*The Distribution of Income* The market system is also oblivious of the distribution of income used to acquire consumer goods and services. A market system operates in an impersonal and computer-like way, avoiding the ethical issues bound up in questions of income distribution. Many observers contend that there is a maldistribution of income, wealth, and economic opportunity, even though the needs of people are approximately comparable. The unequal distribution of income effectively gives certain segments of the population a much larger voice in economic matters, including consumption.

What is produced and how a nation's resources are allocated are decisions that are by no means based upon the one-man–one-vote philosophy of political democracy, simply because men do not receive equal incomes. It is possible, however, to affect income distribution by altering the prevailing rules in any society. The distribution of income is an ethical "should-be" problem and, as we have said before, no scientific answer can be given to questions about how large or small incomes ought to be. Even the utopian conditions of competition that allegedly distribute incomes according to the marginal productivity of resources may not be in accord with whatever a society or its leaders decide is just, equitable, or proper. Having reached some normative guidelines on income distribution, a society can use taxation and transfer payments to rearrange the market's capricious distribution of income in either a more or a less altruistic fashion. Clearly, the complexities involved in achieving "true" welfare are enormous, to say the least.

*Externalities* The third weakness in the market system is the result of social costs and social benefits not taken into account by private markets. *Externalities* are the uncompensated-for cost or revenue spillover effects borne by individuals, firms, or society at large. Externalities exist if there are differences between private and social benefits or private and social costs. Society at large ends up bearing some of the costs of consumption and industrial production via the pollution of air, rivers, and lakes. Still other social costs are associated with the drunken driver. Moreover, various types of social benefits are frequently underproduced in a market system. Certainly the development of the American economy has been enhanced by the provision of public education, hospitals, and highways that benefit society directly and indirectly; yet, a pure market system would not provide these goods in the measure now available at a price that would make consumption possible for millions of people.[17]

*In summary:* The operation of a market economy in the real world can produce results quite different from those envisioned in a competitive model because: (*a*) market power does exist and is used, (*b*) justice in the distribution of income is ignored by markets, and (*c*) a market system is fraught with externalities—social costs and social benefits not fully accounted for by the private sector of the economy.

## D. DEFICIENCIES IN THE THEORY OF THE FIRM

By *assuming* profit maximization on the part of imperfectly competitive firms, the microeconomic theory of pricing has helped explain imperfections in the real-world allocation of resources. We have developed a theory of resource allocation that shows how competitive firms must maximize profits and minimize costs in order to remain viable participants in the economic process. Our analysis also has clearly shown that imperfect competition is the general rule and not the exception. The conventional wisdom of the theory of the firm has survived a barrage of assaults from dissenting economists—if it had not, we would not have labored so long over product- and resource-market pricing. Nevertheless, microeconomic theory has not gone unscathed in the debate over the validity of the profit-maximizing assumption, and it is time we faced this issue head on.

We will briefly trace the history of the dispute over the profit-maximization assumption and summarize the viewpoints of those who have challenged microeconomic theory. This is an important task, but not because either the critics or the proponents of the theory of the firm can be proven wrong. Rather, the critiques of scholars like Adolf Berle, Gardner Means, Robin Marris, Kenneth Boulding, and John Kenneth Galbraith can add important insights to our knowledge about the organization of mixed market economies such as that of the United States. The challenges to conventional microeconomic theory center upon the fact that it ignores competing behavioral motives other than profit maximization. Were the challengers proven correct, all that we have said about pricing and resource allocation would have to be modified or abandoned. Remember, however, our earlier warnings: No theory can hope to correspond fully to reality, and while there is no excuse for embracing a bad theory, some simplifications of economic theory have contributed to economic knowledge.

### A Critic's View of Microeconomic Theory

Critics of the theory of the firm argue that business firms are no longer entrepreneurial in character and that maximization of something other than profits is a goal of the firm. Some critics even argue that firms will

[17] Chapter 20 discusses the question of externalities and public goods in more detail.

not maximize, cannot maximize, and do not care to maximize. The guardians of conventional microeconomic theory recognize the oversimplifications embodied in the profit-maximization assumption, but contend that, despite its abstract character, microeconomic theory does yield worthy results and is the best approximation available for explaining how resources are allocated.

The microeconomic theory of the firm was founded on the works of Adam Smith, Augustine Cournot, and Alfred Marshall. Later (the 1920s) a debate arose over the theoretical firm's cost structure, and this debate ultimately led to examination of imperfectly competitive firms.[18] Edward H. Chamberlin was instrumental in the analysis of monopolistic competition and related forms of imperfect product markets in this period. The analytical structure of microeconomic theory that was retained remained based upon the concept of profit maximization, even though imperfectly competitive firms are not automatically *forced* to maximize profits, as are those under pure competition. The well-known English economist, J. R. Hicks, expressed his reservations about the validity of a profit-maximizing theory of the firm, observing that firms operating in imperfectly competitive markets need not be concerned about efficiency and maximum profits, for monopoly "is a quiet life."[19]

Rumbles of dissent have mounted substantially over the assumption that firms maximize profits, and some critics have raised other serious questions about the evolving nature of large business enterprises in developed countries such as Britain and the United States. The array of challenges are as follows.

## INFORMATION AND UNCERTAINTY: CAN FIRMS MAXIMIZE PROFITS?

Many observers have questioned whether firms can maximize profits. It is difficult if not impossible for a firm to determine marginal cost and marginal revenue—indeed, many businessmen have no idea of what these terms mean. Aside from the difficulty of obtaining marginal data from accounting and financial records, a business enterprise continually faces uncertainty and inadequate information on current market conditions. The likelihood of earning some level of profit may depend on marketing and pricing strategies, but the certainty of realizing a given level of earnings may be small, and business firms must weigh this likelihood against the possible consequences of being wrong. Recognizing these problems, Kenneth Boulding, for example, has argued that business firms attempt to maintain a "balance-sheet equilibrium" among key financial ratios.[20] Furthermore, the difference between maximizing short-run and long-run profits must be considered. Firms may avoid maximizing short-run profits because numerous risky ventures cumulated over the long run can be disastrous.

Empirical research has shown that nonexistent and imperfect informa-

[18] The impetus for this development was distilled from controversy over decreasing-cost industries. See Piero Sraffa's article "The Laws of Return Under Competitive Conditions," *Economic Journal* (December 1926), pp. 535–550.

[19] J. R. Hicks, "Annual Survey of Economic Theory: Theory of Monopoly," *Econometrica* (February 1935), p. 8.

[20] See K. E. Boulding, *A Reconstruction of Economic Theory* (New York: John Wiley, 1960).

tion, uncertainty, and the incentive to minimize risk over the long run may well lead to product-price and output decisions that differ from those predictable on the basis of profit-maximizing behavior. Unfortunately, determining the mix and weight of the different factors that lead to a probability-oriented pattern of pricing has proven to be next to impossible. Thus, such criticism remains negative rather than helpful in improving upon information about business-enterprise behavior in allocating resources.

## FULL-COST PRICING

Other critics have argued that, in view of the difficulties of dealing with imperfect information and uncertainty, firms add some "markup" percentage to full costs in pricing products, offering whatever supply of output the market will bear at the markup price.[21] Once again there is evidence to suggest that business firms do follow markup-pricing principles, especially when only crude information on product demand and marginal revenue is available. However, agreement is lacking about the uniformity of use of this pricing principle, particularly in view of recent trends toward the compilation of records in such a way as to develop marginal-cost data. Moreover, James S. Earley and others have shown that many business firms utilize a loose form of marginalism in making markup-pricing decisions.[22] Still another weakness of the markup-pricing argument is that it does not explain why, for example, a firm chooses a markup of 30 percent over one of 50 percent.

## WHO CONTROLS THE ENTERPRISE: OWNERS OR MANAGEMENT?

The idea that business firms may follow markup-pricing policies or perhaps even attempt to maximize objectives other than profits rests in part upon the widely recognized fact that many business enterprises are not managed by entrepreneur-owners but rather by hired managers. First expressed in studies conducted by Adolf Berle and Gardner Means some four decades ago, the thesis of separation of ownership and control has profound implications for the theory of the firm if the interests of hired managers and owners do not converge on the objective of profit maximization.[23]

While small shareholders normally own most of the modern corporation, the typical stockholder owns a minute portion of any one corporation and has little if any voice in its business decisions. Corporate officers, a few prominent families, or large institutions often hold sizable portions of stock and may control the corporation. It is indeed difficult for dissident stockholders who individually own only small portions of a corporation to unseat hired managers who are supposed to work in the owner's best interests. Management decisions can be and are reviewed from time to time, but barring a major financial calamity, hired managers control the destiny of modern business firms with little or no direct stockholder intervention. Many goals other than profit maximization may rank high in the priorities

[21] For one of the earliest studies on markup pricing see R. L. Hall and C. J. Hitch, "Price Theory and Business Behavior," *Oxford Economic Papers* (May 1939), pp. 12–45.

[22] See, for example, James E. Earley, "Marginal Policies of Excellently Managed Companies," *American Economic Review* (March 1956), pp. 44–70.

[23] A. Berle and G. Means, *Modern Corporations and Private Property* (New York: Commerce Clearing House, 1932).

of hired management, and it is important to see how these goals may conflict with the assumption of profit maximization upon which the microeconomic theory of pricing and resource allocation depends.

## ALTERNATIVE GOALS TO PROFIT MAXIMIZING

The onslaught against the profit-maximizing assumption of conventional price theory has produced other theories purporting to better explain the behavior of the business firm. Among the more noteworthy alternative goals are the following.

*Sales and Growth Maximization*   Professor William Baumol has argued that firms attempt to maximize sales revenues, subject to the achievement of some minimal level of profit.[24] The apparent motive in this behavior is that business firms, perhaps particularly those not controlled by owners, are motivated to maximize total revenues or to attain large size and rapid growth in order to enhance the power, prestige, and salaries of hired managers. If a few firms dominate a market, they may be extremely sensitive to their share of the market, and this sensitivity may reinforce their desire to achieve maximum sales or growth. Like the many other possible explanations for the price and output decisions of imperfectly competitive firms, the sales-revenue and growth-maximization hypotheses are enticing, but as yet not fully tested nor totally accepted. Nevertheless, in the measure that sales or growth are goals of a firm, a theory of pricing based solely upon the profit-maximization assumption is called into question.

*"Satisficing" Behavior and Organization Theory*   Many critics have argued that the organizational complexity of modern corporations is such that multiple objectives and joint decision-making lead to compromise and the dominance of "rules" over one narrow goal such as profit maximization. Thus, it may be that a satisfactory (not maximum) profit is the dominant goal—a thesis closely linked to hired management in the view of theorists such as Professor Herbert Simon.[25] If satisfactory profits are a prominent goal, firms may reach various price-output decisions, particularly if market power allows the maintenance of a monopoly profit. The competing goal of satisfactory profits may well mean that prices and the allocation of resources do not correspond to the predictions of our earlier theories about the operation of a market system.

*Management Preference Ranking*   Recognizing the competing theories of the behavior of business firms, some critics argue for a theory of preference or utility-maximization as an explanation of market prices. Within a preference–maximization framework, it could be said that management opts for whatever combination of goals strikes its fancy—satisficing, some choice between leisure and hard work, achievement of noneconomic goals, maintenance of market power, management security and prestige, salary maximization, and so forth. Of course, the real world is just such a maze of

[24] W. J. Baumol, "On the Theory of Oligopoly," *Economica* (August 1958), pp. 178–198.

[25] See Herbert A. Simon, "Theories of Decision Making in Economics," *American Economic Review* (June 1959), pp. 253–283.

complicated goals and values which shape the behavior of men and the institutions they create. Unfortunately, completely realistic theories that take all factors into account are also unworkable because of their complexity.

*Recapitulation:* We have considered several alternatives to the profit-maximizing theory of the firm. While these alternative theories appear to be contradictory, they are in some ways complementary to conventional price theory. Those critics who have developed alternative explanations for the theory of the firm have improved knowledge about pricing and resource allocation by the persistent challenges they have raised. Economists have been forced to pay considerably more attention to uncertainty, the nature of products and markets, industry entry and market-structure conditions, the state of entreprenurial knowledge, market power, and so on. Despite the bruised status it enjoys, microeconomic theory remains crucial in explaining pricing, output, and resource-allocation decisions, and the reasons for this fact merit consideration.

### In Defense of Price Theory

A critical appraisal of microeconomic theory can give the misleading impression that economists are totally disenchanted with the theory of the firm. However, several formidable pragmatic and methodological arguments have been raised in defense of orthodox price theory.

#### VIABILITY OF THE FIRM

The profit-seeking goal cannot be totally discarded. Even in the large corporation operating in an imperfectly competitive market, for example, hired management does tend to identify its own welfare with the welfare of the corporate entity, despite the fact that personal earnings are not uniformly and directly tied to profits. The success or failure of corporate management is frequently gauged by the profit performance of activities under their control. Indeed, salaries and bonuses are not infrequently tied directly to profit performance, and failure to perform profitably can directly affect the stature, security, and viability of both the firm and hired management. Profits are also important to the future growth of the corporation. While sales growth and market shares may be important, both depend in part on profits, which are needed to acquire capital for future expansion. Moreover, there may be some general workability about competition, including rivalry spread across overlapping product and resource markets, and those firms capable of surviving in the long run must be viable enterprises in the profit context. In other words, something reasonably close to profit-maximizing decisions may have to be made over the long run, even though hired managers do not consciously pursue this objective.

What is suggested here is that business firms may "act as if" profit maximization is a goal, even though uncertainty and poor information plague the environment of business enterprises. Simply because businessmen do not or cannot derive the needed revenue and cost information to maximize at one point in time does not refute the theory that they try to make sound and profitable decisions using intuitive marginal reasoning. "Satisficing" behavior may represent disguised long-run profit-maximizing behavior under conditions of uncertainty. A business firm cannot attach itself irrevocably to markup pricing and remain oblivious to profit control, because it will not survive. Markup pricing may also mask marginal analysis leading to profit maximization as it is approximated through trial and error. Thus there are good reasons for viewing profits as a key feature of business behavior in a market economy. This has become all the more true with the development of increasing numbers of professional consultants and computerized techniques that ease the difficulties of using managerial economics.

### A NOTE ON OPERATIONAL ISSUES AND MICROECONOMIC THEORY

The second fundamental explanation given for the survival of microeconomic theory is that the profit-maximizing framework has provided sufficiently general, and yet useful approximations for the purposes at hand; namely, furnishing an explanation for and testing hypotheses and predictions concerning markets, prices, and resource allocation. Professor Fritz Machlup argued some time ago that conventional price theory is often judged to be in error on the basis of ends it never set out to accomplish.[26] Microeconomic theory is *not* intended to provide a complete explanation of commercial behavior, but rather to explain how prices and markets allocate resources. Even though microeconomic theory may help explain how changes in market conditions affect a firm or how a firm can maximize profits, this is not its basic purpose. Thus, some observers argue that the theory of the firm is a useful *tool* for the economist, and the unreality of its assumptions may be quite unimportant in evaluating its validity. The important characteristic of a theory is whether or not it leads to hypotheses which provide meaningful explanations, not whether or not it is based upon realistic assumptions. There are some intuitive reasons to believe that the theory of the firm does provide an explanation that is as good as or better than those offered by other theories.

Even though much can be said in defense of microeconomic theory, economists can take little comfort in such intuitive assertions because the theory is not fully operational—it cannot be fully tested and applied in the real world. Nevertheless, by assuming profit-maximizing rationality, economists have been able to arrive at determinate equilibrium solutions. More realistic theories of business behavior (such as satisficing or markup pricing) have failed to supplant the profit-maximization premise because the more complete and more realistic theories often turn out to be hopelessly inconclusive. That is, one cannot readily move from a complex theory to a determinant explanation of economic events. Sophisticated models may well embody characteristics more consistent with the information hired managers have, but these theories can be made to work only by succumbing to the tempting (and necessary) crutch of assuming some information or relationships as given. When assumptions are made to accommodate a higher level of specification, it often turns out that criticisms similar to those leveled against profit maximization also apply to some of the alternative theories of business behavior.

The microeconomic theory of markets and pricing has been neither proven nor disproven in its entirety, but the qualifications and criticisms we have reviewed in this chapter are much too important to ignore. There are vast differences between the model and the complexities of pricing and

[26] Fritz Machlup, "Marginal Analysis and Empirical Research," *American Economic Review* (September 1946), pp. 519–554.

resource allocation in the real world, just as economic efficiency narrowly defined fails to describe fully the meaning of economic welfare. Accordingly, the general position of most economists today is one of critical acceptance and continual reevaluation of orthodox knowledge about the way in which markets determine prices and allocate resources. Legitimate criticisms can be directed at microeconomics, and a large number of critics voice them, but there are also a large number of authorities who regard the existing theory of market pricing as a useful framework for understanding what resource allocation is all about and why it is important.

## REVIEW

### Summary

1. Marginal utility describes the additional satisfaction gained from consuming one more unit of a product and is related to product price. Thus, consumers are willing to pay different prices for a good depending upon its marginal utility and relative scarcity. The greater the marginal utility and the greater the scarcity of a product, the higher its relative price. Under competitive conditions, an individual consumer maximizes satisfaction by consuming products until equal marginal utility/price ratios are achieved for all goods.

2. General equilibrium in a competitive market economy provides a broad overview of the linkages among resource and product markets. Competitive economic efficiency is achieved in production when price = marginal cost. Since product price reflects marginal utility—the consumers' subjective valuation of a product—the equality of marginal cost (MC), product price (P), and marginal utility (MU) denotes equal values being placed upon: (a) the opportunities forgone or resources sacrificed to produce, and (b) the subjective values consumers place upon a product in achieving additional satisfaction as reflected by product price.

3. The competitive model of a market economy is only a model, not a description of the real world. It is valuable in describing the achievement of a rigidly defined maximum amount of consumer satisfaction in the allocation of scarce resources. In addition, the simple model of competition provides a useful way of studying economic issues related to resource-allocation questions.

4. Numerous important qualifications must be appended to a definition of competitive economic efficiency. Market power deriving from imperfect competition, the issue of income distribution, and externalities (differences between private and social benefits or costs) limit the meaning of economic efficiency.

5. The theory of the firm as a key dimension to microeconomic theory *assumes* profit maximization. Yet there is evidence to indicate that firms are motivated to behave in many other ways. Business firms are faced with uncertainty and imperfect information which inhibit the achievement of profit maximization. In addition, some observers have contended that full-cost pricing, separation of ownership and management, and alternative goals to profit maximization serve to qualify the validity of microeconomic theory.

6. It is important to remember, however, that firms must be sensitive to profits, which are crucial to the viability of a business unit. In addition, it is necessary to recognize that, even though the theory of the firm is nonoperational, it does help explain how firms, consumers, and markets function. In spite of certain important limitations, then, microeconomics is a useful frame of reference for studying problems associated with resource allocation.

### Identify the Following Concepts and Terms

- diminishing marginal utility
- $\dfrac{MU_{tea}}{P_{tea}} = \dfrac{MU_{beans}}{P_{beans}}$
- production efficiency

- general equilibrium
- economic welfare narrowly defined
- externalities
- full-cost pricing

### Questions to Answer

1. Using the following data, diagram the marginal utility ($MU$) of tea.

| Pounds of tea | Total utility | Marginal utility |
|:---:|:---:|:---:|
| 0 | 0 | |
| | | ____ |
| 1 | 80 | |
| | | ____ |
| 2 | 140 | |
| | | ____ |
| 3 | 180 | |
| | | ____ |
| 4 | 200 | |

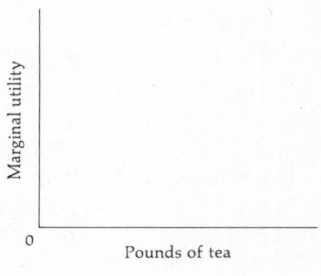

If bread is consumed in a fashion such that $MU_{bread}/P_{bread} = 5/\$1$, and tea sells at a price of \$8 per pound, how much tea would a maximizing consumer with an unlimited income purchase? Why?

2. Explain each of the following statements:
   (a) "Consumers and producers ultimately are the source of supply and demand in resource and product markets."
   (b) "When resources are allocated efficiently, resources and products are equally valued—a condition which suggests that production and consumption efficiency (narrowly viewed) is met."

3. Explain the ways in which this statement is true and/or false: "Technical economic efficiency means that everyone has the best of all possible worlds."

4. The assumption that firms maximize profits has been subjected to extensive and critical review. Give the arguments which have been presented in an attempt to discredit profit maximization as a bulwark of microeconomic theory. Evaluate these arguments.

# APPENDIX B
## Microeconomic Theory

There are certain properties of microeconomic theory which clarify the character of economic efficiency, conflict, and welfare beyond that presented in Chapters 14 through 19. Accordingly, more detailed examination of four topics follows: (a) production efficiency, (b) consumer satisfaction, (c) efficiency in production *and* consumption, and (d) the implications of welfare and warfare under imperfect markets, discussed in that order.

### Cost Minimization and Economic Efficiency

Achievement of *economic efficiency* exists when a product is produced using the least costly combination of resources possible. Just how does a firm reach minimum costs when all resources can be varied in the long run? The answer to this question depends on two things: (a) the productivity of the resources which can be substituted in production, and (b) the price of resources as explained earlier in Chapter 18.

Use of the least costly combination of resources can be explained by logic and intuition. If $1 of costs invested in one more unit of labor results in *more* additional output (marginal product) than $1 invested in capital costs, a constant level of output can be produced at a lower cost by using more of the most productive resource (labor). Costs are minimized when equal marginal products per $1 of costs are reached for additional units of labor and capital.

The least-cost combination of substitutable resources under competitive conditions is important because it reveals the technical condition of economic efficiency. To reach a minimum point on *LRAC*, firms have to employ resources in the most productive combinations at least cost. This point is illustrated in the example below for a firm using two resources (capital denoted by *K*, and labor denoted by *L*) to produce dishwashers.

Several different combinations of capital and labor could be used. Assume that one hour of labor is priced at $3 and the price of one hour of capital is $6. The possible combinations of capital (*K*) and labor (*L*) resources capable of producing one dishwasher might be as shown below. Thus, the firm could produce a dishwasher by using 1 hour of labor and 28 hours of capital

| Resource Combinations Producing One Unit of Output | | | | | | | |
|---|---|---|---|---|---|---|---|
| Hours of labor | 1 and | 2 and | 4 and | 12 and | 24 and | 40 and | (Price = $3) |
| Hours of capital | 28 | 18 | 12 | 8 | 5 | 3 | (Price = $6) |
| Total cost | $171 | $114 | $84 | $84 | $102 | $138 | |

(1L and 28K) and incur a cost of $171, 2L and 18K could be used at a cost of $114, 4L and 12K could be used at a cost of $84, and so forth. Actually, minimum cost is rather obviously achieved at $84 by using 4L and 12K (4 hours of labor cost $12 at $3 per hour, and 12 hours of capital cost $72 at $6 per hour). Note that minimum cost can also be achieved in this example by using 12L and 8K. Operating with either combination of these resources is economically efficient, since one unit of output can be produced at a minimum cost of $84.

The price ratio between these two resources used as factors of production is:

$$\frac{\text{Price capital}}{\text{Price labor}} = \frac{PK}{PL} \quad \text{or} \quad \frac{\$6}{\$3} = 2$$

That is, the price of capital is twice that of labor. If Chapter 18's efficiency explanation is correct, this must mean that capital will be used as long as it is at least twice as productive as labor. Note very carefully that the least-cost resource combination is either 4L and 12K *or* 12L and 8K. In other words, the firm could substitute 8 hours of labor resources (from 4L to 12L) for 4 hours of capital resources (from 12K to 8K) and still produce one unit of output—a dishwasher. If 8L and 4K are substitutable with no output loss, as in this example, then 4 hours of capital which is priced twice as high as labor must do the work of 8 hours of labor. Thus, an hour of capital is twice as productive as an hour of labor, in proportion to capital and labor price.

Without resorting to technical proof here, what this means is that the additional output or marginal product of one hour of capital (MPK) is twice as great as the marginal product of one hour of labor (MPL). In other words, at a least-cost combination of capital and labor resources, the market's price ratio of capital to labor (PK/PL) and the ratio of capital's technical productivity to labor productivity (given by the MPK/MPL ratio) are equal at least cost. On the average, (a) the MPK for one hour is .25 units of output, (b) the MPL for one hour is .125 units of output, and (c) the ratio MPK/MPL is .25/.125 = 2. Least cost exists if:

$$\frac{PK}{PL} = \frac{MPK}{MPL} \quad \text{or} \quad \frac{\$6}{\$3} = \frac{.25}{.125}$$

which is also given by

$$\frac{MPK}{PK} = \frac{MPL}{PL}$$

The earlier data showing the substitution possibilities between capital and labor reveal that these resources are *imperfect* substitutes. For example, at a technological combination of resources using very little labor (e.g., 1L and 28K) one more hour of labor can be substituted for ten hours of capital which is being used very intensively. At the other extreme of intensive use of labor (40L and 3K), it takes 16 hours of labor to replace 2 hours of capital. As one resource such as labor is increasingly substituted for capital, more and more labor is required because of the diminishing marginal productivity of labor as it is used in larger quantities and because labor is an imperfect substitute for capital. That is, labor is increasingly a poorer substitute for capital. Similar imperfections in resource substitution prevail for an increasingly intensive use of capital leading to increasing costs due to the lower marginal productivity of capital used in production.

Least-cost efficiency in production is achieved under pure competition because firms are forced to minimize costs by producing where $P = ATC$ minimum. Firms that do not meet this requirement will not earn a normal profit and while some producers may be inefficient some of the time, ultimately, the least efficient users of combinations of labor and capital resources will be forced out of the industry. As least-cost conditions are met throughout an economy, the marginal product of capital for firms producing one product must be equal to the marginal product of capital in producing all other products. If this were not the case, resources would be bid away from some users. For example, if capital were more productive in producing product X than Y, owners of capital resources could and would sell more capital to profit-maximizing firms producing product X until the equality $PK/PL = MPK/MPL$ exists. Price competition for resources is important precisely because competition ensures that every employer will pay an identical $PK$ and $PL$ as set by market supply and demand, and firms will substitute resources as described above.

## Indifference-Curve Analysis of Consumer Satisfaction

Least-cost production efficiency is an important characteristic of competitive markets, but it is equally as important that production is geared to the wants of society. The way consumer satisfaction is related to the price system can be clarified by closer examination of the problem of consumer choice.

A consumer typically is interested in a bundle of different products and if there is a great deal of one (e.g., 100 pounds of sugar per month), the marginal utility of another unit of that product will be small. At the same time, the marginal utility of one more unit of another good scarcely available at all (e.g., 1 pound of meat per month) will be relatively large. In short, the relative scarcity of alternative goods influences their utility or "value" as perceived by a consumer. The idea that utility must be a cardinally measurable phenomenon (something which can be counted) is not necessary. Instead, the consumer may be regarded as expressing ordinal (or preference-ranking) calculations in acquiring a utility-maximizing combination of goods. Remember, however, that concern for consumer satisfaction expressed in terms of utility abstracts from the income-distribution problem, where inequality may possibly lead to distortions in the marginal utility of money.

## USING INDIFFERENCE CURVES

Let us examine a simple problem in consumer choice for two goods X and Y by using consumer indifference curves. *Indifference curves* show the different combinations of two goods which yield *equal* total utility or satisfaction. An indifference curve reveals that a consumer might be equally satisfied with 35Y and 5X *or* 30Y and 6X as is illustrated below for alternative quanties ($Q$) of these two goods.

| $Q_Y$ | 35 | 30 | 25 | 20 | 15 |
|---|---|---|---|---|---|
| $Q_X$ | 5 | 6 | 11 | 21 | 41 |

These same data representing the relative preferences of a consumer for goods X and Y are shown in diagramatic form in Figure 1. In Figure 1(a), quantities of product Y are measured on the vertical axis, quantities of product X are measured on the horizontal axis, and five hypothetical combinations of these two goods are plotted as points $a \ldots e$. There are four basic features about indifference curves which merit our immediate attention:

1. An indifference curve such as $I$ in Figure 1(a) reveals the relative preferences of a consumer for different quantity combinations of two goods X and Y, and all combinations of these goods yield some constant amount of satisfaction. That is, a consumer is indifferent to any two points on indifference curve $I$ because equal amounts of *total utility* are shown for all different combinations of two goods in Figure 1(a).

2. The location of indifference curves used to reveal consumer preferences is a second important feature. Actually, the relative preferences for goods are given by an entire set or "map" of indifference curves such as $I_1$, $I_2$, and $I_3$ (or any number of other indifference curves) drawn in Figure 1(b). The greater the distance an indifference curve is from the origin in Figure 1(b), the greater the amount of consumer satisfaction represented. Consequently, indifference curve $I_3$ is preferred to $I_2$ because greater quantities of goods can be consumed on $I_3$. In contrast, $I_1$ is less desirable than $I_2$ and $I_3$ because it depicts less consumer satisfaction. Therefore, rightward movement to successively higher indifference curves in Figure 1(b) depicts greater utility.

3. As shown by the figure, an indifference curve slopes downward because the loss of marginal utility from less of product Y is offset by additional utility gained from having more of product X. In other words, in order to maintain a constant level of satisfaction, a negative change in product Y must be offset by a positive change in X and, conversely, less X requires more Y to maintain constant utility.

4. Even though a consumer is equally as satisfied with the combinations of X and Y denoted by points $a \ldots e$ on any one indifference curve such as $I$ of Figure 1(a), note that the rate of substitution of goods varies. Indifference curves are generally concave from above, as the slope of $I$ in Figure 1(a) decreases. When small quantities of X are consumed at point $a$, for example, a one unit increase in the quantity of X consumed provides satisfaction equivalent to a much larger reduction $(-5Y)$ in the amount of Y consumed (i.e., in moving from points $a$ to $b$, $1X = -5Y$). The slope of indifference curve $I$ diminishes because the marginal utility of product X $(MU_X)$ is large relative to the marginal utility of product Y $(MU_Y)$; therefore, relatively small amounts of X can be indifferently substituted for a larger amount of Y at point $a$ where product X is scarce and product Y is abundant.

This substitution relationship of goods in consumption is given by the slope of an indifference curve. Viewed in the discrete quantities of Figure 1(a), the substitution of more X for less of Y is shown by the gain of $+MU_X \div$ the loss of $-MU_Y$, where varying quantities of the two goods provide constant total utility on one indifference curve. In Figure 1(a), for example, consumer preferences allow the substitution of $+1X$ for $-5Y$ between points $a$ and $b$, indicating that the marginal rate of substitution

FIGURE 1    Indifference-Curve Analysis

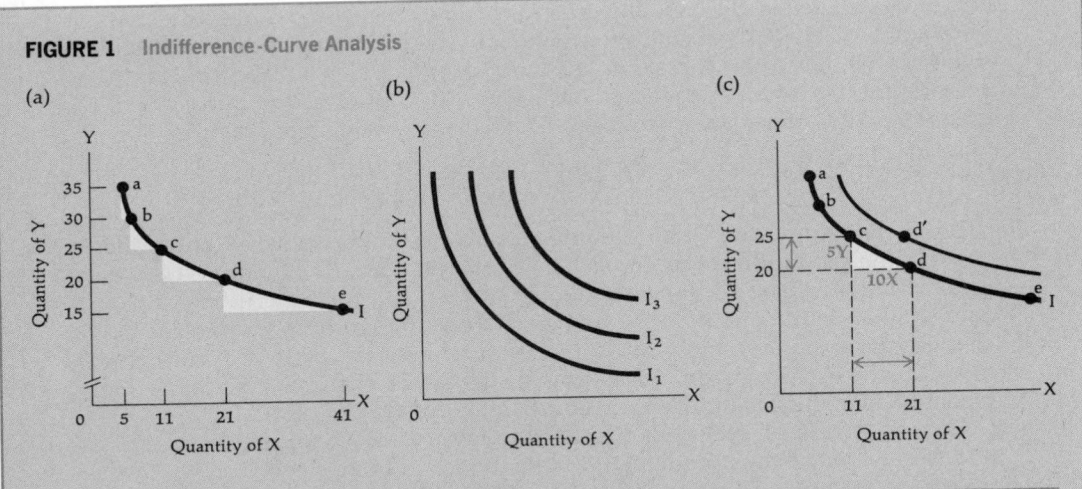

Indifference Curves. The meaning of indifference curves is illustrated in (a) where schedule $I$ depicts alternative combinations of consumption of two goods which yield a constant amount of total utility. The slope of $I$ is $MU_X/MU_Y$ which reveals the rate at which goods are substituted in consumption. Actually, there is not one, but an entire map of indifference curves as $I_1$, $I_2$, and $I_3$ as illustrated in (b). Exchange is mutually beneficial when the rate of substitution in consumption is different for two consumers. Thus, at point a in (a) one consumer will give $-5Y$ for $+1X$ and another consumer at point d in (c) will accept $+5Y$ and give up $-10X$, allowing one or both persons to attain a higher level of satisfaction [e.g., point d' in (c)].

(the ratio $MU_X/MU_Y$ per unit) is relatively large. In contrast, as product X is consumed in larger quantities and less of product Y is consumed between points $c$ and $d$, $+11X$ can be substituted for $-5Y$; i.e., the rate at which $-Y$ is sacrificed for $+X$ declines. Accordingly, *the slope of an indifference curve given by $MU_X/MU_Y$ measures the rate at which a consumer indifferently exchanges one good for another.*[1]

## EXCHANGE AND CONSUMER SATISFACTION

Indifference-curve analysis nicely reveals the importance of economic exchange to the welfare status of individual consumers. For simplicity purposes consider a two-person (party A and party D), two-commodity (good X and good Y) economy. Initially (i.e., before exchange) party A is consuming a combination of goods shown at point $a$ in Figure 1(a), or 35Y and 5X. Party D shown in Figure 1(c) is assumed to be at point $d$ consuming 20Y and 21X. We further assume that each individual consumer is maximizing his own utility, or $MU_X/P_X = MU_Y/P_Y$ for each consumer.

The conclusion shown by comparison of party A to D is that both parties

---

[1] The utility ($U$) from consuming given quantities of X and Y given by one consumer indifference curve is expressed as $U = u(X, Y)$, where indifference curve $U$ is a constant. By taking the total derivative to obtain the slope of the indifference curve at any one point, we obtain $\Delta X \times MU_X + \Delta Y \times MU_Y$ equals zero $\Delta U$. Thus, in consuming $+\Delta X$ and $-\Delta Y$ while moving from points $a$ to $b$ on indifference curve $I$ in Figure 1(a), the gain in utility of $\Delta X$ of $+1$ times $MU_X$ is just offset by a loss in utility of $\Delta Y$ of $-5$ times $MU_Y$ and total utility is unchanged. The slope of the indifference curve is thus expressed as $\Delta Y/\Delta X$ or $MU_X/MU_Y$ which is the marginal rate of substitution of X and Y.

can increase their collective satisfaction through exchange. Since any combination of X and Y consumption is equally as satisfying, party A would sacrifice five units of the relatively abundant good Y in Figure 1(a) to acquire another unit of X. In contrast, Figure 1(c) shows that party D will give up $-10X$ to obtain a gain of $+5Y$. Thus, the exchange potential is:

> Party A: give $-5Y$ and accept no less than $+1X$
> Party D: accept $+5Y$ and give no more than $-10X$

By exchanging goods, one or both parties can increase satisfaction and reach a higher indifference curve. For example, party D could give up as little as $-1X$ to party A in order to obtain $+5Y$ and thereby reach point $d'$ on a higher indifference curve in Figure 1(c). Of course, the reverse exchange circumstances might also prevail, in which case party A would give up $-5Y$ in exchange for $+10X$ and usurp all of the gains in utility by reaching some higher indifference curve in Figure 1(a).[2]

Just what rate of exchange is settled upon depends upon market prices, and to see this we must understand the nature of a budget line.

## THE BUDGET LINE

A budget line is used to reflect the reality that consumer incomes are limited. Accordingly, the hypothetical budget line $BB'$ in Figure 2(a) identifies the area $OBB'$ as all attainable combinations of two goods X and Y which can be purchased with an illustrative budget of $100. If product prices are $P_X = \$2$ and $P_Y = \$1$, a consumer could spend all of his budget for good Y and purchase 100 units ($\$100 \div \$1$). Alternatively, 50 units ($\$100 \div \$2$) of the higher priced good X might be purchased with a constant budget of $100, or various other combinations of goods which absorb a $100 budget might be purchased at these prices as shown below.

| $Q_Y$ | 100 | 80 | 60 | 40 | 20 | 0 |
|-------|-----|-----|-----|-----|-----|-----|
| $Q_X$ | 0 | 10 | 20 | 30 | 40 | 50 |

Three properties of a budget line merit clarification: the effect of price changes, the effect of an increase in income, and the slope of the budget line.

First, consider what happens if the price of one good is unchanged while the price of another good *increases*, perhaps because a $1 per unit tax is imposed on good Y ($P_Y$ is now $2). A price increase lowers the budget line of Figure 2(a) to $BB''$ with a constant budget of $100. That is, a consumer can now purchase a maximum of 50Y at $P_Y = \$2$ and the attainable consumption area is now $OBB''$ in Figure 2(a). In contrast, if $P_Y$ remains $1, and if the government were to offer a consumer subsidy on product X in the amount of $1 per unit and reduce its price from $2 to $1, a maximum

---

[2] Potential conflict in negotiating the rate of exchange exists between two parties. For example, party D could intimate that at any higher price than 1X for 5Y, he will not strike a bargain or perhaps will initiate a second game of war against party A.

**FIGURE 2**   Consumer Budgets and Equilibrium

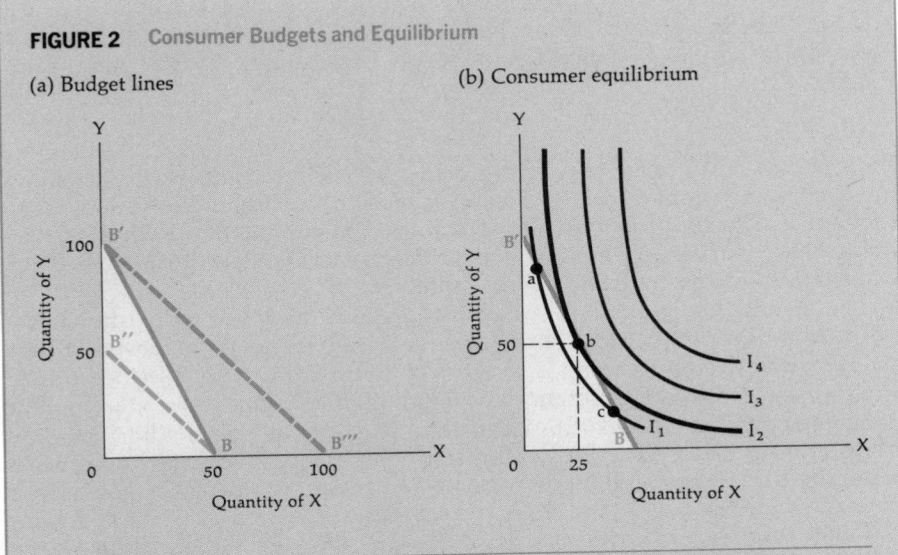

(a) Budget lines

(b) Consumer equilibrium

*Budget Lines.* A budget line reveals the market rate of substitution of two goods which is the slope of a budget line or $P_X / P_Y$. The relative price ratios of two goods are shown by the slope of a budget line such as $BB'$ in (a). As the price of Y rises, the budget line shifts to $BB''$. However, if the price of X declines, budget line $BB'$ shifts to $B'''B'$. In (b) by combining the budget line and indifference curve, the equilibrium point b can be identified as a level of maximum consumer satisfaction. Thus, $I_2$ is the highest attainable level of satisfaction possible given the limited budget, and at tangency point b, $MU_X /MU_Y = P_X /P_Y$ —the consumer's rate of substitution of goods X and Y equals the market's rate of substitution for these same two goods.

of 100X could then be purchased. The rightward shift in the budget line in Figure 2(a) now establishes the area $OB'B'''$ as the area of attainable consumption.

Second, consider the effect of a change in budgeted income, assuming prices remain at \$1 as shown by budget line $B'B'''$. If income decreases to say \$50 for one reason or another (e.g., an increase in income taxes), the budget line shifts leftward to $BB''$, and consumption is reduced. Conversely, as a budget is increased, larger quantities of goods can be consumed as the budget line shifts away from the origin in Figure 2(a).[3]

Third, recognize that the slope of the budget line shows the *market's* evaluation of the opportunity cost of one product in relation to another good. That is, relative market prices taking into account the relative preferences of all consumers for two goods X and Y are revealed by a budget line. Thus, for budget line $BB'$ in Figure 2(a), the market's evaluation of product

---

[3] The relative extent to which a change in per unit taxes (or subsidies) change consumption compared to a change in income taxes varies. As a budget is altered, the quantities of two goods consumed decrease or increase, depending upon product prices or consumer preferences shown by an indifference schedule. Advanced courses in microeconomic theory demonstrate, however, that a per unit tax on one good causes greater distortion for consumer choice than a change in income taxes.

X in relation to Y, is such that the opportunity cost of 100Y is 50X, or 2Y is equivalent in value to 1X. What this means, then, is that the market's value (price) of X is twice the price of Y as shown by the price ratio $P_X/P_Y$.[4]

## MAXIMIZING UTILITY

Indifference-curve analysis can be combined with a budget line to show how a price system and free exchange lead to maximum consumer satisfaction. In Figure 2(b), a budget line is used in conjunction with a map of indifference curves, each of which indicate successively greater levels of satisfaction in moving from $I_1$ to $I_4$, as before.

The geometric solution to maximizing consumer utility is shown by point $E$ of Figure 2(b). Maximum consumer satisfaction is achieved at that point where the budget line is tangent to indifferent curve $I_2$, since this is the highest possible indifference curve attainable. Suppose we start with a consumer purchasing quantities of X and Y to the left of equilibrium, say, at point $a$ in Figure 2(b). By buying less Y and more X and moving toward point $b$, the higher indifference curve $I_2$ can be attained. Or consider a consumer purchasing X and Y in the quantities denoted at point $c$. Again, a higher indifference curve can be attained by moving to point $b$ in Figure 2(b).[5]

Given a constant budget and fixed relative prices, what is it that is unique about equilibrium point $b$ in Figure 2(b)? At this combination of goods, substitution in consumption (the slope of indifference curve $I$ which reflects a consumer's preferences for X and Y) is equal to the market's rate of substitution of goods X and Y (or the slope of the budget line as a measure of relative product prices). As we know, the slope of the indifference curve is an expression of consumer preferences or the relative marginal utility ratio, $MU_X/MU_Y$. Furthermore, the market's values of these same two goods is shown by the slope of the budget line which is $P_X/P_Y$. Thus, at equilibrium:

$$\frac{MU_X}{MU_Y} = \frac{P_X}{P_Y}$$

which is also

$$\frac{MU_X}{P_X} = \frac{MU_Y}{P_Y}$$

Accordingly, a household will alter consumption spending for alternative goods until the quantities purchased yield equal marginal utilities per dollar

---

[4] The slope of the budget line is:

$$\frac{\$\text{Budget}/\text{Price}_Y}{\$\text{Budget}/\text{Price}_X} = \frac{B/P_Y}{B/P_X} = \frac{B}{P_Y} \times \frac{P_X}{B} = \frac{P_X}{P_Y}$$

or

$$\frac{\$100/\$1}{\$100/\$2} = \frac{\$100}{\$1} \times \frac{\$2}{100} = \frac{\$2}{\$1} = 2$$

[5] If the price of one good (e.g., product Y) were to increase, the budget line would swing toward the origin, and some lower indifference curve such as $I_1$ would be attained. In contrast, if the budget line were to swing away from the origin, greater levels of consumer satisfaction could be achieved on some indifference curve higher than $I_2$ of Figure 2(b).

spent for all goods as shown at point $b$ in Figure 2(b) (as discussed earlier in Chapter 19). In conclusion, the precise combination of any two goods consumed depends upon the market's evaluation and the relative marginal utilities provided to individual consumers.[6]

## Efficiency in Production and Consumption

We are now in a position to put together the ideas of least-cost efficiency in production and in consumption. This competitive-efficiency optimum, known as *Pareto efficiency*, can be illustrated by a two-commodity example in which all consumers are collapsed into one—let us say an economic planner bent on seeing that an economy produces efficiently and consumers maximize utility.[7]

Figure 3 illustrates Pareto efficiency or the achievement of efficiency in production *and* consumer maximization of satisfaction at point $E$—a point of tangency between the indifference curve $I_2$ and the production frontier $(PF)$. The maximum possible amount of output is limited by production frontier $PF$ in Figure 3. As explained earlier, to attain a production frontier, resources must be used efficiently. Furthermore, under competition, product price = marginal cost for *all goods produced*. A Pareto equilibrium can be any point on the production frontier, which reflects the relative opportunity costs of producing two goods, or $MC_x/MC_y$. Any point on production frontier $PF$ *could* be a Pareto point, but only point $E$ is as long as market prices and consumer preferences remain as shown in Figure 3. The geometric logic of Pareto efficiency is clear enough. There is no other indifference curve providing greater satisfaction than $I_2$ which is attainable, given production frontier $PF$; point $b$ is inefficient in production since it represents operating below the production frontier. Although point $c$ on indifference curve $I_1$ is on the production frontier, consumer satisfaction is not maximized since there is a higher attainable indifference curve $(I_2)$.

The one particular equilibrium in Figure 3 is unique in that this particular combination of a pair of goods equates the market's substitution of goods shown by the slope of the gold price line $(P_x/P_y)$ with both the substitution of goods in consumption as shown by the slope of indifference curve $I_2$ $(MU_x/MU_y)$, and the opportunity costs of producing two goods which is $MC_x/MC_y$ as shown by the slope of production frontier $PF$ at point $E$. At equilibrium $P_x/P_y = MU_x/MU_y = MC_x/MC_y$; i.e., or the market's rate of substitution (the price ratio), substitution in consumption

---

[6] One further point about equilibrium in consumption: If competitive prices exist for all consumers, we can further specify the conditions required for *all* consumers to be maximizing utility. Utility is maximized subject to a budget constraint set by some given pattern of income distribution when the ratios $MU_x/MU_y$ for both party A and party D are equal to the market price ratio $P_x/P_y$. That is, since competition sets a uniform price to all consumers we can say that A's $MU_x/MU_y$ must equal D's $MU_x/MU_y = P_x/P_y$. If this condition did not exist and one consumer valued Y more highly than another, as occurred in Figure 1, each party could improve upon his position without worsening another's by exchanging goods.

[7] Actually, the marginal conditions necessary for a Pareto optimum are a good deal more complex than is indicated in the following pages. Marginal equalities must exist in production (relative marginal costs for all goods $i \ldots n$ are equal); in consumption (relative marginal utilities from all goods for all consumers $i \ldots n$ are equal); in resource supply, time, and so on.

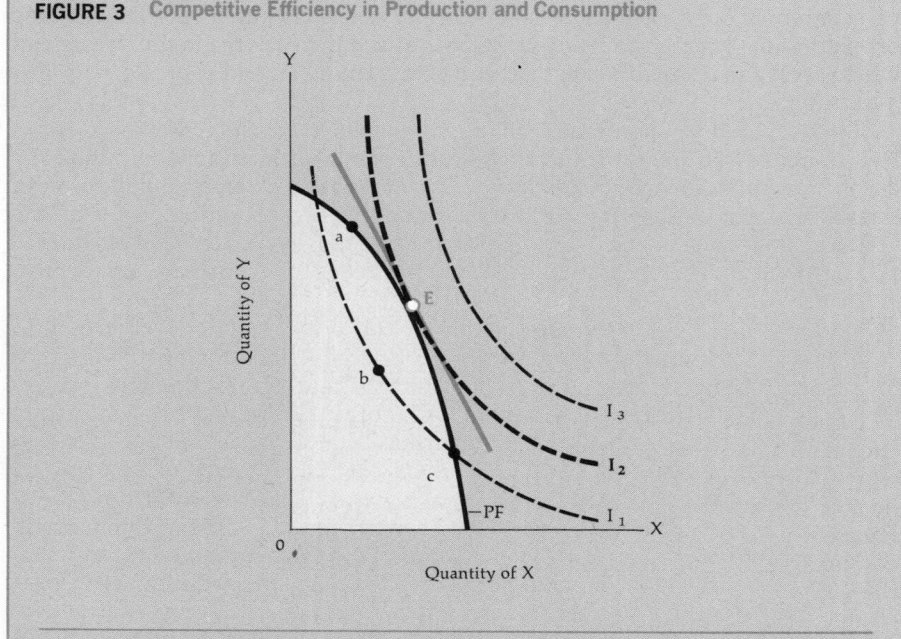

**FIGURE 3**  Competitive Efficiency in Production and Consumption

*Pareto Efficiency.* Efficient production and maximum consumption exists at one point on a production frontier which has the slope $MC_X/MC_Y$, depicting the marginal cost of transforming one good into another. Thus, maximum attainable consumption exists on indifference curve $I_2$ at the tangency point $E$ where $MC_X/MC_Y$ and $P_X/P_Y$ are equal. Point $E$ is Pareto efficient because the gold price line ($P_X/P_Y$) depicting market substitution of X for Y is equal to the slope of the production frontier given by $MC_X/MC_Y$ and the slope of the highest attainable indifference curve given by $MU_X/MU_Y$.

(the marginal utility ratio), and opportunity costs in production (the marginal cost ratio) all are equal.[8]

## On Welfare and Warfare

It is one thing to set forth the conditions for competitive efficiency in production which minimizes scarcity and maximizes utility in a much over-simplified model, and quite another thing to examine the real world in which the pattern of income distribution cannot be ignored. Comparisons of social and private costs and benefits often reveal divergence, and imperfect competition is the rule and not the exception to the rule.

Under such conditions we often find that conflict-choice is prevalent just as it is in considering a move from one point on a production frontier to

[8] Since least-cost efficiency in production of $MPK/MPL = PK/PL$ occurs where price and marginal cost are equal, $P_X = MC_X$ and $P_Y = MC_Y$, which means the Pareto condition is achieved where $P_X/P_Y = MU_X/MU_Y$. There are, however, further marginal conditions which must be met requiring equal rates of substitution in consumption between any pair of goods for all consumers of equal rates of substitution in production between any pair of resources, and so forth. See Chapters 16 and 17 of C. E. Ferguson, *Microeconomic Theory* (Homewood, Ill.: Richard D. Irwin, Inc., 1970).

another. Game theory is a subject which can add more realism to analyses of economic choice. Let us briefly consider game theory as a different way of examining pricing and output decisions by firms with monopoly power which are thus capable of distorting the market's solution to resource allocation.

The basic tool of game theory is the *payoff matrix* which depicts alternative choices or strategies for parties experiencing conflict in which the action of one party influences a rival. The payoff matrix depicting the value or "payoff" of acts as shown in Figure 4 assumes:

1. There are two parties, say, firm B and firm G.
2. Each firm is faced with two alternative strategies. Thus, firm B can select strategy $B_1$ (holding prices constant) or strategy $B_2$ (which involves a price reduction). Similarly, firm G may leave prices unchanged ($G_1$) or reduce them ($G_2$). Now let us see what Figure 4 means.

Two competitive firms are illustrated in Figure 4(a) which uses hypothetical numbers to depict the payoff to firm G (in gold) and the payoff to firm B (in blue). The two strategies shown as columns $G_1$ and $G_2$ are for firm G which can make horizontal moves as denoted by the gold arrows of Figure 4(a). Conversely, firm B can make vertical moves between strategies $B_1$ and $B_2$. Each of four cell values in the payoff matrix show the value of the game to firms B and G. Thus, if firm G selects strategy $G_1$ and B selects strategy $B_1$ (no price changes), each party receives an economic-profit payoff of $1 as shown in Figure 4(a), perhaps because technological changes have lowered unit costs. If this is the initial starting position for both firms, notice that there is an *incentive* for G to lower prices by moving rightward in selecting strategy $G_2$ since the firm will earn $2 (firm B will lose $2). Having done so, however, firm B will also be forced to cut prices by moving downward to strategy $B_2$, and the competitive result will be a normal profit ($0 economic profit) for both firms. If firm B were to select competitive strategy $B_2$ first, this move would also be followed by a countermove on G's part which once again produces the $0 economic-profit payoff as a stable and competitive value to the game.

## THE DILEMMA OF RIVALRY

In Figure 4(b) other facets of rivalry and game playing are illustrated. Suppose that Figure 4(b) depicts two oligopolists, where price cuts by both parties (strategies $B_2$ and $G_2$) lead to total loss of −$2 (each firm loses $1). Now assume that the game begins with both firms at strategy $B_1G_1$ where each earns a profit of $1. The short-sighted and stable solution to this game reveals that firm G has an incentive to move horizontally to $G_2$ where $2 can be earned, but if firm G selects $G_2$, firm B will elect $B_2$ to avoid a loss of $3. Similarly, if the first move belongs to firm B, the same stable equilibrium will be reached where each firm loses $1. Accordingly, each firm can be said to be experiencing what is termed a "prisoner's dilemma"; that is, both parties are locked into an undesirable payoff solution. However, there are four other characteristics of this particular game which merit consideration.

1. Collusion. Actually, the dilemma confronting the oligopolists in Figure 4(b) has a collusive "long-sighted" solution that both firms may well

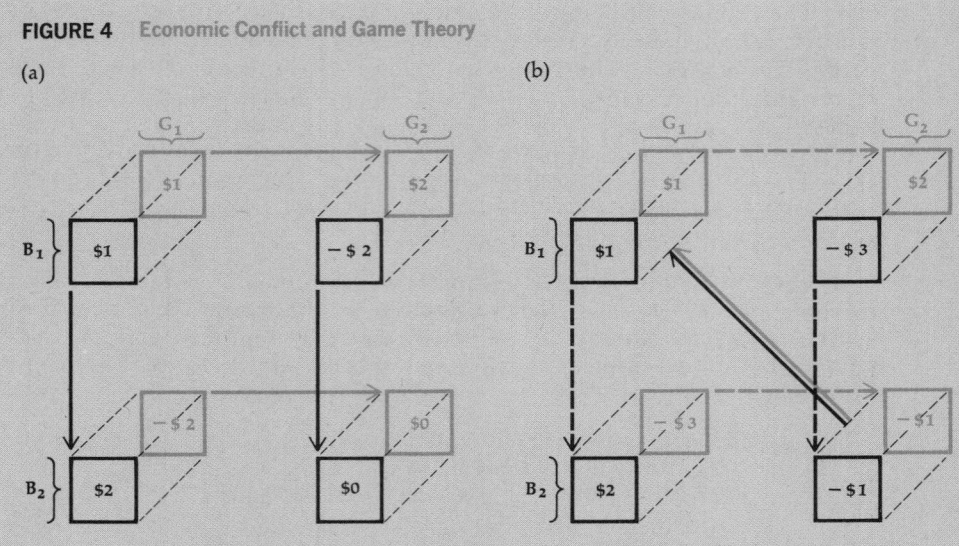

**FIGURE 4**  Economic Conflict and Game Theory

*Game Theory.* Market imperfections qualify the highly impersonal market allocation of resources. When two parties (G and B) compete, the payoff value of a competitive game is the stable equilibrium of $0 in economic profits shown in (a). Rivalry leads to conflict as shown in (b), where each party has a short-term incentive to improve his own position. Thus, interdependent and rival oligopolists can be driven to the prisoner's dilemma payoff of − $1, − $1. However, there are incentives to collude at $1, $1 and the use of threats, promises, and bribes may be important tactics in reaching a collusive agreement.

hit upon after experiencing negative payoffs due to rivalistic price wars. Provided that both firms agree to *not* compete in a ruinous fashion, they can select strategies $B_1$ and $G_1$ in order to remain at the profitable payoff level. Indeed, each firm has an incentive to do exactly this, for it is profitable to acquire a longsighted perspective of the game.

2. Bribery. Still another alternative is for one producer such as firm G, to bribe or compensate a rival. Thus, firm G might "persuade" firm B to always play strategy $B_1$ only and therefore maintain the favorable $1 payoff solution. Actually, firm G can pay a bribe of up to $2 for the − $1 that would otherwise be lost if both parties select price-cut strategies $B_2G_2$.

3. Threats. Another feature of the conflict game consists of making effective use of threats. In Figure 4(b), firm G might make known a threat to move to $G_2$ if firm B plays strategy $B_2$, and may be able to force his rival to stay with strategy $B_1$. Of course, if firm G then selects strategy $G_2$, the effectiveness of a threat is destroyed as long as opponent firm B can move once again. Two vital characteristics of a threat are the ability to communicate with a rival and the credibility of a threat. If firm G can not communicate with firm B or if the threat lacks authenticity—perhaps because similar statements in the past have been enforced sporadically—firm B may regard a threat as a bluff and proceed to seek its larger gain of $2 at strategy $B_2$. In this case, however, there is an incentive for firm G to make good on the threat and opt $G_2$.

4. The Promise. Still another feature of game theory of some importance is trust, or the ability to make a promise. Suppose, for example, that both parties can make one simultaneous move only (e.g., an agreement to make or refrain from initiating massive style changes). Firm B must be able to believe G's promise to refrain from such a costly endeavor. If firm B selects the no-style change strategy $B_1$, firm G could opt for $G_2$ and impose considerable harm on its opponent while gaining itself. Indeed, the difficulty with making a promise is that there are incentives for either party to cheat as is shown in Figure 4(b).

Barring the ability to make enforceable commitments, then, it is possible for noncollusive rivals to remain trapped in a prisoner's dilemma. There are, however, a variety of tactics which may improve upon existing payoff alternatives, including outright collusion on the part of oligopolistic firms which are rivals. Game theory also applies to many different types of economic conflict. Thus, corporate goliaths and powerful labor unions may tacitly make inflationary wage settlements, implicitly knowing all the while that the public at large will pay higher consumer prices which can be administered upwards in imperfectly competitive markets. Or, government authorities interested in promoting greater submissiveness to status quo may tender compensatory bribes to the poverty population, farmers, the oil industry, or the unemployed. Lawmakers may "promise" to refrain from initiating the relatively firm controls environmental pollution needs (an implied "threat"), provided that offenders engage in some form of modest self-policing. In short, many extensions to competitive price solutions are possible in any society which makes rules and fosters institutional ways of coping with economic choice problems.

# PART 4

A wide variety of domestic economic issues and problems arise in any complex economy and the United States is no exception. The chapters of Part 4 examine economic issues of contemporary importance to the American people and to government officials who are charged with promoting the general welfare of all citizens. Public economic policies are not, however, developed and implemented in a sterile vacuum, void of conflicitng values and guided by definitive and proven economic relationships. Rather, a social expression of value judgments is embodied in resolving problems associated with the power of government and corporate institutions, government expenditure decisions, resource-allocation adjustments in agriculture, monopoly power in labor and product markets, environmental debasement, poverty, discrimination, and so forth. These are economic problems of contemporary relevance and the attention they receive in the chapters which follow is well-deserved.

# Domestic Economic Issues

**20.**
**Economic Welfare and the State**
Institutional economics, the
corporation and the state, and
public-welfare and finance
problems in government

**22.**
**Environmental Economics:**
**The Quality of Life**
The impact of income inequality
and environmental deterioration
on the quality of life

**21.**
**The Problems of Monopoly**
**and Agriculture**
A study of public policy
in relation to monopoly power
and the agricultural problem

**23.**
**Labor Markets and Wage**
**Determination**
Markets for human resources,
labor unions and the determination of wages, and the economics
of organized labor markets

**24.**
**Human Resources, Poverty, and**
**Discrimination**
Human capital, the poverty
problem, and the economics of
racial discrimination

# CHAPTER 20
## Economic Welfare and the State

As has been noted (Chapter 4), the public sector influences resource allocation by taxation, expenditures, and administrative rules, which are founded on a system of social values. In this chapter, we will refine our knowledge about market pricing and resource allocation by first placing economic theory in a different perspective and then examining the role of government in the economic welfare of society.

Today aggregate tax receipts and expenditures (purchases of output *plus* transfer payments) in the United States are approximately one-third of a trillion dollars. Indeed, government purchases of goods and services alone account for over 20 percent of final output in the United States each year. Annual government receipts are three times as large as the sum of corporate profits (before taxes) *plus* net farm income—and that is a sizable concentration of economic power. Indeed, only a few nations in the world create a total output equal to the public-sector expenditures of the United States. With no guidance from the price system, government directly allocates resources to national defense or education and distributes output (income) to the poor or to the wealthy, to consumers or corporations. Consequently, the theory of market pricing and resource allocation must be modified considerably.

The first step in this modification is presented in Part A, in which the resource-allocation framework of markets relied upon earlier is briefly reexamined. Part B then presents a rather different set of views about the market system, economics itself, and the public sector—views which have been most ably synthesized by Professor John Kenneth Galbraith. Part C reviews the relation between the welfare of society and selected ideas in public finance that relate to problems faced by government today. Having thus established a frame of reference for government's involvement in the welfare of society, it will be possible to move on in later chapters to discuss contemporary economic issues. Let us begin by taking a hard look at the realities affecting the market system and the state.

## A. THE MARKET INSTRUMENT

Since concentrated and serious inquiry into economic affairs first began approximately two centuries ago, knowledge about economics has progressed substantially. Specialization, exchange, markets, and prices have been shown to be important and very much interrelated factors that involve consumers and producers linked by resource and product markets. Specialization and exchange in markets remain meaningful realities today; what is very much in dispute is the validity and usefulness of the legacy, willed to us by earlier scholars, of microeconomic ideas as an explanation of resource allocation. Part of that legacy consists of a view of markets as an admittedly imperfect, but nonetheless coordinating network of price signals.

### Price Signals and the Market Network

The way in which price signals ration goods, allocate resources, and influence income distribution in a market system is summarized in Figure 1. The orthodox argument is that, as expanding industries experience greater prosperity, they use more scarce resources, whereas firms and industries producing goods which are declining in consumer favor use fewer resources. Similarly, less efficient firms tend to earn lower profits and ultimately must leave the industry. In the utopian state of pure competition, general equilibrium means that producers and consumers are all relatively satisfied—society is said to be squeezing as much satisfaction from its limited resources as is possible, as is suggested in Figure 1. This view of the market system, observed long ago by Adam Smith, depicts an economy as if being led by an Invisible Hand, where consumers maximize satisfaction, producers maximize profits, and resource owners maximize incomes. Changes in the profitability of firms and variations in the pattern of income distribution to households are triggered by resource- and product-market prices.

Resource and product market supply and demand, as well as market prices have a direct influence on the lives of all individuals. Consider the contemporary American economy, in which unskilled labor is abundantly supplied, but subject to a relatively meager demand, while a rather high level of demand for highly skilled human resources is accompanied by a scarce supply. The income result? Based on 1970 income levels, the average 22-year-old male college graduate can expect to earn about $650,000 over a normal lifetime, whereas a 22-year-old male laborer with eight years of

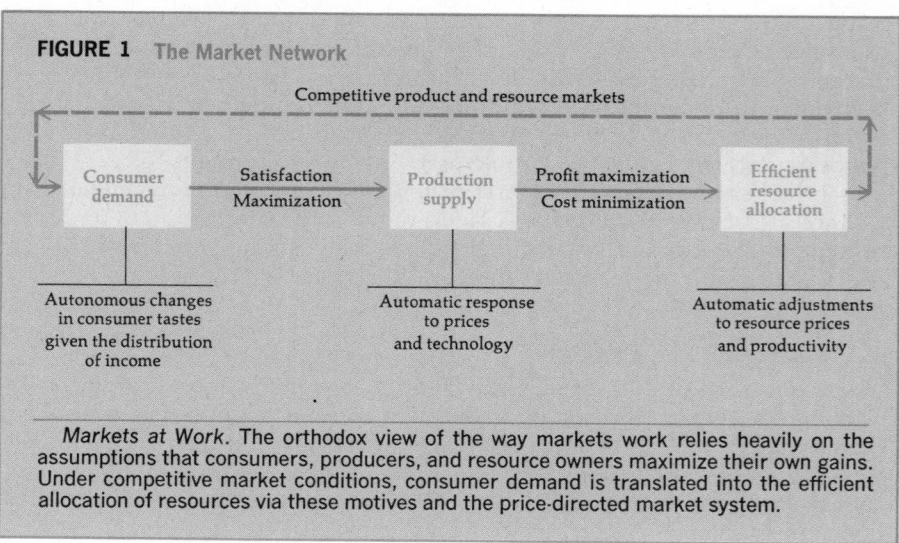

**FIGURE 1** The Market Network

Competitive product and resource markets

| Consumer demand | Satisfaction Maximization | Production supply | Profit maximization / Cost minimization | Efficient resource allocation |

Autonomous changes in consumer tastes given the distribution of income

Automatic response to prices and technology

Automatic adjustments to resource prices and productivity

*Markets at Work.* The orthodox view of the way markets work relies heavily on the assumptions that consumers, producers, and resource owners maximize their own gains. Under competitive market conditions, consumer demand is translated into the efficient allocation of resources via these motives and the price-directed market system.

education can expect average lifetime earnings of about $270,000.[1] And lest you think price is of no consequence in allocating resources, compare what you intuitively know about markets for panty hose vs. those for wringer washers, or just look about you at the enrollment, construction, and rate of growth on college campuses in recent years. Comparisons of supply, demand, and prices for land in rural Illinois relative to metropolitan Chicago reveal the same general tendencies. While the higher price of metropolitan land reflects higher levels of demand relative to a scarce supply, metropolitan land values are by no means uniform. The price of a lot in Harlem is quite different from that of one on Wall Street—again because of supply and demand.

While the orthodox microeconomic view of markets and prices is appealing, how meaningful an explanation of pricing and resource allocation is furnished by the concepts of market supply and demand, which depend upon the assumption of maximization? For example, does the view of markets summarized in Figure 1 explain a large enough proportion of the nearly $400,000 difference in lifetime income between elementary- and college-educated males? What else is involved in the lower price of land in Harlem compared to Wall Street? For that matter, are either a $400,000 lifetime-income difference or ghetto property in Harlem in the best interest of society? Is it meaningful to talk about the price of a Chevy or a Rolls, or are the economics of freeways, smog, highway deaths, and the vast wealth of General Motors (and certain stockholders) more relevant in America in the 1970s? Or, just how do markets relate to college campuses, where most of the direct cost of higher education is subsidized by a "welfare state"?[2] Clearly, it behooves us to see just where orthodox economic theory is most vulnerable to criticism.

## On the "Theology" of Economics

In the process of unveiling several basic economic principles used to explain prices and resource allocation, we have discussed what critics have acidly dubbed the "theology" of economics—the basic assumptions upon which microeconomic theory is based. Economists have assumed that consumers and firms maximize, and this logical assumption is subject to dispute. Similarly, all economic theory presumes certain goals for society, and these too can be debated. While seeming to be articles of faith for economists, often for very good reason, such orthodox assumptions are also subject to critical appraisal.

### THE MAXIMIZING ASSUMPTION

Orthodox theory repeatedly assumes that consumers, business firms, and resource owners maximize. Various critics of microeconomic theory argue, however, that orthodox economists have an irrational passion for assuming

[1] United States Department of Commerce, Bureau of the Census, *Present Value of Estimated Lifetime Earnings*, Technical Paper 16 (1968), pp. 8 and 10; and *Current Population Reports*, P-60, No. 69 (April 1970). (See Chapter 24 for further details on lifetime earnings.)

[2] That the professional economist is uncertain about the answers to these questions should be apparent.

that the maximizing compulsion drives society. Indeed, a few reputable economists are prepared to debunk microeconomic theory because they believe that the maximizing assumption, along with the entrepreneurial concept of the market economy, are meaningless in an economy dominated by mammoth corporations. If the maximizing assumptions upon which microeconomic theory depends are incorrect, the conventional view of the way in which prices allocate resources needs considerable modification. Because economists are not in agreement on this issue, microeconomics remains in intellectual ferment.

## THE GOALS OF ECONOMIC ANALYSIS

Equally important, and also a matter of concern to some economists, is the degree to which the economic problems and goals deemed worthy of study have not varied for decades and even centuries. The orthodox view of economic problems centers upon three basic goals arising from the premise of scarcity and choice, which are considered the central economic problem. These three goals are:

1. The full employment of resources
2. Economic growth and development
3. The efficient allocation and utilization of resources

There are, of course, many other goals and economic issues such as environmental and urban problems, concentration of market power, or the distribution of income—all of which relate more or less directly to the scarcity-choice premise. However much the assumptions and objectives of economics are criticized, it must also be recognized that the framework and tools of economic analysis that have been developed do illuminate important economic problems. Such evidence as can be developed both verifies and vilifies orthodox economics; it does not provide convincing and clear-cut answers one way or another. Even though debate over the assumptions and the goals of economics can revert to an endless argumentative tug-of-war, it is instructive to consider dissenting economic views further.

## B. BEYOND CONVENTIONAL PRICE THEORY

It is one thing to criticize such "conventions" of economics as the assumption of profit maximization or the goals of full and efficient use of resources, and quite another and more challenging matter to reconstruct a useful explanation which adopts assumptions that purport to describe the goals and operations of a large, complex, mixed market economy in the twentieth century. This latter course is precisely the one that Professor John Kenneth Galbraith of Harvard has taken in recent years. Galbraith has bluntly reexamined the nature of American capitalism through the works of past and present scholars.[3] Fire-brand leftists view his synthesis as a sinister sanctification of the status quo; "bible-belt" conservatives view his ideas as those of a left-winger undermining the good life; and economists in both camps accuse each other either of becoming sociologists or

---

[3] A debt readily acknowledged by Galbraith who states ". . . I could not have written without their prior efforts." John Kenneth Galbraith, *The New Industrial State* (Boston: Houghton Mifflin, 1967), p. 402.

of ignoring what may rank as an important contribution to economics. Let us specify.

### A Word on Economic Dissent

Between the late 1800s and the present, economic dissent or radicalism in this nation has both regressed and surged ahead. While it is hazardous to label schools of economic thought, the term "institutional economics" has been used to describe the ideas of dissenting American economists whose individual viewpoints sometimes vary widely.

During the first part of this century, many distinguished American economists returned from studies in Germany under European scholars and advocated what appeared at that time to be radical reforms such as government involvement in labor relations, regulation of selected industries, and progressive income taxes. Scholars such as Thorstein Veblen, Wesley Mitchell, John R. Commons, and Clarence Ayres ranged widely over such topics as the rights of private property, law and economics, the business cycle, and the modern corporate state in their study of institutions and economic systems. The main thrust of institutional economics has been to suggest that various systems of economic organization, including the market-oriented capitalistic economy, are simply large "bundles" of institutions—sets of values, rules, and behavior patterns. Consequently, dissenting economists often stress views of economic relationships that transcend the market-pricing framework which assumes maximizing behavior and accepts such goals as the efficient allocation of resources. In contrast, the orthodox or neoclassical economic approach takes the existing economic order as a given framework and explains economic problems, postulates economic relationships, and develops economic policy *within* that frame of reference. According to institutional economists, economic theory purports to be a "value-free" as well as an "institution-free" body of knowledge and, for that very reason, institutionalists maintain that orthodox economic theory incompletely describes the economic realities of life today.

Institutional economics contends that values and institutions are central to man's economic behavior. Some institutional economists maintain that the entire framework of economic theory needs to be supplanted by the institutional view, but the majority of economists agree that institutional economics is a more or less useful *supplement* to economic theory. Indeed, economic dissent such as that prompted by Karl Marx in the past or more recently by America's "radical economists" have upon occasion held that the market system is not a viable form of economic organization. However, the more moderate dissenters view the market-oriented capitalistic society as a changing and evolving bundle of institutions that cannot remain unaffected by contemporary socioeconomic problems. While a sizable number of so-called "orthodox" economists share these views, it is impossible to declare one group right or wrong. It is important, however, to summarize the dissenting view and see how it fills certain gaps in economic theory.

### THE INSTITUTIONAL FRAMEWORK

The institutional view of social and economic systems deserves systematic consideration on three counts.

First, the institutionalists view economic change in an evolutionary and historical context. The work of Wesley Mitchell on fluctuations in economic activity and Thorstein Veblen's analysis of a technologically determined industrial order exemplify the evolutionary, historical, and empirical methodology used in studying economic change. Second, emphasis is placed on a broad social-science view of economics that incorporates the political, social, and cultural process in explaining the way in which an economic system evolves. The economic process is thus viewed as part of a broader socioeconomic system. This orientation embodies concern for the development of an economic system to serve the broader welfare needs of society and for policies unencumbered by tradition. As social needs evolve, traditions are not to be held sacred, but rather, are to serve as a basis for adapting to change. A third dominant characteristic of institutional economic thought is concentration on the logic and pattern of industrial growth and development. In many nations, certain common elements seem to characterize the process of growth and development. Change has involved increased urban living, declining market competition, separation of the ownership and management of productive resources, conflict over the use of economic power, and a growing public sector charged with both guiding the evolving economy and mediating conflict over economic conflict.

The basic questions which the institutional approach raise are: Where are we headed; why; and what pragmatic adjustments can be made to enable the socioeconomic system to serve mankind better? Thus, the goals or values, and the rules or institutions of society are seen as agents of economic change. How change is initiated, whether change forebodes a better or a worse world, and for whom change occurs are also of obvious importance. And these are far from trite matters, as we shall see next.

### THE TRADITION-CHANGE DICHOTOMY[4]

Technological change is at the center of economic evolution. The differences between tradition and change in the way man has organized economic affairs is shown in Figure 2. Values and goals shape the rules or institutions of a society, which in turn are the basis for organized activities and behavior (e.g., the production and distribution of goods) leading to consequences or outcomes in the economic system. The crucial point about an economic system is the extent to which society responds to new outcomes and needs. Nations may be tradition-bound and unresponsive to change (the lower feedback loop of Figure 2). Or they may be adjustment-oriented if values, rules, and behavioral activities are responsive to a new order as shown by the upper feedback loop of Figure 2.

An example or two may help clarify the implications of Figure 2. A society may revere economic growth as one of several goals because of certain values regarding increased output and, as a result, may develop various institutions or rules (e.g., depreciation allowances that prompt capital investment) to help achieve growth in output. Underdeveloped nations may establish family-planning agencies, government agencies may undertake economic planning, educational institutions may be created for the development of human resources, or the monetary system may be guided by a desire to further the development process. An advanced nation such as the United States could stress growth in quantity while ignoring deteriora-

---

[4] I remain indebted to Lloyal M. Hartman, Louis Junker, and other colleagues past and present for their assistance on this subject.

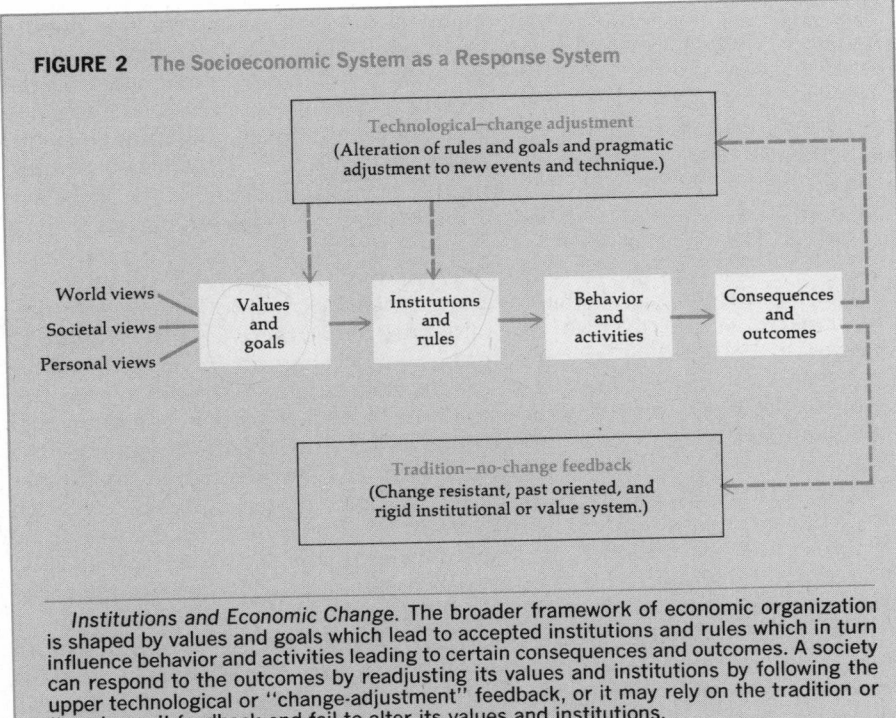

**FIGURE 2** The Socioeconomic System as a Response System

*Institutions and Economic Change.* The broader framework of economic organization is shaped by values and goals which lead to accepted institutions and rules which in turn influence behavior and activities leading to certain consequences and outcomes. A society can respond to the outcomes by readjusting its values and institutions by following the upper technological or "change-adjustment" feedback, or it may rely on the tradition or "no-change" feedback and fail to alter its values and institutions.

tion in the quality of life due to social costs associated with environmental debasement, urbanization, or poverty. Alternatively, development policy in an advanced nation could include such goals as preventing poverty and debasement of the urban environment. Of course, there are many goals in any society, all of which are structured on contemporary values. India values the sacred cow in a literal sense, and rules and institutions exist to implement this value; in the United States, universities value collegiate football, and the institutional system backs this value to the end. Similarly, the family farm, a rather loosely monitored stock exchange, and passage of private property wealth from one generation to another typify contemporary economic values and institutions in the United States. Britain and Sweden value the availability of public health for all on an equal basis and act accordingly, whereas the United States has, for the most part, valued a private medical-care industry above total public-sector involvement.

Countless examples verify the values-institutions-behavior-consequences chain of logic which typifies an organized socioeconomic system, but the crucial features of Figure 2 are the "change" and the "no-change" feedback loops, which are reaction paths traveled in different combinations by different nations. Just what is "acceptable change" depends primarily on values. Values may be classified as world-view values (human survival is an example, usually), societal values peculiar to a group (democracy in a nation), or personal values (racial segregation to some and equality to others). Implementing new values and altering existing behavior require changes in institutions and rules. Thus, while slavery was once an accepted institution, the emergence of different values and consequent changes in the "rules of the game" led to new outcomes as slavery was abolished. Change in the institutional framework is neither a painless nor an automatic event, as the issue of racial balance in public education in America illustrates. Indeed, history is replete with examples of resistance to change, behavior that is tradition-bound and tied to the past, and values embalmed in past norms and taboos.[5]

The implications of the dichotomy between change and tradition are staggering. On one hand, the no-change feedback loop of Figure 2 depicts preservation of the past. At the other extreme, there is a sensitivity to changes in both values and institutions—a receptivity, if you will, to the new. Mankind has formulated economic institutions and rules because of scarcity, the need for economic choice, and the necessity to monitor economic conflict. That is, institutions lend order to what otherwise might be chaos, and in this sense the market system is a key economic institution. Nations are often required to travel the precarious tightrope between change and preservation of the institutions that lend order to man's affairs. While orderly institutions and some constants are needed in any society, change and adaptation are also needed to modernize or update organized affairs, be they economic, social, or political.

It is apparent that it is not the teacher's business to force values and goals onto anyone. Nevertheless, in the measure that economics stresses price stability, full employment, stable economic growth, or economic efficiency, certain precepts, goals, and values are identified and "peddled" even in academia. These are *not* the only economic goals, they are not necessarily the *correct* ones (whatever "correct" is), and they are *by no means unchanging*. He who fails to recognize this has no concept of economic reality, and the recent concern for the subject of political economy illustrates this truth.

It is all well and good to taste the fruits of the economics of dissent, to view economics in its social-science perspective, and to recognize the fundamental role that values and institutions have in society. However, the task of disseminating a vast body of economic knowledge is a pressing one which demands its due from student and teacher alike. In what remains of this chapter we shall narrow our perspective down to problems of economic welfare that involve values and rules which relate to the state.

## An Alternative View of the Resource-Allocation Process

Today, dissenting economic ideas cover a wide spectrum. Perhaps the ablest spokesman for middle-of-the-road economic dissent is Professor Galbraith, whose recent works have served to keep alive the controversy over neoclassical economic theory.

In a dialogue with Galbraithian forces arising from his review of *The New Industrial State*, Professor Robert Solow of M.I.T. paraphrased the essence of the chasm between neoclassical economics and Galbraith's

[5] Interestingly, a staunch institutional view of the subject matter of economics would contend that it, too, is immersed in the now-antiquated taboos created by deceased intellectuals.

emphasis as a difference in "little-think" and "big-think."[6] Much of economics falls in the little-think camp, which stresses economic relationships between taxes and consumption, the production of housing, statistical relations between poverty and labor markets, and so forth. While there are obvious dangers to an excessively narrow focus, the little-think approach remains an integral part of solutions to the economic problems of our age. Those who stress the big-think approach use a broad brush, concentrating on the broader dimensions of change in the social, political, and economic environment.

Discord in economics is generally lively, and it stems in part from the oft-repeated allegation that economic theory has not adjusted its perception of the American system of economic organization to the corporate structure, whose tentacles touch the economy at innumerable points. Thus, in his earlier works, *American Capitalism* (1954) and *The Affluent Society* (1957), Galbraith spoke of the economic-welfare implications of markets overridden by economic power and the failure of the United States to meet social wants. He pictured business enterprise as a commercial giant often controlling instead of serving dozens, hundreds, or even thousands of markets. Galbraith also described the emergence of *countervailing power*, a check-and-balance system that arises when very large buyers and sellers conduct business with each other. The "Big Three" automobile manufacturers may be checked by similar market power represented by trade unions or by monopoly strength in the steel and rubber industries, much as the United States and Russia form a political-power duopoly today. Industrial goliaths render irrelevant the simplified theories of markets and prices. In the corporate environment, even consumer tastes and demand can be swung in favor of more horsepower or frills, perhaps at the expense of a clean environment and habitable cities. These assertions are important to the contemporary economic issues examined in later chapters, and they also suggest a new dimension to government and the public welfare.

## "THE NEW INDUSTRIAL STATE"

In the United States, there is not one type, but rather a variety of "firms," including corporate monarchs such as AT&T and General Motors, two firms whose combined revenues exceed farm income by a wide margin. Not only are large corporations of growing importance in terms of manufacturing output; their capability to wield economic power and merge their own and government's interests is also substantial. In contrast, the entrepreneurial sector of business enterprise is of less importance and operates with a simplified technology. The entrepreneurial firm remains profit-oriented, consumer sovereignty reigns, prices and markets are not tightly controlled, and sizable commercial ties to the broader complex of the public sector are rare. However, this entrepreneurial sector is small. The contention that entrepreneurial conditions no longer prevail for much economic activity in the United States is central to Galbraith's assertions, the most important of which are as follows.

1. Technology—the application of organized, scientific knowledge to business tasks—impairs and destroys the economic functions and operation

[6] Robert M. Solow, "The New Industrial State or Son of Affluence," *The Public Interest* (Fall 1967), pp. 100–108.

of markets. Today, increasingly fixed and specialized techniques require that firms manage markets, because investment in capital resources is a costly, time-consuming, and relatively complex process. Huge capital requirements thus set the stage for large-scale and complex corporate goliaths capable of dominating markets and stabilizing a portion of their own economic environment.

2. Common stockholders, as owners, very rarely run the modern corporation. Rather, corporate enterprise is controlled by a "technostructure" of managers, technicians, and highly specialized experts who form an interchangeable public sector–private enterprise bureaucracy. Moreover, corporate behavior is not firmly guided by the profit motive. Modern industry seeks security in some minimal target rate of return, tending to devote its larger energies beyond that point to the headlong pursuit of corporate growth. This latter goal furthers the status, advancement, and pecuniary returns to professional managers who control the corporation. Thus, the classical assumption of profit maximization, which in theory serves to engineer the resource-allocation process, is abandoned. Profit-oriented producer-supply decisions no longer informally govern a market economy.

3. The orthodox doctrine that production is geared to consumer sovereignty is also held to be an untenable and erroneous assumption in the contemporary market environment of the United States because the large, complex industrial system must manage and regularize consumer demand. It takes hundreds of millions or even billions of dollars and long planning horizons to gear up for mass markets for even a simple breakfast cereal. To supply technical products such as supersonic jets requires even greater management of demand. The customs of our contemporary culture and the planning needs of business enterprises are intertwined on a multi-billion dollar advertising panorama that manipulates the wants and perceived needs of men to "fit" the stability needs of the industrial system. Wants can be molded by irrational institutions and values, and people may reject what is truly needed and acquire what is potentially harmful. In short, consumer decisions may well be a response to a powerful, perhaps irrational, and often capricious industrial system. Thus, the legitimacy of a market system itself is called into question.[7]

4. The chief resource of consequence in the industrial system is the "scientific and educational estate" which forms a technostructure—the raw manpower that governs the modern corporate state. It is this technostructure that plans the American economy by regulating flows of economic activity which synchronize consumer demand and the corporation's utilization and allocation of resources. Corporate economic planning is masked by antiquated concepts of a competitive, private enterprise market system, but planning does occur as surely as it does when government planning boards direct the allocation of resources in other nations.

These four postulates challenge conventional interpretations of the market system of economic organization, they serve as a point of departure for a different view of resource-allocation problems, and they further imply certain conclusions with regard to government policy and economic welfare.

---

[7] The significance of this claim is dramatized in contemporary society which appears to be unwarily led to a private transportation system capable of spawning smog, millions of miles of concrete raceways, and more than 55,000 auto deaths along with billions of dollars of property damage each year.

According to Galbraith, the industrial system is, as a result of its interest, power, and manpower technostructure, closely fused to the state—one is the handmaiden of the other. Modern corporations have shed the shackles of a consumer-dominated, impersonal, and sometimes capricious market. The interests and values of public authorities and the corporate sector tend to merge in what have become joint goals. A few firms do all of their business with government and many (including the university research system) are heavily dependent upon government. Technicians cross the public-private-sector line, and managers trained in one sector freely change to the other over a lifetime.

*The Military-Industrial Complex*  One good example of interdependent corporate-state interests and values is furnished by a new socioeconomic reality in the United States, the military-industrial complex. Emerging and large corporations serving the military system are not subject to markets operated by the forces of supply and demand. These corporations and the federal government plan output in defense markets in which government as the buyer finances its purchases via the somewhat "infamous" cost-plus contracts. That is, according to extensive Congressional hearings, prices and profits are contractually agreed upon through a process subject to vast wastes. Approximately 100 corporations and universities (including M.I.T. and Johns Hopkins University) account for some two-thirds of the many billions of dollars of prime military contracts each year, and several thousand other firms are highly dependent upon the military system. Indeed, in addition to more than 3 million direct military jobs, several million additional jobs are provided indirectly through national-defense expenditures, which topped $80 billion annually in the latter 1960s and remain close to that level today. Top corporate executive positions, particularly in industries serving defense markets, are held by literally hundreds of former generals and admirals. The combination of pork-barrel politics, very loose cost-control systems, cost-plus contracts subject to fat cost overruns, concentrated military contract awards amounting to over $1 billion for selected corporations, and retired military personnel in positions of corporate power have had one dangerous result: A self-perpetuating group with vested interests in military spending has been created.

*Welfarism: Curse or Cure?*  Perhaps the most ominous development in Galbraith's thesis is the possible convergence of public and private interests, goals, and values. That American capitalism is capable of amply supplying quantities of physical output is not subject to question, but any appraisal of an economic system must ascertain how well it serves society's general welfare. Whether the general welfare serves the interest of the industrial-state system rather than the other way around is a pertinent query, and one which is increasingly raised today. Individual and social welfare could be sacrificed unknowingly to the interests and values of the state and the corporation, both of which are run by a common elite technostructure.[8] Welfare goals could be distorted to a set of common ends and values in-

[8] See David Mermelstein (ed.), *Economics: Mainstream Readings and Radical Critiques* (New York: Random House, 1970) for an excellent collection of New Left readings.

creasingly impervious to "people needs." Government might then embrace policies in accord with the wishes of the military-industrial complex; economic activity and consumption demand might well be bent to the needs of the "system"; and the values, beliefs, and rules of social behavior might unwittingly serve this same master. Indeed, even the university could be turned into a crass manpower-procurement system.

*Summing up:* One final word of caution is in order in summarizing these ideas: There is both agreement and discontent with such visions of contemporary society. Most economists recognize that economic theory does not come to full grips with economic reality, including the modern corporate sector. But many also have argued, as we know, that the profit motive is a good approximation in analyzing the resource-allocation process. Research efforts have provided no clear-cut answers to the issue of managed consumer demand. At the extreme, the really difficult issue about a market system of economic organization is simply this: If consumers do not decide "properly" (whatever that means), then what awesome authority is to have that power?

On one hand, various authorities regard *The New Industrial State* as an important treatise that buttresses many of the views of economists who have stressed the significance of social institutions and who sometimes regard economic theory as an exercise in mental ping-pong. Many others disagree with major portions of Galbraith's ideas, and still others find the emphasis on institutions and technology more or less useless. Although it is sometimes alleged that these differences reflect a desire on the part of orthodox economics to preserve economic theory and keep the temple of academia pure from institutionalism, this is a superficial explanation of intellectual ferment.

Though institutionalists present a "big picture" of quite a different hue than conventional economics, the institutional view by no means negates the need for neoclassical economics; rather it supplements it by placing new demands upon conventional tools of economic analysis. The contribution of institutional thought is that it fills out our understanding of economics, and these same contentions have left an indelible mark on economics, particularly in the areas of resource allocation, economic welfare, and the public sector.

## C. THE STATE: WELFARE AND PUBLIC FINANCE

Perhaps the prevailing values and goals of a society are nowhere better reflected than in government's microeconomic decisions to allocate public funds. Decisions to allocate funds to highways, national defense, or urban renewal reflect social values, and public claims on resources also operate within the institutions and rules that government has set up to monitor economic affairs.

Although the issue of government priorities has been in the spotlight in American society in recent years, the public remains poorly informed about government affairs, particularly the composition (not the size) of the federal government's budget. Part of the explanation for this situation may be that the United States is the wealthiest nation in the world (in pecuniary terms) and grows more affluent as each year passes. Increasingly, the average citizen is becoming acutely aware that quantities of real output and monetary riches cannot solve all of our problems. Like any other economic unit, government must solve the problems of choice in the use of scarce resources, and this subject is of major importance today.

## Public Choice

The axiom that people expect more than can be produced identifies the problem of public choice, and seeing that public-sector resource claims are used to satisfy the most urgent needs of society is largely what public finance is all about. The growing undercurrent of dissatisfaction in the United States today suggests that public priorities are not being fully directed toward the general economic welfare. Although economists sometimes appear to have abandoned all normative roles upon entering academia, economics does in fact add much to our knowledge of public welfare and the state. "Choosing" how to use one-third of a trillion dollars of government revenues in the United States is essentially a normative process, and we offer the warning as a prelude to our subject. Now, let us see what economic welfare and the state are about.

Earlier generations in the United States were imbued with a depression psychosis and thus riveted their attention on the quantity of output. In economic circles, "growthmanship" remained very much in style during the 1950s and 1960s—an era that emphasized the differences in national output forthcoming from a modest increase in the growth rate of 1 percent. Economic problems and goals change, however, and in time the possible gains from economic growth were seen to be insufficient if not illusory for meeting the pressing demands placed upon the public sector. Thus, today there is a new concern for the quality of life and the values of society, and this concern has intensified interest in the public sector's use of resources.

Like any private participant in the economy, government needs resources to accomplish its goals, and once a nation is at full employment, additional resource claims must come from higher taxes. If an economy is operating at capacity, government borrowing provides no escape because all it accomplishes is the imposition of the hidden "tax" of inflation. Accordingly, a major dimension of public finance today is to make wiser and better decisions about how to use the public sector's *existing* claims on output.

Unfortunately, the fact that changing needs and problems are inescapable in economic life does not mean that the government machinery for resolving new needs will automatically be forthcoming. Government must pay careful attention to its choices. Existing institutions and rules cannot remain untouched as the aspirations of people are altered. The mammoth institution of government courts disaster when it stagnates or remains impervious to the needs of a new era or is infiltrated by vested-interest groups.

The evolution of economic needs is an endless process and the alienation of youth as well as upheavals on campuses, in cities, and between races will sooner or later evoke the needed public response. Crime, grime, inflation, poverty, and inefficiency in government may be fads in public finance, but they are also economic problems of utmost import to American society today. Social and economic reforms are not automatically made because a society's rules and institutions become culturally embedded in a value system that defends the status quo. Although this is sometimes all to the good, there often is a sense of sterility about the standard fare of government and other institutions. Often the tribal ritual consists of praising the system as it is—a dangerous pastime if it sidetracks attention from emerging social problems, goals and values.

Government must function as an active guide for all goals of society, regardless of its political form. Throughout the "welfare states" that have evolved in the world, the concept that "government governs best which governs least" is as meaningless as the polar extreme that regards the public sector as a universal panacea. The blueprint model of pure and unbridled capitalism is neither a viable nor a realistic frame of reference for a modern society which is required to develop policies to solve major social problems. Similarly, the strict Marxian model of communism offers little in the way of a pragmatic solution to the needs and problems of nations which organize their economic affairs along a very different line. All economic systems must travel a precarious path, cognizant of both public and individual goals and needs, and there are no simplified utopian solutions to income-distribution and resource-allocation problems.

## DISTRIBUTION AND ALLOCATION PROBLEMS

Economics stresses the gains from cooperative behavior in the exchange of goods and services, and yet it is easy to lose sight of the fact that market prices also mediate choice problems. The very act of having prices attached to limited goods serves to determine the distribution of a society's output among different claimants and alternative uses. How well markets perform these functions is a subject of dispute, as the ideas of dissenting economists have demonstrated. How well government pursues the public interest is also a subject of debate, if for no other reason than that a public-sector decision to spend $X billion for some purpose is backed up by values and vast economic power which are not subject to the market. Issues concerning public choice are related to government's welfare role because it is the public sector that is responsible for controlling the market power of business firms and labor unions; enforcing rules to control the debasement of natural resources; and sanctifying or condemning a system that affects poverty, the distribution of income, trade with other nations, and other problem areas. The public sector uses taxes, expenditures, and the law to monitor economic life, and opinions vary widely on the exercise of such economic power. Public authorities face two categories of problems of interest to us here.

The *distribution problem* is related to how government authority should affect limited incomes distributed to different persons and groups. The "system" may operate to provide more or less output for the wealthy vs. the poor. Taxes, transfer payments, subsidies to the corporate sector, and inheritance laws that permit the handing down of vast estates in much the same way that feudal castles and titles were passed from parent to child illustrate government involvement in the distribution problem. From this standpoint, it is easy to see why many observers comment on the conflict inherent in the way a system of political economy makes "choices."

The *allocation problem* also involves choice—conflict choice over the use of resources. A society must resolve to use public funds to build hospitals or satellites, to import goods from other nations or to purchase American goods, to use tax receipts to build schools or roads. When government uses tax funds to purchase goods and services it is diverting resources from a private-sector use (e.g., housing or more automobiles) to other goods and services such as national defense or higher education. The decision of a few years back to allow oil firms to establish ocean drilling sites or implied government approval of the use of the Great Lakes as a sewage-disposal system represent still other resource-allocation decisions, all of which have a material impact on the general welfare. Accordingly, as an image of social values and behavior, the public sector affects both the distribution of income to a populace and the allocation of resources used to meet private and public wants.

## THE RATIONALE FOR GOVERNMENT

Public-sector involvement in various types of distribution and allocation problems stems from three forms of market failures: (a) the failure to maintain fragmented market power, (b) a failure of private benefits and costs to correspond to social benefits and costs in production and consumption, and (c) the failure to distribute incomes in accord with what is deemed "just."[9]

*Market Power* When markets operate imperfectly, the opportunity and temptation to manipulate the market in one's own interest prevail. Thus, government agencies are charged with policing corporate mergers, inspecting the output of food and drug manufacturers, and regulating natural monopolies such as those found in the utility industry. However, government activity in these areas does not necessarily mean that the best interests of society are served. If the product market for buggywhips were oversupplied, one would expect the demand for expert buggywhip-makers to fall, and human resources to seek other, more profitable occupations. This is a correct conclusion if nothing else intervenes, and this is why it is alleged that resources are allocated by the price system. Of course, the intrusion of some "extra-market" force may be important. As a Congressman, for example, you might decide that the buggywhip industry should be preserved or protected, and that government policy should be used to accomplish that goal. This does happen in international trade for so-called "vital industries" (oil, farming, and ship-building are contemporary American examples), and the well-trod path to this end extends straight to Washington. Or consider the consequences if government provides outright subsidies to weapons manufacturers, increases the productivity of resources used in the weapons industry by underwriting scientific research, or simply decrees a labor shortage by drafting human resources. Intervention in any form will have an income-distribution impact and will also cause resources to be reallocated, thus promoting or restraining the achievement of economic welfare for society. *Any* party with sufficient market power can modify the seemingly idyllic operation of the market system, and business, labor, and government units have vast economic power which can work for good as well as ill.

*Externalities* A second type of public involvement in economic decisions is explained by "spill-over" effects (externalities) that affect individuals not directly involved in a transaction. Externalities, which arise from market

[9] Each of these shortcomings of the market system (identified earlier in Chapter 19) poses serious problems under any system of economic organization.

failures, exist if private costs and benefits diverge from social costs and benefits as noted in Chapter 19.

Supply and demand can be equal at some market equilibrium price, but that price may not reflect all social costs. This is precisely what occurs when the chemical or paper industry pollutes waterways. External economies or social benefits exist if the benefits to society exceed private market-valued benefits, as in the case of public-health programs and public education. In other instances, externalities derive from private market transactions which ignore compensation between private parties, as when one party maintains a junkyard adjacent to an outdoor restaurant.

Social benefits are likely to be undersupplied and undervalued in a mixed market economy such as that of the United States, partly because it is impossible to market public goods such as police protection only to those who wish to buy.[10] Public goods generate indivisible benefits that spill over to others. Thus, your "purchase" of police protection may well provide significant benefits to a neighbor who might very well elect not to participate if such services were supplied in a free market. In still other cases, the social cost of producing goods is not fully reflected by the private cost of using resources. When society fails to force producers and consumers to pay for external diseconomies, it is possible for foul air and polluted water to distort the general welfare. Government is then needed to correct understated private costs and to compensate those who are forced to bear them.

*Distributive Equity*  Finally, bear in mind that even idyllic competitive conditions say nothing about the justice or ethical attributes of the distribution of income. Income distribution could be equal—as some utopian thinkers have advocated—if human resources were of approximately equal quality and property resources were equally owned or perhaps held in trust by the state. On the other hand, income distribution might also be severely unequal. Impersonal markets are oblivious to whatever values and concepts of equity or justice may prevail in a society. The public sector is a determining factor in income distribution because it establishes laws, the incidence of taxes, transfer payments, and subsidies. Like any other source of authority, government uses its economic power to shape the personal quality of life each citizen experiences.

Income distribution is a conflict-choice situation subject to the use of power, as can be illustrated by a simple two-person example. Either one of two parties could lay claim to a nation's output in the extremes of egalitarianism or slavery.[11] Under conflict circumstances, either party could force, cajole, bribe, or coerce the other into accepting less and less of a nation's "social product." If one group can be given an inferior education and poorer-paying jobs, or otherwise be "put in place," that group may be forced to take less and less social product (at the calculated risk of ultimate revolt). Without government, the only limitation on the exercise of eco-

[10] However, it is also possible to oversupply a public good—a charge sometimes leveled against the Pentagon concerning national defense.

[11] Of course, there are many instances in which both parties can better their status. Remember, however, that once the competitive ideal is attained and a society is using its resources fully and efficiently, no one party can improve his position without hurting another—that is, maximum output is achieved at that moment in time.

nomic power is whatever ethical and moral restraint prevails in relation to the subsistence need of one's opponent—and people sometimes violate even this. With government regulation, either more or less "justice" can occur, depending on who is licensed to define justice. The ethics of income distribution are outside the domain of economic theory, but the way government and the market system cooperate has a large influence on the distribution of income.

## PUBLIC AND PRIVATE WANTS

Many students of contemporary societies have argued that public goods are vastly undervalued and in short supply in advanced economies such as that of the United States. While poor nations must consume most if not all of their output to meet basic subsistence needs, technologically advanced societies are not so firmly shackled to biological needs. Such societies appear to have greater public needs and can also afford to devote more resources to social output such as education, health facilities, the provision of habitable urban centers, and the aesthetics of life. Public wants may go unmet, however, because of the ideological heritage of a mixed market economy. Existing levels of taxation, advertising by the private sector, and the less visible nature of public goods may further contribute to undervaluation of public wants and thus to underallocation of resources to meet these needs.

There are conflicting opinions about the merit of the claims for more public goods. Many observers have suggested that government bureaucracies are biased in the direction of overspending or of spending to perpetuate the bureaucracy rather than to resolve social problems. Then, too, the public as well as Congressional leaders sometimes fail to recognize fully the opportunity costs of increased government expenditures. Serious questions are often raised about inefficiency in government as well as the failure of public authorities to reflect social priorities accurately in providing public goods. The difficulty here, of course, is the familiar normative problem in which government use of resources is guided by values and political choice.

It is not possible to judge, on positive economic criteria alone, what constitutes the "best" solution to the vast array of distribution and allocation problems with which the public sector contends. Should the state allocate added resources to more weapons or to more farm production? Are government's claims on resources better spent on youth attending colleges by the millions or on the aged? On concrete freeways or swimming pools in urban ghettos? On the investor in oil, cattle, and timber or on the fatherless? Should blacks or whites be favored by the system? You may feel that the rich should receive more of society's output, whereas others could favor the poor. This is normative economics in its greatest glory and should be so recognized. There is seldom one proven "best" answer to these questions, which require social value judgments on the part of all informed citizens. It is possible to identify distribution and allocation problems due to externalities or abusive exercise of market power; however, there are few if any objective or scientific criteria to use in judging the merits of competing claims. Moreover, the competing claims of the public and private sectors also rest heavily upon prescriptive assertions and judgments, all of which reflect social and cultural values.

DOMESTIC ECONOMIC ISSUES

In recent years, both public and private agencies have carefully examined the impact of the public sector upon resource allocation as it is revealed in the federal budget.[12] Information about national goals and priorities for the near future is probably nowhere better represented than in the President's annual budget recommendations to Congress. Private and public agencies such as The Brookings Institution and the Council of Economic Advisers study the proposed federal budget in depth to assess national goals.[13] Even though unexpected contingencies (e.g., war) and Congressional pressures can alter the direction of public finance dramatically, the President's proposed federal budget for 1971 with projections to 1975 offers important insights into near-term public priorities as seen by President Nixon (who underbudgeted 1971 Congressional appropriations by roughly $15 billion).

Figure 3 summarizes federal outlays for selected years since 1960 and suggests the general nature of priorities in the recent past, as well as

[12] Public-sector expenditure patterns described in Chapter 4 indicated that state and local governments spend approximately one-half of their revenues on education and highways with the remainder being heavily allocated to public services such as fire and police protection and health and welfare. The federal government, in contrast, spends approximately three-fourths of its receipts on national defense and income transfer payments for health and welfare (largely social security) purposes.

[13] The discussion which follows draws heavily from Charles L. Schultze, Edward K. Hamilton, and Allen Schick, *Setting National Priorities: The 1971 Budget* (Washington, D.C.: The Brookings Institution, 1970) and the Council of Economic Advisers, *Economic Report of the President*, 1970, ch. 4.

**FIGURE 3**  Trends in Federal Budget Outlays, Fiscal Years 1960–1971 (billions of dollars)

|  | 1960 | 1965 | 1969 | 1971[a] |
|---|---|---|---|---|
| National defense | $46.0 | $ 49.9 | $ 81.4 | $ 75.3 |
| Income transfers and subsidies[b] | 24.5 | 34.2 | 56.8 | 72.7 |
| Education, health, and manpower | 2.5 | 4.1 | 10.3 | 12.8 |
| Space | 0.4 | 5.1 | 4.2 | 3.4 |
| Housing and community development | 0.7 | 1.5 | 3.3 | 6.8 |
| Physical resources | 6.4 | 10.2 | 10.8 | 13.3 |
| Interest | 6.9 | 8.6 | 12.7 | 13.1 |
| Other | 4.8 | 4.8 | 5.1 | 3.0 |
| Total outlays | $92.2 | $118.4 | $184.6 | $200.4 |

[a] Budget estimates.
[b] Includes social security programs, farm subsidies, and veterans' compensation.

SOURCE: Charles L. Schultze, Edward K. Hamilton, and Allen Schick, *Setting National Priorities: The 1971 Budget* (Washington, D.C.: The Brookings Institution, 1970), Table 1-1.

existing public-sector resource claims at the national level. One of the particularly striking changes in budget trends during this period was the large increase in national defense expenditures between 1965 and 1969, a trend which has subsequently been scaled down some to an *estimated* outlay of $75.3 billion for 1971. Transfer and subsidy payments have nearly tripled since 1960, due in large measure to expansions in social security and public-health programs. More modest increases in outlays for education, health, and manpower are shown in Figure 3, while space expenditures have been deemphasized since 1965. Expenditures on physical resources, particularly housing and community-development programs, have also increased, although the outlays remain rather small relative to housing needs and the problems of community development today.

Data on existing expenditures are of historic interest, but they tell us little about the potential role of government and its public-finance problems in the near future. Two major issues in public finance of current and future import merit careful consideration: First, the extent to which government revenues will rise as the economy grows; and second, the choice problem faced in the allocation of limited federal resources.

## THE FISCAL DIVIDEND

The amount by which future growth in the American economy will increase federal revenues to meet new and expanded public wants is the *fiscal dividend* (see Figure 4). It is often assumed that there will be a substantial fiscal dividend that can be used to meet public wants in the near future. Unfortunately, when projected 1975 revenues based on the existing tax base are compared to current federal spending programs adjusted for price and wage increases plus the program expansion already committed, it appears that the federal government will not have a strong capability to meet new public wants.

Estimates of the future course of an economy are hazardous, and calculations of federal revenues and expenditures may be subject to serious error. However, it is instructive to examine public-finance developments to illustrate the outlook for the near future. The basic assumptions which underlie the fiscal dividend shown in Figure 4 are as follows: GNP is estimated as growing 4.3 percent annually between 1969 and 1975, and after 1973 the unemployment rate is assumed to drop to 3.8 percent. The severe inflationary pressures experienced during the 1968–1970 period are assumed to diminish modestly to the point where prices are rising approximately 2 percent annually by 1975. Before adjustments for scheduled and proposed tax changes resulting from the 1969 legislation, federal revenues are estimated as rising to $284 billion in 1975. The increased expenditures shown in Figure 4 are attributable to four factors. First, automatic "load" increases are built into programs existing in 1970. These increases describe higher outlays for programs to cover more people, and a certain amount of known and unavoidable budget expansion (e.g., public-employee retirement and already committed social security benefits). Second, pay increases needed to keep federal government wage and salary levels comparable to the private sector are built into estimated future expenditures. Third, the impact of rising prices is accounted for in federal programs. Thus, expenditures to 1975 are budgeted at constant 1971 levels of real purchasing power or higher if program expansion is a known commitment in 1970 (as is true of the medicare program). Finally, the estimated costs of new programs or program expansions proposed by the President which are scheduled to begin in 1971 are included in the expenditure estimates of Figure 4.

Thus adjusted, the budget estimates of Figure 4 indicate a gross fiscal dividend of revenues in excess of expenditures of $31 billion by 1975. However, these estimates assume that federal expenditure on the Vietnam War will decline from the 1969–1970 average of $20 billion to $1 billion by 1975. Moreover, two additional claims on federal resources that could lower the gross fiscal dividend must be accounted for: (a) Adjustments for already scheduled tax-reform revenue losses ($8 billion in 1975) must be

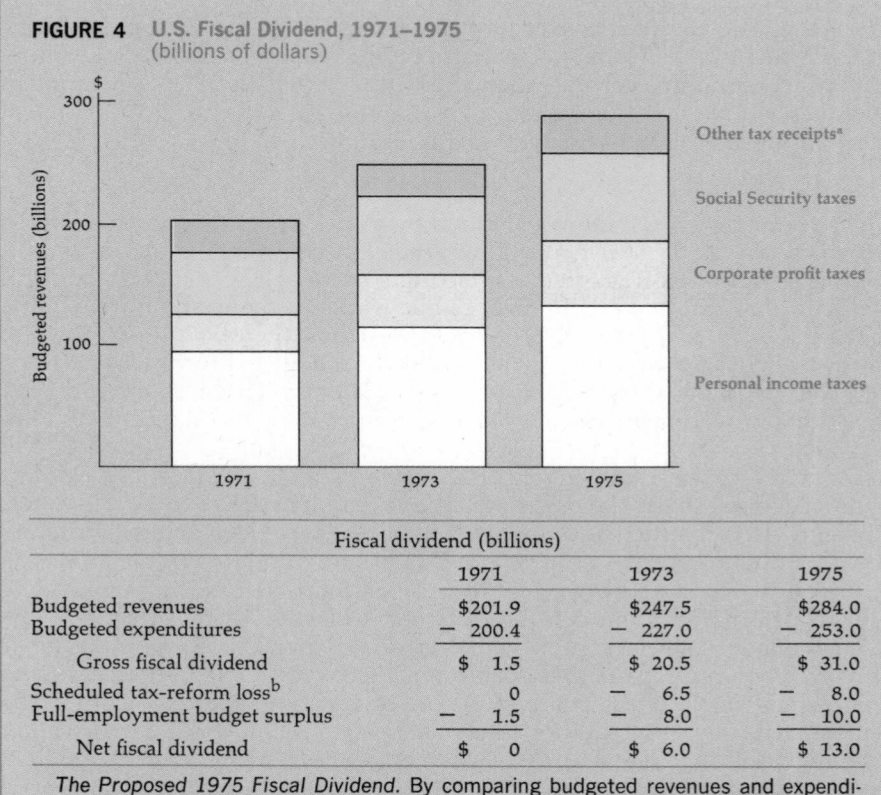

**FIGURE 4**  U.S. Fiscal Dividend, 1971–1975
(billions of dollars)

| Fiscal dividend (billions) | | | |
|---|---|---|---|
| | 1971 | 1973 | 1975 |
| Budgeted revenues | $201.9 | $247.5 | $284.0 |
| Budgeted expenditures | − 200.4 | − 227.0 | − 253.0 |
| Gross fiscal dividend | $   1.5 | $  20.5 | $  31.0 |
| Scheduled tax-reform loss[b] | 0 | −   6.5 | −   8.0 |
| Full-employment budget surplus | −   1.5 | −   8.0 | −  10.0 |
| Net fiscal dividend | $   0 | $   6.0 | $  13.0 |

*The Proposed 1975 Fiscal Dividend.* By comparing budgeted revenues and expenditures for some future period such as 1975, the revenue-expenditure difference, or fiscal dividend, can be estimated. Taking several known factors into account reveals that the estimated net fiscal dividend for 1975 will be only $13 billion, even though tax revenues will rise by an estimated $84 billion over budgeted 1971 expenditures.

[a] Largely excise, estate, and gift taxes.

[b] Revenue loss due to tax reform legislated in 1969 which provides selected tax increases of $7.5 billion and tax relief of $15.5 billion by 1975.

SOURCE: Charles L. Schultze, Edward K. Hamilton, and Allen Schnick, *Setting National Priorities: The 1971 Budget* (Washington: The Brookings Institution, 1970). Data are combined from Tables 6–2, 6–3, and 6–5.

recognized, and (b) a $10 billion adjustment is needed for the probable full-employment budget surplus which will be required to stabilize the economy while maintaining the lower interest rates needed to allow the nation to begin to meet a serious housing shortage. Assuming that these conditions prevail and that taxes otherwise remain unchanged, the net fiscal dividend available for *additional* public wants is estimated at $6 billion for 1973 and $13 billion for 1975. If certain expenditures do not change as assumed, the fiscal dividend will evaporate, and it could disappear altogether (as the projected budget surplus for 1971 already has) if receipts and expenditures were to vary.

## NATIONAL PRIORITIES AND "DIVIDEND" ILLUSIONS

There are numerous reallocation alternatives to those shown in Figure 4 (e.g., further reductions in national defense or a tax increase). The striking feature of the fiscal dividend shown in the figure, however, is the intense pressures placed upon limited federal revenues. Budgeted revenues for 1975 are $84 billion larger than budgeted 1971 expenditures; yet, at best, a comparatively small net fiscal dividend of $13 billion remains.[14] Just how did the vast sum of $84 billion disappear so rapidly?

Figure 5 summarizes the major expenditures that are expected to absorb the added $84 billion in federal revenues between 1971 and 1975 by cause and by program priority. After adjustment for tax-revenue losses, the budget surplus, and the net fiscal dividend recognized earlier in Figure 4, an estimated $53 billion in revenue remains. As Figure 5 indicates, wage and price increases are expected to absorb about one-half of this amount, while increased program-load coverage and already locked-in program commitments will absorb the remainder. Notice that these changes assume a sizable cutback in military spending. In terms of program priorities, increased social security and medicare expenditures loom large in the near future. In addition, federal revenue-sharing grants to state and local governments, welfare transfer payments, and government-employee compensation will absorb identifiable portions of federal revenues.

Figure 5 puts the illusory fiscal dividend into perspective. The $13 billion net fiscal dividend shown in the upper portion of the figure is all that is available to meet added public wants above and beyond those commitments made as of 1970—and that is not a large sum in view of contemporary social problems. It is hard to say whether there will be added tax revenues or more dramatic changes in the use of resources. Given this relative scarcity of public resources, public authorities must weigh alternative programs carefully to obtain the greatest possible mileage from a limited resource base.

## BENEFIT-COST ANALYSIS

Clearly, efforts to use public revenues more effectively must be intensified. Benefit-cost analysis of public programs is an attempt to achieve the most effective distribution of scarce public resources. Benefit-cost analysis relies

---

[14] Many experts, including Charles Schultze, Director of the U.S. Bureau of the Budget from 1965 to 1968, believe the figure of $13 billion to be on the high side because of the countless appeals, claims, and pressures placed on Congress and the President to expand existing programs.

**FIGURE 5** Absorption of Federal Revenues by Cause and by Program, 1975 (billions of dollars)

| | |
|---|---|
| 1975 funds available over budgeted 1971 expenditures | $84 |
| Tax-reform revenue loss | − 8 |
| Full-employment budget surplus | −10 |
| 1975 fiscal dividend for new public wants | −13 |
| Budgeted dollar difference to account for | $53 |

| Absorption of federal revenues by cause | | Absorption of federal revenues by program | |
|---|---|---|---|
| Pay increases | $ 8.5 | Social security | $12.0 |
| Price increases | 20.0 | Medicare and medicaid | 6.9 |
| Program load increases | 19.0 | Highways and urban transit | 2.4 |
| New and committed | | Housing | 1.7 |
| programs | 11.0 | Revenue sharing | 4.2 |
| Other adjustments[a] | 3.5 | Welfare assistance[b] | 5.7 |
| Reduced military spending − | 9.0 | Pay and retirement[c] | 12.5 |
| | | Other | 7.6 |
| Total absorbed | $53.0 | Total absorbed | $53.0 |

[a] Includes financial adjustments such as sale of government-owned financial assets and reductions in selected programs.

[b] Based upon existing programs and the incremental costs of family-assistance programs.

[c] Cannot be allocated by program.

SOURCE: Charles L. Schultze, Edward K. Hamilton, and Allen Schick, *Setting National Priorities: The 1971 Budget* (Washington, D.C.: The Brookings Institution, 1970). Data are combined from Tables 6-2, 6-3, 6-4, and 6-5.

upon estimating present value of the benefits ($B$) of a program compared to the present value of program costs ($C$) in order to help public officials decide on alternative government programs, or weigh alternative methods of accomplishing a given program at least cost. Certain economic principles discussed earlier are useful in benefit-cost analysis. They are as follows.

1. Marginalism. Only the additional or the marginal costs or benefits should be used to evaluate a public decision to construct a dam, build a new missile, provide manpower training for the poor, or what have you. Adoption of the efficiency criterion generally dictates that no program should be undertaken unless the ratio of marginal benefits to marginal costs is equal to or greater than one, or $B/C \geqslant 1$. Moreover, under comparable conditions, implementation of those programs with the highest $B/C$ ratio provides the largest possible net benefits to government. Thus, different programs might be selected according to their rate of return by comparing net benefits to costs.[15]

[15] Actually, the benefit-cost criterion for selecting goverment expenditures is only one of several competing methods of analysis which often gives different priority rank-

2. Present value. Benefits and costs must be evaluated in a present-value context because a dollar of benefits in some future year is worth less than a dollar today (as explained earlier in Chapter 18). This means that an interest rate or some "social rate of discount" must be selected and used to reduce the estimated time-stream of future benefits and costs to their present value. The higher the rate of discount, the less the stated present value of a project over a period of time because dollar benefits due in the future are worth less today.[16] A *near*-equivalent alternative to computing B/C ratios in present-value terms is to compute the annual rate of return of alternative programs and select those that have the largest percentage return, provided that this return exceeds the social rate of discount.

*A case in point:* Suppose a manpower-training project for hard-core unemployed costing $50 million will yield $70 million in discounted benefits. In contrast, a $6 million investment in a college scholarship program is expected to yield $14 million in discounted benefits. Thus:

$$B/C \text{ of manpower training is } \frac{\$70 \text{ million}}{\$50 \text{ million}} \quad or \quad 1.4$$

and

$$B/C \text{ of college scholarships is } \frac{\$14 \text{ million}}{\$6 \text{ million}} \quad or \quad 2.3$$

Using the efficiency guideline of maximum net benefits, it would appear that the state should invest scarce resources in college scholarships. However, the rational distribution of public expenditures is a far more difficult chore than it appears to be.[17]

3. Competing objectives. Some of the problems associated with benefit-cost analysis came into focus in the above example. While the economic payoff measured in terms of increased worker incomes may be greater from expenditures for college scholarships, notice carefully that the income-distribution effect is ignored. By making funds available for higher education, the federal government is contributing to greater income inequality and continued unemployment and poverty problems for another class of citizens. This may or may not be appropriate, depending on the values of society and the many goals of the public sector. What weight does a government official assign to equity? Should benefits for the unemployed be marked up by some multiple or should they be lowered, and if so, by how much? Reasonable men can become quite unreasonable in such discussions.

ings because of differences in using generalized benefit-cost comparisons. A great deal of attention has centered on alternative benefit-cost criteria. The interested reader should consult Otto Eckstein, *Water Resource Development* (Cambridge, Mass.: Harvard University Press, 1958), and Roland McKean, *Efficiency in Government Through Systems Analysis* (New York: John Wiley & Sons, 1958).

[16] At a high rate of discount, $1 due in the future is worth less now because greater amounts of interest are earned each year. Interest earnings are effectively subtracted from future benefits to obtain present values.

[17] One of the less complicated difficulties in using benefit-cost comparisons is illustrated by this example, for the "least efficient" manpower-training program according to the B/C ratio approach actually provides a greater total volume of benefits ($20 million). Nonetheless, the net return *per dollar* of expenditure remains higher for the college-scholarship program.

One can imagine the Nebraska Senator arguing for markup factors being applied to programs helping agricultural interests, while the Senator from New York asserts his right to a markup factor for aid to urban centers. In the end, political power and bargaining suaveness, occasionally nurtured by a pang of national conscience on behalf of the less powerful, dictate early access to the federal purse strings.

4. Distributive and external effects. Income-distribution effects are one often-ignored by-product of public policy, and they pose troublesome issues in rationalizing resource-allocation decisions in the public sector. Another difficulty arises because some benefits and costs are indirect—the case if the probability of ghetto crime or riots is reduced when funds are allocated to training the "hard-core" unemployed. When such effects are ignored and only increased earnings are included as benefits, total social benefits are simply not represented in a benefit-cost comparison. Then, too, many benefits and costs are not subject to market pricing, and often they are noneconomic as well. Just what is the value of 10,000 lives *saved* through fewer automobile accidents, and what is the end (or beginning) of a war *really* worth? What is the "value" of clean air in New York, the amelioration of rural poverty, or a decent existence for Indians on reservations?

Benefit-cost analysis can be helpful, but it can also be abused through Congressional pressures and public agencies which sometimes use sleight-of-hand tactics to justify expenditures and maintain their economic viability. Water-resource agencies have been instrumental in developing benefit-cost techniques, for example, yet by overstating benefits and using unusually low discount rates, agencies long subject to Congressional pressure such as the Corps of Engineers and the Bureau of Reclamation have "justified" questionable public expenditures. Concerning water-resource projects, Charles Schultze has observed that ". . . the $1 billion-plus annual investment is devoted to projects that yield little if anything in the way of net national benefits." Still other authorities like Robert Haveman have also pointed out how such practices divert scarce federal resources into comparatively unproductive uses.[18]

In short, rationalizing government expenditure programs is not a simple task. Nonetheless, benefit-cost comparisons can be useful, particularly if indirect and noneconomic benefits and costs can be identified and gauged in a manner that allows public authorities to look at alternative investments in a "cost-effectiveness" context which remains cognizant of noneconomic factors. Care must be taken to recognize that public decisions are matters of political economy that do not fully lend themselves to dollars-and-cents economic analysis. Whatever values one might place on the indirect, non-economic, and external effects of various activities is a decision that must

[18] Schultze *et al.*, *Setting National Priorities, op. cit.*, p. 163. Schultze notes as an example that federal irrigation projects provide for a ". . . water subsidy to a typical large cotton farmer in Southern California (that) amounts to $40,000 a year" (p. 165). Curiously, government is requiring taxpayers to provide water subsidies to high-income farmers while also paying for a costly farm program designed to reduce total farm output. Also see Robert Haveman, *Water Resource Investment and the Public Interest: An Analysis of Federal Expenditures in Ten Southern States* (Nashville, Tenn.: Vanderbilt University Press, 1965), ch. 5.

be made, but it usually depends on value judgments as much or more than on economy in government.

## REVIEW

### Summary

1. The market system allocates resources through supply and demand which are engineered by consumers' desires to obtain satisfaction and producers' desires to earn profits. Just how much of the price and resource-allocation process is explained by this framework of analysis is a subject of some disagreement even among economists. The presumption that consumers and producers maximize and the conventional theoretical goals of full employment, growth, and efficient use of resources constitute a loose sort of "theology" in economics in the eyes of some observers.

2. Economic dissent has a long and colorful history which is typified today by institutional economists who stress the importance of the values and rules of an economic system. While many dissenting economists simply modify the orthodox view of economics, others adamantly maintain that the frame of reference used to study prices and resource allocation in microeconomics tends to distort our understanding of the economic process.

3. Dissenting economic thought is much too complex and far-flung to summarize briefly, but it is generally agreed that institutional economics stresses a rather broad social-science perspective of the subject of economics. The institutional approach suggests that behavior and economic outcomes in society are the product of the institutions and rules a nation creates. In turn, it is the value system at both personal and community levels which shapes institutions and thus influences economic consequences.

4. Among the more prominent contemporary expressions of institutional economics, Galbraith's assertions about the "New Industrial State" are widely recognized. Galbraith sees the resource-allocation process as dependent upon modern technology which leads to corporate planning of markets. Neither consumers nor producers are seen as maximizers in a meaningful sense, and reliance upon a common technostructure which merges private and public interests is alleged to have a fundamental impact upon the general welfare.

5. Even more important, however, is the industrial state's potential for merging private and public goals and values, as evidenced in some measure by the military-industrial complex. Opinions on the usefulness and legitimacy of ideas about the "New Industrial State" and dissenting economics in general vary widely. Essentially, dissenting economic ideas supplement or round out our understanding of economic relationships by injecting new realities into the subject of economic welfare and resource allocation.

6. The way in which industry-state interests and social values affect resource allocation is shown by examining the public-finance role of

government in pursuit of general welfare goals. The public sector is faced with choice problems for much the same reason that private parties are—limited budgets. In choosing to use resources for some purpose, government has an impact on both the distribution of income to a citizenry and the allocation of resources in an economy.

7. Three general types of market failures typically elicit government involvement in economic affairs: (*a*) the public sector may take steps to monitor the private use of market power; (*b*) government action may be taken for the purpose of remedying external economies (social benefits) or diseconomies (social costs); and (*c*) government policy may be implemented for income-distribution purposes, as when the elderly or unemployed are provided with means of subsistence at public expense.

8. Revenues of the federal government increase each year as income grows, giving rise to the fiscal dividend—added revenues available to meet public wants. However, upon close examination, the fiscal dividend is seen to be somewhat illusory. Price and wage increases, automatic increases in the workload of certain programs, and program expansion already locked into government budgets all serve to reduce the net fiscal dividend (for 1975, for example) to a rather meager amount.

9. Because of revenue limitations, expenditure priorities must be assigned by public authorities. Such decisions are judgmental ones which reflect whatever values and political pressures that guide governmental officials. In addition, benefit-cost comparisons can be made to determine which programs are most effective per dollar of cost. Benefit-cost analysis is a helpful tool in making public decisions affecting distribution and allocation problems, but it must be and is supplemented by normative considerations.

## Identify the Following Concepts and Terms

- present value
- distribution problem
- fiscal dividend
- technostructure
- institutions
- three forms of market failure
- countervailing power
- allocation problem
- economic dissent
- maximizing assumptions

## Questions to Answer

1. How might maximizing assumptions be viewed as a part of the theology of economics? In what way do the conventional goals of economics also comprise a part of the theology for all of economic theory?

2. Briefly explain the ways in which the values and institutions of a society relate to behavior and the consequences of economic life. How do values and institutions apply to the following cases as you understand them at the moment? (*a*) The tradeoff choice between inflation and unemployment. (*b*) The allocation of government resources for medicare vs. national defense. (*c*) The relative incidence of taxes on families by income level.

3. Present and evaluate the "industrial state" contentions of Professor Galbraith. In what ways does this argument deny the basic assumption

of orthodox economic theory? What relationship does it have to the more general institutional view of the economic process?

4. Assume that you are a Congressman able to cast the deciding vote on the allocation of a fiscal dividend equal in value to $1.3 billion. Explain: (a) How your understanding of distribution and allocation problems could influence your vote. (b) What types of market failures would be most appealing to you to rectify and why. (c) Your evaluation of the use of benefit-cost analysis, including an assessment of the ambiguities it may present.

# CHAPTER 21
# The Problems
# of Monopoly
# and Agriculture

In previous chapters we noted the impact of imperfect competition on the allocation of resources and briefly examined the character of various types of market failures. In this chapter we will narrow our investigation down to two different types of resource-allocation problems—monopoly in imperfectly competitive markets and the competitive problems of agriculture. The monopoly power of corporations represents a market failure which has been the object of government attempts to promote greater competition in some industries. At the same time, rapid competitive dislocations in American agriculture also represent a serious but very different type of resource-allocation problem involving political forces as well as the misallocation of economic resources.

In Part A of this chapter a logical background is provided for studying the organization of industry and the problem of monopoly and the public policy toward it. The very different issues associated with economic adjustments in the agricultural sector are examined in Part B.

## A. GOVERNMENT AND MONOPOLY POWER

The American economy is a mixed public-private system of economic organization, as we know. Government's responsibility for stabilizing economic activity and prices at full employment is supplemented by a variety of microeconomic policies related to the allocation of resources. We shall begin our study of problems in American industry by developing an industrial-organizational framework of analysis and then examine the problems of monopoly and market power in the American economy.

### Industrial Organization and Markets

The way in which markets operate depends upon the interaction among the structure, conduct, and performance of these markets. Market structure (ranging from competition to monopoly) is important because it influences the conduct of firms in a market. Market conduct in turn helps determine how markets perform in allocating resources. Whether the organizational nature of markets represents a problem because of monopoly power or because of competitive dislocation makes a great deal of difference. However, public-policy objectives are the same in either case: promotion of markets which will compel performance that is in the public interest.

There are three primary elements to the structure of markets: (a) the concentration of firms in a market, (b) product differentiation, and (c) barriers to entry into a market. Seller concentration, measured by the relative importance of the largest firms in an industry, gives a rough indication of the structure of a market. When the largest four firms, for example, control 70 percent of all assets (or sales) in one industry, concentration in that market is obviously high. Among markets with high levels of concentration (measured in terms of control of more than 75 percent of all industry assets) are: motor vehicles (Ford, General Motors, and Chrysler); telephone equipment (Western Electric); aircraft engines (United Aircraft and General Electric); aluminum (Alcoa, Kaiser, and Reynolds); metal containers (American Can and Continental Can); and computers (IBM). Studies have repeatedly shown that somewhere between 30 and 45 percent of all markets in the United States are subject to the substantial market power which is possible when a few firms dominate a sizable portion of a market.[1]

Figure 1 shows the share of total assets held by the largest 100 and 200 American manufacturing corporations as an aggregate measure of market concentration. In terms of the 200 largest firms, concentration has risen from about 46 percent to more than 60 percent of total manufacturing assets during the last two decades. Aggregate concentration has increased substantially in the all-important manufacturing sector of the American economy, even in the very brief period between 1968 and 1970—a "golden era" in the corporate merger movement. There are now over 100 firms with assets of at least $1 billion, and these firms control nearly one-half of total manufacturing assets and earn more than one-half of total manufacturing profits. The largest 609 manufacturing corporations with assets in excess of $100 million own three-fourths of all assets and earn more than 80 percent of all profits in the manufacturing sector of the American economy. Out of the some 200,000 manufacturing corporations shown in Figure 1, about 2 percent have assets in excess of $10 million and earn more than 90 percent of all manufacturing profits. The conclusion is inescapable: Aggregate concentration and vast size have intensified in recent years, conveying potential market power to a few hundred firms.

Greater aggregate concentration and its potential impact have a direct bearing on the monopolistic conduct of American business firms. Moreover, product differentiation contributes to monopolization of markets by allowing firms to initiate individual price policies in accord with qualitative differences in their products. Many consumer-goods industries are characterized by product differentiation, although markets in heavy manufacturing (e.g., computers and automobiles) are by no means devoid of it. Finally, barriers to entry also shape the competitiveness of a market environment since they shield firms from additional competitors. IBM, for example, dominates the computer industry in part because of its pricing policies, and also because of its size and the market advantages it holds over rivals. Computer leasing and carefully cultivated customer services have become

[1] William G. Shepherd, *Market Power and Economic Welfare* (New York: Random House, 1970), p. 246.

**FIGURE 1**  Concentration in American Manufacturing Assets and Profits

(a) Share of assets held by largest manufacturing corporations, 1930-1970

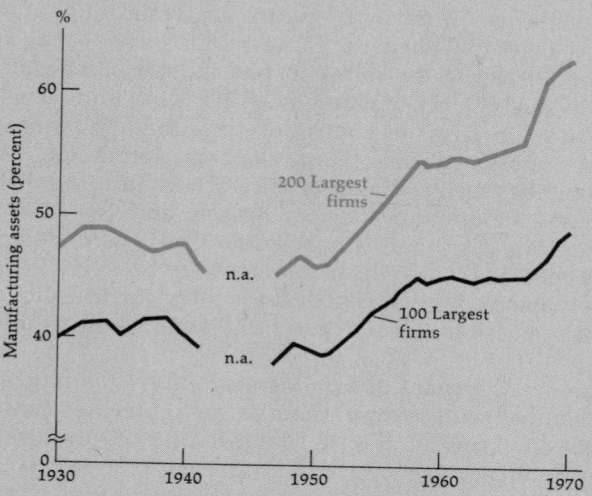

(b) Concentration of assets and profits in manufacturing corporations, 1st quarter 1968, 1970

| Asset size, 1970 | Number of firms | Percent of total assets | | Percent of total profits | |
|---|---|---|---|---|---|
| | | 1968 | 1970 | 1968 | 1970 |
| $1 billion and over | 102 | 43 | 48 | 49 | 53 |
| $100 million to $1 billion | 507 | 30 | 28 | 28 | 29 |
| $10 million to $100 million | 2,101 | 13 | 12 | 11 | 9 |
| Under $10 million | 197,710 | 14 | 12 | 12 | 9 |
| Total | 200,420 | 100 | 100 | 100 | 100 |

*Industry Concentration.* The manufacturing industry is characterized by increasing concentration of assets and profits in the largest firms, particulary from the mid-1960s to 1970. Indeed, 102 of the largest firms with assets of at least $1 billion earn over one-half of manufacturing profits.

SOURCE: Bureau of Economics, Federal Trade Commission, and Securities Exchange Commission.

barriers to entry for rival firms unable to acquire enough financial strength to pose a serious threat to IBM. In short, seller concentration, product differentiation, and entry barriers are key determinants of the structure of markets, tending to maintain or destroy market competition.

## MARKET CONDUCT

The pricing policies of a firm, the way it reacts toward rival producers, and the nature of nonprice competition such as advertising are behavioral indicators of monopoly conduct in markets. Conduct occurs within the environment established by the structure of a market and, as Chapter 17 suggested, the conduct of monopolistically competitive and oligopolistic firms differs in many ways. One common and important outcome, however, is that the market conduct of imperfectly competitive firms is likely to result in the inefficient allocation of resources. Firms that follow "price-leadership" patterns, for example, are able to control markets in a manner symptomatic of oligopoly. Such conduct can also influence the competitive structure of markets by allowing firms to increase barriers to entry, and it may also affect profits and other measures of performance in the industry.

## MARKET PERFORMANCE

The test of "good and bad" performance for a market economy depends upon the goals of a nation. Flat judgments cannot be made about the general performance of the mixed public-private enterprise economy, but there are certain indicators of how well any given market performs. The American economy has provided the highest level of living in the world in terms of per capita output, but it is also important to determine the degree to which a *specific* industry's performance deviates from the best possible economic results. Assessment of market performance concentrates on whatever gaps may exist between *actual* and *potential* market performance in terms of generally recognized economic goals. The goals of an economy are not invariant over time, however. Today, for example, industrial performance in the area of controlling pollution and preserving a clean environment is sadly lacking in comparison to the potential that exists.[2] Other economic goals that are currently important to market performance include the full and efficient use of resources, growth which contributes to the productivity of resources, and a just system of economic organization that does not whimsically favor or discriminate against certain firms or groups.

In establishing public policies designed to remedy undesirable market performance, the market structure in which firms operate is a more important target than conduct because market structure typically is the *source* of the conduct which influences performance in a market economy. For example, if 55,000 annual automotive deaths (performance) are due to automotive accidents (conduct) because of unsafe cars or inadequate freeways (structure), the most effective remedial policies are those that attack the source of the problem. However, this does not mean that laws against speeding or the conduct of drunken drivers are not useful. Similarly, laws against firms that rig prices can be helpful, but remedying the basic cause of the problem by diluting market concentration and monopoly power is a surer way to obtain desired performance patterns.

## THE FOCUS OF INDUSTRIAL ORGANIZATION

Economic facts are organized and theories are postulated in order to explain why things come out as they do and what can be done to improve the existing outcome. Improved knowledge about the structure, conduct, and performance of markets is important if we are to construct a better world and help preserve what we have today. The focus of the study of the organization of markets, therefore, is directed at developing public policies which enhance the functioning of markets in the private sector of the American economy.

---

[2] Chapter 22 further discusses environmental economics.

Economic policies must be directed toward achieving performance standards that are in harmony with the goals of society. Public policy toward monopoly and competition is oriented to the efficient use of resources in a mixed market environment, but public policies are also designed to achieve other economic goals such as an equitable distribution of income or job opportunities for agricultural workers. On occasions policies designed to achieve one goal conflict with others. Thus, if legal measures are used to bring about greater competition, government policy may infringe upon economic freedom in the private sector. On the other hand, if monopolization of markets is ignored, goals such as full employment and price stability may be difficult to achieve, since monopoly power permits the upward administration of prices which leads to cost-push inflation. In such a case, inflationary price increases *and* high levels of unemployment may both occur at the same time. In addition, markets in which firms control prices can erode the competitive base for American exports and bring about problems in international trade.[3] Clearly, the organization and performance of markets are important to many economic goals, both directly and indirectly.

### Monopoly and Market Power

When competition breaks down in a market, the allocation of resources is distorted, leading to higher prices, the underallocation of resources, and a restriction of output. Imperfectly competitive firms with discretionary pricing power also contribute to a variety of social, economic, and political problems which can distort the growth and development of an economy.

### APPRAISAL OF THE MONOPOLY PROBLEM

While the structure of markets and the concentration of assets throughout large portions of the American economy today are excessive in the eyes of many observers, appraising market performance is no easy task. Nevertheless, by observing characteristics such as product differentiation, barriers to entry, price rigidity, profit rates, and so on, economists are able to make tentative appraisals about the performance of markets.

Industry and market studies generally confirm what economic theory would predict, i.e., the conduct of the largest firms in the most heavily concentrated markets is monopolistic. While evidence on economies of scale and the size of firms is not definitive, most authorities agree that there are few or no significant cost advantages attached to the operation of the largest firms.[4] Studies of market concentration within specific industries also indicate that profit rates for firms in highly concentrated industries tend to be high—perhaps one-half again as high as profit rates in modestly concentrated industries. Profits also appear to be related to large advertising outlays as well as to high entry barriers.[5] These generally "most-profitable"

---

[3] As Chapters 25 and 26 point out, inflation may lower sales abroad, hampering the achievement of economic balance in trading with other nations, and contributing to a balance-of-payments deficit.

[4] See, for example, Richard Caves, *American Industry: Structure, Conduct, and Performance* (Englewood Cliffs, N.J.: Prentice-Hall, 1967), ch. 6.

[5] Cabinet Committee on Price Stability, *Industrial Structure and Competitive Policy*, Study Paper 2 (Washington, D.C.: U.S. Government Printing Office, January 1969), pp. 42, 43.

firms and industries are often characterized by high entry barriers, various forms of nonprice competition, and rigid or inflexible pricing behavior. The impact of imperfectly competitive markets on technological change is another important feature of the monopoly problem. Some authorities have asserted that extreme monopoly power approaching oligopoly tends to be conducive to research and more rapid technological advance, but evidence on this issue is not at all clear. Willard F. Mueller, an acknowledged expert on such matters, has suggested that the late Joseph Schumpeter's contention that imperfect markets promote technological advance ". . . is on the verge of collapse."[6] The typical assessment of monopoly power tends to confirm two fundamental conclusions:

1. Production efficiencies demand high concentration in only a very few industries, most of which are already natural monopolies owned or regulated by government. Economic efficiency simply does not appear to warrant a highly concentrated market structure.

2. Technical progress stemming from innovative activity does not seem to be more prevalent in highly monopolized industries than in more competitive markets. Thus, market concentration trends, including the corporate merger movement of the late 1960s and early 1970s, potentially could be harmful.[7]

Indeed, if any economic consideration appears to dictate large size, it is neither economies of scale nor technological change, but rather advertising economies and, as we know, extensive advertising is itself a manifestation of imperfectly competitive markets in which firms have the ability to influence price. The general consensus, then, is that an imperfectly competitive market structure inhibits the potential performance of American industry and is capable of distorting the allocation of resources.

Two cases of monopolized markets deserve individual treatment: (a) the public utility as a natural monopoly, and (b) conglomerates, a new twist to the corporate merger movement.

PUBLIC UTILITIES: NATURAL MONOPOLIES

A natural monopoly results from scale economies, as in the case of firms in the communications, power, and transportation industries. Public-utility industries are characterized by high fixed costs, low unit costs at large levels of output, and the capability of avoiding unnecessary duplication of facilities and services if firms are not forced to operate in a competitive environment. Because it is usually inappropriate to preserve competition under these conditions, government regulation or ownership is usually imposed in the public interest.

Federal and state laws now regulate the business practices of public utilities by granting firms charters to provide services as natural monopolies. States first began establishing regulatory commissions to monitor

[6] Testimony of Willard F. Mueller, "Planning, Regulation, and Competition" Hearings of the Subcommittee of the Select Committee on Small Business (Washington, D.C.: U.S. Government Printing Office, June 1967), p. 19.

[7] For a representative study of the monopoly-technology topic, see F. M. Scherer, "Firm Size, Market Structure, Opportunity and the Output of Patented Inventions," *American Economic Review* (December 1965), pp. 1121 ff.

pricing practices and profit rates nearly three-quarters of a century ago. Unfortunately, state regulation has not been effective, in part because state governments typically do not have the resources or authority to use regulatory agencies effectively. The courts also made state regulation a difficult task by undermining the decisions of the regulatory commissions. As technology and the American economy expanded during the early years of this century, more and more difficulties among state regulations cropped up, contributing to greater involvement by the federal government.

A considerable amount of economic activities generated by a variety of important industries falls under federal regulation. How well regulatory agencies perform in their task is a matter of some dispute, however. The oldest federal regulatory body is the Interstate Commerce Commission, which is empowered primarily to rule on the prices and services of the railways, certain classes of coastal shipping, petroleum pipelines, and highway trucking. A second agency, the Federal Power Commission, regulates telephone and telegraph rates and services. Fares, routes, and services provided by domestic airlines are under the surveillance of the Civil Aeronautics Board, and various other federal agencies monitor selected industries (e.g., the Atomic Energy Commission and nuclear power).

Regulatory agencies often face problems in handling vast numbers of requests for rate changes, disputes over service routes, and similar problems. Difficulties are also encountered in determining whether a given rate of return is a "fair" one. Seeing to it that the regulated natural monopoly remains aware of cost controls and operates efficiently is no easy task, since prices are set by administration authority instead of markets. These problems and numerous isolated examples of ineffective regulation have led many reputable observers to suggest that too often regulatory commissions become servants of the firms they are charged with regulating. Evaluating the effectiveness of regulation over natural monopolies is not simple, however, and most experts acknowledge that regulation, poor though it may be, is probably preferable to other alternatives such as public ownership or competition.

## CONGLOMERATES: PUBLIC EVIL OR PAPER DYNASTY?

Although uneven economic growth among different firms and industries has contributed to increased market power, mergers between firms explain much of today's concentration in economic power. In the mid-1960s, acquired assets of manufacturing and mining firms averaged around $5 billion annually, but by the first quarter of 1969 acquired assets had reached the annual rate of nearly $20 billion per year. The merger rate declined temporarily as the stock market tumbled in 1969 and 1970, but most authorities anticipate that the merger trend will continue in the 1970s.[8] The merger of two or more firms may involve a corporation gobbling up potential competitors, other firms complementary to its operations, or perhaps quite different and unrelated businesses.

The courts and the Department of Justice frown upon merger activities under certain conditions that threaten competition. However, the 1960s witnessed a new form of merger—the conglomerate. The *conglomerate*

[8] The data on firms acquired as reported by the Bureau of Economics of the Federal Trade Commission include only corporations with assets above $10 million.

*merger* occurs when a company takes over another firm which is operating in quite unrelated markets. In contrast, *vertical mergers* are mergers that serve to integrate production markets—the case if General Motors buys a company producing steel, tires, or batteries. *Horizontal mergers* occur if one company purchases another firm selling in the same product market, as when one major retail or computer firm takes over another.

Conglomerates have been characterized as paper-growth dynasties created through financial maneuvers to which stock-market speculators respond like children playing monopoly. The key to the growth of a conglomerate has been "*buy* firms with the stock of a parent corporation, don't build them." The market price of stocks tends to be associated with growth in earnings, a relationship generally shown by the price/earnings ratio a stock supports. A share of stock in an old-line, stalwart corporation growing 3 or 4 percent per year in a not very glamorous industry, for example, might sell at 10 to 15 times per share earnings. Before the conglomerate bubble burst in 1969 and 1970, the faster the rate of growth in earnings a conglomerate could show, the higher its stock price. Accordingly, price/earnings ratios of conglomerates rose to 40, 50, and even higher. This situation allowed the conglomerate to issue its own stock selling at high premiums and use it to buy another firm's stock selling at low price/earnings ratios.

By other shrewd financial maneuvers, including the juggling of accounting records, small companies bought big ones, upped their reported earnings per share, and drove the price of the conglomerate's stock upwards. As the price of a conglomerate's stock rose in value, the acquisition of still other firms was facilitated.[9] Litton Industries, for example, ballooned from a small electronics firm in 1953 to one of the 50 largest firms by the late 1960s. At one time, the reported net worth of Litton was in the multi-billion-dollar category, and its conglomerate status was clear as it operated in some two dozen different industries—including the federal government's poverty program (the Job Corps). International Telephone and Telegraph (IT&T), another good example of a conglomerate, increased assets from

---

[9] Suppose company X (the fast-growing conglomerate) wishes to take over company Y (a staid American corporation). Before merger we have:

|  | Shares outstanding | Earnings | Per share earnings | Price/earnings ratio | Price per share |
|---|---|---|---|---|---|
| X = | 2 million | $2 million | $1 | 40 | $40 |
| Y = | 3 million | $3 million | $1 | 10 | $10 |

Now, fast-growing conglomerate X offers to exchange one share of its stock for every three shares of company Y, giving the stockholders of company Y a net gain of $10 for every three shares of Y held, or a gain of $3.33 per share. After acquisition, and assuming that the conglomerate's spiced-up financial report supports carrying the same *P/E* ratio of 40, conglomerate X could report more than a 50 percent increase in earnings per share and thus drive the per share price of its stock to even higher levels.

|  | Shares outstanding | Earnings | Per share earnings | Price/earnings ratio | Price per share |
|---|---|---|---|---|---|
| X (and Y) = | 3 million | $5 million | $1.67 | 40 | $66.80 |

While it ironically appears that everyone gains, the conglomerate's management team may not be able to manage the newly created dynasty successfully—which is exactly what has happened in some cases (e.g., Litton Industries).

$1 billion to more than $5 billion between 1961 and 1970. IT&T's profits increased sevenfold in this period, and today it produces and sells, among other things, houses, insurance, radios, and books, as well as hotel and rental-car services.

Ultimately, the big-money interests on Wall Street and in major corporate board rooms across the nation grew uneasy. Needless to say, the conglomerate was resented and feared by those in control of the financial and corporate scene who already enjoyed various degrees of monopoly power. The size of a company was no serious obstacle to acquisition in many cases —at least not until Wall Street's financial establishment mounted a frontal attack on "outsiders." In early 1969, the corporate-monopoly establishment crushed an attempt by Leasco Corporation to take over the nation's sixth largest bank (Chemical Bank of New York).[10] Washington quickly joined hands with Wall Street against the conglomerate merger movement, and numerous antitrust suits were filed against conglomerates as the decade of the 1960s closed.

While the attack on conglomerates is now underway, clear evidence that such firms threaten competition in specific markets is not easy to come by. The threat of even greater concentration of economic power is very real in the eyes of many economists. However, others are not unduly concerned about the conglomerate movement, basing their view on the theory that an already monopolized corporate jungle may be driven to greater efficiency and responsibility if the handful of autocrats now controlling vast amounts of economic power are challenged.

In short, the signs of the times do appear ominous; yet, it is easy to ignore the fact that monopoly is far from typical of the aggregate American economy. Much of the economic activity of this nation occurs under somewhat workable competitive conditions. Nonetheless, public policy must be attentive to the awesome amount and growth of financial power that characterizes large segments of the American economy. A concentrated economic system is prone to manipulation and the merging of corporate and state interests of which some observers have warned.[11] Ability to control the economy must remain in the hands of politically elected representatives, not a financial and industrial oligarchy.

### Fostering Competition: Antitrust Policy

The United States government has long had antitrust laws intended to monitor the growth of market power in nonregulated industries. The first of the major pieces of legislation dealing with product-market monopolies was the Sherman Antitrust Act of 1890. More recently, the Clayton and Federal Trade Commission Acts (1914) and the Celler-Kefauver Antimerger Act (1950) have been directed against concentrations of economic power. However, the enforcement of these laws has been quite uneven.

Market power can be checked by breaking up existing monopolies and by policies that negate and reduce barriers to entry. In addition, government can step down hard on price collusion and other undesirable forms

[10] Accounts of this financial ploy can be found in *Business Week* (April 26, 1969) and *Fortune* (May 1, 1969).

[11] Recall Chapter 20's summary of Galbraith's concern for the emerging "industrial state."

of market conduct used by firms to control and avoid competition. A variety of other measures ranging from tariff reductions to better consumer protection have also been suggested as ways to dilute the power of product-market monopolies. For the most part, efforts by the federal government to cope with the monopoly problem have concentrated on mergers—new threats to the competitive structure of American industry—much to the dismay of numerous critics of antitrust policy. A great many economists have encouraged applying an equally stringent antimonopoly standard to existing firms which have excessive market power.

## THE SHERMAN ACT

The question of monopoly and competition came to the fore during the period following the Civil War in an era of economic development marked by rapid technological changes. Business firms merged with increasing frequency into trusts—a legal device under which the majority shareholders of independent companies combined by placing control of a company in the hands of trustees who issued trust certificates and ran the new combine of companies. Along with holding companies and other merger devices, the trust movement resulted in a backlash of public indignation that culminated in the Sherman Act which made monopolization and restraint of trade illegal. Under the Sherman Act, the Supreme Court found two companies (Standard Oil and American Tobacco) guilty of "unreasonable" monopolization and ordered their dissolution into several separate companies in the early 1900s.[12] Sadly enough for "trust-busting" proponents of the Act, the pro-business Court hinged its highly subjective ruling upon tangible evidence of *unreasonable* restraint of trade. Thus, only the monopolization of competitors through unreasonable and unfair practices was declared illegal—not the existence of monopoly itself.

## THE CLAYTON AND FEDERAL TRADE COMMISSION ACTS

Vagueness in the Sherman Act prompted passage of the Clayton Act in 1914, a law which sharpened the antitrust provisions of the Sherman Act by outlawing selected business practices leading to monopoly power, including *price discrimination* (selling goods to select firms at different prices to destroy competition) and *tying arrangements* (firm A forcing firm B to deal exclusively with A as a condition of buying a certain product). In addition, the Clayton Act placed limited regulations on mergers between firms and prohibited the interlocking of corporate directors and officers if it lessened competition. In the same year that the Clayton Act was passed, Congress created the Federal Trade Commission (FTC) for the purposes of evaluating the organization of markets in the American economy and investigating specific business practices which restrained competition. As a result of restrictive court rulings, the FTC proved to be ineffective in monitoring monopoly practices. Since the Wheeler-Lea Amendment in 1938, the FTC has primarily concerned itself with monitoring deceptive advertising practices, although, together with the Department of Justice, it also has responsibilities for antimerger enforcement.

[12] Both companies controlled more than 75 percent of their respective markets at that time. See *U.S.* v. *American Tobacco Co.*, 221 U.S. 106 (1911) and *U.S.* v. *Standard Oil Co. of New Jersey*, 221 U.S. 1 (1911).

Section 7 of the Clayton Act outlawed mergers lessening competition when they are accomplished by the acquisition of stock, but mergers conducted in other ways (e.g., the acquisition of assets) could not be checked until the Celler-Kefauver Act of 1950 was passed. Since that time the Antitrust Division of the Department of Justice has had greater authority to block merger activities that threaten to undermine market competition, including the conglomerate merger movement discussed earlier. Whether or not the the Department of Justice prohibits a merger depends heavily upon the degree of concentration in a market, and on this count the conglomerate merger presents new problems because it may not lead to increased concentration in a specific market. Since it is very difficult to assess the ramifications of multi-billion dollar firms expanding into dozens of markets, the legal guidelines used to determine violation of antitrust laws need to be reformulated. The problem with conglomerates is that it is very difficult to untangle such things as subsidizing one product out of profits from other markets, reciprocity in purchasing decisions, and "tie-in" selling in many different markets.

### The Impact and Direction of Antitrust Law

Since spotty enforcement and legal technicalities have hampered antitrust policies, it is difficult to judge their effectiveness. Government is the chief enforcement agent of antitrust laws, although damaged private parties can seek relief under some provisions of the law. The checkered history of application and enforcement of the antitrust laws is partially an image of the political postures of different administrations in Washington. The vigor with which the United States has pursued the monopoly problem also has depended upon the courts' interpretation of the law, as well as the financial support given to federal regulatory agencies.

For some time after the celebrated case involving the U.S. Steel Corporation in 1920, antitrust law was viewed as inapplicable to existing monopoly power, as long as undesirable forms of market conduct such as price fixing were not engaged in.[13] Some 25 years later, the courts reversed their earlier position when Alcoa was judged to be in violation of the Sherman Act simply because it controlled about 90 percent of the market for aluminum production. Thus, the older standard of requiring illegal market conduct was supplemented by a recognition that present market concentration as an indicator of a monopolized market structure may constitute violation of the law. Still, the thrust of antitrust policy too often ignores markets in which monopoly already exists.

Market power due to monopolized product markets works through a vast web of complex relationships. Monopoly may involve overlapping appointments of directors and officers among major corporations; the concentration of billions of dollars of corporate stock in the hands of a few mutual funds and bank trust departments; or a maze of subsidiary companies spread across the globe, all of which are attached to a major parent corporation. Fragile and tentative though it is, there is evidence to suggest that market power is increasing in many markets in the American economy.

---

[13] This was the view of the courts even though U.S. Steel was the result of earlier combinations of a large number of companies, which at the time controlled about 60 percent of the market. See *U.S.* v. *U.S. Steel*, 251 U.S. 417 (1920).

Monopoly is typically greater than technical efficiency dictates and it imposes costs in the form of waste and inefficiencies estimated to range from 2 to 5 percent of national income. Imperfect competition may also retard economic progress and growth in output and result in a redistribution of income in favor of the persons associated with those firms enjoying such power. The weight of evidence suggests that profits are favorably affected by monopoly power. The monopoly problem is not confined to manufacturing industries alone, although these markets attract attention because of their size and greater public visibility. The significance of monopoly also extends beyond concerns about the efficient use of resources. Market power enables firms to rig prices in order to maintain profit margins, passing price increases on to consumers even though demand and output may be declining. Because of this situation, the effectiveness of monetary and fiscal policies in controlling economic instability is reduced. Monopoly both adds to inflationary wage-price spirals and contributes to the factors that place society in the difficult position of choosing between more unemployment or more inflation. At the same time, however, it is necessary to qualify these conclusions about the severity of the monopoly problem. Technological change may be favorably influenced by imperfect markets, countervailing power may restrain monopoly practices, and the general "workability" of competition also serves to moderate (though not destroy) the case against monopoly.

While antitrust policy can and very well may be enforced more vigorously and more consistently in the future, it is well to remember that the present monopoly-surveillance system has been useful in preserving the degree of competition that exists in American industry today. The law acts as a direct check against monopolistic practices in those cases where prosecution does occur. It also may represent a "deterrent force" of unknown strength in cases not subject to prosecution, in much the same way that criminal laws against pilfering restrain such behavior.

To more fully assure a viable market system of economic organization, it is necessary for the federal government to direct its attention to highly concentrated industries already in existence. Conglomerate mergers also warrant careful scrutiny if a decentralized economy is to be preserved in the 1970s. Large blocks of stocks are controlled by major financial institutions, and pyramiding financial control in bank trust departments, mutual funds, and other such institutions represents as great a potential threat to a market economy as do conglomerates. For this reason it is imperative to subject the merger movement and the entire banking and financial community to continual surveillance. Finally, improving the information available to consumers and creating more effective consumer-protection laws can also be helpful in further checking the excesses of market power.

*Summing up:* Not all public policy has helped control market power, and the government has not always acted as vigorously as permitted by law. Nevertheless, the government has begun to react to the monopoly problem with more vigilance. In recent decades, the tobacco, aluminum, finance, and steel industries all have felt the anger of the Department of Justice. Even though difficulties are encountered in enforcing antitrust policies, the combined efforts of the Federal Trade Commission, the Department of Justice, and a concerned and informed electorate can do much to minimize the ills of imperfect competition. Retaining a viable market economy in which market power is minimized is no small task, but it is a necessary one if the

United States is to avoid centralization of economic and political power. To date, however, government policy has been feeble and much less effective than required to cope with the monopoly problem.

## B. PUBLIC POLICY AND COMPETITION: THE CASE OF AGRICULTURE

Just as government policies have been applied to monopoly, so too has the public sector attempted to facilitate adjustments in instances where there is tangible evidence of *competitive* failures in the market mechanism. While many different problems in competitive markets have attracted government action, agriculture is a striking example which remains an important economic problem today. The agricultural industry is unique in many ways, not the least of which is that it is doomed to decline in importance as an economy develops and prospers. American agriculture has been a key source of economic growth in that productivity in agriculture has increased twice as rapidly as it has in the rest of the economy, and declining employment in farming has released manpower resources for employment in other sectors of the economy. Agriculture is also a vital industry simply because food and fiber are such basic needs of any population. In many ways, public policies designed to cope with competitive market failures in agriculture have been ineffective and even misguided.

Government policies toward competitive markets cover many areas other than agriculture, and the diversity of these policies merits brief consideration.

### The Diversity of Policies to Monitor Competition

The history of the American labor movement furnishes one illustration of the public sector stepping in to alter the operation of private markets—in this case, by restricting competition among workers. The American worker ultimately has been allowed and even encouraged to band together in labor unions in order to "check" the market power wielded by employers over individual workers. In addition, laws have been passed to prohibit or regulate child labor, hazardous working conditions, minimum wages, and overtime payments, among other things. Another example of government policy which alters the operation of markets is the Robinson-Patman Act (1936). During the 1920s and 1930s the chain store came into its own, while "mama and papa" retail operations experienced difficulties. The Robinson-Patman legislation struck at the advantages of volume purchasing by making it illegal for a firm to give quantity discounts to buyers that could not be defended on the basis of cost savings. Price discrimination against selected buyers can be harmful to competition and, in that sense, the Robinson-Patman Act is useful legislation. On the other hand, price-discrimination laws also reduce price flexibility and competition among sellers who can legally hold the line on prices.

Fair trade or resale price-maintenance laws are still another example of government policy that limits price competition. The Miller-Tydings Act of 1937 checks the ability of one retailer to undersell another on certain brand-name products. Once again, many economists regard legislation of this sort as promoting monopoly pricing practices and protecting less efficient sellers. American patent laws also prevent competition by giving innovators exclusive monopoly rights for 17 years. While patent legislation is of obvious importance in protecting innovators and rewarding those who contribute to technological advance, it also leads to monopolized market positions. The list of industrial giants now controlling vast portions of important markets whose power derives partly from patent laws is nearly endless (General Electric and Polaroid are good examples).

Policies to restrict or regulate competition typically are based on a maladjustment or failure of the market in question, but market failures are not always improved by government policies. Unfortunately, agricultural policies, like patent and price-maintenance laws, have had several undesirable side effects. Instead of concentrating on resource markets, and particularly on markets for human resources which represent the crux of agriculture's problem, government policy has tampered with product-market prices and has failed for that reason. At the same time, however, certain aspects of our agricultural policy have had notable success in fostering increased production that has enhanced economic growth.

## Economic Changes in Agriculture

While the agricultural sector of the American economy is the backbone of life, economic activity in agriculture has declined steadily in relative importance in recent decades.[14] Sixty years ago over 13 million persons were employed on farms, but today farm employment accounts for less than 4 million jobs, even though the total labor force has more than doubled in size in this period. The number of farms in America has declined from a high of 6.5 million 40 years ago to less than one-half that number today. Agriculture accounted for 10 percent of total national income in the late 1930s, but produces less than 3 percent of total national income at the present time. While the agricultural sector of the American economy has undergone vast changes in recent decades, it has also remained the leader among all major sectors of the economy in annual productivity gains. Indeed, gross investment in farming has increased 50 percent in the last 10 years! Therefore, although the decline of agriculture is a real event, it is also one that can be misleading.

In many ways the inevitable changes experienced by American agriculture in recent decades are a measure of progress and not of decline. However, agricultural interests have retained disproportionate political muscle and much noise is often generated about the "farm problem." The fact that per capita disposable income for farm residents is three-fourths of the national average is sometimes alleged to be a symptom of the farm problem. While it is true that *average* farm incomes are not on a par with those in the nonfarm sector, to characterize the farm problem in this fashion is an oversimplification, as we shall see. The fact is that there are two agricul-

[14] The importance of agriculture is very evident in that the production of basic food and fiber outputs provides vast quantities of inputs to industries manufacturing clothing, household furnishings, chemicals, and so forth. In this same context of "agri-business" activities, it is apparent that as an economy develops and production becomes more specialized or roundabout, many economic activities once a part of the agricultural sector have been transferred to manufacturing and trade (e.g., meat processing). These development patterns likewise apply to other economic sectors such as construction. Indeed, all modern economies are highly interdependent and one can, for that reason, speak of "manufacturing- or construction-business" as well as agri-business.

tural sectors—a relatively prosperous commercial agriculture and the less prosperous and sometimes very poor "noncommercial" farm.

## COMPARING THE TWO FARMING SECTORS

Among the most significant changes in the structure of the farm enterprise in recent years has been a dramatic shift from the family farm to a large and expanding commercial agricultural sector. Figure 2 shows that wide differences characterize American agriculture, which sold a total output

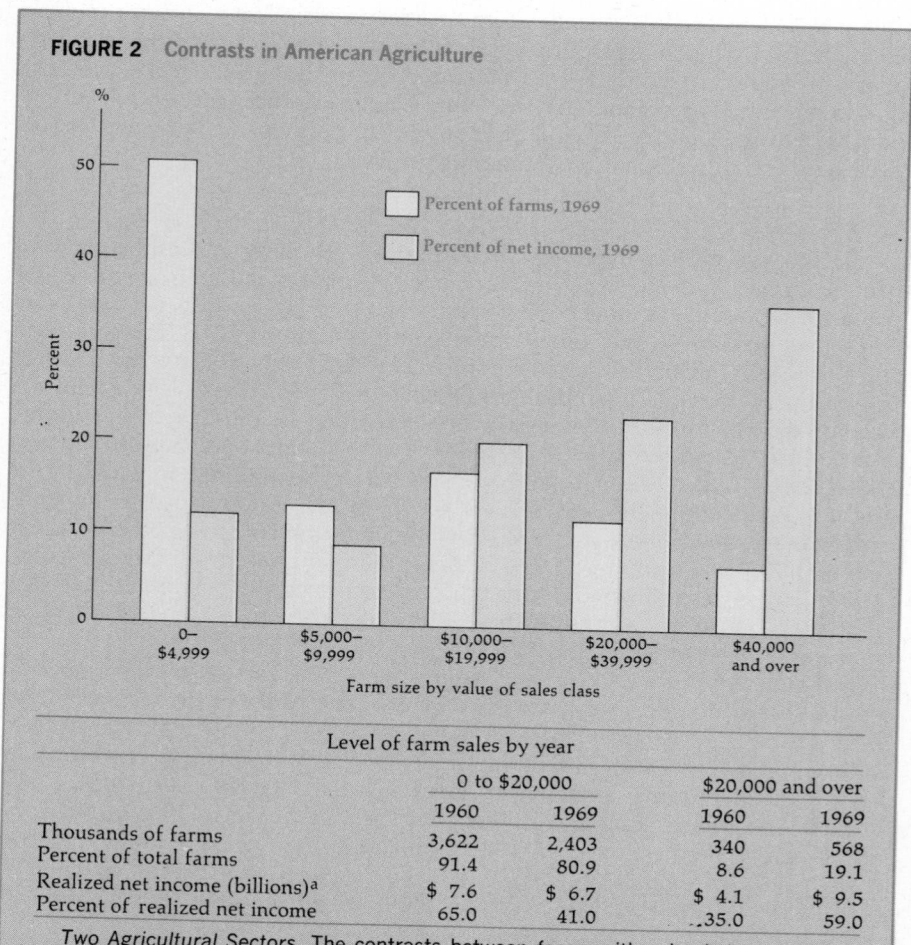

**FIGURE 2** Contrasts in American Agriculture

Percent of farms, 1969

Percent of net income, 1969

Farm size by value of sales class

### Level of farm sales by year

| | 0 to $20,000 | | $20,000 and over | |
| --- | --- | --- | --- | --- |
| | 1960 | 1969 | 1960 | 1969 |
| Thousands of farms | 3,622 | 2,403 | 340 | 568 |
| Percent of total farms | 91.4 | 80.9 | 8.6 | 19.1 |
| Realized net income (billions)[a] | $ 7.6 | $ 6.7 | $ 4.1 | $ 9.5 |
| Percent of realized net income | 65.0 | 41.0 | 35.0 | 59.0 |

*Two Agricultural Sectors.* The contrasts between farms with sales below and above $20,000 per year are vivid. The large commercial farms are growing in number and realizing a large proportion of net farm income, but smaller farms are declining.

[a] Income includes realized net income from farming, government payments, off-farm income, and in-kind (nonmoney) food and housing income.

SOURCE: United States Department of Agriculture, Economic Research Service, *Farm Income Situation*, July 1970.

of $55 billion in 1969—a year when realized net farm income was in excess of $16 billion. The striking characteristic of Figure 2 is the large proportion (just over 50 percent) of farms realizing less than $5,000 of gross sales per year and earning only about 12 percent of realized net income. By way of comparison, the largest 7.1 percent of all farms earned over one-third of realized net income. Clearly, the smallest farm operations selling less than $5,000 of output each year are mere vegetable gardens by comparison to commercial farms.

The data shown in Figure 2 distinguish between smaller and commercial farms—those with gross sales below or greater than $20,000 annually.[15] The commercial-farming operation selling in excess of $20,000 per year is experiencing rapid growth in both numbers and net income. In contrast, the number of smaller and less productive farms declined by one-third, from 3.6 million to 2.4 million, between 1960 and 1969. Net farm income realized by larger commercial farms more than doubled from 1960 to 1969, but realized net income fell from $7.6 billion to $6.7 billion for the 2.4 million smaller farms selling less than $20,000 annually. Thus, there are two distinct farm sectors—one expanding and the other contracting.

## THE NATURE OF THE FARM PROBLEM

But what is the farm problem, what causes it if it does exist, and how severe is it? There are no easy answers to these questions, partly because there are two quite different dimensions to the American agricultural industry. There are certain production and demand problems associated with the expanding and relatively prosperous commercial agricultural sector which contrast sharply with the problems of poverty and absolute as well as relative economic decline that exist in rural America.

The basic farm problem is one of a misallocation of too many resources to agriculture. Along with certain unique characteristics of the markets for farm products, the consequences of this resource misallocation are poverty for one out of five farm families and economic decline for millions of other rural Americans. Excess resources in the agricultural sector have led to depressed farm prices, declining farm employment, and outmigration of human resources from rural America. Upon close examination, then, agriculture is a trouble spot because rural America is in trouble—as is the urban environment for that matter. However, the economic problems of agriculture are peculiar ones.

## Characteristics of the Agricultural Industry

The structural and performance characteristics of agriculture are unique in several ways. Five distinctive characteristics of agriculture are: (a) rapid technological changes, (b) inelastic and slowly increasing demand, (c) competitive and unstable markets, (d) immobilized and excess supplies of resources, and (e) widespread rural poverty and economic decline. The combined effect of the first four characteristics has been poverty and economic decline for many Americans still living in rural areas and millions more who have moved to urban areas.

[15] About one-fifth of all farms were classified in the commercial category in 1969 and these farms produced nearly three-fifths of realized net income from farming.

The agricultural sector has experienced striking rates of growth in output per manhour in recent decades as the larger commercial-farming operations have adopted technological advances which rely upon mechanized, capital-intensive, and scientific farming methods. As Figure 3 illustrates, the food and fiber production of one farmer supports some 45 persons today, compared to 7 persons in 1920—the level of agricultural performance prevalent in other nations today. Indeed, American farm output per manhour has doubled every 7 to 10 years for more than three decades. Fertilizers, pesticides, feed additives, and sophisticated capital equipment are increasingly important inputs to farming. Technological change in agriculture, much of which has stemmed from government-supported research programs in state universities, has transformed American agriculture in numerous ways. Productivity has been translated into rapid increases in supply which, together with a sluggish rate of growth in demand for farm products, have resulted in declining prices.

## DEMAND FOR FARM PRODUCTS

The demand for agricultural products has increased with the passage of time, but its growth is modest compared to growth in income. The major reason for sluggish growth in demand is that food and fiber consumption are dependent upon population growth, particularly in relatively affluent and well-fed nations.[16] Once a society meets its basic consumption needs, a larger share of consumer expenditures tends to be diverted to housing,

[16] When disposable income grows more rapidly than the demand for agricultural products, the demand for food products is said to be *income inelastic*.

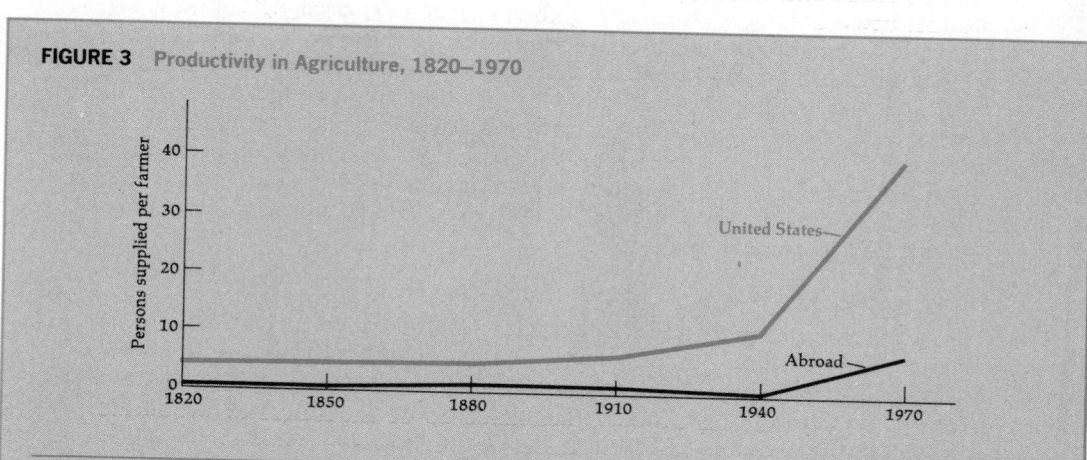

**FIGURE 3**    Productivity in Agriculture, 1820–1970

*Rising Productivity.* Because of technological changes, agricultural productivity has increased significantly in the United States for one and one-half centuries. Consequently, the average farmer in the United States can supply 45 Americans with food and fiber needs today—a performance level that far outstrips agricultural production abroad.

SOURCE: U.S. Department of Agriculture, *Change in Farm Production and Efficiency,* Statistical Bulletin, No. 223.

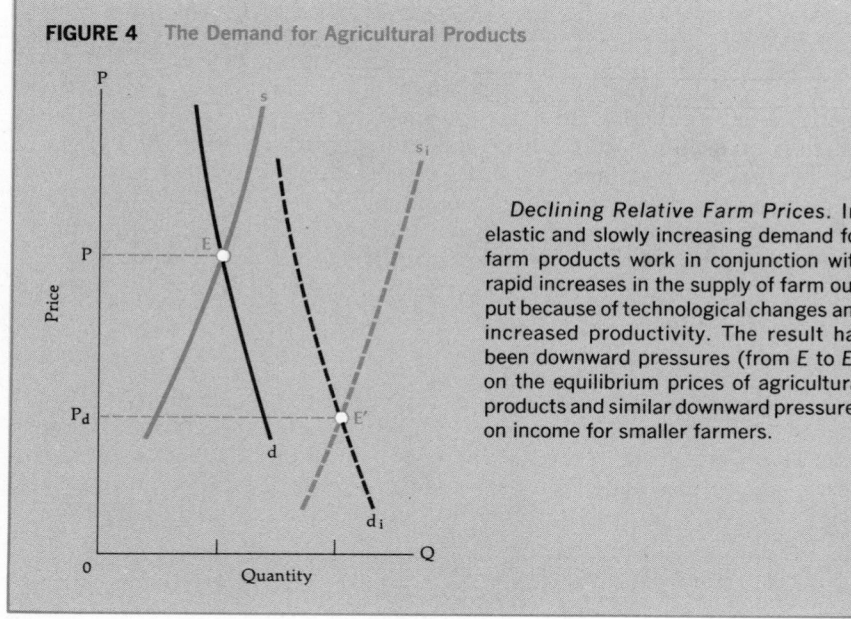

**FIGURE 4**  The Demand for Agricultural Products

*Declining Relative Farm Prices.* Inelastic and slowly increasing demand for farm products work in conjunction with rapid increases in the supply of farm output because of technological changes and increased productivity. The result has been downward pressures (from *E* to *E'*) on the equilibrium prices of agricultural products and similar downward pressures on income for smaller farmers.

leisure, and other less pressing wants. The demand for farm products also is inelastic or relatively insensitive to changes in price. Thus, as the quantities of crops and commodities supplied vary, relatively large variations in product price occur.

Figure 4 shows how the price problems in agriculture can be explained by a simple supply and demand illustration. Slow growth in demand is illustrated as a shift in demand from $d$ to $d_i$ while, because of technological advances, the supply of food increases more rapidly from $s$ to $s_i$. Coupled with modest growth in demand, supply changes have tended to depress farm prices from $P$ to $P_d$, as illustrated in Figure 4. Market prices have tended to decline for farm products relative to price levels in the nonfarm sector, and this in turn has placed income pressures on the smaller and less efficient farmers. Moreover, because demand is relatively inelastic, short-run shifts in the supply of agricultural products are capable of producing wide swings in equilibrium prices.

## COMPETITION AND INSTABILITY

Markets for agricultural products are made up of thousands of producers selling relatively standardized products in a reasonably competitive environment. Even though aggregate farm production is relatively stable by comparison to much of the manufacturing sector of the American economy, any individual agricultural enterprise can experience feast or famine because of the heavy dependency on one or a few basic crops characteristic of most farms. Unlike the nonfarm enterprise, which is more likely to be sheltered in some measure from highly competitive markets, individual farmers cannot exert a significant influence on prices. Consequently, any given agricultural operation may be an unstable and precarious business because of wide swings in output and prices. During good years not subject to the vagaries of weather or natural disasters, supply increases drive farm prices and incomes down rapidly. Because of the unplanned and relatively competitive nature of the industry, too many or too few farmers may alter production plans for a given crop and thus contribute to wide swings in prices. Moreover, if farmers attempt to increase their output to stave off declining incomes due to inelastic demand and lower prices, the increase in supply further depresses farm prices and incomes. Along with supply increases, inelastic demand, and the inability to influence market prices, short-run variations in the supply of a crop often contribute to the farmer's economic difficulties.

## LOW-MOBILITY RESOURCES

Slowly growing and inelastic demand, rapid gains in productivity and supply, and competitive price pressures suggest that resources would be moving out of agriculture into the nonfarm sector. While substantial outmigration from agriculture has occurred over recent years, it has been inadequate, especially in view of recent trends in commercial farming. Even though farm income and employment have declined rapidly in proportion to total employment and aggregate income, excess human resources have remained misallocated to agriculture. Many farmers remain locked into farming because of their age, because job alternatives in the nonfarm sector are lacking, or because they lack the skills and education needed to move into available jobs in the nonfarm sector. In addition, land and capital resources used in farming tend to be immobile and highly specialized, and often they have a very modest value for other uses. Relatively high fixed cost retards exodus from the industry and encourages marginal farming among the least efficient agricultural producers. Indeed, the true farm problem is a surplus of resources, although commercial agriculture does face the special production and marketing difficulties described above.

## RURAL POVERTY AND DECLINE

Many of the problems associated with an agricultural sector in rapid transition are shared unequally by different classes of farmers. It is true that competitive pressures, a rapidly changing technology, short-run instability, and depressed farm prices affect both the commercial and the marginal farmer, but the smaller and less efficient farmer unable to benefit from government aid to agriculture and least capable of migrating to decent jobs in the nonfarm sector is subject to the greatest pressure. Furthermore, rural Americans who do migrate to urban centers far too often find that sporadic work and a ghetto tenement are their only option.

The majority of farmers in the United States receive only a small fraction of net farm income, and within this group poverty is not uncommon. On the average, approximately two out of three nonwhites classified as farmers are poor by 1970 standards. Indeed, the chances of being poor are *twice* as great for a farmer as they are for a nonfarm American, and a total of 12 million persons, or nearly one-half the total poverty population, live in rural America. Many are whites living in depressed regions such as Appalachia, and others are members of minority groups—black sharecroppers in the South, Indian Americans living in barren regions of the country, and Spanish Americans spread across the southwestern United States. Tens of thousands migrate from state to state each year during harvest season and then return to a stony patch of land capable of growing a few beans or a little corn or cotton.

While government policy has been addressed to certain aspects of the agricultural problem, it has been most ineffective in recent years. Let us see how the federal government has attacked the farm problem.

## Implementing Agricultural Policy

For the most part, agricultural policy has concentrated on raising farm income by altering product-market prices. Agricultural subsidy payments depend on the level of output and the size of a farm; thus, almost all government support has gone to the largest farmers least in need of such assistance.

Farm policy in the United States extends back to the early years of the republic, but only in 1929 did government begin formally to erect the complex price and production controls in existence today. Prior to the 1930s, government aid to agriculture consisted largely of land-settlement policies and scientific research in areas such as soil conservation and farm production. Direct cash-payment programs were established to bolster farm prices and incomes in the early 1930s. What farmers initially sought through Congressional friends was a guaranteed *parity price*—a price level for farm products that would provide a level of real purchasing power equal to that which existed in the past—say, in the good years for agriculture of 1910–1914. The rationale for parity prices is simply that if a bale of cotton or a bushel of wheat, for example, sold at a price capable of purchasing a given quantity of consumer goods several decades ago, then, the price of cotton or wheat today should provide equivalent real purchasing power today.[17]

The three basic approaches used to bolster farm prices and income are: (a) the price-support program, (b) programs designed to increase the demand for farm products, and (c) supply-management programs which currently account for the bulk of agricultural subsidies to farmers.

### FARM PRICE-SUPPORT PROGRAMS

Figure 5(a) shows the effect of a government-supported price for farm products. Either by outright purchase of commodities or by a loan guarantee at a given product price, government authorities can hold price at support price $P_s$, which is higher than the market equilibrium price $P_e$. Consumers purchase Q units at the supported price in contrast to the larger quantity supplied (Q'). While farm prices (and *average* incomes) are increased through price support, farmers supply larger than equilibrium quantities of the product, and government surpluses accumulate in the amount of QQ' units. Surpluses may be stored at a cost of millions of dollars per

[17] The essentials of parity pricing remain today for selected crops and commodities, although parity values have been adjusted to world market prices. In a dynamic economy in which technology and changes in scale are reducing costs, the concept of parity has little relevance.

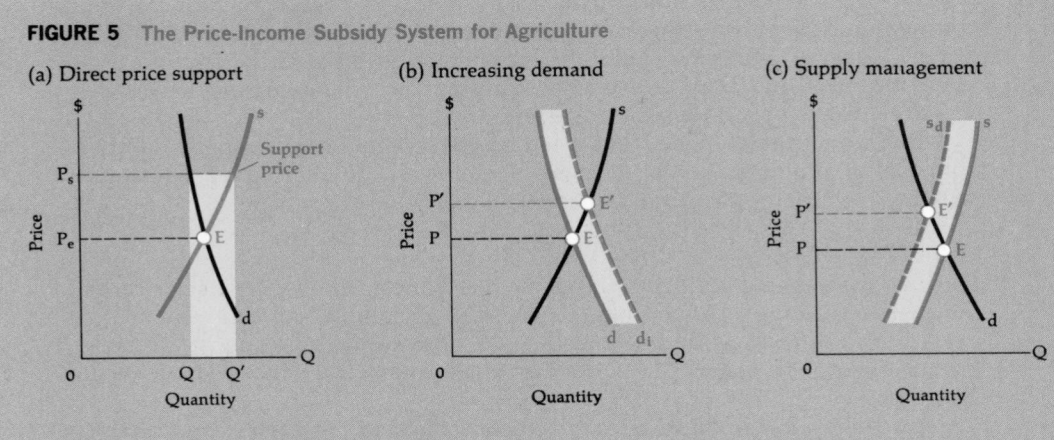

**FIGURE 5** The Price-Income Subsidy System for Agriculture

(a) Direct price support

(b) Increasing demand

(c) Supply management

*Three Ways to Increase Farm Prices.* Government may support a selling price higher than the market equilibrium as in (a) by effectively buying the surplus output QQ'. Increasing the demand for farm products (b) or reducing supply (c), can also be used to raise the price of farm products to some preconceived level which is higher than the market equilibrium.

month or may be channeled to underdeveloped nations as part of foreign aid under the Food for Peace Program (Public Law 480).

### INCREASED DEMAND FOR FARM PRODUCTS

Farm pressure groups also encourage programs such as food stamps for the poor, school-lunch programs, and research efforts designed to find new commercial and industrial uses for commodities. These approaches are illustrated in Figure 5(b) as an increase in the demand for farm products from $d$ to $d_i$ which is designed to increase farm prices from $P$ to $P'$. Public Law 480, providing for the shipment of surplus food products to foreign nations who pay the American government in their own currencies, increases demand in this fashion. While feeding the world's hungry and poor might appear to be a humane way to use the vast productive capacity of the American farmer, it is not costless. The underdeveloped nations of the world typically lack dollars to purchase American goods and as a consequence, the American government must subsidize the export of surplus commodities by agreeing to accept foreign currencies, only a portion of which ever will be used. Moreover, the underdeveloped nations of the world can become reliant on surplus American agricultural production and fail to fully develop their agricultural sector.[18]

---

[18] It is true that foreign aid in the form of food products is very important to the underdeveloped nations, but it must also be remembered that negative effects accompany such efforts. "Dumping" American food surpluses can distort international trade patterns and market prices and thus hamper economic development abroad. Underdeveloped nations which otherwise might compete in world trade markets may be unable to do so because of American overproduction. Also, because of domestic subsidies, the United States may itself import less from other countries. Foreign assistance wisely given (e.g., technical assistance for agricultural development) and not simply aid in the best interests of American farmers is what underdeveloped nations need.

Steady downward pressures on farm prices, inadequate increases in demand in relation to increasing supply, plus vast government surpluses have recently encouraged public authorities to use supply-management policies. If the supply of farm products can be reduced from $s$ to $s_d$ as shown in Figure 5(c), it is possible to establish a price higher than the original price ($P$) while avoiding the accumulation of surpluses which on occasion have been burned or have literally rotted. Land-retirement programs are one widely used method of attempting to control the quantity of farm output. Acreage diversion under the Soil Bank program, as well as agreements by farm operators to limit planted acreage each year to a quota set by the Department of Agriculture have met with only modest success, however. The basic shortcoming of supply-management programs is that they misallocate resources under the guise of bolstering farm income for needy farmers. In fact, however, if income assistance is deemed necessary for low-income groups, it more logically must be given because they are poor—not because they are farmers. Under land-retirement programs, farmers usually "rent" their least productive land to the government and refrain from planting cash crops. As acreage quotas are reduced, farmers use more of other resources such as fertilizer, better seed strains, and pesticides, which result in increased yields per acre and increased total output. Consequently, even though the total acreage of land under cultivation declined more than 10 percent between 1950 and 1970, crop production per acre increased nearly 60 percent and total agricultural output also increased rapidly.

## AGRICULTURAL DEVELOPMENT POLICIES

Public policy toward agriculture also includes research in farm production and rural economic-development policies—developmental goals that have been of substantial benefit to the American economy. However, agricultural policy generally has failed to meet the priority needs of a rural America in transition on many, if not the most important counts. In 1967, the President's National Advisory Commission on Rural Poverty noted that: "Some of our rural programs, especially farm and vocational-agriculture programs, are relics from an earlier era. . . . Instead of combating low incomes of rural people, these programs have helped to create wealthy landowners while largely by-passing the poor."[19] As in past years, well over one-half of the expenditures of the United States Department of Agriculture (which were budgeted at $5.5 billion to $6.5 billion per year in 1969–1971) are earmarked for price-support programs which neither facilitate the transfer of resources out of agriculture nor ease the condition of rural poverty.

### The Effectiveness of Agricultural Policy

Claims for public assistance to agriculture vary in intensity and quality partly because there are two distinct dimensions to the farm problem—one being the all-too-real problem of poverty and rural decline experienced by millions of farm and nonfarm citizens living in rural America, and the

---

[19] President's National Advisory Commission on Rural Poverty, *The People Left Behind* (Washington, D.C.: U.S. Government Printing Office, 1967), p. ix.

second the problems of production and marketing encountered by commercial agriculture. Unfortunately, claims for public assistance for these two very different problems are sounded by one voice—that of the powerful, affluent commercial-farm interest. The small marginal farmer has been ignored for the most part. For example, the approximately $4 billion in cash payments for price-support programs for fiscal 1970 and 1971 was nearly twice the amount spent for unemployment compensation for unemployed Americans. Such comparisons have led many authorities to judge existing agricultural expenditures as a colossal waste. By manipulating market supply and market prices on behalf of the wealthier farmer, farm policy has ignored the employment, income, and relocation needs of millions of rural Americans, many of whom, during the last two decades, have remained locked in subsistence farming or have crowded into burgeoning urban centers.

Public support for agricultural subsidies derives from the contention that farm family incomes are substantially below nonfarm family income levels. What has not been fully recognized, however, is that the statistics purporting to show low farm incomes are in a large measure mythical. Moreover, existing agricultural policy is inefficient and expensive and, worst of all, ignores the problem of excess resources in agriculture, at the same time helping the more rather than the less affluent farmer.

## LOW FARM INCOMES: FACT OR FALLACY?

In order to understand farm policy more fully, we first must consider the "low-agricultural-income" claim. *On the average, per capita farm incomes* are low relative to those in the nonfarm sector—about three-fourths of the national average in recent years.

Numerous agricultural economists, including D. Gale Johnson, who is past President (1965) and now Fellow of the American Farm Economics Association, long ago debunked the low-income argument as a fallacy.[20] Low per capita farm income on the *average* is neither an accurate symptom of agriculture's economic problems, nor is it remedied in any meaningful fashion by current farm policy. Indeed, figures on low *average* farm income are a statistical hoax insofar as government policy is concerned.

In the first place, the statement that farmers have a "lower than average" income is not at all meaningful in deciding if farm incomes "should" be higher or lower, because farm and nonfarm groups are not comparable in many very important ways which more accurately explain low average farm incomes. For example, the classification scheme used to identify a farm operator includes numerous persons employed in off-farm jobs, and this distorts the *overall* average farm income. Second, a larger proportion of the farm population is in the dependent class (e.g., children or workers over 65 years of age), and this too tends to explain why statistics on per capita incomes are low for the farm relative to the nonfarm population. Third, farmers have an educational attainment level which is lower than the national average and, as in the nonfarm sector, lack of education contributes to a lower average income. Furthermore, a smaller proportion of

[20] See D. Gale Johnson, "Government and Agriculture: Is Agriculture a Special Case?" in H. C. Harlan (ed.), *Readings in Economics and Politics* (New York: Oxford University Press, 1966), pp. 28–46.

the female population is in the labor force than is true in the nonfarm sector. Finally, average tax rates are lower for farmers, and the purchasing power of the farm-income dollar is higher than in the nonfarm sector. Factors such as these are vastly more meaningful explanations for low average farm incomes than the simple farm-nonfarm comparison. In evaluating overall differences in average incomes, Professor Johnson has remarked that, ". . . if the per capita income of the farm population was 65 percent of that of the nonfarm population, the returns to workers of similar age, education, and sex would be approximately comparable." Dale E. Hathaway has estimated that a farm income one-seventh below the nonfarm average provides a comparable level of living. Still others have noted that income returns to the quality of labor are higher in agriculture than in nonagriculture, and that on the average United States farmers are now moving into an era in which ". . . they will be above the average national income."[21]

Income statistics based on overall averages also badly misrepresent the nature of the farm-income problem because the expanding commercial-agriculture sector differs from the declining small farm so dramatically. Congressional studies have clearly revealed facts which have led to the conclusion that commercial farms with $20,000 or more in gross farm income ". . . average parity or more than parity returns."[22] The largest 1.5 million farming operations realize almost 90 percent of total net farm income and receive a labor return equal to or greater than that which could be earned in the nonfarm sector (ignoring off-farm income sources). Second, overall returns to management and capital in commercial farming (valued at current costs) are greater than can be earned elsewhere, and returns to *all* farming operations are approximately equal to earnings from investments in securities and other near-comparable investments.[23] Moreover, since these studies were conducted, farm subsidies have increased substantially, adding even further distortions to the distribution of income among American farmers. As a consequence of such investigations, the Council of Economic Advisers and other prestigious research organizations have concluded that farmers with gross sales over $20,000 annually earn *more* from farming than they would with the same resources in the nonfarm sector, and that those farmers receiving most of the benefits from farm-subsidy programs already have net incomes *substantially above* those received in the nonfarm sector.[24]

All of this is not to say there is no farm-income problem. Poverty is certainly a problem for the one-half million farm families with average

---

[21] G. S. Tolley, "Management Entry into U.S. Agriculture," *Journal of Farm Economics* (January 1970), p. 492; also see Johnson, *op. cit.*, p. 42; and Zvi Griliches, "Research Expenditures, Education, and the Aggregate Agricultural Production Function," *American Economic Review* (December 1964), pp. 961–974.

[22] United States Department of Agriculture, *Parity Returns Position of Farmers*, Report to the Congress of the United States, Senate Document No. 44 (90th Congress, 1st Session, 1967), p. v.

[23] Evidence submitted to Congress has shown that "in terms of net return on farmers' equity the sum of these [annual returns plus capital gains] has been slightly less than 12 percent." *Ibid.*, p. iv.

[24] Council of Economic Advisers, *Economic Report of the President*, 1969, p. 116; and Charles L. Schultze, Edward K. Hamilton, and Allen Schick, *Setting National Priorities: The 1971 Budget* (Washington, D.C.: The Brookings Institution, 1970), p. 174.

incomes of approximately $2,000 per year, which is about two-thirds the poverty-income level. Also bear in mind that there are 12 million rural Americans classified as poor and many of these represent discarded human resources once directly employed in agriculture.

## SUBSIDY DISTORTIONS

There are a variety of subsidy distortions in the American economy, many of which emanate from privileged positions of economic and political power. International trade controls and special tax favors, for example, benefit the oil industry which receives subsidies costing the American consumer no less than $4 billion annually, and quite likely much more. Or consider the automotive industry. Between $5 billion and $10 billion in annual costs of model changeovers are incurred each year. Other less visible and indirect subsidies are incurred in the hidden social costs of smog. Some portion of public-sector outlays for highways (which total more than $16 billion per year) is an indirect cost, as are some of the nearly 5,000 automotive deaths and hundreds of thousands of accidents per month—many of which could be avoided. Unlike government regulation of labor markets, however, subsidies to economic sectors such as agriculture do not promote other goals such as equality in the distribution of income which sometimes require deemphasizing efficient resource allocation. Instead, agricultural subsidies have led to greater income *inequality* as well as an *inefficient* allocation of resources.

Farm programs are very complex, involving such items as special tax favors and subsidized water supplies for irrigation as well as the price-support and supply-management programs considered earlier.[25] The two most conspicuous elements of the farm-subsidy system are *direct* cash subsidies and *indirect* subsidies arising from higher-than-equilibrium market prices achieved through supply-restriction programs (e.g., acreage diversion). Increasingly in recent years, agricultural policies have moved toward supply-management methods which generate an indirect subsidy that is not visible as a multi-billion dollar budget item for the federal government. Department of Agriculture economists estimate that *indirect* subsidy benefits for farm programs were approximately equal to the $3.5 to $4 billion spent annually for direct price-support programs each year between 1968 and 1970, meaning that farm subsidies from these two sources alone range from $7 to $8 billion annually.

Figure 6 reveals something about the nature of the income earned by farmers and the distribution of government subsidies. What is clear is that using income received from farming to gauge welfare is statistically misleading because of the large average off-farm incomes earned by farm operators. Fully one-half of realized net income received by the average farm operator (in excesses of $10,000 annually in 1969) is derived from off-farm

---

[25] For example, gross farm investment is in excess of $6 billion annually, while net investment is —$0.5 billion, thus allowing sizable reductions in taxable farm income. When tax loopholes are taken into account along with direct cash subsidies, indirect above-equilibrium price subsidies stemming from supply-management policies, low-interest loans, and international trade policies, the total subsidy to American agriculture appears to be substantially above $10 billion per year.

**FIGURE 6** Selected Summary Characteristic of United States Agriculture, 1969

(a) Income per farm operator, 1969

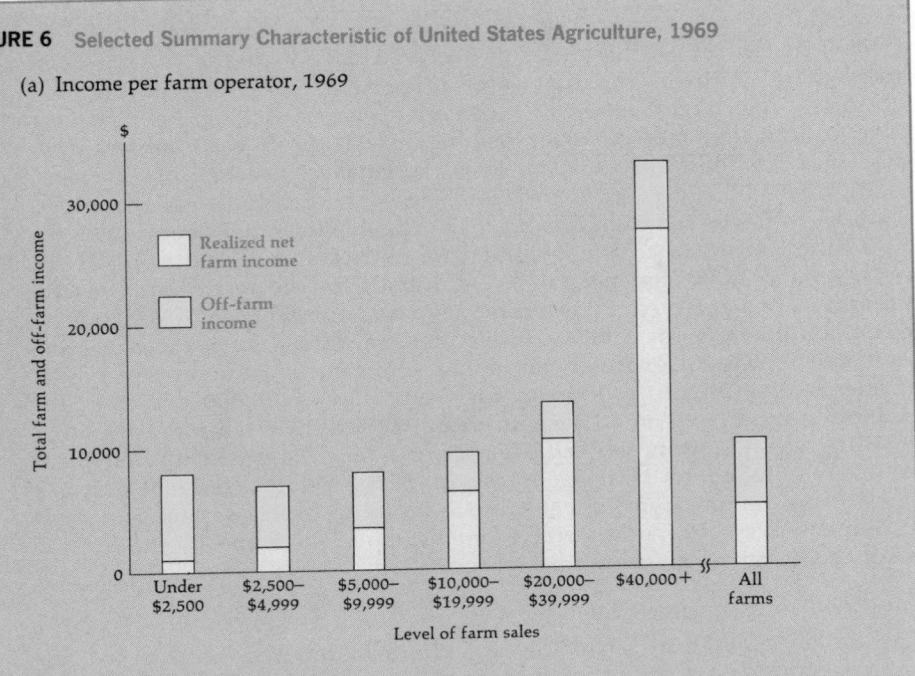

(b) The "dual" agricultural sector

| Farm sales | Realized net farm income (millions) | Realized net farm income (percent) | Distribution of farms (percent) | Distribution of government payments (percent) | Direct government payments Average per farm | Direct government payments Total (millions) |
|---|---|---|---|---|---|---|
| $ 0– 2,500 | $ 1,323 | 8.2 | 41.2 | 7.6 | $ 238 | $ 291 |
| 2,500– 4,999 | 607 | 3.8 | 9.6 | 4.6 | 615 | 176 |
| 5,000– 9,999 | 1,412 | 8.7 | 13.1 | 9.8 | 954 | 371 |
| 10,000–19,999 | 3,273 | 20.3 | 17.0 | 23.8 | 1,788 | 903 |
| 20,000–39,999 | 3,736 | 23.1 | 12.0 | 24.8 | 2,630 | 939 |
| 40,000 or more | 5,803 | 35.9 | 7.1 | 29.4 | 5,280 | 1,114 |
| Total | $16,154 | 100.0 | 100.0 | 100.0 | | $3,794 |

*Farm Income and Subsidies.* On the average, off-farm income is as large as farm income for all operators. Government payments and realized net farm income are directly related to farm production as the larger farm operators realize a much larger share of income and subsidy payments than the smaller farm operators.

SOURCE: Department of Agriculture, *Farm Income Situation,* July 1970, pp. 68–73.

sources. Indeed, off-farm income accounts for more than two-thirds of the average income earned by the 1.5 million smallest farm operators generating less than $5,000 of gross sales annually. Notice, however, that realized net income per farm operator for commercial farms selling $20,000 or more annually is sizable and is composed primarily of net income realized from farming.

The chief distortion in existing farm policy is the result of basing subsidies, which allegedly benefit low-income farmers, on the quantity of output produced by a farm operation. Figure 6 shows that over 1.3 million or the smallest two-fifths of farms received only 8 percent of net farm income and approximately that same proportion of existing government subsidies. The largest 600,000 commercial farms, selling in excess of $20,000 annually, received over one-half of all direct cash subsidies, or more than $2 billion in 1969, whereas the smallest one-half of all farms, selling under $5,000 in farm products each year, received less than $500 million in direct cash subsidies. Subsidy payments range from $239 for the smallest farms to an average payment in excess of $5,000 annually for the largest 211,000 commercial farms. Indeed, in the recent past several hundred farms received government payments ranging from $100,000 to $1 million or more for a few giant commercial farms. Such excesses have prompted repeated Congressional attempts to limit maximum government payments to farmers. A limit on cash subsidies of $5,000 per crop, for example, would have no adverse affect on 90 percent of all farm operators growing wheat, cotton, or feed grains, yet a much larger ceiling payment of $20,000 failed to clear Congress in 1970. While President Nixon's $55,000 maximum payment per crop to any one farm operator is an improvement over the pork-barrel economic policies of the recent past, it hardly represents a meaningful correction.

## SOME UNSETTLED ISSUES

The declining political power of agriculture in recent years has led numerous observers to argue for a more effective organization of farmers—a parallel to collective bargaining for agriculture. Farm interests have succeeded in obtaining some market power through past government programs; however, they are not as tightly knit a group as labor organizations, for example.

In defense of monopoly power for farmers some authorities argue that other sectors of the economy which sell to or buy from the farmer are favored by imperfectly competitive markets. It is also argued by some observers that large surpluses are required for domestic or foreign-aid purposes. In contrast, other authorities believe that greater monopoly power may do more harm than good, just as the inordinate political power of past decades led to abuses already discussed.[26] Many authorities also question the need for larger farm surpluses, which they see as already substantial. Opinions vary on the collective-bargaining issue, but the consensus seems to run against it as a solution to the problem of poverty and the allocation of too many resources in agriculture. More likely than not, bargaining in agriculture will do little for the marginal farmer who produces very little output.

In addition, the preferred way to counter monopoly power and resource misallocation in part of the economy is to destroy it there, not create it in other sectors. Moreover, many observers have noted that the degree of monopoly which exists elsewhere in the American economy is often exaggerated. Farmers have enjoyed considerable market power and privileges through government, as price supports, supply quotas, and marketing agreements demonstrate; yet, such "power" has not resolved the farm

[26] Johnson, op. cit., p. 34.

problem. Instead, these arrangements have left excess resources in agriculture while helping those least in need of assistance. Opinions vary on all of these issues, but most economists agree with Professor Johnson's conclusions that there are no basic considerations which demonstrate ". . . that the present large-scale program of price supports and other subsidies is any more warranted in agriculture than in almost any other part of the economy."[27]

## NEW DIRECTIONS TO FARM POLICY

Current farm policy actually accentuates the maldistribution of income among farmers, since those who receive the bulk of the benefits already have net incomes in excess of the average income level for the American population.

Convincing evidence about the distortion effects of farm subsidies is best shown by the Lorenz curves of Figure 7, which compare (a) the percentage distribution of the American population and the distribution of income with (b) the percentage distribution of farmers and farm-subsidy payments to farmers. The percentage of the total American population (measured on the horizontal axis) receiving different shares of family in-

[27] *Ibid.*, p. 45.

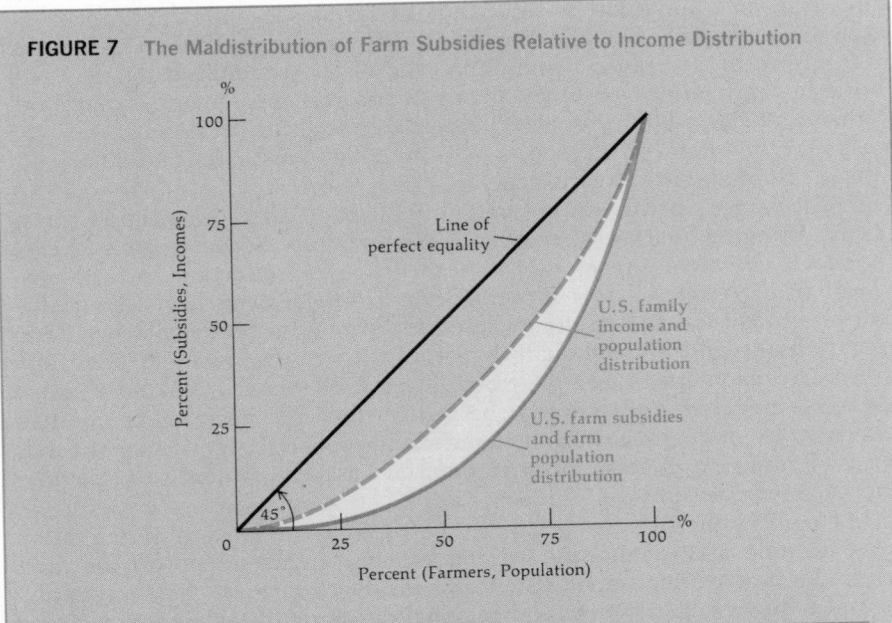

**FIGURE 7** The Maldistribution of Farm Subsidies Relative to Income Distribution

*Maldistribution of Subsidy Payments.* A Lorenz-curve comparison shows how agricultural subsidies are more unequally distributed than family income in the United States. Perfect equality is shown by the 45° line. The percent of American families receiving a given percent of income is shown by the dashed gold Lorenz curve, while the percent of farm operators receiving a given percent of farm subsidy payments is shown by the solid gold Lorenz curve.

come (as shown by the vertical axis) is shown by the dashed Lorenz curve of Figure 7. If income were distributed equally to the population 20, 30, and 60 percent of all Americans would earn 20, 30, and 60 percent of all income, as is denoted by the 45° line of perfect equality in Figure 7. The further one moves rightward or away from the 45° line, the greater the degree of income inequality. Figure 7 also compares the percentage of farmers (the horizontal axis) receiving a given percentage of direct-cash subsidy payments (the vertical axis). The crucial point in comparing the two Lorenz curves of Figure 7 is simply that government subsidies are *more* unequally distributed than family income. While 40 percent of all farm operators receive about 7 percent of total farm subsidies, 40 percent of the American population receive some 18 percent of all family income in the United States. Thus, instead of relieving the all-too-real income problem faced by the least affluent 30 or 40 percent of farm operators, the farm-subsidy program *increases income inequality!*

In view of a continually changing agricultural sector, new directions are needed if public policy is to deal effectively with American agricultural and rural economic problems. Wholesale changes in farm policy are required in three distinct directions.

1. Certain forms of government assistance for developmental purposes (particularly scientific research) should be continued. In the past, research efforts have made the American agricultural sector the most productive in the world, and hundreds of thousands of farmers cannot duplicate these services individually. In addition, continuation of government assistance in the form of insurance to minimize short-run economic instability will encourage agricultural efficiency among commercial-farming operations and is therefore desirable—provided political abuses can be avoided. For the most part, however, other aspects of farm policy must change dramatically from a retarded, bureaucratic snarl to a people-oriented program.

2. The larger need is purposive elimination of farm price-support programs. Bringing market supply and demand into closer balance over a period of a relatively few years is needed if overproduction and the misallocation of resources now in agriculture are to be remedied. Reformulation of agricultural policy along these lines would encourage efficient farm operations capable of making full use of an ever-advancing technology, allowing consumers to benefit from lower food prices. Whatever rather negligible negative effects might be felt by low-income farmers could be alleviated by more direct income maintenance policies as government funds released from the price-support program are used to combat rural poverty and economic decline.

3. Finally, policies must be implemented to accommodate outmigration from farming and fashion decent employment opportunities for the rural poor, many of whom are subsistence or displaced farmers. Income supplements, relocation assistance, and regional-development plans are required to resolve the farm problem and refurbish rural America. Federal aid for education and housing, extensive education efforts to assist in rural community development, and updating of other social services can restore selected rural communities to viable economic units and take some of the population pressure off already crowded urban centers. Public-policy efforts are now beginning to promote rural development, but the most important

resource—human beings—is largely ignored today. For the most part, farm policy continues to be bogged down by government bureaucracy in which direct Department of Agriculture expenditures averaging in excess of $2,000 per farm do remarkably little to remedy the problem of maldistribution of income in agriculture. Whereas public policy has ignored market imperfections and failure associated with human resources, it has intervened unnecessarily in relatively competitive product markets and thereby distorted the allocation of resources and failed for its trouble.

Unfortunately, politics can favor bad economic policy. Those victimized by a declining agricultural sector perceive their plight as excessive competition instead of inadequate outward mobility from the industry. The situation of American agriculture demonstrates that as a competitive sector of the economy undergoes rapid change, public policies to encourage and facilitate the transfer of resources are needed. Protecting the misallocation of resources serves only to intensify rather than solve serious economic problems, and it matters very little whether the source of protection is monopoly economic power or political power in a relatively competitive sector of the economy.

## REVIEW

### Summary

1. Microeconomic policies are applied to problems associated with both monopoly and competitive market adjustments. The degree of monopolization in the structure of one given market is revealed by the concentration of assets and profits among the largest three or four firms in an industry. The proportion of assets and profits controlled by the largest 100 or 200 firms is suggestive of aggregate concentration and monopoly power. When product differentiation and entry barriers are recognized along with concentration trends, it is clear that the structure of the American market economy is by no means perfectly competitive.

2. The conduct and performance characteristics accompanying a monopolized market structure generally conform to the predictions of economic theory. Firms do influence product price and practice nonprice competition leading to market performance characterized by the misallocation and inefficient use of resources. Evaluation of the industrial organization of markets also tends to confirm the fact that firms operating in monopolized markets earn larger profit rates, that monopoly is not necessary to the achievement of economic efficiency (except in the case of "natural" monopolies), and that there is little evidence to support the claim that technological advance is more common in heavily monopolized markets than in a more competitive market structure. However, definitive evidence against monopoly, like that against the recent conglomerate merger movement, is sometimes difficult to come by, even though conclusions drawn from economic theory lean toward disapproval.

3. Public concern for the exercise of monopoly power resulted in the passage of the Sherman Act (1890). Other major legislative measures that have rounded out antitrust policy in the United States include the Clayton Act, the Federal Trade Commission Act, and the Celler-Kefau-

ver Antimerger Act. The effectiveness of antitrust policy is spotty, partially because enforcement has not been consistently vigilant, and also because the law has not been applied fully to existing monopolies. However, most observers concede that antitrust policies have been useful and will remain an important ingredient in avoiding greater concentration of economic power in the future. .

4. There are two sectors in agriculture—the growing and relatively prosperous commercial sector and the sector typified by smaller farms which are declining rapidly in number and importance. Although paradoxical in certain ways, government has established rather elaborate public policies to cope with competitive market failures in agriculture as well as other sectors of the economy (e.g., labor legislation and patent laws). The basic farm problem is the overallocation of resources to agriculture accompanied by economic decline and poverty for the least efficient farm operations.

5. Because of rapidly increasing supply, inelastic and slowly growing demand, and competitive market pressures, farm prices have been subjected to downward pressures. Some human resources remain locked in agriculture at low income levels and rural poverty is not uncommon because of such disadvantages as old age and lack of education, as well as the absence of alternative employment opportunities.

6. Agricultural policy is allegedly directed at raising the low income levels of farmers. Price supports can be implemented through parity-price schemes, programs designed to increase the demand for farm products, and supply-management programs. Developmental programs in agriculture have been useful and effective, although their consequence has been to increase agricultural output and maintain downward pressures on farm prices.

7. Agricultural policy has been misguided and relatively ineffective in resolving the farm-income problem. Moreover, it is not at all clear that *average* farm incomes are disproportionately low. Indeed, the evidence clearly shows that this is not the case for the commercial agricultural sector which receives the bulk of farm subsidies. Overall income averages conceal the maldistribution of farm income and mask poverty for several hundreds of thousands of farmers. The real tragedy of the current agricultural program is that these policies contribute to the overallocation of resources to agriculture and also help those least in need of welfare assistance, while ignoring the smallest and least affluent farmers, many of whom live in poverty.

8. As now constituted, the farm program contributes to *more* rather than *less* income inequality. If agricultural policy is to be effective, it must: (a) continue to provide developmental and economic stabilization assistance to commercial agriculture and rural America at large, (b) gradually but purposively withdraw direct and indirect price-support programs, and (c) aid the transfer of resources from agriculture while fashioning employment opportunities in the nonfarm sector. If income assistance is deemed appropriate for farmers living in poverty, it should be forthcoming because they are poor, not because they are farmers.

- natural monopolies
- market concentration
- tying arrangements
- price discrimination
- supply management
- Lorenz curve
- conglomerate mergers
- market conduct
- Sherman Antitrust Act
- price supports
- parity price and income

## Questions to Answer

1. Explain the meaning of market conduct, structure, and performance. What are some of the indicators of structure, conduct, and performance in a monopolized market? How are these three features of the industrial organization of markets related to each other?

2. Briefly explain the major pieces of legislation which now furnish a legal basis for antitrust policy. Evaluate the effectiveness of the legislation.

3. Using the concepts of supply and demand, illustrate and explain: (a) the nature of downward price pressures on agricultural products, (b) the usage of price supports, and (c) how supply-management policies are used to implement agricultural policy.

4. Explain and evaluate the following statements:
   (a) "Price supports are needed to bolster low farm incomes."
   (b) "The farm problem is one of too many resources allocated to agriculture."
   (c) "All that we have to do to solve the farm problem and use resources efficiently is to set a maximum on the amount of output each farmer can produce."

# CHAPTER 22
# Environmental Economics: The Quality of Life

While it is clear that economic growth has benefited mankind, equality and quality in life are by no means assured by growth in aggregate income. Both the distribution of and the growth in a nation's income are at the focal point of the environmental-quality problem. As President Nixon has said, "At the heart of this concern for the environment lies our concern for the human condition: for the welfare of man himself, now and in the future."[1]

There are two basic dimensions to the quality of life and the environment—the individual and the aggregate. First, if individual incomes are unequal, individual shares of whatever quality of life a socioeconomic system and the natural environment provide are also unequal. Because of the preferential way a society distributes its output to its citizens, the quality of life is vastly different for millions of people, particularly those at the lower and the uppermost extremes. Thus, environmental quality and the "human condition" must be viewed at the personal level.

The total environment is also an important economic problem for society today, as anyone who has experienced air and water pollution will recognize. The quality of man's environment in this broader context is conditioned by growth in GNP, which overstates (perhaps massively) how much better or worse off a nation is as output rises. This overstatement is due to the fact that the production of more output of "goods" also entails the creation of pollutants or "bads," as Professor Kenneth Boulding once chided. Bads assume a variety of overt and subtle forms such as physical pollution of the air and water and urban congestion and blight. The quality of life, then, is the joint product of the personal distribution of income *and* the aggregate level of deterioration of the general environment.

Individual opportunities are determined partly by the personal distribution of income, the subject of Part A. Part B describes the dimensions and magnitude of the pollution problem, and Part C explains the causes of pollution. Finally, Part D reviews the policy implications of environmental-quality issues in the United States, particularly the aggregate environmental problem.

[1] Richard M. Nixon, "Presidential Message to Congress" in *Environmental Quality*, First Annual Report of the Council on Environmental Quality (Washington, D.C.: U.S. Government Printing Office, 1970), p. xv.

Stripped of artifacts of control, it is the philosophy and values of a people that determine environmental quality at both the personal and the aggregate levels. Environmental quality depends upon a healthy functioning of man-made and natural systems of control and, as President Nixon once stated, "While growth has brought extraordinary benefits, it has not been accompanied by sufficiently farsighted efforts to guide its development."[2] Changing the quality of an environment both in terms of personal income distribution and at the aggregate level requires difficult value judgments which are by no means agreed upon. Difficult though such issues may be, they are all too real today. A nation can opt to distribute more or less of its output to the wealthy vs. the poor, or it can elect to use public resources to enhance military security rather than renewing the urban environment. The economics of these decisions are of obvious interest to a society.

Although income inequality is a less conspicuous dimension to the environmental quality of life than air or water pollution, the personal distribution of income does affect mankind's environment by allowing some to bask in luxury while others struggle to survive. Different groups may benefit or may be harmed within the general environment in unequal ways as a society uses its resource base for economic production. Because of extremes in the distribution of income, vast differences occur in the quality of life for different socioeconomic classes—the wealthy can provide themselves with amenities privately, while the quality of life progressively deteriorates for the less affluent.

## Income Distribution

The way a society's income is distributed to the factors of production used to produce goods and services is the *functional distribution* of income. Over the course of this century the proportions of income going to labor and capital in the long run have remained relatively constant, drifting modestly in the direction of a larger income share to labor. The functional distribution of income is important in some contexts, but it is of little value in investigating how income is distributed to family units or to individuals. This is the *personal distribution* of income, and it depends upon the quality and quantity of resources available to an individual and the price those resources command in the marketplace. Families owning few resources or less productive resources which sell cheaply in the market simply do not participate in the economic game on equal terms with those owning vast quantities of high-priced resources.

The bulk of Americans are neither rich nor poor. Although income is more equally distributed in some nations (e.g., Sweden or Great Britain), it is less equally distributed in others (India and many South American nations, for example). Nevertheless, in a nation of some 205 million persons there are bound to be extremes—the "super-rich" whose affluence astounds even the relatively well-off American, and the forgotten Americans who live from hand to mouth. Figure 1 gives some idea of the extent of the inequality in income distribution among family units.[3] Comparisons of in-

---

[2] *Ibid.*, pp. vi–vii.

[3] Family income is not adjusted for taxes and also *excludes* income received from expense accounts, capital gains, and earnings retained by corporations (which add to stockholder equity).

**FIGURE 1**   U.S. Income Distribution by Family

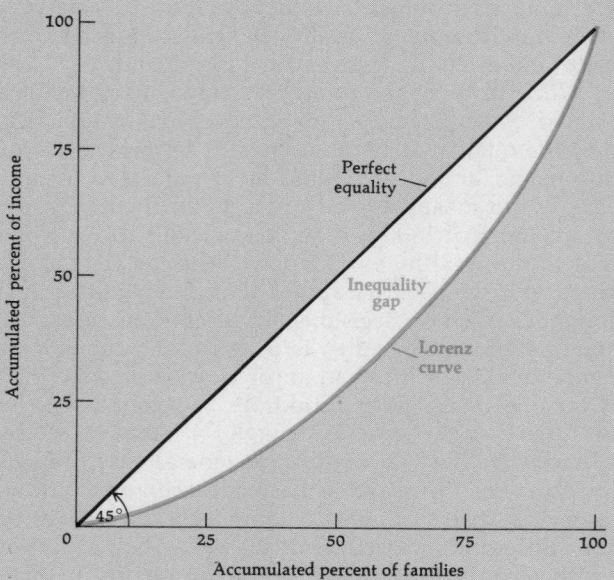

| Millions of families | Millions of persons | Percent of families | Percent of income | | Per capita income | Family income level |
|---|---|---|---|---|---|---|
| 4.0 | 11.8 | 7.9 | 1.2 | | $  500 | $  1,475 |
| 7.3 | 24.0 | 14.5 | 5.7 | | 1,158 | 3,800 |
| 11.4 | 40.8 | 22.6 | 15.2 | | 1,821 | 6,518 |
| 14.0 | 53.3 | 27.7 | 28.1 | | 3,574 | 9,800 |
| 12.5 | 48.7 | 24.7 | 40.1 | | 4,021 | 15,664 |
| 1.3 | 5.3 | 2.6 | 9.7 | | 8,943 | 36,180 |
| Total  50.5 | 183.9 | 100.0 | 100.0 | Average | $2,656 | $  9,670 |

*Income Inequality.* The gold Lorenz curve shows the degree of income inequality. A perfect equality line is a 45° line showing the cumulative percent of the population (the horizontal axis) receiving a cumulative percent of income (the vertical axis). The above data also show the level of income by family on a per capita basis for all persons in families (excluding unrelated individuals).

SOURCE: *Current Population Reports*, P-60, No. 66, 1969. (Data are for 1968.)

come distribution for family units exclude about 7 percent of the household population living as unrelated household units, a large number of whom are single and often elderly persons. Because the average income of such unrelated persons is lower than average family income, the distribution of income by family shown in Figure 1 tends to understate the existing inequality in income distribution.

Average family incomes for the poorest 4 million American families are one-twentieth the family income level of the 1.3 million families at the highest income level. Some 11.8 million persons live in families with an average income of $1,475 compared to a family income of $36,180 for the

5.3 million persons in the highest income groups. At these same two extremes, average per capita income ranges from a low of $500 to a high of nearly $9,000.

As the data of Figure 1 indicate, 7.9 percent of all American families earned 1.2 percent of total family income, whereas, at the upper extreme, 2.6 percent of all families earned nearly 10 percent of total family income. Perfectly equal distribution of income would exist if 7.9 percent of all families received 7.9 percent of all family income. Figure 1 measures the degree of income inequality among American families with the aid of a Lorenz curve. Perfect income equality is shown by a 45° line—the blue line of Figure 1—indicating that 25 or 75 percent of income (measured vertically) would go to 25 or 75 percent of all families (measured on the horizontal axis). The existing pattern of income distribution, shown by the gold Lorenz curve of Figure 1, indicates the percentage of families that earned some accumulated percent of income. It shows that 22.4 percent of all families earned 6.9 percent of all income, 45 percent of all families earned 22.1 percent of all income, and so forth. Movement of the Lorenz curve toward the 45° equality line would indicate the achievement of greater equality in the distribution of income, whereas any rightward change would indicate less equality.

Figure 2 shows a different and needed perspective on changes in the

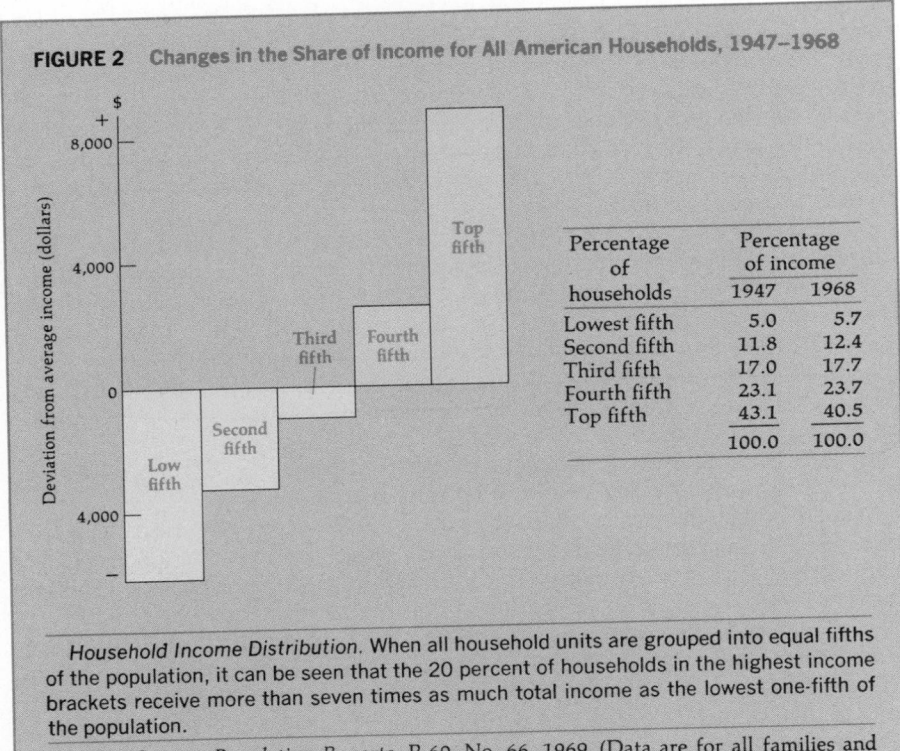

**FIGURE 2** Changes in the Share of Income for All American Households, 1947–1968

| Percentage of households | Percentage of income | |
|---|---|---|
| | 1947 | 1968 |
| Lowest fifth | 5.0 | 5.7 |
| Second fifth | 11.8 | 12.4 |
| Third fifth | 17.0 | 17.7 |
| Fourth fifth | 23.1 | 23.7 |
| Top fifth | 43.1 | 40.5 |
| | 100.0 | 100.0 |

*Household Income Distribution.* When all household units are grouped into equal fifths of the population, it can be seen that the 20 percent of households in the highest income brackets receive more than seven times as much total income as the lowest one-fifth of the population.

SOURCE: *Current Population Reports*, P-60, No. 66, 1969. (Data are for all families and all unrelated individuals.)

distribution of income for each one-fifth of American households during the last two decades. Considerable deviation from perfect equality in the distribution of income prevails, as data for *all* households—both families *and* unrelated individuals—show. The poorest 20 percent of households earn an annual income that is approximately $6,000 *below* the national average. In contrast, the most affluent 20 percent of American families receive an average income that is more than twice the national average. When all households are grouped into equal fifths of the population, as they are in Figure 2, we can see that the wealthiest 20 percent of the population receive about 40 percent of all income and the poorest 20 percent of households receive less than 6 percent of total income. Average income for the most affluent one-fifth of all households provides a level of living (and thus a quality of life) about eight times as large as that of the least affluent group. Note, too, that the distribution of income has not changed appreciably since 1947, in spite of government welfare payments, unemployment compensation, social security, and the like.

## Two Views on Inequality

Viewpoints on the proper degree of income inequality differ substantially, and righteous indignation usually accompanies the arguments for and against greater equality in the distribution of income. Those who support the prevailing degree of income inequality mount a variety of arguments in defense of their position. It is said, for example, that inequality is necessary to a smoothly functioning economy in which productive resources freely flow from one economic activity to others at the behest of market prices, profits, and income. Another argument offered is that work incentives are enhanced because of the unequal distribution of income. A third frequently heard view is that an unequal distribution of income encourages a rapid rate of economic growth and investment because the wealthy consume less and save more.

Proponents of greater equality in the distribution of income feel quite differently. These critics believe less inequality would not hamper the mobility of resources and the operation of the economy. They argue that executives and physicians might well perform their tasks with equal diligence given incomes two or three times the national average instead of the existing multiples of ten or more. While incentives may not be related as firmly to large income differentials as some believe, this is an issue on which we have very little concrete evidence either way. Those advocating less inequality also refute the investment and capital-formation claim as contrary to fact and, in any event, devoid of social purpose.

Debates on such normative matters are bound to continue. Barring definitive research evidence, each person must judge the merit of the cases for and against income inequality. If the distribution of income is excessively lopsided, equal access to education, housing, medical care, and quality in life in general is also distorted. Ownership and control of the industrial sector of the economy essentially rest in the hands of 5 percent of the population; indeed, many observers have noted that one or two thousands families and institutions have effective control over the vast bulk of this nation's productive capacity. It is important to attain a tolerable distribution of income that disperses economic and political power, maintains equal opportunity for all, enhances the productivity of all workers, and achieves social welfare for the poor as well as the rich. Although opinions vary upon just what is "tolerable," most students of income distribution recognize that considerable inequality remains in the United States.

Unequal distribution of income and the consequent inequality in the quality of life are a product of: (a) factors which influence the earnings of human resources, and (b) the distribution of wealth in the form of property resources.

## INEQUALITY, ABILITY, AND OPPORTUNITY

The saying "All men are created equal" may be valid with reference to the spirit of man, but not with respect to his economic fortunes. From the standpoint of what men can garner from an economic system by virtue of their labor, millions of Americans suffer from a series of cumulative disadvantages which do not reflect individual qualities. Disadvantaged, uninformed, and physically or mentally handicapped individuals usually pay a price for what they lack, just as a few very talented artists, athletes, and business leaders reap great rewards for their unique qualities. Discrimination on the basis of race, sex, age, and ethnic background is another unfortunate reality that helps explain income inequality. All persons are not equally motivated or ambitious, nor is equal opportunity available to all. Studies have repeatedly demonstrated that the probability of acquiring wealth, a high income, and a good education is reduced for children coming from poorer homes. Finally, unequal opportunity and income inequality reflects the fact that life itself is apt to distribute fortune and misfortune in capricious ways. The loss of a job, physical disability, or a recurrent illness can and does contribute to income inequality just as good luck and the "right" contacts may lead to higher levels of living for the fortunate.

## THE DISTRIBUTION OF ECONOMIC WEALTH AND POWER

Were wealth distributed according to the natural abilities of different men there would be a great deal less income inequality. Although it is difficult to gauge the reliability of various studies on the distribution of wealth, we do know that the distribution of property resources is even more decidedly skewed in favor of high-income groups than the distribution of income shown by the Lorenz curve of Figure 1. In short, income inequality can be traced back to wealth ownership in significant ways. A second important by-product of the concentration of wealth is the maldistribution of political and economic power in favor of those enjoying privileged income positions. Chapter 5 reported on the surprisingly low income taxes enjoyed by the wealthy in America in the latter 1960s, and this situation is an excellent indicator of the political privileges that emanate from the concentration of income and economic power.[4] Thus, in addition to differences in the quantity and the quality of labor services, the maldistribution of wealth and the concentration of political power provide economic privileges for segments of the American population.

[4] Hundreds of American households with incomes of $100,000 or more each year and even some with $1 million or more income paid no taxes in 1969. See United States Congress, Committee on Ways and Means, *Tax Reform Studies and Proposals of the U.S. Treasury Department*, Parts I, II, and III, 1969.

The most frequently cited studies on this subject in recent years are those of Professor Robert Lampman done for the National Bureau of Economic Research, a series of continuing surveys conducted by the University of Michigan on consumer finances, and more recently the provocative work of Ferdinand Lundberg.[5] Some of the more pertinent conclusions reached from studies of the distribution of private wealth are as follows.

About 1 percent of all household units own between two-thirds and three-fourths of all state and local government bonds and corporate stocks and bonds. The upper 1 percent of the population—the very, very rich—control about one-fourth of *all* personally owned private wealth. Moreover, the concentration of private wealth has not decreased appreciably since the 1940s, but rather has remained steady or increased slightly.[6] At the other extreme, approximately one-tenth of all household units in the United States have zero or negative property wealth. More than one out of four American households have assets equivalent in value to only two to three months' pay and these property assets are usually in the form of "trinkets" of contemporary life (e.g., automobiles, television sets, and other relatively valueless household furnishings). Indeed, fully one-half of the least wealthy Americans can claim assets with an average value of less than the average U.S. family's income for one year. All told, one-half of the American population divides ownership of less than one-tenth of the nation's wealth, whereas one-fiftieth of the population owns one-third of the national wealth.

Because wealth ownership is the handmaiden of unequal income distribution, it also is an indicator of the unequal distribution of the quality of life for millions of Americans. When it is also recognized that substantial economic wealth does no harm to those aspiring to political office, particularly at the national level, the implications for men of ordinary means is clear. The latter rarely, if ever, reach Congress, and many state and local offices are also out of the grasp of those lacking the wealth such "public service" requires. Whether concentrated power and wealth bode ill or well for the nation need not be judged here, but concentrated wealth is as much a fact as is the inequality in the distribution of income.

Perhaps the gravest danger of income inequality in the United States is that it perpetuates unequal opportunities, social division, and very real differences in the quality of life. Most economists agree that while some inequality in the distribution of income is useful, the existing degree of inequality is devoid of any economic merit, ethical issues quite aside. Because the personal effects of inequality pose issues much too complicated to treat tersely here, we shall devote a later chapter to them.[7]

[5] See Robert Lampman, *The Share of Top Wealth-Holders in National Wealth: 1922–56* (Princeton, N.J.: National Bureau of Economic Research, 1962); and Ferdinand Lundberg, *The Rich and Super-Rich* (New York: Bantam Books, 1968). Data from the Survey Research Center of the University of Michigan are reported in annual issues of the *Statistical Abstract of the United States* (Washington, D.C.: U.S. Department of Commerce).

[6] These are Lampman's findings also confirmed in James D. Smith and Stauntan K. Calvert, "Estimating the Wealth of Top Wealth-Holders from Estate Tax Returns," *American Statistical Association Proceedings* (September 1965).

[7] See Chapter 24.

Unequal distribution of income is one aspect of the quality-of-life problem, but personal hardships due to inequality extremes are the unfortunate lot of a minority of the American population. Environmental deterioriation has a somewhat more even, although still unequal impact on a population.

The facts about environmental pollution reveal that "progress" threatens to engulf entire nations. Literally billions of tons of air, water, and waste pollutants are thrust into the environment each year. In the United States, more than 7 million cars are junked annually, along with hundreds of millions of tons of waste paper and sewage. The world's population is growing in a nearly uncontrolled fashion, and even in a nation with moderate population growth such as the United States, each week of the year means that 40,000 additional people must be serviced by an environment with a carrying capacity that is being depleted. The volume of debris and pollution doubles about every 10 years in this country, and people and debris characterize most developed nations of the world. Like large portions of the Great Lakes, Tokyo Bay has become an open sewage system incapable of supporting aquatic life, while Paris rivals New York and Los Angeles in the contamination of air.

There are some interesting quantitative dimensions to the quality of life that are now coming before the populace, and they confirm what most citizens know from first-hand experience: Adam didn't eat the apple core; he threw it in the river which served both as his source of drinking water and sewer. Debasement and pollution of the environment is both a natural and a special by-product of the creation of goods. It is natural in the sense that modern technology and contemporary values have allowed and encouraged environmental decay, and it is special in the sense that preoccupation with *quantity* in life has led nations to ignore *quality*. The reason for such behavior is largely economic, because the "cost" of polluting can often be shifted to others. This is why environmental economics is a crucial subject today.

## Sources of Pollution

The first important fact about the economics of pollution is that the environment is limited in supply, making it susceptible to pollution, degradation, and depletion through abuse and misuse. Professor Kenneth Boulding has called our environment the "spaceship earth"—a limited reservoir that cannot be polluted forever.[8] If it was ever assumed that natural resources such as land, water, and air would absorb indefinitely the waste output that a growing GNP produces, this is now seen as an error. As the population of developed nations has grown, increased quantities of per capita output and consumption have not been matched by efforts to monitor debasement of the environment by producers and consumers. The open luxury of the past—an era characterized by dumping of the residuals of production and consumption—is fast ending as the limits of our finite ecological system are reached. Among the most offensive types of environmental pollution at the present time are: (*a*) air pollution, (*b*) water contamination, (*c*) people

[8] Kenneth E. Boulding, "The Economics of the Coming Spaceship Earth," in Henry Jarret (ed.), *Environmental Quality in a Growing Economy*, Sixth Resources for the Future Forum (Baltimore, Md.: Johns Hopkins Press, 1966), pp. 3–15.

pollution and urban sprawl, and (*d*) pollution due to noise, chemicals, wastes, and radiation.

## AIR POLLUTION

Air pollution is largely a phenomenon of urban living in over 200 densely populated metropolitan centers. While man has proven to be very adept in transforming nature's resources into products ultimately designed for consumption, only very primitive methods of coping with smog and smoke have been developed throughout the world. Indeed, one report alleges that the typical nonsmoking New Yorker absorbs the toxic equivalent of 38 cigarettes a day in the form of air pollutants.[9] In urban centers, the capacity of the air to dilute pollutants is inadequate because of population and industrial concentration, and the death rates from diseases such as lung cancer and emphysema are rising rapidly. About 100 million tons of carbon monoxide, a poisonous but colorless and odorless gas, are discharged into the air annually. In addition, another 100 million tons of four other major pollutants are inventoried in the air each year.[10] Modern transportation systems alone account for 42 percent of the total volume of air pollution, including two-thirds of the pollution due to carbon monoxide. Stationary pollution due to energy production and industrial manufacturing processes plus automotive transportation account for nearly two-thirds of all air pollution today.

The potential importance of automobiles and energy production as sources of pollution is illustrated in Figure 3. Barring any changes in air pollutants attributable to automotive transportation, automobiles may be generating 200 million tons of carbon monoxide pollutants per year within some two decades, as Figure 3(a) shows. If proposed 1975 emission standards are adopted, however, carbon monoxide as *one* form of automotive pollution will decline to one-third the 1970 level of more than 65 million tons per year. Figure 3(b) shows the rapid growth expected in nonnuclear fueled energy production between 1970 and 1995—a growth projected at more than 7 trillion annual kilowatt hours. The production of energy from nonnuclear fuels creates severe air- and water-pollution problems, while nuclear sources of energy pose difficult radiation problems, as we shall see; therefore, energy production also ranks high along with the automobile as a source of pollution.

Air pollution is also influenced by wind speed and atmospheric conditions which may trap polluted air in basins or bay areas via the familiar phenomenon known as "inversion." Known to be a chief contributor to extraordinary numbers of deaths on certain such occasions, air pollution also inflicts substantial damages on materials and buildings.[11] Air pollution can also produce global changes in climate and temperatures. Man does not yet know what such changes in the environment may lead to, but another

[9] See Robert Reenow and Leona Train Reenow, "38 Cigarettes a Day," in Garrett De Bell (ed.), *The Environmental Handbook* (New York: Ballantine Books, 1970), p. 113.

[10] Data cited here and on the following pages concerning the magnitude of various forms of pollution are taken primarily from the First Annual Report of the Council on Environmental Quality, *op. cit.*, chs. 3–7.

[11] The "killer smog" experienced by London in 1952 brought death to an estimated 4,000 Britishers.

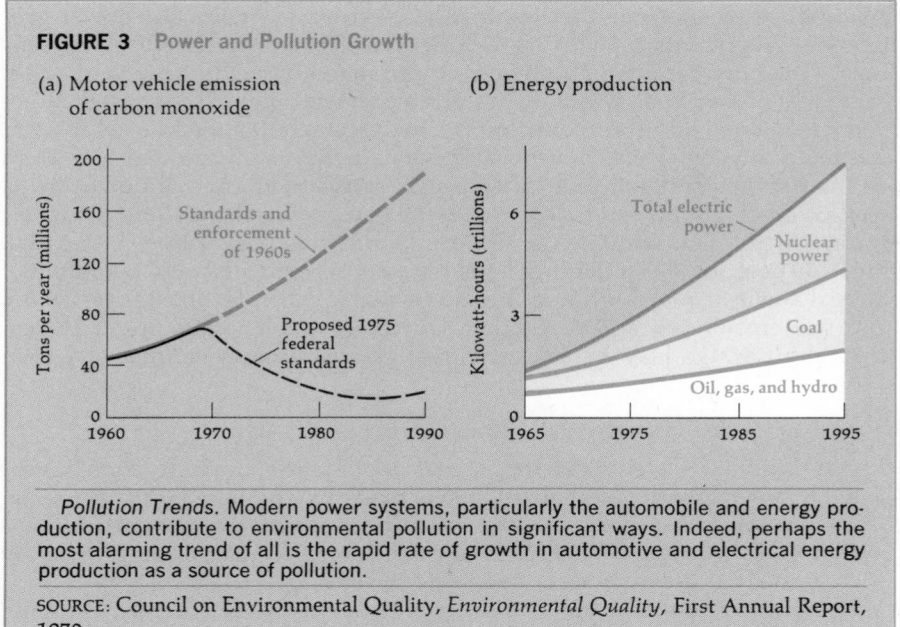

**FIGURE 3**   Power and Pollution Growth

(a) Motor vehicle emission of carbon monoxide

(b) Energy production

*Pollution Trends.* Modern power systems, particularly the automobile and energy production, contribute to environmental pollution in significant ways. Indeed, perhaps the most alarming trend of all is the rapid rate of growth in automotive and electrical energy production as a source of pollution.

SOURCE: Council on Environmental Quality, *Environmental Quality*, First Annual Report, 1970.

disastrous ice age or, more likely, a catastrophic melting of the ice caps may occur because the earth's air and atmosphere have been altered in measurable ways.

## WATER POLLUTION

Over the ages, societies have experienced epidemics and plagues due to polluted and unsanitary water and, even though modern medicines have helped conquer disease, water pollution has recently reached new crisis proportions. According to the Federal Water Quality Administration, about one-third of this nation's waterways are contaminated, and not just a few are open cesspools incapable of sustaining marine life. Fertilizers, pesticides, detergents, human wastes, and industrial sewage have transformed vast bodies of water such as Lake Erie and southern Lake Michigan into open cesspools.

Moreover, the use of vast quantities of water in producing energy and processing industrial products discharges thermal and chemical wastes that harm and even destroy aquatic life. As the waste loads dumped into water are increased, the oxygen required to decompose them is rapidly consumed, ultimately destroying marine forms of life. The final result is dark, slimy water with no oxygen, no life, and an overwhelming odor.

The most important sources of water pollution are industry, municipal power, and agriculture. Some 300,000 factories in the United States discharge three times as much waste into American waters as does the total sewered population, and the electric power, paper, chemical, steel, and petroleum industries rank high among the leaders in contaminating water.

Many observers believe that thermal heat—a waste product of power production—represents the most serious source of future water pollution. Currently the power industry alone uses more than 40 trillion gallons of water each year. Municipal waste-disposal requirements double every ten years and also loom large as contributors to water contamination. Moreover, adequate municipal waste-disposal systems currently serve only one-third of the nation's population. Incidents such as the Santa Barbara offshore oil leak of 1969 and an estimated 10,000 other oil spills also pollute navigable waters in the United States each year. All of this occurs in a nation that must dispose of 350 million gallons of used oil annually plus a volume of animal wastes equal in bulk to 2 billion people. When fertilizers, pesticides, and soil erosion are added to other sources of water pollutants, it is clear that clean water may be an extremely scarce resource in the very near future.

## PEOPLE POLLUTION AND THE URBANIZATION PROBLEM

It has been estimated that the world's population doubled about every 1,000 years to reach one-half billion persons by the mid-1600s. By about 1830 the world's population had reached 1 billion persons, requiring a period of 200 years to double. Today the world population is growing at such a rate that the number of people doubles every 35 years.

The people-pollution crisis is aptly illustrated by the preposterous but simple extrapolation of the current rate of population growth into the future. The world's population of 3.7 billion people in 1970 may expand to more than 7 billion by the year 2000 and to 20 billion a century later (2100). According to biologist Paul R. Ehrlich of Stanford University and British physicist J. H. Fremlin, 600,000,000 billion people would inhabit the earth in 900 years, and that is about 100 persons per square yard of space over the entire planet! The absurdity of such trends is seen by considering living conditions in the one continuous 2,000-story building Fremlin speculates would be needed—a building that would cover all of the space on the earth.[12] Now, that many people *is* absurd, for, according to experts, the world will experience massive famines and plagues long before the population reaches the 600,000,000,000,000,000 mark—which is a body-heat limit to survival in any event. Ignoring the impossible and somewhat amusing prospect of exporting people in these numbers to other planets, the only alternative to a "death-rate solution" for overpopulation is a birth-rate solution. Yet, at the present time, the world's population— most of it desperately poor—is growing at the chilling rate of over 2 percent per year.[13]

Population shifts to urban centers have also complicated environmental-quality and people-pollution problems in developed and relatively low birth-rate nations such as the United States and Japan. At present rates of change, some 160,000 acres of U.S. land is converted into highways and airports each year. Urban centers house three-fourths of the people of this nation who live on 1 percent of the land, and it is in urban areas that

---

[12] See Paul R. Ehrlich, "Too Many People," in Garrett De Bell, *op. cit.*, p. 220.

[13] The world's population expands as long as the birth rate exceeds the death rate. Chapter 27 explains the implications of population growth for the underdeveloped nations of the world.

deterioration in the quality of life is most serious. In addition to air and water pollution, noise, congestion, garbage, crime, and poverty add to the offensiveness of life for millions. Inner cities are stagnant or literally decaying in hundreds of metropolitan areas that are home for millions of Americans whose income levels are often insufficient to lift them above poverty.

Typically, the city has ignored people and parks while bowing to the automobile, freeways, and commercial demands for an even larger concrete and steel jungle. Suburbia has become a magnet for the more affluent and fortunate segment of the population, a migration trend that has caused the tax base of local governments to decline. Only rarely have America's cities been successfully rehabilitated, and far too often efforts by government to renovate urban living have created more instead of fewer problems, especially for the poor and less mobile residents of inner-city areas.

## "PROGRESS" POLLUTION

The quality of the environment has also been debased by pollutants associated with technological progress. Although a better life has emerged because of rising per capita incomes, technological advances have also added waste, noise, pesticide, and radiation pollutants.

Among the variety of elements that pollute the environment, the volume of solid waste and litter is staggering. Solid wastes consisting of 200 million tires, 30 billion jars, 90 billion cans, 75 billion metal and plastic caps, 4 million tons of plastics, and hundreds of millions of tons of other debris, appliances, and autos accumulate each year. An average of about 2,000 pounds of solid waste per person is accumulated each year, and by 1980 the volume is expected to approach 3,000 pounds in the United States. The bulk of solid wastes originates from manufacturing, mining, and agriculture—the latter accounting for one-half of the 4.3 billion tons accumulated each year. In 1970, although almost $4 billion was spent to remove residential waste alone, fully one-fourth of the 250 million tons of such waste was uncollected, and federal agencies estimate that some four-fifths of all incinerator facilities and land-disposal operations are substandard. Litter and solid wastes generate offensive sight and smell pollution and also contribute further to air and water pollution, especially if they are disposed of improperly.

Pesticides and mercury contribute to the pollution problem, but they also are very obvious contributors to environmental debasement. Pesticides have created a better life for mankind in many ways, as have numerous other technological developments that also create pollution problems. At the same time, it is known that imperfectly understood ecological changes have accompanied the widespread use of pesticides and related chemicals. An unknown amount of morbidity and mortality to both human and nonhuman life have obliquely accompanied increased usage of toxic pesticides such as DDT. Indeed, the Council on Environmental Quality has conservatively estimated that as many as 200 human deaths are known to be caused by pesticides in the United States each year. Another major difficulty with these pollutants is that they accumulate in larger and more concentrated doses through nature's food chain, often ending up contaminating food eaten by man (e.g., Coho salmon in Lake Michigan and ocean tuna).

Radiation from everyday electronic devices found in homes and offices as well as from nuclear power and nuclear weapon systems constitutes another recognizable source of environmental pollution. According to the Atomic Energy Commission (AEC), there are 80 million gallons of radioactive liquid wastes stored at AEC sites. Some ten "burial" sites also exist today for disposing of solid radioactive wastes. In 1969, 650,000 cubic feet of such solids were buried at selected sites. The potential hazards of such materials are unknown and could be very great. Indeed, very little is known about the effect of radioactivity on the total environment, although it is known that such materials initiate genetic changes and cause cancer. As the nuclear energy field expands from providing 1 percent of all power in 1969 to the AEC's estimate of 25 percent of total power by 1980, this environmental pollutant will assume much greater importance.

Finally, the din of air and surface transportation, construction activity, and industrial production are increasingly annoying contributors to environmental pollution. Hearing damage accompanies steady exposure to eight or more hours of 80 decibles of sound—a sound level that can be and is generated by the traffic noise in cities and on freeways. Recent controversy over plans for a supersonic transport (SST) typifies the public's concern for noise pollution, in this case the SST's sonic boom. Although the furor raised thus far has led to a temporary Department of Transportation proposal to ban overland flights of the SST, the hundreds of millions of dollars spent on its development may foreshadow its introduction in spite of the hostile reaction of many citizens.

### The Economic Costs of Pollution

Just exactly what it would cost to clean up the environment is as impossible to reckon as is the cost imposed upon society by the several categories of pollution described above. One of the major difficulties in assessing the benefits and costs associated with pollution and pollution abatement is that they are often noneconomic or *incommensurable; that is,* not measurable in terms of some common denominator such as dollars. The social costs of the lives lost through auto deaths, smog, or radiation pollution, can be valued only as life itself. The same is also true of the recreation or aesthetic benefits associated with a lake or an urban environment that is pleasing to the eye. In their attempt to cope with incommensurables, economists have attempted to assign *shadow prices* or proxy values to a day's use of water resources, for example. One way to develop a shadow price is to estimate what people pay for some near-comparable facility or resource (e.g., a day's recreation) supplied privately. Although a hazardous and formidable task subject to great ambiguities, benefit-cost analysis can be used to very roughly approximate certain obvious economic dimensions to environmental pollution.

Using such crude and approximate approaches, various experts on different aspects of the environmental-quality problem in the United States have reached the following conclusions:[14]

1. The total cost of cleaning up existing air, water, and waste pollution

[14] See J. H. Dales, *Pollution, Property, and Prices* (Toronto: University of Toronto Press, 1968); O. C. Herfindahl and A. V. Kneese, *Quality of the Environment* (Washington, D.C.: Resources for the Future, 1965); Harold Wolozin, *The Economics of Air Pollution* (New York: W. W. Norton, 1966); and Marshall I. Goldman (ed.), *Controlling Pollution: The Economics of a Cleaner America* (Englewood Cliffs, N.J.: Prentice-Hall, 1967).

*alone* is estimated at $15 to $20 billion per year for each of the next five years. Commitments to fully meet environmental-quality standards for these three types of pollution could cost as much as $40 or $50 billion a year in the future, according to Senator Gaylord A. Nelson of Wisconsin.

2. For the five-year period beginning in 1970, the costs of coping with water pollution would be no less than $60 to $70 billion. Air-pollution abatement systems would cost somewhere between $15 and $25 billion over this five-year period, while modernization of trash collection and waste-disposal systems would add another $4 to $8 billion to the total bill. And at this, pollutants such as noise and urban decay are being ignored.

3. The costs of *not* remedying these types of problems cannot be fully accounted for because of a variety of incommensurables, including the fact that future generations will have to bear many unknown consequences of our action or inaction today. Nonetheless, the available evidence suggests that cleaning up the environment *saves* more money than it costs. The most readily measured and also conservative cost estimates of polluted air (corrosion, farm losses, and so forth) appear to range from $12 to $15 billion per year, and the costs of continuing to live with water pollution are of the same magnitude. Since nearly all incommensurables are ignored in such comparisons, it is rather apparent that improving upon the quality of the environment by eliminating major pollutants will pay for itself in economic terms.

When all sources of pollution such as noise, radiation, and crowded urban centers are considered, the annual costs of regaining and preserving a quality environment conceivably could exceed the $50 billion level—which is about two-thirds the amount currently spent on national defense. Just how much of a country's resources a citizenry wishes to devote to the quality of its environment remains to be seen, however. We do know that a crisis is around the corner, if not already upon us, and future generations will pay dearly if the values of society fail to change in order to stem the rapid rate of environmental deterioration experienced in recent decades.

One final point is worth noting. Even though various pollutants have had a major impact on the quality of life and our environment, the view that economic development is totally evil is neither realistic nor useful. American society today is considered affluent by many other socioeconomic standards of measurement, and this fact forces some optimism about what might appear to be a dismal future. As a matter of fact, it is economic growth which can provide the means whereby environmental deterioration can be remedied *if a society elects to allocate resources for that purpose.*

## C. MORTGAGING THE "COMMONS"?

The crises brought about by environmental pollution and income inequality as two basic dimensions to the quality-of-life problem are the by-products of market failures, and their specific forms merit identification.

In the case of income inequality, differences in the quality of life are primarily the result of: (*a*) several types of misfortune, which nevertheless are *not* randomly distributed over the population; (*b*) the values of society where, in the United States, a premium is placed on the ethic of work, individualism, and a certain degree of callousness tempered with public assistance; and (*c*) social and economic institutions such as discrimination.

Quality of life is a serious problem for millions of Americans at this personal and distributive level, but it is a special human-resource problem more conveniently discussed later after we have more information on human-resource markets. The aggregate case of environmental pollution is quite different, however, partly because pollution relates first to natural resources and also because the volume of pollution is growing—perhaps doubling every decade or so.

The heart of the environmental-quality problem has been succinctly described by the Council of Economic Advisers as follows: "The existing rules of the game governing the economic system were not primarily designed to deal with our common responsibility for the environment in which we live."[15] The *commons* of New England towns was property owned by townspeople as a community or a society at large. As Garrett Hardin has pointed out, mankind's environment also is a "commons"—a complex of jointly owned man-made and natural resources comprising an environment subject to abuse and decay.[16] Even though many aspects of the environmental commons cannot be evaluated fully in the space available here, economic analysis can provide useful insights into the root causes of environmental decay.

## Economic Causes of Pollution

As societies have developed, populations have grown, and industrial production has transformed resources into goods, a variety of wastes have been inventoried in a finite environment. As noted earlier, increased production has been subsidized by a sometimes irreversible pollution of the environment. Social values and technological bias are key reasons that the environment has been abused, and as long as social behavior patterns indiscriminately revere private material gains the commons will deteriorate.

### VALUES AND TECHNOLOGY

It is important to recognize that the purpose in studying environmental economics is not to change one's values to better fit the precepts held by another. Rather, the purpose is to be exposed to the facts so each person can reassess his own values. It is unimportant whether you or I may approve or disapprove of certain values, but it is very important that each citizen fully recognize the cost characteristics of using the environmental commons as we do.

Knowledge about the economic causes of pollution is necessary if remedial public policies capable of correcting for abusive use of the environment are to be developed. This is so because a certain remorseless working of things economic in nature promotes debasement of the environment. Thus, the quality of the environment deteriorates if the value structure of a society defends individualistic freedoms which are not in harmony with quality in life.

Society subsidizes environmental decay to the tune of many billions of dollars each year. For example, automobiles are subsidized by the public sector which supplies millions of miles of "public" freeways, and also underwrites the automobile by providing tax breaks to the oil industry and by ignoring

---

[15] *Economic Report of the President*, 1970, p. 99.

[16] Garrett Hardin, "The Tragedy of the Commons," *Science* (December 1968), pp. 1243–1248.

polluted air, water, and beaches. Indeed, even the legal process subsidizes the automobile by undervaluing human life damaged through this medium of transportation. As a consequence, the private cost of using the automobile is less than the social cost. Consider another example: As job opportunities and people concentrate in certain areas, pollution problems intensify, and the quality of the urban environment decays while thousands of once viable smaller communities experience economic decline. The enormous sprawling suburban and urban environment faces an almost hopeless battle of trying to keep up with the need for parks, schools, roads, police, and fire protection. Difficult value questions also arise concerning people pollution in the aggregate, for population control strikes hard at personal preferences and religious beliefs. As a result, people may well have to look carefully at their personal and social values in the light of the costs of such freedoms.

Historically, technological change and economic growth have exhibited a "Q-bias"—that is, increasing quantities of goods have been produced while the quality of life has been ignored, and this bias contributes to the current environmental crisis. Bear in mind, however, that this same Q-bias has furnished a level of private and public affluence which now offers a college education in modern facilities to youth by the millions. At the same time, it is instructive to question whether or not bigger boats, four relatively leisure-filled years in academia, or retractable headlights "should" take precedence over clean air, clear lakes, or remedies for the more than 1,100 auto deaths that occur each week of the year.

"Progress" can be and has been thought of in such material terms as computers in space, machines that punch out and assemble appliances, or chemicals that eradicate insects and transform liquids into plastic and synthetic clothing. Technologically, a contemporary economy is a production Goliath which also creates smoke, junk, and litter wastes that are stockpiled in the environment. Unfortunately, the technology of coping with pollutants is badly retarded, largely because the environmental commons have not been priced. A quality environment is a scarce good today simply because the environment has long been regarded as free. Indeed, consumer, commercial, and industrial interests have frequently regarded the act of polluting as a mark of progress and even as a right, just as General Motors and consumers look upon automobile ownership as a right—death and pollutants aside.

## MISMANAGEMENT OF THE ECONOMIC SYSTEM

Far too often people blame industrial and corporate interests alone for inflicting environmental pollution upon society. This simple-minded view of the problem is also in error, for self-interest makes *all* mankind equally guilty of abusing the environment. Environmental decay is the product of a misguided economic system along with retarded government planning and policy. To resolve environmental problems, a clear understanding of the way economic incentives work to encourage pollution is necessary. Pollution damages are an external diseconomy—a social cost imposed on all who use the environmental commons. Furthermore, rivalry in a market system rewards the polluter—or so it seems—because the private market pricing mechanism does not take into account the environmental damages that a polluter inflicts upon others in society. The heart of the problem lies with the short-sighted perspective of self-interest, which encourages one party to heap "bads" upon others and in the process destroy the environment instead of preserving it.

Unfortunately, because the environment is owned and used in common, it cannot be marketed. As a public good, it cannot be purchased and consumed privately. Environmental quality cannot be produced profitably in the private sector because benefits are indivisible, and thus there is no market price to ration existing scarcity. Even though the private market prices paid for swimming-pool facilities, country-club memberships, or penthouses with fine skyline views provide only a crude "shadow price" for the worth of environmental quality, we all know that there are real and substantial prices attached to such qualitative dimensions of life. Indeed, the underallocation of resources to enhance environmental quality also serves to maldistribute quality in life to those with higher incomes. The slum landlord or the auto executive lives in suburbia and purchases what amenities of life he can to enhance his own environment. Life is a good deal more restricted for those who cannot afford to pay what are often very considerable prices for such environmental amenities.

## SOCIAL COSTS IN THE "COMMONS"

Lakes, air, forests, and rivers are environmental resources as are a variety of social goods such as freeways, parks, cities, and educational systems. When ownership and use of the environmental commons are joint, no one party can control usage. As a result, each user of the environment has an incentive to abuse the environment and impose social costs on his neighbors.

Picture, for example, a river in a forest. Each citizen uses these resources in his own best interest—some hunting and fishing, and others building homes, factories, furniture, and the like. Use of resources in the commons implies both a positive-gain component and a negative-cost component, as is illustrated in Figure 4(a). The positive gain—the additional proceeds from using more of these resources—is the marginal revenue product ($MRP$), and users acquire these proceeds privately in using the commons to produce more output.[17] In using resources from the commons, each party will also privately incur some additional or marginal costs, denoted by $MC$ in Figure 4(a).[18] The net gain from use of the commons is the difference between additional proceeds (or $MRP$) and additional costs (or $MC$), shown as the gold-shaded area in Figure 4(a). Any party seeking to maximize private net gains will thus draw upon resources in the commons until additional costs and revenues are equal—i.e., until $MRP$ and $MC$ are equal, as shown at point $E$ in Figure 4(a). Thus, private output produced entails the use of $Q_p$ units, which enterprising users of the commons value at a price of $P_p$.

[17] The added proceeds represented by marginal revenue product decline as output increases in Figure 4 because of diminishing returns, as explained in Chapter 18. Thus, schedule $MRP$ represents the typical down-sloping demand curve for resources.

[18] The negative component consisting of the added costs borne by a private user (shown as marginal cost schedule $MC$ in Figure 4) might be thought of as reflecting the private effort required to exploit water and timber resources in the forest. As the timber is harvested privately, marginal cost tends to rise as increasingly inferior resources are used. For simplicity, schedule $MC$ can be regarded as very much like a supply curve.

**FIGURE 4**   Abusive Use of the Environmental Commons

(a) Private cost and use of the commons

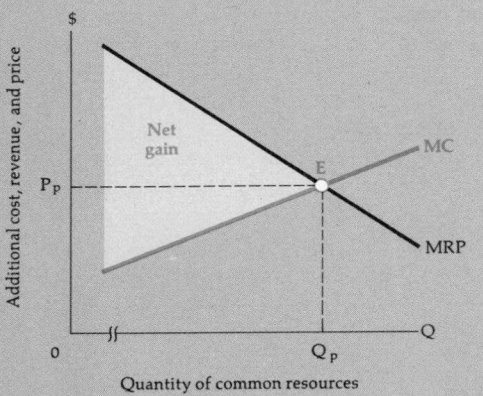

(b) Social cost and losses in using the commons

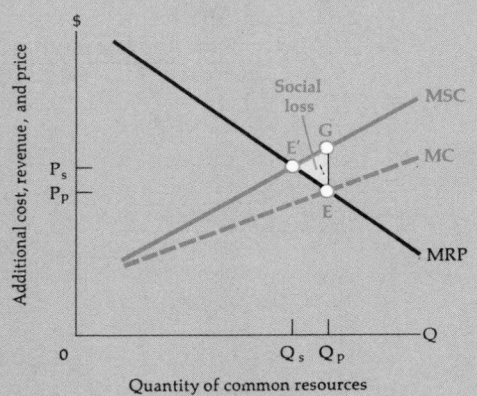

*Overuse of the Commons.* When private costs of using the commons as given by *MC* and private returns shown by *MRP* are compared, users will use $Q_p$ units at an equilibrium price of $P_p$ to maximize net private gains as shown in (a). However, some costs are not privately incurred as shown by the difference in *MC* and marginal social costs *(MSC)* in (b). If the cost of common resources were fully recognized, only $Q_s$ units would be used at the higher value of $P_s$. The area *EGE'* represents a net social loss (the "bads") imposed on society because resources are over-utilized and under-priced in creating a larger output of goods.

The use of common resources by any one party—e.g., cutting timber to build a factory or simply using the river as a residential sewer—imposes some private costs on the user, as shown by schedule *MC*, but the additional cost to society—*marginal social cost (MSC)*—is greater than private costs and rises more rapidly because use of the commons adversely affects other citizens. For example, a house upstream might use the river as a sewer and destroy your water supply, or you might indiscriminately harvest timber and, as your private output rises, deplete the forest leading to erosion, floods, and water pollution. The important point is this: The private costs shown by *MC* are lower than the marginal social costs shown by *MSC*.

As Figure 4(b) demonstrates, it is profitable for the enterprising resident of the commons to do "his thing" until the additional costs he incurs (*MC*) are equal to additional gains or revenues he receives (*MRP*). However, if social costs were accounted for fully, a society would equate *MRP* and *MSC*. Users of the environmental commons do not have to bear the full social cost of exploiting resources in the short run. Rather, the rest of society shares some costs of whatever deterioration in the quality of life a decaying environment imposes.

Note carefully in Figure 4(b) that the private equilibrium quantity of output at point *E* is far in excess of what would be produced with resources from the commons if full marginal social costs were accounted for at point *E'*. Notice, too, that the private price of products produced in using the commons is understated. Abuse of the commons is assured when *MRP* and *MC* are equated, allowing $Q_p$ units to be sold at a price $P_p$, but if full social costs were recognized, a smaller quantity $Q_s$ would be valued at the higher price $P_s$. *Society overproduces goods (and bads) and underprices the private output created by commonly owned resources.* In this example resources would be better allocated and the entire society would be better off if controls on the use of the commons restricted output to $Q_s$ and a price $P_s$ were paid that was sufficient to cover full social costs. Unfortunately, self-interest is at odds with social responsibility and, under such conditions, it is rare indeed that an individual will elect to forgo the private gain which can be realized by abusing the commons.

The tragedy of such external diseconomies is not just that society at large bears a net social loss equal to the gold area *EGE'* in Figure 4(b). In addition to creating this "loss" due to overproduction, self-interest drives a society to self-destruction. A shrewd, enterprising resident can only conclude that his private interest lies in beating a rival by exploiting the commons as rapidly as possible. As long as social rules require that each citizen provide for himself from the environmental commons, it does indeed pay to scramble—and quickly. Those who can somehow acquire title to and harvest the most timber or gain most from the river will be better off personally. Indeed with increased private affluence, enterprising users of the commons may be able to change their residence to another locale (the suburbs) and bar the average citizen from use of a privately owned commons (the country club)!

*To recapitulate:* When one party uses air or water for waste disposal as if it were a free resource, and others bear the cost of environmental contamination, the social worth of the environmental commons is underpriced and its capacity is overused. All users of the environment would be better off if output were reduced to $Q_s$ and the user shown in Figure 4(b) compensated the community for the difference between private and social cost (*MC* and *MSC*). In this fashion the net social loss shown in Figure 4(b) could be avoided. When a community allows some portion of social costs to remain uncompensated for, it is able to sell output at lower prices and thereby increase consumption per capita, but only by absorbing the unaccounted for social costs of Figure 4(b).

In short, *freedom in the commons is capable of temporarily increasing the personal quality of life for the affluent few and ultimately visiting ruin upon all.* In addition, there are perverse private incentives at work against rebuilding the commons. Because it is an indivisible good available to all, any benefits from cleaning up the commons cannot be captured by private investors. It does little good for one slum landowner to clean up his dwelling while others milk ghetto residents in a maximizing sense. Thus, there is little incentive to invest in a pollution-abatement system, short of considerations of sheer survival. Therefore, citizens must act *jointly* to force the preservation of the commons at some desired quality level.

### Pollution-Prone Markets and Cumulative Disequilibrium

The idea that self-destruction is inherent in the environmental-pollution problem as described above is worthy of further elaboration. The fact is that self-interest in a market system characterized by rivalry among sellers *encourages* and *rewards* environmental decay while *discouraging* preservation of the environment. Uncontrolled, the competitive market system does indeed remorselessly drive all participants to foul their commons. Producers are pressured by rivalry and the urge to survive into incurring only those costs which *cannot* be avoided, for if one party can produce more cheaply than a rival by fouling the environment, that party stands to gain in sales, market power, growth, and profits.

Pollution-prone behavior is not, however, peculiar *only* to the market economy where private interests are readily expressed. While it is no doubt correct that private enterprise and the profit motive account for a substantial portion of America's environmental problem, the Soviet Union and other socialist nations have similar problems.[19] Indeed, depending upon the relative priorities placed upon environmental quality, state ownership and accountability for disruption of the environment need not be any more responsible than the private sector.

## THE INGREDIENTS TO POLLUTION-PRONENESS

Pollution-proneness is a behavior pattern conditioned by the several ingredients to environmental disruption, many of which have already received our attention. These contributing factors are, in summary:

1. A limited spacial capacity to carry residual pollutants and an environmental capacity which can be irretrievably damaged or destroyed.

2. The historical attitude that many of the natural resources of the commons are free goods which "should be" subject to unfettered use by mankind.

3. A rapidly growing population with a seemingly insatiable appetite to consume.

4. A value system which has placed a premium upon technological changes which best serve the desire for increased quantities of output and consumption.

5. The combined effects of a strong self-interest motive working in conjunction with rivalry or competition and the unaccountability which characterizes externalities of the social-cost variety.

6. Unaccountability for external diseconomies, or instances in which the external costs not reflected in economic decisions are instead imposed upon third parties, including society at large.

The first five of these ingredients of environmental debasement work in conjunction with failure of an economic system to account for externalities. Taken together they have the potential of degenerating into a cumulative disequilibrium leading to increasingly more intense pollution problems. Whether a collective society ameliorates or exacerbates pollution problems depends upon what combination of the three behavior patterns illustrated next are adopted.

## EYE-FOR-AN-EYE PHILOSOPHY

One alternative is adherence to an "eye-for-an-eye" level of social responsibility, with each member of society or party polluting precisely as much as another rival, returning like amounts of evil for evil.[20] Thus, if party G

[19] See, for example, Marshall I. Goodman, "The Convergence of Environmental Disruption," *Science* (October 2, 1970), pp. 37–42.

[20] Equal amounts of "good for good" would also be returned in the case of the biblical eye-for-an-eye philosophy, for parties could move to zero and even negative pollution.

pollutes the environment in some amount, others respond by providing a like amount of pollution. More pollution might also occur, or perhaps extremely placid rivals might decide to not pollute at all. Would that reality were so kind!

The eye-for-an-eye philosophy is quite uninteresting except that it illustrates why good guys misbehave toward the environmental commons when joint social behavior is called for. Suppose that parties G and B promise each other that they will not pollute, an act requiring costly changes in production methods. Being lean and a little hungry, party G could cheat—indeed, it has a market incentive to do so, for it could then lower prices and beat its rival! Others also have an incentive to cheat, and the chances are that any promises made will be poorly kept—if they are kept at all—at least until some third party (e.g., the law) intervenes or threatens to do so. While it is conceivable that members of society might become altruistic, it is crucial to realize that both are locked into a situation in which the costs of altruism could be high if one party cheats. Social responsibility is unlikely simply because each rival must trust the other, and each has a private incentive to cheat. This may help explain why oligopolists like Ford and General Motors are unlikely to depollute—at least without severe public pressures. It hardly makes *private* sense for such giants to spend millions of dollars on pollution-abatement equipment and lose out to a market rival in the price context. Ford and General Motors could also forgo annual model changes and invest billions of dollars in developing safety features which could save thousands of lives. However, the new auto market might be measurably smaller, and this situation would not be well accepted in Detroit, as you can imagine.

## THE SINNER

Rivalry for private gains (or growth gains in a socialist state) under circumstances in which social costs can be shifted to the community at large characterizes many nations today.

In order to reduce private costs relative to a competitive rival, party G is induced to pollute, perhaps by dumping wastes into the Ohio River or the air (after all, water and air are "free goods" in the absence of social controls). Others then react in a competitive context to preserve their own viability by adding to pollution, perhaps in order to attain lower costs and a modest competitive edge over rivals.

An economy can spin off into increasingly serious pollution-prone behavior, particularly if the cumulative acts of hundreds of thousands of firms and millions of consumers are considered. Of course, pollution-proneness of this sort may be checked by: (a) altruistic values, which have a very poor historical record; (b) physical destruction limits; or (c) laws or other control mechanisms imposed on such behavior. The key point, however, is simply that an unstable and cumulative disequilibrium condition can induce and may even necessitate more pollution.

The current state of the environment suggests that the commercial lions have eliminated the Christians. In far too many cases the "sinner" is a rather accurate prototype of the polluter and usually "eye-for-an-eye" behavior is the best that can be hoped for. Veneer-thin and relatively dangerous autos that foul the air, wrinkle like accordions, and lie in state by the millions in open graveyards illustrate this sort of cumulative pollution-proneness. Cheaper but indestructible aluminum cans, aluminum foil, plastic bags and bottle tops, and throw-away beer bottles likewise represent profit-enticing or cost-reducing options which currently contribute to the pollution problem. Ever ready to serve the short-run consumption whims of a population much impressed with the immediate gratification that "goods" provide, the economic system often is diabolically oblivious to the pollutants it creates.

## THE SAINT

The remedy for pollution-prone behavior lies in achieving a more "saintly" spirit. No matter what the initial level of pollution by one party, rival members of society who use the environmental commons must *lower* the level of environmental contamination for which they are responsible in a saint-like fashion. That is, each party must be "persuaded" or "coerced" to pollute *less* than other rivals do, rather than more.

Although the saint is a utopian ideal, the need for controlled use of the environment is very real. In the past, population increases, individualistic social values, a technological Q-bias, and uncompensated-for social costs have served to reinforce each other and rapidly consume the environment. Instead of permitting unlimited assault upon the environmental commons and cumulative disequilibrium, social and institutional devices must be employed to check, discourage, and disallow pollution-prone behavior on the part of producers and consumers if the quality of life is to be preserved. As long as unrestricted freedom of usage remains, the "mortgage on the commons" well may be foreclosed at some future date.

## D. BUILDING AN ENVIRONMENTAL-CONTROL SYSTEM

State and local government can employ administrative regulations and the law plus government subsidies, taxes, and pollution fees to remedy environmental pollution and to refurbish the environment, but externalities between regions (e.g., upstream vs. downstream interest in water-pollution control) hamper regional attempts to resolve the environmental crisis. Consequently, the federal government will probably have to assume the major burden in regulating usage of the environment.

### The Philosophy of Environmental Rules

The key question underlying remedies for the environmental-quality issue is: Under what conditions does a society agree to limit the freedom of its members? Limitations to the use (and abuse) of an environmental commons requires acceptance of coercive restrictions, and the target of public policy must be uncompensated-for social costs [illustrated earlier in Figure 4(b)]. Efforts to control pollution will require a mutually agreed-upon commitment to monitor and limit certain forms of behavior, and today there is no such mutual agreement. Many formidable equity issues arise in considering questions of control, and their resolution is the key to the preservation of environmental quality for present and future generations. Let us consider some examples.

Today we have laws, rules, and sanctions against my dumping garbage on your doorstep, a neighbor constructing a factory on your property, reckless speeding, pilfering, arson, robbery, murder, tax evasion, and many other forms of "unacceptable" personal behavior in a "social commons." Has freedom thus been restrained? Liberty certainly is restricted for the bank robber and other violators of laws and customs, just as the legal enforcement of private property rights restricts everyone's freedom to use what once was a very much larger "commons." Nonetheless, society has become more, not less, free as certain forms of unbridled behavior have been restrained. Just where one draws the line with respect to using and abusing the environment is a matter of endless debate, however.

From a purely economic point of view, we could say that government policy "should" regulate the commons so that resources are allocated efficiently; that is, it should enforce equality between marginal social cost and marginal revenue product [at point $E'$ of Figure 4(b)]. Of course, the world of reality is not so easily manipulated for many reasons already discussed, such as the incommensurables of life and the "proper" distribution of income.[21] Once the problem is recognized for what it is, about all an individual prescription devoid of normative rhetoric can recommend is that the facts must be fully examined, and that the citizens must collectively decide when, where, and how to "toilet train" American industry and the consumer.

Having recognized the open ambivalence on matters of philosophy and environmental-control systems, let us consider two approaches to environmental surveillance: the law and economic reform.

REGULATION AND THE LAW

In recent years, federal authorities have joined state and local governments in the battle against pollution. The Clean Air Act of 1963 as amended in 1965 represented a major step in the struggle against air pollution, and other legislation affecting various aspects of the environment has also been passed (e.g., the Housing Act and its nearly one dozen formal Congressional amendments). Most notable among recent federal legislative action are the Air Quality Act of 1967 and, even more important, passage of the National Environmental Policy Act of 1970 along with creation of the Council on Environmental Quality. Further proposals have been made to consolidate and coordinate federal programs concerned with the quality of the environment under the Environmental Protection Agency and the National Oceanic and Atmospheric Administration.[22] The thrust of federal efforts to date has been directed to development of acceptable pollution "standards" and the provision of funds for restoring selected parts of the environment.

Most authorities recognize the need for and the many limitations to quality standards, rules, and the law as components of an environmental-control system. Sellers could be forced by law to charge deposit fees sufficient to provide the incentives required to develop markets for reusable containers and encourage private parties to return such containers—the situation that existed some years ago before technological "progress" produced the "throw-away" container. Similarly, air- and water-quality standards backed up by punitive fines would help control pollutants. Air-

[21] Recall that Chapter 20 itemized a battery of factors compounding the problems of public choice.

[22] Adopted by Congress in 1970.

pollution standards, laws banning the use of nonreturnable bottles or indestructible materials (aluminum beer cans) also could be established to monitor the environmental quality of life.

Because so many federal agencies are involved directly or indirectly in environmental programs, it is hard to determine just how much is spent for such purposes. The Council on Environmental Quality has compiled data on direct expenditures (exclusive of urban programs) which are shown in Figure 5. Expenditures on environmental quality are programmed at comparatively higher levels through 1975, but on balance, federal expenditures do not appear sufficient to do the job required, particularly in relation to the sizable public outlays used for other purposes. While programs aimed at urban renewal as well as state and local pollution expenditures augment the limited federal outlays shown in Figure 5, the total public-sector effort directed at pollution abatement for 1971 ($2.1 billion) is small in comparison to the magnitude of the problem.

To date government efforts have focused largely on regulatory actions and quality standards, and have involved a very moderate financial burden. Most authorities now agree that more forceful legal reform is needed if the quality of life is to be improved. In addition, basic economic reforms must be adopted to reduce or eliminate economic incentives to pollute.

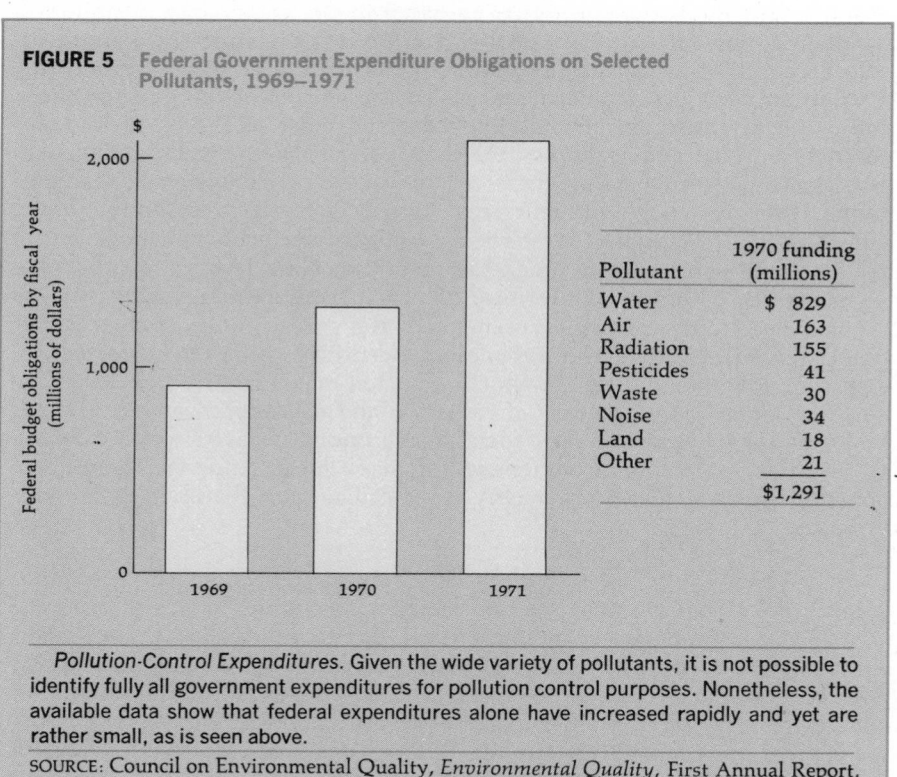

**FIGURE 5**    Federal Government Expenditure Obligations on Selected Pollutants, 1969–1971

| Pollutant | 1970 funding (millions) |
|---|---|
| Water | $ 829 |
| Air | 163 |
| Radiation | 155 |
| Pesticides | 41 |
| Waste | 30 |
| Noise | 34 |
| Land | 18 |
| Other | 21 |
| | $1,291 |

*Pollution-Control Expenditures.* Given the wide variety of pollutants, it is not possible to identify fully all government expenditures for pollution control purposes. Nonetheless, the available data show that federal expenditures alone have increased rapidly and yet are rather small, as is seen above.

SOURCE: Council on Environmental Quality, *Environmental Quality*, First Annual Report, 1970.

Shifting the costs of pollution to the polluter is the central focus of economic sanctions to monitor environmental debasement. Tax credits, direct
subsidies to firms, and pollution-emission (effluent) fees are the most
commonly discussed techniques of correcting misguided economic incentives.

For example, some authorities have proposed levying a tax against automobiles when they are first sold which would be sufficient to provide for
their disposal. The approach of relying on taxes or fees levied against certain products could also be directed at defraying the costs incurred by
government in disposing of waste products. Other observers argue that
pollution fees sufficient to provide bounty payments to private collectors
would be preferable to direct government involvement, and tax credits or
subsidies could also be used to encourage greater private involvement in
pollution abatement.

In some instances, there may be a need for charges sufficiently large
to ban certain pollutants altogether. In addition, government could step up
the pace of research and development efforts in the technology of pollution
control. One of the most crucial needs is to find ways to recycle waste
products, including the many pollutants disposed of in the water and air as
well as the more common forms of litter. Tax proceeds from polluters (or
others) might be used to subsidize research in the technology of pollution
abatement or to finance firms that install pollution-abatement equipment.

Economic reforms can supply powerful incentives to remedy many forms
of pollution, provided financial charges are sufficient to impinge upon those
production or consumption pollutants deemed most offensive. Indeed, research incentives and technological changes may well result in improvements so considerable as to generate pollution-recycling systems capable of
paying their own way. Effluent fees have been used successfully in the
Ruhr Valley in Germany for decades, and certain economic policies are
being used in some regions (e.g., tax credits in New Jersey) to cope with
air and water pollution. Uniformity of control standards over all markets
certainly is required as is measurement of the severity of particular forms
of pollutants in relation to the economic incentives needed to correct them.
Then too, governmental units, which are often major contributors to pollution themselves (as is the case of radiation and electric-power generation),
must also be subjected to new social and economic constraints. Achieving
improvements in the environment will demand more stringent planning of
economic life as well as more massive financial support than has been forthcoming.

## THE EFFICIENCY OF ENVIRONMENTAL-CONTROL SYSTEMS

According to most experts, decisions to remedy various forms of environmental decay should be economical; that is, benefits should exceed costs,
which they usually do by a rather wide margin. Difficult choices may be
required between programs designed to diminish air pollution or automotive deaths vs. water pollution, for example. Public-sector activities are
also limited by a budget constraint, although there are alternative ways of
ameliorating pollution. Decisions must be made as to the most effective
and least costly way to achieve an environmental change. The alternative
benefits and costs of levying fees against polluters compared to granting
tax-credit subsidies which encourage firms to develop recycling processes

do have to be weighed. The problems encountered in measuring benefits and costs associated with environmental quality are monumental because of the incommensurables we noted earlier. However, these are not insurmountable problems, and public authorities are increasingly turning to benefit-cost analysis to help make such decisions.

## EVALUATING ENVIRONMENTAL-CONTROL SYSTEMS

Assuming for the moment that problems associated with noneconomic incommensurables are properly handled, perhaps through the establishment of shadow prices, public authorities may use benefit-cost analysis to weigh alternative programs and methods in order to achieve the maximum net return per dollar of costs. Benefit-cost comparisons of environmental problems raise important issues, however.

Chapter 20 pointed out that in using benefit-cost analysis, public authorities must reduce future benefits to their present value by discounting. A $1 return or payoff 10 years from now is not worth $1 today, but rather a fraction of $1, since some positive interest rate can be earned on each dollar invested for a period of 10 years.[23] The crucial point about the discount rate selected to adjust a stream of benefits to their present value is simply that the higher the discount rate, the lower the present value of estimated net benefits accruing from public-sector investments. At higher interest rates, each $1 invested today earns more in future years. Therefore, the present value of $1 today, which will not be received for several years, is smaller the higher the interest rate.

Debate has raged for many years over the "proper" rate of discount to use in evaluating government expenditures. Some experts advocate using the cost to the Treasury of borrowing, others have suggested the use of a social rate of discount which might be adjusted downward to reflect the collective need for public goods, while still others have advocated using measures of the opportunity cost of displaced private spending. Although we cannot fully investigate the technicalities of this issue here, it is worth noting that after extensive hearings the Joint Economic Committee supported the use of an opportunity-cost discount rate.

In Figure 6(a), the net benefits (benefits *less* costs) of an illustrative environmental-control system are shown for a period of 50 years. Assuming that net benefits equal $1 million per year and no discount rate is used, $10 million of future benefits would accumulate over each 10-year period. A 4 percent discount rate applies to net benefit schedule B and a 6 percent discount rate is used for net benefit schedule B' in Figure 6(a).

The time stream of net benefits discounted to their present value is also important in evaluating government expenditures on environmental-quality programs. Figure 6(b) shows the problem sometimes encountered by government economists in analyzing the choice between two environmental-investment alternatives, or between two different approaches (e.g., taxes

[23] For an excellent and more complete consideration of the problems in discounting public-sector investments, see U.S. Congress, Joint Economic Committee, *Economic Analysis of Investment Decisions: Interest Rate Policy and Discounting Analysis* (Washington, D.C.: U.S. Government Printing Office, 1968); and Allen V. Kneese and Kenneth C. Nobe, "The Role of Economic Evaluation in Planning for Water Resource Development," *Natural Resources Journal* (December 1962), pp. 465–477.

**FIGURE 6**    Investment in the Environmental Commons

(a) The impact of the discount rate on environmental investments

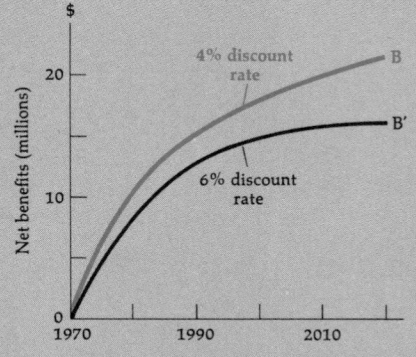

| Period | Discounted net benefits per period (millions) | | |
|---|---|---|---|
| | 0% | 4% | 6% |
| 1970–1979 | $10 | $ 8.1 | $ 7.3 |
| 1980–1989 | 10 | 5.4 | 4.1 |
| 1990–1999 | 10 | 3.7 | 2.3 |
| 2000–2009 | 10 | 2.5 | 1.3 |
| 2010–2019 | 10 | 1.7 | .7 |
| Total | $50 | $21.4 | $15.7 |

(b) Alternative time-streams of net benefits from environmental investments

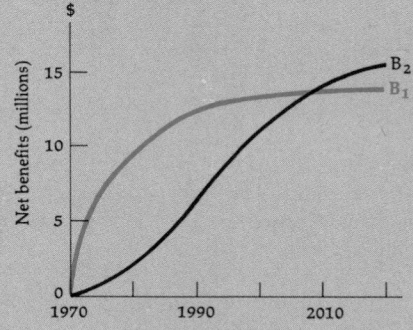

| Period | Net benefits $B_1$ | | Net benefits $B_2$ | |
|---|---|---|---|---|
| | 0% | 6% | 0% | 6% |
| 1970–1979 | $10 | $ 7.3 | $ 2 | $ 1.5 |
| 1980–1989 | 10 | 4.1 | $ 6 | 2.4 |
| 1990–1999 | 5 | 1.1 | $20 | 4.4 |
| 2000–2009 | 2 | .3 | $30 | 3.8 |
| 2010–2019 | 2 | .2 | $40 | 2.9 |
| Total | $29 | $13.0 | $98 | $15.0 |

*Evaluating Returns to Public Investments.* Ignoring the many problems in estimating benefits and costs, (a) shows the effect of the discount rate in evaluating public investments. Using the lower discount rate of 4 percent, net benefits are larger (B) than if a higher discount rate is selected (as in B'). In (b) two different time-streams of benefits are compared. The particular program providing the largest total return after discounting ($B_2$) may not be the "best" since program $B_1$ provides larger returns in earlier years.

or subsidies) used to remedy a specific type of pollution. Suppose that the discounted net benefit stream $B_1$ in Figure 6(b) is generated by the control of air pollution, providing $13 million at the end of a 50-year period. Before discounting, net benefits are large in the initial period ($20 million up to 1990), but they then begin to decline to a low of $2 million during the last 10 years of the 50-year period. Consequently, in initial years, the present value of net benefits is large. However, note carefully that at the end of the same 50-year period the net benefits derived from another program, say water conservation as shown by schedule $B_2$, produces larger discounted net benefits of $15 million. While water conservation provides a greater total payoff, it does not provide as sizable a return as the air-pollution control system until more than 35 years have passed. In this example, public authorities are faced with the difficulty of choosing between a program providing large immediate returns ($B_1$, or clean air) and another program providing a greater but decidedly postponed payoff ($B_2$, or water conservation). As we have noted on other occasions, benefit-cost analysis does not always provide clear-cut guidelines for public decision-makers.

When the vast array of incommensurables and unknowns embodied in estimates of gross benefits and the uncertain nature of costs projected into the future are added to the above difficulties, we gain some appreciation for the dilemma facing government economists in analyzing environmental problems. Whether air or water pollution provide a "better" investment compared to allocating scarce public funds to people-pollution or urban-sprawl problems is not easily determined. Although politicians must and do decide where public-sector priorities lie, these important and complex decisions must recognize the existence of incommensurable social benefits and costs far too often ignored in benefit-cost analysis. If such social objectives are ignored, benefit-cost analysis becomes only a simple-minded tool of questionable relevance. Even ignoring these considerations, the example of Figure 6 shows that when government opts to solve the long-run problem of a future water shortage, untold damage may be done to the air or to the urban commons. On the other hand, if a solution to existing urban problems is sought at the opportunity cost of water conservation, the urban population dependent upon water could face a dire problem in 50 years! Thus, it is clear that economic efficiency and choice in government-spending decisions require much research.

## Pollution and the Future

The consequences of the social costs of environmental pollution are as formidable to assess as is inequality in the distribution of income. There are inexorable links between these two basic dimensions to the quality of life, however. Those least able to purchase or rent a quality environment obviously number among the low-income groups in contemporary society. Greater affluence derived from a favorable distribution of income and wealth permits others to acquire a life style less encumbered by the pollutants attributable to physical environmental factors and the social artifacts of contemporary society such as the inner city. It is clear that the welfare of millions of people is very directly debased by the distribution of income, the decay of the environment, or both. Whether the existing distribution of income is good or bad is very much a normative matter, but the fact that life styles differ substantially for a $5,000- compared to a $20,000-a-year family is obvious and bears heavily on financing remedies for the environmental-pollution problem.

It is often said that the cost of correcting past and present environmental abuses naturally must be borne by the consumer who must pay higher prices for goods. Such a proposal avoids the central issue. It is no more natural to require consumers to pay the costs of cleaning up the environment than it is to ask the corporation to foot the bill from profits.

The argument that consumers should pay for a cleaner environment deserves close examination. First, the raising of product prices to finance a quality environment constitutes the imposition of yet another regressive tax—a tax that absorbs a higher proportion of the income earned by low-income groups than is required from those whose incomes are higher. The consequence, then, is to shift the existing distribution of income even more in favor of the wealthier portion of the population. From the micro perspective of individual families, such a policy could further distort differences in the quality of life. A second consideration relates to determining just which income groups in society have garnered most of the benefits from using the environment as a common receptacle for wastes. Who has derived most of the private benefits of accumulated social costs—the corporation and the more affluent owners of business enterprises or the average consumer?

The answers to these questions are not yet clear, but there are identifiable ways in which various parties have benefited from and have been harmed by the deteriorating environment. Different social and economic classes bear unequal responsibility for the way that man has treated the environment, and the case made for proportional or even progressive taxation to finance an environmental-control system is perhaps sounder than the option of regressively taxing the poorest citizens through higher consumer prices. At the same time, however, it must be recognized that unless prices reflect full social costs, the market mechanism will be distorted in its efforts to allocate resources efficiently. Once again the familiar conflict in goals—efficiency vs. equity—must be evaluated in financing alternative ways to clean up the environment.

## REVIEW

### Summary

1. Not unexpectedly, quality of life varies in predictable directions according to the degree of inequality in the distribution of income. Although average family income approximates $10,000 per year, more than 5 million Americans live in families with incomes averaging in excess of $36,000, and more than twice that number of persons are members of families with incomes of only about $1,500 per year. The top one-fifth of American households receive 40 percent of total income, whereas less than 6 percent of total income is received by the one-fifth of the population in the lowest income brackets.

2. Income inequality reflects the even more unequal distribution of property resources as well as a variety of factors that influence the earnings of human resources. Just what degree of income inequality is proper in a society cannot be determined except by reference to the nation's value system. While neither extreme inequality nor perfect equality in the distribution of income is regarded as reasonable, excesses in the distribution of income can promote unequal opportunities and the unequal distribution of political and economic power.

3. Environmental pollution is a second and more aggregative dimension to quality in life which has increased in severity throughout the world in recent decades. Air and water contamination are two of the most significant pollutants in the American economy. Industrial output, energy production, automotive transportation, and a consumption-bent population that continues to grow represent major contributors to pollution.

Indeed, sheer numbers make people pollution a potentially serious problem throughout the world. In addition, increasing concentrations of people in large urban centers has added to deterioration in the environment and the quality of life. Litter and waste as well as noise, pesticides, and radiation pollutants add to the environmental problems in developed nations.

4. Many of the costs of pollution as well as the benefits of pollution-control systems cannot be reckoned in dollars and cents. What information we do have suggests that cleaning up the environment will cost at least $15 to $20 billion per year, and the total bill could run as high as $40 to $50 billion annually. Most experts have concluded that such expenditures will be offset by equally large benefits gained via arresting environmental decay and improving the quality of life.

5. The environment is finite and incapable of inventorying an ever-increasing quantity of pollutants. Moreover, certain aspects of the environment can never be returned to their natural state. At the same time, most environmental resources are owned and used in common by societies with value systems that have been biased in the direction of preserving the liberty of man to use (and abuse) the environmental commons. Contemporary societies have stressed production of larger quantities of output and have failed to remain cognizant of quality and a limited environment.

6. In the United States (and many other nations) the cost of using environmental resources is inadequately recognized or even ignored. When private costs are thus understated in relation to social costs, self-interest inexorably leads a society to overproduce and to undervalue environmental resources. The real tragedy of the pollution problem is that private parties actually have incentives to debase the environment in order to shift the personal distribution of income (and the personal quality of life) in their favor.

7. Along with the self-interest motive, rivalry in various forms leads users of the environmental commons to reject personal responsibility and abuse the environment. Private parties have a public incentive to react to a neighbor's pollution-prone behavior by polluting still more—provided that the rules and customs of society do not check such reactive behavior. The rhetoric of moral suasion and public pressure may ameliorate these tendencies, but it is rare indeed that self-sacrifice is privately elected when economic viability and gain are at stake.

8. Environmental-control systems based upon the law and public regulation must be supplemented by policies designed to curb misguided economic incentives that contribute to environmental debasement. The ideal of economic efficiency will be more nearly achieved if public policy brings about equality between marginal social costs and marginal private costs. However, inability to deal with (a) the incommensurables of life and (b) the income-distribution consequences of any environmental-control system complicate the use of economic policies. Since the personal impact of environmental control on different firms and groups in society will vary, much debate over equity enshrouds the environmental problem.

9. Federal government efforts to monitor environmental pollution are being intensified, as creation of the President's Council on Environmental Quality and passage of the National Environmental Policy Act of 1970 suggest. However, most authorities recognize that a much larger financial commitment and significant economic reforms are still needed to come to grips with the pollution problem. Effluent fees, punitive taxes, tax subsidies, and direct government expenditures are among the tools which can be used to redress the economic distortions that contribute to environmental decay. While benefit-cost analysis can be useful in evaluating the effectiveness of public investments in the environment, economic comparisons often provide ambiguous solutions which must be supplemented by judgment.

### Identify the Following Concepts and Terms

- personal distribution of income
- "Q-bias"
- incommensurables
- cumulative disequilibrium
- shadow prices
- the "environmental commons"
- goods vs. "bads"
- marginal social costs

### Questions to Answer

1. Explain how the quality of life depends upon: (a) inequality in the distribution of income, and (b) the aggregate environmental-pollution problem. In what ways might the quality in life vary because of the personal distribution of income, quite irrespective of the severity of the aggregate pollution problem?

2. Assuming that you are a member of a Congressional committee charged with identifying the physical forms and the economic costs of polluting, develop a summary report on the subject.

3. Social costs associated with the use of environmental resources are alleged to be a feature of the pollution problem. Explain how this is so in the case of air and water pollution. Illustrate with a diagram.

4. In what context is it possible that social values, technology, and mismanagement of the economic system have contributed to debasement of the environment?

5. How does rivalry lead to pollution-prone behavior and possibly even self-destruction? In what ways are economic viability, survival, and the personal distribution of income related to cumulative disequilibrium and tragedy in the environmental commons?

6. Evaluate the following statement: "Men have become reasonably 'saintly' in terms of personal behavior patterns and personal accountability though the law has little to do with responsible behavior. Therefore, we can expect like social responsibility concerning use of the environmental commons."

7. When government regulations and various types of economic reforms are used to remedy environmental pollution in its many forms, difficulties arise: (a) in evaluating the cost effectiveness of public investments, and (b) in assessing the personal liberty and the income-distribution impacts of public policy. Explain.

# CHAPTER 23
# Labor Markets
# and
# Wage Determination

As a factor of production, human resources are not a mere commodity exchanged in impersonal markets. Human beings are vitally affected by the price of labor, the quality of a job, the work environment, and the opportunity to work or not work. Employers and employees are related in a personal context in which the fairness, justice, and integrity of the work relationship is no less important than the "market transaction."

In this chapter we will become familiar with the operation of labor markets and study the general determination of wages.[1] Our first task (Part A) is to examine the markets for human resources and the evolution of labor organizations. The factors which help determine wages are investigated in Part B. Then in Part C we analyze several current problems and issues related to labor markets and wage determination.

Considerable attention must be paid to institutional factors and to the imperfect operation of markets for human resources. Nonetheless, the marginal-productivity theory of resource pricing developed in Chapter 18 provides a convenient framework for introducing wage determination, where wages are understood to represent payment for all types of manpower services. Wages include the salaries, fees, and commissions earned by executives, physicians, and salesmen as well as the wage payments and fringe benefits paid for the manpower services provided by a secretary or welder employed by a corporation.

## A. HUMAN-RESOURCE MARKETS

In order to acquire some perspective about human resources and labor markets we shall first review the macroeconomic dimension to employment and earnings and then trace the historical developments leading to organized labor markets.

### The Labor Force

The demand for labor is derived from: (a) the productivity of human resources used as factors of production, and (b) the value to society of the goods and services which human resources produce. The labor supply depends upon the size of the population, the number of persons electing

---

[1] The subject of "human-resource economics" is a good deal broader than our momentarily narrow interest in wage determination and will be examined further in Chapter 24.

work over leisure, retirement, and similar factors. Were it not for the fact that increased productivity causes the demand for labor to increase with the passage of time, the simplest comparison of increasing supplies of human resources and a constant level of demand would correctly suggest a declining wage level. However, because of productivity gains, the demand for labor has increased more rapidly than the labor supply and, as a result, real wages have increased.

Figure 1 furnishes a broad overview of the supply and demand for human resources in recent decades. A general constraint on the supply of labor is set by the working-age population—defined today as persons over 16 years of age. The fraction of persons in the working-age population willing and able to work make up the *labor force,* which at the present time includes about three out of every five persons in the working-age population. The *total* labor force consists of military employment, the unemployed, and civilian employment in agricultural and nonagricultural industries, as Figure 1 indicates. In 1929, the total labor force numbered 49.9 million persons and it is expected to reach 92 million persons by 1975.

### EMPLOYMENT TRENDS

The percentage of persons in the labor force unable to find work (the ratio: unemployed/labor force) has varied markedly over the past four decades, reaching all-time highs in the 1930s, as Figure 1 shows. Full employment has by no means been the norm in the past, and this is why economists have been concerned with the relationship between aggregate spending, income, and employment. The structure of employment opportunities has also changed dramatically. Some 40 years ago, one out of five persons was employed in agriculture, but today only one out of twenty-five persons works in agriculture, and by 1975 it is anticipated that only one out of thirty persons in the labor force will be classified as an agricultural worker. Although the trend is not shown by the data in Figure 1, employment has increased rapidly in the service and government sectors in recent decades.

The number of persons participating in the labor force has drifted upward since 1900 from 52 out of 100 persons of working age to about 60 out of 100 today. Curiously enough, as Americans have become more affluent in economic terms, a larger proportion of the population have chosen work over leisure! This rising rate of participation in the labor force is even more surprising once it is recognized that a large proportion of males postpone labor-force entrance to remain in school because of the need for more training, and later withdraw from the labor force as retirement age approaches because of private pension plans and social security retirement benefits. Offsetting this downward trend in male participation in the labor force has been a rapid increase in female participation. On the average, nearly one-half of all women between 20 and 65 years of age work today, more than twice the proportion of females employed in the United States at the turn of the century. A few of the key factors influencing women's decisions to work are the changing attitudes toward the working woman, an increase in suitable jobs as the manual content of labor has declined, and the transfer of human resources from rural to urban centers—all of which have broadened job opportunities. Needless to say, these decisions have enhanced the supply of labor, economic growth, and the standard of living for millions of families.

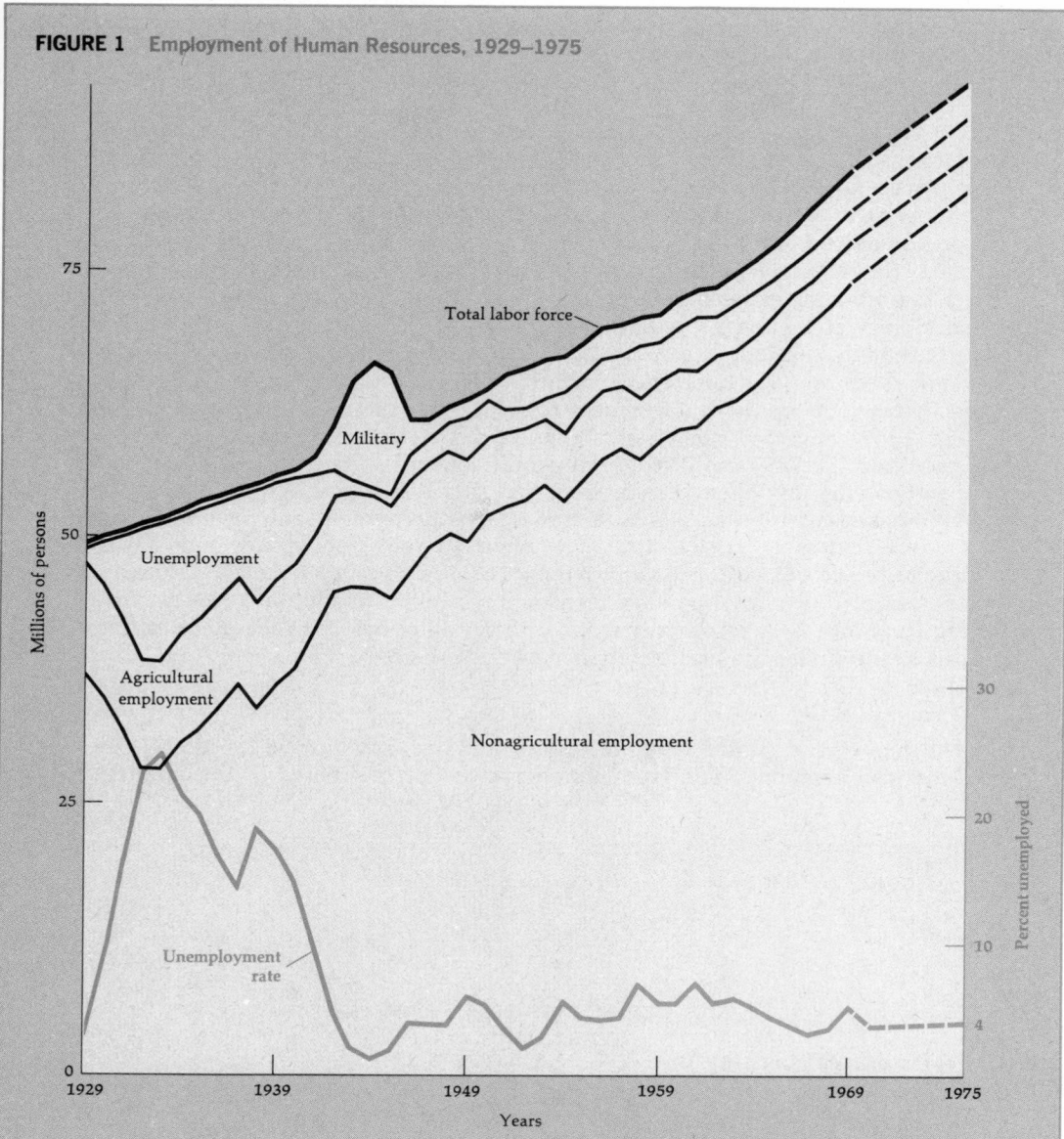

**FIGURE 1**  Employment of Human Resources, 1929–1975

SOURCE: *Economic Report of the President*, 1970, and *Manpower Report of the President*, 1970. Historical data for years prior to 1947 based on persons 14 years of age and older; thereafter, 16 years of age and older. Estimates for 1975 assume pre-Vietnam level of military activity and 4 percent unemployment.

DOMESTIC ECONOMIC ISSUES

From previous chapters we know that the demand for human resources is derived from the demand for goods and services. Not surprisingly, then, when a society demands less output—as was characteristic of the 1930s— the demand for labor (and other) resources used as factors of production slackens. Unemployment rates furnish an approximate estimate of the slack in an economy; however, the consensus among experts is that the unemployment rate tends to be conservative because anyone working part-time (one or more hours) in a survey week is counted as fully employed. Moreover, the number of individuals in the labor force seeking work rises during business expansions, while in hard times, discouragement about the possibility of finding a job drives people out of the labor force.

Although caution is called for in the interpretation of unemployment rates, there are vast differences in the incidence of unemployment. Figure 2 indicates some of these differences for two years of full employment (1948 and 1969) and two other years typified by slack aggregate demand and "recession" (1949 and 1961). The total unemployment rate for married men remains low even in recession, but this is not true for the aggregate unemployment rate, as Figure 2 shows. Unemployment among nonwhites today is twice as great as the unemployment rates for whites, and this is true in periods of both full employment (1969) and recession (1961). Nearly one out of four nonwhite male teenagers was without a job in 1969, according to Figure 2, suggesting that job opportunities are not very plentiful for this group under the best of labor-market conditions.

### Organization of Labor Markets

The move to organize labor resources has had a lasting influence on the American economy. The labor-union movement originated in this country

**FIGURE 2**    The Incidence of Unemployment

| | Full employment 1948 (percent) | Recession periods | | Full employment 1969 (percent) |
|---|---|---|---|---|
| | | 1949 (percent) | 1961 (percent) | |
| Total unemployment | 3.8 | 5.9 | 6.7 | 3.5 |
| Married men | na | 3.5 | 4.6 | 1.5 |
| All white | 3.5 | 5.6 | 6.0 | 3.1 |
| All nonwhite | 5.9 | 8.9 | 12.4 | 6.4 |
| White males 16–19 years | 9.8 | 13.8 | 15.8 | 10.2 |
| Nonwhite males 16–19 years | 9.9 | 16.5 | 27.5 | 22.1 |

*Unemployment.* The percentage of the labor force unemployed varies widely by class of worker. Among those who are most vulnerable to unemployment are racial minorities and teenagers.

SOURCE: *Manpower Report of the President,* 1970; and *Handbook of Labor Statistics,* 1969.

in the late eighteenth century, when skilled craftsmen first joined forces in "workingmen's associations" in Boston and other eastern commercial centers. Unorganized workers faced grave difficulties in bettering their working conditions and earnings because they had little bargaining power with their employers. The ability of employers to dictate working conditions and to withhold work at will far exceeded the power of one individual to shape the conditions under which he labored and, as a consequence, workingmen formed into collective groups to enhance their bargaining power. While civilized societies long tolerated associations among attorneys, physicians, skilled artisans, and shop owners, more than a few eyebrows were raised when the ordinary workingman first organized to further his social and economic well-being.

## THE EARLY LABOR MOVEMENT

The beginning of today's labor movement occurred in 1886 when the American Federation of Labor (AFL) was formed by Samuel Gompers. Labor unions were initially formed for social as well as political and economic reasons, and earlier attempts to organize labor (such as the Knights of Labor) failed in part because of the broad social and political reformism they embraced. Economic objectives, however, have been predominant in union affairs throughout the twentieth century.

Initially, the AFL was organized by crafts or trade occupations. The union movement was organized into *local unions*, which in turn associated with one *national union* representing distinct trades that affiliated with one *federation* (e.g., the AFL) made up of the numerous national unions. The federation serves as the standard-bearer for the union movement. Led by Samuel Gompers in its early years, the AFL abandoned the search for immediate and vast reforms of the political and economic system. In rejecting broad social reform, the AFL embraced "bread-and-butter" goals—an orientation to practical economic objectives including better pay, shorter working hours, healthier working conditions, and so on. Neutrality on the part of the public sector was supported by Gompers under the principle of "voluntarism," which philosophically rejected government intervention in management and labor conflicts. Finally, the AFL supported separate jurisdictions for identifiable occupations among the several national unions which were members of the federation.

As the mass-production factory system grew in the United States, larger and larger numbers of noncraft workers found themselves without representation because of the "trade" orientation of the AFL. It soon became clear that the industrial sector of the economy needed leadership, and the void was filled by John L. Lewis of the United Mine Workers, who formed a new federation in 1935—the Congress of Industrial Organization (CIO). In part because of lethargic competition from the AFL in the CIO's formative years, the new federation was successful in organizing workers employed in the large and rapidly growing mass-production industries. CIO membership, which numbered in the millions in a few short years, was also aided by pro-union legislation passed during the 1930s. After World War II, the union movement attempted to achieve a new unity by combining the industrial and trade-union interests of the CIO and the AFL. In 1955, both federations merged into the AFL-CIO, which today includes all but a few national unions, some of which are large in their own right. Membership in nonaffiliated national unions such as the Teamsters, the United Auto Workers, and the United Mine Workers totals over 6 million individuals today, while AFL-CIO membership is almost 14 million.

The labor-union movement has a colorful past, and today exerts substantial influence on the working lives of millions of persons. Although the unions long were a relatively powerless institutional force in the American economy, this situation changed sharply in the mid-1930s.[2] The membership of officially recognized American labor unions today is approximately 20 million persons although, as Figure 3 indicates, the rate of growth in union membership has stagnated since 1950. Today the labor-union movement (excluding professional associations such as the National Education Association) includes a little better than one-fifth of the total labor force. Although membership in labor unions is less pronounced among white-collar workers, women, workers in the South, and farm areas in the United States, many vital industries such as steel, trucking, automobile manufacturing, and construction are heavily organized. The vast majority of labor-union members reside in a dozen or so heavily industrialized states concentrated in the East; approximately one-half of all labor-union members are employed in manufacturing industries; and one out of every ten union members shown in Figure 3 is an employee of the government at the federal, state, or local level.

GOVERNMENT AND THE UNION MOVEMENT

Much of the history of unions as an economic institution relates directly to their legal status in past decades. While this is not the place to examine government and labor law fully, we would be remiss in failing to sketch the social and economic changes reflected in the legal status of labor unions.

[2] In the 1930s the courts recognized unions as legal economic institutions in the United States, a decision spurred on by the deprivation and poverty common to millions of Americans during the Depression era.

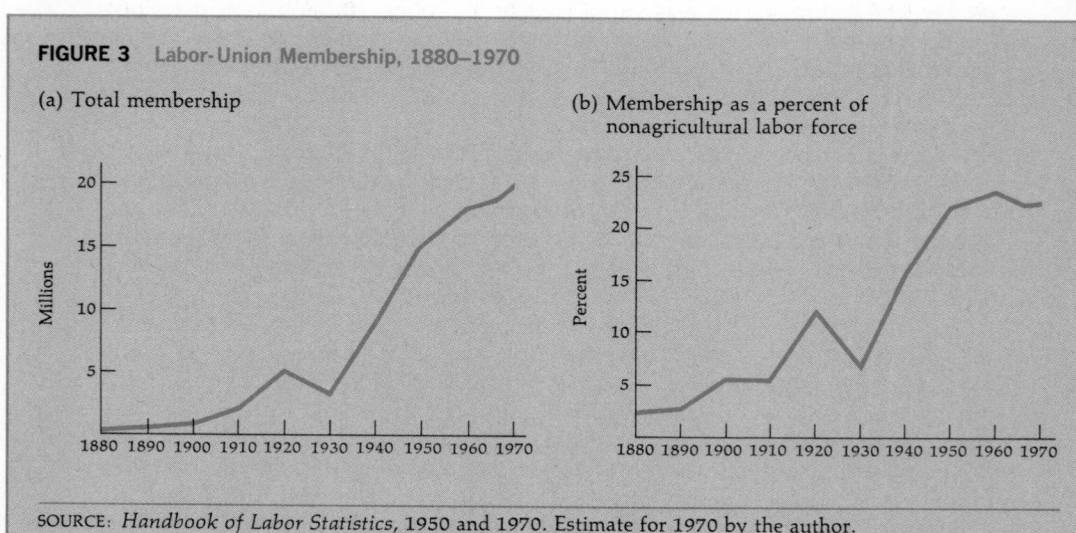

FIGURE 3   Labor-Union Membership, 1880–1970

(a) Total membership

(b) Membership as a percent of nonagricultural labor force

SOURCE: *Handbook of Labor Statistics*, 1950 and 1970. Estimate for 1970 by the author.

The first one and one-half centuries of the union movement were a period of perpetual struggle against powerful business interests, the courts, and Congressional legislation. The law of the land was dedicated to preserving property and employer rights and was thus hostile and reluctant to recognize the rights of organized workers. Like most participants in organized efforts to promote social and economic change, union members were commonly viewed as ungrateful troublemakers and agitators, if not criminals.[3] With the implicit and explicit approval of the highest courts in the land, employers arbitrarily fired pro-union workers, and on numerous occasions plants were simply shut down by employers to stifle strikes or union membership drives. Employers also maintained *blacklists* which identified union workers or union sympathizers. Moreover, employers often required that workers not associate with the union as a condition of employment—an agreement which was termed the *yellow-dog contract*. Because weapons like these received considerable legal support for many decades, the labor-union movement did not appear to have much of a chance to succeed. However, employees were determined to share collectively in employer decisions to establish earnings and working conditions. The advances in this struggle are best illustrated by a skeletal description of the union's drive for legal status.

*The End of Criminal Conspiracy*   Government hostility toward organized labor was first demonstrated by the *criminal-conspiracy doctrine*, which held that any combination of workingmen organized for the purpose of raising wages was illegal. Until the Supreme Court of Massachusetts ruled otherwise in the case of *Commonwealth* vs. *Hunt* (1842), unions were prosecuted under criminal law as a conspiracy against the state. The end of the criminal-conspiracy doctrine did not free the union movement from the heavy hand of the law, however, for the courts continued to regard such activities as strikes and picketing as in restraint of trade and therefore as illegal ways of achieving improvements in wages or working conditions.

[3] The emergence of labor unions is well documented as a revolution marked by violence and death. The Mollie Maguires, an organization of miners in the anthracite coal fields of eastern Pennsylvania, were brought to trial in 1875, and ten members were later executed, while another fourteen were imprisoned. Nearly another dozen persons were killed in the "Haymarket Square Affair" in Chicago as an outgrowth of a strike against the McCormick Harvester Company in 1886. Four union members were subsequently convicted and hanged, and dozens languished in jail, including one person who committed suicide upon receiving the death penalty. In 1913 at "Bloody Ludlow," mining firms controlled by John D. Rockefeller, Sr., engaged in pitched battles with Colorado miners, including an alleged strafing of mining camps with machine guns mounted on trains. In later Congressional hearings on the Ludlow Massacre, one Congressman Foster asked Rockefeller if "You are willing to let these killings take place...," to which this giant of industry replied: "...we expect to stand by the [company] officers at any cost. It is not an accident that this is our position." And then there was Joe Hill, a "troubadour" of the miners belonging to the Industrial Workers of the World (Wobblies), who was arrested, tried, and convicted of what history suggests was a trumped-up murder charge. Despite two appeals by President Wilson to Utah authorities who were anxious to run the Wobblies out of the state, Hill was executed by a firing squad on November 19, 1915. His final words ("Don't mourn for me—organize.") became the rallying cry of labor.

*Unions and the Sherman Act (1890)*   Hostility toward business monopoly resulted in the passage of the Sherman Antitrust Act of 1890, a law intended to restrict and regulate business monopolies that were in restraint of trade. However, the Sherman Act was also applied to labor unions. The courts regarded unions as labor-market monopolies that were in restraint of trade and therefore illegal under the antitrust law. On several occasions, union techniques for achieving their goals (such as the strike) were declared illegal under the broad umbrella of the Sherman Act. One of the important legal tactics used by employers to squash union activities was the *injunction* —a court order obtained at the request of employers forbidding workers to strike or picket to achieve union demands.

*The Norris-LaGuardia Act (1932)*   This legislation outlawed the yellow-dog contract. Another noteworthy feature of the Norris-LaGuardia Act was the severe limitations it placed upon the use of injunctions as a weapon which had proved successful in restraining unions.

*The Wagner Act (1935)*   This legislative hallmark for the union movement came midway in the sharpest economic decline in American history. It gave unions the rights to organize and bargain collectively with employers. In addition, the Wagner Act furnished unions with safeguards by identifying certain unfair practices used by employers (such as discrimination against union members). Finally, the Wagner Act established the National Labor Relations Board—a quasi-legal agency of the federal government which investgates labor disputes and rules upon alleged violations of labor regulations.

*The Taft-Hartley Act (1947)*   Within 15 years after the Wagner Act was passed, union membership increased fourfold, but by 1947 public opinion and the pro-union legislative tenor of the 1930s had dissipated. Postwar labor disputes and an obviously strong labor movement were checked by passage of the Taft-Hartley Act, which spelled out in detail crucial aspects of labor-management relations. Among other things, the 1947 legislation regulated certain internal financial and political affairs of unions and specified controls over the collective-bargaining process. In addition, the law identified unfair labor practices on the part of unions and provided for government intervention in strikes that threatened to imperil the economy. The President was given power to obtain an 80-day injunction, thereby setting up what has been termed a "cooling-off" or delay period. During this 80-day period, government authorities are charged with publicizing and mediating disputes. The significance of the Taft-Hartley Act is that it denotes a redress in the balance of power which had earlier swung in favor of organized labor, and also asserts government's interest in the collective-bargaining process.

*The Landrum-Griffin Act (1959)*   Financial reporting and the management of union fees and pension funds are now closely regulated under the Landrum-Griffin Act. Election procedures are also subject to the scrutiny of federal officials, and restrictions have been placed upon union officials with criminal records and persons affiliated with communist organizations. Union members have thus obtained a measure of protection from undemocratic and corrupt procedures by the authority delegated to the United States Secretary of Labor.

*In summary:* The organized labor movement has a colorful history, marked by hostility and suppression during its first century; a brief period of remarkable growth and expansion; and, more recently, retrenchment and stagnation. This institution has had a profound influence on society, and labor unions remain important today. Many of the weapons used in the struggle between management and organized labor (strikes, boycotts, sit-ins, and injunctions) are also characteristic of more recent social-reform movements such as the civil rights movement and the so-called "student revolutions." Many people still think of labor unions in terms of factory and trade workers; however, today several million other workers such as the teachers, engineers, physicians, attorneys, nurses, and the airline pilots belong to associations or professional organizations—which are comparable in many ways to the conventional labor or trade union. All such groups lobby on behalf of the vested interests of their members and are concerned about wages, working conditions, retirement benefits, and the like. While the labor-union movement as commonly defined is not growing numerically, collective action by economic interest groups is very much a part of American life today.

## B. WAGE DETERMINATION

The purposes of organized associations of workers are very broad. Teachers' associations frequently work toward improving the quality of education by demanding smaller teacher-pupil ratios or better equipment and facilities, the American Medical Association lobbies for public support and medical research funds, and the AFL-CIO promotes health and safety in the work environment and economic security for unemployed, disabled, and retired workers. In addition to nonwage goals, collective action is also directed toward wage improvements—either explicitly or implicitly. While wages are influenced in the most general sense by the supply and demand for labor, there are other important institutional influences (e.g., collective bargaining), as well as qualitative differences in human resources that help explain wage determination. We shall begin by reviewing the competitive determination of wages discussed in general terms in Chapter 18, then examine wage differentials, and finally investigate imperfections in labor markets.

### Productivity and Wages

The long-run relations between wages and productivity are crucial ones that merit remembering. We know from the theory of marginal productivity developed in Chapter 18 that the determination of resource prices under competitive conditions is founded on two ideas:

1. Firms utilize labor resources according to the productivity of labor, where the marginal productivity of labor and product price determine the marginal revenue product of labor. The *demand* for labor is thus given by labor's marginal revenue product schedule.
2. Resources are employed profitably up to that quantity at which the marginal resource cost (*MRC*) and marginal revenue product (*MRP*) of

labor are equal[4]—that is, one firm can profitably employ a resource until $MRC = MRP$.

## COMPETITIVE WAGE DETERMINATION

In Figure 4(a) the intersection of competitive market supply and demand determines an equilibrium market wage of $w$ ($20 per day, let us say), as was explained in Chapter 18. To obtain more labor of a uniform type, *all* firms must offer a higher wage to attract workers from other firms, as is denoted by market supply schedule *s* in Figure 4(a). The market demand for labor (schedule *d*) is obtained by summing individual *MRP* or demand curves for all firms using one homogeneous grade of labor.

Figure 4(a) assumes that there are no immobilities or other sources of friction in the labor market and that there are many buyers and sellers. Thus, no one firm can influence the market wage, and all workers are assumed to compete freely for jobs. Each firm has to pay the competitive wage $w$ to acquire some small portion of the market supply of labor. Therefore, the supply of labor to *one* firm is a perfectly elastic supply schedule at a wage of $20 per day. Labor will be hired by each competitive profit-maximizing firm up to that level at which the additional revenue generated by one more unit of labor (i.e., one firm's *MRP*) equals the additional cost of $w = $20$ for the last unit of labor employed. Under competitive condi-

---

[4] As long as labor is hired competitively by an employer, labor supply to the individual firm is perfectly elastic and each *additional* unit of labor paid the market-determined wage (of, say, $20 per day) costs an employer that wage (an additional $20). If labor's $MRP = $21$, it is profitable by $1 to hire another unit of labor, but if $MRP = $19$ another unit would not be hired by a profit-maximizing firm if the wage (and *MRC*) is $20.

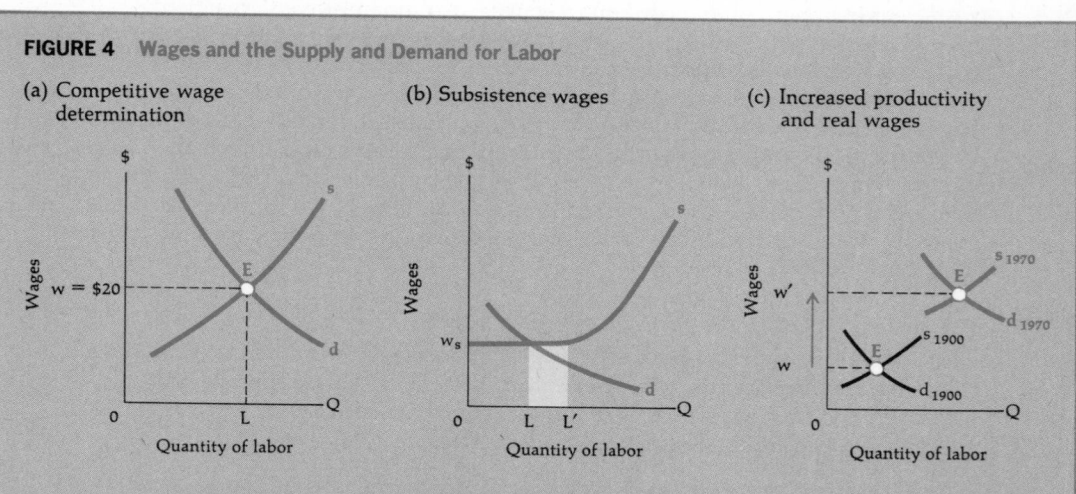

**FIGURE 4** Wages and the Supply and Demand for Labor

(a) Competitive wage determination

(b) Subsistence wages

(c) Increased productivity and real wages

*The Wage Rate.* Market supply and demand for labor determine the equilibrium wage of $w = $20$ as in (a). Marx argued that labor demand would decrease until the relatively low wage level shown in (b) is obtained, the result being a growing reserve army of unemployed workers (*LL'* units). In fact, however, the demand for labor has increased along with supply as shown in (c), allowing real wages *and* employment to rise.

tions, wages cannot be driven to the lower levels employers might desire, nor can they be driven upward to the higher levels which are preferable to workers.

At one time in the not-too-distant past, quite different and rather dismal views of the determination of wages were held by economists. Karl Marx, for example, felt that wages would be depressed to the subsistence level of wage $w_s$ in Figure 4(b) because of an excess supply of unemployed proletariat workers—a condition that would be created by capitalistic business firms continually substituting capital resources for labor in a vain search for increased profits. The Marxian equilibrium wage condition would also lead to a depressed labor market in which a "reserve army" of unemployed and increasingly rebellious workers would be without jobs [in the amount $LL'$ of Figure 4(b)]. Although Malthus and Ricardo cited different causes, they reached similar conclusions about the pervasiveness of a subsistence wage level like $w_s$ in the long run. According to these two Englishmen, wages were maintained at a level at which human resources are just able to survive and reproduce—say at wage $w_s$. Any short-run wage rate above the subsistence level could not be maintained because of diminishing marginal productivity, and because the population will expand in the long run, driving wages down to $w_s$ in Figure 4(b).

Marx, Malthus, and Ricardo were wrong insofar as developed nations are concerned; real wages have increased well above subsistence levels in line with the increased productivity of labor, as Figure 4(c) indicates. Even though the supply of labor has increased significantly over the decades, *both* employment *and* wages have increased in developed economies because of rising productivity. It is true, of course, that the dismal prophecies of Malthus and Ricardo have proven to be more right than wrong for many underdeveloped nations because labor productivity has not increased, but that is a separate problem, as we shall see.[5]

## WAGE DIFFERENTIALS

It turns out upon close inspection that the marginal-productivity theory of wage determination grossly oversimplifies the real world. Markets for human resources tend to conform to pricing on the basis of productivity only in crude and very long-run terms. Only over long periods of time are the rigidities, immobilities, and imperfections of labor markets smoothed out. The reason annual wage earnings of physicians and surgeons are eight to ten times the average for male laborers in the United States extends beyond explanations of competitive supply and demand alone. Let us consider some of the more common explanations for wage differentials.

*Noneconomic Job Attributes*  Wage differentials sometimes represent payments that equalize the qualitative features of a job. Even if labor markets were perfectly competitive for equally productive human resources, wage differentials might be used to equalize the noneconomic characteristics of different occupations. Undertakers may earn a good deal more than persons in equally skilled occupations to compensate for the noneconomic features of their job. Part of the wage premium enjoyed by the medical profession reflects the long and irregular hours of work required in com-

[5] See Chapter 27.

parison to the more placid life of, say, a university-employed biochemist, and most of us know that clerical or banking work is agreeable, regular, and generally more attractive than construction work, which is one reason that construction jobs are characterized by higher wages.

*Human-Resource Quality*   But is it not true that many of the better-paying jobs are also more attractive in noneconomic terms (e.g., dentistry vs. garbage collecting)? It is, and this fact suggests that equalizing differences are by no means the only important determinant of wage differentials. A second partial explanation for differences in wages depends upon differences in the quality of human resources. Systems analysts are qualitatively very different from warehouse laborers or neurosurgeons, and the wages of all three groups will partially reflect the qualitative differences of the human resources in these occupations.

*Noncompeting Labor Markets*   Still another reason that wage differentials are common is that markets are differentiated—that is, innumerable "noncompeting" labor markets exist. Today's technology often demands highly trained and specialized talents, a situation which serves to fragment labor markets into literally thousands of quasi-independent market processes. For example, relatively separate and noncompeting markets exist for engineers, physicists, attorneys, and machinists. When labor markets are fragmented into a variety of skill levels and specialized occupations, the perfectly competitive model of wage determination breaks down; machinists are not good substitutes for physicians, nor are artists good substitutes for electricians. Even individuals of equal innate abilities are affected by noncompeting markets because the opportunity to acquire specialized training is not equally distributed.

*Imperfect Markets*   Markets for human resources are not perfectly competitive for a variety of reasons. Immobilities characterize human resources because personal ties of past training, custom, home, and regional familiarity limit the movement from one job or locality to another. Moreover, human resources are imperfectly aware of alternative opportunities, and job opportunities are not equally available to all. Rigidities and immobilites in labor markets also reflect institutional barriers to work in professions such as teaching (the "union card" in this case is a college degree plus X hours of education courses) as well as to a variety of other occupations (such as those of the electrician, teamster, or optometrist). Rigidities in the labor market also reflect social barriers. Discrimination on the basis of sex or race, for example, handicaps the earnings of women and nonwhites.

In short, the productivity of human resources is one, but not the only, factor that helps explain wage determination and wage differentials. The noneconomic attributes of work, qualitative differences in human resources, noncompeting and differentiated labor markets, and market imperfections all influence wage differentials. Economic power can therefore be used either by workers or by employers to influence wages, a condition which permits and even encourages collective action in the wage-determining process.

### Imperfections in the Labor Market

Labor markets only rarely approximate the competitive ideal because men have developed socioeconomic rules and arrangements that convert markets into imperfect forces in which market power has been institutionalized. Although any generalized models used to depict the impact of market power on wage determination ignore many relevant factors, we can gain some new insights by first examining market power on the part of buyers of labor. We then review four other cases of market power on the part of sellers. While each case is more illustrative than descriptive of the real world, there are elements of reality in each of the five cases which follow.

## CASE I: MONOPSONY POWER IN THE HIRE OF LABOR

Resource supply to *one* firm under competitive conditions is perfectly elastic because no one firm can influence the price paid for competitively supplied labor; i.e., one uniform wage rate is set by the market. Consequently, the market wage is uniform for all firms hiring a given grade of labor. This means, as we know, that the additional cost of hiring one more resource (the marginal resource cost) is equal to the wage rate. Now let us look at the supply of resources in imperfectly competitive markets.

Suppose there is *one* monopsonistic buyer of labor resources in a localized market. The demand for labor is given by the schedule of labor's *MRP* and the supply curve of labor to the employer with monopsony buying power is the upward-sloping supply schedule *s* drawn in Figure 5.

**FIGURE 5**   Monopsony in the Hire of Labor

Case I: Monopsony

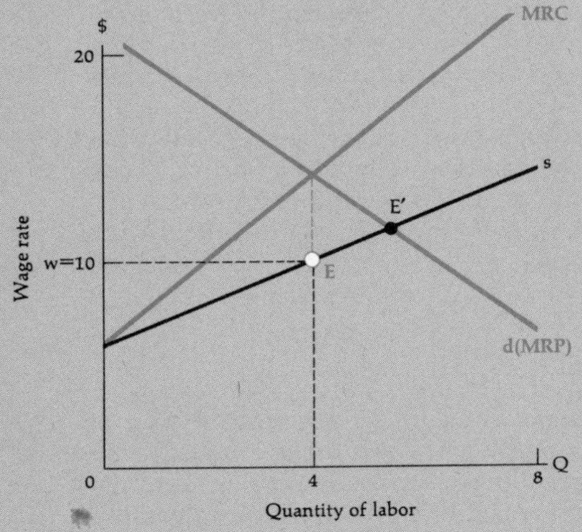

| (1) | (2) | (3) Total resource cost | (4) Marginal resource cost |
|---|---|---|---|
| Quantity of labor | Wage rate | (1) × (2) | △ (3) |
| 0 | $ 6 | $ 0 | |
| | | | $ 7 |
| 1 | 7 | 7 | |
| | | | 9 |
| 2 | 8 | 16 | |
| | | | 11 |
| 3 | 9 | 27 | |
| | | | 13 |
| 4 | 10 | 40 | |
| | | | 15 |
| 5 | 11 | 55 | |
| | | | 17 |
| 6 | 12 | 72 | |
| | | | 19 |
| 7 | 13 | 91 | |
| | | | 21 |
| 8 | 14 | 112 | |

*Monopsony-determined Wages.* If firms have the ability to influence wages through monopsony power, the supply schedule is upward-sloping as s above. Marginal resource cost (*MRC*) exceeds the wage rate given by the supply schedule because additional quantities of labor can only be hired at a higher wage rate. Employers with monopsony power in the hire of labor equate *MRC* and *MRP* to maximize profits at point *E* which results in the hire of 4 units of labor. The monopsony wage of $10 is lower than what it would be under competitive conditions at point *E'*.

Every point on supply schedule *s* represents the *average cost* that must be paid by an employer hiring a given quantity of labor. When the monopsonistic employer hires another unit of competitively supplied labor, the additional cost—the marginal resource cost—exceeds the wage rate; marginal resource cost schedule *MRC* lies above the supply schedule shown in Figure 5. Hiring three workers at $9 per day compared to four workers at a wage of $10 per day adds $13 to total costs ($27 compared to $40). Thus, the *MRC* of the fourth worker is $13. The additional cost of one more laborer is larger than the wage rate because all workers must be paid the higher wage of $10 per day. The monopsonistic employer continues to hire labor as long as the additional cost given by *MRC* is less than labor's marginal revenue product shown by demand schedule *d* of Figure 5, and thus the intersection of *MRC* and *MRP* identifies the equilibrium wage and quantity of labor hired. In Figure 5, *MRC* and *MRP* are equal at four units of labor, and the wage of $w = \$10$ that must be paid to employ four units of labor is given by the supply schedule at point *E*.

The point about employer-exercised monopsony buying power is straightforward enough. By hiring the profit-maximizing amount of labor at which *MRP* and *MRC* are equal, both the wage rate *and* employment tend to be lower than they would be under competitive supply and demand (point *E'* in Figure 5). When a monopsonist attempts to hire more labor, he drives wages up himself. In addition, the monopsonist employs less labor and pays a wage that is less than the marginal revenue product of labor, as Figure 5 also illustrates. The wage rate ($w$ of $10) is less than the value of labor's marginal revenue product because monopsonistic employers are able to influence the wage rate, and not unexpectedly, wages tend to be less than they would be under competitive conditions. Thus, employer monopsony or buying power in the hire of labor resources tends to restrict employment and distort wages relative to the contribution labor resources make to output.

We have seen the impact of employer-exerted market power, but what happens when market power rests in the hands of sellers of labor resources, perhaps because a labor union (the United Auto Workers) or a professional association (the Bar Association) influences the price of labor services? The market-power tactics sellers use to influence wages in each case consist of: (*a*) increasing demand, (*b*) reducing supply, (*c*) administering wages, and (*d*) bilateral monopoly.

## CASE II: THE BAR—INCREASING LABOR DEMAND

In some instances, increasing the demand for labor is an effective way of raising wage rates. Suppose, for example, that the attorneys' "union" (the Bar Association) astutely observes prevailing political institutions and decides to "help" society legislate and organize its affairs by writing complicated laws (in a language suspected to derive from the Anglo-Saxon) which only they can understand and administer. After a period of time and a vast accumulation of laws, demand increases for this specialized type of labor, ultimately leading to the employment of one attorney for every 60 persons in Washington, D.C., compared to one attorney for every 950 persons in Indiana. In the measure that this class of labor is successful in shifting market demand for its services from *d* to *d'* and supply remains unchanged, as shown in Figure 6(a), both wages and employment rise. The wage rate in-

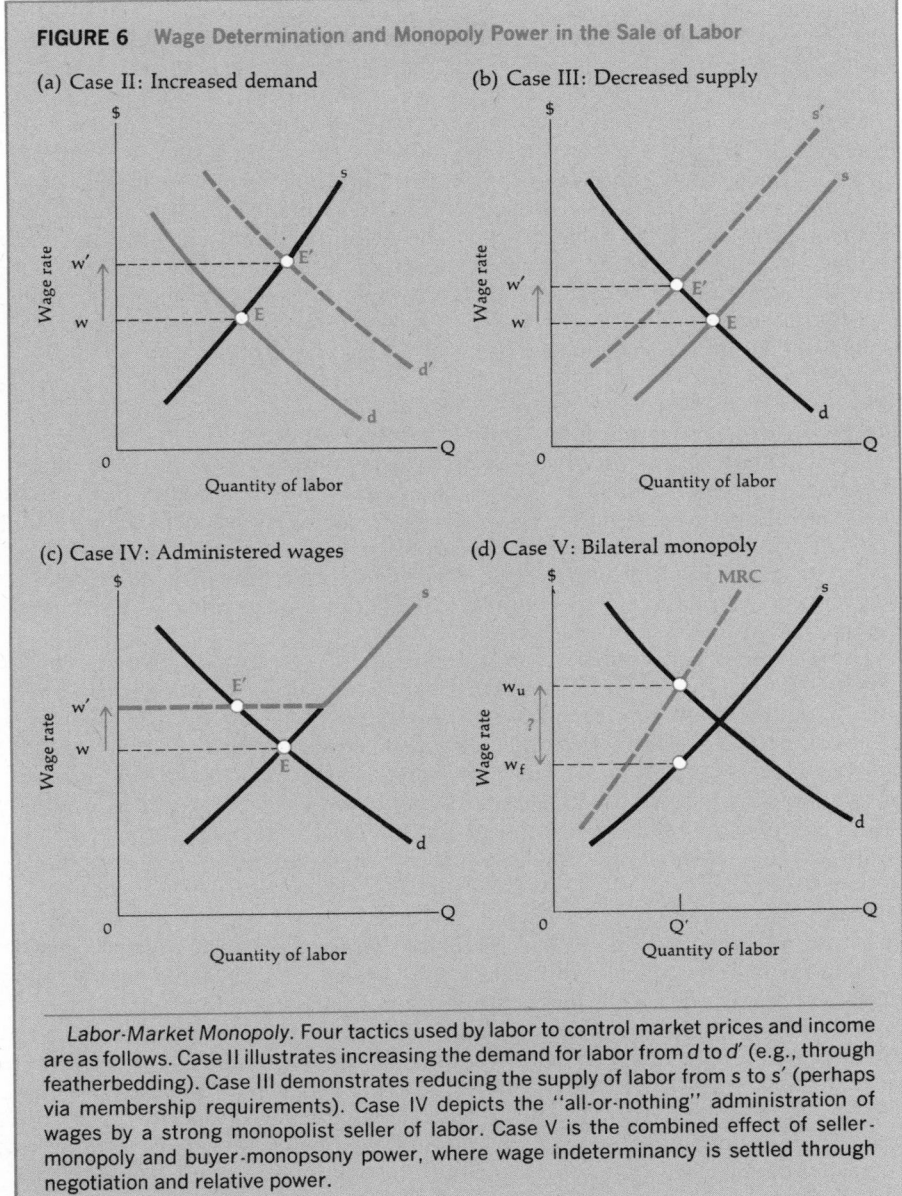

**FIGURE 6**  Wage Determination and Monopoly Power in the Sale of Labor

(a) Case II: Increased demand

(b) Case III: Decreased supply

(c) Case IV: Administered wages

(d) Case V: Bilateral monopoly

*Labor-Market Monopoly.* Four tactics used by labor to control market prices and income are as follows. Case II illustrates increasing the demand for labor from $d$ to $d'$ (e.g., through featherbedding). Case III demonstrates reducing the supply of labor from $s$ to $s'$ (perhaps via membership requirements). Case IV depicts the "all-or-nothing" administration of wages by a strong monopolist seller of labor. Case V is the combined effect of seller-monopoly and buyer-monopsony power, where wage indeterminancy is settled through negotiation and relative power.

creases from $w$ to $w'$ and employment rises to the higher equilibrium level denoted by $E'$.

The opportunity to increase demand for labor services varies, of course, from market to market. Labor unions in the steel industry advocate "buy-American" policies, as well as tariff protection for steel products, in hopes of strengthening the demand for domestic steel, which in turn enhances the derived demand for labor. The "increased-demand effect" may also apply in some degree to course prerequisites established by university professors or to war pronouncements by the Pentagon. The general result is analogous to the situation of the Bar Association illustrated in Figure 6(a)— creation of additional employment and (barring conscripted manpower or other changes in supply) higher wages to boot. In other instances, feather-bedding (make-work) policies illustrate demand-manipulation tactics used to avoid or prolong anticipated decreases in the demand for labor. Thus, the effect of farm subsidies in holding up the price of certain commodities has been to keep more human resources "down on the farm." We have not yet seen the adoption of dental chemicals capable of resisting decay (and reducing the demand for dentistry as well), yet more wondrous scientific advances have made interplanetary space travel a reality.

### CASE III: THE AMA—CONTROLLED LABOR SUPPLY

We now turn our attention to another market imperfection that is characteristic of some sellers of labor—supply restriction. Suppose a trade union is formed for electricians, or a physicians' association is organized which has some ability to restrict supply through licensing procedures. The result is a shift in the "effective" market supply curve from $s$ to $s'$, as shown in Figure 6(b). Equilibrium is thus established at $E'$ because membership restrictions are placed on the number of sellers of labor allowed entry into the market, and wages increase from $w$ to $w'$.

The common requirement for influencing wages in this fashion is to develop exclusion policies. The American Medical Association may have such a policy in mind in chafing at the federal government's involvement in health care. After all, when medical-school training facilities are limited, prospective entrants to such facilities can be "screened" to fill the number of available seats, and thus the supply of physicians is controlled. In addition, control over the substitution of paramedical personnel for physicians is important because paramedical professionals increase the supply of human resources.

Both subtle and obvious supply restrictions are used to boost wages. Craft unions such as the electricians or barbers are prone to support membership-exclusion policies through entry barriers such as licensing and initiation fees, and hostile feelings are quick to arise when nonunion members perform union tasks. The difficulty of the supply-exclusion tactic is in making the entry barriers stick, because the excluded labor supply willing to work at a wage lower than $w'$ in Figure 6(b) just may be able to secure work. To avoid the development of secondary labor markets, it is necessary to have tight control over such institutional barriers as licensing or apprenticeship which restrict job entry—something the plumbers, electricians, and physicians have been much more successful at than have the laborers.

### CASE IV: THE TEACHERS—WAGE ADMINISTRATION

Another tactic typifying some industrial labor unions and professional groups is outright administration of wages to some level like $w'$ shown in Figure 6(c). Workers long ago learned that employers sometimes can be "induced" to accept higher wages by the threat of retaliatory action. Suppose that, in Figure 6(c), the teachers simply make a wage demand of $w'$, insisting on it as an alternative to a strike. To be successful in this tactic, the organization must represent the bulk of a labor market and must be committed to pursuit of the common goal of wage $w'$. To the extent that inclusive membership and a strong organization are lacking, negotiating an administered wage is difficult. The higher costs of $w'$ will exclude some labor from the market, and workers who are not organized may break ranks and accept a lower wage in order to return to work—a situation much more prevalent among teachers than among the more powerful dentists.

## CASE V: THE AUTO WORKERS AND THE "BIG THREE"—BILATERAL

A final and generally more common combination of market power is that of (a) monopoly power in the sale of labor and (b) monopsony power on the part of employers hiring in labor markets. In such instances, imperfect competition occurs on both sides of the market. This is the case for the "Big Three" automotive firms, who hire labor as monopsonists from the United Auto Workers. Similarly, "Big Steel" must negotiate with steel-workers' unions which are monopolists in selling labor. Figure 6(d) shows the demand and supply curves for labor used to determine the wage rate and the amount of labor employed. The equilibrium wage under the circumstances shown in Figure 6(d) is indeterminate, depending on the relative strength of the opposing market powers.

Assume momentarily that the employing automotive firms possess all of the market power as perfect monopsonistic buyers of labor. The units of labor purchased will be determined by equating $MRC$ and $MRP$, shown as demand schedule $d$ in Figure 6(d). In this case, $Q'$ units will be employed at a wage of $w_f$. Now suppose that the union informs automobile manufacturers that the price of labor will be $w_u$—take it or leave it! About all one can say at this point is that the conflict between the two market powers will have to be negotiated, the outcome being dependent on the relative strength and bargaining power of both parties. The wage level will fall somewhere between the extremes of $w_f$ and $w_u$. It is possible that "countervailing" market power (as Galbraith and others have termed bilateral monopoly) will remedy extremes in either direction, but it is clear that there is no competitive market system allocating resources in this situation. Indeed, the reverse of powerless behavior under competition prevails. "Power" now becomes a requisite to survival, as well as a key factor in wage determination.

## C. THE ECONOMIC IMPACT OF ORGANIZED LABOR MARKETS

The power to influence wages which arises from imperfection in labor markets has important practical consequences as well as interesting economic implications. Should nurses, teachers, or any group of workers, for that matter, be allowed to strike or otherwise employ economic power, and how does market power influence the collective-bargaining process? Can we allow the railway workers to halt commercial activities by tying up the nation's transportation system? Are union leaders corrupt, and is it true that lower wages increase employment?

For the most part, bargaining has increasingly become an important technique of resolving disputes over wages and employment conditions. By its very nature, collective action implies the use of mutually shared market power. Three features of imperfect labor markets deserve attention: (a) the way in which collective bargaining operates, (b) the problems and issues in organized labor markets, and (c) government's role in monitoring organized labor markets.

## Collective Bargaining

Personal experiences, knowledge of the history of the labor movement, and the theory of wage determination tell us that control can be exercised over wages as well as over working conditions. In most industrialized nations, collective bargaining over the conditions of employment is widely used to reconcile the conflicting goals of labor and management. When a nation encourages collective bargaining and the monopolization of labor markets by unions, as the United States has done, it is attempting to neutralize and equalize economic power. The rationale behind institutionalization of the labor union and the collective-bargaining process rests in no small measure on the need for monopoly power to counter the monopsonistic power large firms enjoy in negotiating with a single employee. Although bargaining is most commonly thought of in terms of the traditional blue-collar labor union, it is apparent that numerous professional occupations are also moving in the direction of formal negotiations.

Contract negotiation is a mixture of competitive and monopolistic forces relying upon bargaining-power tactics. Labor unions pit their power against corporate employers, while professional groups such as the teachers, physicians, and attorneys are less conspicuous forms of "unions" in imperfect markets where economic "power" tactics are also useful. In these latter instances, subtlety in the use of bargaining power prevails, and much of the time power is not evenly distributed, since the opposition (the public) is usually poorly represented, if it is represented at all. Even though we accept labor-union monopolies as a useful check against large corporations, imbalance in the distribution of market power cannot be justified on grounds of equity. Market power in the hands of a large Teamsters' Union negotiating with small trucking lines distorts the allocation of resources and the determination of wages just as does the use of market power by professional associations which "negotiate" prices with the unorganized consumer. It may well be that the long-standing and subtle use of organized power helps explain why physicians' incomes, for example, have increased more rapidly than average wages in recent decades.

Many issues other than wages are often at stake in collective bargaining. The economic security of both individual workers and union representatives is usually an area of conflict between management and unions. Contractual agreements between labor and management almost always reflect employee concerns for job and economic security, and this goal is normally achieved through seniority systems that define acceptable conditions for promotions, changing jobs within a firm, pension rights, holidays, and the order for layoffs if they are necessary. Collective bargaining is a continuous process, however, not something that occurs every two or three years. Since management and the union work together on a day-to-day basis, minor "grievances" arising from the ongoing work relationships agreed to in contractual form must be resolved. Most contracts spell out how grievances are to be processed. Often, the grievance machinery terminates in arbitration conducted by a third party whose decision normally is binding on both management and labor. Despite the fact that collective bargaining is often thought of as a near-riotous affair culminating in a strike, this is not at all true. During the last quarter-century in the United States, less than one-half of 1 percent of total manhours worked in any given year have been lost because of strikes or related work disputes.

## ECONOMIC CONSIDERATIONS IN BARGAINING

Economic considerations such as the magnitude of unemployment, the level of profits, labor productivity, and changes in the costs of living are important factors in the collective negotiation of wage settlements. If profits have risen rapidly, union leaders will emphasize that fact, along with the real-wage erosion caused by inflation and the increased productivity of labor. Employers, on the other hand, can be expected to emphasize the fact that wage increases contribute to higher costs and inflation, particularly if wages rise more rapidly than productivity. Many labor unions have successfully negotiated *escalator clauses* into contractual agreements with management, providing for automatic wage increases as consumer prices rise. Other important economic considerations are the negotiated wage settlements or key bargains already reached in selected industries, and the going wage rates for similar work skills. Finally, government may also be a factor to contend with in the collective-bargaining process, particularly if a strike threatens to disrupt the national economy.

## BARGAINING STRATEGY

It has long been said that how you play the game is important, and this is certainly true of collective bargaining over wage and employment conditions.

If the union adopts a conciliatory strategy and management a hard-line posture toward negotiation, one might suspect that management would gain the upper hand. Many other factors affect the outcome of conflict situations, however. Management may really be bluffing or the union may think that management is bluffing and not take their threats seriously. The extent to which a party has strength or staying power in a conflict situation is also important, as is its willingness to assume a greater risk of failure. Then, too, both parties may implicitly collaborate on a settlement, knowing that if the firm has the ability to administer prices, any cost increases can be passed on to the public. Furthermore, the credibility of negotiation tactics such as threats is important to the outcome of labor-management disputes. Indeed, the desire to lend credibility to their present and future demands often explains the reason firms shut down and lose hundreds of thousands of dollars in profits and the reason thousands of workers will strike for days or weeks over the equivalent of a few cents per hour.

Under imperfectly competitive conditions such as bilateral monopoly, economic considerations and negotiation tactics produce some degree of bargaining power. If the power of either the buyers or the sellers of labor is unopposed by a "countervailing force," sheer monopsony or monopoly strength may carry the day, as it did for management in the early, unorganized years of the labor movement. Collective bargaining presumes that each party has some power, and settlement depends on the presence of a "bargaining range." The top potential wage the employer is willing to offer must at least cover the minimum wage demand acceptable to the union, thus creating a bargaining range. Normally both parties strive to mask their true settlement positions, however, in hopes of negotiating a better settlement. Just what the wage rate will be within a bargaining range depends on the success of each party in resisting their opponent's demands, persuading the other party of how costly it would be to disagree (perhaps via a threatened strike, proving to them how little it really costs to agree, and so forth. Pure conflict and sheer power may also be needed to resolve conflict. There is no bargaining range if the maximum possible wage offer and the minimum wage demand do not overlap. Provided that both parties possess market power, after a laborious battle of nerves, threats, moves, and countermoves, they may be able to produce a bargaining range and reach a suitable agreement. If this does not occur, more than a threatened use of power may be required and a union, for example, may well strike.

In the case of unorganized markets in which an unequal distribution of power prevails and collective bargaining is not allowed by law, the settlement position may tend to favor the powerful at the expense of the powerless. Thus, before New York City's sanitation workers were organized, they, like the nurses or public-school teachers a few years back, were driven to settlement at or near the employer's terms. On the other hand, if physicians, for example, can exert enough power to hoist their fees substantially because of public apathy or ignorance, or because the increases are masked by private insurance, they may be able to push wages to higher levels pretty much at their own discretion.

## Current Issues in Labor Economics

That there are several controversial economic issues related to labor markets should come as no surprise to the reader. In some instances, these labor issues pose real and serious problems which have no one "correct" answer, while in other instances faulty thinking and myths have confused many people.

### DO WAGE REDUCTIONS INCREASE EMPLOYMENT?

A labor demand curve for one firm implies that, under normal circumstances, a wage decrease increases the quantity of labor employed for a firm, depending upon the elasticity of demand for labor. With very elastic demand, the increased employment resulting from a cut in wages might be large, but if the demand for labor is relatively inelastic, the increase in employment will be small.[6] However, to infer from the *micro-level* experience of one firm or one particular labor market that wage reductions in the *aggregate economy* will increase aggregate employment is in error. If aggregate wages are reduced, the probable consequence is a decline in the aggregate demand for output due to the fall in wage and salary income, which in turn leads to even *lower* future levels of income and employment. As aggregate spending on output declines, business inventories of goods and services accumulate, causing future production to diminish, which in turn tends to create *fewer*, not *more* employment opportunities. One firm or industry may employ more workers in a particular labor market as wages are re-

[6] Generally speaking, labor demand is more inelastic: (a) at higher skill levels, because resource substitution is difficult (as in the case of attorneys); (b) the more inelastic the demand for the product (such as plumbers' services); and (c) the less important labor costs are as a portion of total costs (the situation of airline pilots).

duced without affecting total spending, but assuming that the same is true for *all* firms in an economy is fallacious.

To argue that increased wages will remedy unemployment is equally as questionable. Most experts agree that it is not possible to conclude that aggregate wage changes and employment are related in a meaningful and dependable fashion, with one exception: If substantial amounts of idle capacity prevail, and increased wages result in increased aggregate demand, income and employment do tend to rise. However, it is clear that employment will not rise as wages rise if households save instead of increasing consumption expenditures. Whether income and employment rise in the aggregate depends on consuming compared to saving, investment spending in relation to the demand for output, and a variety of more complicated factors related to aggregate capacity and monetary and fiscal policies.

DO INCREASED WAGES CAUSE TECHNOLOGICAL UNEMPLOYMENT?

The fallacy of composition—reasoning from the part to the whole—is also responsible for the questionable allegation that rising wages result in technological unemployment. At the level of the firm or a localized labor market, higher wages have sometimes encouraged employers to substitute capital for labor, resulting in fewer jobs. Some two decades ago, for example, the magnates of the coal-mining industry and John L. Lewis agreed to automate, to increase wages substantially in the industry, and to abandon union featherbedding practices. The result was a substantial increase in unemployed coal miners. Similar circumstances have characterized other sectors of the economy, including agriculture, meat-packing, and the automobile industries in recent years. In the aggregate, however, the oft-voiced fear of higher aggregate levels of technologically unemployed workers has not materialized. Advances in technology, greater amounts of capital per worker, and continually expanding labor productivity have *enlarged*, not *diminished* aggregate job opportunities. However, these newly created jobs have imposed new skill demands on the supply of labor.

We cannot ignore structural labor-market problems, of course. Hundreds of thousands of jobs are displaced each year, and rising labor costs have encouraged investment that embodies technological advances in more productive capital resources. The obvious response of any interest group to the threat of declining job opportunities is self-protection. Consequently, labor unions engage in featherbedding practices just as agricultural interests lobby for government favors and as college instructors may well resist labor-saving technological changes in the future. Many specific labor markets are plagued with structural imbalances, but it is important to remember that more total jobs have been created than have been destroyed. Even if wage increases in particular labor markets do intensify changes that lead to declining job opportunities, this does not mean that *aggregate* employment opportunities will decline, that featherbedding practices are appropriate, or that a 30-hour workweek is required. Technological advance and the substitution of capital are vital to greater productivity—they are the handmaidens to economic growth. The social bonus provided by economic growth can be used in part to retrain displaced labor resources instead of allowing the least fortunate workers to bear the burden of "progress" individually. When technological unemployment does arise, it can and must be remedied through manpower-retraining policies and the maintenance of stable capacity levels of growth, which can be achieved through the use of fiscal and monetary policies.

### HAVE UNIONS INCREASED REAL WAGES?

A third half-truth believed in some circles is that unions have increased wages mightily. While we cannot settle the issue fully here, it is worth noting that there is little evidence to substantiate this claim because of the many problems associated with statistically determining what *would* have happened to wage levels in the absence of unions.

Leading students of the organized labor movement generally agree that labor unions may have raised wages for their members, perhaps by about 10 percent on the average. According to studies conducted by experts such as Arthur Ross and Lloyd Reynolds, some unions have increased wages by more than this amount, while others have had no discernible effect on wages. Statistical comparisons, which commonly indicate that wages are significantly higher in unionized industries than in nonunionized sectors of the economy, are misleading because unionized sectors tend to be concentrated in the larger, higher-wage, and more profitable industries employing skilled workers. In addition, nonunion sectors in the economy may grant wage increases comparable to those achieved by labor unions to stave off unionization. If union wage settlements establish a "going wage rate" that has spillover effects in other segments of the economy, industry comparisons are meaningless. In short, it is not at all clear that the union movement has increased wages in a very significant way.

This does not mean that unions have had no effects on contemporary economies. Quite aside from their impact on wages, labor unions have helped achieve improvements in working conditions and economic security for disabled, retired, and unemployed workers. Furthermore, we do know that in an imperfect market economy, unions may also administer wages upward and thus contribute to inflation, particularly if business firms have the power to pass price increases on to consumers in monopolized product markets.

### ARE UNIONS CORRUPT AND UNDEMOCRATIC?

One allegation levied against union leadership is that it is undemocratic, corrupt, and even linked to the Mafia or to communism. The governing principles of labor unions as they are written in union constitutions are very democratic and, along with federal legislation, provide extensive protection for voting, worker rights, the financial management of union funds, and so on. However, apathy among the membership of a union does reduce operational democracy just as it does in many other institutions, such as local governments or churches. Union officers are seldom challenged in a spirited election and it is even rarer that a challenger is successful in unseating incumbent leaders. In many ways, the problems of union government are akin to (and probably no more severe than) problems of corporate government. Although corporation shareholders have a theoretical vote, in the pragmatic sense they simply do not control the business enterprise they own. The consequences are somewhat predictable and also understandable. Both union members and corporate shareholders may remain lethargic until the organization fails to produce desired results or a calamity appears imminent. In most cases leaders pursue the interest of their membership; but, when opportunities for deceit and fraud prevail, scandals will occur in both labor unions and corporate enterprise.

There have also been isolated instances in which ideological interests at odds with the American political system have gained control of unions. The labor-union movement as represented by the AFL-CIO has repeatedly denounced organized crime and communism and has cleaned its ranks of these elements on several occasions. In the late 1940s, communist-controlled unions like the Longshoremen were expelled from the AFL-CIO, as were the Teamsters long before Dave Beck and Jimmy Hoffa were granted extended vacations at government expense. The fact is, there is little evidence to indicate that undesirable behavior is any more rampant in unions than it is among the corporate elite, or in Congress itself for that matter! Moreover, laws against union excesses are a good deal more definitive than those applying to Congress and corporations—a fact which may suggest what a concerned citizen might more properly worry about.

### The Public Sector and Organized Labor Markets

Government traditionally has expressed interest in labor markets, as our brief encounter with the legal development of the labor movement revealed. Let us consider next the major issues concerning government and organized labor.

#### THE RIGHT TO JOIN OR NOT JOIN UNIONS

Heated debates frequently occur over individual rights to belong or not belong to unions. The term *union security* describes union guarantees that govern membership conditions. One form of union security, the *closed shop*, is an arrangement under which a prospective employee must be a union member before he can be hired. The *union shop* provides that the employer may hire anyone, but the individual must join the union within a specified period of time (usually 30 days), and the *open shop* provides no union security, since workers may decide whether or not they wish to support the union that represents some proportion of the company's employees. While the closed-shop approach to union security has been declared illegal, union leaders argue that some form of membership security is necessary because: (a) improvements achieved through collective bargaining benefit members and nonmembers alike, (b) it is not equitable for nonmembers providing no support and sharing no risks to benefit from the hard-won gains of organized labor, and (c) nonmembers can be used in place of union members to reduce the effectiveness of the union's chief weapon—the strike. Opponents to union security argue that individuals should not be denied work because of mandatory union membership and should be free to join or not as they wish.

This issue is not easily resolved because different people have different values. The philosophical difficulties of coping with the so-called "right-to-work" issue are illustrated by the now-celebrated Section 14b of the Taft-Hartley Act, which allows each state to pass legislation determining what forms of union security are legal or illegal in that state. About one-third of the nonindustrial states in the Midwest and South have invoked their own right-to-work laws restricting the union shop or other forms of union security. In all likelihood, union security will remain a matter of concern for some time to come, and valid points can be made on both sides. It is curious, however, that professional associations like the AMA and the Bar have maintained the tightest closed shops ever known, without serious challenge.

## PUBLIC-SECTOR INVOLVEMENT IN ORGANIZED LABOR MARKETS

One final issue is the contemporary posture of government toward strikes, collective action, and manpower problems. Even though the power to strike is used infrequently, it is a potent weapon lending considerable authority to the demands of organized labor. Because strikes can affect the economic welfare of the entire nation when they occur in a key economic sector such as trucking or the railroad industry, government authorities have developed legislative means to monitor "national-emergency" disputes. By virtue of national-emergency provisions of the Taft-Hartley Act, the President has authority to obtain an injunction against strikes imperiling the national interest for an 80-day "cooling-off" period, as noted earlier. During this period, fact-finding missions, mediation attempts, and a final opinion poll of union members are conducted in an attempt to settle the key issues threatening to lead to open conflict. If the cooling-off tactic fails, seizure of the industry is the only remaining government alternative. However, previous experience suggests that the national-emergency provisions are relatively successful, in no small measure because unions and employers possess a strong preference to settle disputes privately.

Government is rapidly becoming embroiled in a second and even more difficult issue—that of collective bargaining and strikes in the public sector of the economy. Millions of public employees including nurses, postmen, firemen, policemen, teachers, and office workers are either joining AFL-CIO affiliated unions or restructuring their professional associations to more closely parallel the goals, tactics, and collective action of labor unions. Like the labor-union movement which originated many decades ago, public employees have recently discovered that collective action is needed to more nearly equate the distribution of power between a large and powerful monopsonistic employer and the individual worker. Government officials still lean heavily toward the traditional view that public employees may neither engage in strike activities nor collectively negotiate over wages. The rationale is analogous to the national-emergency provisions of the Taft-Hartley Act; namely, that such freedom can result in concerted action harmful to the public in general. Therefore, it is alleged that the right to free collective bargaining should be limited. What the outcome of this struggle portends for the future is unknown, and once again, an excellent case can be made for either position on this issue. One thing remains clear, however: Efforts to extend collective-bargaining and unionization rights to the public sector are intensifying, and the prospects seem to favor increased power on the part of government employees. Americans no doubt are in for many changes in this area during the next decade, even though public employees are now legally restrained in their rights to strike and collectively negotiate wages.

Many other manpower problems directly and indirectly related to wage determination remain in modern economies. For example, the government has legally set minimum-wage levels which act as price supports for certain categories of less-skilled, youthful, or elderly wage earners. Although it was established partly as a remedy for poverty, many experts believe that the minimum wage serves only to destroy employment opportunities for large numbers of very young, old, and unskilled workers. Most informed observers regard the union as a useful social institution in the American economy. The general consensus is that improvements have accompanied the controlled organization of labor markets and that collective bargaining has been an instrumental force in resolving economic conflict, preserving economic order, and creating industrial democracy. Developed nations have taken steps to mobilize their labor forces and have provided public employment agencies, unemployment compensation, education, training, and retraining opportunities. Nevertheless, there are gaping needs that are only partially met through existing manpower programs, as the following chapter demonstrates.

## REVIEW
### Summary

1. The labor force of the United States has grown steadily as the working-age population over 16 years of age has expanded, and it is expected to reach more than 92 million persons by 1975. Agricultural employment has declined rapidly as the American economy has become industrialized and unemployment is unevenly distributed among different segments of the labor force.

2. The organization of labor markets, which began in this country two centuries ago, was marked by an extended struggle for equal power between workers and large employers. The organization of the AFL in 1886 marks the start of the modern labor movement. Today there are scores of national unions, each made up of numerous local unions. Under the leadership of Samuel Gompers, the AFL stressed economic goals. In 1955 the two federations representing trade unionism (AFL) and the later-organized industrial unions (CIO) merged into one. Several legal developments mark the rise of unions to an accepted social institution. Among the more important are: (a) the criminal-conspiracy doctrine, (b) the Sherman Act, (c) the Norris-LaGuardia Act, (d) the Wagner Act, (e) the Taft-Hartley Act, and (f) the Landrum-Griffin Act.

3. Worker productivity and product price determine labor's marginal revenue product (MRP) or demand schedule. Marginal revenue cost (MRC) and MRP are used to explain competitive wages and employment. Real wages have increased in the United States because of labor's rising productivity, an event that has contradicted the dismal prophecies of Marx and Ricardo. Many factors other than competitive marginal revenue product influence wages which are subject to a variety of market imperfections (e.g., noneconomic job attributes, qualitative differences in labor, differentiated or noncompeting labor markets, and rigidities and immobilities in labor markets).

4. Market power on the part of employers can influence employment and wages, as monopsony power in hiring labor demonstrates. The more interesting cases of market power in labor markets derive from four different sources. Workers or their representatives may take steps to: (a) increase the demand for labor (e.g., the Bar Association), (b) reduce the effective supply of labor (the AMA), (c) administer wages upward

(the teachers), or (*d*) set wages by mutually shared bilateral monopoly powers (the Auto Workers and the "Big Three").

5. Collective bargaining is the formal negotiation of the terms and conditions of work between labor and management, including the handling of grievances. Economic conditions such as profits, prices, and productivity as well as bargaining ability and tactics (i.e., bluffing and the credibility of threats) affect the final outcome of collective bargaining. Even though strikes are not common in labor-management relations, it is possible for a breakdown in negotiations to result if an overlapping negotiation range does not occur. Under these conditions, the important determinant of wages is the relative power of both parties in a dispute.

6. Several contemporary issues and problems are related to the determination of wages under the imperfect market conditions that in fact prevail. It is often said that aggregate employment will rise if wages are reduced —a statement that is in error because lower wages and incomes reduce spending on aggregate output. Moreover, a serious technological unemployment problem has not materialized in the aggregate, although some categories of workers have experienced difficult labor-market adjustments. While the evidence is not very clear, it does not appear that labor unions have increased wages a great deal above what they otherwise would have been. Finally, the charges of corruption are not fully representative of labor unions as a group. Indeed, it may well be that undesirable and deceitful elements are no more or less common to unions than to corporations or to Congress itself.

7. The public sector is involved in the organized labor movement in several ways: (*a*) Federal law has partially avoided the difficult issue of the so-called "right-to-work" by allowing states to decide how they wish to treat different forms of union security; (*b*) government does have the power to intervene in national-emergency disputes by obtaining an 80-day injunction under authority of the Taft-Hartley Act; (*c*) the difficult issue of the rights of public employees to collectively assert their own interests is an open question at the present time, and one that promises to be irksome in the coming decade; and (*d*) minimum-wage laws and a rather wide variety of government programs are used to mobilize manpower.

### Identify the Following Concepts and Terms

- labor force
- AFL
- voluntarism
- yellow-dog contract
- blacklist
- cooling-off period
- injunction
- featherbedding
- countervailing market power
- grievances and arbitration
- escalator clause
- closed vs. open shop
- union shop
- technological unemployment
- right-to-work and Section 14b

### Questions to Answer

1. The historical development of organized labor began while workingmen's associations were treated as criminal activities. Briefly reconstruct

the major legal developments and changes which have led to the contemporary situation, in which 20 million workers belong to labor unions and millions of additional persons belong to professional associations that perform certain functions resembling labor-union activities.

2. In 1994, the moonsters, who bear the responsibility for shuttle flights of cargo and people to the moon, banded together as a collective group of workers with common goals and problems. Diagram and explain how they might improve their economic station: (*a*) by licensing all moonster labor, (*b*) by encouraging Congress to subsidize moon rides, and (*c*) by setting wages as a unilateral authority because they are a highly regarded profession that saves many lives each year by depopulating the earth. How might the moonsters' collective-bargaining problem be different if they are forced to negotiate with one monopsonistic employer (e.g., government)?

3. Critically evaluate the following statements:
    (*a*) "A law should be passed making it unlawful for workers to have to join a union because the union says so. Furthermore, government employees should be barred from union membership because such workers have no right to bargain with government."
    (*b*) "Unions are corrupt, and they cause wages to increase at the expense of unorganized labor, which reduces aggregate employment and leads to massive technological unemployment."

# CHAPTER 24
# Human Resources, Poverty, and Discrimination

The purpose of this chapter is to evaluate the economics of human-resource problems. Income and wealth are distributed unequally, massive pockets of poverty coexist with luxury, and economic discrimination is prevalent in what has been termed "the affluent society." While our orientation is rather narrowly economic in nature, it is apparent that political, sociological, physiological, and psychological affairs also affect human resources in important ways.

Our study of wage determination in Chapter 23 provided no easy and definitive answers to the question of what determines the wages paid to human resources used as factors of production. Indeed, what we have done is open a Pandora's box of human-resource issues and problems. Investments in education and health have been ignored, for example, yet they do help determine wages because of their effects on productivity. We have not considered contemporary economic problems such as poverty and discrimination, but they, too, relate to wage determination and income distribution.

Most Americans are aware that average incomes and living standards in this country are the highest in the world. What is not well understood, however, is the extent to which incomes vary and why. Chapter 22 indicated that at the low end of the income spectrum, one out of every seven American households has a family income less than one-third the U.S. average, or a per capita income level of approximately $800—a level achieved for the *average* American in the United States one-half century ago. At the upper extreme, *per capita* income for three out of one hundred affluent Americans is over $9,000, a level that, at current growth rates, will not be attained for the average American until another *century* passes.

While a full accounting of income differences is very complex, part of the explanation depends upon the level of investment in human resources and the resulting productivity of those resources. Our approach to human-resource economics starts in Part A with an examination of the concept of human "capital." Many aspects of income distribution and wage determination also reflect subtle forms of inequality which lead to poverty for millions of human beings—the topic of Part B. Part C examines the economic aspects of the problem of discrimination, and public policies directed at the economics of human resources are considered in Part D.

The formation of human capital is the result of investments in human resources that develop and enhance the productive capacities and welfare of man. Once this concept is recognized, increases in productivity that engineer economic growth and contribute to rising real incomes become more understandable. Moreover, a view of human resources as "capital" both (a) helps to explain how wages and incomes are determined and why they vary, and (b) adds a new and relevant perspective to the deterioration and ultimate destruction of human resources through unemployment and poverty.

The statement that human capital is the result of investments that maintain, enhance, and develop the productive capacity of human resources is much too opaque to be workable. Therefore, let us begin by examining the costs and returns to such investments.

### Social and Noneconomic Costs and Returns

Much that is important to the formation of human capital is not readily measured in a conventional economic context. The desired end in assessing investment in human resources is to fully reflect *all* costs and *all* returns to such investments. Major problems arise, however, in identifying social, indirect, and noneconomic costs and returns, and many reputable economists look askance at the human-capital concept—largely because the costs and returns to investments in man defy reliable measurement. What, for example, is the return or *social* "worth" of a more rational political awareness stemming from increased education? What social costs are imposed upon society by underinvestment in human resources destroyed through detention in penal institutions? Or how does one measure the *indirect* externality (spillover) return emanating from health investments that curtail the spreading of communicable diseases? For that matter, what is the private *noneconomic* value of human life—the value of 55,000 persons lost each year as a result of automobile accidents? Should investment costs borne largely by public taxes to train physicians or Ph.Ds generate private returns which accrue to individuals—and if so, just how much of the income return from the "socialized" costs of training should be privately retained?

Even casual examination of earnings data by education level suggests that persons who remain in school attain higher average income levels than those who enter the labor force with less training. Other factors such as race and sex, family background, ability, opportunity, and motivation work with additional education to produce sizable income differentials. A few hardy economists have proceeded—with considerable hesitancy—to stake their reputations on estimates of the percentage rate of return to investments in human resources.[1] What these economists have found has, in general, led them to the very tentative conclusion that the rate of return to investments in human capital is equal to or greater than the return on investments in nonhuman (physical-capital) resources. The numerical rela-

---

[1] The collection edited by Mark Blaug, *Economics of Education* (Baltimore, Md.: Penguin Books, Ltd., 1968) provides an excellent survey of current research on this subject.

tions are of some importance, but a good deal less important than the basic idea that an investment in human capital *does* earn a return.

Research on the return to additional health and education expenditures, for example, has been hindered by a poor understanding of how ability and education interact, by inadequate information on what portions of education and health investment can be regarded as investment rather than consumption, and by the severe difficulties experts have in measuring noneconomic and social costs and returns. Educational expenditures yield direct satisfaction, as do purchases of goods and services (the consumption component), and provide productive skills through training and expanding learning capabilities as well (the investment component). Moreover, the concept of human capital is awkward because neither the returns from nor the costs of human-capital formation are restricted to direct economic outlays alone. Needless to say, these questions are very difficult to answer and they have attracted the research interests of many economists in recent years.

## Forms of Human-Capital Investment

Even though social, indirect, and noneconomic costs and returns are more conceptual than measurable, a good deal of valuable insight can be gained from the human-capital concept. The four most important categories of investment in human capital are expenditures for: (*a*) health care, (*b*) education, (*c*) on-the-job training, and (*d*) mobility.

### HEALTH INVESTMENTS

Neither the costs nor the returns to investments in health and nutrition are easily measured, but it is reasonably clear that such expenditures do enhance the productive capabilities and the working life of human resources. Productivity and nutritional intake of human resources in developed compared to underdeveloped countries are directly related; basics such as sound diet, adequate shelter, and decent sanitation do affect the work capabilities and alertness of human resources. In addition, improved health may shorten the time span required for education and training, add several years to the productive lifetime of a human being, and reduce absenteeism on the job.

One of the important explanations for the high productivity of the American labor force is that it is one of the best-fed, best-housed, and healthiest in the world. Investments in health affecting human resources directly and indirectly include greater per capita consumption of health services and research and development expenditures that have led to advances ranging from heart transplants to wonder drugs. Today, because of improvements in health and longevity, the typical American is much more likely to participate in the labor force at higher levels of productivity and for a longer time period than his counterpart of 50 years ago. Individuals living in underdeveloped nations or residents of poverty-stricken regions in this country are less productive because of underinvestment in health.

### INVESTMENT IN EDUCATION

A second important form of human-capital investment consists of expenditures on education. Education provides directly useful skills which increase the productivity of human resources and also provides a basis for future learning, abstract thinking, and logical analysis. Skills and advancements in productivity furnished through educational investments are of particular importance to developed nations whose production process is technologically complex. Persons who lack the education required to operate complex capital equipment and are incapable of filling the growing demand for services in diverse fields such as law, psychology, or finance can be bypassed in the world of work.

## INVESTMENT IN JOB TRAINING

Expenditures for job training constitute a third type of investment in human capital. As a general rule, the more specific the training is to a firm's operation, the more likely it is that the investment will be borne by the employing firm. Transferable kinds of job training generally require investment on the part of individuals. There are numerous exceptions to these generalizations, the most notable of which is the "learning-by-doing" training of managers or the government retraining of underdeveloped human resources. Today many jobs possess the unique characteristic of providing an upward drift in skill level because job training accompanies job performance. The youthful college graduate who rises from an entry-level position in sales or finance to executive status is the beneficiary of learning by doing, as are university professors who are paid to reinvest in their stock of knowledge. On the other hand, millions of jobs, most of which require lesser skills, do not possess learning-by-doing attributes, and with time, these jobs may even contribute to the depreciation of human capital. Technology and machines have displaced once-skilled craftsmen, particularly semiskilled and unskilled workers whose "labor content" is consumed on a job each day. When technological changes alter the world of work many once-valued skills are capriciously antiquated and human-capital destruction occurs.

## INVESTMENT IN MOBILITY

A fourth important category of human-capital investment consists of expenditures that encourage migration and mobility. Although little is known about mobility investments, we do know that manpower mobility is vital to an ever-changing economy. Today nearly all developed nations have extensive government programs which make job-market information available. Indeed, many European countries furnish relocation allowances to enhance labor mobility on an industry-wide, occupational, or geographic basis. Government programs to train or retrain workers also increase mobility when, for example, structural unemployment causes an imbalance between the supply and demand for certain manpower-skill levels. Examples of underinvestment in human-resource mobility can be seen in the pockets of poverty in Appalachia or the rural South as well as in urban ghettos in the North.

### The Investment Costs of Education and Health Care

Although little definitive information is available on job training or mobility investments, several authorities have assembled data on the costs of investment in education and health. These expenditures have expanded at staggering rates in the United States throughout this century and are a primary explanation for economic growth and increasing income levels in the United States.

Figure 1 shows how total investment costs in education have edged upward since 1900. The *direct costs* of education include direct expenditures for buildings, salaries, tuition, and so on, while *opportunity costs* consist of wage income forgone by students of working age who withdraw from the labor force while acquiring an education. These two major categories of educational costs were first developed by Professor Theodore Schultz of the University of Chicago and have since been updated by the Council of Economic Advisers, as shown in Figure 1. Measures of opportunity costs may not be exact, but wages forgone are substantial, particularly for college youth. Direct costs of educational investment are rapidly approaching $100 billion, a level of expenditure that has already been surpassed if opportunity costs are included in the total costs of education shown in Figure 1.

Expenditures for health care also represent a form of human-capital investment which is of growing importance to the American economy, as we can see from Figure 2. Just as expenditures for education have increased

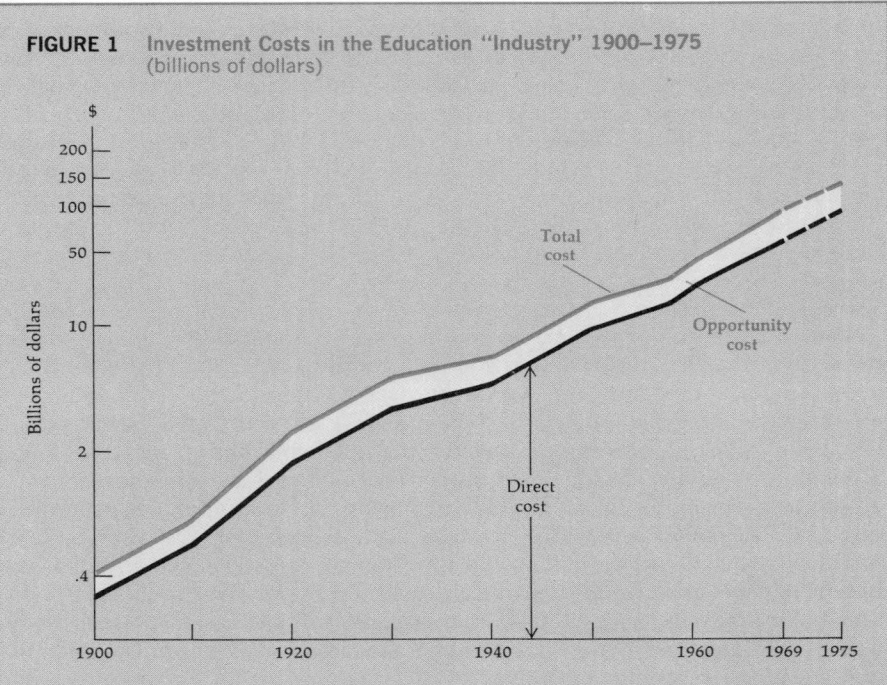

**FIGURE 1** Investment Costs in the Education "Industry" 1900–1975 (billions of dollars)

*The Costs of Education.* Increasing numbers of people attending school for a greater number of years together with price-level increases underly the rapidly rising investment costs in education. Both direct monetary outlays and rising opportunity costs due to postponed entry into the labor force are part of the $100 billion education industry.

SOURCE: *Statistical Abstract of the United States*, 1970, and Theodore Schultz, *The Economic Value of Education* (New York: Columbia University Press, 1963). Data for 1975 are estimated by the author.

**FIGURE 2**  Investments in Health and the Price of Health Care

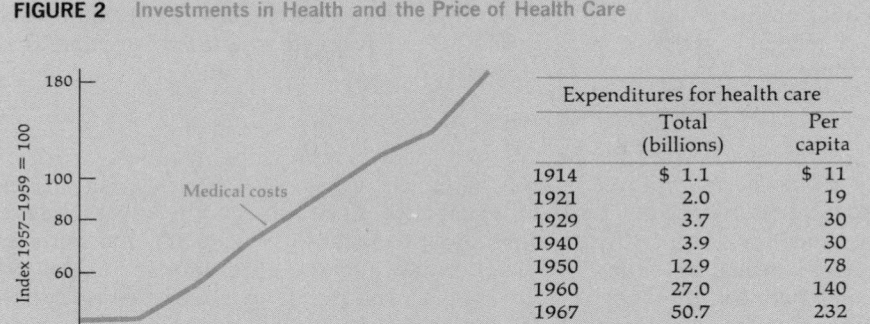

| Expenditures for health care | | |
|---|---|---|
| | Total (billions) | Per capita |
| 1914 | $ 1.1 | $ 11 |
| 1921 | 2.0 | 19 |
| 1929 | 3.7 | 30 |
| 1940 | 3.9 | 30 |
| 1950 | 12.9 | 78 |
| 1960 | 27.0 | 140 |
| 1967 | 50.7 | 232 |
| 1970 | 68.0 | 330 |

*The Costs of Health.* Today Americans spend more than $300 per person on health care. While rising prices have contributed to increased outlays on medical care in significant ways, 1970 expenditures of $68 billion on health care represent some 7 percent of GNP.

SOURCE: *Economic Report of the President,* 1970, and Selma Mushkin, "Health as an Investment," *Journal of Political Economy,* October 1962, pp. 129 ff. Data for 1970 estimated by the author.

substantially during the twentieth century, so have those for health care, from $1.1 billion or $11 per capita in 1914 to an estimated $68 billion or $330 per capita in 1970. Recently, price increases in the health-care industry have become a matter of concern as an important component of the rising cost of living. The overall price level for health care (Figure 2) has increased almost twice as rapidly as the consumer price index in recent years. One explanation for the rapidly increasing price of health is rising hospital costs, which account for one-third of total health-care expenditures. Another explanation is the higher fees charged by physicians and dentists, which represent another 30 percent of the total. On the other hand, despite spectacular scientific advances in the chemistry of health care, drug prices have not been a substantial inflationary force. Even though health-care costs have risen rapidly, it must be remembered that improvements in the "quality" of health care have also occurred in recent decades. Still, while United States citizens spend more than any other nation on health care (nearly 7 percent of GNP), infant mortality is higher and life expectancy is lower here than in some Western European nations such as Sweden.

### The Economic Value of Human Resources

The productive capacity, adaptability, and reasoning ability of man are vital resources to nations. Despite this fact, millions of teenagers enter the labor force yearly without a high-school education. The unemployment rate for dropouts is twice as large as it is for those completing high school. Moreover, two-thirds of all dropouts earn less annually than the average income for their overall age group, whereas nearly two-thirds of all high-school graduates earn in excess of the average for the age group. Education is a primary variable in determining employment opportunities and thus income, and deserves special consideration for that reason.

PRIVATE RETURNS TO INVESTMENT IN EDUCATION

The significance of education as one factor shaping the incomes earned by males in the labor force is demonstrated by Figure 3. Average (mean) income varies by age level, reaching a peak at an earlier age, the lower the level of education [Figure 3(a)]. More significant, however, are income differentials by levels of education. The annual average difference in income for males between the ages of 45 to 54 is as follows: The high-school graduate and individuals with *some* college training respectively have average incomes of $3,000 and $5,300 more each year than males with only an elementary-school education. Males with four years of college in the 45-to-54 age bracket earn an average of approximately $10,000 more each year than those with an elementary education. With continuing economic growth, money-income levels rise at all age-education levels, as Figure 3(a) also indicates; however, during recent years, the income of college graduates has grown at a slightly

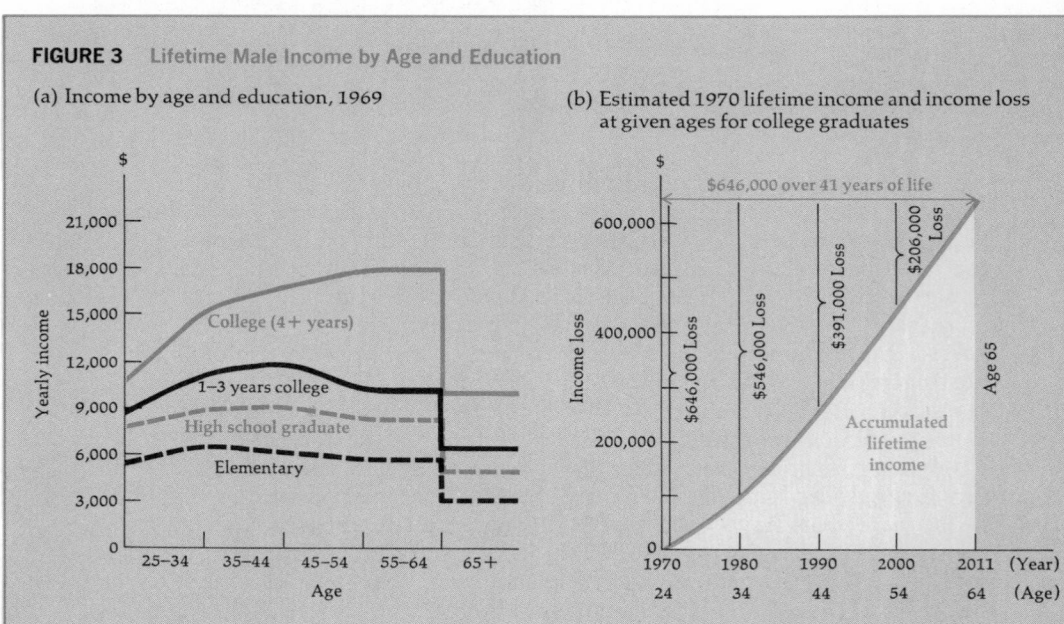

**FIGURE 3**  Lifetime Male Income by Age and Education

*Income Values for Human Capital.* Level of education is an important determinant of income as shown in (a). Estimated lifetime-income values and the hypothetical income "loss" for a college graduate at different age levels are shown in (b) for such a worker entering the labor force in 1970.

SOURCE: *Current Population Reports*, P–60, No. 66 (1969), and United States Department of Commerce, *Present Values of Estimated Lifetime Earnings*, 1967. Estimating procedure assumes retirement at age 65. All data are adjusted for death and unemployment probabilities. Equal growth and discount rates are also assumed to prevail for 1970 income levels.

more rapid rate than the average for all educational levels. Consequently, the income differences between college graduates and workers with less education has increased.

*The Economic Value of Education*   In recent years, information of the sort shown in Figure 3 has been used for various purposes. On numerous occasions the courts, for example, have admitted probable work-life-income data as testimony in personal injury suits that allow compensation for dependent beneficiaries because of the wrongful and untimely death or injury of a household head. Figure 3(b) shows that if a college-graduate, male head of household dies at age 24 in an accident found to be the liability of another party, his estimated remaining work-life-income "value" would be $646,000. Similar "values" for human lives are illustrated in Figure 3(b) for the 41-year period beginning in 1970 at age 24 for a college graduate. The income "loss" at a given age is the difference in work-life income ($646,000) less the amount of earned income [the shaded portion of Figure 3(b)], which varies by attained age.[2]

The concept of the capital value of human resources is also useful in evaluating the return to investments in additional education, or the costs of alternative forms of investment in human capital (vocational vs. academic education). Such comparisons may be of particular importance in evaluating manpower-training and retraining programs (as suggested in Chapter 20). Remember, however, that human-capital investment comparisons involve social and noneconomic costs and returns, and it is well to remember that measurement difficulties are encountered for those reasons.

*Lifetime Incomes*   The private return from different levels of education, which imposes both direct costs and opportunity costs on persons who engage in such an investment, is best shown by comparing expected lifetime earnings as is done in Figure 4. Consider once again the case of a typical male college graduate age 24 who enters the labor market in 1970. Over the course of a lifetime of work ending at age 65, his estimated income is $646,000 after making adjustments each year for the likelihood of death and unemployment. By comparison, each person in this group of workers with a twelfth-grade education average about $359,000—one-quarter of a million dollars *less* than a college-educated male during a working lifetime of 41 years. Moreover, the average difference between eight years of schooling and four years of college is nearly $400,000, again holding other things equal.[3] Note carefully that some unknown amount of these lifetime-income differentials is attributable to unspecified differences (e.g., innate ability) that higher levels of educational attainment do imply. Even so, there clearly are significant private economic returns associated with higher levels of education. As a matter of fact, educational deficiencies are

[2] In addition to adjustments for growth in income and consumption losses, most courts require that the capital value of expected lifetime earnings be adjusted for productivity increases reduced to present values.

[3] These comparisons are very crude, in that numerous other variables that *are not* equal and are of importance to lifetime-income values are ignored. [See R. Wykstra (ed.), *Education and the Economics of Human Capital* (New York: Free Press, 1971).]

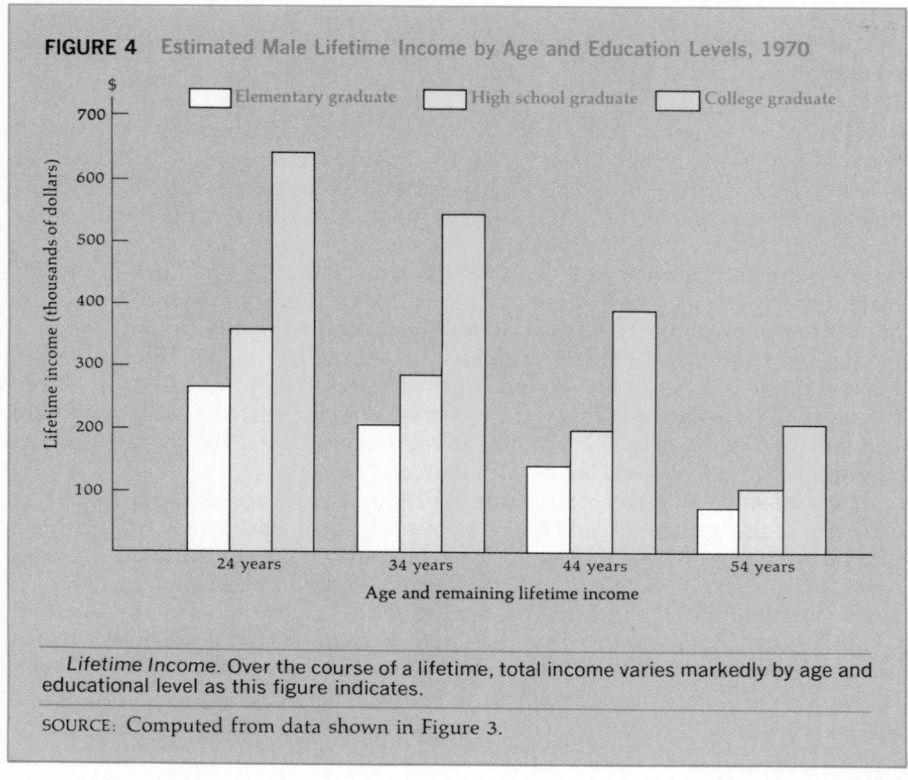

**FIGURE 4**  Estimated Male Lifetime Income by Age and Education Levels, 1970

☐ Elementary graduate  ☐ High school graduate  ☐ College graduate

Lifetime income (thousands of dollars)

Age and remaining lifetime income

*Lifetime Income.* Over the course of a lifetime, total income varies markedly by age and educational level as this figure indicates.

SOURCE: Computed from data shown in Figure 3.

one of a great many social and personal factors which compound in the plight of poor people—our next topic.[4]

## B. POVERTY

Many of the issues facing the world today are controversial because they involve social and personal values. This is especially true of the economics of poverty. Poverty is a frame of social reference that currently engulfs one out of eight Americans. In its broadest context, the problem of poverty is psychological, political, sociological, cultural, and economic in nature. Inferior access to jobs, fatherless families, substandard housing, the problems of urban-ghetto decay, and past government welfare programs number among the numerous elements which have contributed to the dismal world of the poor. Poverty by no means concerns economists alone, but economics can furnish important insights and information on the subject.

### The Anatomy of Poverty

The poor constitute a separate culture with its own institutional environment. There are special sociological and psychological traits that produce

[4] Over one-half of all families who are classified as poor are headed by individuals with less than 12 years of education.

the economic *symptom* of poverty—low incomes. Normal clothing and educational expenditures and even treatment of minor illnesses thrust major economic burdens on the poor, who may be apathetic or hostile and resentful of their deprived status, which is usually acquired through the accident of birth. Moreover, the culture of poverty is often hidden in remote rural areas or crowded urban ghettos which are visited by affluent Americans as rarely as possible, if ever.

## THE INSTITUTION AND CULTURE OF POVERTY

The values and attitudes of the poor differ from those of persons in the mainstream of economic life. In the United States, the majority of poor people are children, the disabled, and persons over 65 years of age. The crux of the poverty problem is best depicted by the 10 million children of poor families who are exposed to a poverty subculture daily. Hostile feelings toward both contemporary social institutions and the power elite as a dominant class are common reactions to the economic and political realities of the poverty subculture. Low levels of self-expectation and motivation may also be common attitudes learned over several years, decades, or generations of futile attempts to hurdle such barriers as discrimination, inadequate education, poor training for jobs, and tenement housing. Lack of family identity, female family heads, inadequate community organizations, and consensual marriage sometimes accompany the behavioral patterns and sociology of poverty. Existence is risky, tenuous, and geared to an environment of deprivation in which human capital is ultimately destroyed instead of created. Sometimes these values and behavioral reactions are conditioned by the "irregular" street economy which provides markets and work for the "hustler," who may deal in the numbers game, hot jewelry or furniture, or even other human beings. The alternatives of a temporary, insecure, and low-wage job of the most menial type are often viewed with contempt by value-conscious members of the irregular economy who have little or no precise hope for the future.[5] Even though there are millions of rural and aged poor who may not experience this irregular street economy, most of the one in seven children under 18 years of age who are classified as poor grow up in this environment.

This does not mean that those who are poverty-stricken are unwilling to leave such an environment, but it does mean that other options must be both available and presented on terms sufficiently attractive to facilitate movement out of the culture of poverty. The major difficulties with the poverty environment are that it is hemmed in on many sides by behavioral and institutional barriers, and that it is its own breeding ground—today's children of the poor are likely to be the next generation of poor. This is the reason that most authorities describe the values, attitudes, and behavior of what we call the poverty subculture as a conditioned reaction to being poor, *not* as a selected nor a preferred life style.

[5] In fact, the irregular economy may help some of the poor by compensating for unavailable jobs or marginal work proffered them by an economy which increasingly demands higher skill levels. The social psychology of the irregular economy gives birth to life styles that accommodate and even relish winning the game with the "system"— perhaps by beating the law or accepting welfare payments illegally.

DOMESTIC ECONOMIC ISSUES

The economics of poverty is concerned largely with the income characteristics of the poor. In addition, it is important to identify the economic institutions and values which have locked the poor into rural marginal farming or urban-ghetto dumping grounds which destroy their capital value as human resources.

A family is typically classified "poor" if its income is inadequate to provide the clothing, food, and other necessities of life needed to meet certain minimum requirements as established by government agencies. While it is not possible to set precise minimum standards for the social and psychological aspects of poverty, the economic standard normally used is based upon nutritional budget requirements adjusted for age, family size and composition, and farm or nonfarm residence.[6] As a general rule of thumb, government officials have found that a poverty budget is three times the cost of the minimum food requirements for a family. The official poverty threshold is an arbitrary, absolute-dollar level which increases in proportion to rising prices. The absolute-dollar poverty level of 1930 is rejected today because of rising price levels, just as today's defined poverty level will be rejected in 1985.

[6] These definitions arose out of the work of Mollie Orshansky [*Social Security Bulletin* (January 1965)], who used household-expenditure studies conducted by the United States Department of Agriculture to establish the poverty budget.

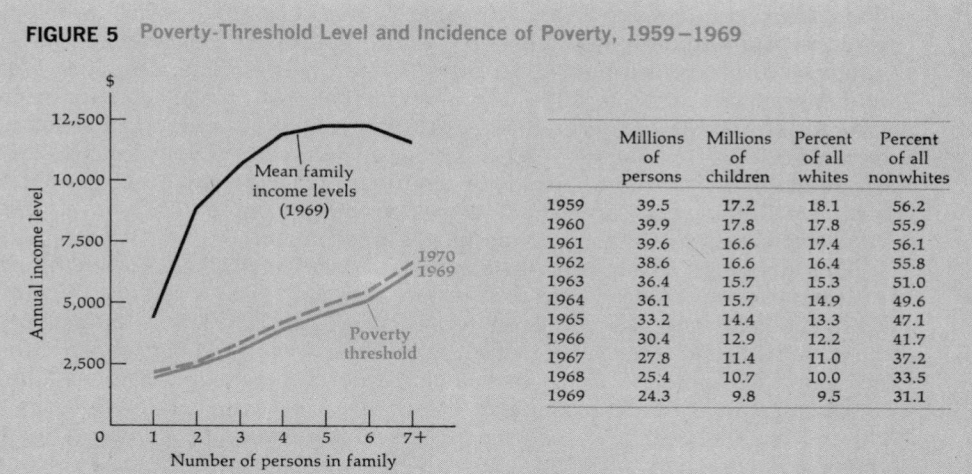

**FIGURE 5**   Poverty-Threshold Level and Incidence of Poverty, 1959–1969

|      | Millions of persons | Millions of children | Percent of all whites | Percent of all nonwhites |
|------|------|------|------|------|
| 1959 | 39.5 | 17.2 | 18.1 | 56.2 |
| 1960 | 39.9 | 17.8 | 17.8 | 55.9 |
| 1961 | 39.6 | 16.6 | 17.4 | 56.1 |
| 1962 | 38.6 | 16.6 | 16.4 | 55.8 |
| 1963 | 36.4 | 15.7 | 15.3 | 51.0 |
| 1964 | 36.1 | 15.7 | 14.9 | 49.6 |
| 1965 | 33.2 | 14.4 | 13.3 | 47.1 |
| 1966 | 30.4 | 12.9 | 12.2 | 41.7 |
| 1967 | 27.8 | 11.4 | 11.0 | 37.2 |
| 1968 | 25.4 | 10.7 | 10.0 | 33.5 |
| 1969 | 24.3 | 9.8  | 9.5  | 31.1 |

*The Poor.* The income threshold level of poverty is designated by family size in (a) for 1969, with inflationary increases estimated for 1970. The incidence of poverty (shown in the table) has declined markedly in a decade, but children and nonwhites are still a large portion of the 24 million persons living in poverty in 1969.

SOURCE: *Current Population Reports*, P–60, No. 68 (1969), No. 70 and No. 72 (1970), and No. 66 (1969). Family income and poverty threshold data are for the total urban and rural population. Children in poverty include persons under eighteen years of age.

Figure 5 illustrates the poverty threshold for American families in recent years. Although the poverty threshold rises each year in amounts equal to price-level changes, it *does not* increase as rapidly as average real income. The real income of a family normally increases more than 3 percent each year due to increased productivity, *in addition* to whatever changes occur because of a rising price level. However, the *real* income represented as a poverty level does not rise each year. In 1969, the poverty level for a family of four was $3,743 annually, or about $75 per week. However, millions of additional "near-poor" persons—those with incomes only one-third above the poverty threshold and less than one-half the national average—hover on the brink of economic disaster.

## IDENTIFYING THE POOR

In the last decade the magnitude of poverty as defined above declined rapidly to about 24 million persons, or 12 percent of the American population in 1969. Although the number identified as poor shown in Figure 5 has diminished significantly since the early 1960s, this fact offers little consolation for the millions still trapped in poverty. Moreover, the absolute-dollar standard used to delineate poverty is an important source of possible bias which understates the incidence of poverty. In many ways poverty may be more accurately measured in *relative* terms (e.g., the percentage of people receiving one-third the median family-income level). After all, it is the *relative* income disparity which creates social distance and dissatisfaction among classes. When viewed in these terms, poverty has declined very little; eleven percent of all families were poor in 1947 and 10 percent were poor in 1969.[7] The disparity of poverty by race is also quite striking; Figure 5 shows that nearly one out of three nonwhite families is poor and that a nonwhite family's chances of being poor are three times as great as those of a white family. (Nonwhites include Negroes, Indians, Japanese, Chinese, and exclude persons of Spanish-American ancestry not of Indian extraction.) Although poverty is not the special plight of one type of American, there are certain characteristics that the poor have in common. Poverty is disproportionately concentrated among minority groups, the fatherless, rural citizens, and other disadvantaged Americans such as the aged.

*Racial and Ethnic Minorities* Poverty is heavily concentrated in minority groups, particularly among the blacks. Even though about two out of three persons in the total poor population are white, the nonwhite incidence of poverty (31.1 percent) is more than three times as large as it is for whites (9.5 percent). (See Figure 5.) Some two-thirds of all American Indians living on reservations are poor, and two other ethnic groups—Spanish Americans and Puerto Ricans—exhibit unusually low incomes and a disproportionately large incidence of poverty.

*The Fatherless and Children in Poverty* Nearly four out of ten families headed by women are apt to be poor, and four-fifths of these families have some children under 18 years of age. The combined impact of being a fe-

[7] These comparisons are based upon a median family income of $3,031 in 1947 and $9,433 in 1969. Still a third alternative measure of poverty is based on the percentage of total income earned by each fifth of the population. The lowest 20 percent of all American families received 5 percent of total income in 1947 and 5.6 percent in 1969.

male plus having young children at home is an important factor in denying a woman the option to work as well as a strong reinforcing condition for a large number of Americans living in poverty. The unavailability and instability of work for women, as well as the problems of dependent children and racial discrimination, hamper many female heads of households from lifting their families out of poverty. It is quite apparent that millions of children in city slums and in rural poverty pockets reach maturity under seriously deprived conditions.

*The Rural Poor*   The incidence of poverty is twice as great in rural America —especially in the South and Appalachia—as it is in the nation as a whole. The circumstances of the rural poor are especially unfortunate in view of the fact that government agricultural programs provide little or no significant aid to more than 2 million low-income rural families, even though the United States Department of Agriculture spends, on the average, $100 million every week of the year, the bulk of which benefits the larger and more affluent farmers.

*The Disadvantaged: Unemployed, Undereducated, Aged, and Disabled*   Disability or illness, recurrent and sometimes prolonged periods without work, and employment in jobs paying poverty-level wages characterize the labor market for many of the disadvantaged poor. Several million poor live in families headed by unemployed persons with an elementary-school education, unable to acquire skills and frequently incapable of obtaining work in a technologically advanced society. Elderly households also frequently number among the poor. In some instances, the income of the aged erroneously indicates a poverty level of living because of supplemental earnings from assets accumulated earlier in life.[8] However, most of the 1.2 million low-income families headed by someone age 65 years or over receive few or no retirement benefits from prior employment in the private sector, and the social security benefits for which they may qualify are not substantial enough to lift them above the poverty level. There are numerous cases of stark poverty among the elderly, especially among those who are disabled. The disabled and ill who are poor also include large numbers of younger persons who cannot take advantage of employment opportunities.

### Destruction of Human Resources

The possibility of being poor increases markedly if the major characteristics of poverty discussed above cumulate. On the average, being *either* aged, fatherless, nonwhite, or a rural resident implies about three chances out of ten of numbering among the poor. Upwards of one-half of all families with two of these characteristics are likely to be poor; and with three or more of the above poverty traits, the poverty odds rise as high as 80 or 90 percent.

For the most part, poor Americans have been poor all their lives. They lack the opportunity for education; they are unskilled, insecure, and poorly prepared to cope with the world today; although work experience is common, such experiences are sporadic, menial, dead-end labor that as often as not produce a below-poverty level of living. Frequently, the poor are frustrated, hostile, and trapped by contemporary socioeconomic institutions that add

[8] This condition is estimated to affect about 20 percent of the elderly poor.

to their disadvantages and reinforce their behavior patterns. In addition to facing income, housing, and education problems, they frequently bear the brunt of crime, and it is clear that they have severe health problems. When Dr. George James was the Commissioner of Health of New York City, he remarked that the condition of poverty represented the third leading cause of death in that metropolitan area. Perhaps the health problem of the poor is illustrated adequately by the fact that the average lifetime expectancy for all nonwhites—who are three times as likely to be poor as whites—is 10 percent (as much as seven years) *less* than the average lifetime for whites! Poverty and death accompany each other in tragic and avoidable ways, resulting in the physical destruction of human resources instead of the creation of human capital. Such destruction is all the more tragic in view of the self-perpetuating poverty culture, which is characterized by hopelessness and despair.

## THE LEGITIMACY OF POVERTY

Low incomes give evidence of, but do not represent the cause of poverty. Nevertheless, economic data add to our knowledge of poverty in important ways. Despite factual data on the poor and the recognition that the subculture of poverty breeds more of the same, poverty remains a subject of debate to millions of Americans. There are two diametrically opposed views on the poverty problem *per se*, and even more disagreement is voiced over human-resource policies to remedy poverty, as we shall see later. Let us consider first the philosophical split over the reality of poverty.

*"Motherhood, Apple Pie, and the Flag"* Value systems underlie views on poverty, and the judgment of some is that poverty is as unavoidable and American as motherhood, apple pie, and the flag. Although most Americans may not hold these views today, there remains a strong tradition of values that forms a basis of sorts for denying adequate help to the poor. Not long ago, well-known and respected Americans argued that the poor deserve what they get. Andrew Carnegie, for example, sanctified poverty as an American institution by stating that ". . . the greatest and best of our race have necessarily been nurtured in the bracing school of poverty—the only school capable of producing the supremely great, the genius."[9] A closely related philosophical tenet likens public support for the poor to condoning survival of the unfittest—to an "anticivilization" law.[10] Another pillar of the view that poverty is right rests on the notion that it benevolently purifies men and society. Deprivation is alleged to be in the best interests of a Darwinian view of humanity. Society weeds out the least fit, incapable, and idle while molding others to accept postponed gratification in the hope of receiving more in the future. The rationale for poverty also derives from the "work-

[9] Quoted from Andrew Carnegie's *The Gospel of Wealth and Other Essays*, 1901, in Robert E. Will and Harold G. Vatter (eds.), *Poverty in Affluence* (New York: Harcourt Brace Jovanovich, 1970), p. 27.

[10] In response to this philosophy, Thomas Huxley once noted that men ". . . who justify such ideas on the grounds of a sanctified cosmic process . . . must rank medicine among the black arts and count the physician a mischievous preserver of the unfit. . . ." See Thomas Huxley, *Evolution and Ethics and Other Essays* (New York: D. Appleton, 1902), p. 36; and A. G. Keller and M. R. Davie (eds.), *Essays of William Graham Sumner*, Vol. II (New Haven, Conn.: Yale University Press, 1934), p. 56.

reward" ethic of the Western culture, which somehow equates the wages and productivity of resources to justice and thus regards rugged individualism as freedom. Holding that wages should equal a man's marginal product is seen as proof of the "poverty-is-good" view in some circles. It proves the fitness of those whose material achievements are high *and* it also proves that the poor are poor because they are indolent and unfit rascals who have chosen to fritter away life's opportunities. Accordingly, a society's responsibility ends at helping the poor to help themselves. After all, admonitions aplenty (e.g., in the Bible) remind mankind that "ye have the poor with you always."

*Social Institutions and the Generation of Poverty*   Certainly the prevalence of a social value akin to Carnegie's "poverty-breeds-success" doctrine does not help the poor. Nor do social values based upon ideas such as "support of the poor equals support of the unfit" or "productivity wages equal justice." These ideas tend to serve one purpose: that of preserving the existing institutional order and legitimatizing the rules of the game already accepted by those in control. In such a context a society can indeed establish and rationalize a breeding ground for poverty.

There is, however, a second view; namely, that poverty is an institutional and cultural result of past and present environmental inadequacies. This view emphasizes the fact that deficiencies in social values and institutions create poverty-ingrained behavior patterns and allow a stacking of the "rules of the game" against lower classes. Consider discrimination, the urban-ghetto housing situation, or government-sponsored freeways which replace housing for low-income families. Or examine the tax laws which allow tax-free income to millionaires and trust-fund accumulations of vast property wealth. The most insidious "rule" of all, and one only recently denounced by President Nixon, is government welfare itself, which had long denied payments to a family if a father or man were present in the home. Of course, institutions and rules work toward both the elimination and the creation of poverty. Turning back to Figure 5 once again, we see that the number of poor has declined from about 40 million to less than 25 million persons since 1959, and this is a mark of substantial progress in one short decade.

The essence of the institutional view is that society and not individuals themselves bears much responsibility for the existence of poverty. The social and economic fabric is seen as both courting and remedying poverty, and thus those who advocate eradication of poverty argue for institutional changes in the environment and the culture that accommodates poverty and lead to the destruction of human resources. Institutional changes are needed to cope with: (*a*) unemployment induced by technological change, (*b*) sporadic or low rates of economic growth, (*c*) inadequate education unequally available, and (*d*) racial discrimination. A complex social and economic system has helped assign more than one-tenth of a nation to the ranks of the poor, the vast majority of whom are children, racial minorities, mothers, and elderly or disabled Americans.

## THE WORKING POOR

No one individual can provide definitive answers to such a question as: What is equity and justice? Nonetheless, everyone must answer that query, either explicitly or by default. Even though convictions and values vary (sometimes markedly), facts and logic about such complex subjects as the economics of poverty demand their due. One last fact about the legacy of the poor is in order—most of them work! In 1969, for example, 30 percent of the heads of all poverty-level families worked full time; another 25 percent worked part-time; approximately 30 percent were officially classified as unemployed, ill, disabled, or keeping house and caring for children; and still others not in the labor force were, no doubt, unable to find work because of age, inadequate training, and other problems. The number of male heads of poverty-level households between 25 and 64 years of age who did not work during any one year over the last decade for reasons other than disability, illness, and unemployment has never exceeded one-half million persons out of a total poverty population of some 24 million persons today. To characterize the poor as lazy, indifferent, and indolent citizens in search of handouts is grossly misleading for the vast majority. It is quite incorrect to equate welfare to a give-away program for the shiftless American, as some are prone to do. Indeed, as the 1968 Commission on Civil Disorders reported, social attitudes and public-welfare programs might very well be criticized for trying to save money instead of people, and succeeding in doing neither.

## C. THE ECONOMICS OF RACIAL DISCRIMINATION

Many American minority groups such as the Poles, Jews, Italians, and Irish have at one time borne the brunt of discrimination, but none have experienced what the blacks, Indians, and Spanish Americans have for decades and even centuries. Millions of people belonging to ethnic minority groups have moved through the gates of Ellis Island into an economic melting pot that today is uniformly American, but the common feature of color is still distinguishable, and blacks and other nonwhites have met lasting, instead of temporary, prejudice.

Racial prejudice is an economic reality in northern cities, the barren southwestern United States, and the warm and lush South. Today, nonwhites comprise approximately one-ninth of the population, but they account for one-fifth of total unemployment. Nonwhites also represent one-third of all persons and two-fifths of all children living in poverty, and these minority groups account for nearly one-half of all female-headed poor families. Irony abounds for nonwhites, especially the blacks, who constituted 10 of the 22 persons founding Los Angeles in the 1780s—a city which now contains some 30,000 black families living in poverty. At the present time, only about 1 percent of all lawyers, 2 percent of all physicians, and 0.3 percent of all plumbers are nonwhite. Despite the fact that 1 of 9 families in the United States is nonwhite, only 1 in 33 families with incomes in excess of $21,000 is nonwhite. History reveals that much of the real problem of discrimination goes far beyond economics, and that while progress has been made in recent years, racial equality is still a goal, not a reality.

### From Slavery to Serfdom

The slave economy was a supply and demand economy which might be one way to suggest that market systems do not always work for good. The

American slave market was an absolute one. In its formative years, plentiful supplies imported from Africa were crucial to the pricing and resource-allocation process. When slave trade was prohibited at the beginning of the nineteenth century, adjustments were required in the slave economy. With supply-import constraints, prices rose rapidly, and the institution of slavery became even more dominated by the intellectual control of humans.

The American slave was a property, not a person. Rights to marry were nonexistent, and thus wives and children could be sold. In a number of border states, after restrictions were imposed upon foreign supplies, slaves were bred for the market. Several observers have held that, unlike the Ancients, who maintained slavery as an institution by threats of death and chains, Americans employed psychological, intellectual, and emotional violence in much the same way that the Germans, Red Chinese, and more recently the Viet Cong have used these forms of control over prisoners of war. The effect of American slavery was to rob blacks of hope and desire just as effectively as brainwashing tactics subdue American GI's in Asia. Slaves were deprived of freedom, ambition, and manhood, while independent family organizations were purged. In essence, this process contributed to the creation of what was long claimed to be the Almighty's original design—an inferior human by the psychological, educational, and cultural standards common to this nation. Many states expressly forbade teaching blacks to read or write, several northern states denied slaves the right to a jury trial, and a few states on the western frontier barred the entry of any black. Judge Taney's decision in the Dred Scott Case in 1857 clearly states what American slavery was like: Blacks had no rights whites needed to respect.

The American system of slavery was a personal system, not a contractual one like that in Latin America (which, incidentally, had black bishops in the 1800s). Because of the total effectiveness of American slavery, the black was hardly emancipated when he was freed physically some 100 years ago. Rather, a serfdom status replete with its own forms of inhumanity replaced the breeding pens of the Old South. Segregation, for example, grew more prevalent in both the South and the North several decades *after* cessation of Civil War hostilities. New York barred blacks from restaurants and other public places in the early 1900s, a decade after segregation began to appear in the South, and about the same time (1912) President Woodrow Wilson first segregated facilities in federal office buildings, ending four decades of common racial use. While the social and economic status of blacks (as well as other racial minorities) has improved in the century since slavery was abolished, much is yet to be gained.

## The Good Life: Fact or Fantasy?

The economic status of racial minorities today reflects the legacy of slavery in all classes of society. The success white minorities have experienced in forcing assimilation into the middle and upper classes required group pressure and political power tactics. What specific forms of social power will be utilized by today's discriminated-against Americans remains to be seen, but it is clear that some form of socioeconomic "push" is here and probably is in order if standardized economic opportunities and racial equality are to be achieved. Where America stands today between the roads to serfdom and to equality and where it wishes to be can best be judged by the reader. What social and economic data we do have seem to indicate that: (*a*) Prejudice and human-resource peonage remain an economic reality for nonwhites, over 90 percent of whom are black; and (*b*) the latter part of the 1960s is striking in terms of the progress that has been made.

INCOME, EMPLOYMENT, AND EDUCATION

Figure 6 shows the maldistribution of family income by race in the United States. Although many factors other than race which influence family income averages are not isolated in the figure, data comparisons reveal sizable income differentials. While the vast majority of all white families earn

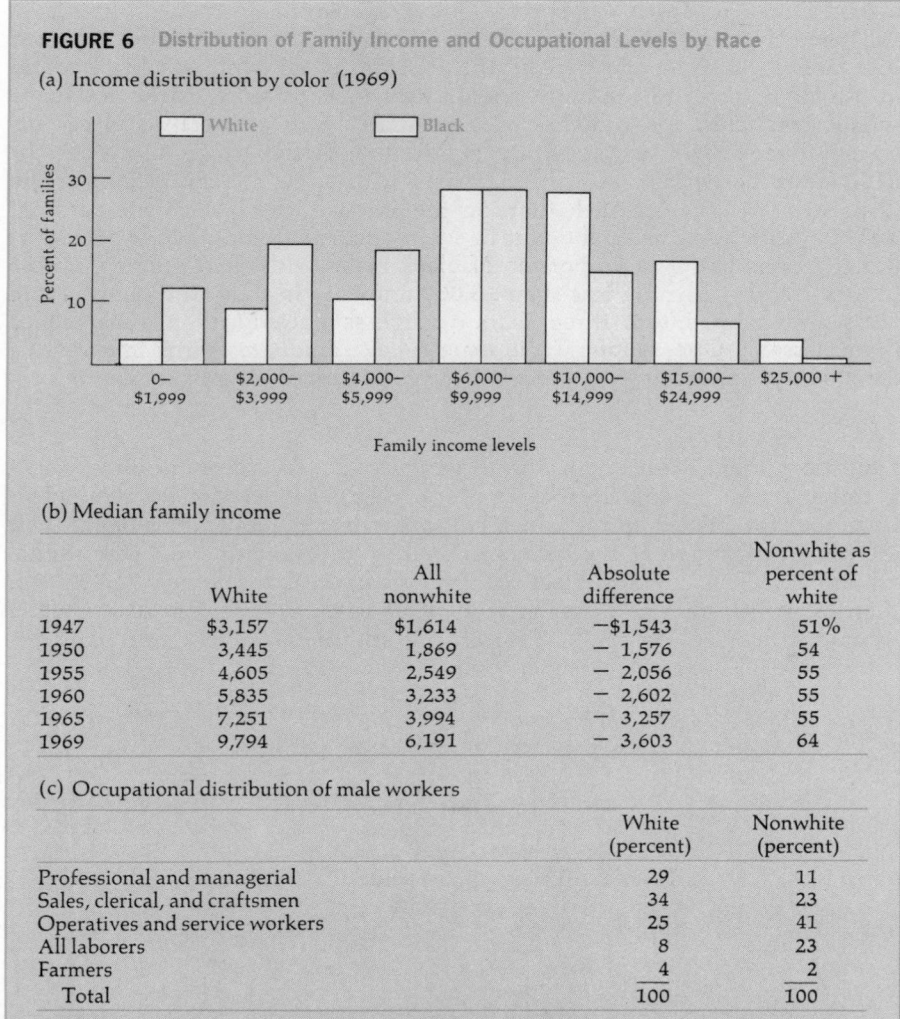

**FIGURE 6**  Distribution of Family Income and Occupational Levels by Race

(a) Income distribution by color (1969)

(b) Median family income

|  | White | All nonwhite | Absolute difference | Nonwhite as percent of white |
|---|---|---|---|---|
| 1947 | $3,157 | $1,614 | −$1,543 | 51% |
| 1950 | 3,445 | 1,869 | − 1,576 | 54 |
| 1955 | 4,605 | 2,549 | − 2,056 | 55 |
| 1960 | 5,835 | 3,233 | − 2,602 | 55 |
| 1965 | 7,251 | 3,994 | − 3,257 | 55 |
| 1969 | 9,794 | 6,191 | − 3,603 | 64 |

(c) Occupational distribution of male workers

|  | White (percent) | Nonwhite (percent) |
|---|---|---|
| Professional and managerial | 29 | 11 |
| Sales, clerical, and craftsmen | 34 | 23 |
| Operatives and service workers | 25 | 41 |
| All laborers | 8 | 23 |
| Farmers | 4 | 2 |
| Total | 100 | 100 |

SOURCE: U. S. Department of Labor and Commerce, *The Social and Economic Status of Negroes in the United States*, 1960; *Handbook of Labor Statistics*, 1970; and *Current Population Reports*, P–60, No. 66 (1969), No. 70 and No. 72 (1970).

$6,000 a year or more, one-half of all black families earn less than $6,000 annually, as shown in Figure 6(a). Income-data comparisons are also shown in Figure 6(b) for all nonwhites. The absolute-dollar difference between median incomes for white and for all nonwhite families doubled from 1947 to 1965 to an average of $3,257 per family in 1965. The better jobs are still biased in favor of white males. Nearly one out of three white males is classified in managerial or professional occupations in Figure 6(c), as compared to one out of ten nonwhites, and two-thirds of all black males are employed in operative, service, and/or labor occupations. One final point is worth noting: Since the mid-1960s there has been a decided trend toward greater relative income equality on a racial basis; that is, average nonwhite incomes have increased as a percent of average white incomes.

The cutting edge of economic discrimination is shown in Figure 7, which compares average income by educational level for all white and black males in the labor force. White high-school dropouts earn more than black high-school graduates, white high-school graduates earn as much as black college graduates, and whites with a high-school diploma earn an average of $100 more per *month* than black males with *some* college training! The disparities by race are such that, on the average, the black male earns at least 30 cents less for each dollar of white income at equal levels of educational attainment. The proportion of black males with one to three years of *college* training earning less than $5,000 annually is about the same as it is for whites with one to three years of *high-school* education—one out of three persons. One in four white male college graduates earns in excess of $15,000 annually, but if you're black, the odds are one out of ten.

### BLACK HUMAN CAPITAL

Education, then, is an important element leading to higher incomes, but it is not yet a racial equalizer to any large degree. Indeed, there are indications that the higher up the education ladder blacks move, the smaller their income as a fraction of the income earned by whites with equal educational attainment. The average black college graduate earns about $4,700 less than his white counterpart each year of his life, or 64 percent of the white income level (see Figure 7). Two crucial additional facts about economic

**FIGURE 7** White and Black Income by Education Level, Males 25 and Over

| Educational level | Mean income | | | Percent earning under $5,000 | | Percent earning over $15,000 | |
|---|---|---|---|---|---|---|---|
| | White | Black | Black as % of white | White | Black | White | Black |
| Elementary (0–8 years) | $ 4,896 | $3,395 | 69% | 58.7% | 74.7% | 1.5% | 0.2% |
| High school (1–3 years) | 6,973 | 5,078 | 73 | 29.1 | 50.4 | 3.3 | 0.5 |
| High-school graduates | 8,319 | 5,737 | 69 | 17.7 | 39.0 | 6.2 | 0.5 |
| College (1–3 years) | 9,559 | 6,615 | 69 | 16.1 | 28.7 | 12.1 | 2.2 |
| College graduates | 13,126 | 8,448 | 64 | 11.3 | 18.9 | 26.8 | 9.6 |

SOURCE: *Current Population Reports*, P–60, No. 66 (1969).

discrimination by educational level are that: (*a*) Only very modest improvement has occurred in the last ten years, and (*b*) racial discrimination of this sort may retard investment in black human capital at a time when more, not less, education is an important need for racial minorities.

When annual incomes by race and education are translated into lifetime-income differentials, the "price of being black" is even more startling.[11] Going back a decade for the moment, 1960 census data have revealed that a nonwhite male age 24 with a college education could expect to earn $209,000 *less* in his lifetime than the total lifetime income of an equally educated white.[12] In addition to discrimination at equal educational-attainment levels, the probable lifetime incomes of blacks are pulled down by higher mortality rates and less rapid rates of advancement into better jobs. A male who has attained the age of 20 years has an average life expectancy of 50 years, if he is white—and if not, 45 years. This is an *average* of five fewer years of working lifetime for black human capital which, in conjunction with racial and job discrimination, combine to reduce expected lifetime incomes by hundreds of thousands of dollars.

When income comparisons are updated to 1970, the average lifetime income for a black male college graduate entering the labor force at age 24 would not be the $646,000 shown in Figure 3, nor could we simply reduce that amount to reflect the fact that black college graduates earn 64 percent of what a white graduate earns, as shown in Figure 7. Rather, the average lifetime income of black human capital today would be approximately 60 percent of $646,000. This would amount to a difference of more than one-quarter of a million dollars for the black male college graduate entering the 1970 labor force at age 24—and that might be called a "bundle of coins." There are important income gains associated with increased education, to be sure, but white-black income differentials are also very real as we turn the corner into the 1970s. Indeed, they are so real that some observers have labeled them a "honky tax."

In view of recent (albeit gradual) trends toward amelioration of these differences, it is doubtful that the magnitude of the price of being black will remain fixed in the next decade. Needless to say, American society will not tolerate and cannot afford to passively observe economic discrimination of this sort in the future.

Income inequalities by educational attainment and race reflect occupational disparities as well as differences in educational quality, but these facts only shift discrimination from the economic to the social and educational spheres. The cumulative impact of past and present injustice plus the personal frustration of blacks endanger all of society. A less-than-equal return on investment in black human capital carries its own diabolical design that works for a deprived, not better, future for blacks. The motivation to learn, earn, and work cannot help but suffer from discrimination. To those bearing the brunt of economic discrimination today, the major issue is how fast the past will in fact disappear, and yesterday is just about

[11] Ignored in income comparisons are differences in occupations and the quality of education, factors that help explain some portion of lifetime-income differences and also suggest job and educational discrimination.

[12] U.S. Department of Commerce, *Present Values of Estimated Lifetime Earnings* (1967), p. 10.

the right timing in the minds of most blacks, other nonwhites, and racial minorities such as Spanish-Americans.

## AN UNDERDEVELOPED AMERICA

Conditions among nonwhites in education, housing, and health confirm what one logically would expect from our review of the economics of poverty and discrimination. It is also a well-documented fact that the non-white consumer ends up paying more for what he does get, particularly if he is poor. Decent credit terms and health-care services are difficult to obtain for the nonwhite poor. The problem of absorbing those persons with educational deficiencies into a labor market that has fewer and fewer semi- and unskilled job opportunities often makes it impossible for them to work steadily, even at menial tasks. Consignment of racial minorities to unstable, menial jobs at lower skill and wage levels cannot help but whet their appetites for rejection of contemporary society.

Housing discrimination cuts several ways. Segregated ghetto housing generates segregation in education, which feeds social and class stratification now and in the future. Segregation in both housing and education remain characteristic of urban America in the early 1970s, all laws to the contrary quite aside—although once again progress has been made since the mid-1960s. Housing problems are particularly acute for the urban non-white poor, who generally live in areas where population densities range up to 100 times the suburban average. Not only is their housing shoddy, they also pay more for comparable shelter than whites because discrimination reduces the available supply of housing. Nonwhite demand for decent housing bids up rents, adding further price pressure for nonwhites because inadequate supplies are available. Competing freeways and business demands for urban space as well as urban renewal (which is still working off a backlog of low-income housing which it has displaced) add even more irony to the minority-housing problem in urban areas. Because health care is auctioned on the basis of markets, purchasing power and not need separate those who consume from others who suffer. Lower incomes depress nonwhite demand for modern health care and inadequate supplies of physicians and hospitals also discriminate against nonwhites, again particularly for that portion of the population living below or near the poverty threshold. These circumstances contribute to a shorter average lifetime for nonwhites and also help explain why nonwhite maternal and infant mortality rates are three times as large as they are for whites.

*Summing up:* The disadvantages facing nonwhite Americans are still quite real. The blacks and other racial minorities are part of an invisible underdeveloped country within America that often is unseen by those who control its institutions. In many ways the human-resource policies discussed next portend a better future for both the poor and racial minorities, but this future is largely dependent upon the attitudes, beliefs, and values of an affluent white majority.

## D. HUMAN-RESOURCE POLICY FOR POVERTY AND DISCRIMINATION

Past and existing facts on poverty, and particularly on economic discrimination, are by no means necessarily indicative of the future. In the mid-1960s America responded to the realities we have been considering. Between 1965 and 1969, for example, the number of persons classified as poor declined by 9 million; median family incomes increased by more than one-half for blacks compared to one-third for whites; nonwhite family incomes rose from 55 to 64 percent of the average for whites; and an average of over 12 years of school are now completed by nonwhites under 35 years of age. Still, the proportion of nonwhite high-school dropouts under 21 years of age is one out of three, or twice as large as it is among whites, and nonwhite unemployment is twice the rate of unemployment for whites. Society has made substantial adjustments, but much remains to be done.

### Eradicating Poverty and Racial Discrimination

Many of the barriers to equal opportunity and a chance to succeed in economic terms are noneconomic in character. Social values must change, institutional barriers (e.g., educational inequality and housing segregation) must be destroyed, understanding and compassion must accompany and distill latent social conflict, and decaying inner cities as well as desolate rural pockets of poverty must be restored to viable substructures of an affluent economy capable of producing $1 trillion of GNP as of 1971.

Poverty and the special case of economic discrimination represent horrible external diseconomies of a larger environment—they are by-products of an impersonal and decentralized system of economic organization fueled by man's selfishness. Both the private and public sectors of the economy bear enormous responsibilities for remedying contemporary injustices—and no one knows for sure whether either sector will do what needs to be done in the time that remains. Government agencies, for example, have blundered in the welfare "industry" on more than one occasion, and until recently inadequate support and a poor understanding of the problems have been common throughout all communities in a world which is, after all, motivated by profits.

As the decade of the 1970s begins, both business and government are coming more closely to grips with the problems we have just considered. At the same time, even a casual observer must recognize that the data we have examined reflect many decades of living with disadvantaged Americans and innumerable public programs allegedly designed to help them. Let us see just what factors impinge on poverty and discrimination.

### THE BATTLE FOR ECONOMIC JUSTICE

Many existing government policies can and do affect poverty, inequality, and injustice. While poverty differs from racial discrimination in many contexts, both problems succumb to common policy measures in significant ways. Let us review the general features of the attack on poverty and injustice which was begun under the late President Kennedy in the early 1960s and has been continued through the Johnson and Nixon administrations.

*Economic Growth and Employment*  Increasing the rate of economic growth and maintaining full employment is a general but very important measure in helping some of the disadvantaged improve their economic stations in life. Between 1965 and 1969 full employment and unprecedented growth provided jobs that broke down discrimination barriers and lifted literally millions above the poverty threshold. Regional economic-development programs sponsored by the United States Department of Commerce and state and local development agencies have also been important to economic growth and the enlarging of employment opportunities, particularly for poverty pockets in Appalachia and other rural regions in the United States which have stagnated while the aggregate economy has expanded. Unfortunately, the aged, the disabled, the very poorly trained who are near-functional illiterates, and families headed by women—groups which represent the bulk of all persons living in poverty—benefit little from full-employment growth. In addition, the inflationary problems encountered in the United States during 1969 and 1970 provided other offsets that intensified poverty and discrimination by pushing the unemployment rate up substantively, thus destroying rather than creating jobs for marginal workers.

*Minority Enterprise* Inequality and racial discrimination have been unusually common in the past for nonwhites interested in establishing business operations. By and large, nonwhite businessmen have had and continue to have difficulty in obtaining such things as financing, insurance, and access to distribution outlets in the complex and often concentrated business enterprise system characteristic of the United States today. Ghetto business operations are particularly risky, and the greater likelihood of fire, theft, uncollected accounts, and even riots makes insurance and financing difficult to acquire. In recent years, Washington policy-makers have begun to provide grant and loan assistance directly and indirectly to encourage black capitalism. While conceptually a noble purpose, black ownership of firms providing goods and services to minority consumers has not as yet received the requisite transfusion of white capital. Moreover, many observers believe that integration in business enterprise, not segregation, is more likely to provide the uplift nonwhites need.

*Education and the Creation of Human Capital* Education and training are a third category of policies directed at the achievement of greater equality by adding to the "capital" content of underdeveloped nonwhite human resources. The 1962 Manpower Development and Training Act (MDTA) authorized the federal government to provide education and training for disadvantaged workers, most of whom are young and undereducated; it also included provisions for retraining older unemployed workers. Under the Nixon administration emphasis shifted in the direction of improving work incentives, enlarging the role of business in providing training, and increasing state and local government responsibility for manpower activities. One million persons had completed MDTA programs by 1970. Many other federal programs have been oriented toward the further development of human resources. Among the more notable efforts are: (*a*) the expanded Work Incentive Program, which is designed to facilitate training and work for welfare recipients; (*b*) the Concentrated Employment Program, which supplies manpower training in poverty and ghetto areas; (*c*) Job Opportunities in the Business Sector—a program in which government subsidizes business firms for training the hard-core unemployed; (*d*) the Neighborhood Youth Corps and the Job Corps, which concentrate on in-residence training for disadvantaged youth; and (*e*) the Public Services Careers Program, which is designed to enhance government employment opportunities for the disadvantaged. On the average, one-half million persons were enrolled in various manpower programs in any given month of the year throughout 1970, and total openings in all federal manpower programs are budgeted at 2.1 million positions for 1971.

*Equal Opportunity*  Equal opportunities in employment, housing, and education are basic antidotes for poverty and economic discrimination. Nevertheless, there is no doubt that the white majority must fully accept the concept of equal opportunity before legally declared policy positions can be an effective arm of social change. As a fourth type of policy measure designed to break poverty and discrimination barriers, equal-opportunity programs are directed at desegregating housing for nonwhites, renewing ghetto environments, providing equal educational opportunities, and eradicating the cultural and institutional disadvantages which now submerge the poor. Laws such as the Civil Rights Act of 1964, as well as legislation concerning housing discrimination, are important to the achievement of equality. Moreover, the Economic Opportunity Act (EOA) has provided new educational opportunities for children from disadvantaged backgrounds through Headstart programs. Several thousand investigations of discriminatory employment practices have been conducted under EOA auspices, and equal employment opportunities are also generated through government projects that require contractors to provide maximum employment opportunities for minority groups on urban renewal, public housing, and similar construction projects.

Unfortunately, legally promulgated guarantees of equality and freedom in reality often translate into the difference between "saying" and "doing." Congress called for a decent home for every American family more than 20 years ago (1949), and once again in the Housing Act of 1969—yet one out of four nonwhites still lives in substandard housing.[13] Moreover, equality is not readily accepted or defined, particularly with regard to providing nonwhite employment opportunities in proportion to the nonwhite population in a labor market. Segregated schooling remained a common experience for over two-thirds of all nonwhite children who attended predominantly nonwhite schools in the fall of 1970. In short, equal opportunity requires changes in values and institutions, a social commitment, and time —not just law. Because the achievement of equality along with racial and social class integration has been laboriously slow and seemingly fought at every turn, some nonwhites are calling for separatism. As a means of achieving group identity, pride, and organized political power—which was also necessary for the Irish, Italians, and Jews a few decades ago—separatist tactics could be successful. It is interesting to note, however, that many minority leaders in this and other nations typically insist that integration, not separatism, is needed.

## ON TREATING CAUSES AND ECONOMIC SYMPTOMS

There are vast differences between dealing with the causes of human-resource problems and treating their symptoms. The measures just dis-

[13] U.S. Department of Commerce, *The Social and Economic Status of Negroes in the United States*, 1969, p. 57.

cussed deal with causes, which is where the thrust is needed today. Symptoms of poverty and discrimination are mirrored by the low income level under which millions of American citizens barely exist.

The magnitude of the aggregate poverty-income deficit incurred by all poverty household units (both families and unrelated persons) for recent years is shown in Figure 8. The total poverty deficit of $10.1 billion for 1969 is the product of the number of poverty households multiplied by the average difference in income received and the poverty threshold for all such households (adjusted for age, region, and family size). Figure 8 also shows that, on the average, there is a $1,000 deficit by household unit which has remained relatively stable for a decade.[14]

While the total poverty deficit rose as unemployment increased between 1959 and the recession of 1961, rapid declines until 1969 reflected growing employment opportunities during the 1960s. As inflation and employment problems developed in 1969–1970, the poverty deficit leveled out at ap-

[14] Remember, the rigidity of the poverty standard defined in absolute dollars provides for no improvements in real income, but is adjusted upward only for higher costs of living. (During the last decade the *real* income of all American households increased by almost one-third.)

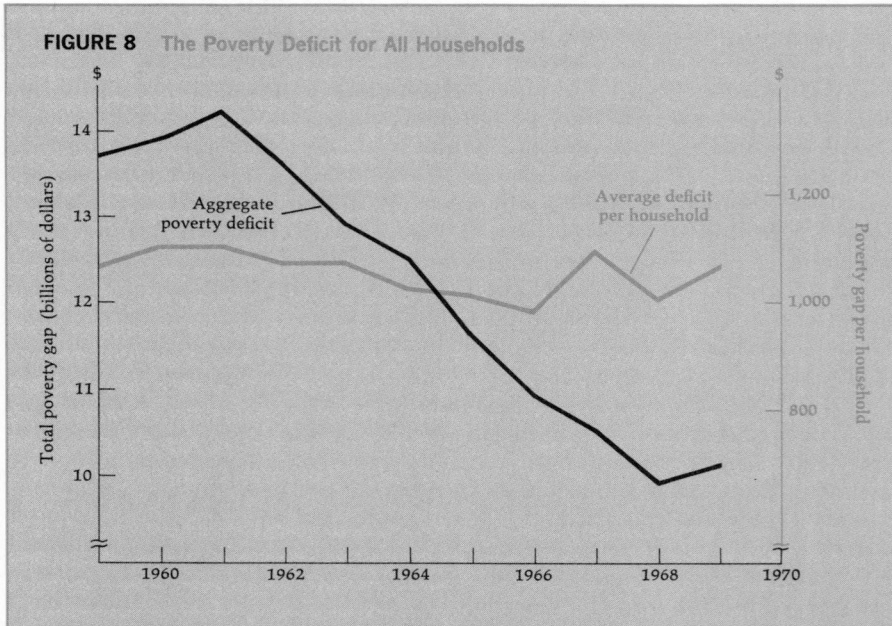

**FIGURE 8**   The Poverty Deficit for All Households

*The Magnitude of Poverty.* Using government defined poverty-threshold levels, the aggregate income required to bring all households up to the poverty minimum has declined from more than $14 billion to $10 billion. However, the average deficit per poverty household has remained relatively steady at $1,000 per year.

SOURCE: *Current Population Reports*, P–60, No. 66 (1969) and No. 71 (1970).

proximately $10 billion. Another important factor in recent improvements is the progress made through the manpower-development and equal-opportunity programs described earlier. Finally, direct government financial aid to the poor has increased since 1960. Today, direct cash payments comprise about 60 percent of total aid to the poor. Even though there has been a shift toward more emphasis on human-resource investment programs since 1960, cash assistance still remains an important need.

### Income Maintenance

Income subsidies to the poor are based in part on normative concepts of morality and justice and in part on the recognition that the vast majority of the poor are unable to work for a variety of reasons. Policies designed to provide full employment do little to assist the hard-core poor unable to work and, in addition, income-maintenance programs may be needed to bring many of the working poor up to subsistence income levels.

The aggregate $10 billion poverty deficit between incomes received and minimal poverty-income levels shown in Figure 8 exists in spite of several government programs providing in-kind and direct income supplements to the poor. Such measures as food-stamp programs, school-lunch programs, rent supplements, and public housing reach some households, but the level of relief provided is still inadequate by the standards which experts have established. Before we look at recent welfare reforms, a brief review of past and present welfare programs is in order.

### SOCIAL-WELFARE PROGRAMS

There are four major categories of public-welfare programs embodied in public policy today: (a) retirement, (b) public health, (c) disability and unemployment compensation, and (d) public relief for the disadvantaged.

Retirement insurance represents the largest income-maintenance program in the United States today, a program financed jointly by employer and employee tax contributions. Provision for public-health assistance (e.g., Medicare) is the second important feature of the current welfare program. Public-health expenditures in 1970 exceeded $10 billion, including new Medicare provisions attached to the social security program, and Medicaid, which provides health-care benefits to the elderly and poor. Although retirement and health benefits (as well as taxes) are raised periodically, the current benefit level by itself is not large enough to lift many aged poor above poverty levels.

Although the social security program is not designed for the poverty problem, it also includes disability payments that vary by state. Unfortunately, in the vast majority of states, disability benefits are too low and eligibility requirements too stringent to provide the assistance the disabled poor need. Unemployment compensation, still another provision of the 1935 Social Security Act, establishes income supplements for some workers unable .to find jobs. Again, however, less-than-poverty income levels are provided (payments are about one-third of average wages for a maximum period of 26 weeks). Moreover, eligibility and coverage requirements are such that millions of workers do not benefit fully when they are unemployed—especially those who are most likely to be poor. Finally, disadvantaged families can often qualify for several different public-relief programs established for the blind, permanently disabled, and dependent children. Aid to Families with Dependent Children (AFDC) is the best-known and probably the most inept welfare program of all. Initially established during the Depression to aid children of deceased or disabled fathers, three-fourths of all AFDC relief now supports deserted, unmarried, and separated women with children. Like the welfare programs mentioned above, AFDC benefits very rarely provide income levels sufficient to raise needy families above the poverty threshold. The controversial "man-in-the-house" rule, which denied AFDC assistance when a male was present in the house, was common in nearly every state as recently as the mid-1960s. Even in 1970, in one-half of all states, families were ineligible for AFDC benefits if an unemployed male were in the home. The effect of such rules is to encourage family disintegration because responsible male family heads are urged to desert their wives and children so that the family can qualify for public welfare.

## WELFARE OR ILLFARE?

Were it not for the existing social security program and allied public-assistance programs in the United States today, poverty would be much more prevalent than it is. Still, the very existence of poverty in the magnitudes discussed earlier in this chapter clearly indicates that much remains to be done. For the most part, current social-welfare programs have been designed for those who need help least in comparative terms. Millions of persons classified as poor receive little or no transfer payments and over two-thirds of all retirement and health benefits paid under social security programs go to households that experience neither poverty nor near poverty.

Nevertheless, rapidly increasing welfare costs have been severely criticized by irate taxpayers, who frequently view welfare as a government dole to persons whose condition is alleged to reflect lack of effort. Well-meaning men have important differences of opinion about poverty, discrimination, and welfare programs, depending on their philosophies and values. Today's culture is searching for meaning and brotherhood in life beyond simply more GNP to count and distribute whimsically through impersonal markets. Consequently, welfare reform looms large as an economic issue.

Professionals associated with social-welfare programs have also been disgruntled, but for different reasons. They note that social welfare is both inadequate and inequitable, and single out such programs as unemployment compensation and AFDC, which are controlled by individual states that specify diverse eligibility conditions and provide widely varying benefits. Heavy criticism has also been levied against the family-disintegration bias of welfare programs such as AFDC. President Nixon's remarks to Congress in presenting his 1970 Family-Assistance Plan summed up public disenchantment as follows:

The present welfare system has failed—it has fostered family breakup, has provided very little help in many states and has even deepened dependency by all too often making it more attractive to go on welfare than to go to work.[15]

Reforms in public assistance for the poor in recent years have emphasized an orientation toward improved job and income guarantees. The best-

[15] Presidential message to Congress, August 11, 1969.

known of these reform plans is the "negative income tax" popularly acclaimed many years ago by Professor Milton Friedman and more recently by Professor Robert Lampman of the University of Wisconsin and Professor James Tobin of Yale University. Indeed, the Nixon administration's interest in overhauling the AFDC program via a Family-Assistance Program for low-income families is founded on basic principles embodied in the negative income tax.

## NEGATIVE INCOME TAXES

The formulas recommended to implement a negative tax on incomes vary widely, but the essential principles of most plans are roughly the same. Family income deficits are calculated relative to the poverty threshold, and some portion of the deficit is then supplemented by government payments. Let us assume that a family of four earning $4,000 in 1971 is at the poverty threshold level. Any family earning a higher level of income would be required to pay a progressively scheduled tax. However, if the family earned less than $4,000 in income, they would receive a government payment (thus the label, "negative" tax). For example, a family earning $1,000 annually, or $3,000 less than the poverty minimum, would receive some percentage of the family poverty deficit ($3,000, in this case) as a government income supplement.

Figure 9 illustrates a hypothetical negative income tax based upon a constant tax rate of 50 percent of the family poverty deficit. If a family received no income, its negative tax transfer payment would be 50 percent of $4,000, or an income of $2,000. As earned income rises, 50 percent of whatever poverty deficit remains is paid to a family. This means that for each additional $1,000 in earned income, one-half or $500 is retained by the family and the other one-half is an offset to the income which the government otherwise guarantees.

The two crucial features of negative income tax plans are: (a) the incentives provided as reflected in the negative tax rate, and (b) the minimal income level supported, which is assumed to be $2,000 in Figure 9. Obviously, the incentive to work is seriously distorted when government assistance is reduced $1 for every $1 of additional earned income, representing a 100 percent tax rate. On the other hand, if a guaranteed income of $4,000 were available and there were a 0 percent tax rate on earnings between 0 and $4,000, poverty households might not have adequate economic incentives to seek work.

One of the difficult and unanswered questions associated with a negative income tax program is the work-leisure path a household might elect under such a plan. In Figure 9, two possibilities are illustrated: If a negative income tax guaranteeing a minimum of $2,000 per year produces large disincentive effects, a family might opt for more leisure and less earned income, as shown by path A. Alternatively, a negative income tax might facilitate an increase in earned income, as is shown in the figure by path B. Studies that have been conducted on the incentive issue are not conclusive, although tests currently underway in the so-called "New Jersey Experiment" suggest that the negative income plan may not significantly reduce work incentives. Much more research is needed before the incentive and tax-rate relationships can be definitely answered.

A second problem with the negative income tax is that it is difficult to

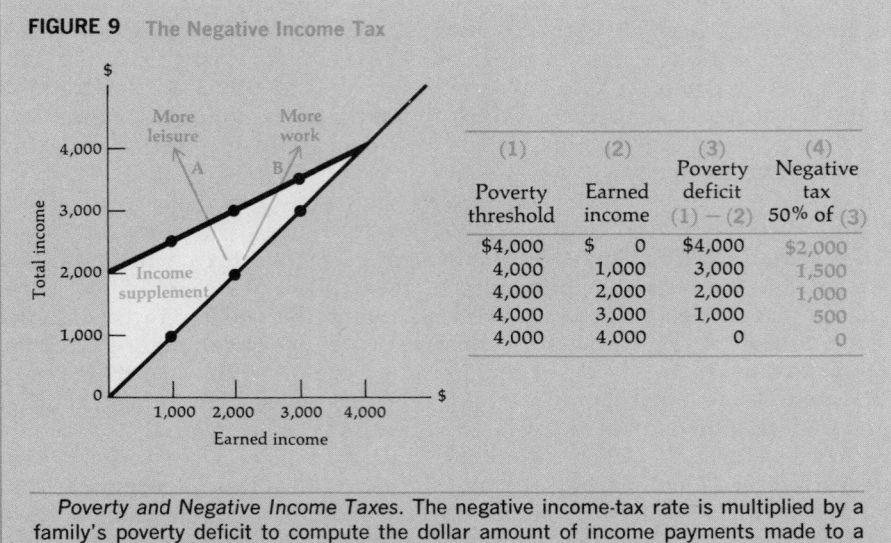

**FIGURE 9** The Negative Income Tax

| (1) Poverty threshold | (2) Earned income | (3) Poverty deficit (1) − (2) | (4) Negative tax 50% of (3) |
|---|---|---|---|
| $4,000 | $ 0 | $4,000 | $2,000 |
| 4,000 | 1,000 | 3,000 | 1,500 |
| 4,000 | 2,000 | 2,000 | 1,000 |
| 4,000 | 3,000 | 1,000 | 500 |
| 4,000 | 4,000 | 0 | 0 |

*Poverty and Negative Income Taxes.* The negative income-tax rate is multiplied by a family's poverty deficit to compute the dollar amount of income payments made to a poverty household. If $4,000 were determined to be a poverty minimum for a family, with no earned income and a 50 percent negative income tax prevailed, that family would receive $2,000. The unknown factor in any negative income-tax plan is the extent to which a poverty household's earned income will fall because of more leisure (path A) or rise (path B).

provide fully for the poverty-threshold income level at reasonable costs. Suppose, for example, that the income-support floor were raised above the $2,000 level assumed in Figure 9. Each family might be provided with a poverty-level minimum income of $4,000, and the 50 percent tax rate would then be applied to all persons whose incomes fell between $4,000 and $6,000. Negative tax payments would then be extended to millions of additional persons with incomes between $4,000 and $6,000, and costs would mount astronomically.

In addition to the difficulties of incentives and poverty-floor minimums, there are other problems with the negative income tax. Many tax-paying citizens feel that people should *work* for subsistence and not receive a guaranteed income. Still others note that a negative income tax will not replace existing public-welfare expenditures, which are designed to get at the causes of poverty and not simply treat the low-income symptom. Certain of these objections can be remedied by complementary human-resource programs such as providing job training, supplying child-care facilities, and providing guaranteed work opportunities. Implementation of food-stamp plans that allow the poor to purchase basic goods and services at less than cost, together with a negative income tax, are still another way of providing for minimum family needs. Indeed, many of these supplementary features can be found in the proposed Family-Assistance Plan noted earlier. Feelings on guaranteed-income plans run high, but most authorities believe them to be superior to existing welfare programs. The negative income tax may be less expensive in the long run than welfare programs such as AFDC, a better way to provide incentives, more efficient in dealing with poverty, less demeaning to the poor, and capable of more nearly providing minimal levels of living.

## REVIEW

Summary

1. Wage and income levels vary among persons for many reasons, including different levels of investment in education and health. It is difficult to determine the return on investments in human resources because social, indirect, and noneconomic costs and returns accompany them. It is likewise difficult to determine the extent to which human-capital formation is an investment or consumption expenditure.

2. The four major types of human-resource investments are expenditures for: (a) improved health, (b) increased education, (c) on-the-job training, and (d) enhanced human-resource mobility. As of 1970, aggregate expenditures on education, including estimated opportunity costs, approximated $100 billion, and total health-care expenditures were about $68 billion. The direct economic value of education is shown by the substantially higher incomes earned by human resources with greater amounts of education. A male college graduate's lifetime income is almost $650,000—nearly $400,000 more than that earned by persons with a grade-school education.

3. Poverty is much more than an economic condition; indeed, poverty is a culture of its own which is reinforced by behavior patterns and institutions such as discrimination. The major victims of poverty are racial minority groups, rural Americans, and the disadvantaged—the aged, disabled, unemployed, and undereducated.

4. Using absolute-dollar standards to define poverty reveals that some 24 million Americans were poor in 1969, which amounts to one out of every eight Americans. Poverty is three times as common among nonwhites as among whites. The values and attitudes of society help explain the prevalence of poverty in an age of affluence. The institutions and culture surrounding the poor often lock them into a never-ending cycle of deprivation, regardless of the fact that nearly all family heads living in poverty work, are mothers caring for children, or are disabled or elderly persons.

5. Racial discrimination against nonwhites is a problem bound up in the history of the black's rise from slavery. Discrimination exists in the form of substantially lower incomes, unequal access to job opportunities, and racial segregation in education and housing. While nonwhite family income has increased since the mid-1960s to about two-thirds the level of an average white family, substantial income discrimination persists for equally educated blacks and other nonwhites.

6. Substantive human-resource policies are required to lessen the severity of poverty and discrimination. Among the major policy measures that may help remedy these social problems are: (a) sustained economic growth in employment, (b) programs to encourage business enterprise

among minority groups, (c) education and manpower programs that create human capital, and (d) equal economic and social opportunities. In addition, the immediate short-run problems of inadequate incomes can be supplemented by social-welfare programs. The negative income tax as a form of guaranteed income represents one of the more sensible approaches to alleviating short-run income deficiencies.

## Identify the Following Concepts and Terms

- human capital
- lifetime incomes
- poverty threshold
- negative income tax
- black capitalism
- MDTA
- causes of poverty
- AFDC

## Questions to Answer

1. According to the data shown in Figure 4 of the text, the *very* approximate difference in lifetime incomes for persons with a high-school, compared to those with a college education is about one-quarter of a million dollars. Taking into account social, indirect, and noneconomic costs and returns, prepare a summary evaluation of the economics of this return to investment in education.

2. Explain the differences between social, indirect, and noneconomic costs and returns associated with human capital. Give examples of each of these types of costs and returns. How is the concept of lifetime income a less-than-adequate measure of the returns to investment in education?

3. As a Congressman about to vote on larger appropriations for the poor, evaluate the following statements:
   (a) "Whether poverty is a serious problem is a normative matter depending on values and judgment, irrespective of the positive information that is marshaled to 'prove' a point."
   (b) "Poverty is randomly distributed throughout the population and is primarily the result of people's unwillingness to better their condition in life."
   (c) "The absolute-dollar standard or threshold for gauging changes in poverty does not differ from relative measures of poverty."

4. Carefully evaluate the economic conditions and facts that pertain to racial discrimination in the United States today. Explain how the existence or the lack of school busing, neighborhood integration, and equal employment opportunities relate to the facts of economic discrimination.

5. Evaluate and *defend* a position on legally enforced school busing, integration, and job preferences or quotas being established for nonwhite minorities.

6. Explain the nature of human-resource development policies common to the United States experience. Evaluate their impact upon poverty and discrimination in the recent past. Just how does an income-support level like the negative income tax relate to work incentives and the total cost of alleviating poverty?

# PART 5

Trade among nations and the development of government policies related to international trade are subjects that have attracted the attention of economists for centuries. The international exchange of goods and services allows further specialization in the use of resources and increased productivity which makes it possible for nations to increase consumption. There are, however, a variety of international financial problems which arise when nations trade. The underdeveloped nations of the world represent still another international problem of great concern to the entire world. Finally, the subject of differences among alternative systems of economic organization is of great significance to the international scene. Among other things, these differences have had a substantial ideological and military impact, particularly in the case of the United States and the Soviet Union.

# The International Economy

# CHAPTER 25
# International Trade

Trade among nations was one of the first economic matters to attract the attention of such early economists as Adam Smith, David Hume, and David Ricardo. Their explanations of the international-trade process have shaped the international economic policies of many countries. The world today is experiencing rapid growth in trade and financial interdependence, and currently over one-third of a trillion dollars of goods and services are exchanged each year. If international trade continues to expand as it has recently, the total volume of trade will double every eight to ten years—a rate of growth that is more than twice the GNP growth rate in such developed nations as the United States and Canada.

The explanation of this rapid growth in international trade is both powerful and simple. Nations gain additional output from the exchange of goods and services because increased specialization accompanies the international division of labor. Real income levels and therefore living standards increase through international specialization and exchange. A more efficient allocation of world resources is thus possible because of international exchange. Exchange also allows the development of vast markets which permit economies of scale on a level impossible in a closed and less specialized economy. International trade is a unique case of specialization, however, because of the importance of political boundaries, different currencies, and domestic economic problems related to international trade.

This chapter explains the special character of trade among nations. Part A is concerned with comparative costs—the economic basis for international trade. Part B investigates the process of international payments, focusing attention on the balance of payments. Many of the public-policy issues involved in international trade relate to trade controls—the topic of Part C. With this background, we can examine international financial matters in Chapter 26.

## A. THE ECONOMIC GAINS FROM TRADE

In a world without international trade, total output and per capita income levels would be substantially reduced. Exchange permits a specialization of resources which makes possible increased productivity. Without exchange, each nation would be forced to be self-sufficient, and productivity as well as per capita output would decline. International trade allows nations to achieve levels of consumption greater than their *domestic* production frontiers because of the diverse resource endowments, differences in productivity and technology, and differences in tastes in the various nations of the world.

Different technologies and resource endowments encourage Argentina to produce beef, Japan to produce electronic products, and Germany to produce steel more efficiently than some other countries. Given their economic and geographic differences, it is not surprising that two economies like Germany and Argentina benefit by exchanging beef and steel. Germany is more efficient in capital-intensive steel production, which it can trade for land-intensive Argentina beef, particularly because of the relative scarcity of land resources in Germany. Once trade is opened up, scale economies may also be realized. Expanded markets contribute to even greater specialization of production, and external economies may lower costs and international prices still further. Because trade among nations is complicated by a variety of factors, we need to examine the nature of international specialization in its own context.

### The Importance of Trade

Trade among nations plays a vital role in many countries. Japan, Great Britain, Switzerland, Canada, France, and the Netherlands, to name a few nations, export between one-tenth and one-third of their GNP. Many of the underdeveloped nations of the world, particularly those that are one-commodity export economies, are vulnerable to international economic conditions. Nations that specialize in primary commodities and products become very dependent on foreign markets, which are often subject to volatile changes in demand and price. A good example is Chile, which relies heavily on its export of copper to Germany and the United States. Similarly, Bolivia depends heavily on tin exports, Venezuela on oil exports, and Cuba on sugar exports.

About one-fifth of all world trade consists of Canadian and American exports, while exports from Germany, Japan, and the United Kingdom comprise another one-fifth of the volume of world trade. All told, seven nations (Canada, the United States, Japan, Germany, France, Russia, and the United Kingdom) account for over one-half of all world trade.[1] For nearly two decades, the volume of trade among developed nations has grown at the rate of 7 to 8 percent each year, largely because barriers to trade have been reduced significantly since World War II. Trade barriers remain in the form of quotas, selective tariffs, and subsidies, but international trade has expanded at an unprecedented rate in the last 25 years nevertheless.

Although the United States accounts for a large portion of total world trade, export transactions make up a relatively small proportion of the GNP of the United States—only about 5 percent in recent years. About two-fifths of the total exports of the United States consist of manufactured goods, particularly machinery, chemicals, and automotive equipment. Some United States imports (such as coffee and certain metallic ores) do not compete with American producers, but other imports do (such as steel, textiles, beef, and oil). In recent years, American export transactions with Canada have been larger than those with any other foreign nation. The underdeveloped nations loom large as customers for exports from the United States, and are also important suppliers of imported goods and services. While international trade is relatively unimportant in terms of the total output of the American economy, the absolute value of American

---

[1] Data on the role of trade are compiled by selected agencies such as the International Monetary Fund and published monthly in *International Financial Statistics* and *Direction of Trade*.

trade is very significant to many other nations.[2] Moreover, because the dollar is used as an international medium of exchange, American trade takes on added significance.

### International Specialization and Trade

Nations can benefit in obvious ways when each is absolutely more productive in one area—that is, has a lower per unit cost of production (and a lower price) than other countries. Comparative advantages in production are the real basis for trade, however. To understand the output gains from trade, we must first understand the meaning of the term "opportunity costs."

#### COMPARATIVE OPPORTUNITY COST: THE BASIS FOR TRADE

In order to clarify the principles of trade, suppose the world economy is composed of two nations, Argentina and Germany, producing two goods, food and steel, with a "bundle" of generally defined resources.

International trade depends upon opportunity cost ratios or, more simply, cost ratios. *Opportunity cost*—the output of one product sacrificed to produce more of another—shows how nations can mutually benefit from exchange. The opportunity cost of more steel is food output forgone. The *cost ratio* simply reveals the opportunity cost of steel to food, or $S:F$.

Thus, in Argentina the opportunity cost of producing one more ton of steel $(+1S)$ may be one ton of food output sacrificed $(-1F)$. In Germany, on the other hand, the opportunity cost of steel shown by the cost ratio may be $+5S$ for a sacrifice of $-1F$; that is, one less ton of food. Germany clearly can produce more steel than Argentina for equal $(-1F)$ sacrifices of food. Because the transfer of a resource unit from food to steel production in these two countries involves unequal cost ratios, trade can be mutually beneficial.[3] Specialization and trade can increase total world output, even though one nation might be more efficient in producing *both* products, *provided that the cost ratios of transferring resources differ between the two goods in the two countries.* To see just how opportunity cost forms the basis for trade, we must dig deeper into the process of exchange.

#### AN ABSOLUTE ADVANTAGE

An *absolute advantage* exists if one country can produce a commodity more cheaply than another. This is often possible because of differences in production conditions and tastes among nations endowed with different resources and technology. An absolute advantage exists if one nation can produce more of some product than another country with the same amount of resources. This is the case below, in which one resource unit (say, one man-day) is used to produce food and another resource unit is used to produce steel in each country:

| Germany produces | Argentina produces | Total output = |
|---|---|---|
| $20S + 1F$ | $2S + 2F$ | $22S + 3F$ |

[2] It has been said that "When the United States sneezes, Europe catches cold and Japan gets pneumonia." The sum of American exports and imports is approximately equal to GNP in Italy, for example.

[3] Ignoring prices for the moment, it is intuitively clear that Germany could produce more steel and less food $(5S:1F)$; Argentina could produce more food and less steel $(1S:1F)$; and the two nations could somehow share more total steel output $(+4S)$.

Output for these two nations is 25 units (say, tons) when they do not trade.[4] Germany, however, is *more* efficient in using a resource unit to produce steel (a resource unit produces 20S compared to 2S for Argentina) and *less* efficient in food production (1F compared to 2F for Argentina). Each nation should specialize in producing according to its *absolute advantage*—Germany in steel and Argentina in food.

Now, what happens if these nations do specialize and trade steel and food? By transferring one resource unit from food to steel in Germany and one resource unit from steel to food in Argentina, total output in the two nations rises, and both nations can benefit. With Germany producing only steel and Argentina specializing in food, and if each country uses two units of resources, total output is 40S plus 4F:

| Germany produces | Argentina produces | Total output = |
|---|---|---|
| 40S + 0F | 0S + 4F | 40S + 4F |

By specializing according to absolute productive-efficiency advantages, the two nations can increase their total output by 19 tons and both can gain—depending on the terms of trade, which will be discussed later.

### THE PRINCIPLE OF COMPARATIVE ADVANTAGE

The previous example masks the reasons nations trade, a deficiency remedied by examining the principle of comparative advantage. Nations can increase output by producing those products in which they are "relatively" most productive—products in which they have the largest comparative advantage (or the smallest comparative disadvantage). The principle of *comparative advantage* describes how gains from trade are possible even when one nation can produce all products more efficiently than another because of different cost ratios between nations.

For illustrative purposes, suppose that German agriculture becomes more productive, allowing one German resource unit to produce either twenty tons of steel *or* four tons of food. A unit of Argentine resources produces either two tons of steel or two tons of food. Thus, with two resource units and no specialization, production is:

| Germany produces | Argentina produces | Total output = |
|---|---|---|
| 20S + 4F | 2S + 2F | 22S + 6F |

In this case, Germany is more productive than Argentina in producing *both* products. Germany is ten times as efficient in steel production (20S to 2S for Argentina) and twice as efficient in the production of food (4F to 2F for Argentina). Nevertheless, it will pay these nations to specialize and trade according to the principle of comparative advantage. Germany's *greatest comparative advantage* is in steel, which it should produce; similarly, Argentina has its *smallest comparative disadvantage* in the production of food. By specializing on this basis, both nations can increase their output, even though Argentine resources are less productive than German resources in producing both products. By producing according to the principle of comparative advantage and reallocating one of two resource units to steel in Germany and one of two resource units to food in Argentina, each nation can produce as follows.

[4] We are indiscriminately adding tons of output and ignoring prices for the sake of simplicity.

| Germany produces | Argentina produces | Total output = |
|---|---|---|
| $40S + 0F$ | $0S + 4F$ | $40S + 4F$ |

Specialization according to the principle of comparative advantage thus increases output by 16 tons (from 28 to 44). Both countries can thus gain from trade by doing what each can do best and more efficiently. It makes no difference that German resources are more productive in both products (Argentina has *no* absolute advantage).[5] What is not so obvious about the principle of comparative advantage is that it is the *relative costs* of producing that make specialization and international trade a viable way of raising output and levels of living.[6] The basic principle leading to increased total output because of specialization and trade under a comparative advantage is that the cost ratios in the production of two goods differ in the two nations involved.

## An Example of Comparative Cost[7]

When a German resource unit produces twenty tons of steel or four tons of food, we can see that the cost ratio is $20S:4F$, or $5S:1F$—Germany sacrifices five tons of steel to produce one ton of food. By comparison, the Argentine cost ratio is $2S:2F$, or $1S:1F$, revealing that one resource unit produces equal quantities of steel and food. A basis for specialization on the principle of comparative advantage prevails when cost ratios for two or more nations vary, as in our example. When $1S = 1F$ in Argentina, and the cost ratio is $5S:1F$ in Germany, unequal sacrifices of steel output are required to increase food output by some amount, and specialization and trade will increase total output.

## THE CONSUMPTION-TRADE FRONTIER

To simplify matters, let us again suppose that the world economy is composed of Germany and Argentina producing steel and food, again with the same cost ratios. Figure 1 shows simplified production frontiers for these two nations to illustrate the significance of cost ratios. Rather than using the usual outward-bowed production frontier, which reflects increasing costs due to imperfect substitution of resources, constant costs are assumed in the production frontiers shown in Figure 1.[8] (This assumption facilitates our discussion of the principle of comparative advantage and does not change the major purpose of showing how cost ratios determine the gains

[5] The corporate executive who is more productive both in an executive capacity and in a secretarial context may serve as an example to clarify this point. The executive will specialize in administrative tasks simply because he has a larger comparative advantage in these tasks. It pays him to perform the function in which his productivity is greatest, since specializing according to his comparative advantage permits him to produce greater total output.

[6] You can see this if you evaluate transferring resources under these conditions: Germany produces $20S$ and $4F$ while Argentina produces $10S$ and $2F$. Even though Germany is more productive in both steel and food production, there is no way to increase output through specialization. Why? Because Germany's comparative advantage in *both* products is equal (Germany is twice as productive in either steel or food). The explanation for this "no-trade" situation relies on the fact that there are no comparative cost differences, as explained next.

[7] This section may be omitted at the instructor's option without loss of continuity.

[8] This oversimplification is remedied shortly.

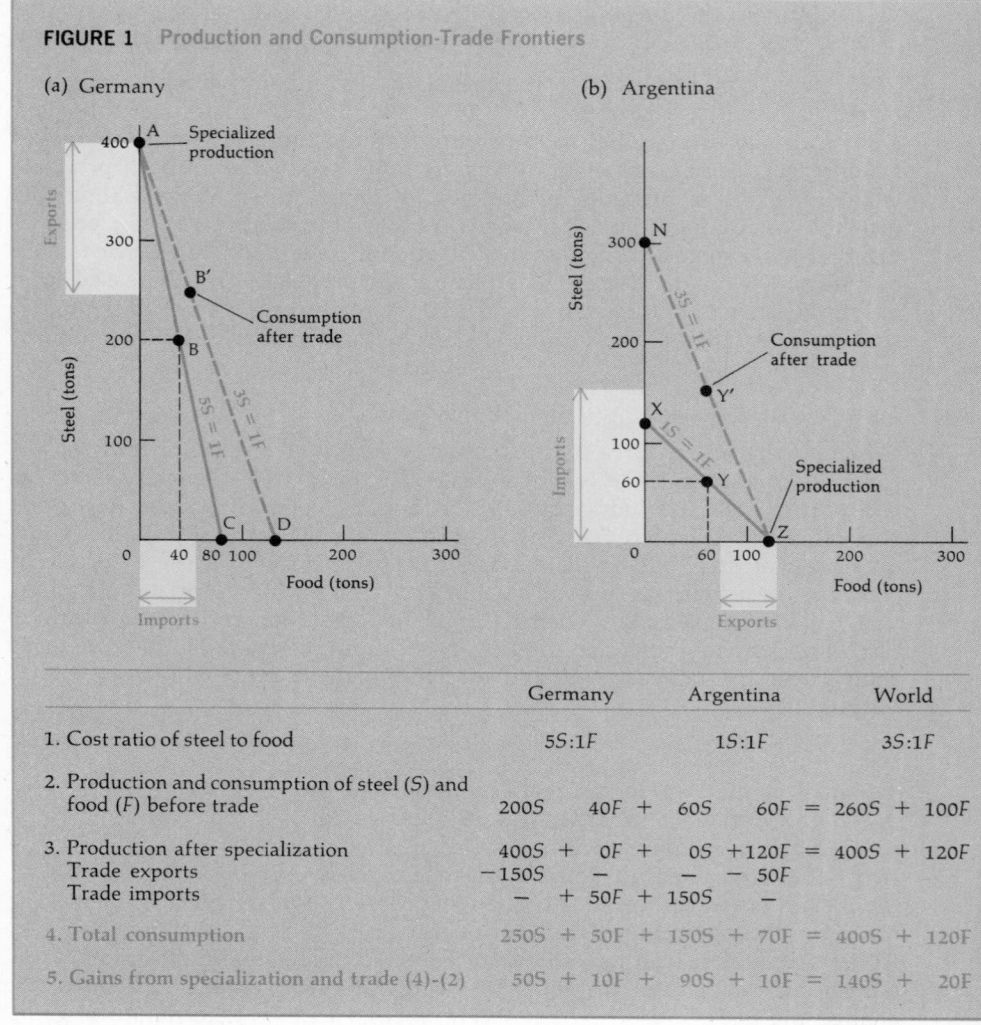

**FIGURE 1** Production and Consumption-Trade Frontiers

(a) Germany

(b) Argentina

|  | Germany | Argentina | World |
|---|---|---|---|
| 1. Cost ratio of steel to food | 5S:1F | 1S:1F | 3S:1F |
| 2. Production and consumption of steel (S) and food (F) before trade | 200S    40F + | 60S    60F = | 260S + 100F |
| 3. Production after specialization<br>Trade exports<br>Trade imports | 400S +   0F +<br>−150S    −<br>−    + 50F + | 0S +120F =<br>−    − 50F<br>150S    − | 400S + 120F |
| 4. Total consumption | 250S +  50F + | 150S +  70F = | 400S + 120F |
| 5. Gains from specialization and trade (4)-(2) | 50S +  10F + | 90S +  10F = | 140S +  20F |

from trade.) Further assume that Germany has 20 resource units available to it, while Argentina has 60 resource units. Each nation is at full employment and is currently dividing its resources equally between steel and food production.

Since Germany has 20 resource units, it could produce nothing but steel (20S × 20 units of resources = 400 tons of steel) at point A of Figure 1(a). Because each resource unit also could produce 4F, Germany can produce 80F with existing resources at point C, or it could produce several other combinations of the two products (e.g., point B) on the production frontier ABC in Figure 1(a). The slope of production frontier ABC is 400S: 80F, which depicts the constant cost of transferring one resource unit between steel and food production based upon the domestic cost ratio of steel to food in Germany (5S:1F). This cost ratio means that the cost of one additional ton of food ($+1F$) is the sacrificed output of five tons of steel ($-5S$), as before. Also observe that food is "expensive" to Germany because so much steel must be sacrificed to increase food output.

Argentina can produce $2S$ or $2F$ with one resource unit and it has 60 units of resources; therefore, total output can be $120S$, $120F$, or any combination of $S$ and $F$ output between these extremes, as shown by the production frontier $XYZ$ in Figure 1(b). Steel is relatively costly for Argentina because if it transfers a resource unit to producing one less ton of food ($-1F$) it gains only one additional ton of steel ($+1S$). Furthermore, food is costly to Germany given its mix of productive resources, and steel is costly for Argentina.

Accordingly, Figure 1 shows that Germany has an absolute advantage in *both* products as well as a comparative advantage in steel, while Argentina's smallest comparative *dis*advantage is in the production of food.[9] The constant-cost production frontier is schedule $ABC$ for Germany and schedule $XYZ$ for Argentina. Now assume that, without world trade, supply and demand in each domestic economy determine an equilibrium price and quantity of both steel and food output such that Germany is using 10 resource units to produce 200 tons of steel, and the remaining one-half of its resources to produce 40 tons of food. Before trade, Germany is on its production frontier at point $B$ in Figure 1(a). Similarly, Argentina is producing 60 tons of steel and 60 tons of food at point $Y$ in Figure 1(b), devoting 30 resource units to each product. Total output in Germany is $200S$ plus $40F$ at point $B$ on production frontier $ABC$, and Argentina is producing a total output of $60S$ plus $60F$ as shown by the data of Figure 1. Total world output is $260S$ and $100F$.

However, we can see by the cost ratios in Figure 1 that there is an opportunity-cost basis for trade. Argentina sacrifices $-1S$ to get $+1F$, but Germany sacrifices $-5S$ to produce $+1F$ (Argentina forgoes $-1F$ for $+1S$, while Germany sacrifices $-\frac{1}{5}F$ to get $+1S$). Now, suppose that Germany specializes in steel, where its comparative advantage is greatest, and Argentina allocates all of its resources to food production. Production in Germany will be $400S$ ($20S \times 20$ resource units) and Argentina will produce $120F$ ($2F \times 60$ resource units). World output is now higher by $140S$ and $20F$, as Figure 1 shows. Clearly, both nations can benefit from specialized production *provided* that trade between them can be arranged.

But on what terms will they trade?

THE TERMS OF TRADE

The cost ratios in each country set the extreme limits to the terms of trade.

Upper price limit for food $=$ Germany's cost ratio of $5S{:}1F$

Lower price limit for food $=$ Argentina's cost ratio of $1S{:}1F$

The maximum possible gain for Germany from exporting steel to Argentina in using the lower price limit is the receipt of five tons of food for five tons of steel: German exports of $-1S$ can then finance imports of $+1F$, whereas domestic production of $+1F$ in Germany "costs" $-5S$. These

---

[9] These production frontiers are based upon our earlier comparative-advantage example in which the output of one resource unit was $20S$ or $4F$ in Germany and $2S$ or $2F$ in Argentina.

trade terms leave Argentina no worse off than it would be if it produced its own steel, since to receive $+1S$ it must give up $-1F$ in domestic production. Argentina would never accept *less* than one ton of steel for one ton of food because it would be less costly to produce steel domestically (remember, $1S:1F$ in terms of resource usage). The maximum gain (and upper price limit) for Argentina, on the other hand, would be the exchange of $1F$ for $5S$ in exporting food and importing steel. Trade on these terms would leave Germany no worse off than if it produced its own food, although it would gain nothing from trade. Germany would never give six tons of steel for one ton of food because it can produce food domestically with a smaller sacrifice of steel output.

The actual exchange ratio will fall somewhere between the limits set by each nation's domestic cost ratio. World demand and supply for steel and food play an important role in establishing the actual international market prices for these products. If steel is in greater demand than food, then its international market price will be relatively high, while food prices will be relatively low—thus, trade terms will favor Germany. Given the opposite price conditions in the international market (food being the relatively scarce product), one ton of food will exchange for a good deal more than one ton of steel and the terms of trade will favor Argentina.[10]

Suppose now that trade opens at the $3S:1F$ exchange ratio, and that each nation specializes according to its comparative cost advantage. Figure 1 indicates that Germany can produce 400 tons of steel at point $A$ in Figure 1(a). Argentina, of course, can produce 120 tons of food at point $Z$ in Figure 1(b). Germany can now profitably export 150 tons of steel, for example, and import 50 tons of food at the international exchange price of $3S:1F$. Total consumption of steel and food rises in Germany to point $B'$ on the new and more desirable *consumption-trade frontier* shown as $AB'D$ in Figure 1(a). Similarly, Argentina exports 50 tons of food and imports 150 tons of steel and thereby achieves higher consumption levels indicated at point $Y'$ on its improved *consumption-trade frontier*, $NY'Z$, in Figure 1(b).

Specialization depends on the extent to which cost ratios for different products vary among different nations. That cost ratios do vary is not surprising because nations have different resource endowments and production technologies. Specialization and trade allow nations to increase consumption by achieving a more efficient pattern of resource allocation—the same process that has greatly expanded the production capacity and consumption of residents of the 50 states in the United States. World output can increase because the opportunity costs of utilizing resources are unequal between the two nations in our hypothetical example. The basis for trade, then, is variance in domestic output sacrificed—differences in domestic opportunity costs.

### INCREASING OPPORTUNITY COSTS AND THE PRODUCTION FRONTIER

The linear production frontiers of Figure 1 reflect the constant-cost assumption—a condition in which each nation sacrifices some constant amount of one product to produce another. When production frontiers are bowed out-

[10] The terms of trade may also be affected by the relative "strength" of each nation. Notice that the greater the differences in relative costs (and economic structure) between two nations, the greater the potential benefits of international trade.

ward, as they typically are, they reflect increasing costs which limit the extent to which nations can specialize. In other words, as Germany moves upward on its production frontier by specializing in the production of steel, the opportunity cost (of food output sacrificed) rises. Thus, while the sacrifice of $-1F$ may initially allow the production of $+5S$, as specialization occurs each ton of food output forgone allows production of less steel because resources are successively less adaptable to the production of steel. Similarly, resources are imperfectly substituted as Argentina increasingly produces more food. As each nation specializes, then, the cost ratio showing the output sacrificed to produce more steel (in Germany) and more food (in Argentina) rises.[11]

## Trade Gains in Review

The crucial points about specialization according to comparative advantage boil down to these three:

1. Germany's comparative advantage (in steel) is a relative cost advantage. Different cost ratios between two nations reflect comparative opportunity costs, which in turn account for production advantages or disadvantages for each nation.

2. When one nation's opportunity cost of producing a given product is lower than another nation's, a comparative advantage exists and it pays the nation to specialize and trade in that product as long as product prices reflect cost differences. Argentina should thus specialize in food, because the opportunity cost of a unit of food to Germany is a very high $(-5S)$, whereas Argentina's opportunity cost is a much smaller sacrifice $(-1S)$. Germany should specialize in steel because it incurs a lower opportunity cost of $-\frac{1}{5}F$, whereas the opportunity cost of an additional ton of steel to Argentina is a higher $-1F$.

3. As a nation such as Germany specializes, it moves on its production frontier toward more output of the product in which it has a comparative advantage, and more and more of some alternative product is sacrificed as specialization occurs. In other words, in our example, Germany's initial cost ratio of $5S:1F$ declines to $4S:1F$, $3S:1F$, and so forth. Continued specialization of resources in steel production results in smaller and smaller additional gains in steel output relative to the opportunity cost of one less ton of food, because increasingly less productive resources are transferred to steel production. Similarly, Argentina cannot fully specialize in food production because of increasing opportunity costs in the form of additional steel output forgone to produce more and more food.

The comparative cost advantages for each nation thus diminish as nations increasingly specialize and world prices change. Specialization of resources is carried to its maximum when relative cost and price ratios are equal in the two countries. At this point, the opportunity costs of steel and food impose ·equal sacrifices on both nations, perhaps at our assumed world-trade price of $3S:1F$. Nevertheless, living standards are higher in both countries after trade. Finally, remember that comparative advantages among

---

[11] Thus, comparative advantages change. Germany goes from $+5S$, $+4S$, $+3S$ for successive sacrifices of $-1F$ and Argentina successively obtains less and less food output for each $-1S$ sacrificed.

nations change as technology, resource endowments, and consumer tastes are altered.

### Prices and the Allocation of World Resources

International trade expands world output by more nearly equalizing the prices of both products and resources among nations. Specialization in given products or industries tends to raise the prices of resources that had been relatively cheap and abundant before trade. Also, the price of relatively scarce resources tends to decline once trade opens, since the products produced by such resources are imported in some quantity. For example, once foreign trade opens, the price of steel rises in Germany because a portion of the domestic supply can be sold abroad at higher prices, causing the domestic supply schedule to decrease. In Argentina, however, the relatively high domestic price of steel falls once foreign supplies become more abundant. Supply shifts also change food prices for both nations after trade opens. With trade, the high price of German food induces Argentine export suppliers to ship commodities abroad, causing food prices to decline in Germany and to rise in Argentina.

Specialization and the international movement of products also tend to equalize *resource prices*. As international prices change for steel and food, resources are reallocated in terms of each nation's relative production efficiencies. Thus, when Germany increases steel production, it requires more of the relatively abundant resources used to produce steel and fewer of the relatively scarce resources used by the food industry (remember, Germany will import some food). Such resource transfers are initiated by product-price changes that are transmitted to price changes in resource markets. Resources used in food production such as land (in scarce supply in Germany) are relieved of market pressures. Thus, the relatively high price of land will tend to decline after trade, simply because less land is needed for food production once Germany imports food. On the other hand, the price of abundant and relatively cheap land resources tends to rise in Argentina as it uses more of these resources by specializing in food production. The comparatively low price of capital used in the production of steel tends to rise in Germany as specialization occurs, and the relatively high price of capital declines in Argentina for comparable reasons. By shifting supply and demand for products, world trade alters resource prices in the general direction of greater equality.

The basis for trade, then, turns out to be differences in domestic output sacrificed—opportunity costs. Specialization and trade benefit nations because they facilitate the achievement of higher consumption levels and a more efficient pattern of resource allocation—conditions which also tend to equalize product and resource prices among nations. There are special financial problems associated with international trade, however, and it is to these that we now turn.

### B. INTERNATIONAL PAYMENTS

Figure 2 is an overview of the international exchange of goods and services which identifies four central ideas about the economics of foreign trade.

First, gross United States receipts from international transactions with all

**FIGURE 2** A Simplified International Balance of Payments

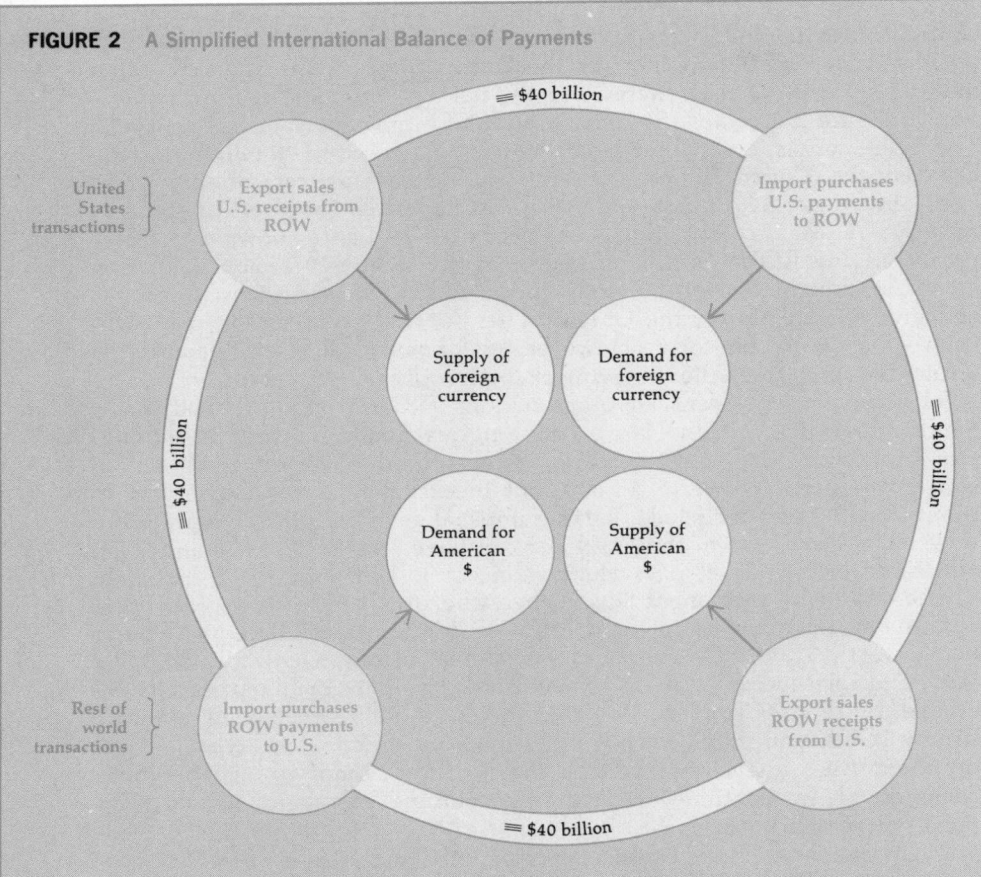

*Trade Flows.* There are four important ideas about international trade: (a) one nation's receipts from ROW are identical to ROW payments to the nation; (b) international transactions create international markets for different currencies; (c) a nation's export sales finance its import purchases; and (d) an "accounting balance" is forced because one nation's receipts from ROW must equal that nation's payments to ROW.

other nations (designated as ROW, or rest of the world) are the same as the gross payments that other nations make to the United States. Just as each coin has a head and tail side, United States gross receipts are the same as gross foreign payments, and United States gross payments to foreign nations are identical to the gross receipts received by other countries. A second idea shown in Figure 2 is that when the United States sells abroad it creates a *demand* for dollars and receives a *supply* of foreign currencies. In contrast, United States imports from foreign nations provide a *supply* of dollars and a *demand* for foreign currencies. Thus, United States transactions with foreign nations create markets for dollars as well as markets for foreign currencies. A third important idea about international finance shown in Figure 2 is that export receipts from sales to foreigners allow the United States to finance import purchases from other nations. Similarly, whatever other nations export to the United States helps finance foreign imports from the United States. Finally, perhaps the most crucial implication of Figure 2 involves the consideration of "imbalance" in foreign trade. The figure conveniently shows that there is a balance of $40 billion in trade between the United States and other nations—American receipts from sales abroad are $40 billion and American payments for import purchases from ROW are also $40 billion. Furthermore, the figure shows that ROW payments and ROW receipts are equal at the same $40 billion in foreign monetary units. The point is that, *in an accounting sense*, gross receipts and gross payments for the United States (or any given nation) are identities—they must be equal. However, just *how* equality or "balance" is achieved is crucial, as the following example will make apparent.

Suppose you represent all other nations (ROW) and I represent one nation (the U.S.A.), and we are exchanging real goods and services—things like food, machinery, and the like. I propose to sell or export goods to you which we agree are worth $4,000, but in exchange I want to import or receive $5,000 of your goods. Barring unusual generosity, you would probably tell me one of two things: that I can have $5,000 of goods either if I will trade for goods of equivalent value, or if I arrange to go into debt to you and make repayment later. When I borrow from you, we both force our financial statements to be identical by treating the IOU I give you as being worth $1,000. Of course, if my annual income were only $3,000 a year, and for several years my expenditures on your goods perpetually exceeded my receipts from goods I sold to you, the difference being made up by my IOUs, you might very well become concerned. I am living beyond my means in a financial sense, and the situation cannot go on indefinitely even though we continue to force an accounting balance of $5,000 when you grant me a loan each year.

In international trade, certain types of imbalances between receipts and payments are known as *international disequilibrium*. Adjustments to disequilibrium in foreign trade is the central theme of international economics. Let us start by learning more about the balance of payments.

## The Balance of Payments

A *balance of payments* is a nation's record of all transactions that generate: (*a*) receipts for items of value shipped abroad, and (*b*) payments to other countries for items purchased. The accounting balance is merely a truism and must not be confused with the "economic balance" that delineates a balance-of-payments surplus or deficit.[12] While receipts and payments always must be equal or "balance" in an accounting context, the way in which this balance is achieved is the crucial item of interest in studying international trade. Disequilibrium in the balance of payments is characterized by a *surplus* if certain types of receipts exceed payments to other nations, and by a *deficit* if certain types of receipts are less than payments abroad. The

---

[12] Accounts for a balance of payments are kept as a double-entry record of transactions between the trading country and foreign nations, and for this reason there is always an accounting balance.

economic balance is important because the economic relationships under-lying certain transactions which force an accounting balance may not be sustainable or may be harmful to a nation.

## FIVE BALANCE-OF-PAYMENTS ACCOUNTS

The components of a balance of payments fall into five categories of trans-actions.

1. *Goods and services traded* record export sales to foreign nations and import purchases from other countries.

2. *Transfer payments* are private payments as well as government re-mittances and pensions paid to persons living in other nations.

3. *Government grants and loans* are official government payments abroad, consisting of transactions in goods and services, foreign-aid grant or loan payments, and certain types of financial transactions.

4. *Capital-account transactions* are investments which denote the ex-change of claims on property and financial assets. Capital transactions are typically broken down into *short-term* (*liquid*) and *long-term* (*nonliquid*) flows of funds, where a maturity of one year or less on paper assets such as bonds represents the difference between liquid and nonliquid invest-ments.

5. *Errors and omissions* are statistical errors which crop up in the bal-ance of payments. These are due to unrecorded transactions such as tourist expenditures abroad, citizens switching bank deposits to foreign branches of American banks, smuggling, and so forth.

Out of these five account categories economists construct records that reveal important characteristics about the financing of international trade. A nation's receipts from transactions with foreign nations are recorded as a + item, whereas payments to other nations are recorded as a − item to indicate the direction of flows of funds. If the United States sells tractors to Venezuela, export receipts may change by + $3 million, but the purchase of copper from Chile will be recorded as import payments of, say, − $1 mil-lion, since funds leave the United States.

The most important feature of the balance of payments is that it can be used to distinguish between autonomous trade transactions and compen-sating financial transactions. *Autonomous* transactions generally are thought of as transactions arising from the exchange of goods and services based on comparative advantage and long-term investment transactions that reflect fundamental economic relationships among nations. By comparison, *com-pensating* transactions record purely financial flows of funds that are used to settle whatever imbalance might exist in the five account categories men-tioned above. It is because compensating transactions are used to "accom-modate" or settle discrepancies in balance-of-payments accounts that they attract much attention.[13] The important point about distinguishing between autonomous and compensating international transactions, then, is that different measures of a deficit or a surplus in the balance of payments can be obtained, depending on how certain transactions are recorded. With these

---

[13] Since compensating transactions are financial in nature, they usually affect capital-account transactions.

definitions of major account categories, receipts (+) and payments (−), and autonomous vs. compensatory transactions in mind, let us examine the meaning of a balance of payments next.

## THE MEANING OF THE BALANCE OF PAYMENTS

Figure 3 shows a consolidated balance of payments for the United States, where + and − items denote receipts [column (1)] and payments [column (2)], respectively, and the net balance [column (3)] denotes whether a category of receipts and payments generates *net* receipts or *net* payments.

*Goods and Services Exchanged*   Merchandise exports and imports measure the value of goods and services flowing between the United States and other nations. Line 1 of Figure 3 indicates that, on balance, we exported (sold) more abroad than we imported (purchased); therefore $2 billion is the net amount due to the United States. Transactions in line 1 involve the exchange of *visible* merchandise such as wheat, machinery, and tea, as well as *invisible* items such as insurance, transportation, travel, and military services. For example, when a German firm purchases insurance or transportation services from an American firm, the United States is exporting a service that generates receipts. Similarly, income earned on foreign investments owned by American citizens or firms is regarded as an "export" item that generates gross receipts of +$8.8 billion. Of course, foreign-held investments in the United States require us to pay for the service of foreign capital "imported" earlier (−$4.5 billion), and the difference of +$4.3 billion simply means that on balance Americans received that much more investment income than was paid abroad. When receipts and payments on exports and imports, investment income, military services, and other services are totaled up and compared in line 1, *net* receipts of $2 billion are recorded. This means that all other nations purchased $2 billion more in American goods and services than were sold to the United States or, what is the same thing, that the United States sold $2 billion more of goods and services abroad than was purchased from other nations. By exporting $53.6 billion of goods and services to the United States, other nations were able to cover all but $2 billion of their $55.6 billion of purchases.

*Remittances and Pensions*   The second account category of Figure 3 shows the transfer payments paid to foreigners, including government pension payments (e.g., social security) paid to American nationals living abroad. The sum of transactions involving goods and services plus all remittances and pensions (lines 1 and 2) is sometimes termed the *current account balance*. Although the net current account balance is a small +$0.9 billion (+$2.0 billion − $1.1 billion) for 1969, between 1950 and 1967 the American current account balance ranged from a low of +$3.5 billion to a high of nearly +$8 billion. Since 1968, the current account balance has shrunk— an event that has contributed to current international financial problems which we will discuss in Chapter 26.

*Government Grants and Loans*   Nations today live in a small world and, like other countries, the United States is actively involved in foreign affairs. Line 3 of Figure 3 shows that public expenditures for foreign aid (economic assistance loans plus grants and loans for military assistance) generated

**FIGURE 3**  United States Balance of Payments, 1969
(billions of dollars)

| Account transactions | (1) Receipts (+) | (2) Payments (−) | (3) Net balance (1)—(2) |
|---|---|---|---|
| **1. Amount of U.S. goods and services exchanged** | **$55.6** | **$53.6** | **+$2.0** |
| a. Merchandise exports and imports | 36.6 | 35.8 | |
| b. Investment income transactions | 8.8 | 4.5 | |
| c. Military services | 1.5 | 4.9 | |
| d. Other services[a] | 8.7 | 8.4 | |
| **2. Remittances and pensions** | | **$ 1.1** | **−$1.1** |
| **3. Government grants and loans** | **$ 1.3** | **$ 5.1** | **−$3.8** |
| **4. Private capital flows** | **$ 4.0** | **$ 5.4** | **−$1.4** |
| a. Long-term outflows (loans −) and inflows (borrowing +) | 3.9 | 4.7 | |
| b. Short-term outflows (loans −) and inflows (borrowing +) | 0.1 | 0.7 | |
| **5. Errors and omissions** | | **$ 2.9** | **−$2.9** |
| 6. Liquidity balance (sum of lines 1–5) | | | −$7.2 |
| a. Increase (−) in United States reserves (gold, convertible currency, IMF borrowings, SDRs) | | | −$1.2 |
| b. Increase (+) in foreign liquid-dollar holdings[b] | | | +$8.4 |
| Official holdings | | | (− 0.6) |
| Private holdings | | | (+ 9.0) |
| 7. Financing for liquidity balance (sum of lines 6a and 6b) | | | +$7.2 |
| **8. Capital transaction adjustments** | | | **+$9.9** |
| a. *Plus* increase in net *private* foreign holdings of liquid United States dollars treated in a manner similar to a short-term capital inflow | | | (+ 9.0) |
| b. *Plus* decrease in net *official* foreign holdings of *non*liquid United States dollars because of reduced long-term foreign claims on United States banks | | | (+ 0.9) |
| **9. Official settlement balance** (sum of lines 6 and 8)[c] | | | **+$2.7** |
| a. Increase (−) in United States reserves (gold, convertible currency, IMF borrowings, SDRs) | | | (− 1.2) |
| b. Decrease (−) in foreign dollar holdings (official liquid and *non*liquid holdings) | | | (− 1.5) |
| **10. Financing for official settlement balance** (sum of lines 9a and 9b) | | | **−$2.7** |

[a] Largely travel and transportation services.

[b] Items consist of *liquid* liabilities only, held in both private and official accounts.

[c] Note that only *official* dollar holdings of *both* a long-term and a short-term nature finance the official settlement balance, whereas *both* private and official dollar holdings, but only those of a liquid nature, finance the liquidity balance.

SOURCE: Federal Reserve Board.

gross payments of − $5.1 to foreign nations.[14] After accounting for $1.3 billion in receipts from scheduled loan repayments, net United States government payments abroad of − $3.8 billion furnished foreign nations with additional dollar balances.

*Private Capital Flows*   Some of the most important transactions for understanding the meaning of a balance of payments are shown in the capital account, which records private capital flows among nations. Lending abroad creates a *capital outflow* (a − payment) because dollars are provided to foreign nations. When the United States extends credit abroad, it does so by importing title to paper assets (securities), purchasing ownership claims on real physical capital (a foreign plant), or perhaps acquiring larger Swiss bank-account balances. In contrast, a *capital inflow*—the result of the U.S. borrowing from foreigners—means that a nation is "exporting" paper claims on its wealth for which it receives payment from other nations. Thus, if Germany lends funds to the United States in return for IOUs representing ownership claims on American assets, Germany experiences a capital outflow and the United States experiences a capital inflow.

The balance on capital account shows whether a nation is, on balance, a net lender (net capital outflows or payments go abroad) or a borrower (net capital inflows or receipts flow in).[15] The sum of long- and short-term capital movements in Figure 3 indicates a net private capital outflow of − $1.4 billion, meaning that the United States lent that amount abroad as private investment. (Remember, capital outflows are treated as a United States import of foreign debts, since dollar payments are made to other nations.)

*Errors and Omissions*   Certain transactions go unrecorded, as noted earlier, and Figure 3 reveals that such transactions amounted to − $2.9 billion in American payments to foreign nations. Much of this amount is in reality short-term capital outflows attributable to Americans transferring deposits to foreign branches of American banks termed *Eurodollars* (as a reflection of the fact that they often involve American branch banks located in Europe).

*The Liquidity Deficit*   Line 6 of Figure 3 indicates a balance-of-payments "liquidity" deficit of − $7.2 billion. This deficit is the sum of all receipts *less* all payments for lines 1–5, or the sum of all "net balance" items shown in column 3. The − $7.2 billion deficit means that payments abroad exceed receipts from other nations, a condition earlier described as balance-of-payments disequilibrium. In short, other nations are provided with $7.2 billion *more* in dollar claims than are used to finance transactions involving merchandise trade, transfer payments, government transactions, capital flows, and the unrecorded transactions showing up as errors and omissions in Figure 3.

[14] In addition to grants and loans, item 3 also contains changes in United States government holdings of foreign currencies and short-term claims on other nations.

[15] Any time individuals in a foreign nation elect to "hold" dollars, their action can be treated as American borrowing (a short-term capital inflow), since other nations are accepting an American IOU in the form of United States currency. The liquidity balance shown in Figure 3 *does not* treat private (nongovernment) holdings of dollars as a short-term capital inflow, for reasons to be explained shortly.

FINANCING THE DEFICIT

Either a deficit or a surplus in a nation's balance of payments is symptomatic of disequilibrium because the autonomous international transactions of lines 1–5 are not in balance. While any definition of the autonomous sources of financing international trade cannot help but be tenuous, economists generally agree that the transactions embodied in lines 1–5 of Figure 3 constitute autonomous sources of payments in defining the liquidity balance also shown in the figure.

The −$7.2 billion balance-of-payments deficit is financed through two types of compensating transactions: The United States must either use its international reserves or allow foreign nations to hold larger liquid-dollar balances—short-term government securities that can be converted into dollar deposits. Either of these procedures is a compensatory or involuntary financial settlement used to "contrive" the accounting balance.

A liquidity deficit can be "accommodated" by selling reserve assets, while if a surplus occurs, a nation may acquire more reserves. International reserves consist of world-wide recognized financial assets. The four types of reserves shown in line 6a in Figure 3 are: (a) a nation's stock of gold, (b) widely held convertible currencies, (c) International Monetary Fund (IMF) borrowing rights, and (d) special drawing rights (SDRs).

Convertible currencies are foreign monies widely held by nations and readily accepted internationally as monetary units. Nations can also borrow gold and currencies from the IMF, an international financial institution that stabilizes trade and finance among the nations of the world. In addition, SDRs—an international form of money—can be transferred from one nation to another.[16] In addition to the use of reserve assets, increased foreign holdings of highly liquid American assets, shown in line 6b, may be used to accommodate a deficit. These "dollar balances" represent short-term foreign claims on American dollars which effectively are claims on United States gold, because this nation is committed to redeeming dollars for gold at the fixed price of $35 per ounce upon the request of the central bank of a foreign nation.

Figure 3 indicates that the United States acquired additional reserves (largely by "importing" gold) that required payments equal to −$1.2 billion. Increased foreign holdings of American dollars loom large among the contrived measures to cover the liquidity deficit shown in Figure 3. Foreign holdings of liquid-dollar assets (e.g., short-term United States government securities maturing in less than one year) increased by +$8.4 billion. In essence, by holding dollars and not cashing them in immediately for gold, other nations are granting a short-term loan to the United States; that is, the United States can be thought of as receiving a short-term capital inflow. Nations hold convertible currencies such as the dollar in lieu of gold because dollars are "as good as gold" and because positive interest and dividend returns can be earned on dollars.

In summary, the combined impact of paying out dollars for increased ownership of reserve assets in the amount of −$1.2 billion *plus* increased foreign ownership of liquid-dollar balances in the amount of +$8.4 billion accommodated the −$7.2 billion deficit shown in Figure 3.

---

[16] These rather complex international financial transactions are more fully explained in Chapter 26.

There are two commonly used measures of the balance of payments, each of which is useful for different purposes.[17] The deficit shown in Figure 3 is a "liquidity deficit" because *liquid-dollar* balances held by *all* (private and official) foreigners are viewed as a potential demand against United States reserves. The rationale for the liquidity balance rests upon the fact that the dollar is widely used as an international currency. Therefore, *all* liquid claims against American reserves are treated as compensating transactions which finance trade, since private foreigners can cash in dollar claims at their banks on very short notice. In contrast, the "official settlement balance" emphasizes *liquid-* and *nonliquid*-dollar balances held only by *official* foreign (central-bank) institutions. In computing the official settlement balance, any increase in dollar balances held abroad by private parties is regarded as a private capital inflow to a nation. In addition, *nonliquid*-dollar balances held by official foreign institutions are treated as a financing item. The official settlement balance recognizes that private foreigners have a demand for dollar balances as an international currency, much as they have a demand for other American services. Therefore, only *official* claims (of both a *liquid* and *nonliquid* nature) are regarded as financing transactions in computing the official settlement balance.

The adjustments needed to derive the official settlement balance primarily affect the capital-flow account. As shown in the lower portion of Figure 3, the official settlement balance (a $2.7 billion surplus) is derived by adding +$9.9 billion in capital transactions to the liquidity deficit. Most of this $9.9 billion adjustment consists of treating $9 billion of increased *private* foreign holdings of liquid dollars as a short-term capital inflow, and the remainder comprises official *non*liquid liabilities held by foreign banks and governments.[18] When changes in *private* foreign holdings of liquid dollars and *official* foreign holdings of *non*liquid dollars are added to the liquidity deficit, an official settlement surplus of +$2.7 billion is derived in Figure 3. The liquidity deficit makes the United States balance of payments appear "worse" than the official settlement balance because, in the latter, private holdings of liquid-dollar balances are treated as a capital inflow into the United States.[19] Because the dollar is widely accepted as an international medium of exchange, many authorities believe that the "liquidity" deficit initially shown in Figure 3 is a more useful measure of the international financial status of the United States.

### How Important Are Reserves?

Nations achieve only temporary solutions to disequilibrium in the balance of payments when a liquidity deficit of the type shown in Figure 3 is financed by larger foreign holdings of a currency or by drawing on reserves.

[17] A third measure—the "basic balance"—is also used for certain purposes.

[18] Much of the difference between the $7.2 billion liquidity deficit for 1969 and the $2.7 billion surplus computed on the official settlement basis can be traced to the Federal Reserve Board's Regulation Q, which set interest-rate ceilings on United States bank deposits. Because interest rates were higher abroad, "Eurodollars" flowed to American branch banks in foreign nations.

[19] Certain net government transactions did occur in 1969, but these are ignored in this explanation for purposes of simplicity.

Nations that end up with larger liquid-dollar balances are, in effect, lending to the United States. Accommodating a balance-of-payments disequilibrium is a contrived solution to a deficit *primarily* because it does not remedy the causes of a balance-of-payments deficit. If nations had inexhaustible supplies of reserves or could endlessly supply other nations with more of their currency, accommodating measures would be a perfectly adequate way of coping with a payments disequilibrium. However, this would be comparable to an individual having an inexhaustible supply of wealth, which is an absurd proposition in all but the rarest of instances.

Financing a liquidity deficit by liquidation of international reserves and larger foreign holdings of liquid-dollar balances is not necessarily bad. Nor is a nation necessarily better off if it acquires more gold reserves. Still, when other nations "sit tight" on billions of liquid-dollar claims, they *are* extending short-term credit to the United States by not cashing dollars in for gold. Under these conditions, just how long international faith in the dollar as a reserve currency is maintained becomes an important issue.

Nonetheless, the argument that nations should strive to accumulate greater reserves is the most naive position of all—one, incidentally, that was popular in the era of mercantilism during the mid-eighteenth century. The prescription at that time was: "Trade policies should be geared to selling more goods abroad and restricting import purchases through tariffs (taxes on imports), thereby allowing nations to acquire precious metals."[20] The consequences of such a policy in the short run could be a positive balance of payments *if* the world were that simple, but the nation would nevertheless lower its own standard of living. Why send goods abroad in exchange for gold—a commodity that is about as useful as red-headed woodpecker scalps? Moreover, the world of international trade and finance is not all that simple. Not unlike a spurned female, trade barriers have a way of begetting retaliation—an event that serves to lower the volume of international trade and average levels of living as well.

In spite of the powerful economic logic in defense of unrestricted trade, many people retain ideas similar to those of the mercantilists. Early classical economists such as David Hume were particularly adamant about abandoning the widespread use of trade controls because they do not provide an appropriate answer to payments disequilibrium. Hume exploded the myths of mercantilism over two centuries ago when he suggested that lower barriers to trade were a good, not a bad thing. After all, the world's supply of gold will not disappear, as if consumed by some horrid Loch Ness monster, if there are no trade barriers. Furthermore, acquiring *more* gold can be harmful if it leads to increased prices when a nation is already at full employment. This does not mean that balance-of-payments deficits and surpluses do not pose international financial problems; it simply suggests that international reserves are not necessarily the only or most important consideration.

[20] Actually, justice is not done by so simple a view of mercantilism. Early in the mercantilist era, a favorable balance of trade was also looked upon as a means toward full employment as well as toward national strength. Favorable trade balances leading to an increase in the supply of gold kept interest rates down, which in turn helped keep employment high, according to the mercantilists. See Myron H. Ross, *Income: Analysis and Policy* (New York: McGraw-Hill, 1964), p. 415.

It has been shown that as long as there are differences in relative production efficiencies, total world output increases if nations specialize and trade in those products in which they have a comparative advantage. In addition, it has been noted that in the course of international trade, nations lose or gain international reserves if disequilibrium exists in the balance of payments.

The use of reserves to settle international accounts is a short-run solution, as has been indicated, primarily because nations are limited in the extent to which they can borrow financial assets. More basic adjustments are therefore needed to equalize payments and receipts. Aside from reserve accommodation of a deficit, there are three other basic solutions (shown in Figure 4) which a nation can use to restore equilibrium in its balance of payments. While not at all desirable, one of the commonly adopted procedures is the use of *trade controls*—the erection of barriers to international trade by: (*a*) imposing physical quotas on the quantities of goods a nation can import, (*b*) artificially raising the price of imported goods through special duties called tariffs, or (*c*) granting subsidies to selected industries to protect their markets from more efficient and cheaper foreign suppliers. Figure 4 also indicates that financial and economic policy adjustments can be used to remedy a balance-of-payments disequilibrium.

In what remains of this chapter we will examine trade controls, which are used allegedly to remedy a balance-of-payments disequilibrium. Since the study of financial and economic adjustment policies requires more knowledge about international finance than we now have, these subjects will be discussed in Chapter 26.

## The Character of Tariffs and Quotas

Given consumer tastes for products, an important limitation to consumer expenditures is product price. A *tariff* is nothing more than a tax applied to

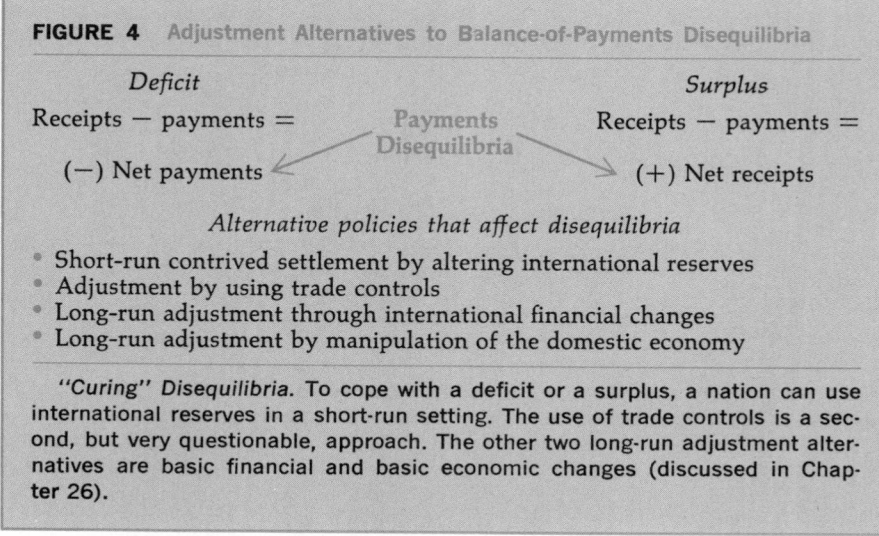

**FIGURE 4**   Adjustment Alternatives to Balance-of-Payments Disequilibria

|  |  |  |
|---|---|---|
| *Deficit* |  | *Surplus* |
| Receipts − payments = | Payments Disequilibria | Receipts − payments = |
| (−) Net payments | | (+) Net receipts |

*Alternative policies that affect disequilibria*

- Short-run contrived settlement by altering international reserves
- Adjustment by using trade controls
- Long-run adjustment through international financial changes
- Long-run adjustment by manipulation of the domestic economy

*"Curing" Disequilibria.* To cope with a deficit or a surplus, a nation can use international reserves in a short-run setting. The use of trade controls is a second, but very questionable, approach. The other two long-run adjustment alternatives are basic financial and basic economic changes (discussed in Chapter 26).

the products a nation imports that raises their price for domestic consumers. By raising product prices through tariffs, nations: (*a*) extract a domestic price higher than would prevail under free trade, (*b*) restrict consumer demand for imported goods, and (*c*) *"protect"* markets for domestic producers who are unable to compete with cheaper and more efficient foreign sources of supply. Under a "protective" tariff, the domestic market price for a product (such as Scotch whiskey) is higher than it otherwise would be, and consumption of the product is restricted to those willing and able to pay the higher "supported" price. Moreover, domestic producers capable of producing and competing at a *cost*-plus-*tariff* price misallocate resources, since some portion of the resources they use would otherwise be used to produce different goods and services. As stated before, free trade enables a nation to attain a consumption point *outside* the domestic production frontier because world resources are used more efficiently.

Tariffs are normally quoted on a "percentage-of-value" (*ad valorem*) basis. Like all nations, the United States has vacillated in the establishment of tariffs. Tariff rates on goods imported by the United States reached peak levels of about 60 percent of the dutiable value of imports in the early 1930s (the Smoot-Hawley Tariff), and have declined steadily since that time to a current average of about 5 percent of the dutiable value of imports.[21] Unfortunately, the long-run trend of lowering trade barriers was broken in late 1970 when the United States selectively raised trade barriers. Even though protective tariffs do not usually fully restrict all imports, they do give domestic producers a comparative price advantage over foreign suppliers and, if a tariff is high enough, international trade may even come to a standstill for certain products.

Import *quotas*, on the other hand, are government specification of the quantities of a good that can be legally imported. Unlike the tariff, an import quota firmly prohibits international trade beyond some specified amount, and quotas do not generate government tax revenues unless public authorities sell import licenses. The higher domestic market price emanating from a quota is pocketed by the favored producing firms or by those importers, if any, who are allowed to market a good. Thus, protected producers may be in an excellent position to hire Washington lobbyists with appropriate Congressional connections to sustain their protection from foreign competition.

Domestic *subsidies* or production "bounties" are similar to tariffs and quotas in that they enable domestic firms to better compete with foreign suppliers. If the government grants a tax advantage as a subsidy and in addition establishes a quota arrangement, as it has for the oil industry in the United States, it offers domestic producers significant protection from foreign competition.

Arguments over the merits of tariffs, quotas, and subsidies have characterized trade among nations for many years, in spite of the potent comparative-advantage rationale underlying specialization and free trade. Even though a large volume of trade does characterize the international economy today, restrictive-trade practices are common to all nations. Arguments in

[21] Since tariffs are sufficiently high on some goods to eliminate trade altogether (prohibitive tariffs), average rates understate the restrictive impact of tariffs as trade-control devices.

favor of trade restrictions are numerous, but often a good deal less valid than they appear on the surface. Those advocating barriers to trade typically base their argument on the idea that, when left to its own devices, a free international market may not be in the best interest of a nation. The reasons for this contention are varied, one of them being the appearance of a balance-of-payments deficit. In the absence of retaliation, import restrictions can enlarge a nation's current account balance and thereby diminish any balance-of-payments deficits that may be incurred. As it turns out, however, trade controls are rarely successful because nations do retaliate.

### An Evaluation of the Trade-Barrier Debate

Most of the arguments in favor of tariff or quota restrictions are shallow, and not a few are requests for special favors to pressure groups at the expense of the citizenry. Moreover, trade controls may inhibit world peace and understanding and intensify international tensions.

### IN DEFENSE OF FREE TRADE

The powerful case for free trade among nations rests on the same argument that applies to unfettered trade between Atlanta, Georgia, and Scarsdale, New York. In a world whose resource endowments and productive capabilities are diverse, trade based upon comparative cost advantages elicits the most productive allocation of resources. Interference through such barriers as a tariff lessens efficiency and lowers average living standards. In the measure that comparative advantages are cultivated under free trade, a more efficient use of world resources increases total world output.

Other benefits from free trade also merit clear identification. First, unimpeded international trade and investment promote the export and import of technological know-how embodied in capital goods which may enhance the growth potential of all nations. Furthermore, as a nation develops along the lines of its particular comparative advantages, benefits associated with specialization may upgrade the productive skills of human and capital resources. Also, international specialization and trade may permit economies of scale. In those instances in which broadened markets allow costs to decline as the scale of production is increased, firms are able to produce at lower costs and nations reap the rewards of using resources more efficiently, given existing technological knowledge. Finally, free trade stimulates the exchange of sociocultural contacts among nations.

These are indeed substantial arguments in favor of expanded trade among nations. Why, then, do nations erect barriers to trade? In some instances, there are *partially* valid arguments for protectionist trade policies, but each argument must be carefully scrutinized for half-truths. Other arguments border on being pure economic myths.

### THE CASE FOR TRADE BARRIERS

Elements of truth and less convincing half-truths are mingled in the case for trade protectionism. The partially valid arguments in defense of trade barriers that are applicable to specific political and economic conditions are national self-sufficiency and resource-mobility adjustments needed to maintain full employment.

*National Self-Sufficiency* Self-sufficiency arguments for restrictive-trade practices fall into two categories: achievement of noneconomic goals and the objective of economic diversification. There are, of course, a vast array of important goals for individuals and nations other than maximum economic output. Political and military strength, for example, may require that the United States nurture and maintain productive capabilities in shipbuilding, watch-making, or the extraction of oil resources, even though other nations might be more efficient producers of these goods. It is difficult to weigh objectively the relative merits of improved national security compared to the efficiency loss emanating from restrictive-trade practices that immunize certain industries against foreign competition. It should be clear, however, that such noneconomic goals are subject to potential abuse, since numerous industries might lay claim to a need for strategic protection under the self-sufficiency banner.

A second related argument in defense of tariffs insists that a nation initially must nurture new or "infant" industries in order to develop a modern and diversified economic base. Proponents of this view contend that protective tariffs which raise consumer prices are needed to develop comparative advantages in industries initially unable to compete in world markets. Tariff protection may also be rationalized as a mechanism to allow certain highly specialized nations in various stages of economic development to reduce their dependence on one-crop foreign markets (Brazil's dependence on coffee is a case in point). International political turmoil, war, technological changes which may antiquate a product, and even economic instability can force a nation to adjust in painful and harmful ways if it is not diversified enough to sustain itself. The infant-industry and economic-diversification arguments are valid in certain respects, but they also demand careful scrutiny.

More highly developed economies such as those of the United States or Great Britain rarely if ever need tariff protection for the reasons given above. Most of the nations of the world are classified as underdeveloped economies, and the infant-industry rationale often makes sense for them, depending upon their particular situation. Underdeveloped economies may need trade controls and may have to tolerate short-run inefficiencies to stabilize and develop their economic potential, but even if this is true, a good deal of ability to see accurately into a hazy and unknown future of comparative advantages is needed. Although underdeveloped economies can often benefit from tariff protection, trade controls and regulation traditionally are subject to abuse. After all, "infancy" can be protracted for many decades by domestic producers.

*Domestic Resource-Mobility Adjustments* As international competition develops and prospers, nations sometimes find that capital and labor resources are temporarily locked into certain industries. Competition from Asia in the electronic and textile markets, for example, has exerted dislocation pressures on workers in these occupations in the United States as well as on firms with fixed-capital commitments to these industries. Immediate resource-reallocation adjustment is not feasible, especially when geographic or occupational immobilities are characteristic of human resources. In a word, there are real short-run resource immobilities, and time may be required to facilitate orderly adjustment to avoid changes that otherwise might wreak havoc in the domestic economy.

The dangers in this argument for trade protection are: First, that such claims may be advanced by almost any industry, firm, or group of workers, since a dynamic economy is necessarily in perpetual motion. For this reason, the rationale of resource-mobility adjustment is subject to potential abuse. Second, remedies for serious dislocation problems may be postponed indefinitely if political pressures build—as they often do in the case of restrictive-trade practices. Consequently, an inefficient pattern of resource allocation may be perpetuated. A short-run protective tariff to accommodate needed adjustment is one possible approach, but it is an inferior approach to government subsidies or bounties, which are a more direct solution to such problems. When public intervention is called for, it is normally preferable to grant *direct* assistance such as retraining and relocation allowances for displaced human resources, or subsidies to allow producers in vital industries to update or otherwise alter their capital resources. Direct assistance that facilitates transition is less likely to remain a permanent cost to society than a tariff, simply because the costs of such grants are a visible item that perpetually prods the memory of political leaders.

One very widely abused argument that is closely related to the resource-adjustment claim for tariff protection is the cry for full employment. When a domestic economy exports *more* or imports *less* because of trade controls, aggregate demand and income rise. Harking back to our discussion of the determination of employment and income reminds us that:

$$\text{Aggregate demand} = \text{consumption demand} + \text{investment demand} + \text{government} + \text{net foreign spending}$$

or

$$DD = C + I + G + (\text{exports} - \text{imports})$$

If a net increment (e.g., $5 billion) is added to aggregate spending through tariff policies that restrict imports or subsidies that increase exports, income and employment may rise by some multiple of the initial change in aggregate demand. Increased net foreign spending supports and creates jobs just as domestic spending does. Thus, if less is spent abroad on imports, new domestic employment opportunities may be generated. Like any autonomous increase in expenditures, foreign spending is subject to the multiplier effect. The multiplier impact is different from the simplified investment multiplier of Chapters 8 and 9, however, because income-stream leakages now include import expenditures as well as leakages to taxes and saving. As a nation's income level rises, there is a tendency for imports to increase; therefore, the final proportion of income consumed and the multiplier effect tend to be smaller once international trade is taken into account.[22]

---

[22] The multiplier effect in taking foreign transactions into account is generally smaller because import leakages from the spending stream ($M$) tend to rise and fall directly with the level of income ($Y$). Therefore, if the marginal and average propensities to import are 0.1 (i.e., $M = 0.1Y$), the multiplier is $m = 1/\text{marginal propensity to save}$ ($MPS$) + marginal propensity to import ($MPM$). (E.g., if $1/MPS + MPM = 1/0.3 + 0.1$, the multiplier is 2.5.)

That there are shortcomings to the full-employment case for trade barriers should come as no surprise. Restricting imports to reduce unemployment has become known as a "beggar-thy-neighbor" policy because it represents an attempt to export unemployment. In the long run, this policy is normally doomed to fail. Nations can purchase the output of another country, but only if they can also export goods and services to maintain a reasonable balance of payments. All countries cannot simultaneously stimulate employment through increasing trade barriers (i.e., reducing imports relative to exports) because both buyers and sellers are necessary to international exchange. Nations that are affected favorably by increased tariffs on goods they export are very apt to retaliate by increasing tariffs on goods they import—the precise reaction of the world economy to the restrictive trade practices of the 1930s. Instead of stimulating a domestic economy, trade controls contribute to the decline of international trade, both eliminating the advantages gained from trade and further intensifying economic decline. Finally, even if trade barriers are raised and retaliation does *not* follow, the cost of artificially achieving full employment is still a less efficient utilization of resources. Economists generally agree that monetary and fiscal policies are much more appropriate solutions to domestic unemployment problems because retaliation and efficiency losses accompany the use of trade barriers.

*Warning:* Much of this critical review of trade barriers applies to both developed and underdeveloped nations. However, underdeveloped nations do encounter special problems in developing a viable economy and in using resources efficiently. The case against trade barriers is less clear when the special problems of underdeveloped nations are recognized, especially if their monetary and fiscal institutions are too weak to be useful in achieving economic stability.

## MYTHS ABOUT TRADE CONTROLS

Under certain conditions, a germ of truth does pervade the self-sufficiency and resource-adjustment arguments for protective trade barriers, but each argument is also laced with half-truths and erroneous reasoning. There are also several fallacious and even ridiculous arguments raised in defense of trade restrictions which deserve brief comment, if only because they are commonly believed in many circles. Much of the mythology about the advantages of trade controls is based on nothing more than an exercise of power by various special-interest groups concerned with their own gain. Consumers are largely unorganized, with the result that narrow producer interest groups can impair the general welfare by unilaterally pursuing their own ends with Congressional friends.

1. "High tariffs produce revenues paid by foreigners." If a nation is the only one or one of a few large buyers of a product, it may be possible to shift a modest tariff to foreign sellers through threats of curtailed demand and lower world market prices. Part of the tariff burden is then absorbed by the exporting nation, which must cope with monopsonistic market power. Normally, however, higher domestic product prices to consumers and less efficient use of resources by domestic producers accompany the use of a tariff. Tariffs impose a regressive tax burden on domestic consumers, who either purchase a more costly domestic product or pay a portion or all of

the duty on the imported product. For instance, suppose the United States imposes a protective tariff of 50 cents per pound on bananas (the principal export crop of Panama) and constructs the requisite hothouse environment to grow bananas domestically. Assuming American and Panamanian bananas are perfect substitutes, domestic consumers, not foreign producers, bear a substantial portion of the cost of this tariff, since bananas now cost 50 cents more per pound than before. The fictitious nature of the increased-revenue argument for tariffs is exposed once it is recognized that tariffs are like transportation costs. Even though cement blocks may be produced at less cost in Japan than in the United States, the costs of shipment more than offsets Japan's cost advantage and no cement blocks are traded. Similarly, as domestic product prices rise because of trade restrictions, less and less exchange occurs. If tariffs are high enough, the product will not be imported at all, causing the revenues generated by a tariff to fall toward zero. Under normal conditions, the conclusion is inescapable: Consumers pay for tariffs to protect the profits of less efficient domestic producers.

2. "Tariffs develop industry by keeping money in our country." This rather popular fallacy is as shallow as any. Since funds received by foreign producers are used primarily to purchase American goods and services exported abroad, why shouldn't dollars momentarily leave the country? Proponents seeking protective tariffs as a means of equalizing foreign and domestic production costs are simply advocating payment of a sales-tax subsidy to compensate for the inefficiencies of domestic industries. We have already seen that while there may be rare instances in which infant industries may legitimately require protection (e.g., in underdeveloped nations), this rationale is often abused and, in addition, there are more effective ways of providing development assistance. Protecting home markets through import restrictions also invites retaliation and, as stated before, its chief consequence is a lower standard of living for all nations. Moreover, some portion of the limited household incomes that might otherwise be used for other goods produced by more efficient domestic industries is absorbed by the inefficient sector of the economy that receives tariff protection.

3. "Tariffs protect our high wages and living standards." The cheap foreign labor which underwrites lower-priced foreign goods imported into the United States is frequently said to lower domestic wage rates and incomes. Proponents of this view are also in error, although the argument is appealing at first glance. The fallacy is obvious if we reverse the argument. The typical resident of Brazil or Japan might respond by asking his government to "protect us from the cheaper mass-produced American goods." It is the abundance of one factor of production relative to other factors resulting in a comparative advantage and hence lower production costs that is the source of this argument.

The point is this: The productivity of labor determines wages and incomes as well as production costs and prices. Highly paid American labor can and does compete with low-paid foreign labor in international markets because of a significant productivity advantage due to capital-intensive production methods. The billions of dollars of American exports amply prove this point. A more productive American labor force reflects the higher quality of human resources and the advanced technology embodied in capital resources, as well as the larger amounts of capital resources employed per worker. Comparative cost advantages explain trade among nations endowed with different productive capabilities, and as long as domestic full employment and high productivity are realities, American workers need not bother themselves with the low wages in Japan or Italy. Real wages per manhour can be higher here and still allow comparative cost advantages, as long as output per manhour is greater here than abroad.

Still, it is true that in some industries (e.g., the production of transistor parts) lower wage rates abroad may contribute to lower unit costs and a cost advantage along typical comparative advantage lines. Import restrictions are not an answer to such problems because employing domestic workers in relatively unproductive sectors (compared to international competition) simply misallocates domestic resources. Once again, the tariffs against transistors, Swiss watches, or what have you are not justified on these grounds.

## A CONCLUDING NOTE

For the most part, the trade-restriction controversy breaks down once it is subjected to a careful appraisal. The defense for protective tariffs in general relies on goals of a noneconomic nature that enlarge social welfare. In other words, when one examines the *entire set* of national objectives (economic efficiency being only *one* goal), it may be possible to conclude for one reason or another (e.g., economic development or national security) that the general welfare of society is enhanced by something less than free trade. Because arguments in defense of protective tariffs are subject to abuse, however, the advantages to be gained from trade restrictions are short-run ones at best.

The case for tariffs is a shallow one and economists overwhelmingly support long-run policies aimed at lowering trade barriers to reallocate resources from the less efficient sectors of a nation's economy to more productive industries. The case for unfettered international trade, based as it is on the principle of comparative advantage, depends on a system of relatively free international markets to allocate resources and take advantage of diverse production capabilities. Trade barriers cause a country to operate below the "best possible" consumption frontier. With rare exceptions, then, it can be concluded that trade controls are not a desirable solution to domestic economic problems, disequilibrium in the balance of payments included. The simple truth is that in most cases there are more direct and desirable policies which can more effectively attain the goals allegedly achieved by trade controls.

There are no points about international trade more fundamental than these simple but pervasive truths:

1. Real output *does* increase if trade is conducted on the basis of comparative cost advantages.

2. Trade controls are built upon the vested interests of a few, they are founded on legacies or myths of the past, and they fail to provide answers to the complex economic problems of the world today.

## REVIEW

### Summary

1. International trade is important to all nations of the world, and particularly to those countries that sell a large proportion of their domestic

output in world markets. Even though one nation may be able to produce all products more efficiently than another, trade is mutually beneficial as long as a comparative advantage exists.

2. The principle of comparative advantage argues that each nation should specialize in those products in which it has the greatest relative advantage or the least relative disadvantage in transforming resources into output. The "comparative" basis for trade is reflected by a nation's opportunity-cost ratio—the amount of one product ($x$) sacrificed relative to the additional output of another product ($y$) produced with a fixed amount of resources. The existence of a comparative advantage is revealed by the existence of different cost ratios in two (or more) nations.

3. The terms of trade are set by world market demand and supply within trade limits whose upper and lower limits are established by the respective cost ratios for two nations. By producing on the basis of different cost ratios which denote comparative production efficiencies, a trading nation can reach a level of consumption on a consumption–trade frontier that lies outside its domestic production frontier. International trade is limited because opportunity costs increase as a nation specializes more heavily in one product; that is, the cost ratios for trading nations become more nearly equal as increasingly inferior resources are used in specialization.

4. The final consequence of unfettered international trade is equalization of world prices for products exchanged. This in turn tends to equalize relative resource prices among nations because each country specializes in those products which are produced with more intensive use of their least scarce resources.

5. International trade also involves financial transactions that are accounted for via the balance of payments, a bookkeeping device that records the flow of goods and services as well as other financial payments and receipts. A balance of payments also depicts compensating transactions used to finance a balance-of-payments deficit or a surplus. Compensating transactions involve: (a) reserve assets (such as gold, the currency of other nations, International Monetary Fund borrowing rights, and SDRs), and (b) foreign holdings of liquid-dollar balances (in the case of the United States).

6. A payments disequilibrium (a deficit or surplus) must be settled in the accounting sense; however, mere accounting settlements *do not resolve* economic imbalance. The economic difficulties associated with a balance-of-payments disequilibrium can present international financial problems. However, trade-control devices like tariffs or quotas are not viable solutions to payments disequilibria. The reason for this is that the effects of trade controls are a diminished volume of trade, lower standards of living, and higher domestic prices underwritten by consumers who in effect are protecting inefficient domestic production.

7. Arguments in defense of trade restrictions are either shallow (e.g., claims for national self-sufficiency or resource-mobility adjustments) or falla-

cious. A domestic economy, not foreigners, pays the price of a tariff, and trade controls diminish a nation's ability to sell abroad. Attempts to restrict imports often fail because of retaliation and, as a result, a nation's most productive use of its own scarce resources is subverted.

### Identify the Following Concepts and Terms

- absolute and comparative advantage
- Eurodollars
- opportunity cost
- terms of trade
- balance of payments
- "visible" and "invisible" items
- reserves
- tariffs, quotas, and bounties

- capital inflows and outflows
- cost ratios
- consumption-trade frontier
- payments disequilibrium
- mercantilist
- infant industry
- liquidity deficit
- autonomous vs. compensating transactions

### Questions to Answer

1. The opportunity cost for Eden is 8 sheep = 1 freezer and for Sodom 2 sheep = 1 freezer. Each nation has 10 resource units and wishes to open trade. How will total output change? What are the limits to trade? What will affect the terms of trade? Diagram each nation's production and consumption-trade frontier assuming constant opportunity costs.

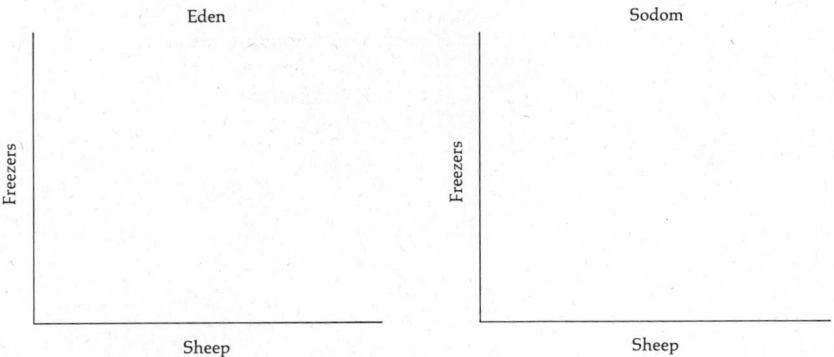

2. Construct a balance of payments for a nation using the following accounts.

| | | | |
|---|---|---|---|
| Capital inflows | = +$12 | Capital outflows | = −$8 |
| Exports | = +$40 | Government loans | = −$1 |
| Imports | = −$32 | Net military services | = −$3 |
| Remittances | = −$ 3 | Net investment income | = −$1 |

Compute and explain the deficit or surplus, assuming the liquidity balance.

3. How is a United States balance-of-payments adjustment to a disequilibrium condition affected by reserves and foreign holdings of liquid-dollar balances?

4. Critically evaluate the following statement of a member of Parliament representing a "steel state": "Now look, unemployment is very high in my district and, in addition, workers' earnings are depressed. There is no question about it—we must raise tariffs on steel imports from Japan and Western Germany. Cheap foreign labor is ruining domestic markets and creating jobs for foreigners while the people who elected me cannot obtain work. Besides, just think of the added revenue we can generate for government."

# CHAPTER 26
# International
# Finance

Our previous discussion of the principles of international trade has set the stage for the topic of this chapter: current international financial problems and policies. Increased output, which has been made possible by a more efficient use of world resources, represents the rationale for the international exchange of goods and services. As we have seen, however, disequilibrium in a nation's balance of payments creates financial problems in that deficits entail the loss of international reserves. Trade controls are the oldest and least satisfactory remedy for a balance-of-payments deficit, as Chapter 25 emphasized, and they are at best only stop-gap measures.

The purposes of this chapter are fourfold: Part A traces the development of international financial institutions, Part B explains foreign-exchange markets, Part C considers the United States balance-of-payments problem, and Part D treats contemporary international financial problems.

## A. DEVELOPMENTS IN INTERNATIONAL FINANCE

There is a good deal of agreement among bankers and economists about the undesirability of trade restrictions. Nations throughout the world recognize the benefits of trade and the negative consequences of tariff barriers and other trade-control devices such as quotas. Today the crucial issues of international trade are financial in nature. To provide the necessary perspective on these issues, we will begin with a brief consideration of the development of the international financial system.

The international monetary system has changed significantly over the decades. In general, we can identify two distinct periods of change associated with: (a) the gold standard and depression, and (b) World War II and its aftermath, including the era of economic integration.

### The Gold Standard and Depression

Prior to World War I, international finance was regulated through automatic adjustments provided by the gold standard. The gold standard defined the value of a nation's monetary unit in terms of grains of gold, and nations stood ready to transfer gold to other nations upon request. For about half a century before World War I and during the brief postwar interval prior to the Great Depression, the major nations of the world were on the gold standard. During that time their currencies' values were tied to gold, which was freely exported and imported. A gold outflow under the gold standard theoretically forced adjustments which restored the payments equilibrium and also maintained stable exchange rates.

The gold standard in theory prompted the following sequence of events: A nation's payments deficit led to a gold outflow, which produced a contraction in the domestic money supply because most domestic monetary systems were tied to gold reserves; monetary contraction in turn spurred interest rates to higher levels; prices, incomes, and employment ultimately declined in the deficit nation; and deflationary pressures helped increase exports and diminish imports to remedy a deficit. Nations experiencing a payments surplus and gold inflows also found their balance of payments being redirected toward a new equilibrium level because of rising domestic price levels, declining exports, and rising imports relative to deficit countries. Accordingly, a permanent adjustment to a balance-of-payments disequilibrium was possible under the gold standard.

Ignoring such factors as transportation costs for the moment, suppose that: (a) Japan experienced a balance-of-payments deficit due to an increased demand for a foreign currency such as the dollar, (b) the *exchange rate* (the price of one currency in terms of another) was 360 yen = $1, and (c) the dollar was worth 20 grains of gold. No Japanese importer would pay more than 360 yen for $1 because he could use his currency—the yen—to buy 20 grains of gold instead and ship it to America in exchange for dollars. Therefore, exchange rates were also stabilized under a pure gold standard within a modest price range tied to costs associated with shipping gold. Furthermore, as gold left Japan (the deficit nation), bank reserves would decline, interest rates would rise as the money supply contracted, and the gold outflow would create deflationary pressures, tending to dampen Japan's price level relative to prices in other nations. As relative prices declined in Japan, exports to foreign nations would rise and imports from abroad would decline. Moreover, the higher interest rates due to the gold outflow would attract foreign capital inflows, helping to restore equilibrium to the balance of payments. Nations experiencing a surplus would be affected in just the reverse fashion, for as gold flowed to nations with a balance-of-payments surplus, interest rates would decline, and their domestic economies would expand, tending to increase their demand for imports from other nations.

On occasions, however, the operation of the gold standard imposed unwanted expansions or contractions on domestic economies even though it did provide the advantages of automatic correction of balance-of-payments disequilibria and stable exchange rates. Historical studies have revealed that the gold standard was never really put to a severe test until the international financial traumas accompanying World War I and the Depression of the 1930s.

One of the difficulties with the gold standard was that the domestic price level experienced only a slow and partial contraction as gold moved abroad. When a nation's domestic money supply did contract, prices tended to remain "sticky," with the result that incomes declined and widespread unemployment increased, particularly in the 1930s. When it was needed most, the gold standard failed because of downward price rigidities and because the classical prescription of deflation to remedy a payments deficit was unacceptable to nations already experiencing a severe economic crisis. Thus, the gold standard was abandoned in the 1930s, when countries could no longer afford to be tied to gold because of the severity of declining incomes and rising unemployment.

Britain first broke with the traditional gold standard in 1931, and devalued its currency to avoid more severe domestic deflationary pressures. Most other nations followed suit. Because the gold standard impaired domestic economic stability, it was abandoned by the United States in the Gold Reserve Act of 1934. The United States discarded the domestic gold standard and devalued the dollar by declaring that it was worth fewer grains of gold (the price of gold was increased from $20.67 to $35 per ounce). Tariff barriers rose as nations attempted to create jobs by reducing imports and exporting unemployment. "Beggar-thy-neighbor" tariff policies failed, however, as every nation turned beggar in an attempt to reduce imports. Both devaluation and increased tariffs turned out to be self-defeating. As uncertainty intensified, the value of world trade declined rapidly and trade barriers climbed throughout the world. Both higher trade barriers and devaluation theoretically can relieve domestic deflation and improve one nation's balance-of-payments position by encouraging exports and discouraging imports, *but only if other countries refrain from following suit*. This was not the case in the 1930s.

Duties on imports into the United States rose to a record high of twice their prewar level with the passage of the Smoot-Hawley Tariff Act of 1930. As the economic chaos continued, however, the United States gradually lowered these trade barriers. The first step toward trade liberalization in the United States appeared with the enactment of the Reciprocal Trade Agreement Act of 1934, which allowed the President to reduce existing tariffs up to one-half of their legislated level on a generalized basis that applied to nearly all nations of the world. Problems continued during World War II, however, as the international flow of goods and services was distorted by the needs of warring economies. Substantial quantities of both human and property resources were expended, and in countries such as the United States the money supply rose dramatically to finance the war effort.

## War and Its Aftermath

World War II dramatically altered the economic problems of the United States. Aggregate levels of spending rose rapidly, pushing the nation up to and beyond full-employment levels of output. As the war drew to a close, however, it became clear to the leaders of many nations that the international monetary system required restructuring. In 1944, representatives from 44 nations, including the U.S.S.R., met at the Mount Washington Hotel in Bretton Woods, New Hampshire, to establish a framework to remedy the financial and trade errors of the 1920s and 1930s. Some 1,000 delegates met at the famed summer resort to rescue the world economy, which had been raked for decades by currency disorders, monetary instability, and trade restrictions. While the delegations from several nations (particularly France) had reservations about the agenda of the conference, two important financial institutions grew out of the Bretton Woods meetings: the *International Monetary Fund* (IMF) and the *International Bank for Reconstruction and Development*.

## INTERNATIONAL FINANCIAL INSTITUTIONS

The IMF was established to stabilize exchange rates for nations faced with short-run balance-of-payments disequilibria and to forestall chaotic devaluations such as those which characterized the international community in the

1930s. Nations became members of the IMF by subscription, which they achieved by depositing gold and currency with the IMF according to quotas set in relation to their economic strength. Today, nations may borrow foreign exchange and use the special international credits called special drawing rights (SDRs) noted in Chapter 25 in order to stabilize their exchange rate and to meet short-run deficits. The IMF exercises advisory control over changes in the official exchange rate for a currency and also controls borrowing. Member countries may change the value of their currencies by as much as 10 percent without sanction of the IMF, but greater adjustments require IMF approval.

The International Bank for Reconstruction and Development, now part of "The World Bank Group," was the second important institution arising out of the Bretton Woods meetings. The World Bank Group also includes the International Finance Corporation and the International Development Association, as well as the original International Bank for Reconstruction and Development. These institutions facilitate long-term capital movements among nations by extending grants and loans to underdeveloped nations. The World Bank Group also underwrites loans made by other nations to developing countries and it can borrow from one nation and lend to others. Needless to say, Bretton Woods did much to create a more orderly international monetary system which has been important to the vast expansion of international trade during the last 25 years.

## AMERICAN TRADE-LIBERALIZATION POLICIES

A variety of trade-expansion policies have also characterized the postwar era. Trade-liberalization policies were implemented in 1947 by the United States and some two dozen other nations in the General Agreement on Tariff and Trade (GATT), later expanded in the "Kennedy Round." The "Kennedy Round" refers to the granting to the President in 1962 the power to negotiate lower trade barriers with selected Western European countries. Signatory nations to GATT continue to negotiate reductions in existing tariffs and import quotas, and recent consideration has been given to extending the President's authority to negotiate further tariff reductions and to establish tariff preferences for underdeveloped nations.

In spite of the fact that trade barriers among nations have not disappeared by any means, the tariff reductions negotiated in the 1960s have been significant in promoting freer international trade, particularly among the developed nations of the world. Today, the average duty on American imports of about 5 percent is less than one-tenth as large as the record levels of the Smoot-Hawley Tariff of 1930.

## ECONOMIC INTEGRATION IN EUROPE

Much of Western Europe was devastated by World War II, creating an economic dilemma that, among other things, contributed to the integration of international trade and finance among more than a dozen European nations. After experimenting with cooperative trade arrangements for selected industries such as iron, coal, and steel early in the postwar era, six nations banded together in 1957 as one European Economic Community, the *Common Market*, as it is generally called. The Netherlands, France, West Germany, Italy, Belgium, and Luxembourg formed this bloc of nations to reduce and gradually eliminate trade barriers among themselves by the early 1970s. In addition, these nations agreed to allow free movement of capital and labor within the Common Market and to establish uniform tariffs and quotas on goods moving into the six-member bloc.

In 1960, a second trade bloc called the European Free Trade Association (EFTA) was established by Denmark, Great Britain, Norway, Sweden, Switzerland, Austria, and Portugal for the purpose of achieving common tariff reductions. While these seven nations originally were not as eager to achieve economic integration as were the members of the Common Market, the theme in Europe today is economic unity. More recently (February 1970) Denmark, Finland, Norway, and Sweden agreed on a draft treaty to establish a customs union to be known as Nordek. Further attempts to achieve economic integration in Western Europe such as efforts to merge the Common Market and the EFTA have as yet been unsuccessful. France's negative attitude toward accepting Great Britain has been one of the major stumbling blocks. Despite French vetoes (in 1963 and 1967), the return of the Conservatives to power in mid-1970 has kept British interest in Common Market membership alive—an event that, if it occurs, will probably herald the entry of several other nations as well.

Economic unity among Western European nations must be regarded as one important ingredient in the recent prosperity experienced by Common Market and EFTA nations. As national economies become integrated, resources are more effectively allocated across national boundaries, and previously undeveloped mass markets are opened, allowing the achievement of economies of scale. However, elimination of trade barriers poses new problems for nonmember nations trading with the Common Market and the EFTA. When West German steel or autos move freely across selected national boundaries while common tariff barriers are maintained against Japanese steel and American automobiles, the latter two nations are at a serious competitive disadvantage. By investing in foreign operations in Common Market nations, however, American business firms have partially circumvented these trade barriers. Indeed, U.S. investments contribute to the persistent American balance-of-payments deficit of the last two decades. These investments also have significant implications for European nations concerned about American domination of their industrial base.[1]

## B. THE FOREIGN-EXCHANGE MARKET

Our next task is to understand the financial complications arising from trade among nations, which requires the exchange of currencies as well as goods and services. Domestic exchange is simplified because payment is made in a common monetary unit, such as the dollar. However, because nations have different monetary units, we must understand foreign-exchange markets—markets in which the currencies of trading nations are purchased, sold, and priced in terms of dollars, marks, and pounds.

The crucial feature of international finance is the idea that achieving

---

[1] These concerns have been succinctly expressed as follows: "Fifteen years from now it is quite possible that the world's third greatest industrial power, just after the United States and Russia, will not be Europe, but American industry in Europe. Already, in the ninth year of the Common Market, this European market is basically American in organization." See J. J. Servan-Schreiber, *The American Challenge* (New York: Atheneum, 1968), p. 3.

equilibrium in the balance of payments (no deficit and no surplus) requires long-term solutions other than trade controls or perpetual reliance on limited supplies of international reserves (such as borrowing from the IMF, or selling gold or convertible foreign currencies). A payments deficit can be cured by allowing the values of currencies to fluctuate freely, and our ultimate aim is to understand how freely fluctuating exchange rates are related to a balance-of-payments deficit or surplus. Let us first consider the meaning of foreign-exchange rates.

## Foreign-Exchange Rates

International trade between the United States and Germany, for instance, requires that dollars be exchanged for marks because American exporters want dollars to pay their domestic production costs. Similarly, German firms selling goods to American buyers typically expect payment in their currency (the deutsche mark, henceforth DM). This means that international trade will normally occur only if currencies can be exchanged, a situation which requires that there be markets for different monetary units. These foreign-exchange markets reflect the supply and demand for different currencies, which in turn determine foreign-exchange rates. Exchange rates between the United States dollar and selected foreign monetary units are shown below.

| Dollar Price of Selected Foreign Currencies | | | |
|---|---|---|---|
| Italy: | 626 lira = $1 | Britain: | 0.42 pounds = $1 |
| Germany: | 3.7 marks = $1 | Japan: | 356 yen = $1 |

Normally, businessmen engaged in international trade need only go to a bank and purchase almost any foreign currency they need—much as an average consumer buys toothpaste at a drugstore. Suppose that a New York auto dealer wants to purchase a Volkswagen and the German export price is quoted at 6,000DM. Upon arriving at the Chase Manhattan Bank, which maintains a market in foreign exchange, the auto dealer might be told that the rate of exchange is 4DM = $1. This means that a check for 6,000DM can be purchased for $1,500—the cost of the Volkswagen to the American importer (ignoring the small commission paid to the Chase Manhattan as a dealer in foreign exchange). When $1 purchases 4DM, it is also true that the mark is worth ¼ of a dollar, or 25 cents. The crucial point is that the "price" or foreign-exchange rate is determined by the supply and demand for a currency. In turn, the supply and demand for a currency is an outgrowth of financing trade among nations.

## THE SUPPLY AND DEMAND FOR FOREIGN EXCHANGE

Suppose the exchange rate is 4DM = $1, and an American importer of automobiles purchases a German auto priced at 6,000DM ($1,500). The American importer goes to his New York bank and purchases 6,000 DM at the current rate of exchange by drawing a check on his account for $1,500. Being a dealer in foreign exchange, the American bank maintains an account with a German correspondent bank, from which it purchases marks to sell to the American auto dealer. The marks are then paid to the German exporter, who in turn deposits the check in his account in the German bank. *In purchasing a German product, the United States is supplying dollars and demanding marks.*

Now consider the case of an American exporter of tobacco selling at $1,500 per ton in the United States (assume the exchange rate remains 4DM = $1). The German importer of tobacco will make payment by exchanging 6,000DM for $1,500 at his bank in Frankfurt which also buys, sells, and maintains an inventory of dollars as a foreign exchange. The German importer pays the tobacco exporter who deposits the $1,500 check in his American bank. *Notice that American exports to Germany create a German demand for dollars and make a supply of marks available to Americans.*

## THE RELATION BETWEEN TRADE AND FOREIGN EXCHANGE

By selling goods abroad, the United States obtains foreign currency to finance purchases from foreign nations, just as German sales abroad earn foreign currencies which can be used to finance German imports. The United States bank is willing to hold marks earned by exports to Germany and sell them to importers such as the American auto dealer at the prevailing exchange rate plus a small commission. Likewise, the German bank will accept dollars earned by goods exported to the United States because it also needs foreign currencies to fulfill its intermediary role of providing foreign exchange (dollars) to German importers.

A balance-of-payments deficit or surplus is related to foreign-exchange markets in the following way. When a nation incurs a deficit, it is buying more abroad than it sells—payments to foreign nations exceed receipts from them. This means that more dollars, for example, are provided abroad than are needed for direct trade purposes. On the other hand, when a nation such as the United States incurs a surplus in its balance of payments, the quantity of dollars provided foreigners is less than the quantity they need for trade purposes. Thus, a balance-of-payments deficit for the United States is synonymous with excess quantities of dollars provided to foreign-exchange markets, while a balance-of-payments surplus for the United States indicates a shortage of dollars abroad. The receipts and payments associated with international trade activate foreign-exchange markets. Accordingly, markets are established for different currencies which determine the rate of exchange among the American dollar, German mark, Swedish krona, and Brazilian cruzeiro, for example.

### Fluctuating Exchange Rates

What happens in markets for foreign exchange is analogous to what happens in any other market: When the quantity of dollars wanted by foreigners is in excess of the quantity available, the exchange rate (price) of the currency is bid up. A second important event also follows from price changes in foreign-exchange markets: As the exchange rate varies, a nation's balance-of-payments deficit or surplus is altered. This happens because a change in the foreign price of a domestic currency (such as the dollar) alters the prices of American goods to other nations and also changes the prices of foreign goods to Americans. Consequently, the terms of trade for exports and imports are altered, affecting the balance of payments.

The current international financial system is based on a system of managed or "pegged" exchange rates; however, fluctuating exchange rates that respond freely to supply and demand have been used to resolve balance-of-payments disequilibria in the past. After mastering the analytically simpler case of fluctuating exchange rates, we will examine the way in which international finance operates today.

## THE EQUILIBRIUM EXCHANGE RATE

The way fluctuating foreign-exchange rates are determined is represented by hypothetical supply and demand curves in Figure 1(a). The quantity of a currency (the dollar) is plotted on the horizontal axis, just as would be done for any good or commodity; the vertical axis depicts the "mark" price of the dollar, for example. Moving up the vertical axis shows *dollar appreciation*: $1 is worth more marks, or it takes more marks to buy a dollar. Moving downward on the vertical axis denotes *dollar depreciation*: It takes fewer marks to buy $1, meaning that dollars are cheaper to foreign nations.

The demand schedule for dollars in Figure 1(a) is downward-sloping, indicating that the quantity of dollars demanded by Germany increases as the dollar becomes less expensive. This is because, as the dollar becomes less expensive, American goods become cheaper and more attractive to Germans. The demand for dollars is "derived" from the demand for American goods and services. In other words, a larger quantity of dollars will be demanded to buy more American goods as the mark price of dollars de-

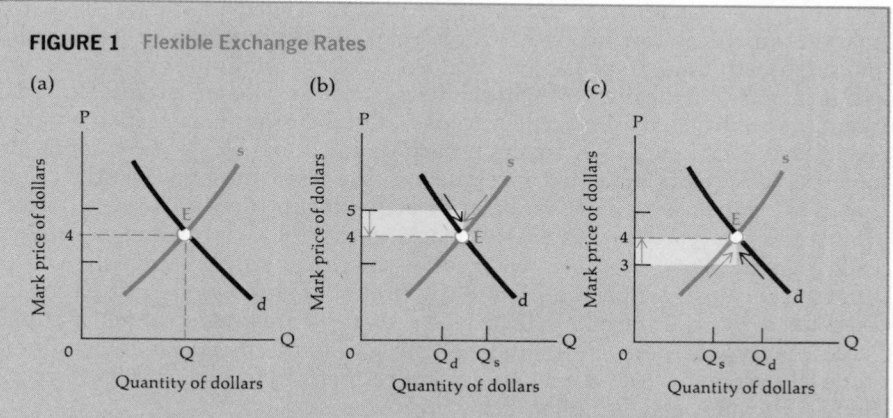

**FIGURE 1**  Flexible Exchange Rates

*Exchange Rates and the Balance of Payments.* The equilibrium exchange rate is determined by the supply and demand for currencies. A currency such as the dollar appreciates or depreciates according to whether it buys more or less foreign exchange. In (a) equilibrium occurs at 4DM = $1 but in (b) the exchange rate of 5DM = $1 cannot be maintained. The dollar depreciates in value, causing American exports to increase (foreign nations demand a larger quantity of dollars), and imports to decline (the quantity of dollars supplied declines). Similarly, the relatively low exchange rate of 3DM = $1 in (c) cannot be maintained. This time, however, the dollar appreciates in value, which means that American exports decline (foreign nations demand fewer dollars) and imports rise (the United States supplies more dollars). Variations in the exchange rate thus lead to trade adjustments which alter a nation's balance of payments in the direction of a new equilibrium.

clines. The supply of dollars slopes upward in Figure 1(a), indicating that a larger quantity of dollars is supplied if Americans can get more marks per dollar. This is because, at a higher price, $1 buys more marks, for example, which in turn will allow $1 to buy more German goods. The *equilibrium exchange rate* is the point at which the supply and demand schedules intersect—at 4DM = $1 in Figure 1(a)—and the equilibrium quantity of dollars exchanged is Q. At this exchange rate, the supply of dollars equals the demand for dollars, and the exchange rate is stable. To verify this, consider what happens if the exchange rate exceeds 4DM = $1 in Figure 1(a).

## ABOVE EQUILIBRIUM EXCHANGE RATES: DOLLAR DEPRECIATION

Suppose momentarily that the current foreign-exchange rate is 5DM = $1, and the United States incurs a deficit in its balance of payments. In this case, the quantity of dollars supplied ($Q_s$) exceeds the quantity demanded ($Q_d$) in Figure 1(b). Because dollars are in excess supply as a foreign exchange, the mark price of dollars will decline to a lower equilibrium value at 4DM = $1. As the value of the dollar depreciates (or the value of the mark appreciates, which is the same thing), the quantity of dollars demanded by Germany to finance imports increases along demand schedule d of Figure 1(b). Since the dollar has depreciated, German goods are more expensive to Americans, United States imports from Germany will decline, and a smaller quantity of dollars will be supplied (along supply schedule s) until the 4DM = $1 equilibrium exchange rate in Figure 1(b) is reached. An initial balance-of-payments deficit is diminished because United States exports (receipts from sales abroad) rise and imports (payments to foreign nations) decline. *Fluctuating exchange rates that respond to the supply and demand for foreign exchange ultimately correct a deficit and restore equilibrium in the balance of payments.*

## BELOW EQUILIBRIUM EXCHANGE RATES: DOLLAR APPRECIATION

Now suppose that the initial exchange rate is 3DM = $1, perhaps because the United States has a balance-of-payments surplus and German importers need more dollars to purchase American goods than are currently supplied. The demand for American dollars thus exceeds supply at 3DM = $1 in Figure 1(c). The consequences now are appreciation of the dollar until the shortage of dollars is remedied at 4DM = $1 as shown in Figure 1(c). As the mark price of dollars rises, the relative prices of German and American goods are altered, tending to make German goods cheaper and more attractive to American importers. Conversely, American goods become more expensive and therefore less attractive to German importers. The American balance-of-payments surplus diminishes because exports decrease and imports rise while Germany reduces the size of its balance-of-payments deficit because exports rise and imports fall.[2]

[2] For example, as the mark price of dollars increases from 3DM = $1 to 4DM = $1, a ton of American tobacco priced at $1,500 increases in price from 4,500DM to 6,000DM to Germans. The consequence is that Germans cut back on purchases of American goods. Conversely, the German Volkswagen priced at 6,000DM declines from $2,000 (at the 3DM = $1 exchange rate) to $1,500, since 4DM can now be exchanged for $1, as Figure 1 shows. Germany now exports *more* to the United States and imports *less*. Changes in exchange rates thus move toward a new international equilibrium and eliminate payments deficits and surpluses.

Essentially, there is no need for international reserves if exchange rates are allowed to fluctuate freely in response to changes in the demand and supply for a currency. Nations add to or draw upon their reserves to the extent that they wish to stabilize the price at which their currency is sold. If nations wish to stabilize or "peg" exchange rates at some value, they can do so by using international reserves as a buffer against shifts in the supply and demand for their currency.

## EXCHANGE RATES AND INTERNATIONAL RESERVES

Suppose that the initial rate of exchange between the dollar and mark is 4DM = $1 and that United States investments abroad increase. This capital outflow shifts the supply of dollars from $s$ to $s'$ in Figure 2. The result is an excess supply of dollars available to foreigners at the initial exchange rate of 4DM = $1. Given the new dollar-supply schedule $s'$, the excess quantity of dollars supplied at a price of 4DM = $1 is $QQ'$ in Figure 2. This excess quantity of dollars supplied at the initial exchange rate of 4DM = $1 is the size of the American balance-of-payments deficit if American financial authorities maintain the existing exchange rate of marks for dollars. When a nation uses its international reserves to cover a balance-of-payments deficit, it is effectively fixing exchange rates at some predetermined level by reclaiming or absorbing the excess supply of its currency (the payments deficit $QQ'$). To peg the exchange rate, the demand for dollars must shift to equilibrium at point $E'$ which maintains the 4DM = $1 equilibrium of Figure 2. This can be accomplished, for example, if the deficit nation demands its own currency by selling gold, or borrows from the IMF in amounts sufficient to reclaim or redeem the excess quantities of currency available to foreign nations.

## EXCHANGE RATES AND THE BALANCE OF PAYMENTS

If nothing changes in Figure 2 and trade occurs only between Germany and America, the United States will experience a deficit equal to $QQ'$ dollars each year. At the 4DM = $1 exchange rate in Figure 2, 100 marks would "purchase" $25, but if the exchange rate were allowed to decline to 3DM = $1, the same 100 marks would buy $33.33. It is not difficult to see that this constitutes depreciation of the dollar—American goods become cheaper to Germans, and, conversely, German goods become more expensive to Americans. Dollar depreciation would contribute to increased American exports (receipts would rise) and reduced imports (payments would decline), and thus would tend to restore equilibrium by reducing the American balance-of-payments deficit. Thus, the original deficit ($QQ'$) evaporates as the dollar depreciates in value, and the exchange-rate equilibrium is established at point $E$ in Figure 2. The reverse developments occur in the event of an initial balance-of-payments surplus in the United States.[3]

The crucial conclusions are straightforward enough. A deficit or surplus can be remedied by allowing exchange rates to vary, or it can be accommodated by using international reserves. The basic connection between ex-

---

[3] As the dollar appreciates, American exports fall, imports rise, and receipts decline for a United States balance-of-payments surplus. (Remember, American goods become more expensive to Germans and German goods become cheaper to Americans.)

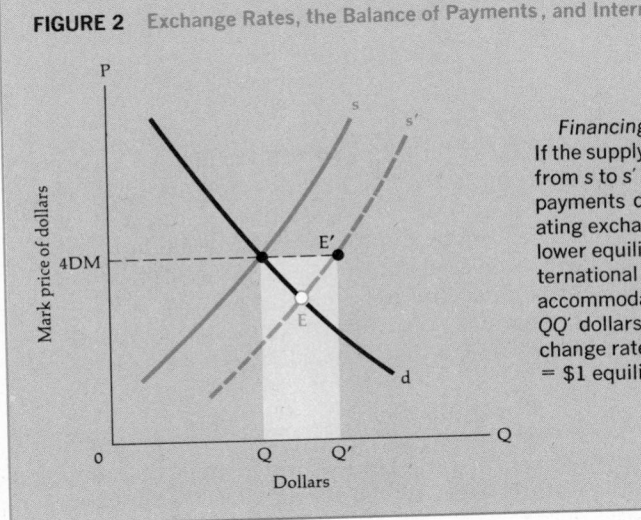

**FIGURE 2** Exchange Rates, the Balance of Payments, and International Reserves

*Financing Deficits with Reserves.* If the supply of a currency increases from s to s' because of a balance-of-payments deficit, the freely fluctuating exchange rate will decline to a lower equilibrium at E. However, international reserves can be used to accommodate the deficit (equal to QQ' dollars), in which case the exchange rate is stabilized at the 4DM = $1 equilibrium level at point E'.

change rates and the balance of payments is that freely fluctuating exchange rates: (a) change the relative prices of goods between two countries, and (b) alter the size of a deficit or surplus by stimulating exports in one nation and depressing them in another. The principal connection between international reserves and pegged exchange rates is that international reserves can be used to stabilize exchange rates, although at the "cost" of diminishing international liquidity.

Although expansion or contraction of exports and imports can be used to correct a balance-of-payments deficit or surplus, there is a good deal more to international financial matters. Nations do use international reserves to peg exchange rates, and this brings us face to face with the need to look at the contemporary international monetary system.

### The Gold-Reserve Standard

Even though gold plays a very nominal role in the domestic monetary affairs of most nations today, the international role of gold is quite different. Essentially, gold remains the ultimate international monetary reserve used to settle deficits and surpluses among trading nations.

Although gold is critical to the current international monetary system, convertible currencies (such as the dollar) and reserve assets held by the IMF (such as SDRs) are also used as reserves by nations. This is why today's monetary standard is termed a *gold-reserve* standard. The dollar is a *reserve currency* today because since 1934 the United States government has fixed the value of the dollar in relation to gold at $35 per ounce. The effect of a fixed-dollar price on gold is to peg the currencies of all nations to the dollar and therefore to gold within a narrow exchange-rate band. Consequently, continual balance-of-payments deficits in the United States potentially threaten to deplete American gold stocks. As other nations acquire larger holdings of liquid-dollar balances as reserves, they are gaining assets that can be redeemed for gold. Thus, any nation holding dollars effectively owns gold as long as the dollar is convertible into gold at a fixed price. Maintaining the convertibility of dollars into gold has been a difficult problem, however, and one which deserves our attention.

## C. THE AMERICAN PAYMENTS PROBLEM

We have already seen how a United States payments deficit can be accommodated by: (a) depletion of reserves (gold, American-owned IMF assets, or convertible foreign currencies) or (b) increasing our indebtedness to other nations in the measure that they willingly hold additional liquid-dollar balances. Because the dollar is a reserve currency, the American balance of payments is important to the international monetary system. With our background knowledge of financial institutions and the contemporary monetary system, we can now look at the United States balance-of-payments problem.

### Chronic Disequilibrium: The Case of the U.S. Dollar

During World War II, the economy of the United States more than doubled its real GNP from the low output levels which typified the waning years of the 1930s. International gold reserves sought American shores, in part because of the political and economic uncertainty accompanying Hitler's European activities, and in part because of the large quantities of goods shipped to our European allies during the war. The United States emerged from the war with a strong, virtually untouched resource base plus vast quantities of gold which had left war-torn Europe. In contrast, the European economy emerged with much of its productive capacity destroyed and a badly exhausted supply of gold reserves. Postwar trade seemed a virtual impossibility because many Western European nations, as well as Japan, lacked the ability to produce goods for export to the United States and thus also lacked the dollars needed to purchase our exports.

Postwar American aid programs were initially developed to assist the economic recovery of Europe and Japan. More recently, American aid has been channeled to the underdeveloped nations to promote economic development and to parry the political thrusts of the Soviet Union. The Marshall Plan was established in 1948, and in 1951 the Mutual Security Program was formed to reconstruct the economies of Europe and enhance political stability. At the close of the ten-year period ending in 1955, for example, over $50 billion had been made available to other nations in the form of economic and military grants and loans provided by the United States government. About two-thirds of this amount went to Western Europe, one-half of which was for nonmilitary purposes. These and other international efforts produced spectacular results: The productive capabilities of Britain, France, Japan, and Germany expanded rapidly and world trade increased significantly.

Whereas the early postwar era was characterized by a shortage of dollars in the hands of foreigners, during the latter 1950s the pendulum began to swing in the other direction. By 1958 reconstruction of the free-world economy was completed, and the era of the so-called "dollar shortage" had ended. Thus, the stage was set for a chronic long-term deficit in the United States balance of payments.

Figure 3 summarizes the American balance-of-payments deficit over the last 20 years, an era in which nations have stabilized exchange rates by agreement with the International Monetary Fund. The sale of gold and foreign currencies, as well as borrowing from the IMF, have helped the United States accommodate its deficit. In addition, the United States has allowed large amounts of liquid-dollar balances to accumulate in the central banks of foreign nations.

The deficit shown in Figure 3 is called a *liquidity* deficit, since both private and official foreign holdings of liquid-dollar balances are viewed as a potential demand against United States reserve assets, as Chapter 25 explained.[4] As of 1970, liquid-dollar balances in the hands of all foreigners totaled $43 billion. Because the dollar is in demand as international reserves, the liquidity deficit understates the strength of the American balance of payments. At the same time, however, when liquid-dollar holdings of private foreign persons are treated as a capital inflow to derive the official settlement balance, the strength of the American balance of payments is overstated.

## CAPITAL FLOWS AND PAYMENTS DISEQUILIBRIUM

Some appreciation for the difficulties associated with remedying disequilibrium in the balance of payments can be developed by considering for a moment the United States deficit of recent years. A current account surplus has occurred, but it has been more than offset by an unfavorable balance on capital account for most of the last two decades. Long-term capital outflows due to private investments abroad have averaged over $3 billion annually for more than a decade, adding to the supply of dollars available because of government grants and loans. Also, short-term capital outflows have contributed to the United States deficit.

Short-term capital outflows (investments in liquid assets maturing in one year or less) have a very volatile impact on the balance of payments. If the central bank of a nation like Japan raises interest rates through restrictive monetary policies, for example, American short-term capital moves abroad in search of higher interest earnings. Consequently, the supply of dollars made available to foreigners rises even more, an event that places further pressures on the American dollar and the payments deficit.

### Reasons for a Recurrent Deficit

There is no one simple explanation for the balance-of-payments deficit shown in Figure 3. Several events have contributed to the recurrent liquidity deficit.

1. *Foreign competition.* As a result of their remarkable productivity increases, Japan and several Western European countries have provided increased competition for American goods. Another source of increased com-

---

[4] The $7.2 billion liquidity deficit for 1969 compares to a $2.7 billion surplus computed on the official settlement basis. Most of this difference is the result of treating $9 billion of private holdings of liquid-dollar balances as a capital inflow and not a financing transaction used to offset the liquidity deficit.

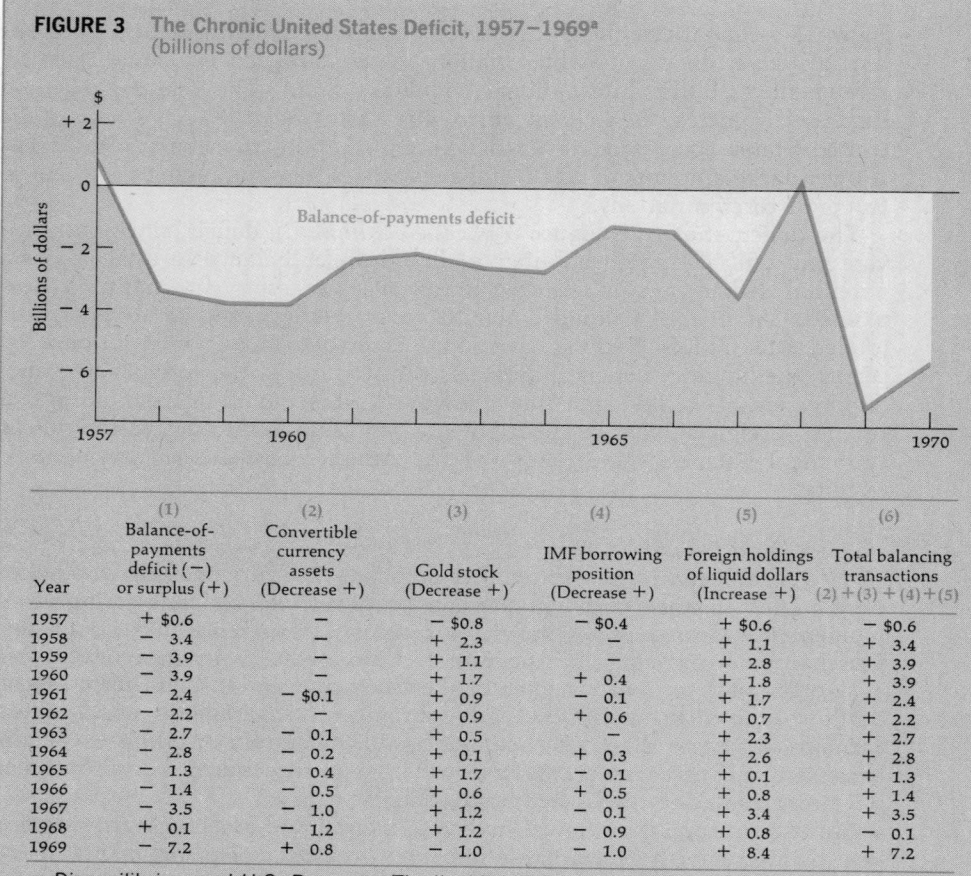

**FIGURE 3** The Chronic United States Deficit, 1957–1969[a]
(billions of dollars)

| Year | (1)<br>Balance-of-payments deficit (−) or surplus (+) | (2)<br>Convertible currency assets (Decrease +) | (3)<br>Gold stock (Decrease +) | (4)<br>IMF borrowing position (Decrease +) | (5)<br>Foreign holdings of liquid dollars (Increase +) | (6)<br>Total balancing transactions (2)+(3)+(4)+(5) |
|---|---|---|---|---|---|---|
| 1957 | + $0.6 | − | − $0.8 | − $0.4 | + $0.6 | − $0.6 |
| 1958 | − 3.4 | − | + 2.3 | − | + 1.1 | + 3.4 |
| 1959 | − 3.9 | − | + 1.1 | − | + 2.8 | + 3.9 |
| 1960 | − 3.9 | − | + 1.7 | + 0.4 | + 1.8 | + 3.9 |
| 1961 | − 2.4 | − $0.1 | + 0.9 | − 0.1 | + 1.7 | + 2.4 |
| 1962 | − 2.2 | − | + 0.9 | + 0.6 | + 0.7 | + 2.2 |
| 1963 | − 2.7 | − 0.1 | + 0.5 | − | + 2.3 | + 2.7 |
| 1964 | − 2.8 | − 0.2 | + 0.1 | + 0.3 | + 2.6 | + 2.8 |
| 1965 | − 1.3 | − 0.4 | + 1.7 | − 0.1 | + 0.1 | + 1.3 |
| 1966 | − 1.4 | − 0.5 | + 0.6 | + 0.5 | + 0.8 | + 1.4 |
| 1967 | − 3.5 | − 1.0 | + 1.2 | − 0.1 | + 3.4 | + 3.5 |
| 1968 | + 0.1 | − 1.2 | + 1.2 | − 0.9 | + 0.8 | − 0.1 |
| 1969 | − 7.2 | + 0.8 | − 1.0 | − 1.0 | + 8.4 | + 7.2 |

*Disequilibrium and U.S. Reserves.* The liquidity deficit for recent years has occurred despite a favorable current-account balance. Large capital outflows have made it necessary for the United States to accommodate this recurrent deficit, largely by the sale of foreign currency and gold, as well as by allowing liquid foreign-dollar balances held by foreigners to increase.

[a] The deficit is computed on a liquidity basis.

SOURCE: *Economic Report of the President,* 1970, and *Federal Reserve Bulletin* (September 1970).

petition has been the development of free-trade blocs such as the Common Market.

2. *Government aid.* Since World War II, government grants and loans for military and economic development purposes have contributed to a substantial capital outflow. The net bill for all foreign assistance (economic and military) hit the $125 billion mark by 1970 and currently averages about $4 billion annually. These funds were crucial to European recovery, as we noted earlier, and in recent years have been channeled to underdeveloped nations. Expenditures for economic development and military purposes have thus contributed to the payments deficit in important ways.

3. *Private capital flows.* Increased private investment abroad has steadily

added to our balance-of-payments deficit since the mid-1950s. Since 1955, private American investments abroad have more than tripled and now exceed $150 billion, an event of no small consequence to the persistent deficit. Both the developed nations of Western Europe and (to a lesser extent) certain underdeveloped nations have attracted American capital. Growth in world markets and profitable investment opportunities abroad have encouraged net private capital outflows and added to the world's supply of dollars.

4. *Price-level changes.* Finally, changing prices in the domestic economies of trading nations have affected the competitiveness of United States goods on world markets. For most of the last 25 years, the general pattern of U.S. inflation relative to other nations of the world was neutral to favorable; that is, price-level increases here were less than those in most nations and hence did not contribute significantly to the American balance-of-payments deficit. Even though we maintained a large and favorable balance on current account for years because American goods were generally priced attractively in world markets, modest deterioration has occurred recently, especially since the late 1960s. As prices have risen in the United States relative to foreign nations, the competitive edge American exports once enjoyed has been diminished, and the current-account surplus has deteriorated. A favorable current account balance must be maintained if the United States is to finance extended net capital outflows in the future.

### Curing the United States Deficit

When transactions on current and capital account reveal a persistent liquidity deficit and foreign nations end up holding larger dollar balances, strains are placed upon the international strength of the dollar under the system of pegged exchange rates which prevails today. Indeed, continuation of the deficit shown in Figure 3 could conceivably prompt a "gold rush" on the United States if the confidence of other nations in the United States dollar were to collapse. Foreign holdings of liquid-dollar balances depend on the Treasury's ability to meet its commitment to maintain the strength and convertibility of dollars relative to gold.

### ARTIFICIAL SOLUTIONS TO A DEFICIT

To guard against such problems, the American payments deficit must be controlled at a sustainable level. However, some control measures are nothing more than artificial solutions. *Trade and exchange controls* are among the inappropriate tactics. We have already seen that restrictive tariffs and quotas invite retaliation (Chapter 25) and typically end up retarding the volume of trade. But what about the possibility of rationing the supplies of the currencies of other nations? The United States could control its level of imports from foreign nations by requiring all exporters who earn foreign exchange to sell their currencies to the United States government. Government authorities could then ration the limited supplies of foreign exchange to American importers, thus controlling the volume of imports. This type of exchange rationing, which is often used by underdeveloped nations, breaks down for several reasons.

In the first place, government authorities must discriminate among importers, deciding which ones will obtain foreign currencies (or who will import what), a function otherwise performed impersonally by international markets and prices. Exchange controls also distort consumer choice because of their impact on the domestic prices of certain goods no longer subject to foreign competition. When a nation uses exchange rationing and refuses to allow certain goods to be imported, the viability and competitive character of domestic markets and industries may be affected. Furthermore, a government-imposed shortage of foreign exchange may result in the development of black markets for currencies if importers want them badly enough. Most damaging, however, is the fundamental truth that exchange rationing controls the volume of international transactions just as a tariff does. In essence, exchange rationing distorts the composition of trade and reduces its volume, particularly if other nations retaliate, as has often happened in the past.

If neither trade controls nor exchange rationing are acceptable, how about simply continuing to use foreign-dollar holdings and reserves to accommodate a chronic deficit? Remember one additional conclusion we reached before: A nation's supply of international reserves is exhaustible and the dollar must remain strong because it is a reserve currency. While using reserves to accommodate a deficit does buy time, it has been likened to bailing water out of a leaky boat rather than seeking a more basic solution (e.g., plugging the holes in the first place). There are vague but finite constraints to the use of reserves to accommodate a deficit. An economy like that of the United States can finance a deficit for many years, but smaller and less developed nations which depend more upon international trade will have fewer reserves and must adjust in more fundamental ways much sooner. Therefore, more basic solutions to a deficit must be sought.

## BASIC SOLUTIONS

There are three categories of basic solutions to a chronic balance-of-payments deficit: deflation, adjustment of exchange rates, and other selective policies.

*Deflation: The Classical Remedy*   If international reserves can no longer be used to accommodate a deficit, a nation can use fiscal and monetary policies to deflate its domestic economy. Restrictive domestic monetary and fiscal policies operate in a fashion similar to a gold outflow under the gold-exchange standard of the pre-1930 era. By adopting restrictive domestic stabilization policies, for example, the United States can engineer the following chain of events.

1. Contractionary fiscal and monetary policies dampen economic expansions, tending to lower domestic prices relative to prices in foreign nations. Such deflationary policies also may raise domestic interest rates.

2. Consequently, foreign demand for dollars increases because United States goods are more attractive, and American demand for foreign exchange (and goods) decreases.

3. Higher interest rates in a deficit nation may also attract a capital inflow, and fewer dollars may be invested abroad where returns are relatively lower.

4. A balance-of-payments deficit is gradually reduced and eliminated because import payments to foreigners decline, export receipts from foreign sales tend to rise, and capital may flow into the United States.

Financial authorities in many nations are reluctant to employ restrictive fiscal and monetary measures to remedy balance-of-payments disequilibria. This is because deflation and the higher domestic interest rates needed to create a favorable current account balance and to induce capital inflows may not be compatible with domestic full-employment policies. In short, the cost of achieving balance-of-payments equilibrium is apt to be a recession. Even though this classical remedy is a basic solution for a chronic balance-of-payments deficit under fixed exchange rates, it is bitter medicine and not necessarily a simple goal to achieve—particularly if other nations counter with higher interest rates to retain short-term capital.

*Restoration of Fluctuating Exchange Rates*    A second class of solutions to a payments deficit involves returning to fluctuating exchange rates and abandoning the managed exchange-rate system or declaring a devaluation of the dollar. It will be recalled that under freely fluctuating exchange rates international markets will depreciate an overvalued currency that is in excess supply because of a payments deficit. As depreciation of a currency occurs, exports rise while imports decline, tending to relieve a payments deficit. Similar adjustments follow devaluation of a currency from one fixed rate of exchange to a lower rate.

Advocates of fluctuating exchange rates contend that problems like the American payments deficit and the continual loss of reserves would disappear if the pegged exchange-rate system were abandoned. Proponents of fixed exchange rates disagree, contending that the "cure" of fluctuating exchanges is worse than the disease of a chronic deficit. Those opposed to fluctuating exchange rates argue that free foreign-exchange markets are destabilizing to domestic economies whose trade sectors are periodically stimulated or depressed. Moreover, if fluctuating exchange rates cause a nation's currency to appreciate during a recession, unemployment may rise even further because of declining exports. Another argument advanced by proponents of fixed exchange rates is that when the rate of exchange is free to adjust to market supply and demand, risks and uncertainties are introduced which tend to discourage trade.[5] The controversy over the relative merits of fixed and fluctuating exchange rates remains unsettled, although many international financial experts have revealed some preferences for a fixed exchange-rate system. However, attitudes are always changing on this point.

Some authorities have called for more drastic measures to solve the payments deficit, such as raising the dollar price of gold, which constitutes devaluation of the dollar—a permissible but not very feasible alternative under existing international monetary conditions. United States authorities have not pursued dollar devaluation, in part because retaliation by other nations could cancel out the gains such a measure might temporarily generate. A major problem in devaluation of the dollar centers upon its use as a reserve currency. Since the dollar is held in lieu of gold in large quantities throughout the world, many nations would be penalized if the dollar were

---

[5] For example, a German importer may contract to purchase American goods with the expectation of paying a price based on one exchange rate (say, 3DM = $1). If the dollar appreciates in value (to 4DM = $1) by the time the exchange takes place, the product will cost considerably more than was anticipated.

devalued by raising the price of gold from \$35 to \$70 per ounce, for example.

*Selective Deficit Policies* | Barring major reforms of the international monetary system, neither of the above-mentioned cures is a totally acceptable solution for the chronic American deficit. However, in hopes of avoiding the perils associated with these basic remedial policies, economists and policymakers have advanced several selective prescriptions.

1. Increased productivity and lower costs in the United States would enhance the competitiveness of American goods in world markets.

2. More effective anti-inflationary policies in the United States compared to foreign nations would also help remedy the chronic deficit.

3. Redistribution of the burden of military and development assistance now carried in large measure by the United States would mitigate the United States deficit, as would careful reevaluation of American national-security policies.

4. Tourist travel and purchases abroad could be subjected to greater restrictions.

5. Government grants and loans could be tied to the purchase of American goods to a greater extent than they are today.

6. Tax penalties on American investments abroad also could be extended and increased. (As it is now, the "interest-equalization" tax on foreign securities purchased by Americans ranges up to 11.25 percent on debt obligations—depending on their maturity.)

All things considered, the use of such measures at least buys a little time and at best might slightly lessen the severity of the chronic deficit. Still, the balance-of-payments problems of the United States and other nations in similar circumstances are not easily remedied, and for this reason, suggestions for reform of the international monetary system have been very much in evidence of late.

## D. INTERNATIONAL FINANCIAL REFORM

The existing international financial system does present certain problems, many of which are crucial to international economic and political tranquility. The history of these problems is important, even though the 1970 reforms leading to enlarged IMF reserves have staved off the threatened collapse of the international monetary system. Three key problems have arisen in the past: (*a*) the persistent American deficit, which resulted in a heavy gold drain; (*b*) the failure of international reserves to provide enough liquid assets to accommodate deficits under a fixed exchange-rate system; and (*c*) the frequent deferment of basic adjustments needed to resolve deficits.

### The "Dollar Crisis"

One way to think of the American balance-of-payments deficit shown earlier in Figure 3 is to regard it as a short-term loan to the United States that must be extended by foreign nations. Indeed, this is exactly what happened in past years when foreign nations decided to hold larger dollar balances.

The data in the lower portion of Figure 4 show how United States reserves have declined from their 1957 highs. The United States has seen its gold reserves decline by more than one-half to some $12 billion in 1970, a trend that has been reasonably steady since the 1950s. Foreign holdings of liquid-dollar balances are more than three times as large as the United States supply of gold today, as Figure 4 also indicates. By inventorying liquid-dollar claims in United States securities, foreign "lenders" have extended short-term loans to the United States to accommodate the chronic balance-of-payments deficit. Using dollars for international reserve financing is not necessarily good or bad, but certain hazards are implicit in this procedure that relate to the stability of the international monetary system. A "dollar crisis" could arise because current gold reserves in the United States are nowhere near as large as liquid-dollar balances in the hands of foreigners. However, financial panic has been averted thus far, in part because of IMF reserves and, more recently, by the creation of special drawing rights provided through the IMF.

In one sense of the term, a *dollar glut* (excess dollar balances) has existed in international money markets in recent years—at least according to recent liquidity deficits and depletion of American reserves. Because the United States has continually increased its indebtedness to foreign holders

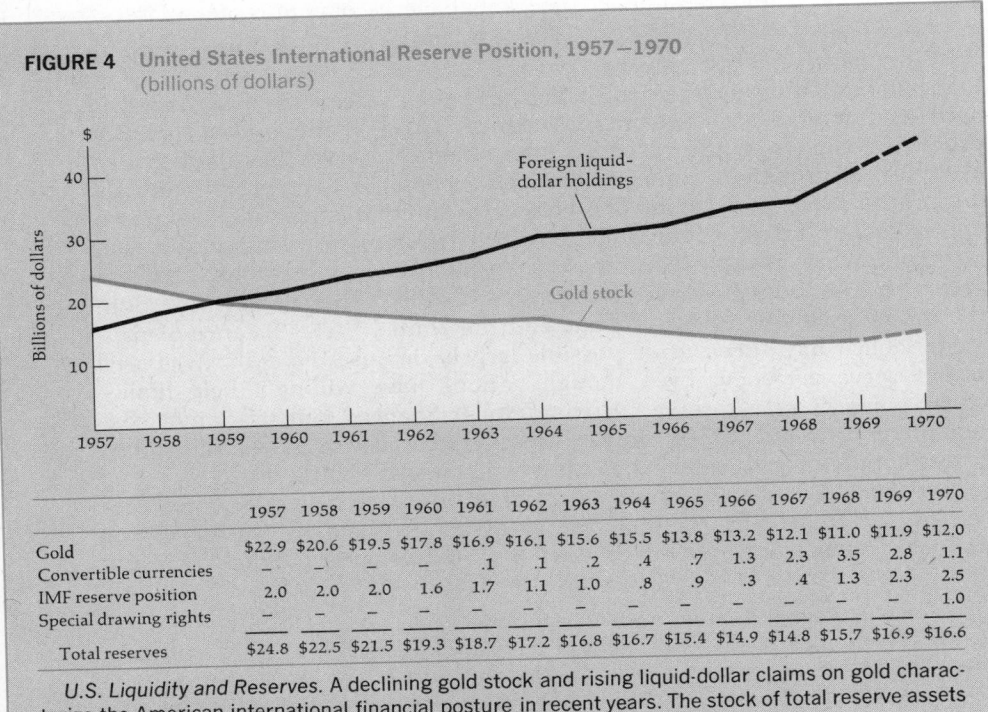

**FIGURE 4**  United States International Reserve Position, 1957–1970
(billions of dollars)

| | 1957 | 1958 | 1959 | 1960 | 1961 | 1962 | 1963 | 1964 | 1965 | 1966 | 1967 | 1968 | 1969 | 1970 |
|---|---|---|---|---|---|---|---|---|---|---|---|---|---|---|
| Gold | $22.9 | $20.6 | $19.5 | $17.8 | $16.9 | $16.1 | $15.6 | $15.5 | $13.8 | $13.2 | $12.1 | $11.0 | $11.9 | $12.0 |
| Convertible currencies | – | – | – | – | .1 | .1 | .2 | .4 | .7 | 1.3 | 2.3 | 3.5 | 2.8 | 1.1 |
| IMF reserve position | 2.0 | 2.0 | 2.0 | 1.6 | 1.7 | 1.1 | 1.0 | .8 | .9 | .3 | .4 | 1.3 | 2.3 | 2.5 |
| Special drawing rights | – | – | – | – | – | – | – | – | – | – | – | – | – | 1.0 |
| Total reserves | $24.8 | $22.5 | $21.5 | $19.3 | $18.7 | $17.2 | $16.8 | $16.7 | $15.4 | $14.9 | $14.8 | $15.7 | $16.9 | $16.6 |

*U.S. Liquidity and Reserves.* A declining gold stock and rising liquid-dollar claims on gold characterize the American international financial posture in recent years. The stock of total reserve assets has also declined as the data in the lower portion of the figure indicate.

SOURCE: *Economic Report of the President*, 1970, and *Federal Reserve Bulletin*. Data may not add due to rounding errors. 1970 is estimated by the author on the basis of June data.

of dollars in order to finance its deficit, it appears that the dollar is "over-valued" in relation to other currencies.[6] However, such labels as "dollar glut" and "overvaluation" are only partially characteristic of international financial affairs. After all, the dollar has been an accepted and, indeed, a badly needed reserve currency which has provided trading nations with a measure of liquidity that otherwise would not have prevailed.

The acceptability of dollars in international circles also suggests that the terms "glut" and "overvaluation" are only partially accurate characteriza-tions of the so-called "dollar crisis." Large amounts of dollars are on deposit in foreign branches of American banks, particularly in London. When Federal Reserve authorities used Regulation Q to impose interest-rate ceil-ings on deposits in American banks in 1969, many United States citizens switched their deposits to foreign branches of American banks where inter-est rates well in excess of 9 percent could be earned. These dollar-denomi-nated deposits in foreign branches (termed "Eurodollars" in view of their foreign location) have become an important source of short-term capital financing throughout the world. Growth in the Eurodollar market in the late 1960s and early 1970s implies continued acceptance of the dollar abroad, and indicates a stronger international position for the dollar than is implied by the sizable liquidity deficit for 1969, for example. In short, Eurodollar markets reveal a basic strength in the dollar abroad and also show how interconnected financial markets have become in recent years.

### The Liquidity Problem

*International liquidity* refers to the adequacy or inadequacy of the reserves used to accommodate payments imbalances among nations. The liquidity problem stems from the fact that international reserves have not grown as rapidly as growth in world trade, which expanded 7 to 8 percent annually during the 1950s and 1960s. The volume of international trade has grown approximately three to four times as rapidly as the world supply of mone-tary gold, which is expected to increase in the future by less than 2 percent each year after adjustment for industrial and other nonmonetary uses. Both the growing volume of world trade and the United States balance-of-pay-ments deficit have been made possible largely because the dollar was used as a reserve currency. Even though nations have willingly held liquid-dollar balances as a reserve currency, dollar-financed deficits cannot con-tinue to expand unchecked forever, especially because drains on the United States supply of gold reserves already have taken a significant toll.

The distribution of international reserves also is a matter of some con-cern. Over four-fifths of total reserve assets are held by the developed nations of the world, which conduct the bulk of international trade but

---

[6] International conversion on a widespread scale would be roughly analogous to the domestic bank runs of the early 1930s in the United States in that the international monetary system most certainly would be severely disrupted and could collapse. When exchange rates remain fixed, and as long as foreign-dollar balances accumulate, con-tinuing pressure is placed on the dollar, and it is increasingly difficult to maintain the rate of exchange at its present level. Continuation of a balance-of-payments deficit year after year imposes continued pressure on the dollar because American monetary author-ities have to accommodate the deficit by selling gold and foreign exchange or by in-creasing the indebtedness of the United States to foreigners.

account for less than one-third of the world's population. Indeed, *all* underdeveloped nations in Latin America, Asia, and Africa together have fewer reserves than the United States (about $15 billion). While the reserve position of the United States has deteriorated since 1949, many Western European nations such as Germany have substantially increased their reserve position. Considering the growth and development needs and the dependence on trade of underdeveloped nations, inadequate liquidity and the distribution of reserves is a serious matter.

## The Basic Adjustment Failure

A third key international financial problem is that the fixed exchange-rate system of today allows countries to defer accepting basic adjustments needed to bring about equilibrium in the balance of payments. When a reserve-currency nation such as the United States exercises its prerogative to delay such changes, the possibility of financial breakdown becomes a traveling companion to the international monetary system.

### SPECULATIVE CRISIS

Toward the end of the 1960s, continued deterioration of the British balance of payments, persistent pressure on sterling as a key international currency, the never-ending liquidity shortage, and the American deficit nearly brought the international monetary system to its knees. The United Kingdom narrowly averted a crisis-prompted devaluation in the mid-1960s. British exports were growing slowly, and capital outflows persisted. As in the United States, a chronic payments deficit continued in spite of restrictive domestic fiscal and monetary policies designed both to enhance the British current account balance and to stem the flight of capital abroad. In 1964, the British government borrowed heavily to shore up its rapidly deteriorating liquidity position. By the fall of 1967 it became apparent that the Bank of England might not be able to repay fully its previous indebtedness. Holders of pounds sterling moved quickly to exchange them, fearing imminent devaluation. Capital account pressures mounted as the Bank of England was forced to purchase large quantities of pounds sterling, and in November the pound was devalued by one-seventh its earlier value (from $2.80 to $2.40).

### TWO MARKETS FOR GOLD

The speculative pressures of 1967 also had an impact upon the dollar, ultimately leading to a two-price system for gold. The United States and half a dozen other nations (Italy, Germany, Britain, the Netherlands, Belgium, and Switzerland) formed the *London gold pool* in 1961 to pool sales and purchases of gold at $35 an ounce. Rising liquid-dollar claims held abroad relative to available American gold supplies, the continued existence of a payments deficit, and heavy losses of American reserves led to speculation that U.S. gold supplies would soon be exhausted, and that the dollar would have to be devalued. Private speculators began buying large quantities of gold at $35 an ounce in anticipation of an increase in the dollar price of gold. By early 1968, the gold drain to speculators reached crisis proportions and the nations associated with the London gold pool formally abandoned support of the private market for gold. Two markets and two prices for gold were thus established.

Central banks of the gold-pool nations agreed not to buy or sell gold in the private market, where prices had soared as high as $41 per ounce. Rather, they confined themselves to exchanging gold only at the official price of $35 per ounce. On the private market, gold prices are now set by speculative demand and supply forces just as are prices for other commodities. Thus, speculators and hoarders can deal in gold as they see fit without the continued price support of $35 an ounce being maintained by central bankers.

An immediate crisis was avoided by the two-market pricing system for gold, but international monetary affairs remained tenuous. The two-market system by no means solved all international financial problems. Rather, it was a stop-gap by which the international monetary system was momentarily patched up; since that time other IMF reforms have stabilized the free-market for gold, although prices do vary from $35 an ounce. In addition, the German mark, which has been a strong currency, was revalued upward and the French franc was devalued in the latter part of 1969. These developments, which were necessary for the two nations involved, also helped strengthen international financial markets.

### International Monetary Reform and the 1970s

With some understanding of the dollar, liquidity, and gold-speculation problems, we can now summarize the policy conflicts inherent in international finance and examine recent developments related to reform of the international monetary system.

### DOMESTIC AND INTERNATIONAL POLICY CONFLICTS

The basic difficulty of remedies for a balance-of-payments disequilibrium is that, if used, they can and often do conflict with the desires for trade expansion, domestic stability, and growth. In essence, international trade and financial relationships make countries more interdependent. Adopting fluctuating exchange rates, imposing deflationary and restrictive employment policies, or devaluing a currency to remedy a deficit may well be in order, but nations remain reluctant to subordinate domestic economic goals to international stability. If balance-of-payments policy is made the master, a contractionary monetary policy, higher interest rates, and lower income and employment levels may be required to reduce capital outflows and imports. Needless to say, nations are reluctant to achieve a payments equilibrium at these costs. On the other hand, a payments surplus requires expansionary measures that increase imports, contract exports, and lower the balance on capital account. But will a nation accept fiscal and monetary policies that conflict with domestic economic growth, anti-inflationary objectives, or the development of a diversified economy relying on capital investment from foreign sources? Frequently the answer to this question is no.

The chronic American deficit is even more complicated because of the reserve-currency role of the dollar. American payments policy has been both aided and hindered because the dollar is at the center of an international monetary system plagued with crises of the sort described earlier. The world's vast liquidity needs are regarded by some as aiding the United States in "covering" its deficit, while others recognize that dollars have been willingly absorbed by foreign nations. A variety of reforms intended to provide additional liquidity and to control disequilibria have emerged, the most recent of which has been the creation of special drawing rights (SDRs).

## THE IMF's "PAPER GOLD": SDRs

At the Bretton Woods Conference in 1944 when the IMF was founded, Lord Keynes recommended the creation of a paper-money substitute for gold. Similar proposals such as the Triffin and Bernstein Plans have also called for transforming the IMF into an international bank which could literally create credit-money substitutes for gold, or "paper gold." After many years of study and debate concerning inadequate liquidity and persistent balance-of-payments deficits in the United States and elsewhere, the IMF increased the borrowing rights for nations and also approved the extension of additional international credit in the form of special drawing rights or SDRs in 1970. Over $9 billion worth of new "paper gold" was authorized for use through 1972.

What this means for the liquidity crisis is that additional amounts of international reserves are available for use (e.g., $3.5 billion for 1970) in the form of SDRs. The striking characteristic of the newly created IMF credit is that these reserve assets are very much like the paper money used domestically by nations today. Unlike reserve currencies such as the dollar or pound, which are the credit-money of the American or British economies, SDRs are an international money backed jointly by all the IMF member nations, who have agreed to accept them as reserve assets. As it currently stands, the IMF can create additional "paper gold" (SDRs) with the approval of the member nations. In short, nations can now use SDRs as reserve assets to accommodate balance-of-payments deficits in the same way that they now use gold, convertible currencies, or IMF loans.

The long-awaited development of an additional international reserve asset capable of expanding at rates comparable to the growth in trade is a notable achievement in international cooperation. However, other fundamental problems remain. It is still necessary to develop ways to correct a chronic payments imbalance. SDRs provide liquidity and allow nations to buy time; they do not solve overvaluation or undervaluation of domestic currencies.

## CRAWLING PEGS: THE BEST OF TWO WORLDS?

Under current IMF regulations, nations are required to maintain a stable rate of exchange for their currency within $\pm 1$ percent of the declared (parity) value. If there is a need to alter the foreign-exchange rate to correct chronic payments disequilibria, up to a 10 percent revaluation can be made without approval of authorities of the IMF, but a larger adjustment must be approved—a regulation designed to prohibit exchange-rate instability and guard against competitive devaluation.

Recently, some monetary experts have advocated revision of pegged exchange rates to allow greater flexibility but still leave a degree of stability. They feel these two goals can be accomplished by a "crawling-peg" exchange-rate system. The crawling-peg proposal does not rely on either the extreme of freely fluctuating exchange rates or the more rigid pegged exchange rate that is maintained by nations reluctant to devalue their currencies to cope with a persistent deficit (or surplus). While the crawling-peg idea varies in certain technical details in various proposals, its two key characteristics are as follows:

1. Over a period of time, the declared parity value of a currency would be allowed to crawl (or slide) to a market equilibrium determined by its supply and demand. The value of a currency as a reflection of a payments deficit or surplus could be allowed to change by as much as 2 or 3 percent per year under the crawling-peg exchange-rate system.

2. A widened short-run fluctuation band around the parity exchange rate would be allowed, perhaps by increasing the present maximum range, and allowing the rate of exchange to fluctuate as much as 2 percent above and below the declared currency value in any given year.

Figure 5 demonstrates how these adjustments might operate. In any given year, the dollar might be allowed to fluctuate 2 percent above or below the parity exchange rate. These widened exchange-rate bands would give short-run relief to financial problems, but they would not resolve a chronic deficit such as that experienced in the United States in the last two decades.

A crawling peg which would allow exchange rates to rise or fall by 3 percent each year, for example, would permit the creeping but orderly adjustments needed to remedy payments disequilibria by shifting the terms of trade among nations, as Figure 5 illustrates. Because it allows exchange rates to adjust gradually to recurrent and pervasive deficits or surpluses, the widened-band and crawling-peg scheme embraces: (a) the stability of a relatively fixed exchange-rate system and also (b) the positive features of fluctuating exchange-rate adjustments to remedy payments disequilibria. Many observers believe that a more orderly international monetary system

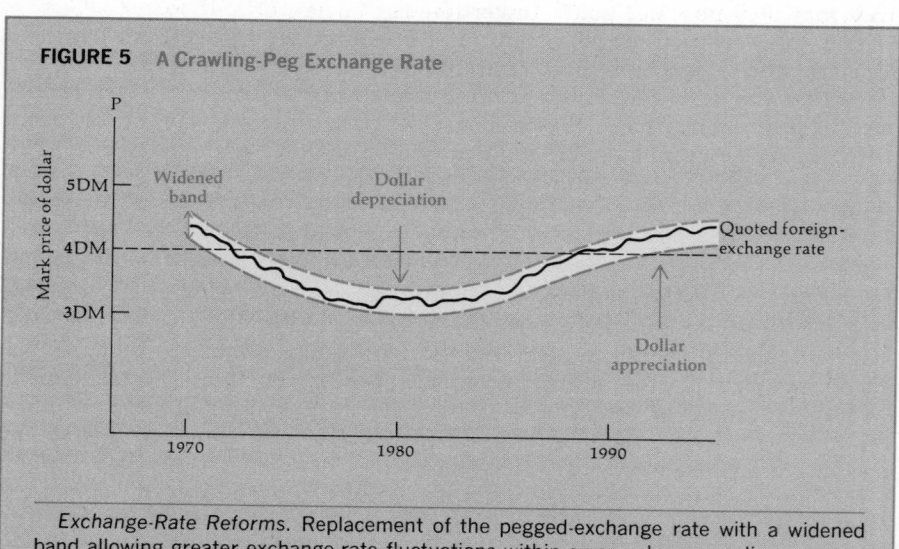

**FIGURE 5**  A Crawling-Peg Exchange Rate

*Exchange-Rate Reforms.* Replacement of the pegged-exchange rate with a widened band allowing greater exchange-rate fluctuations within a year plus a crawling peg permissive of secular slides in exchange rates allow controlled adjustments to payments disequilibria.

may well emerge if a crawling-peg system is adopted in conjunction with the additional liquidity provided by SDRs.[7]

## OTHER PROPOSALS FOR INTERNATIONAL MONETARY REFORM

Several alternatives to the now-realized paper gold and the potential adoption of a widened crawling-peg exchange rate have been proposed at one time or another. At one extreme, some have suggested raising the price of gold from $35 to, say, $70 or $100 per ounce for all nations, thereby doubling or tripling the present volume of international reserves. It is unlikely that a plan for raising the price of gold will be adopted, for several reasons. First, even if the price of gold were raised, gold outflows and deficits leading to devaluation pressures on a currency would continue to force nations into contraction and deflation. However, massive changes in reserves and liquidity would permit extended accommodation of chronic deficits if nations chose to ignore the discipline of gold as they have in the past. Second, gold speculators and hoarders, as well as nations like South Africa and Russia which mine much of the current output of gold, would benefit from enormous windfall profits. In contrast, nations which have willingly held dollars and convertible foreign currencies instead of speculatively hoarding gold would be penalized. Finally, most authorities regard the use of gold as a monetary base as a relic of tradition. Raising the price of gold would allow more gold to be mined profitably, but additional purchases would cost nations more of their current real output. Gold is of limited usefulness except that it perpetuates the myth that money is valuable because of gold when *in fact* gold is valuable largely because it is wanted for monetary purposes. The consensus among experts favors gradual abandonment of this folly in favor of a credit-based international money such as the SDRs now in existence.

As indicated earlier, others argue for a complete restoration of fluctuating exchange rates which would automatically correct payments disequilibria. Under such a system, nations would have no need for international reserves. Adoption of completely fluctuating exchange rates has not been fully tested, but critics have expressed concern about the instability of exchange rates as well as the potential trade restriction which could accompany abandonment of at least a partially stabilized international monetary system. Needless to say, complete success in coping with all of the problems of international finance remains to be achieved. Nevertheless, progress has been made since the stringent trade controls and financial collapse of the 1930s and the speculative crisis of the 1960s. While much has been done to remedy the difficulties of the past, continued cooperation among nations whose economies have become more closely interwoven will be called for in the future.

[7] If a general trend in the direction of dollar devaluation were anticipated in foreign-exchange markets, for example, short-term capital outflows could still intensify a payments deficit. Therefore, parity adjustments of 3 percent per year might require that domestic monetary policies move in the direction of restraint to maintain domestic interest rates above foreign rates and stem a capital outflow. In spite of the fact that some standard problems remain, many authorities believe that gradualism of the kind embodied in the crawling peg is a worthy reform measure.

THE INTERNATIONAL ECONOMY

# REVIEW

## Summary

1. The evolution of today's international monetary system began with the financial crisis of the 1930s. Under the gold standard, balance-of-payments disequilibria resulted in gold outflows (for deficit nations) and inflows (for surplus nations). Theoretically, gold outflows stabilized the value of international currencies and also restored balance-of-payments equilibrium through contraction of the money supply and economic activity. With the advent of a worldwide depression in the 1930s, the major economies of the world collapsed, abandoned the gold standard, and raised trade controls to unprecedented heights.

2. The International Monetary Fund (IMF) and the International Bank for Reconstruction and Development (now part of the World Bank Group) originated in 1944 at the Bretton Woods Conference. The IMF is an international bank that assists nations in maintaining adequate international reserves, whereas the World Bank Group is concerned primarily with lending to underdeveloped nations. As international finance stabilized after World War II, a trend toward trade liberalization occurred throughout the world. The United States lowered tariffs, and several Western European nations have since integrated their economic affairs through the development of customs unions—the Common Market, the European Free Trade Association, and more recently Nordek.

3. Exchange of goods and services among nations creates a demand and supply for currencies traded in foreign-exchange markets. Under fluctuating exchange rates, a balance-of-payments deficit increases the foreign supply of a currency and tends to lower its foreign-exchange rate. As a currency thus depreciates in value, that nation's exports increase and imports tend to decline until equilibrium is gradually restored in the balance of payments. The reverse tendencies prevail for nations experiencing a balance-of-payments surplus. However, achievement of equilibrium will be impeded if nations manage the values of their currency; i.e., if they peg the foreign-exchange rate.

4. Nations use their international reserves to accommodate a deficit or surplus and to stabilize the foreign-exchange rate. The current international monetary system is based upon the gold-reserve standard—a combined use of (a) gold and IMF credit, plus (b) currencies, such as the dollar, that are used as international reserves.

5. An American balance-of-payments deficit has persisted for nearly two decades. Trade controls are an artificial solution to this problem. Three important basic solutions to a deficit are: (a) deflating the domestic economy, which lowers domestic output and prices while moving the balance of payments toward equilibrium; (b) restoring fluctuating exchange rates, which alters the price of a currency, the costs of goods to foreign nations, and the balance of payments; and (c) a variety of selective policies related directly to the causes of a balance-of-payments deficit.

6. Chronic disequilibrium in the American balance of payments has resulted in the long-run loss of gold and an increase in foreign holdings of liquid-dollar assets. Today there are more than $3 in international

claims for every \$1 of Treasury-owned gold. To characterize this situation as a "dollar glut" is only partially correct, because the dollar is still used as a reserve currency and is widely accepted in international circles.

7. International trade has grown much more rapidly than international reserves, creating a "liquidity" problem. In addition, the distribution of reserves among nations can complicate any given country's balance-of-payments problem. Great Britain faced a speculative crisis in the late 1960s, and similar but less intense pressures on the dollar and American gold led to the establishment of two world markets for gold to stabilize international finance.

8. Recent international monetary reform measures have included the establishment of IMF special drawing rights ("paper gold") and other proposals designed to allow greater, but still controlled, variations in exchange rates. By widening the short-term variations in the exchange-rate band and also allowing exchange rates to slide in a secular direction via the "crawling peg," nations would be better able to adjust to payments disequilibria.

## Identify the Following Concepts and Terms

- gold standard
- Common Market
- currency appreciation and depreciation
- pegged exchange rates
- dollar glut
- World Bank Group
- international liquidity

- paper gold (SDRs)
- fluctuating exchange rate
- crawling-peg exchange rate
- reserve currency
- IMF
- gold pool
- gold-reserve standard

## Questions to Answer

1. How do markets for foreign exchange determine the exchange rate? How is the exchange rate related to a nation's deficit in the balance of payments under freely fluctuating exchange rates? If a managed or pegged exchange-rate system prevails, what is the relationship between a payments deficit, international reserves, and the pegged price of a currency?

2. How does the gold-reserve standard of today relate to the so-called "dollar crisis" and to the recent chronic disequilibrium in the American balance of payments? What bearing do these factors have on dollars as a reserve currency?

3. There are several reasons for the existing American deficit, and a variety of policies that might be useful in coping with the problem. Give the causes and explain and evaluate the solutions.

4. Critically evaluate the following statement: "A U.S. gold drain constitutes no threat to the dollar as a currency and in no sense of the word has a dollar 'glut' prevailed in recent years."

5. "Two markets for gold, the creation of SDRs, and a more flexible exchange-rate mechanism as embodied in the idea of a crawling peg will ultimately do much to restore payments equilibria and remedy international financial problems." Is this statement true or false? Why?

# CHAPTER 27
# The Underdeveloped
# Nations of the World

The underdeveloped nations include at least two-thirds of the nearly 4 billion people on this planet. Most people of the world live under conditions of subsistence, disease, and squalor which have not been experienced for centuries in North America or Western Europe. Were this your lot, you would probably live to age 45 or 50 instead of 65 or 70, and your income would be but a fraction of what is expected in this country; indeed, in all likelihood you would exist on a few hundred dollars per year. You would probably be illiterate and tied to primitive customs in a tradition-bound economy. Political concerns such as the encroachment of communism or the existence of freedom and justice might seem unimportant in comparison to starving or watching your brothers and sisters perish in a quagmire of despair. About the only thing that would not change would be the natural human desire to live a full and "good" life. Unfortunately, economic reality is harsh and the prospect of realizing the good life in your lifetime would be bleak. Just how bleak is clear when you realize that about one-twentieth of the world's population—the portion living in the United States—consume something like one-third of the world's output. This is twice as much gross income as is available to the more than 2 billion people living in underdeveloped nations on the three continents of Asia, Africa, and Latin America.

The enormity of the dilemma of economic underdevelopment matches its importance and just what is done about this problem may well determine the destinies of all peoples of the world. In approaching this topic, we will first examine some facts about the problem in Part A, and then in Part B describe the obstacles to economic development. The policy targets for future development will be examined in Part C.

**A.** SOME FACTS ON THE UNDERDEVELOPED ECONOMIES

When the nations of the world are examined over the centuries, one striking fact is clear: Continued economic growth and development are exceptions historically—not the rule.[1] Even in this century, economic development remains the exception for most nations. The chief problem of underdeveloped countries is increasing their capacity to produce more out-

---

[1] It has been suggested by at least one observer that Western Europe and North America did not enjoy the wealth of citizens in the Roman Empire until the nineteenth or twentieth century; however, this observation is not very comforting for the billions of people now living in squalor. L. J. Zimmerman, *Poor Lands, Rich Lands: The Widening Gap* (New York: Random House, 1956), p. 9.

put per capita. These nations are poor in the most general sense because they have remained tradition-bound societies in which neither market nor dictate has launched economic growth. Often they lack a viable resource base and, even more frequently, they fail to use their resources effectively.

### The Character of the International Development and Poverty Dilemma

Underdeveloped nations exhibit one common symptom: low per capita income. However, there are also other indicators of the poverty experienced by an underdeveloped country.

#### DISTRIBUTION OF WORLD OUTPUT

The contrasts between rich and poor are revealed by examining the distribution of national income by broad regions, as is done in Figure 1. If income

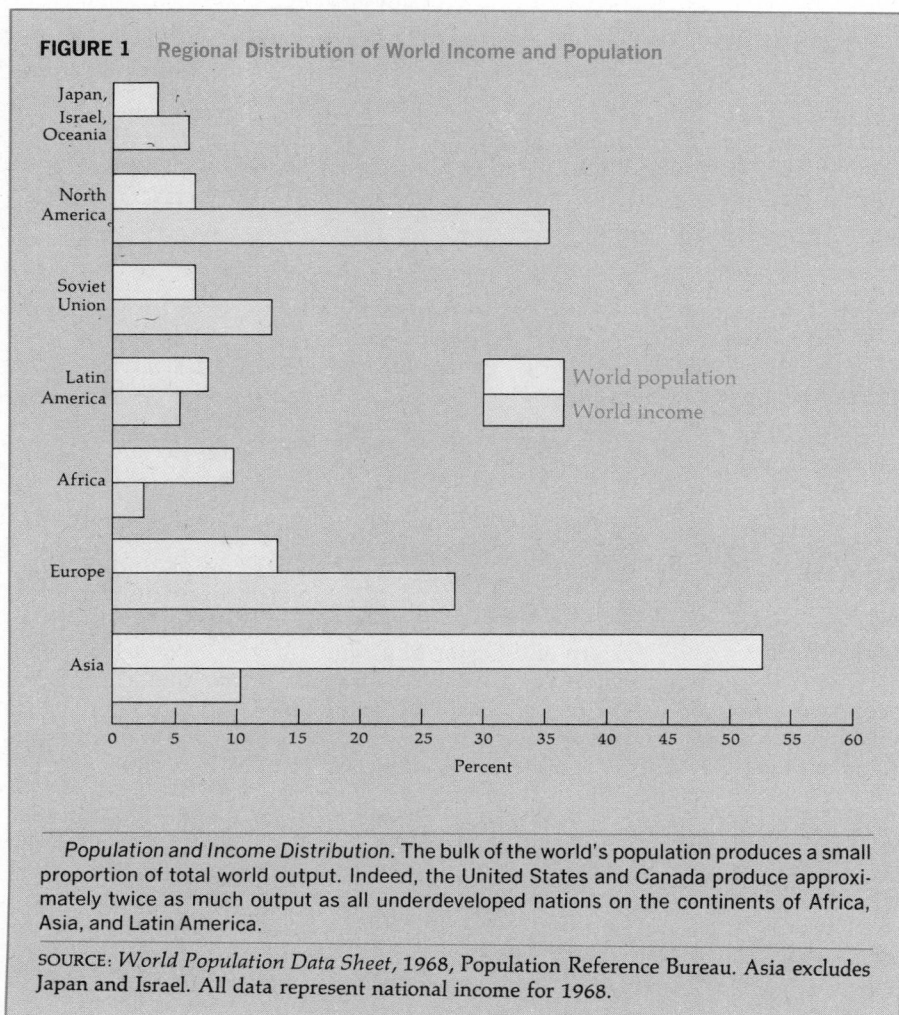

**FIGURE 1**  Regional Distribution of World Income and Population

*Population and Income Distribution.* The bulk of the world's population produces a small proportion of total world output. Indeed, the United States and Canada produce approximately twice as much output as all underdeveloped nations on the continents of Africa, Asia, and Latin America.

SOURCE: *World Population Data Sheet,* 1968, Population Reference Bureau. Asia excludes Japan and Israel. All data represent national income for 1968.

were equally distributed throughout the world, regions with 10 percent of the population would have 10 percent of the income, and so forth. Instead of a reasonably equal distribution of world output, Figure 1 shows very unequal income-distribution patterns. North America, for example, has over one-third of the world's income and slightly over 6 percent of the world's population. In contrast, Asia and Africa alone support over 60 percent of the world's population on about 12 percent of total world income. Some 30 percent of the world's population residing in North America, Europe, and Oceania, plus citizens of the Soviet Union, Japan, and Israel, earn over four-fifths of total world income, while the bulk of the world's population living in Latin America, Africa, and Asia share what remains under poverty conditions that are difficult to comprehend. Japan, Israel, the Union of South Africa, and a few nations in Latin America (e.g., Venezuela and Argentina) are the only nations on those three continents in intermediate stages of economic development. Despite the crudeness of regional comparisons resulting from such exceptions, Figure 1 reveals very clearly the fact that the underdeveloped nations of the world are largely concentrated in three regions: Asia, Africa, and Latin America. Nearly one-half of the world's income is earned by about one-tenth of the world's population, who are citizens of a few advanced economies. In contrast, the least developed economies of the world, which today house most of the population, are experiencing severe economic and social deprivation, a fact clearly revealed by per capita income comparisons.

## LOW PER CAPITA GNP

A crude indication of the strength of an economy is shown by per capita GNP in Figure 2 for some of the nations of the world. Per capita GNP of less than $300 to $400 is generally regarded as indicative of an underdeveloped nation. Although it is difficult to draw a clear dividing line, Figure 2 does indicate that a broad spectrum of economic development is characteristic of the world today. For most underdeveloped nations, per capita output is a mere fraction of the world average, which itself is less than one-fifth of the average for the United States. There is no escaping the conclusion that international poverty is a most important economic problem today. Literally billions of people in such nations as India, Peru, Pakistan, and Indonesia subsist on a per capita GNP of a few hundred dollars or less, a small fraction of the average citizen's personal wealth in North America and Western and Eastern Europe.

There is no one reliable or consistent measure of an underdeveloped economy, and per capita output is no exception. For example, per capita GNP data do not reflect nonmarket exchange, which is common in subsistence-level peasant economies. In addition, output measures for the underdeveloped countries are understated because official exchange rates may not accurately reflect differences in living standards. Moreover, statistical estimates for the least advanced nations of the world are generally crude. Still, time and time again one finds that the expected relations between per capita GNP and other social and economic indicators of a nation's economic welfare do hold up.

## SOCIOECONOMIC INDICATORS OF DEVELOPMENT

Figure 3 gives another and broader view of the facts of economic underdevelopment. Africa and Asia, for example, face an enormous literacy

**FIGURE 2** Per Capita GNP Among Selected Nations of the World[a]

| | Nation | Per capita GNP | GNP relative to U.S. |
|---|---|---|---|
| | United States | $4,121 | 100% |
| | Sweden | 3,130 | 76 |
| | Canada | 2,737 | 66 |
| | Switzerland | 2,702 | 66 |
| Highly developed | Denmark | 2,489 | 60 |
| | France | 2,399 | 58 |
| | Norway | 2,264 | 55 |
| | Australia | 2,190 | 53 |
| | West Germany | 2,154 | 52 |
| | United Kingdom | 2,071 | 50 |
| | Israel | 1,678 | 41 |
| | East Germany | 1,450 | 35 |
| | Italy | 1,358 | 33 |
| | Japan | 1,283 | 31 |
| Intermediate to partially developed | U.S.S.R. | 1,250 | 30 |
| | Venezuela | 928 | 23 |
| | Spain | 866 | 21 |
| | Poland | 850 | 21 |
| | Argentina | 668 | 16 |
| | Chile | 610 | 15 |
| | Mexico | 546 | 13 |
| | Uruguay | 525 | 13 |
| | Portugal | 513 | 12 |
| | Cuba | 380 | 9 |
| | Brazil | 359 | 9 |
| | Peru | 318 | 8 |
| | Iran | 304 | 7 |
| | Colombia | 296 | 7 |
| | Ecuador | 253 | 6 |
| | Philippines | 193 | 5 |
| | United Arab Republic | 185 | 5 |
| Underdeveloped | South Korea | 175 | 4 |
| | Thailand | 157 | 4 |
| | South Vietnam | 135 | 3 |
| | Indonesia | 120 | 3 |
| | Kenya | 120 | 3 |
| | Pakistan | 110 | 3 |
| | India | 90 | 2 |
| | Nigeria | 90 | 2 |
| | Congo | 75 | 2 |
| | Ethiopia | 68 | 2 |

*Per capita GNP.* Crude, but nonetheless indicative economic development comparisons are furnished by examination of per capita GNP for selected nations of the world.

[a] All data are in 1967 dollars. GNP data for communist countries are crude estimates because of differences in income-accounting procedures.

SOURCE: International Bank for Reconstruction and Development, *World Bank Atlas,* 1969; and Agency for International Development, *Gross National Product,* 1969.

**FIGURE 3** Indicators of Development[a]

| | Percent illiterate (percent) | Years life expectancy | Infant mortality per 1,000 | Birth rate per 1,000 | Death rate per 1,000 | Number of years to double population | Per capita national income as percent of world average |
|---|---|---|---|---|---|---|---|
| World | 39 | 53 | 87 | 34 | 14 | 35 | 100 |
| North America | 2 | 71 | 23 | 19 | 9 | 63 | 567 |
| Europe | 5 | 70 | 31 | 18 | 10 | 100 | 217 |
| U.S.S.R. | 2 | 70 | 26 | 18 | 7 | 63 | 190 |
| Oceania | 12 | 71 | 18 | 20 | 9 | 39 | 331 |
| Latin America | 34 | 60 | 66 | 40 | 10 | 24 | 70 |
| Africa | 82 | 43 | 140 | 45 | 22 | 31 | 25 |
| Asia | 54 | 50 | 49 | 39 | 17 | 32 | 26 |

*Social and Economic Indicators.* The relations between per capita national income and other measures of development are generally consistent. Illiteracy, rapid population growth, and shortened life expectancy accompany low per capita income for underdeveloped nations.

[a] Illiteracy applies only to the population over 15 years of age, population growth is based on current rates, and national income for the world averages $493.

SOURCE: Adapted from *World Population Data Sheet* (Washington, D.C.: Population Reference Bureau, 1968), and United Nations data.

problem—about three of every five persons are illiterate. As we mentioned, the people of the underdeveloped world can expect their life span to be shortened by decades. According to Figure 3, 45 years is not an unusual average lifetime in an underdeveloped region. Death rates and infant mortality rates are several times higher than those experienced by more developed regions. However, at current rates of population growth, an underdeveloped nation can expect its population to triple or quadruple in the next 100 years, a fact that will further contribute to per capita income disparities. Generally speaking, the population of Asia, Africa, and Latin America is growing two or three times more rapidly than it is in developed nations.

THE MEANING OF UNDERDEVELOPMENT

The underdeveloped nations are not completely backward, as some might think. Modern cities, plants, and educational complexes may appear on occasion, and rural misery contrasts with urban elegance, as can be seen in the state of Sao Paulo, Brazil. Underdeveloped economies are not uniformly stagnant, densely populated, or short of food and natural resources, but often some or all of these problems do prevail. Among the common symptoms of underdevelopment are a large portion of workers (frequently as many as seven or eight of every ten) engaged in subsistence and low-productivity farming, and heavy reliance on human and animal power as the basis for production. People in underdeveloped nations have a meager chance for an education, and the opportunity for improvement in their economic future is bleak. There may be several thousand persons for each physician instead of the 700 to 800 persons per physician common in Western Europe and North America, and people subsist on a nutritive food intake per person that is two-thirds (or less) as much as that of their affluent neighbors abroad.

Underdeveloped nations vary dramatically, but the common symptom is poverty for the masses. Even though we cannot have much faith in an arbitrary per capita income measure of development and underdevelopment, underdevelopment is unmistakable when encountered. The one-room shacks, huts, and shanty towns in Peru; the bloated stomachs of children in remote Indonesian villages; and women rummaging in garbage and beggars dying in the streets of Calcutta are surely symptomatic of underdevelopment—an international economic disease of scandalous proportions.

Just how have the people of the underdeveloped nations responded to their station in life? Although many millions live in ignorance and apathy, there is an increasing awareness of the almost unimaginable affluence of other nations. Aspirations for a higher living standard have risen dramatically in underdeveloped nations while nationalism has intensified, in part because advances in transportation and communication systems have shrunk the world. At the same time, the frustration and hostility of the world's poor have intensified. As the years have worn on and underdeveloped nations have failed to realize improvements in their standards of living relative to developed nations, worldwide social and political unrest has escalated. Unfortunately, breaking the international poverty barrier is no simple task.

## The Poverty Cycle

The record of both the long-term and recent past sheds some light on the magnitude of the underdevelopment problem. In addition, the record seems to confirm the decades-old prophecy of Thomas Malthus that population growth would exceed the world's ability to feed its people. If living conditions in underdeveloped countries are to improve, their economies must experience more rapid growth in productive capacity than has been realized previously. Closing the per capita income gap between rich and poor economies requires that underdeveloped nations grow faster than developed nations. Just how dismal the recent growth record is can be seen by examining Figure 4, which summarizes percentage changes in per capita GNP since 1960. The growth "gap" shown in the figure is reasonably typical of patterns of economic development during the last quarter of a century. Although total GNP for developed and underdeveloped nations grew at roughly comparable rates in the 1960s, Figure 4 indicates that *per capita* GNP grew more slowly in the underdeveloped countries. Per capita output in these nations has generally grown two-thirds as fast as it has in developed nations. One culprit (on the surface, at least) is the rapid rate of population growth in the underdeveloped nations of the world. Many underdeveloped nations fail to generate economic growth rates even close to these levels, and a growth gap comparable to that shown in Figure 4 has persisted in some nations for a century or more.

There is no simple explanation for such patterns of underdevelopment, nor does the past necessarily represent a good indication of future trends. Still, the message of Figure 4 is ominous, to say the least. So many ingredi-

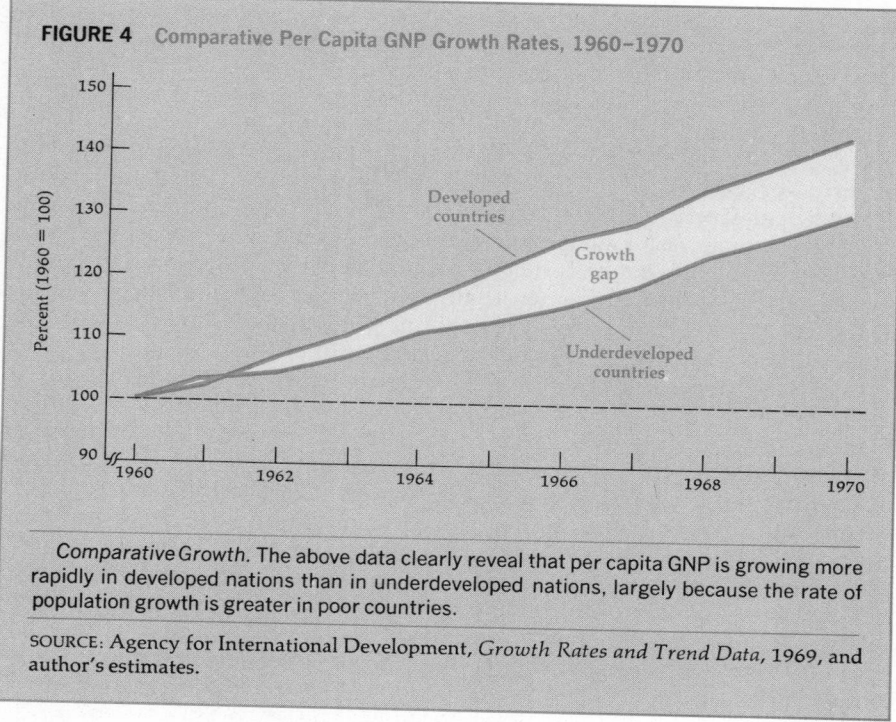

**FIGURE 4**  Comparative Per Capita GNP Growth Rates, 1960–1970

*Comparative Growth.* The above data clearly reveal that per capita GNP is growing more rapidly in developed nations than in underdeveloped nations, largely because the rate of population growth is greater in poor countries.

SOURCE: Agency for International Development, *Growth Rates and Trend Data*, 1969, and author's estimates.

ents to economic growth are lacking, and the interrelations among the elements that induce growth and development are so complex, that observers like Gunnar Myrdal have suggested that poverty simply begets perpetual poverty. It appears that past poverty has a long history of anchoring the present and future of poor people and nations. This vicious circle of enslavement to subsistence and economic stagnation hinges on low rates of capital formation, rapid population growth, tradition-bound behavior, and a host of other impediments to progress. Economists like W. W. Rostow talk of the need for a growth "take-off"—a stage of economic activity in which a nation mobilizes and energizes its resource base. But where does the "big push" come from and how is it accomplished? As we noted in our earlier discussion of the development of the United States (Chapter 13), the role of capital goods in the economic development process is certainly crucial. One major difficulty, however, is that economic development demands a shift from consuming to saving and investing, an exceedingly onerous task for a nation whose population is eking out a minimal existence at the outset. It is indeed possible for the poor to be poor because they are poor—they are unable to consume less today in order to invest in output for the future. Thus, it is possible for nations to remain trapped in a poverty cycle.

## The Rich and the Poor Forever?

Growth *rates* tell a very important story, but perhaps the cruelest twist of fate is the low per capita income levels from which underdeveloped nations start. The point is simply that a 2 percent growth rate applied to a per capita GNP of $2,000 generates a $40 increase in one year, but it results in only a $6 increase when applied to a nation with a per capita GNP of $300. Clearly, a low income base and a sluggish growth rate combine to perpetuate poverty.

Consider an example: Today the per capita income gap between Peru and West Germany is in the neighborhood of $1,700 per person. If per capita GNP in both nations grows 1 percent per year, 100 years from now Peru could raise per capita GNP from $318 to $870. At the same time, West Germany would be producing nearly $6,000 per person, thus widening the absolute output gap from $1,700 to some $5,000 in one century. Thus, the gap between rich and poor could widen enormously in the future, particularly if we consider the even more affluent American economy. When an underdeveloped nation doubles its level of GNP from $300 to $600 per capita, a measure of progress has been made. However, underdeveloped nations aware of their low levels of living are also aware of the absolute differences between rich and poor nations.

Suppose we ignore current and past rates of growth in per capita GNP, which reveal that developed nations are growing as much as one-half again as rapidly as the poor nations. Instead, let us optimistically assume in Figure 5 that the least developed nations, with a per capita GNP of $300, grow at the rate of 2 percent per year, or *twice as fast* as more advanced nations, whose per capita GNP is assumed to grow 1 percent annually from a base of $2,000. On one hand, the relative per capita disparities will diminish. However, the data in Figure 5 indicate that the output gap between rich and poor will not disappear for some two centuries! In short,

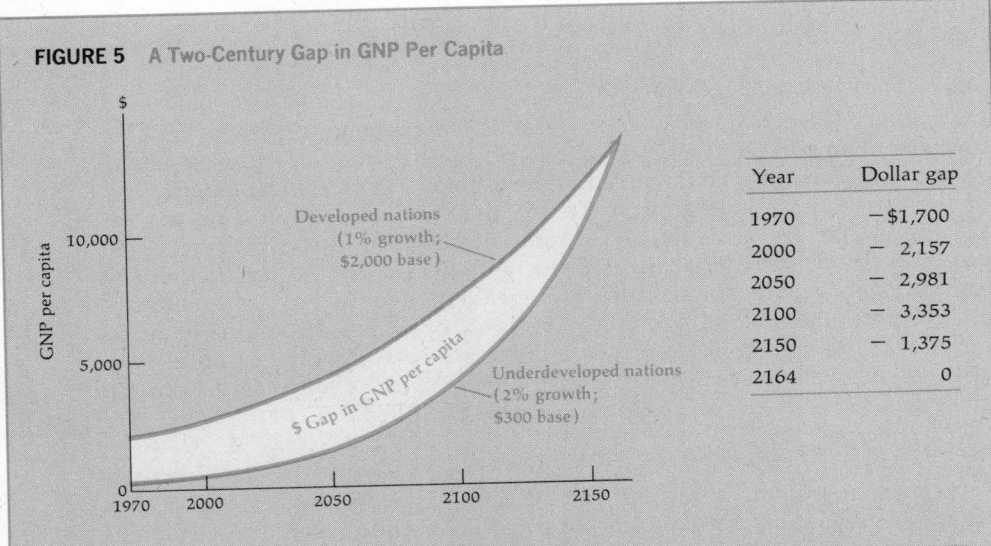

**FIGURE 5**   A Two-Century Gap in GNP Per Capita

| Year | Dollar gap |
|------|-----------|
| 1970 | − $1,700 |
| 2000 | − 2,157 |
| 2050 | − 2,981 |
| 2100 | − 3,353 |
| 2150 | − 1,375 |
| 2164 | 0 |

The "Haves and Have Nots." Even if underdeveloped nations experience a 2 percent growth rate and the developed nations experience a 1 percent growth rate in per capita income over the next 100 years, the absolute size of the income gap will widen making equal levels of livings some two centuries away.

even if economic growth occurs in a *most* unlikely fashion, the absolute international differences between rich and poor promises to double in the next century. Moreover, if advanced and underdeveloped nations alike do not mobilize quickly and forcefully, the underdeveloped world will do very well to grow at rates *equal* to those of the advanced nations, and all of mankind will be poorer for that.

## B. OBSTACLES TO ECONOMIC DEVELOPMENT

Just as there is no single social or economic indicator that fully defines an underdeveloped economy, neither is there any one factor responsible for economic backwardness. The barriers to development encountered by different nations vary widely. While one underdeveloped nation may have abundant natural resources and a severe population problem, another may lack natural resources. However, there are several common obstacles to development, some or all of which may apply to a given nation. Future economic growth depends on a nation's success in developing and applying policies designed to overcome these barriers.

Underdeveloped nations must be especially concerned with increasing the capacity of their productive resources and using these resources efficiently. In a general sense, economic development depends upon: (*a*) the resource base (natural, capital, and human resources); (*b*) the institutional environment; and (*c*) technology, which influences resource utilization and allocation. Even though the critical factors in the economic development process fit generally within our threefold classification of growth elements (see Chapter 13), an assessment of the obstacles to economic development must be more specific. Our task here is to identify the chief reasons why nations are underdeveloped. Clearly we are faced with a special case of the process of economic growth.

### Capital Formation and Technological Change

Economists have, for very good reasons, long emphasized the lack of investment in capital resources as one obstacle to economic development. Saving and investing from current consumption is one central determinant of the rate of economic growth. Today, the more rapidly growing nations are those that are achieving high rates of capital formation. The output produced by $1 of capital investment, as reflected by the productivity of capital (the output/capital ratio) is dependent upon a host of qualitative and vaguely understood growth factors, all of which are mutually interdependent. Poor nations do not have a large stock of capital resources relative to labor, however, and because *technological change is very often embodied in capital resources*, progress may be stifled.

### NET INVESTMENT AND CAPITAL FORMATION

Any level of output or income can be used, as we know, in one of two ways: A population can consume or it can save and invest. The consumption-goods sector uses resources to produce for current sustenance, and the capital-goods sector uses resources to produce physical capital for indirect consumption and future production.

But what is investment, other than the obvious "absence of consumption"? A narrow, but perfectly valid, view regards net investment as the accumulation of physical-capital goods such as shovels, machines, and factories—the formation of a stock of *physical-capital resources*. Physical-capital formation is just as characteristic of primitive societies, in which equipment such as hoes and shovels are produced, as it is of more modern economies which produce computers, machine-tool lathes, and diesel trucks. The more complex and advanced economy, however, devotes a good deal of investment to physical capital that is capable of reproducing itself. Thus, for example, machine-tool industries are useful in producing physical-capital as well as consumption goods. Without physical-capital resources, a society would revert to a peasant agrarian economy unable to transfer human resources out of subsistence farming. Moreover, in the absence of investment, it would be virtually impossible to transform resources into output efficiently using technological processes which now dominate such activities as farming, building boats, or mining—all of which are simple handicraft industries in certain nations. Net physical-capital formation allows a society to perform more tasks more efficiently with man-made aids to production. Thus, by adding to the quantity and quality of its capital resources through investment, a nation can enhance its growth potential. For this reason, investment represents a focal point in the study of economic development.

Economists also focus on investment as an ingredient of growth because a growing society must devote substantial amounts of resources to the elements that work together to further growth. A portion of a nation's resources are "invested" in educating human resources and human capital is formed. Vast amounts of resources may also be invested in scientific research and development efforts to find new ways of improving life through technological change. Investment also reclaims once-deteriorated natural resources such as eroded and barren soil or depleted fisheries, and aids in the discovery of new resources such as timber, oil, or minerals—a fact Queen Isabella and Columbus well knew. Furthermore, investment in *social-overhead capital*—communication and transportation systems, schools, and medical clinics—also facilitates economic development.[2]

*The crucial point is this:* Investment (whether in physical capital, human capital, research and technical change, exploration for natural resources, or the improvement of institutions) is a key requirement in the enlargement of a nation's productive capacity. This does not mean, of course, that investment is *the cause* of economic growth; rather, investment is one of several crucial *elements* in the growth process.

Low rates of saving and investment and rapid population growth are major dimensions to the economic ailment called "underdevelopment," and the way in which these factors interact is vital to understanding the problem. Before we discuss the many other interrelated variables that act as obstacles to economic development, it is worthwhile to see how investment, the output/capital ratio, and population growth interact to help determine growth in per capita income.

[2] Consuming the entire proceeds of current output simply prohibits using resources for schools, shovels, or what have you. Of course, much of what we have regarded as investment "broadly defined" is in part consumption, but that is also true of physical-capital resources such as buildings. The capital-consumption breakdown of investment is an academic matter which we can ignore for now.

*Rate of Saving and Investment*   Capital resources are one ingredient frequently lacking in underdeveloped nations because the rate of domestic saving and investment is low, despite foreign trade and grant and loan assistance from other nations and international agencies. Social-overhead capital facilities such as roads, schools, and dams for harnessing power or irrigating land are in short supply, and even the simplest farming implements as one form of private capital are frequently lacking. The problem is simply this: A nation currently living at subsistence levels faces grave problems in postponing current consumption to save and invest in much-needed capital resources.

*The Output/Capital Ratio*   The dollars of GNP created by new capital resources ($K$) is a crude reflection of the productivity of capital; in fact, it is a capsule summary of how the forces contributing to economic growth such as human and natural resources and technological change interact to create higher levels of output. Domestic saving and funds invested from abroad create new capital which engineers growth and development.

Investing in different types of capital facilities—an irrigation dam, a steel mill, or schools—will increase output in varying amounts, depending on the productivity of capital resources. With an output/capital ratio of $GNP/K = \$1/\$3$, which is a fairly typical average, it takes $3 of capital resources to increase GNP by $1. Thus, it is important to channel scarce investment funds into those projects in which capital is most productive. Suppose, for example, that some amount of new investment can be channeled into either steel mills or agricultural seeds and implements. Further assume that the output/capital ratio of a steel mill is $GNP/K = \$1/\$4$, while investment in agricultural implements yields an output/capital ratio of $GNP/K = \$1/\$2$. It appears, in this instance, that the allocation of capital resources should favor agriculture, since such agricultural capital is considerably more "productive"—it takes $2 of investment in agriculture to produce $1 of new output, but $4 of investment in steel mills to produce $1 of new output.[3]

*Population Growth*   An expanding population is often a negative element in underdeveloped nations because, if living standards are to improve, total output must grow faster than population. Remember that when *both* total GNP and population grow 5 percent per year, per capita GNP remains unchanged. Thus, it is possible for an increase in output to be absorbed in maintaining new members of the population at the old standard of living.

THE POPULATION-CAPITAL ACCUMULATION DILEMMA

Given these growth factors, what are the development prospects for poor countries? Suppose that a nation saves and invests $10 of every $100 of income (or 10 percent of current output), and further assume that each $3 of capital increases output by $1 (the output/capital ratio is 1/3). Under these conditions, ten dollars of investment will add $3.3 of new GNP to a $100 income base: that is, $\$10 \times \frac{1}{3} = \$3.3$, or 10 percent $\times$ 1/3 = a 3.3 percent annual growth in total GNP.[4]

[3] The resource-allocation problem is a crucial one which will receive more attention in our later discussion of development policy.

[4] The output/capital ratio as a measure of GNP capacity created by increments of

That is, the capacity rate of growth equals the portion of income saved and invested *times* the output/capital ratio as described in Chapter 13. The underdeveloped nations, plagued as they are by bare subsistence, are victims of a low *absolute* level of saving and investment because of low total GNP. In addition, they generally save and invest a smaller portion of total income than the developed nations. Moreover, as we have noted, these nations are plagued by rapid population growth which stifles growth in per capita income. Consider an example.

Suppose developed nations invest at the rate of 12 percent of current output, population growth is 1 percent per year, and the output/capital ratio is held constant at $GNP/K = 1/3$. Each $12 of investment yields $4 of new GNP; total output grows by $4/$100, or 4 percent; and output per capita grows 3 percent per year (4% − 1% population growth). In some underdeveloped nations, the rate of saving and investment is one-half or two-thirds that of advanced and growing economies—more like 6 percent of GNP is saved and invested, rather than the 10 or 12 percent invested in advanced economies. With an output/capital ratio of 1/3, total GNP will expand about 2 percent per year in the underdeveloped nation as each $6 of investment creates $2 of GNP. Now consider the impact of population growth. Growth in total GNP of 2 percent annually may be just about enough to maintain the already bare subsistence level of per capita income if population also grows 2 percent each year. Instead of doubling levels of living every generation, as would occur at a 3 percent growth rate in per capita income, the economy remains almost stagnant. This is just what has happened to *most* people and nations for the last several centuries. Even if GNP grows 3.5 percent annually and population expands 2.5 percent per year (a not uncommon rate of population expansion for Latin America, Africa, and Asia), per capita output increases by only 1 percent per year. At that rate it would require one and one-half centuries to push $300 of per capita income up to $1,200.

## CAPITAL AND THE EMBODIMENT OF TECHNOLOGY

Advances in technology known and used for decades in developed nations frequently can be adopted only if a nation is capable of acquiring new and more productive capital goods. Agricultural mechanization, transportation systems, food and commodity processing, and the exploitation of mineral resources are all desperately needed in subsistence economies. But technological methods that require large amounts of capital in the production process must be forfeited in favor of projects requiring little or no additional investment to capture modern technology. Such projects make more intensive use of the vast amount of underutilized rural labor available and

---

investment is $GNP/K = \$1/\$3$, and the rate of saving to output is $S/GNP = \$10/\$100$. Growth in total GNP is:

$$\%\Delta GNP = S/GNP \times GNP/K$$
$$= \$10/\$100 \times \$1/\$3$$
$$= 10\% \times 1/3$$
$$= 3.3\%$$

This assumes, of course, that a constant marginal propensity to save for a nation and a constant output/capital ratio that does not change as investment and capital formation takes place.

thereby increase the productivity of capital. Modern crop rotation, for example, requires little or no capital. Similarly, improved seed strains, fertilizers adapted to a nation's climate, or the use of simple tools and implements such as metal plows can replace an old technology and economize on the use of capital. There are limits, however, to the extent to which current low levels of investment can more intensively use labor by adopting capital-saving technologies. Even though eradication of certain inefficiencies is possible, contemporary technological processes often require heavy investment in capital equipment.

Two additional features of capital and technology are important:

1. Capital formation is cumulative. Once a nation embarks upon investment and the accumulation of capital resources, capital formation and technological improvements accumulate. Productivity and incomes rise and, if population growth lags behind growth in output, capital formation from domestic saving is increasingly possible without restricting per capita consumption.

2. Technology can be imitated. Today, the innovations known and used throughout the developed world represent a backlog of potential progress for the underdeveloped nations. Germany, the United States, Russia, and Japan are good examples of nations that have practiced technological imitation at one time or another in the past, and many of the underdeveloped nations are in a position to do so today. However, capital formation is a prerequisite for imitation, and that obstacle is not easily overcome by poor nations for several reasons.

### BARRIERS TO DOMESTIC CAPITAL FORMATION

In an underdeveloped nation, capital formation may originate from internal or external sources. Internal capital accumulation requires that a nation allocate resources to future goods by saving and investing from what otherwise would be current consumption. Prospects for domestic saving in underdeveloped countries are often limited, as we have seen. Then, too, saving is difficult when income is unequally distributed, as it is in many poorer countries. Wealthy landowners as well as the political and industrial elite with large saving potentials often hoard property or precious metals instead of investing. They may also spend vast sums for a standard of luxury which contrasts sharply to the poverty of the masses. The wealthy often invest their savings abroad where safety and stability are more assured, and this is one reason that social and political factors have an important bearing on a nation's prospects for economic development. Yet another important impediment to domestic capital formation is the instability of and frequent lack of faith in domestic banking institutions and government. When the value of a domestic currency or a monetary system is questioned, funds are quickly channeled abroad or into assets such as property or gold instead of risky capital equipment. In essence, domestic capital formation is meager because both incentives and opportunities to invest are poor.

### FOREIGN SOURCES OF CAPITAL

Underdeveloped nations also rely on capital from abroad. Foreign capital accounted for much of the progress of the United States during its first century of development. In recent years, increased grants and loans from the governments of more highly developed nations and international agencies, as well as private capital flows to underdeveloped nations, have aided the capital-formation process. However, the United Nations estimates that total funds annually made available to *all* underdeveloped nations are less than one-fifth of gross domestic investment in America alone. In addition, foreign sources of capital are not very stable, nor are they entirely acceptable to poor nations.

Underdeveloped nations often impose restrictions on capital from abroad to avoid foreign control and well-remembered colonial exploitation. Pre-World War I imperialism brought advantages and disadvantages to underdeveloped regions of the world, and one of the decided disadvantages was the imbalanced economy created in some countries. Foreign capital inflows conflict with the spirit of nationalism so prevalent in the underdeveloped world today, partially because foreign capital moves into the most profitable economic activities, a situation which may not favor the economic independence and future growth of an underdeveloped nation. When a nation needs to diversify its economy and develop stronger domestic markets, foreign capital will not be beneficial if the lopsided economic base common to past imperialism is perpetuated.

The risks associated with political and social instability, as well as the not infrequent threat of nationalization, discourage investment by foreigners. Other barriers to foreign investment are the absence of developed markets and the lack of the leadership and organization skills common to the risk-taking, entrepreneurial middle class found in developed nations. Without a class able to mobilize and administer the use of capital resources, an element vital to the process of economic development is missing.

*To summarize:* Capital formation and technological improvements that are vital to economic growth are a serious problem in the poorer countries of the world. Subsistence consumption and many other barriers to domestic and foreign investment retard capital formation in underdeveloped nations. Potential technological improvements are thus passed up because of the shortage of capital. Since the rate of saving and capital formation help determine growth in total GNP, impediments to capital formation are indeed serious.

## Human Resources

The human-resource problems faced by underdeveloped nations today include runaway population expansion, underinvestment in human resources, and labor subject to widespread underemployment. Reasonably good information is available concerning population growth trends in the developed and underdeveloped segments of the world, and the evidence is less than comforting to most experts. Let us see why.

### POPULATION EXPLOSION: FACT OR FICTION?

There is not much doubt about the population problem in the have-not nations. Figure 6 shows that extremely rapid rates of population growth have occurred only in comparatively recent times. At current growth rates and with a current population approaching 4 billion persons, the number of people on this planet will double in less than one-half a century. As the figure clearly shows, doubling the world's population was a centuries-long process until very recently. Should these estimates of population growth materialize, economic development and growth in per capita income

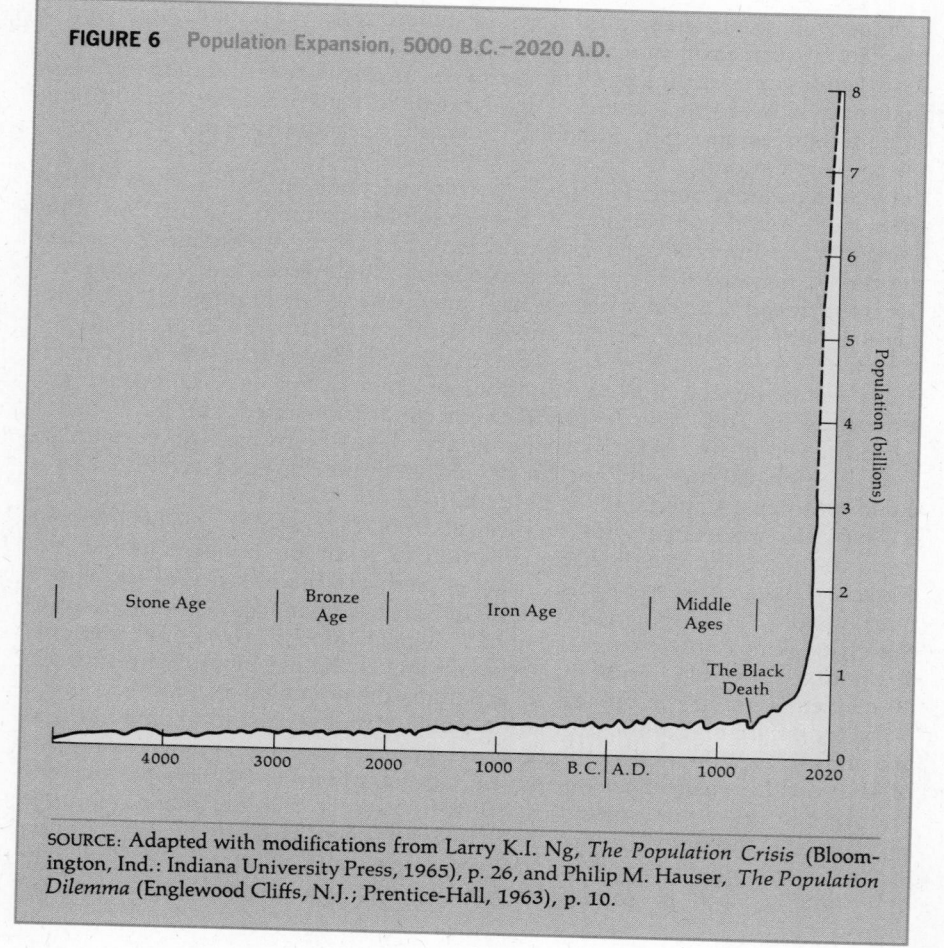

**FIGURE 6** Population Expansion, 5000 B.C.—2020 A.D.

Stone Age | Bronze Age | Iron Age | Middle Ages

The Black Death

Population (billions)

4000    3000    2000    1000    B.C. | A.D.    1000    2020

SOURCE: Adapted with modifications from Larry K.I. Ng, *The Population Crisis* (Bloomington, Ind.: Indiana University Press, 1965), p. 26, and Philip M. Hauser, *The Population Dilemma* (Englewood Cliffs, N.J.; Prentice-Hall, 1963), p. 10.

are not promising. Simply finding productive employment today is a dream for hundreds of millions of persons in the labor force of underdeveloped nations. We need hardly mention the enormous difficulties that could arise half a century hence for another 4 billion persons. Increasing income more rapidly than the population in order to raise the per capita level of living may turn out to be no mean task; indeed, how to properly feed billions more people is disturbing to many authorities. With some 1.5 billion persons estimated by the United Nations to be undernourished *today*, a subsistence problem of crisis proportions may be around the corner, if it is not already upon us. However one appraises the population-food race of the next few decades, renown authorities like Gunnar Myrdal and the ex-president of the World Bank, Eugene Black, bluntly warn of an unthinkable, but menacing calamity. To many, an optimistic view does not project growth, but simply the capability of underdeveloped nations to subsist at present levels. Vast numbers of persons will be affected dramatically by our success or failure in meeting this challenge.

Much of the concern for population expansion is a reflection of where vast numbers of people are located. Although Figure 7 is only an approximate identification of the developed and underdeveloped regions of the world, it nonetheless indicates that the number *and* proportion of persons living in underdeveloped regions (Africa, Asia, and Latin America) have increased and will increase in the future. While three out of five persons lived in underdeveloped nations in 1900, it is estimated that four out of five, or some 5.5 billion persons, will live in these nations by the year 2000. Whether real economic progress, subsistence at today's level of income, or a social catastrophe is the future for the world's poor depends very much upon overcoming a variety of barriers to economic development, including simply having too many mouths to feed.

## UNDERINVESTMENT IN HUMAN RESOURCES

Overpopulation, low per capita incomes, and a paucity of social-overhead capital resources such as schools and hospitals are interrelated features that contribute to the low *quality* of human resources in underdeveloped nations. Just as modernizing machinery and plants requires the diversion of resources from end uses such as consumption to investment, so does improvement in the quality of human resources require investment in man, or human-capital formation. Inadequate sanitation, the absence of sufficient medical care, illiteracy and poor education, and inadequate or nonexistent training facilities all characterize the poor nations of the world. Poor diets, including a lack of sufficient protein that can lead to brain damage, compound the problem of the quality of human resources.

In recent years, vast reductions in death rates have augmented the quantity of human resources, but comparatively short life spans and extremely low levels of quality and productivity remain typical. As a result of inade-

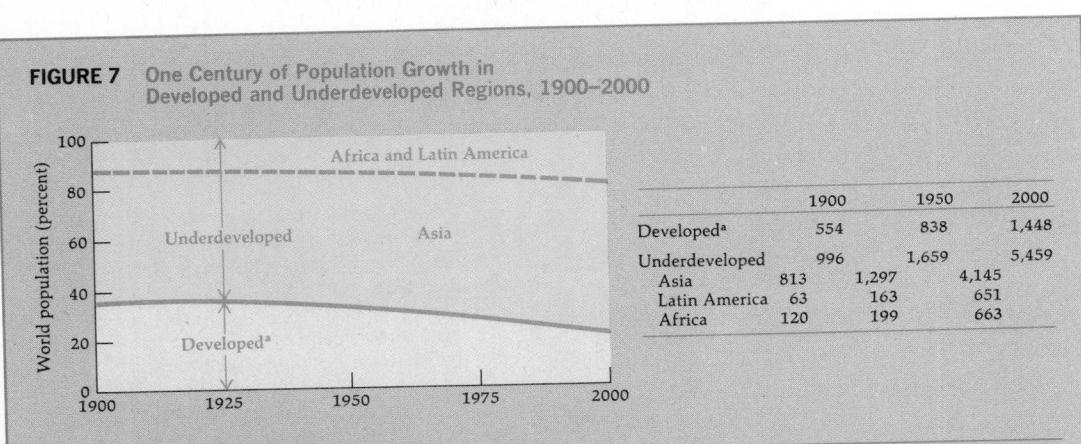

**FIGURE 7**  One Century of Population Growth in Developed and Underdeveloped Regions, 1900–2000

|  | 1900 | 1950 | 2000 |
|---|---|---|---|
| Developed[a] | 554 | 838 | 1,448 |
| Underdeveloped | 996 | 1,659 | 5,459 |
| Asia | 813 | 1,297 | 4,145 |
| Latin America | 63 | 163 | 651 |
| Africa | 120 | 199 | 663 |

*Future Population Changes.* The underdeveloped countries of the world are expected to contain an ever larger proportion of the world's population in the next 25 years.

[a] In millions of people: Includes North America, U.S.S.R., Europe, Japan, and Oceania. The region designated as Underdeveloped Asia—is adjusted for U.S.S.R. and Japan categorization.

SOURCE: Benjamin Higgins, *Economic Development* (New York: W. W. Norton, Inc., 1968), p. 39.

quate investment in education and training, illiteracy and cultural fetishes continue to hinder both the use of technological improvements and the mobility of labor. Underinvestment in education also helps account for the lack of an entrepreneurial middle class capable of fully developing business activities. Finally, the problem of human-resource quality also contributes to a labor force subject to underemployment in a primitive agricultural sector.

## THE LESSONS OF HISTORY: DIMINISHING RETURNS

We first learned in Chapter 13 that the principle of diminishing returns describes a condition in which total output increases less and less rapidly as a variable resource is added to other factors of production which are fixed in supply. Even though the principle of diminishing returns applies to all nations, underdeveloped countries are saddled with the special limitation of being unable to offset diminishing returns. The adoption of technological changes and qualitative improvements in their resource bases have not contributed to rising per capita output to the degree that has occurred in developed nations. Diminishing returns arising from relatively fixed supplies of arable land and scarce capital resources, in conjunction with a burgeoning population and labor force, help explain low per capita output.

Assuming that the population and labor force grow at equal rates, Figure 8 illustrates the diminishing-returns and population-explosion dilemma, causing the labor/land ratio to rise. With a growing labor force already intensively using fixed land resources, total product (TP) increases at a decreasing rate in the tradition of Malthus and Ricardo. As labor increases, underdeveloped nations have tended to move on a relatively constant total-product curve like TP. Of course, we are assuming that other growth elements (e.g., technological improvement) are absent, which is an oversimplification. However, improvements in other growth factors have not been sufficient in underdeveloped nations to allow per capita output to

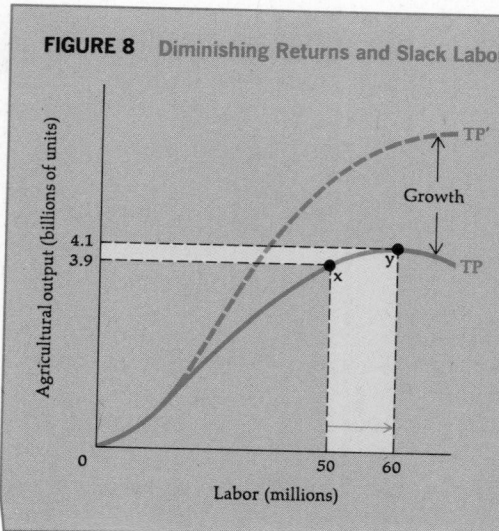

**FIGURE 8**    Diminishing Returns and Slack Labor

*Slack Labor.* Because of diminishing returns associated with intensive use of land, slow rates of growth in capital, and little technological change, labor increases more rapidly than output, causing per capita output to stagnate. While total output rises along the expansion or growth path denoted by points *x* and *y*, low productivity (slack) labor is growing more rapidly. In this instance, the marginal product (additional output) created by 10 million additional workers is nearly zero (as is the case for true "surplus" labor).

grow at rates comparable to growth in most developed nations. Although the assumption of a constant *TP* schedule oversimplifies the problem, it is indicative of underdevelopment. The forces which could cause growth and shift a production schedule to *TP'* have not been very active in underdeveloped nations.

If all growth elements except the supply of labor are held constant, Figure 8 shows how a nation might use less labor (e.g., 50 million instead of 60 million) with very little decrease in total product.[5] This can occur because the relatively large labor force is intensively applied to fixed factors; that is, the productivity or additional output of labor is low, a situation that has enticed some experts to speak of "slack" (low-productivity) labor. *If labor could be released for more productive purposes, the 10 million workers now trapped in subsistence farming might well enhance development prospects.* Transferring underutilized human resources engaged in subsistence farming to the production of social-overhead capital or to the more modern industrialized sector could aid in stepping up the pace of growth and development. Unfortunately, more efficient use of slack labor is not a simple task.[6]

The most vicious, self-perpetuating circle in the underdeveloped world may well be the barriers to the transfer of slack labor to the industrial sector, which lacks capital and does not offer adequate job opportunities. Another relatively scarce resource, however, is rural land, which is frequently operated with an antiquated technology and on too small a scale. Slack rural labor is locked into farming without modern technology. Underemployed labor is often unable to transfer into productive employment in sectors which lack capital resources. Inadequate investment in capital and human resources has resulted in the perpetuation of the cycle of underdevelopment in which rural labor cannot obtain more productive employment in industry.

### Natural Resources

The quality, quantity, and utilization of natural resources also contribute to the low productivity in the agricultural sector which is so typical of many underdeveloped nations.

### THE STOCK OF NATURAL RESOURCES

In several underdeveloped countries, a sparse natural-resource base is a constraint to future economic progress. Without sufficient arable land, minerals, timber resources, or reasonable climatic conditions, hopes for future growth and development are diminished. However, it is important to recognize that many highly developed nations also have an extremely poor natural-resource base in relation to population size. Japan and Western

---

[5] The "marginal product" of the last 10 million workers is close to zero (0.2 billion units of output) in Figure 8.

[6] Some authorities speak of "surplus" (zero marginal product) labor. While surplus labor is a subject of heated debate among students of development economics, it is clear to most observers that much of the manpower in underdeveloped nations is low-productivity labor because of relatively fixed supplies of productive land and capital resources. Whether labor is "slack" or "surplus," low productivity and the spectre of diminishing returns are too frequently a reality.

European nations such as the Netherlands are adversely affected in this sense and, in contrast, many of the African and South American nations ranking low on the economic development scale are abundantly endowed with natural resources. Although one cannot attribute failure to develop to scarce natural resources alone, geography and climate do shape economic progress. Poor natural resources are not nearly as amenable to corrective social and economic policies as are some of the other obstacles to development.

A nation's natural-resource base is affected by conservation and technological progress. Harvesting mineral or timber resources without due regard for soil erosion, water pollution, and timber depletion may strip a nation of a promising future in a few short decades. New discoveries and technological changes can enhance the resource base of an underdeveloped nation, as the discovery of oil in Libya suggests. However, changes in technology are also an ever-present threat to the value of resources and the economic prospects of underdeveloped nations—many of which rely upon one or a few minerals or crops. Technological change has reduced demand and exerted downward price pressures on rubber and silk, once highly prized natural resources, and volatile world market prices for basic commodities and minerals also threaten the stability of many underdeveloped economies.

The important point is that the future progress of nations now in formative stages of economic development may be limited by the inadequacies of their natural resources. These inadequacies can be overcome to some degree, but candor demands that we recognize that the more amply endowed with natural resources an underdeveloped nation is, the brighter are its prospects for future development. The natural-resource base complements or hinders future economic development, but a strong natural-resource base does not assure a nation of future development.

## LAND REFORM

Land reform is of utmost importance in many underdeveloped nations, which often concentrate a large population on relatively small and fixed quantities of arable land. At one extreme, century-old traditions have led to a few extremely small parcels of land being held by a large number of peasant farmers. Over the centuries, family plots have been passed on to successive generations, resulting in the emergence of an increasingly fragmented agrarian economy. Agricultural production is thus conducted on a scale that is much too small to allow efficient use of resources and the modern production methods that today's agricultural technology can provide.

Several Western European nations such as Britain overcame the problem of land fragmentation centuries ago, whereas the Soviet Union, for example, collectivized agriculture only five decades ago. At the other extreme, some underdeveloped nations are characterized by excessive concentrations of land in the hands of an elite class which is often far removed from agricultural production. Not infrequently, vast landed estates are utilized for prestigious crops instead of for priority farming. Thus, one can find in Argentina estates of several thousand acres used for ranching which could be much more productive in raising agricultural crops that would also use more rural labor. Such vast holdings may be too large to permit efficient operation and effective control. The landless peasant masses till the soil with little incentive to innovate and to work to capacity on behalf of the wealthy landholder.

If land reform were a reality, and peasants became landowners, strengthened attachments to democracy and government would enhance the viability of underdeveloped nations. Purposeful and forceful pursuit of land-reform policies could lead to enormous improvements in agricultural productivity and vastly improved incentive systems. Unfortunately, the economic need for land reforms frequently runs afoul of vested political landowning interests, which often control the government. Progress on this front has been extremely modest, and the agricultural sector has remained a bottleneck to development in hundreds of nations.

### The Cultural and Institutional Environment

Traditions and customs which stifle initiative, diminish the integrity of business and government, and retard the development of a risk-taking entrepreneurial class present enormous problems in an underdeveloped country. Individuals and societies must want change badly enough to alter the behavior patterns that choke off growth. In some societies, business affairs are dominated by social class distinctions, favoritism based on past associations, or family ties that take precedence over individual performance. The culture of work, based upon individual incentive and reward, characterizes nearly all highly developed nations today; yet, in many underdeveloped nations, incentive and reward are not customarily accepted behavior patterns. Indeed, in some of the more primitive nations, manual labor is not considered a fitting task for men or educated persons. In many underdeveloped nations, the bulk of the population is illiterate and often apathetic, seeing little potential advantage to be gained from working harder or further commercializing their environment. In many nations not only are governments unstable; they also may be prone to corruption in public and commercial affairs. Business leaders and owners not infrequently spend time and money attempting to influence governmental authorities in order to secure favors. Primitive tax systems and sporadic compliance with tax laws are also frequently characteristic of underdeveloped nations. Weak governments dominated by the elite and economically powerful sometimes control a nation's productive resources. Their interest too often is in preserving the prevailing traditions in order to protect the privileges of the powerful few. Thus, economic and social change that threatens the status quo may be blocked.

Remedying the inertia in such an environment requires sociocultural changes that alter both institutions and behavior. Today economists such as John Kenneth Galbraith, Benjamin Higgens, Sir Arthur Lewis, and Everett Hagen have joined the camp of those who stress cultural and institutional problems in an interdisciplinary approach to economic development.

Not all students of the subject agree with Max Weber's inference that private incentive and initiative plus an orderly commercial, legal, and governmental system are prerequisites to economic development.[7] Still, all of

---

[7] See Max Weber, *The Protestant Ethic and the Spirit of Capitalism* (New York: Charles Scribner's Sons, 1930).

these features are characteristic of the more highly developed nations today. Honest and efficient administration of a tax system is important to underdeveloped nations that often lack many of the social goods so important to development, such as education, health, and transportation systems. Reforming institutions or remolding them in the image of the Western world is not an easy task, nor for that matter is it necessarily desirable. In recent decades, Japan, for example, has developed on an impressive scale, but much of its cultural and institutional heritage has remained intact. Still, social, cultural, and institutional changes appear frequently to be lacking in the underdeveloped world. Disorganization, acceptance of the status quo, and socioeconomic disorientation among the masses must be replaced by a spirit and will to develop, and this process depends in part on changes in behavior and institutions.

Coping with the many pressing problems that encumber economic development brings us to the special topic that bears heavily on the future economic welfare of billions of people—selected targets for government policy. The public sector is a key ingredient in dealing with a wide variety of problems, such as the population explosion, the quality of human resources, investment and capital formation, and particularly the administration of change.

## C. TARGETS OF ECONOMIC DEVELOPMENT POLICY

The impediments to growth and development are such that the success of an underdeveloped nation in increasing per capita output depends to a large extent on its government. A stable government committed to the goal of development is the first prerequisite to enhanced standards of living in the underdeveloped nations. Most experts agree that underdeveloped nations will have to rely on public-sector involvement in economic affairs in different ways and to a larger degree than was true during the early stages of the development of such nations as the United States, Canada, or the United Kingdom.

### The Direction of Government Policy

Governments of underdeveloped nations must confront their problems directly and forcefully, especially since they seek rapid growth and near-term improvements. The need for rapid growth has increased as the gap between aspirations and living standards has widened, and as differences in income levels and growth rates between the developed and underdeveloped nations have increased. Let us consider some directions that underdeveloped nations might pursue in formulating development policies.

### SOCIAL AND PRIVATE CAPITAL NEEDS

You will recall that low-income countries are trapped in a circular web of low per capita income, low saving ($S$), low investment ($I$), and low productivity. The circularity of the dilemma depends upon these chain relations leading to low productivity, which reinforces low GNP through the feedback loop illustrated on page 709. Income is low because saving, capital formation, and productivity are low, a situation which turns around again to stifle growth in income, and so forth.

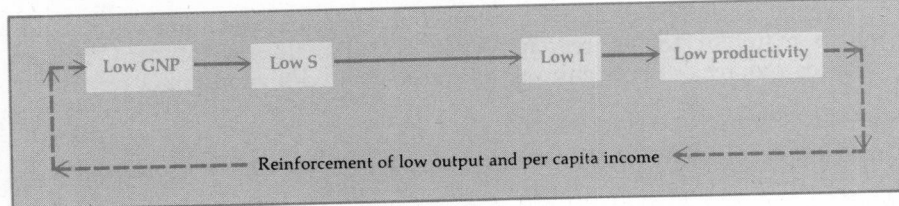

Because shortages of physical-capital resources are a critical restraint to development, it is vital that underdeveloped nations augment domestic markets and improve investment incentives in the private sector of the economy. In addition, vast amounts of social-overhead capital are required. Domestic saving is severely hampered by low consumption standards; however, provided that an efficient and operable tax system is developed and fairly administered, government can directly tax its populace in order to invest in needed social-overhead capital.

Another alleged alternative to the acquisition of funds for social-overhead capital is to force saving through inflation, although there are grave dangers associated with such efforts. An inflation that is "expected" by consumers and firms and is induced by credit expansion, is apt to weaken or distort private investment incentives, with the result that funds may flow abroad or may be directed into land accumulation. Moreover, rampant and chronic inflation tends to lower domestic exports if the prices of the goods exported rise above international market prices.[8] Inflation may also increase a nation's imports from other countries because foreign goods will become cheaper. When exports decline and imports rise, underdeveloped nations often encounter serious balance-of-payments problems. Many authorities agree that, while some inflation may be appropriate, chronic price-level pressures do more harm than good in terms of the need for capital formation.

### HUMAN-RESOURCE POLICIES

Human-resource control is a necessary precondition to the achievement of a higher standard of living, which in turn can release the saving needed for the capital formation that undergirds the economic development process. The "Malthusian misery" doctrine is all too real in much of the underdeveloped world and, in many ways, human resources are a serious barrier to development. Control of runaway birth rates through family planning remains a priority need if the underdeveloped world is to increase per capita income. However, family planning for millions of illiterate people has not turned out to be an easy task, despite such technological wonders as the pill. In addition to lowering birth rates, steps must be taken to remedy illiteracy as well as the low skill level and the immobility of labor. Urban centers such as Calcutta are teeming with both the unemployed and underemployed because industrial jobs are lacking. Illiteracy and the tradition-bound way of life common in rural regions further inhibits the mobility of human resources.

The task of reaching and communicating with vast numbers of people

[8] This assumes that fixed exchange rates prevail.

is a crucial need which underdeveloped nations are attacking with vigor. Like so many of the ingredients vital to economic development, human resources require overt attention and purposively designed policies.

## ATTACKING INSTITUTIONAL OBSTACLES

Government plays a crucial role in coping with a variety of social, cultural, and institutional barriers characteristic of nations experiencing slow economic progress. An entrepreneurial class needs to be formed, the large extended families deemed necessary to support the elderly must be replaced by social insurance programs, and substitutes must be found for sometimes corrupt and frequently inefficient or poorly trained government administrators. Above all, the people of poor nations must develop a spirit and will to adapt to change and to pursue a better future. All of this means that the modernization of underdeveloped economies requires the conversion of individuals and entire societies from tradition-bound ways of life to modern social, economic, and political systems. The enormity of this task is such that government intervention on a broad scale is usually regarded as crucial.

The implications and magnitude of the underdevelopment problem are startling. Many of the barriers to development that nations must hurdle in a few short decades may well require a system of political economy alien to the market economy common to the early development of Western nations. As a matter of fact, numerous underdeveloped nations have already turned their attention to economic planning, partially because of structural economic problems.

## STRUCTURAL ECONOMIC PROBLEMS

Attempts to increase per capita output continually bump into a ceiling in the form of inefficient use of resources, perhaps best illustrated by the low productivity of labor in underdeveloped nations often described as "dual economies." The *dual economy* describes the existence of a backward, rural, and largely primitive agrarian sector which contrasts sharply with an industrial sector located in a few urban centers which may be relatively modern. Poor communication, the absence of roads, and the hinterland's failure to acquire capital resources fragment underdeveloped nations into two sectors which often are rarely linked together at all.

When subsistence is the norm and malnutrition or starvation is a near neighbor, as is true in many underdeveloped countries, food and fiber production dominate economic needs. In fact, such production accounts for the use of more than one-half of all resources in most underdeveloped nations today. Agrarian life in an underdeveloped nation, often burdened with unrealized land reform, is a simple and bare subsistence that absorbs redundant manpower unable to find more productive employment elsewhere.

A dual economy is two different worlds where people are linked only by the poverty common to all, plus whatever spirit of nationalism might prevail. Even though potential productivity gains are greater in agriculture than in the industrial sector, capital does not flow readily to the rural environment. Transfer out of the primitive agricultural sector to the alien urban world is difficult, if not impossible, for many people.

Today, some experts argue that embodiment of a modern technology in capital resources is inappropriate for underdeveloped nations whose resource base is biased in the direction of underutilized labor. For the most part, the technology known in the West is *capital intensive;* that is, it uses large quantities of capital and relatively small amounts of labor resources. Developmental economists sometimes suggest that an underdeveloped country should adopt less modern production technologies that tend to be *labor intensive,* particularly if underutilized labor is a problem. Capital-intensive methods tend to maximize output (and perhaps skew income distribution in favor of the wealthy elite), but labor-intensive methods tend to maximize employment (and conserve scarce capital resources). Social and political considerations make it important to weigh the advantages of both methods carefully, particularly because the people of underdeveloped nations have not realized their rising expectations.

### Development Policy and the Advanced Nations

Only a twist of fate separates the average Canadian, Western European, or American citizen from the disease and misery common to the resident of an underdeveloped country. The latter is increasingly aware of the "good life" which the minority enjoy, and when the GNP yardstick used for measurement of economic progress is translated into starvation or years of longevity forgone, the matter of development policy becomes serious. The economically advanced nations cannot remain oblivious to the intense struggle currently being waged against the poverty, ignorance, and disease that characterize the lot of most people of the world today. There is an ongoing revolution against economic backwardness, and the destiny of all mankind may be affected by its outcome.

Developed nations like the United States have humanitarian, economic, and political interests in prompting institutional changes that will push back the barriers to development. The humanitarian or moral aspect of this interest is obvious, although it is not an obligation agreed upon by all governments and peoples because of different values and goals. The underdeveloped nations are also of direct economic importance to developed nations as suppliers of important raw materials and as buyers of billions of dollars of exports. From a political viewpoint, underdeveloped nations loom large in the ideological struggle between West and East. There are very real differences in alternative systems of political economy, and the role of the uncommitted nations in national security is of no small consequence to developed nations. These interests are generally recognized by major nations now in a position to provide economic development assistance. Unfortunately, all nations capable of providing significant economic aid, including the United States, have not overextended themselves in the eyes of impartial observers and the underdeveloped nations alike. Moreover, on numerous occasions American economic development efforts have generated hostility instead of good will.

### ECONOMIC DEVELOPMENT POLICY OF THE UNITED STATES

When the total of all forms of American aid to all nations is adjusted downward for post-World War II assistance to Western Europe and further adjusted for political and military aid, the funds allocated for economic development amount to less than one-half of 1 percent of United States GNP for any given year. United States economic aid to the underdeveloped countries assumes many forms, including: (*a*) government grants and loans,

(b) technical assistance, (c) development assistance extended through international agencies such as the World Bank, and (d) trade and private capital investments.

*Grants and Loans*   Over one-fourth of United States aid in recent years has consisted of food grants based upon surplus agricultural commodities generated by the agricultural price-support program. Outright grants or low-interest loans from the United States government are often used to provide social-overhead capital such as educational programs, dams and irrigation facilities, or transportation and communications systems.[9] Despite the fact that social-overhead capital often is a precondition to private investment, most underdeveloped countries are sadly short-changed on this count.

The United States Agency for International Development (AID) was established in 1961 to coordinate economic assistance to underdeveloped nations. An important institutional link between United States economic development programs and underdeveloped nations, AID's efforts are augmented by the Export-Import Bank, one of the oldest United States government agencies providing economic development assistance. Export–Import Bank loans make both a higher level of living *and* increased productive capacity possible in underdeveloped nations.

*Technical Assistance*   After innumerable frustrating economic-aid failures, due in part to inadequate worker skills, illiteracy, and unstable host governments, advanced nations have turned to technical-assistance programs in such areas as agriculture, family planning, public health, and education. Originally established in 1950 under the "Point Four" program initiated by former President Truman, technical-assistance programs have been expanded because of their success. Technical assistance is sometimes provided on a full-grant basis, and at other times it is financed on matching terms, under which less developed nations underwrite a portion of the cost.

*International Development Agencies*   Several international agencies exist for purposes that complement the needs of underdeveloped countries. One important international agency is the International Bank for Reconstruction and Development (the World Bank), an agency founded during the closing years of World War II. Today, the major function of the World Bank is to grant loans to underdeveloped countries, an objective underwritten by the more than 100 nations which have provided capital to the bank in proportion to their own economic strength. Other international agencies participating in economic development assistance include the International Development Association, the Organization for Economic Cooperation and Development, and several agencies operating under the auspices of the United Nations. Unfortunately, the total aid available to underdeveloped nations from these international agencies is far from adequate.

*Private Capital and Trade*   Private investment in underdeveloped countries is not an official form of economic aid, but it can be an important source of capital formation that complements the growth and development process.

---

[9] Social goods like roads, public health, and educational facilities normally do not attract private capital because the returns to such investments are indivisible and widely diffused.

In recent years, private investment from the United States to underdeveloped nations has averaged some $2 billion annually. Foreign intervention, expropriation, and tax laws subject private-capital formation to the special risks of political instability, as we have said before. Still, the rewards of potential growth continue to attract private capital.

International trade is important to underdeveloped nations. Often their growth potential is related to their ability to export basic commodities and materials to developed nations in order to import the machinery and equipment required to diversify. The more that underdeveloped nations export to advanced nations, the less they need to borrow to finance import purchases of capital resources. Even though underdeveloped nations can benefit substantially by obtaining access to larger foreign markets for their exports, they cannot rely on trade alone. Some four-fifths of all exports from underdeveloped nations consist of basic raw materials such as oil or staple commodities, and several underdeveloped nations are one-crop export economies. In many instances, foreign trade accounts for from 10 to as much as 50 percent of GNP, a feature that hinders economic stability and diversified growth in these nations. Because underdeveloped nations depend upon export markets, it is important that the developed nations of the world reduce trade barriers which now limit their export sales. International agencies such as the Organization for Economic Cooperation and Development and the International Monetary Fund, along with several Western European nations and the United States, have begun to seriously consider the establishment of tariff preferences to help underdeveloped nations expand trade and develop a modern and viable economic base. While stabilization and enlargement of international trade on many fronts is important, it is also clear that underdeveloped nations need more direct assistance to achieve their development goals.

## WORLD CONFLICT OR "GREEN" REVOLUTION?

Although economic conditions in the underdeveloped world are bleak in many ways, startling gains in the production of certain food grains have occurred since 1965 in nations such as India, Pakistan, and the Philippines. Crop yields can be doubled or tripled by the use of high-yield and climatically adapted seed strains, regularized irrigation, fertilizer, and pesticides. This technological breakthrough—labeled the "Green Revolution"—economizes on the use of scarce investment capital and may also provide for more employment for slack labor.[10] If the Green Revolution in agriculture is realized, instead of constraining growth and development, agriculture may contribute significantly to victory in the international war on hunger and bring hundreds of millions closer to their economic goals. Green Revolution or not, the world's poor remain in dire need of assistance in overcoming the many obstacles to development noted earlier, including a shortage of capital resources.[11] Without capital and technical know-how, the much-heralded Green Revolution is no more than a dream.

[10] Clifton R. Wharton, Jr., "The Green Revolution: Cornucopia or Pandora's Box?" *Foreign Affairs* (April 1969), pp. 464–476.

[11] For example, uniformly controlled irrigation is one of many factors crucial to achieving vastly improved yields, and while a $2 billion irrigation project appears small by American standards, that amount is about one-fourth of total annual national income for the four nations of Laos, Cambodia, South Vietnam, and Thailand.

Most of the developed nations of the world relied heavily on other nations as a source of capital in their early stages of development, and the United States is no exception. Capital investment in the United States from Britain and other Western European nations during the nineteenth century was many times as large as total United States investments in underdeveloped nations to date. Although the problems faced by underdeveloped nations today are by no means the same, capital from foreign sources is a nearly uniform need for all poor nations. The need for increased economic development assistance is large, and the developed nations of the world have failed to provide adequate foreign aid.

## REVIEW

### Summary

1. Economic growth and development is not an automatic process. Many nations have not developed, but have instead remained tradition-bound. While there is no single adequate measure of economic development, it is generally conceded that measures such as total and per capita income, death rates, literacy, and life expectancy are reasonable guides in spotting the ailment called "underdevelopment."

2. Two-thirds of the people of the world live in underdeveloped nations characterized by low levels of per capita income and consumption. Even though the continents of Asia, Africa, and Latin America house nearly two-thirds of the world's population, the countries in these regions produce only about one-twelfth of measured world output (GNP).

3. Economic development depends in the general sense upon a nation's resource base, institutional environment, and technology. Low rates of saving and capital formation are common in underdeveloped countries. The population often lives at subsistence levels of per capita income, much as the principle of diminishing returns to labor predicts. Rapid population growth in conjunction with low levels of investment lead to low, stagnant, and sometimes even declining levels of living.

4. The proportion of income saved and invested times the output/capital ratio denotes the rate of growth in total output. Capital resources are often necessary to utilize modern technology, and capital formation is cumulative as per capita income rises. Moreover, growth in the stock of capital through saving and investment allows technological imitation. Internal sources of capital are impeded by subsistence-consumption needs, uncertainty, hoarding, and political instability. Moreover, foreign capital is meagerly supplied relative to investment needs and, in some instances, not readily accepted.

5. Human resources are in excess supply and underinvestment in people often characterizes the underdeveloped nation. Slack labor exists in the sense that significant quantities of human resources often could be withdrawn from subsistence farming and more fully employed elsewhere if employment opportunities were available.

6. Natural resources are plentiful in some underdeveloped nations and scarce in others. Land reform represents a pressing problem in many countries. Cultural and institutional barriers often inhibit economic

development. Tradition and custom bind behavior to the past, while unstable and weak governments also inhibit improvement of the economic situation in underdeveloped nations.

7. In underdeveloped countries, the barriers to economic development require that government play an active role in such diverse areas as the formation of social-overhead capital, population control, health, and education. Major difficulties are encountered because the traditional and modern sectors of underdeveloped economies are separated by generations and even centuries of change. Developed nations of the world, including the United States, have extended aid to the underdeveloped nations in the form of grants, loans, and technical assistance, as well as expansion of foreign trade and private investment, all of which are important to underdeveloped nations. In general, however, economic development assistance has been rather meager in relation to the enormity of the problem, even though numerous international agencies have been created for the purpose of assisting underdeveloped countries.

### Identify the Following Concepts and Terms
- GNP/$K$
- social-overhead capital
- human capital
- embodied technological change
- slack labor
- labor-intensive investment
- the dual economy
- the "Green Revolution"

### Questions to Answer

1. How may diminishing returns assign the population of an underdeveloped nation to declining levels of per capita income? What are the prospects for capital formation under these conditions? If the output/capital ratio is $1/$4, how much of an output increase is generated by $1 billion of net investment? Given the above output/capital ratio and assuming that all saving is invested, what rate of growth will be generated if 9 percent of income is saved and invested? What happens to growth if saving rises to 10 percent of income and the output/capital ratio changes to $1/$2? Why?

2. Critically evaluate the following statements:
   (a) "Underemployment, underinvestment in human resources, and resistance to change loom large in any explanation of underdevelopment."
   (b) "The output/capital ratio masks many forces that condition economic development."

3. A variety of structural problems bear heavily on economic development problems and policies. Assuming that you are responsible for guiding economic development in an underdeveloped nation, explain each problem and analyze its policy implications.

4. Explain the various measures which developed nations have taken to assist underdeveloped countries. Based upon your knowledge of the problem of underdevelopment, how would you assess aid to underdeveloped nations? What improvements would you suggest?

# CHAPTER 28
# Economic Systems and International Conflict

While examination of contemporary economic conditions in the under-developed nations is a sobering experience, it affords only a partial perspective on international economic issues. Economic systems have, in recent years, increasingly moved in the direction of a larger economic role for government. In some nations there has been a surge of interest in socialism and communism—systems of political economy which have their genesis in the work of Karl Marx as reshaped by Lenin, Stalin, Tito, Mao, Che, and many others.

All nations face scarcity-choice problems in making decisions about the allocation of resources, yet the market approach to economic organization is far less common than many Americans think. Today, alternative systems of economic organizations are very real. The rather rigid centralized economic decision-making characteristic of communism is the dominant form of economic organization for about one-third of the world's population who live in Russia, China, and other Asian and Eastern European nations. In addition, state ownership of selected resources and some centralization of economic activity—known as "democratic socialism"—is common to many Western European nations. In less developed nations such as some of those in Latin America, rigid authoritarianism is a product of a political dictatorship and a capitalistic system of economic organization.

The goals of economic growth and development and military security loom large for all nations of the world, no matter what their system of political economy or degree of development. If we are to fully understand the international economy, it will be necessary to step outside our study of mixed market economies. We shall begin with a brief survey of Marxian economics in Part A, examine alternative economic systems in Parts B and C, and direct attention to the economics of war and peace in Part D.

## A. MARX AND COMPARATIVE ECONOMIC SYSTEMS

Unfortunately, "ism" labels fail to convey fully and accurately the libertarian or totalitarian flavor of a political or economic system. Socialism and modified capitalism differ in both subtle and distinct ways, but political freedom or tyranny can and does coexist with either system. Any system of economic organization is a man-made device—a complex set of institutions, rules, and goals—designed to facilitate the use of resources and the distribution of output.

Laissez faire capitalism, long defunct, has been modified as described earlier in this book. Two alternative forms of economic organization are socialism—characterized by government planning of evolutionary change and de-emphasis of private property, and communism—which more forcefully and often ruthlessly pursues the political and economic goals envisioned by Marx's scientific socialism. Differing and sometimes conflicting economic ideologies contribute to the international political tensions which militarily absorb nearly 10 percent of the productive capacity of the United States, and 15 percent of that of the Soviet Union. We can best begin to appreciate these tensions by quickly surveying the challenges and ideas set forth by Marx.

### The Marxian View of Capitalism

The literary works of Karl Marx (1818–1883) and his colleague and benefactor, Friedrich Engels (1820–1895), first materialized fully in Russia with the Bolshevik Revolution of 1917. Since 1945, the United States has been engaged in "cold" and "hot" wars with nations espousing Marxian ideas as they have been refined by leaders such as Lenin and Mao.

Like the utopian socialists, Karl Marx was angered by the contrasting abundance and poverty that characterized an Industrial Revolution that was insensitive to even young children laboring in factories 10 or more hours a day. Much of the work of this meticulous German scholar is of philosophical, social, and political interest, but our immediate concern is with Marx as an economist. Although cognizant of capitalism's accomplishments, Marx was an unyielding critic who stressed the need for vast economic, social, and political reform.

Most of Marx's work consisted of a critique of capitalism, which, as he knew it, was fundamentally an act of robbery. At the same time, however, Marx recognized the achievements of capitalism, noting in the *Communist Manifesto* (1848) that: "The bourgeoisie [the owners of capital as a means of production] during its scarce rule of 100 years has created more massive and more colossal productive forces than have all preceding generations together." What he deplored was the personal costs and injustices this process created, which could only end, he thought, in a communal dictatorship by the proletariat working class. The notion of *dialectical materialism*—emphasis upon change inherent in the material and physical environment of societies—constitutes the basis of Marxian philosophy. Just as tradition-bound feudal societies were reformulated into the market system, further economic, social, and political changes were seen by Marx as inevitable.

Marx saw the capitalistic market system as a device which enslaved and exploited the proletariat class, who labored on behalf of capitalists when, in fact, their past and present labor was the sole source of value. By paying labor a subsistence wage which was less than its full value, capitalists received a profit. This unearned increment—the difference between what workers produced and what they were paid—was termed *surplus value*. To obtain title to what was "rightfully" his whole labor value, Marx felt the worker would have to change the social and political structure.

Marx further stated that the capitalists' lust for surplus value would lead to competitive expansion of output and the increased accumulation of capital. In contrast, the worker would find jobs more difficult to obtain as capitalists substituted machinery for labor. Poverty increasingly was to be the lot of the unemployed masses subject to the intensifying forces of "misery, oppression, slavery, and degradation." The consequences would be sharpening class distinctions and the growth of an unemployed *reserve army* of proletariats ultimately driven to rising up and abolishing capitalism's superstructure—private ownership of the means of production.

Capitalism would, in fact, destroy itself because of the self-interest, economic instability, and greed upon which it was based. The competitive struggle among firms would lead to monopoly capitalism as the search for profits intensified in an environment agitated by severe swings in economic activity. The embittered proletariat class then would (and "should," according to Marx and Engels) finally rise up in revolt. Periodic economic crises would grow more intense, but the freedom to exploit the proletariat so cherished by the bourgeoisie would culminate only in the victory for the common man under communism.

On these precepts, Marx was unyielding and intolerant. He had no use for those socialists who advocated tolerance of varying viewpoints, less revolutionary change, or the destruction of all doctrines. His theory of the economic process was to be the new dogma to replace the competitive "religion" penned by Adam Smith.

### The Marxian Influence on Economic Organization

The all-too-terse survey presented above provides little information on the "new" communist society—and this failure is also characteristic of Marx's chhief work, *Das Kapital*. His major goal was a description of the inevitable self-destruction of capitalism and a presentation of the means to this end. On what was to come, Marx was less precise.

In many Western European countries several of Marx's predictions have materialized, and today there are only a handful of nations in which capitalism is flourishing (e.g., the United States). Economic instability and crises, free public education, taxation of the wealth of capitalists, monopoly capitalism, state control over monetary systems, national planning, and state ownership of selected sectors of the economy (e.g., transportation and communication) are among the Marxian predictions which have materialized to some degree in many nations. Marx also foresaw the emphasis that is now put upon economic and social change and the need to restructure and develop new institutions. Economic fluctuations certainly have made life difficult for market economies, and growth in monopoly capitalism has surfaced again and again over the decades. But Marx failed dramatically by underestimating the resiliency of the institutions and rules of the mixed market system—its ability to accommodate itself peacefully to the emerging needs and values of an advancing society.

His final prediction of the demise of capitalism cannot be totally ignored, however. Nations in much of Europe and Asia have experienced a withering away of reliance upon the market system. Among the underdeveloped nations, more centralized forms of economic organization are popular, and even in Western Europe there has been a partial abandonment of reliance upon the market system. The changes have been dramatic in nations such as Britain, the Netherlands, France, and Sweden, which are more heavily committed to socialism than is the United States. Much of the trend toward a planned market system cannot be explained by war, dogmatism, nationalism, or international tyranny, although these have taken their toll. Rather, it is because of socioeconomic failures that the once-viable market systems of Western Europe have undergone vast transformations along the lines foreseen by Marx. Hardened social class distinctions and the inability of governments to right wrongs have resulted in gaping differences between "haves" and "have-nots," and the consequence has been political changes that have de-emphasized the economic role of the market in some parts of the world.

To survive, the market mechanism must remain capable of developing in new directions. In contrast to Western Europe, social and economic resiliency—a willingness to question old values—have accommodated needed changes in the United States. Where Marxian economics has been proven wrong, it has been because governments have found the will and means to head off class stratification, deny misery for the working class, and correct the excessive concentration of wealth. Private-property interests have survived and prospered for their trouble, a situation which can also be attributed to the basic postulates of Keynesian economics which are now used to stabilize the market economy. In short, mixed market capitalism has survived thus far because of its ability to adapt to change and its willingness to meet the needs of people in ways quite unforeseen by Marx and Engels a century ago.

## Other Systems of Economic Organization

The world of reality is not so easily divided into distinguishable camps as a simplistic view of the Marxian doctrine would suggest. Today, the goals and values of socialism are more dominant in Iron Curtain countries than elsewhere in Western Europe. Most economic systems are a mixture of central direction or "command" and markets, some being more liberally sprinkled with Marxism and others more heavily capitalistic in nature. In much the same way that capitalism has been revised in both theory and in practice, modern events and men have modified the Marxian socialism of old. Thus, distinctions between economic systems are nowhere as clear as labels would imply and the institutions and methods of economic organization in Canada, France, Sweden, Russia, Switzerland, and the United States vary on counts too numerous to mention.

In Great Britain, for example, political power has vacillated between the Conservative and Socialist Labor parties for a quarter of a century. Welfare services have been greatly expanded, income has been redistributed, economic planning has been implemented, and certain basic industries have been nationalized. Similarly, socialism has found political expression in France, Sweden, the Netherlands, and several other Western European economies. While each of these nations rely upon a system of economic organization different from that of the United States, our attention in what follows will be confined largely to the communist nations of the world. This is because at this extreme, clear differences in economic organization arise and, in addition, sharp ideological competition has led to disconcerting military developments.

## B. THE BASIS FOR ALTERNATIVE ECONOMIC SYSTEMS

In drawing admittedly ill-defined distinctions between alternative systems of economic organization, the most apparent differences relate to the status of private property and the degree of economic planning. Planning strategies in Western Europe combine the market system of pricing in allocating resources with planned constraints established by the state. Among communist nations elsewhere, even greater reliance is placed upon state-controlled economic planning which requires sophisticated knowledge of the inter-industry relationships of an economy.

### The Command Economy

While a matter of degree, the centralization of economic authority is a foremost distinction between market capitalism and planned command economies. At the foundation of centralized authority rests (a) the public ownership of productive resources, (b) the predominance of social values, and (c) de-emphasis of the profit incentive.

#### OWNERSHIP OF PRODUCTIVE RESOURCES

Under democratic socialism, economic planning is combined with private-enterprise markets and a guided evolution toward public ownership of productive resources. Even more centralization characterizes communism where the private ownership of property is banned, and command planning supplants free markets. Socialism *envisions* state ownership of property as an evolutionary and *ultimate* target, but in the strict Marxian context, public ownership of productive resources is a *revolutionary* goal which is a must (and a fact in nations such as the Soviet Union).

Thus, there are marked differences among nations concerning the degree of private and public ownership of property, and there is no pure form of capitalism or socialism. The United States, which perhaps best symbolizes a relatively high degree of reliance on private property and markets, is also characterized by public ownership of land and productive resources in the utility and education industries, for example. Similarly, the Soviet Union still retains remnants of private property (admittedly of a very different proportion) in agriculture, housing, and trade. Off again-on again public ownership of certain industries also prevails under democratic socialism in Britain and under mixed market and socialistic systems in Norway, Denmark, and Sweden, as do less dogmatic variants of communism in Yugoslavia and Czechoslovakia.

#### SOCIAL AND PRIVATE VALUES

One important consequence of public ownership of property is the greater emphasis upon social expression of values. Centralized decision-making by public authorities tends to reflect the goals and the values of the state, while the privately expressed interests of consumers and producers are de-emphasized. As the public sector becomes more dominant in the ownership of resources, government can assume a larger responsibility in determining what and how much is produced, the prices of products and resources, and ultimately the allocation of resources as well as the distribution of income among citizens. The public sector in a market economy can also influence resource allocation through taxation, subsidies, and expenditures, but given the predominance of private property and markets, consumers and producers remain relatively free to express their personal values in making economic decisions affecting the allocation of resources.

## ECONOMIC MOTIVES

The economic incentives of a society may also vary according to the degree of public and private property ownership. Value and incentive systems differ in some real ways, depending upon the degree to which a state moves toward or away from the operational and philosophical tenets of capitalism or socialism. Capitalistic governments can and do limit private property rights. They also may modify private values through the provision of social goods and may control incentives through regulation or taxation. In contrast, the Soviet Union relies less upon monetary incentives and a self-interest value orientation to organize economic activity. What limited evidence we have suggests that relative *wage* differentials by occupation and skill level in the Soviet Union, for example, are at least as large as they are in the United States. However, larger *income* differentials may prevail under capitalism because private ownership of productive resources is permitted.

Nations which rely more heavily upon the public ownership of productive resources tend to face difficult problems in maintaining incentives and in allocating resources efficiently. Public ownership of productive resources can blunt the producer's response to official appeals for efficiency since profits accrue to the state, although bonuses or nonmonetary incentives (e.g., force) can be substituted for the profit motive. Then, too, when product and resource prices are set by government decree instead of by the market, consumer demand may or may not be adequately met. As a result, other resource-allocation devices must be developed; thus, economic planning occupies a strategic role in allocating resources in a command economy.

### The Role of Economic Planning

Most of the advanced nations of the world developed and prospered spontaneously without formal economic planning. However, in the Soviet Union, economic planning has been used for one-half century and, since World War II, numerous nations (including many of the emerging underdeveloped countries) have moved in the direction of utilizing economic planning to identify priorities, achieve national goals, and implement industrialization and economic-development policies. When highly centralized control dominates a nation, as it does in the Soviet Union, economic planning must be introduced to coordinate an economy. In such a case, government modifies the profit motive by setting production goals, and allocates resources by overt decisions. Thus, government achieves its stated goals by command rather than through the market system. Economic planning can also be used as a more general guidance mechanism in conjunction with markets and the profit motive, as it is in several planned market economies in Western Europe (e.g., Germany, France, the Netherlands, Britain, Italy, and Scandinavia).[1] Under such circumstances, nations can rely upon privately expressed consumer demand in order to fulfill planned economic objectives.

In some instances, economic planning is a mere facade, but in others it consists of firm commitments which (a) establish investment and output goals; (b) involve detailed analysis of a nation's resource base, including consideration of international trade flows, income distribution, consumption, and investment in human and physical capital; (c) rely upon command-established prices in the selection of priorities and the allocation of resources; and (d) set production targets for economic sectors, regions, and perhaps even plants. Realistic and useful economic plans also address attention to such areas as the growth and level of aggregate income, saving, and investment; the mobility and employment of human resources; and the use of monetary and fiscal policies. Economic planners also give attention to the development of the infrastructure of social-overhead capital needed to mobilize, develop, and fully employ resources.[2]

Economic planning has had its failures and successes, and more often than not there is good reason to suspect that the overall resource base and the institutional structure of a society are more important than planning in explaining growth and development. Underdeveloped nations face a critical choice concerning the degree to which they wish to rely upon private direction compared to the more centralized authority allowed by economic planning.

Planning experts recognize the importance of self-interest and personal incentives, but at the same time the worldwide prevalence of five- and seven-year plans resoundingly indicates rejection of the loose, market-directed solution to organizing economic activity that characterizes the economy of the United States. In most underdeveloped nations, the notion that a loosely directed market system is needed to decide how resources are allocated and what is produced simply is not regarded as a sufficient basis for economic development, whether this position is approved by our values or not.

### Input-Output Models and Economic Planning

In order to implement detailed production and price plans, it is necessary to know how innumerable markets, industries, and even firms relate to each other. Studies of the interindustry relationships are very valuable to economic planning agencies, and they also are useful in understanding a market-oriented economy.[3]

---

[1] Different nations in the communist bloc also rely upon the profit motive to varying degrees, as we point out later.

[2] An *infrastructure* (such things as power facilities, roads, transportation systems, and the like) is needed to produce and distribute goods and to develop internal markets. Whether nations will grow faster by investing in capital for direct production activities in agriculture and industry, or by allocating resources to the social-overhead capital required to develop an infrastructure is an unsettled issue. The general consensus seems to be that economic plans must accommodate both types of capital investment, perhaps in a modestly unbalanced fashion favoring direct production. See Albert O. Hirschman, *The Strategy of Economic Development* (New Haven, Conn.: Yale University Press, 1958), p. 92.

[3] Viewed generally, economic planning covers a wide spectrum of government involvement ranging from the general approach used in the United States to the detailed

The easiest task for planning agencies is to establish five-year targets and goals which are then broken down into short-term (one-year) plans by region, industry sector, and plants. More difficult decisions are encountered in coordinating a totally planned economy, since planners must develop subplans which provide for industrial output used as input by other industries. For example, labor and other resources must be coordinated with production plans for the steel, clothing, automotive equipment, and numerous other industries. Because a complex economy is so interdependent, state planning agencies must continually monitor output and pricing, for if production plans in one sector fail to materialize or if a bottleneck arises in some resource market, aggregate-output goals will not be achieved.

Central to the planning process is a form of general-equilibrium or "input-output" analysis which measures the interrelations between various sectors of an economy. Input-output analysis allows identification of the impact of a change in one sector of the economy upon other sectors. If an economic plan calls for increasing the output of, say, steel by 20 percent, planning authorities must know by how much the output of other sectors will increase. They must also identify required new investment, provide for added manpower requirements, identify the relationships of such plans to international trade, and so forth.

Figure 1 is a much simplified illustration of how an input–output model reveals the planning problems arising from interdependence among different sectors of an economy. The three basic "tables" show (a) total transactions, (b) direct requirements, and (c) total requirements.

1. Transactions table. In Figure 1(a) each industry or sector in an economy is shown as purchasing inputs from other sectors to produce its output. In reading down a column of the simplified input-output model in Figure 1, we can see that sector 1 purchases $80, $40, and $40 from sectors 1, 2, and 3, plus $240 of all primary resource inputs. Why? To produce $200 of final output shown as the sales of sector 1 to final demand in Figure 1. Reading horizontally by row shows that some portion of each sector's output is sold to other sectors in the economy as well as to final demand (GNP). The final output or GNP for all sectors (of $540) is smaller than gross transactions because some portion of production is used up in intermediate stages of the production process.

2. Direct requirements. The gold portion of Figure 1(a) includes internal or endogenous transactions which are converted into the direct requirements table shown in Figure 1(b). The direct requirements are each sector's purchases (by column) as a percent of gross payments for all inputs. Thus, for every $1 of output of final demand produced, sector 1 buys $80/$400 or $.20 from itself, $40/$400 or $.10 each from sectors 2 and 3, and $240/$400 or $.60 of resource inputs. These direct requirements, sometimes called "input coefficients," reveal in percentage terms the "first-round" increase in output needed to increase sales to final demand.[4] If the output for final de-

---

consumption and production plans used in the Soviet Union. Input-output analysis (described earlier in Chapter 6) is used in both market and planned economies.

[4] For simplicity, input-output analysis assumes constant returns to scale, fixed production techniques, and constant relative prices. Although the assumption of fixed input coefficients is a limitation, it is not unduly restrictive for relatively small changes in demand over short periods of time.

# FIGURE 1    An Input-Output Illustration of Economic Planning

## (a) Transactions table

|  | Sector 1 purchases | Sector 2 purchases | Sector 3 purchases | Final demand | Gross output |
|---|---|---|---|---|---|
| Sector 1 sales | $ 80 | $ 60 | $ 60 | $200 | $400 |
| Sector 2 sales | 40 | 20 | 10 | 230 | 300 |
| Sector 3 sales | 40 | 30 | 20 | 110 | 200 |
| Resource payments | 240 | 190 | 110 | $540 (GNP) | – |
| Gross inputs | 400 | 300 | 200 | – | 900 |

## (b) Direct-requirements table

|  |  | Purchasers | | |
|---|---|---|---|---|
|  |  | Sector 1 | Sector 2 | Sector 3 |
| Sellers | Sector 1 | $ .20 | $ .20 | $ .30 |
|  | Sector 2 | .10 | .07 | .05 |
|  | Sector 3 | .10 | .10 | .10 |
|  | Resources | .60 | .63 | .55 |
|  | Total | $1.00 | $1.00 | $1.00 |

## (c) Total-requirements table

|  |  | Purchasers | | |
|---|---|---|---|---|
|  |  | Sector 1 | Sector 2 | Sector 3 |
| Sellers | Sector 1 | $1.34 | $ .34 | $ .47 |
|  | Sector 2 | .15 | 1.12 | .11 |
|  | Sector 3 | .17 | .16 | 1.17 |
|  | Industry multiplier | $1.66 | $1.62 | $1.75 |

*Input-Output Model.* The transactions table [Figure 1(a)] depicts the purchases and sales between sectors in an economy, including payments to resources and sales of final output. Input coefficients (sector purchase/gross inputs) indicate the direct percentage requirements for a $1 increase in output to final demand [Figure 1(b)]. Because each sector also purchases from other sectors of the economy, indirect increases in output are also required. The sum of direct and indirect requirements are total requirements as shown in Figure 1(c). In addition, the sum of total requirements equals the industry multipliers of 1.66, 1.62, and 1.75 for sectors 1, 2, and 3.

mand in sector 3 is increased by $100, for example, sectors 1, 2, and 3 must initially supply $30, $5, and $10 of output, and $55 of additional payments will be made to resources.

In short, when the output to final demand is increased for any endogenous sector of the economy, this prompts an initial increase in the output of all sectors selling inputs used in producing. Notice carefully, however, that we have only begun to trace through the effect of an increase of $100 in final output. When the output for sector 3 increases by $100, $30 of additional output is directly required from sector 1. The input coefficients indicate that to increase output sector 1 indirectly requires more output from itself and from all other sectors in the economy in the amounts shown in Figure 1(b): 20 percent from itself, 10 percent from sector 2, and so on. More indirect output from these sectors requires the use of still more inputs and resources in the production process. To take account of all indirect requirements in successive spending rounds, economic planners use computers and matrix algebra to compute the total-requirements table shown in Figure 1(c).

3. Total requirements. Each column of Figure 1(c) gives the sum of all direct and indirect production requirements when, for example, the final output of any sector is increased by $100. Thus, if sector 1 is to increase sales to final demand by $100, it must produce a total amount equal to $134 (1.34 × $100) because $34 of output is used up in producing for final demand. In addition, sector 1 requires $15 of additional output from sector 2 and $17 of additional output from sector 3. The sum of all total-requirement coefficients shown in Figure 1(c) gives an illustrative multiplier for each sector; that is, as the output of sector 1 increases by $100, total output for this sector rises in the amount of $166. Accordingly, increasing the output of each sector by $1 yields a multiplier effect of 1.66, 1.62, and 1.75 for sectors 1, 2, and 3 in Figure 1(c).

Input-output techniques have proven to be very useful in understanding the operation of modern economies whether economic planning is relied upon or not. The United States, for example has used input-output analysis to study industrial development, regional growth, and manpower problems. Input-output analysis can also be invaluable for economic planning, but as can be imagined, it is also a very complex and elaborate process for an economy containing thousands of sectors, hundreds of thousands of firms, and millions of consumers. Various sources of final demand, taxes, government spending, international trade, and a host of resources dispersed over many regions must be coordinated to avoid bottlenecks. While much more detailed input-output analyses than shown in Figure 1 are helpful to economic planning agencies, this method of analysis is by no means a cureall, as we shall see.

## C. COMPARATIVE ECONOMIC SYSTEMS AT WORK

Nations which rely heavily on economic planning (e.g., the Soviet Union) set and manipulate product and resource prices to ration output and allocate inputs, but they can encounter grave problems in using resources efficiently. To see more clearly what planning involves, let us consider selected economies of the command variety.

### The Soviet Economy

In allocating resources, the Russian economy (whose leaders are members of the Communist Party) relies on state ownership of productive resources. Economic planning complements state ownership of resources, which is nearly complete in the industrial, agricultural, and commercial sectors of the economy. Private enterprise is very rare, although a modest proportion of agricultural output is produced privately on small farms or plots of ground more nearly like gardens. In addition, certain services are privately provided, but private ownership of productive resources (particularly on a scale requiring the hire of labor) is virtually banned in the Soviet Union.

After the socialist victory in 1917, Soviet leaders were faced with structuring the ill-defined Marxian ideal of a "planned socialist economy." After a full decade of inept administration and disjointed economic organization under the revolutionaries Lenin and Trotsky, Josef Stalin assumed command in the latter 1920s. Shortly thereafter, the first centralized economic plans for industrialization and economic development were initiated. Since then, Russian authorities have relied upon one-, five-, and twenty-year plans in striving to reach short- and long-term goals. Under economic planning, much of the early economic development of the Soviet Union was harsh and ruthless. Heavy-handed authoritarianism and a relentless use of power held consumption down, while the laboring masses were exploited and controlled as the state ruthlessly pursued its objectives of capital formation and industrial development. Irrespective of the costs, totalitarian control and economic planning did allow the Soviet Union to develop into an industrialized economic power in a few short decades.

Initially, economic planning in the Soviet Union was highly centralized under the direct control of top administrative officials. As the Russian economy developed, however, its complexity and interindustry relationships expanded prodigiously. In recent years, the problem of planning the production goals and patterns of resource allocation for thousands of industries has required movement toward decentralization, and new stress has been placed upon consumption. Essentially, however, economic control remains in the hands of the government and GOSPLAN—the economic planning agency. Numerous intermediate planning agencies at regional and industrial levels along with Communist Party organizations monitor the planning and state financing of business operations. The Soviet banking system (GOSBANK) is a key control mechanism through which the state finances production enterprise and accounts for the revenues and costs of state-controlled firms.

In order to coordinate consumption with production plans, Soviet authorities apply a *turnover tax* (which is like an excise or sales tax) as a markup factor to the production costs of consumer goods. The Soviet government uses the turnover tax to coordinate state-directed production with consumption. By varying the turnover tax from product to product, the government can control consumer demand and consumption for selected commodities. This same tax also redistributes income and consumption among the more and less affluent, and ultimately allocates scarce resources to those production efforts planned by the state.

## SOVIET ECONOMIC REFORMS

In a complex economy in which product and resource prices are centrally administered, it is extremely difficult to settle upon prices which reflect the scarcity of limited goods and resources. Together with the absence of the profit motive, command-established prices can lead to the misallocation of resources, production inefficiencies, and unsatisfied consumer demand. These problems have prompted certain reforms in Russia.

The "Liberman Reforms" first surfaced in 1962 when Evsei G. Liberman, a Soviet professor at Kharkov University, published an article in *Pravda* urging modification of economic planning. These reforms, sometimes described as a move toward "market socialism," have involved the de-emphasis (but not abandonment) of highly centralized planning from the top down in favor of regional and local economic plans allowing more autonomy at lower levels, including the level of plant production managers.

Liberman Reforms also involve a modified form of the profit motive under which pecuniary incentives for workers and managers are linked to the economic efficiency and profitability of productive enterprises. Although some observers have speculated that this trend may herald a "convergence" of capitalism and communism, there are vast differences between paying profits to the private owners of productive resources and linking variable wage and salary payments to the profit incentive. Moreover, the central Soviet planning agency, GOSPLAN, still retains firm control over the economy of Russia.

### GROWTH AND DEVELOPMENT IN THE SOVIET UNION

Just how has the economy of the Soviet Union fared under a form of economic organization so unlike our own? Although the Soviet Union was classified as underdeveloped not too long ago, it has experienced rapid economic growth during the one-half century since the Russian Revolution.[5] Its impressive growth rate makes the U.S.S.R. an interesting comparison to the United States.

The fundamental conclusion reached by authorities on Russian economic growth are threefold.[6] First, the Soviet economy grew about twice as fast as that of the United States over the 40 years ending about 1960. Real GNP in the Soviet Union has expanded about 5–6 percent per year more recently, compared to 3.5–4 percent in the United States. Second, total GNP in the Soviet Union is approximately one-half as large as total GNP in the United States and per capita output is about one-third the American level at the present time. Finally, like many countries, economic growth in Russia has been punctuated by expansionary spurts and periods of less rapid growth due in part to wartime invasion as well as to changing development emphasis and economic problems in the industrial and agricultural sectors.

Prior to 1960, the Soviet Union expanded very rapidly in the industrialized sector while agricultural development languished at a near-zero rate of growth, in part because the collectivization of Soviet agriculture was fraught with massive problems. Economic planning was directed toward heavy capital investment in factories and machinery while increased output for consumption was more modest. Increased supplies of labor were also important in the earlier period of Russian development, and women became an especially crucial component of the labor force at all skill levels. Since the late 1950s, the Soviet economy has not grown quite so rapidly

[5] While available data confirm the fact that Russia has indeed changed from a peasant economy to an industrial power in a short 50 years, bear in mind that other mixed market economies (Japan and Western European nations such as West Germany) have also experienced rapid and sustained economic growth in the last 25 years.

[6] The growth record of the Soviet Union is documented in United States Congress, Joint Economic Committee, *Soviet Economic Performance* (Washington, D.C.: U.S. Government Printing Office, 1968); and Abram Bergson and Simon Kuznets (eds.), *Economic Trends in the Soviet Union* (Cambridge, Mass.: Harvard University Press, 1963).

which helps to explain interest in the Liberman Reforms noted earlier. While increases in the total supply of labor have tapered off, capital formation has continued at a high rate. The Soviet Union devotes about one-half again as much of its GNP to investment as does the United States. Moreover, the Soviet agricultural sector has experienced a modest turn-around in recent years through productivity gains associated with mechanization and technical advances. Although production in Soviet agriculture still lags far behind that of the United States, improvements in this sector during the last two decades have released millions of Russian workers for industrial employment.

The primary factors contributing to prospects for future growth and the solid economic-development achievements of the past are related to three features of the Soviet economy.

1. The Soviets are blessed with a wealth of natural resources. Moreover, expansion of investment in capital resources has continued and significant improvements are apparent in the quality as well as the quantity of human resources. Perhaps the greatest achievement of this nation has been its ability to transform a backward, peasant society into an industrial power with a literate and generally well-educated populace. The Soviet's ability to deploy its agricultural labor force to the industrial sector has been, and will continue to be, an important determinant of future economic growth.

2. There is little doubt that the Soviet economy grew rapidly in the past by effectively applying known technological processes, and presently many sectors of the industrial sector are nearly equivalent in technological terms to other developed nations. Continued growth, however, will depend in large measure upon pushing technological knowledge forward instead of borrowing it, particularly since the knowledge gap of a few decades ago has diminished on most fronts.

3. Centralized economic planning has allowed the rulers of the Soviet Union to dictate how resources are to be allocated. While economic planning has complemented the development needs of mobilizing resources and maintaining heavy investment expenditures in physical- and human-capital formation, new problems are arising for economic planning. The Russian economy is no longer relatively simple. Only time will tell if such tactics as the Liberman Reforms, in conjunction with computers and mathematical advances, will be sufficient to resolve the complexities of economic planning on as broad a scale as is used in the Soviet Union.

## A Note on Other Communist Economies

The economies of other communist nations exhibit significant diversity even though they rely heavily on economic planning. Some nations within the communist bloc (e.g., China) have moved toward revolutionary Marxist-Leninist doctrines, whereas others have embraced even greater decentralization of economic authority by more firmly incorporating elements of the market system.

Economic reform swept the more heavily industrialized communist nations of Europe during the early 1960s for much the same reason that the Soviet Union began to experiment with decentralized economic planning. In many ways Yugoslavia—which first broke with the Soviet bloc in 1948

—foreshadowed these events by adopting what has become known as *market socialism*—an economic system which retains decentralized planning and the broad goals and characteristics of socialism but allows production, pricing, and decision-making authority to be influenced by the market at the level of the firm. Market socialism as described by Oskar Lange and Abba Lerner uses the capitalistic microeconomic criterion of economic efficiency, with the profit motive and planning, at the level of the firm.[7] Typically, however, central planning agencies retain some measure of control in allocating state-owned resources.

## YUGOSLAVIA

Although the state owns most productive resources, for about two decades the Yugoslavian economy has used the market-price mechanism together with decentralized economic planning and investment control to avoid the microeconomic inefficiencies and cumbersome controls associated with centralized planning. Government retains broad control over investment, which is financed through profits earned by state-owned enterprises, but individual firms borrow and bid for financing for capital resources. Workers' councils are elected for each plant and these in turn select managers who are relatively free to hire resources and produce what they think can be sold. The typical Western concern for cost controls and profits are important to the operation of Yugoslav firms, which can reinvest earnings and distribute a portion of after-tax profits to workers and managers as incentives. Despite these modifications, state control over investment decisions, communal property ownership, and public identification of economic targets and goals remain dominant under Yugoslav market socialism. Consequently, economic planning continues to be important to the economy of Yugoslavia.

## CZECHOSLOVAKIA

As in many Eastern European nations, economic reforms were the subject of much controversy in Czechoslovakia during the mid-1960s, largely as a result of the frontal attack on central planning launched by Radoslav Selucky, a Leningrad-trained Czech economist. Like Russia's Liberman experiments, the "New Economic Model" of Selucky called for greater discretionary authority to be given to the managers of firms within broad planning confines. In addition to these reforms, greater flexibility in setting prices (some of which are market determined) and in distributing a portion of "profits" to workers and management has emerged. Unlike Yugoslavia, the Czech economy has never attained independence from the Iron Curtain bloc. In 1968, when Czechoslovakia did threaten to establish closer economic ties with the West, a Soviet-led invasion quickly quelled such notions. For the most part, however, this invasion was prompted by the surge of political and ideological liberalization in Czechoslovakia, not by its economic experiments.

[7] The concept of market socialism described by Lange and Lerner saw individual firms operating as profit maximizers even though they were owned by the state. Oskar Lange, a Polish economist and government official until his death in 1963, first developed these ideas, which were further explained by Abba Lerner in *Economics of Control* (New York: Macmillan, 1959).

OTHER EASTERN EUROPEAN NATIONS

Experimentation with economic reform is also occurring elsewhere among Iron Curtain nations including Poland, East Germany, and Hungary. However, no one clear blueprint describes economic reform in all of these countries. Thus far, economic reforms in Poland, East Germany, and Hungary have not moved as far toward market socialism as have those in Yugoslavia, but they do represent a substantial departure from the highly centralized planning of earlier eras. Poland is moving cautiously toward decentralization, while Albania and Rumania have departed very little from Stalinist reliance upon a highly centralized system of economic planning. The trend toward decentralization tends to be more prevalent in the more industrialized communist economies. Reforms are more likely to be initiated first in the domestic consumer-goods sector, which has less impact on the growth potential of these nations. At the present time it is impossible to judge how acceptable the departure from highly centralized planning will be politically, since such reforms are fraught with ideological overtones.

## CHINA AND CUBA

Centralized planning and more forceful authoritarianism is generally more common in agrarian nations in the early stages of industrialization, and China and Cuba live up to such expectations.

China regards the communism of the Soviet Union and other Eastern European nations as a deviation from the basic principles of Marx, Lenin, and Stalin in social, political, and economic affairs. The Chinese stress on "cultural revolution" and "moral" instead of pecuniary incentives does not accept the emphasis upon economic efficiency that underlies economic reforms in Eastern Europe. Indeed, in both China and Cuba, maximum efficiency is rejected in favor of social consciousness. Reforms which rely upon making capitalistic methods such as markets and profits serve socialist ends are regarded as a hopeless contradiction. Thus, China and Cuba along with North Vietnam and North Korea continue to disregard the values of capitalistic materialism, which are seen as serving capitalistic goals. These nations remain comparatively underdeveloped peasant economies which stress social and political cohesiveness along with more highly centralized economic planning.

## Conflict Between Alternative Systems

The differences between the American version of market capitalism and the planned economy of communist countries would fill volumes; yet, we do know that there are basic conflicts between East and West. In the context of economic ideology, the primary difference centers upon state vs. private ownership of property and productive resources. There is no reason why under socialism the market cannot be used for purposes of resource allocation, since the state can respond to market surpluses and shortages by price and production changes within the loose confines of overall economic plans. Markets work under socialism or communism *if* the state wishes to serve the preferences of consumers instead of those of central planners.

In 1957, when Russia's Nikita Khrushchev stated "We declare war upon you," he referred to a war of production and trade between two competing systems of economic organization. As an important source of economic conflict, the "growth war" stems in part from the ideological implications of planned communism and market capitalism and a host of terribly complex factors centering upon very costly and real concern over national security on the part of both types of economies. Although opinions vary about the causes of this conflict, it is a problem in international politics which is placing severe strains upon world peace and the American economy.

## D. THE ECONOMICS OF WAR AND PEACE

While systems of economic organization reflect the social goals and values of different nations, such diversity does not necessarily imply persistent conflict. Yet war, preparation for it, and its aftermath have plagued man since history was first recorded. While ancient civilizations often engaged in war for economic conquest, the militarism of today which is common to both communism and capitalism is based in part upon conflict over political and economic ideology. In recent decades, the ideological overtones of capitalism and communism with their differing systems of economic organization have contributed to a political power struggle of enormous proportions. Thus, it is important to recognize and weigh the price of conflict —the cost of waging war and of maintaining peace.

### Defense Economics

Many realities are discomforting, but to peoples of an allegedly civilized age in which so-called "reason" guides the destiny of all, perhaps nothing is quite so galling as war. Yet, throughout history, real or imagined insecurity has led to the need for national defense, and hot and cold wars have imposed enormous costs on nations and contributed untold harm to the environment. The average citizen seldom comprehends the economic magnitude of war and peace. Although the economic dimension to international conflict is admittedly a very small part of the full story, it deserves telling, particularly in the context of reviewing economic systems which are so often regarded as our foe.

At the outset, it is crucial to realize that using resources for national security can both destroy and enhance the quality of life. For one thing, there are opportunity costs accompanying the very process of securing a nation's defenses. Vast amounts of resources which would be used for other purposes are instead absorbed in providing national security. On the other hand, the opportunity costs of domination by another power are high; thus, national security does enhance the welfare of all *if* and *when* it is needed. Assessing the "if and when" is a timeless and unanswered question—particularly in an age of competing "isms" and thermonuclear war.

Not surprisingly, the economic impact of war has attracted the attention of scholars for centuries. In the seventeenth and early eighteenth centuries the mercantilists revered economic strength partly for reasons of national security. The economic impact of war and its aftermath attracted considerable attention during the 1940s, and since that time government expenditures on the "cold war" have been the subject of much additional study.[8] Throughout the 1950s and 1960s the economics of war and peace has remained prominent, and for good reason—it is a costly business!

## THE COSTS OF WAR

There are substantial direct and indirect costs associated with preserving the national security of the United States, in terms of both economic outlays and the indirect effects war has on the institutions and the economic structure of society. Figure 2 depicts total U.S. government expenditures in relation to military spending. Defense expenditures during war years reached the $1 billion level for the first time in 1865 at the height of the Civil War (excluding unavailable data on Confederacy spending). Military expenditures for the four war years 1861–1865 totaled $3.5 billion, nearly four times as much as all defense expenditures during the previous 70 years.

The major upsurge in expenditures for national defense came during World War I, and not long thereafter the outbreak of World War II resulted in the United States spending more than one-third of its GNP for military purposes. Since World War II, the price of peace has remained relatively high; military spending has absorbed nearly one-tenth of GNP during each year of the cold-war era since 1950. Military expenditures in each year during the last one-quarter of a century have accounted for from one-third to more than one-half of total federal expenditures. All told, annual federal expenditures for military purposes are as large or larger than state and local government expenditures for all purposes; they also exceed by a small margin total public-sector outlays on education and health; and military spending is almost twice as large as the net profits of *all* American corporations.

Since the Korean War, directly related defense activities not included as military expenditures in Figure 2 have become increasingly important. Foreign aid, the space program, and other miscellaneous expenditures on national security added another $10 billion per year to the 1969 peak in direct military outlays of $81.2 billion. Among other expenditures not shown in Figure 2 is the interest on some two-thirds of the national debt which can be attributed to war, a figure which adds still another $10 billion or more per year to federal expenditures for national security at the present time. Also among the readily identified costs of national security not shown in Figure 2 are expenditures for veterans' benefits which presently exceed $8 billion per year. Finally, the manpower costs of war must be reckoned with. Beginning with the Civil War, military conflicts have resulted in some 2.5 million American casualties which cannot be evaluated in economic terms. Furthermore, the draft system allows the procurement of manpower

[8] The American Economic Association devoted much attention to the topic of war in its annual meetings during 1940 and 1941. See the proceedings issues of the *American Economic Review* (February 1941 and February 1942). Also see James L. Clayton (ed.), *The Economic Impact of the Cold War* (New York: Harcourt Brace Jovanovich, 1970), for an excellent collection of readings; John J. Clark, *The New Economics of Defense* (New York: Random House, 1966); Cabinet Coordinating Committee on Economic Planning for the End of Vietnam Hostilities, "Report to the President," *Economic Report of the President*, 1969, pp. 187–211; and Kenneth E. Boulding, *Conflict and Defense: A General Theory* (New York: Harper & Row, 1963).

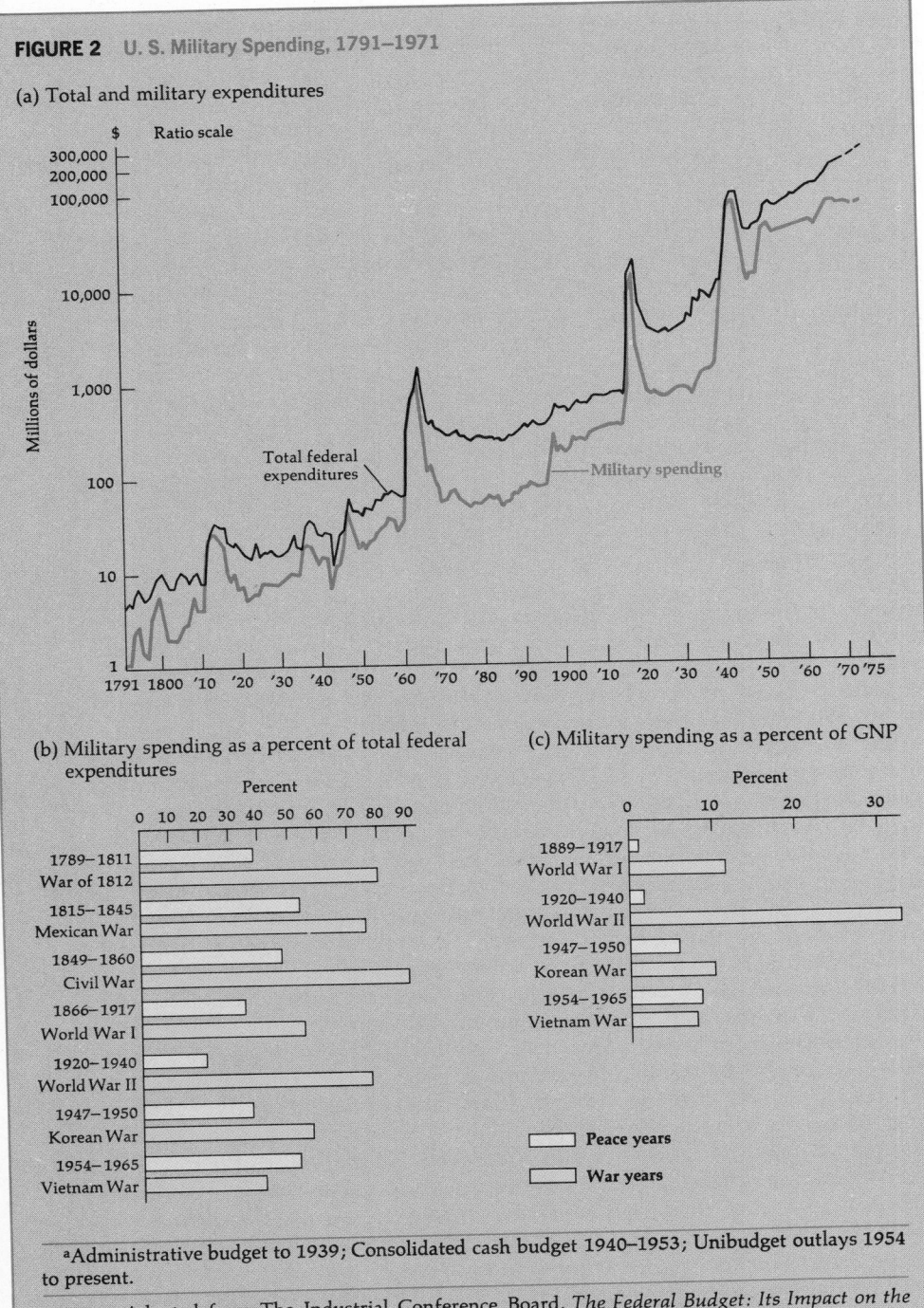

**FIGURE 2** U. S. Military Spending, 1791–1971

(a) Total and military expenditures

(b) Military spending as a percent of total federal expenditures

(c) Military spending as a percent of GNP

aAdministrative budget to 1939; Consolidated cash budget 1940–1953; Unibudget outlays 1954 to present.

SOURCE: Adapted from The Industrial Conference Board, *The Federal Budget: Its Impact on the Economy* (1970), p. 23.

for military activity in the United States at lower than market wages. According to those who have studied the problem, a volunteer army would increase defense expenditures by as much as $5 billion to $8 billion more per year to maintain total military manpower strength at 2.5 to 3 million persons.[9] In effect, the draft system is a subsidy to national defense, and one which is paid by those persons who serve in the military. Clearly the cost of war or the price of peace entails sacrifices much too great to ignore.

Military expenditures also impose indirect costs and benefits on an economy. Thus, World War II was beneficial in the sense that it stimulated aggregate demand and income following the Great Depression. In contrast, the Vietnam hostilities overheated the economy which resulted in persistent inflationary pressures for a period of several years. Then, too, concern is often expressed for the economic adjustments required in returning to a peacetime economy. Structural adjustments are required among different industries as a nation makes the transition from war to a peacetime economy. However, if fiscal and monetary policies remain attuned to the goal of economic stability, unemployment and depression are by no means natural outcomes of transition. In order to maintain aggregate demand, a nation could annually spend considerable sums on social goods instead of on war "capital" which is purposively destroyed.

### THE PRICE OF PEACE?

Clearly direct military expenditures are quite distinct from (and only a portion of) the total costs of war and peace. For all years during the cold-war era between 1951 and 1970, cumulative military expenditures have amounted to $1.1 *trillion*. More than $450 billion of this amount was spent during 1964–1970 as the Vietnam conflict intensified.

The *military-industrial complex*—a large arms industry and the military establishment—is another hidden cost which has influenced the economic, political, social, and psychological fabric of life. On this subject, the late President Eisenhower warned a decade ago that "The potential for the disastrous use of misplaced power exists and will persist."[10] The magnitude of defense expenditures has had just this impact upon the structure of the American economy. For example, between one-half and two-thirds of total United States expenditures for research and development (approximately $35 billion in 1970) are financed by the federal government, and during the 1960s some 90 percent of these funds were allocated to defense and defense-related research.[11] During the peak of Vietnam military activity in the latter 1960s, at least 1 out of 25 civilian workers in about a dozen states was supported by defense employment. A few dozen major corporations (e.g., General Electric, Boeing, and General Dynamics) have received multibillion-dollar defense contracts and, in not a few cases (e.g., Lockheed Aircraft), defense contracts account for more than one-half of the total sales of a corporation. Literally dozens of universities secure annual Department of

---

[9] See, for example, Anthony C. Fisher, "The Cost of the Draft and the Cost of Ending the Draft," *American Economic Review* (June 1969), pp. 239–254.

[10] President Eisenhower's Farewell Address to the Nation (January 18, 1961).

[11] "Defense-related" activities include the Atomic Energy Commission and the Space Administration, which themselves account for 40 percent of all federal government research outlays.

Defense research and development grants in amounts which may reach $1 million each, and defense grants for some institutions range up to and beyond $100 million per year. By all standards, the economics of national defense is of profound economic importance. Militarism has had a decided impact upon the structure of our economy, technological change, and the institutions and values of American society.

## A VIETNAM SPENDING SCENERIO

Since mid-1965 when American troops first entered combat in Vietnam, the imprint of conflict in Southeast Asia upon federal government budget priorities and aggregate military spending has been enormous. Estimates of military expenditures in Vietnam from 1965–1970 and projections to 1975 are shown in Figure 3. Cost projections for the 1970–1975 period presume that troop withdrawals will proceed at such a rate that a military manpower force of 540,000 men in 1969 will have been reduced to 50,000 in 1972 and 0 thereafter. Two different bases for cost estimates have been developed by different authorities. Aggregate-cost data shown by the blue curve of Figure 3 contain estimates for (a) deferred deficits in equipment supplies, which have lowered overall military capabilities in the eyes of some au-

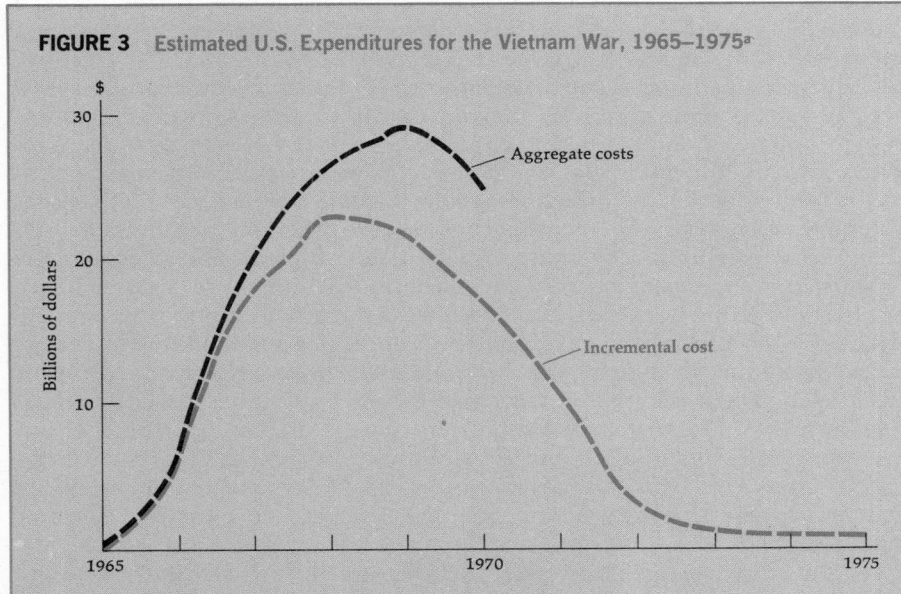

**FIGURE 3**  Estimated U.S. Expenditures for the Vietnam War, 1965–1975[a]

*Estimated Vietnam Military Expenditures.* The additional or incremental expenditures for the Vietnam War are projected as shown above. If the costs of other deferred expenditures are included in these estimates, aggregate Vietnam military expenditures are increased substantially.

[a]Estimates prepared as of 1969 and 1970, excluding the deferred expenditures for the non-Vietnam Department of Defense operation.

SOURCE: Charles L. Schultze, Edward K. Hamilton, and Allen Schick, *Setting National Priorities: The 1971 Budget* (Washington: The Brookings Institution, 1970), Chapter 2.

thorities; and (b) incremental costs, which presume that there have been few if any military needs that have gone unmet because of Vietnam hostilities. While opinions vary on the relative accuracy of these two alternative measures, it is clear that the direct costs of the Vietnam War have been substantial.[12]

The estimated expenditures on the war in Vietnam shown in Figure 3 are somewhat imprecise; however, signs of moderating activity first appeared during 1970. The costs of the Vietnam War rose from $1 billion in fiscal year 1965 to a peak of nearly $30 billion in fiscal 1969 according to Bureau of the Budget calculations which recognize backlog deferrals or cutbacks in defense department programs adversely affected by the war. As military expenditures on Vietnam rose to 3.2 percent of GNP in 1969, defense expenditures for other national security purposes declined, indicating that some backlog or accumulation of unmet defense needs may have occurred. Using incremental costs alone, Vietnam expenditures have been estimated at $85 billion through 1970, and adding in deferral costs pushed the aggregate outlay above $110 billion since 1965.

### The Modern Economy and Defense Economics

The cold war era and the ascension of thermonuclear power have changed traditional concepts of economic war potential.[13] Whereas 20 years ago "economic war potential" typically referred to a nation's ability to mobilize resources for national security when needed, the cold war has placed an ominous stress upon continual "preparedness." Two great nuclear powers —one capitalistic and the other communistic—have felt a need to maintain deterrent and strategic forces at the ready because a cold war turned "hot" might well end before resources could be diverted and economic war potential developed. One consequence of this situation has been a wide diversity of opinion concerning the wisdom of continual preparedness.

Many citizens regard reduced expenditures on national security as badly needed, while others express concern for the adequacy of national security. Along with the instability resulting from uncertain and continually changing international developments, a dramatic shrinkage of the shield earlier afforded by geography has occurred as missile capabilities have increased. Consequently, the major world powers have unrelentingly pursued an ever-increasing updating of military capability. As might be expected, the competitive search for security (or supremacy) by one nation has been matched by the opposing nation, the consequence being the escalation of militarism and insecurity in the world.

It is next to impossible to ascertain the direction of actual defense expenditures from 1970 to 1975. However, the federal government gives careful consideration to alternative objectives of war (macrostrategics) as

[12] These data and related information on defense expenditures, taken from Congressional testimony, also can be found in Charles L. Schultze, Edward K. Hamilton, and Allen Schick, *Setting National Priorities: The 1971 Budget* (Washington, D.C.: The Brookings Institution, 1970), ch. 2; and United States Congress, Joint Economic Committee, Subcommittee on Economy in Government, *Hearings* (91st Congress, First Session, 1969).

[13] See Charles J. Hitch and Roland N. McKean, *The Economics of Defense in the Nuclear Age* (Cambridge, Mass.: Harvard University Press, 1960).

well as alternative efficiency patterns (microstrategics) in reaching any given level of capability to provide national security.

## MACRO-ALTERNATIVES IN THE NATIONAL DEFENSE UNIVERSE

The macrostrategic alternative to the very high price of war and national security is to pare back aggregate outlays. Figure 4 estimates three alternative levels of military spending projected for 1971–1975 for strategic-nuclear and general-purpose forces, excluding the estimated incremental costs of $11 billion for Vietnam in 1971 and $1 billion thereafter. Although the costs of maintaining a strategic-nuclear force for *deterrent* purposes is widely debated, Figure 4 shows that such expenditures represent only one-third of non-Vietnam defense costs. Non-Vietnam defense expenditures can be planned to range from a low of $48 billion in 1971 and $57 billion in 1975, to the alternative high of $77 billion in 1971 and $91 billion in 1975. The substantial differences in the three budget alternatives reflect different assumptions as to nuclear and general-purpose defense needs in the future. Within the context of rapidly escalating costs, national leaders do not face an easy task in assessing future defense needs, as can well be imagined.

One of the difficulties in selecting a given budget is that the cost of

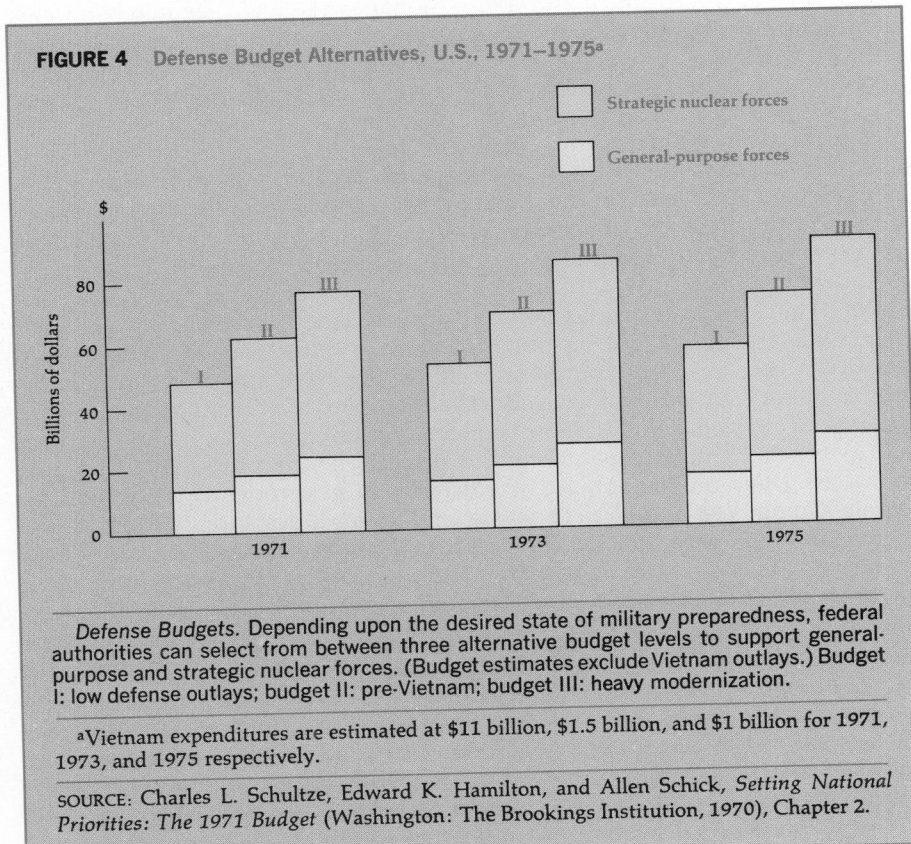

**FIGURE 4** Defense Budget Alternatives, U.S., 1971–1975[a]

☐ Strategic nuclear forces

☐ General-purpose forces

*Defense Budgets.* Depending upon the desired state of military preparedness, federal authorities can select from between three alternative budget levels to support general-purpose and strategic nuclear forces. (Budget estimates exclude Vietnam outlays.) Budget I: low defense outlays; budget II: pre-Vietnam; budget III: heavy modernization.

[a]Vietnam expenditures are estimated at $11 billion, $1.5 billion, and $1 billion for 1971, 1973, and 1975 respectively.

SOURCE: Charles L. Schultze, Edward K. Hamilton, and Allen Schick, *Setting National Priorities: The 1971 Budget* (Washington: The Brookings Institution, 1970), Chapter 2.

strategic-nuclear strength changes rapidly in response to the technological and military advances of one's opponent. Budget I in Figure 4 typifies a low defense posture—a relative reduction in nuclear capability over time in the United States, and a national defense stature dependent upon some 1,700 ICBM and Polaris missiles, 300 heavy bombers, and the sophisticated electronic surveillance system now existing. Additionally, this budget posture assumes general or conventional military manpower and arms forces capable of waging one major land war and a minor conflict simultaneously. The "pre-Vietnam" budget level II of Figure 4 concentrates on the restoration of defense objectives achieved during the early 1960s.[14] Even greater nuclear strength is represented by budget III in Figure 4, although much of the added strength would depend on the outcome of an even more intensified strategic arms race between the United States and Moscow. General-purpose forces under budget level III would be augmented by greater firepower, a much more mobile state of preparedness, and the adoption of even more advanced conventional weapons systems.

### WAR EFFICIENCY AND ECONOMIC INEFFICIENCY

Controlling aggregate expenditures for national defense forces difficult choices on government authorities who must remain subject to the influence of public sentiment and international conditions. The microstrategic approach to the problem of massive defense expenditures relies on increasing the efficiency of waging war. Considerable planning and analysis is carried out by the Department of Defense to determine military goals and the optimal way to achieve given war objectives.

For purposes of maximizing "damage" with scarce dollars, for example, it has been determined that 400 one-megaton bombs can "wipe out" something like 30 percent of the Soviet population (74 million people) and three-fourths of Soviet industrial capacity. Yet if expenditures for megaton-delivery capacity were doubled, damage inflicted would increase by a mere 9 percent.[15]

On the surface, it would appear that efficiency in rendering environmental destruction could be obtained via cost-effectiveness comparisons. However, cost overruns and gross inefficiencies have appeared with alarming frequency in the military-industrial complex. Overruns amounting to billions of wasted dollars are not uncommon on contracts, many of which are awarded on noncompetitively bid projects. During extensive Congressional hearings on the subject of efficiency in government, the Joint Economic Committee found vast waste and even gross intimidation of the Pentagon employees they asked to testify. The conclusions reached in these hearings called for careful re-examination of national priorities concerning defense and civilian budget needs. In commenting on economic inefficiency, the Joint Economic Committee observed that: "In recent years numerous instances of inefficiency, excessive profits, and mismanagement in defense

---

[14] This implies a general-purpose force sufficient to wage two major wars (e.g., one in Asia and one in Europe as in World War II) plus one smaller conflict elsewhere; nuclear retaliation capability assured of destroying 20–25 percent of the Soviet population and over 50 percent of their industrial capacity; and development of the ABM defense force.

[15] Schultze et al., op. cit., pp. 45–46.

contracting have been revealed by this subcommittee, other committees, and the General Accounting Office. The wasteful, inefficient practices uncovered in the course of the hearings raise basic questions concerning the Defense Department's management of its own affairs."[16]

## A Concluding Note

Harsh though these conclusions may be, they point out the realities of international conflict and the costs of such behavior. That the United States and the Soviet Union are cognizant of the explosive character of the competitive arms race is symbolized by their attempts to hold strategic arms limitations talks. Simultaneously, however, ABMs (and no doubt the Russian counterpart) plus a host of "more effective" offensive and defensive weapons systems continue to emerge from advancing military technology. Simplistic theories about the need for national security and military power are not sufficient to fully evaluate the issues immersed in the economics of war and peace, but to go further is beyond our purpose here. If trends in military expenditures of the sort we have explained are ever to be reversed, conscious efforts by the leaders and citizens of many nations, particularly the people of the U.S. and U.S.S.R., will be required.

## REVIEW

### Summary

1. The differences between capitalism, socialism, and communism are partly a matter of degree, although at the extremes these differences are substantial. All economic systems are mixed, relying on different degrees of public vs. private ownership of property, markets vs. centralized economic decision-making, and so forth. The contemporary international community has both accepted and rejected the substance of Marxian thought.

2. Karl Marx foresaw the end of capitalism as an inevitable as well as desirable goal for nations to pursue. He argued that capitalism enslaved the proletariat by usurping "surplus value" from the real value created by labor. As capitalists unrelentingly sought to bolster profits by oppressing the working classes, Marx felt capital resources would be substituted for labor and the masses of unemployed workers would increase. Economic instability in conjunction with exploitation, a growing industrial reserve army, and sharpening class distinctions were seen as means to the avowed Marxian end—destruction of capitalistic society, which was to be replaced by communism.

3. Although many of his predictions have materialized in some nations, Marx failed to recognize fully the resiliency of social and economic institutions in a mixed market economy such as that of the United States. However, the underdeveloped nations of the world face more difficult choices in forming systems of economic organization. More advanced nations which rely on very different systems of economic organization (e.g., the United States and the Soviet Union) cannot ignore the

[16] United States Congress, Joint Economic Committee, Subcommittee on Economy in Government, *Report on the Economics of Military Procurement* (May 1969), pp. 1–2.

economic-development assistance needs of these nations and concerned with the ideological and political choices of these nations.

4. The contrasts between capitalism and communism center upon private compared to public ownership of productive resources, expression of private compared to social values, and the extent to which economic incentives remain oriented around private self-interest. Economic planning is vital to a centrally directed system of economic organization, although different degrees of economic planning also characterize other systems of economic organization, including several nations of Western Europe which are planned market economies.

5. Decentralized economic planning can be combined with a market system of economic organization. Economic planning can also be rigidly directed from the top (i.e., centralized). It requires that the state coordinate production, resource-allocation, and pricing decisions. Input-output models used in all advanced nations today show the interaction among the industries in an economy and are of importance to a planned economy. These models reveal the total output requirements placed upon particular sectors of that economy when the final output of one sector is increased. Input-output analysis helps a nation to use economic planning to carefully set and monitor prices, production goals, and the use and flow of resources.

6. The Soviet Union and other communist nations represent systems of economic organization which are least like the mixed market economy of the United States. Although it has moved away from highly centralized planning in some measure, the Soviet Union still relies on planning controls furnished by GOSPLAN and guided financial controls achieved through GOSBANK. In planning and setting prices, the turnover tax allows government authorities to influence consumption expenditures and the allocation of resources.

7. With the Liberman Reforms in the early 1960s, economic planning has become more decentralized and production for profit has played a larger role in the Soviet Union. Since 1917, the economic growth rate of the Soviet Union has been greater than that of the United States, although the difference between these nations has diminished in recent years. Other nations behind the Iron Curtain have also participated in economic reforms. Yugoslavia perhaps best illustrates the use of decentralized planning along with a controlled but more liberalized market system than is used in other Iron Curtain nations. Czechoslovakia, Poland, and East Germany number among the other communist nations which have moved in the direction of decentralization. Nevertheless, private property and profits accrue for the most part to the state in these countries. China and Cuba have placed less emphasis on the efficiency goals of capitalism and have rejected the profit motive as a means to this end.

8. Many factors are responsible for international conflict, and different systems of economic organization contribute to hot and cold wars. The cost of war and peace is high for both the United States and the Soviet Union. Direct military expenditures in the United States absorb nearly one-tenth of GNP and indirect military costs (e.g., foreign aid, space exploration,

Quantity, competitive demand, price and, 387–388
loss-minimizing, 369–371
profit-maximizing, 369
Quantity demanded, change in, 317
Quantity response to price change, measures of, 327–333
Quantity theory, 250
Quesney, François, 37
Quotas, 650–652

Racial discrimination, economics of, 611–616
eradicating, 617–621
slavery to serfdom, 611–612
Racial minorities, 607
Radiation, 549–550
Rates, foreign-exchange, 666–667
balance of payments and, 670–671
equilibrium, 668–669
fluctuating, 667–669
international reserves and, 670–671
pegged, 670–671
restoration of fluctuating, 677–678
growth, economic, 694–695
savings and investment, 698
Real assets, 194
Real (or constant-dollar) earnings, 60
Real income, adjusting for inflation, 106–107
money income vs., 105
Reality in deference to pure competition, 364
of imperfections, 379
theory and, 22–23
Reasoning, economic, 18–26
approach to, 18–21
problems in, 23–26
Reciprocal Trade Agreement Act (1934), 663
Reform, international financial, 678–685
basic adjustment failure, 681–682
"dollar crisis," 678–680
liquidity problem, 680–681
1970s and, 682–685
proposals for, other, 685
land, 706–707
Soviet economic, 726–727
Regressive tax, 86–87
Regulatory agencies, 512
Remittances, balance of payments, 644
Rent, economic, public policy and, 423
significance of, 422–423
transfer earnings and, 420–424
Required reserves, 205, 228, 231–232
changes in, 231
Research, 278
technology and, 279–280
Reserve-city banks, 202
Reserve equation, 235–236
Reserves, 204
balance of payments and international, 648–649
commercial-bank, new, 206
excess, creating money with, 208–209
maintenance of, 214–215
fractional, 204–205

free, 233–235
required, 205, 228, 231–232
changes in, 231
sources of, 235–236
total, 205
uses of, 236
Residual of ignorance, 280
Resource-allocation device, price as, 44–45
Resource-allocation process, alternative view of, 486–490
Resource base, 274–276
Resource demand, 412–419
derived, marginal productivity and, 412–416
elasticity of, 417–419
interdependence and, 417
marginal-productivity theory of, 411–419
monopoly in the sale of output and, 426–428
shifts in, 416–417
Resource-development policies, 279
Resource market, 36, 312–313
competitive pricing in, 424–430
differentiation in, 430–431
labor, 435–436
prices and, 48, 411–438
perspective on, 426–430
production factors and, 431–436
reasons for study of, 411–412
Resource-market pricing, meaning of marginal-productivity theory, 424–430
note on, 430–436
Resource-mobility adjustments, case for trade barriers, 653–655
Resource pricing, justice and, 428–430
Resource supply, 419–424
Resources, economic, 15–18
allocation of, see Allocation of resources
capital, 17–18, 432–434
investment and, 275–276
common, mortgaging, 551–559
social costs in, 554–556
demand for, 412–419
entrepreneurial, 16
human, see Human resources
inefficient use of, 393–395
labor, 16
low-mobility, 524
marginal cost of, price equals, indicator of economic efficiency, 363–364
natural (land), 274–275, 431–432, 705–707
stock of, 705–706
physical-capital, 697
production, ownership of, 720
products and equally valued, 448–451
profit-maximizing use of, 414–419
property, 16–18
Restraint, voluntary, 263–264
Restrictive monetary policy, balance sheet, 228
Retirement insurance, 621
Revenue, federal, absorption of, by cause and by program (1975), 500
marginal (MR), see Marginal revenue
total, 365
Reynolds, Lloyd, 590

Ricardo, David, 250, 283, 284, 285, 286, 421 n., 579, 631, 704
Risk, 276
redistribution of, 76–77
Robertson, D. H., 110 n.
Robinson-Patman Act (1936), 518
Rockefeller, John D., Sr., 575 n.
Ross, Arthur, 590
Rostow, W. W., 694
Roundabout production, 432
Rural poor, 608
Rural poverty and decline, 524–525

Salaries, 16
Sales, maximization of, 458
Satisfaction, consumer, see Consumer satisfaction
Saving, discrepancies, 156
investment and, rate of, 698
propensities to save, 134–135
Say, J. B., 122
Say's Law, 122
Scale, diseconomies of, 352–353
economies of, 283, 352
technology, 377–378
Scarcity, economic organization and, 31–40
human-resource, 16
overcoming, 15–18
Scarcity-choice dilemma, 13–15
Schedules, aggregate demand, 129
aggregate supply, 128–129
consumption, 133
cost, for a firm, 344–347
demand, product substitution and, 318–319
marginal-efficiency-of-capital, 221
supply, 313–315
Schultz, Theodore, 600
Schultze, Charles, 499 n., 502
Schumpeter, Joseph A., 57, 110, 377, 407, 511
Sectoral inflation, 260
Secular exhilaration, 292
Securities and Exchange Commission, 56
Security markets, 56–57
Segregation, 616
Selective credit controls, 232
Self-sufficiency as a case for trade barriers, 653
Selucky, Radoslav, 729
Serfdom, 611–612
Servan-Schreiber, J. J., 665 n.
Sherman Antitrust Act (1890), 514, 515
unions and, 576
Short run, competitive firm in, 367–372
optimum output for, 364–372
Short-run costs, 340
relationships, 347–350
structure for a firm, 344–350
Shubik, Martin, 450 n.
"Shut-down" cost level, 349–350
Simon, Herbert, 458
Slavery, 611–612
Smith, Adam, 5, 35, 37–38, 40, 46, 57, 74, 282–283, 407, 453, 456, 480, 631
Smoot-Hawley Tariff Act (1930), 663, 664
Social balance, 78
Social costs, 339–340
in the "commons," 554–556
modification for, 339

71 72 73 74   7 6 5 4 3 2 1